P9-DDF-774

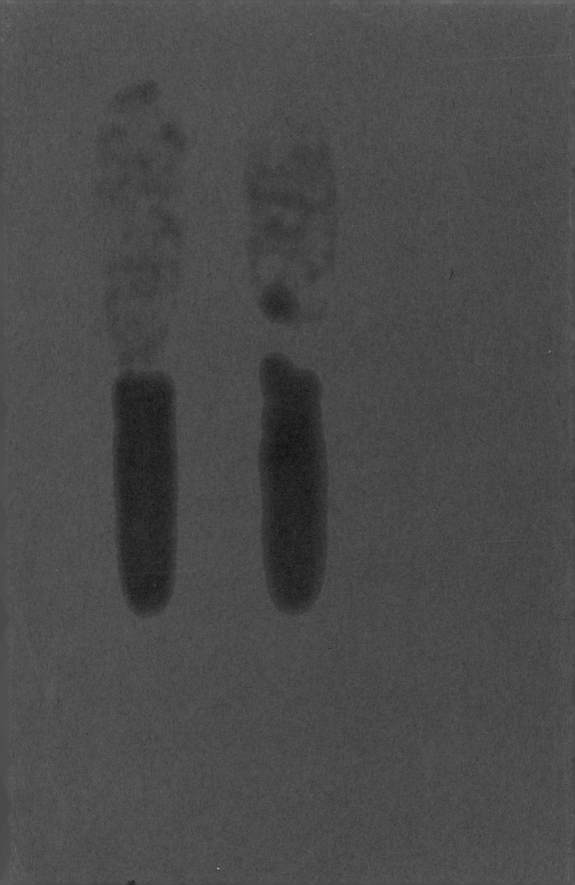

Literature of
the People's Republic
of China

CHINESE LITERATURE IN TRANSLATION

Editors

Irving Yucheng Lo, Joseph S. M. Lau, and Leo Ou-fan Lee

Literature of the People's Republic of China

Edited by Kai-yu Hsu

Co-editor, Ting Wang

With the special assistance of
Howard Goldblatt, Donald Gibbs, and George Cheng

Indiana University Press
Bloomington & London

Library of Congress Cataloging in Publication Data
Main entry under title:

Literature of the People's Republic of China.

(Chinese literature in translation)
Bibliography: p.
Includes index.
1. Chinese literature—20th century—Translations into English.   2. English
literature—Translations from
Chinese.   I. Hsu, Kai-yu, 1922–   II. Series.
PL2658.E1L55   895.1'08'005   78-24807
ISBN 0-253-16015-4 1 2 3 4 5 83 82 81 80

To The Translators

to you
the unsung, the uncrowned,
the poet, the aerial artist walking on a tightrope
          between two words—two worlds,
the ventriloquist virtuoso speaking others' dreams in your own voice,
          or speaking your own dreams in others' voices,
the bridge builder, working with syllables and commas and periods,
the unrecognized academic producer whose scholarship
          is appreciated only by the most cultivated.

                                   Kai-yu Hsu

CONTENTS

vii

PART TWO: The Hundred Flowers Movement and the
Anti-Rightist Campaign (1956–1958) / 195

PART THREE: The Great Leap Forward and
Anti-Revisionism (1959–1961) / 389

PART FOUR: The Socialist Education of the People
(1962–1964) / 559

Part Five: The Great Proletarian Cultural Revolution (1964–1970) / 747

Preface

The Yenan Forum on Literature and Art in 1942 firmly established the inseparability of Chinese literature and politics. Since then, whenever political aims and emphases have changed, the direction of literature has changed accordingly. This relationship between literature and politics in the People's Republic of China dictates that any representative anthology of contemporary Chinese literature must also reflect the political fortunes of the writers and their works. Thus, the readings in this volume have been selected and organized in relation to the major controversies that have shaken the politico-literary scene in China since 1949. Most scholars in the field agree on the utility of this approach in the study of modern Chinese literature.

With very few exceptions, all duly identified, the translations have been specially commissioned for this book, and the translator's name appears at the end of each work or group of works. A headnote has been added to each selection or group of selections to provide biographical data on the author and to allow the translator or editor to make other essential comments on the work. A chronology of major events relevant to the development of contemporary Chinese literature follows the general introduction. A brief glossary of Chinese terms that are frequently used without translation, and of organizations, campaigns, and movements mentioned in many of the works, appears at the back of the book. Also included are a list of Chinese references, a list of the translators and contributors, an author index, and a title index.

An effort has been made to avoid duplicating the information in such readily available sources as Kai-yu Hsu, *Twentieth Century Chinese Poetry* and *The Chinese Literary Scene,* and John Berninghausen and Ted Huters, *Revolutionary Literature in China.*

Acknowledgments

Professor Joseph S. M. Lau of the University of Wisconsin was chiefly responsible for persuading me to undertake the development of this anthology, and my friends at the East Asian literature program of Indiana University enthusiastically supported the plan. The project came to fruition with the patient, prompt, and dedicated collaboration of sixty contributors, bolstered by efficient, knowledgeable help from friends at the Library of Congress, the Harvard-Yenching Library, and the libraries of Columbia University, the Hoover Institute on War, Revolution, and Peace of Stanford University, the University of California at Berkeley, San Francisco State University, and other institutions in Australia, Europe, Hong Kong, and Japan.

In addition to translating their respective selections or doing other related research for the project, Ting Wang, Howard Goldblatt, Donald Gibbs, and George Cheng gave me special assistance and worked closely with me throughout the year. Hsü Yü, novelist and literary scholar now in Hong Kong, aided me in designing the framework for this book. May Shih did much of the typing, and Yi Yü dispatched many necessary chores that are too seldom noticed or acknowledged. I want to express my gratitude to all of these, and to many others too numerous to be listed here.

Kai-yu Hsu

Literature of
the People's Republic
of China

Introduction

The awesome energy of eight hundred million people, when finally harnessed for a unified purpose, burst forth in many startling ways. Scattered creative forces, long handicapped by the stringencies of a protracted war and kept underground in most areas of China until 1949, burgeoned soon after the Liberation. Nationwide campaigns to increase production on the literary front and corresponding drives to improve literacy spurred the publication of thousands of volumes in all genres. Some of these works had ephemeral lives, some had stormy careers, and others traced a rather curious course of disappearance and reappearance.

What is in these thousands of volumes? The stories, plays, and verses of modern China portray a human drama of astonishing magnitude. Their settings range from the heart of Peking to the frontiers of Tibet and Sinkiang. Their action might center around victory over enemy secret agents or the participation of intellectuals in physical labor. But the numerous variations generally stem from five major historical themes:

1. *The Communist revolution up to 1949.* This category includes works about the early underground urban struggle (for example, Ou-yang Shan's saga *A Generation of Noble Souls*), the guerrilla war against the Japanese and the Kuomintang in the 1930s (the Peking opera *The Red Lantern*), and the war in the 1940s (Chün Ch'ing's "Dawn on the River").

2. *The land reform experience, shortly before and after 1949.* This era, which was as violent as the first, is the focus of works such as Ting Ling's Stalin Prize–winning novel, *The Sun Shines over the Sangkan River,* and Liu Ch'ing's *The Builders.*

3. *The Chinese Communist participation in the Korean War—the early 1950s.* Liu Pai-yü's "On the Dusty Road" and Yang Shuo's *A Thousand Miles of Lovely Land* are two of the works that depict the men and women involved in combat or in support of the war effort.

4. *The socialist reconstruction of the country—an ongoing process since 1949.* The feverish activities of building up a new socialist society on the agricultural and industrial fronts have inspired by far the largest group of works, including Sha Ting's "Try and Catch Me" and Hsiao Chün's *Coal Mines in May.*

5. *The continuing need for socialist education of the masses.* "Be Alert Against Enemy Spies," screams a ubiquitous poster in the People's Republic of China. And numerous stories and plays, particularly those aimed at younger readers, also concentrate on the need to guard against imperialist (American) and counterrevolutionary (Kuomintang) spies, like the one in Malchinhu's "On the Kolchin Grasslands." The need to maintain the fight against the corrupting influences of urban life has been equally important, and multitudinous works

1

have been written to exhort junior high school students to settle on the communes as peasants or to work in frontier areas. Ch'en Yün's *The Young Generation* is an example.

Despite Mao's 1942 decree that all works must be written for the proletariat, not all the literature that followed was aimed at the amorphous masses of barely literate peasants, workers, and soldiers. Some works were clearly intended for the cadres and students—a more sophisticated segment formerly known as the "petty-bourgeois intellectuals." In the post-1949 works, complications along the road to socialist success provided themes for the development of complex characters, both heroic and villainous, and enabled authors to demonstrate their awareness of what real life entailed, although their attempts at in-depth realism often brought them political misfortune. The waxing and waning of the writer's political fortune follow a course that at times seems tortuous and bizarre; the history of literature in the People's Republic of China has certainly been no less tumultuous than that of Communist politics, wherein one leadership has replaced another as rapidly as meetings could be held.

WAVES OF CONTROVERSY

Politico-literary arguments in Communist China have covered the entire range of socialist theories, reviving at different times all the pertinent issues ever raised by Engels, Trotsky, Stalin, and Mao Tse-tung. Once the old society began to crumble, literary and artistic energies heretofore spent on exposés, criticism, and satire were put to the service of the revolution and its guiding light, the Chinese Communist Party (CCP). The creation of a proletarian literature became the subject of intense debates. What should be considered an acceptable degree of realism? How much emphasis should be placed on the positive side of life? To what extent should a work adhere to Engels' interpretation of typicality? Clearly, political dicta had to be formulated to guide literary activities.

Every writer in China accepts the socialist goal as the ideal for a new Chinese society and agrees that his duty is to work toward that goal. But the authorities cannot always make specific assignments, and the writers themselves cannot always agree precisely what and how they should write in support of the revolution. Many writers see imperfections in reality; political authorities, on the other hand, insist on the need to be positive, to exhort readers to follow an infallible Party and its ideology. Hence the recurrent argument concerning the "depth of realism." Many writers see human nature as complex—nonstereotyped, but with some fundamental traits that are universal; the Communist Party, however, insists on the social class theory as the only correct, true, and adequate explanation of human nature. Hence the quarrel about "middle characters" in literature—those who are neither heroes nor villains. While the writers see the reality of man in such a way as to preclude the existence of perfect heroes, proletarian or not, the Party insists on presenting models for the masses to emulate; the result is the quarrel over whether all heroes should be "red-faced"—suntanned, fearless, almost superhumanly powerful—as they are in every revolutionary opera. Many writers feel impelled to write about the unhappiness of their characters, which they see as the result of the uncertainties and contradictions that can exist in any society. Thus, even though their characters are supposed to be living in a new and more perfect society, the exposure of their unhappiness is not intended as a criticism against communism. But the Party insists on drawing a sharp line, saying that any innuendo, however subtle, that casts a shadow over the Party's perfect wisdom immediately makes the writer an enemy of the people. The theory of two kinds of contradiction was first proposed by Mao Tse-tung, who made a distinction between a contradiction within the people (a difference of opinion to be peaceably resolved among comrades all devoted to communism) and a contradiction between the people and their enemy (an irreconcilable difference that must be struggled against without reserve). Since only the Party Central had the power to make such distinctions, many serious writers who had tried to decide the issue for themselves were charged with sedition, despite the fact that they had been veteran Party members and had even risked their lives time and again for the Party.

In short, these issues revolve around three basic questions—the same questions Mao Tse-tung dealt with in his talks at the Yenan Forum on Literature and Art back in 1942. Which comes first, political ideology or literary art? Besides the life of the proletariat, what else is permissible in literature? Can there be characters whose behavior and motivation are more complex than what is easily explained by the class theory? In 1942 Mao's own answers to these questions were already quite explicit, but, typically, not without tactical flexibility. Since then, Party-appointed literary authorities have interpreted the Yenan Talks to suit changing political needs, implementing a now more, now less, rigid policy based on "revolutionary realism plus revolutionary romanticism." The former allows realism only to the extent that it will aid the revolution; the latter encourages exaggeration of the hero-villain contrast only so long as it, too, serves the revolution.

The controversies during the past three decades have arisen like waves in a troubled sea, repetitive and persistent, with only brief lulls in between. The first campaign against dissident writers began almost immediately after the establishment of the People's Republic, as one facet of the Party's effort to eliminate all opposition and to consolidate power. It was an extension of the quarrels that the Yenan Talks had failed to settle once and for all. No new major literary work was involved; the fire was mainly concentrated on the influential critic and essayist Hu Feng and his advocacy of a broader realism. The campaign culminated in his arrest in 1955.

The second major campaign gathered momentum in 1957 in the wake of the short-lived thaw known as the Hundred Flowers movement. Many well-established writers who survived the Hu Feng case, such as Ting Ling, Ai Ch'ing, and Hsiao Chün, came under attack for their earlier works, published mostly during their residence in Yenan, which had expressed dissatisfaction with the Party's arbitrary literary policy and with the corruption of some elements within the Party. Two new novels drew considerable criticism. Hsiao Chün's *Coal Mines in May* ran afoul of the authorities for its failure to uphold the Party's infallible wisdom. Fang Chi's *The Visitor* incurred the ire of the official critics for its emphasis on the seamy side of urban life and the implication that the main character's failure was due more to the imperfection of the new society than to his own bourgeois class background.

Following the Eighth Plenum of the Central Committee, Eighth Party Congress (September 1959), which ordered a drive to take a Great Leap Forward and to eradicate rightist opportunism and revisionism, a third major campaign was launched against those writers championing broad humanism and objective truth. Chao Hsün's *Homecoming*, a play describing the heartrending disappointment of a veteran Red soldier with what he finds when he returns to his native village, was condemned for its antiwar spirit, despite its hopeful ending. That the soldier did not behave like a red-faced hero on stage, but rather gave in at moments to despair, could not be tolerated by the Party-directed critics. Even "Gazing at the Starry Sky," a rather innocuous poem by the veteran Communist poet Kuo Hsiao-ch'uan, who for years shared the political stewardship of the national Chinese Writers' Association, did not escape blame for its expression of "pessimism stemming from a frustrated individualism."

The fourth intensified campaign to correct capitalist revisionism in literature was a response to the Party's call for socialist education of the people, which was enunciated at the Tenth Plenum of the Central Committee, Eighth Party Congress, in September 1962. This time the CCP was intent on refuting the more open literary policies laid down by Krushchev in the Twentieth Russian Party Congress and amplified during the Twenty-Second Russian Party Congress in 1961. The CCP was particularly critical of the Russian literary trend reflected in the writings of Nobel Prize winner Mikhail A. Sholokhov, whose *And Quiet Flows the Don, Virgin Soil Upturned, Fate of a Man,* and other works—all very influential among Chinese writers—present complex characters and issues not easily explained by the CCP's simplistic dogma.

The most severe berating was directed at the topflight Communist critic and literary leader Shao Ch'üan-lin (secretary of the Party branch of the Chinese Writer's Association and concurrently holding half a dozen other leading literary positions in the government), who dared to advocate the importance of "middle characters" that are neither red-faced heroes nor ashen-faced villains. The campaign spread from Shao down to the popular novelist Ou-yang Shan, who was severely attacked for his unfinished saga, *A Generation of Noble Souls.* His assailants claimed that in the 1920s Ou-yang Shan allowed his principal revolutionary characters to indulge in sentimental romances. Even worse, the female objects of the hero's attention were all bourgeois young ladies from a rich family! These offenses, the critics charged, distorted the typicality of underground Communist revolutionary cadres.

THE CULTURAL REVOLUTION

Li Hui-niang, a dramatic piece first published in August 1961, brought trouble for its author, Meng Ch'ao. The work was based on a Ming dynasty legend about the ghost of an aggrieved young woman returning to seek revenge against her tormentor-murderer, a corrupt prime minister. Meng was charged with leading his readers and audience back to feudalistic superstition and viciously instigating the masses (or the unreformed reactionaries) to seek revenge against authority. The play was condemned as an anti-Party piece. Beginning in mid-1962, criticism of *Li Hui-niang* served as a prelude to the theater reform led by Chiang Ching, Mao Tse-tung's wife. A series of historical plays all fell under the charge that the authors criticized the Communist government through the thin disguise of re-creating history. Wu Han's *Hai Jui's Dismissal from Office,* T'ien Han's *Kuan Han-ch'ing,* and other works all joined the ranks of the disgraced. The Great Proletarian Cultural Revolution, officially launched in June 1964, was in fact well under way.

Ostensibly aimed at correcting all undesirable tendencies in the new society, the Cultural Revolution was primarily motivated by factional politics in Peking. In literature this fifth major campaign carried on the unfinished drive for socialist education of the masses, for which the theater appeared especially suited. Chiang Ching and her chief spokesman, Yao Wen-yüan, reviewed the theater programs popular at the time and proscribed all of them because, as Mao Tse-tung pointed out, the shows contained only Confucian scholars and delicate maidens, emperors and generals—all feudal dregs reflecting values of the worst bourgeoisie. As such, these traditional programs were "poisonous weeds" that had to be eradicated. The metaphor of poisonous weeds had been in circulation since the end of the Hundred Flowers movement; now it regained currency. Weeded out of the theater along with the old works were the plays of Hsia Yen, T'ian Han, and Yang Han-sheng. Hsia Yen's *The Lin Family Store* was faulted for its lenient treatment of the store-owner and the warm feeling of the apprentice toward his master. Yang Han-sheng's *Northland and South of the River,* though based on his own experience of learning from the peasants, was condemned for its emphasis on the negative side of the rural situation, and all his earlier popular plays were also condemned.

These three playwrights, along with Chou Yang, the Party's literary czar since the late 1930s and the man who had himself been responsible for all past literary purges, were unceremoniously removed from the limelight and labeled as the Four Villains. Finally, only about a dozen revolutionary operas designed by Chiang Ching remained on stage; all the writers had been ordered to the countryside to learn from the peasants; the students were turned loose as Red Guards to assail Party Headquarters in Peking with wall posters written in large, bold characters; the press ground to a halt; the bookstores and libraries boarded up their doors. The Cultural Revolution swept over China like a hurricane. In the desolate aftermath, there was only a whisper here, a murmur there, of what could be considered the voice of an underground literature.

THE FALL OF THE GANG OF FOUR

There was never an official closure of any movement launched in the People's Republic. By 1970 Mao Tse-tung had indicated his wish to curb the Cultural Revolution, but not to end it forever. In fact, in the fall of 1973 there was an effort to rekindle the Cultural Revolution with a campaign to attack, once again, Confucianism. Much printer's ink was spilled over a reexamination of China's Confucian tradition, but very little creative writing was involved. A handful of officially sanitized writers, such as the peasant-novelist Hao Jan, the worker-poet Li Hsüeh-ao, and the woman writer Yang Mo, began to write a little, but mostly they revised and republished their earlier works.

The deaths of Chou En-lai and Mao Tse-tung in 1976 threw the country into another spell of political upheaval. Now those who ten years ago acted as the literary executioners of the Four Villains have themselves become the anti-Party Gang of Four, and some works and authors previously condemned are being brought back into circulation. At the Third Session of the Third Congress of the All-China Federation of Literary and Art Circles, held in Peking in May 1978, the roster of delegates made it clear that the silenced and exiled had all been resurrected—all except the tragically unfortunate, like Lao She, Chao Shu-li, and Shao Ch'uan-lin, who died either under the Red Guards' brutal beatings or under suspicious circumstances in political prison. The scenario of a political thaw seems quite complete at the moment, including a change of literary guards, reversal of verdicts, and public rituals to vindicate Lao She and many less famous than he, restoring honor to their memories. Only one question remains—how long before the next upheaval?

THE NEW FOLK HERO: AN EASY PATH TO SUCCESS

In thirty years the significant changes in Chinese literature have been so extensive that most readers familiar with pre-1949 works can hardly bring themselves to countenance Hao Jan, or Feng Ching-yüan, or even Tsang K'o-chia. The latest works present a different world, expressed in a virtually different language. We can best observe this new phenomenon through its new heroes, through their actions, and through their view of reality around them.

The principle of proletarian literature dictates that the new hero hail from the common folk—the peasants, workers, or soldiers, who, with the advances of socialist education and the leveling of the classes, should include the entire Chinese populace by now. The new hero differs from the traditional Chinese folk hero in some important ways.

There have been several types of folk hero in traditional Chinese literature, but the general reader could truly identify with none of them. Kuan Yü (Kuan Yün-ch'ang), the sword-wielding general of the Three Kingdoms, must be ranked among the most popular. He had a humble family origin, with which the common folk could identify, but his unbelievable physical prowess could only be explained by a divine origin, to which the reader could not aspire. Sun Wu-k'ung, the monkey king in *Journey to the West* (or *Monkey*), is another folk-hero model. His defiant caprices, tempered by his blunt but commonsensical handling of human frailties, have won immortal admiration, but his magical power lies beyond any reader's realistic identification. Judges and magistrates with the wisdom of Solomon and the deductive powers of Sherlock Holmes are also folk-hero models. Their clever judgment and shrewd perception may inspire much admiration, but few readers see themselves as being so wise.

Perhaps the folk-hero model with whom the Chinese reader can identify most closely is a combination of the Kuan Yü type, with his loyalty to a sworn brotherhood *(Romance of the Three Kingdoms)*, and the Robin Hood type, with his readiness to take the law into his own hands *(Water Margin)*. The heroes of the kung-fu stories satisfy this formula, which accounts for that genre's great popularity in China until 1949, when these folk-hero qualities were translated into a new code of conduct.

Post-1949 Chinese writers have created a new folk-hero model in the Kao Ta-ch'üan of *Broad Road in Golden Light,* the Kuo Chien-kuang of *Shachiapang* (actually, I think his female counterpart, Ah-ch'ing Sao, is the real hero of that work), and the Yang Tzu-jung of *Taking Tiger Mountain by Strategy.* The hero hails from a proletarian background, as does the reader. The hero possesses no supernatural powers; thus his accomplishments are within the reader's reach. The new heroism is achieved with only two qualities: an ability to follow the Party's dictates, and an undying loyalty to the proletarian brotherhood, translated into the state and the Party. No reader in the People's Republic today would find it hard to meet either requirement.

The new folk-hero model is a success; it has to succeed because it is realistically easy to emulate. All it takes is determined dedication to surpass the assignments, which usually require physical labor on the production front. The hero does not have to die a martyr, even though there are such models of supreme self-sacrifice—Lei Feng, Wang Chieh, and Chang Ssu-te—whose images are paraded in public in the repeated campaigns to inculcate dedication to the Party. The new successful hero does not die, however; he or she is supposed to succeed, emerging triumphant and unscathed from difficulties. Therein lies the attraction. The heroic quality of the new production-brigade captain in Wang Wen-shih's story is solely his courage to face, with the Party's official support, the entrenched reactionary forces in the village. The old peasant in Chao Shu-li's story distinguishes himself only with his pair of toughened hands and his insatiable appetite for hard physical work. The Mongolian girl in Malchinhu's story is attractive simply because she is alert enough to take notice of a suspicious character, a Kuomintang spy, and foolhardy enough to spur her horse across a blazing prairie. With the new literature the reader may miss a dimension of daydream and wish-fulfillment, but he gains an identity with the hero, which is a powerful incentive to readership.

THE NEW SUBJECT MATTER: ELEVATION OF THE ORDINARY

The traditional Chinese tales were tales of the wondrous. From T'ang and Sung dynasty tales to *Strange Stories from a Chinese Studio,* all the short fiction told of something extraordinary. Fairy-tale romance, supernatural intervention in the affairs of man, crimes of passion, historical wars, and unusual experiences and strange coincidences were fit materials for traditional Chinese fiction. Then an influx of various literary theories and new ideas into early twentieth-century China stimulated a tremendous diversity in Chinese writings that lasted until 1949. During this period themes ranged widely, from exposés of social evils (a theme that dominated), to in-depth psychological probing, to allegorical exploration of the meaning of life and the nature of reality. However, it was only after 1949 that writers affirmed the validity and upheld the supremacy of one type of subject matter—that of making an honest living or doing an honest job.

If we were to examine the pre- and post-1949 treatments of fighting a flood, a frequent theme in Chinese literature, we would find that Liu T'ieh-yün's

Travels of Lao Ts'an (1907) makes use of this subject, but there is no description of how people actually fight the flood. T'ien Han's *Flood* (1936) and Ting Ling's *Water* (1933) also use this theme, but these works are mainly concerned with the tragedy aggravated by government abuse and the evils of the rich, rather than with the drama of fighting the flood. The task of fighting a flash flood becomes a *central* scene only in such a story as "Carry On," by a People's Liberation Army soldier, Yang Hsing-wang.

The construction of a factory, the development of frontier lands, a survey for ore deposits, or just the daily routine of digging dirt and manufacturing wheel-barrows has never before constituted the main subject matter in any recognized work in Chinese literature, and yet today's writers in the People's Republic are using these subjects, almost to the exclusion of others. This is a new literary phenomenon created by the new generation of writers in China; it could have been created only by them.

THE NEW LANGUAGE: FROM INTELLECTUAL TO VISCERAL

How the new folk heroes express their responses to the world around them can best be seen in their use of imagery and other rhetorical devices. The traditional Chinese poet has excelled in using images from nature to elicit the reader's emotive and aesthetic response. Take, for instance, two lines from Wang Wei's "Clear Stream," a poem with the kind of nature imagery that evokes a feeling of joy about life:

> Sounds arise among strewn rocks,
> Colors hush in deep pine woods.

Writing over a thousand years ago, Wang Wei (701–761) evoked a beautiful world of nature in these two lines: the sound of a creek bubbling through strange-looking rocks; shades of green, all subdued and quiet, melting into the deep blue of a pine forest. We can enjoy the picture as it is even without turning to the next level of meaning suggested by *sheng* (sound) and *se* (color), the first words of the two lines. For *sheng* and *se* are the phenomenal world, which, to Wang Wei, has been subdued by what is noumenal in nature. The *sheng* is heard only among the inanimate, unchanging rocks; while the *se* surrenders to the pine trees by becoming hushed. There is joy in such a world—quiet joy, to be experienced through one's intellect in calm contemplation, a joy never accompanied by physical exuberance.

The Chinese poets after 1949 turn to nature images in a fresh way. To them, aesthetic responses are directly connected to man's most basic needs. The beauty of peach blossoms lies not in their ability to remind the viewer of the cheeks of his beloved lady but rather in the fact that they herald a bumper crop of peaches. We discover a new evocative power in the nature imagery of post-1949 mainland Chinese poetry like Yen Chen's *Songs South of the River:*

> I love this patch of intense green,
> For many happy dreams lie in its rich fold;
> Who won't like to pick treefuls of ripe fruit,
> When autumn mellows into rich gold?

Traditionally, the image of the spring tide has connoted irrevocable seasonal change and the passage of time, or, taken a step further, the ruthless dictates of history and the futility of man. The Mongol poet Sa-tu-la uses this image in a poem from *Pai-hsiang tz'u-p'u:*

> Listen—late at a lonesome night, assailing this
>   deserted city wall—
> The spring tide rushes.

Chang Jo-hsü of the Tang dynasty describes a beautiful, serene, moonlit scene on a riverbank where poets gather to enjoy the view:

> The tides in the spring river level it with the sea,
> And over the sea a brilliant moon ascends along with the
>   rising tide.

But let us look at the way the same image is used in the poem "Every Calendar Page, A Victory Poster":

> A journey of three thousand miles glowing in red sunlight,
> Thousands of wood shavings curl up a spring tide under the plane,
> In long strides we fly across the threshold of 1971,
> Every leaf from the calendar a victory poster.

In the eyes of this poet, a Shanghai factory worker, spring tides promise a rewarding planting season, or a good catch for the fishing fleet, or smooth sailing for the seamen laboring on a loading dock. No doubt he is doing carpentry at the moment, and he sees all these possibilities as the curling wood shavings repeat the exciting pattern of the whitecaps on surging water, a spring tide. Both the post-1949 poet and his reader share the kinds of experiences symbolized, in a concrete way, by the spring tide.

The new use of old images and themes creates a different kind of evocative power not only in poems and songs but also in some stories. Wang Chia-pin's "The Whale Trough" presents something more than just a heroic proletarian conquest of the sea. When Szu-ma, the skipper, leaps on the back of a fish-filled net that twists and tosses in black, twenty-foot-high waves, there is as much drama as when Wu Sung grapples with the tiger in *Water Margin* or when the legendary battle takes place between the folk hero Chou Ch'u and the marine monster. There is also a touch of the allegorical significance of man's struggle to overcome a superhuman force, just as we find in *Moby Dick* or in *The Old Man and the Sea.* But there is a difference. While Melville's white whale and Hemingway's blue marlin are not hunted for their meat, the young comrade in "The Whale Trough" is trying to haul in that net full of gleaming fat garfish because each fish is enough to make a hefty meal that will bring smiles to ten hunger-haunted Chinese faces. In Chinese aesthetics today the visceral has taken over from the intellectual; materialism is now king.

Several stylistic traits characterize post-1949 prose. The principal innovation is the liberal use of familiar elements from the fiction and drama of the Ming and Ch'ing dynasties, combined with a rich technical vocabulary from factory, farm, and military life. The adoption of traditional narrative techniques has been selective, to be sure; the dominant style tends more toward the hard-line clichés of *Water Margin* than toward the finesse of *Dream of the Red Chamber.* The characters are often formally presented, as in traditional theater: when important figures first appear, they are required to recount their family background, their present position, and, most likely, the problem at hand. To these traditional techniques has been added a vocabulary enriched by the experience of the proletariat. To a reader unfamiliar with such modes of life, the terms could amount to an inconvenience, but in most cases they are not so esoteric as to be a barrier. Liu Pin-yen's "At the Bridge Site," though generously endowed with technical material, remains more a story for the general reader than a technical report.

From the *pai-hua* (vernacular) literature of the May Fourth era (the 1920s and 1930s), the new writings, particularly when they involve political and social ideas, have inherited many syntactical features and terms with European origins. These terms have been translated either directly into Chinese, or indirectly, via the Japanese. When the foreign elements are mishandled, the writing has a droll ring, but in the adroit hand of such an author as Hao Jan, the imported syntactical features have acquired a Chinese polish. Chao Shu-li demonstrates how the effective use of colloquialism not only adds touches of authenticity to the setting and characterization but also enhances the flow of the language: his works are rich and vibrant, nearly always fast-paced, and frequently sprinkled with delightful humor. Folk metaphors and proverbs are also being used heavily—and to good advantage—by most authors. Particularly popular is the unique Chinese figure of speech called *hsieh-hou-yü,* a proverbial phrase with its last word omitted, for the reader to supply. In descriptive prose, phrases with reduplicative and onomatopoeic sounds are in vogue, a technique that stems from the tradition of oral narrative. Although this technique is a worthy one, it is sometimes used excessively, as in Yang Shuo's *A Thousand Miles of Lovely Land.*

As the leaves began to fall in 1978, the history of literature in the People's Republic of China seemed to have turned a new page. The resumption of most of the major literary journals led to a flood of reports on new signs of life on the literary scene. Veteran writers talked about their grand schemes for *chefs d'oeuvre,* most of them not yet started. Yao Hsüeh-yin has now resumed work on his multivolume historical novel *Li Tzu-ch'eng,* and Ts'ao Yü has just completed his five-act historical play, *Wang Chao-chün,* which he started at the beginning of the Cultural Revolution. A group of new writers (Liu Hsin-wu, Tsung Fu-hsien, Lu Hsin-hua, and others), some very young, have provoked nationwide discussion with their bitter and tragic stories of life under the Gang of Four. They write with convincing realism, and their characters show a measure of complexity that would not have been tolerated during the Cultural Revolution. The late Premier Chou En-lai's speech of June 19, 1961, which called for relaxation of control over writers, was released in its entirety with fanfare on February 4, 1979. A flood of responses followed, all clamoring for greater freedom in literature. New magazines, literary and general, are being published, including one that is the equivalent of *Good Housekeeping.* Writers are experimenting with new genres: the first science fiction to appear in the People's Republic was published in the August 1978 issue of the prestigious *People's Literature.*

Since millions have learned to read and write in the last thirty years, speculations on the phenomenon of unleashed creative energy in the People's Republic of China are hard to resist. Meanwhile, the creative writing that has already accumulated in the thirty years since the revolution begs to be recognized. Let us experience it in all its variety—some of it robust and sanguine, some skeptical and critical, and some trying to convey the bitter and the sweet in due proportion—a reflection of life in the People's Republic of China.

Chronology of Major Events
Relevant to PRC Literature

1949

Mar. 23   Second Plenum, Seventh Central Committee, CCP, directs all cadres to start participating in cultural struggle

July 1   Mao Tse-tung publishes "On People's Democracy," stressing need to reform intellectuals

2   National Assembly of Literary and Art Workers starts meeting in Peking

7   Chou En-lai reports before the Assembly, urging writers to accept CCP leadership, reform themselves, and strive to serve the people

19   All-China Federation of Literary and Art Circles (FLAC, with branches in major cities) formed, with Kuo Mo-jo as chairman, Mao Tun and Chou Yang as vice-chairmen; many other literary and art associations also formed at about the same time

Aug. 22   First campaign to question the appearance of bourgeois characters in literature begins in Shanghai publications

Sept. 25   *Literary Gazette,* organ of All-China FLAC, formally starts publication

Oct. 1   Mao Tun appointed minister in charge of Department of Cultural Affairs (DCA) in the State Council; Kuo Mo-jo chairs the Cultural and Educational Commission

1950

Feb. 14   Peking-Moscow treaty of alliance signed; influx of Russian literature begins

18   Poet Tai Wang-shu dies

Mar. 29   Kuo Mo-jo chairs Association for the Study of Folk Literature, with Lao She as vice-chairman

Mar.   Sometime in this month Mao Tse-tung condemns Yao K'o's *Malice of Empire* as betraying China and calls for nationwide denunciation of the play

Apr. 19   Party Central decides to launch criticism campaigns in mass media

May   DCA pushes for publication of a large number of literary works, including classical, modern, and translated works, performing arts, and literary theories

June 6 Third Plenum, Seventh Central Committee, decides on large-scale reform campaign (*cheng-feng* movement)

26   Korean War begins

July 11 Chou Yang appointed head of Central Commission for Theater Reform; Mao Tun in charge of Central Commission to direct motion picture industry, with Chiang Ching as a member of the Commission; DCA issues five-point directive on film-making

29   Shanghai FLAC established, with Hsia Yen as chairman; Pa Chin, Feng Hsüeh-feng, Mei Lan-fang, and Ho Lü-ting as vice-chairmen

Sept.   Tientsin FLAC established, Fang Chi and Lu Li among committee members

Oct. 25 Chinese Communist volunteer troops enter the Korean War

28   All-China FLAC calls upon writers and artists to support the Korean War

Nov. 27 DCA holds two-week national meeting on theater programs

29   *People's Daily* republishes Mao Tse-tung's "On Practice" and exhorts all writers and artists to study it

Dec.   Campaign to suppress counterrevolutionary elements spreads throughout the country

1951

Jan. 2 Central Institute of Literary Research established in Peking, jointly directed by DCA and All-China FLAC, to train literary workers

Mar. 5 All-China FLAC's Standing Committee announces survey showing seventy-four literary magazines in operation

Apr. 25 *Literary Gazette* starts drive to criticize the motion picture *Wu Hsün chuan*

May 5   State Council directive on theater reform issued

12   Chou Yang's speech at Central Institute of Literary Research urges adherence to Mao Tse-tung's literary policy

20   Mao Tse-tung's signed editorial in the *People's Daily* orders close critical attention to the movie *Wu Hsün chuan*

June 6 *People's Daily* calls for effort to maintain purity and health of the Chinese language

15 *Liberation Army Literature* (monthly) starts publication

16 DCA holds meeting of cultural work groups assigned to all parts of the country

July 23 *People's Daily* starts publishing historical documents related to the life of Wu Hsün

Oct. Folk Literature series published

10 *Selected Works of Mao Tse-tung*, Vol. 1, published

Nov. 17 All-China FLAC meeting decides on program of political education for writers

24 Chou Yang and Hu Ch'iao-mu start reform *(cheng-feng)* movement in literature and art

Dec. 20 Kuo Mo-jo awarded Stalin International Peace Prize

1952

Jan. *Drama* (monthly) published

Jan. Three Antis movement starts; writers respond with works on this theme

5 The People's Political Consultative Conference releases resolution to involve intellectuals in thought reform

Mar. 5 First group of writers goes to factories, farms, and army to learn from the proletariat

May 10 *Literary Gazette* calls for nationwide discussion on creating new heroes in literature

23 Reform *(cheng-feng)* movement spreads among writers and artists

Oct. 6 DCA sponsors first national drama festival

Dec. Second wave of writers goes to factories and farms to learn from the proletariat; land reform completed; literary works concentrate on land reform themes

26 DCA issues directive on improving the work of dramatic troupes

1953

Jan. First five-year plan begins

11 Chou Yang, second in command in Party Central's Propaganda Department and in DCA, publishes "Socialist Realism—the Road Ahead for Chinese Literature"

30 Lin Mo-han and Ho Ch'i-fang begin attack on Hu Feng in *Literary Gazette*

Feb. 22 Literary Research Institute established at Peking University (transferred to Academy of Science in 1956)

Mar. 24　National Assembly of Literary and Art Workers meets on literary productivity, reorganizes All-China FLAC, and creates mechanism to guide writers

28　Writers organized to go to the Korean front

July　*Literature in Translation (I-wen)* published, later renamed *World Literature (Shih-chieh wen-hsüeh)*

27　Truce in Korean War

Sept. 23　National Assembly of Literary and Art Workers meets again to organize Chinese Writers' Association (CWA) with branches in major cities

25　General Line (of national policy during the transition to a socialist state), designed by Party Central a year before, announced; drive begins for entire populace to study it

Oct. 9　Kuo Mo-jo chairs All-China FLAC; Mao Tun and Chou Yang serve as vice-chairmen; Mao Tun heads up national CWA, with Chou Yang, Ting Ling, Pa Chin, K'o Chung-p'ing, Lao She, Feng Hsüeh-feng, and Shao Ch'üan-lin as vice-chairmen

Dec. 24　State Council announces "Decisions on Strengthening Motion Picture Work"

1954

Jan. 19　All literary and art associations announce plans for activities to support the General Line

20　*Theater Journal (Hsi-chü pao)* starts publication

Mar. 1　"Literary Heritage" page starts in *Enlightenment Daily* (Peking) for purpose of critically restudying Chinese classics

May 3　Chinese People's Association for External Cultural Relations established, with Ch'u T'u-nan presiding and Ting Hsi-ling, Yang Han-sheng, and Hung Shen (three noted playwrights) as vice-presidents

June　Criticism campaign against Lu Ling's novels begins, later condemning him as a supporter of Hu Feng

7　DCA and National Federation of Labor Unions issue joint directive on strengthening cultural and artistic activities in the industries

Sept. 1　Li Hsi-fan and Lan Ling start attacking Yü P'ing-po's studies on *Dream of the Red Chamber*

Oct. 16　Mao Tse-tung sends letter to Politburo, supporting Li Hsi-fan's criticism against Yü P'ing-po over *Dream of the Red Chamber;* national campaign to criticize Yü and Hu Shih starts

28 Feng Hsüeh-feng, editor of *Literary Gazette*, criticized by poet Yüan Shui-p'ai because of Feng's negative comment on Li Hsi-fan; this starts the *Literary Gazette* Case leading to Feng's downfall

Dec. 2 Kuo Mo-jo chairs special committee appointed by Academy of Science and national CWA to criticize Hu Shih's thought

8 All-China FLAC and CWA jointly decide on criticism agains Yü P'ing-po and reorganization of *Literary Gazette*

1955

Feb. 5 CWA announces decision to criticize Hu Feng

Mar. 10 FLAC announces decision to criticize Hu Feng and Hu Shih and to expand struggle against bourgeois thought in literature and art

21–31 Second session of CCP's Seventh Congress adopts resolution on anti-Party clique of Kao Kang and Jao Shu-shih

May 13 *People's Daily* leads in national campaign to attack Hu Feng accused of leading an anti-Party clique
(Over 81,000 persons, many of them writers, accused of involvement in anti-Party activities during 1955)

Aug. 18 FLAC and CWA hold joint meeting on the Hu Feng case and other hidden anti-Party elements

Oct. 4 Literary activities respond to call for cooperativization of agriculture announced by Sixth Plenum of Seventh Central Committee, CCP

1956

Jan. 14 Chou En-lai speaks to special Party conference on intellectuals, urging relaxation of control

30 Chou Yang directs *Literary Gazette* to begin campaign against Ting Ling

Feb. 27 Chou Yang speaks at CWA conference defining the "mission to develop socialist literature"

Mar. 1 First national spoken drama festival begins in Peking

13 CWA adopts resolution on how to strengthen screenplay productivity

15 National conference of young writers begins

May 26 CCP's Propaganda Department chief Lu Ting-i issues call, "let a hundred kinds of flowers bloom together and let the hundred schools of thought freely contend"

Sept. 15 CCP's Eighth Congress convened, calls for carry-
          ing out the Hundred Flowers policy
Nov. 21   Ten-day conference of magazine editors begins
          in Peking to plan response to Hundred Flowers
          movement
Dec.   CWA Leadership reshuffled: first secretary, Mao
          Tun; secretaries, Lao She, Shao Ch'üan-lin, Liu
          Pai-yu, Ts'ao Yü, Tsang K'o-chia, Wu Tsu-
          Hsiang, Chang Chin-i, Chang Kuang-nien,
          Ch'en Pai-Ch'en, Yen Wen-ching

1957

Jan.   *Poetry Journal (Shih-k'an)* inaugurated with
          eighteen poems by Mao Tse-tung
Feb. 27   Mao Tse-tung addresses Supreme State Council
          on "How to Properly Handle Internal Contra-
          dictions among the People"
May 1   Party Central directs another reform *(cheng-
          feng)* movement; writers boost activities in
          Hundred Flowers movement
June 6   Struggle against rightists begins among writers;
          silenced and exiled by September: Ting Ling,
          Ch'en Ch'i-hsia, Feng Hsüeh-feng, Ai Ch'ing,
          Wu Tsu-kuang, Liu Pin-yen, and others
July 12   *People's Daily* calls for correction of the bour-
          geois tendency of *Literary Gazette*
24   *Harvest (Shou-huo)* begins publication, edited
          by Pa Chin
Sept. 1   *People's Daily* urges continued struggle against
          rightists among writers to protect socialist lit-
          erature

1958

Jan.   Second five-year plan starts
26   *Literary Gazette* repeats attack on Wang Shih-
          wei, Ting Ling, Hsiao Chün, Lo Feng, and Ai
          Ch'ing
Apr. 14   Large-scale campaign to collect and encourage
          folk songs begins
May   Second session of CCP's Eighth Congress issues
          new General Line calling for accelerated
          buildup of socialism; writers respond
June 1   Chou Yang writes "New Folk Songs Have Blazed
          a Trail for Poetry" in inaugural issue of Party
          organ *Red Flag (Hung-ch'i)*
9   *People's Daily* announces, "A cultural revolution
          has started"
26   *Literary Gazette* starts criticism campaign
          against revisionist literary policy of Yugo-
          slavia

Aug. 1 First national folk theater festival begins in Peking

Sept. 27 FLAC calls for encouragement of literary creativity among masses

Oct. Collections of local theater pieces first published

Nov. 28 Sixth Plenum of Eighth Central Committee decides on People's Commune movement, announces   Three   Red   Flags   campaign:
Commune, General Line, Great Leap Forward

Dec. Literary Research Institute of Academy of
Science publishes *Mao Tse-tung on Literature
and Art*
During 1958 many authors, including Pa Chin,
are criticized, largely because of K'ang Sheng's
campaign to "Pull out the White Flags"

1959

Feb. Campaign against Yang Mo's *Song of Youth* begins

June Wu Han's "Hai Jui Upbraids the Emperor" published

Aug. 2–16 Eighth Plenum, Eighth Central, meets at Mt. Lu
(Kiangsi Province) to condemn Marshal P'eng
Teh-huai, member of Politburo, vice-premier,
and defense minister, as a rightist opposing
Great Leap Forward

Sept. FLAC meets to support the anti-rightist decision
reached at Eighth Plenum; celebrated actor
Chou Hsin-fang stages the opera *Hai Jui Me-
morializes the Emperor* in Shanghai (Chou is
later condemned for it during Cultural Revolution)

Dec. 11 *Literary Gazette* criticizes Kuo Hsiao-ch'uan's
"Gazing at the Starry Sky"

1960

Jan. 11 *Literary Gazette* starts anti-revisionism campaign, resulting in the disgrace of Chao Hsün,
Jen Chün, Hai Mo, Yü Hei-ting, Ch'ien Ku-
jung, Chiang K'ung-yang, Li Ho-lin, Wang
Shu-ming, Wang Jen-shu, etc.

26 Yao Wen-yüan's essay attacks Wang Jen-shu's
theory of human nature

Feb. 25 48-day meeting of Shanghai Writers' Association
criticizes the revisionism of many leading
writers in that area

June CCP holds conference of leading writers and
educators from all over the country

July Chou Yang reports to the Third National Assembly of Literary and Art Workers on "The Path

of Socialist Literature and Art in China"; the month-long meeting decides on important measures to improve the writers' socialist awareness and eradicate bourgeois thought

Aug.   CWA leadership reshuffle: Mao Tun, Chou Yang, Pa Chin, K'o Chung-p'ing, Lao She, Shao Ch'üan-lin, Liu Pai-yu in power; FLAC leaders: Kuo Mo-jo, Mao Tun, Chou Yang, Pa Chin, Lao She, Hsü Kuang-p'ing, T'ien Han, Ou-yang Yü-ch'ien, Mei Lan-fang, Hsia Yen, Ts'ai Ch'u-sheng, Ho Hsiang-ning, Ma Szu-ts'ung, Fu Chung, Saifuting, Yang Han-sheng

Sept.–Oct.   Repeated directives denouncing bourgeois humanitarianism, upholding Mao Tse-tung's theory of struggle against revisionism in literature; Pearl Buck criticized

1961

Jan. 14–18   Ninth Plenum, Eighth Central, urges "readjustment, consolidation, reinforcement, and elevation" to salvage the Three Red Flags movement; Wu Han's play *Hai Jui's Dismissal from Office* published in *Peking Literature*

Mar.   Teng T'o starts column "Evening Talks at Yenshan" in *Peking Evening News,* continuing until September 1962

26   *Literary Gazette* calls for expansion of literary themes and styles

May   CCP's Propaganda Department issues ten-point directive to correct extremist leftism in literature

June 8   Month-long meeting on story films begins in Peking, drafts 32-point directive

19   Chou En-lai addresses the above meeting, urging democracy in literature

Aug.   *Drama* publishes T'ien Han's *Hsieh Yao-huan* and Meng Ch'ao's *Li Hui-niang,* both later denounced

1   CCP's ten-point directive handed to literary and art circles to study

31   Liao Mo-sha, Teng T'o's associate, publishes "No Harm to Have Ghosts in Literature," later denounced

Sept. 19   DCA urges development of folk drama

Oct. 10   Teng T'o, Wu Han, and Liao Mo-sha start column "Three-Family Village Notes" in Peking's *Frontline* magazine

Dec. 7   CCP Propaganda Department head Lu Ting-i revises ten-point directive into eight points

1962

Jan. CCP Central Work conference begins, 7,000 at-
      tending; Mao Tse-tung presents self-criticism
      and reveals author Wang Shih-wei's death in
      jail in Yenan back in the 1940s; failure of the
      Three Red Flags movement examined

Apr. CCP issues eight-point directive on literature
      and art

May   *People's Daily* urges "Serve the People" to com-
      memorate the twentieth anniversary of the
      Yenan Forum

July 6 Chiang Ching demands banning the play *Hai
        Jui's Dismissal from Office*

28   Historical novel *Liu Chih-tan* serialized in Pe-
        king's *Worker's Daily*

Aug. 4 Mao Tse-tung orders suspension of *Liu Chih-tan*

Sept. 21 Dramatist Ou-yang Yü-ch'ien dies in Peking

24   Tenth Plenum, Eighth Central, Mao Tse-tung ad-
        monishes the country "never to forget class
        struggle," and attacks *Liu Chih-tan,* resulting
        in removal of Vice-Premier Hsi Chung-hsün
        and others; K'ang Sheng and Chiang Ching de-
        mand DCA to ban theater programs featuring
        ghosts, followed by another demand to ban all
        traditional theater pieces

Aug. 2–16 Shao Ch'üan-lin chairs writers meeting in
           Dairen, discussing "middle character" issue

1963

Jan. 1 Politburo member, Shanghai CCP's first secre-
        tary, K'o Ch'ing-shih calls for bold writing for
        ten years; dispute follows; Mao Tse-tung per-
        sonally criticizes DCA as a bunch of "emperors
        and generals, feudal scholars and dainty maid-
        ens" for failure to push revolutionary operas
        organized by Chiang Ching

Mar. DCA bans theater programs featuring ghosts;
      Chiang Ching announces intention to reform
      literature and art

Apr. CCP's Propaganda Dept. criticizes Shanghai's K'o
      Ch'ing-shih; *Literary Gazette* attacks historian
      Chou Ku-ch'eng

27   FLAC meets to strengthen revolutionary line in
      literature and oppose revisionism

May   Mao Tse-tung orders "Socialist Education" move-
      ment, calling it the most important movement
      since land reform

6   Chiang Ching and K'o Ch'ing-shih criticize
      "ghost drama," attack cultural offices in Peking

Sept. DCA and Dramatists' Association meet on policy about the theater; *Literary Gazette* advocates equal emphasis on traditional theater, new historical plays, and contemporary (revolutionary) drama; the last prevails

Nov.   *Red Lantern* produced

26   *Literary Gazette* criticizes Russian films and "modern revisionist art"

Dec. 12 Mao Tse-tung comments on the lack of socialist reform in all literary genres

1964

Jan. 3 Liu Shao-ch'i, Teng Hsiao-p'ing, and P'eng Chen cool toward Mao-Chiang directives about literature, but still hold meeting to encourage more revolutionary operas

Mar. 31 DCA sponsors theater contest

June 5 Contemporary (revolutionary) opera festival in Peking, including *Red Lantern, Taking Tiger Mountain by Strategy*

24   Mao Tse-tung decries refusal of literary organizations to carry out CCP's directives

Aug.   Mao Tse-tung orders denunciation of films *Northland and South of the River* and *February, Early Spring*

Oct.   *Literary Gazette* attacks Shao Ch'üan-lin's "middle character" theory; Ou-yang Shan's novel, *Three-Family Lane*, criticized

1965

Jan.   CCP Propaganda chief Lu Ting-i replaces Mao Tun as minister of Cultural Affairs

30   *Literary Gazette* attacks Shu Ch'ün's story "Beyond the History of the Factory"

Feb. 16 *Literary Gazette* criticizes Ch'en Hsiang-ho's historical novels

May   Hsia Yen dismissed from office, his screenplay *Lin Family Store* denounced

June   K'o Ling's screenplay *Nightless City* criticized

Nov. 10 Yao Wen-yüan starts campaign to destroy *Hai Jui's Dismissal from Office* in Shanghai's *Wen-hui Daily;* Great Proletarian Cultural Revolution begins

1966

Feb. 2 Chiang Ching, by Lin Piao's order, holds conference in Shanghai on literary work in the armed forces; Mao Tse-tung edits the proceedings before publishing them

    3   P'eng Chen heads up a five-man committee on cultural revolution in Peking, prepares report on intellectual tasks; Liu Shao-ch'i approves and releases the report

Apr.   Shanghai faction of cultural revolution winning; P'eng Chen disappears

   14   Kuo Mo-jo publicly criticizes himself

   16   Criticism of Teng T'o begins; Teng soon dies of harassment

May 7   Mao writes letter to Lin Piao, ordering every Chinese to learn other productive jobs in addition to his or her own carrier (the May Seven directive)

   18   Lin Piao reports to Politburo meeting on struggle against P'eng Chen, Lo Jui-ch'ing, Lu Ting-i, and Yang Shang-k'un

   18   *People's Daily* reorganized with Shanghai faction winning

June–July   Red Guards start storming universities and other government agencies; Peking intellectuals subjected to physical abuse in struggle meetings

July 1   Chou Yang attacked

   18   Mao Tse-tung returns to Peking from Shanghai

Aug.   Mao Tse-tung writes big-character poster, "Bombard the Headquarters"

   8   Eleventh Plenum, Eighth Central, approves Mao's sixteen-point decision on Cultural Revolution

      Sometime in August Liu Shao-ch'i's downfall begins; Red Guards run rampant

   24   Lao She's body found in Peking creek, two days after being beaten severely by Red Guards; several other top literary leaders beaten at same time

Nov. 16   CCP and State Council order closing of schools to allow Red Guards to travel around the country

Dec.   Fighting surges between Mao followers and Liu supporters: literary journals suspend publication

   4   P'eng Chen arrested and abused by Red Guards; most leaders in Peking harassed

   10   T'ien Han dies in jail

   24   Red Guards arrest Marshal P'eng Teh-huai in Chengtu and take him to Peking for trial

1967–1969

      Supporters of Mao and Chiang Ching take over all offices and institutions throughout the country; Liu Shao-ch'i and Teng Hsiao-p'ing physically abused by Red Guards; mob action, civil war conditions, and confusion prevail; Chiang Ching and supporters urge "three dominances principle" in literature (*san-t'u-ch'u:* positive characters, heroic characters, central heroic figure—in ascending order of importance) and condemn all writings between 1949 and Cultural Revolution; literature completely paralyzed

1970–1973

Cultural Revolution simmers down slowly; some noncontroversial technical magazines gradually resume publication; writers sent to learn from the proletariat slowly return to cities; Shao Ch'üan-lin dies in jail on June 10, 1971; poet Tsang K'o-chia returns to Peking from countryside in Hsien-ning, Hupeh

1972

July 25 Wang Jen-shu (Pa Jen) dies doing hard labor in hometown as result of Red Guards' persecution

1974

Apr. 4 Playwright Ting Hsi-lin dies in Peking

1976

Poet Ai Ch'ing returns from Sinkiang to live in Peking; Feng Hsüeh-feng, disgraced in 1957–58, dies

Jan. Fifth five-year plan begins

Jan. *People's Literature* resumes publication, edited by poet Li Chi, still upholding revolutionary operas and Mao's directives on literature dated Dec. 12, 1963 and June 27, 1964; *Poetry Journal* resumes publication featuring two new poems by Mao Tse-tung, with Yen Ch'en as chief editor, and Tsou Ti-fan and K'o Yen as associate editors; *People's Drama* resumes publication

8 Chou En-lai dies

Apr. 5 Riot at the Heavenly Peace Gate in Peking: police clash with supporters of Chou En-lai and Teng Hsiao-p'ing

Sept. 9 Mao Tse-tung dies: Hua Kuo-feng succeeds him; Teng Hsiao-p'ing returns to power

Oct. Poet Kuo Hsiao-ch'uan dies

Oct. Gang of four (Chiang Ching, Chang Ch'un-ch'iao, Wang Hung-wen, and Yao Wen-yüan) officially denounced

1977

During the year, over thirty new full-length novels published; many old novels once condemned during the Cultural Revolution
republished, including *The Builders*, *Li Tzu-
ch'eng*, *Red Rock*, *Hurricane*, *Sea of Forest on
Snow-covered Plain*, *Song of Youth*, *Wildfire
and Wind Vie in an Old City*, *Heroes of Lü-
liang Mountains*, *New Romance of Heroes and
Heroines*; Lin Mo-han returns to Peking to
prepare annotated edition of *Complete Works
of Lu Hsun*

July 24 Poet Ho Ch'i-fang dies

Oct. Chou Yang, one of Four Villains, reappears in
public

Nov. Liu Hsin-wu's "Class Monitor," exposing evil of
Gang of Four in education, appears in *People's
Literature*; *Kwangtung Literature* criticizes
Hao Jan

25 Mao Tun resumes writing; his critical essay
against the Gang of Four appears in *People's
Daily*

Dec. 28 *People's Literature* sponsors four-day conference
to discuss new policy after the fall of the Gang
of Four

1978

Nearly all literary organizations resume operation; Mao Tun and Chou Yang resume leadership; *World Literature (Shih-chieh wen-
hsüeh)* resumes operation; twenty-two world
literature masterpieces in translation scheduled for reappearance

Jan. *Poetry Journal* publishes Mao Tse-tung's July 21,
1965, letter to Ch'en Yi discussing poetry; other
major publications also print it; *People's Literature* prints Hsü Ch'ih's "The Goldbach Con-
jecture," a report on mathematician Ch'en
Ching-jun, drawing nationwide attention

10 Works by Ma Feng, Chün Ch'ing, Liang Pin, Sun
Li, and others, condemned during Cultural
Revolution, scheduled for republication

Feb. *Literary Criticism* (*Wen-hsüeh p'ing-lun*, a bi-
monthly) resumes publication

Mar. Li Hsi-fan, whose attack on Yü P'ing-po forshad-
owed Cultural Revolution, criticized in *Literary Criticism*

Apr. 30 "Red Flag," first poem by Ai Ch'ing in twenty
years, appears in *Wen-hui Daily*, Shanghai

June Novelist Liu Ch'ing dies

12 Kuo Mo-jo dies

28 Wu Tsu-kuang announces plan to write play based on life of Mei Lan-fang

July *Literary Gazette* resumes publication

Aug. *People's Literature* publishes first science fiction

Nov. Poems collected during the Heavenly Peace Gate riot published; Ts'ao Yü's five-act historical play, *Wang Chao-chün,* published; death of Chao Shu-li under Red Guard torture reported by novelist Ch'en Teng-k'o in *Literary Gazette*

1979

Jan. Novelist Hao Jan, former CCP propaganda chief Lu Ting-i, playwright Yang Han-sheng (one of Four Villains) reappear in public; P'eng Teh-huai's case reversed

16 Wu Han posthumously restored to honor; P'eng Chen's case reversed

17 *Liu Chih-tan,* the novel banned by Mao Tse-tung for sixteen years, scheduled for republication

Feb. Pa Chin publishes account of his and his wife's suffering during Cultural Revolution; Hsia Yen, disabled, appointed advisor to DCA; Ting Ling back in Peking

4 Chou En-lai's June 19, 1961 speech urging more democracy in literature reissued

Mar. Hsiao Chün seen in Peking

26 Liu Hsin-wu and Wang Ya-p'ing (two new writers) and Chou Li-po win top recognition in 1978 short story review

Apr. 21 T'ien Han posthumously restored to honor

24 Liu Pai-yü appointed head of cultural affairs in the Political Department of the People's Liberation Army

May 20 Irony over *Dream of the Red Chamber:* Yü P'ing-po and Li Hsi-fan, two ideological enemies, drink toast at dinner celebrating establishment of *Dream of the Red Chamber Journal* in Peking

PART ONE

From Yenan to Peking

(1942–1955)

The literature of the People's Republic of China began not with the thunderous applause that greeted the founding of that new nation in October 1949 in Peking, but with the Yenan Forum on Literature and Art in May 1942.

Following in the wake of the May Fourth movement of 1919,* itself a dramatic release of creative energy, and nurtured on nineteenth-century liberalism, humanitarianism, and social consciousness, Communist and other leftist writers in the early 1940s were still laboring under illusions of a socialist utopia where a writer was free to—indeed, obligated to—criticize any established order for its imperfections. Hence the disputes between Zola's realism and Gorki's realism (see Hu Feng, below), between permission to criticize the Party and need for a unified force to support the Party (see Mao Tun and Chou Yang), between presenting the complexity of man to mirror real life and upholding socialist heroic models for the masses to emulate (see Shao Ch'üan-lin).

In 1942, just over six years after the Long March,† with the end of the war against the Japanese and the struggle against the Kuomintang still nowhere in sight, the writers and artists assembled in Yenan, veteran Communists and new converts alike, had already shown enough divergent views on what literature and art should be and do in China's Communist society to forecast the controversies and literary purges that were to take place in the following decades. These issues were causing sufficient turmoil on the literary front for

---

*On May 4, 1919, students in Peking demonstrated against the Versailles decision to give to Japan former German possessions in Shantung. It was a dramatic expression of widespread dissatisfaction with China's intellectual, political, and social ills, and the beginning of intensified movements to seek reform and revolution. [K.Y.H.]

†An 8,000-mile trek to escape Kuomintang siege and to consolidate scattered Communist forces in China, the Long March started in Juichin, Kiangsi Province, in October 1934 and ended in Yenan, Shensi Province, in December 1935. [K.Y.H.]

27

Mao Tse-tung to call a three-week conference in Yenan in May 1942, with Mao himself delivering the charges at the beginning and making the summary at the end (see below).

When the new socialist nation was born in Peking on October 1, 1949, the dust had not yet settled from the conflicts of the preceding years. The fresh experiences of land reform, the Korean War, and memories of the bloody struggle to power understandably dominated the writing of this period, but the call to socialist reconstruction had already stirred such new and old writers as Fei Li-wen and Ai Wu to depict the positive. Cheery tunes, focusing on spring growth and autumn harvest, were sung by the poets; Liang Shang-ch'üan lavished his lyricism over the beauty of his old but new motherland, and Shih Fang-yü struck what must have been central in everyone's heart at the time: let there be peace in the world. Meanwhile, Ho Ch'iu's comedy poked fun at the emerging evils of a new bureaucracy that repeated much of the old malpractice.

MAO TSE-TUNG

(1893–1976)

The following excerpt from Mao's "Talks at the Yenan Forum on Literature and Art" is taken from the 1965 official English translation published in Peking. Subheads have been added.   —K.Y.H.

---

from Talks at the Yenan Forum on Literature and Art

THE PURPOSE OF THE CONFERENCE

The purpose of our meeting today is precisely to fit art and literature properly into the whole revolutionary machine as one of its component parts, to make them a powerful weapon for uniting and educating the people and for attacking and annihilating the enemy and to help the people to fight the enemy with one heart and one mind. What are the problems to be solved in order to achieve this objective? I think they are the problems of the standpoint, the attitude and the audience of the artists and writers and of how they should work and how they should study.

Standpoint: Our standpoint is that of the proletariat and the broad masses of the people. For members of the Communist Party this means that they must adopt the standpoint of the Party and adhere to Party spirit and Party policies. Are there any of our artists and writers who still lack a correct or clear understanding on this point? I think there are. Quite a number of our comrades have often departed from the correct standpoint.

Attitude: Our specific attitudes toward specific things arise from our standpoint. For example: Should we praise or should we expose? This is a question of attitude. Which of these two attitudes should we adopt? I should say both and it all depends on whom you are dealing with. There are three kinds of people: the enemy, the allies in the united front and our own people, namely, the masses and their vanguard. Three different attitudes must be adopted towards these three kinds of people. With regard to our enemies, i.e. the Japanese imperialists and all other enemies of the people, the task of revolutionary artists and writers is to expose their cruelty and chicanery, point out the tendency of their inevitable defeat and encourage the anti-Japanese army and people to fight them with one heart and one mind and overthrow them resolutely. In our attitude towards our various allies in the united front, we ought to promote unity as well as criticism, and there should be different kinds of unity and different kinds of criticism. We support their resistance to Japan and commend them for their achievements. But we ought to criticize them if they do not put

29

up an active resistance to Japan. We must resolutely combat anyone if he opposes communism and the people and moves farther down the path of reaction with every passing day. As to the masses of the people, their toil and struggle, their army and their party, we should of course praise them. The people also have their shortcomings. Many among the proletariat still retain petty-bourgeois ideas, while both the peasantry and the urban petty bourgeoisie entertain backward ideas—these are the burdens handicapping them in their struggles. We should spend a long time and be patient in educating them and helping them to remove the burdens from their backs and to fight against their own shortcomings and errors so that they can take big strides forward. In the course of their struggles they have remolded or are remolding themselves, and our art and literature should depict this process of remolding. We should not take a one-sided view and mistakenly ridicule them or even be hostile towards them unless they persist in their errors. What we produce should enable them to unite, to advance and to stride forward with one heart and one mind, discarding what is backward and promoting what is revolutionary; it certainly should not do the opposite.

Audience: For whom are the artistic and literary works produced? Since the audience for our art and literature is made up of workers, peasants, soldiers and their cadres, the problem arises of how to understand these people and to know them well. [Our writers and artists] failed to understand language, i.e., they lacked an adequate knowledge of the rich and lively language of the masses of the people. Many comrades love to talk about "transformation along the popular line," but what does that mean? It means that the ideas and feelings of our artists and writers should be fused with those of the broad masses of workers, peasants and soldiers. If you want the masses to understand you and want to become one with them, you must be determined to undergo a long and even painful process of remolding. In this connection I might mention the transformation of my own feelings. I began as a student and acquired at school the habits of a student; in the presence of a crowd of students who could neither fetch nor carry for themselves, I used to feel it undignified to do any manual labor, such as shouldering my own luggage. At that time it seemed to me that the intellectuals were the only clean persons in the world, and the workers and peasants seemed rather dirty beside them. I could put on the clothes of other intellectuals because I thought they were clean, but I would not put on clothes belonging to a worker or peasant because I felt they were dirty. Having become a revolutionary I found myself in the same ranks as the workers, peasants and soldiers of the revolutionary army, and gradually I became familiar with them and they with me too. It was then and only then that a fundamental change occurred in the bourgeois and petty-bourgeois feelings implanted in me by the bourgeois schools. I came to feel that it was those unremolded intellectuals who were unclean as compared with the workers and peasants, while the workers and peasants are after all the cleanest persons, cleaner than both the bourgeois and the petty-bourgeois intellectuals, even though their hands are soiled and their feet smeared with cow dung. This is what is meant by having one's feelings transformed, changed from those of one class into those of another.

THE PROBLEMS

What then is the crux of our problems? I think our problems are basically those of working for the masses and of how to work for them. If these two problems are not solved, or [are] solved inadequately, our artists and writers will be ill-adapted to their circumstances and unfit for their tasks.

Problem 1: For whom are our art and literature intended?

This problem has, as a matter of fact, been solved long ago by Marxists, and especially by Lenin. As far back as 1905 Lenin emphatically pointed out that our art and literature should "serve the millions upon millions of working people." It might seem that this problem has been solved by our comrades working in art and literature in the anti-Japanese base areas and needs no further discussion. But actually this is not the case. Many comrades have by no means arrived at a clear-cut solution of this problem. Consequently their ideas concerning the guiding principles of art and literature have been more or less at variance with the needs of the masses and the demands of actual struggles.

Quite true, there exist art and literature intended for the exploiters and oppressors. Even today such art and literature still retain a considerable influence in China. The art and literature for the bourgeoisie are bourgeois art and literature. People like Liang Shih-ch'iu, whom Lu Hsün severely criticized, may talk about art and literature as transcending the classes, but in fact they all uphold bourgeois art and literature and oppose proletarian art and literature. So far as we are concerned, art and literature are intended for the people. We have said that China's new culture at the present stage is an anti-feudal, anti-imperialist culture of the broad masses of the people under the leadership of the proletariat. Everything that truly belongs to the broad masses of the people must now of necessity be under the leadership of the proletariat. Naturally the same applies to the new art and literature in the new culture. We should take over the rich legacy and succeed to the fine tradition of Chinese and foreign art and literature of the past, but we must do this with our eyes upon the broad masses of the people.

Who are the People?

The broadest masses of the people who constitute more than 90 per cent of the total population are the workers, peasants, soldiers and the urban petty bourgeoisie. So our art and literature are first of all for the workers who form the class which leads the revolution. Secondly they are for the peasants who form the most numerous and steadfast allies in the revolution. Thirdly, they are for the armed workers and peasants, i.e., the Eighth Route and New Fourth Armies of the revolutionary war. Fourthly, they are for the working masses of the urban petty bourgeoisie together with its intelligentsia, who are also allies in the revolution and are capable of lasting cooperation with us.

In theory or in words, none in our ranks would consider the masses of workers, peasants and soldiers less important than the petty-bourgeois intellectuals. I am speaking of their deeds and actions. In deed and action, do they regard the petty-bourgeois intellectuals as more important than the workers, peasants and soldiers? I think they do. Many comrades are concerned with studying the petty-bourgeois intellectuals, analyzing their psychology, giving emphatic expression to their life and excusing or defending their shortcomings, rather than with leading these people, together with themselves, to get closer to the masses of workers, peasants, and soldiers. Many comrades, because they are petty bourgeois in origin and intellectuals themselves, take the stand of the petty bourgeoisie and produce their works as a kind of self-expression of the petty bourgeoisie. As to the masses of workers, peasants and soldiers, they seldom come into contact with them, do not understand or study them, do not have bosom friends among them and are not adept at describing them. Thus they have not yet solved or unequivocally solved the problem "For Whom are art and literature intended?" And this refers not only to the newcomers in Yenan; even among those who have been to the front and worked for a few years in our base areas and in the Eighth Route and New Fourth Armies, many have not solved this problem thoroughly. To solve this problem thoroughly, a long time is required, say, eight or ten years.

Problem 2: How to serve the masses? Elevation or popularization?

Since our art and literature are basically intended for the workers, peasants, and soldiers, popularization means extending art and literature among these people while elevation means raising their level of artistic and literary appreciation. We must popularize what is needed and can be readily accepted by the workers, peasants and soldiers themselves. Consequently the duty of learning from the workers, peasants and soldiers precedes the task of educating them. This is even more true of elevation. There must be a basis to elevate from. It can only be raised from the basis of the masses of the workers, peasants and soldiers. This means not that we raise the workers, peasants and soldiers to the level of the feudal class, the bourgeoisie or the petty-bourgeois intelligentsia, but that we raise them up along their own line of advance, along the line of advance of the proletariat.

The problem facing the workers, peasants and soldiers today is this: engaged in a ruthless and sanguinary struggle against the enemy, they remain illiterate and uncultured as a result of the prolonged rule of the feudal and bourgeois classes and consequently they badly need a widespread campaign of enlightenment. Under the present conditions, therefore, popularization is the more pressing task. It is wrong to despise and neglect this task.

But popularization and elevation cannot be sharply separated. Elevation does not take place in mid-air, nor behind closed doors, but on the basis of popularization. It is at once determined by popularization and gives direction to it. Thus our elevation is on the basis of popularization while our popularization is under the guidance of elevation. This being the case, the work of popularization in our sense not only constitutes no obstacle to elevation but affords a basis for our work of elevation on a limited scale at present, as well as preparing the necessary conditions for our far more extensive work of elevation in the future.

All the [expert] comrades should keep in close touch with the popularizers of art and literature among the masses, help and guide the popularizers of art and literature as well as learn from them, and through them draw nourishment from the masses to develop and enrich themselves and to prevent their specialities from becoming empty, lifeless castles in the air detached from the masses and from reality.

The source of art and literature

What after all is the source of any kind of art and literature? An artistic or literary work is ideologically the product of the human brain reflecting the life of a given society. In the life of the people itself lies a mine of raw material for art and literature, namely, things in their natural state, things crude, but also most lively, rich and fundamental. This is the only source, for there can be no other source. All revolutionary artists and writers of China, all artists and writers of high promise, must, for long periods of time, unreservedly and wholeheartedly go into the midst of the masses, the masses of workers, peasants and soldiers; they must go into fiery struggles, go to the only, the broadest, the richest source to observe, learn, study and analyze all men, all classes, all kinds of people, all the vivid patterns of life and struggle and all raw material of art and literature, before they can proceed to creation.

The relationship between life and art/literature

Though man's social life constitutes the only source for art and literature, and is incomparably more vivid and richer than art and literature as such, the people are not satisfied with the former alone and demand the latter. Why? Because, although both are beautiful, life as reflected in artistic and literary works can and ought to be on a higher level and of a greater power and better focused, more typical, nearer the ideal, and therefore more universal than actual everyday life. Revolutionary art and literature should create all kinds of characters on the basis of actual life and help the masses to push history forward. For example, on the one hand there are people suffering from hunger, cold and oppression and on the other hand there are men exploiting and oppressing men—a contrast that exists everywhere and seems quite commonplace to people; artists and writers, however, can create art and literature out of such daily occurrences by organizing them, bringing them to a focal point and making the contradictions and struggles in them typical—create art and literature that can awaken and arouse the masses and impel them to unite and struggle to change their environment. If there were no such art and literature, this task could not be fulfilled or at least not effectively and speedily fulfilled.

Problem 3: Criteria of art and literary criticism

Art and literary criticism presents a complex problem which requires much study of a special kind. Here I shall stress only the basic problem of criteria in criticism.

a) Political criterion

According to the political criterion, all works are good that facilitate unity and resistance to Japan, that encourage the masses to be of one heart and one mind and that oppose retrogression and promote progress; on the other hand, all works are bad that undermine unity and resistance to Japan, that sow dissension and discord among the masses and that oppose progress and drag the people back. And how can we tell the good from the bad here—by the motive (subjective intention) or by the effect (social practice)? Idealists stress motive and ignore effect, while mechanical materialists stress effect and ignore motive; in contradistinction from either, we dialectical materialists insist on the unity of motive and effect. The motive of serving the masses is inseparable from the effect of winning their approval, and we must unite the two. In examining the subjective intention of an artist, i.e., whether his motive is correct and good, we do not look at his declaration but at the effect his activities (mainly his works) produce on society and the masses. Social practice and its effect are the criteria for examining the subjective intention or the motive.

[Some say] "It is not a matter of standpoint; the standpoint is correct, the intention good, and the ideas are all right, but the expression is faulty and produces a bad effect." Is the question of effect not one of standpoint? A person who, in doing a job, minds only the motive and pays no regard to the effect is very much like a doctor who hands out prescriptions and does not care how many patients may die of them. Of course a person is liable to mistakes in estimating the result of an action before it is taken; but are his intentions really good if he adheres to the same old rut even when facts prove that it leads to bad results? One who has a truly good intention must criticize with the utmost candor his own shortcomings and mistakes in work, and make up his mind to correct them. That is why the Communists have adopted the method of self-criticism. Only such a standpoint is the correct one.

Under the general principle of unity and resistance to Japan, we must tolerate all artistic and literary works expressing every kind of political attitude. But at the same time we must firmly uphold our principles in our criticism, and adhere to our standpoint and severely criticize and repudiate all artistic and literary works containing views against the nation, the sciences, the people and communism, because such works, in motive as well as in effect, are detrimental to unity and the resistance to Japan.

b) Artistic criterion

According to the artistic criterion, all works are good or comparatively good that are relatively high in artistic quality; and bad or comparatively bad that are relatively low in artistic quality. Of course, this distinction also depends on social effect. As there is hardly an artist who does not consider his own work excellent, our criticism ought to permit the free competition of all varieties of artistic works; but it is entirely necessary for us to pass correct judgments on them according to the criteria of the science of art, so that we can gradually raise the art of a lower level to a higher level, and to change the art which does not meet the requirements of the struggle of the broad masses into art that does meet them.

c) Relation between political and artistic criteria

We believe there is neither an abstract and absolutely unchangeable political criterion, nor an abstract and absolutely unchangeable artistic criterion, for every class in a class society has its own political and artistic criteria. But all classes in all class societies place the political criterion first and the artistic criterion second. Some things which are basically reactionary from the political point of view may yet be artistically good, but the more artistic such a work may be, the greater harm will it do to the people, and the more reason for us to reject it. What we demand is unity of politics and art, of content and form, and of the revolutionary political content and the highest possible degree of perfection in artistic form.

As I see it, the political side is more of a problem at present. Some comrades lack elementary political knowledge and consequently all kinds of muddled ideas arise. Let me give a few instances found in Yenan.

Problem 4: Muddled ideas stemming from lack of
political knowledge

a) The theory of human nature

There is only human nature in the concrete, no human nature in the abstract. In a class society there is only human nature that bears the stamp of a class, but no human nature transcending classes. We uphold the human nature of the proletariat and of the great masses of the people, while landlord and bourgeois classes uphold the nature of their own classes as if—though they do not say so outright—it were the only kind of human nature. The human nature boosted by certain petty-bourgeois intellectuals is also divorced from or opposed to that of the great masses of the people; what they call human nature is in substance nothing but bourgeois individualism, and consequently in their eyes proletarian human nature is contrary to their human nature. This is the "theory of human nature" advocated by some people in Yenan as the so-called basis of their theory of art and literature, which is utterly mistaken.

b) The fundamental point of departure for art and literature is love, the love of mankind

Love is a concept, a product of objective practice. Fundamentally, we do not start from a concept but from objective practice. Our artists and writers who come from the intelligentsia love the proletariat because social life has made them feel that they share the same fate with the proletariat. We hate Japanese imperialism because the Japanese imperialists oppress us. There is no love or hatred in the world that has not its cause. As to the so-called "love of mankind," there has been no such all-embracing love since humanity was divided into classes. All the ruling classes in the past liked to advocate it, and many so-called sages and wise men also did the same, but nobody has ever really practiced it, for it is impracticable in a class society. Genuine love of mankind will be born only when class distinctions have been eliminated throughout the world.

c) Objectivity of art and literature

Art and literature have always described the bright as well as the dark side of things impartially, on a fifty-fifty basis. This statement contains a number of muddled ideas. Art and literature have not always done so. Many petty-bourgeois writers have never found the bright side and their works are devoted to exposing the dark side, the so-called "literature of exposure"; there are even works which specialize in propagating pessimism and misanthropy. On the other hand Soviet literature during the period of socialist reconstruction portrays mainly the bright side. It also describes shortcomings in work and villainous characters, but such descriptions serve only to bring out the brightness of the whole picture, and not on a "compensating basis." Bourgeois writers of reactionary periods portray the revolutionary masses as ruffians and describe the bourgeois as saints, thus reversing the so-called bright and dark sides. Only truly revolutionary artists and writers can correctly solve the problem whether to praise or to expose. All dark forces which endanger the masses of the people must be exposed while all revolutionary struggles of the masses must be praised—this is the basic task of all revolutionary artists and writers.

d) The task of art and literature has always been to expose

This sort of argument, like the one above, arises from the lack of knowledge of the science of history. We have already shown that the task of art and literature does not consist solely in exposure. For the revolutionary artists and writers the objects to be exposed can never be the masses of the people, but only the aggressors, exploiters and oppressors, and their evil aftermath brought to the people. The people have their shortcomings too, but these are to be overcome by means of criticism and self-criticism within the ranks of the people themselves, and to carry on such criticism and self-criticism is also one of the most important tasks of art and literature. However, we should not call that "exposing the people."

e) No more need for satire?

[Some say], "This is still a period of the essay, and the style should still be that of Lu Hsün." Living under the rule of the dark forces, deprived of freedom of speech, Lu Hsün had to fight by means of burning satire and freezing irony cast in essay form, and in this he was entirely correct. We too must hold up to sharp ridicule the fascists, the Chinese reactionaries and everything endangering the people; but in our border region of Shensi-Kansu-Ningsia and the anti-Japanese base areas in the enemy's rear, where revolutionary artists and writers are given full freedom and democracy and only counterrevolutionaries are deprived of them, essays must not be written simply in the same style as Lu Hsün's. Are we then to give up satire altogether? No. Satire is always necessary. But there are all kinds of satire; the kind of [emanating from] our enemies, the kind for our allies, and the kind for our own ranks—each of them assumes a different attitude. We are not opposed to satire as a whole, but we must not abuse it.

f) Reluctance to praise and eulogize

[Some say], "I am not given to praise and eulogy; works which extol the bright side of things are not necessarily great, nor are works which depict the dark side necessarily poor."

If you are a bourgeois artist or writer, you will extol not the proletariat but the bourgeoisie, and if you are a proletarian artist or writer, you will extol not the bourgeoisie, but the proletariat. You must do one or the other. Those works which extol the bright side of the bourgeoisie are not necessarily great, while those works which depict the so-called "dark side" of the proletariat are certainly poor—are these not the facts recorded in the history of art and literature?

Excerpted by Kai-yu Hsu

MAO TUN
(Shen Yen-ping, 1896–)

Mao Tun, in whose life is reflected the entire history of China's new literature, has a bibliography rivaled in length and variety perhaps only by that of Kuo Mo-jo, and an international reputation challenged only by Lu Hsün. Except for a short eclipse during the Cultural Revolution, Mao Tun has maintained his position of prominence in Chinese literature—he shared the gavel with Kuo Mo-jo at the Third Congress of the All-China Federation of Literary and Art Circles in May 1978 in Peking.

High school in Hangchow, college education at Peking University (1913–1916), and ten years of editorial apprenticeship and practice in the Commercial Press, China's largest, prepared Mao Tun for his eventful literary career. Between leading literary movements in Shanghai, editing several of China's most influential literary magazines, and a trip to Yenan in 1940, he published diligently. *Disillusionment, Spring Silkworms, Autumn Harvest, Lingering Winter, Decay, Rainbow,* and the *Lin Family Store* are among his successful novels.

He is best known and will be long remembered for his part in founding the Literary Research Society to promote in-depth realism in the 1920s; for *Midnight,* his mature and complex novel (some say the greatest in twentieth-century China) reflecting the nightmarish world of Shanghai in the early 1930s; for his volumes of thoughtful literary criticism, collected over the decades; and for his literary leadership, which, though quite clearly identified with Marxism, maintained a sense of sobriety even during the darkest days of ideological purges.

Unfortunately, his post-1949 official duties as Minister of Cultural Affairs in the State Council have kept him from creative writing, leaving us only a huge quantity of semiofficial pronouncements, such as the sample translated below.

—K.Y.H.

We Must Still Prepare for a Long and Determined Struggle

*In Commemoration of the Thirtieth Anniversary
of the May Fourth Movement*

The May Fourth Movement was a mass movement as well as an ideological movement. That it was also a political movement goes without saying. Ideologically, opposition to feudalism (opposition to traditional Confucian morality) and advocacy of the emancipation of individuality became its main thrust during those years. As a mass movement it swept over the entire nation like

37

wildfire, and we cannot but acknowledge the fact that petty bourgeois intellectuals, i.e., student youth, were its main strength at that time. The political slogans of the May Fourth, as we all know, were "oppose feudalism," "oppose imperialism," and "liberate the oppressed classes" (even though we were not too clear as to that latter slogan in those days).

The leading figures of the May Fourth were divided mainly into two ideological camps: one was the Marxist faction, and an excellent representative of this group is Li Ta-chao, whose martyrdom of twenty-two years ago we have so recently commemorated here. The other faction can be called, albeit not without stretching the term, the bourgeois liberals (at that time they were still hiding their true identity behind the mask of liberalism). They have now degenerated into stupid and shameless lackeys of Chiang Kai-shek and America. The war criminal Hu Shih is a most typical representative of this faction. The prestige and grass-roots support given to bourgeois liberal values in those days exceeded that given to Marxism, and this is a fact which we need not gloss over. However, in terms of the ideological movements of the past thirty years, it has been the Marxism-Leninism of the working class and not the liberalism of the bourgeoisie which has given real substance to the ideas and strengthened the fighting spirit of the May Fourth. At each crisis period confronting the nation during those same thirty years, it was never the bourgeois liberals who pointed out the historical trend towards national liberation, who resolutely and correctly led the people forward. No, instead it was the vanguard of the working class—the Marxist-Leninist party.

This year [1949] marks the thirtieth anniversary of the May Fourth. During this "Red May," an old semifeudal, semicolonized China passes forever from the scene, and a world-shaking new China comes into being; only now is the historical mission of the May Fourth fulfilled. Is there anyone who would deny that this indisputable fact [that the Marxist-Leninist party, not the bourgeois, ushered in a new China] has proved, once and for all, with whom the truth lies, whose star is on the rise, as distinguished from those trying to swim against the tide of history and whose destiny is on the decline?

There was a time during the initial period of the May Fourth when China's national bourgeoisie* did demonstrate some enthusiasm and toyed with the idea of throwing itself into the fray. But that same national bourgeoisie just did not have what it takes. Those bourgeois intellectuals, frightened out of their wits by the laboring masses' demands for liberation, proved only too willing to make their peace with imperialism. Under the threats and blandishments thrown up by the forces of reaction, domestic and foreign, our national bourgeoisie's short-lived enthusiasm quickly expired as it swung to the right and proceeded, promptly, to turn reactionary. One segment of the national bourgeoisie went so far as to fall into the embrace of the feudalistic landlord and compradore class and got itself enrolled on the payroll of imperialism. The analogous manifestation of this same thing in the cultural realm was the

---

National bourgeoisie refers to the moneyed class of Chinese which arose toward the end of the nineteenth century. Its members were nationalistic, as distinguished from the equally moneyed compradore class which rose by collaborating with and serving the interests of foreign capitalists. [K.Y.H.]

vacillation and shilly-shallying of the liberals and the eventual descent into decadence by a certain percentage of them. Such examples are too numerous to require mention here. It may be said that in the early days of the May Fourth, the liberals still carried the banner of opposition to feudalism. In any case, they at least did not yet dare to support imperialism openly, and the young petty-bourgeois intellectuals at the time could still harbor some illusions about liberalism. Even so, it was not long before they either became disillusioned and demoralized or else crossed over resolutely to join ranks with those who marched under the Marxist banner. This was something we all personally witnessed or experienced and there is no need to mention further examples.

At that time, Marxism-Leninism in China was still in the process of developing. China's revolutionary movement committed some errors and suffered some setbacks. For the demoralized educated youth, there was a brief period of ideological chaos. Petty-bourgeois youth sought refuge in decadence—heavy drinking with girl friends in garden pavilions, fist-pounding on the tables, hysterical shouts of "Go among the people! Live among the people!" Enraptured with individualistic anarchism, these sons of déclassé families, who wore faded, unconventional clothing and had already exhausted every cent of their wife's dowry and personal savings, would "passionately" and self-righteously yell: "Down with everything! After everything has been destroyed, utopia will then appear!" The metaphysical crazies, the sleepwalkers, the advocates of "art above all else" hiding out in their ivory towers at the crossroads, the futurists, the *fin de siècle* melancholiacs, the traditionalist reactionaries hoping to restore the past, the advocates of total Europeanization, etc., all came tumbling onto the stage at once. Finally, the shining light of Marxism-Leninism gradually brought order and clarity to all this ideological chaos. And was this not something that we all experienced, something that seems as if it happened only yesterday?

From Darwinism to Marxism, from Ibsen to Gorki, from "experimentalism" to the dialectic, from critical realism to socialist realism, from the wholesale adoption of Europe's recent artistic and literary forms to raising the whole issue of national forms, steady progress has been sustained over the course of the past thirty years. The path has been one that required a constant struggle on two fronts, and although it has veered and twisted at times along the way, it was never merely a cyclical course leading us back into the past. "Thirty years makes a generation." Today, Mao Tse-tung Thought—the Chinese form of Marxism-Leninism—has won a victory on the cultural front just as decisive as the great victories won on the political and military fronts.

It is not true, however, that the enemies of the New Democracy culture which is guided by Mao Tse-tung Thought have been completely disarmed and completely eliminated. Among the enemies of the culture of New Democracy are imperialist culture, feudal culture, and compradore culture. Today, thirty years to the day since the May Fourth incident, Shanghai, the greatest cultural center of South China, is either on the eve of liberation or has just been liberated. During these thirty years, Shanghai has been the forward outpost along the cultural battleline, the site of the most intensive struggle. Just as it has been the "Coexistence and Coprosperity Sphere" for imperialist culture, feudal culture, and compradore culture all along, it will, I fear, also prove to be the most intractable area in the whole country. Just as we cannot expect the forces of reaction to disappear immediately once the revolution is victorious throughout the entire country, so also the liberation of Shanghai will not spell the annihilation of these three types of reactionary culture. The residual evil of imperialist culture, feudal culture, and compradore culture will still lurk in every part of the nation and we must still carry out a long and determined struggle.

We are opposed to imperialist culture, but that does not mean that we will indiscriminately reject the constructive scholarship and thinking, the classical art and literature, the critical realist art and literature which can be found even in the imperialist countries. No, the things to which we are opposed and which must be completely cleaned out from our cultural sphere are those which function as the assault troops for imperialist aggression and have a spiritually corrupting and numbing effect on the Chinese people—things such as individualism, decadent values, all the so-called "modernists" in art and literature characteristic of the European bourgeoisie in its declining period. I refer particularly to that which is termed "American-style democracy," "the free life-style of the American way of life," and the art, literature, and philosophy of commercialism, which have all flooded the market neatly packaged under the label of "Americanism."

It is true, of course, that our Liberation Army has been delighted to receive the American equipment and weapons which our large-scale importer, Chiang Kai-shek, has been so kind to present to us. Nonetheless, our warriors on the cultural battlefront will certainly mop up all those things which carry the trademark of "Americanism," no matter how beautifully packaged, which came into China ahead of or accompanying the American equipment and quickly spread far and wide across the nation. All such things will be sent back to their original owner, since we have no need of the democracy of "Americanism" or of its "free life-style." By the same token, we can do very well without its philosophy of commercialization and its pornographic art, which seeks to bedazzle the eye with exposed thighs and breasts.

Nor do we mean to say that we will indiscriminately lock up all of our national art and literature in some deep dungeon, even though we do intend to resolutely eradicate feudal culture. Contrary to what some may fear, we must carry on the outstanding cultural legacy of our people and develop it even further. This line of reasoning has become almost a truism by now and needs no more elaboration here. It should be noted that the creeping tendrils of feudalistic culture extend everywhere and have insinuated themselves deep into our daily life. I fear that chopping our way out of these entangling tendrils will be even more difficult and will take longer to accomplish than land reform.

Compradore culture, which might well be termed the godchild of imperialism, has relied on our big cities as its base camps and has sent out its probing attacks from there. The petty bourgeoisie is the hothouse soil most conducive to compradore culture, a soil in which it will always take root. The worshipping of Western people, the intoxication with European and American life, the notion that "the moon shines brighter abroad than here at home"—or, to put it most succinctly, the sowing of the seeds of an inferiority complex in the minds of our people—this is the specialty of compradore culture. Most odious are those who carefully select out some of the decadent and unsavory feudalistic customs of China (adopting the approach of those who traffic in phony antiques) in order to write whole books merely to win a laugh and earn some paltry largesse from their Western masters; and all this for the purpose of satisfying their material desires! Lin Yutang is a stereotypical example of this kind of producer of compradore culture. But the Chinese people are a great and heroic people. In the eight years of our war of resistance against Japan and in the three years of our war of liberation, countless numbers of our people sprang forth to perform acts of great valor and self-sacrifice which deserve our homage and our tears of mourning. There is no people in the whole world now (save the people of the Soviet Union during their war of defending their motherland) who have equalled the record of our people. We must sing the praises of our people's heroism and honor and foster our race's self-respect. We must totally expunge both compradore culture and the compradore class from one end of China to the other.

The victory of the revolution throughout our entire country is now imminent. Nevertheless, we shall have to continue to work very hard indeed to sweep away the residual evils of imperialism, feudalism, and the compradore bourgeoisie from every part of the nation. The extirpating of imperialist culture, feudal culture, and compradore culture on a national scale may perhaps require as much or even more time and effort. I do believe that we *shall* be able to completely sweep away these three interrelated enemies of New Democracy culture! It is precisely because our cultural troops have now had the experience of thirty years of struggle that neither are we so green at the game nor are we so disorganized as was the case back at the time of the May Fourth thirty years ago; we have learned not only how to vanquish our foes but also how to unite all friendly forces with us. However, we must continue to study and learn in order to safeguard our successes, to change ourselves for the better, and to arm our minds with the most progressive thought of all mankind.

April 30, 1949

Translated by John Berninghausen

TING LING
(Chiang Ping-chih, 1903–)

Ting Ling's career began in 1927–28 when she published a series of short stories focused on female characters. Inspired by reflection on her own experience, on that of other rebels and bohemians she knew, and by her interest in anarcho-feminism, her stories examined passion, sexuality, and femininity openly and critically. After the execution of her lover, Hu Yeh-p'in, Ting Ling's flirtation with left-wing politics broadened into commitment. She spent the years between Hu's death and her own arrest in 1933 as a Communist activist and literator. The style she pioneered during these years is considered the precursor to Chinese socialist realism. Among her best remembered works are: *In Darkness* (1928), *The Diary of a Suicide* (1929), *A Woman* (1930), *Wei Hu* (1930), *The Birth of a Person* (1931), *Flood* (1932), and *Mother* (1933).

Following her escape from the authorities in 1936, Ting Ling made her way to Yenan, where she began, in the late thirties, to produce war literature. Ting Ling's first, spectacular brush with Party censorship and discipline occurred in 1942. The famous essay "Thoughts on March 8" resulted in her immediate purge from all positions of authority on the grounds that she had overstepped the limits (drawn up subsequently by Mao in his "Talks at the Yenan Forum") set for creative literature and had advocated individualist rather than socialist feminist objectives in the struggle to emancipate Chinese women. Publication of *The Sun Shines over the Sangkan River,* a novel about land reform, brought Ting Ling back into favor. She obtained a Stalin Prize for this novel, and by the early fifties she sat in executive positions in a number of leading Party literary and women's bureaucracies. Her prominence was, however, short-lived. Escalating discontent over Party control and factional infighting with Chou Yang led to her final purge in 1958. In that year, after a series of stormy open meetings and behind-the-scene maneuvering, Ting Ling was proclaimed a political nonperson. Her disappearance from the public scene was followed by rumors about her demeaning experiences in reform-through-labor camps. She reappeared toward the end of 1978, and a public exoneration was made in March 1979. However, though back in Peking now, Ting Ling has refused to discuss her lengthy silence.

The following selection from *The Sun Shines over the Sangkan River* was chosen, in part, for the light it sheds on Ting Ling's sensitivity both to male/female relations and to the class factors which separated rural women from one another. The novel documents Ting Ling's shift from a very personal, urban, class-blind feminism to a socialist feminist position which recognizes the specific ideological and economic factors determining individual experience. Li Tzu-chün's wife stands out as a strong figure whose character is determined not by her sex, an assumption which had occupied much of Ting Ling's early fiction, but by her position of privilege and her desire to protect it. There is no common ground between Li's wife and the poor peasant Chou Yüeh-ying, who makes a brief appearance here. But, as this excerpt also makes clear, Mao's criticism of Ting Ling had in no way dulled her characteristic sensitivity to the problem. Te-lu's complaints about his "backward" wife, the Peasant Association's facile assumption that Li's wife would be easy to deal with because she was "just a woman," and the funny, vulgar exchange which follows Chou Yüeh-ying's attempts to participate in the fruit harvest illustrate Ting Ling's continuing concern that Chinese women of all social positions be emancipated and be granted full equality with men. —T.E.B.

from *The Sun Shines over the Sangkan River*

Li Tzu-chün's sudden disappearance started the rumor mills grinding. Pao-t'ang, the old orchard-keeper, got curious when Li's daughter, Lan-ying, showed up at the orchard with her daddy's meal.

"He was here at the fifth watch," he said to the child. "But I haven't set eyes on him since the fruit buyers left. I just figured he'd gone home, Lan-ying. Well, so he didn't go home after all." Lan-ying waggled her head furiously. All along the way people noticed how the child raced for home, as though she'd taken leave of her senses. The sight raised eyebrows.

"Sure looks like somebody's mama is dying—kid must be rushing off to the funeral," someone remarked.

Pao-t'ang left for the village too. When he got there he told his nephew, who told the neighbors, and slowly the word traveled. A number of tenant farmers got very upset and crept off to let the cadres know what had happened. Loiterers filled the road, and the door of the cooperative was jammed with people, none of whom had come to shop.

"What kind of a fucking land reform can we have with the landlord gone," some complained. "We've got meetings day in and day out, but it's all talk and no action. Who ever heard of an uprising that didn't spill a little blood?"

"Hey brother, hey Cheng-kuo," came the quip. "Looks like your militia took the day off for a little fun and games with the girls." [The militia was supposed to keep an eye on the landlords during the land reform.]

"Li Tzu-chün's a coward," some muttered under their breath. "He can't take it. Somebody must have told him we were going to get to work on his land first this time, and scared the living daylights out of him. Once he got wind of that he must have panicked."

"Well, we heard the same thing," came the rejoinder. "We heard that this time the struggle was going to start with him."

Everyone's rage at the landlord intensified.

"That fucker. Who ever said that little son-of-a-bitch was for real. Shit, he's been hiding out in the orchard for days selling fruit, ever since he heard that the land reform was going to go to work on his land. It didn't use to bother him a bit to hand over fistfuls of money to agents or traitors and rich people. But when he hears we're going to reform *his* holdings he decides to take a little walk. Well, take that little walk, man, but don't ever decide to come walking back. You can't take the land with you, so let's see if you have enough brains to keep a hold on it now. Don't think that there's going to be any hands-off policy for you just because you've left town."

A number of people, however, had gone to the Peasant Association. "It's very possible," they pointed out, "that he took the title deeds with him."

This threw the Peasant Association into a panic. The Association wanted to send some tenant farmers posthaste to get the deeds and had summoned Kuo Fu-kuei's father, Kuo Pai-jen, for some of the tenant farmers still did not want to appropriate the deeds. Previously, when the Peasant Association issued a directive, they'd all agree to it, but then each one would just go on back to his own plot. So the Association was going to have to work on them one at a time. Now the elder Kuo sat, expressionless, on the *k'ang* in an inner room of the cooperative, while Ch'eng Jen, chairman of the Peasant Association, strode back and forth on the floor below him. Every now and then Ch'eng Jen would pour himself a drink from the porcelain water jug. Then he asked Kuo:

"Uncle, how many years have you spent farming that same eight *mu* of Li Tzu-chün's?"

"Twelve years," Kuo replied, after lengthy calculations on his fingers.

"How much rent do you pay a year?"

"Well, the land I farm is irrigated but mountainous, so the rent isn't much. Years back it was three pecks of grain for every *mu,* but in the last few years it got upped to four and a half."

"And why was the rent increased?"

"Because the land is better than it used to be. My bit is up on the mountain, so when I first rented it it was full of stones and the soil was as hard as a rock. I've turned it under twice a year since I started, and I've worked a lot of manure into it as well. Then of course I toted a lot of rich topsoil up for filler and hoed out all the weeds, so the yield is a lot heavier than it used to be."

On his way in from one of the outer rooms, Chang Pu-kao, the organizational officer for the Peasant Association, glanced over at the gullible tenant farmer.

"So," he couldn't help snorting, "as far as you're concerned that's grounds enough for raising the rent."

Kuo just looked at him.

"How much grain do you get out of a *mu*?" Ch'eng Jen continued his patient questioning.

"You really don't understand, do you?" the old man said. "How can there be a norm? I get six to seven pecks in a good year, but if there's a drought I'm lucky to get four or five."

"Uncle Kuo," Ch'eng Jen asked gently, "what's your life like?"

"Oh, so-so, so-so," replied Kuo, a forced smile plastered on his face.

"Pa!" Kuo's son Fu-kuei had just come in and now stood in the doorway staring at his father. "Pa, have we ever had a year that wasn't a famine year? When's the last time you ate any real grain? All we get is bean husks, bran, and rice chaff. That shredded up old mat we have on our *k'ang* won't even cover enough space for the two of us to lie down at the same time. And you say 'oh, so-so, so-so.' We live worse than animals!"

"You, you ... watch what you say...." The old man seemed about to reprimand his son, but suddenly gulped back the reproach, his lips trembling.

"Uncle, think it over," Ch'eng Jen said. "Every day when you start work there're still stars in the sky, and you don't leave the field until the stars are back again. Where does that grain you grow get off to? Do you really think it's right that some people sit around in the cool shade, never lift a finger, and end up eating rice and noodles?"

"But it's their land," old Kuo stuttered, his watering eyes fixed on Ch'eng Jen.

"Their land," his son exploded. "Would that land go on growing grain all by itself if Li Tzu-chün didn't have us farm animals to do his work for him? My pa has the mind of a plow horse. He won't even go listen at the Poor Peasants Association. Ask him to and he'll say his back hurts. What's there to be scared of now that Li Tzu-chün's gone?"

"But it's his land, isn't it?"

"His land! His land! You rented it for twelve years. Don't you think you've paid that land off by now just in rent?" By this time a number of Li's tenants were standing around outside and it wasn't clear just which one had interrupted the old man. They'd all known for quite some time that when the land reform was carried out the land was going to be given to the man who farmed it. They'd waited all that time for the cadres to give the land to them. Now, since hearing of Li's flight, they'd gathered to wait for word of what the Peasant Association's next move would be, apprehensive that if Li had taken the titles with him their hands would be tied.

"You men all out there?" Ch'eng Jen asked when he saw them gathered.

"No. Some got scared and some are related to Li, so they don't want to come."

"Related to him!" Chang Pu-kao had a quick temper. "What do they mean, 'related to him'? Did that ever get them a lower rent?"

"That's fine. There's enough of you to get the job done." Ch'eng Jen acted quickly, stressing the orders of the Peasant Association to the gathered men. "Go wrangle the title deeds out of Li's wife yourselves. If she won't hand them over, settle accounts with her. And be sure you say it was the Peasant Association that sent you."

"Don't leave if she hasn't got them." Chang Pu-kao had his two cents to add. "Make her hand over Li Tzu-chün. Got it?"

"Right. That's what we'll do. Come on, Kuo, let's go."

"But, but ..."

"Pa," Fu-kuei said, as he pulled his father onto his feet, "you aren't going all by yourself, so what are you scared of? It's the Peasant Association that told us to."

"But, a woman ..."

"Aw, come on. A woman's just as big a leech as a man." And with that everyone started talking. The courtyard was jammed with people who had come to see what the confusion was all about. When the tiptoeing, gawking crowd saw the men coming out it parted swiftly to the side. From the rear came Pu-kao's shout.

"Don't get scared if the woman puts on some big act." Then, under his breath, he said to Ch'eng Jen, "They're bound to have taken those deeds to Cho-lu County, so we better send somebody out to get them back."

"You've got to go, Pa," Fu-kuei said. "The Peasant Association said so. When we get those title deeds, that eight *mu* is ours!" And with that he pushed his father into the band of tenant farmers.

The crowd thronged to Li's gate. Those who had come along just for the ride stood by at a distance while the tenant farmers talked things over among themselves.

"You don't dare go in, huh?" someone in the rear said. "She's just a woman. What's there to be scared of?" In they slipped, Kuo Pai-jen thrust through the door by his son.

Three children, playing under the arcade, stood stock still and stared at them. Then Lan-ying, who realized what was going on, swiveled around and ran, screaming "Ma, they're here, they're here," at the top of her lungs. Dogs, tethered on the veranda, began barking. The men stood in the open courtyard, looking at one another, no one quite knowing what to say. Bamboo blinds rattled in the master bedroom. Out stepped Li Tzu-chün's wife. She wore a light blue shirt and trousers of imported cotton. Her disheveled hair hung in two black mats over her temple, and her eyes started out of her pale, full face; crying had inflamed the rims so badly it looked as though they'd been smeared to excess with rouge. Against her bosom she clutched a red lacquered box. A voice —who knows which one—rang out:

"Madame!"

The woman rushed down the steps. Tears streaming down her face, she groveled on the ground near a porcelain pot of evergreens.

"Gentlemen, I beg of you," she said in a voice punctuated by sobs. "Help us, oh, help a woman and her children. This box belongs to their father. I entreat you, masters, please accept it. There's a hundred thirty-six and a half *mu* here altogether, and a house. But you know that, don't you, my dear, dear friends, my neighbors. Their father's always been such a big disappointment. We can't expect a thing from him. Now all I can do is deliver myself into your hands, gentlemen, since we've been friends for so long. We are feudal landlords. I know it, and our land should be divided up among the poor peasants. I don't have a thing against that. I only beg you, please, remember that I'm just a woman, all alone here. I beseech you, find some mercy in your hearts for these children. Look, look, I'll kowtow to you!" Box proffered, tears scalding her face, the woman prostrated herself repeatedly to the men. Lan-ying knelt at her mother's side. Lost somewhere in the crowd, the two younger children bawled.

The tenant farmers, who had made such a brave entrance, were speechless. They stared at the woman on the ground at their feet. Never in her life had she suffered for anything, and they had long since become accustomed to thinking of her as royalty. Their thoughts turned to her past acts of petty charity. In a sudden turnabout they found themselves touched by her plight. Not one of them reached for the box. They had forgotten why they had come. Her act had worked its narcotic effect.

A sigh escaped from Kuo Pai-jen as he turned and retreated into the far recesses of the courtyard.

"Madame," said a man, who in all probability was related to the Li's and had never intended to confiscate his title deed anyway. "Madame, if you want to say something, get up off the ground and say it."

The woman fabricated an effort to stand, made a great show of weakness, and then resumed her position on the ground.

"You give that box to the gentlemen," she said to her daughter and slapped the child.

Lan-ying took the box, rose, and stepped forward. The men retreated a step.

"This is all your father's fault," the woman said and broke into fresh tears.

One man left, followed by a second. The battle was over. Slowly the defeated troops dispersed, until Kuo Pai-jen stood alone, looking totally ridiculous. He wanted to say something, but didn't know how to start. The woman got up off the ground.

"Uncle, rest a while before you go," she sobbed. "You've known us an awfully long time, Uncle. We let you down, I know, but please find it in your heart to be a little forgiving. Have mercy, Uncle. I'll pay you back for your kindness bit by bit. It's all my husband's fault. Look how he ran away and left us, and without a second thought. Oh, what a cruel blow fate has dealt us. Please, Uncle, please, take these deeds to the Peasant Association and remember to put in a few good words for me and my children. Uncle, we're in your hands now."

"Don't cry." Kuo looked terribly distressed. "We're all faithful tenants. Things will work themselves out. Anyway, it was the Peasant Association that told us to come over. Come, come, you take your deeds. I'll be going now, so you go on in the house and rest up."

None of the men who had slipped away from Li's place went back to the Peasant Association. One by one they returned to their fields or simply went home. Ch'eng Jen and the others waited for a while. When no one came back they sent a man out to scout around, but all was quiet at the Li's front gate. And all was quiet in the courtyard. The Li children sat by the drying screens, their mouths crammed with luscious, fresh red fruit, as though nothing had happened. Finding it very peculiar that no one was at Li's, the messenger redoubled his efforts. The matter-of-fact response he got when he went to their houses to inquire from the tenants themselves was:

"It would've been all right if Li Tzu-chün had been there himself. But how could we do it to a woman, and drag her kids into it too. How could we look her in the face again? Let's just let the Peasant Association get the deeds."

. . . .

The cooperative was in an uproar. The village cadres liked to meet there since there was no other space in the village for an office, and now they were hashing over the Li fiasco.

"What the hell happened?" Ch'eng Jen asked Yü-min bluntly, and the other cadres echoed his question. "Why didn't the peasants want their deeds?"

"The farmers still haven't managed to stand on their feet," was Yü-min's reply. [Yü-min, founder of the village Party cell, was the most experienced of the local cadres and so it was only natural that the others would turn to him.] "They're still so scared they don't dare take the deeds."

"Scared of a woman?"

"Come on," said Yü-min, "women may not use their fists, but when it comes down to a fight they have their hidden talent. You know the old saying, 'a pretty woman can make a brave man quake.' She really pulled one over on them this time with her sniveling and bawling. That woman's a real snake in the grass, a wolf in sheep's clothing. She's even worse than her old man. In a word, we lost. We were routed! The Peasant Association is too impatient. Before we even get ourselves organized we pitch the tenant farmers into a fucking damn fight."

Yü-min knew the people wanted land, but he also knew they were unwilling to take any initiative. Their fear ran so deep that unless the old powers were toppled, no one was really willing to get involved. There were several strong-men in the village, and crushing them was going to be difficult. The cadres had made sure they chose one of the weaker ones for the spring struggle; Hou Tien-k'uei was a bedridden old man, and no one could be afraid of him, or so the cadres thought. But in the end, only scattered activists had jumped up to shake their fists at the old man.

"Speak up! Speak up! Say something!" the Association members in the crowd had shouted, and the people shook their fists and shouted, but their eyes had shifted stealthily to the rear where Boss Ch'ien Wen-kuei [the most powerful and corrupt of the local strongmen] was squatting. Hou Tien-k'uei ended up having to pay forty *mu* in lieu of the hundred-peck grain fine imposed at the struggle meeting, and it was parceled out to about two dozen people. Some of the recipients were delighted with their shares. Some were so suspicious of their good fortune that they couldn't bring themselves even to walk past Hou's front gate. The old tenant Hou Chung-ch'üan simply returned his to the land-lord in secret. Yü-min was absolutely certain, despite the fact that the district government had approved their struggle against Hou, that in this drama only the same few would be on stage, act after act. . . .

So Yü-min had made his decision. He had seen that the arrival of the com-rades from county Party headquarters and the subsequent demand for land reform had raised everybody's expectations. But he had also seen that their indecisiveness over which strongman should be chosen as the target of the struggle, and the various rumors that were circulating through the village now, had sent enthusiasm plummeting. He had kept his anxiety private but had ended up spilling his guts to Yang Liang.

[Yü-min wasn't the only villager who felt he could trust his most intimate thoughts to Yang Liang. Everyone liked the young cadre. Yang was the only one of the men sent in by headquarters who could put everyone at ease, men and women alike. Because the villagers found it so easy to confide in him, he was rapidly becoming very sensitive to underground currents in village social life, currents which both bound the villagers together and prohibited them from making any radical changes in their social relations: years-old vendettas; sexual tensions; secret debts; family quarrels; class tensions which threatened the newly instituted mass organizations, particularly the Women's Associa-tion; and finally, the ubiquitous, paralyzing insecurity the poor felt in the face of the powerful. Yü-min's confession to Yang Liang had focused on the weak-nesses he saw developing in the local village Party cell. Chang Cheng-tien, cadre in charge of village security, had been thoroughly corrupted by Ch'ien Wen-kuei, his father-in-law. Ch'eng Jen's loyalty was suspect because he har-bored a secret passion for Hei-ni, Ch'ien Wen-kuei's niece. And Te-lu, well Te-lu . . . Everyone, it seemed, was implicated in one way or another. Still . . .]

Their conversation in the orchard had strengthened Yü-min's sense of mission and fueled his enthusiasm. Land reform would never get off the ground if they stuck to the methods they had used last spring.... Yü-min had already done a lot of groundwork with the other village cadres, trying to win them over to his side. He had already had it out with Li Chang and Cheng-kuo. Chao would probably not oppose them, since he always followed the majority anyway, so gradually their ideological outlook was beginning to shape up.... Ch'eng Jen and Te-lu were the last two he needed to talk openly with now....

As Yü-min turned into the alley [after leaving the bull session at the cooperative], he noticed a lot of people hanging around Te-lu's gate. He heard yelling, so he ran over. People surged forward as they caught sight of him, as though there were something they wanted to tell him, but he didn't stop to find out what it was. The rest moved aside to let him through. He barged into an empty spot in front of the house. From where he stood he could hear Te-lu's brutal imprecations.

"You've ruined my reputation forever. How can I ever open my mouth in this village again."

Just as Yü-min moved to go inside, a woman charged furiously out of the house. She gave a start when she caught sight of all the people standing around in the yard, then turned her head and pointed a finger at the window.

"Motherfucker! You think you can go around slandering people this way. You're going to pay through the teeth for crossing me, you motherfucking beast!"

Yü-min knew that the tiny, slender creature with sleepy eyes and her hair streaming down her shoulders was a well-known village temptress who belonged to Chiang Shih-jung, one of the minor landlords. She had been a whore in a neighboring village and had moved in when Chiang became head of a security unit in the village, but they had never been formally married. She spent her time going from door to door, gossiping and pimping for people who needed fovors done so they could get illicit affairs going on the side—affairs in which she was frequently not just an innocent bystander. Yü-min was not interested in delving into petty detail, but she was still making an ugly scene, pointing and stamping around. Two quick strides brought him face to face with her.

"What the hell are you up to now?" he shouted angrily.

The woman had fully intended to continue her abuse of Te-lu, but when she realized she was confronting Yü-min, she stopped abruptly, turned her head, and started to weep.

"The good people of this world never get what they deserve," she said to the gathered crowd as she walked off. "People really have to put up with a lot of injustice. How can we live like this, oh my, oh my ..." She did pick up a lot of speed as she went, however, and, weeping and wailing, she was soon out of sight.

The staccato sound of blows now came from inside the house. A piercing voice screamed: "Help! Help! He's killing me!"

Before Yü-min could reach the door, Te-lu's wife, her hair in total disarray, came hurtling out. She stumbled with fear as she fled, screaming "help, help, help," like a banshee. There wasn't time for anyone to intervene. Naked to the waist, Te-lu burst out in pursuit and, with one kick, toppled her to the ground; heedless of Yü-min's restraining hand, Te-lu struck her again. There was a loud sound. The flowered shirt Te-lu's wife wore tore open from the neck down, exposing her belly and two dingy breasts. She sat sobbing brokenheartedly on the ground, secure in the knowledge that Te-lu had been pinned down by some of the men. She kept yanking at the short, tight, pretty shirt, but try as she might she could not hide her breasts from view. Te-lu exploded from where he was pinned.

"Look at that shameless whore. She's destroyed my reputation. For better or worse, I'm still the deputy chief around here."

A number of sympathetic neighbor women surrounded Te-lu's wife to comfort her. "Oh, that Chao Te-lu, he scares us! He's just the kind of person who can't work things out without resorting to violence. How can a man who's supposed to be a cadre beat up his own wife! And she, the mother of his children!" But it was hard not to burst out laughing when they took a look at how tightly the flowered shirt fit her.

The shirt was a gift from Chiang Shih-jung's woman. Chiang had been sending his harlot of a wife to Te-lu's place every day to bribe Te-lu's wife over to his side, and since he'd given the children little goodies to eat and sent her the shirt, she'd begun to think they must be pretty nice people. Very pleased with herself indeed, she'd put the shirt on and told her husband what lovely people the Chiangs were, right to his face. And she'd gotten a beating in return. Sadly, she looked at the ripped shirt, her heart aching.

"Ah, I haven't had a shirt on my back all summer because he won't let me have any clothes," she said. [Everybody knew there was truth to her complaint: she'd been almost completely naked all summer.] "When I say anything, he just tells me he's the deputy village chief. So what does that mean? That his wife can't even have one shirt? Oh, what a shame."

Te-lu left her and went home with Yü-min. The east room that Yü-min rented wasn't particularly large, but it felt spacious enough. Two grimy pillows lay on the deserted *k'ang,* and heaped in one corner was a jumbled pile of clothing and bedding. Next to that were a little stove and a pot; leaning against the wall was a rickety chest, upon which bowls, chopsticks, and cooking things were laid out. Directly in front of the chest was a water urn. Te-lu walked over and helped himself to a dipper of water. Then he rubbed the sweat off his head with a bare arm.

"Men don't fight with women," Yü-min said from his perch on the *k'ang.* "It's not right for an old married couple like you to squabble. People laugh at you."

"Well, what's there to say," was Te-lu's reply. "Poverty just takes everything out of you. My idiot wife is so damned backward that if I didn't slug her every once in a while she'd never behave herself. Anyway, it was the only way I could make sure that witch of Chiang's would never have the guts to come around the house again."

Te-lu sat down on the *k'ang,* stretched his legs out, and accepted the cigarette Yü-min handed him.

"Look, old man," he said, checking the window to make sure no one was around. "I'm not going to lie to you. I borrowed two *piculs* from Chiang Shih-jung this spring. I mean, who could've known that land reform would heat up again . . . Chiang's seen that we have meetings without inviting him. [Look, he knows he's village chief only because we forced him into it, and he knows none of us trust him as far as we could throw him.] He may not have said anything yet, but he also knows which end's up, so he invited me over to dinner. Oh, I didn't go. He can't really think he can buy me for two lousy *piculs*. As a matter of fact, if I was that easy to buy off, my wife wouldn't be crying her eyes out over other people's fancy clothes. The way I look at it, no matter how the chips fall from now on, I've chosen my side and I'm sticking to it. I was village head during the Resistance War—all me and my wife got out of that was a couple of fucking brats to feed. So what's more to talk about? I say we cadres haven't put enough energy into organizing things this time around. Nobody's opened his mouth and said so, but inside they're all worked up, don't you think?"

"Te-lu!" Yü-min leaped up from the *k'ang* and paced around, unable to conceal his delight. "That's exactly what I was coming over to see you about." He was about to explain, but Te-lu launched back into his monologue.

"Well, you got me just in time, because I was going to come find you. An awful lot of people have come over and told me how big a thing this could be! You know what I mean? The village harvest this year is big, and I mean big. Think it over. There's over a hundred *mu* in this village tied up in fruit orchards. Go on, walk around and look. The trees are loaded with fruit. Listen, now that land reform's reared its head again, there's plenty of people that can't sleep nights just thinking about it. The land reform's dragging on and on and we can't really split the land up overnight. But by the time we finish with the land, there's going to be nothing on those trees but leaves! Man, the rich are selling fruit like their lives depended on it, and it's driving the poor people crazy. They keep coming over to me to see if there isn't something we can do about it. So what are we going to do! I think, starting today, we shouldn't let the rich sell any more fruit, and we should slap a watch on all the orchards. This is big business! Do you know how much money's involved?"

Several days before, the same thought had occurred to Yü-min, but he'd been so busy that it had remained just a passing thought. The last few days, as he'd rushed around getting ahold of people to talk with, the thing had slipped his mind completely. Now, with Te-lu jogging his memory, it came back to him in all its urgency. He leaped up.

"Absolutely! This is important. Only I don't think just putting a watch on the orchards will do the job. When the fruit's ripe it can't wait for us to do a slow land reform! So how are we going to get around that!?"

"Well, let's go get Ch'eng Jen. I think we'd be better off if the Peasant Association took charge. This isn't something just a few men can manage on their own. What do you think?" Catching Yü-min's nod of assent, Te-lu continued. "We better find some people who can figure accounts. I think the Peasant Association should take control of all fruit sales. Then, later, whoever gets orchard land in the land reform will get back the money for their own fruit."

"We better get a lot of people," Yü-min said on his way out the door. "And wc should let all the village cadres know about it. But first we better go talk things over with Yang Liang."

. . . .

Yang Liang, however, had gone out to the fields to help hoe weeds that day. He was just getting back to the village and was barely around the mud wall when suddenly somebody whacked him hard on the shoulder. Yang looked around and saw that it was Liu Man. Liu Man's skin was dark, his hair was long, and his wide eyes sparkled with nervous anxiety. He wore a pair of black cotton pants but was bare-chested.

"Yang," he said, "I've been waiting, but I'm the only person you haven't gotten around to."

"Well, I guess that's true," Yang Liang confessed. "It's only because I couldn't find your house. Is this where you live?" Suddenly he recalled somebody having told him that Liu Man's elder brother, Liu Ch'ien, had once served as chief of the old village security system.

"Come on, come on. My house is a little dirty, but dirt never killed anybody," Liu Man said, as he shoved Yang Liang down the little alley.

"How come you never came and got me?" Yang asked him.

"Well . . ." A deep sigh escaped from Liu Man. He strode along silently, then stopped and said, "This is my house. My brother isn't here now. Come in."

Yang Liang followed him into a long, alley-like yard, where the rooms on the east and west sides crowded in almost on top of one another. Liu Man stood in the middle of the yard staring around, unsure where best to direct his guest.

Out of the easternmost room came a woman with a bad eye infection. She was carrying a child. Flies buzzed around the baby's head and its eyes were glued completely shut with mucus.

"Where have you been all day?" the woman said to her husband. "I left some food for you. Are you going to eat now, or what?"

Liu Man looked right through her as though she didn't exist.

"It's even hotter inside," he said anxiously. "Let's sit out here, Yang."

Yang Liang walked over to the door of the east room to take a look.

"Is this room yours?" he asked. "It's kind of hot still to be cooking inside. Why haven't you moved the stove outside yet?"

"Oh, he never bothers with the family," she sighed, swatting at the flies on the child's head. "Sometimes he doesn't even bother to come home at all, and I'm too busy to do it. The room's unbearably hot, but when he does come home he's so sullen. Look, aren't you going to have something to eat?"

Just then a young woman came out of the west room, walked hesitantly over to the men and said in a low, fearful voice, "Uncle, you can go sit in my room."

Yang Liang followed along behind his host. The west room was somewhat cleaner than the other. Tacked on the wall were a pair of faded scrolls and a cheap commercial print of a pretty girl. The quilt was rolled up neatly on the *k'ang*, the sleeping mat still looked fairly new, and on the mat lay two worn, but not yet shabby, blue embroidered pillows. A mirror and two vases were set out on the chest. Yang's surprise and delight showed through in spite of himself. He was just about to compliment Liu Man on the beautiful room when the man said abruptly:

"Don't condescend to me, Yang. I haven't always been this poor. I'm not even all that upset about the way they forced me into this poverty. What really gets to me is this grudge I have; I just can't seem to get rid of it." Liu Man's eyes bulged and he stared at Yang, trying to take his measure.

"Take it easy." Yang took a seat on the *k'ang*. "We're equals here and I'm not going to give you away to anybody. Go on, say whatever you want."

But Liu Man was silent. He didn't know how to say what he wanted to say, so he paced around the room, clenching his fists and, from time to time, rumpling his thick, luxurious head of hair.

His wife brought in a bowl of millet gruel and a dish of salt pickles. She gave Yang Liang a cigarette and light and then stood by the door, rubbing her inflamed eyes, waiting for her husband to finish eating, oblivious to all else.

"Go on, Liu Man, eat," Yang said.

"I'm going to level with you." Liu Man confronted him. "Ever since the day Nuan-shui Village was liberated, I've been waiting for a day of reckoning. How could Ch'ien Wen-kuei manage to use the Eighth Route Army for his own purposes? [He forced his son to enlist so he could get an "army dependent" classification and now nobody wants to touch him.] This is my chance to see if you're made of the same stuff as they are, Yang. I want to know if you're going to go for the hard ones or just play around with the pushovers."

"Slow down if you have something to say." Liu Man's wife was afraid of her husband but she had her own stubborn streak. "Let him have his way, Chairman," she said to Yang. "They drove his brother crazy ... Come on, eat your millet."

"She's right. Let's talk when you finish eating."

"If you don't get rid of this bowl I'm going to smash it." Liu Man moved away and flashed a brutal, vicious look at his wife. Her gaze swept back over him, but she didn't yield an inch.

"You never stop to think how hard it is on me," she said in a voice of boundless reproach. The aggrieved woman left the room, but her sighs could be heard even through the wall.

"Liu Man, now is the time for peasants like us to stand on our feet," Yang said. "We've been exploited and oppressed in the past, but now is the time to settle the scores one by one. The worse a man is, the more important it is to crack him wide open and crush him, so why should we just take on the pushovers? Don't be scared. If you've got grievances you'll get your revenge, because the Communist Party is backing you up."

"Oh sure, sure, that's fine. Only things aren't like that. I'm not lying to you, Yang, you're not going to make it here if you only listen to what that bunch of village cadres has to say. They're cowards, Yang. They don't dare offend anybody. Think about it. You and the other [county cadres] come here and you stir things up: you've got nothing and nobody to fear. Then you leave. But the village cadres can't think in those terms, because they're going to stay in the village. They have to figure out whether or not they're going to be able to win the fight and then they have to have a way of retreating if they don't. Yü-min used to be a pretty good guy, but he's been dodging me lately, and I know why. He's afraid I'll expose him. So now whenever I see him I yell, 'Hey, Chairman of the Resistance Union, whose ass are you licking now?' One day it made him so mad he wanted to slug me, but he didn't because you were in the village. All he said then was, 'Liu Man, I've treated you good. How come you want to plow me under now?' Well, he did treat me good. He even got me introduced into the Party."

"Into the Party?" Yang found this bit of information perplexing. Since his arrival in the village he'd met all eighteen of the local Party members, but he had never heard Liu Man included. He questioned the man further.

"Oh, I'm an old-timer. I joined up even before Liberation. I did all the dirty grass-roots work, but they threw me out this spring. Still, it was Yü-min who spoke up for me and made them change it to a suspension; so now I'm a cadre with clipped wings. The reason I just can't accept it is because they're all lined up on Ch'ien Wen-kuei's side. Then, on top of ruling against me, they got me criticized by the local district government. What I really want now, Yang, is to have my case reversed. Not just to quibble over a few *mu* of land, but so I can get even and rub Ch'ien Wen-kuei's nose in it. You know who Ch'ien Wen-kuei is, don't you, Yang?"

Liu Man had delivered a lot in one breath. He didn't address himself to whether Yang was really catching him or not, for he appeared to assume that the other man was familiar with all the details. All he really wanted was the chance, finally, to right the wrongs that were causing him so much anguish. Nor did he seem any more relaxed after he finished. On the contrary, he stood gazing at Yang, careless of his surroundings, like a soldier fresh to the battle and quivering with tension.

"Well." Yang Liang let his breath out gently.

Once again Liu Man rushed over and out poured another torrent of words. [Liu Man claimed that Ch'ien Wen-kuei's influence spread like a web through the village. By manipulating the ignorant and blackmailing or eliminating the more capable, Ch'ien had secured a monopoly over local affairs. It had been Ch'ien's idea that Liu Ch'ien, Liu Man's brother, take on the job of village security chief; once he had them within his grasp, Ch'ien had ruined the brothers financially and pressured Liu Ch'ien into irreversible madness. It was Ch'ien Wen-kuei who had, through his son-in-law Chang Cheng-tien, involved Liu Man in the bitter, embarrassing quarrel over a few *mu* of land. The dispute had resulted in Liu Man's censure and final ouster from the village Party cell. Ch'ien had, in fact, successfully divided village leadership and was close to defeating efforts by the more independent cadres to topple him from power. Yang Liang was beginning to piece together all the information he had gleaned since his arrival in Nuan-shui. Liu Man was not the only person who had suffered at Ch'ien's hands, though clearly in Liu Man's case the outcome was proving particularly brutal. An undercurrent of hatred surged everywhere throughout the village. It was stemmed only by fear of Ch'ien Wen-kuei's power.]

Sometimes Liu Man's wife would come rushing in, drawn by the shrillness in his voice, fearful of trouble, to stand for a moment and watch as he raged on without respite. Yang Liang watched him dispassionately, interrupting him only to say "Slow down" and "What else," until finally Liu Man had finished. At last she watched her husband stretch out on the *k'ang*, panting but still obdurate, and heard Yang say, "Now I understand, now I understand. Take it easy, Liu Man, don't get so worked up. We'll find a way somehow." Then the woman came and stood in the doorway.

"Chairman," she said to Yang Liang, "if you could only help us get even we could start living again. They drove his brother out of his mind, and now look at him, he's almost crazy himself. The roots of the bitterness go so deep."

Yang Liang sat with him for a long time. When he saw that Liu Man was gradually calming down, he signaled the woman to bring a bowl of millet gruel. Liu Man rose from the *k'ang* to escort Yang out. His eyes were as scarlet as those of his wife, the rims wetter by far, but he was calm.

"You're right." Liu Man's voice was resonant as he placed his hand on Yang Liang's shoulder. "When it rains the ground gets slippery, but if you fall down you're the one that has to get up again. We're not going to get up on our feet except by our own effort. You were even more right about all the peasants being one family. We have no strength unless we unite; we will never stand on our feet unless we unite. You've shown me the way, Yang, and now we're sworn to loyalty and brotherhood."

. . . .

All over Nuan-shui Village people were passing the word.

"Hey, eleven landlords have watches on their orchards. Members of the Poor Peasants Association are standing guard."

"Oh, yeah, which eleven? Looks like we're going to 'liquidate' all of them."

"Well, not all of them. I heard they're only taking fruit away from the ones who lease out some of their land. The rich peasants still get to sell their own fruit."

"That's no good. Can't we liquidate the rich peasants?"

"They said we couldn't do it all at once. Some people are going to get liquidated, but we'll bleed the others dry when their turn comes around. We'll make them cough up cash. There's no problem there."

"Good. If we put the squeeze on everybody in the village the Peasant Association would be so busy selling fruit it'd never get around to land reform. The land still has to be divided up, right?"

Along came old Red-nose Wu, chanting and banging his gong. He announced the names of the men on the fruit committee and the decisions the committee had already made.

"That's good. It'll be a good committee with Jen T'ien-hua on it. He's a sharp guy and he'll look out for us. Look at how well he runs the co-op. Any farmer in the village can get credit from him and the place still makes money!"

"Pao-t'ang's on the committee too. He'll be good. He knows every inch of those orchards like the back of his hands. After all, he's been walking around under those trees for twenty years. Nobody's going to be able to pull the wool over his eyes about who owns what trees. He can reckon how many *catties* you'll get off every one of them. He's got the long and short of it all stored away in his head."

"Looks to me as though this time they're giving all the power to the poor peasants. . . ."

People did not confine themselves to conversation snatched in the street, or chats at the neighbors' house, or information gleaned through calls on relatives. Nor were they content merely to crowd the doors of the co-op to pass along word of the action. People went right down to the orchard to check things out for themselves. Some had actually been assigned work there, but scores of women and children had come along just for the excitement.

The faces of Nuan-shui's seventeen rich peasants and five middle peasants, who'd heard earlier that no one who owned fruit would be spared, were now plastered with grins.

"I told you so," they said to each other, fears allayed. "The Communists will live and let live. They're reasonable, they're not going to cut their noses off to spite their faces." They and their entire families left, en masse, for the orchard, to pick the ripe fruit. They couldn't fall behind now. The fruit must be dispatched as quickly as possible.

The eleven whose fruit had been impounded by the Association had their people in the orchard along with everyone else. They came asking to be spared a part of the harvest, but they were also there to keep their eyes on the peasants. They meant to ensure that the Peasant Association did not under-calculate the amount of fruit or sneak any out on the sly. Parents sent their children to snatch whatever fruit they could—any time they could exploit the pandemonium— and bring it home. A single apple was better than no apples, and nothing should be released without a struggle! ...

Ladders were propped against the tree trunks. Men scaled the ladders, and as the fruit began to fall into their rough, coarsened palms, and from their hands into the baskets, a fresh scent drifted up into the shimmering light. Now who owned this orchard! Pao-t'ang directed the work. For twenty years he had watched as other people picked the fruit, or had actually picked for the owners himself. He had always remained a silent, taciturn man, working without pause as though what was going on around him did not register, as though the sweetness and fragrance of the fruit made no impression on him at all. He had appeared to work without joy, handling the fruit as if it were clods of earth or pieces of stone. But today Pao-t'ang's sensitivity to the fragrance had, like the very ground he stood on, come back to life. The blinders had fallen from his eyes for the first time in a very long time, and he saw the verdant, luxurious foliage around him the same way a beggar would see a pile of gold he had stumbled upon. The glittering fruit dazzled his senses.

"There are twenty-eight white pear trees, fifty regular pears, nine apples, three cherry apples, thirty jujubes, and a walnut. Way back in Li Tzu-chün's father's day there were a lot more white pears, but when the property came into Li Tzu-chün's hands he cut down a few that hadn't been well cared for and put in regulars instead. Li wasn't good for much of anything else, but he sure did know how to grow pears. He'd read up on it from a book, so he told us how to fertilize and how to get at the worms. It's a real shame that there's only eleven and a half *mu* of them left. The five *mu* in the northwest corner lot got sold to Chiang Shih-jung. The southern half a *mu* he gave to Wang Tzu-jung even though he never did get paid a cent for it. He got a good price for the three and a half *mu* over by the well—bought up by old Ku. The other seven and a half got sold off piecemeal to four or five other locals. None of them knew much about keeping up pears, and they only had a *mu* or so apiece anyway, so they've just left everything up to fate. Even so, they did pretty well this year."

Some of the men were charged with carrying the baskets, packed with fruit, over to the collection station. As the pickers in the trees moved from one branch to the next, and gradually reduced the number of fruit, the foliage seemed even more lush. Some found it impossible to contain their exuberance and tossed huge fruit to the men picking in the next trees. When the fruit was caught midair, they roared with laughter; when it fell, the people on the ground ran to grab it. Some crammed the fallen pieces into their mouths, but others were always standing by to shout at them:

"You're breaking the rules. We're not supposed to eat any. This stuff now belongs to the poor!"

"Ah, come on," was the response. "Can't we eat the ones that get smashed on the ground? Who cares if we eat one of Li Tzu-chün's, anyway?"

Some of the men teased old Pao-t'ang. "Hey, Uncle, what's got you so heated up? Once we carve up Li Tzu-chün's orchard you're going to lose a cushy job. You going to be so happy then?"

"Orchard watchman's a pretty good job, isn't it, Uncle. It's nice and quiet and shady. An old man can just sit and smoke all day. If you get thirsty you stretch your hand out and eat anything that drops into it. You can kiss that bed of clover good-bye, Uncle."

"Actually, you're absolutely right." Suddenly the old man started to babble. "But I've had enough of that kind of clover. This time they should distribute two *mu* to me and put me to doing some real work. I've been a bachelor for so long, been drifting around with no one to answer to for decades. Now," he chuckled, "if they'd distribute me a wife and set me to listening to her nag, that would be even better."

"And all this time we've been saying that you were sleeping with the orchard fairy. If it wasn't her that put a spell on you, how come you looked down your nose at all the pretty girls, and how come you never got a go-between to make the rounds for you? Everybody knows how much those sex-crazed orchard fairies go for old men!"

There was a roar of laughter and then another. The laughter spread. Everyone was high from all the horsing around. . . .

Li Tzu-chün's wife came down after breakfast, dressed in nice clean clothes, her hair brushed to a sheen. The woman's face was wreathed with smiles, her manner was timid, and her attitude frankly obsequious. Everyone ignored her, including Pao-t'ang, who pretended he hadn't noticed she was there. In her presence, however, his face resumed its former blank expression.

"Our orchard isn't very big now," she said as she sidled over to Jen T'ien-hua with a diffident smile. "Only eleven and a half *mu* left. Of course Uncle Pao-t'ang knows more about that than I do. Every single year my husband sold off a piece."

"Why don't you just get lost," said the fellow holding the scales. He worked at the beancurd mill. "Why don't you trust us—the poor people do. Anyway, you already sold off a lot of fruit."

"Let her stay," said Jen T'ien-hua.

"It's still going to be a gouge," she complained. "We were counting on that fruit to pay the spring wages."

"Hey," one of the pickers high in a tree shouted to another. "Who said Li Tzu-chün could only grow regular pears and didn't have any luck with the whites? Get a load of the huge one he's got himself over here—white, soft, plump, and sweet smelling." A healthy gust of laughter swept through the trees.

The woman moved away and sat down on the ground. She gazed at the trees, at the scarlet jewels clustered on the green boughs. That fruit had been hers. In the past all she'd have had to do was look at anyone she found walking around under those trees and he'd have come over, shuffling and grinning, to explain what he was doing there. How could they close their eyes to her now? Her orchard was filled with men who were deliberately climbing her trees and trampling her soil. And there she was, like some inconsequential beggar woman; no one would even toss her a piece of fruit out of charity. Swallowing her humiliation, she sized them up one after another, taking note of their exuberance and the contempt they were aiming at her.

"Even that old Pao-t'ang's turned on me," she thought with naked emotion. "All these years, and we ended up feeding an ungrateful dog. Oh, it's true, you never find out what people are really like until something really big happens."

No one had any sympathy to spare.

Li's wife was not a timid soul. Since her own family had been dealt with the previous year, she had sensed that the storm was gathering, the crisis imminent. She had spent a lot of time working out escape plans in the event of any sudden turn of the tide. It was because she was so convinced that things would not remain the same forever that she had become generous and had gotten into the habit of giving away old clothes and lending out grain. She had actually begun chatting with the hired hands and cooking decent meals for them once in a while. Whenever she met a cadre—for she had become very friendly of late and spent a lot of time visiting around in the street—she would insist on inviting him over for a drink. The greater change by far, however, was her newfound industriousness. Li's wife had taken over all her own housework, had begun carrying meals out to the laborers in the field herself, and had even helped out with the weeding and threshing. "Well, she's not so bad," people had begun remarking to one another, "it's her husband that's no good." A number of people really believed her stories, even her tall tale that if the Li's didn't sell more land this year they would never get through the winter; they figured she must actually be going through hard times. But the disaster was upon her now and there was no escape. She had no choice but to tough it out, endure, and try to steer herself clear of the maelstrom. She could never, never let her relentless hatred and galling resentment of these men show through. All that was left was to assume the pose of a soft little woman to put them off guard, and then appeal to their generosity. . . .

At noon everyone went home for lunch. [Li's wife walked through her own trees to the orchard owned by Ku Yung, a wealthy middle peasant.]

Ku Yung's orchard was quiet. His trees hung heavy with fruit, and windfalls had already begun piling up on the ground. He was short on regular pears but his whites were particularly large, for he didn't begrudge his trees labor or manure. Still, the fruit of that labor was going to end up in somebody else's pocket. As this thought flashed through her mind, Li's wife allowed herself a feeling of immense pleasure, for she was under the impression that Ku Yung's three and a half *mu* had been impounded like her own. "If they're going to sell fruit," she thought happily, "let them sell everybody's fruit. Since they think they have to divide up the land, let's hope they make a total botch of it."

As she lingered over this thought, Li's wife heard the sound of girlish laughter. A figure dressed in light blue flitted past her. Now who could that be? Racking her brains, she walked to the edge of the ditch. A willow from the far side of the ditch had toppled over onto a pear tree on her side. Only one bough on the half-dead tree was still alive, but that one branch had produced an astonishing number of pears.

"So, it's her." Li's wife knew very well that the orchard on the far side of the ditch belonged to Ch'ien Wen-kuei. She could see Ch'ien's niece, Hei-ni, dressed in light blue, hanging onto the trunk of a tree like a woodpecker, nodding to someone below. The trees surrounding Hei-ni on every side made her look as though she was trapped in a huge cage. Behind her the fruit hung in a brilliant galaxy while a steady stream of vivid stars flowed through her hands into the basket which hung on the branch below. Suddenly, her trousers a whirlwind of white, Hei-ni slipped down off the ladder. Her cousin's wife bounded to her side like a rabbit and snatched the basket out of her hands.

"Hei-ni," Ch'ien's daughter T'a-ni shouted from a distance. "You're always playing around.". . . .

"You damned sluts! You whores! You fucking whores!" Li Tzu-chün's wife could no longer bite back the vulgarities that sprang to her tongue. "That crook! Ch'ien Wen-kuei makes his girls suck up to the cadres, those fucking bastards, and they think they can push my family around. What kind of a shit-hole is this Communist Party! Big talkers, going around all the time lighting fires under people to settle accounts and get revenge. Then they go right on, not just protecting a traitor and a gangster like Ch'ien, oh no; they actually get right down on their knees and pray to his holiness. Nobody dares lift a finger against Ch'ien Wen-kuei! But we get in trouble just because we have a few extra *mu,* no one to join the army, and nobody to stick her twat in the air for the cadres. Yü-min, you son-of-a-bitch, one day I'll find out why you're so soft on that bastard!"

She couldn't tolerate the sight another minute. Half crazed, she ran toward home but was forced to wheel and scramble away to the side when she saw the men, their meal finished, coming her way, and heard them driving the draft animals in. Not them! She couldn't face them. She loathed them all. There was no way she could let her true feelings out and she was terrified she wouldn't be able to hold the hatred back any longer. Like a whipped dog, tail between its legs, she fled from them, wrestling to subdue the fear and vengeance in her eyes.

People flocked back to the orchard. Hou Ch'ing-huai led the transportation crew. Two large carts with iron wheels waited by the roadside to be loaded. Even Hu T'ai's rubber-wheeled cart was hitched nearby with an extra mule. Li Chih-hsiang, reins in hand, was there with his long whip, his old cringing expression replaced by a smile, for now wherever Li looked he saw signs of hope. Row after row, the men emerged from the depths of the orchard carrying their baskets to the carts. . . .

Yang Liang saw a young woman coming in his direction and watched her lower a heavy basket of fruit from her shoulder to the ground.

"Uncle Kuo," she cried, "get over here and take this."

She was a skinny woman with a ruddy complexion and delicate, sweeping eyebrows. Her hair was combed back severely and piled into a sober bun at the back of her head. Out of her white man's-style sleeveless jacket stuck a pair of long arms, and on her wrists she wore a number of eye-catching red artificial bead bracelets.

"Woowee, this one must've flown in by airplane!" cracked a young peasant as he approached her. "What a woman! What a woman among women! What a pile of donkey shit in a sheepfold!"

The woman was not about to be intimidated. Her head spun around: "Your mother passed you down one filthy mouth," she shot back.

"How right you are," the young man said when no one paid any attention to his grimace. "My mouth is so stupid it still can't even sing 'From the red east the sun rises' ..."

Everybody broke up when they heard that crack.

"So come on, sing us a little song," someone suggested slyly.

"You men are something." The woman turned on her heel. "Take your big fat mouth to the struggle session if you're so talented. Just make sure you don't lose your soul to old you-know-who," she said [veiling the reference to Ch'ien Wen-kuei in her taunt]. "No man on this earth frightens *me!*" And off she strode, quickly and gracefully.

"Whew! Who's that?" Yang Liang thought he recognized her but couldn't remember her name, so he asked Kuo Ch'uan.

"Oh, that's Chou Yüeh-ying," Kuo said, trying at a wink. "The shepherd's wife. Everybody knows what a shrew she is. Oh, she's a regular spitfire, though. Not afraid of anything in this world—or in the next. She gets up and shouts even louder than the men do at our meetings. Chou Yüeh-ying's the vice-chairwoman of the Women's Association; all the Association women are here today."

"Look at her," somebody snorted. "One basket of fruit—that's enough to make her stagger around screaming and bawling for help. And she thinks she wants to be king of the mountain."

"King of the mountain! King of the pricks! Huh, not a chance. She still doesn't have that one little thing you just gotta have!" And with that they all started to chortle.

In time the carts were piled high with the fruit and tied securely down. Bursting with satisfaction, Hou Ch'ing-huai called up the mules. Li Chih-hsiang cracked his whip. Slowly the carts moved out. One after another, the three carts moved down the road, and behind them, filing one behind the next, their loads secured previously in the orchard, came dozens of mules and donkeys. On either side of the pack animals walked the escorts. People pressed against the mud walls at the roadside, rubbernecking, following the raucous band with their eyes. Other people, not yet willing to go back into the orchard, crowded the gates, pointing, admiring, and applauding. The mule train had stirred up more excitement than the January lantern festival, more excitement than a bridal procession—for a bride was unusual but this was unique. Kuo Ch'uan stood against the wall, gently stroking his long moustache, and when he had watched the procession out of sight, he asked Yang Liang very softly:

"It is really all for the poor people?".... .

The uproar in the orchard continued, especially when the sun began to set in the west and all the old ladies came out leaning on their sticks. This was something totally unheard of—for poor people to seize control of the fruit which belonged to the rich and then actually take that fruit to market and sell it. The crowd swelled. Even the timid ones who had been afraid to come out before—because deep in their hearts they felt there was something wrong about the whole thing—even they lost their scruples. People who had just dropped by to watch, rolled up their sleeves and plunged into the work. Everybody had caught a little of the spray, so why be afraid of the water? If they all dove in together then everybody would be in the same shape and no one would have to be afraid. Now all there was to fear was that you might get left out and all the best things would be taken by other people. The affair in the orchard had the whole village every bit as keyed up as Te-lu, Yü-min, and the other cadres. The cadres were pleased with the peasants' determination, and they were satisfied with their own growing prestige among the masses. They were also satisfied with the talk that was going around the village, for people were all saying that the cadres had handled things very well. Quite naturally the cadres were hoping that from here on everything would be smooth sailing. In any case, confiscation of the fruit was a good omen. No one was anticipating any big complications or trouble ahead.

. . . .

[The cadres' hopes proved premature. The village later exploded in a bitter struggle against the kingpin Ch'ien Wen-kuei. Psychologically, the struggle was brought to its climax through the efforts of Liu Man, whose entire family had been destroyed by Ch'ien, and, unwittingly, by Liu Man's insane brother, Liu Ch'ien.]

Translated by Tani E. Barlow

HU FENG
(Chang Kuang-jen, 1903–)

Hu Feng was one of China's most intelligent and best-known Marxist literary critics of the 1930s and 1940s. A native of Hupeh Province, Hu enrolled in Peking University and engaged in a variety of revolutionary activities in the mid-1920s, in Naking and later in Japan. In 1933 he returned to China to become one of Lu Hsün's most important followers when the once powerful Shanghai League of Left-wing Writers was beginning to fall apart. From 1937 to 1945, when Shanghai was occupied by Japanese forces, Hu Feng was among those leftist writers who fled south and eventually settled in Kuomintang-controlled Chungking to carry on political and literary activities during the second United Front. Others sought refuge in Yenan, the center of Communist wartime resistance.

"Realism Today," written by Hu Feng in December 1943, was one of Hu's major position statements. It caused an uproar in China then, and its echoes are still audible today. It is difficult to appreciate the significance of this short essay without knowing something about its contemporary political environment. Although Hu Feng was a prominent Marxist literary thinker, he never joined the Communist Party. Moreover, he had a reputation as an independent and often controversial literary personality. Although Hu had clashed in the 1930s with a number of Marxist literary figures whose first allegiance was to the Party, the Party itself had no clearly articulated policy toward the arts in the prewar era. Most scholars agree that leftist literary life in the 1920s and 1930s was quite diversified. In the early 1940s, however, Party leaders in Yenan made several attempts to organize the leftist literary movement by setting forth policies and programs designed to guarantee a high degree of ideological unity among Party cadres and left-wing intellectuals like Hu Feng. In early 1942, for example, a highly publicized *cheng-feng* or ideological rectification movement was launched in Yenan. Among other things, intellectuals and cadres were expected to study the works of Lenin, Stalin, Mao Tse-tung, and Liu Shao-ch'i. In May 1942, Mao himself delivered his famous "Talks at the Yenan Forum on Literature and Art," in which he spelled out the Party's policies toward the arts, including the principle of absolute Party leadership in the cultural realm. In 1943, Party officials in Yenan decided to extend the rectification movement to include cadres and intellectual supporters working in Chungking and other Kuomintang areas.

"Realism Today" is only one of many essays written by Hu Feng and his associates in response to the new trends. It is not especially well written and is worded rather hesitantly in some places, but its main thrust is quite clear. To be sure, there is nothing particularly original about Hu's call for a realistic literature that combines subjective and objective elements, or his rejection of literature that is excessively idealistic or deterministic. Of greater interest is his choice of specific targets of attack. The problem of transcendental escapism from the harsh realities of life and war, the first "new trend" discussed by Hu, was not a serious problem in the early war years. One suspects that by condemning such literature Hu was actually attempting to draw attention to his own materialist credentials. There can be little doubt that the real target of Hu's essay is the second trend he mentions, the theory that requires writers to stress "positive characters." This was nothing less than Hu's way of expressing alarm about the sort of ideas contained in Mao Tse-tung's "Talks at Yenan." "Do not force writers to tell lies, and do not malign real life," Hu pleaded at the end of his essay.

Hu Feng's "Realism Today" is significant because he sensed that important steps were being taken by Party literary leaders to redefine the role of the writer in the Chinese revolution. Hu believed that May Fourth literature was great (and revolutionary) precisely because writers insisted upon being an independent force in society and because they believed their primary role was to criticize contemporary society. Thus he was alarmed about the "positive character" trend, not because he was unwilling to write about positive developments, but because he believed such theories threatened the independence and integrity of Chinese writers. To be a critic of Chinese society, he implied, it was necessary to immerse oneself in the reality of society. Like others of his generation, including Mao, Hu Feng believed that literature and art played an extraordinarily important role in the Chinese revolution. But unlike Mao, Hu insisted upon the autonomy of literature from the state, regardless of whether the state was Confucian, Nationalist, or Communist.

Hu Feng continued to debate these issues with his Marxist colleagues throughout the 1940s, mostly via the influential monthly *July,* which he edited. Upon Japan's surrender Hu returned to Shanghai, where he stayed until 1953, when he moved back to Peking. Though he held several important cultural positions after the establishment of the People's Republic, he remained a controversial figure at odds with the Party. In 1955 a major campaign was launched to criticize Hu Feng. Among other things, he was accused of actually organizing a counterrevolution. On July 18, 1955, he was arrested and jailed. There was no word about him until July 1979, when it was reported that he had been released from prison in 1965 and had been living incognito in Szechwan.

Hu's major works include five volumes of essays and one book of poems.
—P.G.P.

Realism Today

From the beginning, the new literature has been inspired by the hope that real human life can be liberated. The notion that "words must have substance" reflects this basic spirit. More specifically, it means that "most of my material is *selected* from the lives of the unfortunate who live in our sick society. My motive is to *expose* the illness in order to induce people to pay attention to its cure" (Lu Hsün, "How I Came to Write Fiction"). It is in this way that the real content of history is given expression; the "substance" to which I refer is not something obscure. To do something "for the sake of life" means "improving life."

To do something "for humanity," one must, on the one hand, be sincere about doing it "for" humanity, and, on the other hand, have profound insights into the humanity "for whom" one is doing something. The material that is *selected* and the illness that is *exposed* must deal with the truth about the human condition. The one who does the "selecting" and "exposing" must have a mind keenly sensitive to both the "sickness" that afflicts the "sick society" and the "misfortunes" of the unfortunate. This unity or combination of subjective spirit and objective truth has produced a militant new literature. We call it realism.

Of course during the new literature movement there have been occasions on which the element of subjective spirit has been exaggerated. The liberation of the individual is, however, a requirement of history, and the need to transcend life has long been an important aspect of creative work. Actually, realism originally embraced these ideas. It is only when subjective spirit departs from the essence of reality and drifts into emptiness that it becomes a disease that is repugnant to realism. During the new literature movement there was also the tendency to chase after the ephemeral bubbles of life. The tendency, at the beginning, had been the result of an effort to face squarely a newly born reality. But if the subjective will is frozen or consumed by the object of study, true realists will protest. In the course of the new literature movement, aestheticism, mysticism, symbolism, satanism, and other trends have appeared from time to time, but they were merely reflections in the literary realm of corrupt forces in society itself and, as such, each could have no more than a fleeting existence in the development of realism.

If one looks back upon the history of the new literature it becomes apparent that, despite having labored under difficult circumstances and having experienced weakness, the basic spirit of the new literature has always been to reflect the demands of national and social liberation and to exert great effort in the bloody struggle for these goals. It took a stand against darkness and pursued light; it spoke on behalf of those who groaned beneath a legacy of suffering and reached out to the souls of those decent, steadfast, and industrious people who inherited this yoke of oppression. It observed with due dignity the past that was cold and dead, and sang praises to the first glimpse of dawn. . . . Because of this spirit, sparks have been scattered in the hearts of thousands upon thousands of people. These sparks have now ignited and are emitting a brilliant radiance in the sacred struggle of the present day, a struggle that finds our nation unyielding, unwilling to accept a meaningless existence, and believing firmly in victory and the bright future. What accounts for the rise in this spirit? It is the devoted will and benevolent affection of writers. It is a result of their thorough and correct understanding of real life and their total lack of self-deceiving hypocrisy. We call it realism.

This foundation of realism permits the new literature to develop further and to display its fighting qualities on those occasions when war breaks out.

Why do its fighting qualities become even more pronounced when hostilities erupt? It is because during wartime people are immersed in a surging tide of enthusiasm and excitement. They insist upon acquiring an understanding of life and they are sensitive to the feelings of life. Once they are exposed to the new literature it will be like fire igniting fire: not only will the fire burn with greater ease, the light it radiates will be stronger and its heat more intense.

Why will the new literature be able to develop even further? It is because the changes brought about by war have forced all segments of society, in varying degrees, to take a stand, and to show their true colors. Under such circumstances the objects studied by literature have become more diverse and conspicuous, and the writer is better able to penetrate deeply into human life. Because of the changes caused by war, writers have been liberated from their narrow circles. They have thrown themselves into the self-directed movement of life and experienced its exciting fervor. Consequently, their powers of cognition and their creative vigor are able to take great strides forward.

Such are the facts. But under the pretense of demanding "great works," some people have said that literature has not been sufficiently serious and has made no progress during the war of resistance, or, even worse, that the new literature has been moving down the wrong path. They are slanderers with ulterior motives, who have maligned not only writers and literature, but also our great nation and people. The new literature, whose lifeblood is realism, has become a national artery, a national nerve, and serves as a spiritual weapon of the people.

But it is necessary to point out that the new literature now finds itself in a most difficult situation, and is confronted with a serious crisis. Naturally, this distressing situation has social origins: it is a social phenomenon, not something developed just in the past day or two. The problem, as manifested in literature, is so acute that it has become a question of whether or not literature should exist.

First, there appeared facts which virtually amounted to elimination of literature, and then "theories" were produced to support the practice. These "theories" defy enumeration. Here I wish to cite only one or two as examples.

The first one seeks to create literature out of certain modes of thought, divorced from real life as much as possible. Why? Because real life is perceived as a bottomless swamp incapable of being reclaimed, whereas thought is viewed as something "lofty," as a priceless treasure. Of course, this theory is exceedingly "lofty," and those writers who comply with it are able to extricate themselves from Hell and summarily ascend into Heaven. No one doubts that there is plenty of happiness in Heaven, but the writer there is limited to writing about the Jade Emperor's Golden Dragon Palace and the moon goddess's powdered face. Do the theorists want to make a rebuttal? A debate of this sort would be like demons in Hell bickering across the immense space with fairies in Heaven and would thus produce no results, but there is no harm in "talking off the top of my head" and carrying on a bit. If thought could be irrelevant or even contrary to real life, that would be the end of the argument. But if thought is for the sake of or beneficial to the liberation of the nation, or to victory in the war, how can it be divorced from real life, and how can it not be truth that flows, like blood, through real life? If thought is divorced from real life or from the life and struggle of the broad masses, how can the nation be liberated and how can the war be won? Thought that is for the sake of or beneficial to the liberation of the nation and victory in war must, of necessity, derive its flesh and blood content, its richness, and its health from real life. A great thought is always a synthesis or refinement of tendencies in the development of real life and never a burdensome fetter pressing down on the shoulders of humanity or a cloud floating in the sky. Is it not true that in the bloody struggle waged by the people, thought provides great strength and leads the way? Is this not because the new literature of the past twenty years and the literature of the war of resistance have emerged from the depths of real life and produced the sweet aroma of the truth of life—which is thought itself?

The second theory requires writers to write about light or positive characters. Dark characters and those living in negative social environments should be ignored or, at best, be mentioned only in passing to embellish the text. Why? Because literature about light or positive characters is believed to produce virtuous people, while literature about dark characters and those in negative social environments is believed to cause readers to become depressed, corrupted, and even suicidal. Following such a theory could produce only one result: all writers will only daydream, with their eyes closed to reality. Think of it! If we surrender when facing violence or retreat when observing darkness, how can mankind's persistent reform movement continue to develop? How can our bitter struggle of the past six years, one in which our blood has flowed like rivers, continue to develop? Unless one is a slave by nature or through long-term practice, one need only observe the manner of the various bloodsucking brutes and unscrupulous charlatans to have one's disgust aroused. One need only see the expressions on the faces of those innocents who are killed in cold blood and the oppressed who have nowhere to file their complaints to have one's grief and indignation aroused. If this was not the case, the history of humankind would forever be subject to the reign of darkness. Think of the vast number of images contained in the new literature of the last twenty years and of the war of resistance that portray various oppressors and brutes as well as those who have suffered and been sacrificed at their hands! Did this sort of literature lead us to depression and corruption, or did it instead lead us to sobriety and action? Why should our new literature be an exception to the great works of world literature? Some say that the people Lu Hsün wrote about were all negative characters and thus conclude that there was no light in Lu Hsün's heart. The fact that some "theorists" think in this manner proves that they are but cowards before the power of darkness. I approve of writing about the bright aspects of life, and I disapprove of exposing darkness just to peddle something exotic. But where does light come from and where do we find positive characters? Light must break through the layers and layers of darkness that surround it. Positive characters are besieged by negative characters, in constant battle against them, and victimized by their barbarous slaughter. This is reality. This is the truth. Only by recognizing these truths can the works written by writers be true to life and educate and encourage their readers. If readers are armed with works of this sort when they return to the battlefield of life, they will not feel that writers are insane or destestable liars.

Although a theory like this claims to promote literature that is "bright" and "lofty," in reality it does not want literature to exist at all; it wants to strangle literature. It wants literature to take leave of real life and it wants writers to tell lies. It seeks to kill the spirit of realism. If this path is followed, literature will have to surrender its arms in the struggle for the liberation of the nation.

Of course, history will advance and realism will triumph. This sort of "theory" is nothing but a chloroformic perfume that puts you to sleep. True, the perfume may not kill you, but the enemy can more easily put you to death with one thrust of the knife when you are under its influence. We are engaged in a fierce struggle for the liberation of the nation, and our enemies are baring their fangs all around us, so we must rally all the forces latent in us.

I call the situation a crisis and I make an appeal on behalf of literature: do not force writers to tell lies, and do not malign real life!

Contrary to what some people think, this problem is not the exclusive concern of writers and literary workers. The list of those who must choose their destiny—to be enslaved by the power of darkness or to be citizens of a state of freedom, equality, and happiness—extends far beyond the ranks of writers of the present and future.

—December 3, 1943, at the "Villa to escape law," suburb of Chungking

Translated by Paul G. Pickowicz with the assistance
of Chang Chiu (Chiang Ch'ao)

YANG SHUO
(1913–68)

As a young man, Yang Shuo left his home in the Shantung Peninsula to study English and English literature in the Manchurian city of Harbin. He did not, however, give up his reading in classical Chinese literature. He even practiced writing classical Chinese poetry, which contributed to the development of his prose style. The invading Japanese drove him from the northeast to Canton in the south, where his first novella, *The Foothills of the Pamir Plateau,* was serialized in the Communist-sponsored *National Salvation Daily*.

After a brief stay in Yenan in 1939, Yang Shuo spent the next several years working with the Eighth Route Army in North China. His experiences there contributed to his many stories later collected in the *Moonless Night*. He returned to Yenan in 1943, and thence to Hopei, where he collected materials for his *Red Rock Hill,* a novel about coal miners struggling against capitalist mine owners. A series of war zone dispatches followed as he joined the army in its last push to control the whole of China in 1946–49; these stories have been assembled in the *Peian-Heiho Line,* and in *Mount Wang-nan*.

His first post-1949 assignment with the National Railroad Workers Union and his transfer to the Korean front in 1950 explain much of the background against which Yang Shuo wrote his *The Land Beautiful as Brocade* and *A Thousand Miles of Lovely Land*. Several terms of service with delegations abroad took him to a number of South Asian and African countries. He died of illness in August 1968.

He agreed with his critics that his best writing was in short sketches and reports, feature articles that he worked over with meticulous care before releasing them for publication. "I wrote every one of those short pieces," he said to a critic, "as though I was writing poetry—polishing each line until I was satisfied . . . I revised them again and again." There is much evidence of his patient polishing in *A Thousand Miles of Lovely Land.* The use of reduplicative phrases and onomatopoeic devices may be somewhat excessive, but it sets a style which many of his contemporaries imitated.   —K.Y.H.

---

from *A Thousand Miles of Lovely Land*

[The 212-page novel depicts North Koreans and Chinese volunteers fighting against the Americans in 1950–52, across the Yalu River.

A prologue spreads a rather poetic view of a Korean farmhouse near the Yalu River border. Across the river, near the bridgehead on the Chinese side, lives a Yao family. Yao Ch'ang-keng, a People's Liberation Army veteran now in charge of the maintenance of the bridgehead section of the railroad, is apprehensive about the war. His wife is worried over the marriage, only three days away, of their daughter, Chih-lan, to a lively, trustworthy young man, Wu T'ien-pao, a locomotive driver in the rail transport corps. The loss of the Yaos' two sons to the Japanese has made the only daughter that much more precious to the parents.

One morning in August 1950, Yao Ch'ang-keng and daughter Chih-lan start for work, he to the railroad station, she to the railline's telephone office . . .]

On his way to the station, Ch'ang-keng saw a train on a siding. Beside it a dozen soldiers were squatting in a circle, taking a hearty meal. They wore cotton-padded uniforms, but with neither red-star badges on their caps nor any other insignia. They were not our own People's Liberation Army at all. Getting suspicious, Ch'ang-keng slowed his pace and pricked up his ears.

"Let's have a good feed!" shouted a soldier who was as solid as a cannonball, filling his bowl. "This is newly reaped kaoliang. Just smell it!"

"If we had left home a few days later we could have reaped our crops," a soldier with thick lips said slowly. "For a whole year we busied ourselves in the classes and all kinds of exercises, and it was only during the intervals of study that we managed to sow and plough. Now that the crops are ripe, the Americans won't let us reap them. What a pity to leave them all in the fields!"

"You think just like a peasant," the cannonball chuckled. "So long as there are people to reap the crop and eat the grain, everything's all right and you have nothing to worry about. As the old saying goes, the old ones plant trees for the young ones to sit in the shade. Opening up waste land is our speciality."

Somehow the conversation turned from crops to the local produce of the various places they came from. The new topic being introduced, all the men struck in at once, each insisting that the produce of his native town was the best. One bragged that in the wind the immense wheat fields on the Hopei plain looked like boundless heaving seas; another sang the praises of the natural scenery and inexhaustible store of rice and fish in areas south of the Yangtze; a third expatiated upon the rich coal mines in Shansi, which lay near the surface of the earth. A Szechwanese boasted about the limpid water flowing from the "heart" of the Yangtze and the tea leaves on the top of Meng Mountain, while a boy from the northeast pointed to the gigantic factories thick as trees in a wood.

Being a keen fellow, Yao had already gathered something about these people from their talk. Gazing at these robust and plain young fellows, he felt indescribably happy. "O these people! . . ." he thought to himself, unable to hit upon a happier expression. For the moment, he could not yet recognize in them the bulwark of world peace and justice, the heroic volunteers of the Chinese people.

Someone hurried up from behind and patted Ch'ang-keng on the back by way of greeting. It was Chin Ch'iao, the Korean secretary of the railway administration bureau, who had come to Yenchi when a boy and had become a Chinese citizen. To Ch'ang-keng's surprise, Chin was in the same queer uniform as these soldiers.

"Don't you recognize me?" Chin said, smiling. "What are you looking at? I've joined the Chinese People's Volunteers, you see."

"What volunteers?" Ch'ang-keng inquired.

"Volunteers to aid Korea!" Chin answered. "We railway workers have formed a detachment of volunteers and very soon we shall cross the Yalu River. Comrade Wu Chen, director of the railway administration bureau, is the commander as well as political commissar of the detachment. Are you going to join up?"

This was the first Ch'ang-keng had heard about it. He smiled and parted from Chin without saying anything. Presently he stopped walking; for a few moments he stood rapt in thought as if rooted to the spot.

He came home early that evening. For many nights he had sat up late and hadn't got much sleep, so he returned early this evening after the basket weaving was over. Upon his arrival, he found his wife giving their daughter a dressing down. Chih-lan was leaning over the table, her chin on the back of her hands, her eyes full of tears, and her cheeks puffed.

Mrs. Yao thought that her husband had come to her rescue. Instantly she sang out: "Well, you should do something about this precious daughter of yours. She is vexing me to death. I have done everything for her, brought her up and fed her, haven't I? And now the only thing she does is to do mischief and get me into one set of trouble after another. What sort of a daughter is she? What mortal sins have I committed for God to punish me now by giving me a daughter who's always disgracing me? Oh, what a shame it all is!"

Ch'ang-keng was shocked, but he could make no head or tail of the matter. Again his wife shouted to their daughter: "Your father is to blame for having spoiled you so. I don't know what you're coming to. Now that the trousseau is ready and the wedding will soon be here, you declare you won't get married. Is marriage some sort of a game? Aiding Korea is your own lookout; but I won't let you go unless you get properly married."

"I don't want to get married! I don't want to!" Chih-lan muttered sulkily.

"I'll flay you alive if you don't," Mrs. Yao said, fuming. "If you're lost to shame, I'm not. Was there ever another girl like you in the world? I never heard of such a thing!"

In the last few days Chih-lan and some others had dipped into the history of American aggression against China and had got a clear notion about American ambitions. It would be too disgraceful for her to bother about her wedding at a time when everybody was talking about and working for the movement of opposing American aggression and aiding Korea. It was for this reason that she had been restless the last few days. What is more, those girls at the telephone office had very sharp tongues; to her dismay, they liked to make fun of her and T'ien-pao. One of them, Young Chu, was particularly malicious. She was always ready to catch people on the raw and hold them up to ridicule. Like a sparrow, she would chirrup on and on, sparing nobody.

When Chih-lan went to the office that morning, Young Chu was chatting with somebody downstairs. Chih-lan was in a new coat and Chu, cocking her head on one side, took her in with mocking deliberation. "What a smart dresser!" Chu remarked ironically. "No wonder people say clothes make the man; your new coat certainly makes you much prettier. Well, tell me, who are you all dressed up for?"

"Don't let your high spirits run away with you, or you won't know where or who you are," Chih-lan said, blushing and giving Chu a hostile look.

"I won't forget who I am or what my name is, though somebody I know may soon be forgetting hers. She will have Yao for surname today and Wu tomorrow without knowing which fits her better," Chu said with a giggle and set the others roaring with laughter. "Chih-lan, I suppose you're going to join the detachment," Chu said maliciously. "I'm too backward—not a patch on some other people."

Chih-lan blushed in embarrassment. Presently she turned her head, shut her mouth, and walked away. She enlisted that day, the first one in her section.

The news threw Mrs. Yao into a fury. When her threats proved of no avail, she began to coax and wheedle her daughter. "I know," she said, "you don't care much for your poor mother. But as I am older and have had more experience than you, you might have asked me first. It's all very well for you to talk about going to Korea; but what could your father do if T'ien-pao came and asked for you when you were gone?"

"What does T'ien-pao think?" Ch'ang-keng asked.

"I don't know," Chih-lan said sulkily. "He's on his train and I've sent him a letter."

"What nonsense did you put in your letter?" Mrs. Yao asked quickly.

"I made a challenge and said let's see which of us crosses the Yalu River first," Chih-lan replied.

"Just listen, the wench is out of her senses!" Mrs. Yao cried out, striking the couch with the palm of her hand. "A young girl wanting to go into war and leave home and comfort behind! Well, I never heard of such a thing. Do you mean to go to your death?"

Ch'ang-keng cast a glance at his daughter, his heart glowing with admiration. He felt very proud of her pluck. But very soon a faint sadness stole upon him as he thought of the separation and long journey she had to take. He wanted to say something but all that he managed to say in a husky voice was: "It's getting late, you'd better go to bed."

. . . .

The detachment set up its headquarters on Chenkiang Hill on the Yalu River. Chih-lan was in deep distress. She had been the first one in her section to enlist but she was not even allowed to move into the detachment compound. To her chagrin, she had witnessed Young Chu triumphantly packing up her things at the office that morning, ready to move into the detachment headquarters. What sense could one possibly make of that? Was it because she was not qualified? She flushed crimson with shame at the thought. She became awfully fidgety. With a sudden turn of her head, she ran to the headquarters. She wanted to ask Wu Chen about it. Leaning stiffly against the door, she gave Wu a look of hate and sulked in sombre silence.

Wu knew what she had on her mind. "What has bitten you?" he asked, smiling. "Fancy coming in the cool of the morning with such a long face, looking for a quarrel!"

Chih-lan broke into a laugh in spite of herself. "Commander Wu," she said eagerly, still with her eyes cast down, "when shall I move in? I have volunteered but am not permitted to come. What sort of 'volunteer' am I?"

Wu suppressed a smile and said, while washing: "It's splendid, of course, that you should want to come. But on second thought, I think you'd better not. You're too young, and a woman, too."

"What, a woman? Is Young Chu a man, then?" Chih-lan interrupted vehemently. "And you know, she is even younger than I. Why should she be called into service but not I? What sort of justice is that? It's enough to make a deaf-mute shout!"

"But yours is a different case," Wu said. "Isn't it true that you're going to get married?"

This made Chih-lan blush like a pomegranate flower. She jerked her head to one side and clenched her fists. Then she said angrily, "Marriage, marriage, always marriage! What if I don't want to get married?"

"What a stubborn girl!" Wu thought to himself with a smile. "Comrade," he drawled, "don't be in such a hurry! Hurrying won't help matters. You're a member of the Youth League, and the first thing you should do is to observe discipline."

A pang shot through her heart and two tears rolled down her cheeks. She hurriedly wiped them away with her sleeve. She felt so utterly wretched. Yet to whom could she tell her grievances? Mother was unsympathetic, and the commander tried hard to put her off with the magic word "marriage." "What sort of girl would I be if I were thinking about marriage at a time like this," she thought bitterly. "Everybody treats me like a child, but I'm not a child any longer! Indeed I would rather die than get married; you people can just wait and see."

Wu was searching for a soothing word or two to say, when his breakfast was brought in. "Stop crying, Chih-lan," he said. "What are you crying about? Have you had your breakfast? I guess not. Let's share what we have here and continue our talk."

Chih-lan didn't answer. "Come on, please," Wu urged, "you can't go on sulking at your stomach's expense!"

Chih-lan burst into a laugh. "You'll let me go to Korea, won't you?" she pleaded, smiling. "You see, I'm so anxious to go that I don't even care for my meals. You don't mean to keep me fasting, do you?"

"Help yourself, help yourself," Wu said repeatedly, pointing to the food with his chopsticks.

They were just about to start when suddenly a bomb exploded. The walls shook and a big lump of lime fell from the ceiling and was scattered all over the table.

Wu jumped to his feet, throwing away his chopsticks. "It looks as if we'll indeed go fasting," Wu said angrily. Then he opened the window and looked out.

Bombs had fallen in some sections of the town and flames darted up into the air in quick succession. Over the river a big fire was burning and smoke spread a thick screen over the bridge. Large puffs of black smoke mushroomed, blocking, for the moment, the sunshine from the earth. Bullets swept whistling through the air and fell in a shower. It had been a fine day, dry and refreshing; but in the twinkling of an eye darkness came.

Wu jumped out of the window into the jeep outside the gate and started for the bridge. "Comrade Chin," he shouted back, "send some men to the bridge, quick!" Then a wind rose. Sinuiju on the other side of the river became a hell of fire. The ceiling-paper of dwelling houses was reduced to black ashes. It was blown across the river, fluttering over the streets. On arriving, Wu began to notice a hubbub of screams and groans gathering volume from the southern end of the bridge. In an instant a crowd of Koreans emerged from the smoky haze, men and women, old and young, their clothes torn, their faces badly burnt, some hugging bed-quilts and some carrying children, all crying and cursing, puffing and blowing, madly surging towards the street.

Pale and stern, Yao Ch'ang-keng dashed down the bridge in Wu's direction, exclaiming that the bridge had caught fire.

After the smoke dispersed, they saw the flames gutting the boards of the bridge. With ropes, clubs, hooks, and buckets in their hands, the whole volunteer detachment and local railway workers rushed from all directions to save the bridge. "This is risking our necks. The enemy planes are still overhead. Who'll be held responsible if anybody gets killed?" Yao heard someone grumbling behind him. He looked back at him with hatred.

"All the women comrades go over the bridge with the medical units to help the victims," Wu Chen called out. "No one can tell what is happening in Sinuiju!"

Yao Chih-lan ran onto the bridge with the other girls, following those who carried sacks marked with the red cross.

Young Chu was naive and talkative. She kept on chattering to Chih-lan all their way to the bridge.

"Can't you be quiet for a while?" Chih-lan asked. "What are you talking about before such a horrific air raid?"

"Do you mean you're afraid?"

"Quite so. But I hope you're not," Chih-lan replied angrily. "Don't talk big, my girl," she said to herself, "we'll see who'll get scared."

Smoke on the bridge assailed their faces and made Chih-lan cough and weep. The bridge was hit; the rails became crooked and the boards were scattered in all directions. Looking through the glaring gap between the sleepers, one could see water whirling past below.

Dead fish of all sizes drifted down the river with their white bellies turned up. Water splashed on the bridge, froze and became slippery and shiny as glass. The workers rushed into the smoke, knocking down the burning boards into the river and fetching water from below to put the fire out. Wherever water was poured, black smoke curled up, hissing. But in a minute flames rose again and the workers had to stamp them out with their feet. In their excitement, they did not even feel pain when their heels were scorched.

Chih-lan was worrying about the difficulty of getting the wounded over the damaged bridge when Wu Chen's crisp clear voice rang out, "Get some smart fellows to put the footway into shape so that the wounded can be sent over." Quick-witted and courageous, Wu was as resourceful in ideas as he was resolute in action. "He could pluck stars from the heavens if he wanted to," Chih-lan sometimes thought in amazement.

The air over Sinuiju was murky with smoke. The sun had disappeared and even the sky looked burnt. Here and there shells of incendiary bombs were scattered. The uncropped rice had been reduced to smoldering cinders which flew up into people's faces when the wind blew. As far as one's eyes could see, heaps of Koreans lay dead.

Chih-lan's heart stood still. Glancing backward, she found Chu's face ghastly pale, her bloodless lips all atremble. Chih-lan wanted to speak, but she felt her tongue tied beyond her control. She shivered with fear but was not able to utter a word.

Suddenly a little Korean girl rushed up barefooted, her torn apron fluttering in the wind. Chih-lan stepped forward to meet her. The little girl hugged Chih-lan with a heartbreaking cry as if she were her nearest and dearest in the world. The girl dragged Chih-lan along to her home.

It was no longer a home. The house had been knocked down and the furniture burnt. Only heaps of cinders were left smoldering. Though there was nothing left to burn, the red flames rose steadily.

In the flare of the fire Chih-lan found the girl's mother lying prostrate in the mud. What a sight she was! Her head was turned to one side, her big rough hands lay on her bosom, which was gory with blood. She lay motionless but her face looked soft and her limbs alive. A doctor who had come along with Chih-lan knelt down beside her, tore open the blood-soaked garment, and whispered, "She is still alive!" Yes, she was alive.

The doctor gave Chih-lan a glance and asked her to help dress the wound. Blood soaked through the dressing and stained her hand. Chih-lan's heart thumped, her face went white, and her fingers trembled in spite of herself.

"What's the matter?" the doctor inquired.

"I don't know," Chih-lan said, wiping her face with her arm and biting her lower lip.

The Korean woman came to herself with a deep sigh. She looked painful and exhausted. For some time, she fixed her eyes upon Chih-lan, her mouth twitched on the verge of a smile. She raised her hand and stretched it out for nobody knew what. As Chih-lan drew closer, the Korean woman smiled sadly. Softly her hands wiped away the beads of sweat on Chih-lan's face and caressed it.

What hands she had! They were chapped, blackened, and hardened through work. But their touch was gentle and soothing. They were hands that had sewn and knitted, sown and planted for a whole lifetime. They were the hands of a woman who never had the heart to crush even an ant. Like a swallow, she had devoted her whole being to building a nest and planning a future for her fledglings, fetching now a mouthful of clay and now a mouthful of straw. The imagined future would become reality one day but the mother, its creator, had fallen in a pool of blood spilt by the American fiends.

Again the enemy planes made a raid over the Yalu River. Shells whistled past and smoke rose from the banks. Suddenly, a great splash of water leaped over the bridge. Hurriedly Chih-lan straightened up and saw someone dashing down the bridge through the dust and disappear. Then he came out again on the embankment. Another bomb exploded and the man rolled over and over.

Looking at the man's back, Chih-lan recognized her father.

Yao Ch'ang-keng was bowled over and buried under heaps of earth. He crawled out and felt as if he had just turned a dozen somersaults, his head swimming and stars before his eyes. For a moment he couldn't even remember what he had come for.

Why, of course, he had come to Li Chun-san's rescue. During the air raid a moment before, Ch'ang-keng thought he saw him clinging to the rails of the bridge. Then an explosion came and shook him down into the river, fortunately not very far from the bank. Perhaps not a heavy fall, if his luck was in.

Gradually Ch'ang-keng recollected this. He turned his eyes to the river bank and saw that Li was no longer there. He must have crept to somewhere else, he thought. Ch'ang-keng called him but there was no response. Then he came to a part of the bridge with no water under it.

"Anybody there? Help! Help!" a voice rang out from under it.

The voice struck Ch'ang-keng as strange, and he walked down and asked, "Is that Li Chun-san?"

"No. I'm Cheng Ch'ao-jen," came the reply.

"Who's he?" Ch'ang-keng wondered. As he approached and peered at him, he found it was the man who had complained when they were crossing the bridge over the Yalu River. Pale with fear, the man was clinging to the bridge as if he wanted to squeeze his body into it to be out of danger.

"What's wrong with you?" Ch'ang-keng asked with deep disgust.

"I don't know," Cheng said gloomily, "I can't stand."

Ch'ang-keng examined his legs and found nothing wrong with them. He tried to help Cheng to his feet. Whining piteously, Cheng slightly raised his right leg, his left leg still laying on the ground. Then he sank down with a thud and broke into a cry.

"You seem to have been frightened out of your wits," Ch'ang-keng said grimly after taking a long look at him. "Be a man and don't behave like a blubbering old woman! Pull yourself together."

"I'm not afraid of dying, you know, but only of being disabled," Cheng complained. "I'm young and I've lots to do; if I were disabled, it would have been a waste for the country to have brought me up."

Ch'ang-keng had no time to talk. Raising Cheng's arm and putting it round his neck, Ch'ang-keng carried him up to the embankment and hurried towards the bridge.

At that moment Wu Chen was supervising the repair work on the bridge. His dark square face glistened with sweat. Quickly taking charge of the wounded Cheng, he said to Ch'ang-keng: "You look tired."

"You're the technician of the detachment, aren't you?" he asked, taking Cheng in. "What's wrong with you?"

"Something wrong with his legs," Ch'ang-keng said, panting.

With Wu Chen's help, Cheng moved a few steps forward. He could walk, though clumsily.

"You have probably got convulsions," Wu said and called Ta Luan to help Cheng take a little walk.

"I'm really worried about my legs," Cheng murmured. "Even sleeping on the cold floor is bad for them."

"Maybe you've been frightened into a fit of convulsions," Ta Luan said jokingly.

Wu glared at Ta Luan. Turning to Ch'ang-keng, he asked: "Any more people falling behind?"

"There is still Li Chun-san," Ch'ang-keng replied. Turning back, he shambled away.

"Where're you going?" somebody said, trying to stop him. "Do you want to tire yourself to death?"

"I'm forty already and it won't matter much if I die," Ch'ang-keng said, "but Li's a youngster, and it would be a shame if something happened to him."

Somehow Wu managed to stop him. "Don't you bother," he told Ch'ang-keng, "I'll send somebody to look for him."

All the way along Ch'ang-keng felt his heart thudding violently. His legs were like heavy weights. He reached the northern end of the bridge in a daze. He sat down on the ground, unable to move any further. His cotton coat was soaked through with sweat. Wu Chen knew that Ch'ang-keng was utterly exhausted. He asked some of his men to send Ch'ang-keng home for a good rest.

"This is no time for rest, there's work for every one of us," Ch'ang-keng said, smiling weakly and shaking his head. "Comrade Wu, you know me. For years I've lived near this bridge. For more than ten years I saw the Japanese crossing the bridge to murder our people. Now that things are just beginning to pick up, the Americans want to do the same. I can't look on and let them do that. We must never allow the bad old days to return."

Wu Chen fixed his gaze on Ch'ang-keng, his head on one side, not knowing exactly what he meant.

"There is only one thing for me to do, I must join the detachment," Ch'ang-keng said without lifting his eyes.

"Your daughter is coming," someone said, pointing to the southern end of the bridge.

Chih-lan arrived on the scene with another worker. They came up at a snail's pace, dragging Li Chun-san along. Chih-lan thought the raid must have killed her father and tore towards the embankment. But there she found Li Chun-san instead. She was tired out and smeared all over with mud and blood. Her plaits were scorched and looked yellowish, the tips of her hair were all singed.

Wu Chen looked from the father to the daughter. The past years flashed over his mind. A course of more than ten years is not an easy one to travel. When the force of darkness seemed to have reigned supreme, and when struggles were at their bitterest, Wu Chen saw such fathers and daughters—such people —coming to the fore, fighting shoulder to shoulder through wind and rain, fog and snow. Before such great and plain people, what brute force could hope to prevail or to avoid a crushing defeat? He admitted the Yaos into the detachment right on the spot.

By this time, the northern sky had cleared up and the sunshine was dazzlingly bright. But in Korea, south of the river, the smoky haze still shrouded the sky. Then, as the northern wind rose and the smoke began to disperse, the sunshine gradually reached the bridge, the river, and the southern bank, and lit all of them up.

That day, under the cover of dark night, Wu Chen and his detachment crossed the Yalu River.

. . . .

[A war saga unfolds with the Chinese volunteer detachment plunging into battle alongside the North Koreans, involving more than just the few characters already identified thus far.

An old army cook, Old Pao, stubborn to the point of the humorous and the comic who sticks to the group through thick and thin, scolds the young and foolish, but always cheers them on in the battle. A Korean stationmaster tries to make life a little easier for the detachment members; he has no knowledge of the spoken Chinese but an excellent command of classical Chinese literature, hence he communicates with them by passing written notes back and forth. Another Korean commander, fluent in Chinese because he had fought for the Eighth Route Army against the Kuomintang troops in North China, is now receiving his due reward through these Chinese volunteers. All along, the college student turned volunteer, Cheng Ch'ao-jen, undergoes a slow, sometimes painful, political and physical metamorphosis to come gradually closer to the true revolutionary.

The story follows many subplots, but the telephone girl Yao Chih-lan and her fiancé Wu T'ien-pao remain central. Her interaction with her co-workers, girls from different backgrounds with different temperaments, particularly the outspoken and teasing Hsiao Chu (Little Chu, or Young Chu), brightens up their otherwise hard and bleak life, in mountain caves, along railroad beds, in the woods, braving blizzards and windstorms. More than once they have to chew snow along with the dwindling ration of dry cornmeal just to survive. Suddenly a time-bomb falls right in front of the entrance to their cave, sealing them inside. When they finally manage to escape, Young Chu has lost an eye.

Wu T'ien-pao, whose duties separate him from the telephone girls, keeps the train running, under American air attack. He achieves narrow escapes by speeding for shelter in tunnels.

They run into suffering old Chinese who have settled in North Korea; they also visit the same Korean family, whose son had gone to war for the revolutionary cause, first introduced in the prologue. They witness the ridiculous state of affairs of American prisoners of war, and participate in some lighthearted moments in a field hospital where Chih-lan tries to cheer up her wounded comrades. All the while, American planes seem to be hovering overhead; in an actual bombardment of a bridge, a loyal North Korean comrade and by now good friend to the Chinese volunteers, Ch'e Ch'ang-chieh, loses his life, and Yao Ch'ang-keng is wounded.

Meanwhile, young love continues to smolder, causing moments of pain . . .]

So far Yao Chih-lan had heard nothing from Wu T'ien-pao. Every time the home mail arrived, people trooped up to get their letters, and every time

Chih-lan was disappointed. She would mutter dazedly, "Why no letters for me?"

To her exasperation, T'ien-pao hadn't written her a single word. "Is he angry with me—why doesn't he write?" she brooded in fury. "Let's break if off if we must; I'm not afraid. But nothing would make me go back to you after that, even if you grovelled in the dust and kept on kowtowing till there was a hole in the ground."

After seeing her father to the door, Chih-lan again turned her thoughts to T'ien-pao. She simply couldn't get her mind off him.

Drifts of snow in the courtyard had thawed into small pools of black water. The foot-long icicles hanging from the eaves also melted. Drip, drip, drip, went the sound.

Chih-lan felt her head itching. She fetched a basin of water and unbraided her two little plaits, getting ready to wash her hair. Kneeling down on the brick bed, she began slowly to comb her hair.

Chih-lan hated herself for being constantly troubled by petty personal feelings. Commander Wu was never like that, she pondered with envy.

She remembered Wu Chen had once told her quietly: "A man should never care too much about himself. He should always serve the people and love them. Excessive self-love makes one selfish, calculating, and cowardly. Cowardice, you see, has its ideological basis. It is nothing but a form of selfishness."

Young minds are like spring soil; you can expect to reap from them whatever you have sown. Wu's words took root in Chih-lan's mind, and she followed him as her example in all respects.

Wu Chen gave a savor to everyday meals, he put spice into the life around him; he was a true Communist. Unobtrusive wherever he went, friendly to whomever he met, he served as the standby for all and sundry.

Talking about Wu, Ta Luan once observed, "It's just not his nature to care about himself."

True, Wu Chen never bothered about his own affairs. He was surprisingly careless about his food and clothing. Sometimes work kept him busy all night, and the next morning, when his head began to swim and his voice grew husky, Ta Luan would suggest sending for a doctor. "Too much of a nuisance!" Wu would say, stopping him. "I can sleep it off; no need for medicine."

His attitude towards others, however, was a different matter. Chih-lan learned much about Wu's life in the army from Ta Luan. In the old days, no matter how long the march they were making, Wu Chen never rode his horse. It was used to carry either the sick or supplies. One summer day he and Ta Luan set out alone on an errand and came across a soldier who was very ill. They made a stretcher with small birches and carried him over a mountain path for seven miles until they finally reached their camp.

Wu's self-sacrificing spirit was always an inspiring example, though Chih-lan so far hadn't always followed it. Not infrequently, personal troubles engrossed her mind. That was why she hated herself.

Slowly doing her hair, she pondered on absentmindedly.

Young Chu was washing clothes in the kitchen. The door opened with a click, and she came in with a basin full of clothes which she had wrung out; her mouth crackled like a string of firecrackers. "This Korean weather, just a moment ago the yard was full of sunshine. Now it's all clouded over, before you know where you are. Where am I going to dry these clothes I've washed?" Muttering to herself, she stretched a rope across the room and hung up the clothes.

"I wish you'd be more careful hanging up those wet clothes," Chih-lan said, turning around. "You're splashing water all over my face. Something must have gone wrong with your eyes. Everything seems to strike you as strange in Korea, except yourself."

"Why, isn't it strange? Look at Kang Mum Jai. When we met her for the first time we all thought there must be an old man in her family. Now we've got to her house, all we find is Achimani and Kang's little nephew, Kangkunni. Nobody has ever hinted that Achimani has got a sister-in-law. There's something fishy about it all, if you ask me."

Chih-lan parted her hair in the middle and let it drape over her shoulders. "Oh, shut up," she said, cocking her head on one side as she braided the hair. "You'd better mind your own business. We don't know Korean; we may have misunderstood them. You're all right except for that loose tongue of yours. When are you going to take yourself in hand?"

"Oh, God," Chu shrieked, "open your mouth and let me see how many teeth you've got. Other people have thirty-four at most, but you must have more to be able to talk so beautifully!" With a gesture of her hand, she went out.

"Ha! Wu T'ien-pao is here," Chu shouted with a laugh, out in the yard. "When did you arrive?"

Chih-lan suppressed a laugh and ignored her. She wouldn't be taken in by this mischievous imp again. Last time when Chu had played the same trick on her she was foolish enough to rush out to meet T'ien-pao and made a spectacle of herself.

"Chih-lan, come out, quick," Chu called again, in real earnest. "What're you so shy about?" She ran toward the door and pushed it open.

Chih-lan blushed to the roots of her hair. The plait she was making slipped out of her hand.

At the door stood T'ien-pao, dark and cheerful, his eyes and lips smiling. He looked strong, fresh, and happy, his cap pushed back and a shock of hair sticking out.

Upon T'ien-pao's appearance, the anger and hate that had been brewing in Chih-lan's breast all went up in smoke. Happy as a lark, she completely forgot her previous determination to give him the cold shoulder. In spite of everything, T'ien-pao remained the same wonderful person. But when she came to realize that he had come from China, T'ien-pao appeared in a new light. In her mind's eye he had now become a completely new man. Without waiting for him to sit down, she plied him with all sorts of questions while smiling sweetly at him.

T'ien-pao told her that after the conclusion of the second campaign the lights had again come flooding during the night, on the northern bank of the Yalu River. The volunteers, people said, were like stars in the sky, giving people light wherever they went. As usual, T'ien-pao's answers sparkled with wit, though there seemed to be no end to Chih-lan's questions. He remained undaunted even when her questions became more and more pointless.

"Is the Yalu River as blue as ever? What're our folks doing every day?" she asked.

"Oh, lord, how could it change its color?" T'ien-pao laughed, pushing back the cap and scratching his head. "It's the Yalu River, not the Yellow River, you know. What's wrong with you today? You used to talk good sense, but now you chatter as if you had lost your wits."

But Chih-lan felt differently. She thought many momentous changes must have taken place in her country during the months since she had left, and they must be most exciting. She hadn't realized until this moment how anxiously she had yearned for news from her country. Her heart had dwelt not only on her own home but on her country as a whole.

At home, she mused, you could walk about in the daytime and turn on lights at night; you could do whatever you liked and get what you wanted. But strangely enough, she had always taken these things for granted, utterly unaware of their significance. Only after her arrival in a land of suffering did she really understand the happiness—the great happiness—these everyday things meant.

The first rush of excitement over, Chih-lan calmed down. She asked T'ien-pao why he hadn't written to her.

"What's the use of writing letters?" T'ien-pao laughed. "I joined the detachment the moment I received your letter challenging me. I thought I had to cross the Yalu River anyway and we would meet and be able to talk our heads off. So I might very well be spared the trouble of writing and save ink and paper. Besides, I didn't have time. All the workers were speeding up production and my crew was completing 150,000 kilometers of safe-running and trying to set a new record at the same time. We had to put everything we'd got into it, you see, and I had no time to write. Are you angry with me for that?"

"Have I got such a bad temper?" Chih-lan said with a toss of her head. "You needn't write me for the whole of your life if you don't want to! That's your lookout, and it has nothing to do with me."

"As long as you're not angry with me, I'll be happy," T'ien-pao laughed, fumbling in his pocket. "You see, you've been making such a fuss that I forgot to give you my little gift."

Chih-lan peered into the pocket and caught a glimpse of a book. Without waiting for T'ien-pao to produce it, she stuck her hand into his pocket, and dug out a number of interesting articles—a harmonica, a diary, and a carefully folded picture. T'ien-pao snatched the picture away and hid it behind his back, just when Chih-lan was starting to unfold it.

"I don't want to keep it. Just let me have a look at it," Chih-lan pleaded, knitting her brows and swaying her body.

"You may look at it but you mustn't touch it," T'ien-pao said. Then, unfolding the picture, he held it up at arm's length. It was the same colored portrait of Chairman Mao that he had shown Chih-lan the first time he went to her house.

She held the book in her left hand and flipped the pages over. It was a travel book about North Korea and it instantly aroused her interest.

T'ien-pao watched her and smiled. "What a bookworm you are," he whispered. "You seem to give up your whole life to books. You never think of me, do you?"

"Why should I?" Chih-lan said, hiding her face with the book. "Every day I've got so much to think about and so much to do. You simply have no time to bother about such trifling matters."

"Is it a trifling matter?" T'ien-pao pressed, grasping her hand.

"Don't touch me," whispered Chih-lan, struggling to get her hand out of his and eyeing the doorway. "What would people say if they caught us?"

"How timid you are," T'ien-pao said. "Don't be afraid, I'm not a tiger. I won't eat you up." Instantly he stood up, seized his cap, and started spinning it on his finger.

Chih-lan peered at him from behind the book, smiling quietly. "Now it's you who's losing your temper!" she said to herself. "Well, you may go on sulking until you burst with anger." Burying her head into the book, she deliberately ignored him.

This really got under T'ien-pao's skin. He had come to Korea and had passed the previous night in a big cave. He had come to the detachment headquarters on business and then he had gone to visit Chih-lan to show how he felt about her. But apparently she didn't enjoy the visit.

"Don't read now," he cried, snatching the book away. "What's the good of reading now?"

"Nothing wrong with it," said Chih-lan, suppressing a smile.

"I'm no fool!" T'ien-pao said. "What about our getting married?"

For some time Chih-lan fixed her eyes upon him. "Don't always harp on that," she said quietly. "This is no time for marriage. You know that. I won't forget you and I believe you won't forget me. So long as we love each other, we can leave that to take its course. What's the use of talking about it now?"

T'ien-pao riveted his eyes upon Chih-lan in great astonishment. Outwardly, of course, she remained the same as ever, limp and slender, with heavy eyelids and liquid eyes and two little plaits hanging down her back. But her bearing and her talk had something different about them. She had almost become a new woman, he thought.

"A man should not just care about himself; that's selfish," Chih-lan began to lecture, assuming Wu Chen's tone. "He should always serve the people and love them. What happiness will marriage bring us when the enemy is pointing his bayonet at our throat? Everybody knows how a slave lives. You have had the experience, and so have I. So if you love me, love your country."

"What's going on?" somebody chuckled outside. "Enemies one moment and friends the next."

Chih-lan recognized Young Chu's voice and dashed out to deal with her.

Halting in the middle of the yard, Chu turned back and pleaded: "Now don't make a fuss, please. I only came for my overcoat. Please give it to me. I'm looking for a place where I can get some sleep. I'm on duty this evening, you know. I'm no eavesdropper and I'm not interested in your talk at all."

Outside the sky was overcast. From time to time, a cold draft surged into the room. It looked like snow. The air in the yard was filled with drifting chimney smoke. Quite imperceptibly, the hour for supper had come. T'ien-pao had night duty to perform and could stay no longer. When he rose to say goodbye, Chih-lan's hard heart suddenly softened. She would very much have liked to walk a little way with him, but Chu was there and shyness held her back. To hide her embarrassment, she hastened to sweep the bed with a broom as soon as he went out of the house.

From the distance came the sweet songs of grey thrushes and Mongolian larks. "He is whistling. What a clever mouth he has," Chih-lan thought, quietly smiling to herself.

[Nearly eighteen months have passed since the volunteers first crossed the Yalu River. Now, against a North Korean landscape that is once again in full bloom, the hero reaches his fateful destination . . .]

When Wu Chen's men were working hard on the Chong-chon bridge, a heavily loaded train ran across the Yalu River and raced towards the front. The driver's cab was heavily curtained so that no light should show. From between the blackout curtains a head poked out, looking forward, and the dim moonlight revealed the lean face of Yu Liong Tal, guide on Wu T'ien-pao's train.

Yu was a man of few words and always said only what was necessary: "Going uphill . . . going downhill . . . slow down . . . stop . . ." And the driver would act accordingly.

As the train approached a station, the stationmaster on duty would come out to greet it, hiding a small signal-lamp inside his coat. Opening the coat for a brief moment, he would flash a green light to the train, which rushed past without stopping.

T'ien-pao sat in the driver's seat, looking from the water indicator to the steam gauge. He steadily increased the speed and the train tore cheerfully on, shaking and rattling over the bumpy, war-damaged roadbed. T'ien-pao remembered how Kao Ch'ing-yün had said he wished they had more antitank grenades. The train now carried not only antitank grenades but heavy tanks. Before starting off, T'ien-pao had walked up and down the train, itching to lift the tarpaulin draped over these tanks and touch them. But to his regret, the train escort wouldn't allow him to. "What's he afraid of?" T'ien-pao said to himself. "I don't mean any harm. What's wrong with touching them?"

T'ien-pao smiled at his own thoughts.

Liu Fu-sheng was shoveling coal. Straightening up, he saw T'ien-pao smiling and asked: "What are you smiling at?"

"Guess," T'ien-pao answered, still smiling.

Liu, being a straightforward man, had little patience for guessing. He never could hide anything from anybody. He hated to keep anything to himself. When he woke up in the morning he would tell what he had dreamed the previous night.

The train pulled up at a big station to take on coal and water. T'ien-pao leapt down, a small hammer in one hand, and started tapping the rails. He felt the axletrees with the back of his hand and tested the screws. Liu stood on the step, blocking the entrance to the cab with his bulk, folding his sinewy arms. "It's chilly," he said. "Autumn only chills one's flesh but spring chills one to the bone. It's really too early to leave off your padded clothes. In my home in Shantung, the ears must have formed on the wheat by now."

"Oh, have you got a home?" T'ien-pao asked casually, still hammering.

"Why shouldn't I have a home? I didn't just spring out of thin air, when I was born," Liu said. "I wonder what my wife's doing at home just now."

"Oh, I expect she's thinking of you," said T'ien-pao with a laugh.

"I must admit she is a good wife, all right," Liu said. "She's a hard worker. Every night she sits by the lamp doing needlework after getting the kid to sleep. That child was born at the right time all right. When I was a boy of six, you see, I had nothing but water and gruel to live on. I was just a skeleton with a big belly. My son has things different. He's not only got plenty to eat, but can go to school. Do you know, he's the first one in our family for three generations who ever had a chance to go to school? All this time while I have been here fighting Americans and helping Koreans, my son has been at school. I would have insisted on coming even if Chairman Mao didn't like it."

Beyond the hills lights flashed up now and again. They were the enemy's flares.

"None of your nonsense, now!" T'ien-pao said. "Have you raked out the ashes? Get everything ready, we've got to get a move on."

"Pooh! They're only trying to scare us!" Liu said, spitting contemptuously at the flares. "It would be up with us if we let you frighten us with those things!"

The train rumbled forward once more. Time and again T'ien-pao poked his head out of the curtain, looking ahead.

The night was far spent. The damp wind gently swept over T'ien-pao's face. To his annoyance, the half-moon was still there as if glued to the sky.

Only after they had started did Liu's question once again come to T'ien-pao's mind: "I wonder what my wife's doing now?" It was a good question. T'ien-pao wondered what people at home were doing. "Having a good rest after a day's hard work? But Chairman Mao wouldn't have gone to bed yet. People say he always works late into the night. He has brought happiness to the people yet he takes little rest himself. Chairman Mao, you mustn't overwork yourself."

While such thoughts rushed through his mind, he instinctively raised his hand to feel Chairman Mao's portrait in his shirt pocket and recalled Chairman Mao's instructions which were printed at the bottom of the picture: "Love for the motherland, love for the people, love of labor and of science, and respect for public property should be cultivated in the country as the common virtues of the people." "I always want to do as you bid," T'ien-pao thought, "though I still have to make more effort." In the past four months or so he had only performed one meritorious deed which had won him a medal. He wanted to perform more. "I must win enough medals to decorate my coat, when I return home in triumph." He wanted to live in glory as Chairman Mao taught.

When he went home, T'ien-pao thought, he would have a few days' rest. But first of all, he would give his engine a good cleaning. His heart always ached at the thought that it had got so dirty. He was determined to make the copper parts shine so that you could see your face in them. As for himself, he would have a really good dinner and a good sleep.

He was very tired because he hadn't had enough sleep. He often heard Liu Fu-sheng say: "After I get home I'm going to sleep for ten days and ten nights. And I won't let anybody wake me up even at mealtimes."

"Then there is the question of getting married," said T'ien-pao to himself as his thoughts turned to his own affairs. "Chih-lan's really wonderful. She always said, don't run after pleasures at this moment. What happiness can marriage bring us when the enemy is pointing his bayonets at our throats? What she says is right. When victory is won, we shall live together as man and wife and never part again. After the day's work, we'll have supper at the same table and study by the same lamp. She is a great lover of flowers. She used to plant balsam under the window and rouged her fingernails with the petals. We'll surround our house with all sorts of flowers so that we can pass every day among them."

In the moonlight dark ranges of lofty mountains loomed in the distance. Suddenly, a great noise leapt out of the sky right over T'ien-pao's head, and a black cloud skimmed over the train.

"An enemy plane!" Yu Liong Tal called out.

It was one of the enemy's "black widow" fighter planes, specially designed for night raids. An idea flashed across T'ien-pao's mind: "Get into the ravine ahead."

But it was too late. A napalm bomb fell and lit up the rice fields in a blaze of light. Wheeling round, the "black widow" swooped down again, its machine guns barking.

"Quick, the train's caught fire!" Yu yelled.

"Stop! Let's go and put out the fire first," Liu called out anxiously.

Shutting up the steam port, T'ien-pao jammed on the brake. The train came to a sudden halt and he jumped down to the ground. But he had only run a few steps when there was another explosion. He was thrown up into the air and then fell to the ground unconscious.

Close by, Yao Chih-lan was helping Young Chia, an electrician, set up telegraph poles. Just a little before, Chia had rung up from the working site for more wire. As no one was free except Chih-lan, who was off duty, she came up with a coil of wire on her back and was helping him out.

This was the second time that Chih-lan had met Chia. He had the knack of making friends with anyone after exchanging a few words with him. Chou Hai had told Chih-lan about his ability, his mischievousness and his fooling of the enemy. As Young Chu had knit a pair of gloves for him and spoken nicely about him, Chih-lan had suspected that something was going on between the two. She had pried Chu with questions about it, but Chu swore there was nothing between them. Now the mystery unravelled itself. It turned out that Chu had been writing Chia quite often, telling him that her wound wouldn't matter very much, for only one of her eyes had been burnt and her only regret, Chu said, was that she couldn't come back to Korea again. "I'll have it out with her when she does come," Chih-lan said to herself, "so as to stop her making fun of T'ien-pao again."

Chia was at the top of the pole when the enemy plane hit T'ien-pao's train. He saw it clearly and yelled: "That's a train from the north. It must be carrying important things. Let's run to the rescue."

People rushed up from all directions, men of the rear service and the engineering brigade, and Korean peasants, all shouting. Chih-lan and Chia ran forward in the middle of them all.

The car that was hit was second from the last. It was loaded with antitank shells. Flames went up as more napalm bombs exploded. Several telegraph poles along the railway caught fire and burned like huge candles.

Chih-lan dashed through the flames to the train, her face and clothes badly scorched, her rubber shoes smoldering. Paying no attention to all this, she concentrated on helping to put the fire out. The men stripped off their clothes, soaked them in water in the rice fields, and beat them against the flames. Others poured sand or threw mud on the fire.

"Push the last car away!" Liu Fu-sheng yelled. Instantly someone uncoupled it and, with hands and shoulders, it was pushed away from the fire.

Liu also wanted to separate the second car, which was burning, from the rest of the train. But the antitank shells were exploding right and left. The men dashed off, no longer daring to go near the train. Someone was hit by splinters and several people called for nurses in a chorus. Then came the shout: "Here's someone lying on the ground. Come and help!"

Chih-lan ran up and saw it was T'ien-pao. She had often been awakened at night by raids. And as she heard trains rumbling past in the distance, she naturally thought of T'ien-pao. At such moments she would toss about in bed, worrying and fretting. When at last she managed to overcome her fears she would feel ashamed of herself. "Isn't it selfish of me only to worry about T'ien-pao? Every train driver has someone dear to him, and they are all running the same risk. Why should I care about nobody but him!" Thinking such thoughts, she would calm down.

Now, the moment she saw her lover lying wounded, her heart ached. But she bore up under the sorrow, calm and unshaken. She seemed to have inherited from her father his indomitable spirit. As there was no blood to be seen anywhere on T'ien-pao's body, she grew less strained. She took down the water bottle from her shoulder and gave him a drink.

T'ien-pao had come to by now, but his mind was still very confused. "What's wrong with me?" he murmured.

"You were knocked out," Chih-lan said, with relief.

"How did that happen? Where're we going?"

"To the front. Don't you remember?" said Chih-lan, wiping his forehead with a wet handkerchief.

"To the front?" he said, still at a loss.

"Yes, you were taking munitions to the front," she explained, bending over him. "You've forgotten all about it."

T'ien-pao swept a hand over his forehead and felt better. Yes, he began to recall, he had come with munitions. What kind of munitions? He couldn't tell. Had he been sleeping and dreaming all this time? Then a glance at the burning cars brought it all back to him. He had come up with antitank grenades and heavy tanks. How had he come to be lying here? He sat up at once and tried to get to his feet.

Chih-lan at once clutched his arm. What a strange man! Extremely lively in his movements, he wanted to be up and about when he had only just regained consciousness. That would never do!

"Take your hands off me!" T'ien-pao cried out, struggling to free his arm.

"What do you want to do?" Chih-lan asked impatiently.

"Take your hands off me, please!" T'ien-pao said, "I must go pull that burning car away from the rest, otherwise the fire will spread."

Liu Fu-sheng and Yu Liong Tal had gone before T'ien-pao had time to get up.

What a fire it was! Half the sky was red and the bombs in the train were exploding, with pieces of shrapnel whistling in the air. Liu and Yu had brought their cotton coats with them. Covering their heads with the coats, after soaking them in water, they dashed up through the haze of smoke.

Big flames were engulfing the train. While the iron boards were licked by the fire, the comrades heard a booming sound that became louder and louder. They knew the enemy plane was coming back.

As a matter of fact, the enemy plane had been circling high in the air all this time. Now it swooped down again, its machine gun chattering. Some of the men were about to run away but were stopped by a voice shouting: "Don't run away! Fight the enemy to a finish!" The enemy pilot kept pouring bullets into the car which was already on fire. Had he aimed at the other ones, he would have set all of them ablaze.

Liu and Yu continued to crawl forward even though the plane was right above their heads. As Liu put aside the coat protecting his head, a lump of mud hit him in the face. He was angry but he wanted to laugh. "Damn you, you stupid devil!" he cursed.

When he reached the car which had been blown up, Yu Liong Tal went round and crawled along under the train. He stretched out his hand to uncouple it from the one next to it, but the couplings were so hot that he burned his hand as soon as he touched them. Protecting his other hand with his coat, he tried again, without success. Then Liu came to his aid. Striking a club against the couplings, he finally got them apart.

In a few minutes, the whole crew climbed back on the train. Mustering all his strength, T'ien-pao also ran up.

"Are you hurt?" Liu called out to him. Yu was ready to drive the engine for him.

"Nothing serious," T'ien-pao yelled, pushing Yu away.

Settling himself into the driver's seat, he started the engine, leaving the car which was on fire to the others. The train sped forward. T'ien-pao's chest was aching but he didn't mind. The most important thing was to get moving again.

Yu stood leaning against the door, his legs stretching apart. He looked grim and constantly urged the driver to speed up.

The train raced forward at full speed, and a cold wind blew in against T'ien-pao's chest. He wanted to button up his coat but found that the buttons had all been torn off. His fountain pen, too, had slipped through a hole in his pocket.

Damn that moon still leering up there in the sky, he thought.

The "black widow" spotted the train as soon as it got underway. Its machine guns barked, pouring out a hail of bullets at the whirling wheels. Some hit the stones beside the rail, sending up a shower of sparks.

Yu drew back a few steps from the door. Then he went up to it again and shouted, "Speed up!"

T'ien-pao felt exhilarated as he let out the throttle. Kao Ch'ing-yün's image flashed into his mind. He could see him pouring antitank grenades into the enemy tanks. Now he had run short of the grenades and all the time the enemy tanks were pressing forward. Kao shouted for more antitank grenades.

"I'll bring them, don't you worry," T'ien-pao thought, and the wheels rolled faster.

The "black widow" was hot on their trail, determined not to let its prey escape. It reminded T'ien-pao of how, once when he was a small boy, he had climbed a tree to pick apples, and had stirred up a hornets' nest. The bursts of machine-gun fire brought back to his mind the angry buzzing of the insects.

The "black widow" flew almost on a level with the engine, raising a great cloud of dust. Sweeping past the train, it would immediately turn back and fire, belching flashes of bright flame from its guns.

How T'ien-pao wished that he could drive the train straight into the ravine! He stuck his head out. A bullet whistled past his ear. His left thigh trembled, and he felt a hot wave running through it.

Liu Fu-sheng, stripped to the waist, was busy shoveling coal. Unscrewing the water pipe, he doused water over himself. Then he took up the shovel again.

Once more the machine guns rattled and bullets plowed up the ground.

"There's a fog coming up!" Yu Liong Tal called out suddenly.

In Korea fog is liable to rise at any moment. Now, coming out of the ravine, it was spreading a veil over the hills and the sky. It surged forward like a cloud of dust. T'ien-pao knew that they would be out of danger as soon as he could get the train into the ravine, for then the "black widow" would no longer be able to fly low. And what luck to be aided by fog at a time like this! Opening the throttle wide, he dashed towards the fog.

Once the engine was hidden by the fog, T'ien-pao shut off the steam and let the train slide into the ravine. Now all the cars were in except the last one.

The "black widow" seemed mad with fury. Four times it swooped down, strafing, but the train remained undamaged. The enemy pilot seemed to realize that the train was loaded with important munitions and must be destroyed at all costs. The "black widow" made a fresh attack from the rear.

But the last car had gone into the ravine too and the new attack was fruitless. The "black widow" gave up after a lot of aimless shooting. Suddenly a red light flashed over the misty top of the hill and was immediately followed by a big crash.

Liu Fu-sheng's eyes opened wide. Then he realized what must have happened. "The 'black widow' has crashed against the hill!" he yelled.

It was true. The plane had crashed. The "black widow" had become a dead widow. By his courage and skill in making use of the favorable conditions, T'ien-pao had won the battle against the enemy plane.

Yu Liong Tal gave T'ien-pao a joyful hug. For the first time since war began, this Korean, weighed down by great sorrows, gave out a hearty laugh.

The train went on. T'ien-pao was tired, but he struggled against fatigue. Dimly he saw flames burning in the southern sky, across which the searchlights were sweeping back and forth. He was worried about the Chong-chon bridge and kept on muttering: "Is the Chong-chon bridge being bombed again? I hope nothing'll happen to it." He knew that on the other side of the river, the Korean crew was waiting for his train.

From station to station the train was given the green light. But as it drew near to the river bank, a red light appeared before it glimmering in the fog.

"Damn it!" Liu yelled, putting down the shovel. "After all our efforts, we still can't cross the river."

The train came to a halt. "So you've come!" the man with the red lamp shouted. It was a familiar voice.

"Yes, we made it all right," T'ien-pao replied.

"Get ready to cross the river," the man said.

"So we can go across after all?" asked T'ien-pao, poking out his head.

"Yes," came the answer out of the fog. The man climbed up into the train. He held up the lamp and let the light fall on the crew's faces. It was Wu Chen himself.

He was in high spirits. "You've done a good job!" he said, with a grin. "The dispatch office has sent me a report and I know all about what's happened to you. . . . So you brought down an enemy plane, eh! Good work! Let me thank you on behalf of the people. Commander Ching rang me up several times inquiring about your train. Thanks to your efforts, it got through. You'll have to go across slowly; they've only just finished repairing the bridge. I'll guide the crossing myself."

Holding a lamp in one hand and placing the other hand on the railing of the engine cab, Wu Chen led the train slowly onto the bridge. A thick fog hung over the river and the bridge was quite invisible. When they reached the middle of it, it began to creak as if it might collapse at any moment. Hurriedly Wu Chen ordered them to stop. The people on both banks held their breath. What if the bridge suddenly gave way?

Worried about Wu Chen rather than about the bridge, Liu Fu-sheng popped his head out of the cab and said: "Commander Wu, get off now. Don't risk your life that way. We can go ahead by ourselves."

Wu jumped down from the train and carefully examined the bridge. Then he came back and climbed up onto the engine, as if he had not heard Liu's pleading. Swinging the lamp, he cried: "Go ahead!"

The train started again and crept slowly on, with the wooden bridge creaking under it all the way.

Finally they reached the southern bank. With a heavy puff of its steam the train drew in at the station. The new crew took it over and were ready to drive on to the front with a new engine.

Wu T'ien-pao took a deep breath and relaxed on the foot-plate of his engine. He wanted to get up but his legs failed him. Suddenly, with a flop he fell down.

"Come on, you! Get up!" Liu said.

But T'ien-pao couldn't move. Liu bent down to help him. His hands touched T'ien-pao and became sticky with blood. A strong smell of blood assailed his nostrils. In the light of the furnace fire, he saw that T'ien-pao's trouser-leg was drenched with blood. A good horse, it is said, will run like the wind even when it has been hit by a bullet, until it reaches the destination. It was the same with T'ien-pao. He had suffered a severe concussion in the explosions a while back, and now his left leg was also injured, but with his whole heart in his task he had forgotten the pain and himself. His strength did not give out until he had fulfilled his task and began to relax.

Ignoring the pain in his own hand, Liu tore open T'ien-pao's trousers and bound up the wound. Then he went out and called at the top of his lungs to the men at the station: "Send for a doctor!"

A doctor came and with him Wu Chen. T'ien-pao could hardly talk for loss of blood. "What're you shouting about?" he asked Liu feebly, forcing a smile. "Even Commander Wu has come . . ." Then he turned to Wu Chen and asked:

"The loads'll reach the front in time, will they? They must be sent on without delay. These tanks're as big as hills . . . our men are waiting for them."

"It's all right. There won't be any delay," Wu Chen answered, bending over T'ien-pao. "You don't need to worry about that. How do you feel now?"

"I'm all right. Just tired," he said quietly, closing his eyes. After a while, he opened his eyes and said, "Do me a favor. I want to have a look at Chairman Mao's portrait."

Liu understood and took the portrait from his pocket and handed it to him.

T'ien-pao held the picture up before him. A red light glowed out of the furnace and lit up his own face as well as the portrait. Both the colored picture and T'ien-pao's face gleamed in the light. For a long time he looked at the portrait with a smile. "Good-bye, Chairman Mao," he said softly, "I've done the job the people gave me."

Wu Chen's eyes became moist and he choked back his tears. Liu began to weep.

"What're you crying about?" T'ien-pao said, with a smile. "Tell Chih-lan not to cry, but to give her love for me to our country . . ."

T'ien-pao's eyes began to wander; a smile hovered round the corner of his mouth. "I'm so sleepy," he muttered. "I'm done in. Let me sleep a while . . . just a little while . . ." Gradually his voice grew softer and softer, his eyes closed, his hands still clasping the portrait. . . .

At last he slept the sleep that knows no awaking. He died peacefully, like a man who, having finished his day's work, stretches his legs, yawns, and dozes off in comfort.

Complete text translated by Yuan Ko-chia, Peking, 1957;
excerpted by Kai-yu Hsu, Tiburon, 1978

LI CHUN
(1928–)

Li Chun came from a Honan village family. A completely self-taught man, he became a teacher after the Liberation. His career in creative writing began in the early 1950s.

"Can't Take That Road" is Li's first work, published in the *Honan Daily,* November 20, 1953. It immediately received favorable attention from the provincial Cultural Affairs Bureau. The story was chosen as a study guide for all workers by *Honan Literature,* a monthly, and was quickly reprinted in *Ch'ang-chiang Literature,* January 1954, and in *People's Literature,* February 1954. Numerous adaptations and rearrangements of the story soon surfaced, and a dramatic version was performed a few months later in over fifty places.

His novella, *As the Ice and Snow Melt,* appeared soon afterwards. By 1957 his short stories had filled a volume entitled *When the Elephant Grass Blooms Turn White.* Then he turned his attention to movie scripts; his *An Old Soldier's New Biography* was chosen to represent the People's Republic in a 1959 Moscow film festival. Remaining silent during the Cultural Revolution, Li Chun reappeared in public in 1977 to complete his movie script *Up and Down the Great River.* Other collections of his short stories include *Cart Wheel Tracks* (1959) and *The Story of Li Shuang-shuang* (1961).

Rural life is of primary concern in his writings. Critics have said he enjoys success mainly because he follows the Party line faithfully; they see much stereotyping among Li's characters, but they also commend him for his effective use of peasant language, both simple and folksy.

An earlier English translation of this story appears in *A New Home and Other Stories* (Peking, 1959). The present translation is based on the revised version in Li Chun's 1959 short story collection of the same title, also in the anthology *Selected Short Stories* (Peking, 1956). —M.K.H.

Can't Take That Road

I

For the past few days, everybody has been talking about Chang Shuan selling his land.

"Just keep fooling around and soon enough you'll lose your shirt." Such a common saying contains rather uncommon perception. Actually Chang Shuan could have maintained a decent living for a family of four, had he properly farmed his land, which was over ten *mu.* If he had worked his land well, he would have had enough food to eat, but he had to mess around with animal trading. And he was the type of man who just loved to do that. Last spring, he traded away his chestnut ox for a young donkey. After keeping it for less than ten days, he found it could not keep up with the farm work, so he sold it. By doing this, he lost over 200 thousand *yüan* and could not even afford to buy a young calf afterwards. A cadre in the village said to him, "Chang Shuan, don't mess around. As the saying goes: 'Cutting a long gown longer only makes it a short lined jacket.' You'll just make a fool of yourself by being too smart." However, Chang Shuan refused to admit his failure. He borrowed a million *yüan* from the husband of his wife's sister and immediately bought two old oxen from the Chou-chia-k'ou Market. Unfortunately the wheat crop was damaged by frost at that time, so he could not get a good price for the oxen, and he had to borrow feed for the oxen until it was time to plow the winter field. Only then did he finally sell them. After this deal, he lost practically every single *yüan* that he got for the donkey and, in addition, he was in debt for several hundred thousand *yüan* to the husband of his wife's sister.

As the saying goes, "The deficit in one's collapsed finance and the debt on one's back—it's like medicine plasters sticking to the body—very hard to get rid of." Chang Shuan was only a small-time farmer who could not overcome such a crisis. Day and night, no matter how he tried, he could not get out of it. Furthermore, his sister-in-law's husband came every day for the money, and this often resulted in long, red faces between the two relatives. Finally, Chang Shuan did not want to go on begging any more and, in desperation, he made up his mind: "Sell the land! I'll sell my 'Banner' plot! I'll pick the best to sell and see if there will be a buyer!"

This Banner plot was the best land in the village. Shaped like a triangular banner, it was next to the irrigation ditch. Known to everyone as the village granary, it yielded two harvests a year; everyone was just green with envy because of it. In his clenched-teeth decision to sell this plot, Chang Shuan figured that it should be easy to sell, and that he could sell this two-*mu* plot for over one million *yüan*. After paying all his debts, he would still have enough money left over to have one more try at some ambitious undertaking. Besides, he had not been able to farm well; and he also felt that farming could never quench this thirst he had.

Once people began talking about Chang Shuan selling his land, everyone in the village started making guesses. One speculated this family would buy it; the other suspected that family instead. Yet, no one could say for sure. Several families had become more active since the Liberation, but it was not sure if they would buy any land at all. There were two middle peasant families that could actually afford the land. However, they had been complaining frequently about feeling the pinch; the people figured that they would not be so conspicuous as to put out so much money. Finally, the people focused their attention on Sung Lao-ting. They all knew he had taken a turn for the better during the last two years. Furthermore, his second son, Tung-lin, a carpenter, had been sending him money every month in the sum of several hundred thousand *yüan*. Besides, Lao-ting himself had been clamoring for a long time about wanting to buy some land. Nevertheless, there were others who did not believe that Lao-ting would be the buyer, because his elder son, Tung-shan, was a member of the Communist Party.

II

"Seeing is believing." There is indeed some truth in this saying. This year Sung Lao-ting received eight registered letters in a row from Tung-lin. There was money in every single one. With all that money, he was somewhat worried and did not know what to do. He had never once in his whole life tried on a pair of knitted socks, and even now he was still reluctant to buy a pair. He just put away the money without spending it. Last spring his son Tung-shan wanted to buy some soybean cakes, and asked him once for some money. The old man refused. There was another occasion when the mutual aid team planned to pool the resources to drill a well at the village hollow; Tung-shan again asked him for financial support. The father said, "I have use for the money. You'll see later." Tung-shan was a proud man and did not want to squeeze this money from his father's hands. It was only recently that he realized his father was actually contemplating buying land.

As soon as Sung Lao-ting heard about Chang Shuan wanting to sell the Banner plot, he felt both excited and anxious, just like on his wedding day when the bridal sedan chair arrived at the front door of his house. It was a kind of excitement that he could not share with anyone else. For the past few days he had been running around making inquiries. At breakfast he called Tung-shan to his room in a serious manner and asked him excitedly, "What's the latest on Chang Shuan selling his land?"

Tung-shan replied with a simple statement: "He's not going to sell it."

Lao-ting did not say a word for a long time. Tung-shan took his rice bowl and left the room.

Tung-shan returned home late that night. He saw his father puffing incessantly at his pipe and his mother dozing off beside him.

Lao-ting saw him and said, "Someone from the district office was looking for you. Did you see him?"

"I saw him." Tung-shan wanted to say more, but he could not figure out how to put it.

Lao-ting was waiting for him especially to discuss buying the land. He figured that since Tung-shan was stubborn, it would be wise to talk with this young man smoothly and with patience.

The house was dead silent as if there was not a soul around. Finally Lao-ting spoke first; he said hesitantly, "I saw Wang Lao-san today. He said that Chang Shuan swore he's going to sell that land. I know all about that Banner plot. The soil is dark and rich; once soaked with rainwater, there's more fertilizer there than there's in manure." He paused for a short moment, took a deep draw on his pipe, and went on. "It was given to Chang Shuan during the Land Reform. I was wondering why it wasn't allotted to us. But then, we were cadres, so naturally we couldn't fight with him over this plot of land. Now that he's going to sell it, we shouldn't miss this chance." He looked straight at Tung-shan's face and added, "Do you know what we farmers want the most? Nothing—just to own some land!"

Tung-shan knew all along that that was what his father would say to him. He was just about to answer, but Lao-ting went on with a sigh, "What do I need the money for anyway? I just want to have something for both you and your younger brother. I can't be with you for the rest of your lives, you know."

Smiling, Tung-shan said, "Chang Shuan's land isn't for sale now. Don't listen to Wang Lao-san's nonsense."

"Not for sale?" Lao-ting laughed. "I wonder! He has for himself an ass full of debts! Who's going to pay them off for him?"

"He doesn't owe people that much money," Tung-shan said with his spirit aroused. "I've talked it over with him this afternoon. Selling the land isn't a solution at all. Chang Shuan doesn't own thirty or fifty *mu* of land. He only has those ten-odd *mu*. What will happen after he sells his land? His family and ours were all poor peasants in the old days. Now he's got a problem; we should help him. How can we buy his land?"

The old man grew impatient listening to all this. He had heard through the grapevine: "Tung-shan is a Party member; he will never buy any land or lend any money with interest." He figured that because of such talk, his son would probably not dare buy the land. Thus he said indignantly, "Why can't we buy it while others can? As the saying [from the *Romance of the Three King-doms*] goes: It's Chou Yü beating Huang Kai—one's willing to do the beating while the other's willing to take the beating—it's mutually willing. It isn't that we're using your Party membership to bully him into selling. Why can't we buy it?"

Tung-shan did not expect his father to come up with such words. Stunned, he hurriedly said, "Dad, you can't put it that way. It's true, Chang Shuan was selling his land. But he'll be all right even if he doesn't sell it. All he needs is to borrow a few hundred thousand *yüan*. We just can't watch him go bankrupt. I have already promised to lend him 500 thousand *yüan* ..."

Before Tung-shan could finish, Lao-ting interrupted, "When did you promise him that?" His bloodshot eyes glared out.

"I promised him this afternoon."

Tung-shan had barely uttered these words before Lao-ting suddenly jumped to his feet, his face reddened and his veins bulging around his neck. As if in a state of hysteria, he exploded, "This money belongs to Tung-lin; you didn't earn it. And you lend it out? You do that? Why don't you lend me out? Why don't you lend your mother out?" Furious, the old man threw on a coat and left the house.

Tung-shan's mother woke up and grumbled, "Your sister is getting married soon and I have asked him several hundred times for some money. I want to buy something for her. He never gave me any money. He just wants to buy land. And you're arguing with him over that? What for?"

III

As far as the quarrel between father and son was concerned, it was not that serious. Nevertheless, it scared and worried Tung-shan's wife, Hsiu-lan. First she went to the wheat-threshing ground to soothe the father-in-law, trying to persuade him to go home. The old man said coldly, "I'm not going home. I want to sit here for a while." Then he told her slowly, "Don't you make a big scene out of this! And don't let anybody know about this either!"

Hsiu-lan hurried home. Tung-shan was lying in bed, fuming.

"Still angry, huh?" She sat on the edge of the bed with a smile.

"Angry at what?" Tung-shan pretended to be at ease.

Hsiu-lan teased him and said, "Don't you know by now what's in your Dad's mind? He has it all figured out. If he wants to buy land for your younger brother, let him. Why are you butting into his business?"

Hearing these words from Hsiu-lan, Tung-shan immediately sat up and said, "Why are you talking like this? Right now we aren't talking about whether we or someone else should buy the land. The problem is that I can't stand aside and watch Chang Shuan sell all his land away.... What will he live on afterwards? I'm now faced with this problem and I have to think of a solution. Being a member of the Communist Party isn't for the name only." Then he went on slowly, "I know I haven't done my job well enough. Before wheat harvest time, I walked by Chang Shuan's field. When I saw his wheat growing as thin as incense sticks, I felt so bad. We were all poor peasants in the old days. I know darn well that he doesn't know how to farm properly. Yet, I didn't offer him any help. Whenever people walked by his field on their way to the market, they would say, 'Look at the wheat in the field. What a waste of seeds!' I just felt as if it were a slap on my face. And now you say that I should just mind my own business. What kind of Youth League member are you?"

That made Hsiu-lan talk back. "Well, well. Aren't you using fancy words in front of me! Why didn't you say all this in front of Dad? If you can say it in front of me, why can't you say it to him?"

With an uneasy grimace Tung-shan said, "He left before I could finish. What could I do?"

Hsiu-lan was all seriousness when she said, "I have to give you some criticism also. You never talk with your father whenever you see him. You two, father and son, have never really sat down together in one place and talked things over. Once you finish eating, you go out. Then, jacket on your shoulders, you're on your way to the village office. You keep to your Party membership, he sticks to his farmer's business. Then when there's something to be done, you want him to do as you say. It's only natural that he'd have a fit with you!"

Tung-shan said, laughing, "So you're giving me a lecture, huh?" Nevertheless, deep inside he knew she was right.

Hsiu-lan was about to say some more when Lao-ting's footsteps were heard in the courtyard. Tung-shan motioned Hsiu-lan to stop. The old man went to his room. Tung-shan listened attentively, but with the doors closed he could not hear clearly what his mother said. He only heard the old man responding, his voice loud and deliberate: "He wants to lend money? Let him lend as long as he has it to lend! Who cares if he lends away the whole country!"

Hsiu-lan gave Tung-shan a nudge and chuckled, "That's meant for you to hear!"

IV

The sun was just showing its bright red face. The morning in the village was tranquil. From the field, there was the distant noise of commands to the oxen.

Lao-ting did not go to the field. He did not have a good night's sleep at all. Tossing and turning all night long, he kept thinking about buying the land. The moment he got up in the early morning, he went to Wang Lao-san's house.

Wang Lao-san was a bookkeeping manager for a landlord before the Liberation. In those days, he ran all around the village. One might say that he was a "middleman of all things." For the past few years, the villagers had not paid much attention to him at all. Nevertheless, he knew his way around with people. Whenever he met a cadre, he would rack his brains, figuring ways to talk with progressive expressions. In the old days whenever he met Sung Lao-ting, he would not bother to look at Lao-ting even from the corner of his eyes. Now that he saw that the villagers were rather supportive of Tung-shan, he would be extra friendly whenever he saw him. Sung Lao-ting had talked with him about buying land, and ever since he had been running around like a weaver's shuttle to arrange and deal.

Lao-ting was just walking through the front door. Wang Lao-san went up to greet him. "Hey! Older Brother, I was going to see you yesterday. There's good news about Chang Shuan's deal."

"I've heard that he's not going to sell; is it true?" Lao-ting asked him slowly.

"Well, a couple of days' delay isn't a big deal. You still have me around! He did think of borrowing some money instead of selling the land. But I told him, 'You're no fool! Sell it when you have to. Don't pick up that foreign habit of always borrowing on credit! Besides, you have to pay back whatever you borrowed!' After that, he started to change his mind again." Then he whispered into Lao-ting's ear, "I guarantee that you can buy it. This plot is a real bargain. In one wheat harvest next year, you'll get back more than half of your investment."

Lao-ting was somewhat annoyed by Wang Lao-san's manner of talking, making faces, winking his eyes, and all that. He said, "If he really isn't going to sell, we're not going to force him."

In response, Wang Lao-san patted his shoulder and said, "Older Brother, a chance like this doesn't come often. Don't miss it! Look, you've got about twenty *mu* of land now. Buy ten more! And, if you can afford a year-round farmhand, get one too!" With an affected smile, he added, "Besides, you've been sweating all your life. It's about time to take a rest."

Lao-ting listened to him and did not say a word for a long time; his head sank, his mind buzzing with thoughts. He thought, "Do I really need to hire a farmhand? I've been a farmhand myself for eighteen years!" As he was leaving Wang Lao-san's house, he recalled that in the past Wang Lao-san showed the same kind of zeal whenever he was running around to buy land for the landlord. He also recalled the days when he was working for the Chu family. During the wheat season the managers would come to watch the farmhands, soiled in sweat and dirt, working hard in the field. Wang Lao-san was there also, standing to one side and cooling himself with a fan. In great disgust, Lao-ting spat out a mouthful of saliva and cursed, "Go to hell, you Wang Lao-san! You always know how to kiss asses to stay on the winning side."

Slowly he strolled to the wheat-threshing ground. A row of wheat straw stacks appeared before his eyes. He looked at one and compared it with another. He thought, "If I buy that plot of land from Chang Shuan, huh! Then we'll see whose stacks will be the biggest of all in the wheat harvest next year." He saw his stacks gradually getting bigger and bigger; there semed to be a group of people working in his own field. . . . Then, he looked over to the other side at Chang Shuan's stacks; they were becoming smaller and smaller, so small that they were barely the size of straw baskets. He suddenly thought of Chang Shuan's children. Appearing before his eyes, they were thin, with only skin wrapped around their bones. They all ran towards him. . . . Lao-ting hurried home.

Hsiu-lan and her mother-in-law were toasting steamed bread and chatting in the kitchen. Lao-ting heard his daughter-in-law say, "I'll say, Dad is still so old-fashioned . . ." He stood in the courtyard, tilted his head, and cocked his ears to listen to what they were talking about.

"He's doing all this only for you young people. He's almost halfway to his grave. What else would he be thinking of if not for you people? The family is growing every year. He can't help but try to plan something for you." The old woman talked along. However, Hsiu-lan chuckled, "But who needs him to plan for us? Really! We now have a mutual aid team, and by next year, if our village forms a co-op, we'll join it. In the future we can plow the fields with machines! And I don't think we need to worry about food at all." Upon hearing this, Lao-ting was enraged; even his beard bristled. He knew he had a stubborn son. Now he realized he had a good-for-nothing daughter-in-law also.

At lunch time, Hsiu-lan set the table and put out the food. Lao-ting turned his face to one side and refused to look at her. Hsiu-lan said, "Dad, the food's getting cold, please eat."

He did not seem to hear her. After a while, he suddenly said to his wife, "I'm not eating. I'm going to the market and eat some meat!" While talking, he took a few pieces of bread and angrily said, "Whom am I saving the money for? Like a mule, I've been pulling the plow and wearing out all eight harness cords. What good do I get in return?" His angry eyes glared at Hsiu-lan. Hsiu-lan turned her face to the wall, chuckling to herself.

Indeed, Lao-ting did go to the market and eat a meal there, but no meat. It was only a bowl of beancurd soup with slices of steamed bread tossed in it.

V

There was something unusual about the quarrels between Lao-ting and Tung-shan. The angrier they got at each other, the harder they worked. Even if they worked together, one furrowing the field for seeding and the other helping to sow the seeds, they could remain silent for half a day. Nevertheless, neither would sit idle at home and ignore the work.

Last spring they had a quarrel over a cart. Lao-ting was not willing to lend it out to anyone. Tung-shan, on the other hand, promised it to someone and kept his word. Because of this, they had a fight and did not speak to each other for ten solid days. Lao-ting figured that this fight would cause silence between them for at least half a month.

It was getting dark. Tung-shan came home from a Party Branch meeting. Lao-ting was feeding the ox. He pretended to be fixing the feed, avoiding his son. However, Tung-shan asked him unexpectedly, "Dad, after the grain harvest, let's grow peas in the plot. What do you think?"

Lao-ting did not think his son would speak to him at all. He took a look at Tung-shan's face; the latter smiled. Although the smile was forced, he knew that his son had come to make peace. Thus he said slowly, "Fine, we should rotate the crop in that plot anyway." Then he sat on a rock that was used for doing the laundry in the courtyard. He thought the son was probably willing to buy the land now. So he said hesitantly, "You are still young. Nothing beats owning a few *mu* of land. Land is our roots. If I can't buy some land for you two brothers while I'm still alive, I'll never rest in peace. What are you afraid of, anyway? I'm the one who's buying. I dare people to say anything against it. We just can't keep eating only mixed flour for the rest of our lives. We should think of eating bread made of nice white flour! I dare say, we'll be able to plant a few more *mu* of winter wheat every year in the future." He swung his fist in the air and added, "We'll harvest more wheat than we can eat!"

"We aren't short of food and we've got enough to eat now," said Tung-shan, squatting down.

"Sure, we have enough, but never enough to spare."

Realizing that his father was still as persistent as ever, Tung-shan changed the subject and talked about the crop. He said with a smile, "Dad, how much do you think we can harvest from our four-*mu* plot on the east side?"

Lao-ting figured silently for a long time and replied, "We can get at least 1300 to 1400 *catties.*"

Tung-shan knew his father would be green with envy whenever told about someone else's better crop. So he said, "Lin Wang's plot produced 500 *catties* per *mu* this year. Each of the nineteen *mu* of crop from the other team in the village is better than the others. Their crops are taller than ours by at least one chopstick's length."

Lao-ting became indignant every time he heard such a comparison. With a huff, he said, "If you're willing to pour enough stuff into the field, any field can become a land of plenty."

"That's right," Tung-shan said. "It's just that we didn't do it! Had we spent a couple of hundred thousand *yüan* and bought some good manure for the field, we could've harvested more than 300 to 500 *catties* of grain in addition."

After a long while of talking, Lao-ting realized that he was caught by Tung-shan over last spring's incident. He tried switching the topic and said, "Just pouring manure into the field alone won't do any good. You should also take into consideration the quality of the soil. Lin Wang's field belonged to us before. I know all about that plot. The soil's dark and rich. It can be used for sprouting!"

Tung-shan had hoped that he would get into this subject. Delighted in hearing this, he cut in and said, "How in the world did we end up selling that plot to Ho Lao-ta, the landlord?" There was a note of complaint in his voice.

Lao-ting looked at his son's face, heaved a sigh, and said, "You can't blame me for it. Every time I think about it my whole body shivers all over. That was the thirty-second year of the Republic. Besides two crop failures one after another, your mother was stricken with child-birth complications. I was laid off by the Chu family at the time. I came home and could only push a cart, selling coal to earn a few coins for some medicine for your mother. You were still little then. Did you know how your younger sister died? Your mother was lying in bed. Every day I took the baby girl to all the families in the village begging for a drop of milk for her. I wanted to ask your maternal grandmother to come over, but we didn't even have enough to feed ourselves! Every day I had to prepare food and take care of the sick. Before the crack of dawn, I had to push the coal cart out to make some money. As a result, your little sister simply died of starvation."

Lao-ting's eyes turned red as he talked. He paused for a moment, gritted his teeth, and went on. "By the time your mother got well, I had for myself an ass full of debts. I borrowed half a peck of grain during the off-season and I had to pay back a full peck by harvest time. When I sold that four *mu* of land to Ho Lao-ta, I didn't even know how much I got after subtracting all the debts I owed him. The money left over was just enough to pay for the medicine." He lowered his head and added, "That was the year I sent you away as an apprentice to a coppersmith. You were barely thirteen years old." He glanced at Tung-shan's face, which had been scarred by a childhood disease.

"Didn't anyone give us any relief?" Tung-shan asked.

"Relief my foot! The only thing the village office didn't do was to make buttons out of us poor peasants' bones. The rich only worried that we weren't poor enough for them yet." With his teeth clenched, he added, "It's not like today ..." But he held back immediately.

Tung-shan read his father's mind. With a sigh, he said slowly, "Because Chang Shuan messed around, he too has to sell his land now. But this is a new society. If that problem of ours were to happen today, we wouldn't have to sell our land at all. Under the present leadership of the Communist Party, as long as you work properly and hard, the government and the people will all come to your aid whenever there's a need. We want to improve everyone's life gradually. We can't just watch and let anyone go bankrupt."

Lao-ting did not utter a sound. He felt the blue veins on his forehead bulging and jumping, and his mind, just like the Yellow River, rushing with thoughts whirling like the waves.

Tung-shan saw his father's expression and said, "Dad, in the old days it was the landlords who resented the fact that the poor people weren't poor enough for them. Now it's up to us to help each other. You have experienced that hardship. You know that bitter taste. We can't take that road which was taken by the landlords before."

Lao-ting still did not utter a word. He just heard a buzzing sound in his mind.

VI

It was autumn; the persimmon trees were lined up in rows along the fields. The green leaves entwined together as if they were weaving out a green curtain. The ripening persimmons hung on slender branches.

Sung Lao-ting took off one of his shoes and sat on the edge of a dirt mound under the persimmon trees. He looked up at the sky; it was blue and there was not a trace of cloud. He looked out at the fields, where the autumn crops grew exuberantly, as if they were competing against each other to reach the sky. He especially noticed a plot of kaoliang in front of him; the tassels on the plants were spreading outward like tiny little open umbrellas. Below them, each ear was filled with full, round kernels like clusters of pearls.

"A well-planted one-*mu* plot is really as good as two *mu*." As Lao-ting mumbled to himself, the thought of what had happened the past few days came to his mind. Regardless, he thought to himself, it would still be a wise move to buy a few more *mu* of land. Later when Tung-lin had his own family and separated from his elder brother, wouldn't it be nice if each of them could get a share of twenty *mu* of land? Someday the grandchildren would say, "Grandpa bought lots of land!" They would also learn that grandfather was the builder of the family fortune. He also recalled the words of Wang Lao-san: "In one wheat harvest next year, you'll get back more than half of your investment." Who could complain about owning too much land anyway? Furthermore, the Banner plot in this deal was the best piece of land in the entire village. He should never miss this opportunity. While thinking about all this, he got up and walked in the direction of the Banner plot.

Chang Shuan planned to grow wheat in the plot. It was near sowing time, but the soil still needed a second plowing. The field was grown with foxtails. Looking at the weeds, Lao-ting gave out a sigh.

He took a pinch of the soil from the field. The dark, rich soil caught his eyes. "I'm going to buy this piece of land, no matter what!" While talking to himself, he looked around. Since no one was in sight, he started walking around the plot, trying to see if the plot was really two and a fourth *mu*.

He carefully paced his steps from the corner of the plot. Just as he turned around, he suddenly caught sight of a pile of yellow dirt in the plot. It was grown with thorns and brambles. That was the grave of Chang Shuan's father.

His heart started to pound heavily. He really did not want to look at it, but his eyes were fixed in that direction. The image of Chang Shuan's father, who died the year before the Liberation, surfaced in his mind. When he died, after working a whole lifetime with a carrying pole, he did not even have a piece of land for his own burial. Chang Shuan had to put his coffin in an abandoned cave for two years. It was only after the Land Reform that he could bury his father at this site. Lao-ting knew all this very well. He remembered what the dying father said to Chang Shuan: "Someday we will have our own land. Only then bury my bones. No land, don't bury me! I don't want to hog up a corner of the landlord's property." He remembered these words. He also recalled the hardship of the last few years before Liberation. Feeling these emotions, he began to sniffle; he could not hold back the tears in his eyes. Before he could finish pacing around the plot, he hurried home to the village.

Near the village gate, he met Old Man Ch'ang-shan, who was pushing along two half-filled sacks of wheat. He said to the old man, "Going to the market to sell them?"

Old Man Ch'ang-shan smiled. "No. I'm lending them to Chang Shuan. I hear he's preparing to weave mats. I'm lending them to him so that he can sell them to the co-op and buy reed for weaving."

"My, you must have a bumper crop this year!" Lao-ting could not help but slip out this comment.

"No bumper crop, just enough to eat. What's the use of storing these at home anyway? Besides, I'm not thinking about buying any land."

Lao-ting's face instantly flushed with embarrassment. The old man pushed the sacks of wheat to the east side of the village. Lao-ting looked at his back and wanted to catch up to him and talk back. But somehow, he felt he himself was in the wrong. Finally, he murmured from far away, "What a brag! You're burning your money!"

VII

After dinner, the courtyard was covered by a blurring white under the moonlight. Several crickets chirped under the cedar tree. Lao-ting was sitting in a daze in the courtyard. He felt as if tons of noises were bothering him. At one time it was the crickets; at another time it was the clink-clank of the dishes being washed. Then it was the conversation and laughter of Hsiu-lan and her mother-in-law from the kitchen.

"What a mess!" he uttered. However, his mind was soon occupied with the things he saw during the day, and all the disrupting noises did not reach his ears anymore.

At this moment, someone came in from the front door and called, "Tung-shan!"

Lao-ting recognized that it was Chang Shuan's voice; he answered, "He's gone to the village office." Then he got up and said, "Chang Shuan, come over and sit for a while."

However, when Chang Shuan heard that Tung-shan was not home, he said nervously, "No, no, thanks anyway." In big steps, he ran off.

"Damn it, this guy treats me like he's seen a wolf!"

Lost in thought, he found his way back into the house. His wife asked him, "Is Chang Shuan still going to sell his land? Are you going to lend him the money?"

"I can't make up my mind," he answered absentmindedly.

Footsteps sounded again from the courtyard. He tilted his head to listen; he heard Tung-shan and Chang Shuan's voices. Tung-shan was saying in a low voice, "Let's go to my room and have a seat." The two went inside. Lao-ting heard whispers from his son's room. He was unable to keep still any longer. He glanced at his wife and quietly walked out of the room. Then he felt that his shoes were making too much noise, whereupon he took them off outside the doorstep. On his bare feet, he stood beneath his son's window in the courtyard. From inside his son's room came high-spirited talking.

He heard Chang Shuan say, "When a man gets desperate, he doesn't know what to do. I really couldn't think of a way out in the last few days. As the saying goes, 'You can't be afraid of scraping the flesh if you want to cure a sore.' So I thought of selling the land. Besides, I thought to myself: there won't be much left to make anything out of anyway. With the money, maybe I can go to the Chou-chia-k'ou Market and try once more. With some luck, I can earn back everything."

"Look how terrible your idea is!" This was Tung-shan's voice. "All you think about is profiteering. How can you make it without settling down and working hard? Nowadays it is different from the old society of the past. You'll be better off weaving mats for a few months. Later on, do some decent farming. Don't ever try to mess around with animal trading again."

"After you criticized me that day, I've decided to do according to what you've said and I've decided not to sell the land. My wife's talking to me again. Once you've figured out a solution, there seems to be a way out everywhere. I guess the worst that one can get is to have no one to talk to when in trouble. You've really helped me by getting Uncle Ch'ang-shan to lend me those five pecks of wheat. He said to me, 'Chang Shuan, everybody needs help now and then. I'll loan them to you.' He brought me the wheat this afternoon."

"Can you borrow the 200 thousand *yüan* from the credit union?"

"The manager of the credit union said there shouldn't be any problem. They fixed it on a three-month term. All that's left now is to see if I can borrow some money from you. I'm about 200 to 300 thousand *yüan* short."

Lao-ting took a deep breath as he listened under the window. He heard Tung-shan say, "I have yet to get through to my father. He's over sixty now and I really don't want to make him angry. He's suffered all his life. The money he has saved up is of course precious to him. But, don't you worry. Under the leadership of the Communist Party, we won't let you lose your land and your home. We won't let you and your family wander out on the streets. I plan to call a meeting among the members of our mutual aid team. We'll get together and get you some help."

Lao-ting always thought his son was cold to him. He really did not expect Tung-shan to worry about him getting angry. Then he heard Tung-shan speak again, "Just don't worry. Uncle Ch'ang-shan has lent you some; the credit union will lend you some; and I'll get some other people together to chip in some more. Then you can start on some sort of side job. I'll find someone to talk to your sister-in-law's husband, to tell him that once you have an income, you'll pay him back in installments. Then you'll get by all right."

"Tung-shan," Lao-ting heard Chang Shuan say, full of emotion, "I know you don't want people to talk behind your back. You've got nothing to worry about. Every one of us in the village, old and young, knows what kind of man you are. You're a Communist. Whoever mentions you always has good things to say. Everyone in the village knows who's fair and who really cares for the people all the time." Then he added quietly, "We all know you've got a mixed-up father. No one's going to blame you." Chang Shuan's voice was especially low, but Lao-ting heard every single word distinctly.

"My father's been changing for the past two years, too. As you know, two years ago when I first joined the mutual aid team, we had a fight. Well, now when there's some minor thing that's needed to be done in the team, he won't complain about being taken advantage of anymore. He works very hard, too. I was just thinking, it has served no good purpose in the past for me to confront him directly. Like in this incident about him wanting to buy your land, after I talked to him, he's changed his way of talking quite a bit since yesterday. He now says, 'We can't buy that plot of land which belongs to Chang Shuan's family. In the old days his father and I pushed coal carts together for several years. We're all poor people. We just can't buy off his land.' He's just afraid of letting it out that we've got money to lend," Tung-shan said with a chuckle.

Chang Shuan said, "I know Uncle Lao-ting. He's a straight man. In the old days he also signed the cross* to the landlord. He knows the taste of selling land. My father had always said, 'What a pity; when your Uncle Lao-ting and I die, we'll probably end up looking after someone else's land inside our graves!' But the Communist Party came! If only my father were still alive today . . ."

---

*An illiterate farmer in old China drew a cross or used his fingerprint as his signature on any legal paper, most often an agreement to sell his land or property. [K.Y.H.]

Lao-ting could not continue listening to them any more. He tried to use his hands to hold back the tears. He walked back to his room and, like a bundle of firewood, he fell on his bed.

VIII

The morning in August was clear and fresh, just like the running water of an autumn stream.

The ripe autumn crop emitted a fragrance in the wind, which tenderly carried this fragrance to the smiling faces of the farmers and to their hearts.

After Sung Lao-ting heard what Tung-shan and Chang Shuan said the night before, he got up early in the morning and went to the fields to look for Tung-shan. He wanted to talk it over with him, to decide first to drill a well in the village hollow and, later after the autumn harvest, to install a water-wheel. He walked along a kaoliang field and met Chang Shuan heading his direction. He wanted to go up and say hello to him, but Chang Shuan seemed to be avoiding him intentionally as he hurriedly disappeared into the kaoliang field.

"Chang Shuan, Chang Shuan! I want to talk to you!" he yelled loudly. Chang Shuan then surfaced from the field. Lao-ting said, "Come to my house this afternoon. I'll give you the 300 thousand *yüan.*"

"You mean you're lending me the money?" Chang Shuan was startled, his eyes wide-open.

"Why, you think I won't lend you the money so that I can still buy land? Just remember this: from now on, shape up and work hard on the farm. Otherwise, you won't be able to face anybody here at all."

After he finished, he walked, step by step, straight to the east toward the sun.

Translated by Marlon K. Hom

AI WU

(T'ang Tao-keng, 1904–)

Born to a Szechwan family of declining fortune, Ai Wu attended the First Provincial Normal School in Chengtu in his early years. In 1925, influenced by the new thought which upheld the value of manual labor, Ai Wu journeyed south to Yunnan, where he worked as an errand boy for the local Red Cross. Two years later he proceeded further south, traveling along the Yunnan-Burma border, doing whatever odd jobs were available to him. He also taught school and edited publications. While in Burma in 1931 he was accused of sympathizing with a peasant revolt and the British police arrested him and sent him back to Shanghai, where he began his serious writing career. He published in quick order three anthologies of short stories which won him immediate recognition as a very promising writer in this genre. In World War II he took to the road again, heading west, back to Szechwan. The dozen volumes of fiction, including *Southern Journeys, The Night in the Southland, The Night View,* and *Homeland,* which he produced between 1931 and 1948 established his reputation. He wrote simply but sensitively. His pen captured the life and pulsation of the large variety of characters he came to know so well in the countryside.

His prolific creativity sagged after 1949. In the past thirty years his publication list includes only two novels (*Mountain Wilderness* and *Steeled and Tempered*) and three small collections of short stories (*A New Home, Return by Night,* and *Southern Journeys, II*). The story "Return by Night" has retained the plain but persuasive style that distinguished Ai Wu's earlier works, but cannot be compared with his pre-Liberation best. During the Cultural Revolution he remained silent, though there was no report of his being in any difficulty. In May 1978 he reappeared in public for the first time in years, among many veteran writers at the Third Congress of the All-China Federation of Literary and Art Circles meeting in Peking.   —K.Y.H.

Return by Night

By the time he came out of the main gate of the factory compound it was already pitch dark, yet the white of the snow-covered road was still just visible. There was nobody about but K'ang Shao-ming, who was walking along by himself. The snow on the road had already been trampled into ice—hard, uneven, and slippery—making it difficult to walk on. A moment before, at the end of the meeting, his team leader, Teng Ch'ing-yüan, had said to him with a pat on his shouder:

"K'ang, my lad, it's too late to catch the train. What are you going to do?"

"That doesn't matter. I've still got my two feet."

"Isn't it about fifteen or sixteen *li?*"

"What's there to worry about? I'll make it in an hour or so."

He had replied in a brave, gay tone for he felt that a young man worthy of the name should be able to put up with such minor hardships. Besides, since he was applying for membership in the Youth League he could hardly appear a shirker in front of the Party branch secretary. He had been on this road a good many times, for it was the main route from the town into the country, with carts passing up and down it all day long. When he went to town on his day off and missed the train, he would hail one of the cart drivers, exchange a few words, and clamber onto the back of the cart, and that would send him back, jolting and bumping, across the country. This was the road he had in mind while talking to the branch secretary a moment before, remembering it as it had been two months ago: parched earth, with dead weeds showing on both sides, so that when carts passed they left a cloud of dust behind them. But the road which stretched before him now was covered with slippery frozen snow and, besides, there were no carts to give him a lift. He just had to make do with his own two feet; one false step and he would take a spill. He could not but begin to worry over this in the back of his mind, and he frowned deeply.

The moon had risen by the side of the trees and cast a cold beam on the snow-covered fields, making them even whiter and aggravating his feeling of coldness. The leafless trees with bare branches were as dark as charcoal, standing without a sign of life, silent and still. The stars in the blue sky, as if afraid of the cold, winked restlessly. There was no wind, but the air was bitterly cold, hurting his nose and the parts of his face not covered by the flaps of his fur hat. He could not help sighing as he thought of how it would feel in the heated train, where it was warm enough to send one off dozing.

Fortunately, the meeting had gone well tonight. They had examined each other's work. In light of the present work-drive, the month's task could certainly be completed, with four days to spare. As for beating the "B" team in the contest, there was no longer the slightest doubt about it. Seeing such fine prospects ahead, they had started shouting and dancing and embracing each other, as if they had already won that red flag in the union office and had clearly seen the words "Model Concrete-Mixing Team" written in large characters. It was this spark of happiness burning in his heart that enabled him to pluck up his courage to face the cold moon in the freezing sky, the snow-covered fields and the slippery road, and to press on quickly.

He had not gone far when the sound of someone urging a horse on came from a branch road leading to the marketplace. Although the moon was shining on the white snow, it was nighttime, and so the horse and its driver were just vaguely discernible. But at a glance he could tell from the petite figure and the dark shadow of the two plaits that the driver of the cart was a young girl.

K'ang Shao-ming dodged to the side of the road, his plimsolls sinking into the loose, crisp snow. Without feeling the cold at all, he waved his aluminum lunchbox and shouted gaily:

"How about letting me have a ride on your cart, little girl?"

The driver of the cart made no reply; she just churned straight past him noisily as if she had not heard anyone calling.

Naturally, K'ang Shao-ming did not want to miss this chance of a ride on the cart. Even if it was only for a short ride, he felt that it would be worth his while; he started to run after the cart at once, shouting at the top of his voice:

"Didn't you hear me, little girl? Won't you just give me a lift?"

"There's no little girl round here."

The driver of the cart replied in a high-pitched voice, obviously angry. The rubber-wheeled cart drove on without the slightest sign of stopping.

K'ang Shao-ming ran behind the cart and, changing his form of address, called: "Comrade," and then implored her: "I'm a worker returning to my village from work, please let me have a ride on your cart."

The rubber-wheeled cart now slowed down to a halt. The horse snorted loudly. The girl was sitting to the front left-hand side, her feet dangling over the edge. She was holding a whip stuck up in the air as if it were a short fishing rod. She sat there and did not move, only turned her head and said coldly:

"Get on, comrade."

K'ang Shao-ming climbed up swiftly. He was delighted, but purposely laying on his suffering, said:

"It's terribly cold, I'm frozen stiff."

He felt that the girl driving the cart was not exactly friendly, and he wanted some sympathy from her.

With a flick of the wrist the girl gave the whip a sharp crack in the air, and the horse started off again at full speed. K'ang Shao-ming put his empty aluminum lunchbox down beside him. It immediately bounced up high, and he hurriedly held it in place. As the horse trotted, the wind mingled with the smell of sweat from off his back and swept towards them. There was nothing in the cart except a pile of empty sacks which smelt faintly of grain. Whether it came from sorghum or wheat he did not know, but in any case the smell at once reminded him of a granary in the country. Under the light of the moon he could see the body of the girl sitting upright, facing straight ahead with her chin slightly tilted up, and her skillful handling of the horse. He sensed that this was a person not to be talked to lightly, and accordingly told himself to be careful.

In fact, K'ang Shao-ming was extremely fond of playing jokes on people. The women ticket collectors on the train disliked him intensely; when they had clearly asked for his train ticket, he would produce his worker's meal ticket instead and hold it out for them to inspect, thus getting a good laugh from the other passengers. This sort of behavior had finally been "reflected" to the leadership in the factory, and, consequently, he had been criticized on the blackboard newspaper. Now that he had met this girl he was again itching to joke with her, to say, "What fine business drove you to town?" or "Aren't you afraid to travel all alone at this time of night?" But when he remembered the criticism he had received, he again put himself on his best behavior. He sat there, one hand holding onto the board framing the side of the cart, the other hand pressing his lunchbox, his mouth tightly shut. The girl went on driving without even looking at him, as if he were not on the cart at all. He began to feel a bit uncomfortable and could not help asking:

"Comrade, what village are you from?"

Fearing that she might take offence he put the question with the utmost caution.

"Ying-hsia Village."

Having given this brief reply the girl said no more.

"Ha, that means I can go ten *li* on the cart!" K'ang Shao-ming cried out in the best of spirits: "I'm from K'ang-chia T'un and I work in the basic construction department of the Anshan Steel Company. At first I worked in the seamless tube factory, then at the No. 2 sheet mill, and now . . ." The cart now passed over an exceptionally rough patch, jerking him up and down, and for the moment he had to break off. He particularly wanted to tell her that his team was expecting to beat the "B" team in the competition, for this spark of happiness never ceased to warm his heart.

The girl seemed not to have heard what he had been saying. She just waved the whip in earsplitting cracks and sent the horse on at an even faster trot.

When he saw that she was not listening at all, K'ang Shao-ming lost interest in talking. It was only when the jolting of the cart became so rough as to make him extremely uncomfortable that he asked timidly:

"You're going too fast, comrade. Why not slow down a bit?"

"Do you go home every day?" asked the girl abruptly, without answering his question.

K'ang Shao-ming wondered why she answered him like that, but seeing that she was at last talking, he replied cheerfully:

"Yes, I go home every day."

"If you go home every day, why don't you know there is evening school in the village?" scolded the girl harshly. "Do you mean to say your village hasn't got that?"

"Yes it has. Who says it hasn't?"

K'ang Shao-ming replied promptly, his high spirits now gone. He felt that her rebuke was most unreasonable.

"Don't you go to evening school?"

This time she half turned her head and gave him a look, but there was still heavy reproof in her tone.

Seeing that she had at last given him a glance, K'ang Shao-ming explained: "Comrade, you've no idea how busy we've been lately." Then he sighed cheerfully: "Why, tonight, for instance, I even missed the train. We were working ourselves to death."

"It's not like that with us. However busy, we still have to get to evening school," replied the girl proudly, and cracked the whip again, sending the horse flying full gallop.

Suddenly K'ang Shao-ming realized why she was driving the horse so quickly. He hurriedly explained as though he would never be able to clear himself unless he produced an explanation now.

"You see, comrade, we work in three shifts. Sometimes we're on in the morning, sometimes in the afternoon, and sometimes late at night, so we're bound to miss classes if we go to evening school. We aren't like farming people, we can't even rest at night."

Seeing that she was concentrating on driving, he went on consolingly.

"I'm afraid you won't make it, no matter how fast you drive."

His real aim was to get her to slow down a bit so as to put up with less jolting, for he was truly tired after a whole day's work and the long meeting that followed.

"Whatever time I can make up is better than nothing, at least," spoke the girl with determination, her voice full of confidence and pride.

K'ang Shao-ming felt that this girl was really too haughty. Although none too pleased, he still said in a mild tone:

"Comrade, why didn't you set out a little earlier? Going like this, it's the horse that suffers."

"What else could I do, having run into such a crowd of people?" countered the girl. She sighed aloud as if the temper which she had been in while in town was coming back. However, she did slow down slightly, her sympathy for the horse obviously aroused. As the horse began to go slower, it immediately stole a lick at the snow drifts by the side of the road.

K'ang now realized that there had been another reason for the girl's rude behavior this evening, and his dislike of her vanished completely. Now in full sympathy with her, he could not help asking in amazement:

"Comrade, what crowd was it you said that caused you so much trouble?"

"Ai-yo! Such a big event, and you haven't even heard about it?" She was surprised, and rebuked him severely.

"What big event?"

K'ang Shao-ming broke into uneasy laughter, hardly knowing how to handle this girl whose surprise attacks made him feel vulnerable all the time.

"Really, you people seem to have lost your senses with all your hard work," she scolded in a raised voice which carried a jeering note. "Everywhere people are talking about the General Line.* Don't you even know that?"

"Don't we know?" retorted K'ang Shao-ming quickly. "It's precisely because of the General Line that we are going all out for the contest." He felt that he must not be jeered at for no reason at all, and that it was essential to make the matter clear. As he spoke he naturally became a little excited.

But the girl disregarded his words and continued:

"Go to the Grain Company and take a look, then you'd understand. There are ever so many people taking their surplus grain to sell."

"Ah, so you were taking surplus grain to sell?" Pleasantly surprised, he cried out: "Comrade, you've really done something great . . . What an honor! . . . Then even if you do miss your lesson tonight it will be for a good cause." He was now praising her wholeheartedly.

Still indignant, the girl said: "It was just those damned women. It's all right to take their grain to sell, but why must they bring their kids too! When you see their kids crying from the cold, what can you do but let them get their grain weighed first? Now that's fine—once you've given your place to one, you've given it to all the others, and you're kept waiting until it's dark."

K'ang Shao-ming glanced at her in the moonlight. Her face was stubbornly exposed to the cold air. She appeared to be very angry, so he said to her tactfully and with a smile:

*General Line of the State, a guideline pronounced by the government in 1953 for the period of transition to socialism, roughly parallel to the first five-year plan. [K.Y.H.]

"I think you were quite right to let them go first. It's really commendable, only you shouldn't get angry after you've done it."

The girl could not help breaking into a laugh and then she sighed happily: "It was only because I didn't want to miss the evening class that I went there early. How was I to know that I still wouldn't make it! Just think, you've missed a lesson, you're one step behind, and you won't be able to catch up with the others; the more you think about it the more angry you'll get!"

"You could still make it up tomorrow."

"Are you trying to say we're idlers? We've got other things to do tomorrow, and by tomorrow evening, ah, there'll be another lesson!"

After going rather slowly for quite some time—the horse licked the snow drifts by the side of the road now and then—the girl suddenly cracked her whip again, making a deafening noise. The horse jumped forward and once more began to gallop along the slippery, icy road. Now that it had had time to regain its wind it was going even faster than before and the jolting of the cart became even more violent. K'ang Shao-ming steadied himself with one hand on the board and pressed the lunchbox with his other hand, keeping his mouth shut for the time being. The cold wind, mingled with the smell of the horse's sweat, brushed past his face and the tip of his nose with its needlelike sting.

The cart crossed over a stone bridge and immediately entered a narrow lane. Feeble lamplight came from the houses on either side and fell onto the dirty snow-covered ground. The cart stopped abruptly in front of the door of one of the houses, and the girl jumped off smartly. She opened it and went in. After a short while she reappeared carrying a square glass lantern and a bucket of water.

Realizing that she wanted to water the horse, K'ang Shao-ming hurriedly jumped down from the cart and held the lantern for her. The white frost which had formed on the whiskers round the horse's mouth gradually melted as the horse dipped its mouth into the water. The girl's fresh, delicate cheeks, frozen into the deep red color of an apple, were shining with a beautiful glow. It seemed he had never seen such prettiness on a girl before, and he stood in a complete daze.

When she had finished watering the horse the girl raised her head and looked at him and, as though she had noticed something, broke into a smile. Only with some effort was she able to prevent herself from laughing out loud.

Now it was K'ang Shao-ming's turn to feel embarrassed. He waited until the girl had returned the lantern and the bucket and climbed back onto the cart, then asked self-consciously:

"Why did you smile at me like that just now?"

It was only after the cart had begun to move again that the girl burst into loud laughter. As they came out of the narrow lane, she half turned her head and gave another look at K'ang Shao-ming, but she did not answer him.

Suddenly K'ang Shao-ming understood; it must be something to do with his face; a face covered with muddy water from the concrete mixing, with dirty greasy patches here and there, must look very funny indeed. Normally after work he would have had a quick wash, but tonight, busy with the meeting and in a hurry to get home, he had not been able to do any washing. Whereupon with an apologetic smile he said:

"Comrade, if you only take a look at my ugly mug you'll see just how hard we workers labor."

"That may be so, but you've been able to raise production!" She seemed to feel sorry for laughing at him, and now earnestly tried to show her good will. "I heard a report recently that Old Hero Meng T'ai of the Anshan Steel Company produced as much as seven hundred and seventy-two peasants did in one year! That's really marvelous!"

"Of course he's marvelous!" At the mention of Meng T'ai's name K'ang Shao-ming shouted cheerfully, as if he shared the glory too. "He has been elected Model Worker Extraordinary every year since our company started."

"What's he like? I should really like to see him!"

The girl spoke dreamily. The horse had now slowed down but she forgot to urge it on.

"If you worked for our company you would see him every day." As he said this he suddenly thought how good it would be if he could see her more often, and could not help asking: "Don't you want to work in a factory? We're getting more and more girl comrades every year."

Suddenly the girl reverted to her proud and confident tone, and said in a loud voice:

"I'm used to working on the land. I like flowers and birds, and I like driving a horse and cart on the road. The other day when we heard that we'll be using tractors on the farms, I was so happy that I couldn't sleep the whole night."

Having said this she suddenly tilted her head and asked with a smile:

"Comrade, when are you going to turn out tractors? Don't just keep us waiting."

Seeing that the girl had become so cheerful, K'ang Shao-ming had an urge to give some hint of what he was hoping and say: "If you really want it, I'll speed it up for you even if it means working day and night!" But he immediately sensed that this would not be the right thing to say; quite apart from being somewhat rash, it would also sound frivolous. He also remembered the criticisms which had been made of him on the blackboard newspaper, so he had to restrain himself and instead said seriously: "If you could produce more grain then we could sooner make tractors! Haven't you noticed that we've been working day and night building the new factory? That's because we want to bring out the tractors as soon as possible."

"You can count on our cooperative to produce more grain, there's no question about that."

The girl shouted this out in her confident, proud tone and promptly urged the horse to go faster.

The flow of snow-covered fields and bare trees receded, but the moon, casting a cold beam, rushed forward all the time as if it were racing the big cart.

K'ang Shao-ming wanted to carry on the conversation. Even listening to her voice gave him inexplicable pleasure, so he asked with great interest:

"Did you produce a lot of grain last year?"

"Of course we did; otherwise, how could our production cooperative have been selected as a model?"

The girl reverted once more to her earlier tone of reproach, as if to say that since he lived in the district it was really unthinkable that he should not know about a model cooperative.

K'ang Shao-ming very much wanted to say, "Our team is also a model team in the factory." But when he thought of the monthly self-examination meeting, he suppressed himself, and could only say, "At the end of this month our concrete mixing team may also be chosen as the model team." However he blushed as soon as he had said this, feeling that it was pointless to talk about something that was still to come. He was even more ashamed when he saw that the girl said nothing and merely replied by cracking the whip. He had the feeling that she thought he was boasting.

The cart came to a halt at a fork in the road and the girl said coldly:

"Comrade, you can get off now, we go different ways from here."

Clambering off the cart, K'ang Shao-ming said lingeringly:

"Thank you, comrade. If you hadn't given me a lift this evening, I would probably have had to walk till midnight. Do you mind if I ask what your name is?"

"Don't bother to thank me, it's all right. My name is Lin Yun."

K'ang Shao-ming had hoped that the girl would also ask his name. Seeing that she had no intention of doing so, he wanted to tell her himself. But giving him no chance, the girl immediately cracked her whip hard and drove off swiftly down another road. As his legs were stiff from sitting, making it difficult to walk at once, he stood dazedly for a while on the snow-covered ground. He stared after the cart, which became a small black dot and finally disappeared along the snow-covered road in the dim moonlight. Only then did he begin to walk.

As a rule, when he returned from the railway station to K'ang Village, K'ang Shao-ming always accompanied his cheerful strides with some singing as he completed the three *li* of the unpaved road. Now, walking all alone in the night, he should find the time just right for a song, but he was simply not in the mood for it. He only thought dejectedly, "That little thing is certainly stuck-up; she refused to look at anyone who isn't a Model Worker Extraordinary."

It was very quiet in the snow-covered village. Lights had gone out in many households. His mother opened the door to let him in and hurriedly brought him water to wash his face. She put his heated dinner on a low table on the *k'ang,* and asked him lovingly:

"Why are you so late getting back in this cold weather?"

"There was a meeting at the factory this evening," replied K'ang Shao-ming briefly, without mentioning that he had missed the train. He sat down by the table on the *k'ang* and began to eat.

It was very warm inside the house, but ice had already formed on the windowpane that was lit up by the lamp.

His mother sat beside him and watched him eating for some time before saying:

"Were you criticized again at the meeting?"

"What makes you think that, Ma? No one criticized me."

"I can see you aren't very happy tonight."

K'ang Shao-ming gave a sigh. "It's nothing . . . just that, when I come to think of losing the red flag to another team last time, it's very hard to take."

"Why worry about something that's already over? There's still plenty of time. Starting from this month, you should really get down to it."

K'ang Shao-ming made no reply, but went on eating with his head lowered.

From far across the snow-covered fields came the noise of a passing train; and then, once or twice, the wailing sound of its whistle.

The night was as quiet as ever.

Renditions, no. 7 (Spring 1977), 39–44

Translated by Raymond S. W. Hsu

CHÜN CH'ING
(Sun Chün-ch'ing, 1922–)

Chün Ch'ing, a native of Shantung Province, was one-time assistant secretary to the Party unit of the Chinese Writers' Association in Shanghai. During the war against Japan, he joined the Communist movement and worked in east Shantung. Later he studied at the Lu Hsün Academy of Art in Yenan. When the army marched south, he went with it and traveled extensively in the southern provinces.

His first short story appeared in 1942, and a collection of short stories was published shortly after Liberation. "Dawn on the River" is the title story in his second anthology (1954), which received high critical acclaim for his effective depiction of the resistance movement during the war. Another story of vivid description and strong characterization is his "Old Daddy Water Buffalo," in which he presents some dramatic scenes of fighting a flood. His later works include *East Shantung Stories, The Petrel,* and *The Bloodstained Clothes.* He also published two collections of essays, *On the Writing of Short Stories* and *Autumn Rhymes.*

Chün Ch'ing disappeared from public view during the Cultural Revolution, but has returned to the writers circle since 1973. In May 1978 he was a delegate to the Third Congress of the All-China Federation of Literary and Art Circles held in Peking. –E.Y.

---

from Dawn on the River

[Yao Kuang-chung, leader of an armed partisan unit—organized and directed by the Communists in the guerrilla warfare against Japan in the early 1940s— was acclaimed hero for his role in the battle of the Ch'ang-wei Plain on the Shantung Peninsula. He was commended for his tenacious courage and strong organizing skills in carrying out his mission behind enemy lines. However, whenever Yao was requested to speak of his exploits he would tell the story of Hsiao Ch'en, the young scout, and his family, and how they had assisted him in making that dangerous but crucial crossing from enemy territory to the east bank of the Wei River. Without their help Yao could not have regrouped the armed partisan unit on the east bank and the battle would have been lost.

Hsiao Ch'en, a lad of about eighteen, was assigned to guide Yao and his assistant, Lao Yang, to the river and ferry them across on a small rowboat. On the way to the river they ran smack into a small group of enemies but managed to fight their way through. Then they were caught in a storm and almost lost their bearings. Finally, they arrived at the edge of the Wei River at daybreak.

To their consternation, they found that the hidden boat had been washed away by the rising river water. Hsiao Ch'en suggested that they seek help from his father.]

V

It was very quiet in the orchard.

After the storm, the leaves on the trees seemed a fresher green than usual. Ripening apples and hawthorn berries, shiny and red, looked exceedingly inviting. Raindrop-laden leaves swaying in the early morning breeze released the drops in showers onto the loose sandy soil. Treading on the sand, we went down a small path into the deep part of the orchard. After traveling for a short while, we came upon a small house surrounded by thick green layers of grape and calabash leaves. Then came a growl like rumbling thunder, and a big, ferocious yellow dog came charging at us, breathing hard. But as soon as he saw Hsiao* Ch'en, he immediately stopped snarling, and, with his tail wagging vigorously, began to frolic beside him.

Fondly, Hsiao Ch'en stroked the yellow dog's head and called his name with pleasure:

"Tiger, Tiger."

The door of the house creaked open, and a white-bearded old man poked his head out. He peered at us for some time through narrowed eyes, but when he saw Hsiao Ch'en, his mouth flew open in surprise.

"Dad!" Hsiao Ch'en cried out in a low voice.

The old man looked around him warily, and, motioning with his hand, ordered:

"Quickly, into the house!"

As I stepped across the threshold, I was aghast at the shambles which greeted me. It was as if a bull had strayed into the hut and had charged at random. The pot on the oven was broken; so was the water urn in the corner. The cupboard was toppled over, the storage bin turned upside down, and the floor littered with bits of pottery, food, grass, and cloth. . . .

When Hsiao Ch'en saw this, his face turned pale and swiftly he went inside to check. He returned, looking very worried.

"Dad, where's Mother?" he asked.

Silently the old man sat down on the threshold and glumly lowered his head. Finally he burst out angrily:

"She has been taken by the Repatriates.† Your brother, Hsiao Chia, too, was taken."

Hsiao Ch'en slumped down dejectedly on the ledge of the oven, his breathing becoming short and fast.

"When were they taken, Old Uncle?" asked Lao** Yang, anxiously.

*Hsiao: meaning "small," prefixed to a name as a form of friendly address, generally denoting youth. [K.Y.H.]

†Repatriates: landlords and village bullies who had fled their villages at the advent of the Communist forces. After the Nationalist forces had retaken the areas, they returned to their villages. [K.Y.H.]

**Lao: meaning "old," prefixed to a name as a form of friendly address. [K.Y.H.]

"Five days ago." The old man heaved a sigh. Then he told us what had happened: During the past months, Hsiao Ch'en had been continuously helping comrades cross the river from the spot nearby. This secret was betrayed by a traitor named Ch'en Hsing. Five days ago, Ch'en Lao-wu, who was the head of the Repatriates in Ch'en Village, arrested Hsiao Ch'en's family and brought them down to the village police station to be tortured. Finally they released only the old man, giving him instructions to go home and wait for Hsiao Ch'en. If Hsiao Ch'en should come by with other people, the old man was to coerce his son to secretly hand over his comrades to the Repatriates. Otherwise the old man would never be able to ransom the rest of the family.

When I heard this, my heart began pounding. Lao Yang looked at me, apprehension written on his face. Hsiao Ch'en, on the other hand, bit his lower lip tightly and did not utter a single word. After a time, he raised his head abruptly and asked:

"Dad, what were you going to do?"

"I? I was planning to go and bring you back here," said the old man, flatly.

"Bring me back here?" Hsiao Ch'en was alarmed.

"Right!" The old man nodded. "For five whole days your mother and Hsiao Chia hung suspended from the beams. I looked everywhere for you but I couldn't find you . . ."

"Why were you looking for me?" Hsiao Ch'en interrupted the old man.

"Why was I looking for you?" sneered the old man. "Huh, you ask me why? Don't you care at all about the three of us? And don't you want to avenge the death of those twenty to thirty village cadres and their family members? Why do you think I consented to let you join the army in the first place? Eh?" As he spoke, the old man grew more and more agitated and his thick white beard shook. His accusing glance flashed at us like lightning. It was then that I finally understood what he was saying. Hsiao Ch'en gave me a look full of meaning and smiled. Suddenly he gripped his father's hand and said excitedly:

"Dad, but I've come back, haven't I?"

"I searched for you for two days," continued the old man, stroking his son's head, "but I couldn't get any news of you. I couldn't wait any longer, so the day before yesterday, even before the sky was light, I went to the east bank of the river intending to seek out Captain Ma. I heard that they were stationed at the village. But before I got there I heard gunfire. The enemy had them hemmed in. There were more than a thousand enemy soldiers surrounding them, many layers deep on all sides. Even the Fourth Brigade stationed at Ch'ang-i came. The battle went on till dusk. Captain Ma and Liu, his assistant, died. I heard that at the very end, after they had used up all their ammunition, they killed themselves with their own hand grenades. When I went into the village their bodies were still lying in the street. Ai, my brave captain. He used to help people cross the river to this side. Now he's finished. The armed partisan unit is finished. The territory occupied by our forces on the east bank is also finished." The old man's voice grew softer and softer. Then he heaved a deep sigh and let his tears flow.

My eyes experienced a prickly sensation and my lips trembled violently.

Filled with emotion, Lao Yang grasped the old man's hand.

"Old Uncle, be comforted. The armed partisan unit on the east bank is not finished yet; neither is the territory across the river. The two of us are going there to continue Captain Ma's work."

"Eh?" the old man looked at us in astonishment. "Really? You're going to the east bank of the river?"

Hsiao Ch'en nodded. "Yes, Dad. That's why I'm here. But the rowboat hidden among the willows by the river has been washed away. What are we going to do?"

The old man stood up and studied us from head to foot. Then he nodded his head.

"Good! It's good that you've come. You must hurry. Since the death of Captain Ma, the Repatriates have become worse. Yesterday, two comrades separated from their troops hid in the forest south of here, but they were discovered by the Repatriates. Those two comrades were really something. They resisted for over half a day. Then finally they smashed their guns and jumped into the river. It's good that you've come. The people will have someone to place their trust in again. You must cross the river as soon as possible. Eh, what? The boat has been washed away?"

"Yes," I said. "The boat has been washed away and the river is rising. But it's imperative that we make the crossing today. . . ."

. . . .

The old man quietly opened the door and went outside. He looked up at the sky. Then he turned and asked:

"Can you two swim?"

"A little, but not in such high water," Lao Yang and I replied.

The old man did not speak but walked back into the house. He took out a bottle, and tilting back his head, gulped down a few mouthfuls. Then he offered the bottle to us, saying:

"Come, have some. The water is terribly cold."

We took a few draughts. It was potent kaoliang wine.

"Let's go," the old man ordered.

We looked at him in bewilderment. Hsiao Ch'en gave us a merry wink and spoke softly:

"Go. He's going to help you swim across. The old man is a fine swimmer."

When he spoke, Hsiao Ch'en's voice was full of pride and confidence. That made me feel better and my spirits rose. Then suddenly I remembered Old Auntie and Hsiao Chia suspended from the beams of the police station in the village. What would happen to them?

"Why have you stopped?" The old man was surprised to find me deep in thought.

"I was thinking. Old Auntie . . ."

The old man's beard trembled and he turned away abruptly. Then, beckoning with his hand, he said sharply:

"Let's go! Hurry!"

VI

Dawn had come.

In the eastern sky rays of crimson light penetrated the cracks in the thick layers of clouds. The dark outline of villages far off was becoming more and more distinct. On the surface of the river a strong wind was blowing. The river was full of rolling white swells so that it looked like a rocking field of snow. At the foot of the river embankment, wave upon wave charged repeatedly at the wall with terrifying roars while the wind swept up spray and bits of grass toward us.

"What strong wind!" said the old man, inhaling sharply. "Come, I'll see you across one by one. But let's agree on one thing first: Once we're in the water, don't thrash around. Now, who'll go first?"

I gave Lao Yang a push, saying:

"You and Hsiao Ch'en go first. I'll stand guard."

"No, you go first," said Lao Yang. He looked up at the sky.

"No, it's better that you go first," I insisted.

At that moment, a shot rang out from the west. Lao Yang was going to speak but the old man pulled him and, with a splash, they were in the river.

"Hsiao Ch'en, go down. Quickly!" I pushed him with my hand.

Angrily Hsiao Ch'en turned and ran up the embankment. I followed him to the top and looked toward the west. We saw seven or eight people emerging from Ch'en Village and coming up the main road, covered with swirling morning fog. They were not in any hurry at all. It would appear they had not seen us yet.

"Duck!" I ordered.

On the embankment there was a winding trench which had been dug a month before when our army was resisting the enemy on the banks of the Wei River. Now the edge of the trench was overgrown with reeds. Hsiao Ch'en and I hid there. Tiger had been trailing us and he too hid in the trench. I turned and looked toward the east. The old man was towing Lao Yang with one hand and pushing water with the other, swimming swiftly toward the east among the hillocks of water. At times they would disappear beneath and at times they would surface among the white-crested waves. Then I turned and looked toward the west. Those seven or eight ruffians had suddenly left the main road for a small path which ran at an angle into the orchard. My heart skipped a beat and I turned to look at Hsiao Ch'en. He was biting down hard on his lower lip, and with his rapidly heaving chest and short, quick breathing, he seemed like an infuriated lion.

Quickly I evaluated the situation: When the enemy discovers that the old man is missing, they will come to the edge of the river to look for him. In that case we will be forced to fight with our backs against the river. A very risky situation. But regardless of the risks, we must cover Lao Yang so that he can get to the opposite side of the river. If Lao Yang can reach the east bank it will mean victory for us. All right, I thought: for the preservation and expansion of the territory and for the survival of the armed partisan unit and the people of the east bank, Hsiao Ch'en and I will give our all. I glanced at Hsiao Ch'en. He kept looking back and forth impatiently, first in the direction of the orchard and then the river. I knew that his heart must be very heavy. I wanted to comfort him, but before I could speak, he instead offered me words of comfort.

"Captain Yao, look! My father has already reached the middle of the river. What a fine swimmer the old man is. He'll be back in no time and will get you across the river."

What a good and honest heart! I thought.

Suddenly, Tiger sprang up and, poking his head above the trench, barked wildly in the direction of the orchard. I looked up and saw those seven or eight ruffians with guns in their hands emerging from the orchard. They were following the path we had taken and heading straight toward the river's edge.

Woof, woof, woof! Tiger barked furiously, as if he was going to charge.

"Be quiet! Get down!" Hsiao Ch'en quickly grabbed him by the scruff of his neck and forcibly pushed him into a corner. Tiger whimpered with an injured air, but sat down obediently.

By this time the sky had lighted up.

From the villages around, smoke from breakfast cooking rose. In the sky above the Wei River an eagle appeared, his jet black wings sweeping against the clouds, which looked like pieces of worn cotton. At times he would emerge from behind a cloud, stopping motionless in midair, gazing down for a long time at those fields washed by the recent storm and at that majestic river. Then at times he would dip his wings as if startled, and, like a flash of black lightning, he would dive into the dark ocean of clouds.

The river's edge at dawn was not peaceful at all. A violent storm would soon be breaking.

The enemy was advancing, nearer and nearer.

We could clearly see their faces and their clothes. This mob in disorderly attire was made up of the landlords and village bullies from the Repatriates. In their hands they held shotguns and handguns of varied sizes and brands.

"Ah!" Hsiao Ch'en gave a low cry of discovery and nudged me with his shoulder. "That traitor!"

"Which one?" I asked.

"That short man who's walking at the head. That's Ch'en Hsing. He used to be the head of our village. After the enemy came he teamed up in secret with Ch'en Lao-wu. The arrest of my mother and my younger brother was all his doing . . ." So saying, he picked up his gun. I looked in the direction where Hsiao Ch'en pointed his gun and saw that brazen traitor. He was about forty or fifty years old. Short. His face wearing an obsequious yet somewhat worried smile, he strode toward the foot of the embankment. I could clearly hear the squelch his feet made in the mud and the drone of his voice as he spoke.

"His mother's ——!* That old bastard must have gone over to the side of the Eighth Route Army," said Ch'en Hsing. Then he turned and talked to the dark fat man behind him. "Brother Hsiang-k'uei, as far as I'm concerned we should have buried the whole lot of them alive there and then. But Uncle Lao-wu insisted on trying out his plan of playing out the line to hook a big fish . . . So now, we've ended up not hooking any fish but losing the bait instead."

*A common coarse curse, with the four-letter word often unsaid but clearly understood. [K.Y.H.]

"What the hell do you know?" the fat man sneered. "Your mother's ————!
You only know how to call struggle meetings* and divide the spoils."

"Ah, brother Hsiang-k'uei, why must you bring that up? Didn't I give you
my word? I said that I would get back all your property which has been
distributed among the different households, so why are you ..."

"I'm tired of listening to your droning," the fat man snarled. "A whole month
has passed already. How many of my possessions have you gotten back? I'm
giving you ten more days. If you don't get them all back, I'll bury you alive."

"Stop bickering," said another ruffian, who was wearing a straw hat. "Last
night Uncle Lao-wu said: The district office has sent word that during these few
days we must be extra watchful in guarding the river because they think that
the Eighth Route Army to the west will definitely dispatch cadres to the east
bank. The order from above is that we must prevent them from getting across
at all costs. Once they cross the river, it will be disaster...."

"Allow me." Ch'en Hsing didn't even wait till the man in the straw hat had
finished, but in an effort to curry favor, broke in: "I'll stand guard here at the
river's edge at night. Just let them come this way ... Ugh, it's slippery on the
embankment." Hunching his body, he started up the slope of the embankment.
Then he slipped and grabbed at the reeds with both hands....

"Fire!" I signaled with my hand.

Hsiao Ch'en stood up in the trench and whipped out his gun so that the gun
barrel almost touched the chest of Ch'en Hsing. For one split second the traitor
was so terrified that his eyes almost popped out of their sockets. His face turned
ashen, then his grip loosened and he fell backwards. Down the slope his body
tumbled till it landed with a big splash in the ditch at the foot of the embankment.

At the same time, my automatic pistol also sputtered, and the dark fat man
and the man in the straw hat fell down one after the other. The ruffians were
thrown into utter confusion by the surprise attack. They didn't even have time
to level their guns. Falling and crawling they scattered down the embankment.
Tiger, who had been cooped up in the trench for so long, could restrain himself
no longer. He jumped out of the trench and sped down the embankment in hot
pursuit. He ran swiftly, the hackles on his back rising, and, like a flash of
lightning, caught up with one of them. Tiger sank his teeth into the ruffian's
leg and held on, bringing him to the ground. The other bandit, taking advantage of this lucky break, fled. Like a hare, he ran down the kaoliang patch
toward Ch'en Village.

VII

The scorching sound of gunfire had ceased and the wind had dispersed the
gun smoke on the embankment.

I looked back toward the river. Two men, looking like black dots, bobbed
among the waves. They had almost reached the east bank. My heart felt lighter,
as if a thousand-kilo rock had been lifted.

*Struggle meeting: a public meeting called to disgrace someone or to punish an
offender. [K.Y.H.]

"They've made it across the river," I said, heaving a sigh of relief.

Hsiao Ch'en nodded, but his expression did not relax.

Suddenly from the direction of Ch'en Village came the sound of bells clanging. Then the same sound emanated from the villages to the south. Soon, one after another, many of the villages of the west bank rang with the urgent peal of bells.

A more violent storm was approaching.

After appraising the situation, I decided that it was impossible to cross the river. In a few minutes the enemy would be rushing us from three directions. Come then and let's fight, I said to myself. If I can't fight my way out I will do what those two comrades did. I'll jump into the river. I had experienced my share of danger, but never before had I to make such a desperate decision. But the situation was clear. I could not swim, and I was greatly outnumbered. There was no other alternative....

I felt inside my pocket. Inside were some secret documents soaked through by rain. I tore them to shreds and threw the scraps into the river. Hsiao Ch'en looked at me with the wondering gaze of a child. My heart stirred and the thought that I should compel him to go down to the river crossed my mind again. Since it was impossible to make a break for the west, and since Hsiao Ch'en could swim, what then was the point of his staying and dying a needless death? So I said:

"Hsiao Ch'en, you can swim. Before the enemy charges, hurry and get down to the river."

Hsiao Ch'en fixed a surprised look on me. Then he frowned and said:

"What? Are you bringing that up again?"

"Isn't it obvious?" I said. "I shouldn't even need to explain. Hurry, get down there."

Offended, he turned his face away and remained motionless and silent.

"Well, didn't you hear me?" I knew he was not going to respond to reason so I was prepared to use pressure even though my heart was not in it.

Still he said nothing, nor did he turn his head.

"Do you or don't you understand what is meant by following orders?" I shouted, in exasperation.

"I understand," he finally answered in a low voice. But immediately he turned and looked at me steadily. Then, slowly and distinctly, he spoke: "It is precisely because I'm following orders that I won't go down to the river."

"What nonsense is this? What kind of orders are you following?"

"I'm following the order which says I have to see you across the river, and not to abandon you to save myself."

Ah, I would never have thought that this usually quiet young man could speak in such a manner. I was speechless, and then, despite myself, I began to laugh.

Hsiao Ch'en did not laugh. Instead he looked at me with his large, deep-set eyes and said solemnly:

"Captain Yao, you're not calm enough and you don't have enough faith in the masses."

I was taken aback.

"What do you mean?"

"Just what I said," he said slowly. "Besides, you have insulted me." As he spoke he angrily turned his face away, but not before I caught a glimpse of tears in his eyes.

For a long time I was quiet while my face grew hot. It was only then that I fully understood what Hsiao Ch'en was saying. It was only then that I really knew Hsiao Ch'en. I was deeply touched. I turned and looked at the river. Lao Yang was already on the east bank and the old man was swimming back to us. I also looked toward the west. A large swarm of people had emerged from Ch'en Village and were coming swiftly toward us. In the north, and in front of the villages farther away, enemies also appeared. From all three directions—north, south, and west—came the sound of gunfire, and bullets whizzed past our heads.

"All right, Hsiao Ch'en. Don't be angry with me," I said. "Let's prepare ourselves for battle. Do you still have bullets?"

He did not answer but patted the bullet belt which he had retrieved from the foot of the embankment. A ghost of a smile flickered across his face.

The sound of gunfire came nearer and nearer.

Enemies to the west of us had wound their way to the edge of the orchard and had taken up position behind a sand ridge not far from us. Their bullets flitted by us like locusts, sending up dirt from the edge of the trench and snipping off blades of reeds.

We remained still and did not return a single shot, but waited till the enemy drew nearer. However, they were cunning and would not leave the protection of the sand ridge. Suddenly, they stopped shooting. One ruffian poked his head out from behind the dune and, waving a red cloth, shouted:

"Don't shoot, don't shoot." I recognized that the speaker was the one who had just made the lucky escape.

"Hsiao Ch'en, take a look. Who is this?" he shouted.

Then, from behind the ridge two people were pushed out.

Hsiao Ch'en's face turned as white as snow. Standing on the ridge were an old woman and a fourteen- or fifteen-year-old boy. Even without being told I could tell that they were Hsiao Ch'en's mother and his younger brother, Hsiao Chia.

Old Auntie stood on the ridge, her hands tied behind her back, her face streaked with blood and her hair falling about her face. Strong gusts from the river whipped up her hair and caused her to sway. But with an effort she stood up straight and, lifting her head, looked in our direction. Hsiao Chia was not bound but his pale face attested to the ill-treatment he had suffered. With one hand holding a cane and with the other supporting his mother, he also looked in our direction. When Tiger saw them he jumped up, darted out of the trench and friskily ran toward his mistress. Behind the ridge, the enemies began to raise their heads, some of them straightening up but shielding themselves behind the old woman and Hsiao Chia, and peering at the embankment. Among them was a dark fat man, his big belly exposed, who kept close to Old Auntie as he stood up. Then the ruffian waving the red cloth shouted:

"Hsiao Ch'en, you'd better listen. Master Wu wants to talk to you."

"Hsiao Ch'en," the dark fat man's voice sounded like a duck's. He pointed to Old Auntie and Hsiao Chia. "Hsiao Ch'en, do you see? You have two alternatives right now: The first one: die with your mother and your brother here! The second one: put down your gun and return home with your mother. As for those Eighth Route Army men with you, we'll guarantee them mercy. All right, I have laid everything out clearly for you. You have to choose between the two alternatives. Whether you want to live or die, you only have to say the word."

When I heard this I was so furious that I seethed. I looked at Hsiao Ch'en. His ashen face had turned a fiery red. Without a word he leveled his gun and took aim at Ch'en Lao-wu. But, his whole body began to shake and the muzzle of his gun wavered among the reeds. He could not take aim. I grasped his shoulder and spoke gently.

"Hsiao Ch'en, keep cool. Don't shoot, you'll hit your mother."

He sighed and tears welled up in his eyes. He brushed them away fiercely with the back of his hand and leveled his gun again.

Just then, Old Auntie spoke:

"Son!" Her voice was clear and calm. "Where are you? Why is it I can't see you?"

"Over here, Mother," Hsiao Ch'en answered loudly from among the reeds.

"Son, you stand up and let me take a look at you.—Oh, no, no. Don't stand up, Son. You mustn't stand up. Just call me once more."

Tears streamed down Hsiao Ch'en's face.

"Mother!" he called in a quavering voice.

"Ah, good boy. You're my good boy. Can you see me and your brother?"

"Yes, I can see ..." Hsiao Ch'en could not continue.

"Good boy, that's good enough. Shoot!" Old Auntie suddenly raised her voice. "Shoot! Don't listen to that old dog of a Lao-wu. Kill all these ruffians. Shoot, my son! Shoot in my direction."

"Brother, go on, shoot! Quickly, shoot!" Hsiao Chia also shouted urgently.

Commotion reigned on the ridge as all the ruffians scampered behind it like hares. Right then, Hsiao Ch'en's gun roared. The hapless ruffian waving the red cloth did not have time to take cover, and as the shot rang out, he fell down at the feet of the old woman.

"Well done! That's my boy." Old Auntie, who was on the ridge, looked down at the dead man at her feet and nodded her head in approval.

Suddenly from behind the ridge came the sound of a shot. Old Auntie gave a cry of pain. She swayed and then slowly sank to the ground. . . .

"Mother!" Hsiao Ch'en screamed.

My body was shaking and hot tears spilled down my cheeks. I leveled my gun but there wasn't a single person left on the ridge. The ruffians were all crouching behind the ridge and they had pulled Hsiao Chia down with them. I glanced at Hsiao Ch'en. His lower lip was bleeding from his biting down on it, and his eyes seemed to emit sparks. Motionless he stared at the crumpled form of his mother on the ridge.

Just then a head appeared above the ridge. I was going to raise my gun when the man's head exploded with a bang. Hsiao Ch'en had shot him. Then after a while another head appeared and exploded in the same manner. This time it was I who fired. Then the two of us stared in silence at the ridge, firing at any moving shape. In this way we remained for more than ten minutes. The enemies just didn't have the courage to come up from behind the ridge. They fired blindly. After some time, someone shouted again:

"Don't shoot, don't shoot!"

Following the shouts, Hsiao Chia was pushed out again. After that, four or five ruffians in a line closely followed Hsiao Chia, and using his body as a shield rushed toward the foot of the embankment.

Caught by surprise, I unconsciously lowered my gun.

Hsiao Ch'en also stopped shooting.

Hsiao Chia, who was propelled forward by the ruffians, got nearer and nearer, his chest in the direct path of our guns. . . .

The enemies behind the ridge raised their heads, preparing themselves for the charge. The river bank had become astoundingly quiet. The guns of the two camps were silent. One could hear the rapid breathing of Hsiao Chia, the approaching footsteps of the ruffians hidden behind him, and the roaring of the waves in the river . . . Suddenly, the clear, resolute voice of a young boy broke the tense silence.

"Brother, why have you stopped? Shoot! Go on, shoot! Shoot in my direction."

My body trembled and my blood boiled.

Breathing hard, Hsiao Ch'en leveled his gun, but I tugged at his arm.

"Don't shoot."

"Shoot, shoot!" Hsiao Chia shouted urgently. "Avenge our mother. Quickly, shoot, my brother. Ch'en Lao-wu is right behind me. Fire in my direction. Shoot! Avenge our mother . . ."

Hsiao Chia broke off. At that moment I saw Tiger dash out from the side and bite the leg of the ruffian who was pushing Hsiao Chia along. He screamed with pain, loosened his grip on the boy and fell. Seizing the opportunity Hsiao Chia turned around and pounced on the man, and managed to snatch a hand grenade away. Holding it high above his head, he pulled out the pin. The ruffians, stunned by this unexpected turn of events, all froze and stood stock still beside the boy, staring at the white smoke coming from the hissing fuse on the grenade. . . .

My heart was pounding hard and I closed my eyes tightly.

The grenade went off with a loud boom.

When I opened my eyes, white smoke was surging upwards from the foot of the embankment. One ruffian, who had miraculously survived, half rolled, half crawled his way back. Immediately our guns spat long tongues of flames in the direction of the escaping man. . . .

VIII

To tell the truth, despite the numerous battles I had been through, I had never experienced such violent emotions. A few minutes before, I had been considering how to conserve bullets and to buy time until the old man returned. Then I forgot everything. I pushed the lever on my gun to FAST and bullets shot out like raindrops. Though the enemies from the south were forced by our gunfire to take cover behind the dunes, the enemies from the west and the north swarmed toward us like bees. But they did not register at all in my mind. I just kept firing and firing. I was obsessed with one single thought:

Revenge! Revenge for Old Auntie! Revenge for Hsiao Chia! Revenge for the masses slaughtered by Chiang's bandits on the Ch'ang-wei Plain.

But during a lull in the bloody battle, I discovered that Hsiao Ch'en was not as crazed as I was. He was saving bullets, seldom firing double shots. He kept turning around and looking toward the river. Suddenly he grabbed my arm and gave a cry of joy:

"Captain Yao, look! My father is back."

I turned and looked. Swift as an arrow, the old man was swimming toward the foot of the embankment. Overjoyed, Hsiao Ch'en stood up and shouted:

"Hurry, Dad. Hurry!" He stopped, and clutching at his chest with one hand, sat down. Blood was spurting from his chest. I dropped down beside him and, gripping his shoulder, called his name loudly:

"Hsiao Ch'en, Hsiao Ch'en."

He did not respond, his head lying limply on the edge of the trench. I felt an unbearable stabbing pain in my heart.

Seizing this opportunity, the enemies rushed forward.

My blood was bubbling fiercely in my veins. I leveled my gun and shot in a sweeping arc at the foot of the embankment. My gun jerked repeatedly and the shiny shells scattered like grasshoppers. I was drowning in the thrill of revenge . . .

Suddenly, a strong hand clamped down on my shoulder. Alarmed, I turned and saw that it was Old Uncle.

"Come quickly down to the river."

"No!" I said stubbornly and continued shooting at the enemies.

Old Uncle crouched down beside me. When he saw the bleeding Hsiao Ch'en, his thick beard trembled, and, taking his son's hand in both of his, he said:

"My son, my son."

Hsiao Ch'en opened his eyes a crack. When he saw his father he gave a weak grin and said in a hoarse voice:

"Dad, you've come at the right time. Hurry. Take him down to the river."

The old man did not speak. His face had turned deathly pale. Then he saw the bodies of the old woman and Hsiao Chia lying at the bottom of the embankment. His large beard trembled even more violently and his tears flowed silently. But immediately he raised his hand and wiped his eyes. Then he gripped my arm and said in a loud voice:

"Come quickly. Come."

"No," I said, "I won't go. I want to stay with Hsiao Ch'en."

"Hurry. You must hurry," Hsiao Ch'en cried, "I will cover you." His gun began to sound like peas popping in a roasting-pan.

"No, no . . ." Before I could finish what I was saying, the old man grabbed me around my waist and we plunged into the river. . . .

"Hsiao Ch'en, Hsiao Ch'en!" I shouted in the water. A wave broke over me and water flowed into my mouth choking me so that I was breathless for a time.

The wind churned up the tumultuous waves and the air reverberated with the howling of the wind and the waves.

I turned my head and looked at the embankment. I did not see Hsiao Ch'en. I only saw thin wisps of faint blue smoke circling above the trench. Up on the embankment Tiger was jumping and snarling, venting his anger and growling at every bullet which landed on the embankment sending up bits of dirt. Hsiao Ch'en was still fighting. He was holding back the enemy so that I could cross the river. My heart felt as if it was on fire and I struck out with my arms.

"Be still. Don't move!" the old man said harshly. His arm around me grew tighter. I could feel it trembling and I sensed that he was forcing himself not to look back at the west bank. He swam with all his might. . . .

The sun rose from behind the layers of clouds, shedding its golden rays on the stormy surface of the river. One white-crested wave after another pounded at us, lifting us high into the air and then dropping us into deep valleys. My head was reeling from all that rocking, and yet I strained to look back toward the west. I felt as if I had left my heart behind in the trench. Suddenly an awesome spectacle held me spellbound: The sound of gunfire from the west embankment stopped. The faint blue gunsmoke was dispersed by the wind. Against the azure blue of the lightened sky in the west a human form stood facing the golden sunshine. Ah, it was Hsiao Ch'en. He got out of the trench and threw his gun into the river. Then he wheeled around, and, throwing his arms around a ruffian who had rushed up to him, jumped into the swiftly flowing Wei River. . . .

Dark silhouettes appeared on the west embankment. They fired at us but the bullets fell short. We had broken past the swift currents in the middle of the river. At that moment, shots also rang out from the east embankment. It was Lao Yang covering us. Ah, the east bank at last, but what of Hsiao Ch'en . . .? I took one last look at where he had jumped but I could see nothing except the turbulent waves, churning, churning. . . .

[Captain Yao and Old Uncle reached the other side of the river, but the old man received a gunshot wound in his shoulder. Hsiao Chen's body was found the next day down the river. It had been washed ashore. A few feet away lay the body of Tiger. After the old man had recovered, he joined the armed partisan unit under Captain Yao's command.]

Translated by Ellen Lai-shan Yeung

LIU PAI-YÜ
(1916–)

In the summer of 1977, Liu Pai-yü was elevated to the post of chief of the cultural department, political bureau of the People's Liberation Army, a recognition he earned with his long and successful years of writing about military life.

Starting shortly before the war against Japan with sketches of life and guerrilla warfare he witnessed in North China, he developed his writing career while working and traveling with the army. He went to Manchuria with the military mediation team in 1946, then he joined Lin Piao's Fourth Field Army fighting in North and Central China. His best-known works, including *Flames Ahead* and *Battle Fires Spread,* were based on his experience of this period. For a dozen other collections of reportage already published and well received, and for his participation in writing movie scripts to glorify the Liberation of 1949, he won a Stalin Prize in 1951.

The decade immediately following the Liberation kept him busy doing political and administrative work as first secretary of the Party branch in the national Writers Association. But by the late 1950s and early 1960s there came another outpouring from his pen. No less than eight collections of short stories and reports were published, including *Pledge to Peace, The Morning Sun,* and *Morning Lights.*

Even the titles of his books indicate his style and mood. The gusto of military action, the bloody struggle for what to him is a just cause, strike stirring notes in the ears of his readers. The wild enthusiasm for the future of a new nation cheers his readers. His sanguine style and crisp pace are superbly suited to the demands of the time.

Though responsible for the severe setbacks of many veteran writers during the series of literary purges in the 1950s and 1960s, he himself became a target of Red Guard attack in 1967 at the height of the Cultural Revolution, but the storm seems to have left him unscathed. He played an active role in the Third Congress of the All-China Federation of Literary and Art Circles meeting in Peking in May 1978.   —K.Y.H.

On the Dusty Road

It was tense and all abustle on the highway near the Front as dusk approached. At this time in June, it was soothingly cool and dry in Korea; dust was flying like rolls of smog, and the trucks drove right through it. The tree branches stuck on the truck for camouflage were rustling. The sky darkened;

125

like a small golden fireball the first star suddenly popped out in the distance. When the headlights of the automobiles were suddenly turned on, an extraordinary scene of amazing images appeared: countless vehicles dashed toward us, their lights resembling pairs of eyes blinking brightly. The vehicles followed along the winding highway, linking themselves into a shiny long chain. Light shone on the tree trunks along the highway. Leaves, each heavily laden with dust, revealed their burnt countenance; as soon as the headlights flashed past, the leaves vanished. Here, at the battlefront, everything was speed. The scenes on this highway were like an accelerated motion picture.

It was on such a day that I headed for the Front in a jeep. Our driver was a lively and courageous youth. He was merely a driver's assistant when I met him in the icy snow last year. He took me through what the enemy called "The Iron Triangle"—Ch'orwon, Yonch'on, past the Hant'an River—dashing toward Seoul. We were heavily strafed by enemy planes. With the headlights off, we fumbled in the dark on the icy muddy road. At the point where it was most difficult to drive, the lights were momentarily turned on. (The lights were draped over with black cloth, leaving only a slit through which seeped a line of yellowish light.) Blinking even such a thin line of light would immediately cause reprimands from the pedestrians.

The enemy planes were extremely bloodthirsty. Suddenly the flash from the planes appeared. Look! The airplane followed the bullets in a killer dive. Those brave young people, like this driver—wasn't it they who cut a path through these difficulties? Now the driver decided to turn on the headlights full-blast, as if he was using this action to inform me, "Look! This is not last year!"

Thus he took me racing over the highway. One by one he overtook the trucks ahead of him by driving on the shoulder of the road. As he passed them he looked very pleased, clacking his tongue as he bragged about the small jeep under his command. He also hummed a Korean song continuously, halting only when he discovered another vehicle. He would then concentrate on his driving. Almost brushing the side of the other car, he passed it like a gust of wind and resumed his lighthearted singing.

As I watched him, I became indescribably cheerful—when you are with such a person, regardless of how dangerous the situation might be, you can't help but feel instantly uplifted and you become as expansive and carefree as he. I looked up at the road ahead. Vehicles came toward us in a steady flow. Their headlights shone so brightly that the highway looked like a bustling main street. The jeep flew past the convoy sentry as the guard quickly waved his white flag, and our driver solemnly waved his left hand in response. Suddenly gunshots were heard, and all the lights vanished. The enemy planes returned with a rumble; the earth was a sweep of darkness. When the planes left, all the truck lights were turned on again as if erupting from underground. The driver resumed singing the Korean song; we were on our speedy journey again. At the crack of dawn, we found the camp in a village nestled against a red-earth hill.

It was almost noon when we awoke. It was awfully hot, and the flies clinging to the cool wall had no intention of stirring. The driver and I sat on top of a great pile of bright yellow straw bags in front of the cowshed, chatting. I don't know whether you have begun to like this young man. As for myself, I certainly meant what I said when I praised him. But, he said to me, "I haven't done anything, really. You ought to see our Yang Ts'ung-fang! If you see him, you will know what a man of the Mao Tse-tung era is! You'll know how we feel when we fight the enemy."

This is what he told me about his buddy, Yang Ts'ung-fang:

"That was last year, during the Fifth Campaign ... Our comrades on the firing front were fighting with the enemy from hilltop to hilltop ... At the most crucial moment, a volley of telegrams came, asking for ammunition, ammunition, and ammunition. That was quite an emergency situation. It was already midnight, but the commander sent for a group of us drivers. There was not a sound at his place; the frowning commander had been slowly pacing the floor. He halted when he saw us. 'It's very hot on the Front,' he said, looking at all of us. 'They're out of ammunition. They're ready to use rocks.' He looked at us, his eyes bloodshot from many sleepless nights, as if he were testing us. Finally he said, 'If we can't hold this position, the entire army will be in trouble. You must deliver the ammunition by daybreak.' He walked over and shook hands with us one by one: 'All right, go! I'll wait to hear from you.' Before long our thirty trucks, fully loaded with ammunition, set out toward the battlefront. How did I feel then? Well, I knew that whether we could deliver the ammunition to the Front would determine not only the fate of the positions on each hilltop, but also the life and death of our comrades out there. In our hearts we all understood this clearly. Nobody said a word, but we all dashed toward the Front.

"I remember it was April weather; we were still wearing padded jackets. Late at night it was quite chilly as the wind rushed in through the truck window.

"The trucks in front stopped. Someone got out to signal: 'Look at this spot. Is it all right to refill the radiator and gas tank here?' Everybody parked the trucks alongside the road, one after another. With this section of the highway winding around the foot of the hill, and with the heavy night fog, we felt this spot should be rather well protected. We huddled: if we went any further, we would be in extensive flatland and might not find such terrain as this, so we might as well refuel here and then make for the Front in one dash. Someone sitting on the fender said, 'After we reach the Front, if we can't turn back by daybreak, we should hide the trucks. Each of us can carry two boxes of ammunition and deliver them to the firing line!' Our captain nodded, and we decided to make the fuel stop there. There was not a sound in the sky. Everyone hurried to make the best use of the lull, and soon the once-still air was filled with all kinds of sounds. Some were taking the empty gasoline cans to the riverbank for water, some were standing high on their trucks pouring water into the radiator, while others hit the gasoline tank caps with pliers and checked the engine from under their trucks with the help of a flashlight. Still others walked over to the roadside to strike a match for a cigarette. Suddenly the planes came—riding on a menacing rumble, they came.

"The air-raid alarm sentry on our small hilltop fired.

"In the blinking of an eye, not one flicker was seen. Even the smokers hastily shoved the cigarettes under their feet and crushed them.

"From the thick forest behind the hill there arose a string of red tracer bullets —tu, tu, tu. Comrade, you were in Korea last year. You know that the enemy often air-drop their secret agents to hide in sheltered places where they signal to the airplanes. When this happened that night, the situation became tense.

A couple of hotheaded ones picked up their guns to go after the agents behind the hill. But what about the thirty carloads of ammunition? In an instant the airplanes flew over to the spot illuminated by the red tracer bullets and a storm of gunfire poured down, with the planes themselves diving immediately after for the kill. Fortunately, the whistling bullets all landed in the deep ravine along the road, hitting the leaves like a hailstorm. We were most scared by the airplane dropping flares. If the enemy discovered this group of ammunition trucks, they would not leave until they had dumped all their bombs on them, and they would definitely send for more planes to reinforce their attack!

"It was really nerve-wracking. The planes actually circled back. I climbed into the cab in a hurry. I only knew that I should, under no circumstances, leave my post. I was so tense that my heart was pumping out fiery stars.

"I heard the truck behind me, for some unknown reason, start its motor.

"I stuck my head out, and I yelled ...

"I was afraid he would drive out without headlights at this crucial moment. What if the truck turned over? That would be disastrous!

"In the wink of an eye, the truck with the motor running started to move. The driver turned his steering wheel to pass near the side of my truck and proceeded on. For an instant the truck pulled up parallel to mine; I looked— isn't that Yang Ts'ung-fang? He flashed past in a swoosh!"

The young man telling me the story became excited as he related the incident. He stopped, breathed heavily, then continued:

"That's it! I can never forget it. At that moment I saw Yang Ts'ung-fang sitting high in the driver's seat, his hands grasping the steering wheel. In a flash—it was truly dark, but the truck was so close—I could see his face. He also took a hard look at me and turned his head to stare straight ahead. I remember the tension on his face. But his truck sped past us and raced away.

"No one could understand why Yang Ts'ung-fang wanted to do such a thing. I thought he must have planned to dash out of danger. Indeed, the airplanes would be returning at any moment. What to do? ... Should I dash out with him? It was too late. There was no time to think; the aircraft roared and swooped down on us.

"Suddenly a flash of glaring light appeared before us. I thought it was a flare bomb, but when I looked again, that light was not in the sky; it was on the ground. It was Yang Ts'ung-fang ... He had driven no more than a hundred yards, but as soon as he felt he had left us behind, he swiftly turned on his headlights. ... "

I could not help but interrupt: "Wasn't that very dangerous?"

He looked tense; his voice became lower than usual: "Sure, extremely dangerous—I was so alarmed that I jumped up in my seat. Did he want to kill himself? You know the aircraft is looking for you to bomb you, and yet you turn on the lights, exposing yourself like a sitting duck. What more is there to say!

"I saw clearly the headlights flickering and the lone truck speeding toward the plain ahead. Immediately a battery of machine-gun fire flashed and chased the truck. That was some terrific strafing. But the danger over our heads was gone—the planes were lured away by Yang's glaring lights. We all came out from under cover and stared, our hearts in our throats, at the fleeing headlights. The airplanes screamed fanatically, shooting red fiery stars across the entire sky. Yet that truck's headlights were still on. Their beam flashed upward; that was when the truck was dashing up the hillside. And in another moment it was gone; that was when the truck was descending the other side of the hill. In a short while it reappeared, further away. An airplane dove to shoot again, then pulled skyward, and banking sharply it swung back to shoot again. Now the lights disappeared. It was pitch dark everywhere; one could hardly see a thing. The plane shot around blindly, hitting nothing; but, as soon as it pulled up in the sky—the lights were on again. The truck was still speeding along the highway! Again and again it went; the American in the airplane became totally insane; the plane dove lower, so low that its wings were caught in the truck's headlights. As the plane brushed close to the top of the truck, fiery streaks of bullets pursued. Later—no one knew whether Yang's truck was hit or had gone over to the far side of another hill—anyway, the headlights disappeared. I thought they would come on again but they didn't. There was only thick darkness. We could not tell what had happened. Then we heard two loud explosions . . . A flash of red glow shone on our faces. My heart sank to the very bottom. Finished. Now it was all finished. We heard the plane droning around a couple of turns and flying away. Gradually the rumbling hushed.

"There was even less sound where we were; we heard only the rustle of the pine trees in the wind on top of the hills.

"I calmed down, except my innards were twisted in knots.

"All the comrades got together quietly behind our captain. All looked at that distant place; no one made a sound. Now, everybody understood. If it had not been for Yang Ts'ung-fang's bravery, his risking his life, the enemy would have dropped flares to discover our trucks, and we would not have been able to stand on that plot of land anymore. These truckloads of ammunition were a giant powder keg. If even one case of ammunition had exploded, all the trucks would have been reduced to shattered metal scraps. Even the cliff there would have been leveled; the pine forest would have caught fire, and by daybreak that spot would have been nothing but a giant pit. With this thought in mind everybody took another long look at that distant place. Now if we only knew what actually had happened to that truck?! After a while, some comrades came up in the dark and asked, 'Who was that?' I said, 'It was Yang Ts'ung-fang.' Everybody came over around me, all thinking of this Yang Ts'ung-fang.

"Comrade! I haven't introduced this man to you yet: he is twenty-four years old, sturdy, and doesn't say much. His disposition is completely different from mine: he doesn't like to sing, and as he drives he stares straight ahead. As for me, my habit of driving fast has had something to do with him. Wherever he goes, don't expect anyone to pass his truck. He often says, 'Bullets won't hit the first one.' When you ask him why, he says, 'There's reason in this: speed. When you get that much faster, you are that much safer. Don't you think so?'

"However, comrade! At that moment I was only thinking of Yang Ts'ung-fang. It was as if he had been standing before me; I thought of the moment he drove out and took one hard look at me—he was saying something to me, perhaps a last farewell. I can never forget such a man as he: I can't forget that time during the Fourth Campaign, in particular. I was his assistant driver. Our troops shifted from the Han River front; we were the last batch of trucks to retrieve the ammunition. The enemy's long-range cannon had already shot ahead of us to barricade the Hant'an River. We drove into the Civic Center; the entire street was burning like a fiery dragon, with billowing smoke and fumes. As the flames leapt, one could hardly see the road.

"Suddenly, making a turn, I caught sight of a Korean child standing in front of a house that was howling with flames. This child stood there motionless, with his back to us. Yang Ts'ung-fang asked me, 'Do you think the enemy tanks will get in here right away?' 'I think they aren't far now.' Yang said, 'He must be an orphan . . . No one to take care of him!' Saying this he stopped the truck, clicked the door open, and jumped off. He ran straight to the child and, in a moment, carried him back to the truck. The child looked about ten years old; his clothes were all burnt and torn, and his bare feet were planted in a pair of shoes more than double the size of his feet. I took him over and placed him between Yang and me. Yang hopped in, and we sped away. At first the child kept crying and looking out of the truck. But soon he leaned his head on my shoulder and fell asleep. Yang Ts'ung-fang let me cuddle the child comfortably in my arms.

"Ever after that, wherever Yang went, he took the orphan with him. To feed him, Yang saved up his own dry ration, clothing, and pocket money. Whatever he had, he gave to him. The child was often asleep when we reached camp; Yang would carry him off the truck. He loved the child as much as he did his own brother. Yang Ts'ung-fang did not part with the child until this year when the condition in the rear area of Korea had improved, and the authorities made such a decision. He led the child by the hand and handed him over to the teacher at the orphanage. The child has not forgotten him; he has been writing Yang frequently to tell him about his study. As for Yang, he has also taken to writing to the child seriously. He is a lovable and intelligent boy indeed."

This strong young man realized that he had diverged a bit. He smiled bashfully and hurried back to his subject:

"That night, from beginning to end the tense experience lasted only about ten minutes. The airplanes had gone, and we all boarded our trucks to proceed.

"I was in the lead. I drove the truck full throttle, for I wanted to hurry and see what had happened to Yang Ts'ung-fang.

"Passing over a hilltop I saw the dark motionless shadow of a truck under several pine trees on the roadside. My heart skipped a beat—but what was all this? I jammed on the brake, pushed open the door and ran, shouting at each step, 'Yang Ts'ung-fang! Yang Ts'ung-fang!' But nobody answered. With each step I ran, my heart sank that much lower. Then I saw one of Yang's arms on the steering wheel and the other at the window; his head was leaning on his arm over the window, his face looking toward the rear as if he had been reaching out to look before he passed out. There was no trace of his cap, and his hair was dancing in the wind.

"The trucks all stopped. All the comrades came up around him. I embraced his shoulders. My face brushed against his left shoulder and I felt a wet patch —he was wounded and he was still bleeding! The stir brought him back to consciousness.

"I asked, 'Yang Ts'ung-fang! How do you feel?'

"He did not respond to my question; instead, he raised his head to look up at me and at the others, asking, 'Have all the comrades come up?'

"The captain pushed his way up close to Yang, and with one foot on the running board he answered, 'All here, Comrade Yang, not one missing, all here.'

"'No damage to the ammunition?'

"'None. Don't you worry!'

"At the time all our attention was focused on Yang; his questions reminded us that it was getting late, yet our urgent mission was not accomplished. We turned to look in the direction of the Front. There, in the distance, the cannon fire flashed like the flash of the morning dew at the summer daybreak. Immediately following that a muffled rumble could be heard through the wind. It reminded us how anxiously our comrades on the firing line were awaiting the ammunition! There was a saying: water and fire have no mercy for each other. Wars are much worse than the merciless clash between water and fire! The captain turned from the running board, waved, and shouted, 'Comrades! Let's go! They are waiting for us on the Front!' He pulled open the door and darted into Yang Ts'ung-fang's cab. I turned the ignition on and looked in his direction —I saw the light turned on in the cab; the captain was bandaging Yang's head and shoulder. Then the captain himself sat up erect in the driver's seat and, with the light off and the exhaust pipe coughing a few times, his truck led the way heading for the Front."

When the driver reached this point in his story, he took a cigarette from his pocket and started to smoke.

"What happened?" I asked anxiously. "Was the ammunition delivered on time?"

"You want to know how it ended? Certainly, it was really nerve-wracking. As half of the eastern sky was turning purplish and dawn was approaching, we delivered the thirty truckloads of ammunition to the Front. The comrades on the firing line said, 'If you had come an hour later, it would have been awful.' They stood up from the midst of smoke and fire to throw hand grenades at the enemy. You know, what I'm telling you took place last year. At that time it was really tough for us. But that didn't stop us. You must have seen it last night. You saw the bustle on the transportation route! The enemy bombed out dozens of cities, but we really changed North Korea into one big city. If you don't believe me, look; aren't the vehicles on these highways similar to those we have in the big cities back in our own country? They run so happily! We've even installed traffic lights at each crossroad.

"But ... You mustn't ask me. I haven't done much. Comrade, you understand what I mean. Just take our Yang Ts'ung-fang. Later, I visited him at the hospital. He was sitting on the bed. I asked him, 'How did you ever think of pulling out?' He replied, 'At first I drove hard, with nothing else in my mind except that I must lure the airplanes away. When the bullets began to bounce off my cab left and right, I thought again; then I felt there was something wrong—I'm not scared of dying, but ammunition cannot withstand fire. What if the gas tank gets hit? Whatever you do, if you give it careful thinking, then you grasp the problems. I thought further: since the target has been shifted over this way, I'd turn off the headlights. So all the bullets hit the roadside. I heard the plane pulling up. Then I said to myself, "Now, that's not right! You can't leave, since it has taken me a great deal of trouble to invite you over here!" So, I turned on the headlights again.'

"I said, 'Yang, old pal! Honestly, at that moment, didn't you worry about anything?' 'Of course I worried! I'm human, not carved out of wood. Don't you think I know a bullet will make a hole in my head when it hits? But . . .' He stopped. His entire left shoulder and arm were immobilized because of the bandage. With only one hand he held onto the matchbox and struck a match to smoke. No matter what I asked, he had nothing to tell me. Finally he waved his hand, saying, 'Just think of our comrades on the line of fire. What happened to me was nothing!'

"Our chief of staff told me later that the commander never closed his eyes a wink that night. He just waited at the command post. He kept calling to inquire about the trucks. You will understand this; after all, to be a soldier is easy, but a commanding officer must bear the load of thousands of us. Whenever there's a problem it's the problem of an entire battlefield. The chief of staff said that at daybreak he received a message from the Front reporting the safe arrival of the ammunition. After the commander read it, he put it on the table and turned to tell the chief of staff, 'Thank them for me.' Then he bent over the table and went to sleep. Poor man! The commander was exhausted. See, I'm easily sidetracked from my story. Actually I was talking to you about Yang Ts'ung-fang—Yang Ts'ung-fang."

As I looked at this young man, so brave and strong, he rose, picking up the flat, empty gasoline can beside him, and walked toward the well, swinging his short sturdy body. The sunlight penetrated a verdant chestnut tree and shone on his body. My eyes never left him. He had just said to me, "You're asking me? What happened to me was nothing!" His Yang Ts'ung-fang also had said, "What happened to me was nothing!" Right, Comrade! You see how simple, how lighthearted these words sound as they come from the mouth of this young man! But pause a moment and think: every day and every night, under the flares, the cannon shots, the flying bullets, each minute, each second, there is danger, grave danger. Then, you will know how much weight there is in what they say.

Now he had gone into the chestnut woods. In Korea there were many such giant chestnut trees, with long outstretched branches from which the carefree, lush, big leaves drooped. The driver was standing on the well platform; a few Korean children in pink, white, and lavender frocks stood around him. These girls were all very fond of him. As for him, after a brief exchange, he had made friends with them. He asked them to dance; right away they started to dance. As he was filling the gasoline can with water, he spoke in his half intelligible Korean. In a moment he started to sing his pleasant Korean song again.

That night we reached the Front, and I parted with my likeable companion. As for Yang Ts'ung-fang, I never had the opportunity to meet him. Once I almost saw him, but instead I received a wire, saying, "Yang Ts'ung-fang was seriously wounded in action." I haven't received any news of him since then. But every time I sit next to the driver of a jeep or a truck, I can always see the spirit of Yang Ts'ung-fang in him. I know, just at this moment, that on highways near the Front, young men are singing, as they dash ahead in the rolling dust.

Translated by Lucy O. Yang Boler

FEI LI-WEN

(1930–)

Fei Li-wen was born in Shanghai. With very little formal education, he was employed as a drill operator in a diesel engine manufacturing plant. His first writings were news articles published in 1952 in Shanghai's *Labor News,* where he later worked as reporter and editor.

In 1953 Fei was writing short narratives and essays reflecting the life of the working people; these earned him a name among the worker-writers. He has also written movies and plays. "One Year" is the title story in Fei Li-wen's 1956 short story anthology. His other narrative collections include *The Two Brothers* and *Early Spring,* which are both very popular in the People's Republic of China.

The subject matter of Fei's writings is confined to activities in factories and to the lives of the workers. Because of his own personal experience and understanding, he is able to portray realistically the emotions of the workers in connection with their everyday lives in a socialist world.   —L.Y.

One Year

Leaving the personnel office, I once more fondled the working permit that I held in my hand. My heart swelled with joy, as though it was filled with honey, so very sweet.

To be truthful, a year's rest because of illness had seemed to me as though I were being punished and confined in jail for a year. Living in the country, lying in bed, my mind was constantly occupied, day and night, with thoughts of the factory . . . the machines, production, and my many apprentices. Now I had just learned about the recent proclamation of the five-year plan, and my heart was bursting with joy. I felt I must run back to work as fast as possible, as though my legs had wings, because I knew that the minute I arrived the workshop would gain a senior skilled worker, and the apprentices would again have a master. I felt I must work harder now and contribute more toward the goal of socialism.

Thoughts surged in my mind. My steps were getting longer and faster. After passing a wooden bridge I walked past a neatly arranged flower garden and made a turn. From there I saw the honor roll bulletin board, which is built in the style of the Tien-an Gate in Peking, at the entrance to the workshop. This board was quite familiar to me. A year ago my photo was often posted there, because I had been an advanced worker for five quarters in a row before I fell ill.

"Who could that person be now?" I walked to the front of the board, stood still, and took one look at the photo on the board. When I saw that it was a photo of a girl with short hair, a fine oval face, and thin lips, I thought my eyes were fooling me. I wiped my eyes with a handkerchief and recomposed myself. But after I looked at it twice, I couldn't help slapping my thigh hard and I cried out, "Ah! Is it true? Has the girl Ai-hua really become an advanced worker?"

Huang Ai-hua was an apprentice I did not like very much. There are reasons for my not liking her. Although ordinarily she was polite to me, at work her manner was quite unlike my attitude toward my master. On the surface she followed my instructions when I gave her work to do, but she occasionally would waste time finding fault. She seemed not entirely satisfied with my method. She did not understand the tradition that once a master, always a master, and once an apprentice, always an apprentice. During the years when I was an apprentice I would never look to the west, not even once, if the master told me to face the east. Even though this tradition was no longer in practice, still, as far as technique is concerned, it is I who taught her, not she who taught me! I recall that just two days before I became ill, I had scolded her a little bit because of a piece of work she did. She said nothing at the time. But the following day, much to my surprise, her new method had a successful try-out. Later, at the group meeting, she actually criticized me. She said that I still had conservative ideas. It was unprecedented for an apprentice to criticize a master. I certainly had never encountered anything like it before. Because of these incidents, frankly, I paid very little attention to the letters she wrote to me when I was convalescing. Although the apprentice Hsiao Shen in his letter had told me that Ai-hua had become the group leader, that her work was excellent, and that she would soon be rated as an advanced worker as well, somehow all this just didn't register in my mind.

While I was still standing in front of the bulletin board in a daze, suddenly someone pulled on my arm from behind and said, "Master, you have really returned! This time the director did not kid us." I turnéd my head and sure enough it was Ai-hua. I looked at her face closely. She appeared a little bit heavier than she did in the photo on the board. Nothing about her had changed; the brisk manner, the clarion voice, were all the same as before.

Ai-hua was holding my hand and, without waiting for me to say anything, she continued, "Master, you must have completely recovered! To tell you the truth, master, if you are not recovered by now your apprentices will surely be worried sick and lose their minds."

"So, you mean that I have turned into a devil to cause all that trouble!" I replied, pretending to be angry. Ai-hua realized that I was purposely picking on her slip of the tongue. Her face turned red. She twisted her head about and started laughing softly.

"Foolish girl, of course I am fully recovered." I patted her shoulder. "The doctors nowadays are so stubborn. They would rather quarrel with you, but they'd never allow any unrecovered patient to return to factory work. Look here, my legs are just as strong as before, like two iron bars. Tomorrow, we'll go to the soccer field. I definitely must score a few points . . . Ha ha!" So saying, I pulled up my trousers and patted my legs several times.

"I can well imagine what a fuss you would have made if they had prevented you from coming back to the factory any longer. It would be a wonder if you didn't get so mad at them that you'd glare at them and your beard would curl up with anger!" While Ai-hua was saying this, she took a step backward and made a face at me.

"You, little girl, how dare you get naughty with me!" I said with a straight face, pretending that I was serious. I shook my finger at her several times. Actually, she had guessed my mind.

" ... Then are you returning to our group?" Ai-hua asked me. She stared at me with wide-open eyes.

"Certainly! Staying away from the lathes will surely bore me to death. That's right. I have already had a long talk with the director about it." I stepped towards Ai-hua, put my hand on her shoulder, and said, "Let's go!"

We walked into the factory. I saw that things were all changed. Everything was new and novel to me. I cocked my ears and listened to the voices of the machines. How very familiar these noises sounded! When I caught sight of some of the lathes which I had handled before, I hurried toward them. Standing in front of the machines, I mumbled, "Lathes, my old friends, Chin Chao-kang has returned!" I don't know whether it was because I was overly excited or whether something else led me to act that way.

Many people nodded warmly to me. From their happy faces I could read that they were glad to see me return. I kept waving my hands in answer to their greetings. I thought to myself, "You are a senior. You must work hard and be a model for these youngsters!" But when I carefully examined the machines they were using, and the boxes and boxes of new products, I became perplexed and muttered to myself, "These lathes, are they all new designs?"

"These are new lathes," Ai-hua heard my comment and answered. At the same time, she pulled my arm to direct my attention and continued, "You see that high-speed machine over there? It revolves twenty-eight hundred times per minute. These are all new style lathes ... Master, nowadays, more and more we have been made to realize that our technology is not sufficient for our needs! Yesterday you learned one thing, today you have to learn something else. There is so much to learn you need more than two heads."

"Twenty-eight hundred rpm?" I was astonished. I have worked many years but this was the first I had heard about such a high-speed lathe. I felt as though someone had thrust a chunk of something into my chest. I thought to myself, how much things have changed! Yet I still believed that I should be able to cope with the situation. Without revealing how I felt, I spoke to Ai-hua: "In order to fulfill the quotas of the first five-year plan, everything has to accelerate, faster and faster. You youngsters must listen more to those who are experienced when you don't understand."

"That is so right!" Ai-hua replied. "When I worked the thirty-five-hundred-rpm extra-high-speed lathe, which just arrived, I not only used the experience of others but also consulted books."

"You worked a lathe with thirty-five hundred revolutions a minute? Is it really that fast? Are you sure you are not mistaken? Wow! It's more than three times faster than the speed at the time I left. Can your hands keep up with the speed?" I stopped walking and took two deep breaths.

"The others helped me to figure out a way. I just struggled along to stay with them." Ai-hua answered in modesty. She twisted the corner of her jacket and her face was red.

I knew her disposition well. By the way she acted, I could guess that her work was probably very praiseworthy.

"Ah, Master Chin. Are you really back?" someone suddenly called out. But when I turned around I found no one.

"Master, I am here." Again I heard the voice. This time I saw him. It was Hsiao Shen. He was standing on a platform over ten feet high, manipulating a vertical lathe which was more than four times his height. He was calling me, his neck stretching forward.

"So, it's you," I said. "Watch out for the thing. Hold the handle tight. Ai-ya! How come he was put to work on a lathe that is so difficult to handle. Are you trying to make him look foolish?" Truly, I was really worried for him.

"Master, you don't need to worry about him. He has already worked on that machine for over three months. Moreover, he has exceeded the quota every month. He has turned out over one thousand flywheels. By the way, his photo was in the papers, didn't you see it?" Ai-hua explained.

"These flywheels, were they all lathed by him?" I lifted my head and looked at Hsiao Shen's thin face again. There was nothing more that I could say. I walked a few steps forward, turned my head around again, and added, "Be careful, and be sure to read the blueprints a few more times, especially where the dimensions are marked." But after I said it, even I, myself, felt that it sounded silly. He already had apprentices and I was treating him as though he was still an apprentice of mine.

"Master, I have thought of a new method. Please come and take a look." A girl in a T-shirt, upon seeing us, called out in a squeaky voice.

"Ah!" I stepped forward. But, before I put my foot down, I knew I had made a mistake, because I did not know the girl at all.

At this moment, Ai-hua walked forward from behind and answered, "Fine, I'll be right there." She pulled my arm and turned to me. "Master," she said, "let us go take a look together."

I realized then that the girl in the T-shirt was in fact Ai-hua's apprentice. Again I gazed at my former apprentice at my side. I said, half in jest, "Not bad! You really act like a master."

"It is all because Master Chin educated me so well!" Ai-hua replied. She seemed to have sensed my thoughts, yet she continued, "I was always terribly worried that if I could not handle the job at any time, it would tarnish the reputation of Master Chin."

"Little girl, that tongue of yours will never yield to anyone." In spite of my words, my heart was joyous, because I knew the young plant I had nurtured in the past had blossomed and borne fruit.

Presently, we arrived at a lathe. Immediately the girl started talking: "Master, look, I'll install one more cutter here to drill holes and round the exterior at the same time. Wouldn't this double the speed? Do you think it would work?" She gestured as she went on.

"That way, it would cause the thing to vibrate," I said, shaking my head.

"Ah!" The girl stood there transfixed.

"Oh," Ai-hua rubbed her hands. She stretched her neck and took a look at the blade. Then, with chalk in hand, she made repeated sketches on the floor.

Finally, she looked up and said to me, "Master, suppose we reduce the size of the cutter blade. Do you think that would eliminate the vibration?"

I was greatly surprised. I never dreamed that she would be able to figure out a solution before I could. She was correct. By reducing the size of the blade there should be no vibration to speak of. But why didn't I think of that?

Circumstances have really changed. How quickly Ai-hua's technical ability had improved. And yet I was still treating her like a snotty little girl. As my thoughts raced, I scolded myself secretly. I should not have been in such a hurry to pour cold water on the young right after my arrival. Fortunately Ai-hua was calm and self-assured, and did not become flustered upon hearing my comments. She was still able to think out good solutions. Otherwise my remarks could have had unfortunate consequences.

"Master, do you think it would do?" When Ai-hua saw that I didn't reply, she asked again.

"Fine! Fine! If we advance the cutter slightly and speed up the lathe chuck a little bit, the result will be even better." I wiped my perspiration with a handkerchief and nodded my approval.

"You are right, Master." Ai-hua turned around and told the other girl, "Try it out just as we said. Should there be questions, we will study it again together."

In the meantime, a group of people had crowded around me. My former apprentices had seen me from a distance. They all brought their own apprentices over to meet me.

I patted the shoulders of some and shook the hands of others. No words could have expressed the happiness in my heart. As I looked at the more than twenty young men and women standing there surrounding me, I thought, "How could anything compare with the pleasure of seeing with one's own eyes the blossoms and fruits in persons that one had cultivated oneself!"

I straightened my jacket, smiled, and said, "Hm . . . , go back to your lathe. Don't delay the work because of me! Go on, I too will be at a machine soon. Let us work together and fight a good battle."

"Fine!" They responded together and all went right back to their lathes like a puff of smoke.

I walked slowly along with Ai-hua.

"Ah! Back up the cutter, quick, you fool. The cutter is going to hit the chuck." I saw the whirling chuck on the lathe in front of me just about to collide with the cutter, but the little fellow at the machine did not even move. I was so frightened that I rushed over. But before I could get there, somehow the cutter stand made a noise and then moved back steadily. My heart was still beating violently.

"Don't worry, Master. There is a device installed on every lathe that automatically withdraws the cutter," Ai-hua explained.

"Where did the automatic withdrawing device come from?" I asked.

"Master Huang invented it," the little fellow working at the lathe said, looking at me and pointing to Ai-hua. "Quite a few factories have come here to learn from her."

"You thought of this new method?" I asked Ai-hua.

"No. It was with the help of others. It was everybody's effort that made it a

success. Master, won't you please examine it and give us your comments!"
Ai-hua replied cheerfully.

I stooped, touched the part of the machine with my hands and wondered how
it worked. It was not more than five inches in diameter and the same in length.
What was it that made it capable of withdrawing the cutter automatically?
What could the principle be? It was quite beyond my comprehension. While
I was deep in thought, Ai-hua, standing behind me, explained it to me in detail.
She pointed to this and that and made all kinds of gestures as she spoke. But
my mind was confused. I did not understand what she had said at all. Utterly
frustrated, I drew a deep breath and abruptly stood up.

"Master, would you like me to bring the blueprints for you to examine?"
Ai-hua asked. It seemed that she did not sense the mood I was in at all.

"Fine!" I replied; my voice was gruff.

"Master, look! These are thirty-five-hundred-rpm lathes. This is the one I use.
That one is reserved for you." Ai-hua pointed at the machines.

I composed myself, and then examined the lathe in front of me, feeling it
with my hands again and again. How strange this machine seemed.

"Master, this is how this machine works." Without waiting for me to ask any
questions, Ai-hua, like a museum guide, described how the various moving
parts of the lathe operated.

"You see, over here, if you operate the levers in the wrong manner the cutter
will be damaged and the operator may also be hurt." As Ai-hua explained about
the operation of changing the speed she made a mischievous face, tossed her
head and said, "I for one was hurt once. Would you like for me to demonstrate
the whole procedure for you?"

"Mm . . . " I responded. I was not sure whether I meant acceptance or refusal.

She demonstrated the operation of the machine at different speeds. Skillfully
she performed the stopping, cutting, and several other important operations
repeatedly. I was standing behind her. At first I paid little attention, but soon
my eyes started to follow her hands. I looked at her back, and I felt tears
threatening in my eyes. I grasped my shirt tightly near the chest. My heart
ached, as if I had been stabbed by a knife.

"Master, these are the drawings of the lathe which I did with the help of the
technicians. These are the blueprints of those seven parts of the lathe which
I improved, including the automatic cutter withdrawal device. After you look
them over, let me have your comments." While I was lost in thought, Ai-hua
had turned off the lathe and had gone to get those two sets of blueprints, which
she now handed to me.

"Do you know how to make mechanical drawings?" I was surprised.

"I learned it at the night school recently, but these are just like children's
exercises. Don't laugh at me when you see them." Ai-hua tossed her head and
said, "Go ahead, Master, look at the drawings. I'll go get some material for you."
She turned around and went away, running and jumping.

I waited until she was out of sight, then I threw the blueprints on the toolbox
and sat down on the stool. Discouraged, I bowed my head. There was so much
on my mind, yet no words would come out of my mouth. The truth is, there
was little for me to say. People were looking forward to my return as an
advanced worker. They wanted me to be working with them, beating the clock,

in order to complete the five-year plan ahead of time. "Now that I am back here," I thought, "I have become a useless figure. It seems as though everyone is riding on a horse and galloping ahead. But I am like a carriage with broken wheels, which has fallen down to the bottom of a hill. The distance between the others and me is immense now. Ai-hua has overtaken me. I do not understand the tools she has invented. I cannot work the lathe she handles." As I was thinking, I panicked. Suddenly, I grabbed my hair with rage and grumbled, "Chin Chao-kang! What is the matter with you?"

A cool breeze blew across my face again and again with increasing force. Slowly I lifted my head. My eyes met the embroidered flag on the wall beyond. The two characters "Ch'ien-chin" [Forward, march!] on the flag flashed across my eyes. They startled me. I shivered. With trembling hands I fondled the left pocket on my shirt where the five red characters "Hsien-chin kung-tso-che" [Advanced Worker] were printed.

A long time passed. Finally I realized how mistaken I had been. I jumped up from the stool and mumbled to myself, "Shame on you. How could you ever have deserved the honor of being an advanced worker. You should have known that any knowledge and skill you possess was not born in you. They were acquired from other people. If you always stick to the old methods of doing things, how can socialism ever be achieved. It is about time that you quit acting like a master. If your apprentice has progressed to this point, then you should learn from her. . . . " As these thoughts churned in my mind, I grabbed the blueprints which I had thrown on the toolbox. I opened them up and examined them page by page.

I pulled out a handkerchief, wiped my eyes, and read the blueprints carefully over and over again. Without stopping, I studied three times the drawings of those seven parts which Ai-hua had improved. Before I had finished reading all of the blueprints, Ai-hua returned. She brought a pushcart with the material in it for me to work on. As soon as she saw me she shouted, "The director was very happy to hear that you want to start to work immediately. He said that he will come to see you very soon. Hey! Master, why are your eyes red?"

"Ah . . . Ah! It's nothing. It's the wind." I was startled and quickly turned my face away from her.

"You better put on the face visor." Ai-hua passed hers over to me.

I accepted the visor, and then with great effort I said, "You . . . you stay here beside me and watch. I'll make a try, and you must let me know if I do anything wrong."

I installed the cutter, clamped the work in the lathe, and turned on the switch. Following the instructions which Ai-hua had just given me a while back in her demonstration, I began to work. The accustomed rhythm of the machine began to put me at ease. It seemed like a heavy weight had been lifted from my heart.

"That's right, Master. Try to run the machine faster," said Ai-hua.

"All right!" I wiped the perspiration from my forehead.

"No! Master! Both levers must be turned to the right simultaneously." Ai-hua called out and pulled my arm as soon as she saw that I made a mistake with the operation of the speed levers. She expertly turned the levers to the correct position for me.

"Right! Right! How forgetful I am." I recalled the way she had just shown me. I nodded toward her, blushing a little.

As the speed of the lathe increased, the color of the shavings turned from blue to purple. My heavy heart received a lift.

"You are really running it fast, Master. Like the old general Huang Chung, you certainly deserve your reputation!" Ai-hua rushed over and seized my hand, as I stopped the machine.

"Ai-hua . . . " I held her hand tightly. There were tears in my eyes. There was a great deal that I wanted to say to her, but I was practically speechless. I only managed to say, after a long struggle, "Ai-hua, will you explain the construction of the automatic cutter withdrawal device to me tonight? I want to learn its operation well. To tell you the truth, I don't understand what's involved!". . . .

Translated by Lucia Yang

WANG YÜAN-CHIEN
(1929–)

Wang Yüan-chien, a native of Shantung, joined the Eighth Route Army when he was fourteen. Later he served at one time or another as correspondent, editor, and reporter for army newspapers and journals. It was in the army that he sharpened his pen and polished his style.

His first short story, "Party Membership Dues," appeared in print in 1954 and won him sudden fame. It was later made into a movie.

Because of his talent, hard work, and loyalty to the Party, Wang was sent to the National Institute of Literature for advanced studies. Before he was purged as one of Chou Yang's "loyal disciples" during the Cultural Revolution in 1966, he had at least eight short story collections credited to him, including *Party Membership Dues, The Offsprings,* and *An Ordinary Laborer.* Several of his short stories were adopted by high schools throughout China as text materials.

The main theme of his stories is invariably that of the life and struggle of the masses and the Red Army against the Nationalists during the 1930s, a subject treated by relatively few other contemporary writers.

Wang was rehabilitated in 1977 and has taken up his pen again. Two of his short stories and one of his essays appeared in recent issues of *People's Literature.* —G.C.

Party Membership Dues

Whenever I received my special allowance, with which I went to pay my Party membership dues, as soon as my local leader registered the amount under my name on the list, a strong feeling rose from the bottom of my heart. Events of the fall of 1934 suddenly flashed back into my mind.

The year 1934 was just the beginning of a hard struggle for us in the border regions of Kwangtung, Fukien, and Kiangsi provinces. Part of the main Red Army units joined the anti-Japanese vanguard forces and moved to the north; others joined up with the central Red Army for the Long March and left in April. We were part of a tiny force left behind to continue behind-the-lines struggle. Right after the main force's departure, the Nationalist Army assaulted us with their "siege-and-destroy" tactics. In order to avoid unnecessary sacrifice and to continue our struggle, we were forced to retreat into the mountains.

Even though we were in the mountains, we were still the guiding force of the underground struggle in the region. Comrade Wei Chieh, the political commissar of our unit, served also as the district Party secretary. Under his leadership, we attacked enemies whenever we had the chance, and at the same time maintained communication with all the underground Party organizations through clandestine channels. After we had adopted this strategy for only a short while, the enemy realized that they could no longer get the upper hand, so they designed their "resettle-residents and combine-villages" policy, forcing all the people in the out-of-the-way small villages near our mountain base areas to move to big villages on the plain. This scheme was very effective; it cut off our communication with the masses and paralyzed our underground organizations. We had to regroup to continue our struggle.

Before we retreated into the mountains, I was a scout for our unit. I spent most of my days roving about in enemy territory. Wherever I went, the masses would always take care of me. At every opportunity, we would make a clean sweep of the enemy, often wiping out a small unit of their security force. That was great. But once the enemy initiated its new strategy, my free-roving days were ended. I grew desperate and helpless, not because of personal hardships such as food and shelter, but because I could not endure my isolation from the masses, with whom I had fought and struggled, shoulder to shoulder.

While I was in one of these depressed moods, comrade Wei summoned me to his office. He asked me to be a courier—to go down the mountains and contact local Party organizations.

I accepted this assignment with heartfelt thanks. I knew well that this mission was quite different from my scout days. My mission was to reestablish contact with all the underground Party organizations which had been paralyzed during the "resettlement," to facilitate communication between village Party organizations and the county Party committee—the guerrilla forces in our mountain base area—so that we could mount an organized struggle. My destination was Pa-chiao-yao, a big village not too far from the mountains, a place receiving people forced to move out of several small villages nearby. My contact was Huang Hsin, a housewife in her mid-twenties and a Party member since 1931. During the Red Army Expansion Campaign, she set an example by sending her own husband to join the Red Army. Later he followed Chairman Mao on the Long March. She had only a five-year-old daughter with her at home then. When the enemy started the "village-combining" tactics, they burned her village to the ground, so she moved to Pa-chiao-yao with her fellow villagers. It was said that she had always been a loyal, dependable comrade, who actively continued to carry out Party functions even after the move. That was why I was sent to contact her and deliver to her our district Party secretary's directives to gradually develop Party activities in the area.

Commissar Wei had told me all this in his briefing. I actually knew only the general terrain of Pa-chiao-yao, and had never met Huang Hsin. Because of this, Commissar Wei specifically instructed me, "You have to remember carefully that Comrade Huang Hsin has a black mole on one of her ears."

I packed a few things, changed into civilian clothes, and went down the mountains as the dusk deepened.

Pa-chiao-yao was about ten miles from our mountain base. Since I had to take winding paths, I arrived there after midnight. I had been to this village before, but things had been quite different then: a big village like Pa-chiao-yao in the base areas used to have meetings, classes, drums and gongs, shows and songs all over the place after a day's work. Now everything had changed: there was a deathly silence everywhere, and no lights in the village. It was so dark that it looked more like a deserted graveyard than a village. Only occasionally could I hear a couple of "white devils" yelling half-heartedly, thinking that all the villagers in the base area were kept well in line under their village-combining strategy. But I knew that the darkness of this dismal village concealed sparks of revolution. In time, the sparks would spread into a huge conflagration burning across the land.

I slipped quietly into the village. Following Commissar Wei's instructions, I began from the east side of the village and counted to the seventeenth shed, then I tiptoed to the door. Strangely enough, even this late at night there was still light inside the shed. But it was covered so that I couldn't see it until I walked up to the door. Someone inside was softly humming a folksong. It sounded like a woman's voice, very low. The tune was so very familiar that I knew immediately she was humming "Seeing My Love Off to Join the Red Army," a very popular song during the Red Army Expansion Campaign.

> Seeing my love off to join the Red Army;
> Be brave on the battlefield.
> If you die for the cause of revolution,
> I'll shoulder all the burden.
> Seeing my love off to the Red Army,
> Please remember what I said:
> I am so happy you enlisted,
> And don't you worry, I'll till the land.

I had not heard this song for quite some time, and it was heartening to hear it at this moment. I had been correct in thinking that the masses were still with us deep down in their hearts; even during these trying days they were thinking about our Red Army, thinking about those glorious days when our red flag flew and our revolutionary struggle surged. Could she be Comrade Huang Hsin, the person I was looking for? It had to be her; otherwise, how was it that her singing was a little bit off tune? Her mind must have drifted miles away with her husband on the Long March, and she was not concentrating on her singing. I stood outside listening, not having the heart to interrupt her thoughts. But it was almost dawn and I could wait no longer. I stood by the door and gave the prearranged signal, knocking three times on the upper part of the door, three times on the bottom, and once in the middle.

The humming stopped and I repeated the knocks once more. I heard the footsteps coming, then the door opened.

I entered, and was stunned by what I saw; there were three people there, two women and one old man, crowding around a basket of vegetables, picking leaves from the basket without looking up. They appeared so calm and relaxed that no one seemed to notice my entrance. That made it hard for me, for I could not tell which one was Comrade Huang Hsin. If I made a wrong move, not only would my own life be in danger, which was not my major concern, but our Party organizations would suffer. I hesitated for a second or two, then my nimble mind came to my rescue. I said to them, "Oh! Have I entered the wrong house?"

It worked. They all looked up at once. With a quick glance I saw that the woman sitting on the mat had a black mole on one of her ears. In one step I walked up to her and said, "Mrs. Lu, do you remember me? Brother Lu asked me to bring this letter to you." The last statement was also prearranged. Ever since the Kuomintang forces occupied this area, Comrade Huang had let it be known that her husband, Lu Chin-yung, was working at an incense shop in another area.

I had to admire the tact and alertness of this ordinary village woman, Comrade Huang. Smiling, she handed a wooden stool to me as though we were old friends, and then said to her company, "Well, that's all for today. You people take the vegetables home and divide them among yourselves; as for salt, we'll divide it among us whenever we get some."

The two looked at me with broad grins, then each picked up a bundle of vegetables and quietly left the house.

Comrade Huang followed them out, probably to see whether everything was all right. From my scout training, I took a good look at the house where this Red Army wife and underground Party member lived: the two-room home was made of bamboo and mud. The bed on the floor by the corner of the north wall consisted of nothing more than a pile of straw. A child slept under a tattered cotton coverlet on the bed. Her quivering little nose showed that she was sound asleep. This was probably Comrade Huang's daughter. There was a sooted earthenware pot supported by three stones at the corner of the wall; that was Comrade Huang's cooking pot. Looking up, I saw a small attic supported by several sticks; a few pieces of broken furniture and some bundles of dried sugarcane tips were stored there.

While I was still looking around, she came back. After closing the door and covering the oil lamp, she sat down opposite me and said, "Those two are comrades. We only met recently." She must have remembered my puzzled look as I entered the room, for she pointed at the hole in the corner of the wall and said to me, "Next time when you come, please check through the hole first to see whether it's all right to come in, lest something go wrong."

She appeared a little older than Commissar Wei had told me, more like in her thirties than her twenties. Her hair was combed into a round bun on top of her head, but it was so short one could still sense that she must have joined in "cutting one's hair to join the Red Army" not too long ago. Although her face was not robust, her kind, calm eyes were alert and full of energy. Probably she was too touched at the moment, for time and again she lifted a corner of her clothes to wipe tears from her eyes.

After quite some time, she began to talk again. "To lose contact with one's Party is like being a kite separated from its string. It's an awful experience! When I see our people suffer and our Red Army experience problems, I know we should fight back. But how? Now everything is all right. We have reunited with our district committee: we have you and you have us, and we'll surely raise the red flag again."

Before I left the mountain base, Commissar Wei had instructed me to comfort her and I had prepared a lot of nice things to tell her as soon as I saw her. But judging by how strong she was and how she talked about struggle and paid no attention to hardships and problems at all, what was there for me to say? I figured I had better come right to the point.

As I was about to convey Commissar Wei's directives, she suddenly remembered something. "Look at me. I am so excited that I forget everything. I should fix you something to eat." She opened the pot and took out two hard Chinese rolls made of sweet potato strips and vegetable leaves. Getting out another chipped pot, she searched in it for a while and fished out one preserved turnip. As she gave these to me she said, "Ever since the village-combining strategy, the white devils keep a very close watch on us, so we have been unable to send you people anything. You must have suffered a lot there; I have nothing good to offer you, so please eat what little I have here."

After a long night's walk, I was really hungry. Besides, I had not tasted salt for quite some time, so when the preserved vegetable was offered to me, it actually made my mouth water. I gulped the food down without the slightest formality. Although the vegetable was a little sour because it lacked salt, it still tasted fine to me. The flavor of a little salt reminded me of all my comrades in the mountains; I began to see their pale, wan faces—they needed salt badly there.

While I was eating, I delivered Commissar Wei's directives regarding our underground Party activities. The directives included, among other things, getting a clear understanding of the enemy's activities; organizing the anti-rent and anti-land-confiscation campaigns; and some anticipated problems and their solutions. She nodded as she listened, and she raised questions every once in a while. Finally she said to me, "What Commissar Wei said was right. We do have problems. But I have seen the world. Since 1929, the year I joined the revolution, I have been through several enemy siege-and-destroy campaigns. If I could survive those, I surely can take on any new assignments given me." She showed great resolution and confidence and took the tough assignments on her own shoulders without the slightest reservation.

After we exchanged some information we heard the crow of a rooster. Since this was our first meeting, I could not stay too long; I wanted to get back under the protection of the morning fog. She stopped me as I was leaving. Tearing the lining of her clothing, she pulled out an envelope. In it was her worn-out Party membership card, with the sickle and hammer and the district commissar's seal still in vivid red colors. Inside the card folder, there were two silver dollars; she weighed the dollars in her palms for a while, then handed them to me saying, "Comrade Ch'eng, these dollars were left for me by the child's father before he went to the Front. I have not paid my dues since the enemy put its village-combining strategy into effect. Please take these to the commissar. If one takes care of the pennies, the dollars will take care of themselves, right? Hope these will help the Party a little."

How could I accept these dollars? I had not received any instruction to collect dues in the first place. Secondly, she was by herself and had to take care of her child. With no job and nobody to rely on, she still insisted on working for the Party under such hard circumstances. She needed these dollars badly. So I said to her, "As for dues, I have not received any instruction to collect them. I cannot take these with me. You'd better keep them."

Seeing that I refused to take the money, she thought for a moment and said, "You're right. Under the present circumstances, supplies probably would be more useful than money."

She knew what was needed, therefore she would rather pay her dues in useful goods instead of money. But who could tell then that this was a fatal mistake?

After a couple of weeks, we received information that the enemy had been alerted to all the underground activities after their village-combining strategy. They tried to undermine our efforts by using some of the waverers among the masses. Several of our organizations in the villages had suffered losses. To meet this new challenge, I was sent to Pa-chiao-yao again with new directives.

As I arrived at Comrade Huang's doorstep, I first looked through the hole in the wall to see if everything was all right, as she had told me to do. I saw that she was busy under the light of the lamp. There were a few piles of preserved vegetables on the floor, the broken pot from which she had taken a pickled turnip for me last time, some preserved cabbages, turnips, and broad-beans, some yellow, others green. She was sorting these vegetables into piles and then putting them into a bamboo basket, while trying to soothe her child by saying, "My darling, you don't want these, do you? Ma is going to sell these. After Ma sells these and gets some money, she'll buy you a big flatcake, buy you anything you want. Tell me you don't want any of these, tell me."

The little girl apparently could not endure the long hardships; she was even thinner than her mother. Her tiny neck held up her small head, as she leaned weakly on her mother. Probably she had not tasted things like these in the basket for quite some time. With her big eyes staring at the vegetables, her mouth watering, she would not listen to her mother but instead stubbornly grabbed her clothes, asking for some preserved vegetables. Then she crawled over to the empty pot, stuck her skinny arm into it, dipped her fingers into the salty water and sucked them. She finally could stand it no longer. Grabbing a bean-pod she stuffed it into her mouth at once. Her mother, turning her head, saw this. Looking first at the child, then at the basket of vegetables, she snatched the bean-pod away from her. The poor little child started howling.

The tragic sight propelled me. I knocked on the door and entered. "Comrade Huang, I don't think you're doing the right thing. Even if you want to sell these vegetables, one bean-pod won't make that much difference. Don't be so hard on the child, please."

Seeing that I was already there and that I had witnessed the whole thing, she said to me with a sigh, "Old Ch'eng, do you really think I am going to sell these? Nowadays salt is even more valuable than gold, so how could I afford to make preserved vegetables to sell? All these were contributed by our members to send to our comrades in the mountains as our Party dues. We hope these will help a little. I was just trying to put them in order for you."

I suddenly realized that these were the vegetables they had been picking during my first visit here not too long before.

She glanced at me, then at the child, and said, as though to herself, "If we have our Party, our Red Army, millions of children may be saved."

The child stopped crying but still circled around the empty pot. I picked up several bean-pods for the child and said to Comrade Huang, "A few bean-pods won't matter that much even during such hardships. I'd rather not eat for ten days than to see the child suffer."

The words were still on my lips when I heard hurrying footsteps at the door.

Somebody knocked and said, "Comrade Huang, please open the door; open it quickly, please."

As I opened the door, the woman I saw the first time in the room stood there. She gasped out a few words. "News has been leaked out that someone from the mountain base is here. The white devils are searching for him. Please do something. I have to warn the others." She left quietly.

When I heard this, I said: "I'm going."

Comrade Huang grabbed me and said, "If they are searching for you, they'll surely encircle this place so well that not even a raindrop could get through, won't they? Where can you go? Just try to hide somewhere. Quick!"

I could figure this out too, but I didn't want to get her involved. So I tried to pull away from her and walk out of the room. Suddenly she grew very serious, and her face became rigid. Her tender voice changed into a forceful, authoritative tone as she said, "According to our rules for underground operations, you are under my command here. You'd better listen to me. For the Party you have to live and fight." Then she pointed to the attic. "Go and hide there quickly. No matter what happens, don't make a move. Just leave everything to me."

At that moment, there was a commotion on the street—yelling and footsteps were very near. I climbed up into the attic and peeked through the cracks. I saw Comrade Huang cover the vegetable basket with straws, and hold her child up and kiss her. She then put the child down on the mat, turned toward me and said, "Comrade Ch'eng, since the enemy has already found out, I don't think I can make it this time. Even if the worst comes, our organization in Pa-chiao-yao is still in operation; the anti-land-confiscation campaign has been arranged. I guess we can succeed. From now on, you probably have to make contact with Comrade Hu Min-ying, the girl who just warned us. Remember, she lives on the west side—the fourth shed counting from the north. There is a little banyan tree by her door ... " She pointed to the basket of vegetables and said, "Please take these to the base. The vegetables are the dues from our members here."

She stopped for a moment and listened to what was happening outside; tenderness returned to her voice as she spoke again: "The child, if you can, please take her to the base or some other place. When our Red Army comes back, please deliver her to Comrade Lu Chin-yung." She was overcome by emotion for a moment and then continued: "Remember, last time I asked you to turn in two silver dollars as dues? I used one of them to buy salt; the other one is in the pot. Please take that one and my membership card with you. Don't forget."

The white devils rushed up to the door as she finished her reminder. Holding her child, she turned back and sat down, leisurely straightening her child's hair. As I looked through the cracks again, she appeared very calm and serene, exactly the same as when I saw her the first time.

The white devils were knocking at the door. She slowly walked to the door and opened it. Several of them rushed in and grabbed her clothes at the chest, asking, "Where is the man from the mountain?"

"I don't know," she said, shaking her head.

They searched all over the place and were very disappointed at not finding anything. As they were about to give up, one of them suddenly saw the basket of preserved vegetables. He kicked it over and the vegetables spread across the floor. He used his bayonet to poke around the vegetables and sensed something wrong, so he asked, "Where did all these vegetables come from?"

"I made them," she answered.

"You made them! Why are they so neatly arranged by color? Haven't you collected them to send up the mountain?" He looked around the room, then ordered the others, "Turn this place upside down."

With such limited space, if they really meant it, they surely would get to the attic, wouldn't they? At this very moment, Comrade Huang yelled out: "Since you know everything, why bother asking any more questions?" She broke away from their grasp and ran to the door, where she called out, "Comrade Ch'eng, run to the west!"

Two of the bandit soldiers ran out and headed west, the remaining two seized her and forced her to walk to the door.

At first I thought everything would turn out all right. But now that they had arrested her, how could I let her suffer for me. I had to face them. With my strength, I could at least get even with them. As I was about to jump down, she turned her head back, her eyes looking straight at her frightened child and said to her, slowly, "My child, do as Ma told you." That was the last time I heard her.

Her last words reminded me of what she had said to me before the soldiers had entered her house, and I held myself back. I was probably the only one who could figure out their real meaning: do as Ma told you; Ma was the Party organization.

After everything quieted down that evening, I managed to stop the child's crying, collected all the vegetables from the floor, and got Comrade Huang's membership card and dollar from the pot. Then I put the child in one basket, the vegetables in another, and carried them with a bamboo pole back to our mountain base area.

Commissar Wei held the child in his arms and heard my report. After a thorough examination of the situation at Pa-chiao-yao, as usual, he neatly wrote down in his notebook:

Comrade Huang Hsin, October 21, 1934, turned in her dues....

He could write no more. With the pen still in his hand, he stopped. An unusual solemnity appeared on his face as he rubbed the child's head. He glanced at Comrade Huang's membership card, then at the preserved vegetables. He took out his handkerchief, dabbed it with some dew from the grass, then tenderly wiped off the tear streaks on the child's face.

He had not put down the amount under Comrade Huang's name.

Sure, a basket of preserved vegetables can be measured, but how can anyone measure the value of a Party member's affection for his Party? How indeed can anyone count a Party member's devotion and sacrifice?

Translated by George Cheng

HO CH'IU
(1921–)

In his early life, Ho Ch'iu tried to pursue a career in art, then developed an interest in theater. He started writing while he served as a teacher in a normal school in Kwangtung, his native province. His one-act satirical comedy, *Before the New Bureau Director Came,* rocked the literary world of China in 1954. It was filmed and won a first-class citation during the national drama festival of that same year. The object of the satire, a low-level Communist functionary who places the winning of the new boss's favor above national and public interest, was a fresh and welcome theme. The comic elements in the villain are sufficiently exaggerated for stage effect, but remain altogether believable. In this play, Ho Ch'iu handles his stage direction and his dialogues with polish.

For some years Ho Ch'iu was active in the writers' circle in Kwangtung. His second play, in five acts, *Luck upon the Grand Opening,* failed to measure up to his earlier prize-winning work, however, and he has been silent since the early 1960s.   —K.Y.H.

Before the New Bureau
Director Came

Time: A late-spring morning
Place: The director's office of a government bureau
Characters:
Lao Li, a janitor in the General Affairs Department, fifty years old
Liu Shan-ch'i, Chief of the General Affairs Department, in his forties
Tai Wei, a clerk in the General Affairs Department, in his thirties
Chu Ling, a female comrade in the Construction Department, in her twenties
Comrade Chung, a working comrade in the government bureau, in his mid-thirties
Chang Yün-t'ung, the new director of the government bureau, about fifty
Setting:
   In the middle of the stage is a door which opens to a hallway. Through the translucent glass of the door is seen the back face of the words "Bureau Director's Office" in black. On the left side of the stage a door leads to the office of the General Affairs Department. On the right side of the stage is a series of glass windows. The office is furnished with a desk, a swivel chair, a file cabinet, and a conference table and chairs. On the desk are some stationery, a telephone, a small desk clock, and a call bell. As the curtain rises, the center door is closed, the left door is open. Lao Li is sitting at

the round table, reading a book in deep concentration. He jots down notes as he reads. There is a dustpan and broom next to him. Outside the windows the sky is overcast, a sign of impending rain.

After a moment, urgent rapping sounds on the center door. LAO LI *puts down the book and hurries to open the door.* LIU SHAN-CH'I *rushes in with a bulging briefcase under his arm. He throws it onto the table and hurriedly peeks through the left door, then turns to ask* LAO LI:

LIU SHAN-CH'I   Where is everybody?

LAO LI (*Puzzled*)   Who are you looking for?

LIU (*Motioning with his head toward the left door*)   Where is everybody? Hasn't Clerk Tai come yet?

LAO LI (*Glancing at the desk clock*)   Chief, it's still an hour before office hours!

LIU   Office hours! Office hours! That's the mercenary point of view! The new director will be here this afternoon; how can you still be waiting for office hours to begin, with so many things to do? (*Picks up the book on the table and thumbs through it*) Whose is this?

LAO LI   Mine.

LIU   Oh? You studying the General Line too?

LAO LI (*Nodding his head*)   Um!

LIU (*Throwing the book back onto the table*)   You janitors could fulfill the requirements of the General Line by cleaning up the offices and serving tea on time. (*Pointing to the dustpan*) Look at the way you throw your broom and dustpan around. That's not in accord with the General Line. Why haven't you removed them? (*Without a word,* LAO LI *takes the dustpan and broom and turns to leave*)

LIU   Come back here!

(LAO LI *stops*)

LIU   Did you clean up the director's office?

LAO LI   Yes.

LIU   How about the curtains?

LAO LI   I already fetched them.

LIU   Are they hung?

LAO LI   Yes.

LIU   I'll take a look later. That'll be all.

(LAO LI *takes the dustpan and broom and exits, left*)

LIU (*Sits down and wipes his perspiring forehead with a handkerchief, then dials the telephone*)   Hello, Chien-hsin Furniture Shop? I want to talk to your manager . . . (*Angrily*) Never mind who I am, just call him to the phone! (*Bangs the call bell on the desk; when no one comes, he calls to the left*) Lao Li! Lao Li!

(LAO LI *rushes in*)

LIU   Tell Clerk Tai to come here.

LAO LI   Yes, sir. (*Walks over to the left door*)

LIU   Come back here!

(LAO LI *stops*)

LIU (*Someone has answered the phone, so he quickly talks into the receiver*)

Hello! This is Department Chief Liu. (*Motions with his head to* LAO LI) Go on! (LAO LI *exits, left*)

LIU   Hello! Why haven't the sofas that we bought yesterday been delivered yet? . . . What? No, nothing doing! They have to be here before nine o'clock . . . before nine o'clock, and not a minute later! (*Slams down the receiver, then dials again*) Hello! Who's this? . . . Oh, it's you, Lao Lu. Say, you know that spring bed we bought yesterday for our director? Well, you'd better deliver it to us right away!

(*Sounds of loud arguing can be heard to the left, disturbing* LIU's *phone conversation; he covers the mouthpiece and shouts toward the door to the left*)

LIU   Hey! Hey! Who's arguing out there? Who's making all that racket?

(TAI WEI *sticks his head through the door*)

TAI (*Timidly*)   It's me, Chief.

LIU   What are you yelling about? Can't you see that I'm on the phone?

TAI   Comrade Chu of the Construction Department . . .

LIU   It would be. Tell her she'll have to wait.

TAI   Yes, sir. (*Draws his head back*)

LIU (*Into the telephone*)   Hello! Hello! Hello! Hello!

(*Nobody answers*) Damn! (*Slams down the telephone*)

(*Arguing can still be heard outside the door to the left.* LIU *bangs hard on the call bell.* TAI WEI *enters*)

LIU   What are you arguing about?

TAI   The people at the Construction Department . . .

(CHU LING *enters on* TAI WEI's *heels*)

CHU   Chief, take a look at the sky. There's going to be a heavy rain today for sure. We can't leave our three hundred sacks of cement outside any longer.

LIU (*With a forced smile*)   Comrade Chu, isn't your cement already covered with oilcloth?

CHU   What good does that do? The rain we had the day before yesterday already soaked seven or eight sacks . . .

LIU   But there isn't any storage space. Now, you tell me, what am I supposed to do?

CHU   Even if there isn't any storage space, you still have to do something. That cement is state property, and we can't just stand by and watch it be destroyed.

LIU   I've studied the General Line, so I know that. But finding storage space is a problem too.

CHU   If we have problems, aren't we supposed to overcome them?

LIU (*Frustrated*)   Ai! Overcome them, you say! Of course we'll overcome them! (*Looks at his watch*) Wait till everybody starts to work, then I'll talk it over with them.

CHU   You sure do observe working hours closely.

LIU   That's in conformity with the General Line, which requires an increase in production, but doesn't require overtime.

CHU   The rain doesn't fall according to your schedule. If the cement is lost, your General Affairs Department has to bear the responsibility.

LIU   Sure, sure! We'll bear the whole responsibility. (*Looks at his watch*)

Comrade Chu, would you please do me a favor: give me half an hour, and I'll resolve this problem of yours.

CHU   All right, I'll be back in half an hour. (*Exits, left*)

LIU   Those people in the Construction Department have all kinds of problems, but they've no consideration for the problems of others.

TAI   That's the truth! Yesterday she came by five times. We kept trying to reason with her, but nothing satisfied her. All she can see is her own three hundred sacks of cement; she doesn't give a thought to our difficulties.

LIU   When she comes back, just tell her there's nothing we can do for the time being. And make sure you don't let her get through to me again.

TAI   A moment ago she said that she wants that room downstairs turned over to her.

LIU   That's absurd! I left that room vacant for the new director. Can't she see that it's just been done over?

TAI   I told her, but she said it was a waste of money, since there's already a director's office.

LIU   You tell her that this one is too small to be suitable for the director's use. Besides, with the heavy work load of the General Affairs Department, how could we get anything done without a department head's office?

TAI   She said that there's no room left for the cement because we want more office space for our section.

LIU   Opinions! Opinions! All we ever hear is opinions! (*Points to the lettering on the glass of the center door*) Why hasn't that been changed yet?

TAI   It'll be done right away. It's easy; all we have to do is change "Bureau" to "Department."

LIU   No. Add the three words "General Affairs Department" at the top.

TAI   Yes, sir!

(LAO LI, *carrying a wooden sign with the words "Bureau Director's Office" written on it, enters, left*)

LAO LI   Chief, here's the new sign.

LIU (*Takes the sign and examines it carefully*)   Hm! Sung dynasty style characters. Not bad! Not bad at all! (*Hands it to* TAI WEI) Hang it up right away.

TAI (*Takes it*)   Yes, sir. (*To* LAO LI)   Lao Li, scrape the word "Bureau" off the door. I'll send somebody over to paint in the new words later.

LAO LI   Yes, sir.

(TAI WEI *and* LIU SHAN-CH'I *exit, left*)

LAO LI (*To himself*)   The Chief is sure full of zest. He even concerns himself with hanging up the signs.

(*While he is talking, he looks for a knife to scrape the word off the glass*)

(*Enter* COMRADE CHUNG, *left*)

CHUNG   Lao Li, where's your chief?

LAO LI   He went downstairs.

CHUNG   Please go find him for me.

LAO LI   Comrade Chung, it isn't time to start work yet. What is it you want?

CHUNG   The roof of our dormitory leaks. Is the General Affairs Department going to repair it or not?

LAO LI   Yes, of course we will! But Comrade Chung, our chief ...

CHUNG   Your chief only knows how to put things off. All he ever talks about is "budget" or "bureau rules." When you see him, tell him that we already got a repairman to fix the building. He'll be here shortly. We want the General Affairs Department to see him and settle on the cost. If your chief won't go the expense, then we'll foot the bill ourselves.

LAO LI   What does the man look like? What's his name?

CHUNG   He's a tall fellow, named Chang. He's the manager of the Hsiang-t'ai Construction Company.

LAO LI   All right. When he comes, I'll take him to see the chief.

CHUNG   Thanks very much. (*Exits, center*)

LAO LI   (*Shaking his head*)   What good will it all do? This change of directors has turned the General Affairs Department upside down, so how could anyone find time to take care of these sorts of things? (*Picks up the scraping knife and recommences scraping the word*)

(*After a pause, someone knocks on the center door.* LAO LI *stops working and opens the door.* CHANG YÜN-T'UNG *enters*)

CHANG   Excuse me, is this the director's office?

LAO LI   Well . . . (*Taking a look at the words on the glass*) It was, but now it has become the General Affairs Department head's office.

CHANG   Where is your chief?

LAO LI (*Looking him over carefully*)   Why? Do you want to see him?

CHANG   Yes.

LAO LI   Your name, please?

CHANG   My name's Chang.

LAO LI   Oh, yes! Manager Chang.

CHANG (*Puzzled*)   Manager Chang?

LAO LI   Yes, I know. Comrade Chung was just here. (*Kindly*) I'm afraid it looks bad, Manager Chang. Why beat your head against the wall? Our new director is assuming his official duties this afternoon, and our chief is busy getting the new director's office ready right now. He's really got his hands full. Where would he find the time to take care of building repairs?

CHANG (*Even more puzzled*)   Building repairs?

LAO LI   That's right! The dormitory building was a bit old to begin with. Then, during the windstorm last week, quite a few tiles were broken. Now when it rains, the room turns into a quagmire. But, what can we do? The director's office needs whitewashing, matching curtains, new flooring, new sofas, and a spring bed. In no time at all, we've disbursed more than four hundred dollars. So where's the money going to come from to repair the building this month?

CHANG   But since the roof leaks so badly, something has to be done.

LAO LI   I couldn't agree with you more! It's rained a lot recently, and whenever it does, everybody just lays aside his work and goes back to catch the leaks. If it happens at night, no one gets any sleep. They've practically declared war on the General Affairs Department over this matter, but our chief is a man who sticks to the rules and keeps a tight hold on the purse strings. So the comrades will just have to suffer for a while longer. We'll see what happens next month.

CHANG   Where is the dormitory? Can you show me?

LAO LI   You can go on over there yourself. Go downstairs, take a right, and you can't miss it. Come to think of it, Manager Chang, once you've had a look, you might as well make an estimate, since when it's repaired next month, the job will be yours anyway.

CHANG (*Nods his head with a smile*) Oh, all right. Thank you. (*Exits, center*)

LAO LI (*Taking a look out the window*) Ai! We're in for another downpour. I'd better hurry up and close the windows so the floor doesn't get wet again. (*Closes all the doors and windows. Then he recommences scraping the word off the glass*)

(CHU LING *and* LIU SHAN-CH'I, *in the midst of an argument, enter, left*)

LIU Enough! That's enough, my dear Comrade Chu! You promised me a half hour, but then you just turn around and come back to bother me. If everyone were like you, how would I ever get any work done?

CHU Now that's funny, how can you say that I'm here to bother you? I'm here on official business.

LIU Fine! Since it's official business, we'll handle it strictly according to the rules! Comrade Chu, it's still too early for office hours.

CHU But didn't you hear the thunder? Have you seen the black clouds in the sky?

LIU Yes, I know. But have you forgotten that the General Affairs Department provided you with oilcloth?

CHU I haven't forgotten. But the oilcloth is so old that it lets the water in.

LIU (*Troubled*) Well, what is it you think you'll accomplish by arguing with me all day long?

CHU We want that room downstairs.

LIU Which one?

CHU The one where the cement used to be stored.

LIU My dear comrade, that room is now the director's office. Do you plan to store cement in the director's office?

CHU Since you can't make any other space available, then give us half the room, and we'll make do.

LIU Give half the room to you?

CHU That's right! For three hundred sacks of cement half the room should be enough.

LIU Ha! You put it so nicely! Your cement occupies half the room, and the other half is left for the director's office!

CHU But our cement is important, and we think you should be doing something about it.

LIU Which is more important, the Construction Department's cement or the director's office? The director arrives this afternoon, and what would it look like if his office was in a big mess?

(*Another distant roll of thunder*)

CHU (*Worried*) Listen! It's thundering again. It's going to rain any minute. What are you going to do?

LIU (*Calmly*) Comrade, you've studied the General Line, haven't you? In this period of general austerity, even supplying you with several pieces of oilcloth was no easy task.

CHU But, the cement; do you mean to tell me that . . .

(*The thunder grows louder*)

CHU Look, it's going to start raining any minute!

(CHANG YÜN-T'UNG *enters, center*)

CHANG (*To* LAO LI) Comrade, where is your chief? I must see him.

LAO LI (*Anxiously*) Manager Chang, don't ... you'd better not ...

LIU (*Disturbed*) What is it now?

LAO LI Oh! Um, Manager Chang, this is Department Head Liu.

LIU (*To* LAO LI) Who is he?

LAO LI He ... he's Manager Chang, who's here to repair the roof. Comrade Chung sent for him.

CHANG Hold on! I'm ...

LIU (*Interrupting*) Who wants the roof repaired?

LAO LI It's the workers' dormitory roof. It's leaking badly.

CHANG That's true, I've checked it myself.

LIU So! A few small leaks have got the whole place in an uproar. There are procedures to follow in taking care of such matters. If everyone can go and get a repairman whenever he wants, what do you need me, the head of the General Affairs Department, for?

CHANG Granted they haven't followed procedures, but who is responsible for what has happened?

LIU Listen to me: you go talk to whoever sent for you to repair the roof. (*Looks at his watch, then turns to* LAO LI) There's still half an hour before we go to work. I'm going to rest, and I don't want to be disturbed. (*Grabbing his briefcase, he turns to leave*)

(CHU LING *hurriedly bars the way*)

CHU No! Our three hundred sacks of cement cannot be left out in the rain again.

LIU Then what do you propose to do?

CHU I want to use the room downstairs. Chief, since the new director won't be here until this afternoon, why don't you let us move the cement in for now, then once the rain has stopped, we'll clear the room out for you.

LIU What's that! My dear comrade, can't you see that the room has just been whitewashed and the floor waxed? If I let you put the cement there, do you think the place would ever get cleaned up again?

CHU You've got an answer for everything. I'm no match for you. Chief, I'm going to get someone to move the cement right this minute! If I make the office dirty, and the new director is unhappy about it, I'll take the consequences. (*She starts to go off, left*)

LIU (*Gaily*) Sorry, Comrade Chu, but the door is locked! (*He takes a key from his pocket, tosses it into the air nonchalantly, then throws it to* LAO LI) Here, you are responsible for the key. When they deliver the sofas, have them moved inside. (*He turns to leave, but after one or two steps, he stops and says to* LAO LI) No one is allowed to open the door without my permission. (*After a sweeping glance around the room, he exits, center*)

CHU (*Angrily*) Look at him, just look! ... What's in that head of his? (*So enraged that she can't speak, she sits down to catch her breath*)

LAO LI (*Sympathetically*) Ai! I'm afraid that he's got a heart of cement!

CHANG (*To* CHU LING) Comrade, are those sacks piled downstairs the cement you've been talking about?

CHU Yes, but if it rains, it'll all be ruined! What good are the few flimsy pieces of oilcloth that he gave us?

CHANG Why do you have to leave it outside?

CHU It used to be stored in the empty room downstairs. But with the change of directors, the General Affairs Department told us to move it out so that they could decorate and repair the room and convert it into the director's office. Department Head Liu promised that he would do something about the cement, but we never imagined that "something" would be a couple of pieces of flimsy oilcloth!

CHANG What's wrong with this office? Why move to another one?

CHU This room is too *small!* He's our *director!* He's got to show how high and mighty he is!

CHANG High and mighty? Do you really think so?

CHU What other reason could there be?

CHANG The whole thing's preposterous!

CHU Preposterous, you say? I say that he's a damned scoundrel! What would you call a director who's so concerned about the way his own office looks that he doesn't care about state property?

CHANG (*Grinning*) If that's the way he is, then he certainly must be a scoundrel.

(*Another roll of thunder*)

CHU Oh, no! It's going to rain!

LAO LI It sure looks that way.

(CHU LING *walks to the window, opens it, puts out her hand, then shuts the window quickly*)

CHU It's raining! It's raining! The cement! The cement's going to get wet! (*Rushes to the door, left*)

LAO LI Comrade Chu, where are you going?

CHU I'm going to my office to see if there's someone who can figure out what to do.

LAO LI If there were someone who could figure out what to do, you wouldn't have had to come here all those times just to beat your head against the wall!

CHU (*Exasperated*) Then what shall I do? (*Pauses for a moment, then gets an idea*) I've got it! Let's get the bed quilts. We can use them to cover the cement. (*Starts to run off*)

LAO LI Comrade Chu, do you know how many quilts you'd need? And what's everyone to use tonight? Here, I've got the key to the room. Let's move the cement.

CHU Move the cement? You mean into the director's office?

LAO LI That's the only place that's empty. Let's move it in for the time being, anyway.

CHU But your chief . . .

LAO LI Never mind him! I may be a mere janitor, but I've studied the General Line, and my mind is clearer than his. Come on, let's move it! I'll take the consequences.

CHANG (*To* LAO LI) Comrade, you're doing the right thing.

CHU (*Shakes hands with* LAO LI *excitedly*) Good for you, Lao Li.

LAO LI Let's go. There's no time to waste.

(*They take a few steps, then* CHU LING *stops suddenly*)

CHU Oh, no! Once it started raining, everyone will have gone back to the dormitory to catch the leaks. Who'll we get to help us with the moving?

CHANG Don't worry. I'll go too. Let's all go together.

CHU That's still not enough! How long do you think it will take the three of us to move three hundred sacks of cement? When it starts raining hard, the cement will still get ruined.

CHANG Then go and round up everyone to save the cement. Tell them it's on orders from the new director.

CHU The new director? Do you expect me to lie to them?

CHANG Go ahead. I'm sure they'll believe you.

CHU You . . . you really expect me to lie to them?

CHANG No, you won't be lying to them. I am the . . .

CHU (*With a start*) Oh! You . . .

LAO LI (*Speaking at the same time*) You? Just who are you, anyway?

CHANG (*Smiling*) I'm not the roofing contractor, if that's what you mean. I am your new director.

(*Both* CHU LING *and* LAO LI *are dumbfounded*)

CHU The director! The new director! (*Beside herself with excitement*) Come on, Lao Li, let's move the cement!

CHANG That's it! You go round up everyone, and I'll be right along.

CHU Yes! Yes! (*Excitedly pulling* LAO LI *along, she runs out, center*)
(CHANG YÜN-TUNG *takes paper and pen from the desk, scribbles a few words, and follows them*)
(*Lightning flashes outside; the rain is coming down more heavily*)
(*Before long,* LIU SHAN-CH'I *and* TAI WEI *enter, left*)

LIU That won't do! Call him and tell him to deliver them immediately.

TAI Yes, sir! (*Takes up the receiver*)

TAI Hello! Is this Chien-hsin Furniture Shop? I want to speak to your manager. Oh, you are the manager. Good morning. Chief Liu has asked me to call and see if the sofas that we bought are on their way. Not yet? Why not . . . you're waiting for the rain to stop? (*Covering the receiver he speaks to* LIU) He says he'll deliver them after the rain stops.

LIU Damn him! Ask him if he's a meteorologist, and can predict when the rain will stop.

TAI (*Into the receiver*) Hello! Our chief wants to know if you're a meteorologist, and can predict when the rain will stop . . . that's right! Then you'd better think of something . . .

LIU They must be delivered within half an hour.

TAI (*Into the receiver*) Hello! Our chief says they must be delivered within half an hour . . . what? Um-hm, um-hm. (*Covering the receiver, he speaks to* LIU) He says he'll deliver them as soon as he's wrapped them with oilcloth.

LIU Nothing doing! Oilcloth's no good. (*He grabs the telephone*) Hello! Let me ask you something: have you studied the General Line or not? Those sofas were bought by the government, so they're state property. We have to protect . . . no! That won't do! Oilcloth's no good. You'll have to get a van . . . what's that? Transportation charges? We have to pay transportation charges? All right, all right, send them over right away. (*He hangs up the phone*) You can't get any more tightfisted than these tradesmen. They even fight you for a few dollars' transportation charges.

(CHANG YÜN-T'UNG *enters, center. He is soaking wet, mopping his face with a handkerchief*)

LIU What, you still here? Go on, get out! We don't want any building repairs.

CHANG Why not? The dormitory leaks like a sieve! Why don't you repair it?

LIU Well, isn't this something! Whether we repair it or not is our business, and I fail to see what concern it is of yours!

CHANG Why don't you go have a look at it yourself? Do you have any idea what state the dormitory is in? Buckets, wash basins, and spittoons all over the place to catch the leaks, and still more leaks are popping up all the time. Everyone's bedding is completely soaked. Doesn't that concern you at all?

LIU Now look here. You've no right to lecture me! I should have known better than to try to deal with a tradesman like you! The movement against the Five Corruptions is barely over and you come digging around. I've been wondering what you're up to here.

(*While they are talking,* TAI WEI *finds the note on the table. He reads it and, with a start, passes it to* LIU)

TAI Chief, the new director . . .

LIU (*Takes the note, but doesn't look at it*) That's right! Our new bureau director detests you tradesmen. If you have any sense, you'll leave before you're kicked out. If you're unlucky enough to run into him, he won't treat you as courteously as I have.

TAI (*Pointing at the note in* LIU'S *hand*) But . . . but, the new director has arrived . . .

LIU Once the new director has arrived, I'll make a full report to him and tell him how much trouble I've been put to by a tradesman.

CHANG Trouble *you've* been put to? Whenever it rains, everyone has to lay aside his work and rush to the dormitory to catch the leaks. What effect do you think that has on work productivity? And with the dormitory all mildewed and damp, what about the workers' health? Why do you have to stick so closely to your budget and your rules, and always put things off till "next month"?

LIU (*Angrily*) Damn you! Do you realize where you are? This is an office, a government agency, and I won't allow you to hang around and carry on like this. (*To* TAI WEI) Throw him out!

TAI (*Pushing* CHANG YÜN-T'UNG) Go on, now, go on! My dear manager, you've lost the job for sure now. Don't get him really mad or, as the saying goes, you'll lose your catch and the bait as well.

CHANG (*Shouting*) Comrade! You ought to be a little more tolerant of other people's criticisms. It will benefit you greatly!

LIU (*Stamping his feet*) Get out of here! Get the hell out of here!

TAI Come on! Let's go! (*Pushes* CHANG *out, center*)

LIU Preposterous! This is absolutely preposterous!

TAI Chief, the director has already arrived.

LIU What? He's here already?

TAI (*Pointing to the note in* LIU'S *hand*) Look, there's the note he left you.

LIU (*Hurriedly opens the note and reads*) "To Department Head Liu: The Director's Office downstairs is to be reassigned to the Construction Department to store cement; the roof of the workers' dormitory is to be repaired within two days. Chang Yün-t'ung." Damn! When was this note delivered?

TAI   I don't know.

LIU (*Toward the door to the left*)   Lao Li! Lao Li! Damn! Where's he disappeared to?

(CHU LING, *holding a set of clothes, enters, center*)

CHU   Chief, where is Director Chang?

LIU   Director Chang?

CHU   Yes! He told me to meet him here.

LIU   Why haven't I seen him then?

CHU   Hm! I guess I'd better go look for him. (*Turns to go*)

LIU (*Stopping her*)   Say there, Comrade Chu, do you know Director Chang?

CHU   We just met. Why?

LIU (*Hesitantly*)   Nothing, I was just wondering.

CHU   What about?

LIU   You see ... he left this note. (*Passes the note to* CHU)

CHU (*Takes the note and reads it*)   That's right! He was very unhappy that the cement was left outside.

LIU   Oh? Did he say anything else?

CHU (*Bluntly*)   He was also very dissatisfied with you. He said that you were careless with public property and unconcerned about the comrades' well-being. You didn't even care that their dormitory leaks.

LIU   But that's the fault of regulations—there's simply no money left this month. The repairs have to be postponed till next month.

CHU   The director wanted to know how regulations allowed for the white-washing of the office and the laying of a new floor, and where the money came from to buy matching curtains and sofas.

LIU   What? He knows that we bought sofas?

CHU   Of course he does. And he's very angry. He said that these things cannot be charged to government accounts. He proposed that you pay for them and take them home.

LIU   Me? He wants me to pay for them? Why, that would take three months' salary!

CHU   Well, if you put a sofa set here, don't you think that would make this room look more like a department head's office? (*Exits, center, still holding the clothes*)

LIU (*Holding his head*)   Oh, what am I going to do? (*To* TAI WEI) Hurry up and get that roofing contractor back!

(TAI WEI *rushes out, center*)

(LIU *paces back and forth nervously. Suddenly he walks to the phone and dials*)

LIU (*Into the telephone*)   Hello! Who is this? Let me speak to your manager ... Hello! This is Chief Liu ... No, no, no! I'm not rushing you. In fact, I don't think I want that sofa set after all ... What? The van's already left? Then call it back! ... What? You can't? It drove off a long time ago? In that case, after it arrives, I'll send them back with the sofas ... Now, look here, won't you do an old friend a favor? ... Fine, that's fine. We'll pay the transportation charges. (*Hangs up and dials another number*) Hello! Who is this? Oh, it's you, Lao Lu. Say, about that spring bed I bought: well, since our director isn't used to sleeping on a spring bed, I'd like to return it ... What? It's already been sent out? Hello, hello, hello! (*Line is dead*) Damn! (*Slams down the receiver and bangs on the call bell*) Lao Li! Lao Li! (*Walks toward the left door*) Damn it! Not a soul in sight!

(TAI WEI *pushes open the center door and politely shows* CHANG YÜN-T'UNG *into the room*)

TAI   After you, Manager Chang. Please come in and have a chat.

(CHANG *enters*)

LIU   Please have a seat. (*Takes out a pack of cigarettes*) Smoke?

CHANG   (*Refuses with a smile*)   No, thanks, I don't smoke.

LIU   I am so forgetful; your name is ...

TAI   Chang, Manager Chang.

LIU   Yes, of course, Manager Chang.

CHANG   No, I am ...

LIU (*Interrupting*)   Let's just forget what happened a while ago. That was just a slight misunderstanding. (*To* TAI WEI) Go keep watch at the front gate. If the spring bed or sofas are delivered, have them all sent back.

TAI   Sent back?

LIU   Sent back! All of them!

TAI   But ...

LIU   But what?

TAI   But the transportation charges, and the delivery fee ...

LIU   Pay them whatever they ask, but see that you don't let them move the things in.

(TAI WEI *hurriedly exits, left*)

LIU   Manager Chang, I'm a blunt, outspoken man. I hope we can forget what happened a while ago.

CHANG   Chief Liu, I'm not here to repair the building. I ...

LIU   I understand! You didn't come looking for this job; they sent for you. It makes no difference one way or the other—the job is yours. It's not a very big job, but you'll make something on it.

CHANG   But I ...

LIU (*Interrupting*)   Don't worry, now, I'm an understanding man. Just name your price, and we'll pay it. But the job must be finished today. If you have to skimp a little in order to finish in time, that's all right with me.

CHANG   You mean you'll meet my price, and I can skimp on the job?

LIU (*Passes him the note*)   See, that's what our new director wants. He wants the repairs finished in two days. If the boss-man wants it that way, then that's the way it's got to be.

CHANG   I see!

LIU   Just one more thing: if the new director brings up the matter, please tell him that I requested an estimate a long time ago, but your busy schedule kept you from starting work until today.

CHANG   Why's that?

LIU   Well, there are too many wagging tongues around here, for one thing. The new director has just arrived and is unfamiliar with things around the office. If he should hear any idle rumors, it could easily cause some misunderstanding.

Chang Oh, I see!

Liu Actually, I have nothing to be afraid of. The new director and I are old friends. He knows how I work.

Chang Oh! You and the new director are old friends, you say?

Liu That's right, old, old friends! We fought as guerrillas together; we worked on Land Reform together; we were ... always together ... (*His tone grows sentimental*) But I haven't seen him for years, and he must be quite old now. He's a fine man, except that he has a bit of a temper, and he particularly dislikes tradesmen. If you meet him, you'd better keep your distance; that'll keep you out of trouble.

(Lao Li *and* Chu Ling *enter, left*)

Lao Li (*To* Chu Ling) See! I told you he'd be here!

Liu (*To* Lao Li) Where have you been? You've been gone for a long time.

Lao Li I went to give a hand with the cement.

Liu The cement? What have you done with it?

Lao Li We moved it into the director's office.

Liu What? Who told you to do that?

Lao Li The new director. Director Chang told us to move it. He even pitched in and helped.

Liu What? The director's downstairs? Lao Li, hurry, come with me! (*Picks up his briefcase and prepares to leave*)

Chu Chief Liu, what's the matter with you? The director is standing right next to you; why would you want to go off looking for him?

Liu (*Stupefied*) The new director? (*Points at* Chang Yün-t'ung) Him, he's ...

Lao Li That's Director Chang.

Liu Oh! Oh! So, he ... (*To* Chang) Director, Director Chang, I, I'm Liu, Liu Shan-ch'i of the General Affairs Department.

Chang Hm! Nice to meet you.

Liu No, you flatter me. Lao Li, what are you waiting for—serve the tea!

Chang Don't bother, Lao Li, you've worked hard enough with the cement. You must be awfully tired. Why don't you rest a while?

Liu Right, right! You rest a while.

(Lao Li *exits, left*)

Chu Director Chang, be careful not to catch cold. You really ought to change your clothes now!

Chang That's all right, Comrade Chu, I'm used to it. I often went around like this when Chief Liu and I "were guerrillas together."

Chu Oh, so you were guerrillas together?

Chang Isn't that right, Chief Liu?

Liu (*Extremely embarrassed*) Yes! Yes! But, I ... I ... um ...

Chang Comrade Chu, did you finish moving all the cement?

Chu Yes, all of it.

Chang How many got wet?

Chu Not a single sack.

Chang You're quite something! As soon as you called, thirty or forty people came.

Chu Thanks to you. I just told them: "The new director is moving cement for our Construction Department, so why aren't all of you out there helping?" And they all came.

CHANG   Why did you say that I was moving cement for *your* Construction Department? Am I not part of the Construction Department? Don't I have a share in the cement?

CHU   You're right, of course. The cement is state property, and everybody has a share.

LIU   Right, right! Comrade Chu has gained a sense of civic awareness through her studies of the General Line. Cement is state property, and everyone definitely has a share.

CHU   Hmph! What share did you have in those three hundred sacks of cement? You didn't even seem to want any share.

LIU (*Embarrassed*)   Comrade Chu, you're going too ...

CHU   Too what? Too far? Not at all! Your mind's full of decadent bourgeois thoughts. You're not concerned about the leaks in the dormitory, and you don't care how wet the cement gets. All you're worried about is getting in good with your superiors. You've been spending all your time buying matching curtains and sofas for the new director in order to get yourself promoted.

CHANG   I'm used to sitting on a hard bench. Won't what you're trying to do just spoil me?

LIU   No, that's the last thing ... that was only because ... because there was some money left over in this month's General Affairs Department budget.

CHANG   Then why didn't you repair the dormitory roof first?

LIU   I was going to repair it, and in fact I've already got an estimate.

CHANG   It's just because of the repairman's "busy schedule" that he wasn't able to start work until today, right?

LIU (*Embarrassed*)   Not exactly. That was a slight misunderstanding. Please don't let that bother you.

CHANG   Bother me! There are many things that bother me, and I wouldn't call them slight!

LIU   Yes, of course.

(LAO LI *enters, center*)

LAO LI   Chief Liu, the spring bed has arrived. Where do you want it put?

LIU (*Confused*)   Spring bed? Oh! Where is Clerk Tai. Doesn't he know?

LAO LI   He's out by the front gate waiting for someone. The bed was delivered to the back gate, so he didn't see it.

LIU   Oh! Very well. Tell them to deliver it to my house.

LAO LI (*Pointing to the bill in his hand*)   Then, what about this bill ...?

LIU   Ask ... ask my wife to pay it.

(LAO LI *turns to leave*)

LIU (*Calls him to a stop*)   Wait! Get Tai here on the double!

(LAO LI *exits, center*)

LIU (*Hastens to explain to* CHANG)   It ... it was something my wife bought ... she's a bit spoiled, I'm afraid.

(TAI WEI *sneaks in, left*)

TAI (*Softly*)   Chief!

LIU (*Quickly pulling him aside to whisper*)   Get out to the back gate right away and wait there; the sofas will be delivered soon.

TAI   The back gate?

LIU Yes, the back gate!

TAI But the front gate ...

LIU (*Anxiously*) Back gate! Back gate! They are using the back gate!*

(TAI WEI *hurries toward the exit*)

CHANG (*To* LIU) Only a person who works sincerely and hard will be a good cadre welcomed by the people. A person who knows only how to take advantage of people and get by with flattery will be the object of the people's scorn. Chief Liu, you have to bear the consequences for any losses the state has sustained because of your bourgeois thinking!

LIU Yes ... yes, sir.

(LAO LI *enters, center*)

LAO LI Chief Liu!

LIU What now?

LAO LI The sofas have arrived.

LIU (*Embarrassed*) Sofas?

LAO LI Yes. A big one and two small ones.

LIU Yes, but why didn't Tai ... ?

LAO LI Didn't you order him to wait for them at the back gate? They were delivered to the front.

LIU (*Extremely uneasy*) Oh, I see! Very well, then.

LAO LI Shall I bring them in?

LIU No, no! Let me see ... let me see ...

CHU Say, why don't you have them taken to Chief Liu's house! His wife is spoiled, or so he says, and they'll be just the thing for her.

LIU No, please, Comrade Chu, Director; I've already made arrangements with the shop to take them back.

LAO LI (*Hands him a bill*) But, the transportation charges ...

LIU (*Snatches it away from* LAO LI) Give it to me, I'll pay it! Director Chang, I'm going to take a look; I'll be right back.

CHANG All right.

(LIU *exits, center, in great embarrassment*)

CHANG Comrade Li, you have demonstrated considerable responsibility in protecting the state's property. You've done your job well and done it bravely. Speaking on behalf of everyone at the bureau, you have our sincere appreciation. (*Goes to shake hands with* LAO LI)

LAO LI (*A bit shyly*) No, please ... I only did my duty. Director Chang, are you starting work today?

CHANG It looks like I've already started.

LAO LI But your office ...

CHANG What's wrong with this office?

LAO LI Then I'll just move Chief Liu's things back where they were.

CHANG Hold on a moment. I think that your Chief Liu needs to be reassigned to a more suitable job.

CHU You mean you're going to ...

CHANG I feel it's my duty to the people and to him.

---

*There is a pun here: "using the back gate (or door)" implies gaining something by improper means, or "pulling strings." [H. G.]

LAO LI (*Takes out the key*) Director Chang, this key . . .

CHANG Let the Construction Department keep it. But since the room is so large and sunny, and has just been fixed up, it would be a shame to use it to store cement. I think if we changed it into a workers' dormitory, it would be a distinct improvement over the one they're using now. We can have the roof of the old dormitory repaired and turn that building over to the Construction Department. Comrade Chu, does that arrangement suit you?

CHU Suit me? It sure does! Director Chang, you, you're wonderful.

CHANG (*Jokingly*) Don't be so quick to flatter me. I hope you won't have need to call me a damned scoundrel again soon.

CHU (*Quite embarrassed*) Director Chang, please forgive me . . .

CHANG That's quite all right. In the future, if you find me making mistakes, I expect you will be calling me even worse names.

LAO LI (*Looking out the window*) The rain has stopped!

(CHANG *and* CHU *also walk to the window. The sky is bright and clear; sunlight streams into the room, lighting up their happy faces*)

CHANG The rain's stopped and the sun is out.

CHU Let's open the windows! It's really stuffy in here.

LAO LI Good idea. Let's open the windows and let in some fresh air.

(LAO LI *and* CHU LING *throw open all the windows*)

CHANG That's fine, open all of the windows and let out this stale air.

(*The three of them face the sunlight and happily breathe the fresh air*)

(*Slow curtain*)

Translated by Doris Sze Chun and Howard Goldblatt

TS'UI PA-WA

(1929–)

Son of an impoverished peasant family in Shensi, sold to the landlord to pay family debts as a child, press-ganged into the Kuomintang warlord army in 1948 but later captured by the People's Liberation Army, who taught him to read and write, Ts'ui Pa-wa does not even have a name of his own. Pa-wa is but a childhood pet name, meaning "child number eight."

Small wonder that his stories are imbued with bitter recollections of past suffering. The remarkable thing is that he can tell them straight, without getting emotionally stymied. At moments there is even a touch of the light-hearted in his writing, indicating that his crowded nightmarish memories have not completely blotted out his ability to see joy and excitement in life. His language is earthy, his characters rough but strong, and his plot movement swift. He has been cited as one of the most representative proletarian writers the nation has produced.

In the late 1950s he worked in an army hospital while continuing with his writing, but he has not published anything in recent years.   —K.Y.H.

A Wine Pot

We had a copper wine pot in our family, and everyone who saw it couldn't help saying something in its praise: "Ah, such a lovely wine pot, just like a golden melon!" Since we didn't even have anything for the cooking pot, we naturally couldn't afford anything to fill the wine pot. Dad often polished it until it gleamed bright and shiny, filled it with water and drank out of it. One day Dad again filled it with water and sat down by the table, smiling at it. I thought to myself, "Dad is admiring his old antique again." Sure enough, he stroked his beard and started: "This pot of mine looks lovelier each time you look at it. That potbellied Kuo and Sheriff Hsu have been trying hard to lay their hands on it, but their money can't buy what is not for sale. I won't sell it! It's been handed down in our family for generations, and when I die, I'll leave my children something to remember me by." Mom paused in her sewing, threw a scolding glance at him, and said, "Aren't you ashamed of yourself! Repeating the same dreary things all day. Don't you get tired of it?" "I say it because I feel good about it," Dad said. "You could sew up my mouth with that needle of yours. Ha ha ha . . . " This made us all laugh. The whole family loved the wine pot, and although we were never sure where the next meal was coming from, there was harmony and cheer, and even just plain water tasted sweet. Ah, but who would have thought that in time our troubles would come just because of the pot!

I remember it was the third year after I was sold into the Ching family. Three years! Of eating leftovers, of being people's whipping post. Wounds and scars never left my arms and thighs; tears never stopped flowing in my eyes. All day I cried when people weren't looking, and I wondered how long it would be before the suffering and pain would come to an end. Finally I made up my mind that I would run home.

It was early in the Seventh Month. The sky was darkening. I had just carried into the yard the hay I had cut and the Big-mouth opened itself and said, "Pa-wa, go get some water!" Since the day I made up my mind to run away, I felt that they had been watching me rather carefully, and that day, even Big-mouth seemed to speak more gently than usual. I thought, "All right"; I wiped the sweat from my face, put on a bit of cheerfulness, and called out, "Auntie, let me have your leftover rice, and in a moment I'll fill the jar with water." Big-mouth brought out a bowl of corn gruel for me to eat. I went into the room, put on my straw sandals, put the buckets on the carrying pole, walked up to her, brushed my sandals on the ground a couple of times, and said, "The slopes are ever so slippery!" I was thinking to myself: "Big-mouth, and Big-head Cheng, I've had enough of you all these years." As I walked my heart beat like hammer blows. When I got to the well, I looked around and saw that nobody was about. My heart settled a little. I gnashed my teeth: "Damn you and yours!" I shook my shoulders, and the carrying pole and the buckets rolled rattling down the slope. I came away from the well, crossed over the rice fields, and ran toward the forest.

It got dark. The moon, two fingers wide, hung on the western horizon. I couldn't pick my way in the gulch. A patch of mud here and a puddle of water there, and so, tripping and stumbling, I ran groping in the direction of home.

Just as I got to the main road, I heard a rattling in the bushes behind me, and then voices calling: "Hurry up and catch him. He can't have got very far!" That was Big-head Cheng's voice. Just my luck! They were giving chase. I looked around. There was a dark clump of pear trees not far ahead; I bent down and dashed into it. "Keep your eyes on him!" Big-head Cheng shouted. He and his two lackeys were behind me. "I'll find you if I have to strip bare all the trees." The lackeys looked behind every tree one by one. Big-head Cheng stood high on the slope and said, "Pa-wa-tzu, come out of there! Nothing will happen to you if you come home with me." I said to myself, "Shit!" I saw that the men were coming close to where I was hiding. I took advantage of the rattling of the branches and slipped by between them. Big-head Cheng was again blabbering: "Well? You won't come out, eh? Do you think I can't see you? If you don't come out, I'll chop you up!" One of the men chimed in, "Boss, no need to get mad. It's all right. He'll come out." He then changed his tone and called out to me, "Pa-wa, come out." Those sons-of-bitches jabbered on like that. After a while, Big-head Cheng said, "All right, let's go home!" I poked my head out to see; they were squatting down. The sons-of-bitches squatted for the time it takes to smoke two pipes of tobacco. I heard them whispering; then Big-head Cheng picked up a stone and threw it in my direction: "Damn you, you little bastard, whether you are there or not. You can run away now, but you can't run away forever." He went away, followed by his lackeys.

The moon had gone down. I made for home cautiously. When I saw the old locust tree in front of my house, my heart felt like fire. The yard was pitch black and still. I knew that Big-head Cheng had not gone there, so I climbed over the low wall. The old black family dog barked once and came leaping toward me. When it saw it was me, it shook its head, wagged its tail and licked my hand, and ran ahead of me to paw the door. I fell on the door, calling "Mom!" and started to cry. Mom opened the door, I rushed into her arms, and only then did my heart settle down in peace. Little Tung-wa-tzu came out without his pants; he held me and cried "Brother, brother!" I told Dad and Mom how I ran away and how Big-head Cheng gave chase. Mom said bitterly, "Even if I have to die ... I can't let the boy go back to suffer at the hands of such whores' sons as Big-head Cheng and Big Mouth." Dad sat thinking for a long while, then suddenly said, "Quick! Get the boy's things together for him to go to his aunt's place in town to hide for a while. Big-head Cheng is bound to come looking for him." He picked up his shoes. "You get the boy something to eat. I'll see if I can get a few dollars off Old Wang. Hurry!" So saying, he went out.

Not long after Dad left the house, the dog started barking again. Mom blew out the lamp. At that moment the beam of a flashlight shone on the window. Mom held me and said, "Something ... " Before she could finish, Big-head Cheng was calling at the door. Mom was all flustered, and hid me in the hay in a corner of the room. I peered through the hay and saw Mom getting back to her bed, and then she asked, taking her time, "Who is it, in the middle of the night?" She got out of bed, unbuttoned her jacket and then buttoned it up again, lit the lamp, and went slowly, grumbling all the while, to open the door. "What's the matter?" The door opened and the sons-of-bitches rushed into the room like a pack of hungry wolves. Without a word, they searched the room all over. Mom repeated, "What's all this?" Big-head Cheng cocked his pig's bladder of a head, sneered, and pushed Mom aside. "Don't play dumb!" They looked in and under the bed without finding me. Big-head Cheng shone the flashlight straight into Mom's face, stared at her a long while and said, "Where have you hidden your Pa-wa?" Mom said, "What? Pa-wa-tzu? I haven't seen ... " "Damn it. I knew you would lie in your teeth." He went to the side of the bed and grabbed hold of Tung-wa-tzu's arm. "Tung-wa-tzu, where's your brother?" Mom interrupted, "Don't know! Pa-wa-tzu hasn't come here." "Get away! Don't interrupt!" Cheng yelled. "Drag her out of here!" The lackeys dragged Mom outside. Big-head Cheng pulled out two banknotes and said to Tung-wa-tzu, "Tell me, where is Pa-wa? Tell me, and I'll buy you sweets, and peanuts ... " "Don't know," Tung-wa-tzu said, shaking his arm free. Big-head Cheng controlled himself, waved the money again and said, "Money! For meat ... " Tung-wa-tzu turned round and pulled the blanket over his head. Big-head Cheng's eyebrows rose in anger; he grabbed hold of Tung-wa-tzu. "Talk, you little bastard! Where is he? If you don't tell me, I'll slaughter you!" Tung-wa-tzu burst out crying and screamed, "Don't know, don't know. Your old woman sells herself ... F—— your mother ... " Mom heard Tung-wa-tzu crying; she fought with all her might and rushed in. "Hey, you! What law have we broken? You come in the middle of the night to rob us like this?" "Don't try to fool me," said Cheng. "A moment ago there was a light in the house." "A light?" Mom said, "So, the rich can set fire to people's houses but the poor are not even allowed a light! And what sort of crime is that?"

As they were shouting, Old Wang and Dad came back. Without giving Dad a chance to say a word, Old Wang rushed into the argument. "What's all this? And in the middle of the night!" Big-head Cheng ignored him, but turned to Dad: "Old Ts'ui, where have you been?" Dad said, "Where've I been? Here and there!" Big-head Cheng said, "I don't know who's been giving Pa-wa ideas. He ran back here when it got dark." Dad said, "Haven't seen him!" Old Wang added, "The boy couldn't have gone far. Look for him tomorrow!" Big-head Cheng glared at Old Wang, but turned and shouted at Dad, "Old Ts'ui ... the boy is young, I'll let it go. Just tell him to come with me and everything will be all right." Then cocking his head, he added, "Otherwise, later you'll have to listen to me!" "You said he has come back here," Dad said, sitting down on a stool. "Look for him then. I don't have to argue with you." Old Wang said, "I think Mr. Cheng should go home first. Tomorrow we'll look around, and if we find him we'll tell him to go back to you." Big-head Cheng was impatient. "Dogs catch rats—none of your business!" he said. "Shit on a barge—what kind of precious cargo do you think you are?"

This touched Old Wang to the quick. He put his hands on his waist and glared at Big-head Cheng. "Look, I'm trying to treat you like somebody," he said. "Guess there's no point lifting a dog in a soft seat; he doesn't appreciate it. Okay, suit yourself!" Cheng said to his men, "Go on, look again!" The men started searching again. Mom gave Dad a look, but Dad didn't understand it. The black dog kept snapping at them. Old Wang shouted at it: "Go on and bite! Damned dogs think they can do anything because there's powerful people to back them up! One of these days, I'll skin you alive!" He pulled out a staff next to me and shouted, "I'll knock out your teeth!" and went at the dog. The hay all round me came crashing down. I tried to curl up to hide myself. "Aha! Over here." The men saw me and crowded round. Old Wang saw me in the hay. He shook his arms and held back the men. "Pa-wa-tzu, don't be afraid. I'm here." Big-head Cheng was shaking with rage, "You little bastard, you've got a nerve." He came up to drag me out, but Old Wang stopped him; "Just a minute, Mr. Cheng. You can't take him." Cheng said, "This is my boy, I bought him for three *tan* of corn." Dad and Mom crowded round me. Seeing that there was little he could do, Cheng said, "If you won't let me take the boy, give me back my corn this minute! If you give me neither the boy nor the corn, then it's you who are damned unreasonable!" He signaled to his lackeys, "Grab the blankets!" But Old Wang waved his stick and said, "If you touch so much as a hair here, you'll have to be helped off your knees when I'm through with you!" The men looked at each other and sidled away. The row went on and on. Our neighbors, like Ch'en Mao-yung, heard the racket and hurried to our house. First they spoke to Old Wang, then they pacified Big-head Cheng. Cheng saw that he wasn't getting anywhere, so he backed down. He let Ch'en Mao-yung guarantee to return three *tan* of grain the next day. Big-head Cheng glared at us one by one. "Three *tan*. Not a grain less!" He snorted and walked out of the house sideways, like a crab.

For a long while after Big-head Cheng left, all of us bowed our heads and stayed silent. Dad squatted in a corner with his chin on his palm. Ch'en Mao-yung said, "Let's think of something!" "Something?" Dad said, eyes staring at the wall; "What is there? At a time like this, we haven't as much as can be carried on a rat's back, let alone three *tan.*" Ch'en Mao-yung said, "That's just it. Poor people like us—who has food even for the next day? Old Wang, you look up Old Chao tomorrow, and I'll get Man-wa-tzu. 'More hands lighten chores.' Let's all try to get something together. Besides, this year's harvest will be ready soon." Then he turned to Dad: "Hey, you try too to get something together tomorrow." Old Wang slapped his thigh and said, "Damn it! A man cares about his pride just as the Buddha cares about his incense. We're not tried and true friends if we don't go through the thick and thin together. We'll try our damndest to make up the sum. In the old days when I got mixed up in that damn trumped-up court case, Old Ts'ui sold his clothes and things to help me. I'll make up the balance after you men." He stood, saying, "Old Ts'ui, better send the boy away. Big-head Cheng may come again tomorrow and make trouble. Besides, you may be able to get something from your relatives in town to help out. Officials look after officials, and the people fend for the people; and we poor folk have ourselves to turn to." Ch'en Mao-yung said, "If we pull together, see if Big-head Cheng can come up with any of his monkey tricks!" He got up to leave; "Time's getting on, Old Wang, let's be going!" So, they all left. Mom cooked some rice for me to eat, patched my clothes, and told me to take care of myself. Dad gave me five dollars, and took me to my aunt in town. My aunt got together three pecks of corn for Dad to take home.

I spent half a month at my aunt's place, knowing very little of what was happening at home. One day Dad suddenly turned up. He looked rather cheerful. When I asked him, Dad stroked my head and said, "My boy, I got you back for a wine pot!" At the time, I didn't understand what he said. Only after Dad had explained it to my aunt did I know what he meant. It was like this:

That day, Dad carried the three pecks of corn home, and found Ch'en Mao-yung waiting at the house. Ch'en had managed to rustle up five pecks. When Dad learned of this, he was distraught and paced up and down. Ch'en Mao-yung said, "It is very clear. Big-head Cheng knows that we haven't got the grain, so he can come and take the boy away. No, Old Wang is right, we can't let him get away with that." Dad asked, "What about Old Wang?" "Well, he hasn't come yet ... " said Ch'en. Just at that moment they heard Old Wang shouting, "Big-head Cheng! I —— your mother! You may try to get other people but people don't give up and drop dead that easily! Don't be so mean! You just wait and see ... " Ch'en Mao-yung hurried out to meet him. "Old Wang," Ch'en said, "what made you so mad?" Old Wang plonked himself down on the bed, his eyes all red, and started swearing again; "I —— his ancestors all eight generations back! Big-head Cheng has passed the word round that he'll take care of anyone who dares to loan corn to Ts'ui ... That son-of-a-bitch is so damn mean!" Dad asked, "How much have you got together, then?" "Enough!" Old Wang said. "Enough?" Dad didn't dare believe his own ears and asked again, "What are you saying?" Old Wang said, "Enough! We won't give him a chance to make fools of us!" But for a while no one there believed Old Wang; they all thought he said things in anger just to boost his pride. Ch'en Mao-yung was about to ask Old Wang again, to make sure, when Mom came in from outside; she fixed her eyes on Old Wang. "Old Wang," she said, "we can't take this lying down! These damn bastards are driving us up the sharp end of a knife." Old Wang went on blustering, "F—— his ancestors! Go ahead and do us in. But there's always a way out if we're not meant to die." Everybody was confused by Old Wang. Dad asked Mom, "What is this all about? Go on, tell us." "I'll tell you," Mom said, heaving a sigh. "Old Wang's piece of land next to Potbellied Kuo's property—he sold that. Potbellied Kuo had his eye on Old Wang's land for some time—offered twenty *tan* of corn for it once—but Wang wouldn't sell it. Now we need grain in a hurry, Wang went to see that damn bastard again. Do you know what he said? 'These are not fat times. I'll give you three *tan* for it, and not a grain more.' Old Wang hardened his heart and sold it. I got wind of it at Man-wa-tzu's place and hurried home. Isn't that driving people up the sharp end of a knife!" Dad said, "Old Wang, the land is your livelihood, it's all you have. Why did you sell it?" Old Wang stamped his foot; "And you ask me why I sold it? I ask you what will you do when Big-head Cheng gets here? When you sold your things for my sake, did I ask you why?" Old Wang broke down and cried like a child. Dad said, "It's not the same. When you've got your family, you aren't poor. When the children grow up, there's hope." Ch'en Mao-yung turned away and wiped his eyes, and nobody said a word.

Outside, the dog was barking. There seemed to be people walking behind the house, and there were people jabbering outside the door. Dad took a look. Big-head Cheng and his lackeys had arrived. Outside the house, under the tree, and along the wall people had gathered to watch the confrontation. Big-head Cheng came up. "Old Ts'ui," he said, "women mince their words but we men come straight to the point. Give me the grain now!" Dad said, "Mr. Cheng, please come into the house. The grain, thanks to everybody's help, is ready!" "All ready? All seven and a half *tan?*" "What? What seven and a half *tan* are you talking about, Mr. Cheng?" Dad asked. Big-head Cheng narrowed his eyes; "Ah! Old Ts'ui, you can't play dumb with me. Surely it's not too much to ask for fifty percent interest a year!" Old Wang and Ch'en Mao-yung heard him; they came out of the house. Old Wang asked, "Mr. Cheng, didn't you say three *tan?*" Big-head Cheng smiled from the corner of his mouth and said, "You buy a hen, and she lays an egg for you. The three *tan* is only the capital. Old Wang, smart people need no explanations, and you are a smart man. Fifty percent interest is not too much to ask." "Why didn't you say so yesterday?" "Well, heaven knows, yesterday I . . . " "Yesterday you talked shit!" "Old Wang, don't you dare get rough with me." "Get rough? I'm going to beat the hell out of you!" Dad held on to Old Wang, but Old Wang was hopping with rage. "Big-head Cheng," he shouted, "Pa-wa-tzu worked for you for three years. Give him his wages!" Turning to Dad he said, "Go on! Tell that son-of-a-bitch to work out the wages. If he has no money, strip his hide!" Big-head Cheng was so frightened that he backed up a few steps. "Old Wang," he said, "you're scaring nobody. If there is no corn, I'll take the boy. It's all within the laws of heaven and earth." He signaled to his lackeys, "Go get him!" Old Wang slipped aside, grabbed a hoe under the eaves. "If anyone dares to come near the house, I'll break his bloody leg!" Big-head Cheng let loose his rage on his lackeys like a mad dog, but they were too scared to move.

Ch'en Mao-yung was standing near the door; he shouted to the people gathered there; "Folks, now we all see it with our own eyes. Yesterday Big-head Cheng told us not to loan Old Ts'ui any corn. Now there is enough corn, he goes back on his word. Isn't it clear that he is bent on driving us to hell!" Before Ch'en

Mao-yung could finish, there was an uproar in the crowd. "No way! Let's beat up the liar ... " Old Ts'ui and Man-wa-tzu whipped off their shirts and jumped forward. Ch'en Mao-yung quickly restrained them. "Hold on," he said. "We'll find a place and reason with him." "That's right. Sue that son-of-a-bastard!" the crowd roared.

Seeing the people around him rolling up their sleeves and clenching their fists, Cheng was terrified. His face turned ashen white. Like a dog with its tail between its legs, he slinked away, calling out, "All right, I'll see you at the sheriff's office. I'll wait for you at the sheriff's. He who doesn't turn up is a whore's son!" Old Wang made after him. "I'll beat up that son-of-a-bitch first!" But the people held him back. Ch'en Mao-yung said, "We'll go to the sheriff's with old Ts'ui, and see if that wretch can fill a sieve with his piss!" Another one said, "Let's go. If they chop off our heads it'll be no more than that many scars!" Someone else said, "This isn't just bullying old Ts'ui, it's riding on the shoulders of us poor folk and shitting on us!" And so, with a curse here, an outburst there, the crowd jostled on with Dad to the sheriff's.

At the sheriff's office, Big-head Cheng was already seated. Dad told the whole story to Sheriff Hsu from beginning to end. Big-head Cheng didn't even open his mouth. The sheriff told Cheng he was in the wrong, and ordered us to pay just the three *tan* of corn to settle the matter. Everybody was happy at the way things had turned out, and everybody was saying, "Even ants can move a mountain. Sheriff Hsu saw how many of us were there and got scared." Ch'en Mao-yung said, "There is a trap somewhere." Dad said, "What trap? Even the stone I pick up to throw at a dog belongs to somebody else. What else can he get from me?" They went home. Old Chao, Man-wa-tzu, and many others helped to deliver the corn to Big-head Cheng, and the whole matter settled.

A few days passed. Sheriff Hsu suddenly turned up at my house. Dad and Mom greeted him. After the usual casual chat, Sheriff Hsu mentioned the affair again. "To tell the truth, Old Ts'ui, if it weren't for my taking the matter on myself, you wouldn't have heard the end of it from Big-head Cheng." Of course, the sheriff was trying to claim credit, and Dad and Mom had to humor him by saying a few polite things like: it was thanks to him, and the whole family would not forget the favor he had done us, and so on. Hsu cocked his head, smiled, and said, "Oh, it's nothing really. We're all sort of like one family. As they say, 'among us there's nobody whose help doesn't come handy; within the village there's no road we won't step on some time.' It was the right thing to do." When he got to this point, he paused, and then said hesitantly, "Old Ts'ui, today, I ... well, it's the same old thing. Lend it to me! You name your price!"

As soon as he mentioned it, Dad knew it was the wine pot. So he thought, "I'd rather offend ten gentlemen than offend one mean man. Especially if he has really helped me out. Why don't I just go along with him and return a favor. As to the price of the pot, he once offered two *tan* of corn, and he won't take it now without paying something." He glanced at Mom and said, "The sheriff has really put himself out for us." Turning to Hsu, he said, "If you like the pot, take it with you!" When the sheriff heard it, his nose and eyebrows twitched with joy. He moved a little closer to Dad and said, "You're still troubled in your mind. These are busy days. Why don't you send for Pa-wa-tzu to come home and give you a hand? The whole thing has blown over now. If you have any more trouble, come to me. I am after all a sheriff and can handle a few things." He took up the pot. "Well," he said, "with our own people, we only say what we mean. I'm taking it now. Tell Pa-wa to come home and not waste his time out there getting up to no good." The family watched the sheriff walking away with the pot.

Dad told my aunt all this in one long breath. "They've got everything off me now," he sighed, "down to my eyelashes." Aunt said, "Don't be upset. In these hard times, some people can't even manage to survive. It was a good thing there was the wine pot. Let's hope the boy will be safe and sound." Aunt asked us to stay for a meal before we set off for home. Dad said there was a lot of work to do at home and so we left.

As I followed Dad home, my heart felt as happy as a bird just let out of its cage. When I got into the yard, the sparrows were twittering under the eaves, and the fine-feathered cock was standing by the gourd trellis. The big black dog was stretched out comfortably by the door. When it saw me it came prancing toward me, making happy noises and wagging its tail. Tung-wa-tzu called, "Mom, brother is home!" and ran into the house. Mom came out, her hands covered with flour. "My boy," she said, "you are home!" I was so happy that I wanted to cry. I turned round and saw that there was no water jar; I picked up the buckets to get water. I thought, Mom has been through a great deal because of me. I must help out in every way I can. I filled the water jar. After dinner I went with Dad to the fields to pick corn. That night, at supper, Mom said to me, "Take a little time off and pay the sheriff a visit. This time he did help us." Dad was not happy about it. "Don't you go!" he said. "Whoever gets up early does it just to get his own worms. Didn't he find an excuse to gyp us out of our wine pot?" Mom said, "Anyway, you might as well go find out how much he is prepared to pay for it." Dad gave in, and agreed to go see the sheriff the next day.

At night, Tung-wa-tzu shared my bed. He told me how Big-head Cheng came for the corn, and how Old Wang tried to beat him up. Tung-wa-tzu went on and on, and that mealy face of Big-head Cheng turned round and round in my mind. I tossed and turned and couldn't get to sleep. It was past midnight before I began to doze off. Suddenly I heard Mom say, "The dog is barking outside. Get up, quick." Dad put on his clothes. Somebody was moving around outside the window. I put on my clothes in the dark. There was a knocking on the door. "Open up, Old Ts'ui!" It was the voice of Ho-ch'ing, one of Big-head Cheng's lackeys. Dad and Mom knew immediately that there was trouble. Dad said, "Quick, hide the boy somewhere." Mom hid me in the wardrobe, and Dad went to open the door.

Dad said, "What's the matter?" "Looking for a draft-dodger," Ho-ch'ing said as he came in. Dad said, "We've not seen any." "If you haven't then you needn't fear a search!" The gang of lackeys worked over our house, making a racket and turning the place into a mess. They searched over the beams and in the corners and everywhere, and then stood round the wardrobe against which Mom was sitting. "Open the wardrobe." "Just a few clothes in there for the children," she said. "Who wants your clothes!" Ho-ch'ing said. One of the lackeys cocked his rifle and aimed it at the wardrobe, Dad stepped up and stood before it. "Put it away!" he said. "There's no need for pulling out guns and knives to scare people." He turned to Mom; "We are not hiding draft-dodgers. Look how scared you are. Open the wardrobe and tell our boy to come out." Mom opened the wardrobe. I looked out. Those sons-of-bitches crowded round me with their gleaming rifles. When he saw me, Ho-ch'ing squealed like a ghost. "Cheng Tzu-lai! So you're hiding here! Come out and let's go!" The lackeys rushed up and grabbed me. Dad clutched Ho-ch'ing's collar. "Ho-ch'ing, what the hell are you talking about? What Cheng Tzu-lai? We're under the protection of the sheriff." "Cheng Tzu-lai is Mr. Cheng's son," Ho-ch'ing said. "He's drafted. I have my orders from the sheriff. Take him away!" Dad clung to Ho-ch'ing with all his might. "We'll go to the sheriff," he said. "You've got to be reasonable." "Get away," Ho-ch'ing shouted. "Here's reason for you!" Dad crashed to the ground from a blow of Ho-ch'ing's rifle butt. I saw Mom rushing to Dad. The lackeys grabbed me and fled, my feet hardly touching the ground. I heard Mom crying after us, "Sheriff, you took our wine pot but gave us shit for protection. You've all got your damned schemes to trap us! Greedy dogs! Savage wolves!" ... Then I heard nothing more. That night I was locked up in the county jail.

Translated by Jane Lai

CHANG YUNG-MEI
(1925?–)

When most writers were silent during the Cultural Revolution, Chang Yung-mei was able to maintain some public literary activities. One of his collections of poems, *The Conch-shell Bugle Call,* was among the first to be brought back into circulation after the long lull.

College-educated, Chang spent most of his adult years in the People's Liberation Army, performing political-cultural duties wherever he was assigned. His poetry reflects these experiences of the 1950s and 1960s. Among his well-received anthologies are *Early Spring* and *Poems of the Seashore.* His revolutionary opera, *Fighting on the Plain,* appeared in the authoritative journal *The Red Flag* (July 1973), accompanied by laudatory reviews, including favorable comments by Chiang Ching herself.

Chiang Ching's support of Chang Yung-mei, however, turned out to be a kiss of death; early in 1978, Chang was publicly denounced for his writings that flatter Chiang Ching. —K.Y.H.

Early Spring

On the tree once destroyed by cannon fire,
Young shoots have issued, tender, green;
In the creek, yesterday still sealed by severe cold,
Now flows warm water, breaking solid ice.

Moisture has returned to the scorched land,
Cuckoos call from morning to dusk;
Ox-carts ply village roads nonstop, and there is no rest
For those busy sowing seeds.

Each morning new buds turn into blossoms,
Each morning rice sprouts that much taller and stronger;
Everything dons a new dress in the cheery sun,
Which defeats winter, dispels the chill.

Cannon reports continue to rumble beyond the hill,
Fire flashes nearby again and again;
On and on intense battle surges, all because
The American bandits are enemies of spring.

All the newly born will grow, stubbornly grow;
Who can halt the approach of spring?
Guns of fine steel grasped in our hands,
We greet the beginning of another embattled year.

February, 1951, on the bank of the South Han River
Conch-shell Bugle Call, pp. 1–2

Translated by Kai-yu Hsu

HSÜ CH'IH
(1906–)

In his early poetry of the 1930s, Hsü Ch'ih, a native of Kiangsu Province, strove for modernity so much that some critics called his a private language. He taught in high schools, practiced writing on the side, and even attempted to translate Stendhal's *La Chartreuse de Parme*. During the 1940s, his works were dramatically transformed, as he began to use a plain, more communicative diction. In addition to verses greeting the promises of a new era, he also wrote satirical short stories for leftist publications. Some of the very effective works went into his 1946 anthology, *The Night of Orgy,* which reflects the corrupt life of the rich and influential in the wartime capital, Chungking. Later he traveled extensively on various assignments which took him to the battlefront of Korea and back to the production front, in the factories and on communes, until the editorial office of the *Poetry Journal* kept him more stationary in Peking in the 1960s. Most of his poetic products of this period are collected in *War, Peace, and Progress* and in *The Beautiful, the Miraculous, and the Resplendent.*

During the Cultural Revolution, he was sent back to the countryside again to learn from the peasants; he stayed mostly in the Hankow area, until 1977, when he returned to active writing. He has recently been publishing journalistic reports and character sketches. —K.Y.H.

South of the River

Outside the bus window spread the fields, the cradle of my youth.
Their golden mustard blossoms dazzle my eyes;
Tender green buds have sprouted on mulberry branches,
Velvety bean flowers spread their wings of butterflies.

From Hangchow, we passed Chia-shih, stopping at Chia-hsing,
Perhaps also past K'un-shan and nearing Soochow;
Rooftops in the foreground feature pickle urns,
And houses nestle in lush bamboo groves.

The bus hobbles and dances on its jolly way,
To where peach blossoms burst open, like fire.
Everywhere stands a cow's shed, and a waterwheel turns.
Here you see a little village—a cluster of bridges.

Bridges built of single logs on rice paddy partitions,
Bridges of stone slabs over narrow, narrow creeks;
Villagers reckon distance by a three-*li* bridge or a nine-mile bridge,
Bridges arching like rainbows, bridges under covers.

Countless are the reflections of bridges around the village,
Bamboo rafts from the mountains pass under them;
A basket-size moon rises to perch on the bridgehead—
Oh, how I wish my feet could step on homeland soil again.

Lake T'ai, deep dark blue, lies like an elephant
On its back, scratching its itch, its legs spread out.
Two or three tiny sails in sunset slip quietly by;
The gentle rumble of a small steamboat accompanies me home.

South of the river, red flags roll and unroll in the wind;
Forever my heart will overflow with your charms.
One day I shall return to your fold and sing
Aloud and in joy on your collective farms.

1950
War, Peace, and Progress, pp. 27–29.

Spring Thunder

Spring thunder explodes, rocking the world.
Up and down the great river, ice has thawed.
The season of frozen mountains is over,
And the era of frozen mountains has come to an end.

Rivers and lakes are swollen with muddy water,
Huge loads of lumber come downriver in peals of songs.
Look at us. Look at how we till the land and build the country
With everyone decked out in light clothes, new gowns.

We open our bright eyes wide, very wide,
To take in our colorful life with infinite joy.
Spring has arrived in a brand new China,
To be followed closely by a spring for all men.

Willows everywhere are swaying in the wind,
Even quiet and solemn wu-t'ung trees have sprouted.
Azaleas bloom, covering the lush mountainsides,
And birds sing their songs to summon travelers.

With a bag on my shoulders and a song on my lips,
I shall go far to the country, to the work sites, and sing
For this world, and look at valleys from hilltops,
And cover me with fallen petals and soak me in rains of spring.

1965
War, Peace, and Progress, pp. 66–67

Translated by Kai-yu Hsu

LI CHI
(1922–)

The son of a poor peasant in a Honan mountain village, Li Chi had barely finished junior high school before war and revolution swept him along and delivered him in 1938 to the Resistance War College, a Marxist institution in Yenan. Soon afterwards he served in the Red Army as a political commissar. From 1942 on he taught in village schools, worked for the Party at the county level, and edited local papers. He began his writing career in 1943, publishing mostly tales in a style that caters to common folks. *Wang Kuei and Li Hsiang-hsiang*, a long ballad depicting the life and love of two young poor peasants, brought fame to Li Chi in 1946.

After the Liberation, Li took over the editorship of *Yangtze River Literature*, an influential monthly. Four years later he went to work at an oil field in Yümen, Kansu Province. Subsequently he divided his days between the literary circles in Peking and his worker friends in northwest China. By 1960 he had published ten volumes of songs and ballads, including *The Story of Yang Kao, The Songs of Life, The Chrysanthemum Rock, Poems of Yümen,* and the *Beloved Tsaidam.*

After the years of silence imposed by the Cultural Revolution, Li has re-emerged as editor of the *Poetry Journal* and, more recently, as chief editor of *People's Literature*, the nation's leading literary journal. —K.Y.H.

Short Song on Autumn Harvest

As far as you can see, all is glittering gold,
Wind sweeps over the rice field, the rice scent is sweet;
They say rice fields are better than gold—
Huh, how can gold grow year after year, like rice?

> Hurry with the cutting, hurry with the threshing,
> Let bumper crops
> Appear on our land year after year.

Suntanned fellows from mutual aid teams, stout and strong,
They harvest along, they sing along;
They say we've got muscles, tough as iron—
Huh, our collective strength, better than anyone anywhere.

> Hurry with the cutting, hurry with the threshing,
> Let bumper crops
> Appear on our land year after year.

Bundles of rice hauled to the threshing ground
Turn into food, white and tasty;
They say put the best in our storage first—
Huh, we ship the choicest to our government as our patriotic grain.

> Hurry with the cutting, hurry with the threshing,
> Let bumper crops
> Appear on our land year after year.

Abacus in hand, let's figure it out,
Each *mu* yielded over a thousand *catties;*
They say this happens to be our best year,
Huh, it's because of the good leadership of Chairman Mao.

> Hurry with the cutting, hurry with the threshing,
> Let bumper crops
> Appear on our land year after year.

October 1952
Seventeen Short Poems, pp. 117–119

Translated by Kai-yu Hsu

LIANG SHANG-CH'ÜAN
(1930?–)

A relative newcomer in poetry, Liang Shang-ch'üan, a native of Szechwan, did not begin his writing career until 1953. Yet, within ten years he published eight volumes of verse, including *Bubbling Highlands, Flowering Country,* and *The Mountain Stream,* which won him a considerable following.

Most noticeable is the lyrical quality in his works. They exhibit a good measure of polish without losing spontaneity. The influence of classical Chinese poetry is strong, and the effort to capture the charm of folksongs is quite successful. Critics have commended Liang for his ability to present a farm scene, a view of the frontier, or an image of simple people, all with equal magic.

After the silent years of the Cultural Revolution, Liang has produced a new anthology, *Songs Flying over the Great Liang Mountains* (1976). His works have been appearing regularly in the magazine *Szechwan Literature.*

—K.Y.H.

The Great Wall, Within
and Beyond

The Great Wall, so tall.
Thousands of mountains look small.
White clouds ply the frontier sky,
Blocking the flying birds.
An iron wall ten thousand *li* long,
Still stands straight today.
Two thousand years of wind and rain
Have not knocked it down.

Within the wall the hills roll like waves.
Ears of grain,
Sprouts of crops.
How much has ripened, ready to drop?
And how much turns green again?
Combat fieldworks turned into irrigation ditches,
Silvery water skirts the villages.
Forts turned into granaries,
Already filled with golden grains.

Beyond the wall, boundless grassland.
All kinds of flowers,
All kinds of grass.
How many of them have turned red?
And how many of them have turned green?

Cattle and sheep, like jewels
Glittering in the sun;
Mongolian tents, like buds,
Each one ready to burst into bloom.

No smoke of war rises again on the beacon tower.
A rainbow floats in the eyes, a smile in the heart.
Men ride on lithe horses,
And horses race like birds in flight.
Freely they run under the blue sky,
Listening to the wind whistle by.
From the top of the wall, all the mountains look small.
The planting songs and the pasturing songs
Rise higher than white clouds.

October 9, 1955, north of the Yen-men Pass
The Mountain Stream, pp. 76–78

Translated by Kai-yu Hsu

T'IEN CHIEN

(T'ung T'ien-chien, 1916–)

In May 1978, T'ien Chien reappeared at the Third Congress of the All-China Federation of Literary and Art Circles in Peking, apparently not much worn or worse for his years of imposed silence during the Cultural Revolution.

T'ien came from Anhwei Province, attended a Shanghai college, and began writing poetry under the influence of the Crescent School, which flourished in the 1920s and 1930s. Some of his earliest works had long lines in neat stanzas. A dramatic change took place in him when he went north at the outbreak of the war in 1937 and plunged into feverish activities among leftists and anti-Japanese underground workers. In Yenan he became a close associate of Ting Ling. Acknowledging his admiration of Mayakovsky, T'ien now wrote with a particular flair for the strong, the nervy, and the wholeheartedly lyrical. Hu Feng said that T'ien's "poetic mind has become intensely united with life as it truly is," and Wen I-to, a leading Crescent poet, praised T'ien as "the Drummer of Our Time," because of the breathless drumbeat effect in T'ien's new poems. By 1949, T'ien had already published a score of well-acclaimed volumes, including *It Is Not Yet Dawn, Chinese Ballads, Sea, To the Fighters, Poems of the War of Resistance, To the Sentries Who Brave the Wind and Sand Storms,* and *She, Too, Wants to Kill.*

From 1949 to the eve of the Cultural Revolution, T'ien held important cultural and editorial posts in Peking. Some of his works during this period were collected in *Songs for the Horse-headed Fiddle* and *Pledge.* After 1976 his poems began to appear again in the revived *Poetry Journal,* and currently he is working on a movie script.

The first installment of his *Carter's Story,* a multi-chapter poem, was published in 1943, but the last six chapters were not released until 1949. At that time he was planning a sequel to the poem. The following excerpt may not do justice either to the original accomplishment or to Cyril Birch's rendition, but until publication in its entirety some day, this much-abridged version must suffice to present T'ien Chien at his very best.   —K.Y.H.

---

from *The Carter's Story*

Chapter One: *Forced Marriage*

Nineteen thirty-six,
A bad year, crops were thin,
The Lord above helped the landlords
Dragging men to their death.

No knowing: the seed went in
But the seedling you transplanted
Was your root of poverty.
No telling: a mouthful of corn
Too much for a man to expect.
This year then, after harvest
Flinty Stone sat in his field,
Sat in his field
Empty-handed.
By his side an empty cart
An old ox hitched in front.
On his back a few poor rags
Not enough for a man.
He picked up a stone from the ground,
Beat his sickle, cried out,
"Flinty Stone, who's it all for?
Who's it for—
Who's it for?
Hard work, hard gathering in,
All given up in rent,
And still not enough for that.
Can't afford to rent my field,
Pig of an owner, dog of an owner,
Skins his tenants alive,
Strips us for rent and leaves us in chains.
You break your back in the field,
He reckons up in his house.
Work as hard as you like
You never catch up with his figures.
There he sits and counts,
Wealth and a soft life for him.
Here you toil and slave
And pay what you owe with your loved ones!"

Flinty had a daughter, Lannie.
Lannie took up his cry,
Called to the Lord above,
"Lord above, you're an old old man
Your ears are deaf, your eyes are dim.
You see no suffering,
You hear no suffering.
The people who fast and pray,
Hungry bellies for them.
The killers, the plunderers
Have more than they can enjoy.
Lord, you've lost your place up there,
You've fallen, fallen down!"
Lannie was eighteen

Quick-witted, quick to please the eye,
Face like a smooth round grape,
Cheeks healthy red, not tanned and swarthy,
Two bright eyes like gems,
Shining and round, round and shining.
Crimson shoes she wore,
Light blue jacket and trousers.
Though born in a poor man's home,
As pretty as a piece of jade.
What's more she was the right sort
She could work with a will.
Could she work, in the hard times?
To her father, she was like one of his hands.
Half of all to be done at home
Could be left to her,
Half of all the work in the fields
Lannie could do alone.
They said she was like a flower
And she deserved the name,
But this was no fragile blossom
She had her father's strength,
No melting woman-weakness
But toughness of tempered steel,
She was no water lily
But a flower of the mountainside.
Flinty Stone said to his daughter,
"Time I found you a husband!"
Lannie asked her father,
"Who've you got in mind then?"
Flinty asked another question,
"What sort of husband do you want?"
A laugh came from Lannie at this.
"I've no time for wealth and show,
I want a good honest lad.
Never mind if his clothes are tattered
As long as he's steady and true."
Flinty asked his daughter
A question with something behind,
"What if rich Mr. Pigg
Carries you off?"
She answered crisp and short,
"That old pig, Crabapple Pigg,
He'll get nothing out of me.
You don't wear your best shoes to walk through dog dirt,
You don't wear your best clothes to fetch foul meat.
I want a good name while I live
And clean earth for my grave when I die!"
As evening came

And the sun hung on the hillside
Lannie called to her father,
"Let's hitch up the ox and go back."
Flinty Stone hitched up his ox
And breathed a weary sigh.
"Twelve months' labor done
For a bundle of dried-up straw.
This is what they call 'dogs eating men.'
—Men! You're better-off a dog!"

As they finished talking
Black-face Pigg came up.
He brought the cart to a halt,
Stood there blocking the way,
Marriage contract in one hand
Jar of wine in the other.
"Congratulations, brother,
Here's a marriage contract.
Drinking the toasts tomorrow
Don't forget old Black-face Pigg."
Flinty's eyes went bloodshot then,
He tore up the forced contract.
"Can't pay our rent
It's death for all of us.
Not at any price
Do I sell this girl of mine.
If Pigg's prepared to snatch her from me
Let him try.
He won't get her alive,
He'll have to take her corpse!"
Black-face Pigg gave a laugh,
"What are you talking about?
For your Lannie
To marry our landlord
It's a match for her and a lucky one too."
They say 'When a dog bites a poor man
He doesn't need a tongue to argue with.'
This dog of a Black-face Pigg
Like a two-edged knife
Now red-faced bully
Now white-faced cheat,
If wheedling doesn't work
He tries real force.
Just about to go
Out comes his last word,
"Crabapple Pigg
Has heated the wine,
Slaughtered the pig.

Two days' time
He's going to take Lannie
Into his house as his wife."
Lannie when she heard these words
Fell forward on the cart, and cried.
Flinty Stone
Driving his cart,
It wasn't a cart he was driving
He was driving disaster and hate!
It wasn't a cart he was driving
He was driving a human life!
It wasn't a cart he was driving
He was driving a tower of fire!

[Flinty Stone goes to court, but is kicked out because the landlord has been working in cahoots with the magistrate. Flinty Stone has to cart his daughter to Landlord Pigg's house to be his concubine. After one abortive effort to avenge the wrong, Flinty leaves the village, driving a cart for a living, to look for the Communist army. He finds them, and he returns to the village to organize a peasant uprising. Time passes. They hold a mass meeting to force the landlord to reduce rents.]

Chapter Thirteen: *Straightening Things Out*

Section Two

A wrong must be righted
A debt must be paid.
Shouts from the east and west
Joined in a stew of sound,
Poor man Chang, poor man Li
The peasants, a swarm of bees
Few feet touching the ground
Surged through the temple gate,
Some with sack over shoulder
Some with measure in hand,
Fists that were brandished skywards
Fists that pounded the ground.
The two friends Steel and Stone
Two men of the carter's trade,
One of them clasping a stout stick
Strode down from the tower, steady and calm,
One with a fish-handled knife in his hand
Strode down from the tower with flashing eyes.
The two men, shoulder to shoulder
Marched at the head of the crowd,
One the chairman
One the marshal

Like a pair of burning candles
Ruddy glow on their faces
Like a team of chestnut horses
Drawing a wagon behind them.
The crowd was like a bow
The two men like two arrows
The arrows fitted to the bowstring
Ready to fly any second.
Flawless Steel roared out,
"Work till we've straightened things out!
If we can't get straight in one day
Take two days
If we can't get straight in two days
Take three days,
Work till the Yellow River runs clear!"
Flinty Stone sang out,
"Now's the time, welcome this hour
The savior of the country stands at the gate
Everywhere the courts are opening
The judges scour the land.
Chairman Mao! Your program
Comes like kinfolk to live in our homes
Like the red sun up there
Lighting our faces all day!"

[The peasants win; their life is enormously improved. Lannie, now liberated, goes home to rejoin her father.]

Translated by Cyril Birch;
excerpted by Kai-yu Hsu

SHIH FANG-YÜ
(1930?–)

Shih Fang-yü was born and educated abroad, but returned to China in time to greet the arrival of the Mao Tse-tung era. "The Mightiest Voice of Peace," a poem of over 700 lines, catapulted Shih Fang-yü to fame in 1950. It captured the euphoria of Liberation and gave robust expression to a new nation's genuine yearning for peace and reconstruction. It captured the hearts of nearly the entire population of China, then said to number 470 million.

Following that meteoric rise in new poetry, Shih Fang-yü published several other equally long poems, but none of them earned him additional recognition. Nothing has come forth from him since 1963. —K.Y.H.

---

from The Mightiest Voice of Peace

I

The sound that spread from Stockholm
was the mightiest voice on earth
like a hurricane spinning
from Baltic breakers
into the flying sands of the Gobi.

Men in the mines of Donbas,
Liberation Army in China,
dark-skinned peons on South American plantations,
fishermen from the fjords of Norway—

We are common people.
The Wall Street bosses
never heard
        our names
but we signed our names
        on the Peace Petition.
We pointed at their noses,
forbid them to use their customary cannon shell
to ladle out our blood
        as thirst-quencher,
forbid
        the farmers along the Mississippi
        to raid peasant collectives in the Ukraine.

We are common people,
but we are
        unconquerable people.
Because our name is
            people,
we are the vast majority
            on earth,
our voice is the mightiest voice
            on earth.
We are not beggars for peace,
we order them,
            "End the war!"

                    II

We must halt them—
    the robber
    in swallow-tail coat,
    assassin
    with cross on his chest.
They take odds on the lives of mankind,
in blood they reckon up their holdings.
At the Pentagon in Washington
their military maps
        stake the Pacific Ocean out
                as a private American lake,
        reduce Japan and the Philippines
                to bases for B-29s.

    . . . .

America
is still the same country
but Jefferson, Lincoln, where are they now?
Once I read
            a Declaration of Independence to the world,
            the fiction of Mark Twain,
            the poetry of Whitman.
Naively I thought
            when one captain falls
            another will come.

But America,
when I set Hollywood slicks
            against *Leaves of Grass*
when I set the *Bill of Rights*
            against Truman's speeches,
I hear your forefathers
            mourning in their graves.

. . . .

Ah, America,
Your people are warning you.
Housewives come
to the bank counters
        with their underfed babies
and no banknotes.
The stacks of paper they present
are slogans written in blood and tears:
they won't be taxed
        for police dogs and atom bombs;
their sons
        are not to die on mountains and fields
        of a foreign country.

. . . .

Your volcano,
America, must erupt.
If Truman and Marshall
        dare to burn and kill,
miners will come climbing from their pits
        and bring their coal-blasting dynamite with them,
railwaymen will head all locomotives to Washington,
soldiers will return from the front,
blacks will smash the electric chairs,
housewives will abandon their kitchens.

If today you want war,
America,
your people will storm the White House
        and the Pentagon;
just as, toward the finish of World War One,
Russian workers
forced the gate of the Winter Palace.

III

Wind blusters,
ocean roars,
reefs stud the Pacific.
Recall your ships, America:
tough Tagalog men
have been digging graves for you
among the Philippine coconut palms;
Ho Chi Minh and Nguyen Giap
will bury your bodies
        beside the French;

the flames of Mount Fuji
will shoot through its cap of snow
                and you will die by fire.

Don't, no, don't go anywhere.
If you dare
                invade China,
five hundred million people
will use you as they use the fox
                for fox-skin souvenirs.

Truman's inferno
rages in Korean wheatfields.
The old blood in Korean ravines has not yet dried
                before they're awash in new blood.

. . . .

Along the banks of the Han,
from a thousand abrupt mountains and ranges
Korean people
rush on like the tide
and guerrillas spring from the bush
blazing away at you;
peasants are smashing your heads
                with their hoes.

. . . .

End the war!
Korean radio broadcasts
                the cry of American prisoners of war,
American soldiers based in Japan
                desert by platoons and by companies.

End the war!
Let the many Tanyas go on with their grade nine schooling.
Let the many Liu Hu-lans live on as model workers.
Let the People's Liberation Army get involved in production.

End the war!
The people's choice is tractors and ears of wheat
and not atomic bombs or Colorado beetles.

. . . .

Girl student on a street in Damascus:
when you were dragged to the police station,
the Peace Petition you had in your hand
was passing through other hands.

Mothers of Vienna:
when you were outside the American Embassy
              arrested for shouting for peace
had you heard from the mothers of Paris
              in front of the same sort of building
              shouting the same slogans?

Peace leaders of Ankara:
when the military court tortured you
Turkey's cities and villages
blossomed like spring with peace groups.
Fighters for peace,
fight harder;
in the name of peace
declare war on war.

IV

The eyes of the people
have turned toward the Soviet Union,
a rainbow spanning heaven
after a long dry spell.

. . . .

Let the hawks recall the history
linked to those ancient steppes.
The armies of the King of Sweden once
surged like the flood;
the defeat of Charles XII
was like the ebb
leaving stranded shells—
the beached bones of a million crack troops.
Once Napoleon stood
              on the Alps close to the sky
but in the Russian snows
his mountainous troops
turned to gravel.

All this history
was history lost on Hitler,
but Hitler's defeat and death
are fresh in the memory
of Soviet heroes
who went to the front.
Any assault from the east will be
           buried in Siberian forests.
Any attack from the west will go
           to the bottom of the Baltic.

. . . .

The heroic people of Stalingrad have taken their uniforms off.
Shchabulov, the Major, did not die;
he went to school again and became a teacher of history.
When the moon reached the tips of the trees
he strolled with Anya, her wounds newly healed,
through streets of dazzling light
to the ballet theater
                    to see Swan Lake.

. . . .

People listen the world over
to the sound that comes from the Soviet land,
to the music of factory motors
                    the movement of collective tractors,
to the people singing about a new life
                    and the Volga calling for peace.

                    V

. . . .

In our land
things have happened to shake the earth:
the birth last year of the People's Republic
sealed the fate of wars planned
for the Asian continent.
Peaceful people,
with fresh flowers and cries of long life to us
welcomed as brothers a quarter of the globe

. . . .

The sunshine of our country is so warm
because her nights
                    had been haunted by funereal winds;
The people of our country are so jubilant today
because their yesterdays
                    had been stunted by catastrophe.

. . . .

Give peace to us
who treasure every bit of material resource that belongs
                    to the people
who keep marauders from spewing fire
                    on our cities and villages.

The People's Liberation Army
took up guns, then took up hoes, now take up pens.
Our trains are running from Manchuria straight to
          Kuangchou Bay;
a new bridge
will cross the Yangtze
from Hankow to Wuchang.

Our people give it all they have:
here
the turn of every single machine,
the growth of every single ear of wheat,
the run of every single train,
voyage of every single ship,
every pair of rough hands
every drop of steaming sweat
contributes to the peace.

I can only wield a journalist's pen:
I want to put the news that we have overcome a thirteen-year
          inflation into front-page headlines;
I want to put the news that production in northeastern
          industry increased six-fold
the news that every kind of grain in the land now has
          a bumper harvest,
the news that children from the working class are now in school
                    into front-page headlines.
I want to fill my paper
                    with the people's work,
                    with their creations.
May it spread around the earth
and the enemy tremble
and friends applaud.

What I want
is simply this,
an equation adding up
to peace.
I never knew how to sing
but I will sing forever
the mightiest voice of peace.

People's Literature, October 1950, 9–15

Translated by Shu-ying Tsau;
excerpted by Kai-yu Hsu

PART TWO

The Hundred Flowers Movement
and the Anti-Rightist Campaign

(1956–1958)

The years immediately following 1956 saw the flowering of economic reconstruction in China. With the whole nation concentrating on recovery, material productivity peaked around 1957. Conversion of agriculture to the commune system was almost complete. Public order and security, availability of consumer goods, and confidence about the future in general all reached a new high level. However, memory of the Hu Feng case lingered on the literary front. Writers were not as eager to produce as the peasants and workers were. To stimulate literary productivity, in early 1956 Party authorities announced the Hundred Flowers campaign—let a hundred kinds of flowers bloom together, let the hundred schools of thought contend.

The responses were enthusiastic and, to Party authorities, a little too overwhelming. A newcomer, Wang Meng, published his "The Young Man Who Has Just Arrived at the Organization Department" (Sept. 1956) to criticize senior Party cadres for their corrupt life and work-style. Liu Pin-yen joined Wang with a report, "At the Bridge Site" (1958), showing how an idealistic engineer was prevented from carrying out his duty by bureaucratic indifference and inertia. These exposés, together with demands for political democracy by some non-Communist leaders who had been influential before Liberation, brought about a prompt reversal of Party policy. The result was a counteroffensive, an "anti-rightist" campaign. Wang Meng and Liu Pin-yen were criticized and silenced. This reversal in political policy went further, to clear accounts with some veteran writers; Ch'in Chao-yang was denounced, not because of his own stories (such as "Election"), but for his part in publishing Wang Meng's story in *People's Literature,* then under Ch'in's editorship. An established writer from Northeast China, Hsiao Chün, was punished for his novel about coal miners; his critics charged that Hsiao failed to uphold the Party's leadership in overcoming the "practical difficulties."

195

Other veteran writers fared better with their upsurge of creative energy. The ambitious were after epical works that chronicled the past three decades of revolution and dramatic change in the countryside and in urban centers. Liang Pin's long novel *Keep the Red Flags Flying* starts with revolutionary undercurrents in the early 1930s and follows a number of colorful characters all the way through Liberation. Chou Li-po wrote about land reform and the far-reaching change it brought about in village life in the late 1940s and early 1950s. Chou Erh-fu treated the struggle between labor and management in Shanghai soon after Liberation. Fang Chi, a versatile writer more deeply involved in Party politics than most other writers, produced a surprise story about an idealistic intellectual's downfall because of his love for a folk theater singer enslaved by her stepmother-owner and the old society. These works enjoyed popularity until their denunciation during the Cultural Revolution in 1966-67.

Ju Chih-chüan's "Lilies on a Comforter" portrays a young Red soldier whose childlike innocence is most disarming; the young bride in the story who develops such a strong feeling for the dying soldier is depicted persuasively and with economy of words. By contrast Tu P'eng-ch'eng's village characters in "The Natives of Yenan" exhibit traits more typical of the proletarian image the new literature tries to foster. Yang Mo's novel *The Song of Youth,* written in 1957 with a setting in the mid-1930s, presents another social stratum—college students involved in the underground Communist movement.

In poetry Mao Tse-tung himself encouraged more verse writing by publishing his own; he allowed eighteen of his early poems, all in classical form, to appear for the first time. Symbolist poet Pien Chih-lin, very quiet after Liberation, wrote several of his rare stanzas since 1949. Short lyrics yielded to longer narrative poems. Tsang K'o-chia and Tsou Ti-fan joined Li Chi in presenting characters in long verse with a story line. Ai Ch'ing and Ho Ching-chih developed their type of long songs with lines of irregular length but sustained with strong feeling. Only Li Ying continued to write mostly short lyrical poems.

HSIAO CHÜN
(Liu Chün, 1907–)

Hsiao Chün's proletarian origins are well known. Born in Northeast China (Manchuria) in 1908, he led the life of a vagabond jack-of-all-trades until joining a militia outfit in his early twenties. After the September 18th Mukden Incident in 1931, which led to the Japanese annexation of Northeast China, Hsiao Chün began his literary career in the city of Harbin. In 1933 he and his common-law wife, the writer Hsiao Hung, left their homeland and traveled first to Tsingtao in Shantung, then south to Shanghai, where they came under the wing of the renowned literary figure Lu Hsün.

Village in August, Hsiao Chün's first novel, was published under Lu Hsün's aegis in 1935; it and its author became overnight sensations. This novel also has the distinction of being the first modern Chinese novel to appear in English translation (New York, 1942). Following the death of Lu Hsün in October 1936, and the opening of war with Japan less than a year later, Hsiao Chün traveled to the interior of China, moving from place to place until his arrival in 1940 in Yenan. By then he had written another novel (*The Third Generation,* 1937) and several collections of stories, essays, and poems.

It did not take the abrasive, egocentric, and basically humanist Hsiao Chün long to get into trouble. His essay "Love and Patience Among the Comrades," published in the *Liberation Daily* in 1942, was one of the articles by Yenan literary figures which spurred Mao Tse-tung into calling his Yenan Forum on Literature and Art. Hsiao Chün and his fellow "malcontents" were criticized, but for Hsiao Chün, at least, the matter was closed. Four years later he returned with the People's Liberation Army forces to Manchuria, where he published a Party-supported newspaper, *The Cultural Gazette.* In a rash of articles and editorials he strongly censured the Communist Party's land reform programs and Chinese and Soviet attitudes toward the Northeastern Chinese. In 1948 a major rectification campaign was launched against Hsiao Chün, and resulted in the closing of the newspaper and his incarceration in a labor reform camp at the Fushun Coal Mines in Liaoning Province. He returned to Peking in 1951. Over the next four years a revised version of *Village in August,* the first part of an expanded and greatly altered version of *The Third Generation* (retitled *The Past Generation*), and a new novel, *Coal Mines in May,* were published.

Coal Mines in May is a fictional tale of the author's experiences during his period of reform through labor; it is, to all appearances, an exemplary piece of socialist realist writing. However, in the author's zeal to glorify the proletariat, he has inadvertently placed them above the Party; having portrayed the people themselves as the motive force of the revolution, it could only be a matter of time before this advocate of individual heroism was once again under attack by Party critics. Indeed, it took but a few months for the first critical article to appear. The final blow came during the Anti-rightist Campaign of 1957–58, and Hsiao Chün disappeared without a trace for twenty years. He quietly re-emerged in public in 1977. There is, however, no word on what he may be writing these days.

The following excerpt is taken from chapter seven of the novel *Coal Mines in May*. Although by no means a microcosmic view of the entire work, it is representative in many ways. Themes of patriotism and dedication to the Party and the masses; attacks against the vestiges of Nationalist Chinese control; individual heroism; the workers' coarse language; and descriptions of production in the socialist naturalist mode are all in evidence.   —H.G.

---

from *Coal Mines in May*

CHAPTER SEVEN: THE GREAT WORK CONTEST

A calamity struck at about midnight on the eve of the great work contest to produce more for the nation. The explosives storage shed for the entire strip mine was rocked by a blast. The news of the incident shocked not only the people at the strip mine, but the entire Black Gold mining region as well.

The word going round had it that it was all the doing of underground counterrevolutionary Kuomintang agents who were bent on sabotaging the people's mine, and who were even more intent on disrupting the great work contests being held in May and June. The warnings that the administrators and certain responsible Party cadres had frequently issued in the past for everyone to be on constant guard against the Kuomintang counterrevolutionaries and their clandestine schemes to sabotage the mines were now revived for the first time among the working masses. There were some among them who recalled the words of Lu Tung-shan at the First Workers' Representative Assembly:

"...Comrades, we must produce, but even more importantly, we must guard against our enemies! We toil hard to produce, to repair and build, and if we allow those bandits to run off with the fruits of our labor, or to destroy them, it's a bad bargain! Those counterrevolutionary Kuomintang agent dogs are nothing but bandits; in fact, they're more shameless than bandits—no deed is beneath them. If we're not careful they'll put sand in our rice and dog turds in our food. They even poison our food ... they can't get anything good to eat, so they don't want us to either. They want to starve us, or poison us!..."

At the time, few people had paid any attention to Lu Tung-shan's warning. Some were of the opinion that the Kuomintang counterrevolutionaries had been frightened out of their wits and wouldn't have the guts to do anything; others believed that this fellow Lu Tung-shan was merely currying favor with the Communists, and that by taking a couple of swipes at the Kuomintang counterrevolutionaries he was showing how progressive he was. As far as the others were concerned, he was just making noises by reeling off some stock phrases. They weren't really listening to him, since no one felt the need to remember what he was talking about. Yet at that very time, underground agents were making plans against Lu Tung-shan's life, plans that, fortunately, were never carried out.

But on this day every word that Lu Tung-shan had uttered came flooding back into their memories: not only were the secret agents bent on throwing sand into the people's rice, they were intent on smashing their ricebowls as well—they truly wanted to destroy this mine upon which thousands of people depended for their livelihood. Even the people who normally thought of nothing but their own monthly wages were now in a restive and angry mood. They wanted to know just who these people were who would stoop to such despicable acts. Why would these bad elements want to break everyone's ricebowl? What was it that drove them to throw sand into the ricebowls of people who had finally been able to sit down to a peaceful and secure meal? Just what was it that made such bad elements tick? And so the people kept their eyes peeled and went from place to place asking questions; with their ears pricked up, they surreptitiously listened to the talk around them wherever they went. Gradually those among them with shadowy pasts and those who had exhibited something less than upright tendencies fell under a cloud of suspicion.

The entire incident, as was to be expected, proved a hard nut to crack.

But the great work contest went ahead on schedule. That was possible because sufficient amounts of explosives and detonator caps for the contest had been handed out by the mine administrators to each unit during the first few days. And so the incident had no direct effect on the implementation of the work contest. On the contrary, the explosion had served to increase the people's sense of outrage, which had a measure of revenge and a measure of something resembling a show of force. As a result, those who were planning to participate in the great work contest were filled with such enthusiasm they seemed about to burst.

It was only four o'clock in the morning—there were still two hours to go before the third unit of the previous day was scheduled to end its shift—but the first unit, which was to relieve them, seemed today to be under the effects of a marvelous "elixir of unity." They were already mustered at the place where they were to begin their shift. Some had shown up even earlier.

Yang P'ing-shan and Lu Tung-shan had spent half the night at their respective work stations, their eyes opened wide like owls as they flew from one place to another. Otherwise, they could be found on their haunches carefully examining every spot where something untoward might happen, and were constantly making any necessary repairs.

The third shift of the previous day seemed unwilling to quit, so the men of the first unit rode herd on them, which led to some half-serious quarrels and shouting matches just about everywhere:

"What the fuck is making you so eager about the work! Are you trying to squeeze two days' production out of a single day's work? What kind of contest is that? To do it right we're supposed to knock off work at the regular time and change shifts on schedule. You're trying to cheat . . ." The men of the third shift, unwilling to leave and feeling somewhat jealous, cursed the others, airing their own complaints. Since their shift was unable to participate in the work contest, they were frustrated, unhappy.

"You guys get the hell out of here! You and your damned grumbling! You don't appreciate the fact that we showed up two hours early. Since your old ladies are still at home keeping the mattresses warm, now's your chance to go get a couple of hours in bed. But no, you don't have the sense to understand that."

Though the quarreling, cursing, and ridiculing continued uninterrupted, the work went on in all earnestness. In the end it was the oncoming shift that won out, as they finally drove off the men from the previous unit.

It was not even 4:30 when Lu Tung-shan and his crew had filled a train of coal cars at their work area; it was being pulled by motor and cable to the ground above. And so, on the first day of the contest theirs was the first crew anywhere in the strip mine to have filled a train of cars with coal. The second trainload was produced by Hsieh Chih-ching's crew in the western sector. Following them, more winch-powered trainloads rumbled up to the ground as the other crews filled theirs. The coal cars snaked their way quickly down the tracks, looking like long millipedes in motion. At every site they wriggled their way up and down the hills, seemingly in competition with one another. Some of the hookmen* aboard them broke into song; they were singing snatches of local opera in high-pitched voices, which floated on the winds to distant places; from time to time their songs were smothered by the cacophony of sounds from the locomotives, electric excavators, punches, and explosives. The combination of sounds—metallic and human—was a symphony that naturally and harmoniously pervaded the entire mine site, and even drifted far off to greet the coming dawn.

The western sky was covered with a layer of light purple, then the eastern sky, with its dark-gray layered clouds, was rent by the slicing silver-red rays of the morning sun. In no time at all that great fiery red ball of an early-morning May sun broke free from the craggy horizon and leapt noiselessly into the sky. The lamps at the top and base of the mountain were still lighted, but they were no longer as radiant nor as inviting as they had been during the night, and soon they were extinguished.

The strip mine was divided into three major sectors: the eastern sector, the western sector, and the sector called the "deep hole," which was at the bottom of the mine and was excavated through a deep trench. It was this shaft where they dug the coal residue at the bottom of the large deposits. All the sectors were located on the southern slope of the mountain. At appropriate places flat areas had been hewn into the side of the mountain, so that from a distance it resembled a man-made rice paddy terraced out of the slope, and men were working on this terraced paddy. Temporary rail lines that served each of the leveled areas could be extended or shifted around as the need arose. Each of these separate transport routes was linked to a major loop, from which a 300-horsepower or smaller winch moved the coal up to the collecting area at the top of the slope. From there it was transferred into larger transport cars that moved horizontally to the coal-washing station or some other place. Throughout the strip mine there were more than twenty sites served by the small winches, which were the transport facilities that connected the ground level with the lower reaches of the mine. In addition, there was at the western sector

---

*A note elsewhere in the original text explains that the hookman's job is to control the cable hookup between cars as they travel up and down the mountain. It is a dangerous job, requiring agility and calm, steady movements. [H. G.]

a 1300-horsepower double-capstaned winch powerful enough to hoist and lower coal cars weighing twenty-five tons—one round trip every five minutes. There was also a large winch in the eastern sector, but it was single-capstaned, and less powerful, managing 1100 horsepower. At these two major transport areas alone, 12,000 tons of coal or rock could be moved daily; they were like two gigantic drinking straws!

The entire Black Gold coalfield was some ten miles long by four or five miles wide, and from ten to more than a hundred feet thick, making it an enormous leaf of coal. From the south to the north it cut into the ground at thirty-degree angles. Few coalfields in the world could boast a layer of such pure concentration as this one. And it was located in the heart of the fatherland! In times past it was sealed up for many years by ignorant emperors; then it was forcibly occupied by the Czarist Russian and Japanese imperialists; and along the way it was ravaged and subjected to insane destruction by the Kuomintang. Now for the first time it was truly controlled by the Chinese people. It was now part of the great wealth belonging to the great people of the great Chinese state, and, reasonably mined and managed, it would, of course, prove its even greater worth. The pride of the Chinese people, it was also a test of the Chinese people's will, particularly the working-class people of the Black Gold mining region. This day—May fifth, 1949—was the opening page of this genuine test.

The workers' production fervor gushed from their political fervor. It initially lacked substance and order, and was, for that matter, somewhat wasted. When the work first began, one could still hear clamorous and chaotic shouts, quarreling among the workers, lighthearted laughter and banter back and forth, and even the sound of jolly singing. But after the work was well under way, these sounds were seldom heard. Outside of the rhythmic clanging and moaning sounds of the machinery as metal struck rock, there was only an almost eerie silence. An atmosphere of leaden seriousness seemed to have settled over the entire mine. The sun's rays burned stronger by the minute. No wind, no clouds in the sky. And yet the people's working fervor was like amassing summer clouds, which grow thicker and darker by the minute, which grow heavier by the minute, which gather and roll faster by the minute, and which grow more beautiful by the minute. This fervor also resembled the twisting winds that come sweeping off the vast desert or off the ocean: at first they are dispersed, light, and warm as they swirl along. But they grow thicker, bigger, and denser; they swirl faster and faster, until at last they begin to suck sand and water up from the ground and form a towering pillar of wind, swirling and twisting, leaping over the deserts and oceans, and rolling up to the heavens.

This wind pillar of the people's fervor, though invisible to the eye, nonetheless swirled more and more rapidly by the minute, and twisted more and more violently; this was the impression one got from looking at the people's faces and watching the motion of their limbs as they worked. At first their faces were filled with boastful smiles born of excitement, and as the men set to work they seemed almost indolent or in a joking mood. But before long this mirthful appearance had disappeared. So, too, had any other discernible expression. By then, whether it was their facial features—their noses, their mouths; or each individual wrinkle; or every hair on their heads, in their beards, in their moustaches, in their eyebrows—everything seemed to have been newly etched with an air of solemnity, and was clearly set off from everything else. It then seemed that the thousands upon thousands of eyes had but one expression: stern and spirited. Limbs and muscles that had been put to work gave one the impression at this moment that they were made not of flesh and blood, but of dark-hued metals—machines in perpetual, unremitting motion.

Lu Tung-shan's eyes were sunk in sockets that seemed like two black pits. His cheeks were hollow, his nose protruded in a sharp curve, and his lips were drawn so tightly inward they had disappeared from sight. His mouth was but a thin slit. His customary loud laughter and shrill yells were no longer heard; he had grown so silent it was almost as though he no longer existed. And yet he never paused in his coal-digging work or in his walking from one place to another. One moment he would drop from sight, the next he would reemerge from somewhere else.

"How many lines of cars have they filled over there?" Chin Ta-liang asked Lu Tung-shan, who was coming out of the wooden shed alongside the winch. The telephone linkup was located in this shed, and from there one could be apprised of the production situation anywhere in the mine site.

Lu Tung-shan answered him without saying a word: he raised two fingers, then picked up a coal shovel from the ground and savagely dug up a heaping shovelful of coal, which he emptied into a coal car.

"How about us?"

Once again Lu Tung-shan answered by using his fingers.

"What? We're only two lines ahead of them? God damn it! 'It's no big deal for a fatso to be girded by a big belt!'* They won't be calling us the 'rabble-rouser unit' anymore; instead, we'll be known as the 'lazy fart unit'!" Chin Ta-liang asked no more questions, but busied himself with shoveling the coal. He shoveled it with such speed that the coal dust formed a black cloud over the area, enveloping him and the men around him. Like the others, he was stripped to the waist, and his dark-brown skin was covered with a layer of coal dust mixed with sweat, glistening in the sun's rays.

The mute, Yen Pai-sui, was standing nearby, mouth agape and staring wide-eyed, with his coal shovel resting idly in his hands. He was scolded by a small, thin coal digger standing alongside him:

"You dumb jackass, what are you listening to? We're only two lines of cars ahead of them, so speed it up."

It finally dawned on the mute that his unit might be swamped under by the "scorpion unit" of the western sector. This was no laughing matter; no wonder Lu Tung-shan had stopped his customary shouting. This was a life and death struggle between the "rabble-rouser unit" and the western sector that would determine who was to be covered with glory. One could not afford to be sloppy. No one could decipher the strange sounds that he uttered at that moment, but they all witnessed his almost crazed burst of activity as he shoveled the coal, raising a cloud of gray dust. In no time at all he had neatly filled another line of cars to the top.

Just then a line of empty cars came hurriedly snaking down the mountain

---

*The meaning here is that for them to be ahead of the others is expected, and that only by increasing their lead can they gain any real praise and satisfaction. [H. G.]

slope. Standing in the rear of one of the cars was the master hookman, Wang San the Swallow. He had, for that day, managed to find a bright red silk bandana, which he had wrapped around his head. It was flapping in the wind, looking like a banner; it also resembled a flaming torch, its tongues of fire dancing in a strong wind. His dark-skinned, tall, erect body was the banner's pole, or the handle of the torch. As the line of cars neared the branch of the track, Wang San, with his customary lightness and agility—he was more agile, even, than a swallow—jumped down from the car on which he was riding and unhooked the steel cable at the rear of the car. The small coal car that was then freed of the cable glided over to another track obediently and all by itself. Wang San dragged the cable over to the line of coal-filled cars and rang the bell as a signal to those above; the line of cars began to move gently as it was slowly towed up the hill by the cable. As for Wang San, he sprang up onto one of the cars with the ease of motion of a sparrow or a chimp. This time, however, he looked like a flag standard placed in the very first car.

"Hey, Wang San, you're just as shameless as ever—now you're even dressed like a young woman! Give us a harvest-song dance!" someone jokingly shouted, breaking the silence. This lighthearted banter was caught up and partly obliterated by the constant *sha-sha* of coal digging and the hollow *tung-tung* of the coal as it hit the bottoms of the coal cars. But Wang San heard it, nonetheless. He turned his head around and opened his mouth, exposing a row of teeth. His hooked, almost aquiline nose, with the sun behind it, presented a forbidding silhouette, like a paper cutout framed against the clear blue sky —crisp and beautiful. Then, as the line of cars began to move, he actually stretched his arms out wide and began to sway in concert with some unheard melody. A loud chorus of laughter rocked the whole western face of the mine and the entire valley.

Suddenly from off in the distance came the intermittent sounds of gongs and drums, causing everyone's spirits to rise sharply.

"It's a harvest-song brigade!" shouted Chin Ta-liang, the first to recognize the sounds. He stood up straight and looked over to the western sector of the mine.

"What harvest-song brigade? Keep digging the coal. You've broken the mood for the others! You big son-of-a-bitch, you only know how to piss around!" Lu Tung-shan cursed him. Chin Ta-liang said nothing more, but bent over and dug up another shovelful of coal.

But the crash of gongs and the thud of drums grew clearer by the minute. And that wasn't all: amidst the usual gray, pale atmosphere of the colorless coal mine, to everyone's surprise, flags—bright red, looking like a bed of flowers— appeared among the concealed bends and curves of the mountain ridge. Then the resplendent brigade itself came into view, though it was creeping along very slowly.

At this moment Lu Tung-shan, too, felt that his heart was like a piece of melting ice, and his eyes began to grow moist.

It was indeed a harvest-song brigade, one made up of young workers from the electric factory attached to the mine. Since their work contest was not scheduled for that day, they had come to the mine to entertain and cheer their coal-digging brothers.

"Are there any women?" Once again it was Chin Ta-liang. Unable to restrain himself, he broke out laughing.

"Damn it, what if there are women? You're a real problem with those thoughts of yours. You're like a dog who can't stop eating turds! We ought to make you the target of a struggle ...," the short coal-digger reproved Chin Ta-liang. This fellow was called "The Sage" by his fellow coal-diggers, since he had studied in school for seven years.

"Is it an ideological problem just to ask if there are any women? You little monkey, you'd better not fool around with your old dad here! Who are you to give lessons to me? What are you? Some kind of petit bourgeois? Well, you ... you'll never be the equal of a Communist. Before a fox spirit can become an immortal, he has to take human form first, and then practice the moral teachings for five hundred years! Your old dad here is a true Communist, so I'm five hundred years of moral conduct up on you ... you ...!"

This time, uncharacteristically, Chin Ta-liang showed signs of an anger born of embarrassment, for he and this young coal-digger often had their differences, and held one another in low regard. But as he scolded he continued to scoop out coal.

This young coal digger was the son of a small landlord. After the Land Reform of 1947–1950 he had drifted over to the mine and had begun digging coal. Since no one else had been willing to take him on, he had been assigned to Lu Tung-shan's "rabble-rouser unit."

"Even if you are a landlord's son, it makes no difference," Lu Tung-shan had told him. "As long as you work hard, don't engage in any counterrevolutionary activities, and make no trouble, we can reform you. You're a cultured man, so you can teach all the ones who haven't had any schooling how to read and write and do figuring. You have our guarantee that we'll do a good job of reforming you!"

Now, on normal occasions this young man was the silent type who read books and newspapers when he had nothing else to do. He also taught the men how to read, and was a good worker, so that as time passed the others began to look upon him as a fellow worker. Chin Ta-liang alone among them looked down on the man, and he in turn was afraid of Chin Ta-liang. Inexplicably, today he had somehow screwed up his courage and was defiantly critical of Chin Ta-liang.

"I'm not merely a petit bourgeois, I'm a landlord's son! But now I'm sincerely trying to turn myself around, and I am a genuine member of the proletariat. In the future I'm going to strive to become a model worker!" the young man said, making a point of keeping a lighthearted and conciliatory tone to his comments.

"You young snip ... you think you're worthy of ...? You young snip!" Aroused by a growing sense of anger, Chin Ta-liang scooped out a large shovelful of coal and heaved it into the coal car. This was followed by yet another. "What makes you think you're worthy of being a model worker? How can you possibly become a model worker when your long-legged old dad, Chin, is around? If thirty-six-goddam-thousand drops of 'model' rain fell, not a single one would land on your runt of a head!"

"You can't go around cursing people out," the young worker said, having grown earnest in his protest. It was clear to the others from the tone of his voice that he was close to tears.

"Curse you? If this were happening in earlier days, your old dad here would have flattened you out. Then after you were all flat, he would have stuck a reed in you and puffed you up into a warty old toad ... humph! ... you're only getting off easy because we live under a democratic government!"

Scattered laughter from those within hearing distance of this shouting match served to momentarily break up the excessively heavy, somber atmosphere. Those who were at too great a distance to know the cause of this raucous laughter only glanced over this way in astonishment, without letting up for a moment the work they were engaged in.

The harvest-song brigade had already arrived at the foot of the slope beneath the flat area in the western sector. They formed a somewhat uneven circle at a spot that was comparatively level and spacious, and began to turn round and round. A man standing in the center of the ring brandished above his head something shiny and silvery that was shaped like a mallet; his other hand was also raised in the air above him. The man was wearing a white coat over a pair of bright blue workpants. A bright red, round flower had been placed in front of his chest, from which hung two long red streamers. As he moved and turned, the streamers fluttered back and forth in the air. This man was the leader of the harvest-song brigade.

The sound of gongs and drums resounded for a moment, then stopped. From his spot in the center of the ring the leader was the first to start the singing; his was a booming, sonorous voice, and his singing seemed to rock the entire valley. Without realizing it, the men digging coal nearby stopped working simultaneously. With the exception of the constant din produced by distant coal trains, electric excavators, and other mechanical objects, the only sound to be heard anywhere in the mining area was this song:

> The fifth day of the fifth month,
> > The great work contest moves along,
> The fifth day of the fifth month,
> > The great work contest moves along ...
> The Chinese nation has produced
> > A Mao Tse-tung!
> The Chinese nation has produced
> > A Mao Tse-tung ...
> Mao Tse-tung, a hero among men!
> > Mao Tse-tung, a hero among men ...
> We've also got Commander Chu Teh!
> > We've also got Commander Chu Teh ...
> The Great Liberation Army
> > Crosses the Yangtze! Hu-ah-hai!
> The Great Liberation Army
> > Crosses the Yangtze ... Hu-ah-hai!
> A single drum call,
> > Nanking is ours!
> A single drum call,
> > Nanking is ours ...

Another burst of gongs and drums, as the men slowly began to twist their bodies, following the rhythmic movements of the silvery mallet in the leader's hand. The pace was suddenly quickened, and streamers of various colors danced in the air. Another high-spirited burst of gongs and drums, then they stopped again, and the frenzied whirling of the men slowed to the original pace. As the second chorus of singing began, once again it was the leader who sang, and each line was repeated by the others:

> The great contest, step up your efforts,
>> The great contest, step up your efforts . . .
> The fruits of our labor
>> Sustain the front lines.
> The fruits of our labor
>> Sustain the front lines . . .
> At the front lines blood flows,
>> At the front lines blood flows . . .
> Behind the lines sweat flows,
>> Behind the lines sweat flows . . .
> Everyone join hearts! Hu-ah-hai!
>> Everyone join hearts! Hu-ah-hai!
> Strike down Chiang Kai-shek's bandits,
>> Liberate Taiwan.
> Strike down Chiang Kai-shek's bandits,
>> Liberate Taiwan . . .
>   . . . .

Translated by Howard Goldblatt

CH'IN CHAO-YANG
(1916–)

A native of Huang-kang, Hupeh Province, Ch'in Chao-yang first prepared for a teaching career at the elementary school level. He switched to art and went to Yenan in 1938. By 1943 he found himself involved in political organization work in central Hopei villages, and in writing short stories about his experiences. His best-known work, *Village Sketches* (1954), collects some of his most refreshing pieces, written in a simple but effective style. *In the Countryside, Forward—March!* (1956) demonstrates further his skill in full-length fiction.

But he is most remembered for his outspoken advocacy of "engaged realism" in opposition to the Party-directed socialist realism which had degenerated into mimicry of political formulae. His essays, represented by the one entitled "Realism—a Broad Road," stirred up a storm in 1958 and brought about his political downfall.

Before his silence, however, as an editor of *People's Literature* he published such controversial works as Wang Meng's "The Young Man Who Has Just Arrived at the Organization Department" (excerpted in this anthology), Liu Pinyen's exposés (see Liu's story "At the Bridge Site" in this anthology), and others, all of which were later condemned in the Cultural Revolution. In 1974-75 there were talks about his return to public light, but he has not yet joined those writers rehabilitated after the Gang of Four.   —R.C.

Election

At the election meeting people were discussing candidates. According to population ratio, this village was to elect three representatives to the district people's congress, and three candidates had already been nominated. The first, Chin Shih-hsüeh, had been secretary of the Party branch for six consecutive years. Next was Wang Shun-te, an old herb-medicine doctor and a model medical worker in the county. The third one was Chin Chia-kuei, a young man in his twenties, head of the county's model mutual-aid team. Now the women nominated another candidate, Chang Ch'iao-feng, Chin Chia-kuei's wife.

Yin Hsiao-chen, a young girl, was explaining in a silver bell-like voice why they had nominated Chang Ch'iao-feng: ". . . Without Chang Ch'iao-feng, is it possible for her man Chia-kuei to do well on the mutual-aid team? Two years ago in the spring, when the team had just been set up, we women were not yet used to working in the fields. Who was it that influenced the rest of us to go to work in the fields by quietly going first? Later, who was the first to endure the hardships, chose the heaviest work, and moved us so much that we forgot our fatigue? When it came time for work evaluations and point allotments, who confronted male members with the facts, fought and won for us 'equal work

207

for equal pay'? Last year, all the work on our team's five *mu* of cotton, from planting to harvest, was done by women. The men were thus free to do other work—and we also had a good crop of cotton! Who was our leader in all that? ... Fellow villagers, Ch'iao-feng's good points are countless. But because she works without talking, or bragging of her achievements, there are still those in our village who are unaware of her good work and know only of Chin Chia-kuei as leader of the model team...."

"I have something to add," spoke up another woman, Li Kuei-hua. She blushed with excitement. "A little over a month ago, I went to the county model laborer's rally and heard Chin Chia-kuei report on his good work, taking all of Ch'iao-feng's credit. He said, 'I talked it up with the women on our team, and mobilized them to join in the hard work.' Afterwards the people who were with me recalled that he had said the same things at two previous district mass meetings. When I came back and talked it over with the chairman of our women's association, I was told that Chia-kuei had been reprimanded by the Party cadres and had admitted his mistake. But this time, he again forgot about Ch'iao-feng and thought only of himself. I had to bring this up today and could not let Ch'iao-feng be ignored again." She looked at Chin Chia-kuei, swung her pigtail and sat down.

There was dead silence, all eyes were on Chin Chia-kuei.

If at this time Chin Chia-kuei had stood up, mentioned some good things about his wife and some of his own shortcomings, people would certainly have supported him. It was a pity he did not do so. He was used to being in the limelight and was so confident the people would elect him and welcome him to make a speech that he had put on new blue cotton clothes for this special occasion. Now, under the scrutiny of the people, the new clothes made him even more uncomfortable, too nervous to even look around, and his face became redder. He stole a glance at Ch'iao-feng, sitting at his side, hoping she would say something, something like, "Fellow villagers, please don't blame Chia-kuei ... it is with his help that I have made such progress." But Ch'iao-feng merely bent over, lowered her head and let her hair drop down over her face. She had never spoken before a crowd.

"Fellow villagers," Chin Chia-kuei finally had to speak for himself. His voice was hoarse and low. "What Li Kuei-hua just said is not true ..."

"Yes it is!" shouted Li Kuei-hua. "Chia-kuei, I admit you are a good team leader; you have played a leading role in our village's production. I also support you as a candidate. But this meeting today is too important. I must bring out Ch'iao-feng's good points and your shortcomings too; I have to speak the truth."

"I agree with Kuei-hua completely," spoke up Wang Ts'ui-jung, the chair of the women's association. "This is an election meeting. We should exercise fully our rights as citizens. We can not let Ch'iao-feng pass unnoticed. Furthermore, Comrade Chia-kuei is a little vain and loves to brag about his achievements."

There was another silence. Only a few old folks in the back were mumbling: "These women are too serious; look how embarrassed Chia-kuei is. After all, he and Ch'iao-feng are husband and wife. What difference does it make which one is elected?"

The chairman called for a vote. At this point all raised their hands, cried out with joy, and unanimously elected Chang Ch'iao-feng as a candidate.

It had never, even in his dreams, occurred to Chin Chia-kuei that people would give Ch'iao-feng such support. At first he was surprised, then he became bitter, especially toward the women of his own mutual-aid team. "Huh! I led you to progress, but now here you are criticizing my shortcomings. Shame on you!" He wanted to leave the meeting posthaste . . . He did not hear the people welcoming the Party branch secretary, Chin Shih-hsüeh, to speak, nor did he hear the old doctor, Wang Shun-te, speaking. He was not aroused until the chairman had called his name twice.

He pulled himself together, cleared his throat with a cough, and went up to the rostrum. If he had taken this opportunity to review his shortcomings and had urged everyone to vote for Ch'iao-feng instead of himself, people would certainly have praised him; unfortunately, he did not. Instead, he tried to gain back his prestige with a touching speech.

"Fellow villagers, my mutual-aid team was the first in the whole village . . ." He started the same old story again, covering the year before last, to last year, and then to the present. It was a long speech, but lacking anything new.

"Same old story, bragging again!"

"You don't have to chant that 'model liturgy' of yours, we all know it by heart."

Chin Chia-kuei, unaware of these hushed criticisms, continued on. When he finally finished, thundering applause and yelling burst out, but not in response to his long speech, rather to welcome Chang Ch'iao-feng to speak.

Chang Ch'iao-feng was humble and shy. She tried to get away from several women who urged her on, but, giggling, she was finally dragged to the rostrum. This is what Chin Chia-kuei saw: Ch'iao-feng suddenly raised her head, straightened her back, and calmly stood there. Her beautiful rosy face shone brightly, as did her large eyes. She even seemed a little taller. With her finger she brushed back a lock of hair from her forehead and, surprisingly enough without hesitation, she began to speak.

"Fellow villagers, today several things came to my mind that trouble me. First, during the peak wheat season last fall I was planning to mobilize the team members to organize a nursery, this to enable the womenfolk who were tied up with children to work in the fields. However, I was a little sick at that time and feared problems I might encounter. I didn't make a wholehearted effort, and it was all because I was not resolute enough to face the challenge. Secondly, after three years our mutual-aid team still has not become an agricultural cooperative. Here again I haven't worked hard enough. I shall accomplish these two things in the future, whether I'm elected as a representative or not. Furthermore, some women in our village are still abused by men or oppressed by mothers-in-law. I shall do my best to elevate the status of women and fight against such oppression."

Her last words were especially forceful. The whole meeting again burst into stormy applause.

"It's still our Ch'iao-feng who looks ahead instead of chanting that same ancient liturgy!" yelled the straightforward Li Kuei-hua, who ran up, grabbed Ch'iao-feng's shoulders, and laughed herself breathless.

Suddenly, Ch'iao-feng's mother-in-law stood up, clapped her hands and started to mumble.

"This is awful! We only need three representatives for our district, and you have elected four candidates. Who wouldn't vote for the Party branch secretary Chin Shih-hsüeh? As to the old doctor Shun-te, won't everyone vote for him too? That leaves a man and woman from the same house. Who shall we vote for?"

What she really meant was that if her daughter-in-law were elected, her son would certainly be upset; she knew her son well. Many others had also considered this point, but the chairman had adjourned the meeting and nobody wanted to bother with such insignificant matters. Moreover, this, being an election, should be fair. Vote for the best person, regardless of whether it's a man or a woman.

Chin Chia-kuei quickly walked home and sat down dejectedly on the *k'ang*. After a moment he heard Ch'iao-feng talking happily with his mother in the front room, as she helped her with the cooking.

"So, you! . . ." he gritted his teeth angrily and muttered. Suddenly he yelled in a rude voice:

"Ch'iao-feng, come here!"

Ch'iao-feng came in, her hands covered with flour, her face still beaming with joy.

"You, what did you think you were saying a moment ago at the meeting?"

"What did I say?" Ch'iao-feng was startled.

"You said you would fight against the oppression of women by men. Who's oppressing you?"

"I didn't mean you . . . What's the matter with you?"

"Why did you have to say those things at today's meeting? You also said that in three years our team has not yet become a cooperative. What are you trying to do to me?"

"So, this is the kind of person you really are!" said the gentle, guileless Ch'iao-feng, also becoming angry.

The two argued back and forth, both becoming so upset that they did not eat.

The old woman also became too disturbed to eat. She could not say that her daughter-in-law was wrong, nor could she stand to blame her son at that moment. All she could do was wring her hands, stamp her feet, and sigh. Finally she could stand it no longer and ran out looking for someone to talk to, heedless of the consequences.

She first found the chair of the women's association. "Oh, chairman, I told you not to nominate them both as candidates. Since they've been married, they have never had such a quarrel. They won't even eat . . ." Next she went to look for Li Kuei-hua, and rattled off the story in detail again from beginning to end.

Wang Ts'ui-jung and Li Kuei-hua were both angry. In addition, Yin Hsiao-chen, who lived next door to the Chins, had heard the quarrel distinctly, especially Chin Chia-kuei's loud voice as he purposely tried to outshout his opponent. Before long, all the women of the village plus some of the men were outraged, and were blaming Chin Chia-kuei.

That night a formal election was held. The results surprised even those who had been anticipating. Chin Chia-kuei, who was defeated, got only three votes. Chang Ch'iao-feng, on the other hand, was elected almost unanimously.

This was too heavy a blow for Chin Chia-kuei and he left the meeting before it was adjourned. His mother followed him sighing . . . When Wang Tsui-jung and Chin Shih-hsüeh came to the house with Ch'iao-feng, Chia-kuei was lying motionless on the *k'ang*, his head buried under the quilt. They called him, but he did not answer. He was like a person who had been crushed by overwhelming public opinion.

His mother, who obviously had given up pacifying him, also went to sleep. She tossed and turned, sighed and mumbled to herself on the *k'ang* in the opposite room.

Chin Chia-kuei still did not utter a word, so Ch'iao-feng asked the chairman and the secretary to go home; she wanted to talk to Chia-kuei alone. After the two had left, she pulled the quilt back from his face and saw tears in his eyes. She kissed his cheek, and said softly,

"I'm not angry with you, but you must realize . . ."

"I . . . realize . . ." He spoke hoarsely, tears falling from the corners of his eyes.

Translated by Richard I.F. Chang

LIU PIN-YEN

(1920?–)

In April 1956, a report entitled "At the Bridge Site" appeared in the monthly *People's Literature.* It stirred up a storm because, as editor Ch'in Chao-yang commented, the report revealed the complex forces contributing to conservatism that bred a decaying Party bureaucracy. The author, Liu Pin-yen, a Party member since the mid-1940s, was then one of the editors of the *Youth Daily* —an assignment he had earned with his reputation as a translator of several Russian plays.

Not long after the publication of "At the Bridge Site," Liu followed with two reports supposedly dealing with confidential information restricted to the editorial office of a certain important publication. All three reports were received as exposés baring some of the deep-rooted political problems in the People's Republic.

Denounced during the Anti-rightist Campaign of 1957, Liu remained in obscurity through the Cultural Revolution. The verdict against Liu was reversed, however, in January 1979.   —K.Y.H.

---

from At the Bridge Site

[The line between reportage, what may be called the feature story in Western journalism, and the short story as fiction is rather thin in the People's Republic. Theoretically, the former is supposed to be true to facts, but the ideological guidelines for both remain the same.

The present story is a report, hence its characters and events are meant to be real. It starts with a long flashback, about two-fifths of the entire report, recalling the author's visit to a bridge construction site on the Yellow River a few years back and presenting three main characters: Lo Li-cheng, the chief of the construction crew and a veteran Party member who had been through the War of Liberation with the author and later became an expert in bridge construction, but also became conservative in his work style and life; Chou Wei-pen, director of engineering services at the construction site, who shares Lo's conservatism; and Tseng Kang, a younger engineer who dares to assume responsibilities and make decisions. Episodes are related to portray these three different personalities and the conflict between them.]

Two days after I returned from the great bridge at Ling-k'ou, Crew Chief Lo and Engineer Tseng had a talk. It began as a personal talk, but ended by becoming strictly business—one might even say, political.

Perhaps because he had not been to Crew Chief Lo's home for a long while, as soon as Tseng Kang walked in he felt tense all over, like a young student entering the examination hall when he can't count on the test going well.

Crew Chief Lo was nevertheless still the same as he had been when Tseng Kang was last there two years before. With affable naturalness he bade Tseng Kang sit in his own broken-down swivel chair, and then went to make tea.

They exchanged platitudes about the weather and the news of the crew, and then Lo Li-cheng smoothly led their conversation to the topic at hand.

"It's not simple, no, not by any means," said Lo Li-cheng in a drawn-out voice, "but accomplishments in the building up of our fatherland these past few years have been nothing short of astounding. Do you still remember the time when we were building wooden bridges? Just compare then to now. Really! In those days we would not even have ventured to imagine it. . . ." He swallowed half a cup or more of cold tea in one gulp, and then continued: "Of course, it's not as though there are no shortcomings. Sure there are. Take you and me, for example. For us, with our levels, to take on such responsibilities . . . who would dare to claim no deficiencies? There are deficiencies, sure there are. . . ."

From Lo Li-cheng's tone of voice, Tseng Kang knew that these words were a conversational opening, and that the denial would follow immediately to negate what had just been said. First confirm, then deny; a pro and then a con: this formula was exceptionally strong. As expected, Lo Li-cheng's glance became even more sincere and moving, and his tone grew even more forceful:

"But no matter how many defects there may be, accomplishment is still the main thing. Whoever overlooks this point is making a mistake. Take bridge-building—take our crew, for instance. Some have criticized us, citing our waste and our cost overruns; and these are undeniable facts. If we lost money, we lost money, that's all. But the bridge? The bridge construction is progressing! Before we came, there was no bridge along this stretch of the Yellow River, but when we have gone, there will be a bridge here. From nothing to something—that's accomplishment. Sure, we've spent a little more money. But we will have built the bridge! . . ."

As he went on and on, he fished from his pocket a thin sheet of white paper, a galley proof of an article, and handed it to Tseng Kang. As soon as he saw it, Tseng Kang understood. It was an article written by a correspondent from the Third Team. So all this talk had been because of this! He laughed.

His laugh didn't really mean anything, but Lo Li-cheng's expression suddenly changed; he stood up and paced back and forth on the dirt floor, and then said sternly:

" 'The leadership is conservative!' 'Conservative!' Based on what? That our production goals have been lowered a bit? That we've fallen behind quota? But this was approved by the Bureau! And it's the same for all the sections and crews under the Engineering Bureau. Calling the bridge crew leadership conservative is the same as calling the leadership of the Engineering Bureau conservative. Such things shouldn't be said so blithely. . . ."

Tseng Kang knew that this debate could get them nowhere. He had long been planning to lay these questions out for thorough discussion, but this was not the right place; it would be best done at a Party Committee meeting. Wanting to wind up this conversation, he remarked casually:

"This article mainly commends the workers' enthusiasm for their work. Isn't the title 'Young Vanguards of Bridge Crew's Third Team Launch Quota-Doubling Campaign'? The conservatism of the leadership is only mentioned once. . . ."

Lo Li-cheng suddenly planted himself right in front of Tseng Kang, looked him straight in the eye, and said very sternly:

"Yes, yes, that's precisely the problem. Think about it carefully, pal. The workers want to undertake a doubling of quotas: isn't that the same as saying that the official quota is too conservative? Aren't conservative quotas the same as saying that the leadership of the Engineering Bureau is conservative? Any discerning person can see that at a glance. OK, that's number one. What's even more important is that some of the other teams cannot meet even a single quota. What will happen if our superiors in the Ministry find this out? They'll order the Engineering Bureau to push the same campaign in all the teams. And that would really put the chief of the Bureau on the spot, since it clearly couldn't be done. But of course the Ministry would be bound to say that if the bridge crew can do it, then why can't the other crews? And that's the least that would happen. If the comrades in charge at Party Central found out about this, things might be rough even for the Ministry's leadership—they'd have to instigate the same drive nationwide. . . ."

"What's wrong with that?" Tseng Kang asked. Though he felt his anger rising, he couldn't help feeling that Lo Li-cheng's manner of speaking was laughable. "Let's all exceed our quotas: what's wrong with that?"

"No," Lo Li-cheng extended a hand, as if to block the other's mouth, "the problem is that it's not feasible! Ten fingers have never been of equal length. I know that there was such a campaign in the Soviet Union—called 'Double Quotas'—but that's the Soviet Union. No, it just wouldn't work. It's no good importing Soviet gimmicks to China. China has her own unique points. For example, in the Soviet Union one can criticize the leaders, but not in China. When a major movement like the 'Three Antis' or 'Five Antis' is to be undertaken, and when there is a directive from the Central Government, it's OK to criticize. Normally, when there is no directive, we cannot criticize the Bureau; if we want to criticize, it has to be authorized by the Bureau. In the Soviet Union they have a penchant for rushing things, but in China we prefer stability. That's another unique feature of China. If we pay greater heed to China's uniqueness in all things, we won't make mistakes. Do you understand? . . ."

Now it was Tseng Kang who stood up. He had heard such talk more than once, and it was precisely because he had heard it more than once that he could bear it no longer. He wanted to pour out to Lo Li-cheng all those opinions which he had pondered so often, but he didn't know where to begin. If he spoke, it would have to be forcefully, so that the other would be unable to retaliate. Thus he hesitated for a moment before speaking his piece:

"Enough, Crew Chief Lo! The things you don't like you say run counter to China's uniqueness and therefore can't be implemented. The things you like you say must be done this way because of China's uniqueness. No, that just won't wash. Answer me this, Crew Chief Lo: can it be that these are China's only unique characteristics? Production conditions are backward, there aren't enough machines, the leaders give no encouragement, and yet the workers still want to undertake double quotas. Isn't this a feature of China? You speak only of the characteristics of backwardness; do you mean that these characteristics don't need to be changed at all? Since the workers aren't highly skilled, the machinery frequently breaks down, and when the machinery isn't working, the only thing we can do is to use human labor. Granting that this is a characteristic of China, then what harm to China if we raise the workers' skills? The cadres' education is at a low level, and the workers are culturally limited, so all we can do is to have more meetings, long meetings; this is a characteristic of China. But if you have meetings every day, meeting after meeting, the cadres needn't think, and the workers have no way to learn; how can they advance? . . ." He wanted to go on, but he suddenly saw that Lo Li-cheng's eyes were already heavy with sleep, as though he hadn't heard these words at all, and so he did not continue.

Lo Li-cheng hadn't the slightest interest in these abstract questions. He had always limited his concern to tangible problems. At that moment what he was thinking about was how this conflagration could be squelched . . . Don't let the article get in the press, don't let this troublesome quota-increasing campaign get started. He also considered the possible reactions of the Bureau Chief and his deputy to all of this in the event that it could not be quashed. . . .

As always, just when Tseng Kang's anger was at its height, Lo Li-cheng led the conversation to a more peaceful topic; he quite seriously began to discuss with Tseng Kang how the various preparatory tasks could be completed before the coming of high water, what to do about the outdated cement and the substandard rock, and even how the next crew work meeting should be conducted. By that time, flocks of cawing crows were flying over the roof, and in the tiers of caves on the loess hills opposite the house the lights of many homes were already lit. As for Tseng Kang, he was so tired he wanted to yawn; with one hand he was lightly rapping the table. Lo Li-cheng wrapped up the last subject. He stood up and shook Tseng Kang's hand very warmly, saying:

"Things are always a lot more complicated than we think. I think it would be best not to publish this article in a hurry. We should go over it with the Party Committee secretary. . . ." Only upon seeing no opposition in Tseng Kang's eyes did he venture to add, "As for the matter of the quota-doubling campaign, it's not that I'm against it, but how can we not discuss such a big undertaking with the Party Committee? I think the best thing to do would be to try it out first with the two vanguard groups, and then consider the question of expanding it. . . ."

They had already walked out the door, and Lo Li-cheng had already seen Tseng Kang up to the road when he said in a low voice, as if to one of his own men:

"I'm telling you this only because we're old comrades. Some comrades at Crew Headquarters are saying that you're too narrow-minded, and that you see only shortcomings and not accomplishments. And some of the cadres in charge have asked whether or not this is a kind of anti-Party feeling; if it isn't, then why are you going to such lengths to find fault with the leadership? . . ."

Tseng Kang had been walking toward the riverbank, but when he heard this last remark he suddenly halted. The sky was already quite dark, and the wind blowing across the river made it hard to catch one's breath; it was obviously not the time for conversation. He turned his back to the wind and stood there several seconds; then, without saying a word, he walked away. . . .

On the wall outside the crew chief's office there hung a large wooden box on which "Suggestion Box" was written in large letters. The lock was rusted shut, and no one put any suggestions in. The workers passed Crew Headquarters twice a day going to and from work, yet very seldom did anyone enter the office and sit down to talk. And it was no wonder: since even the opinions and suggestions which had been put into effect were subject to rejection, what was the use of talking? There was an altogether different atmosphere in Crew Headquarters.

The expression used most often at Crew Headquarters was "normal." "Normal" was what was uttered by the heads of the various sections when they reviewed the work of the past seven days at the weekly planning sessions: "normal" was what appeared in the telephoned instructions and in reports to the Bureau.

This so-called "normal" meant that everything that should have been transmitted, disposed of, discussed, and calculated had indeed been done. But any difficulties or problems that remained after all this had been done, or any requests or proposals from the masses were not mentioned.

Crew Chief Lo recognized only the decisions, instructions, regulations, and rules which came from the Bureau; as for all the ideas, suggestions, or procedures coming from the masses, he ignored them, even though they might be just what was needed to implement a directive. And if a suggestion or proposal went beyond the confines of planning or regulations, and Crew Chief Lo had not had time to think of it himself, he would view it with commingled tension and repugnance. If they imprudently violated the status quo of the crew, if they threatened the state of "normalcy" in the crew, or contravened some regulation laid down five years previously, or—and this is especially important—if they didn't happen to pertain to what was currently being advocated by the Bureau, or if they might run counter to "the intentions of the leadership," then they would be regarded with consternation as dissident, and would be deemed "risky."

At every opportunity, Lo Li-cheng would deliver repeated enjoinders to the cadres of the Crew Headquarters and the various teams:

"With us, the most important thing is grasping the intentions of the leaders. We must be understanding with regard to the difficulties of our superiors. At times you might think that the leaders are careless, or that they are dragging their feet, but you can rest assured that they do know what they're doing; there's a purpose to it all. . . ."

In implementing the regulations which came down from above, Lo Li-cheng had always spared no effort, sometimes even at the cost of favorable working conditions. I myself saw one such strange incident.

The original specification of the Engineering Bureau for the square-dressed stone used in masonry arch bridges allowed a tolerance of no more than two centimeters. This was what the Technical Office required of the stonemasons, and anything exceeding two centimeters was simply regarded as waste. After working for half a month and cutting several thousand blocks of stone, of which seventy-five percent did not meet this requirement, the workers were unable to obtain their base pay. The older workers and the technicians had mentioned on numerous occasions that such precision was unnecessary for the

square-dressed stone of a stone arch bridge. Moreover, the texture of the stone
was actually too coarse; either the corners fell off, or it split. The dispute became
quite heated, and Director Chou of the Engineering Office went to the work site
for an on-the-spot look. Actually, it was not that the workers were lazy or their
skill inadequate; this kind of stone was just unsuitable for fine work. Returning
to Crew Headquarters, Chou reported the situation to Crew Chief Lo, the two
exchanged views, and then Crew Chief Lo signed an order to the stone-working
team:

"... In order to guarantee the quality of the stone arch bridge, specifications
for square-dressed stone shall not be changed arbitrarily; it is necessary to
adhere strictly to the stipulations of the Engineering Bureau and work according to the original specifications. ..."

This matter subsequently caused a commotion in the Engineering Bureau,
which sent someone to make an inspection. The specified tolerance for square-
dressed stone was broadened fourfold to eight centimeters, and it was felt that
this would have no effect whatsoever on the sturdiness of the bridge. Then they
went to find the several thousand reject stone blocks, but they had disappeared
without a trace—they had been used by the Municipal Construction Bureau to
pave roads.

In this respect, Lo Li-cheng had always done too much rather than too little.
If the Bureau wanted everyone in the crew to be reminded of safety, then Crew
Headquarters would have the workers discuss it three times. If the Bureau said
that a study session would have to be organized to discuss safety, then the
bridge crew would be making reports and holding all kinds of discussions
every night for a whole week. But after that week had passed, Crew Headquarters could forget all about the matter of safety. This is what is known as
"dissemblance."

Director Chou Wei-pen of the Engineering Office was the first to catch on to
this "spirit." No harm done if one frequently utters the words "not enough" in
all matters. For things such as the technical proposals and procedures submitted by the various teams, the Engineering Office would always increase the
assurance factor by twenty percent over the original base. Several hundred tons
of concrete, steel, and lumber were absolutely wasted under the demand of
"striving for safety." But no one could pin the blame on Director Chou; "Safety
First" was the directive from above, you know, and of course not one cent went
into Chou Wei-pen's own pocket! ...

There was one occasion in the Party Committee office when I spoke with
Party Committee Secretary Chang Chih-hua about this problem of "dissemblance." Having heard what I had to say about conditions I had witnessed
during this period, he shredded a leaf of tobacco into his pipe, which was worn
shiny from use, and laboriously drew on it awhile until the tobacco leaf was
more or less alight. A sardonic smile suddenly appeared on his face, as though
he had thought of some past unpleasantness:

"Outsiders as well as the people in the Bureau say that as for the chief of the
bridge crew, he's really strong in organization and discipline. Nobody else asks
for instructions as often as he does, and the bridge crew carries out the instructions of the Bureau with the greatest resolve. That is indeed a fact. But after
all, what is organization and discipline? He doesn't study the policies of the

Central Committee, and if the decisions and instructions of the Central Committee aren't accompanied by orders from the Bureau, he doesn't pay attention to them. He seldom reads the editorials in the Party paper; he says that they are written with a view toward 'conditions in general,' whereas the crew is a 'specific case' and is thus not the same. . . ." He drew fiercely at his pipe, choked and coughed a bit, and then said: "He has one guideline: if someone doesn't do things according to the newspaper editorials, even under the worst circumstances he would not be punished for that. That doesn't count as a mistake. And if the Party's policy is contravened by adhering to administrative orders, well, the lower levels wouldn't be held responsible. That's his logic. . . ."

Listening to the words of this emaciated comrade, whose face was pale due to anemia, I could more or less understand what the major difficulties were in his daily work.

The crew chief was a member of the Party Committee. He had never opposed the majority resolutions at the Party Committee meetings, and he ordinarily respected the opinions of the Party Committee secretary. But the right conditions had to exist in order to implement any resolution or view. Many of these conditions could not emerge without administrative support and action, and the administrative leader—the crew chief, in this case—could always point out scores of concrete difficulties as excuses for postponing things with which he was not totally pleased or things which he did not consider urgent. And yet no one could reprimand him, because he of course did not oppose the resolutions of the Party Committee.

When the Party Committee secretary had been there for three months he could see that things were not moving ahead properly, and so he put his main effort to the task. Relying on his political savvy, acquired through lengthy political work, he spotted the third team right away. Tseng Kang of the third team assisted the Party Committee secretary in three ways: as an administrative leader and chief engineer, he did his best to create conditions in his own team, organized true competitions in accordance with Party Committee resolutions, and put into practice every feasible and rational proposal from the workers; as a member of the Youth League Committee, he first established three watchdog posts in the third team, which was a major impetus to reforms in administrative management and construction organization; and lastly, as a comrade, he spent a month's time helping the Party Committee secretary, a layman, to become thoroughly acquainted with the theory of bridge construction and the fundamental principles of organizing construction work.

What Chang Chih-hua originally had in mind was to first set an example in the third team and have the other teams follow it, and this would impel the leaders at Crew Headquarters to improve their own work. But this task turned out to be a lot more complicated than he had imagined. It was easy to teach the other teams a couple of the experiences of the third team, but it was a lot harder to effect a turnaround in the basic attitude of the crew chief and the strong influence it had upon the various divisions and teams. If this influence were not changed, then even good innovations would soon deteriorate. When the Youth League watchdog posts of the third team were extended to the fifth team, they suddenly became "commendation" posts; each time one person was criticized, five others were praised on the blackboards and in wall posters. This was an idea suggested by the crew chief after he had come, saying that it was necessary to do more praising and complimenting lest the watchdog posts became alienated from the masses. The watchdog posts had been established in the second team for only five days when thirteen instances of procrastination, negligence, and irresponsiblity in the work of the team and of Crew Headquarters were revealed. On the seventh day, the secretary of the Youth League branch returned from Crew Headquarters and with knit brows relayed the opinion of Crew Chief Lo: the main task of the watchdog posts was to supervise issues among the workers, and they should not level attacks at the leadership; if this were to continue, it might threaten the leadership's authority. . . .

. . . .

The Lo Li-cheng I remember was the man who came south with the army in 1949, carrying a heavy pack and traveling at night beneath the moon and stars along the route of the Peking-Hankow railway. Our job then was truly difficult: we had to recruit and train the workers ourselves, and to find our own tools and materials. And the deadlines for rush bridge-building were very tight.

How many evenings we sat by the fire outside our tent, drying our drenched clothing and chatting idly about everything under the sun! How can young people gazing into a burning fire not think about anything and everything?

"After the war's over, I want to keep on building bridges," Lo Li-cheng said. "I'll study up on the technology, get a group of men and some machinery— there'll be machinery then—and go to the Yellow River and the Yangtze and build one bridge after another! . . . Without bridges, there can be no roads. And when the bridge-builders have gone, those who come after needn't fear big rivers or gorges; they can all just zip right on across. . . ."

Our conversation drifted from building bridges to building cars, tractors, tanks, and cannon, and then returned to building bridges.

"Have you ever seen an arch bridge?" Lo Li-cheng asked the men around the fire, and then answered himself, "They're the most magnificent. Just like ribbons. Now we can only build stone arch bridges, but wouldn't it be great if we could build steel arch bridges across the Yellow River and the Yangtze? . . ."

Seemingly somewhat abashed at his own fantasy, he grinned. The firelight shone on his ruddy face, on his shining eyes. . . .

In six years' time, what had formerly been a dream had now come to pass. It was none other than Lo Li-cheng who had already built more than one bridge across the Yellow River, and China's first large arch bridge was being erected under his command. The strange thing was that Lo Li-cheng was not excited by any of this. Of course, in reviewing the achievements of the past few years, it wasn't that he felt no pride; his tired face would reveal a smile, but in a moment it would be gone.

Yes, Lo Li-cheng had changed. The tempering of these past few years had made him much more mature than before, but time had seemingly imbued him with something else as well. I am at a loss to give a clear account of this change, yet I remember the old Lo Li-cheng as being interested in everything, and always wanting to have a hand in things himself. But now, he had a dislike for concrete, complex matters. At several Crew Headquarters planning meetings, the various section chiefs would bring up questions—for instance, questions like the irrationality of quotas following the implementation of piecework wages, and workers' opinions—and what I saw in the face of the taciturn Lo Li-cheng was always a mixed expression of indifference and impatience. . . .

Speaking of his change, there's one other thing. When he saw something that didn't jibe with his own view, or something he didn't understand, he never doubted himself, but would often disparagingly pick it apart, or even ridicule it:

"Did you see? Engineer Tseng Kang is reading *Dream of the Red Chamber*," he suddenly said, his mouth next to my ear. Seeing that I was perplexed, he repeated himself: "A member of the Youth League Committee and an engineer, reading *Dream of the Red Chamber*! Interesting! Most interesting!"

I wanted to ask him what was so strange about that. The strange thing to me was a bridge crew chief and Party Committee member who didn't pick up a newspaper for weeks and who never read novels. . . .

One evening at the end of April, I caught a ride with Crew Chief Lo from the Ling-k'ou bridge site back to Crew Headquarters. He was driving the car himself, and I sat in the seat next to him. It was a blustery day, and the car was creeping forward through vast clouds of yellow sand. The little flagstaff on the front of the car was quivering, whipped by the gale. Grains of sand entered the jeep through every crack, and I seemed to sense the sand gradually piling up between the roots of my hair.

My friend was in a very strange mood that day. He said nothing from the time we got into the car, but frowned out through the windshield at the swirling sand, turning the steering wheel carefully with both hands.

After we had traveled about ten minutes or so, he suddenly spat vehemently. I thought he was trying to spit the sand out of his mouth, but then he said: "A bunch of firebrands!"

Then I knew that he was thinking about the meeting he had just had with the workers of the third team. A misunderstanding had arisen: Crew Chief Lo had originally come to give a report to everyone, but the workers had inundated him with a clamor of suggestions. Naturally he was less than pleased.

"Have you ever led troops?" he asked, inclining his head slightly toward me, but keeping his eyes ahead. "There's an old saying, 'Leading soldiers is like leading tigers.' I think that leading workers must be a lot harder than leading troops. I really envy the troop cadres. In the army, there's no need to have the soldiers discuss battle plans, let alone offer suggestions to the commander. . . . But here, the fact that there are a lot of talkers is the least of my problems. There's no telling but that one of these days they'll stir up a real mess for you. And if something happens, the leaders are right in the line of fire. . . ."

I disagreed, saying that even though the workers liked to make suggestions, they still had respect for specialized knowledge and labor discipline. I had been with the bridge crew for more than half a month and had yet to see subordinates fail to carry out any order from Crew Headquarters.

"But they're so full of opinions! They're asking for the sky, and I can't just completely ignore their demands." Lo Li-cheng shook his head vigorously.

"Also, do you have any idea how many opportunities there are for us bridge workers to make mistakes? What with wind and rain, floods and ice floes, and Ol' Man Heaven not bothering to solicit your opinion in the matter. That's number one. And there's no way to see or fathom how things are beneath the water. That's number two. And we can't neglect policies, decisions, or instructions from above. That's number three. And now there's a fourth—the people's inspectorate, supervision by the construction banks, the opinions of the workers. . . ."

"I often think that since we have the correct leadership of the Party, what else do we need to do?" He paused for a moment, as though giving me a chance to think of how to answer this question, and then after a bit he continued in measured tones: "There's only one requirement: Don't make mistakes! If you avoid making mistakes, you have won a victory! That's the only requirement, but it's very hard to fulfill. . . ."

These words did sound reasonable, but they were not completely correct. Only when I had connected these words with all I had seen and heard during my time with the bridge crew did I understand their meaning. Assume that at that moment we were riding not in a car but on a ship. This sailor was saying: Alright, let's stop here; this way we'll be safe, and not run aground. . . . No, the purpose of sailing is not to avoid running aground, and the purpose of working should not be to avoid making mistakes!

Watching Lo Li-cheng, his lips pinched in deep thought, I felt that now I finally understood him.

. . . .

At the end of April, the waters of the Yellow River darkened. This was a warning of high water soon to come. The bridge men here had to face the threats of Nature twice a year: high water in spring and ice floes in winter.

As they watched the water level rise day by day and the flow grow swifter and swifter, the workers' anxiety mounted even faster. If they didn't rush to keep the piers built up higher than the water level, they would be throwing away half a year's time, and would have to wait until fall, when the high water receded, before they could resume construction. The pace of work suddenly accelerated.

The flood was relentless. It wanted to win. It descended on the bridge project, rushing and surging every which way and seeking to upend the sheet-steel pilings which stood in the middle of the river.

The hydrographic station telephoned several times a day to report on the water level and flow rate. The number of days left for safe construction could not be counted on the fingers of one hand. But construction of two piers of the two great bridges on the Yellow River continued. There was a danger that the sheet-steel pilings would collapse.

On May 7, the sheet-steel pilings of pier 1 of the arch bridge began to lean backward on the upstream side. Should construction work continue? Or should the sheet-steel pilings first be strengthened? The engineer in charge couldn't decide, so he asked Crew Headquarters what to do. Crew Chief Lo ran over to the bridge to take a look, and then ran back again, his brows furrowed in intense concentration and worry: If we go on, we might not be able to make it, and if the steel pilings collapse or someone is drowned, what then? If we stop, the high water might rise too fast for us to keep the piers built up above the water level, and who could assume that responsibility? A decision has to be made, and right away. But it's too difficult. No matter how I decide, success is uncertain, and there's a seventy percent chance of making a mistake. I'll have to be responsible, but how can I bear such a responsibility? . . .

Yet in a crisis there sometimes arises wisdom: Ask the Engineering Bureau for instructions! There was no better way. If only the division chief or the bureau chief would pass judgment on the matter, then all problems, all difficulties would cease to exist.

So Crew Chief Lo picked up the phone. The division chief was out, and so was his deputy. They were still out the second time he picked up the phone. The third time, the operator went to call the division chief out of a meeting. But Crew Chief Lo had been to the riverbank to see things for himself, while the division chief had no idea how the water situation was. Of course he had to think it over. They agreed that he would call back that night to give the division's considered opinion on the matter.

At five in the afternoon, when Crew Chief Lo had only just gotten through to the division chief on the phone, the round steel piling was flattened to an ovoid shape, and the whole thing was lying over on its back. The workers on shore were making ready to go save the machinery in it, but it was already too risky and no one would let them go. At half past five, the timbers of the catwalk began to creak and groan, and by six o'clock that evening the catwalk in front of the steel piling had been swept asunder by the current. Around seven, Director Chou was still in his office waiting for a phone call when there came from outside cries of alarm and sounds of confusion. Without looking, Lo Li-cheng knew what had happened. But he walked with the crowds toward the riverbank. By the time he got there, the steel piling was gone without a trace. A worker next to him was crying:

"A piling of more than a hundred sheets of steel! How can we dredge for it?"

"We've got to dredge it up; the bridge pier has got to be built at this spot. . . ."

"The pumps have been swept away, too. . . ."

The workers were discussing the damage caused by this disaster. The crew chief knew more clearly than they; he had thought of it long ago. Dredging expenses, material expenses, the expense of lost working time . . . if you wanted, he could have figured it all out within ten minutes. But he was thinking of something else:

"Oh, how fortunate, how very fortunate, that I had already gotten through on the phone—no matter what, I did ask for instructions. . . ."

. . . .

During that same period, another thing happened at the Ling-k'ou bridge.

The Ling-k'ou bridge was some several miles distant from the great arch bridge. The high water which beat against the piers of the great arch bridge would reach the piers of the Ling-k'ou bridge just several minutes later.

On the morning of May 7, when Tseng Kang emerged from his tent near the bridgehead, the water of the river was sweeping almost level with the top of pier 5, and down below, the foundation was only six inches or more short of being finished. But the high water might knock out the catwalk at any time, cutting off the workers' retreat, and it might at any moment force its way into the pier works and bury the workers inside.

"If the pier doesn't stay above water, no train could use this rail bridge."

"Look at that head of water! It'll soon be as tall as you!"

"No matter what, we've got to get it up!"

There was a hubbub of debate among the workers. Tseng Kang immediately assembled the activists to hold a discussion: Was it possible to continue construction work? If so, how could safety be guaranteed?

Before the meeting was over, the foundation workers who had come on shift that morning established an assault team. When this bunch of husky young fellows put on their rubber suits and walked across the trembling catwalk to work, they were not without apprehension: the high water had but to lash out in a sudden fury and they would surely be stranded out there. But everyone knew how vital these next eight hours were to be, and they had faith that the engineer in charge and the veteran workers knew what they were doing and would not leave them in the lurch.

Preparations had been made the day before. The catwalk had been repaired and all the steel cables inspected. The pumps at the bottom of the sheet-steel piling had been replaced, an extra row of braces had been added to the piling's midsection, and a ring of sandbags had been placed around the top. And numerous other procedures had been thought up at the meeting that day. The plan was to hold out till the last second if they could, but if water conditions changed drastically, work would be halted at once. . . .

Beneath the water, the crusher bored through the rock at a faster pace, making a continuous roar. A man had been stationed atop a ladder to watch the shore, his hand clutching a switch. At a wave of the flag on the bank, he would kill the green light and turn on the red light ordering the workers to retreat. But none of the workers had time to look up and watch the lights.

Every slight rise in the river water was noticed immediately down in the sunk shaft. By noon, the water was above the workers' knees, and by two in the afternoon the braces of the sheet-steel piling had buckled under the flood, and water was gushing in through the seams of the piling. The workers did not dare to stand upright—if they did, they would get water all down their necks. In surge after surge the water flooded in, and the large pipes of the pumps could not draw it off fast enough. The workers stuck to their tasks as the sunk shaft slowly sank. . . .

At that moment, the phone rang in the team office. No one was there to answer it. A few minutes later it rang again, and still no one answered. The phone went on ringing insistently, and finally a worker passing by on his way to work went in and picked up the receiver. The voice at the other end said that according to their understanding the catwalk at the Ling-k'ou bridge was no longer serviceable, and it would have to be torn down immediately. The worker told him that the catwalk had already been repaired yesterday, and that it couldn't be dismantled now—how would the men down in the sunk shaft get back? The voice at the other end was silent for a moment, and then said that construction must be halted, that they should wait for instructions from the Bureau, and that he wanted Engineer Tseng to come to the phone. The worker put down the receiver and walked off toward the work site. He saw Engineer Tseng at the end of the bridge and was going to tell him to come answer the phone, but on second thought he decided not to. The rush job was more important, and right now no one would be willing to drop what he was doing if asked. So he took off his cotton coat, donned his rubber jacket, and mounted the catwalk. . . . The phone lay there in the office, and no one paid it any heed.

Down in the sunk shaft, the water was still rising. The men had been working for four hours, and they were weary; the grit was choking, and the air was foul. Tseng Kang ordered that the system of three eight-hour work shifts be changed to four six-hour shifts, and that a group of men be on constant standby to relieve the overtired workers.

. . . Dawn had just broken when the sunk shaft was finished. When the last shift of workmen filed up the ladder above water level, their ears had been deafened by the pounding, but in their hearts there burned the torch of true elation. Upon reaching the top, without heed for the fact that the catwalk was already awash, they shouted toward the shore at the tops of their lungs:

"We made it!"

"It's all done!"

"No problem here!"

The men on the bank had long been awaiting this news. . . . Everyone breathed a sigh of relief: these past twenty-four hours had been really dangerous. But they didn't stay happy for long. A few minutes later they received some discouraging news: pier 1 of the arch bridge had collapsed under the flood.

. . . .

Before leaving the bridge crew, I came to the edge of the river to say goodbye to the unfinished arch bridge. . . . I said goodbye to Crew Chief Lo and Director Chou. It was already twilight, and the work site was bathed in silence. Usually at this time the workers would have been moving back and forth changing shifts; it was the time of greatest activity. After the collapse of pier 1, the various projects had all been halted, and the entire work site went into mourning over this misfortune. Viewing this scene, I could not help sighing. Lo Li-cheng sighed along with me. But I knew from his most recent report to the Bureau that he didn't consider himself responsible for the pier 1 incident. The high water had come too early, and what could one do in the face of natural calamities! . . .

I suddenly thought of one of Director Chou's favorite sayings, and said sardonically, "It's not easy building bridges, you know!"

"That's right, it's not easy," echoed Director Chou at once; "It's fortunate that this time no one was killed or injured. Such a great flood! And it came so suddenly! It wasn't simple, to avoid losing life. . . ."

Crew Chief Lo immediately raised the question to a philosophical level, saying, "Yes, yes, unavoidable. And why didn't Ol' Man Heaven consult us? It never works when you try to do things based only on subjective desires. Unavoidable, simply unavoidable. . . ."

I wanted to ask: Wouldn't it have been better not to let the pier collapse and still avoid personnel accidents? The Ling-k'ou bridge of the third team was on the same river as the arch bridge, and weren't they able to avoid an "unavoidable" disaster?

Throughout my journey, my thoughts revolved incessantly around this question.

. . . .

[Five months later, in October 1955, Chairman Mao's report "On the Question of Agricultural Cooperation" was published. There followed a wave of rectification in the nation's economic reconstruction efforts. The kind of bureaucratic conservatism exemplified by Crew Chief Lo was exposed and erased case after case, replaced by a high tide of labor enthusiasm.]

In February I went to the Northwest on a reporting assignment, and on the way I suddenly thought of my old friend Lo Li-cheng and his bridge crew. What was this old fellow up to now? Was he still his old imperturbable self? Or had he had to sweat through reading a much-revised self-critique at a mass rally? Thinking of all this, I couldn't help wanting to laugh.

I decided to stop off and pay him a visit on the way.

A twenty-minute bus ride from Kao-lan Municipality brought me to the township of Hsi-kang. From there I still had to cross several mountains to get to where the bridge crew headquarters was.

A heavy snow had just fallen. Walking along the level stretch of road was easy, but going up the mountain was a bit taxing. The old sheepskin coat I was wearing suddenly seemed to have gained fifteen pounds, and by the time I had crossed the second peak I was tired and sweaty. . . .

From behind me there came the crunch of footsteps in the snow. Looking back, I saw that two workmen had caught up with me. The shorter of the two was wearing a brown cotton overcoat covered with grease and grime. Seeing me, he suddenly stopped, and then came running over in great strides to shake my hand. It turned out to be Chang Kuang-fa, the crane worker who had taught me to recognize all the knots. We walked off toward Crew Headquarters together. During this walk of about a mile, he filled me in on all that had happened in the bridge crew during the past six months, first with excitement, then with indignation. His face was flushed and was steaming in the cold, and there was an exceptional contrast between the whites and pupils of his eyes which displayed a certain youthfulness. I wondered why he made no mention at all of Engineer Tseng, whom he thoroughly revered. When I asked about Tseng, he suddenly halted and, staring at me in astonishment, asked:

"What? You didn't know that Engineer Tseng was transferred away a long time ago?"

Now it was my turn to be astonished. Then he said:

"That was in June, more than half a year ago. . . ."

His companion, who had said nothing all the way, now suddenly spoke up to correct him:

"What do you mean, June? It was at the end of May. We were still wearing our quilted cotton clothes...."

"That's right, it was the end of May," Chang Kuang-fa continued seriously. Evidently they regarded this personnel transfer as a major event in the bridge crew. "It was only a few days after the rush job on pier 5 when he was transferred. That's what we heard. During those few days, there were continual meetings at Crew Headquarters, and we thought that they were investigating the collapse of pier 1. Later we found out that they were discussing the problem between Engineer Tseng and Director Chou. They said that neither of them was perfect; Engineer Tseng was haughty and complacent, and Chou Wei-pen had his shortcomings, too.... Finally the leaders decided that they would have to transfer one or the other of them. But I didn't believe that Engineer Tseng had any faults, and I never thought they'd transfer him away...."

"No, that's not exactly right," said the other, slightly taller worker, and only then did I realize that he was a good deal older than Chang Kuang-fa; he must have been at least forty. "Engineer Tseng was not without shortcomings. Arrogant? Yes, he was probably a bit arrogant. But he was a young man, and how could he have avoided making the least little mistake? Take you, Chang Kuang-fa: if it's faults we're looking for, I could find a basketful of yours. Don't you laugh.... What I mean is, you can't look at it just from that one angle. In anything, you have to first find out who is in the right and who is in the wrong. The director and the engineer weren't getting along; you can't say that both of them were in the wrong. Like the old peacemaker's saying, it takes two hands to clap, but this is something different from an argument or a fight...."

"Let's say they were both in the wrong: then how come they only transferred Engineer Tseng? I just can't figure it out!" said Chang Kuang-fa; he then closed his mouth tight, and his face was even redder.

"What Secretary Chang had in mind was not to transfer either of them; if someone had to be transferred, it would be the director. But the Bureau said that if the two of them couldn't get along, they'd have to be separated. It just so happened that the cement products plant had a vacancy to fill. And oddly enough they just had to have someone like Engineer Tseng...."

We had already come to the last slope. We could see the water from melted snow dripping off the roof of the Crew Headquarters office quite clearly. Bidding my two companions farewell, I walked toward Crew Headquarters.

I pushed open the door and walked into the crew chief's office. Lo Li-cheng was bent over his desk in concentration, as though writing something. A closer look revealed that he was repairing a wristwatch! Seeing me enter, he gave a startled gasp and came over to shake my hand with his left hand—his right hand was covered with oily dirt.

Smiling expansively, he chatted with me. He hadn't gotten any thinner at all; his face was as round and ruddy as ever, and in fact he had put on a little weight. Suddenly his face took on a stiff, stern expression, and he asked in a low voice:

"Have you heard of the Central Directive?"

Without waiting for me to reply, he began to brew up some black tea, and said emotionally:

"So wise! Party Central is really infinitely wise! Tell me, how come we're so blockheaded? I guess we're just old dogs who won't learn new tricks!"

There followed a few words of praise for the wisdom of Party Central, and then he looked at me, and suddenly in an indescribably delightful way began to roar with laughter. He took a sip of black tea, and then said:

"Shrinking violets! Ha! We are the shrinking violets of industry! Ha! We had no gumption, no gumption whatsoever! . . ." After his fit of laughter had passed, he wiped away his tears, and said expansively, "Suddenly it all becomes clear, so clear indeed! Who says we aren't conservative? Who says China has no bureaucratism? Huh? Aren't *we* the conservatives, the bureaucrats? . . ."

Lo Li-cheng then went on to mention many instances to prove how conservative "we" had been in the past. He said "we" so many times that from the sound of it his "we" included not only himself but all the cadres and workers as well, as though everyone but Party Central was conservative, and that Lo Li-cheng was merely one among the multitudes.

I reminded him that not long before, people in the bridge crew had come out in opposition to conservatism, but that the conservatives not only had no gumption themselves but would not tolerate gumption in anyone else. They had rebuffed all opinions and suggestions.

He stopped laughing, and without the least concern, casually remarked:

"At that time, wasn't everyone the same? There hadn't been any directive from Central, you know. . . ." He pondered for a moment, and then, as if moved by something, said with sudden agitation:

"That's what Party leadership means, you know! With the leadership of the Party, what need we fear? Huh? What have we to be afraid of? Whatever the problem, Central will think it over from every possible angle, and sooner or later it'll be solved." When he had finished, he laughed again. . . .

It had already become meaningless to sit here any longer; yet I casually asked him a question:

"What kind of progress is the crew making against conservatism?"

"From the bottom up"—it seemed that he was extremely happy to reply to this question—"we're doing it from the bottom up, on a mass scale. First the workers and technicians examine their own conservative thinking, the leaders criticize it, and then the squad leaders and work leaders start examining—the problem of conservative thinking is most severe with these cadres. Then the cadres of each team and each section make self-examinations . . ."

I interrupted him by asking, "When does it become the crew chief's turn?"

Again he laughed. Opening a drawer, he took out a thick document and handed it to me. Then, as though he had it all figured out, he said, "Now, it's all in here, a two-year plan." He walked over and put his hand on my arm, and said warmly, "Write an article and report about us. Write! And if you call us conservative, that's all right . . . Oh, yes! I can find a typical example for you: Director Chou! Director Chou of the Engineering Office!"

A feeling of intense disappointment suddenly rose in my heart, and I was assailed by despair and anger. I had thought that as this upsurge formed throughout the nation, the rejecting of conservatism would at least bring the conservatives to their senses; that shouldn't be too difficult. But I was wrong.

The difficulty lay precisely in the fact that people such as Lo Li-cheng put up no resistance to this tide; the difficulty lay in the fact that this was not solely a question of conservative thinking. . . .

Outside, the gale roared and swirled across the night-clad Yellow River. Through the window one could smell the scent of spring, replete with the breath of life. The northern spring had sent ahead a tempest to clear its path.

My friend was still sitting there, his eyes bleary with sleep.

Oh, Spring Wind, when will you blow into this office?

February 1956

Translated by Philip Robyn;
excerpted by Kai-yu Hsu

WANG MENG

(1934–)

Published in *People's Literature* in September 1956, "The Young Man Who Has Just Arrived at the Organization Department" quickly attracted widespread attention as a manifestation of the Hundred Flowers spirit in literature. Its realistic portrayal of the clash between youthful idealistic revolutionaries and older entrenched Party bureaucrats was viewed by many as an example of how literature could be utilized as a critical tool to improve the existing system. The author of this story, a little-known, twenty-two-year-old Communist Party member named Wang Meng, was praised for his insight and his artistry.

With the end of the Hundred Flowers movement in early 1957 this situation changed dramatically. New interpretations described "The Young Man Who Has Just Arrived at the Organization Department" as fundamentally anti-Party in nature and a large-scale, officially sponsored campaign was mounted against it. During the campaign the story was widely condemned as an example of the excesses committed by those trying to take advantage of the Hundred Flowers movement to weaken Party discipline and promote individual freedom. The editor of the *People's Literature* was attacked for publishing the story and was compelled to recant. Wang Meng himself was sent to the countryside to reform his thought through labor with the masses. He returned to active writing in 1977. His second novel, *Long Live the Youth,* which had been serialized in the *Wen-hui Daily* of Shanghai in 1957, was republished in 1978. More recently his short story "The Most Precious," built on the theme of the lack of moral commitment among the young generation during the Cultural Revolution, has provoked nationwide discussions.   —G. B.

---

from The Young Man Who Has Just Arrived at the Organization Department

CHAPTER I

It was March, with a mixture of rain and snow in the air. Outside the door of the District Party Committee office a pedicab drew to a halt, and a young man jumped down. The driver looked at the large sign above the door and said politely to his passenger, "If you're coming here, there won't be any charge." One of the message center workers, a demobilized soldier called Old Lü, came limping out. After asking why the young man had come, he moved quickly to help unload his bags. This done, he went off to summon the Organization

Department's office secretary, Chao Hui-wen. Chao Hui-wen grasped both of Lin Chen's hands tightly and said, "We've been waiting for you for a long time."

Lin Chen had met Chao Hui-wen while in the teachers' Party Branch in primary school. Two large eyes sparkled with friendliness and affection in her pale, beautiful face. Under those eyes, however, were dark circles caused by a lack of sleep. She led Lin Chen to the men's dormitory, placed his bags in order, and opened them. She also hung his damp blanket up to dry and made the bed. As she was doing these things she continually reached up to arrange her hair, just as any other capable attractive female comrade would do.

"We've been waiting for you for such a long time," she said. "Half a year ago we tried to have you assigned here, but the Cultural and Education Section of the District People's Council absolutely refused to agree. Later on the District Party Committee Secretary went directly to the District Chief and said he wanted you. He also made a fuss at the Education Bureau's personnel office. After all of this we finally got you transferred."

"I only learned about this the day before yesterday," Lin Chen replied. "When I heard that I was being transferred to the District Party Committee I didn't know what to think. What does this District Party Committee of ours do?"

"Everything."

"And the Organization Department?"

"The Organization Department does organizational work."

"Is there a lot of work?"

"At times we're busy. Sometimes we aren't."

Chao Hui-wen took a hard look at Lin Chen's bed and shook her head. "Young man," she said indignantly, in the manner of an older sister, "you haven't been keeping yourself clean. Look at that pillowcase! It's gone from white to black. And look at the top of your blanket. It's completely saturated with oil from your neck. Your sheet is so wrinkled it's like seersucker."

Lin Chen had the feeling that just as he was entering the doors of the District Party Committee and beginning his new life, he was also meeting a very dear friend.

Lin Chen was in an excited holiday mood as he rushed over to the office of the first vice-director of the Organization Department to report his arrival. The vice-director had a peculiar name—Liu Shih-wu.* As Lin Chen knocked nervously on his door, Liu Shih-wu was looking upward, a cigarette in his mouth, thinking about the work plans of the Organization Department. He welcomed Lin enthusiastically, but with a sense of propriety. After offering Lin a seat on the sofa, he himself sat down on the edge of his desk, pushing aside some of the papers that were piled high on the glass top. In a relaxed voice, he asked: "How are things going?" His left eye narrowed slightly. His right hand flicked his cigarette ash away.

"The secretary of the Party Branch told me to come here on the day after tomorrow, but since my work in the school was already finished I came today. Being sent to the Organization Department has made me anxious about my abilities. I'm a new Party member and I was formerly a primary teacher. The work of a teacher in primary school is quite different from the organization work of the Party."

*Literally, Liu, the world and me. [K.Y.H.]

Lin Chen had prepared these words well in advance and spoke them very unnaturally, as if he were really a primary school student who was meeting his teacher for the first time. The room began to feel very warm. It was mid-March. Winter would soon be over. Yet, there was still a fire burning in the room. The frost on the window had melted and turned into dirty streaks. Beads of sweat formed on his forehead. He wanted to pull out a handkerchief and wipe them away, but he could not find one in his pockets.

Liu Shih-wu nodded his head mechanically and, without watching what he was doing, pulled a manila envelope out from a large pile of papers. Opening it, he removed Lin Chen's Party registration form and scanned it rapidly with a keen look in his eyes. Fine lines appeared across his broad forehead and he closed his eyes for a moment. Then, placing his hand on the back of his chair for support, he stood up—as he did so the jacket that had been lying across his shoulders slipped to the floor—and in a skilled effortless voice said, "Good. Fine. Excellent. The Organization Department is short of cadres now. You've come at the right time. No, our work is not difficult. With study and practice you'll be able to do it. That's the way it is. Also, you did a good job in your work at the lower level, right?"

Lin Chen sensed that this praise was given somewhat in jest, so he shook his head and replied apprehensively, "I didn't do my work well at all."

A faint smile appeared on Liu Shih-wu's unwashed face. His eyes sparkled with intelligence as he continued. "Of course, there is the possibility that you will have problems. It is possible. This is very important work. One of the comrades on the Central Committee has said that organization work is the housekeeping work of the Party. If the house is not properly cared for, the Party won't be strong." Without waiting for any questions Liu added an explanation. "What housework are we doing? We are developing and strengthening the Party, making the organization solid, and increasing the fighting power of the Party organization. We are establishing Party life on a foundation of collective leadership, criticism and self-criticism, and close ties with the masses. If we do this work well, the Party organization will be robust, lively, and will have the strength to fight. It will be up to the task of unifying and leading the masses. It will be better able to complete the work of socialist construction and fulfill the various duties of socialist transformation."

After each phrase Liu cleared his throat, except for those expressions which he knew well through repeated use. These he spoke so rapidly that he seemed to be saying one word. For example, when he said, "Let's anchor the life of the Party on . . .," it sounded as though he were saying, "Let's anchor the life of the Party on rata-tat-tat-tat." With the skill of someone manipulating an abacus, he handled concepts that Lin Chen thought were rather obscure and difficult to understand. Even though Lin listened with extreme intensity, he still could not grasp everything that Liu was saying.

Liu Shih-wu went on to assign Lin Chen his work. Then, just as Lin was opening the door to leave he called to him, and in a completely different, easy-going manner asked, "How are you getting along, young man? Do you have a girl friend?"

"No," Lin Chen replied, a touch of redness sweeping across his face.

"A big fellow like you still blushes?" Liu Shih-wu asked with a laugh. "Well, you're only twenty-two. There's no need to hurry. By the way, what's that book you have in your pocket?"

Lin Chen took the book out and read him the title, *"The Tractor Station Manager and the Chief Agronomist."*

Liu reached for the book, opened it to the middle, and read a few lines. "Did the Central Committee of the Youth League recommend this book for you young people to read?"

Lin Chen nodded.

"Lend it to me so I can take a look."

Glancing at the papers piled high on the vice-director's desk, Lin Chen asked in surprise, "Do you have time to read novels?"

Liu Shih-wu placed the book in the palm of his hand and gauged its weight. His left eye squinted slightly as he answered, "What do you mean? I'll read through a thin volume like this in half an evening. I read the four volumes of *And Quiet Flows the Don* in a single week. That's the way it is."

By the time Lin Chen went over to the main office of the Organization Department the sky had already cleared. Only a few clouds remained along the clear bright horizon. Sunlight streamed into the large courtyard of the District Party Committee. Everyone was busy....

Lin Chen stopped for a moment in the portico and looked at the dazzling courtyard. He was very happy about the beginning of his new life.

. . . .

CHAPTER III

Lin Chen had graduated from normal school in the autumn of 1953 and had been sent to serve as a teacher in the central primary school of this district. At that time he was an alternate Party member. Even after becoming a teacher he maintained the practices of his middle school student life. Early in the morning he lifted dumbbells. At night he wrote in his diary. Before every major holiday —May 1, July 1, etc.—he went about asking people for their opinions of him. Some people predicted that within three months he would be "converted" by the older adults whose lives were not so regulated. However, in a short time several teachers were praising him and saying with admiration, "This lad doesn't have any worries or family cares. All he knows is work."

Lin Chen proved himself worthy of such admiration. Because of his accomplishments as a teacher, during the winter recess of 1954 he received an award from the Bureau of Education.

People may have thought that the young teacher would continue on in this steady fashion, living his youthful years in contentment and happiness. But this was not to be. Simple, childlike Lin Chen had worries and concerns of his own.

After another year, Lin Chen was anxiously berating himself even more frequently. Was it due to the press of the high tide of socialism? Was it the result of the convening of the All-China Conference of Young Socialist Activists? Or, was it because he was getting older?

Lin Chen was now already twenty-two. He recalled how in his first year of middle school he had written an essay entitled "When I Am XX Years Old," and how in that essay he had written, "When I am twenty-two I want to . . . " Now he really was twenty-two and the pages of his life history still seemed to be blank. He had no meritorious achievements. He had not created anything. He had not braved any dangers or fallen in love. He had not written one single letter to a girl. He worked hard, but if the amount of work he did and the speed with which he did it were compared to the accomplishments of the young activists or the swiftness with which his life was flying by, of what possible comfort could this be to him? He set forth a plan to study this and study that, to do this and do that. He wanted to cover a thousand things in one day.

It was at this time that Lin Chen received his transfer notice. Now his history could read, "At twenty-two I became a Party worker." Was his real life going to begin from here? Suppressing his love for primary school teaching and the children, he kindled great hopes about his new job. After the secretary of the Party Branch discussed his transfer with him, he stayed up all night thinking about it.

Thus it was that Lin Chen excitedly climbed the stone steps of the District Party Committee, *The Tractor Station Manager and the Chief Agronomist* stuck in his pocket. He was filled with a sacred reverence for the life of a Party worker.

. . . .

[Lin Chen's assignment in the Organization Department is in the Factory Organization Development Section. His section chief, Han Ch'ang-hsin, makes a very favorable first impression on him (Lin Chen thinks to himself, "He's more like a leading cadre than the leading cadres themselves.") and he enthusiastically prepares for his first trip to a factory.

Four days after his arrival, Lin Chen rides his bicycle to the T'ung Hua Gunny Sack Factory to study Party recruitment work. What he finds leaves him shocked and confused. The factory director, a man named Wang Ch'ing-ch'üan, who is concurrently serving as Party Branch Secretary, is domineering, dogmatic, and obviously not very interested in his duties. Worse yet, when Lin suggests to the Party member in charge of recruitment, Wei Ho-ming, that a report on the situation be made to higher authorities, he is told that this has already been done several times with no effect. In Wei's words: "I don't know how many times I've talked to Han Ch'ang-hsin about this. Old Han didn't do anything. Instead, he turned around and gave me a lesson, telling me about the need to respect leadership and strengthen unity. Maybe I shouldn't be thinking like this, but I feel that we may have to wait until Factory Director Wang embezzles some money or rapes a woman before the higher echelons finally sit up and take notice!"

Lin Chen cannot understand how such a situation can be permitted to exist, and he reports excitedly to Han Ch'ang-hsin about what he has learned. Han is unconcerned. He informs Lin that he knows all about Wang Ch'ing-ch'üan and tells him not to worry about matters that are beyond the scope of his duties. This fails to satisfy Lin Chen and he goes to talk to Han Ch'ang-hsin's superior, Liu Shih-wu. Liu openly acknowledges that Wang Ch'ing-ch'üan has made some serious errors, but he asks Lin to be patient, saying that conditions are not yet ripe for resolving the situation.

Lin Chen's talk with Liu Shih-wu eases his mind temporarily, but subsequent visits to the gunny sack factory revive his indignation over Wang Ch'ing-ch'üan's performance. Thinking that he will hasten the "ripening of conditions" mentioned by Liu Shih-wu, he gives his approval to Wei Ho-ming's idea of organizing the workers into a discussion group that will submit complaints about Wang Ch'ing-ch'üan to higher authorities. However, after Wang learns of this plan and accuses Lin of encouraging antileadership activity, it is Lin, not Wang, who receives most of the criticism. At a meeting convened to discuss this matter, Han Ch'ang-hsin complains about Lin's "unorganized and undisciplined activity." Liu Shih-wu notes that Lin, as with most youth, is overly idealistic and reminds him pointedly that he is "definitely not the only person who has principles."

After being subjected to such criticism, Lin Chen is uncertain about what he should do. Should he continue to struggle resolutely on behalf of his high standards? Or, should he put aside this struggle temporarily and wait until he is more knowledgeable and more experienced? A chance meeting with Chao Hui-wen on the following Saturday evening helps him decide which path to follow.]

CHAPTER VII

On Saturday evening Han Ch'ang-hsin was getting married. Lin Chen went into the assembly hall, but he disliked the thick irritating smoke, the candy wrappers scattered about the floor, and the steady roar of loud laughter. Without waiting for the ceremony to begin he made his departure.

The Organization Department office was dark. Lin Chen turned on the light and saw a letter on his desk. It was from his fellow teachers in the primary school. Enclosed inside was another letter signed by the children with their little hands. It read:

"Teacher Lin, how are you? We miss you very very much. All of the girls cried, but they are better now. We have been doing arithmetic. The problems are very hard. We think them over for a long time, but in the end we work them out."

As he read the letter Lin Chen could not refrain from smiling to himself. He picked up his pen, substituted a correct character for an incorrect one, and prepared to tell them in his reply not to use a wrong character when they wrote him again. It seemed as though he was watching Li Lin-lin, with the ribbon in her hair, Liu Hsiao-mao, who loved watercolor painting, and Meng Fei, the one who often held lead pencil tips in his mouth. Abruptly he lifted his head from the letter. Only the telephone, the ink blotter, and the glass desk top were there to be seen. The child's world that he knew so well was already far away. Now he was in an unfamiliar environment. He thought about the criticism leveled at him at the Party committee meeting two days earlier. Was it possible that it was actually he himself who was wrong? Was he really rude and childish, full of the cheap bravery of the young? Maybe he really ought to make an honest self-appraisal. Couldn't he do his own work well for two years or so and wait until he himself had "ripened" before intervening in all of these things?

An explosion of applause and laughter burst from the assembly hall.

A soft hand fell upon his shoulder. Startled, he turned his head and felt the glare of the light pierce his eyes. Chao Hui-wen was standing silently beside him. All women comrades had a talent for walking without a sound.

"Why aren't you over having a good time?" she asked.

"I'm too lazy to go. What about you?"

"I've got to be getting home," Chao Hui-wen replied. "How about coming to my place and relaxing for a while? It's better than sitting here brooding by yourself."

"I don't have anything to brood about," Lin Chen protested. He did, however, accept Chao Hui-wen's kind invitation.

Chao Hui-wen lived in a small courtyard not far from the offices of the District Party Committee. Her son was sleeping in a pale blue crib, sucking contentedly on his fingers. She gave the baby a kiss and drew Lin Chen to her own room.

"Doesn't his father come home?" Lin Chen asked cautiously.

Chao Hui-wen shook her head.

The bedroom looked as though it had been arranged very hastily. The walls were completely bare and because of this they appeared excessively white. A washstand huddled alone in a corner. On the windowsill a flower vase held its empty mouth open like a fool. Only the radio on the small table at the head of the bed seemed capable of breaking the stillness of the room.

Lin Chen sat down on the rattan chair. Chao Hui-wen stood leaning against the wall. Lin Chen pointed to the flower vase and said, "You should put some flowers in it." Pointing to the walls, he asked, "Why don't you buy some paintings and hang them up?" "Since I'm hardly ever here, I haven't given it any thought," Chao Hui-wen replied. Indicating the radio, she asked, "Would you like to listen? There's always good music on Saturday evening."

The light on the radio came on and a dreamy gentle melody floated in from afar. Slowly it became an emotional stimulant. The poetic theme played by the violin seized Lin Chen's heart. He laid his chin on his hands and held his breath. His youth, his aspirations, and his failures all seemed to be transmitted through this music.

Chao Hui-wen leaned against the wall with her hands behind her back, oblivious to the whitewash rubbing off on her clothes. She waited until the movement was completed, and then, in a voice that was itself like music, she said, "This is Tschaikovsky's *Capriccio Italien.* It makes me think of a southern country and the sea. When I was in the Cultural Work Troupe I heard it often, and gradually I came to feel that the melody wasn't being played by someone else, but was boring its way out from my heart."

"You were in the Cultural Work Troupe?"

"I was assigned there after attending the Military Cadre School. In Korea I used my poor voice to sing for the soldiers. I'm a hoarse-voiced singer."

Lin Chen looked at Chao Hui-wen as if he were seeing her for the first time.

"What's wrong? Don't I look like a singer?" At this moment the program changed to "Theater Facts," and Chao Hui-wen turned the radio off.

"If you were in the Cultural Work Troupe, why do you hardly ever sing?"

Chao Hui-wen didn't answer. She walked over to her bed, sat down, and said, "Let's have a chat. Little Lin, tell me, what's your impression of our District Party Committee?"

"I don't know. That is to say, I'm not sure."

"You do have some differences of opinion with Han Ch'ang-hsin and Liu Shih-wu, don't you?"

"Maybe."

"When I first came I was that way, too. Having transferred here from the military, I was making comparisons with military strictness and precision, and there were many things that I couldn't get used to. I made many suggestions and had one spirited argument with Han Ch'ang-hsin. But they made fun of me and said I was childish. They laughed at me for making so many suggestions before I was doing my own work well. Slowly I came to realize that I didn't have enough strength to struggle against the various shortcomings of the District Committee."

"Why not?" Lin Chen exclaimed, leaping to his feet as if he had been stabbed. His eyebrows came together in a deep frown.

"That was my mistake," Chao Hui-wen answered, taking a pillow and placing it on her lap. "At the time, I felt that with my own lack of experience and my own imperfection I certainly wasn't strong enough to be thinking about reforming comrades who were much more experienced than I was. Moreover, Liu Shih-wu, Han Ch'ang-hsin, and some other comrades actually do many things very well. If you scatter their shortcomings among our accomplishments it's like throwing dust into the clear air. You can smell it, but you can't grab hold of it. This is what makes it so hard."

"Right!" Lin Chen responded, smashing his right fist into the palm of his left hand.

. . . .

[After this Chao Hui-wen and Lin Chen discuss what they see as the faults of several leading cadres, including Han Ch'ang-hsin and Liu Shih-wu. The plodding approach of these cadres toward their duties has troubled Chao Hui-wen for a long time and caused her many sleepless nights. Now at last she has an opportunity to vent her frustrations. Lin Chen is deeply moved by what she tells him.]

"Then, . . . what's to be done?" he asked. Only now was Lin Chen beginning to realize how complicated everything was. It seemed that each and every shortcoming was attached to a whole series of causes that ran from the top to the bottom.

"That's true," Chao Hui-wen answered, deep in thought, her fingers tapping on her legs as if she were playing the piano. Looking into the distance, she smiled and said, "Thank you."

"Thank you?" Lin Chen thought that he had heard incorrectly.

"Yes. When I see you I seem to be young again. You often fix your eyes on something and don't move. You're always thinking, like a child who loves to dream. You get excited quite easily and blush at anything. Yet, you are also fearless, willing to struggle against every evil. I have a kind of woman's intuition that you . . . that a big change is on the way."

Lin Chen blushed deeply again. He had simply never thought about these matters and was completely embarrassed by his inability to do anything. "Well," he mumbled, "I hope that it's a genuine change and not just some blind confusion." Pausing a moment, he asked her, "You've thought about this for so long and have made such a clear analysis. Why have you kept everything to yourself?"

"I've always felt that there was nothing I could do," Chao Hui-wen answered. She put her hands across her chest and said, "I look and think, think, and look again. At times I think all night and can't fall asleep. I ask myself, 'You're doing routine office work. Can you understand all of these things?' "

"How can you think such thoughts? I feel that what you've been telling me is absolutely correct. You should tell this to the secretary of the District Party Committee. Or, write it up and send it to the *People's Daily.*"

"Look, there you go again!" Chao Hui-wen's teeth glistened as she said this with a smile.

"How can you say 'There I go again'?" Lin Chen stood up unhappily and scratched his head hard. "I've thought about this many times, too. I feel that people should correct themselves through struggle instead of waiting until they're perfect before they enter the fray."

Suddenly Chao Hui-wen pushed open the door and went out, leaving Lin Chen alone in the empty room. He smelled the fragrance of soap and then in an instant she was back carrying a long-handled saucepan. She skipped in like one of those little girls who comb their hair into three braids, took the cover off the pan, and said dramatically, "Let's eat some water chestnuts. They're already well cooked. I couldn't find anything else good to eat."

"Ever since I was a child I've loved boiled water chestnuts," Lin Chen responded, happily taking the pan with his hands. He selected a large unpeeled one, took a bite, and spit it out with a frown. "This one is bad, both sour and rotten." As Chao Hui-wen laughed, Lin Chen angrily threw the squashed sour water chestnut to the floor.

When Lin Chen prepared to leave it was already late at night. The clear sky was completely covered with shy little stars. An old man singing "Fried dumplings fresh from the pot" pushed his cart by. Lin Chen stood outside the doorway. Chao Hui-wen stood just inside, her eyes sparkling in the darkness. "The next time you come there will be paintings on the wall," she said.

Lin Chen smiled understandingly and said, "I hope that you'll take up singing again, too." He gave her hand a squeeze.

Lin Chen breathed in deeply the fragrant air of this spring night. A warm spring welled up within his heart.

. . . .

[Shortly after his lengthy conversation with Chao Hui-wen, Lin Chen talks to Wei Ho-ming and convinces him to send a letter describing conditions in the gunny sack factory to the *People's Daily.* The letter is published with an editorial note advising the appropriate authorities to look into the matter. Now, Liu Shih-wu moves quickly. He initiates a thorough investigation, and as a result of the findings, Wang Ch'ing-ch'üan is removed from his administrative posts in both the factory and the Party.

Lin Chen, however, is still not satisfied. When the standing committee of the District Party Committee meets to discuss the situation in the gunny sack factory, he tells the committee that Liu Shih-wu and Han Ch'ang-hsin should bear responsibility for not solving the problems there sooner. "Indifference, procrastination, and irresponsibility," he states, "are crimes against the masses." In a loud voice he calls out, "The Party is the heart of the people and the working class. We do not permit dust on the heart. We should not allow shortcomings in Party organs." He persists until the District Party Secretary tells him bluntly, "Comrade, you get excited too easily. Reciting lyrics is not appropriate to the conduct of organization work."

This is a frustrating moment for Lin Chen. Once again his superiors have ignored his views and called his idealism into question. But this is not the only challenge Lin Chen faces as the story now moves to its conclusion. He must also contend with the complex emotions that his relationship with Chao Hui-wen have provoked.]

After the meeting adjourned, Lin Chen was so angry that he didn't eat supper. He had never thought that the District Party Secretary would have such an attitude. His disappointment bordered on hopelessness. When Han Ch'ang-hsin and Liu Shih-wu invited him to go for a walk, as if they were unaware of his dissatisfaction with them, it made him even more conscious of how impotent he was compared to them. He smiled bitterly and thought to himself, "So you had the idea that speaking out before the standing committee would accomplish something!" Opening a drawer, he picked up the Soviet novel that Han Ch'ang-hsin had laughed at, and opened it to the first page. At the top was written, "The Model Life of Anastasia." "It's so hard," he said to himself.

CHAPTER XI

The next day after work Chao Hui-wen said to Lin Chen, "Come over to my place for supper. I'll make some dumplings." He wanted to decline, but she was already gone.

Lin Chen hesitated for some time, and then ate in the dining hall before going to Chao Hui-wen's home. When he arrived her dumplings were just ready. For the first time Chao Hui-wen was wearing a deep red dress. She had on an apron and her hands were covered with flour. Like an attentive housewife she told Lin Chen, "I used fresh beans in the dumplings."

"I . . . I've already eaten," Lin Chen stammered.

Chao Hui-wen did not believe him and rushed off to get chopsticks. But after Lin Chen repeated for a second and a third time that he really had eaten, she discontentedly began to eat by herself. Lin Chen sat nervously to one side, looking first one way and then the other, rubbing his hands together, and shifting his body. Those inexpressible feelings of warmth and anguish were once again welling up within his heart. His heart ached as if he had lost something. He simply did not dare look at Chao Hui-wen's beautiful face, shining red in the reflection of her red dress.

"Little Lin, what's wrong?" Chao Hui-wen asked, pausing from her meal.

"N. . . nothing."

"Tell me," she said, her eyes not moving from him.

"Yesterday I presented my opinions at the meeting of the standing committee. The District Party Secretary didn't pay any attention to them at all."

Chao Hui-wen bit on her chopsticks and thought deeply for a moment. "That's not possible. Perhaps Comrade Chou Jun-hsiang just didn't want to give his views too lightly."

"Perhaps," Lin Chen replied, half believing, half doubting. Fearful of meeting Chao Hui-wen's concerned gaze, he lowered his head.

After eating several more dumplings Chao Hui-wen asked again, "Is there something else?"

Lin Chen's heart leaped. He raised his head and looked into her sympathetic, encouraging eyes. In a low voice he said, "Comrade Chao Hui-wen . . ."

Chao Hui-wen laid down her chopsticks and leaned back in her chair. She was a little taken aback.

"I want to know if you're happy," Lin Chen asked in a heavy, completely serious voice. "I saw your tears in Liu Shih-wu's office. Spring had just arrived then. Afterwards I forgot about it. I've been going along living my own life, not caring about others. Are you happy?"

Chao Hui-wen looked at him with a touch of misgiving, shook her head, and said, "At times I forget, too." Then, nodding her head, she smiled calmly and said, "Yes. Yes, I'm happy. Why do you ask?"

". . . I want so much to talk to you or listen to symphonies with you. You're wonderful, of course. But maybe there's something here that's bad or improper. I hadn't thought about this, and then all of a sudden I began to worry. Now I'm afraid that I'm disturbing someone."

Chao Hui-wen smiled and then frowned. She raised her slender arms and vigorously rubbed her forehead. After giving her head a toss, as if she were casting aside some unpleasant thought, she turned away and walked slowly over to the oil painting that had just recently been hung on the wall. She stood staring at it in silence. Its title was "Spring." It depicted Moscow at the time when the first spring sun appears, with mothers and their children out on the streets.

After a few moments Chao Hui-wen turned back and sat down quickly on her bed, holding onto the railing with one hand. In an exceptionally quiet voice she said, "What are you saying? Really! I couldn't do anything so rash. I have a husband and a child. I haven't told you anything yet about my husband." She didn't use the more common term "loved one," but emphasized the word "husband." "We were married in 1952 when I was only nineteen. I really shouldn't have married so early. He had come out of the military and was a section head in a central ministry. Gradually he became rather slick, competing for position and material rewards, and failing to cooperate with others. As for us, all that seemed to be left was his return on Saturday evening and his departure on Monday. According to his theory love was either exhalted or it was nothing. We quarreled. But I'm still waiting. He's now on assignment in

Shanghai. After he returns I want to have a long talk with him. So, what is it that you want to say? Little Lin, you're my best friend. I have great respect for you. But you're still a child—well, perhaps that's not the proper term. I'm sorry. We both hope to lead a true, real life. We both hope that the Organization Department will become a genuine Party work organ. I feel that you're my younger brother. You wish that I would become more active, don't you? Life should have the warmth of mutual support and friendship. I've always been frightened by cold indifference. That's all there is to it. Is there anything more? Can there be anything more?". . . .

Chao Hui-wen opened her briefcase, took out several sheets of paper and leafed through them. "I have some things that I want to show you this evening. I've already written up the problems that I've seen in the work of the Organization Department over the past three years and have put down my own thoughts about them. This . . ." She rubbed a piece of paper in embarrassment. "This is probably pretty laughable. I've set up a system for competing with myself, a way to let myself see if I've done better today than I did yesterday. I've drawn a table and if I make an error in my work—such as copying a name incorrectly on the notice of admission to the Party or adding up the number of new Party members wrong—I put down a black 'X.' If I go through a day without making any mistakes I draw a little red flag. If the red flags continue for a whole month without interruption, then I buy a pretty scarf or something else as a reward for myself. Maybe this is like it's done in kindergarten. Do you think it's funny?"

Lin Chen had been listening in a trance. "Absolutely not," he said solemnly. "I respect your seriousness about yourself . . ."

When Lin Chen prepared to leave it was again already late at night. Again he stood outside the doorway. Chao Hui-wen stood just inside, her eyes sparkling in the darkness. "This is a beautiful evening, isn't it?" she asked. "Do you smell the sweet scent of the locust tree blossoms? Those common white flowers are more refined than peonies and more fragrant than peach or plum blossoms. Can't you smell them? Really! Goodbye. I'll be seeing you early tomorrow morning when we throw ourselves into our great but annoying work. Later, in the evening, look for me and we'll listen to the beautiful *Capriccio Italien.* After we're done listening I'll cook water chestnuts for you and we'll throw the peelings all over the floor."

Lin Chen stood leaning against the large pillar by the door of the Organization Department for a long time, staring at the night sky. The south wind of early summer brushed against him. He had arrived at the end of winter. Now it was already the beginning of summer. He had passed through his first spring in the Organization Department.

A strange feeling surged up in Lin Chen's heart. It was as if he had lost something valuable. It was like thinking about his inadequate accomplishments and slow progress over the past several months. But no, it was not really any of these . . . Ah, people were so complicated! Nothing fitted Liu Shih-wu's expression, "That's the way it is." No, nothing was the way it appeared, and because of this, everything had to be approached honestly, seriously, and conscientiously. Because of this, when unreasonable or unendurable things were encountered they were not to be tolerated. They were to be struggled against, one, two, or even three times. Only when a situation was changed could the struggle stop. There was definitely no reason to be disheartened or downcast. As for love, well ... All that could be done was grit one's teeth and quietly suppress these feelings in the heart!

"I want to be more active, more enthusiastic, and certainly more strong," Lin Chen said quietly to himself. He lifted his chest and took a deep breath of the cool night air.

Looking through the window Lin Chen could see the green desk lamp and the imposing profile of the late-working District Party Secretary. Determinedly and with impatience he knocked on the door of the leading comrade's office.

Translated by Gary Bjorge

CHOU LI-PO
(1910–)

Chou Li-po chronologically is of the May Fourth generation, but as a writer he belongs entirely to the post-Yenan Forum era. Indeed, his career as a major novelist is really a success story for Mao's insistence at the Forum that writers genuinely penetrate and participate in village life and reflect the positive aspects of the new society in their writing.

Born in 1910 in I-yang, Hunan Province, hometown of Party theoretician Chou Yang—some say they are cousins—Chou Li-po, like many revolutionary youth of his time, made his way from the countryside to Shanghai for college in 1927. His two brothers remained behind and are said to be middle peasants on a rural commune. In 1932 Chou Li-po participated in a labor strike, was arrested by foreign police in the International Concessions, and remained in jail until 1934. He started working for the League of Left-wing Writers, which placed him among the close associates of Chou Yang. Later, he went north to do cultural work in Communist-dominated areas. The winter of 1938 found him back in Hunan Province editing the *Resistance War Daily*. Then, in 1940, he returned north to lecture on foreign literature at the Lu Hsün Academy in Yenan.

Between 1946 and 1949, Chou Li-po served on land reform teams in the Northeast, and his three years of village experience there went into his first major novel, *Hurricane* (1948), which won a Stalin Prize in 1951. The novel describes the fury of peasants wresting power from armed landlords and the aftermath of land reform. After the publication of *Hurricane*, Chou was elected to the All-China Federation of Literary and Art Circles, of which Chou Yang was the deputy director. In 1952, Chou Li-po was promoted to the editorial board of the prestigious magazine *People's Literature*.

His second major novel, *Great Changes in a Mountain Village*, in two volumes, was based on his 1955 experience in a remote mountain town in Hunan Province. Volume one is constructed around a young woman cadre assigned to help the village after the first attempt to establish an agricultural cooperative failed. Several crises overcome, she leaves at the end of volume one and does not reappear. Volume two begins with the village now struggling on its own to make a success of the cooperative against the resistance of the non-joiners. The episode translated below is part of the long struggle to win over the holdouts.

Chou Li-po was criticized in 1966 and his works were withdrawn from circulation on the charge that he overemphasized peasant dependence on Party leadership and gave disproportionate attention to those who resisted collectivization. The downfall of the Gang of Four brought him back in circulation, as a delegate to the People's Political Consultative Conference in February 1978, and as a member of the Third Congress of the All-China Federation of Literary and Art Circles meeting in Peking in May 1978. His works are scheduled for republication.   —D.A.G.

from *Great Changes in a Mountain Village*

Volume Two

CHAPTER 6: COMPETITION

At first, when he heard that the Cooperative was getting ready to clean the mud out of pond bottoms to spread over the low-yield fields to enrich the soil, Gold-biter was green with envy, but then he decided to do the very same thing himself. The two parcels of dry land he owned near the hills, where the soil was so thin that if you plowed it deep water would run right through it to the rocks underneath, were ideal for this project. So Gold-biter put down what he was doing, picked up his tools and, leading his wife and daughter, went off to the pond near his upper parcel. A good number of people were already gathered there. Members of the Co-op were at that very moment carrying out to the fields, basket by basket, the rich, damp mud from the bottom of the drained pond.

"So you've come too," Liu Yü-sheng called out in greeting as he packed out a load of mud. "Well, that's fine. This stuff is even better than manure, you know. Get a whiff of it. It's pretty strong."

"It is," said Gold-biter, nodding to him. "This pond hasn't been cleaned out for a good long time now." But as he moved forward to go down inside to start digging, he ran into Ch'en Meng-ch'un, who blocked his way.

"What do you mean, standing in my way like that?"

"You're not going to dig here," answered the weather-burnt Meng-ch'un, displaying all the brashness of his older brother, whom he had not yet quite overtaken in height.

"And just why is that? Maybe you don't know that I also own a share in this pond?"

"That doesn't mean anything to me. You didn't help drain the pond, so you're not going to dig."

"I don't have to deal with you anyway. Let's go see your Party branch secretary."

"Go get the secretary. You're just wasting your time."

Just when the two of them had locked horns and the exchange was heating up, Liu Yü-sheng rushed up to pull Meng-ch'un away.

"Let him dig. You think a whole pond full of muck like this doesn't have enough for him too?"

"I just can't see why a miser like him can get off so cheap at other people's expense," grumbled Meng-ch'un as he walked away.

Liu Yü-sheng, seeing Gold-biter still standing his ground, not budging an inch and his eyes bulging in anger, went over to smooth things out.

"Go right ahead with your digging and don't mind him."

With this, Gold-biter muttered an oath or two, and then, not wanting to lose any more time, turned immediately to start digging in the muck.

Deep down inside, Gold-biter wanted to compete with the Cooperative, for he always felt that if he could get the better of them there would somehow be something in it for him, and as a loner who refused to join the Cooperative, at the least, at the very least, it would help him to hold out on his own just that much longer. On the first day of digging, his own efforts exactly followed the pattern set by the Cooperative. When the others dug and carried, he dug and carried; when the others took a break, he took a break. But on the following day he went his separate way. At two in the morning, when the moon went down and there was only the weak starlight shining dimly over the outline of the pond, Gold-biter, leading his wife and daughter, groped his way down into the drained pond bottom and had his daughter start digging while he and his wife did the hauling. By dawn, when the Co-op members came to work, the Gold-biters had each already carried away some twenty or so loads of muck.

"From the looks of things, they're going to beat us," Liu Yü-sheng pointed out to the members during a break while they all sat around together on a threshing ground under a camphor tree.

"Not necessarily. There are more of us," Meng-ch'un pointed out, full of confidence.

"Sure, but he's not competing with us in numbers; he's trying to outdo us in performance and in per-acre yield. He's put a lot of fertilizer on his other land, and now here he is fixing up this parcel that's so porous and bony it's like a fish without flesh. Our parcels are uneven in quality—an awful lot of it is full of hollow spots—and look how much is just bone-dry land that you can't improve no matter what you do." This, from Liu Yü-sheng, caused Meng-ch'un to lapse into silence.

"When it comes to farming, he's always been first-rate," Li Yung-ho put in.

"Well now, you can't say we don't have first-rate farmers on our side too. There's Meng-ch'un's father, Hsien-chin, there's Sheng Yu-t'ing, and there's Old Hsieh. They're at least as good as Gold-biter. It's just that none of us, young or old alike, puts as much into it as he does."

"That's right," Meng-ch'un agreed, discomfited by the thought. "Each and every one of us just isn't putting out as much as he is."

"I talked it over with the Party branch secretary," Liu Yü-sheng went on, "and it seems the best thing to do is form a Youth Task Force."

"Count me in," Meng-ch'un put in without hesitation.

"Put my name down," added Shu-chün.

"Put mine down, too," Ch'en Hsüeh-ch'un chimed in, imitating the older girl to the last detail.

"Hey, all the activists are from the same family," Li Yung-ho observed, laughing at his allusion to Shu-chün's wedding plans that would make the two girls sisters-in-law. "Before you know it the whole Task Force will be a family enterprise."

"Now don't go changing the subject," cautioned Liu Yü-sheng. "Li, old fellow, you've already finished your stint as bookkeeper, so now you're ready for another assignment. How about getting the Task Force organized? Take old Gold-biter as your target and then surpass him. Can you handle that?"

"Of course we can!" shouted all the young people at once, with Meng-ch'un's husky voice heard above all the rest as he added, "We'll be damned if we don't beat him!"

Liu Yü-sheng's heart swelled with pleasure as he stood up and said, "Well, I see the beginning here of a real effort." Even when he was extremely pleased, there would only be the slightest trace of a smile creeping into his expression. "But then, of course, so far this is all nothing more than talk, isn't it?"

"Now there's a dig from our Co-op leader." Ch'en Meng-ch'un always liked to roll his sleeves up to get down to work, but now his sleeves were already rolled up. "I suppose you think all we're good for is just hot air and nothing else, huh?"

Liu Yü-sheng turned to Li Yung-ho to ask, "Well, what do you think? When can the Task Force get organized? By tomorrow?"

"What's this about tomorrow? After all, it isn't a wedding we're planning so that it would need to have a specially picked day and all that," retorted Ch'en Meng-ch'un agitatedly.

"You're thinking about a wedding?" cracked one of the younger members.

"Hey, no joking around," Meng-ch'un said with a new seriousness in his voice.

"When we quit work tonight, after supper, we'll get together, all right?" Li Yung-ho said to Liu after some thought.

"What's the point of waiting until tonight?" Meng-ch'un persisted. "If we're going to do it, let's do it now. Why put if off till after supper?"

"Meng-ch'un here is right," Liu Yü-sheng agreed. "If you begin now, the young people can get together in that shed over there." Then, turning to the older people, he added, "You folks are invited too, to give them some direction."

"You flatter us, Mr. Liu, but we won't take you up on that," one answered, puffing on his pipe.

Meanwhile, Gold-biter continued to carry his mud, but his attention was drawn to what the young people were up to. As he watched Liu Yü-sheng lead them along the path to the shed, he thought to himself, "This must have something to do with the competition."

Wave after wave of applause and shouts of enthusiasm issued from the thatch shed, together with gales of laughter and merriment. Half an hour later, one by one, the group streamed out. As they walked toward the pond, Liu Yü-sheng said to Shu-chün:

"Only a very few of the Women's Association showed up today. Run over and get them all together. Explain it to them and see if we can't get a better turnout."

"I'll do that right away," agreed Shu-chün, who took off at once. But before she got far, she turned back toward the Co-op leader and, cupping her hands over her mouth, shouted, "Can you come too and give us a pep talk?"

"I'm tied up. Can't make it," he called back. "Get the Women's Association head to do it."

After she left, he turned to Li Yung-ho.

"This Women's Association head we have isn't as good a manager as she ought to be. All she does is stay home and look after her children."

"I hear she's got another one on the way, too," Li Yung-ho agreed. "It seems to me somebody ought to replace her. Somebody like Sheng Chia-hsiu."

Li's suggestion of the woman Liu Yü-sheng would soon be marrying could not help but be calculated to put Li on the best of terms with the Co-op leader.

"Her political awareness is too low. And there's that pig of hers she's raising. If we get her to do it, it's still just one shoe of a pair, getting things only half-done."

"Then how about Sheng Shu-chün?"

"Come to think of it, she would do just fine, but that's something that has to be taken up with the Party branch secretary. And then he's got to clear it with the Party leadership above him."

At this point a messenger came up from the District Office reminding Liu to call a meeting.

"This would be a good time for you to take it up with Secretary Li," Li Yung-ho suggested.

"All right. I'll do that," Liu replied, as he started off.

After the Task Force meeting and the Women's Association meeting, the work force turnout was much greater than before, so that even Chang Kuei-chen and Sheng Shu-chün's mother, who normally almost never joined in, also turned up. On this day everybody put in a good, full day's work.

That night, Li Yung-ho borrowed a three-barreled fowling piece from the security chief, Sheng Ch'ing-ming, and loaded powder into all three barrels, set the fuses in place and laid it beside his bed. The next morning, at the first rooster crow, probably around two o'clock, Li rolled over, pulled himself out of bed, and, before dressing, put the gun over his shoulder, fumbled around for a box of matches, and went out to the threshing ground in front of the house, where he fired off each barrel, one after the other, into the night sky only faintly lit by starlight. Concussion from the huge roar rattled the paper windows of the house and startled into flight the birds that had been roosting on the tree behind the house. But even before the echoes had settled, as he straightened up after the firing he was astonished to see a lantern hanging from a willow by the side of the pond, telling him that someone was already at work.

"Which of them can that be?" he asked himself as he hurried off to have a look. But the person he discovered hard at work was no Co-op member; it was the Gold-biters, man, wife, and daughter.

"You're really early today. Been up long?"

"Not long. Just got up." This was how Gold-biter replied, but in fact, as Li Yung-ho's later investigation would reveal, he had gotten up at midnight. Now, fearing that the Co-op would follow his lead, he intentionally misled them.

It was early spring when frosts were liable to return at any time, and although there was none this morning, nor any breeze either, still, there was no sun at all. When the three-barreled fowling piece had gone off, everybody was startled awake. Even though they started work well after the Gold-biters, nevertheless everyone's spirits were up for the occasion so that they put in another solid day's work.

On the third day, Li Yung-ho pulled himself out of bed at midnight and raced outside, where at once he could see that there was no lantern. Gold-biter wasn't up yet! Delighted, he fired off three quick charges in succession.

Now on this particular night the weather had changed sharply, and with the rise of a north wind, it was biting cold.

"Is a cold front hitting us again?" wondered Li to himself. When he had the gas lantern started and hung from the willow tree, he could see all around him, wherever the light shone—the weeds on the bottom of the empty pond, the bamboo fencing around the vegetable patch—it was all white with frost! The shallow water in the puddles down in the empty pond had frozen into sheets of ice. The young men and women of the Task Force filed up to the pond carrying their wicker baskets and tools. One of the youths who wasn't wearing a quilted jacket was so cold he shivered. He hastily gathered up some straw from around the edge of the pond and with some dry kindling got a fire going, which the others quickly gathered around. Some of the mischievous ones, seeing this, went over to the thatch shed to take it easy. In no time at all no one was left to go down to the pond bottom.

"What do you think of this! They get us up early just to light the lantern and stand by the fire!" one of them complained.

Li Yung-ho, without a word, slipped out of his shoes, picked up his rake, and like the first horse in the water, took the lead as he stepped down into the cold mud on the pond bottom, where he used both feet to crack the thin sheet of ice over the puddles. His teeth chattered as the ice crackled under his feet. He shouted to the others:

"Ta . . . ask For . . . rce Mem . . . bers! Forget the fire! Be like the PLA! Remember the heroes of Shangkanling. They weren't afraid of dying. Are we afraid of the cold? Hurry up! Let's get going!"

He began digging at the muck with his rake while shouting at his comrades. Ch'en Meng-ch'un, who was toasting himself beside the fire, leaped up at once, grabbed his rake, and ran to the pond.

"Hurry up. It's not cold. Not cold at all!"

"Who cares even if it is cold?" said Sheng Shu-chün, who rolled up her pant legs and went down into the pond. Right behind her were Sheng Chia-hsiu and Ch'en Hsüeh-ch'un. The latter, a short, stocky young girl not yet fully developed, rolled up her pant legs and pushed back her sleeves, looking for all the world like a little bundle of energy.

Seeing the women get started prompted the other young people still loitering by the fire so that they too all came over to the pond. Soon the carriers were carrying, the diggers digging, and some of them were even singing folk ditties.

No more than two loads had been taken out when the three Gold-biters appeared. Gold-biter himself carried their lantern, but when he saw that the Co-op's lantern lighted the whole area he blew out his own.

"Hey, don't go borrowing our light there, old buddy," Ch'en Meng-ch'un shouted over to Gold-biter, partly meaning it, but partly only as the kind of smart crack young people are always making.

"What light of yours are we borrowing?" the daughter replied testily.

"The lantern light. What's the matter, no eyes?"

"Who told you to go light your old lantern, my father I suppose?" she fired back sharply.

The two of them, you say one thing, I say something back, soon were in full swing. At the outset, the conflict was limited to just the two of them: on the one hand, a youth of 18 or 19, always known for his brashness, and on the other hand, a little know-nothing slip of a girl, maybe 12 or 13 years old. Their insults, though fierce, were not of any grave import. Twice Li Yung-ho cautioned Meng-ch'un to stop quarreling, and Gold-biter, for his part worried about losing time from work, time and again scolded his daughter: "Can't you learn to shut up!" However, when it came to this annoying Gold-biter family, the hot-tempered Meng-ch'un not only was unable to give up the fight, he actually felt dissatisfied at trading insults only with the daughter and dearly hoped the flames of battle would spread to Gold-biter himself. But seeing Gold-biter, so far from entering the fray himself, actually scolding his daughter for her part in it, Meng-ch'un felt annoyed and let slip a phrase that was more serious than he realized:

"The seed makes the plant, that's for sure. No seed, no growth. That's what we always say, and it's as right as right can be."

Gold-biter's wife caught fire at this and, throwing down her carrying pole, stormed over to the young man shouting, "Damn you, Meng-ch'un! Just what does that mean?"

"Whatever you think it does," Meng-ch'un fired back.

His baskets hanging empty from his pole, Meng-ch'un took a step closer to her, all the while thinking that while it wasn't Gold-biter himself, it was better, at least, than just the girl.

"Clean up your mouth a little and don't make other people have to come over here to teach you manners. I'm telling you, you hear?" warned the wife.

"I never asked you to come over here to teach any manners," sneered Meng-ch'un. "I never went to your house, and I never went to your fields. I'm just standing here by the pond that's our own Co-op property, that's all. Now just what pigs in the night are they who come running over to our place, taking up our lantern light, getting something for nothing. They're the lord and masters, I suppose?"

"So this pond is your Co-op's, is it?" Gold-biter's wife took yet another step forward.

"Of course."

"Well let me tell you, I've got water shares in this pond," injected Gold-biter himself. When a quarrel got around to the subject of his own property he found it impossible to remain silent.

"That tiny share of yours, compared with our Co-op, is like holding a sesame seed up to a watermelon." Ch'en Meng-ch'un turned to face Gold-biter squarely, "And it's even less when you consider how you didn't drain any of the water and you don't even light your own lantern. All you know is how to get off cheap by sponging off other people." Ch'en Meng-ch'un exchanged a significant glance with the others. Some had stopped working and had come over to see the excitement, while others kept at their job of digging or hauling. Ch'en Meng-ch'un then went on, "We're just going by the Party branch secretary's and the Co-op director's say-so and being generous to you, letting you dig here, but if it were up to me I wouldn't let you."

"And just who do you think you are, to *let* me dig?" Gold-biter was now fully into it, his eyes bulging in fury.

"Me, that's who." Meng-ch'un threw down his baskets and held up his flat carrying pole in one hand and put the other defiantly on his hip.

"You? Who the hell do you think you are?"

"Member, Evergreen Cooperative, that's who. You can't see that, I suppose. Some dog got your eyes, has he?"

"So. Member, Evergreen Cooperative! Well, that's really something, isn't it?" Gold-biter looked him over disdainfully as he said this. "Well I'm telling you something, you sprout. This is Wang Chü-sheng here, and I'm one fish who's been to the ocean, you hear? I've seen a thing or two in my time. No sesame seed of a Co-op member is going to push me around. Bring on your brigade leader, your Co-op leader, your district chief, your county head. Bring them all on, and what's that to me?"

"Old Wang, my friend. Your argument is with him. Why do you have to drag the cadres into it?" This was Li Yung-ho rushing over to break things up as soon as he saw the turn things had taken.

"Listen to him talk, would you. Let's smash those straw baskets of his!" Li Yung-ho's remarks had only encouraged Meng-ch'un to go even further. Flinging down his carrying pole, he reached out to grab the ropes on the baskets hanging from Gold-biter's carrying pole.

"You dare, do you? You and who else?"

"Say that to me, will you?" Meng-ch'un released the ropes and bent down to retrieve his pole.

"You're damned right I do." Gold-biter likewise threw down his baskets and took a good hold on his own carrying pole.

"Curse me and you're going to take a licking."

"Come on, come on." Gold-biter by now had his own stick in the air and was about to rush him when his wife grabbed one of his hands and held on with all her might.

Under the bright glare of the lantern their two poles locked together with a loud "crack!"

Everyone rushed over, surrounding the combatants. Gold-biter's wife, thrown to the ground, quickly jumped back up. The daughter cried in fright. A militiaman jammed his own carrying pole between the two of them, forcing their poles up into the air. Hsüeh-ch'un rushed over to hold back her brother, Meng-ch'un, by the hand. Some of the young people who despised Gold-biter shouted encouragement to Meng-ch'un. Sheng Shu-chün ran off to the village at top speed.

The two plow masters, Ch'en Hsien-chin and Flour-paste T'ing, hearing sounds of the fracas from far off, abandoned their plows and oxen and rushed over with their whips. As soon as the bearded Hsien-chin saw that it was his son Meng-ch'un who was causing the ruckus, he rushed into the fray and bellowed:

"Meng-ch'un! You addleheaded no-good. Is this any way to behave? I'll teach you a lesson." He raised his whip. "So. You still don't drop your pole?" He stepped forward and wrestled the pole away. Now, on the one hand, this old fellow had always had an air of authority, and on the other hand, he was stouter than this second son of his, so once he got his hands on the pole he was able to wrestle it away without meeting much resistance. Gold-biter, seeing both of Meng-ch'un's hands empty and, being at the height of his rage, bore down all the more on Meng-ch'un, brandishing his flat pole to show his intention to give the boy a good clout, all of which served only to further outrage the young man.

Ignoring his father's wrath, Meng-ch'un lunged forward, pinning Gold-biter's pole so that the two of them were pressed together. Gold-biter's daughter was now shrieking and Hsüeh-ch'un's face had gone pale. His sharp rebuke having no effect, the father now threw down his whip and leaped in to try to pull the two of them apart. Just when they had reached this impasse, Party Branch Secretary Li Yüeh-hui and Liu Yü-sheng arrived on the scene, followed by Sheng Shu-chün. There were now more and more people urging the pair to break off the dispute, and finally several strong militiamen managed to wrest the pole away and pull the combatants apart.

Li Yüeh-hui said a few words to the group and then with Liu took Li Yung-ho aside to the thatch shed, where he remained until he found out exactly what had happened. They reemerged only to find the two men still cursing each other.

Li Yüeh-hui went straight over to Gold-biter and said:

"Old Wang, go right ahead with your digging. There's more than enough mud here for everybody. Don't pay any attention to the boy. He's just a youngster and hasn't any sense to him yet."

Then, walking over to where Meng-ch'un stood, he led the boy off to the shed and patted him on the shoulder, smiled, and said, "My boy, how can it be that you're so much like your older brother?"

Meng-ch'un sat on the doorsill, head bowed, silent. Li Yüeh-hui, seating himself on a bamboo chair, went on:

"In our society everybody is undergoing change. I can tell from your older brother's letters that he's changed a lot. Now, do you still want to be just like he used to be?"

Meng-ch'un, head still lowered, said nothing.

"Why do you want to stir up trouble with him? The loam in the pond isn't something so precious that we had to spend money to get it, so why not let him have some?"

"I just got so mad I couldn't stand it." Meng-ch'un's head was still lowered.

"And to think that you want to be admitted to the Party, and with a temper like that!" Li Yüeh-hui was using the opportunity to give the boy some direction.

"Once you're in the Party you become a member of the vanguard of the leadership. Do you think it's easy to be part of the vanguard? There behind you will be hundreds and thousands of the masses, and you must always be inseparably one with them. You can't go too fast or too slow. Lose your temper, give in to yourself, and it only makes things worse."

"He's just a go-it-aloner, so how does that make him any member of your masses?"

"Just like you and me, he's a mud-hauler, and there he is, even now, still hauling the muck. You pack it out with a pole over your shoulder and he does exactly the same. What gives you the right to say he isn't one of the masses? If he isn't, then what is he?"

When it was clear Meng-ch'un had nothing to say to this, Li Yüeh-hui went on:

"All right. Go on with your work."

The two of them went out together, but Li Yüeh-hui went directly over to where Gold-biter was shoveling muck into the carrying baskets. He addressed Gold-biter in a light, friendly tone:

"Wang, old fellow, keep up the good work. The Evergreen Co-op still wants to keep up the competition with you."

"You give me too much credit," Gold-biter replied, showing unmistakably that he still had a lot of anger bottled up inside. "There are more of you, so you're stronger, but you still can't get the better of me, so you use your raw authority to come right out and beat on me."

"You know the old saying, 'You only know each other when you fight each other.' There's been a little squabble, so now we know each other better and can be better friends for it."

"I don't dare compete with all of you. And I admit it—I'm afraid of you." Although in his expression it was clear just how angry he was, still, Gold-biter was sounding the drums for a cease-fire.

"Don't bear us a grudge. We're all in the same village here, so that won't do. Hey, Meng-ch'un! Come over here." Li Yüeh-hui wanted to be a conciliator. His pleasant round face and his ready smile made him ideally cut out for this role. Pulling Meng-ch'un forward with one hand and Gold-biter with the other, he calmly said:

"Once when I was in the city for a meeting I saw a ball game where both sides were about to begin the competition and the referee blew the whistle. One team got together in a huddle and then with a big shout rushed over to the other team. The other team ran out to meet them halfway and it really scared me. I thought they were going to start brawling with each other before the game had even begun. How could I know they were just going to shake hands and that it was part of the pregame ceremony. Somebody there explained it all to me saying 'It's called friendly competition.' So now let's have friendship here, too, and then we can have competition, all right?" Without giving either of them a chance to protest, he pushed Ch'en Meng-ch'un's right hand into Gold-biter's right hand. Carefully avoiding each other's eyes, they forced themselves to shake hands and then separated. By now the early dawn had given way to the brightness of a new day. Just then someone could be heard at some distance shouting.

"Hey, hey! Hey, hey! You son-of-a-gun. Run away from me, will you!" Li Yüeh-hui saw that the one shouting was Flour-paste T'ing. The slightly stooped old man was cursing his ox and shaking his whip as he ran down one of the narrow dikes separating the paddy fields. You could tell from the way he scolded the ox that he thought of it as an errant child and scolded it accordingly. Everybody looked across the fields at him and could see that the ox he had been plowing with took advantage of his absence and had joined Ch'en Hsien-chin's ox for a romp. Dragging their plows, they had drifted over to the edge of the paddy, where it was pretty clear their goal was to graze on the green grass growing there. By the time the two men reached the animals, they had already achieved their goal and were bent on increasing the scope of their appropriations. Relieved to see that the plows were undamaged, the two men were now bringing the oxen back to the abandoned furrows to resume the plowing.

Those who had been squabbling and their spectators all gradually dispersed. Some were already at their digging or hauling, still discussing the issue. Li Yüeh-hui extinguished the gas lantern, and turning to the few who had not yet gone back to work, remarked:

"Next time you light up the lantern for a fight I won't stop you, but I'll send someone down to take up a collection for lamp fuel."

Just then the chief of security came up. Glancing up at him, Li Yüeh-hui teased him, "Well, now, you got here right on time, didn't you?"

"I missed all the excitement. Too bad. I really love a good fight. Next time you have someone notify me a little earlier and I'll get my licks in."

"Which side will you be on?" someone asked.

"Oh, any side will do. I'll put in something for both sides."

Saying this, he took the arm of Li Yüeh-hui and spoke to him as they walked off.

"As soon as I heard there was trouble I went right over to keep an eye on Kung's place.* When I saw he was sound asleep I took it easy, so I'm a little late getting here."

The sun now had completely dispelled the morning chill and melted the ice crust. People were digging vigorously and carrying their loads of mud out in quick order. It was hard work, and out in the warm sun their faces became bathed in sweat. Under their padded cotton jackets, which they peeled off, their undershirts were soaked through, and in this respect, the Gold-biters and the Co-op members were indistinguishable. This was one thing they all shared in common that could have served as a basis for their all getting back on good terms with each other again. But Gold-biter, although he had in word indicated retreat from his indignation, still, in fact, down deep inside remained furious and intended to go as far as he could in his competition with the Cooperative. And what's more, in terms of work output and per-acre yield, he was bound and determined in his secret desire to put the Co-op to rout in the competition.

To get out of the pond bottom where they were digging the mud, it was necessary to climb up the slippery bank. For those carrying the loads of muck, it was hard work, slow going, and if you weren't careful then you would stumble. The women were taking somewhat more falls than the men. In her debut performance with the Task Force the petite Chang Kuei-chen was carrying half-full baskets of the mud when she slipped as she climbed up the steep bank and fell flat over on her back, with baskets, pole, and her four limbs all sprawled out in the thick mire.

Someone laughed, saying, "Didn't break your can, did you? If you had, your hubby would raise hell with us when he gets back."

"It's not right. Somebody takes a spill, gets muddy as an old ox, and you think it's all right to laugh at them," Sheng Shu-chün scolded. She put down her carrying pole and ran over to help Chang Kuei-chen to her feet, meanwhile thinking to herself, "This won't do at all. Something should be done about this."

Immediately afterward she and Sheng Chia-hsiu put their heads together, and then had two of the stronger of the young women go with them to the yard of one of the nearby houses. Before long, the four Mu Kuei-yings† singing in unison, "Hey-ho, hey-ho," muscled a long, thick plank over to the pond where

---

*A counterrevolutionary element. Security Chief Sheng has been told by upper echelon authorities that Kung and others are plotting something. [D.A G.]

†Mu Kuei-ying: A woman warrior of the tenth century who created a legend with her military feats. [D.A.G.]

they put it down so that one end was on the pond bottom and the other on the bank. Because it was too steep, they raised the lower end a little by putting some rocks under it, and they lowered the upper end somewhat. They then placed rocks at the low end to form steps up to the plank. This way, men and women alike could step onto the stones, then up the plankway to the level ground around the pond, all the while walking on a path that was steady and easy-going. Someone praised Sheng Shu-chün for this, but she didn't linger to listen. Shouldering her pole, she disappeared again almost immediately. This time, when she returned she was carrying two baskets full of husk sweepings from the threshing ground.

"What's that for?" queried Sheng Chia-hsiu.

"Wait a second and you'll see."

One by one as they all crossed over the plank the slime from their feet had made the board slippery. Sheng Shu-chün used both hands to spread the husk dust over the plank so that it became much better.

"Hey, Sheng Shu-chün," one of them shouted to her, "you deserve a medal for this."

Another joined in laughing, "We'll have to report this good news to Ta-ch'un. This is something your young man ought to know about."

"What do you mean, 'a medal'? Nonsense," she retorted, without pause as she spread the material over the plank.

"It's just a little trick, but not everybody would think of doing it," yet another pointed out.

They all went about their work, chatting and laughing in a merry atmosphere, completely oblivious to how tired they were, and they kept at their work for long periods between breaks. In contrast to the Co-op members' lively scene, the three Gold-biters, toiling on in isolation, could not help but appear grim and cheerless. Gold-biter, leading his two women, avoided the plank to head off derision from anybody who might lay new charges against him for taking a free ride, and also to avoid tangling with Ch'en Meng-ch'un again. The Gold-biters were still struggling up and down the steep, slippery bank.

"Old Wang! Go right ahead and use our plank," shouted Li Yung-ho. Taking a leaf from the Party branch secretary's book, he made the invitation in a friendly and concerned tone of voice.

Addressing herself to Gold-biter's daughter, Sheng Shu-chün shouted, "Hey, come on over and use our plank." She was thinking of what the Party branch secretary had said: "Even with those who resist collectivization and try to go it alone, in competition one is always to maintain good will."

"Come on over. Don't hold back. We're not going to charge you for it!" one of the militiamen called to her.

The face of the exhausted girl broke into a smile, but the smile disappeared the minute she looked over and saw her father returning.

"Come on over. Let's work together. We can have a labor exchange with you if you want. It's awfully grim over there, just the three of you. What's the fun of that?" Sheng Shu-chün's enticements were, in fact, loaded with political implications.

Gold-biter's daughter gave them a warm, friendly smile, but when she shot a glance toward her father, who had just turned his back, she again shook her head. Judging from her smile and from the way she shook her head, it was clear that the girl's heart was already half won over to the Cooperative, while the other half was held sternly in check by her father so that she just didn't dare come over.

"Don't be so mean; you shouldn't undermine a man like that," chided Li Yung-ho when the Gold-biters had moved off some distance. "The general there has only got two soldiers in his command. One woman soldier and one girl scout. That's pitiful enough, don't you think?"

Ch'en Meng-ch'un remained aloof from this merriment. He was still unwilling to get on with Gold-biter. Our die-hard go-it-aloner also said nothing, just keeping his head bent to the hard work at hand, carrying out load after load, his stout chestnut carrying pole bent like an archer's bow under the two-hundred-some *catties* of his loaded baskets.

"Poor old fellow. Look at him, slaving like an old plow ox," Li Yung-ho could not help but marvel.

When the Co-op members took a break, Gold-biter also put down his carrying pole and baskets, but he didn't rest, nor did he have a smoke, though certainly he liked a smoke as well as the next person. Instead, he raced home. Moments later he reappeared shouldering a board, which he placed against the bank to form a plank walk of his own.

When Sheng Shu-chün saw what he had done she again got her girls together and brought over yet another plank. This one, placed next to their earlier plank, broadened the platform so traffic could go up and down at the same time. The Task Force members now were shouting their "Hey-ho, hey-ho," as they broke into a trot under their heavy loads.

Gold-biter likewise broke into a trot, but when he saw his wife and daughter falter, he lashed out at them:

"You dying pigs. Hurry it up. You going to stay there till New Year's?"

"Father. Honestly, I just can't move," the daughter begged.

"Just good for stuffing your belly, that's all you ever think of, isn't it?"

"I've got a blister on my heel," the daughter explained, limping along, tears welling up in her eyes. This time, her appeal was directed toward her mother.

"Then go on back home. No sense staying out here letting others see how miserable you look." Gold-biter's wife said this to protect her daughter. There was also a blister on her own heel, and she was feeling a little dizzy, too.

"You night-swilling pigs. You'll be the death of me yet. You expect everything to be done for you, right?" cursed Gold-biter as he saw his daughter turn back for home and his wife limp like a wounded soldier as she tried to keep up with him.

"Hey, Gold-biter. Now you're down to one pawn and the king."

"Let's work together. Or, if you want, we can do a labor exchange. We'll give you a hand with the hauling and later you can do something for us."

"For us it's as easy as a hunchback making a bow—it's easy as can be to get up a work force."

"This is where a cooperative has all the advantages. Lots of people and lots of strength. Like we always say, plenty of wood makes the fire hot, right?"

Hearing everybody chime in this way so incensed Gold-biter that he turned grey with anger, but he said nothing and continued to carry his baskets just the same. When the Co-op members rested, he skipped the break and went right on with his hauling.

It was during one of their breaks that Sheng Shu-chün and Ch'en Hsüeh-ch'un sat talking beside a haystack, where they together composed a new song, so that when work resumed the two girls sang it. The words went something like this:

> Co-op comrades sure do well,
> With baskets and poles they trot pell-mell.
> Happy-as-can-be, and lively you can tell,
> But somebody else is mad-as-hell!

The last line, "Somebody else is mad-as-hell," was Hsüeh-ch'un's, but she originally had it, "And this makes Gold-biter mad-as-hell," until Sheng Shu-chün talked her out of it, saying it went too far. It was first changed to "This makes the lone-goers mad-as-hell," but that also was thought to be too obvious.

But no matter how it was modified, the last line was clearly aimed at Gold-biter, and it got under his skin.

Gold-biter was very disquieted. Li Yung-ho saw this and made it a point to fall in behind him and engage him in conversation.

"I see your daughter is already worn out, and it looks like your wife is about done for, too. Why punish yourselves so much? You don't have much help, and yet ... Aren't you being unreasonable?" Although he realized Li Yung-ho's counsel sprang from well-intentioned impulses, still, Gold-biter kept his silence.

Li went on, trying to reason it out for him: "Here you are, run ragged like this just to improve the soil. Think how it's going to be when we start the double-cropping and you'll have twice as much to do at the same time. Do you really think you can keep up with it?"

"Well, I'll cross that bridge when I get to it." Gold-biter hazarded this one-sentence reply.

"It's predictable even now. When that time comes there will be the harvesting of the first crop, then the replowing, and then transplating the sprouts for the second crop. Old fellow, even if you grow three heads and six arms it still won't be enough. The way I see it you'd do better joining the Co-op now. Don't wait until it's too late when you'll have to carry on alone something that's just hopeless."

"I've made up my mind not to join," replied Gold-biter, determinedly.

"And in the future?"

"Then too."

"All right. We'll wait and see what happens." Li Yung-ho let his pace slacken so Gold-biter could go on ahead. Then, shaking his head to a Co-op member who had just come up, he said, "That's the way people are. They won't see something obvious until they're staring it in the face."

Noting that it was late and that he was worn out, Li Yung-ho realized the others must be, too, so he blew his whistle to signal that they could call it a day.

Gold-biter's wife kept on with her digging and hauling, staying with it until nightfall, not shuffling back home to get up some supper until it was pitch-dark.

After supper, when Gold-biter stood on the stone slab in front of his door and looked out toward the pond he discovered the gas lantern was lighted; the Co-op people were at it again! He rushed back to the kitchen and told his wife:

"Let's go. They've all started work again."

"Let it go for today. Our daughter's so tired she can't even eat, and I'm not much better off myself," she replied, washing the supper dishes.

"If they can do it, why can't we?"

"But look how many more of them there are. The few are never any match for the many—what do you think you can do about that? The way I see it, let it go and don't let them get you all worked up over it."

"You going or not?" Gold-biter never was one to stand around for much talk.

"Well, if we go, we go." His wife was seasoned to obedience. Her back was hurting her and she felt a little dizzy, but she still couldn't bring herself to come right out and say "no."

The two of them, man and wife, went all the way over to the pond before they realized that except for Li Yung-ho and Sheng Shu-chün, all the others were fresh troops. They had simply changed shifts! Gold-biter's wife wanted to go back home, but when she saw her husband already starting to work down in the pond bottom, she had no choice but to start rolling up her pant legs.

They went over as far away as they could from the gas lantern for fear of a second encounter with someone as impudent as Ch'en Meng-ch'un. After about an hour of toil, just when Gold-biter's wife had shouldered a load of the black muck, it suddenly appeared to her as though the lantern off in the distance was somehow floating around, and right after that everything went black; the carrying pole slipped away, and down she went, baskets and all, into the mire. Gold-biter hurriedly dropped the rake he was gripping and rushed over to her, while a number of young Co-op members, Sheng Shu-chün among them, also threw down their tools and ran to her.

Translated by Donald A. Gibbs

JU CHIH-CHÜAN
(1928–)

At thirteen, with very little formal schooling, Ju Chih-chüan started traveling around the country with her brother, at times finding shelter in orphanages
and other Christian missionary charitable agencies in Shanghai. In 1943, the
brother and sister together joined Communist-led cultural propaganda teams
in Kiangsu Province, working closely with the Red New Fourth Army units.
Ju Chih-chüan also went on stage, at least once portraying the White-haired
Girl, the heroine in a 1945 folk opera which won a Stalin Prize in 1951.

Ju Chih-chüan's short stories have been praised nationally for their finesse;
their structure is polished and their characterization is very persuasive. "The
Lilies on a Comforter" reflects these fine qualities. In the 1960s, while active in
the Shanghai branch of the Chinese Writers Association and editing a major
literary journal, *The Harvest,* she published several well-received collections
of short stories: *Auntie Kuan, Before Daybreak, The Quiet Maternity Ward,
Towering Poplars,* and others.

Because the quiet and refined tone of her writing, however effective it may
be for a talented storyteller, does not lend itself to the bombastic heroism
advocated by the radical left, she came under attack during the Cultural Revolution. Her critics accused her of exhibiting bourgeois tastes.

By 1973, she had already emerged from the shadow of persecution to work
on motion picture scripts. Her new writings appeared in 1977 and some of her
earlier stories were reissued in a new anthology in 1978. —K.Y.H.

The Lilies on a Comforter

Midautumn, 1946.

The troops were getting ready for a night attack on the coastal area. Several
comrades in the writing section of our Cultural Work Corps received orders
from the regimental commander to go separately with different companies.
When it came my turn for assignment, the commander scratched his head for
a long and embarrassing minute before he summoned a courier to run me over
to a first-aid station on the Front. He must have found it difficult to decide
where to put a woman during an offensive.

First-aid station or any station, it's all right with me, so long as they didn't
put me in a safe with multiple combination locks. I tossed my knapsack on my
back and followed the courier on my way.

There had been a spell of drizzle early in the morning. Now it had cleared
up, but the road, muddy and slippery, challenged any unsteady feet. The autumn crops on both sides of the trail, however, proudly displayed their green
foliage, fresh and lush, bejeweled with glittering raindrops. The sweet scent of

257

the soil filled the air. It was like going to a village market with all sorts of exciting anticipations, I thought, until scattered enemy fire pulled me back to reality.

The courier made long strides from the very start; in a minute I was left way behind. My feet, covered with blisters new and old, simply could not keep up with his, no matter how hard I tried. To ask him to wait for me would make him think I was scared; but I must honestly admit I don't think I could have found my way to the first-aid station without him. But he kept getting farther and farther ahead of me, and that did not make me happy.

Did he have eyes in the back of his head, or did he read my mind? Without turning to look at me, he halted on the roadside, still looking ahead to the far end of the trail. Just before I caught up with him, he took off again, and again left me way behind. I gave up trying to catch up with him. Somehow he sensed my deliberate, slow steps and he too slowed down, but never enough to let me walk side by side with him.

His funny way of walking me to our destination began to amuse me.

When the commander called him to give him the assignment, I did not pay attention to how he looked. Now I had ample opportunity to study him—from the back, of course. He stood quite tall, not broad, but sturdy, with solid, sinewy shoulders. His khaki uniform had faded with washing; the leggings reached up to cover his knees. The twigs inserted in the barrel of the rifle slung across his shoulder were more decorative than protective as camouflage, I thought.

I gave up completely and called for him to stop and rest for a while; my feet were killing me. I sat down on a roadside stone. He too sat down, but a couple of dozen yards away, his rifle balanced on his knees, his eyes still staring ahead. I had never seen anyone behave quite like that before, but I knew it had something to do with my being a woman. Women among soldiers in the field created problems. A little annoyed, I moved over to sit down facing him, in defiance. For the first time, I discovered his round, youthful face; he could not have been over eighteen. My closeness made him fidgety, as though he were sitting too close to a time-bomb. He wanted and yet didn't want to turn his face away or stand up. It was hard for me to suppress my chuckle, and when I managed that, I asked him where he was from, just to make conversation. He said nothing in reply for a long time, his face blushing pink, until finally he muttered something about the Tian-mu Mountain. Ah, we were fellow villagers!

"What did you do at home?" I asked.

"Hauled bamboos for others."

His muscular shoulders brought me a vision of the immense bamboo groves in our home village area. There, in the midst of that sea of green growth, appeared a narrow mountain trail, winding upward in stone-paved steps. And there he was, a piece of worn blue cloth between his shoulder and the huge bundle of bamboos on it, their slender tips and untrimmed foliage brushing the ground behind him as he picked his way on the trail. That was a most familiar scene to me, and brought me close to this fellow villager.

"How old are you?" I asked.

"Nineteen."

"How many years has it been since you joined in the revolution?"

"Just one year."

"How did you get involved in the revolution?" I felt I was not striking up any conversation, but conducting a one-way interrogation, but I carried on.

"When the Red Army pulled back north, I followed them."

"Who did you leave behind at home?"

"Mom, dad, brother and sister—and one aunt also lives with us."

"You aren't married, are you?"

The blush on his face darkened and his tongue glued down stiff. He played with the holes on his leather belt for a long while before he decided to shake his lowered head and answered me with only a bashful smile. I swallowed the rest of my question about whether he had a girl in mind.

In awkward silence we sat a while, then he looked up at the sky and glanced at me as though urging me to get going. As I stood up to move on, I noticed that he stole a moment when I wasn't looking to remove his cap and wipe his head with a towel. He had not perspired during the long walk, but he did when trying to answer my questions; that made me feel guilty.

It was past two in the afternoon when we reached the station, which was set up in a village school only about a mile from no-man's-land. The school's six rooms formed a triangle. The open space in the middle encouraged the growth of weeds, evidence of disuse of the school for quite some time. Several medics were arranging supplies. Boards placed on stacked bricks served as beds, using up all the space under the roof.

Shortly after our arrival, a village cadre çame in; his eyes, bloodshot from strain and fatigue, peered from behind a makeshift sunshade tucked under his old felt cap. A rifle and a weighing scale occupied his shoulders, while in his hands he carried a basket full of eggs and a cooking vessel. Panting hard, he dropped everything and dove for a bowl of water. Between gulps of water he took a rice cake from his pocket and started chewing it, while trying to talk at the same time. I watched his movements—he was doing so many things all at once—but I could not catch everything he said. He seemed to be complaining about something, and telling us to manage the necessary blankets ourselves. The medics told us that army blankets had not yet arrived, and yet we had to have them; the wounded would feel chill from having lost blood. We had to borrow blankets from the villagers. Even if they were only a dozen or so old cotton quilts, they would do. I had been wondering what I could do to help, so I volunteered for this requisition mission. Time was pressing, and I casually inquired if my escort, the courier comrade, would go on the mission with me. He hesitated only a brief moment, then we walked out together.

We divided our route in the first village we approached, he going east and I west. Within a short time, I had signed out three slips for borrowed articles, which filled my arms with cotton quilts and my heart with warm satisfaction. I was carrying them back to the station so I could return for more when the courier comrade walked up, empty-handed.

"How come you haven't gotten any?" I was surprised, since I discovered that the villagers in this area seemed to be politically very aware and easy to approach.

"Woman Comrade, you go borrow from them ... these villagers, hopeless, feudal ..."

"Which family? You show me," I said, thinking that his clumsy way might have offended the villagers, which would be much worse than the failure to borrow a few quilts. I asked him to show me where he had found those stubborn villagers. But it was he who was stubborn, standing there, head low, as though transfixed with a nail. I went up to him and explained in a low voice the importance of maintaining a good relationship with the people. He cheered up and turned back with me.

We walked into the yard of a farmhouse. There was no sign of anybody in the main room facing the entrance, but a pair of fresh, cheerful, red paper scrolls adorned the jambs of a door opening to an inner room. On that door hung a curtain of blue cloth with a red overhang.

We called for "big sister," then "big sister-in-law," then back to "big sister" again, but nobody responded. In a little while, someone stirred inside, and in another while the door curtain stirred and out walked a very pretty young woman, with a straight nose, gracefully curved eyebrows, and a sweep of a bang. Her clothes were coarse, but new. One look at her hair done up in a bun made me call her "big sister-in-law," apologizing for whatever offense she may have taken a while back at the presence of our courier comrade. She listened, keeping her face averted from us and having difficulty controlling her giggle. After I finished my bit of pacifying explanation, she still had nothing to say, still bit her lips to hold back her giggle. I was at the end of my tricks; what else could I say now? The courier stood next to me, blinking his big eyes and taking in earnest every word I said as though I were the company commander giving him a demonstration of how to handle a difficult situation.

I paused a second, swallowed hard, and began my pitch for borrowing blankets. I went through the whole works—how the Communist Party was the people's savior and why we were fighting ... Now she stopped fighting her giggles. She turned serious. As she listened, she kept glancing at the door. When I finished my prepared speech, she looked at me, then at the courier comrade, as though sizing us up against what I had just said. Then she went in, presumably to get what we had come for.

The courier comrade seized the opportunity to tell me, "A while ago I said exactly what you just said. But she just wouldn't budge. Isn't that strange ..."

I tried to hush him by glaring at him, but it was too late. The young woman had reappeared with a quilt in her arms—which immediately explained why she had not been ready to loan us that particular piece. It was a brand new comforter, brand new inside and out. The cover featured a wine-red brocade with patterns of white lilies. She shoved it toward me, as though purposely taunting the courier comrade. "Take this," she said.

My arms were already full, so I signaled to the courier comrade to accept it from her. But he pretended he did not see my signal, and I had to call him and tell him in so many words before he reluctantly walked up to the young woman for the comforter. Then he quickly turned and rushed away.

He turned a little too fast; his sleeve got caught on the door latch. We heard a ripping sound, and there was a dangling piece of cloth and a huge gaping tear on the shoulder of his jacket.

The young woman this time could not control herself anymore. She burst out laughing and insisted that she get her sewing kit to help him fix it up. But he would have nothing of the sort. Turning around, he resolutely walked away, the new flower-adorned comforter under his arms.

A few steps further on, we ran into another villager, who told us that the young woman was a bride of only three days, and the comforter was her only dowry. That made me feel awful, and the courier comrade felt even worse. His brow knitted in a tight knot, wondering what to do with the thing under his arms. Then he started to mutter, "We didn't understand the situation; we took away her wedding comforter. That just doesn't seem right. . . ."

"You said it," I said, both touched and amused by his serious air. "Perhaps before her wedding she had worked extra mornings and nights to save up enough for this thing. Perhaps she had even lost some sleep worrying about it. And yet somebody still called her hopeless, feudal. . . ."

He stopped, looking lost. Then he said suddenly, "In that case . . . in that case, let's take it back to her."

"She has already given it to us. If we returned it to her now, that would worry her, making her wonder what it's all about," I said. His youthful naiveté disarmed me; right there and then I decided I was very fond of this fellow villager.

He tossed the situation over in his mind, then said with determination, "All right, we'll keep it, and after our use we'll wash it carefully before giving it back to her." That decided, he took from me all the comforters and quilts we had borrowed, throwing them one upon another over his shoulders, and headed toward the first-aid station.

Back at the station, I told him to return to his regimental headquarters. As though set free after a prolonged imprisonment, he became suddenly very jolly. He bade me goodbye with a military salute, but his feet were already running.

He suddenly seemed to have remembered something, for he swiveled around in the road, reached into his pocket and produced two steamed buns. He waved them at me, left them on a stone by the roadside and said, "This is your dinner." Then he left, without once looking back.

I went over to pick up the buns; I could see that to the twigs stuck in his rifle barrel one sprig of wild chrysanthemum had been added. It danced in rhythm with his long strides.

When I realized that the torn shoulder of his jacket was still dangling and fluttering in the wind, I regretted that I had not insisted on fixing it up for him, but he had already disappeared around the bend of the road. Too bad; his shoulder would have to stay bare for some time.

The first-aid station was understaffed. The village cadres mobilized several women from the neighborhood to help us with the small chores, carrying water, cooking. The young bride was among them, still looking the same, still biting her lips often to hold back her giggles. Occasionallly she would eye me, but only for a moment. I sensed she was looking for something, then she confirmed it for me.

"Where did that young comrade go?" she asked.

I explained to her that he was not assigned to the station and that he had returned to the Front. She smiled in embarrassment and said, "Guess I wasn't too nice to him when he went along to borrow blankets from us a while back."

She moved about nimbly, separating and folding the borrowed quilts and comforters, placing one neatly on each makeshift bed. Some beds were made with two children's classroom desks pushed together. The new lily-patterned comforter was spread on a bed under the overhang outside the room.

A full moon rose in the sky, and yet our attack had not started. The enemy, as usual, disliked night operations. They built bonfires here and there to light up every possible trouble spot, and their airplanes blindly dropped bombs and flares. The night was turned into broad daylight. Removal of the night cover rendered our operation difficult and called for greater sacrifice. I began to resent the beautiful moon.

The village cadre returned, bringing us a number of homemade mooncakes. I had forgotten it was the Midautumn Festival.

The Festival! If I were at home, I would see, set out in front of every house, a bamboo tea table on which there would be plates of fruit, melons, and mooncakes. Children would be eagerly watching the incense sticks, hoping they would burn over soon so that they could help themselves to the goodies supposedly left over after treating the moon goddess. They would hop around the table, singing "Moonlight bright, candies tonight . . ." And I thought of that courier comrade, my young fellow villager, who used to haul those bamboo trees on his shoulders. Perhaps he was singing songs like that only a few years back. I bit into a mooncake; it tasted delicious. What's he doing now, I thought. Perhaps keeping a prone position in a pillbox, perhaps taking orders at the regimental headquarters, or walking the miles of trenches under enemy fire. . . .

Several red flares whined across the sky; our attack began. Before long the wounded started trickling into the station, and the whole place was plunged into tense action.

My job was to record their names and units. Those with light wounds could simply answer my questions, but the serious cases required my own effort to unbutton their jackets to search for their identifications. Then I came upon one. The word "courier" leapt at me from the ID card, and I shivered, but the rest of the identification, which showed that the soldier was from a certain battalion, saved me from a heart attack. He could not be my courier comrade, for he was assigned to regimental headquarters, not to a battalion. I wanted to ask somebody if by chance any wounded soldiers failed to get picked up by the litter bearers; I wanted to know what else a courier was supposed to do besides deliver messages on the front line. I didn't know why these questions, which could appear irrelevant under the circumstances, rose in my mind.

For an hour or so after the attack began, things moved very encouragingly. Along with the wounded came the good news that we had smashed the enemy's first line of defense, then we broke through the second wall of barbed wire, then we pierced the enemy's next belt of fieldwork and actually engaged them in street combat. But suddenly news stopped coming. The wounded would only say that fighting was in progress, or that they were fighting in the streets. The mud and caked blood on them, however, told a different story, which did not bode well.

There were not enough litters. Quite a few serious cases could not be sent to the field hospital further on and had to be taken care of right there at the station. We were not equipped to do much for them, not even to ease their pain somewhat. We could only try, with the help of those women villagers, to wipe blood and dirt off them, feed something to those still able to swallow, or ease them into a set of clean clothes, if they still had their clothing in their knapsacks. For the last job we had to remove their torn and bloodstained clothes and then wipe the injured men clean.

I had done enough of that before; it did not bother me. Those village women were different; they shrank from it, embarrassed and scared. They dodged the job, preferring to do the cooking instead. The young bride was particularly awestricken. I had to talk to her for a long time before she agreed to try, and then only as my assistant. She would not handle the wounded soldiers alone.

It was still midnight, but the gunfire was thinning, which created the illusion that it was getting close to dawn. The brilliant moon was in the middle of the sky now, brighter than I had ever seen it. Yet another heavily wounded man reached us from the Front. There was no more room inside; we had to place him under the overhang outside of the room. The litter-bearers eased the wounded man onto the makeshift bed, but would not leave him. One older bearer must have mistaken me for a doctor, for he grabbed my arm and pleaded with me, "Doctor, you must try everything to save this comrade. You save him, and we ... all of us bearers, will deliver a plaque to thank you for it ..." As he delivered his earnest plea, his fellow bearers all fixed me with their stare; they seemed to think that I only needed to nod my head and lo and behold their friend would be healed right away. I was just about to try to explain to these supplicants who I was when the young bride, standing in front of the makeshift bed with a basin of water in her hands, suddenly let out a muffled scream. I pushed my way to the bedside. There on the bed lay the wounded soldier. His round youthful face had lost its original suntan and had turned ghastly pale. His eyes were closed, very peacefully. On the shoulder of his uniform was a long tear, a piece of torn cloth still dangling from it.

"It's all because of us ..." said the pleading litter-bearer. "Over ten litters were crowded in an alley, ready to move forward to the Front. This comrade followed us. We couldn't tell where the damned reactionary sons-of-bitches tossed a grenade from. It rolled around in our midst, smoking and hissing. This comrade yelled for us to take cover, but he ... he himself ... he jumped right on top of it...."

The young bride let out another muffled scream. I don't know what I said, but I managed to hold back my tears and sent the bearers on their way. When I turned around, the young bride had already moved an oil lamp close to the soldier and had removed his clothes. No longer bashful now, the young woman proceeded to wipe the soldier's bare body, solemnly, almost with piety, while he lay senseless. I watched them, spellbound.

Then I woke from my trance and darted out to look for the doctor. When I returned with the doctor and his equipment, the young bride was sitting on the edge of the bed, her head bent low, her hands busy with needle and thread mending the soldier's torn jacket.

The doctor listened to the soldier's chest. Standing up quietly he said, "No use doing anything now." I went over to touch the soldier's hand; it was cold and stiff. The young bride, however, didn't seem to have heard anything or seen anything. She kept busy with her needle and thread, and, stitch after stitch, she sewed that tear, carefully, neatly. I couldn't stand it any longer. I whispered to her, "You can stop now."

She looked at me, her eyes full of incomprehension. Then she lowered her head and resumed her stitching. I felt like dragging her away, or tearing to pieces this choking thing in my throat, or perhaps he would sit up from his makeshift hospital bed, would smile his bashful smile. These things did not happen; only my hand inadvertently touched something, which turned out to be those two dried, cold buns, the dinner the soldier had given me a few hours before.

Several medics had a casket brought in. They started to fold the comforter aside to drop the body into the wooden box. As though seized by a spell, the young bride glared at them. Snatching the comforter away from them, she spread half of it on the bottom of the casket and gently pulled the other half over the dead soldier. The medics said, "The comforter . . . was borrowed, from a villager . . ." "It's mine! . . ." she said, but her angry voice choked off, and she hurriedly turned her face away.

The corner of the wine-colored silk comforter adorned with white lilies, those exquisite symbols of purity and compassion, fell over the face of an ordinary young man who used to carry bamboo trees over a mountain path.

March 1958
from *Tall, Tall Poplars,* pp. 54-63

Translated by Kai-yu Hsu

CHOU ERH-FU
(1912–)

Chou Erh-fu was born in Nanking around 1912. In 1933, while a student in the foreign language department of Kuang Hua University in Shanghai, he was jailed for involvement in Communist activities. He went to Yenan in 1938 to work in the Lu Hsün Academy. During the ensuing years, Chou established a name for himself as a writer of reportage literature, and in 1944 he was sent to Chunking to edit a collection of literary works from the Communist-controlled border region. In late 1945 and early 1946 he served as a reporter in Northeast China. In mid-1946 he traveled to Hong Kong, where he worked for nearly three years on the staff of the Communist-sponsored magazine *Wild Grass.*

Chou returned to Shanghai in 1949 and assumed a number of official posts. He was also active in literary circles and became increasingly influential within the Communist literary apparatus in Shanghai. During the Anti-rightist campaign of 1957, however, he himself was attacked as a rightist, and it was apparently only through the intercession of Chou Yang that he was saved. In 1959, again with the help of Chou Yang, he moved to Peking, where he worked in various capacities until he fell victim to the Cultural Revolution in 1969.

The fall of the Gang of Four brought him back into circulation. He was a delegate to the Third Congress of the All-China Federation of Literary and Art Circles in Peking in May 1978. Among his publications are the short story collections *Spring Famine* (1946), *Short Songs on the Highland* (1949), *Spring in the Valley* (1955), and the full-length novels *Swallow Cliff* (1954), *The Children of Hsi-liu-shui* (1956), and *Morning in Shanghai* (1958). —G.B.

---

from *Morning in Shanghai*

[*Morning in Shanghai* is Chou Erh-Fu's best-known and most widely read literary work. Based on material he gathered while living in Shanghai in the 1950s, it describes the changing situation in Shanghai's textile industry during the years following the establishment of Communist rule. Broad in scope and filled with vivid details, it resembles in numerous respects Mao Tun's major work *Midnight*, a portrayal of the Shanghai industrial scene in 1930. Unfortunately for Chou Erh-fu, however, the complexity of his well-developed characters and his faithful reflection of the spirit and events of the times provided openings for certain critics to claim that he had failed to adhere to the standards of socialist realism in his writing. Thus it was that in 1969 this work, which had been widely acclaimed by Communist literary authorities in the late 1950s and early 1960s, was labeled a "poisonous weed" and used as prima facie evidence of Chou's rightist tendencies.

Chou intended *Morning in Shanghai* to have four volumes, but he only finished three volumes before Chiang Ching's literary rectification drive of the mid-1960s led him to set aside his pen. Volume one, from which the following excerpts were selected, covers the period from the arrival of the Communists in Shanghai in 1949 to the eve of the Five Antis campaign in 1952. As these excerpts show, this was a time of vigorous plotting by the capitalists to maintain their power and privileges in the face of increasing government regulation and growing worker militancy. By the end of the volume, however, their efforts have proven to be in vain. Their ranks are in disarray and they have scant hopes of continuing effective opposition to the emerging new economic order.]

EPISODE I

[This first excerpt from volume one encompasses the latter part of chapter one and all of chapter two. It begins with the central capitalist figure in the story, Hsü I-te, the general manager of the Hu Chiang Cotton Mill, and his trusted assistant Mei Tso-hsien, the deputy director of the mill, discussing how to neutralize the new worker's union. It ends with Mei Tso-hsien's successful effort to enlist the help of a factory mechanic named T'ao Ah-mao in their scheme.]

"Tso-hsien, you're right," General Manager Hsü said in a low voice, as if he feared being overheard. "Now that we've been liberated it won't be so easy to move our spindles about. From now on the workers will be on top. Without any of our men in the new trade union, things will be hard to manage. How do you see it?"

"I think that we should gain control of the union," Mei Tso-hsien replied. Slowly lifting his cup of superior grade Mountain Peak Lungching tea from the low round table, he took a sip. Then, concerned that he might have spoken too strongly, he discreetly sought General Manager Hsü's own idea with the question, "What do you think, sir?"

"I say that it's not that easy."

"Oh, it would actually be very difficult. However, if we don't gain control, nothing will ever go the way we want it to."

"Well, think about it and see what you can come up with."

General Manager Hsü did not say any more. The gaze of his piercing fishlike eyes lay fixed on Mei Tso-Hsien, as if to say, "Now we'll see what you're made of." In a single glance Mei sensed what the general manager was thinking, so he boldly set forth his plan.

"Of course it won't be easy to gain control of the union. That's only my way of describing the situation. How could a capitalist lead a labor union? Would the Communist Party permit it? Absolutely not. The Communist Party quite naturally wants to direct the unions, so we'll change the prescription but not change the medicine. On the surface the union will be theirs. But in actuality those inside will be our own people, doing as we wish."

"That's excellent. Tso-hsien, you really deserve to be my deputy director."

"It's all due to your care and guidance."

"Well, who is going to infiltrate the union?"

At this moment Old Wang entered the room and announced to General Manager Hsü, "Sir, the coffee and sandwiches are ready."

"Yes, I know. You can go now. I still have a few things to discuss with Director Mei. We'll be coming soon."

Mei Tso-hsien listened until the sound of Old Wang's footsteps had receded into the distance before moving over next to Hsü and whispering, "How about T'ao Ah-mao? He's clever, capable, and daring. He likes to drink, and for a couple of bottles of liquor he'll do what we want."

"He would do," Hsü responded, tapping his right temple with his fat fingers. Then, turning toward Mei Tso-hsien, he said anxiously, "But he was the deputy chairman of the old union!"

Seeing that the general manager was worried, Mei immediately changed his tone of voice. "This is true. Sir, do you see a way to work this out?"

Actually, Mei had already thought of a way to handle it. But, just as he could not look helpless in front of the general manager, Mei also could not appear to be brighter than he. He deliberately held back, waiting for Hsü to speak.

The general manager thought for a moment and then said reflectively, "Of course there's a way. We did give him a little work to do for us in the past, and he also had his differences of opinion with the chairman of the old union. The workers know about this and his standing among them is quite high. If we could now give him a little capital, that would just about do it."

"Capital?"

Seeing that Mei Tso-hsien did not understand, Hsü I-te laughed and said "Political capital. We will express our dissatisfaction with him and he will think of ways to oppose us."

Mei Tso-hsien gave the "thumbs up" sign and exclaimed, "Ingenious! Positively ingenious!"

"You have to be careful, however," the general manager warned. "There must be no evidence of any contact between us and T'ao, and he must be just like he was before. He should seek opportunities for standing with the proletariat in opposition to us and for leading the workers in struggle against us. In this way he'll have political capital and working for us will be easier."

"Sir, you're brilliant, just absolutely brilliant."

"Handle this yourself. Don't let anyone know."

"Yes, sir. It will be done just as you wish."

"Come, let's go have a cup of coffee."

. . . . . .

CHAPTER II

Although it was broad daylight, with the sun high in the sky, the light inside DD's Cafe was dim. Mei Tso-hsien climbed the spiral staircase and turned toward the ballroom on the right. With the windows covered by black cloth that completely cut off the sunlight, the weak lamplight coming from the booths along the dance floor gave the impression that it was already late at night. As Mei strode into the room his eyes moved from side to side searching for something. Quickly he saw a man seated in the last booth on the west side of the room raise his right hand and beckon to him. Mei nodded his head in return and walked over to him.

The young fellow seated at the booth looked to be about thirty years of age. He was wearing a coffee-colored Western-style pinstripe suit and a red silk necktie with a gold dragon embroidered on it. The sleeves of the suit were too short and it fit poorly around his body. Its appearance was that of something from a used clothing store on Woosung Road. The young man stood up as Mei approached, shook hands with him, and said, "This place is really great."

[This young man is T'ao Ah-mao, and after some initial small talk, Mei Tso-hsien apprises him of his plan to have him infiltrate the union. T'ao is willing to undertake this task, but he is also very much aware of the difficulties and personal dangers involved. Picking up the action near the end of chapter two, we find T'ao telling Mei:]

"I wouldn't say that there's no way of doing this, but it will be very very difficult."

"As long as there's a way, Ah-mao, don't worry about the difficulties. If you run into any problems let me know and I'll help you resolve them."

"Things can't be done now like they were in the old days," Ah-mao responded and then stopped.

"That's true."

"As far as openly leading the workers is concerned, how could I keep up with the Communist Party? They wouldn't permit me to lead, either."

"I know."

"I would have to limit my activities to a small number of people."

"Right."

"There would even be times when I couldn't tell anyone anything and would have to work alone. If Yü Ching and her friends learned about this, it would be very bad."

"Indeed it would!" Mei Tso-hsien agreed completely with all of T'ao's comments, but they lacked substance. Anxiously, he asked, "Well, then, just how are you going to proceed?"

"As you know, I work in the maintenance department. This means that I have a chance to go around the mill and pass the time of day with the workers."

"This approach sounds good."

"But not everything can be discussed in the mill, because there are too many people. It will be necessary sometimes to go to their homes to talk."

"Of course. You want to be careful. In some cases you might even want to meet them elsewhere."

"If there were a lot of family members around it wouldn't be easy to talk, and we would naturally have to go out."

Two dimples appeared on Mei Tso-hsien's long rectangular face. Looking directly at T'ao Ah-mao he leaned forward and asked in a low voice, "Who are these people? Who are you going to start on?"

"I'll start in the maintenance department. There's a worker there by the name of Chang Hsüeh-hai. He's very simple and honest and we get along well. His wife, T'ang Ah-ying, works as a spindle operator. She's also a good person. She quietly does her job and doesn't involve herself with other things. She's popular, too. Talking with her won't be a problem, and through her I'll be able to influence other women working in the spinning shop. If each person brings along several more, when the total is added up it will be something to look at."

"This is a very good plan. Why didn't you mention it earlier?"

"It's just that it's not easy to do," T'ao answered and stopped. He obviously wanted to say more, but nothing would come out. Finally, after a long hesitation, he blurted out, "It will take time, and it will also take money."

When Mei Tso-hsien heard this last word he suddenly realized that he had been playing the role of a fool. T'ao Ah-mao had been toying with him all this time and he hadn't even sensed it. This, however, was no time to become angry. Despite his great abilities and resources, Mei had no way of influencing the upcoming union election. He was a representative of the capitalists. Not only was there no use talking about his being elected to a union office, he couldn't even acquire a red union membership card. He put on his tortoiseshell rimmed glasses, looked very closely at T'ao Ah-mao for a moment, and then said in an agreeable, generous manner, "Money is no problem. Whatever you want you can get from me. Just get elected to the union committee and we'll be able to work everything out."

"I'll try."

"Ah-mao, there's nothing to worry about. I believe that you'll be able to do it." Mei Tso-hsien spoke with great certainty. Without a trace of doubt in his voice he added, "Be quick about talking to Chang Hsüeh-hai, T'ang Ah-ying, and the others."

T'ao Ah-mao's voice also had a confident tone as he answered, "That won't be a problem. I'll look for a chance to approach them tomorrow."

EPISODE II

[This episode takes place in the early autumn of 1950, about a year after the events of episode I. By now the People's Government is starting to implement policies that are encroaching from above on the freedom of the textile magnates. As in the case of the rising threat from the workers below, the capitalists meet to work out their responses. This episode begins with Hsü I-te telling his colleagues at the highly select Tuesday Dining Club, a group whose membership includes the most powerful and influential figures in Shanghai's textile industry, what he thinks needs to be done to meet the latest goverment challenges.]

"Our discussions today have been very good. Our textile industry needs a place like this where we can speak freely. However, there are certain matters that the Dining Club cannot undertake directly, but which must instead be handled through the Textile Association. I have a personal view—I don't know whether it's right or not—that I'd like to put forth. Please tell me where I'm wrong. I feel that the leadership role of the Association is not very strong at present, and that the more capable men in the industry should be freed to manage the Association, as is the case in the Textile Workers' Union. Every single department in our Textile Association should be headed by a millowner.

Then we would present a stronger front, and it would be easier to get things done."

Chiang Chü-hsia was the first to voice agreement. "I feel the same way. I've always felt that it was hard to get something done in the Association. Many members of the executive committee are absent on a regular basis, and many of the subordinate committees within the Association exist in name only. Some committees do have millowners listed as members, but they never exercise control. As is the case with the representatives of the state-run enterprises, they seldom attend. Because of this, those who perform the actual work feel utterly useless."

"That's true," said Feng Yung-hsiang, as he picked up a fried chicken leg. Eating as he talked, he added, "The Association must be strengthened. Since Liberation everything has become dependent upon organization. With a poor organization it's very difficult to accomplish anything. The textile industry has occupied an important position in Shanghai for a long time. At present, however, the situation is one of impressive strength, but confused ranks." Pointing his chicken leg at Ma Mu-han, who was seated at the end of the table, he asked, "Mu-han, how do you feel about this?"

Ma Mu-han took a swallow of Coca Cola and replied thoughtfully, "Our strength is somewhat diffuse, and it is true that only by organizing can we really be strong. But after invigorating our organization we must also improve our study and strengthen our leadership. Since we're operating our mills under the overall leadership of the Communist Party, we must learn more about the Communist Party. We must keep in step with the times. We must look ahead. If we do this our futures will be brighter."

After he finished speaking, Ma stole a glance at Hsü I-te, as if to say, "Everything must be viewed from a higher level now. If you continue to manage your mill in the old way, you'll fail."

Hsü understood what Ma meant by this look and he responded, "Of course. With the communists leading us it would never do to be out of step with the Communist Party. However, we businessmen also have our business position. We can't demand too much from ourselves." In his heart he was thinking that this young fellow Ma Mu-han was, after all, nothing more than a university product with an overly simplistic way of thinking. He had not established himself by managing a mill and did not understand the difficulties involved. He had never tasted the bitter and the sweet, so he had no idea of their flavor.

Hsü's remarks continued. "We are members of the bourgeoisie and always will be. The Association should serve our privately operated mills. If we could change the Textile Association into a bureau of private textile enterprises we would have some power."

"A bureau of private textile enterprises. Brilliant! Absolutely brilliant!" With his father, P'an Hsin-ch'eng, out of the room, P'an Hung-fu became quite lively. His effusive praise was accompanied by animated gesturing.

"Who would be the director of this bureau, I-te?" Feng Yung-hsing asked enthusiastically.

Before Hsü I-te could answer, Chiang Chü-hsia interrupted, "I think that the best person would be Shih Pu-yün, who is in Peking right now attending a conference. Or, the chairman of our board of directors, P'an Hsin-ch'eng, would be fine, too."

"Have father serve as director?" P'an Hung-fu could not restrain his sense of pleasure and began to smile. But then the fear that the others might see what he was thinking made him control himself and he ended up with only half a smile.

Ma Mu-han laughed coldly and said sarcastically, "Then we'll have two textile bureaus and two directors."

"When that happens our Miss Chü-hsia can take charge of the office in the bureau of private textile enterprises," interjected Feng Yung-hsiang.

Chiang Chü-hsia gave Feng Yung-hsiang a sidelong glance and said, "You're making fun of me again."

"Don't worry," Feng Yung-hsiang countered, "the director hasn't been announced yet, so for the time being you won't have to take over the office."

Everyone laughed heartily. P'an Hung-fu called out to Chiang Chü-hsia, "Chief Chiang," but then he saw his father coming back and fell silent.

P'an Hsin-ch'eng came in hurriedly, and without taking a seat or even resting for a moment, he announced excitedly, "That was a long-distance call from Shih Pu-yün, who's in Peking attending the National Textile Conference. He has heard that the government wants to stabilize cloth prices and has decided on the unified purchasing of cloth. He knew that our Dining Club was meeting today, so he called to solicit our opinions in preparation for representing the attitude of the textile industry in Peking. Gentlemen, what are your ideas? How do you feel about this? He's waiting for me to call him back today."

As soon as this news was announced the lighthearted banter and laughter disappeared without a trace. A deep silence fell over the dining room. From outside the window came the sound of falling leaves rustling in the autumn wind.

Hsü I-te's mood was like that of a leaf being blown from a tree. He felt a touch of disappointment. If the government adopted the unified purchasing of cotton yarn, the free market would cease to exist. There would be no way to freely buy and sell the cotton yarn produced by the Hu Chiang Mill system. Even if Fang Yü, the tax office representative in the mill, sent him better information about tax collections, it would be impossible to make a big profit on a single transaction. Normal profits would also have fixed limits. Hsü felt that they should oppose unified purchasing, but businessmen could not struggle against government officials. If this were a proposal of just the Shanghai State Cotton, Yarn, and Cloth Company they could still find a way out. Relying on the Federation of Industry and Commerce, they could unite with the Bureau of Industry and Commerce, win over the Textile Administration Bureau, and then attack the Shanghai State Cotton, Yarn, and Cloth Company. If unsuccessful, they could still appeal to the Central Government. But this proposal was from the Central Government, which made it a thorny matter.

For a long time no one uttered a sound. Hsü I-te stared silently at the plate of fried chicken before him. The chicken was tender and delicious, but he seemed to have suddenly lost his appetite. He couldn't eat another bite.

Seeing that no one was going to speak, P'an Hsin-ch'eng said to Hsü I-te, "You're our 'iron abacus.' Figure this one out. Just what attitude do you think we should take toward unified purchasing?"

Hsü I-te heaved a deep sigh and said dejectedly, "It doesn't matter whether you have an iron abacus or an electric adding machine, or figure a thousand times or ten thousand times. Nothing can match a solitary calculation by Him who rules the heavens."

Feng Yung-hsiang noticed Hsü I-te's look of despair and tried to be encouraging. "Don't exaggerate the determination of others or belittle one's own importance. We in the Shanghai textile industry should, after all, have a set policy. I-te, give us your ideas first, and then we'll have a general discussion."

Hsü I-te thought for a moment, his fat fingers tapping his temple. Then he said slowly, "If the Central Government has decided to introduce unified purchasing, in my view there is no way for us at the local level to oppose it. Ninety percent of the things the Communist Party brings up for consultation and discussion are carried out. Their method of operation is more intelligent than that of the Kuomintang. Before undertaking something, they give us a thorough briefing, seek our consent, and expect us to do it willingly. This is a very formidable approach. As I see it, we should take the initiative in proposing the idea of unified distribution and marketing. At present every factory is experiencing a shortage of new materials, capital is hard to obtain, and our markets are restricted. Let's place the burden of responsiblility on the government. We'll ask the government for raw materials and ask the People's Bank for capital. With marketing given over to the government, we'll concern ourselves solely with operations and management. Since the government is always saying that it wants private enterprise to develop, we won't worry about the government not taking care of us. We'll just watch and see what it does. How do you feel about following this plan?"

Chu Yen-nien listened to Hsü I-te's reasoning with respect. He wanted to voice his support as soon as Hsü finished talking, but then he saw Ma Mu-han glaring at him and didn't feel that he should say anything. All he could do was keep his complete agreement to himself.

Mei Tso-hsien had been listening to these high-flying, wide-ranging discussions of the big bosses in silence. But after listening to this lengthy discourse by Hsü I-te, he leaned toward him and said softly in a flattering manner, "This chicken is very good. You must be hungry. Have a piece before it gets cold." He also servilely passed the small glass peppershaker to Hsü with the question, "Would you like this?"

Hsü I-te shook his head. He had no heart for eating chicken.

Chiang Chü-hsia also admired Hsü I-te's analysis. "I-te's idea is right. He really deserves his standing as our 'iron abacus.'"

T'ang Chung-sheng, "Mr. Brilliant," raised his hand in support and said, "This is an ingenious approach!"

This time Ma Mu-han was in agreement with Hsü I-te. "I agree with I-te's plan, too. Since the government has already made its decision, we might as well go along graciously. We'll leave it up to the government to set the profit and see how much they give us. Whatever amount they give, we'll take."

"Right. We want to look good." This was Feng Yung-hsiang speaking.

Seeing that everyone was more or less in agreement, P'an Hsin-ch'eng silently added up the number of spindles controlled by the members of the Tuesday Dining Club. The total came to about seven hundred thousand, which meant that if Shih Pu-yün acted as a representative of the Shanghai textile industry in agreeing to unified purchasing and marketing at the National

Textile Conference in Peking, there would be no major problems after he returned. P'an then asked if there were any other ideas in the group, and when everyone replied that there was none he said, "Well, in that case we'll take the initiative in accepting unified purchasing and marketing, and we'll have Shih Pu-yün express this position for us in Peking. Agreed?"

"Yes," came the unanimous reply.

Hsü I-te made an additional comment. "We have yielded on the issue of unified purchasing and marketing. But on the question of payment we must take the offensive. Tell Pu-yün that he can raise the subject of the eight percent rate of return that was fixed by the temporary regulations on private enterprise. In this way we'll be able to stress the fact that current profits in the textile industry are too low. We must seek a decision on the formula for calculating payment and struggle to obtain a victory for ourselves on this question."

"This is a very important point, as I'm sure you all agree." P'an Hsin-ch'eng looked at each person for their reaction. No one had a different opinion, so he called the waiter in and said enthusiastically, "Place a long-distance call for me to Shih Pu-yün in Peking. Do it quickly. I have something urgent to discuss with him."

"Yes, sir," the waiter answered and hurried out.

EPISODE III

[The events of this episode occur in the first part of 1951, some months after China's entry into the Korean War. Here Hsü I-te faces a severe challenge from the representatives of the new workers' union. It is interesting to note that T'ang Ah-ying, the spindle operator whose miscarriage in the mill has now resulted in greater worker militancy, was considered earlier by T'ao Ah-mao as someone he could use in his scheme to infiltrate the union.]

The time was two o'clock in the afternoon.

At the labor-management meeting, Yü Ching was just concluding the detailed report she had made as union representative. "According to our union's information and analysis, the primary reason for the work in the mill becoming difficult of late is the raw cotton. I hope that this problem can be resolved once and for all at today's meeting. If we continue on in this way, production in the entire mill will be affected, as will the quality of our products and the health of the workers. It is because of the difficulty of the work that T'ang Ah-ying became exhausted and gave birth prematurely in the spinning shop. The child died and Ah-ying has still not recovered her health. I believe that if we don't clear up this problem there will be a second and then a third T'ang Ah-ying."

When Kuo P'eng heard Yü Ching mention the problem of the raw cotton, he turned his face toward the window and stared at the great smokestack thrusting into the sky. General Manager Hsü was very calm. He avoided looking Yü Ching in the eye and with an unobtrusive glance indicated to Director Mei Tso-hsien, who was seated a little in front of him on one side, that he should respond to the issues raised by Yü Ching.

Director Mei nodded his head ever so slightly to indicate to the general manager that he was prepared to say something, but he did not begin to talk immediately. He first picked up his cup and took a sip of tea. Then, with a very troubled look on his face, he started to speak in a slow halting manner: "This problem has been of concern to the general manager for some time. The quality of our products has been poor recently, and this has affected the reputation of the Hu Chiang Mill in the marketplace. The general manager has come to me on a number of occasions and asked why our goods are so bad. I have been thinking about this for a long time. I know that a problem definitely exists, and I was about to approach the union to discuss it. Now today Comrade Yü Ching has raised this topic. I think that this is excellent. However, I see this problem differently."

When Chao Te-pao heard this he became somewhat annoyed. "The problem is obviously in the raw cotton," he thought. "What kind of game is he playing with his other viewpoint?" Leaning his chin on his left hand, he stared intently at Director Mei.

Director Mei realized that Chao was reacting against what he had just said, but he pretended not to notice. His tone, however, became much more mellow. "I don't know if my opinion is right or not. That is something for everyone to look into. I am especially hopeful that the comrades in the union will provide more direction." He glanced at Yü Ching and then proceeded. "I think that the major problem is with the machinery. Our mill has not had a general overhaul for a long time. If the maintenance department has not been making detailed inspections, this would affect production, make the work more difficult, and cause our quality to decline."

Chao Te-pao stood up immediately and objected. "Your idea is wrong. Two days ago Comrade Yü Ching and I went to the spinning shop and looked things over. The maintenance department also made an inspection. In general, the machinery is very good, with no defects to speak of."

Director Mei asked skeptically, "Well, then, what is wrong?" Continuing on he answered his own question. "Of course not every machine is defective. I'm just saying that some machines should be overhauled. Is that better? *Some* machines are defective. In addition, the task of keeping the spinning shop clean hasn't been done well lately either. Naturally, this has an affect on product quality. That's right, isn't it, Kuo P'eng?"

Kuo P'eng had been watching the black smoke issuing from the tall smoke-stack. Curling up and down in the damp sea breeze of winter's end, it resembled a long, long wisp of hair. The sound of Director Mei calling his name left him startled. He hadn't been listening closely to what Director Mei had been saying, and had only heard the final question, "That's right, isn't it, Kuo P'eng?" Without thinking he answered hurriedly, "Yes. Yes."

Director Mei was very pleased at obtaining Kuo P'eng's support for his idea and his tone hardened immediately. "The work supervisor probably wouldn't be wrong, would he Comrade Yü Ching?"

"What's important is the facts. The cleanliness of the spinning shops recently has really been quite good. But even if the cleaning work in certain shops had been a little below standard it couldn't have affected things this much."

"Not necessarily. The impact of cleaning work is significant. If you don't believe me, ask our own Engineer Han."

Engineer Han had not yet said a word. He had not wanted to attend today's labor-management meeting, and when Director Mei had asked him to come he had declined. When General Manager Hsü called him on the telephone, however, he didn't feel that he could say no a second time. He had foreseen what today's meeting would be like and the difficult position that he would be in. No matter what he said he would be in trouble. From the very start of the meeting he had held a teacup in his hand. On one side was written the number 13, which he considered a bad omen. He tried to turn it away from him, but it was soon back in front of his eyes again. And just as he could not avoid the number 13, so it was that this difficult situation appeared before him. He had not intended to speak, but now he had to say something. He said, "The cleaning work does have a certain effect."

General Manager Hsü now took advantage of this favorable situation to comment. "I have heard reports very recently that the cleaning work in the shops is, in fact, rather poor. This is a clear indication that our worker comrades have a poor attitude toward their jobs. The rate of absenteeism now exceeds thirty-five percent. I hope that the union will give more consideration to this point."

Director Mei was afraid that these words were not strong enough, so he added some of his own in an attack upon the union. "I think that the work style of the workers in our mill is bad. If not, why is the work always done poorly? Perhaps the union will want to consider this point, too." He looked intently at Yü Ching as he spoke.

Yü Ching recorded each problem that they raised, but she made no response other than to ask, "Does management have any other comments?"

Chung P'ei-wen could not refrain from rebutting General Manager Hsü's remarks. "I don't think that there's anything wrong with the work style of the mill workers. As I see it, I would still ask management to give this matter more thought. Perhaps the problem really lies with them."

General Manager Hsü feared that Engineer Han and Work Supervisor Kuo P'eng might give a different view, so he spoke again: "I think that the problem is primarily with the workers themselves. We have no other opinions on this."

Chung P'ei-wen did not give an inch. Pointing directly at General Manager Hsü he said, "You can't be so arbitrary and hold fast to the judgment that the problem is with the workers. You should listen to all sides with an open mind." After he finished speaking his eyes came to rest on Engineer Han. He was thinking that Engineer Han knew where the problem lay.

Engineer Han was devoting his attention to turning his teacup. He did not want to join either side and had been sitting back watching Hsü I-te and Yü Ching face each other with crossed swords. This was not his problem, and he was afraid of being drawn into it. He feared being asked any questions, and deliberately avoided Chung P'ei-wen's hopeful gaze.

For a while no one said a word.

Yü Ching arranged the notes she had written down, stood up, and said in a calm, deliberate manner, "We cannot look at the problem just on the surface. Neither can we discuss it in bits and pieces. We must get to the heart of the problem. First, let's talk about the work style of the workers in our mill. Generally speaking, it's good and proper. The cleaning work is not bad either.

We invite General Manager Hsü, Director Mei, and the engineer to personally visit the spinning shops for a look. Of course, the cleaning work could still be done a bit better, and as Engineer Han just said, the cleaning work does have a certain impact on things. However, it does not have a decisive impact. The worker comrades have been doing their very best on the job. To show this I need bring up only one example, namely, the female worker in the spinning shop whom I mentioned earlier, T'ang Ah-ying. Even though she was more than seven months pregnant she continued to come to work regularly. Due to exhaustion she gave birth prematurely in the shop. Is it possible to say that she did not have a good attitude toward her work? Yes, there are times when the absentee rate reaches thirty-five percent. I acknowledge that this is a serious situation. But what has made the situation so serious? It is the difficulty of the work. If you don't believe me you can look at the rate of absenteeism for the period when the work wasn't hard. What was it? Supervisor Kuo knows. At most it never exceeded twenty-five percent. Why the change? The difficulty of the work. Why has the work become difficult? The webbings on the carding machines are completely covered with flying cotton. There are too many impurities in the laps and slivers and the rovings are not of uniform thickness. Going back to the beginning, it's a problem of the raw cotton. I hope, General Manager Hsü, that we can all lay our cards on the table and have a frank and open discussion of this problem."

General Manager Hsü was taken aback by Yü Ching's pointed remarks, but in an experienced manner he quickly regained his composure and responded, "Comrade Yü Ching, this is my greatest hope, too. I think that our views can be described as exactly identical."

Yü Ching waved her hand in disagreement. "No. Our views are different as a matter of principle. My way of viewing things is completely different from yours."

"Totally different," interrupted Chao Te-pao. "You say that the workers are at fault. This is not in keeping with the facts."

General Manager Hsü asked in amazement, "Do you think that the raw cotton is the problem?"

Without any hesitation Chao Te-pao replied firmly, "Yes, the problem is with the raw cotton."

General Manager Hsü feigned a bewildered look and inquired of Director Mei, "Is there something wrong with the raw cotton? Could this really be it?"

Director Mei knew what General Manager Hsü was thinking. He wanted Mei to stall for time while he himself thought of a good way to respond.

"In general there's nothing wrong with the raw cotton," Director Mei said slowly, thinking as he spoke. "We use even more cotton than other mills. For every lot of yarn we use 418 *catties*. The State Cotton, Yarn, and Cloth Company, however, only allots us 410 *catties*. This isn't enough. Before the yarn is scheduled for delivery the cotton is already running out. The Joint Purchasing Agency can't buy cotton for us either, so we have no choice but to add some Chingyang seconds. Chingyang seconds is comparatively low in quality, but even at this we're losing money. If we added the best cotton we would lose still more money. The general manager wouldn't agree with that, and I would be out as director of the mill, ha-ha." Director Mei looked at Yü Ching and laughed.

As if struck by a great revelation, General Manager Hsü suddenly responded, "Oh, so that's the way it is."

As Engineer Han listened, it seemed as though General Manager Hsü was reading the script of a play. He felt sick to his stomach, but could not bring himself to say anything. His eyes were fixed on the number 13 on his teacup.

"Adding just 8 *catties* of Chingyang seconds shouldn't make the work that difficult," Yü Ching observed. "Is it possible that there's a problem with the blending proportions? If so, please be honest about it."

When General Manager Hsü heard the words "blending proportions" his heart skipped a beat, but outwardly he remained very composed. He said firmly, "The blending proportions are something that I'm well aware of. There's no problem there, absolutely none at all." Turning to Director Mei, he asked, "Isn't that right?"

Director Mei leaned forward slightly and replied, "There's not a single problem, not one single problem. I, Mei Tso-hsien, can give a complete guarantee of that."

Yü Ching sensed that Director Mei was a bit nervous and thought that perhaps this was the key to the whole problem. Seizing this opening, she sought to widen it. "This is an engineering function. How can you guarantee that there are no problems whatsoever? On this question we should allow Engineer Han to speak."

"Right. Ask Engineer Han to speak," added Chung P'ei-wen. He had been thinking from early on that Engineer Han might know something about this. Now that Yü Ching felt this way, too, he was more certain than ever.

Director Mei was unsure of how to answer. He did not dare let Engineer Han talk. If by chance he mentioned the secret of the raw cotton, would not everything be uncovered? General Manager Hsü saw that Mei was having difficulty responding. He had been checkmated by Yü Ching. Now they had to take a chance and allow Engineer Han to speak. If they did not, it would appear that there must be a problem here. Only by encouraging him to speak could they retrieve this desperate situation. Hsü prepared an answer for Engineer Han. "Of course there's nothing wrong with the blending proportions. Everything is done according to the regulations of the State Cotton, Cloth, and Yarn Company. Engineer Han handles this himself, so there's not the slightest problem. Engineer Han, tell Comrade Yü Ching about this."

Once again the teacup in front of Engineer Han was turning round and round. If he didn't tell what he knew, and went along with the lies of General Manager Hsü and Director Mei, he would be going against his conscience. Science should seek after truth, and he should not violate his conscience. But what if he did speak up? It wouldn't help either the mill or himself, and he would be turning his back on General Manager Hsü. No matter what else was true, he was, after all, an engineer in the Hu Chiang Mill and Hsü I-te was the general manager of this mill. Han's conscience wanted him to tell the truth, but his job and friendship were telling him to keep quiet.

General Manager Hsü waited a few moments. Then, seeing that Han was not saying anything, he suggested, "Just tell them the facts; that there's nothing wrong with the blending proportions."

"That's right. There's nothing wrong with the blending proportions." After Han said this his neck felt hot and he flushed slightly.

"Absolutely nothing wrong at all? Engineer Han, tell us the truth." Chao Te-pao put further pressure on Han. But having finally spoken, Han now felt at ease. He replied very quickly, "Naturally there's nothing wrong at all."

"Then why is the work so difficult?" interrupted Yü Ching.

Director Mei was afraid that Engineer Han could not withstand direct questioning by Yü Ching, so he stepped in with an answer. "Recently the raw cotton from the State Cotton, Yarn, and Cloth Company has not been very good. Many other mills have been complaining that the work is difficult. I think that this is the major reason. Just a moment ago Comrade Yü Ching said that the key to our problem lies with the raw cotton. As I think about this now I feel that there's some truth in what she says."

"Then we must approach the State Cotton, Yarn, and Cloth Company tomorrow and formally request that they provide us with more good quality raw cotton."

General Manager Hsü had actually been in a cold sweat these last minutes. Engineer Han's comments had made him feel somewhat relieved, but he was still afraid that things could go the wrong way and get out of control. Then Director Mei, a man experienced in the ways of the world, placed the responsibility on the State Cotton, Yarn, and Cloth Company, and gave him a ready-made way out. Hsü I-te naturally took it. He assumed a very serious, earnest posture and said, "This problem must be resolved soon. Otherwise we won't be able to face our worker comrades. Director Mei, send someone from the mill tomorrow to look in on Comrade T'ang Ah-ying, and send along some things to help nourish her back to good health."

"Of course. It will be done in the morning."

Turning to Yü Ching, General Manager Hsü said warmly, "Comrade Yü Ching, if we are to increase production and thereby keep pace with national construction and meet the needs of the people, we must depend completely on the leadership of the working class. There is no one from management in our mill I can rely on. If our mill is to run well we must rely totally on the Communist Party and always follow Chairman Mao. Only by doing this will we have a bright future. Now you have conscientiously raised this serious production problem. This is a great service to our mill and we're very grateful to you. I hope that after this you'll give us more guidance." After he finished speaking he nodded his head to express his gratitude.

"There is no need to thank me. Furthering production is the primary duty of our union. I hope that management will improve its administration and work positively for production."

"There's no question about that," General Manager Hsü said effusively. "No question at all."

After the labor-management meeting was over and the others had all left, General Manager Hsü and Director Mei stayed behind. Director Mei walked over and closed the door. Then he turned back to General Manager Hsü and said softly in his ear, "Sir, you've committed yourself. What are we going to do now about the blending proportions?"

General Manager Hsü had already settled on an idea, and after wiping his face he said with great satisfaction, "With a young girl like Yü Ching, all it takes is a word or two to shut her up."

This time Director Mei disagreed. "No, you made a commitment."

"That's true. I said that we would soon be contacting the State Cotton, Yarn, and Cloth Company about resolving this problem. Right?"

"Yes. But the cotton that they have been giving us lately has been quite good."

"I know."

"Then what's the solution?"

"Notify Engineer Han and Supervisor Kuo that they can make a slight improvement in the blending proportions. This will mollify the workers and the union will think that the negotiations were successful. As the work becomes less difficult the rate of absenteeism will decline, and soon the feelings of discontent will disappear. After a while we can slowly come back to the present blending proportions. Isn't that a solution, Tso-hsien?"

"Yes," Director Mei replied with a nod of his head. But after thinking for a moment he added apprehensively, "I'm afraid that we can't go on like this for very long. Won't the complaints start up again?"

"A day delayed is a day gained," Hsü I-te responded. Then, whispering in Mei Tso-hsien's ear, he said, "The Peoples' Volunteer Army won't be able to hold out for long against the Americans in Korea. The whole government might collapse completely at any time. If the Communist Party falls and the workers lose their backstage support, who will dare make trouble again?"

Mei Tso-hsien listened with rapt attention, nodding his head in agreement and saying, "Yes. Yes. Yes."

"Won't that take care of everything?"

Mei Tso-hsien replied elatedly in a loud voice, "Yes. That will really solve everything."

EPISODE IV

[This final excerpt, which is taken from near the end of volume one, describes events occurring in the late autumn of 1951. The Three Antis campaign aimed at rectifying shortcomings within the Chinese Communist Party is reaching its climax and the Five Antis campaign against bourgeois corruption is about to begin. Hsü I-te is shocked by the news that several high-ranking CCP officials have been dismissed from the Shanghai Municipal Council for hindering the Three Antis campaign. His own future now seems very much in doubt.]

"One can see from today's paper that the Communist Party is capable of managing the nation's affairs. China certainly has a bright future." Engineer Han's eyes sparkled with joy as he spoke, but looking around the room he noticed that General Manager Hsü's eyes were fixed on the door. His face was still and rigid. He seemed to be deeply troubled.

General Manager Hsü turned toward Engineer Han and said, "Of course China has a bright future. But what about our future? If the Three Antis campaign within the Party is so harsh on their own people, think of what the Five Antis campaign against the bourgeoisie will be like. The Three Antis campaign is a living model for the Five Antis campaign."

General Manager Hsü's remarks spread like a dark shadow across everyone's heart. Even the enthusiastic glow on Engineer Han's face faded away. He could not find a good way to respond. It was as if he were back in school doing arithmetic; his teeth bit tightly on his right thumb and he sank into deep thought searching for an answer. Mei Tso-hsien knew now why the general manager had been so silent. He sensed the excessive tension in the room and thought hard for a way to ease the atmosphere.

General Manager Hsü took the newspaper on the table and turned it over for another look, as though he disbelieved the news he had just read and wanted to verify it. But there it was in black and white. It was true. Hsü could see from the newspaper that the Five Antis campaign would definitely be fiercer than the Three Antis campaign, especially after the office staff and the workers began to participate. Then it would become more savage, like an unstoppable sharp spear. Yet, for now the Five Antis campaign was still only a dark cloud before the storm. Its total effect could not yet be calculated. Hsü felt uneasy and apprehensive. As he looked at the *Liberation Daily* he murmured to himself, "Such high-ranking cadres in the CCP have been dismissed. Cadres who have been in the CCP for so long have been expelled from the Party. We in the business world will be in even greater difficulty. Ah, why haven't they formally begun the Five Antis campaign? Start it! Start it! Let's get going! The sooner the better! It's so hard to be kept hanging like this."

He felt regret about having stayed in Shanghai. . . .

Translated by Gary Bjorge

FANG CHI
(1919–)

Political independence and conformism run together through the life and works of Fang Chi, a poet and novelist who has enjoyed considerable standing in China. In such diverse writing tasks as travel reportage (1957) and art criticism (1963), translated into English in *Chinese Literature,* the author speaks in an aesthetic voice almost totally divorced from politics. To the Western reader not inclined toward socialist realism, "The Visitor" (December 1957) may provide evidence enough of Fang Chi's artistic talent and social conscience. Taut, suspenseful, and full of the racy Hopei dialect which Fang Chi loves but uses here to reveal a social underworld, the story features a compelling monologue by a broken young intellectual who still struggles, half incoherently, to rationalize his life before authority.

Born into a declining Hopei landlord family in 1919, Fang Chi joined the Communist war mobilization effort in Yenan, after participating in left-wing student organizations and the anti-Japanese demonstration of December 9, 1935. He served in Yenan as reporter, author, and editor of literary magazines. The *People's Daily,* on March 12, 1950, attacked the ascendancy of romance, and even lust, over serious politics in his story "Let Life Become More Beautiful," but Fang Chi criticized himself (and later Hu Feng) and continued to write. Vice-Chairman of the Tientsin Branch of the China Peace Committee and Secretary-General of the Tientsin Sino-Soviet Friendship Association, he visited the Soviet Union in 1954. From this came several pieces lauding the Russian approach to communism, which Fang Chi evidently has admired since his Yenan days, when he wrote "Dr. Orlov." In "The Visitor," the main character's name, K'ang Min-fu, which means Communist, may itself betoken a romantic link to the early, idealistic days of Chinese communism, when names ending in *-fu* (transcribing the Russian final *-ov, -iev,* etc.) were much in vogue.

In 1958 a host of critics accused Fang Chi of having written "The Visitor" to "indict" China's new social system. They asked if K'ang Min-fu was the one criticized, or an "anti-feudal hero" whose fate was meant to chastise those in authority. If he was a victim, had he suffered from social interference, or neglect? Some ideological repugnance on the part of Fang Chi toward the social irresponsibility of K'ang Min-fu's extreme self-indulgence or individualism would seem as hard to doubt as the author's long-standing commitment to the ideals of communism. But Yao Wen-yüan, who has since gained notoriety as a Cultural Revolution extremist and member of the Gang of Four, was surely correct in observing that Fang Chi's plot does not turn on the class struggle. The story indeed projects a fairly chilly bureaucratic atmosphere, and conveys romance in romance's own language. And no modern Chinese could fail to wince at the dark aspects of society portrayed in "The Visitor," whether "feudal" liaisons with actresses and prostitutes, or "bourgeois" cohabitation. Was this a slander of the new order sufficient to drive readers into bourgeois despondency and political vacillation, as Yao Wen-yüan proclaimed, or realistic and well-meaning exposé?

On the other hand, when Fang Chi wrote, he was Deputy Director of the Propaganda Department in the Party's Tientsin Municipal Committee, a "Party member responsible for cultural affairs," like the cadre who hears K'ang Min-fu's story. In the summer of 1957 he had been as busy as his cadre criticizing rightists—including those in "Tientsin theatrical circles" (who do not appear favorably in "The Visitor"). Chairman of the Federation of Literary and Art Circles, Tientsin Branch, and Vice-Chairman of the union in Hopei from October 1958, as well as editor of the literary monthly *New Harbor* into the early sixties, Fang Chi may not really have suffered for his own authorial individualism until 1968, when he was finally named an "out-and-out counterrevolutionary revisionist shielded by Chou Yang." If "The Visitor" reveals a Chinese writer's private conscience from beneath a public mask, perhaps its most tortured passages confess what Fang Chi perceives to be his own burden as a protected intellectual—and manager of the public life.

Although reported to be suffering poor health as a result of political persecution, Fang Chi has reappeared in public and has published several new poems since the fall of the Gang of Four in 1976.   —J.K.

The Visitor

The Information Center notified me that I had a caller; he claimed to be a college student. His visitor's appointment form had been filled in to read: "K'ang Min-fu, age 28, origin Liaoning, unemployed ... " Thinking it over, I simply could not remember having known such a person. Was he one of our readers? Had he submitted an article? Or was he a resident seeking assistance, one of the masses who wanted a Party Committee office to solve a problem for him? I hesitated a bit, then followed the courier downstairs and went into the reception office to wait....

I was genuinely startled when I got a good look at this caller of mine. I thought at once of the peculiar name on his appointment form: K'ang Min-fu —Communist. Such names had been popular, in the twenties and thirties, among those who considered themselves revolutionary intellectuals. Most of them had really been sons of the rich who played at revolution, self-styled nihilists. I rarely get to see such names or people again in the course of my life today. Yet, somehow, such a one was seated before me. What startled me was that his appearance and name were of like peculiarity, and his hair was so long as to suggest the artists of an earlier era who had called themselves decadents. But their hair had streamed down to their shoulders, while his stood erect, with each hair distinctly visible. Truly it brought to mind the well-known figure of speech, "so angry that his hair stood on end, pushing off his cap"—only he had no cap. His face, like the shirt he wore, had lost its original composition. It was dirty—filthy—with a bottomless pallor showing through under a layer of oily sweat. And, perhaps because of the lighting, a green, phosphorescentlike hue flitted across his face.

I could not see his eyes, for he kept his head bowed. As I waited for him to speak, I looked at his appointment form—the name at the top, his age, his place of origin ... the handwriting, very clear, seemed not at all like the strange caller before my eyes, except that it appeared similarly pale, weak, and perfunctory.

"What business brings you, ... Sir?"

I simply could not get out such an elevated form of address as "comrade" before a person like this. A tortuously pronounced "Sir" was preferable.

He remained still, with head bowed, and said nothing. But his eyelids suddenly flew open at the sound of my voice. ... The lunacy, despair, and distrust of humanity that his eyes betrayed were frightening.

You must realize, moreover, that this incident took place early in June of this year. It was just at the time of "Great Blooming and Contending," when rightist elements were launching wild, unbridled attacks. The anti-rightist struggle had not yet begun. As the papers often described it later, dark clouds were welling up. In such times, anything could happen, however strange. My reaction may have been oversensitive, but one cannot say it had no basis. I even started to become wary.

His head was still drooping. He simply raised his hand: trembling fingers swished through his shirt pocket, groping for something. Finally he fished out a wad of papers. After laying them down before him and fixing his eyes there, he pushed the papers toward me, forcefully.

I grabbed the documents and went through them quickly. I was anxious to know just what this was all about. First were vouchers, one after another, for things he had sold off. Among the items were a suitcase, a bicycle, a suit, and an overcoat. There were also women's things, jewelry and so forth. Finally, there were two documents certifying periods of hospitalization. On the first was written:

K'ang Min-fu, 28, Liaoning, unemployed, attempted suicide by poison, cause awaiting investigation....

On the second:

K'ang Min-fu, 28, Liaoning, unemployed, attempted suicide by poison, cause awaiting investigation....

Except for the fact that the dates were different and that two different hospitals and doctors had affixed their signatures and seals, the documents were, word for word, the same!

I was even more mystified! I raised my head to look at him. He, too, was observing me; having met my line of vision with his own, he lowered his head again. From another pocket he pulled out a four-inch photograph. He fixed his eyes on it as before, then forcefully shoved it in front of me.

It was of a couple, a man and a woman. The woman—how can I describe her? She couldn't be called pretty, but she was radiant. One could see it even in the photograph. ... She had just put her head on the man's shoulder, and wore a slightly melancholy smile. The man, although likewise smiling, bore an equiv-

ocal expression. . . . I could not help comparing him with the person before me
—indeed, it was he, the visitor sitting in front of me. But he had already
changed greatly.

I understood, and nodded.

He smiled ironically, in a way that was a bit unsettling. Then he began to
get stirred up. He told the story below, speaking fluently and without pause.

. . . .

You must think it strange that I've troubled you with my purely personal
affair. Let me state in advance: I don't come to you in your capacity as novelist
—although I know you often take to writing stories and the like. I'm approaching you as a staff member in a Party Committee office, one, moreover, who was
once responsible for the administrative work of cultural affairs in this city. This
is to remind you of your past work. For example, your oversight of those in the
performing arts . . . have a look, do you recognize this person? Yes, the woman
in this photograph. Look carefully, she's a singer of some reputation who falls
within your domain—she's a drum singer.* Ah, it's hit you, you've recognized
her. Yes, you ought to. In that case, I need not tell you her name. I refuse to
speak it. My memory is filled only with her—her existence and everyting about
her—not her name. Names have no significance. Take mine. You seem to have
found it strange from the first. Indeed, it has no meaning! The year Peking was
liberated, I was in my second year of college. As with many youths, Liberation,
and temporary fanatical enthusiasm, led me to take my name from some novel
or other. Now I realize that this was merely absurd and farcical.

You shake your head. You don't care to hear what I have to say. All right,
I'll get to the heart of my story at once. This is how it was—excuse me, I've
sought you out without even bringing a letter of introduction . . . but where
could I have gone to get one? I burned all my papers early on, before my first
suicide attempt—my college diploma, my employment papers, and the like.
Fortunately there are still these two records of my hospitalizations. I have no
acquaintances in this city, other than her. In fact, there are very few who are
close to me in this whole world. My mother is old and sick. She'll die soon. She
awaits me on her deathbed at my old home in Mukden, but I cannot go to see
her. Besides her, I have a teacher, a professor of philosophy, in Peking. I read
philosophy with him for four years, and then assisted him in compiling the
course syllabus for three years. Now, because I've taken leave of my senses, he's
declared that he has no such student as I. Anyone else? No one, save her. And
she, too, swears she'll never see me again!

This is how it was. Judge for yourself, who in this whole world can vouch
for my identity? I've tried to commit suicide twice—you consider that equivalent to a crime, don't you? I cut myself off from mankind, but each time
someone turned me over to the local public security substation, which in turn
took me to the hospital. The doctors saved my life, and the Bureau of Civil
Affairs supported it. Even the kindhearted public security station chief, seeing

*A singer in one form of East China folk theatre. She accompanies her singing with
a pair of clappers and a small drum. [J.K.]

me famished, shelled out money from his own purse. But why must people be like this? It's really comic!

Perhaps people pity me. I dread that most of all. You'll see why as I continue. Perhaps I really ought to go on living, you think? Yes. I have no reason not to go on. None. I finished my four years of college after Liberation. The school then assigned me to the south, to participate in land reform. Two years later I returned to my alma mater and became a teaching assistant to my philosophy professor . . . it was only because of her . . . do you see? It was she! Originally my work went pretty well. After the Party announced the March Forward to Science campaign, I even wrote a qualifying doctoral thesis. I was young and unmarried, with prospects for a brilliant future . . . but after I came to know her, this woman——

It was during the winter last year, at the winter vacation, that I returned home to see my sick mother. She was once a middle school teacher. My father, an engineer, had died. It was then that I met her, at a theater in Mukden.

You've heard of her, haven't you? In all fairness I must say she's a good woman. Even though it was on account of her that I twice attempted suicide, I'm grateful to her. Only because of her have I now come to know myself. . . .

You wouldn't call her pretty, would you? Or, to put it another way, she isn't "pretty" in the way people ordinarily speak of. But those eyes of hers—look. You can see to her heart in a glance! So candid, and profound. And have you heard her sing? From the first note, all the excellent and brilliant things within her eyes unfold in train with her voice. Her voice is crisp and clear, like the waters of a brook in autumn. . . . I was overpowered the first time I saw her and heard her sing.

Performers must have a special magic to attract people, don't you think? You ought to understand that. For in addition to the qualities they display themselves, there are those of the heroic personalities they personify, which move men's hearts . . . but I don't know, this is only a guess on my part. In any event, I was moved, and attracted.

Don't laugh at me! My arousal was entirely proper. That is to say, her performance was successful. She has a talent for performing. But the others? They liked her as much as I, but . . . threw catcalls. Catcalls—do you understand? I have come to know now, myself. I felt that this was an insult to her, and to me . . . do you see? I was enraged, simply beside myself with anger, and ran backstage directly. But I . . . when I saw her . . . how laughable it was! I didn't know myself what I meant to do! I oh-so-respectfully bowed to her, begged her pardon, and comforted her. In short, I offered her a torrent of mindless praise.

Yet she shook her head, simply mystified, as she listened to me go on. Then she laughed, and her laughter was so full of innocence. She said:

"Thank you, comrade. Thank you for looking out for me. But what's your business? We're backstage, so comrade, please don't let me keep you."

She turned around to go.

I didn't understand her meaning in the slightest. Nor had she understood me. I felt I had been wronged, and nearly cried. I hastened outside. Turning around as I reached the door, I saw that she had followed me. She was smiling at me. I stopped.

"Thank you for your kindness," she said. "If you ever come to Tientsin, drop by and see me, at the South Market ..." And, would you have guessed it, she even extended her hand.

I hesitated a bit. Hurried and flustered, I reached out my hand and squeezed her soft, delicate fingers.

That's how it began. Do you think it odd?

Yes, and so I say, I do not understand such people. As I see it now, the whole affair was entirely misconceived—absurd! ... Yet I quickly returned to Peking, and just as quickly found an excuse to beg a leave of absence from my professor. I came to Tientsin and found her.

Are you familiar with the kind of life these people lead? Performers? ... No, I don't mean her, but her mother. She has a mother, a foster mother. I found out that she was her foster mother only later. Since Liberation, she's been an "element under surveillance." The local public security substation—the very station chief who gave me money out of the goodness of his heart—told me so. He also advised me not to go to her house. But how could I not. . . .

She had an "elder sister"—this is another chapter of her life, which she told me about later, after we'd been living together.

". . . When we had matured a bit more ... " she said. Tears filled her eyes but would not stream down her cheeks. She was always that way. "Mama, whip in hand, brought us to our knees before her, and forced Big Sister to receive customers. She was only fifteen that year. I ... being too young, took up the performing arts. It came about only some time later, after a string accompanist who often came to our house discovered that my voice was pleasing. Then, only because of Liberation was I spared having to go the way of Big Sister. . . . Now she is long dead, from disease!"

How could I have known this in the beginning? When I went to her house the first time—I had learned her address in a theater at the South Market—her mother happened to be away. She greeted my shout as I stood in the courtyard. Her look of astonishment when she discovered it was I really astonished *me.* At first she looked without seeming to recognize me. Then she evidently remembered, but still seemed unable to believe her eyes. She blushed, and smiled—it was a very beautiful smile, not at all like the smile backstage in Mukden—or so I thought.

Flustered, she hurriedly let me into the little room where she lived. In the same flurry, she dusted off a stool so that I could sit, and poured tea. Then she stood to the side, looking at me, and whispered, as if talking to herself:

"This is really a shock. So you've come to find me ... "

Looking back on it now, I failed completely to understand her reaction and her words, just as I had had no comprehension of the words she spoke to me backstage in Mukden.

Moreover, she already seemed to have said everything she had to say, for she didn't speak again. She only sat opposite me, on the edge of her little wooden bed. Leaning toward me with her arms about her knees, she carefully scrutinized me with those profound, candid eyes. I had no idea what she was thinking. She looked at me until my face burned, my heart leapt continuously, and my fidgety hands and feet could find no place to hide ... but she continued to look at me that way, as if she wanted to see through to my heart!

I let her look: I wasn't afraid to let her see my heart. I even wanted her to look at it, and see it clearly. I ... loved her.

But comrade, this is how I explain it now. At the time, I was truly in a quandary. Who knew why she was looking at me like that? Was she really so earnest, and fearless?

I don't want to shirk my responsibility. It's true, when I ran backstage to see her at the theater in Mukden I was only acting from an impulse—in part it was because of her voice, and her eyes. And there were those men who had thrown catcalls. When later I came to Tientsin to seek her out, I myself didn't know what force ultimately was propelling me. I only felt that I must come; and what was more, she had invited me . . . but when I pushed open the door of her home, called her name, and she ran out and stood before me, I knew not what I had come to do.

Now, as she looked at me like that, I understood: I loved her.

Yes, I loved her, and she, too—loved me.

Indeed, that was it. For this insight of mine—this lucid insight formed by emotions which had never been clear to me since I first saw her in Mukden, and which I had never understood—definitely arose on account of her—her looking at me in that way, and her silence. Oh-h-h. Later, when I asked her about it, she said that if she had spoken, she would not have been able to hold back her tears.

But in the end, when we were about to separate, she said: No, that wasn't love, it was only . . . gratitude! Toward my sincerity, my ardor, my willingness to come any distance to see her. . . .

Do you believe it? Sometimes I think perhaps she was correct . . . but perhaps she said it only to console me—to fool me. When we were finally on the verge of separation, she wanted me to forget her—to think of her no more, even to hate her, in order to lessen my bitter suffering.

Yes, she was simply too good; she could have done this.

And I . . . oh, all of this is past now.

Just at that moment, while she was looking at me that way, a middle-aged woman entered. She entered quietly, as a cat treads the street. Neither of us had discovered her. When we did, she was already standing beside me, carefully sizing me up through slanting eyes narrowed to a slit.

When I raised my head and saw her, a chill ran through my body—although her eyes were barely open, they instantly made me feel like trembling with fear. As I stood up, she spoke—

"Ai-yoh!" she cried. Her voice, although very loud, was quite gravelly, and carried with it a heavy nasal quality. It created an impression of stickiness.

"Who is this!" she yelled. "Ai, so there's a guest! Look at this, our Number Two works very cleverly. Even I didn't know about it. So . . . you two have already got something going. Ai, Number Two, don't act like your wits have left you, quickly, pour the tea and bring cigarettes, . . . all right, then, you two sit, I'll do it, I'll . . ."

She went out but came back immediately. Standing in the doorway, she cast a searching glance at me, then slowly walked away. Her look was horrible. I'll never forget it for the rest of my life. When her eyes were fully open, instead of slitted, they flashed a chilling light like a knife-point that made you shiver! Have you seen eyes like that? No, you can imagine my astonishment and chagrin at the time. I could never have anticipated it. . . . I went from terror and loathing to rage! I stood up. I wanted to chase her, to ask her: Who are you to look at us like this, and to speak to us like this!

But *she* . . . she grew pale. Tears welled up in her eyes but would not flow. She went to the doorway. Hanging on to the door frame with both arms, she called out—

"Mother!"

So this was her—her mother! I was simply too amazed to speak. I grabbed my hat and went outside. She withdrew one of her arms to let me pass. I strode across the threshold, but she clasped my hand from behind.

I stopped and turned around. She had already buried her face in her other arm. Too choked up with tears to make a sound, she kept hold of my hand and would not let go.

. . . .

That's how it was at our first meeting.

How strange it was! I returned to Peking feeling puzzled and insulted. Yet I was powerless to shake off the impression that meeting had made on me. And I continued to feel that in tightly grasping my hand, she had been like a person drowning, who will grab at anything at all. I pitied her. She was just too pitiful!

Moreover, these sentiments grew ever stronger, until I could bear them no longer. Finally—not long after, although I still felt that it had been too long— I had to see her, deliver her, even take her by force—from her mother's arms. Tortured by these fantasies, I came again to Tientsin.

This time it was in the evening, in a small theater at the South Market. I had come by night train. I bought a *New Evening News* at the station, and at first glance saw her name. She was performing in a South Market theater; I ran there directly from the station. After buying a ticket, I took a seat near the stage and waited. My heart was aflutter. I wanted to enjoy again the bliss I had known on seeing her in Mukden. Yet, for some reason I can't explain, I already felt uneasy as I thought about it then. Her home, her mother, and the words she had spoken, all changed into a screen of smoke that enshrouded her—now hiding her from view, now letting her reappear. . . .

Now, after the announcer had read her name, a round of applause welcomed her onto the stage. My heart pounded violently, like the clapping that surrounded me. Quietly she walked on, stopped, and bowed to the audience. As the drum sounded, she lifted her head, and those candid, profound eyes smiled at the whole house.

I felt as if my heart had stopped beating—why was I so excited? Was it love? Or something else?

It was just then that the following conversation invaded my ears from behind——

"Look at that—that young chick—what a snob! Night before last her ma dragged me off to play cards, fully hoping that the girl could spend some time with me when she got off. What do you know, but as soon as she showed up from the theater, the girl chased everybody away. . . ."

"Isn't she pretending to be hoity-toity! Time was when those stinking drum singers would go to bed with you, not to mention play cards . . . Now no matter how nice you are to them, they won't even look at you. See that slit dress she's got on? Bet one of her pretty young clients bought it for her!"

Their talk wasn't loud, but it was right up against my ears. No, I should say it was right in my heart. My head seemed as if suddenly hit by a hammer, my ears buzzed, I saw stars, and my body was paralyzed . . . to the point that I no longer heard her singing. I only saw her, very indistinctly, as if from a great distance—no, as if through smoke. Her lips and hands were moving, but I could not see her eyes or hear her voice.

I stood up and staggered out of the theater by hanging onto the chair backs on both sides of the aisle.

That night I bedded down at an inn and ran a fever all night long.

The next day, I went to see her.

She ran out immediately in response to my voice. She appeared to be very happy. She held my hand tightly, and looked at me openly.

But I was looking at her dress with the slits. Light green, with an embroidered hem, it set off the symmetry of her figure. It was really very beautiful. . . .

She looked into my eyes, and then at her dress, as if she had been splashed by something dirty and was an object of ridicule.

"What are you looking at?" she finally couldn't keep from asking.

I said nothing.

"Is there something on me?"

While speaking, she whirled in front of me as nimbly as a little bird. Then she tilted her head to look at me. . . .

I felt myself blushing, and inwardly scolded myself for behaving so impolitely. But still I said nothing.

"Are you looking at these clothes?" she said, still in an exultant tone. "I got paid last month. It's new—pretty, isn't it? Does it suit me? It's nicely tailored, don't you think?"

How refreshing her manner of speaking—artless and candid, just like a child.

I almost wanted to slap myself! But of course I didn't. I only grasped her hand tightly, after which she led me toward the main rooms of the compound. When we reached the door, she whispered to me:

"Mama is inside."

I started. I wanted to beat a retreat, but it was too late. The door opened. There, in front of me, stood her mother.

"Ha, Mr. K'ang . . . or Comrade K'ang! Last time you left without saying goodbye! I brought back some cakes for us, but you'd vanished without a trace. It may not have meant much to you, but our Number Two cried herself sick! She wouldn't eat and she wouldn't go to the theater. She was mad at the world, and blamed her old lady! . . . Now that we've got you back, you mustn't go! I'll leave now, to let you two . . ."

So speaking, she actually grabbed her cape, threw it over her shoulders, and went out the door.

This time, she didn't talk in the funny tone of voice she had used before, but with a smile, as if there were a special meaning to it. This thought struck me particularly as she narrowed her eyes to a slit, in order to observe me.

Puzzled, I stood in the doorway, my heart beating fast.

The girl, for her part, turned around, her face against the wall.

Suddenly her mother returned. Walking up to me with quick footsteps, and narrowing her eyes, she lowered her gravelly voice and said, intimidatingly:

"We're liberated now. It's not like it was before. . . . We sell our artistry, not our bodies!"

In a split second, my whole body quaked! If *she* had not run up immediately and called out, "Mother, Mother," imploring her to say no more, I can't guarantee what might have happened next!

But her mother ignored her completely, and walked away at once. Now only the two of us were left. We stood, neither of us speaking. After a good while, she suddenly rushed up against my breast. She cried bitterly, too choked up to make a sound.

What could I say at that point? I told her, simply and directly, that I wanted her to leave this place immediately and come with me. And never to enter the theater again! . . .

Comrade, judge for yourself! Surely I wasn't wrong to have said that? No, she ought to have left such a filthy place, such a disreputable life, and followed me. . . .

Perhaps my manner of speaking and tone of voice, and my irrepressible feelings of loathing and anger were too extreme, do you think? In short, I hadn't anticipated that—perhaps *you* understand people like them—she answered me this way:

"I know, I've expected this for a long time." She stopped crying, stepped back, and looked at me from a great distance, as if she didn't know me. "You look down on us—our kind, us performers—drum singers! You want me to leave this place and follow you, and you would never let me go to the theater again . . . you! How must you see us! We've been liberated. Now we're literary and artistic workers; we've joined the union—we're of the workers' class. Do you look down on that, then? You're a college student, one notch above other people, so we drum singers aren't fit for you . . . Well you've misjudged us! You get out of here now, while the going's good! Careful, you might stand here too long and get your shoes dirty!"

She rushed into her own little room as she spoke, without even looking back. She locked the door, leaving me to my bitter entreaties, but refusing to come out.

I could only go back. At the inn, I ran a fever for another whole night.

I shut myself up in my room the next day and skipped eating. I wrote her a very long letter.

That evening, I went again to the theater where she performed, but she was not there. A ticket seller said that she had asked for sick leave. I could only give him the letter to pass on to her.

I suffered through another day and evening. That night, after the performance, I waited for her under a power pole along her route home, according to the arrangements I had suggested in the letter.

She did come. But she said nothing. She only stood before me, silently. I took her hand, and she did not refuse it. I insisted that she come with me and she pliantly obeyed.

That night, she slept in my hotel room.

. . . .

Look comrade, I've told you about everything, including my crime.

Yes, I've committed a crime. Nevertheless I feel blessed—don't frown, what I refer to is that night—when we returned to the inn together. It was a quiet, deserted night, with no one out on the streets. There were only the street lamps, reflecting our shadow as a couple. I made it clear to her that I had never looked down on her; on the contrary, it was all because I was too much in love with her. It was on this account that she couldn't go on living as she did now. She ought to be with me, and lead a respectable life. Thank heavens, with her intelligence, and goodness, she understood on the whole. She said that she simply could not relax under the strain of living with her mother. She was not in the dark about that. . . . Although since Liberation her mother no longer beat or scolded her—indeed, she even curried favor with her—she was icy cold. Her face was smiling, and her lips were sweet, but her heart—it was cold! No matter what, the girl never felt a glimmer of warmth. She was isolated and afraid. The joy of her day lay in going to the theater. With her transparent, sparkling voice, which flowed like the waters of a brook in autumn, she poured out all the zest concealed within her heart, before the multitudinous audiences. When she made others happy, she, too, was happy. Thus she could not leave the theater, nor the audiences with whom she exchanged forms of encouragement. Yet there were still those in the crowd who were insulting: after the performance they would follow her, even to her home—mostly they were old acquaintances of her mother. They drank and played cards, and wanted her to stay up with them all night long. After that, this mother of hers was never in want of anything; even her breakfast and daily fare were provided—this was through the shopkeeper of a little odds-and-ends store across the street from her home!

She said she used to think she deserved a better life, someone to care for her, show her warmth, and put an end to her constant anxiety. Since she had come to know me, and seen me come such a long distance just to see her, these hopes had rested with me. . . .

Ai, do you understand? You can imagine my excitement and happiness as I listened to her tell all this . . . don't look at me like that. You don't understand. No—*you* couldn't understand it. But I understood everything—she loved me —yes, she did.

How blissful was that day. I had won her! And I felt that, like Columbus discovering a new continent, I had discovered love, understanding, and hope, within the person of an entertainer.

But now? Now, after I've twice attempted suicide, I've discovered something else—that all this only proved my foolishness and degradation!

Don't laugh, let me continue. The next day, at her insistence, I returned to Peking. Yes, at her insistence. She didn't want me always hanging on to her, not only because of her mother, but because I needed to work hard, and study, for her. . . . I agreed, and this time I went home bearing great happiness and satisfaction.

But I couldn't keep my promise. I had to come back, and come back again, until she became displeased, and fearful. Still I could not restrain myself.

Indeed, when we were not together, she wrote to say—although writing was not very easy for her—that her mother's treatment of her was rotten. She was always scolding her in an unfriendly and sarcastic manner, and gave her no freedom at all. She made it very difficult for her to meet with me. At the same time, she said, with more and more clarity as time went on, they could not live together any more. She must leave, for she was pregnant. Moreover her mother had found out, and would force her to have an abortion!

How full of remorse I felt, on receiving that letter. I was both shocked and pleased. This was *my* child, yes, mine! An abortion—how could she possibly? I would not allow it. I bore responsibility myself. I made for Tientsin that very day.

How enthusiastic the hopes, and great the courage, I bore as I went to the rescue of my wife—it was now my right to call her that. But—imagine for yourself, how her mother dealt with me!

Truly even now when I think of the way she looked at me, I feel my whole body run cold. . . . Her mother was like a poisonous snake, hypocritical, greedy, and cold-blooded—but this time when she saw me, she really seemed happy that we were having a child, and said:

"Ai-yoh-yoh, congratulations, congratulations! So soon—even I was fooled!" . . . "What will you do now?" she asked.

What would we do? Marry! That was my only answer. She was mine, and so was the child. . . .

"Is it as easy as that?" This grandmother-to-be suddenly looked stern. "What kind of air have you inhaled that makes you talk about it so lightly?"

I looked at her, amazed.

She squinted up her eyes to look at me.

"How much money do you have?" she asked.

True, I ought to have considered that point. My salary was sixty-eight dollars a month. Hereafter three people would have to live on it. But I also had a few things at home, such as my mother's clothing, and jewelry. . . .

I told her my actual state of affairs.

She laughed out loud, sarcastically.

"However you want to live," she said, "it makes no difference to me. What I mean is, once you've carried off my girl, how much money will you leave me?"

What? To think that she could actually say such a thing! It was eight years after Liberation—foster mother or not!

I even began to suspect that the two of them, my wife included, had purposely set me up!

A chill ran through my body and my head felt giddy. There, before her, I felt completely sapped. I told her that such a demand was unreasonable and illegal. It violated freedom of marriage. . . . But my voice was hollow, and seemed inaudible even to myself.

"Cut it out—sir." She paid no attention to me at all, but said to me, still narrowing her eyes and smiling with that strange, frightening expression:

"Since you dared to come here to take advantage of us, it's evident that you're no novice at this. This old lady doesn't have sand in her eyes, so don't play-act with us. This affair, so far as we're concerned—let me tell you, it doesn't mean much to us. At worst, our girl might not get married. But you have a public image. When the time comes, you'll find yourself stuck with more than you reckoned on! . . ."

"What, are you saying that . . ." I yelled. "How dare you say that! I want to marry her, to make her my wife. I'm not afraid of . . ."

"Ai-yoh-yoh." Now she began to laugh. "What now, do you take it so seriously, my son-in-law? You're marrying her? Fine, but it's too late. You've fooled around with a performer—insulted an entertainer—the union won't stand for it. . . ."

"I love her. . . ."

"I know. If you didn't, would there be a child to boot? I don't mean that. You wait for me."

I did in fact sit down.

"Number Two, come here!" She called out.

She—my wife—appeared in the doorway. She was wearing only a blouse and pants, and her hair was dishevelled. She cried like one who had gone to pieces.

My heart simply broke! I jockeyed to take a step forward, to embrace her, kiss her, and comfort her. . . . But her mother shifted her body across the doorway, blocking it. Two words rolled softly from those lips, from which a cigarette drooped:

"Hold it!"

She, my wife, lowered her head and sobbed. She knelt on the steps outside the door, without looking at me.

I said nothing. What could I have said? I had only one thought: to wind it all up and get out. At that point I, too, knelt down behind her mother.

This mama was a real terror. Without looking at either of us, she gave a quiet, sarcastic laugh, threw her cigarette butt on the floor, and stamped it out hard, saying:

"Enough! Get up, both of you!"

I stood up. She turned to face me:

"I raised this child. Although she isn't my own, if I don't care for her, who does? Just don't be hardhearted. Don't forget about me afterwards. . . ."

She actually began to cry as she spoke. She lifted a corner of her blouse to wipe the tears.

. . . .

Ai, comrade, look what a price I paid—it was the price of my happiness! We had finally reached our goal—she returned to Peking with me, and we lived together.

This was on the condition that I send her mother fifty dollars every month, for the rest of her life.

Ai, if only it could have stayed that way, and nothing else happened . . . what difference did this monthly payment make? It was all very appropriate. Don't think that the mother was really a bad person. No, what was she to do? She herself had been raised from childhood by a foster mother. Later she became a prostitute, and when she grew older, a procuress. She had raised two girls, and now only one was left. And since Liberation, she had been under surveillance. She had to have some way of living. . . .

You're shaking your head again. You think I'm defending her, don't you? Then why didn't you deal with her during the period of Democratic Reforms?* Why did you only put her under surveillance? No, I'm not defending anything. I don't study the law. My field is philosophy. I only affirm the truth. The facts being thus, I am obliged to find an explanation for them. . . .

Stop shaking your head at me! I know you don't appreciate my philosophy. That's fine, I'm only talking about the facts—the facts are, when she, my wife, left her mother, she also left me.

Yes, she left me, too. Do you think that strange? Then I'll tell you right away —I frankly admit it, she was good to me. Our life of cohabitation was blissful. She was sweet-natured and kindhearted, and she did what I wanted. Despite the environment in which she had grown up, she restrained herself fully and led a simple life. She skimped and saved on our meager salaries so that we could send her mother fifty dollars each month, to clear that unjustly imposed debt, and to make ready for the child . . . but I, on the other hand, did not understand her sentiments at all.

I was not satisfied with her depriving herself of everything, and my increasing dissatisfaction fully had its basis.

For instance, I wanted to have clothes made for her, but she was unwilling; to buy her a watch—but she would not have it . . . now I wasn't doing these things for myself! I only thought that since she was my wife, she ought to dress a bit more appropriately, so as to look like an educated person. And so as not to let those around me know . . . her origin.

You're frowning at me again—yes, this is where we were different. It was because of this that our lives diverged more and more from what we had first anticipated. My temper grew worse as time went on, and she cried with increasing frequency. Finally, I took the occasion to speak to her frankly: she ought to get used to her new life and completely forget the past. What's more, she must never again think of "going to the theater"! . . .

She quietly listened to me.—This was at night, two months after we had begun living together. Tears welled up in those profound, candid eyes and finally coursed down her cheeks.

"K'ang . . ." she said softly, standing before me, still holding my hands. "When all is said and done, you still look down on us! You despise professions like ours, and people like us! Why won't you let me go to the theater? You're a person with education. How can you fail to understand that under the new society, the performing arts are no longer disreputable? I left my mama behind and followed you. That was because of her. . . . But I can't give up the theater. You don't realize how restless I've been these days, not able to perform despite having you. Since I feared upsetting you, I didn't sing a note. I didn't even dare to warm up my voice. Now I feel my throat becoming taut. Soon it will be through. I really fear that I'll never be able to sing in the theater again! I can't give up the theater—nor the audiences, nor the plucking of the strings, nor my singing. Don't you remember what you said to me in Mukden, when you ran backstage after hearing me sing for the first time? Wasn't it only my singing

*The campaign to reform and rehabilitate prostitutes, beggars, and the like, immediately after Liberation. [J.K.]

that attracted you? And brought you to Tientsin to find me? And, has now, . . . brought me to live with you? I beg you—I obey you in all things, and already belong to you—I carry your child . . . just don't look at me like that. Let me go to the theater, to be with the audience, and sing!"

. . . .

Not long after this conversation, because I disregarded her wishes and had a coat made for her that pleased myself, I ran out of money at the end of the month. Even with my past savings, we could not raise the fifty dollars to send to her mother. I didn't consider it important at the time. I wrote a letter of apology, and mailed forty dollars.

But was my being short ten dollars the sole factor that decided our fate? No. . . . It happened precisely three days after I had mailed the letter and money, in the evening, as I was returning from work. She, my wife, was gone!

. . . I went out on the street to look for her, scouring all the shops in our neighborhood. Where had she gone? I heard a radio broadcasting drum singing in Pekingese cadences. Oh, "gone to the theater"! I thought. I went through every theater in Peking.

Just before dawn, I returned home, dragging along a pair of numbed legs and a numbed heart—ai! How could it be a home any more? Without her, there was nothing. It was quiet and deserted; everything had become unfamiliar and detestable. On entering, I kicked over a pot that had been placed by the stove, so I went all the way and smashed the stove itself.

I sat, alone, without even turning on a light. I could see and hear nothing. Everything was empty. It was as if our two months of life together had never happened, as if they were a dream. . . .

When the first train of the day passed by in the early morning, the thundering of the wheels on the rails reminded me. I went to the station.

. . . .

Comrade, is it really because of interest in my story that you've listened so long, without once interrupting me? Or is it because in your profession you've cultivated a calm and collected disposition? Are you not aroused in the least by my happiness? Don't you sympathize at all with my misfortune? Perhaps as you listen you're laughing inwardly at my foolishness, selfishness, and bewilderment . . . but think as you please, I must continue, since I've come this far.

I arrived in Tientsin and ran directly to her house. The door was half open; I strode into the courtyard and stood before her door.

It was locked. I wrenched the lock hard, rattled the wings of the door, and pounded on the door with both fists. It was as if she were sleeping within, but had purposely locked the door from outside so as not to have to see me.

The door to the main rooms opened, and out came her mother. Clothes thrown on and hair disheveled, she was uglier than ever.

"Who is it?" she wrapped her clothes around her and went in back of me, as if she didn't really recognize me. "Oh, so it's . . . you, K'ang. . . ."

I suddenly turned around and stared at her. She drew back a step.

"It's me!" I screamed. "Where is she?"

She narrowed her eyes into slits again, and a strange smile flitted across her face. I could not help but feel a cold shiver in my heart.

"Who? Who are you looking for?" she said, without a trace of anger. "Here you come at the break of day, to break down my door . . ."

"Don't play dumb!" I shouted angrily. "Who am I looking for? Your daughter, of course! You've brought her back—where is she hidden?"

"Number Two?" She withdrew another half step. That strange smile was gone from her face, but her eyes emitted a peculiar light. "My daughter?"

"Yes, your daughter. She's gone, run away. You've brought her back and hidden her. . . ."

Unmindful of everything, I screamed and closed in on her. She retreated, step by step, appearing frightened, but her eyes were blinking slyly. Suddenly she sat on the floor, as if I had pushed her down, and began to sob.

"I haven't. Number Two hasn't come back . . . she's not here! . . . My luckless child, I thought you'd found a good man, educated and well-mannered. For that you cast aside your mother and went on to enjoy your good life. Now, hardly more than a few days later, you've been thrown out yourself. . . . Where can you have fled? This is your home! My poor child . . . "

I looked at her without speaking.

" . . . I thought we'd been liberated, that there was a new society, in which we, too, could hold our heads high! You would perform, and your mother could have a peaceful life with you. How could I have known that you would let me down? . . . A good man is not to be found on this earth!"

She cried and shouted. It was early morning, and there was no one to come mediate. . . .

At that point I didn't know what to do.

She loved me—from beginning to end, I believed this to be so. If not, would she have made my dinner and put it on the stove for me, as she was about to leave? . . . It was only through my own carelessness that the pot had been kicked over.

Yes—I must have been mistaken—if she were here, she could not have kept from coming out to see me.

While thinking it over, I backed up to the doorway and turned around to leave. Someone was standing outside the door.

"What's going on, my good woman?" he said. But his eyes were fastened on me. "Why this, so early . . ."

Seeing him, the woman screamed more fiercely still.

"Grab him!" she shouted, lunging forward unsteadily. "It's him, the one who degraded Number Two, and now he's forced her to flee! I want to get him, no matter what . . . don't let him run away, Proprietor Wang!"

I didn't hear what else she said. It was as if the two words "Proprietor Wang" had struck me on the head like a club. I thought of the conversation I had overheard the other time in the theater, and the part about "he plays cards with her, and even sends breakfast over. . . ."

My rage now turned on him. I lunged forward.

"You," I roared, and grabbed him.

"Ah ... me." He forced the two words out through the space between his teeth, his expression and tone of voice unchanged. Then he squeezed my wrist in his hand, and I fell down on the floor.

"Young punk, did you think this was another place where you'd get away with something?"

He stepped over me to go inside. There followed the sound of the door as it slammed.

I lay there for a long time before I stood up, with great effort. I looked around and saw the tightly closed door behind me—it seemed then that all my hopes and plans had been definitively cut off.

. . . .

I staggered forward, weaving back and forth. There still was no one in the alley. Only the door of Proprietor Wang's general store in front of me was open, so that I could see the various supplies and daily necessities arranged on the shelves. Among them, I suddenly discovered DDT!

Yes, DDT. Isn't it chlorophenophane? A single bottle, or two perhaps, would suffice. Yes, I ought to put an end to it all.

I went on, not daring to stop. More people were out on the street by now. I warily took note of each one, fearing lest I be seen.

Later, I gradually realized that I was seeking *her.* But she was not there.

Not there. I had lost her forever. I had lost everything—my life, my happiness, my beautiful dreams. . . .

I saw another general store, and entered. I stood there for a long while, until someone asked me: "What do you want?" I pointed to the DDT on the shelf.

Yes, I had lost her forever, and everything that was mine. I had nothing else to consider, nothing I could not part with. Everything had been settled, just like that. I needed quickly to . . .

. . . .

When I awakened, I was lying in a hospital.

Need I go into this in detail? There's no need, it's a bore. If I must speak of it, there is just this one point: DDT could not resolve my problem.

I was in the hospital five days.

I lay there, looking up at the snowy white ceiling, and the bedsheets, the bed, the stands and trays—all snowy white. My mind seemed just as white—hollow and empty. . . .

But on the day I was to leave the hospital, a nurse told me that someone had come to see me.

I could not imagine who it might be. No one knew I was there. Not even my dearly beloved mother and honored teacher. I had cut myself off from the world, so that no one would know of my shameful life, nor would anyone come to see me, or pity me. . . .

But the one who entered—was she!

She appeared at the door of the hospital room. Her eyes threw panicked glances in all directions, searching. Yes, she was looking for me. She had not forgotten me.

When she saw me, her eyes glistened, and she came over, slowly.

She was thinner and pale, but she looked more beautiful than ever. She moved carefully, because she was pregnant, or perhaps through indecision.

She sat in front of my bed and lightly touched her fingers to my face—it was really strange—these fingers, delicate and soft, were the same as the first time we touched, in Mukden. Now, as if the fingers of a magician had touched my face, my memory, feelings, thoughts, and desires were instantaneously and completely revived.

In particular, when she began to speak, her voice, transparent and sparkling, seemed like the flowing waters of a brook in autumn.

I truly felt regret! With such a voice, how could I have not allowed her to go to the theater? Could it have been because it was too beautiful—too moving; that I had wanted to possess it all alone? . . .

She said that when she had left our home that day, she had not done so willingly. Proprietor Wang and a "maternal aunt" of hers had suddenly appeared, saying that her mother was seriously ill, and wanting her to return immediately. Although she felt it was a little funny, she still went with them.

"I thought it wasn't the truth," she said, "but I felt pity for my mother. Because you—you wouldn't let me sing. When it comes down to it, we're not the same kind. . . ."

She looked at me. Her eyes were full of tears, but she held them back.

I hated myself! I was selfish, really mean, despicable to the extreme!

"Go. Sing." I wanted to say to her. But I could not. I was afraid to.

"But they tricked me." She was preoccupied with herself. She didn't look into my feelings at all. "Mama was not sick. They tricked me. . . . Why, what was the point? . . . I'm leaving them. I won't ever live with Mama again. . . ."

I nearly jumped for joy.

"Come back! Come back with me!" I grasped her hand at once.

"No!" As she continued speaking, she wrenched her hand free and stood up. "I'm not going anywhere. Alone is how I want. . . ."

At this point, she lowered her head and looked at me—what eyes she had! As candid and profound as before. What I had not recognized there before was an unyielding strength, which saw through to my heart in a glance! I immediately closed my eyes and shrank up on the bed.

How long she looked at me like that I don't know. When I slowly opened my eyes, she was already gone. . . . I was both ashamed and angry—and regretful. In her eyes I had seen my own worth. Yes, what parted us was not just her mother and Proprietor Wang. The most important factor was still she herself. She . . . looked down on me!

From that moment on, I was possessed by a frightening thought. I left the hospital, but did not return to Peking—I wasn't going anywhere, to borrow her words. I found a small inn. I wanted to see her again. I also wanted to look at her in that special way, so as to restore our positions to their former order, proving the value of my existence. . . .

I didn't go to her house again, but I looked for her daily. I followed her and traced her, waiting for my opportunity. I wanted to give her that look! The highways and the alleys, the parks, the markets, and the department stores . . . naturally, the theaters were most important . . . I went to all of them. I went every day, to sit, to listen, to watch, to hope, and wait.

Later I gradually came to like that kind of life. I learned how to throw catcalls —how to stamp my feet, hiss, whistle, and all manner of similar things, just like a thug.

But can you understand my suffering? While I was living like this, my heart was both pained and satisfied—for I had tasted the happiness of vengeance!

. . . Suddenly one day. . . . Yes, I finally arrived at that day—it was she, my wife. She had come out on stage. This was about three weeks after I left the hospital.

Concealing her condition, which had been becoming daily more evident, she sidled up to the front of the stage. The candid and profound eyes were sunken. Her cheeks were pale. Their dazzling adolescent rosiness had entirely vanished. Only her voice was left—transparent and sparkling, like the flowing waters of a brook in autumn.

My heart burst into flame again as I listened to her voice.

If you've ever experienced it, how would you react, if that which you loved, which you longed for, and which could only belong to you, was loved and admired by everyone else?

At that point I stood up. My body was numb, probably because my heart was pounding too hard. As I had the time before, I left the theater by supporting myself on the chairs lining the sides of the aisle.

I had seen her. But I could not look at her in that way—I didn't have the courage. I had fallen too low—there was no way that I could look at her . . . from above.

I walked down the street, skimming the shadows that the street lamps cast beneath the power poles. And I secretly recalled the numbers of the poles. Counting from the first, outside the theater entrance . . . 97, 98, 99 . . . I was there, at the location of our previous meeting! . . .

A tram went by in front of me, roaring and thundering; behind me, pedestrians passed, crowding and jostling. I saw them, but did not take them in. Later the vehicles and pedestrians slowly thinned out, and the active street became quiet and deserted. But I leaned against the pole, motionless.

She came, as expected. I knew that it was she from the sound of her footsteps.

Her gait was very determined; only one who was full of self-confidence, or whose spirit was elevated, could walk that way. Her high-heeled shoes struck the cement pavement one click after another, making a loud, clear sound in the still night.

I turned around.

What I saw at first was a short, fat man behind her, who wore a long gown and was following on her heels. "Proprietor Wang. . . . " The thought of him flashed quickly through my mind, but I stuck my hot face to the icy pole.

Then, from behind me—she paid me no heed and perhaps did not recognize me—she passed by and continued far into the distance, confidently and with determination, her high heels clicking against the cement sidewalk.

I left the power pole only with a great burst of effort. Half my face was icy cold; the other half was burning feverishly.

Hatred burned in my heart. Yes, hatred! I wanted revenge. I followed closely behind her, and immediately felt possessed of sufficient courage and strength.

She ducked into an alley, where the light was dimmer. The door of her house was beyond. She stopped and turned around, and said loudly to the man:

"I'm here, Uncle. Please go back!"

But he, Proprietor Wang, without making a sound, suddenly unfolded his arms and embraced her—my wife!

I felt giddy; my head spun around and around.

"How dare you . . . Help! . . ."

It was she yelling, and resisting. But her voice was immediately stifled by a powerful hand—the brook waters were sobbing.

Next I heard a sharp slap in the face. It was not very strong, but rang out loud and clear; her delicate fingers, slapping that fat face in the dead of night, sent reverberations into the alley.

I came alive. My heart full of joy, I ran out immediately. My strength was so great that I toppled Proprietor Wang, and almost brought my wife down with him. I quickly steadied her, but Proprietor Wang had already got up; I let go of her, again turned toward Proprietor Wang, and before he could get a firm footing, I hit him in the face.

My blow was accurate and sonorous, as if I knew how to fight from practice —I was extremely satisfied with myself.

But at this point my wife recognized that it was I—how fortunate, I thought! I went to her, wanting to speak . . . but she stepped backwards, as if she didn't recognize me, or feared me. She looked at me with loathing and terror. Within an instant she seemed to have become so frightened that I even suspected that I had mistaken her.

I had not. As soon as she spoke, I understood—it was finished! "When it comes down to it, we're not the same kind!" I recalled her words.

But now she no longer spoke in that vein.

"You—*you!*" she said, her voice suddenly gravelly, unlike ever before. "You! Why do you cling to me!. . . . Who am I to you? Surely I don't have to suffer through a lifetime founded on error, just because I was once mistaken about you. You follow and watch me, as if I were a thief. . . . Who am I to you! You hurt me, but you still won't let me go. Go! Leave me. Get away from me. I don't ever want to see you again. . . ."

She hid her face in her hands—as if to confirm her oath never to see me again. She quickly turned around and, almost running, rushed into a deep corner of the alley where she couldn't be seen. She did not in fact enter her mother's doorway.

Now only the two of us were left: I, and Proprietor Wang of the little general store. I felt that we would have to fight it out to the death. And I prepared to die. . . .

Ai, comrade, if we had fought and he had given me a good beating, wouldn't that have been great? But no, he wasn't willing. His eyes were stronger than his hands.

I dared not look at him. I turned my head and looked in the direction she had run. Just then a peal of laughter suddenly broke out behind me—have you ever heard an owl's laugh in the middle of the night? They say that to hear such a laugh is to die. It's absolutely true. I've heard it and it's even more terrible than that.

His laugh sent a chill through my heart. My whole body trembled. Even my bones went soft, so that I could no longer stand.

But he laughed and went away. He entered his store.

. . . .

Comrade, you must be tired. I ought to conclude my story. In fact there's nothing left to say. That's how it was.

Would you still like to hear about my second suicide attempt? Actually it was the same as the first. It was a little prettier, is all. I returned to my hotel, that small inn, and gave away all my possessions, leaving eight dollars in my pocket. Then I wrote my mother a letter by lamplight—when bidding farewell to the world, I had of course to say goodbye to her first. She had already been confined to her bed for a year and had long wanted me to come back to see her, but I could not do it. Now it was still more unthinkable. Next I wrote a letter to my professor, telling him goodbye, too. I confessed that I was truly unworthy of being his student—moreover, I was returning all of his philosophy to him— it hadn't been a bit of help to me. Then day broke. I washed my face, ate breakfast out on the street, and then went to every pharmacy there was, buying as much phenobarbital as they could sell me. By noon, surprisingly, I had accumulated enough sleeping pills to put me to sleep for a long time. I entered a restaurant—perhaps the Spring in P'englai? I ordered a a bottle of wine and two dishes. As I drank, I stealthily swallowed all of the sleeping pills. I left the restaurant, hailed a pedicab, and asked to be taken to the district of Hsia-wa-fang.

The driver was a sturdy fellow, and cheerful. He pedaled very fast, without having the slightest idea of where he was taking me. As we threaded through Taku Street, tall buildings flashed by quickly on either side. The displays in the store windows for once exerted an attraction on me—I'd never paid them any attention before—except for the time when I'd bought her the overcoat. Now there was another overcoat, the same color as hers, and the style, too, was . . . but we had already reached the suburbs. Before my eyes were newly built factories and workers' dormitories. The laughter of children sounded from within—how wonderful it was! But it was too late. I began to spit blood, one big mouthful after another. At first I did so quietly, but later I could not help groaning. The driver looked around and stopped. His very peculiar expression showed both loathing and anger. I was afraid, and began to pity myself. I wanted to say something to him, but already I was unable to. As soon as I opened my mouth, blood spurted forth. I knew it was all over. I forced my eyes open and looked at the driver's robust face. It displayed both anger and dis-gust. . . . *

*The ending of the story as follows has been abridged. [K.Y.H.]

. . . .

The conversation terminated abruptly. Before I knew it, my visitor had seized his "documentary evidence" and departed without so much as a good-bye. I felt both excited and tired, as if I had just awakened from a bad dream. Who was this person? Did his plight deserve much sympathy? What did his story illustrate?

I inquired about the drum singer from a woman comrade in charge of work in literature and art, and was told that she was really pretty good—on the up-and-up, talented, and desiring to progress. She'd been assigned to a choral work brigade by the Union of Workers in Literature and Art, and had left the foster mother who'd prevented her from entering the Communist Youth League. The woman comrade frowned and interrupted me as I started to speak of K'ang Min-fu. "Stop, I know all about him," she said. "A bourgeois playboy through-and-through, self-seeking and self-centered, quite willing to give up his work—his family, too—for a woman—just one *more* person ultimately headed for his list of victims. Treats women like playthings, as his private property. Men like him are hopeless!" I was a little angry, although I knew the woman comrade's heart was in the right place; this seemed to be completely from a woman's viewpoint. I wanted her to see the problem from the political standpoint. I asked her to investigate the matter further.

Only a few days later, on the eighth of June, the *People's Daily* published a memorable editorial. The workers began to speak; the anti-rightist struggle had begun. The intensity of the campaign gave me so much work to do that I could not get through it all. That really was an extraordinary summer! Even now, as heavy snow falls while I write the postscript to this story, I need only think back to those days, and to the vehement and combative scene at the time, to feel myself break out in a fever. As I learned more about the rightists, I began to see how similar to them my visitor was; his goal was only to live for himself. I came to loathe him, but gradually he faded from my memory.

When the woman comrade returned to brief me on K'ang Min-fu in October, after the anti-rightist struggle had won a complete victory and everyone bore a new and healthy joy, I reacted as if I had swallowed a fly at the mere mention of his name. He had gone to be rehabilitated through labor,* it turned out— had requested it himself. His school had not permitted him to return, and after going through the Anti-rightist campaign, he too seemed to feel that this was the only road he could take. After my initial shock I felt immediately that it could have turned out only this way. This was the sole possible, and necessary, outcome. I sighed, relieved.

The drum singer now had a baby girl and was getting by very well. She had freed herself of her foster mother's influence by making accusations against her to the Union, and by making her the object of a struggle session out on the street. Proprietor Wang had been reprimanded and warned he would be dealt with if he ever committed another offense. K'ang Min-fu, on the other hand,

---

*The detention of rightist near-criminals in work camps for rehabilitative labor and political education; slightly less serious than the "reform through labor" assigned to counterrevolutionaries and other out-and-out criminals. [J.K.]

had visited the drum singer in the hospital and pressed her hard to marry him; otherwise, he would take the child! "That woman comrade really had determination and courage," my woman colleague concluded. "She gave him a slap in the face and he fled."

She laughed as she spoke. So did I.

Translated by Jeffrey Kinkley

LIANG PIN
(1914–)

Liang Pin came under Communist influence when he was young. As a student at the No. 2 Normal School in Paoting, Hopei Province, he participated in the anti-Japanese movement directed by the Communist Party in 1931. This resulted in his expulsion from the school. Thereafter Liang spent time in Peking, and was jailed briefly in 1934. Released from prison, he entered a drama school in Shantung Province. His literary career began in 1935. By 1943 he had published a dozen novels and plays, but his reputation as a major author did not spread until the appearance of his *Keep the Red Flags Flying.* This novel was highly praised in the early 1960s, and then condemned by the Proletarian Cultural Revolutionists a few years later. He resumed publishing in 1977 and his new novel, *Turn Over,* has been greeted with enthusiasm.

Keep the Red Flags Flying, conceived in 1953, was published in 1958 as the first of a projected six-volume work (only the first three volumes have been published) depicting the early Communist struggles in China. The novel, set in Hopei Province in northern China, portrays the peasant struggles in the 1920s and the student movements of the early thirties. In center stage are the Chu and Yen families, which for three generations have suffered at the hands of the local landlord, Feng Lao-lan. But the young hero, Yen Chiang-t'ao, having been nurtured by class oppression and subsequently motivated by Communist ideology through Chia Hsiang-nung, rises to lead the peasants to oppose the pig tax. The following is the climax of this episode. —E.Y.

---

from *Keep the Red Flags Flying*

CHAPTER 37

On that day, with the cloudless blue sky above and the yellow earth beneath, after breakfast Chiang-t'ao walked over to Ta-yen Village to call for Yen P'ing. Quietly they slipped out of the house together, Yen P'ing carrying a small bamboo basket stuffed with leaflets and posters hidden under her red scarf. Passing the pond, Chiang-t'ao said, "That will never do. You've got to change."

"Change into what?" Yen P'ing asked.

Chiang-t'ao, looking her over, observed, "Even though we are going to the New Year's bazaar, hardly anyone else will be dressed like you. Look at you, wearing a long dress and leather shoes."

Yen P'ing pulled up the corner of her dress a little, glanced to the left and then the right. Without a word she ran back to the house and put on a pair of canvas shoes, a plain blue jacket, and replaced the red scarf with a coarse hand towel. Then she ran out breathlessly shouting, "Look! How's this?"

"That looks more like a village girl, but not quite," Chiang-t'ao replied.

"Why not?" Yen P'ing anxiously stared at him as if to force him to tell her what else about her did not look exactly like a village girl.

"Your face is too pale, your hair too black, too long and shiny." He shook his head, then added, "You just don't look like a village girl."

Yen P'ing became angry and punched him on the back. "You tell me," she demanded, "what do I look like?"

"A lady, a student!" He ran, with her in pursuit. Catching him by one of his ears, she asked, "What are farmers like?"

"Farmers work hard, live simply, and have a straightforward disposition. All year round they labor under the sun and expose themselves to the wind. They eat nothing but husks and vegetables. Their faces are ruddy and their bodies strong. But you?" He turned around to look at her. Yen P'ing's face was perspiring freely in her effort to keep up with him, but, pouting, she said, "I'd like to be like that!"

Chiang-t'ao said, "In that case, you're okay. Hurry up, comrade, try to catch up with the revolutionary ranks!" Yen P'ing listened and felt that what he said had a double meaning which eluded her.

The two of them walked single file along the highway leading to town. Entering the city gates, they saw that this year's crowd was larger than ever. The butchers and vegetable vendors cried out, trying to attract customers. Peddlers of New Year's pictures sang at the top of their voices to get attention. Chiang-t'ao and Yen P'ing elbowed through the crowd, pushing this way and that until they reached the firecracker market on the south side of the city. There Ta-kuei, with a red-tasseled spear in hand, was standing atop a cart, gesticulating and shouting. Meanwhile, Wu Lao-pa and Erh-kuei set off an assortment of firecrackers and rockets, shooting them high into the sky. The smoke filled the air with excitement. The crowd swelled. Mounting the cart, Chiang-t'ao blew a whistle. People in throngs rushed out from livestock, cotton, and vegetable markets, shops and restaurants. Ta-kuei, standing next to Chiang-t'ao, raised his sturdy arm with fist clenched and declared, "The meeting to oppose the pig tax will now begin...."

Swirling red and green leaflets and posters appeared in the streets and lanes. Yen P'ing, carrying her bamboo basket, went around distributing them. She would toss a bundle of leaflets high into the sky, then watch as they soared in the wind and slowly drifted down. Some in the crowd reached for them with outstretched hands and read them aloud, while others, their faces glowing, looked up, eager for the speech to begin. Chiang-t'ao shouted at the top of his voice, "Friends and fellow villagers, we slave all year round just to make ends meet. Now they even want to tax our New Year's pig."

For a while he spoke to them about resisting the pig tax, then he said, "Rent for land and soaring interest rates are sucking our blood. Surtaxes imposed on land levies are grinding our bones. And now this pig tax is more painful than being skinned. We work like cattle and horses, struggling in the mud, water, wind, and fire....

"When we weed the fields, hunched over and hands on the hoe, we bend double. The hot sun bakes dirty oily sweat out of our backs. We toil from spring to fall. After we pay the rent, what else have we got but empty pockets? By late autumn, we still don't have padded jackets. Even in winter, when it is freezing cold and snow is piling up, there is no smoke coming from our chimneys after dark. We borrow money. In three years the interest equals the principal. We pay interest in advance! We pay compounded interest! We pay compounded over compounded interest. It gets higher and higher and we sink deeper and deeper in debt. . . .

"When the new year arrives, creditors crowd around. They break down our doors to demand payment. We get up before daylight, there is no food in the wok. A cangue* weighing a thousand *catties* on our back. How we tillers suffer!"

He stopped, panting for air. Chia Hsiang-nung, dressed in an old sheepskin jacket, was sitting on the cart with his snow cap pulled down. Only his eyes were visible. No one recognized him. Chiang-t'ao bent down and whispered a question. Chia Hsiang-nung whispered back. Chiang-t'ao straightened up to resume his speech. "Warlords are constantly fighting among themselves; how long will this last? Corrupt officials! They only care to fatten their pockets. They couldn't care less whether the peasants live or die. They scrape every last penny from us. They scrape and scrape. They won't stop even after they have scraped away three feet of dirt!"

Panting as he spoke, he noticed Yen P'ing standing near the base of a short wall. Her glowing eyes were fastened upon him. His heart skipped a beat. Blinking, he saw golden spots dancing in front of him. "My poor and suffering compatriots," he cried out, his voice rising to a metallic shrill, "what can we do to overcome all this?"

Chu Lao-chung, eyes wide open, was watching Chiang-t'ao in the crowd. "This child has grown up," he thought. "What he says makes sense." Suddenly shaking his arm, he shouted, "Let's get organized and act!"

"Right!" Chiang-t'ao shouted back. "When sorghum sprouts are planted close together, neither wind nor rain can knock them down; if they stand apart, they will be leveled by strong wind. So we must get organized and be strong. Now we propose to fight against the pig tax and to knock down Feng Lao-lan. Do you agree?"

Yen P'ing was watching him from below. He usually struck her as being a little feminine—when he sat down, he was demure; walking, he was graceful. With his fine-featured face, well-defined eyebrows, and big black eyes, he was a model of refinement and composure. But today he was standing in front of this large crowd. Each word he spoke struck at their hearts like lightning. He stirred their thoughts and caught their attention. She could not understand what kind of strength he had.

Suddenly she felt her face burning; she trembled and her heart throbbed with happiness. She blushed as she secretly whispered, "Chiang-t'ao." She realized that in the history of China, many a hero had come from among ordinary people. The young man standing before her might very well become a future heroic figure. Her heart swelled with pride while perspiration dotted her forehead. She could no longer control herself. Like everyone else in the crowd, she shook her fist and shouted: "Long live the Chinese Communist Party!"

---

*A wooden collar three or four feet square used to confine the neck and sometimes the hands of a criminal for punishment. [N.A.M.]

Thousands of hands were being raised in front of her; thousands of flags were waving. And the crowd cried out like the first peal of spring thunder.

Yen Chih-ho, from his place in the crowd, was watching his son become a hero in everyone's eyes. Tears coursed down his cheeks as he remembered Yün-t'ao. "If he were here," Yen Chih-ho thought, "he would do even better; but what a pity, he is locked up in prison for life."

When Chiang-t'ao raised his hands, the crowd raised thousands more in response. With tears in his eyes. Yen Chih-ho jumped up and shouted, "Good boy, right you are."

Chu Lao-chung nudged Yen Chih-ho and said with a smile, "You watch, this boy is going to get somewhere!"

"You never know from whose family outstanding sons will come," Yen Chih-ho said.

Ta-kuei, a broad-nosed, thick-lipped young man, leapt three feet into the air. Landing with a thud, he shouted, "Down with the pig tax. Down with that bully and bad landlord, Feng Lao-lan!" Under the glaring sun, the crowd shouted in unison, sounding like the current roaring down a great river. "We want to settle old scores with Feng Lao-lan! We want to settle old scores with Feng Lao-lan!" Waves of shouting reached places far away.

Chang Chia-ch'ing, Chu Lao-chung, Yen Chih-ho, Wu Lao-pa, Ta-kuei, and others formed a cordon protecting Chiang-t'ao and Chia Hsiang-nung. They were in high spirits and prepared for battle. Their spears and swords glistened, threatening to drink the blood and devour the flesh of their enemies.

Chiang-t'ao directed the demonstration according to Chia Hsiang-nung's plan. Vendors stopped doing business as thousands of people watched the imposing ranks marching down the main street. The entire street was filled with farmers marching along in great strides and students singing the *Internationale.* When the first ranks reached the Tax Bureau, the last had not yet left the firecracker market. Chiang-t'ao ran to the head of the column, with Yen P'ing at his heel. He blew his whistle; the demonstrators rushed forward, knocked down doors, smashed windows, and broke into the Tax Bureau. Hearing the commotion, Feng Lao-lan turned pale. He jumped over the wall and fled. Feng Kuei-t'ang also scrambled over the wall and ran through alleys leading to the back door of the county government building, losing his shoes and hat along the way. The door was locked; he climbed over a low wall and ran to the office of the magistrate. Wang K'ai-ti asked, "What happened? You lost your shoes and hat."

"The Communists have started a riot," he answered. "They have broken into the Tax Bureau."

"What?" asked Wang K'ai-ti, his eyes wide open.

"The opponents of the pig tax have rioted!" Feng said.

Wang K'ai-ti rushed to the door shouting, "Send out the police and security guards at once."

Meanwhile Chiang-t'ao was directing the demonstration from the rooftop. "Fellow villagers," he shouted, "the landlord has escaped. Now what?"

Ta-kuei, glaring, shook his muscular arm and strong fist, and screamed hoarsely, "Now the oppressive landlord is down; let's go to the county government building and root out the corrupt officials!"

"We've not yet overthrown the cruel landlord," Chiang-t'ao shouted back. "We must continue to hit him hard."

He blew his whistle again and gave directions. The crowd surged toward the county government building. Chang Chia-ch'ing and his monitors kept close to Chiang-t'ao and Chia Hsiang-nung. Ta-kuei and his young companions, today, under the leadership of the Communist Party, spoke their minds for the first time in their lives. Talking, laughing, running, and jumping, they were intoxicated with joy. This was Yen P'ing's first experience with the masses rising in revolt; there was something sacred about the scene which moved her to tears. She was wiping them with her handkerchief. Because she was slender and being swept from side to side by the crowd, Chiang-t'ao quietly took her arm.

No one but Chang Chia-ch'ing noticed this. He placed his lips close to Chiang-t'ao's ear and whispered, "Who's that?"

"A comrade."

"A comrade like that?" Chang Chia-ch'ing grinned and patted him on the shoulder.

Chiang-t'ao took hold of his hand and said, "Don't talk rubbish, eh?"

"Protecting you is okay," said Chang Chia-ch'ing. "But I can't protect her."

The demonstrators moved on, then they stopped. Chiang-t'ao rushed to the head of the column to see what had happened. Mounted police in black uniform and security guards in yellow military uniform were lined up, blocking the way. They flashed their shining bayonets and snapped the safety catches on their rifles. They looked like mad dogs with bloodstained snouts ready to devour their prey. The crowd panicked and halted. Wu Lao-pa signaled Chiang-t'ao to climb up onto his shoulders. Chiang-t'ao pounded his chest and shouted, "Don't be afraid! Don't be afraid! If troops come, we'll fight back. If water comes, we'll dam it. You with the guns, you take aim at me here!" He continued pounding his chest. When the people saw that the police and security guards dared not fire at Chiang-t'ao, they regained their confidence.

Yet the security guards did not retreat; the demonstrators could not move on. Chiang-t'ao jumped down from Wu Lao-pa's shoulders and shouted, "Comrades, follow me!" And with defiance in his eyes, he led the demonstration forward. Suddenly two sparkling bayonets were pointing at his face blocking his way. Chiang-t'ao, with his hands behind his back, opened his eyes wide and fearlessly glared at the glittering tips of the bayonets. His courage struck home and the demonstrators followed suit.

Chu Lao-chung saw that the bayonets leveled at Chiang-t'ao would soon be thrust into his eyes. He ripped off his padded jacket, and rushed over with a stick.* With one blow he knocked both bayonets to the ground. At once five or six more bayonets descended upon him. He fought back. Soon he was surrounded by countless bayonets, and he was losing ground. He shouted, "Charge, comrades! Even if it's a mountain of swords, we shall overcome!"

Ta-kuei, with his thick neck thrust forward, shook his arms and shouted, "Down with the thugs of the corrupt officials!" The crowd echoed. Their cries shook heaven and earth.

*A stick in three sections, chain-linked together—a traditional Chinese weapon. [E.Y.]

Chang Chia-ch'ing, Ta-kuei, and other young monitors of the demonstration picked up their spears and rushed forward. Because the troops did not have any order to shoot, the monitors soon broke their ranks and drove them into the courtyard.

Chu Lao-chung shouted, "Comrades, let's go in!"

They rushed into the courtyard, they crowded into the hall, they climbed all over the roof.

Chu Lao-chung stood in front of the crowd, shook his fist and shouted, "Corrupt officials, come out and meet the public." The demonstrators echoed his shout. The police and security guards made threatening gestures and held their ground.

"Comrades!" Chu Lao-chung continued, "If they hurt one of us, what shall we do?"

"Kill them all!" the crowd responded.

"Very well," Chu Lao-chung shouted, "get your weapons." The demonstrators armed themselves with hoes, bricks, and rocks and took up combat positions like tigers out on a hunt.

When the magistrate saw such a multitude of petitioners, he dared not show his face. The security guards and police formed a cordon around the building. The demonstrators waited for a long time before the magistrate sent out a message: "For the time being, no pig tax will be collected." Chiang-t'ao demanded that he repeal the tax outright. The magistrate said he did not dare without instruction from the provincial government.

Chiang-t'ao noticed that it had been a long day for the demonstrators, who had had just one meal and were all exhausted. He asked Wu Lao-pa to give him a push to get onto a stone stele nearby. He talked from his perch; "My fellow countrymen, my old fellow townsmen! Now you have seen our power, haven't you? We scared the daylight out of those bad landlords and corrupt officials. But if they come again to collect the pig tax, what shall we do?"

"Kill them right there and then!" Shouted Chu Lao-chung, again jumping up, and again yelling at the top of his voice.

"Down with the bad landlord Feng Lao-lan!" roared the crowd.

Chiang-t'ao tilted his head to one side and imitated Chia Hsiang-nung's gesture as he shouted, "Abolish the license fees! . . . Oppose the salt price hike! . . . Abolish usury! . . ." But his raised right arm was trembling.

"You want to get rid of all the bad landlords and corrupt officials? Then join the Peasants Association!" said Chiang-t'ao. And the crowd responded, "We want to join!"

"Comrades," said Chiang-t'ao, "don't walk home alone. Watch out for the bad landlords. They are out to get you. Watch out for the police; they are waiting to arrest you!"

[The demonstrators' victory is short-lived. Feng Lao-lan soon files a lawsuit against them. Meanwhile, Chiang-t'ao and his schoolmates at the No. 2 Normal School are absorbed in another issue—protesting the Kuomintang government's nonaction against Japanese invaders. The closure of the school does not drive away the student demonstrators, but a police blockade threatens them with starvation, which becomes effectively divisive among the students.]

CHAPTER 54

During the past several days the Kuomintang branch at the city mobilized the students' parents to keep a vigil in front of the besieged school, where they tearfully demanded to see their children. Their soft talk undermined the students' resolve. Some of them secretly negotiated with the police, sneaked out, and went home. The enemy's political offensive showed its effect.

The wavering of some students during the past few days had given Lao-hsia reason to be concerned. He could neither eat nor sleep. One night he went up to the dormitory to look for Chiang-t'ao, but he could find neither him nor Chang Chia-ch'ing. Alone he paced back and forth in the corridor. After a while he stopped, resting both his hands on the railing. The noise of the city had subsided. Everything hushed. Thousands of twinkling stars above matched the thousands of gleaming city lights below like red flags strewn all over the sky and below. . . .

While standing there he remembered the high price he had paid during the past few years at the No. 2 Normal School. For the sake of the revolution and freedom, many comrades had even had to sacrifice their own education to make this school what it was now. In the course of the revolution the No. 2 Normal School had written a glorious page, but today it was facing disaster. It appeared that they would have to abandon it for a life behind bars. Distress filled his black eyes.

There he stood, with his hands behind him. By and by he felt a warm hand reaching for his. He turned to find Chiang-t'ao placing an arm over his shoulder. In the darkness, Chiang-t'ao noticed a sad smile on his pale, thin face. "Are you feeling well?" he inquired.

"It's nothing," Lao-hsia replied, shaking his head.

The magnificent Milky Way and the quiet city at night captured Chiang-t'ao. "Well, we may have to leave this dear school," he said with a sigh.

Any young person, particularly during his school years, would cherish the school that nurtured and educated him—its buildings, trees, ponds, and wells —with the same feelings that he had for his home. The thought of leaving would melt his heart; no matter how many years had passed, he would still recall with fond memories many meaningful events that had occurred there.

"I don't want to leave," Lao-hsia mumbled slowly. "I cannot bear such a thought."

"For the revolution," replied Chiang-t'ao. "But as for our struggle, the aim ought to be clearer."

"It's very clear." Lao-hsia was surprised. "Having armed ourselves, we wait for negotiations."

"Wait for negotiations?" Chiang-t'ao asked. "Isn't that rather opportunistic?"

Taken aback, Lao-hsia started blinking. After a long silence he nodded. "Perhaps. But I still don't quite understand. Paoting is an important center of communication and the heart of revolution of this entire region. The No. 2 Normal School is the revolutionary fortress in Paoting and a fulcrum in student movements. We can't just let the enemy take it. Our heroic action already has had influence on the people in Tientsin and all over North China." His subtle tone revealed the determination of the Party leadership. His heart was afire as he, with his hands behind him, paced back and forth, and his calm eyes shone with confidence.

Chiang-t'ao, with his questions somewhat frustrated, hesitated for a moment. "Yes," he said. "In our demand for resistance against Japan we should be more resolute." He was watching Lao-hsia, trying to gauge his feelings.

Then Chiang-t'ao's thoughts became clearer. To be sure, the young people of this region had all supported this movement and extended its influence, but because of the shape the struggle had taken now the students could no longer wait; they must act at once. "The revolutionary tide has risen all over the country," he maintained. "The establishment of the Chinese Soviet Republic and the expansion of the red areas ought to inspire the people." Frowning in deep thought for a moment, he continued; "We are not cooperating with workers and peasants but fighting alone with our strength exposed. Wouldn't such action harm the revolution?"

He started pacing with Lao-hsia. Lao-hsia's face became grave. "Your question is very much to the point!" He gazed into space, unblinking. After a considerable pause he conceded, "Yes, there may well be an element of opportunism in this." He did not finish. The present situation could well be compared to a drum, which, if punctured, can no longer work. They had underestimated the cruelty of their adversaries. When the enemy announced the list of political criminals, they did not run away. On the contrary, they assembled themselves in the school as if to wait for arrest. At this point he was not prepared to bare this thought, but said, "Right now, our job is to prevent right-wing sentiment among the revolutionary ranks and to fight courageously and stubbornly. If we waver, there's going to be trouble. Once we leave these walls, we will be arrested immediately." He slowly raised his head to look at Chiang-t'ao.

At that time, the enemy, the Kuomintang, was marshaling its forces in preparation to attack the red areas in the south, and actively suppressing anti-Japanese movements and arresting the young activists in the north. After the students had maintained ten days of stubborn resistance on campus, their schoolmates off campus held press conferences in Tientsin and Peking to publicize their cause. But the authorities showed no sign of coming to terms. . . .

To Lao-hsia, for years student movement had been this way: closing schools, demonstrations, petitions, and extensive propaganda; when those who were in authority decided to save face, they would initiate negotiation. Yet today the situation was different. "I understand what you mean," he said. "But have you thought through how we can break out? The enemy has regular troops out there, but we have neither an inch of iron on hand nor support from the outside. That to me is risky."

"The way I see it," commented Chiang-t'ao, "it's better to break out than to wait, because waiting amounts to suicide."

"Waiting is opportunism, while breaking out is adventurism." Lao-hsia said after a pause, "If you agree to this logic, either way it's suicide. There is no hope!" Chuckling humorously, he led Chiang-t'ao downstairs.

They stood hand in hand in front of a map. This had become their old habit in recent years. Whenever they discussed revolution, they would draw red lines on the map around the regions occupied by the Red Army and circle the abandoned areas with blue lines. . . .

When the comrades working in the Kuomintang areas saw the red regions on the map, it warmed their hearts as if the red ones were their home and motherland.

Lao-hsia made a circle on the map. "Look," he said. "Whose territory is this?"

Chiang-t'ao's feelings became mixed. He always had respect for Lao-hsia, who had come from Ching-hsing, where his father and elder brother were miners and members of the Communist Party. From the very beginning he was simply taught by his social class background, and did not come to the No. 2 Normal School until he joined the Party. Though sparing in speech, he loved to ponder questions deeply. All year round he wore a pair of shoes and socks made by his mother and a faded gown of homespun variety. He was a simple but compassionate fellow and a responsible Party member. The victories won by several student protests at the No. 2 Normal School could not have been without his leadership. Because of his ingenious strategies, the second student protest from start to finish lasted for only three days but succeeded in having the Department of Education remove the corrupt principal—an unprecedented victory! But now that the enemy had devised different tactics, Lao-hsia continued to follow the old line and could not leap a single step forward.

As the question of line entered into his mind, Chiang-t'ao regretted that when they were opposing the "Leftists' Adventurism," they did not grasp the new spirit, nor did they purge the attitude of wanting instant success. At the moment the wisdom of the comrades had not caught up with the new line of thought, which caused their struggle to face the present predicament. He no longer wanted to continue this line of thought. "I'll go to stand guard," he said and walked away.

Lao-hsia, from his place by the door, watched Chiang-t'ao's shadow until it completely disappeared in darkness before he returned to sit on his bed to rest. He thought: the prospect of leaving the school and handing it over to the enemies would never get the group's approval; in fact he himself could not bear to agree.

A student who had been on guard brought a letter to him which had been thrown in from the outside. After one quick glance at it he backed up a few steps to lean against the wall, his hand trembling. He placed his other hand over his eyes for a moment, then began to read the letter.

The Provincial Party authority had decided: "Anti-Japanese guerrilla activities will be expanded on both sides of the Hu-t'o and Chu-lung Rivers on the plain of Hopei Province. The Special Party Committee has decided to withdraw the student protesters from the No. 2 Normal School and reassign them to the countryside to support the guerrillas in Kao-yang and Li-hsien." Lao-hsia heaved a long sigh and said resolutely, "It shall be done!"

Alone, Chiang-t'ao had continued to wonder whether or not he was guilty of right-wing reaction in his thinking. But after reading the directive from the Special Party Committee he immediately said with conviction, "This is right!"

His frowning forehead suddenly relaxed and a smile appeared on his face. With the letter in hand he went to the northern building to look up Chang Chia-ch'ing, who was sleeping in his bed. He put the letter in his hands.

Without waiting for Chang Chia-ch'ing to finish reading, Chiang-t'ao said, "I'm one hundred percent behind this excellent strategy." His eyes shone as he paced around the room. "What happens to this school is less important than the affairs of the nation. Being boxed in within these school walls is not as good as expanding guerrilla warfare in the countryside. . . ."

Chang Chia-ch'ing finished reading the letter.... He sat up abruptly and glanced at Chiang-t'ao. "Beware of defeatism!" he said. "We must protect the anti-Japanese fortress and the interests of young students." He waved his arm, chopping up and down. "Do reactionaries want to starve us? So long as one of us is alive, let's break out and charge the Public Security Police Office." Tears came to his eyes as he shouted breathlessly.

When Chiang-t'ao saw Chang Chia-ch'ing's rousing anger, he understood that even though the time for the old line had passed, the old line of thought still remained. Yet how noble was his revolutionary zeal! "We ought to have a broader view," he said. "We can't grow grain on the school playground...."

Chiang-t'ao said, "This is the new line! We must consider problems according to the new spirit. In order to preserve the revolutionary seeds, we should conserve our strength. We must recognize that in a revolution sometimes we advance and sometimes we retreat; at other times we may go in a circle or take a detour. The enemy, seeing this superficially, may think that we have withdrawn in defeat. Yet when the seeds sown on dry ground receive spring rain, they will germinate and become thousands of seedlings. In the sun and wind they will blossom and bear fruit. On the other hand, if we lose these seeds ..." He proceeded to explain in considerable detail the importance of preserving the anti-Japanese strength and the seeds of revolution.

Chang Chia-ch'ing stood up, cutting Chiang-t'ao short, "Oh, my God! You and your circles and detours again! Why can't we take the straight path? Afraid of bloodshed? Fear death? I have no fear of anything, not even the corrupt power which placed this cangue upon me." He was thinking: If you went this way, he would say that way is correct; if you went that way, he would surely say this way is correct. If not too much to the left, then too much to the right— this revolution is surely tough business!

"Our struggle is to fortify further the revolutionary foundation," he said thoughtfully. "We are not to sell ourselves short; we cannot put all the eggs in one basket." He sat down and continued, "What if you break out, charge the Public Security Police, and land in jail? The revolutionary ranks will only lose a comrade, that's all!"

They could not reach an agreement. They had to wait until they held a meeting to reach a decision.

[The students accept the Party directive. They prepare to break out for the countryside to join the guerrillas. But the Kuomintang army takes them by surprise. In the course of violent struggle many students are wounded, arrested, or killed. The first volume of this long novel ends with the imprisonment of Chiang-t'ao and the escape of Chang Chia-ch'ing, his comrade-in-arms.]

Translated by Edmond Yee

TU P'ENG-CH'ENG
(1921–)

Tu P'eng-ch'eng was born in Han-ch'eng of Shensi Province to a family of poor means. Since his father died while he was young, Tu was brought up by his mother and had to work while attending school. His formal education ended upon graduation from a junior middle school in 1937.

In the following year, at the age of seventeen, Tu joined the Chinese Communist Party and became involved in its revolutionary activities. Shortly afterwards, he went to Yenan, where he enrolled for further training at the University of War of Resistance against Japan. Upon completion of his schooling, he was assigned to work in a rural area and engaged in the development of the frontier. In 1942 he was transferred to work in a factory.

In 1947 he was attached to the Northwestern Field Army as a war correspondent for the New China News Agency. During the numerous campaigns he witnessed, he gathered voluminous material, which became the reservoir for his creative writings.

His full-length novel, *Defend Yenan,* was published in 1954. This work of more than 350,000 words earned him great acclaim throughout the People's Republic of China and was hailed as an outstanding novel of military life. Tu gave a fictionalized account of several major battles in the defense of Yenan and favorably portrayed a number of leaders in the Chinese Communist Military High Command, including P'eng Teh-huai, Wang Chen, and others.

In Peacetime, his second major work, was a medium-length novel about the life and times of workers during the construction of the Pao-chi to Ch'eng-tu Railway. Published in 1958, it also brought him widespread critical praise. He was generally regarded as having excelled in his in-depth presentation and analysis of the "contradictions" among people.

Tu's best-known short stories include "The Natives of Yenan" (1958) and "Traveling through the Ling-kuan Gorge at Night" (1959).

Defend Yenan, nationally recognized in the 1950s, was labeled a "poisonous weed" in the 1960s because it upheld the heroic image of Marshal P'eng Teh-huai, an outspoken critic of the Great Leap Forward movement. However, both the memory of P'eng (who died in the mid-1960s) and *Defend Yenan* were officially restored to honor in 1978, and Tu P'eng-cheng has since resumed his writing. —M.H.T.

The Natives of Yenan
—*Old Hei and His Wife*

1. THE OLD COUPLE

Lü Yu-huai had, by order of his superior, come to a project office of the railway to assume his post as Party committee secretary. Upon his arrival, he found none of the comrades in charge were present at the office. He put down

314

his luggage and went out to tour the area. The hills both in front of and behind the office were work sites; next to the office were dormitories for workers and staff, a motor pool, and a row of warehouses. In front of the warehouses was a parking lot, where five or six workers were unloading cement from a truck that was parked at one end of the lot. As they were unloading, they yelled, "No. 400 cement, 250 sacks! No. 200 cement, 700 sacks!"

An old man, who had just directed the unloading operation, sat by the gate of the warehouses. He had a dark and long face. On his slightly upturned chin was a bushy beard that looked both curly and yellowish, as if it had been singed. His blue uniform was full of oil stains and rust spots. The most eye-catching feature about him was his shoes, which must have weighed two catties. There was a piece of paper on his knee. He was exerting great efforts to note some figures upon it. With a tobacco pipe in his mouth, he looked rather clumsy, and he moved so very slowly that he looked like a mentally retarded person.

The workers shouted, "Old Chief, don't get the figures mixed up!" The one who was addressed as "Old Chief" removed the pipe from his mouth and knocked it against his shoes. That was his answer. This "Old Chief" would probably not lose a single screw if he was to take care of supplies, Lü Yu-huai thought. But to put him in the position of chief of supplies would never do. Those who take up the position of chief of supplies at construction sites must all be the most capable and the most patient people. They must have long legs, long hands, sharp ears and sharp eyes; they must be able to handle complaints and endure hardships and at the same time be articulate and diplomatic. Other-wise, they could never hope to secure the supplies the others could not secure. "They've assigned the wrong man!" Lü Yu-huai lighted a cigarette, walking away aimlessly while musing upon the subject. "Comrade, I see you are walk-ing quite spryly. Are you going to the market or to the temple?" a woman shouted. Lü Yu-huai took a careful look and saw a woman about fifty who was sitting in the lotus position by the entrance of a cave-house near the motor pool. She was stitching a shoe sole. Lü Yu-huai smiled and walked toward the old woman.

"Haven't you got eyes?" she asked, with her shoe sole pointing at the wall in front. Lü Yu-huai saw the words on the wall, "Smoking Strictly Prohibited!" Quickly he extinguished the cigarette with his fingers. Pulling a long face and sewing the sole, she pulled the thread so hard that it screeched. It was obvious that her anger had not yet dissipated. Lü Yu-huai said, "Auntie, you sound like you are from Yenan. Perhaps we're from the same hometown!"

"From the same hometown, what's so good about it? Can you eat it? Look, that was very close, wasn't it? —You dare to smoke right in front of a gasoline dump." Although she was reprimanding Lü Yu-huai, her tone was much softer and she was trying to size up Lü to see if he was really from Yenan. Lü Yu-huai sat by the old woman and asked, "Are you, Auntie, a warehouse guard?" She broke into a smile and said, "I am really an emperor!"

Some ten or more supply trucks were driven into the parking lot in front of the warehouses, with horns honking and dust flying. A hundred or more movers were rushing about to unload the supplies. Shouting and calling rang out everywhere all at once. Hei Ch'eng-wei, the old chief, suddenly turned into another person. He shot up, stuck his pipe between his neck and his collar, and shouted, "Hey, you! Little Hei's mother, come on, give me a hand!"

As if she had just gotten an emergency order, the old woman threw down her sole, dusted herself, and hurriedly walked toward the parking lot. The words "Come on, give me a hand" may not mean much to others, but to this old woman, they would always stir up strong feelings.

A long time ago, the chief of supplies, Hei Ch'eng-wei's father, exchanged two pecks of corn with a refugee for a child bride for his son. Later, this couple, with their four shoulders, carried the burden of poverty. During those years when they might have a cooking pot but no rice to go into it, there was hardly any joy and hardly any love. Since they were sworn in under the Red Flag by Liu Chih-tan, however, they began an extraordinary life. During the twenty years that followed, the words "Come on, give me a hand," once uttered by Hei Ch'eng-wei, could make this woman carry out any mission with all her might and her life. It might be that she had to disguise herself as a beggar in order to sneak into the very center of the White Army to gather intelligence; it might be that she had to travel through a territory fraught with imminent danger in order to transmit an urgent message to the Red Army under the command of Liu Chih-tan; it might be that she had to carry a spear on a patrol so as to let her husband lead a unit of red guerrillas, under the cover of night, to attack the enemy, who were sound asleep.

Once the old woman walked into the parking lot, the movers exchanged glances among themselves, as if they were saying, "Be careful! The old lady has come to the front line!" At this time, some drivers had their engine hood open and were doing some repairs. Movers were running back and forth; members of the supply staff were shouting. Hei Ch'eng-wei, chief of supplies, fully energized, looked like a young man. With a notebook in his hand and a half-length pencil behind his ear, he jumped onto a truck, as though he were directing an assaulting army advancing from all directions, and shouted, "You young fellows, don't you drop the parts!" "Don't get the No. 400 cement mixed up with the No. 200 cement!" "Say, Hui, you little rascal, if you don't listen to my instructions, I'm going to twist your ears!" His voice sounded like thunder that drowned out the roaring of trucks and the noise of about a hundred workers. He frequently sent his strong and efficient wife to the most important post, saying to her, "Hey, you, Little Hei's mother, take charge of those moving the cement!"

The old woman, like a combat-seasoned soldier, would immediately run to the cement-movers and very speedily straighten out whatever chaotic situation there might be. None of the young workers dared to make trouble or disregard the old woman's directions. Lü Yu-huai cried "Bravo!" in secret. He had been running from one construction site to another for five or six years, yet he had never seen an old couple who were as well coordinated with each other as they.

As the old woman had just helped her husband with the unloading of supplies, a group of women yelled, "Old Comrade, hurry up! No. 203 is due!" What a busy day! The old woman quickly went to the other side, where she tidied up the soles and threads and withdrew into the cave-house. She then emerged with a black kerchief wrapped around her head and locked the door with a bang. She walked over and threw the key to the chief of supplies, saying, "Old Hei, I may be coming back at midnight or when the cock crows; there are some steamed buns in the steamer and some pickled greens in the jar. Go get them yourself when you're hungry!"

Hei Ch'eng-wei, the old man, simply sat there, speechless, and caught the key in his hands. Once again he had that clumsy, spiritless look. Holding the already extinguished tobacco pipe in his mouth, he was slowly filling in some figures.

"Take me to the Forty Kilometers!" The old woman crossed an irrigation channel and reached the highway. As she waved her hand, a supply truck came to a sudden stop. "Hurry up and get in, Old Comrade!" The driver was full of smiles. He let the old woman sit in the cab, as though the fact that she would ride in it was the greatest honor to him.

As the truck zoomed away, a cloud of dust blocked Lü Yu-huai's vision. He hit his palm with his fist and said aloud, "What a capable old woman!" Admiration, respect, and excitement now so overwhelmed him that even when the dust stirred up by the passing trucks blanketed his face and body, he did not feel it at all.

He turned to those women who were standing by the entrance of the cave-houses to find out more about the old woman. They said that although she was a housewife of a staff member, she was a very important figure, holding more than ten positions: secretary of the Party branch for the workers' families, chief of the family association, committee member of the union, head of the resource conservation squad, volunteer midwife . . . whoever's wife was to give birth to a child, the old woman would be on call to render service, rain or shine. Her services were not only hygienic but also safe. Besides, she would not accept compensations. "No. 203 is due!" meant that she was called upon to take care of the birth of child No. 203. Along the hundred-some *li* stretch of railway work area, she was one of the most senior Party members, thus she was called "Old Comrade." Since she had been called by that name for so long, most people had forgotten her real name. Even at the time of the union's committee membership election, her name appeared on the roster of candidates as "Old Comrade."

Having heard what the staff and workers' wives had said, Lü Yu-huai reflected upon it for a while and thought the whole thing most interesting. He turned around and looked into the cave-house through a window crack. He saw that the cave-house where the old woman lived had been expanded from a small cave. There was a large *k'ang*, at the head of which was a stove. The stone slab on the stove was rubbed gleaming bright. Beside the stove was a small wooden rack, upon which were placed bowls, chopsticks, ladles, basins, jars, and a small wooden steamer for steaming buns. The smell of pickled vegetables drifted out through the window cracks.

All this reminded Lü Yu-huai of those hills and mountains in northern Shensi Province, of the old pagoda and the ancient city walls of Yenan, and of those hamlets in the mountain gulches. It was the place where he was born and the place where he fought. He was familiar with and loved every tree and every blade of grass. Now it was the seventh month of the lunar calendar, when the rice and millet plants in the Yenan area had grown waist-high. One could, from time to time, hear the sonorous and melodious folk songs from the farms and woods.

2. OLD FRIENDS MEET AGAIN

At night, when Lü Yu-huai heard that the project director had returned, he walked toward the office. As he walked, he wondered what the director, with whom he was to work, was like, how his disposition was, and how well he could work.

As he entered a workshed, he saw a man bending low over some reports, now quickly scribbling a few lines on paper, now hurriedly working an abacus, and now making a telephone call. When he saw Lü Yu-huai enter the room, he stood up, shook Lü's hand, and said, "You are . . .? . . . I . . . am Hei Yung-liang."

Lü Yu-huai was dumbfounded. He gazed at Hei Yung-liang's face for a while, stepped back a little, looked at Hei again, up and down, and said, "You . . . let me think . . . you are . . . Comrade Hei Yung-liang! Isn't your childhood name Little Hei? You are from Li's Gulch of Tung-ch'uan in Yenan? Say, am I right?" It was Hei Yung-liang's turn to be surprised. Holding the reports above his head and with his eyes blinking in confusion, he couldn't recall anything at all for a moment. Lü Yu-huai stared at Hei Yung-liang. He thought of a hometown saying, "Tall mountains produce handsome looks." It had been ten years. Little Hei might have gone through all sorts of struggles, yet his cleancut air, his handsome looks, and his intelligent eyes remained the same as before. Lü said, "Little Hei, how forgetful you are! Don't you remember that in 1947 . . ." It suddenly dawned upon Hei Yung-liang. "Oh, yes, you are Lü . . . Lü . . . LÜ YU-HUAI! Gee, I really didn't expect it was you!" He pushed aside the forms and abacus, handed Lü a cigarette, grabbed a tea mug to pour some drinking water, and said, "Old Lü, let me tell you, my dad and mom are both here!"

It was late at night when Lü Yu-huai emerged from the home of the chief of supplies. After he returned to his quarters, he couldn't fall asleep, no matter what. Events of the past presented themselves vividly before his mind's eye.

It was in the latter part of April 1947, after the bandit troops of Chiang had occupied Yenan for more than a month, that the Northwestern Field Army destroyed one division of enemy troops in the vicinity of Yenan. As the battle concluded, the Field Army had to move quickly to another front, preparing themselves for continuing battles, and consequently left Lü Yu-huai, who carried four wounds on him, and ninety some other wounded personnel to a guerrilla unit. The leader of that guerrilla unit was known as Little Hei.

The moon was shining upon the wavelike hills. Scattered rifle reports disturbed the tranquillity of the night. Red signal flares flashed across the distant sky. Lying here and there on the hills were twelve wounded people. Most of the wounded had been carried away by members of the guerrilla unit. Little Hei was waiting for their return to move the last batch. The situation suddenly turned tense. Gunshots came closer and closer, gradually pressing in from the east, the west, and the north.

Little Hei, clasping the rifle in his arms, stamped his feet in desperation. Then he remembered that among the wounded was Company Commander Lü Yu-huai, who might have some idea about what to do. Little Hei went to

Lü Yu-huai's stretcher. He squatted down and lifted the quilt; he saw Lü's face, ashen from excessive loss of blood. Lü did not say a word; he merely touched the hand grenade that was placed beside his head.

As time went by, the situation became worse; bullets were whizzing overhead. One could see many vague human silhouettes moving atop the northern hill. Needless to say, they were the enemies. Little Hei felt his heart pressed against his throat! He loaded his rifle, prepared to shoot.

Suddenly, a human silhouette appeared on the slope. Little Hei felt chills all over him. Swiftly he took the prone position, stuck his rifle barrel out, and shouted, "Who's there?"

The man who was walking along the path on the slope not only did not stop but walked even more slowly and more steadily, as if he were counting the steps while he was walking. Little Hei shouted, "Who's there? Halt!" He was breathing hard and was about to pull the trigger. The man spoke up, "Who! Who! You, good-for-nothing, lived twenty some years for nothing. You don't even recognize your own dad!" Little Hei jumped up. He was at once delighted and anxious. "Hurry up! Listen, bullets are whizzing by!" As he walked, Hei Ch'eng-wei said, "Little Hei, your dad is about halfway through his life, and he's made friends, you know, particularly with those bullets."

When he reached the hilltop, he stood there erect like a wall. Little Hei grabbed him by his arm and said, "Dad, it's terrible. I don't have even a single stretcher-bearer. This . . . this . . ." Hei Ch'eng-wei drew his chin in, his forehead jutting out. With his eyes bulging like those of an ox, he said, "I really feel like slapping you! What are you afraid of? If the sky should fall, you have big guys to hold it up!" He turned around, tilted his hat backwards a little, raised his head, inserted two fingers into his mouth and whistled loudly. The sound of whistling provoked some fierce shooting from the enemy. Upon hearing the whistling, a woman around forty with a couple of dozen other women ran up the hill from the gulch. Excitedly Little Hei shouted, "Ma, you are really a life-saving Bodhisattva!" Hei Ch'eng-wei said, "Little Hei, without your ma, the fighting general, I imagine you're going to flop today!" He turned around. Pointing at the wounded, he said to his wife, "Little Hei's mother, come on, give me a hand!"

As Little Hei's mother waved her hand, the couple of dozen women carried away eleven of the wounded; she herself and three other women carried the stretcher on which Lü Yu-huai was lying. Little Hei with his rifle marched in front of the stretchers; his father carried his rifle in one hand and walked behind. A long column of silhouettes under the moonlight along the ridge speedily and quietly headed toward the south. A moment later, enemies appeared on the hill where they had stayed. Bullets were in hot pursuit of the stretcher-bearers.

After midnight, they reached the wide riverbed, east of Yenan. Immediately before their eyes were the highway and the Yen River. Enemy trucks were running on the highway. Every single hamlet along the Yen River seemed dead. One could not hear any dog's barking, nor could one see any lights.

Hei Ch'eng-wei watched a fleet of enemy trucks pass; he went around to reconnoiter the surrounding area. Then he ordered, "Little Hei's mother, I'm going to run with my gun. You lead the stretcher team and follow me closely.

Even if the sky falls and the earth caves in, don't you stop!" The old Mrs. Hei, looking intently at her husband, nodded.

Hei Ch'eng-wei gave the second order, "Little Hei, you stay behind to cover us. No matter how many enemies come up, you must hold them for half an hour! Have you got the guts?" Little Hei said, "Okay!" With a hand on his son's shoulder, Hei Ch'eng-wei shook him a little and said, "Listen to that, you sound like your dad all right!" Hei Ch'eng-wei led the stretcher team away. They crossed the highway, waded through the Yen River, and climbed the mountain.

Once Hei Ch'eng-wei led the stretcher team to the top of a hill, they stopped to rest. Everyone felt a little more relaxed, for they had finally left the enemy behind. The young women were still panting and cursing, "Old Hei, we followed you on this run; it will cost us ten years of life!" "Old Hei, you are the death of us—you, old devil, you are killing us!" Old Hei didn't hear a thing. He and his wife were looking at the roads down the hill, looking at the Yen River, and looking at the East River of Yenan. One could see that the enemy machine guns on the opposite hill were sticking out their fiery tongues. Enemy trucks were flying, one after another, along the highway at the foot of the hill. Their headlights illuminated the dusty air. Under the moonlight, one could clearly see Little Hei in silhouette, lying prone by the bank of the Yen River, shooting.

Suddenly, Little Hei fired off several rapid rounds, got up, and ran toward the rear. After a few steps he fell. At this crucial moment, the enemies came down the hill, crossed the highway, and ran toward the river bank in pursuit. Bullets whistled over the heads of Old Hei and his wife. The women who were resting on the ground stood up in a hurry and ran toward Old Hei to watch the river banks. They saw the enemies in groups of thirty to fifty moving toward the banks. Machine guns and rifles were spitting fire. No one made any noise except the sound of heavy breathing. Bullets screeched in all directions. Old Hei waved his hand and angrily yelled, "Hit the ground!" Everyone except his wife lay down at once.

Old Hei kicked the ground and said, "Quick! Move the wounded forward quickly. There is a woods two or three *li* ahead. Once we get in there, everything will be okay!" Little Hei's mother tugged at her husband. "You dead old man," she said, "don't you want our son?" Old Hei said, "You womenfolk have long hair but short vision! Let's get the twelve comrades out of danger first, then come back to get Little Hei!"

"How mean you are!" she said, "Isn't Little Hei your own flesh and blood?" Old Hei became angry. With his chin in, his forehead out, and his eyes bulging like those of an ox, he asked, "Which is more important, one life or twelve lives?"

She rushed over and snatched the rifle from Old Hei's hands. "You people get away! If I could bring him to this world, I can save him too." Old Hei blocked her way. He thought, if he hadn't been concerned about the wounded, he would have long ago rushed down, and now there was no way for him to get away. On second thought, he reasoned with himself, "If she goes to get him, that should solve the problem all right. I'll get the twelve wounded moving first. If we run into bad guys in the woods, I alone can handle eight or ten of them." He took a look around and listened carefully. "Little Hei's mother," he said, "let me ask you, how are you going to save Little Hei?" Hugging the rifle, she looked at the river without saying a word. Her hair fluttered in the wind.

Old Hei took the gun from his wife and pushed her to the ground. He then dropped to the ground on his belly and fired off more than ten rounds in a stretch. That provoked the enemy to shoot back rapidly. After a while, the enemy saw no more gunfire or movement from this side, so they stopped shooting and seemed to be groping along the bank. Old Hei took out a box of matches and ran to the east, where he struck a match and blew it out. Repeatedly, he struck about a dozen matches. The enemy resumed shooting, not only with machine guns but with 60-mm cannon as well.

Old Hei handed the rifle over to his wife. "The enemy," he said, "will not dare to advance within a couple of hours. Strike when the iron is hot. Hurry up and go!" She carried the rifle and, braving the heavy fire, rushed down to the gulch and groped toward the river bank. Old Hei, armed with some hand grenades, took the twelve stretchers to the dark woods.

After he came to, Lü Yu-huai in the stretcher felt unbearably thirsty. Through the tree branches he saw a bright moon and a few stars in the sky. He saw the silhouettes of those women who were on guard around the stretchers. Then his vision fell upon Old Hei. Old Hei had his small tobacco pipe out, but he seemed uninterested in smoking; he looked around and listened. Lü Yu-huai said, "Say, fellow-townsman, hurry up to help your old partner and your son!"

Old Hei felt as if he were being deep-fried or burned. How he wished to have a pair of wings so he could fly to the river bank! But when he heard the groans of the wounded, he couldn't bear the thought of leaving them. Just to cover up his anxiety and to give some comfort to the wounded, he responded to keep the conversation going. "Company Commander Lü, you sound like a person from right here."

"I'm a native of Kao-ch'iao-ch'uan, west of Yenan," Lü said. Old Hei stood up, carrying the hand grenades. Absent-mindedly, he asked, "A native of Kao-ch'iao-ch'uan? What is your father called?"

"My father was called Lü Shih-teh. He . . ." Old Hei was surprised. He asked, "Say it again. Who's your father?" Lü Yu-huai repeated what he had said. Old Hei ran over to Lü, lifted his cover, and said, "Gee . . . You're Lü Shih-teh's kid? Your father was . . . ! Your father sacrificed his life in 1936 when the Red Army was in the Eastern Expedition! In the old society, your father peddled charcoal carried on a donkey and I worked as a blacksmith. The two of us were sworn brothers. It was he who sponsored me and my wife to join the Party in 1933. My good nephew, you . . . you . . . Gee! This is really one of those opportunities which you bump into but can never find if you start looking for it!"

If he hadn't been badly wounded, Lü Yu-huai would have jumped up right away to give Hei Ch'eng-wei a good hug. He had not met Hei Ch'eng-wei before. But when he was just old enough to understand a few words, he would climb upon a neighborhood old man's knees, listening to people's stories about Old Hei's superman feats. There was the story about how Hei Ch'eng-wei—he must have consumed a tiger's heart and a leopard's guts that time—bare-handedly fought his way through a huge army of enemy troops. They said that he once disguised himself as a poor cripple and carried a basket of chicken eggs for sale. A group of officers of the White Army jumped him for the eggs; he merely took out a hand grenade with which he effortlessly took five of them captive. There was also the story that as soon as the Central Red Army advanced to northern Shensi Province, Liu Chih-tan transferred this Red warrior of extraordinary courage out of his unit and made him the captain of Security Guards for the Party Central.

Suddenly, it seemed that something had just happened. Old Hei stood up and ran back, tracing his steps. The women followed him. Lü Yu-huai and the other wounded ones who were able to move a bit all struggled to lift their heads to watch. Sure enough, it was Little Hei and his mother, both wounded, holding on to each other and staggering along slowly. Their blood dropped on the road all the way. . . .

3. THE WHOLE FAMILY

After dinner, on the second day after Lü Yu-huai's arrival, Chief of Supplies Hei Ch'eng-wei and Project Director Hei Yung-liang took Lü to tour several major work sites. As they walked, Hei Yung-liang briefed Lü Yu-huai on his experience in the construction of railways through the mountainous region. Pointing to an already completed tall stone arch bridge in the distance, he further explained the merits of securing materials locally during the construction and summarized the history of stone arch bridges in China. Not only Lü Yu-huai looked to Hei Yung-liang with envy, but even the old man Hei Ch'eng-wei regarded his son, who had started as a shepherd, with respect.

Once they got on the slope, they were stopped by a cadre. In a matter of moments, a crowd surged around Hei Ch'eng-wei and Hei Yung-liang: director of the work district, chief engineer, supply staff—all in a water-tight circle around the father-and-son team. Knowing that he was not going to get away in a hurry, Old Hei sat himself squarely upon a rock, inserted the little tobacco pipe in his mouth, and began to smoke. As he finished one pipeful, he knocked the ashes out against the edge of his shoe, loaded up the pipe again, and continued smoking. With a broad smile, he glanced at the pipe and from time to time looked at the work sites in the distance. All those who were present knew that once Old Hei assumed that pose, even if you should jump three feet high and curse his ancestors of the past three generations, you would not be able to make him angry.

The cadres tried to talk all at once:

"Old Chief, no matter what, today you must give me 500 catties of explosives!"

"People handling supplies are always being treated unfairly. If you don't give me a ton of steel rods, I'm going to take 2,000 workers to your home for dinner!"

A tall work-district director angrily said, "Explosives! If you don't give me 500 catties of explosives, I'm going to resign!" Without moving his eyes away from the little tobacco pipe, Old Hei said, "If you resign, you don't get paid. You'd better figure it out! As for the explosives, not until eight o'clock tonight will I be able to distribute 300 catties to you." As if he had gotten hold of a treasure, the tall work-district director hurriedly said, "I'll settle for 300 catties. A verbal statement is no proof. You sign a statement." Again without moving his eyes away from the little dry tobacco pipe, Old Hei said, "The few characters

I know were picked up during my manure-gathering years. They don't look good when I write them on paper. We might as well let the director of the Seventh Work District sign it for you."

The director of the Seventh Work District acted as if he had just been burned. He said, "Are you, dead old man, picking on me? I can't even produce one catty of explosives!" Old Hei said, "No explosives? I've already sent people to your warehouse and moved away 300 catties." The director of the Seventh Work District turned pale, as if an incomparable disaster had fallen upon his head. He demanded, "Who gave you permission?" Old Hei tugged a bit the jacket thrown on his shoulders, and said with a mischievous smile, "Head of the supply section." The director of the Seventh Work District said, "This is outright anarchy! I'm going to fire him!"

Old Hei removed the jacket from his shoulders; he carried it in his hands and straightened his back. His face, which was as black as the bottom of a cooking pot, turned very serious. With his chin drawn in, his forehead jutting out, and his eyes bulging like those of an ox, he stared at the director of the Seventh Work District and said, "You can't fire me, nor can you fire him. Right now, we can only dig something out of the eastern wall to patch up the western wall. I know, you people will manage through tomorrow. The day after tomorrow, if you can't get through the day, you will come to see me all right. I, Old Hei, am not going to run away!"

Seeing that the chief of supplies was not going to budge, the crowd besieged Project Director Hei Yung-liang, making all sorts of complaints, cursing the manager of the supply depot and cursing the supply office of the engineering bureau. All along, Lü Yu-huai was standing nearby, listening, sizing up each one of the cadres. Then he took out a notebook and made a few notes.

After the cadres had left, Hei Yung-liang said, "We're not going to the project area. Let's return to the team office!" Lü Yu-huai and Hei Ch'eng-wei, together with Hei Yung-liang, returned to the workshed, which the construction team used as their office.

Lü Yu-huai, with his hands crossed behind his back, was looking at the wall charts and was thinking about something. Old Hei took out a pad and a pen, waiting for instructions. Hei Yung-liang paced back and forth for a while. Suddenly he pounded the table with his fist and said, "If I can be used as steel rods and explosives, then just chop me up and use me!" Old Hei said, "What a temper! I've told you many times: It's easy to take on a hard job, but it's difficult to deal with complaints!" Hei Yung-liang said, "It doesn't matter whether you take on a hard job or you deal with complaints, it's tough to go through it these days!" He did not at all hide his feelings before a subordinate like the chief of supplies. Old Hei said, "If you can lead me, you've got something better than what I have. But, I might ask you: Are supplies of every unit in this project area or just the supplies of our project difficult?" Noticing that Hei Yung-liang did not respond, Lü Yu-huai turned around and said, "I guess it's probably difficult every day and every year. None of the units will find it easy!" Old Hei said, "Right! All day we fight about supplies. It reflects the whole situation of the country. We started out empty-handed." Lü Yu-huai said, "Well put! Our business is to make progress in spite of difficulties, and to make progress quickly." Hei Yung-liang nodded toward Lü Yu-huai and in a more relaxed tone said, "Dad, since you've explained it so clearly to me, you ought to repeatedly explain it to the cadres!" Old Hei knocked the table with his little tobacco pipe and said, "What do I say? Do I say that our lack of supplies is no fault of this chief of supplies but the fault of our superiors? Yung-liang, if we don't do the difficult things, who will? If we don't face up to difficulties, who will?"

Lü Yu-huai suddenly straightened out his back and looked at the chief of supplies. Through this tall figure he saw a history that covered a period of several decades—no, not just decades but quite a few great historic eras! Hei Yung-liang turned his head; he was touched. He took a look at his father and saw that his weathered face had become darker than ever before and his eyes all bloodshot. Yes, this old man had suffered more than anyone else: all year around, day and night, he traveled from one work site to another—from the project area to Sian, to Chengchow, to Szechwan, to the blazingly hot South, to the lumber mills in primitive forests—in order to secure supplies, to which he had totally committed himself, body and soul. Even this very night he was to travel, under the moon and the stars, to a railway depot fifty kilometers away, to crowd himself aboard the train so that he could reach Sian by daybreak. He would be walking back and forth in front of a certain office, waiting for dawn, and waiting for people to come to the office. . . .

At this moment, Hei Yung-liang's mother came in. She was carrying a small bag and a red rubber hot-water bottle in her hands. She took a look at the Party committee secretary, her husband, and her son Hei Yung-liang and asked, "Have you finished talking about your official business? Right. If you've finished, let me talk about a little private matter."

The old woman had obviously stood outside the door for a while before she came in. She respected very much her son's office; while in there she would never talk loudly, nor would she call Hei Yung-liang by his childhood name. She asked Old Hei, "Must you go to Sian tonight?" Old Hei smiled and said, "Is there still any question about it? I was born a busy man!" The old woman said, "You've been complaining about a stomachache all day long. When you board the train, get some boiling water from the attendant and pour it into the hot-water bottle to warm up your stomach. I've packed a few cakes in this kerchief for you. Gee, a man full of beard still can't take care of himself."

After Old Hei and his wife had left, Lü Yu-huai and Hei Yung-liang looked at each other and exchanged a few thoughts.

Intermittent sounds of explosion came from the distance like a rainless thunder. On the opposite hill several hundred workers were chanting while working. The dispatcher in the office next door was calling his colleagues at various work sites through a bullhorn to find out their work progress of the day. His voice was from time to time interrupted by the roar of the machines. All this sensitized the people in the office to how the whole project area was breathing, how it activated itself, and how the people were making progress at high speed.

Lü Yu-huai said, "From my point of view, hard-working people like Uncle Old Hei . . ." Hei Yung-liang smiled gently. Pointing through the window, he said to Lü Yu-huai, "There is another hard-working person!" Following the direction Hei Yung-liang was looking, Lü Yu-huai saw that the old woman, with her back against the wall of a warehouse, was standing there. She would sometimes look at the lights in the distance, sometimes at the moon above, and sometimes toward the left and then the right, like an alert and duty-conscious sentry!

Lü Yu-huai asked, "Yung-liang, what's the matter with the old lady?" While contemplating his mother's presence out there, Yung-liang gave Lü Yu-huai the following account: The supply warehouse was being watched by members of the supply staff, and, as the rule went, had very little to do with her as the wife of a staff member. Yet, whenever Old Hei had an occasion to leave his office, which was next to the warehouse, the old lady would go there beside the warehouse and stand guard. She wasn't very clear about the supplies stored in the warehouse, their quantities, or their uses. She only knew that the warehouse meant life or death to her husband, to her son, and to all those involved in the project.

As our fellow townsmen in northern Shensi would say: A person who worries too much about anything will become mentally ill and turn a restless soul. At one time, Old Hei was home. In the middle of the night, the old woman roused him from sleep and said, "Say, Little Hei's dad, go out and take a look. I don't think the warehouse is secure. It might have caught fire!" He said, "Do you think I must go out and take a look?" She said, "You must go out and take a look!" "In that case, I'll go out and take a look!" He well knew that if he should contradict her at this time, it would surely lead to a violent squabble. He threw his clothes over his shoulders, went out, and walked around. She relaxed and fell sound asleep.

At another time, she woke up from a dream and hurried out of bed. He asked, "What are you going to do?" She said, "I'm afraid guards at the warehouse drank again today!" He shouted impatiently, "I think you're out of your mind, or else the devil must have got you!" The two of them sat up face to face, each threw some clothes over their shoulders, and pointing at each other's chests, had a good quarrel. During their exchanges, she pulled a quilt and covered his leg with it for fear that he might catch cold. In the end, however, it was he, as always, who apologized and brought the dispute to a close!

4. FOREVER SO

On the third day after Lü Yu-huai's arrival, Hei Yung-liang took him to several tunnels to find out the work situation there. When they emerged from Tunnel No. 2, the two of them were perspiring all over. They sat down under a large tree on the riverside to cool off.

At this moment, the resource conservation squad, composed of twenty some women and led by Hei Yung-liang's mother, came over. Every Monday, Wednesday, and Friday, the old lady would punctually take these women to pick up the discarded supplies all over the project area. As they came to where Hei Yung-liang and Lü Yu-huai sat, the old lady told the other women to go ahead, while she herself put down her basket; it rested on top of Hei Yung-liang's foot. Seeing that the basket was full of scraps of iron, screws, and various machine parts, Lü Yu-huai smiled broadly and said, "The resource conservation squad is really useful!"

She ignored Lü Yu-huai's remark and angrily said to Hei Yung-liang, "Your wings are strong now. You can leave your father, but I can't leave that bunch of old bones of his!"

"Ma, what's the matter?" The old lady said, "Last night, you went to talk to your father? You even lectured him in that self-righteous manner of yours?" Hei Yung-liang said, "I was talking with the chief of supplies." The old lady said, "You don't say! What a fine distinction between the public and the private!" Hei Yung-liang said, "Ma, it doesn't matter whether or not it's a fine distinction between the public and the private. Anyway, we are all Party members and are all responsible to the Party!" He looked at Lü Yu-huai, as if asking for support. Looking at the mother and the son, Lü Yu-huai kept chuckling.

The old lady said, "Responsible to the Party? How many days have you been responsible to the Party? Your father's got a very strong Party character. Don't you think he is easy to take advantage of! Even the Central authorities, your father knows twenty some of them, let alone the sesame-size officials like you! All right, let me test you, the bureaucrat, how much supplies did the resource conservation squad of the workers' families pick up during the first half of this year?" Hei Yung-liang said, "Nails, machine parts and the like came to a total of more than 8,000 catties." He recited the figures without hesitation, thinking that would shut up the old lady. She asked, "Isn't it a lot?" Hei Yung-liang said, "A lot! A lot! Do you mean to tell me that an old lady of your age would want people to praise you every day?" The old lady said, "A lot? Is a lot good or bad?" Hei Yung-liang said, "Good! Good! If it wasn't good, why would the union commend you?" The old lady said, "Good! How shameless! If we picked up a lot, it proves that you discarded a lot. Yet, you are pompously managing production and are not embarrassed!" Hei Yung-liang said, "Ma, why are you fighting me? Do you think that I am so happy about everything that I feel like singing every day?"

The old lady saw her son's work-worn, thin face and turned softhearted. Seizing this opportunity, Lü Yu-huai said, "Auntie, Yung-liang has been busy enough and has suffered enough hardship! Forgive him this time!" The old lady said, "Since the Party committee secretary says to forgive you, I'll forgive you! Don't think that your mother can't think straight. Good or bad, your mother has been in the Party for twenty-four years. You ought to treat your father nicely. I'm really not afraid that your father might be working too hard." She picked up her basket and walked off a couple of steps. "If we don't work hard, who will?"

At this moment, a dust cloud rose and four or five trucks arrived at the supply warehouse on the riverbank. As the dusts gradually settled, Old Hei appeared. He was standing on a truck, looking all around for people to unload the supplies. When he spotted his wife, he was delighted and called out, "Little Hei's mother, come and give me a hand!"

The old lady saw those full-loaded trucks; she knew Old Hei did not make the trip in vain; she knew that at this moment Old Hei was the happiest man in the world. She hurried toward the trucks. Hei Yung-liang looked at his mother's strong back and said, "Ma, let me also give you a hand!" The old lady said, "Get away! Does your mother need help from you?" Hei Yung-liang looked at Lü Yu-huai and smiled. The two men followed the old lady.

As Lü Yu-huai helped Old Hei unload the supplies, he said, "Auntie, you've helped Uncle Old Hei step by step. You ought to help me and Yung-liang a little." She cast a glance at Hei Yung-liang and said, "Hmm, this dead old woman is rapidly getting out-of-date!" Lü Yu-huai said, "Hey, Auntie is treating me like an outsider." The old lady burst into loud laughter. She said, "Outsider? You've long been a member of the family. When we finish unloading, I'll make some fried cakes for you and Little Hei! You've been traveling all these years but probably haven't forgotten the yellow wine our fellow townsmen like to drink!" She turned to helping Old Hei, directing a hundred or so workers in the unloading of supplies.

Those sturdy and strong young fellows were once again exchanging eye-signals among themselves, as though they were saying, "Be careful! The old lady has come to the front line again!"

Old Hei looked at the several truckloads of supplies. He seemed twenty years younger. His physique was robust and his movements were agile. He would now leap onto a truck with a whiz, and now jump down from it with a bang. With a half-length pencil behind his ear, he waved his writing pad in the air and was incessantly hollering, "Got to be careful moving those explosives!" "Say, you dumbbells, put those steel rods in Warehouse No. 3!" The voice of his hollering overpowered the noise of machines, the work-chant of the crew tamping the dirt foundation, and the fracas of the movers.

Watching her old companion, the old lady felt that he was the only hero in the universe.

While looking on at his father and mother, Hei Yung-liang felt incomparably excited and proud.

Lü Yu-huai observed Old Hei, the old lady, and Little Hei. He realized that it was these broad and sturdy shoulders that had been supporting this vast nation. It had been so in the past, it is so at present, and it will be so forever!

Sian, April 1958

Translated by Maurice H. Tseng

YANG MO
(1915–)

The Song of Youth (1958), having gone through three editions, the last in 1977, is possibly as popular today among the youth of the People's Republic of China as it was in the early sixties, before the Cultural Revolution when it came under severe criticism. Its author, Yang Mo, came from a middle-class, intellectual family. Her father, a traditional scholar, was once president of a private university in Peking. Declining family fortune and a family decree that she marry against her wishes forced Yang Mo to leave home. She worked as a store clerk for a brief period, then taught grade school in a rural area in Hopei. By 1935 she was in Peking working with underground Communist revolutionaries. During the war against Japan, she worked with guerrilla units in North China. Liberation brought her back to Peking to concentrate on writing, for the press and for the screen. She was one of the very few writers active in 1973, though her work had been criticized at the height of the Cultural Revolution. With the downfall of the Gang of Four, she continued to be in public circulation, leading delegates of writers to travel abroad and appearing at literary gatherings, sometimes with her celebrated movie actress sister, Pai Yang. In 1979 Yang Mo was completing her new novel, *Dawn Is About to Break in the East*.

Yang Mo's *It Happened in the Reed Pond* (1950) is a collection of short stories recording her wartime experiences of 1937–45. *The Song of Youth* apparently has made autobiographical use of much of the author's background. It tells of the struggles of underground Communist workers in the 1930s when the Nationalist government refused to fight against Japan after Manchuria was seized. The plot focuses on the young heroine, Lin Tao-ching, whose bourgeois background parallels the author's. The story begins with Lin Tao-ching running away from home to avoid an arranged marriage to a corrupt Kuomintang agent, Hu Meng-an (who shows up later in the story as her persecutor). In her attempts to escape further snares in her personal life, she becomes involved in a liaison which plunges her into deeper despair, until she is politically awakened by a young Marxist, Lu Chia-ch'uan. Through his tutelage, Lin Tao-ching finds herself and her faith in Communist ideology. But before she confesses her love for him, Lu, betrayed by a Party renegade (Tai Yü, who appears in the following episode as the lover of Wang Hsiao-yen, Lin's closest friend), is captured, tortured in jail, and finally killed. However, Lin Tao-ching's faith in the Party gives her courage to carry on. Having proved her loyalty to the Communist cause through many tests and persecutions, she is finally granted Party membership at the recommendation of Comrade Chiang Hua (who becomes her lover in the end). She undertakes the assignment to agitate student movements in Peking. The story ends on a triumphant note, signified by the Communist-inspired mass student demonstration of December 9, 1935, protesting the ineffectual Nationalist government during national crises.

—A.P.

from *The Song of Youth*

CHAPTER 39

One night in late November, heavy snow was besieging the inclement northern region. Huge snowflakes, rolled up by the cold wind, danced continuously in the silent night along the deserted, empty streets. Braving the blizzard, Chiang Hua came to Lin Tao-ching's lodging and knocked.

Tao-ching was writing under the lamp, a coal stove burning warmly by her side. Seeing Chiang Hua, she quickly helped him brush the snow from his clothes and poked the coal in the stove.

"Still snowing? It must be terribly cold!" She rattled merrily and poured a cup of boiled water for him. "Do you know, Chiang, that the Student Government at Peking University was established today? What's more, it has decided to join the Peking-Tientsin Student Union."

Chiang Hua was warming himself by the fire. He watched Tao-ching and smiled in silence as if he had already known the facts. But Tao-ching continued: "Thanks to your help and encouragement, the work at Peking University has really turned out better than anticipated. After years of lethargy, the masses are being activated again. I don't know how it is on other campuses, but to realize the principle of a united front against Japanese aggression at Peking University is not going to be simple. Even some of the Party members can't understand it—they regard it as a policy of surrender. In the past, the progressive students only talked among themselves about saving the nation; they called conservative students traitors and would not have anything to do with them. The situation has now changed. All the middle-of-the-roaders are being organized and mobilized, and the reactionaries are isolated. Wang Hsiao-yen appeared crushed at the second election assembly of the history students. She bowed her head and did not dare look at anyone when that monkey, Wang Chung, was exposed for base treachery by Li Shao-t'ung, who read aloud in front of all those fellow students the evidence showing that Wang Chung had been receiving funds from the Kuomintang. It was a receipt discovered by Wu Yu-p'ing, a classmate of Wang Chung. The students were so aggravated that our success at the election became a sure thing. Oh, it was great." Realizing that she was over-enthusiastic, she caught her breath and stopped. She began to wonder why she always turned into a babbling child whenever she was with this handsome staunch comrade with a large frame. Why the difference between talking with him and talking with others? Suddenly she felt embarrassed. Trying to calm herself, she said slowly in a low voice, "I am sorry, Chiang. Didn't you say a while back that you had something to tell me? But I haven't been home much the last few days, and now I am monopolizing the conversation. Talk to me, and I'll listen."

Now it was Chiang Hua's turn to become shy. Should he tell her or not? His dark face reddened. He wrung his large hands again and again over the fire, as if by this movement he could conceal his surging emotions. Except for a brief infatuation during his high school years, this twenty-nine-year-old man had never experienced so strong a power of love as he did now. He had learned to live without love. But he must not waste any more time. Why must he deny himself and continue to suffer and perhaps cause the suffering of his beloved? So thinking, he raised his head and gently held Tao-ching's hand. Suppressing the tremor in his voice, he whispered, "Tao-ching, it is not about work that I came to see you tonight. I want to ask you a question. Do you think this relationship between us can be something more than comradeship?"

Tao-ching watched Chiang Hua's worked-up, flushed face, so unfamiliar to her. Suddenly she recognized the love and suffering hidden in his eyes. It became very clear to her now. Her suspicion had been confirmed. Now was she feeling ecstatic, joyful, or sad? She could not tell how she felt exactly. But she sensed a quickened heartbeat, dizziness, and a weakness in her knees. Tears welled in her eyes. Could this steadfast comrade, whom she had admired and respected, soon become her lover? Yet it was not he who had occupied her dreams all these years. But she should not hesitate any longer. A Bolshevik like Chiang Hua was indeed worthy of her love. Could she find good reason to refuse this man who already loved her? She raised her eyes and looked at Chiang Hua silently for a while, and then answered meekly:

"Yes, Chiang, I like you very much."

Chiang Hua, who gazed at her expectantly, stretched out his arms and embraced her.

The night was getting late. Chiang Hua had no intention of leaving. Tao-ching, nestling next to him, finally reminded him:

"Aren't you going? It's already one o'clock. Come back tomorrow."

Chiang Hua watched her with elation. He drew her closer and whispered in a shaky voice, "Why chase me away? I am staying."

Tao-ching rose to her feet and walked outside. Suddenly she felt confused and even experienced pain at hearing Chiang Hua's words. Outside it was still snowing. The roof, the ground, the trees, and the entire universe were enveloped in white. Tao-ching stood in the quiet courtyard, her feet planted deep in the snow, her thoughts rising and falling like tides between excitement and self-doubt. In her anticipated happiness she was also feeling an unexpected pain. The image of Lu Chia-ch'uan, blurred by the passage of time, suddenly and unexpectedly invaded her mind with an extraordinary force. She could not forget him. No, never. But why must the memory of him come back at this particular moment to disturb her? Right in front of her floated his deep, flashing eyes, floated the image of him crawling stubbornly on the jail floor, with broken legs. . . . Tears streamed down her face. The snowstorm only heightened the complex, conflicting emotions warring in her breast. And she had hoped to drive away her entangled emotions with the cold air! Before she was herself again she returned to her room, feeling cruel about having left Chiang Hua waiting alone for so long.

Once inside, she moved toward him with visible excitement and said tremulously, "Are you really staying? . . . Then stay." Embarrassed, she threw her head against his broad shoulder and locked her arms around his neck with all her might.

At daybreak, when the two were still roaming in their sweet dreams, they were aroused by the sound of rapid knocking—it was not loud, but rapid with urgency. They sat up simultaneously, exchanging questioning glances in the gray dawn.

"Do you have any important document? Give it to me, I'll swallow it." Tao-ching whispered anxiously, while searching under his pillow.

"Calm yourself!" muttered Chiang Hua, who picked up his clothes and went toward the window. Standing sideways, he peeped out through the crack of the door.

Following the knock came a thin, female voice: "Tao-ching, open the door! It's me—Hsiao-yen. . . ."

"Hsiao-yen?" Chiang Hua turned from the window and quickly dressed. Without taking time to put on her jacket, Tao-ching ran to open the door. Hsiao-yen staggered inside as soon as the door was ajar. She was not wearing her glasses; her hair was disheveled. She paid no attention to the man standing behind Tao-ching, but fell into her friend's arms at once and wept uncontrollably. This gentle, levelheaded young woman had lost her usual restraint. She sobbed and sobbed, all tears and no words, as if her heart were torn to shreds with grief and despair.

"Hsiao-yen, calm down, and tell me what happened." Tao-ching's voice was gentle and sincere, as if there never had been any rift in their friendship. Hsiao-yen, whose tears had dampened Tao-ching's shoulder and back, did not answer. Tao-ching said no more, but quietly held Hsiao-yen's shaking body and gently stroked her convulsing chest.

"Tao-ching, I . . . I have wronged you. I tell . . . you," Hsiao-yen finally blurted out, trying hard to control herself. But her words were choked by sobs again. After another long wait, she wiped away her tears and resumed:

"That rascal Tai Yü is the real traitor, a running dog . . . I just found out!" To speak aloud her discovery caused a flood of new tears. At last she was composed enough to tell Tao-ching and Chiang Hua of her shocking experience.

Tai Yü had told Hsiao-yen that he was the Communist Party secretary in charge of the Peking area. Hsiao-yen was in love with him and believed in him, so that when she lost contact with Tao-ching, she was completely under his deceptive influence and had painfully made a 180-degree turn in her opinion of Tao-ching's loyalty to the Party. Gradually, however, her impression of Tai Yü began to change. She found him erratic in behavior and frequently despondent. Sometimes he could still speak convincingly, commanding her respect; at other times he would hem and haw, and was full of contradictions. Frequently he also reeked of liquor and smelled of women's perfume, and his excuses were flimsy when he was put on the spot. Hsiao-yen's suspicion of his private life led her to question his political credibility. Was he really a Party-designated secretary of the Peking area as he claimed? Was her own Party membership authentic? Were Wang Chung and his lot, who sabotaged the Student Association of the Peking University, good or bad guys themselves? What exactly was Lin Tao-ching's political stand? Puzzled, Hsiao-yen became more vigilant over Tai Yü's behavior.

Having made up her mind to get to the bottom of Tai Yü's secrecy, Hsiao-yen proceeded in all directions. To begin with, she never knew where Tai Yü lived, nor met any of his friends or relatives. It would not be possible to find out anything about him through Wang Chung and company. Hsiao-yen became more and more uneasy. But love—her very first love and youthful dream— would not allow her to sever their relationship, but drove her to prove to herself that all her doubts were but a figment of her imagination resulting from her own narrow-mindedness. She would be so happy if only she could confirm what he said he was—a good and loyal comrade, dedicated to serving the Party. She was not destined to have such luck, however. Evil fate had plunged her into the abyss of despair; the magic mountain created out of her life's blood collapsed and melted away like thin ice, leaving hardly a trace.

On the first occasion when she secretly followed him into an alley off Ch'eng-hsiang Lane outside Hsüan-wu Gate, she saw him knock at a vermilion door. A middle-aged woman, skinny but seductively dressed in a fur coat, came out. He tried to hold her hand, but she pushed his hand away. Instead, she pinched his cheek and said, "Go in and wait for me." As she sauntered away, Tai Yü abjectly went inside.

Hsiao-yen was beside herself with rage. What was that woman to him? His wife? His mistress? Why, then, did he tell her, Hsiao-yen, that he loved and adored her? Moreover, she saw genuine passion in his eyes.

After her discovery, she would have nothing to do with him for days. Tai Yü showed suffering and shed copious tears. When Hsiao-yen asked him about the woman, he said she was a comrade who had to be in such a disguise to elude the enemy, and that their relationship was confined only to business. Hsiao-yen was not fully convinced, but in her misery she continued to accept his "guidance" and helped him to undermine innocent fellow students at Peking University.

It was not until the meeting of the History Student Association, when Li Shao-t'ung read aloud the content of the receipt which proved that Wang Chung was on the payroll of the Kuomintang, that Hsiao-yen fully realized that she had been deceived. A few hours before she came to Tao-ching, Hsiao-yen was feeling at her lowest. Tai Yü, thoroughly intoxicated, called on her. Before he could sit down steadily, he muttered something unintelligibly and fell over on her bed, dead to the world. Now came Hsiao-yen's opportunity. She searched his pockets and found a letter, a document of some sort in secret code, and a list of names of students from various campuses. She read the letter. Suddenly she was thunderstruck and felt as if she were being electrocuted.

The letter was from Hu Meng-an in response to his "Brother Yü" (such was the salutation). In it Hu told Tai Yü to put his mind to his work in Peking, and if he carried out Hu's order faithfully, he would be assured of a bright future. As to the request of a transfer to Nan-ch'ang, it could not be done at the moment, since it would disrupt the network of the system. Everything became crystal clear to Hsiao-yen now. Obviously, the list contained names of leftist students and revolutionaries targeted for arrest. That document proved Tai Yü to be a secret agent for the Kuomintang. He was the real traitor and renegade who had falsely accused others, such as Tao-ching, of betraying the Party. In an insane rage, Hsiao-yen struck Tai Yü's face with her trembling hands again and again until they became numb. But Tai Yü could not be aroused.

With the evidence she found on Tai Yü in her hands, Hsiao-yen stumbled to the courtyard. Supporting herself against a bare lilac tree, she stood in the bleak winter night until the wee hours of a new day. Between two and three A.M., Tai Yü appeared in front of her. Still drunk, he grasped her and carried her half-frozen body into her room. Kneeling beside her, he wept and said that he was unworthy of her and of the Party. Shamefaced, he accused himself of being weak, and admitted his crime. Hsiao-yen, lying stiffly on the bed, cold and numb to the core, no longer felt for him. She did not utter a single word. To her the whole world had come to an end, and her life was over. But Tai Yü would not let her alone. He wept and swore that his love for her was real, that if there was any human feeling left in him, it was his love for her, that the only ray of sunshine that remained in his sullied soul was her love, her goodness, her noble image.

To his pleading, Hsiao-yen felt numb and unmoved. To get away from him, she paced back and forth. And back and forth Tai Yü followed her. Crazily, he pleaded, begged, cajoled. He admitted that his cowardice had done him in and that he had failed to live up to the Party's expectations. The enemy, he said, had taken advantage of his cowardice and had forced him to the evil abyss from which there was no return, and that he had betrayed his comrades out of necessity and self-preservation. He told her that the woman she had seen was a secret agent who had a hold on him and demanded that he satisfy her lust; that he could not help but obey her, or else he would be eliminated; that when he fell in love with Hsiao-yen he wanted to free himself from his evil bondage and lead a life of freedom with her and shun the perilous path of cloak and dagger; and that was why he had written to Hu Meng-an asking for a transfer; that if only he could escape from that woman's grasp, he would marry Hsiao-yen and be her loving husband and never leave her side. . . . Hsiao-yen did not listen any more, but tried hard to think of a way to get away from people like him. . . . She lay her head on the desk, feigning sleep. Tai Yü rambled on and on for a long time and finally stumbled away in his drunken stupor. The minute he was gone, Hsiao-yen ran over to see Tao-ching.

At this point, Hsiao-yen concluded her narration with another flood of tears: "My life is over. It is finished. Please help me!"

"No, Hsiao-yen, your life is not over. You can start afresh." Tao-ching responded calmly and softly, as she wiped away Hsiao-yen's tears. "Odd, how did you know my address?"

Hsiao-yen held Tao-ching's hand, her tortured face showing a glimmer of a smile: "I also followed you secretly in the past . . . but I never told him, that . . . that fraud, that swindler! Oh, Tao-ching, please tell me, what am I to do? And what should I do with him?" She looked at Tao-ching and then at Chiang Hua, wiping her red, swollen eyes.

"Let me ask you, Hsiao-yen," Chiang Hua cut in for the first time. Nodding to her, he added, "We have met before, haven't we? Now, tell me, where are the papers you found on him?"

"He took them back," Hsiao-yen sobbed.

"Oh." Chiang Hua fell silent. A little while later he said, "Hsiao-yen, I must remind you that the problem with Tai Yü doesn't concern your personal fate alone. Your grieving is not going to help the imminent danger. Do you understand what I mean?"

"What are you saying?" Hsiao-yen opened wide her tearful eyes. "I did not think of anything else; I simply wanted to tell Tao-ching that I was wrong about her ... and that I wanted her to forgive me."

"Oh, forget it," Tao-ching said, squeezing her friend's hand. "You are exhausted, Hsiao-yen. You had better lie down for a bit," said Tao-ching and, with Chiang Hua's assistance, she supported Hsiao-yen to her own bed.

"Possibly this is what will happen," Chiang Hua speculated quietly. "After Tai Yü sobers up, he will regret what he said in his drunken delirium. His confession will become a burden to his mind. Besides, those important documents had gone through your hands. Then, based on logical deduction, Hsiao-yen, if you are no longer willing to be used by him, he will be afraid of you. He will even hate you and treat you like an enemy. Have you thought of that?"

"No," Hsiao-yen responded, with her eyes closed, her face deathly pale. "He wouldn't ... he couldn't ... He loves me...."

Tao-ching, leaning by Hsiao-yen's pillow, could no longer restrain herself. "Hsiao-yen," she interrupted, "haven't you changed your opinion about him yet? Can you still hope for his love and pity even now? This is really preposterous."

Hsiao-yen did not respond; tears flowed from her closed eyes.

Chiang Hua, standing by the bedside, finally broke the silence; in a low voice, he spoke gravely: "Hsiao-yen, no matter what, it is best to be on the alert. Not only you, but all the progressive students on every campus. Judging by the blacklist you saw, the secret agents must have prepared even more drastic measures to deal with us. I think you and Tao-ching should both find a place to hide for the time being. You had better tell your parents to go into hiding too ... By the way, do you remember any of the names on that list?"

"No," replied Hsiao-yen, wiping her eyes. "Except those of Li Shao-t'ung, Hou Jui, Li K'uei-ying, and, of course, hers," pointing at Tao-ching.

Tao-ching drew close to Hsiao-yen and said gently, "See, even such a person as Li K'uei-ying is on their list, which goes to show you how mean and vicious they are. You must be convinced of that ... So take Chiang Hua's advice, and let us hide ourselves." And, wiping Hsiao-yen's tears with her own handkerchief, she continued, "Hsiao-yen, you have no idea how much I suffered when we drifted apart.... Now that we are together again, I can't tell you how happy I am. But enough of this. Right now we had better talk about what to do next. You must go into hiding with me for a few days."

"I would like to talk with him just once more," Hsiao-yen said to Tao-ching with a pleading look. "Believe me, I won't ever trust him again. I'll be back shortly."

"No, I can't let you do that. We are leaving right now!" Tao-ching's tone was firm. "In case he knows my address, he just might come here to look for you." Pulling Hsiao-yen up by the hand, Tao-ching turned to Chiang Hua and said, "Why don't you go first? Hsiao-yen and I will leave right after you. We'll be staying with a schoolmate for a while."

Chiang Hua looked at Tao-ching with tenderness, as he whispered something into her ear; then he shook hands with Hsiao-yen and left.

"You two have to be separated because of me," Hsiao-yen murmured despondently, as she watched the retreating backview of Chiang Hua. "Come, let's leave. I won't see Tai Yü again."

CHAPTER 41

December 8, 1935—the eve of the tremendous, historical December Ninth Movement! This day Tao-ching was in bed with a high fever. She was sleeping in a wooden bed in a newly rented room. At dusk, in this cold, dreary, small room, Hsü Hui, Hsiao-yen, and Hou Jui were huddling over a coal stove talking softly.

"When did she get sick?" Hsü Hui asked Hsiao-yen. "Did she see a doctor?"

"Yes," Hsiao-yen whispered. "The doctor says she has influenza. Also she has been working too hard. Day and night she held discussions, instigated struggles against reactionary students, and aften skipped meals. No wonder her health has suffered as a consequence."

"She simply overextended herself," Hou Jui shook his head.

"You people should have taken better care of her!" said Hsü Hui, as she looked uneasily at the feverish girl, deep in slumber.

Tao-ching stirred. She opened her eyes and smiled at the three people near her bed. "When did you get here?" she asked, then turned to Hsü Hui; "Has the plan for tomorrow been fixed? Will there be any changes?"

"No, I don't think so," answered Hsü Hui, smiling. "But don't worry about anything. You just take it easy." And, stretching herself, she asked Hou Jui, "How many people from Peking University do you think will be at the demonstration?"

"Hard to say," replied Hou Jui. "We are still recruiting tonight, and there will be others who can be aroused at the spur of the moment tomorrow. I reckon there will be three to four hundred."

Suddenly Tao-ching sat up in bed and said excitedly, "I think as soon as we start to move tomorrow, the suppressed volcano will erupt. A great number of Peking University students will take part in the march."

"Hsü Hui just told you not to worry; what's the matter with you?" chided Hsiao-yen, as she forced Tao-ching to lie down.

"Although northern China is large, there is no room for a peaceful desk! This is a powerful phrase in the leaflets we are going to distribute tomorrow," Hsü Hui told the others in the room. "It reflects the anti-Japanese fervor of the masses. This time the Party's slogans are all geared to the masses' demand and their awakening. . . . I'm sorry, but I must go now. Hsiao-yen, go out with me for a while and then come back to look after Tao-ching." After a couple of steps, Hsü Hui turned back to Tao-ching and said solicitously, "Take a good rest, and don't get out of bed. I'll see you tomorrow . . . Oh, I almost forgot: I have a message for you from Chiang Hua; he'll come to see you tomorrow after the demonstration. Now be patient."

Before leaving, Hsiao-yen tucked Tao-ching in, while Hou Jui poured her a cup of hot water and put some more coal into the stove. Left alone, lying under her quilt, Tao-ching said to herself, "Ah, the volcano will erupt and tomorrow will soon be here." At the thought of the coming struggle, she became excited. In her delirious condition, she kept shouting, "Volcanic, volcanic eruption."*

*This paragraph is one of the few passages revised in the 1977 edition. The 1960 edition has: "Ah, tomorrow, he will be able to come to see me . . ." Tao-ching, lying under her quilt, thought of Chiang Hua, and she was happy. For they had not seen each other again since the night of their marriage. [K.Y.H.]

Hsiao-yen soon returned. She slept next to Tao-ching to look after her. Before daylight, she rose quietly so as not to disturb her friend. While Hsiao-yen was groping for her clothes in the dark, Tao-ching awoke, and shakily she sat up and turned on the light.

"Tao-ching, you can't get up." Hsiao-yen tried to stop her. "You still have a fever—I just felt your forehead. You must not go out."

Dressing herself, Tao-ching laughed. "My fever is gone. And I feel fine. I'll feel even better when I start marching."

Hsiao-yen flushed with anxiety. She held Tao-ching's hand and said gravely, "Now you listen to me. Hsü Hui left you in my care. I have to answer to her. You really must not go out."

"You have to answer to her, but who should I answer to?" retorted Tao-ching. "Now be a good girl, and let me be." While washing herself and combing her hair, Tao-ching coaxed Hsiao-yen like a naughty child: "My dear sweet Hsiao-yen, don't be so strict. Let me go! So many things need to be tended to. I've got to go. Do a good deed, and let us both be a part of today's great event." So saying, she dragged her friend by the hand and ran into the courtyard. Hsiao-yen had no time to wash up but helplessly followed Tao-ching outside. In her weakened condition, Tao-ching could hardly suppress her trembling. When she opened the gate a gust of bone-piercing wind hit her in the face and a sudden dizzy spell seized her. She reeled backwards. Fortunately, Hsiao-yen was alert and caught her in time. In the dark wintry dawn, with her arms around the unconscious girl, Hsiao-yen panicked, her heart pounding against her ribs, her limbs limp. When Tao-ching finally came to, Hsiao-yen tried to put her back to bed. But the sick girl refused to budge. Tearfully Hsiao-yen pleaded with her, "Please go lie down. If it is the success of the demonstration you are worried about, I'll double my effort to make up for your absence. In case I shed blood, there will be your share too." Tao-ching, leaning against her friend's shoulder, was just about to say something, when suddenly in the silent dark sky of the cold dawn burst forth loud singing, sad and heroic, full of heartfelt fervor. Both listened attentively with solemn expression, to the moving, heroic song:

> Laborers, peasants, soldiers, students, and merchants,
>   rise and defend our country!
> Pick up your weapons—knives or guns.
> March out of the factories, fields, and classrooms!
> To the battlefield—and fight for our liberation.*

They had heard the same song numerous times; thus it was no longer fresh. Yet now, in the early morning air, before the burning flame of struggle ahead, they listened as if it were heard for the first time. It aroused them like the bugle call to advance in battle; their blood began to surge in their veins. Tao-ching wanted to speak, but her heart pounded so much that she could not utter a word. Steadying herself, she freed her arm from Hsiao-yen's grasp and shouted urgently:

*The 1960 edition has Peking's pre-1977 national anthem instead of this song, a popular wartime tune. [K.Y.H.]

"Get going, hurry! I'll wait for your good news ..."

After Hsiao-yen left, Tao-ching lay awake in bed all day. She listened to the voices that rose from the streets—earthshaking shouts of demonstrators' slogans mingled with the roaring wind. They seemed to have come from the end of the world, and shook her heart and her small room. It was like a dream, and yet she felt sober in the middle of a wild storm.

It finally began to get dark; the wind was still roaring in the subzero temperature. Exhausted, Tao-ching curled up under the covers. She was just about to doze off when she was awakened by a sudden cold draft. She opened her eyes, switched on the light, and saw Li Kuei-ying and Wang Hsiao-yen in front of her bed, their teeth chattering as they hugged themselves from cold.

"Oh, you are back at last! How was it?" Tao-ching excitedly grasped their hands and struggled to sit up.

"D ... d ... don't get up. We are too ... too cold ... ," came the trembling words from their trembling bodies. Their faces were the color of a purple turnip; ice hung from their hair like icicles on the eaves in front of the house. Li Kuei-ying's fur coat was also caked stiff with ice. But their spirits were high, almost ecstatic, especially Li Kuei-ying, who smilingly opened wide her mouth, although she was unable to form words in her frozen condition.

"How did you get into this state? Exactly what happened to you today? I am dying of curiosity." She picked up her own padded jacket from the bed and handed it to Li Kuei-ying, saying, "Look at your coat, it's a sheet of ice! Quick, change into this."

At first Li Kuei-ying smiled. Now she suddenly fell onto Tao-ching's neck and began to cry: "Oh, Tao-ching, I have been living in a dream all these years. Only today did I come to understand ... understand how a person should live on this earth ..." She was too overcome with emotion to continue. Laughing and crying at the same time, she let tears stream down her beautiful face without restraint.

[There follows a detailed description of the day's events related by Wang Hsiao-yen. When she is about done with her story, Hsü Hui comes in.]

[Hsü Hui] had changed into dry clothes, but on her forehead still dripped fresh blood. She went to Tao-ching's bed and asked, "Hey! Feeling better? Has the fever broken?"

Tao-ching stared at the blood on Hsü Hui's head, grasped her hand and said, "Hsü Hui, why didn't you go to the hospital to have it treated? It is dangerous to leave the wound exposed."

"Don't be a mother hen," smiled Hsü Hui, who deftly straightened out Tao-ching's bedding. "It's really not very serious. I haven't had time yet. But tell me first if you feel better."

"Oh, much better. But how was it? Was our loss great today? Did anyone get arrested?"

"Yes. Two co-eds from the Normal University are in critical condition from bayonet wounds. Many students from Peking University are injured too. One fellow student's nose and lips were cut open. As to the arrests ... so far there are more than a dozen that we know of."

"What's to be done now?" Tao-ching was staring at Hsü Hui with visible anxiety.

"That is what I would like to know, too," rejoined Hsiao-yen.

Hsü Hui rose. She looked for some water to drink. Seeing the teapot empty, she shook her head and asked, "Has your landlady gone to the march also? Not even leaving water for you to drink . . . You wanted to know what to do next? We must stir up the masses even more widely and deeply. Make the student movement penetrate into every walk of life so that all the laborers and peasants will join the struggle. Now that the volcano has erupted, let it burn away all the evils and darkness in the world."

Hsü Hui's voice, at once melodious and solemn, made those words ring like poetry as well as a resolute pledge. The three women comrades raised their heads toward the dawning sky beyond the window.

Translated by Angela Palandri

K'ANG CHO
(Mao Chi-ch'ang, 1920–)

A native of Hsiang-yin County, Hunan Province, K'ang Cho came from a well-to-do peasant family. He attended the Lu Hsün Academy of Art when it was founded in 1938. From 1938 to 1949 he worked with the guerrillas operating in Hopei and Shansi. Doing propaganda work as a writer of popular stories, plays, and songs, he took an active part in agricultural production and land reform with the peasants and experienced their hardships and heroism during the war years. After 1949 he served in various positions of influence, including an editorship with the *Literary Gazette*. In 1957 he was criticized for "distorting the image of Communist Party members" in his novel *Dripping Water Wears Away the Rock*, and he lost the editorship. In 1965 he was attacked for his advocacy of a literature depicting the negative aspects of Chinese society, for his support of theories proposed by Shao Ch'üan-lin, especially those on "middle characters" and "the deepening of realism," and for his association with Chou Yang. Little was known about him after 1966, until *People's Literature* published his "A Pledge to Study Anew" in October 1977. In it he recalls a series of meetings with Chairman Mao from 1938 through 1958 and vows to resume writing after a decade of silence.

K'ang Cho established himself as an important writer with the publication of his short story "My Two Landlords" in 1946. Kuo Mo-jo welcomed it as a nearly perfect work, equal in artistic merit to Chao Shu-li's "The Rhymes of Li Yu-ts'ai" and "The Marriage of Hsiao Er-hei." When a collection of K'ang's stories, *Spring Planting, Autumn Harvest*, appeared in 1956, the well-known critic Li Hsi-fan* praised its "refreshing uniqueness and simplicity of style" and its successful application of traditional forms and techniques. Noting the psychological penetration K'ang achieves in characterization, Li attributed it to the influence of Western literature. Li also spoke approvingly of K'ang's effort in showing the negative traits of his positive characters.

In reading K'ang Cho, the reader is likely to be impressed by the deliberate manner in which he fashions his prose and portrays his characters. *Dripping Water Wears Away the Rock* contains some truly remarkable descriptive passages, and few contemporary Chinese writers have explored the psychology of their characters as fully and painstakingly as K'ang did that of the heroine of this novel, Shen Yü-chih. At times it even appears that K'ang would purposely impede the flow of a dialogue to underscore the complexity of a character's thoughts and feelings.

Besides the two books mentioned above, K'ang has published two other novels, *Coal Mines on Black Stone Hill* and *East Is Red*, and another collection of short stories. —W.K.M.

---

*In 1954 Li's first criticism against Yü P'ing-po's study of the *Dream of the Red Chamber* won Mao Tse-tung's personal support and started the campaign against Hu Feng. In August 1978 Li himself was criticized in the official press. [K.Y.H.]

from *Dripping Water*
Wears Away the Rock

[The story focuses on the love that a beautiful and capable widow, not yet thirty, leader of the agricultural cooperative movement in a village on the border between Hopei and Shansi provinces, develops for a quiet, honest, hard-working but diffident neighbor widower, a veteran Communist serving as the accountant and manager of the supply and marketing co-op operated by the same village organization. Equally central to the story is the effort of the heroine to fight off the lusty advances of the Village Head, also a veteran Communist and a widower, who is sharp and competent, but shrewd, and who keeps his selfishness well disguised.

Much of the story's color is derived from the various villagers' reaction to the heroine, and their suspicion, or lack of it, of the villain's evil deeds. All the actions in the story are propelled by the villagers' effort to improve their life through the collectivization of farming—and the actual farm work itself, of course—and by the joyful revival of an ancient village festival called strike-iron-fire. The villagers compete at night, striking ladles full of molten iron to see who creates the best fireworks with the splashing spray of red-hot metal against the dark sky. It used to be a festival to facilitate meetings between boys and girls.

The setting is a village where a murmuring mountain spring flows all year long. The dripping water from a high cave has worn a hole in the huge flat stone below—a symbol of the patient farmers' steady work to create their own life, the patient love of the heroine to win her man, and his patient dedication to the cause of socialism. This symbol is well observed by the heroine and others in the story; hence the title of the novel.

Before the episode presented here, the story has already introduced the following characters:

Auntie Fu and Yang the Ninth, a twice-widowed woman and an old bachelor, both around fifty. They remain very close to the heroine, Shen Yü-chih, throughout the story. They like to joke with everybody. Since they share the same compound with Shen, they look after her and her ten-year-old son's welfare.

Little Liu, a high school graduate who disdains farm labor, and her boyfriend, Yang Chi-chi, vice-chairman of the agricultural cooperative and a newly inducted Party member. Later she leaves him and the village to seek better life and work in the city.

Old Uncle Jen, another veteran Party member since the War of Resistance and an old friend of Shen's late father-in-law, whom she continues to look up to for comfort and guidance. He has heard the Village Head say that Shen is looking for a man to marry, and, at a meeting of the village's Party branch leaders, he publicly announces this and Shen's pending application for admission into the Communist Party. Shen is surprised by the news of her private life, and even more stunned by the way these two items of her private business are linked together. After the meeting, the Village Head follows Shen to court her, show himself off, and hint that he alone can help her join the Party. They have been walking and talking for a long time. . . .]

Far and near, here and there, the rays of the sun scattered, worn and listless; before long, right before one's eyes, they would quietly disappear. It would soon be dusk. An imperceptible cold wind cooled off the hot sweat on the travelers; they began to notice that the fur and cotton they wore could no longer resist the wind and the chill. But Shen Yü-chih did not feel cold. She kept hurrying in great strides as she started the climb up the slope.

"Uh, Yü-chih." Village Head Chang Shan-yang, trailing Shen Yü-chih, climbed the slope. Suddenly he said, "That second thing your Old Uncle Jen talked about a while back, it seems to me, is probably something as important as your admission to the Party! What do you think?"

All this time Yü-chih had been as perturbed as she could ever have been by the matter. Hearing the Village Head actually speak about it again, she couldn't help noticing a clump of thorn creeper on the roadside and felt at heart just as distraught as those tangled weeds. She stepped heavily on them; she pulled up a blade of withered grass and, tearing it up bit by bit, tossed it into the air. Then, picking up a rock, she flung it so hard on the slope that it tumbled all the way down. Finally she said, "That Old Uncle Jen of mine, it's just like him! Why in the world should he bring up such nonsense?"

"But that is really serious business! Yü-chih, why do you talk like that?" The Village Head appeared extremely solemn. "You see, why didn't we think of this important business of yours! Really . . . hasn't it been almost three full years since that Chun-wa's Dad of yours [your husband] sacrificed his life? Ai, fact is I have never even thought of this!"

"As for me, this important business of mine, even I myself have never thought of it!"

"It's just that ordinarily you wouldn't have thought of it." Once again as if face to face with Yü-chih, the Village Head stroked his fur hat and, stretching his face into a smile, said, "It's just like your Old Uncle Jen said. We can already see the happy occasion of strike-iron-fire taking place right before our eyes. Would you still not have thought of it?"

"This is no longer the old days. Strike-iron-fire is only for the celebration of collectivization. It has never occurred to me that it could have any other meaning."

"Look at you, how can you say anything like that . . ."

"What do you want me to say?"

"Didn't Old Uncle Jen say that you had already mentioned it to somebody else?"

"Whom did I mention it to? Have you heard about it?"

"Oh, my." The Village Head widened his eyes, raised his brows, and cheerfully said, "Yü-chih, though I cannot claim to have treated everybody with affection, though I cannot say that I would have given you any concrete help, if I had heard about it, wouldn't I have at least expressed some concern one way or another long before this! Yü-chih, you should understand me this much at least!"

"You sure have gone too far off the subject! Village Head, let's not talk about this!"

Suddenly Chang Shan-yang looked startled, as though he were at a loss. Then all at once he worked himself into a peal of laughter. "Ha, ha, ha! Yü-chih, you are not a little girl; you are also a labor model; one would never have thought that you were still so backward and didn't want to discuss the question of marriage with a man!" Smiling rouguishly he said, "Yü-chih, for better or for worse, I am a village head. Sooner or later you'll have to register. I can certainly give you a hand! Now you . . ."

"One, I am not backward; two, I am not afraid of men; three, I also know you are the Village Head." Yü-chih was obviously somewhat agitated but she only shook her hair and, lifting a face that continued to shine—her face not changing color, her eyes not dodging any stare—she said in a perfectly calm manner, "I just do not wish to talk about such things!"

For a brief moment the Village Head was taken aback. Then suddenly he once more worked himself into roars of laughter. And leaping two steps, he rushed in front of Yü-chih. With one arm barring her way and a hand pointing at Yü-chih's nose, he feigned pouting and cried out, "You, you look at you . . ." Then, as if helpless and begging forgiveness he said, "OK, if you don't want to talk about it we won't talk about it. Heigh . . . Yü-chih, no wonder some people say behind my back that I'm afraid of you! To tell you the truth, even though I wouldn't admit it openly, at heart I really am a bit afraid of you! You are really . . ."

"Village Head, what is the matter with you today . . .?" For the first time Yü-chih blushed. Holding the skirt of her coat and turning swiftly, she scurried in front of the Village Head and strode on with the same big steps. "Why should you be afraid of me? That's really odd!" she said. The Village Head continued to follow her, mumbling all the while. And flashing a self-satisfied smile, he made it look like he and Shen Yü-chih had always been on such familiar terms, that they had always been in the habit of joking and bantering together.

Shen Yü-chih, though steady and composed as usual, felt prickly all over. Her desire to differentiate between good and evil and her feelings of joy and hate intertwined in such confusion that it all became more difficult to sort out than thousands of skeins of hemp. The content of Old Uncle Jen's talk today had certainly come as a total surprise, but it nevertheless fitted the old man's habit of doing things. All the talk and action of the Village Head, however—the way he laughed and the cockiness with which he barred her way—not only caught her completely unprepared, but even made her, for the very first time in her life and in a way utterly unknown to her, feel fearful. She then thought of the possible reasons behind the Village Head's concern for her, which she had dismissed a while back. Suddenly she raised her head and saw, not far off to the northwest of her village, the gloomy rock cliff and steep slope. And as if all at once that slope toppled on her, she, shaking all over, suddenly remembered that the wife of the Village Head happened to have died a little more than two years ago. But in her daily fleeting contacts with the Village Head, she had never even once felt that the death of his wife would have anything to do with her. Was the Village Head actually such a person? If he was such a person, what on earth ought one to say about him? . . . Could it be that there was really something in the attitude he usually took toward the criticism she raised in village affairs? . . .

Though Shen Yü-chih had never been in love, all these years she had known the joy and sorrow of love-stricken young girls in the village, the entangling, spellbinding, finer-than-needlepoint musings over a word, a glance, etc.—the kind of musing that causes one to lose one's mind day and night—all these things she knew by the hundreds and thousands. Those butterfly-like maidens, on the *k'ang* at night, in the cool shade of a tree during the noontime break in the busy farming season, how they opened their hearts and bared their secrets in telling her countless stories and heartaches! In them there was the greatest glee and happiness, which sent tremors through one's heart; there were sadness and hurt, which brought down tears unawares; there were incidents that aroused one's hate to the point of madness and drove one to vomit in disgust; there were also events that others told with excited interest or streams of tears, but which left the listeners utterly unmoved. Some of these human concerns were strange and odd in myriads of ways; even though she could not fathom their mystery, most of them she could in an undefinable fashion understand. She had, moreover, helped others to analyze and speculate; she offered ideas and came up with solutions, which were almost always right on the mark. But, in this sort of thing, she had never heard, or seen, or thought of the kinds of advances that the Village Head had confronted her with! Would she really be afraid of them? That would be odd indeed! Well, she would deal with them as they came! Hadn't she dealt with numerous situations so dangerous that she was on the verge of losing her life? Afraid? Humph . . . but, ah, how much strain would that again place on her! Why was it that she had to expend so much of her thought and feeling on nothing?

As if calamity were hanging overhead, Shen Yü-chih went on walking for a while. Suddenly she saw her village, and as nothing had happened yet, she couldn't help but let out a deep breath. And, turning the whole thing around, she even felt that the premonition she had just had was really self-torment to no purpose. How foolish! Turning her head she took a look at the Village Head. He was still the same as she had seen him over so many years and months in the past—solid, clean-cut, with a little of that put-on air of an old cadre, smoking a cigarette. Unconsciously she said, "We've arrived!"

She started to trot. But the Village Head abruptly called her to a halt, saying, "Yü-chih, just put your mind at ease about that problem of your admission to the Party! I'll certainly ask for a speedy discussion. As soon as there is news I'll stop by." Then, catching up to her, he grabbed hold of her, and in low voice said, "Oh, I've forgotten another thing! You see, didn't I start a mutual aid team recently? I've been considering that it didn't really add up to much and have been thinking about joining your co-op with my whole team! Do you have any objections? You think about it for a while. The two of us will talk about it again in detail when we have time. Ah, there is, moreover, the problem of planning for increased production in your co-op. I also want to stop over to talk about it."

This again was an unheard of, unexpected turn of events. But things like that could not upset Yü-chih. She nodded her head, agreed to talk about it later, and continued to run toward the village. But then remembering something, she said, "Ah, Chief, don't forget to make proper arrangements for the strike-iron-fire!"

The Village Head slowed down his steps and steadily climbed up the slope. When he went past Shen's village, he saw that she had not gone home right away but was chatting with her fellow villagers by the stream. He saw her dip her handkerchief in that icy water, rub it a couple of times, and, without wringing it dry, wipe her face with it. He couldn't help sucking in a mouthful of cold air, thinking to himself, "Why is it that this woman is so unafraid of the cold?"

[After Shen returns home, she learns from Yang the Ninth how kind Chang Yung-te, the supply and marketing co-op manager, is toward her son, and how Chang's own motherless child is neglected because Chang has been totally devoted to his job and service to the whole village. She begins to feel tenderly toward him, and the feeling is accentuated when, in preparing for the coming strike-iron-fire festival, the whole village wants to involve Chang, the champion at the last such festival fourteen years ago. Then she and Chang have a chance of talking together as they walk toward the neighboring village.

All the villagers admire and respect and are perhaps secretly in love with Shen, and because of that feeling Shen's intention to marry someone, even if just a rumor, disturbs everybody. Even Old Uncle Jen hints that she should be careful about her reputation. Shen cannot sleep. She thinks of her late husband, who married her partly as a result of the last strike-iron-fire festival, and wonders what could be wrong with her wanting to get married again. Come the strike-iron-fire festival night, the fifteenth night of the lunar new year, the Village Head fails to score anything, but Shen and Chang Yung-te strike the molten iron and the sprays touch each other.

The Party branch secretary for the village, who theoretically outranks the Village Head, half suspects the latter's lack of determination and enthusiasm to work for the village, despite his proven ability, but they are old comrades and have been through much hardship together. When the Village Head blocks Shen's admission to the Party saying that her "style" is in question, meaning that her interest in remarriage is less than model behavior, the Party branch secretary acquiesces.

Meanwhile the Village Head continues to pressure Shen into marrying him. He passes word on to that effect through some of his close friends and then proposes to her himself but is turned down. The tension builds up within Shen as the villagers remain unaware of the Village Head's scheme.

Shen and the one she likes, Chang Yung-te, have a second chance to talk in private when they both are called to the same meeting in the city, which is the county seat.]

The next day, Shen Yü-chih went to the city for a meeting. She started a little late. As soon as she got up early in the morning, she was tied up with Little Liu. Since Little Liu had quarreled with her boyfriend, Yang Chi-chi, a few days ago, her anger for some reason had still not died down. Actually what happened between them this time was at first the same old story. Seeing that Little Liu was making mistakes in farm work, Chi-chi criticized her for impatience; she then turned the tables on him and told him off for bad attitudes. Chi-chi then attacked her for not accepting criticism; she again retorted and charged that his criticism was not well intentioned, but an outright attack. Chi-chi held back for a moment, and began to point out patiently to her the various technical mistakes she had made in grafting the fruit trees. But perhaps because of her devil-may-care attitude, plus the fact that the mistakes discovered this time were bigger then usual, Chi-chi couldn't help raising his voice and sounding a bit harsh as he spoke. Terms he was in the habit of using, such as "standpoint" and "attitude toward life," slipped off his tongue a bit too readily. All of this once again provoked her. Well, the two of them soon found themselves arguing back and forth. Little Liu accused him of putting false labels on her, of looking down on and lording it over her, and of despotic thinking. In the end, she even said that she couldn't take this kind of abuse anymore, that she didn't want to have anything to do with this darn forestry technique, that she might just as well work as an accountant and that accounting was also a lofty form of labor. Chi-chi charged that she didn't want to temper herself through labor, that deep down she lacked the determination to do so, that all she did was talk big and that even though she volunteered to learn the techniques, she in fact preferred ease and leisure. He even went as far as saying that being the way she was, what kind of intellectual could she be, and that if she kept this up there would be no future whatsoever for her. When their quarrel reached this level, it departed from the old routine and almost developed into a fist fight. And afterwards, even though the Party branch secretary and Shen Yü-chih talked the whole thing over with her many times, and even though Yang Chi-chi offered his apologies, Little Liu from beginning to end was unwilling to repair the rift. She really didn't even want to go work in the field and even revealed in certain things she said a glimpse of her thinking that she didn't want to waste her life in the village.

This was a sudden, startling change in Little Liu; it was also a startling change in the relationship between her and Yang Chi-chi. How did it start? Neither Shen Yü-chih nor the Party branch secretary could sort it all out. Shen Yü-chih even sensed that perhaps the cause could never be sorted out, because Little Liu had become rather unreasonable—no matter what you said she wouldn't listen. It was just like that early this morning; if Shen Yü-chih didn't have to leave in a hurry, it would be hard to say how long that girl would have kept pestering her. Ai, all this mess; in the final analysis, from which mountain did this wind blow? From which spring did this water flow?

After Shen Yü-chih set out on her way, she pondered the whole time on this piece of romance so full of twists and turns. Since there was a distance of fifty *li* from her village to the city, she used a wooden pole to carry her travelling gear and walked very fast, afraid that she might arrive too late. Coming down the mountain slope, up the west highway, and crossing the river, she was totally oblivious to everything around her, paying no attention to the scenery or people on the road. However, by and by she became aware that someone was driving a donkey, walking in front of her all that time, but she couldn't care less about something that was none of her business. Not till she had covered a distance of almost ten *li* did she notice the donkey was stopping at a crossroads by the river and the man was fixing up the stepping stones in the crossing; then she saw that he was Chang Yung-te, and she remembered that the supply and marketing co-op manager, Chang Yung-te, had also been notified to attend the meeting in the city. . . . She had originally wanted to ask Chang Yung-te to set out together with her today, but she had missed him. Therefore, she hurried several steps and ran over to help Chang Yung-te fetch stones and lay them out as stepping stones.

After the two of them finished fixing up the crossing, they set out together. Shen Yü-chih thought up a couple of things to chat about, but before she said anything, he suddenly spoke first; he said, "Now spring has begun, and the water in the river has risen, but no one would fix up even something as little as the stepping stones." As usual he was speaking in a tone neither cold nor warm, as if talking to himself. Only later did he actually turn to face Shen Yü-chih. "You see, this stretch of land, believe it or not, all belongs to our village. It seems that our village and your co-op ought to take charge of the road repair work for this section."

"That sounds good." Yü-chih realized that this was indeed something that ought to be done. "When we get back home, I'll speak to the Party branch secretary about it. We'll make some plans, then do it."

"What's more, this counts as sideline production! Fixing up bridges and repairing roads, I don't know whether it's the Department of Civil Administration or a separate Department of Transportation, there are special funds set aside for it," Chang Yung-te said. "Ch'un-wa's mom, this time why don't you talk to them at the county office and vouch for the maintenance of a section on behalf of our village!"

"Yeah! That sounds good!" Yü-chih hurriedly said. "But I'd rather you talk to them!"

"I won't do!"

"Ah? Why is it you won't do?"

"Nowadays when you want to get things done, it's still necessary to have a name!" Yung-te said. "It is hard to say whether I can talk them into it!"

"Then I'll give it a try. But neither have I any . . ." Yü-chih said, swallowing the word "name." "Also, I had not even thought of this thing! Ai, when all is said and done I'm still not a . . ."

Shen Yü-chih also swallowed the term "Party member." For some time now she had somehow imperceptibly developed a certain feeling toward this man Chang Yung-te, that is, a solid respect for a Communist Party member. But now, cherishing this most unadorned respect toward him, in spite of herself, she thought of something and asked, "Brother Yung-te, you have already discussed the problem of my induction into the Party, haven't you?"

"Oh, that. It was still only that several of us had an exchange of views. At the same time we've been gathering views among the Party members." Chang Yung-te said, "Last night didn't you come asking for me? I was going my rounds gathering the views of the Party members." Yü-chih said, "Can you give me some of their opinions?"

"The Party branch secretary will give them to you," Yung-te said. "Ch'un-wa's mom, please don't be anxious. Just go about your work as usual. Work as hard as you can! Even though it's true that your problem has been delayed for a bit too long . . ." He halted his step, stretched his arms and shoulders a little, and taking his time as usual said, "The Party will not wrong anyone! Even if it wrongs you now and then, in the long run it will not wrong you forever."

Shen Yü-chih had lost count how many times she had heard this kind of commonplace talk. The Party branch secretary alone had encouraged, comforted her countless times. And she had indeed derived no small encouragement and comfort from this kind of talk. But now, more than ever before, she was touched by what Chang Yung-te said. In the past she did not know him; of course, there had been no reason for her to think that he would not say such things. But now that she had gained some knowledge about him, she would less expect someone in as worrisome a circumstance as he to be so solicitous to others. Besides, the tone and manner of his speech made one feel all the more that he was like a stream flowing deeply and softly over a great distance from the spring on the back mountain, on a quiet and clear night. . . .

Only now did Shen Yü-chih discover that Chang Yung-te had a full load of mountain produce on the animal; he also carried a sack on his own shoulder; and even the roll of bedding she was carrying had at some time been transferred to the back of the animal. "You're going to a meeting, aren't you! Why bring the animal as well?" Shen Yü-chih asked.

"These are things which sooner or later I have to deliver to the county supply and marketing co-op. I'm going anyway; why not bring some!"

"But then why should you yourself also carry a sackful?"

"I'm used to carrying things! If I don't, I'll be going empty-handed. How awkward! How wasteful!"

Nimble of tongue as Shen Yü-chih was, suddenly she could not utter a sound. And Chang Yung-te went on to tell her that every time he went to the city it was like this. Going back to the village would still be the same, with a load on his shoulder and a load on the animal. Besides things he brought back for the supply and marketing co-op, families here and there in the village would ask him to bring back something. At any rate, it was really quite convenient; he was simply doing what he could. Then he said, "But I'm still a bit bureaucratic. I've rarely made any effort to work closely with your village. From now on, I'll have to do better. If there is anything your village and co-op want to buy or fetch, by all means just let me know."

They were now on the small path at the foot of the mountain slope. Yü-chih was, without thinking, picking the varicolored wild flowers by the slope; she was wondering how on earth could someone like the person directly before her have turned his family into such a mess? How on earth could it be that he hadn't thought of joining the agricultural co-op? Last night she had already asked her son, Yu-ken, about these things; but even such an outspoken and open youth as Yu-ken was also hemming and hawing, unwilling to tell her why they did not join the co-op, unwilling to say anything about his family and his father. . . . A strong feeling of sympathy surfaced in Yü-chih. She couldn't help asking, "Brother Yung-te, you are so concerned about everybody's life; why don't you join the agricultural co-op and help us make it better?"

"Hmm, this . . ." Yung-te seemed to be a bit alarmed and confused; even that tone and manner of his which was, like a warm spring breeze, neither too fast nor too slow suddenly took on the qualities of the frosty sky of late autumn.

Sighing, he said, "With a family as messed up as mine, how can you take heart for a better life?"

Now they had gone down to the beach of the river. Yü-chih said, "But contrary to what you just said, when it is someone else's livelihood, you take it very much to heart indeed! Why can't you yourself choose a wider path?" They had reached the head of a single-plank bridge. After crossing the bridge, Yü-chih went on again, "In this day and age, so far as the livelihood of us peasants is concerned, we certainly ought to be doing our best to get from narrow to wider places! We first crossed on the stepping stones, then the single-plank bridge, further ahead there will be the big bridge wide enough for mules and horses to pass through."

Chang Yung-te was silent for what seemed a very long time. Then he said, "Most of us are surely heading for a wider path. I for my part earnestly hope that all of you will reach there soon. I'm more than willing to fix up the roads for all of you. But as for me myself"—he shifted the sack he was carrying from one shoulder to the other—"that family of mine is really so messed up that you can hardly carry it on your back. Ai, I'm already thirty-seven or thirty-eight; truth is I'm going backwards! I have crossed the big bridge and the single-plank bridge, and now I'm afraid I'm about to tread on the stepping stones!"

"Eh! Look at the kind of talk an old Party member like you has come out with . . ." A moment of sadness overtook Yü-chih, as she let this remark slip. She wanted to retrieve it, but it was too late. Hastily she looked for his reaction, but since her view of him was blocked by the sack on his shoulder, she couldn't see it. She only heard him say, "Your criticism is quite well-taken. But it's difficult to be a Party member like me! Out in the village, you're a Party member; back home you are still a peasant. When this one screams and that one curses you cannot even talk to them about principles! Besides, even within the Party, at times, principle cannot flow as freely as the water in the stream!"

When Chang Yung-te had finished speaking, he too felt that he had let his tongue slip; he should not have talked to her about things inside the Party. But concerning that family of his, that family about which he had never poured his heart out to anyone else, at this moment he actually felt that he had not yet spoken enough; he wanted to talk to her some more about it. All along he had been shy with women. Particularly with a woman as capable and beautiful as Shen Yü-chih—a woman whose behavior was said to have been less than perfect in the past—all along, he had kept himself even more aloof. Now that there had been circulating in the village the rumor that Yü-chih was looking for a mate, this naturally compounded his wariness. But then, she was so concerned about him—made shoes for his daughter, little Chiu-niu; even went so far as to let his son, Yu-ken, a non–co-op member, herd sheep for the co-op. And every time they saw each other she did her best to cheer him up with comforting words. He could see how she wished that she could help him reform that rotten family into something harmonious and attractive. . . . When in his entire life had Chang Yung-te ever received such solicitude? Besides, in looking for a mate, would she, in spite of all odds, come to him? Even if you wagered your head, no one in the village would believe this—just as no one would believe that the spring water in their village could be smelted into ironware of the neighboring town! One has to act according to one's conscience;

even a Communist Party member should respect feelings. . . . Therefore, Chang Yung-te picked out, after obtaining Shen Yü-chih's consent, a spacious area on the beach with trees and rocks, to take a rest and to talk to her some more about the situation in his family. Shen Yü-chih helped him take the load off the animal; he untied the hemp fodder bag from the load and took care of the animal, and the two of them, one on the luggage roll and one on the big cotton jacket, sat down on the rocks under the trees.

The warm sun shone and the spring breeze fluttered caressingly. The waters in the stream were leaping and bouncing forward in glee; a fresh scent wafted from the beach, which was covered with wild flowers. There were very few travelers on the road; farmers were busy working on and below the slope. Once in a while a few robust youngsters burst into lines of folk songs in a falsetto so shrill that it seemed to bounce off the high heavens. While Shen Yü-chih was aimlessly picking the wild flowers by her side . . . Chang Yung-te recounted for her the situation in his family.

He said that everyone knew that he had a finicky, snappy daughter-in-law, but the older that good-hearted mother-in-law of his grew, the more wearing she became. Already that Granny Hua of his could hardly do anything, but still everything had to be done her way. She was like a despot, leaving no room for you to give a hand or put in a word. Still, these two years things had improved a bit! Heavy chores, like working in the field and getting water, she no longer concerned herself with, but in everything else all you could do was watch her drag things out every which way. If you should say a word, or do a chore, the moment she found out she would threaten death and suicide, saying that you had given her up for old age, for being a good-for-nothing, and that you were hurrying her into the coffin!

But before she had gone into the coffin, who should come along but that finicky, snappy daughter-in-law as well! She was altogether something else, in no way like the young daughter of a farming family; all she cared about was her own eating, drinking, and powdering-up, and, worse yet, she wanted you to bring everything right to her. That old mother-in-law, who was forever afraid of being left out of doing things and was always taking charge of every-one's business whether or not she herself would actually do it, made this finicky, snappy daughter-in-law the only exception. She treated her like an outsider. At every meal all the daughter-in-law did was sit there and eat, not lifting a single finger to help; the old lady would chew her out and cuss her under her breath. Then the daughter-in-law would retaliate and bawl the old woman out; but she would still be dissatisfied because the old lady was so deaf that they could not fight it out to a decision. The young woman then directed the flame of her fury toward her husband, Yung-te's son, Yu-ken. He was a good son, but he also had his resentments, and it was also on account of this wife of his that the son nursed his resentment against his dad. This young woman was a wife arranged for the son when he was barely twenty by inflated count and eighteen by actual count, by his dad, who, in a fit of folly, trusted the words of a friend. The dad, Yung-te, had at the time asked the son for his opinions, and the son had personally gone to meet her face to face and agreed to the marriage. Only then did this arrangement bear fruit! How could you put the blame of bearing this blighted fruit entirely on your dad! Dad made a mistake, but neither could you totally blame your dad for wrapping up your marriage for you 100 percent, for violating your freedom of choice in marriage! Ai ... the son would not forgive the dad and he carried his resentment to the point of not speaking to him ... Ai, this was how it was!

For the first time Shen Yü-chih understood a little of the situation in Chang Yung-te's family. The hurt and sympathy she had felt for this man deepened. She recalled the conversation she had with Yu-ken, Yung-te's son, the night before, and she asked, "Brother Yung-te, about Yu-ken's sheepherding for our co-op, he must have told you about the terms I went over with him, hasn't he?"

"There are also terms? He only told me one thing and that is you had given him the job!"

Smiling, Yü-chih said that because she had had a talk with Yu-ken's wife, Yu-ken should, as much as possible, not sleep at the sheep farm but go home for the night. And at home, with heavy chores like hauling water and firewood, if both Yu-ken and his dad were not there, the young woman would get someone from a co-op member's family in the village to give her a hand. Later on a little something would be deducted from Yu-ken's wages to pay the helper back. Apart from these items, because the young woman was unhappy for lacking new clothes for the New Year's holidays, Shen Yü-chih also promised that the co-op would buy a length of flower-print cloth for her to make a dress.

"This ... this ... you ..." Chang Yung-te exclaimed in a manner that was very rare to him. He was truly touched, but somehow still had some reservations. "Isn't this making too much of a concession to that daughter-in-law of mine?" he said.

"Ah, a child who has not yet learned to walk, Brother Yung-te—how can you expect her to start running right off!" Yü-chih said. "She had also promised another thing! She said that if only Yu-ken would give her 80¢ or $1.00 each month for spending-money, and if only Granny Hua would ask her to do chores like pushing the millstone, she guaranteed she would do them! You should, in the same way as crossing the single-plank bridge, step by step, steady and firm, mobilize her to take part in labor!"

Chang Yung-te laughed. Who had ever seen him laugh! On that dark-red face of his, there seemed to shine forth a spark of noble, golden luster. He glanced at Yü-chih and saw that her bright red cheeks were glowing under the sun, reflecting a patch of the radiance of the clear, sunny sky. Chang Yung-te was feeling that this woman right before him was, if that were possible, even clearer and brighter than the spring waters in the village; he couldn't help saying with gratitude, "The way you see it, perhaps that family of mine can still be reformed?"

"Well, that will have to depend on how you go about it! How can I say anything for sure?" All of a sudden, Chang Yung-te felt quite awkward. He saw the animal spill some of the fodder on the ground; he hurriedly stood up and went over to tidy things up. Yü-chih discovered that on the shoulder of that cotton jacket which passed for his luggage, the hole which was burned by her during the strike-iron-fire festival had not yet been mended, but was rent even bigger through wear and tear. She wanted to sew it up, but then it occurred to her that mending it in the city might not be that convenient; and back at the village, she could not be certain about an appropriate opportunity to do something as uncalled for as this.... She also noticed that the shoes he was wearing were worn beyond recognition and at the spot where he had just sat on that soft, loose soil before the rock, there appeared a pair of clear and noticeable shoe prints. When he was paying no attention she reached her hand over to measure the length of the sole. As if fearful that it might not be accurate enough, she picked up a twig, lined it up with the shoe prints for measurement once more, broke off the right length, and quickly put it in her pocket....

The two of them once again went on their way, walking along the ever-widening beach.... He told Yü-chih that the reason he had not joined the co-op was precisely because his daughter-in-law would not agree.... Yü-chih promptly promised to talk to the young woman again about it. Yung-te then added that the hilly land around here was too poor, and to get the co-op going would therefore have to depend on planning on all sides.... Forestry definitely still had to be developed a great deal more. They could find wild medicinal herbs in the mountains around their village. With so many travelers passing through the village, the co-op should open up a little rest stop for mules and horses. And on the mountain northwest of the village there was a stream of spring water flowing away to the back slope, which should be tapped by the co-op.

"Brother Yung-te, join the co-op fast!" Yü-chih was so excited she could only come up with these words. "You help me get that daughter-in-law of mine to join the co-op!" Yung-te too was saying, ever more earnestly. "You and I both spend a lot of time going to meetings outside the village, and we both know that the co-op itself is our future. It looks to me that before too long we could more than likely start up village-wide, more advanced collectivization!"

"That's it!" Yü-chih said, but then she started to sigh, "Ai, it's only that more and more I am feeling my ability is not great enough...."

"How could it be that your ability wouldn't be great enough! But, Ch'un-wa's mom, let me say this ... ai, ai, this tongue of mine, how clumsy ..." He was straining so hard that his face got all red, and ... after repeated urgings, he said, "Let me ... say something stupid, Ch'un-wa's mom! I was going to say that later on, even when we start up a village-wide co-op, there won't be many in the village who will not support your leadership. But, but you know, I ... Now aren't there people tossing, tossing around the rumor that you, you are looking for a man ... We, the several of us, have been talking it over. We are thinking that it would be better if you just, just quickly find a county or district cadre and go away, go away to work! People all say, come what may, you, you will in the end more likely than not have to find a ... find a respectable cadre; only then will it be fitting. Ai ... But then, there are many, many of us who ... all together ... nevertheless cannot bear to see you leave ..."

As Yü-chih was patiently listening to him, she was at the same time so agitated that she very nearly couldn't lift her legs. She pulled out her handkerchief, wiped her face once. "Why should I leave?" she said with difficulty. "I'm still not sure whether I'll look for a man! Besides, if I do, who has laid down the rule that I must find a county or district cadre? Which county or district cadre have I picked? All right, even assuming that I have found some big-shot cadre, I will not go away. Brother Yung-te, I will never leave the village! I must, together with all of you, keep the co-op going! Till the day I die, it will still be 'keep the co-op going' for me!"

Yung-te was so startled that the sack on his shoulder nearly fell off. Like reciting a spell, he said over and over in his mind: It's all over! It's all over! Have I gone mad or something? How have I become so wicked, so wicked that I have babbled things as unseemly as these! . . .

Much later, he thought of something totally unrelated. "Ch'un-wa's mom, I heard that Little Liu of your village doesn't much want to stay in the village anymore . . ."

"Oh." Abruptly Yü-chih also awoke from the troubling confusion and said, "How come you too have heard about it?"

"That's right. I've heard it from the Party branch secretary." Yung-te was still trying hard to get a grip on himself. "Ch'un-wa's mom, as you know, the postman has all along been delivering mail to the supply and marketing co-op. I discovered that in the past Little Liu hardly had anyone sending her letters, but recently, there have been quite a few for her! She even has it all worked out, asking me to hold them for her, so that she can pick them up herself every two or three days!"

"Oh! That . . ." for some reason Yü-chih exclaimed.

"They all come to her from someone in a high school in the provincial capital!" In a flash everything became clear to Yü-chih, and abruptly she recalled that the change in Little Liu's attitude toward Yang Chi-chi seemed to have begun gradually after she had entertained the guests from the provincial capital at the time of the strike-iron-fire during the Lantern Festival. Yü-chih threw everything else to the winds, only saying silently to Chang Yung-te's back: You, ah, you are truly a good man!

They crossed a big wooden bridge, and, under a sun that had suddenly appeared even more radiant and boundless, along a beach that had become even wider and more open, they walked on toward the city only a short distance away.

[But the budding romance is hindered by the village elders' (also Party leaders') official warning against her move to become romantically attached to anyone, at least until she is formally admitted to the Party. She is certainly not to get involved with Chang Yung-te, who seems so diffident and meek. Though much of this is engineered by the Village Head with an ulterior motive, nobody except Shen herself knows it and she is honor-bound not to divulge it (each time after the Village Head approaches her and is rejected, he is always shrewd enough to exact a promise from her to keep the whole thing secret). Perhaps because everybody likes her too much, nobody wants to see her marry someone outside the village—and yet nobody, or very few can see her marrying beneath herself, to such a person as Chang Yung-te.

Then the Village Head strikes; he tries to rape her at night. She fights him off but is rather severely injured by a stone that the assailant flings at her. During the recuperation everybody becomes more sympathetic to her private wishes, and since the dreadful incident has speeded her formal membership in the Party, she gains enough confidence and succeeds in persuading her diffident boyfriend to be brave about the future. The whole village plans another strike-iron-fire to celebrate their wedding.

Two dark clouds continue to linger on the horizon, however. One is the fact that the Village Head remains unpunished, even though Shen has accused him before the Party branch secretary and Old Uncle Jen, because the higher-up in the city values peace and harmony within the Party ranks more than justice and exposure of corruption among village cadres. The other cloud is the un-reformed minds of people like Little Liu, who returns defeated because she cannot find a job or schooling in the city. The story closes on a thoughful note as Shen listens to the running stream and wonders how long it will be before the whole village can be as thoroughly joyful as the strike-iron-fire festival should be, and the music of the murmuring water can sing a happy song forever.]

Translated by Wong Kam-ming

AI CH'ING
(Chiang Hai-ch'eng, 1910–)

The study of poetry and art in France, imprisonment on political charges in Shanghai, and extensive travels in North China prepared Ai Ch'ing for his literary career, which was launched in 1936 with his first widely acclaimed poem, "Ta Yen Ho," addressed to an illiterate nurse who had raised him. In plain but powerful language, Ai Ch'ing spoke of his love for the humble, suffering people in his motherland. He was consciously urging a revolution in Chinese poetry along the paths blazed by Whitman and Mayakovsky, and his own writing had the irresistible rhythm and emotional impact of those two poets.

In spite of his attachment to his native town in Chekiang, eastern China, by the time he reached Yenan in 1941 to work with the Communists on cultural assignments and to teach at the United University of North China, he had already adopted North China as his home. There was something about the bleak, harsh, ice-clad land of the north—something paralleling the "Mother Russia" image—and the decent, stoic people who tried to survive there that attracted Ai Ch'ing. It came through clearly in his landmark poem, "The North-land."

He sang of the unself-conscious heroism of a plain soldier who fought for his country and for a great cause in "He Died a Second Time," of man's yearning for warmth and light in "Toward the Sun," and of the promise of victory ahead in "The Bugler." Such outpouring in the late 1930s established his position as one of the foremost poets in modern Chinese literature.

But he had also been steeped in Verhaeren, Apollinaire, Baudelaire, and Rimbaud, and when he published his critical work *On Poetry* (1940) he had developed a well-argued poetic theory, which had a significant impact on his generation of writers. His more complex and professional ideas about literature could not be tolerated by the Party's strict policy of making literature serve politics and politics alone. The 1957 campaign to discredit him was among the bitterest and most protracted ever launched by the Communists, but by that time he had already produced over a dozen volumes to testify to his stature, including *Wilderness, Herald of Dawn, Red Star—A Jewel,* and *Spring.* He remained silent for twenty-one years, until his reemergence in 1978.

Since his return from the labor camps in Heilungkiang and Sinkiang, he has been publishing poetry again. His new works, such as "The Red Flag," retain much of the earlier style that brought him fame and made him a much-imitated model in the 1940s. —K.Y.H.

The Atlantic

Leaving West Africa,
I fly towards South America;
Underneath the plane,
A vast, boundless Atlantic . . .

Today, no breeze blowing over the ocean,
The peaceful Atlantic,
Vast as a piece of ground glass,
Its surface, grey and white,
Not a ship, not a fleet,
Not even a single fishing boat,
As if we had returned to primordial times,
Lonely, desolate, and no signs of human beings;
The Atlantic sleeps deeply,
Uninvolved, unattached,
As if time did not exist,
And the world were not in turmoil.

Of course,
It's not just as simple as that.

In faraway, obscure places,
Beyond the reach of sight,
Lies danger everywhere.
The Atlantic in calm disguise
Is like the mythical Sphinx,
With a mysterious smile on its face,
Watching every traveler.
As she lifts up one of her front legs,
From her mouth comes a cryptic question.
Anyone unable to guess her riddle
Will drop dead before her instantly.

I seem to have come to a primitive jungle,
And I guard against a sudden ambush.
My head leans against the window,
My eyes stare down at the Atlantic,
Following the flight of the plane.
And I follow the flight of my mind.

Then, I see
The real Atlantic—
Wild waves dashing,
An Atlantic spreading its violence.
In this Atlantic ocean,
There are hostilities on every coast,
Polarities from island to island,
And hatred on every reef.

On the other side, I see in every corner of
The east and west coasts of the Atlantic,
Nerves that are more minute and complex
Than human nerves;
If we could slice a small piece from space

Like a piece of head cheese;
If every invisible, flowing wave of electricity
Were a line in space,
Then in this thin slice of space
Would be lines entangled,
Harder to unravel than a crazed woman's hair.
Inside these colorful lines
Are concealed the plots of war,
And cruel, treacherous plans
Involving thousands of lives;
Or a scheme of
How to strangle a newly emerging nation
With a dexterous diplomatic deal.

Oh! Atlantic,
For how many years
Have you become the home of daring pirates,
The origin of colonialism,
And the hotbed of world wars!

In those faraway seaports,
We can see
Innumerable fleets at anchor,
From faraway, they look like cities at sea;
Every warship is waiting
For the crucial moment
To leave the seaport
And take off the cannon covers.

And on both coasts of the north Atlantic,
Inside the skyscrapers of some
Clamorous cities,
Many people are busy calculating
The selling of loads and loads of fire arms ...

At night, in a lighted conference room
Of a certain building,
People hold secret meetings,
On how to invade a young republic,
And whether to arm a battalion
For Ngo Dinh Diem's troops
Is more economical
Than to arm a battalion
Of Chicago's jobless workers.

The airplane is flying over the Atlantic,
My heart beats with the plane engines ...

Life originally was a priceless treasure;
But in the eyes of the warmongers,

Life is not worth a single penny.
In their scales,
Each weight has to balance
A thousand-page book, full of names.

Imperialist warlords and financial magnates
Have become world catastrophes,
Their greed and ambition
Are larger than any king's;
They want to hold the globe in their fat palms
Like a three-year-old child
Holding an apple;
They want to start a war at any time,
Like lighting a firecracker;
They want to take the fates of other nations
To start a large-scale game,
And they proclaim, "This is the will of the Lord,"
While chuckling in secret, knowing that they
      themselves are the Lord.

But all these are about to pass beyond recall.
From Europe to North and South America,
From Africa to Asia,
And far-flung Australia,
Everywhere are fiery volcanoes exploding,
Cries for liberation and freedom
Higher and rougher than the Atlantic tides . . .

We are facing a new era,
People's relationships are changing,
Many concepts are given new interpretations,
Thousands of new people are reborn . . .

We are workers from the factories, dockyards,
Railroads, and mines,
We are workers from the workshops, both big and small;
We are the cultivators of the land,
Men with sickles and hoes,
And men tilling virgin soil, ranching cattle.
Since the day we awoke,
We became the mind and blood of our country.
We are men creating a new history.

Some ask:
What is our wish?

We hold no fancy of wolves' kindness,
Nor would we beg sympathy from bandits,
Hundreds and thousands of experiences proved to us:
Only through struggle shall we become victorious.

We work and create according to our wish,
What we have created belongs to us.
Like stacks of hay, we are many and simple,
Like a precipice, we bear the onslaught of the storm,
Like coal, we are quiet and hard,
And when the time comes, we burst into flaming fire ...

We are digging a grave for the old world,
Oh, listen, the giant is tolling the bell ...

We are the people working on the land,
We are the people turning capstans,
We knock down those who want to step on us,
We burn the idols who cheat us,
Our numbers increase,
There is nothing that can divide us,
We spread out to every corner of the earth,
To both coasts of the Atlantic,
And to the scattered archipelagoes.
We are everywhere.
We unite our labor with wisdom,
Leading us on are the shining truths;
"We have nothing, but will attain everything!"
All wealth will forever belong to us.
We've already built ourselves a new palace,
Our great labor has changed the appearance of the earth,
Marvels will be created from our hands,
All parasites will turn to dust.
Our will is as solid as rock:
We want no war.
Like a train, peace and friendship
Roar with laughter, rumbling forward ...

The riddle of the Sphinx is solved.
At this hour,
A new Atlantic appears before us—
Shining in golden ripples.
There are waves of songs
Coming from the coasts and the islands,
Softly and yet steadily
They sing of the greatest wish of our age,
Following the ripples, they float afar,
To every man, in every place.

July 1954, first draft
October 1956, revised
People's Literature, 11 (1956): 20–22

Translated by Dominic Cheung

FENG CHIH
(1906–)

The life and times of Feng Chih, who has been hailed by Lu Hsün as "the most distinguished lyric poet in China," can be divided into three periods, which coincide with three prominent stages of modern Chinese history: the prewar period (1921–32), the war period (1932–46), and, finally, the postwar period (1946 to the present). Born in Cho-hsien, a small rural community in Hopei province, Feng went to study in Peking and started his poetic career as a lyricist, excelling in narrative poetry. During the war years in Kunming, Feng wrote his famous sonnets, which revealed his ambition to adopt a Western form for Chinese subject matter. After Liberation Feng's poetic image changed drastically, from that of pure lyricist to that of people's balladeer. The writing of the new ballads reflects the poet's serious intention to accommodate himself to the needs of society and to the new demands made on poets.

During the Cultural Revolution, Feng continued to direct the Research Institute of Foreign Literature in the Academy of Sciences but ceased publishing serious poetry. Since the fall of the Gang of Four, he has brought out his translation of Heine's *Deutschland, Ein Wintermachen* (1978) and a series of articles on "How to Adopt Western Materials for Chinese Use."   —D. C.

Ascending the Wildgoose Tower

Countless visits have been made
To this old tower of T'ang;
Famous lines of the T'ang poets
Still vibrate in our minds.

The scenery of "the verdancy of the ages,"*
The sorrow of "a sudden collapse of the Ch'in Mountain,"†
They linger on this tower for thousands of years,
Directing the visions of the ascenders.

But when I, like the ancients,
Ascend to the top floor,
So charming is the scenery around me,
So bright the tower shadow on the ground!

*A line from Ts'en Shen's "Ascending Tz'u-en Temple Tower." [Author's note]
†A line from Tu Fu's "Ascending Tz'u-en Temple." [Author's note]

In the green fields, there are red houses,
Beside the red houses, the green trees grow;
Nearby are fields and gardens, and schools,
Faraway are shops and factories.

People point to the course of the Ch'ü River,
All dried up for a thousand years,
Soon it will be filled with clear running water,
And then, its old countenance will return.

The Wei River to the north will turn clear,
The Ch'in Ranges to the south will bow down to us,
The Pao-Ch'eng Road* breaks through ancient dangers,
No more worries over horses unable to advance.

Our country is intact—
No one will ever again stand on the ancient plain
Facing the lovely setting sun,
Regretting its final fall.†

The sun sets and rises incessantly,
Sian becomes fresher each day,
Magnificent is the people's Sian now—
Surpassing by far the imperial Ch'ang-an of T'ang.

The T'ang poets left eternal lines
For the magnificent but desolate Ch'ang-an;
We will write the new poetry of socialism
For the people's city of Sian.

July 1956
Poems of the Last Ten Years, pp. 54–56

Translated by Dominic Cheung

---

*From Pao-Chi in Shensi Province to Chengtu, capital of Szechwan. [D. C.]
†Refers to Li Shang-yin's lines on his visit to the ancient plain: "The sunset is marvelous / but it's close to nightfall." [Author's note]

HO CHING-CHIH
(1924–)

Ho Ching-chih achieved fame when he and Ting Yi transformed a local legend into the opera *White-haired Girl* (Yenan, 1945), which won a prize from the Communist authorities and was awarded the Stalin Prize in 1951. In that work as well as in his poetry, he demonstrated an adroitness with *shun-tien-yu* or *hsin-t'ien-yu* (literally "follow the drift of the singer"), a folk-song style popular in North China. The form is exemplified by the rhymed couplets of his "Song of the Landscape of Kweilin" (see pp. 534–35).

Next to *White-haired Girl*, Ho's best-known work is the 1200-line poem "Song of Lei Feng" (1963), the life story of a young model soldier with boundless devotion to Chairman Mao. The image of the hero remained untarnished through the Cultural Revolution, and so did Ho's song, which was among the first to be reissued after the Cultural Revolution in 1972 and was again reprinted in 1977.

The son of a poor peasant of Shantung, Ho was one of the few nationally established literary figures who avoided disgrace during the 1960s. He dropped out of sight for a short period around 1975, but since 1977 he has been serving as vice-minister of cultural affairs in the central government.   —K.Y.H.

The Rock in Mid-Torrent

1

Oh, not to remember the past
I come to the Gorge of Three Gates
    Straddling over where King Yü jumped his horse:
See, yellow water rolling, rolling
    Hear, excavator thud-thud.
Makes my
    Eyes full
        of hot tears welling,
    Body full
        of blood boiling, a thousand degrees!

Oh, oh—
Upon the Gorge of Three Gates
    Hold tight
        the sky-breaking, earth-breaking
            Heroes' arms

Beneath the Gorge of Three Gates—
        For millions of years unmoved
                Rock in mid-torrent!

2

Oh, the past, where to?
Torrents: a million horses come.
        Heroes of the past, innumerable!
See, sky-filled war-fires
        Hear, earth-shaking war-drums

Pointing into the distance
        The Great Wall
                Ten thousand miles of sharpened bamboo-poles. . . .
        Chingkang Mountain:
                Red flags fling into dance!

Oh, oh—

The past goes, the present comes
        How many
                wind-bracing, wave-breaking
                        heroes and worthies

Mid-torrent in the Yellow River—
        Erect, immortal for millions of years,
                The backbone of a nation!

3

Oh, today is not the past!
        Red flags descend upon Chingkang
                Change the entire landscape of the nation!
See, new makeup of the Yellow River
        Hear, thundering footfalls
I call
        Ancient men
                To startle them from their dreams
To sigh:
        No match to these heroes!

Oh, Oh—

Since five thousand years ago
        Who has seen
                The working-class
                        Magic axe of celestial skill!

One shout across a million miles:
> For Socialism
>> To raise a skyward monolith!

March 1958
Singing Aloud, pp. 22–24

Translated by Wai-lim Yip

Return to Yenan

I

My heart, don't pound so hard,
And the road dust, don't block my view....

I grab a handful of the yellow dirt, and won't let it go,
Clutching it tight, close to my bosom.

... Many were the times when I dreamt of returning to Yenan,
In dream my arms embraced the Pagoda Hill.

A thousand, ten thousand times I've been calling you,
—Mother Yenan is here now, right here!

The Tu Fu Creek sings, and Willow Grove Village smiles,
The fluttering red flags are beckoning me.

White towels around their necks and waistbands red,
My dear people meet me, taking me across the Yen River.

I fall into their arms, arms stretched wide,
Too much to say at once, my tongue is tied....

II

... Past Twenty-*li* Village, Willow Grove nears,
I'm home again, after ten long years.

The trees have tops, branches, and deep, deep roots,
My kinfolk live in these familiar rivers and hills.

When the lambs suckle they look at their mother,
It's the millet here that fed me and made me grow.

Eastern hills' grain and western hills' rice,
The books in my hand, the red flag on my shoulder.

She taught me all that, holding my hand in her hand,
Then, she sent us to cross the Yellow River.

The road of revolution ran endless miles,
Wherever I went I always thought of you....

III

Rice wine, wheat fritters, and charcoal fire,
On the warm *k'ang* we all sit around.

People crowd into the cave, packing it tight,
Footsteps are still sounding outside the gate.

Old Grandpa enters, still panting hard,
"Dreamed of a letter ... and woke up to find you here!"

The dear ones have come together again face to face,
Tears of joy well up in everybody's eyes.

In defending Yenan you've had much strain,
Look at your hair, greyer now than then.

Youth Corps Party secretary shows in the commune director,
A shepherd boy in those years, a grown-up man now.

Clean white paper on windowpanes, red paper flowers,
Children push forward to shake hands with me.

Thousands of words accompany each mouthful of wine,
Like the surging waves on the Yellow and Yangtze Rivers.

The revolution has developed much in the last ten years,
How can one finish telling about these many long days?...

IV

Even if I had hundreds of eyes and thousands of legs,
It wouldn't be enough for me to see with and walk with.

A big mirror is the clear sky above my head,
Reflecting the whole city of Yenan in my heart.

Street upon street, each wide and smooth,
Building after building draped in colorful banners.

Strings of electric lights shining bright,
Rows of green trees greet spring breeze....

In contrast to the past I can't recognize you,
Mother Yenan you have put on a dress brand new.

V

Red flags on Yang-chia Peak are flying high
And revolution surges across the land, reaching the sky.

His footprints are still fresh below the Pagoda Hill,
Chairman Mao has ascended the Gate of Heavenly Peace.

The lamps in the Jujube Garden light up men's hearts,
The rolling Yen River keeps shouting "Forward, March!"

Red Guards, Youth Corps, and the Red Scarves,
One after another march the generations of heroes.

In long strides we walk on the road of socialism,
The glorious Yen River will continue to march ahead,

Then wings will grow on my body, and clouds under my feet,
I will come back again and see Mother Yenan again.

March 9, 1956, Yenan
Singing Aloud, pp. 1–5

Burial

He didn't come back until very, very late.
The casket carriers, grave diggers had all left,
But he sprawled on the newly dug grave, weeping.
Even those trying to comfort him had gone, long gone,
He still stayed there, his voice hoarse for all that crying.

He didn't come back until very, very late.
The owls in the woods were stirred up by his weeping.
Night had descended over the wilderness,
No stars, no moon,
November, winds howled like wolves.

He didn't come back until very, very late.
Cold gusts of wind whipped him. He struggled up
From the newly dug grave, and walked out of the woods.
Cold wind pushed him, he couldn't see the road.
November, a night in the village, a night of unending sorrow.

He didn't come back until very, very late.
The burial was over, forever underground lay the dead
That had been his brother, his only kin.
Now the debtors were waiting for him at his hut,
To divide up his property, that half-*mu* of land.

He didn't come back until very, very late.
Passing in front of his hut, he kept going,
Going through one stretch of wilderness, and another.
The November cold wind howled—
He walked on, toward a faraway place, far from his homeland.

The Night in the Village, pp. 13–14

Translated by Kai-yu Hsu

LI CHI
(1922–)

(For a general note on Li Chi, see p. 178.)

The 2000-line poem *May Festival* tells the first part of the life story of Yang Kao, an orphan shepherd. Abused by landlords, he runs away to live with a blind storyteller, from whom he learns the arts of storytelling and balladry. The blind minstrel is also an underground Communist cadre. Thus the boy is brought up as a "Little Red Devil," working for the Red Army during the 1930s and 1940s in North China, fighting against the Japanese and Kuomintang troops. The title, "Wu-yüeh tuan-yang," literally "Dragon Boat Festival of May," is taken from the name of the heroine, a girl born on the festival day. The poem is based on a true story. The following two excerpts are chapters 33 and 40 of the last section.   —K.Y.H.

---

from *May Festival*

Convalescence

Since the liberation of the city of Chen-ching
All the white bandits disappeared from that area.
Green Willow Village, no longer a ghetto of the poor,
People received land, horses found grass, everyone happy.

Though liberated, one couldn't forget past sorrow,
Black cloud still covered over one-half of the sky.
Millions upon millions of poor brethren in white area,
Continued to be fried in boiling oil.

Thus young men, one after another, joined the army,
And women made shoes and socks to aid the war effort.
They milled rice, prepared flour, delivered food,
To support our Red Army to march on the Heng Mountain.

That day people were in the middle of a meeting,
A stretcher was carried to the front of the village.
Folks gathered around to look and inquire about it,
They saw a wounded red soldier lying in the litter.

With the stretcher also came a letter to Village Chief,
Asking the villagers to keep and nurse the wounded.
Every family wanted to take him, they nearly quarreled,
As the old lady and Tuan-yang insisted on their turn.

"Too many people in your house, too noisy," they said.
"Our house has only two of us, just right to keep him;
Village Chairman, you say, isn't this only fair?
Please let us take him home, for we would never give up."

Village Chairman nodded, and the old lady smiled,
Little Tuan-yang ran ahead to get blankets ready.
The stretcher was carried to their cave-house door,
And the old lady placed the wounded on their *k'ang.*

When she carried the wounded, she suffered a shock,
This heavily injured one was no bigger than a child.
She studied him carefully again and again, but he was
Blood-smeared all over, and was beyond recognition.

Cold, cold were the little man's hands and feet,
His eyes closed, no motion at all, no speech.
Tears flowed from her old eyes as she watched him,
From her heart flowed curses on the white brutes.

She put her ears close to his ashen face,
He was still breathing, and his heart throbbed.
She hurried to call Tuan-yang to heat some water,
And with a cotton swab they washed his bloodstains.

Cuts and holes covered his body up and down,
A big gaping one replaced one of his knee caps.
Her heart skipped a beat as she dressed the wound,
The little man lay unconscious under her blurred eyes.

But the more she looked, the more he looked familiar,
Yet she just could not recall where she had seen him.
Could not recall, no, she couldn't, though she tried,
And wondered if he was the one seen on Tuan-yang Day.

Fight the Japanese

No word from Yang Kao, since he left,
Green Willow Villagers waited and worried.
Even water in the creek sometimes dried up,
Yet their waiting seemed to have no end at all.

Some say Yang Kao had seen Chairman Mao,
And the latter had sent Yang Kao to a hospital.
And there he had his leg completely cured, but
Immediately he returned to his outfit on the front.

Some say Liu Chih-tan* knew he could tell stories,
Thus ordered him to work with the propaganda team.
He could tell stories and sing songs, so he moved
From rear to front, urging support for the war.

Some saw him, actually saw him, with their own eyes,
Amidst the red troops marching in the Eastern Expedition.
When Liu Chih-tan died in action against the Japanese,
Little Yang Kao was with him, right at his side.

The Eastern Expedition led the Red Army back to northern Shensi,
A Drama Corps for Resistance War replaced the propaganda team.
Some saw him on stage then, performing such hits as
"Twelve Sickles" and "Checking Safe-Conduct."

Clever as ever he was, and his voice ever clear,
Everybody cheered his shows, applauded his songs.
Those who had seen him said he had grown up now,
But still like a rubber ball, lively, and bouncing.

"Why didn't you ever write us?" some asked him.
"That's not true!" he complained, eyes popping out.
Upon each transfer I wrote and sent a lengthy letter,
Even asked people to bring books to Tuan-yang!"

Others had a different story to tell, they said,
During the Eastern Expedition he was wounded again.
As the Red Army withdrew from Shensi, Yang Kao died,
Leaving, on the Yellow River bank, his dried bloodstain.

All these are but hearsay, don't know which to believe,
Or which is completely false, which more or less true.
The old lady refused to accept the death of Yang Kao,
A tall tree with deep roots, her faith hard to shake.

In August 1937 the Red Army was reorganized
Into the Eighth Route and marched to the front.
Boats busy ferrying the troops across the Yellow River,
Rushing the red soldiers eastward to stop the Japanese.

*Red Army commander and hero; a city in Shensi has been named in his memory.
[K.Y.H.]

As one of the boats reached mid-river with a load of troops,
Suddenly one heard someone sing aloud on board.
Ah, it's a "Little Red Devil," he sang really well,
Sitting on the boat's edge, with a carbine on his shoulder.

A cheerleader led the group, he started shouting—
"Good or not good?" The crowd yelled, "Good!"
"Great or not great?" he asked again, and the crowd
Responded with repeated requests of encore and encore.

"Little Red Devil" could not refuse any longer, he
Put down his carbine, and he pushed straight his cap.
He opened his mouth to the wind, to the roaring waves,
Like a red flag unfurled, his voice fluttered in the wind.

"The whole nation involved in a total war," he sang,
"All of us, everyone of us, march to the front.
Two great commanders stand at the rampart on city wall.
Who are they? Standing majestic are Chu Teh and Mao!"

The song over, the boat approached the other bank.
Leaping off the boat, the troops were like tigers
Swooping down from the hill. Here came the Eighth Route Army
To raise the red flags all over the Tai-hang Range.

This song fills a volume, entitled *Tuan-yang of May*.
Let me pause a minute, let me have a smoke.
If you want to know what later happened to Yang Kao,
Next time we'll make a fresh start on a new chapter.

July 7, 1958, Lanchow, Kansu Province
May Festival, pp. 106–108, 132–35

Translated by Kai-yu Hsu

LI YING

(1930?–)

College-educated Li Ying turned to a military life with gusto. He emerged as a most promising army poet by the end of the 1950s. The first collection of his poetry, *Field Combat Verses* (1951), fared well; it was followed by several more volumes of poetry, culminating in *Red Willow,* which brought him nationwide praise.

The soldier's voice in his works carries a good measure of refinement, and yet it remains robust enough to flatter the proletarian readers. His lines invite the reader not so much with action and heroism as with his fresh response to the wide horizon ablaze with a rising sun over the Gobi desert, or to the shimmering blue that spreads around Hainan Island and stretches to infinity. In his poetry there is much joy of life made worthwhile by the growth of a new nation; there is also a wonderment about nature that comes close to the classical standard.   —K.Y.H.

The Clouds Race on the Sea's Face

The clouds race in long strides over the sea's face,
And on the sea's face rises a sweep of noisy fog,
And the rain falls—the rain, an impenetrable wall,
Tightly, ever so tightly seals all the roads.

Braving the high waves our fleet is ready to depart,
Under signals from the lighthouse that show comradely concern.
But no roadblocks raised by the waves could trip us,
No cables tossed down by the rain could hold us back.

October 1956
Red Willow, p. 5

After a Gun Duel at Quemoy

The guns are hushed, after roaring at Quemoy,
Now louder we hear the roar of the sea,
And the gunners leap off their firing positions,
Wiping their sweat of pride.

371

A drop of sweat, thousands of pounds heavy,
For it nurses the flowers on the battlefield;
Heavier still are the artillery shells
That explode to rock the islands off shore.

Camouflage nets, swinging in the breeze;
Singing voices rise high from the trenches.
They take a sip of warm boiled water,
And in laughter they watch Quemoy ablaze.

At the third night-watch, falling stars like rain;
How many of them drop in the soldiers' bosoms?
A disc of moon hangs on the gun's lips—
A round lantern for the victory herald.

Late 1957
Red Willow, pp. 19–20

Translated by Kai-yu Hsu

MAO TSE-TUNG
(1893–1976)

Very few of Mao Tse-tung's poems were known before the official release of nineteen of them in the *Poetry Journal* in January 1957. By now about forty of his poems have appeared in complete or partial English translations, including those by Robert Payne and others (1947), by Kai-yu Hsu (1963), by Jerome Ch'en (1965), by Wong Man (1966), by Barnstone and Ko (1972), by Paul Engle and Nieh Hua-ling (1972), by Wang Hui-ming (1974), and by the editors of *Chinese Literature* (1958, 1963, 1966, and 1976).

On the occasion of the official publication in 1957, Mao wrote an injunction against the imitation of classical Chinese verse forms by young Chinese poets. He discussed poetry with a few people, such as Ch'en Yi (who was foreign minister until his death in 1972), stressing the need to adopt "thinking in images" as the only effective approach to good poetry, whether classical or modern. He did not persist in warning the poets against writing in classical Chinese verse forms, however; neither did he actively promote their doing so, except by his own demonstration—his verses were all in the mode of T'ang *shih* (quatrains or eight-line regulated verse) or Sung *tz'u* (lyrics of irregular meter), mostly the latter. More specifically he stated that *pai-hua* poetry had been a failure during the past decades, and that the future seemed to lie with folk songs completely free of esoteric, cryptic allusions.

The following are fresh translations, noticeably different from all extant versions. —K.Y.H.

Changsha

Before me in chill autumn
The Hsiang flows north
Past Orange Isle.
A thousand hillsides one red blaze,
Layered woods dyed through,
Wide river green to the depths,
Bucking the current, a hundred sail.
Hawks attack the open sky,
Fish leap in the shallows,
All Creation strives for freedom, battling the frost to prevail.
Space overwhelming:
Across the vastness of earth
Who decides, win or fail?
We were a hundred once roamed these trails.
I recall the crowded years, the towering ideals,
Students together, young,

373

In the time of our flowering,
Spirited intellects
Quick to rant and rail,
Setting the land to rights
With stirring words—
Plain dung to us were the lords of ancient tale.
Remember
Flying against the midstream current
Our oars like flails?

1925

Tapoti

Violet indigo blue green yellow orange red—
Who waves this silken banner high overhead?
Slanting sun after rain,
Mountain verdure fresh again.

That year's battles were hard,
Farm walls still bullet-scarred.
Hillside and pass, adorned by war
Lovelier now than before.

1933

Loushan Pass

West wind strong
Wild geese honked across the sky; frosty morning moon,
Frosty morning moon.
Broken clatter of horses' hooves,
Bugles' mournful tune.

They said this pass was iron-bound
But striding out we took it in one,
Took it in one.
Green crests like a sea,
Blood the setting sun.

1935

Peitaiho

Drenching rain on northland Yen,
White waves dash the sky.
Off First Emperor's Island, fishermen
Lost to sight in the sea's infinity—
What course for them?

Trace back millennia to when
Ts'ao Ts'ao whipped legions by
"Eastward to Tablet Rock": his poem then
Sang of a wind that still "whines drearily";
What's changed is men.

1954

Reply to Madame Li Shu-yi

I lost Yang, the "poplar"; you, the "willow" Liu:
Poplar and willow lightly floated through the nine heavens' blue.
They sought a gift from Wu Kang, captive in the moon;
Wu Kang bore them in his hands a cup of cassia brew.

Ch'ang O, the lonely goddess, her sleeves to full width drew
And danced through endless realms of sky for two souls just and true.
Then swift report arrived from earth of the tiger overcome,
And sudden tears as flying rain drenched the firmament through.

1957

Swimming

I drank the waters of Changsha,
Now enjoy fish of Wuchang;
Ruled a bar across river's miles,
Stretched sight horizon-long,
Preferring beat of wind and wave
To aimless stroll in idle court:
These hours to me belong.
The Master's words at stream-side:
"Thus ever does it run."

Wind-sway of masts
Repose of Tortoise and Snake
And a great plan begun:
North and south across nature's moat
Bridged by a soaring span.
West, we erect new cliffs of stone
To block the rains of Witch's Gorge:
Calm lake from sheer walls sprung.
If still the Goddess flourish,
What changes since she was young!

1956

Snow

Northern grandeur:
Hundred leagues locked in ice,
Thousand more of whirling snow.
Within the Great Wall and beyond
Vast without end;
Yellow River, upstream and down
Suddenly quelled in its flow.
Mountains, writhing silver snakes,
High plateaus like waxen mammoths
Strive the heights of heaven to outgrow;
Then the sky clears,
Brightens the gown of banded white
With crimson glow.

By hill and stream enchanted so
Gallant suitors in throngs came bowing low.
But the Lord of Ch'in and Wu of Han
Lacked cultivation,
The founders of T'ang and Sung
Had wits too slow,
The favored master of the world,
Genghis Khan, could win
No prize but eagles with his mighty bow.
All went their way;
Figures truly grand
Our age alone will show.

1936

NOTES ON SELECTED POEMS BY MAO TSE-TUNG

"Changsha" (1925): All the poems in this short selection use metrical patterns of the genre known as *tz'u*, "lyric." These patterns were widely used by poets of the Sung dynasty (tenth to thirteenth centuries), and Mao learned them as a schoolboy in Hunan. Each pattern has a "tune-title" based on the wording of the original song. So, although Mao titles this poem "Changsha," the name of the metrical pattern is *Ch'in-yüan ch'un,* "Spring in the Ch'in Garden." The poem "Snow" (below) uses the same pattern. The number of lines and their varied lengths, the tonal pattern, and the rhyme scheme are all strictly prescribed. The present translations retain the original rhyme schemes and attempt to indicate typographically the metrical patterning of short and long lines.

Mao had studied in the Teachers' Training College at Changsha, capital of his home province of Hunan, and returned there on a revolutionary errand some seven years later. His poem of reminiscence is now inscribed on a huge tablet in a park on Orange Isle, which parts the waters of the great Hsiang River as they flow north past Changsha to join the Yangtze. The first stanza is typical Mao, full of vigorous action. The poem ends with a wry recollection of idealistic young students "rowing against the current," which is still very much his own situation as a young revolutionary in 1925.

"Tapoti" (1933) and "Loushan Pass" (1935): Most traditional Chinese poetry about war, from the classic *Book of Songs* on, stresses hardship and human waste and yearns for peace. But these poems are in a heroic vein, celebrating hard fighting against Chiang's Nationalists around Tapoti in Kiangsi Province in 1929 and the crossing of Loushan Pass in 1935 during the Long March. The first line of "Tapoti" lists the colors of the spectrum, familiar to every schoolboy. It was a brilliant stroke on Mao's part to recognize this as the metrically perfect opening to one of the most common lyric patterns, *P'u-sa man,* "Strangers in Saint's Coif." The pattern of "Loushan Pass" is *Yi Ch'in O,* "Remembering Ch'in O." The three-syllable first line recalls "Great wind rises," the opening line of a celebrated poem by Liu Pang, founder of the Han dynasty in the third century B.C.

"Snow" (1936): Mao's most majestic poem offers a panorama of China's winter landscape in the first stanza and of her long history in the second. The poem is organized around the image of a bride, red-gowned, in the Chinese fashion, by the glow of sunlight on snow (and also by the red flags of Communism). The warrior-emperors of the second stanza, beginning with the First Emperor, the Lord of Ch'in, who built the Great Wall, all sought the hand of this bride but proved unworthy and "went their way." Bridegrooms "truly grand" will be found only in the present age, when the people (under their Communist leaders) have become masters of their own country.

"Peitaiho" (1954): To the tune *Lang-t'ao sha,* "Wave-washed Sands." Ts'ao Ts'ao, mighty general of the third century, after establishing himself as Emperor Wu of Wei, rode through the coastal settlement of Peitaiho to the defense of his northern frontier. He composed the following poem, to which Mao here alludes:

> East to Tablet Rock
> To gaze on the mighty sea:
> How the waters toss,
> The mountain-isles rise sheer.
> Thickly clustering trees,
> Herbs in rich array;
> Drear whine of autumn wind,
> Giant billows rear.
> From this place begin
> Journeys of sun and moon,
> Milky Way's shining stream
> Seems to flow from here.
> Let this joyous song
> Make my great purpose clear.

Mao's purpose in this allusion is to contrast the harshness of unchanging nature, and of the northern territories' brutal history, with the advances under his own leadership in the world of men.

"Reply to Madame Li Shu-yi" (1957): To the tune *Tieh lian hua,* "Butterflies Woo the Blossoms." Yang, meaning "poplar," is the surname of Mao's first wife, K'ai-hui, executed by the Nationalists in the 1930s; Liu, meaning "willow," refers to Liu Chih-hsün, who died in action with the Communist forces in 1933. Liu's widow, Li Shu-yi, wrote a poem on his death and sent it to Mao, who wrote this reply. Mao deftly relates the two martyrs to Wu Kang and Ch'ang O, figures of ancient legend who achieved immortality only at the cost of exile to the moon. Then he tempers the sorrow of the old bereavements with a celebration of "the tiger [i.e., the Nationalists] overcome," so that the tears of the last line represent the martyrs' joy at the success of their cause.

"Swimming" (1956): This poem, to one of the great lyric meters, *Shui-tiao ko-t'ou,* "Water Music Prelude," is full of allusions. Lines 1–2 refer to a third-century folk ditty that protested a transfer of the capital: "Rather drink the water of Chien-yeh," it ran, "than taste the fish of Wuchang." Mao substitutes his own Changsha, which has a famous old well, for Chien-yeh (modern Nanking), and brings out the symbolic nature of his swim across the Yangtze (at Wuhan in May 1956): he has unified the land and can rejoice in both water *and* fish. "Nature's moat" (second stanza, line four) is a historic epithet for the Yangtze, but the moat is now reduced by the new Wuhan bridge. Another proud achievement is the new reservoir, taming the storms of Witch's Gorge on the upper Yangtze, whose willful and wayward "Goddess" was described by the poet Sung Yü in the third century B.C. The "Master" quoted in stanza one is Confucius, whose words suggest a changelessness that Mao refutes: "Tortoise and Snake" (hills on either bank of the Yangtze at Wuhan) may sit there forever, but his new regime is actively rebuilding the landscape.

Translation and notes by Cyril Birch

PIEN CHIH-LIN
(1910–)

One tends to associate Pien Chih-lin, a fine poet who brought much of Verlaine and Valéry into Chinese poetry, with the academe of a bygone era, but he is still in Peking and continues to be active in his own way. To be sure, the pace of life since 1949 has not allowed him to return to his quiet musing about the universe and his own position in it: so far he has not found a comfortable bridge between the feverish building of irrigation ditches and the symbolist world of his *Leaves of Three Autumns*, *Fish's Eye*, or *Han Garden*.

Fortunately, his interest in translating Western literature can be, to some extent, accommodated in the present scheme of things. For some years now, he has been on the staff of the Research Institute of Foreign Languages and Literature, a division of the Academy of Sciences. When I saw him in Peking in 1973, he looked even healthier to me than he had thirty years ago. He told me that he was translating Shakespeare for a politically sanitized college edition. What he really wanted to write, he said, was a full-length novel depicting the metamorphosis of the Chinese intellectual from a pre-1949 bourgeois into a member of the new socialist nation. Although he had vowed as early as 1940 to write such a novel, he has yet to complete it.

Meanwhile, a few lines occasionally take shape in his mind. When he writes them down, they still exhibit the compact syntax and condensed imagery of his earlier work, as shown in the following selections. In December 1978, he drastically screened his own poems for a new anthology, which he preferred to call his collected works rather than selected works. He intended to save a total of less than a hundred poems, and he wrote a long preface analyzing the process of his own development as a poet. —K.Y.H.

A Gift for the Reservoir Project

On the way to the Reservoir, first plunge into the sea of humanity—
Blue tide crashing through the barren pass!
Men come from a thousand households: the movement
Of a hundred streams converges on the sea.

Throwing off your overcoat, grab a carrying-pole;
In the sea of humanity, take a bath in a sandstorm.
Offer a drop of sweat for the Reservoir—
Happy hearts beating like fish frolicking.

Poetry Journal, no. 3 (1958): 10

Dialogue of the Earth Movers

"What's that you're doing,
Spadeful after spadeful?"
"Don't think I'm just digging—
I'm shutting off the roar of mountain floods!"

"What's that you're doing,
Shovel after shovel?"
"A quarter million irrigated *mu*
Are welling up in my palm!"

"And you, you too, shouldering
Basket after basket?"
"I'm raising a lakeful of live fish,
Lighting the villages with electric glow!"

"Each hand joining a thousand hands,
Each step joining a step further,
Each man has become a giant—
We are building the Ming Tombs Reservoir!"

Poetry Journal, no. 3 (1958): 10

Embracing the Flood

Fish shouldn't float into houses;
Thickets are for birds to nest in.
Know, Great Water: you will never again go berserk,
Knocking the flowers off young branches.

Move! The fish don't want a crystal palace;
The birds will go uphill—into paradise.
We'll fix up a lake-bed in the valley
And embrace the Great Water—make it our mirror.

Today we work the soil beneath the lake.
Tomorrow we'll climb the slopes, plant saplings,
Build houses, install electric lights, water the soil;
We'll set out fish nets in the Great Water.

You, Great Water, will have it all:
Houses shining in your bosom,
And trees, trucks, airplanes,
Smiles of labor and of leisure.

Poetry Journal, no. 3 (1958): 12

Goggles and Telescopes

Building a reservoir, should one wear goggles?
Where the River of Sand comes from, sandstorms are heavy!
In the hollow of the storm, a Reservoir is appearing—
Just as we had planned!

Every spadeful starts a small sandstorm;
The sandstorm of a million spades has covered Heaven!
Actually, these goggles are telescopes:
Blue mountains, green waters before our very eyes!

Poetry Journal, no. 3 (1958): 12

View from the Ming Tombs

The Emperor, having analyzed the *feng-shui*,*
Returned to his court and designed a vista:
"Let my bones be enclosed by four mountains;
All future tombs to extend from here!

The Wen-yü River is Dragon's vein! Established here,
Our sovereignty will stand for countless generations.
Even in death we shall command awe:
Once loose these waters, and the commoners will be as prawns!"

But the People turned the tables, penned in the waters.
Household on household they opened up the mountains,
Putting trees on every mountain, green in every tree,
Sending a fragrance of grain south over the countryside!

*Geomancy: speculations on the prophetic significance of topographical features.
[K.Y.H.]

The Emperor said, "Thanks to my foresight,
Adding a lake will be auspicious"—
Not realizing his thirteen little curios*
Would serve to decorate the People's vast garden!

Poetry Journal, no. 3 (1958): 12

Translated by Lloyd Haft

*There are thirteen Ming Dynasty imperial tombs in that valley, which is now a public park. [K.Y.H.]

TSANG K'O-CHIA
(1904–)

Tsang K'o-chia, who had been the most influential voice in *pai-hua* poetry in the 1950s and 1960s and a major force behind the national *Poetry Journal* until the Cultural Revolution shut it down, returned to the revived *Journal* in 1976, but his published works have been restricted to a few unoriginal, politically appropriate short pieces.

Nurtured by the Crescent School poets, Tsang struck out in a direction all his own. By the 1930s his plain, almost gaunt, but strong lines, crying out man's humiliation in a tormented era, had already left their mark on the development of modern Chinese poetry. In the late 1930s he turned to a search for the earthy, honest notes that vibrated among his homeland villagers in Shantung, and for the subdued but true color of the subsoil of China.

He has devoted his life to poetry—editing it, writing it, helping others to write it. The long list of collections to his credit includes earlier works such as *The Brand* and *The Zero-Degree of Life* and more recent ones such as *Cheers* and *Triumphal Return.*

Like most other writers, during the Cultural Revolution Tsang was out in the countryside of Hupeh, digging dirt (but in small quantities because of his poor health). He returned to Peking in early 1973, claiming to be much healthier than ever before. He still looked, as he always had, very much the image of his own gaunt, tense verse. He was watching and waiting for a chance to give his remaining years to poetry, and at that time he spoke with some hesitation. But he should be much more open now—now that he has reemerged on the scene, at such a glittering assembly as the Third Congress of the All-China Federation of Literary and Art Circles in Peking in May 1978. Some of his earlier works are being reissued. —K.Y.H.

Old Man Fu Kuang-heng

Your seventy-year-old form, like an old tree,
In feudal mud buried for sixty years,
Now is left with a crippled leg,
An everlasting, painful remembrance.
Sitting upon a red wooden stool,
You mix dung ladle by ladle into water,
And watch it flow from one plot to another,
Making the vegetables in the plots grow green and tender.
You are used to hearing the sad song of the pulley,
Which has calloused your palms.

383

Today, the well is still the same one as then,
But now the Liberation-brand waterwheel sings out another kind
　　　of tune.
Old man! When I look at you,
It is like seeing a green shoot sprout from a bare tree in spring.
You, old member of the cooperative,
Supported by one leg, still you continue on toward socialism.

The Countryside, On High Tide, pp. 204–205

Translated by Kenneth Koziol

TSOU TI-FAN

(1917--)

Tsou Ti-fan was born in Hupeh Province, where he spent his childhood years in extreme poverty. At the outbreak of the Sino-Japanese war, he left to study in Chungking. It was at this time that Tsou aligned the style of his lengthy poems with the narrative poetry of Tsang K'o-chia and T'ien Chien. His poetry collections during the war years included *The Carpenter Shop, The Determined Gambler, River, Blue Sky and the Forest,* and *Snow and the Village.* After 1945 his new collection, *Across,* marked a transition from the simple narration of events to the expression of dissident feelings of social injustice. In his "political poems" Tsou arrived at a preference for socialist ideology, and after Liberation he emerged as a socialist writer. In his poetic themes he now emphasizes the existence of the "middle characters," who are neither heroes nor petty people, but representations of an "intensified reality." Through the study of these village characters in Tsou's poems, we come to know the real, positive, silent contributors to a better China. —D.C.

A Village Actor

By the water trough,
The production brigade leader introduced me to a grey-haired villager:
"This is the cultural education head of the village."
He put down his hoe,
And gripped my hand,
"What head?
Compared to you people,
I'm just an illiterate.

"Look here, 'Production's Great Leap Forward,'
Yesterday, I took it for 'Production's Great Importance,'
Aye, to read is harder than to act,
I studied the whole winter long, but learned only a few words."

"But in acting, you're number one!"
"Ah—in the old days,
A little song-and-dance gave relief to the poor people.
We worked like dogs all year round
Earning not even a winter jacket for our back,
Nor food to fill up our empty belly.
To stage a show
Was fun;

But the inhuman landlord,
Demanded heavy stage rent from us poor people ...
Oh, tonight we have a show,
Why don't you come and see."

At night,
Kerosene lanterns hung on the stage,
Tobacco pipes glowed in the crowd—
A wintry night, cold wind, out in the open,
Freezing!

He starts to sing on the stage,
In this spacious, open-air theater.
He sends his voice
South of the mountain,
To the faraway forest,
To all the lighted windows in the village ...
He is singing "Hanging the Picture,"
The charming voice of a maiden.
His head, covered with flowers,
His sideburns, pasted with dark wiglets ...
In the daytime, I see his manly labor,
At night, I see his graceful silhouette, singing and dancing.

When he finishes a tune,
The audience roars with applause.
Suddenly he takes off his flowery headgear,
And tears off his sideburns,
Speaking loudly:
"Comrades,
Today, let us have a meeting,
To exterminate the Four Evils,*
and about hygiene ..."

How fascinatingly he speaks;
Although he sings about the ancients,
He speaks of the people's affairs.
He says:
"Without hard work,
No success in irrigation;
Exterminating the Four Evils,
Healthy people to do the harvesting ..."

*The four pests: mosquitoes, flies, sparrows (or bedbugs), and rats. The campaign took place in the late 1950s and early 1960s. [K.Y.H.]

He speaks only of
The bumper-crop village,
A clean village ...
When the spring breeze blows over the willow-covered river banks,
The earth's flowers spread fragrance,
Colorful clouds float in the sky.
In this peaceful village,
This happy village,
There is our builder—
The cultural education head.

Poetry Journal, no. 3 (1958): 20–21

Translated by Dominic Cheung

PART THREE

The Great Leap Forward
and Anti-Revisionism

(1959–1961)

Encouraged by the rapid economic improvement of 1957, the Party announced the second five-year plan in January 1958, and in November initiated a Great Leap Forward as one of the Three Red Flags (the other two being the People's Commune and the General [policy] Line). The official goal was to overtake Great Britain and America in certain aspects of material wealth within a limited number of years, and for that purpose every effort was to be redoubled. Grain yield was to be increased tenfold and steel was to be manufactured in every backyard. While the self-reliant, heroic spirit was admirable, the net result was a near famine in 1960–61. But any opposition to the Great Leap Forward on the ground that it was not realistic was ruthlessly crushed; even the powerful voice of P'eng Teh-huai, one of the ten most meritorious generals, was silenced, and he died in ignominy.

In support of the Great Leap Forward, a nationwide campaign was launched to encourage and collect folk songs; literally thousands of them were printed and distributed in 1958–59. They praise the glory of the new society and the Party, and rejoice in the productive labor of the people. Hsieh Ch'i-kuei's "More" is an example. Other poets, old and young, wrote on a large variety of subjects, ranging from Chang Yung-mei's tale of some peasants recalling their past grievances against cruel landlords and discussing the power in their hands now, to Kuo Hsiao-ch'uan's musings over the immensity of the stellar universe. The forms range from Chao P'u-ch'u's classical *tz'u* to Ch'en Yi's short and nimble quatrains.

Chou Yang, the Party's spokesman for cultural and literary affairs, urged the writers to advance toward a truly proletarian literature, and some models of it were created during these few years. Liu Ch'ing's *The Builders* describes the cooperative movement in the countryside around 1953, showing the correctness of the Party's agricultural policy. Chao Shu-li's old peasant hero, whose

389

hands are invincible and indestructible, and T'ang K'o-hsin's young factory worker, elated by his ability to teach his expertise to his superior, are labor heroes to be emulated.

But again, as the writers began to feel expansive and started writing with less restraint, their works also reflected imperfections in the new society. Chao Hsün's play highlights the problems of a discharged army officer who, upon returning to his home village, finds his wife married to his brother by order of the village chief, and the entire village poor and backward as ever. The play, completed in 1958, was held up by the editor of the national *Drama* monthly for two years, and then printed with a call for criticism of its erroneous viewpoints. A wave of denouncements followed, condemning the play as an antiwar and anti-Party expression. To add fuel to the fire, the critics went on to bring back earlier works with similar flaws. Yüeh Yeh's play, first published in 1956, now became another "poisonous weed" to be eradicated, because the principal character in it, a high-level cadre, divorces his peasant wife to marry a more educated woman, a nurse he has met in the hospital. The play's artistic competence and the fact that the plot involves a universal problem of marital alienation were not enough to redeem it. Sun Ch'ien's story, published in 1958, was also picked as a target. It is a story of another discharged soldier who finds his home villagers extremely backward. His effort to spread the Communist message among them meets only frustration and resistance. The story moves at a fast pace; the characters are very convincing. But these qualities did not win the critics' favor.

Chao, Sun, Yüeh, and other writers like them were labeled revisionists because the Party considered them to be advocates of modification of the current policy.

YÜEH YEH
(1925?–)

The publication of *Together through Thick and Thin* in 1956 won popularity for Yüeh Yeh, because the play treated with considerable artistry the tragicomic entanglements of life that awaited the Communist cadres who had just emerged from peasantry to an elite status. Unfortunately, the author's effort to be faithful to what he saw as real—the human foibles to which all, including the Communists, are susceptible—could not be tolerated by the Party orthodoxy. In 1960, when the campaign against revisionism in literature gained intensity, Yüeh Yeh's works were severely condemned. The charge was that he championed the universality of human nature, which defies the class theory.
—K.Y.H.

from *Together through Thick and Thin*

ACT ONE

SCENE ONE
Five o'clock P.M. in March 1955. In the capital city of a province in North China.

On stage we see a fairly good-sized living room, which is on the second floor of the newly constructed dormitory for cadres in the Provincial Party Committee. This is the new residence of MENG SHIH-CHING, *Assistant Director of the Rural Work Department under the Province's Party Committee, and his family. Almost anyone would judge these quarters to be quite good, with the possible exception that the walls and woodwork have been painted in colors a bit too loud. It is not known which "high class" decorator deserves the credit for this "contribution." The living room also serves as the dining area. Slightly left of center on the back wall (upstage) is the door to the hallway, which functions as the main door to this apartment. There are two other doors on the right side of the back wall, one to the room used by the servant (who takes care of* MENG HUA, *their eight-year-old daughter) and the other to the kitchen. The door on the right-hand wall leads to a bedroom. The sofa, dining table, chairs and stools, etc. are scattered about the living room at random. Furthermore, every piece of furniture is piled high with unopened luggage, books, picture frames, dolls, and all kinds of household articles, indicating that the occupants have just moved in and have yet to get things settled.*

391

CHIA HSIU-LING, *the governess (and housekeeper) in this family, enters from the door to the kitchen carrying a large white porcelain bowl filled with steaming soup. The bowl is so hot that she comes on stage gasping and sucking in air through her teeth. No more than eighteen or nineteen years old, she's quite pretty with glossy black hair, a peaches-and-cream complexion, large eyes and lips; her eyebrows are a bit on the thick side.*

(Someone is knocking at the main door)

CHIA HSIU-LING (*Carrying the steaming tureen of soup in both hands, she yells out toward the door*) Whew—. Come in please! (*As she speaks, some soup spills onto her hands and is so hot it stings them. This makes her all the more unsteady and more soup spills over the edge of the bowl to her hands. She can't control it enough to be able to set it down, and finally she cries out from the pain*)

(*The person outside in the hall has heard her cries and, pushing the door open, enters. This is* CHI TA-CH'ENG, *a messenger boy for the Provincial Government. He's a clumsy and impulsive young fellow and hurries right over to* CHIA HSIU-LING. *Taking the large soup bowl from her he sets it down on the dining table. She waves her hands up and down through the air just like a raven beating its wings and blows on them.* CHI TA-CH'ENG *turns back toward her and also helps blow on her smarting hands*)

CHIA HSIU-LING (*Hurriedly hiding her hands behind her back*) Thank you. Who are you looking for?

CHI TA-CH'ENG (*Without looking carefully at the person to whom he's speaking, quite respectfully*) I take it you must be Comrade Hua, wife of Director Meng?

CHIA HSIU-LING Hua . . . no, she's not at home.

CHI TA-CH'ENG Then you are . . .

CHIA HSIU-LING I'm the governess here.

CHI TA-CH'ENG The governess? I know all the governesses around here. How is it I've never seen you before?

CHIA HSIU-LING I've only arrived today.

CHI TA-CH'ENG There, you see? I knew I hadn't seen you before. (*He sits down to chat with her*) What street are you from?

CHIA HSIU-LING I . . . uhh, no, that street of ours doesn't have any name.

CHI TA-CH'ENG That's funny! What street in this city doesn't have a name? How could the mail be delivered? Do you mean to say that we now have some unauthorized streets?

CHIA HSIU-LING (*Blowing on her hands again*) I'm from the country.

CHI TA-CHEN Oh! You're one of those who are "drifting into the cities without permission or good reason."

CHIA HSIU-LING No, I'm not! I have a letter of introduction from the village government and I'm not "drifting in"! I have a "good reason," which is that they've disbanded the Agricultural Producers' Cooperative in our village and that's why I came here to find a job. Do you want me to show you that letter of introduction?

CHI TA-CH'ENG That's all right, no need to trouble yourself over that.

CHIA HSIU-LING (*Keeping the conversation going and very much on equal terms with him*)   Where do you work?

CHI TA-CH'ENG (*Points back over his shoulder [at the satchel on his back] with his thumb*)

CHIA HSIU-LING (*Not understanding his gesture, looks behind him and sees a chair there*)   In a ... in a carpenter's shop?

CHI TA-CH'ENG (*Perturbed*)   Huh, what do you mean a carpenter's shop? I'm a messenger for the Party Committee. I work with Director Meng. (*At this he recalls his own job and hurries to swing the bag he's carrying on his back around in front of him; now he takes out a large envelope and another small one*)   Here's one stamped with the word "urgent"—you understand that means it's something that can't wait, don't you? Right, that's this big one. I just took it over to Director Meng's office and they told me he had already left for home. Now I'm giving it to you to give to him. As soon as he gets home, you will give it to him immediately, instantly, and without any delay, okay? If Comrade Hua Yün, Director Meng's wife, comes home first, you can just hand this over to her right away and she'll know how to deal with it. This small one is an ordinary letter, just a regular piece of mail; all you have to do is to see that they get both of them, all right?

CHIA HSIU-LING (*Taking the letters from him*)   Okay.

CHI TA-CH'ENG (*Expertly slinging his letter bag back around to where it normally hangs behind him, tugs on his cap and is about to depart, when he feels thirsty*)   Would you happen to have some water here?

CHIA HSIU-LING   Yes, of course!

CHI TA-CH'ENG   Where?

CHIA HSIU-LING   In the water pipes; you can have as much as you want.

CHI TA-CH'ENG   No, I meant boiled water, to drink. I'm thirsty.

CHIA HSIU-LING   Uhhh, I can have some for you in a jiffy. How would it be if you just sit down for a minute and I'll put some water on to boil for you?

CHI TA-CH'ENG   Forget it, I wouldn't want you to go to all that trouble. (*As he heads out the door*)   Be seeing you, Comrade Chia Hsiu-ling.

(*He exits*)

(HSIU-LING *looks at the letters she's holding, unable to decide where to put them, when she suddenly remembers she has left something cooking on the stove and runs into the kitchen, taking the letters with her*)

(*A brief pause*)

(HUA YÜN *comes in from the main door looking very tired and leading her daughter,* MENG HUA, *in by the hand.* HUA YÜN *at thirty-one still looks no more than twenty-four or twenty-five. She is tall, full-figured, and pretty. The spring outfit on her is of good material and well tailored but conservatively colored. Her hair has been given a permanent but so subtly that it looks completely natural. She has large eyes beneath slender eyebrows with very long eyelashes and teeth as lustrous as white jade behind those gleaming red lips. Her manner of expressing herself is just as crisp and adroit as her way of doing things. Because she is more gifted than most people in many aspects, she frequently betrays a certain sense of superiority. She tends to find fault with others for being too slow or clumsy precisely because of the quickness of her mind and deftness of her hands. Her personality inclines toward impatience; she doesn't like to play second fiddle to anyone and she is stubborn and unyielding on the surface, but actually she's relatively fragile and willfully unpredictable.* MENG HUA, *eight years of age, is very bright and pretty, just like her mother, but also has something of her father's masculine temperament. She has the best and prettiest clothes of anyone in the family*)

HUA YÜN (*Heaving a sigh and taking off her scarf, she sits down on the sofa*) Aiya! Well, that's one more thing taken care of anyway. (MENG HUA *takes off her jacket, folds it neatly and lays it to one side*) Aiya, just look at all this stuff heaped up around here! That Hsiu-ling, I told her to get all this picked up and she hasn't even touched it. Hsiu-ling, oh, Hsiu-ling!

MENG HUA (*Looking about the room, then pushing open the door to the bedroom*) Mommy, Daddy still isn't home yet!

HUA YÜN (*Glances at her watch*) I knew he wouldn't get back ahead of us. Hua, my pet, please sit down and rest a bit, won't you?

MENG HUA It's really no fair! We agreed everyone should be back here at six o'clock. Mmmm, I'm so hungry. (*She sees the soup and other food on the table*) Mommy, the soup's already on and everything!

HUA YÜN What? She made the soup first? What about the other courses? (*Walks over to look*) And nothing's been covered up, it's all getting cold. Just look at what a mess we're in, getting transferred to a new job, having to move, changing the governess, it's such a bother!

MENG HUA I'm happy!

HUA YÜN You little imp, you're just saying that in order to be contrary, aren't you?

MENG HUA No, tomorrow I get to go study in a new school, Mommy. Aren't you happy? (*She pulls at her mother*) Aren't you, Mommy?

HUA YÜN I'm happy, I'm happy. Hmmph! In order to get you enrolled in a new school, Mommy's run her legs off today until they're ready to break, but your father hasn't lifted one little finger in this.

MENG HUA He's busy!

HUA YÜN So? Mommy's not busy too? As soon as he's transferred to a new position, our whole family's sent into a tizzy and we have a thousand and one things to do too: you have to be admitted to a new school and I have to tag along in Daddy's footsteps and also get myself transferred to a new job here. Oh, I hope to heaven this time we will settle down and stay in one place!

MENG HUA Not me, I hope Daddy will get transferred every day!

HUA YÜN What's that?

MENG HUA Then I could go traveling with Daddy (*Making grand sweeps with her arms and declaiming like a poet in recital*) to every part of China.

HUA YÜN Heh, this father and daughter pair certainly are made for each other! Nonetheless, Little Hua, come over here and sit by Mommy. I want you to know that this time we're going to stay put right here for a few years! Your Daddy worked in eastern China for more than four years, but he's a northerner and he missed his home area and Grandma a lot. His home village is not far from here.

MENG HUA Grandma, Grandma . . . (*Her little mouth starts to pout*) I'm already eight years old and I still don't know what Grandma Meng looks like. It's no fair!

HUA YÜN   You? Even *I* have yet to meet Grandma!

MENG HUA   How come Grandma has never come to live with us?

HUA YÜN   Your father wrote so many letters to her, asking her to come, but she never did. She said she couldn't bear to leave her old home and also objected to the weather in the south being too hot and rainy. She said she wouldn't ever get used to it.

MENG HUA   I got used to it. Mommy, I got used to living everywhere we lived, didn't I? You count 'em up! Harbin, Shih-chia-chuang, Tientsin, Shanghai, Nanking, Hangchow . . . Uhh, oh, yes, yes there was also "Ch'i-ch'i-ha-erh"?

HUA YÜN (*Laughs*)   What do you know about Ch'i-ch'i-ha-erh? After you were born we stayed there only two months before we moved away.

MENG HUA   But that still counts as having been there, Mommy, I've been there too. Isn't that right, Mommy?

HUA YÜN (*Laughing*)   Yes, you may count it as your hometown.

MENG HUA   Hopei is Daddy's home province, Kiangsu is Mommy's home province and Ch'i-ch'i-ha-erh is my home town. Mom, since joining the revolution how many places have I been to?

HUA YÜN   What? What? Joining the revolution?

MENG HUA   That's right, Mommy, haven't I been growing up right along with the revolution?

HUA YÜN (*This time really having a good laugh*)   Yes, yes, if you figure it up like that, starting from when you were born, you already have a revolutionary history of eight years and two months.

MENG HUA   Aiya! I'm dying of hunger! Why in the world hasn't Daddy come home for supper yet? It's just too mean of him! (*The sound of someone knocking on the door*)

MENG HUA (*Jumps up*)   Daddy's here! (*She runs over to open the door*)
(CHANG LAN-O, *an accountant in a department store, slowly sticks her head in the door. She's forty-two years old, quite plump, and a believer in helping nature out with heavy applications of all man-made resources available for beautifying oneself. Waved hair, painted eyebrows, rouged lips—there is nothing subtle about her use of cosmetics. She is forthright and outspoken in character, quite contented with her lot in life, "zealous in pursuit of the public interest," and always ready to socialize*)

CHANG LAN-O (*Halfway in through the door*)   Is this the place? (*She discovers* HUA YÜN *there*) Oh, Hua Yün, can it be that I've actually tracked you down?

HUA YÜN (*Peering a moment to make out who it is*)   Lan-o? Is that you, cousin?

CHANG LAN-O   Aiya, I heard you had arrived. I've been saying how I must come see you but have been so busy. It's been years since I've seen you, Hua Yün. You're looking healthier than ever and have put on some weight, haven't you? Ah, look here at me, Hua Yün, wouldn't you say I'm a bit thinner than before?

HUA YÜN (*Constrained by politeness*)   Yes, I'd say so. How are you?

CHANG LAN-O (*Noticing* MENG HUA)   Who have we here? Is this your daughter? What's her name?

MENG HUA   I'm Meng Hua. How do you do, Auntie?

CHANG LAN-O   Very well, thank you. Such a good little girl! (*Cupping* MENG HUA'S *face in her hands*) If you aren't just a little replica of your mother! (*Turns back toward* HUA YÜN) She's just as pretty as you!

(HSIU-LING *enters with a hot dish of food*)

HUA YÜN   Hsiu-ling, Little Hua is hungry, would you serve her some food ahead of us so she can have something now?

MENG HUA   Mommy, I'll go wash my hands first and maybe Daddy will get back right away.

HUA YÜN   That's fine, dear, you go do that.

(HSIU-LING *sets down the dish of food and exits with* MENG HUA)

CHANG LAN-O (*Sitting down, she notices* HUA YÜN'S *scarf draped over the sofa*) My goodness, Hua Yün, are you still so partial to green? (HUA YÜN *gives her a noncommittal smile.* CHANG LAN-O *scrutinizes her*) What's this, are you pregnant again?

HUA YÜN (*Laughs, partially at the question and partially because this older cousin on her mother's side is still the same as ever*)   No! (*She pulls her jacket smooth and sits down, now changing the subject*) You and your husband are both very well, I take it?

CHANG LAN-O   He's just fine except he's never at home.

HUA YÜN   Where does he go?

CHANG LAN-O   He's still in that same old line of work—he works in commerce, has to travel all over the place, you know.

HUA YÜN   Are the two of you still getting along as well as ever?

CHANG LAN-O (*Tickled pink at this*)   Hmmph! Every time he has to go off on business he says he can't bear to leave me, simply can't do without me, but when it comes time for his departure he somehow manages to do just that. Who knows what he really feels? To tell you the truth, I'm beginning to have my doubts about him.

HUA YÜN (*Laughing*)   How can you say that? After being happily married all these years?

CHANG LAN-O   No, Hua Yün, according to what I've seen and figured out, there are men who are just terrible, they get married one day and divorced the next, married then divorced, divorced and then married, just like casually changing partners in a dance hall. On the other hand, my old Chao is not so bad. He's not brave enough to pull anything like that.

HUA YÜN (*Doesn't want to continue in this vein*)   How's your job? Are you still working in accounting?

CHANG LAN-O   Yup, accounting! At first I worked at the People's Bank but now I've been transferred to a department store. (*She looks around*) This apartment's pretty nice. Aiya, things are still in a mess, it really looks like you just moved in. (*Walks over to a mirror and turns first one way and then another, all the while admiring herself*) Hua Yün, that outfit you're wearing is too plain. Now's the time of our happy, new society, we should get a little more dressed up. Oh, yes, where's your husband?

HUA YÜN (*A bit lonely and downcast*)   He still hasn't come back. Haven't I just been waiting and waiting for him to get back so we can eat dinner? By the way, have you had dinner?

CHANG LAN-O   I've eaten, thanks. Actually, I'm on my way to the theater but since it's still early I thought I'd drop by and see you. Also I'm waiting for someone else. Hua Yün, you'll never guess what! Who do you think is taking me to the theater this evening?

HUA YÜN   How should I know?

CHANG LAN-O   Liang Shang-chün! Do you remember him? You certainly must remember him. He still isn't married.

HUA YÜN   I thought I heard a couple of years ago that he had gotten married.

CHANG LAN-O   No, he's never married. Gosh, he surely has come up in the world. He's an editor at a newspaper and also is a writer. Now, there is someone whose star is on the rise! He simply pulls money in by the bushel for his manuscripts and is quite the man about town. And when he holds forth on some subject, I can't even understand him.

HUA YÜN   Yes, when it comes to writing, we'd have to say he is talented. I read one of his pieces somewhere recently.

CHANG LAN-O (*Laughing*)   You see, you still do notice him. Did you know that he, Liang Shang-chün, asked me about you? He told me that there had been a time once when he was ardently pursuing you and that it was a very heavy blow to him when you hit it off with old Meng and then got married to him.

HUA YÜN (*Tries to stop her*)   What's the point of going into all that?

CHANG LAN-O   He's heard that you've come here to work and he'd very much like to see you. We arranged to meet here first this evening in order to see you and then we'll go on from here to the theater. He'll probably be here any minute now.

HUA YÜN (*Somewhat uneasy*)   Oh?

CHANG LAN-O (*Lighting a cigarette*)   Ai, human relationships are all so hard to figure out.

HUA YÜN   But this room is in such a state. (*She begins to arrange the chairs when there's a knocking at the door*)

CHANG LAN-O (*As if she were master of the home*)   Please come in.

(*As the door opens*, LIANG SHANG-CHÜN *walks in with a winning élan, a smile playing at the corner of his lips. He's thirty-nine years old, of medium height, as natty as can be, with a lightweight coat worn over his beige-colored Sun Yat-sen suit. His face has the shape of a melon seed, wide at the brow with a pointed chin, and if you look very closely you can detect a few shallow pockmarks pitting his cheeks. These are, however, not at all ugly and actually add that little something to an already handsome visage. Upon seeing* HUA YÜN, *he quickly transfers the books and magazines to his left hand and extends his right one to shake* HUA YÜN's)

LIANG SHANG-CHÜN   Hua Yün, Hua Yün, how are you?

HUA YÜN (*Her face a bit flushed for some strange reason*)   Very well, and how are you, Shang-chün? (*She tries to pull her hand back but it is still held tightly in his grip*)

LIANG SHANG-CHÜN   I'm just fine, too. Aiya, it's been such a long time, hasn't it? (*After repeatedly squeezing and shaking her hand, he finally releases it*)

HUA YÜN   That's for sure. Please have a seat, won't you? We've just moved in and things are in quite a jumble.

CHANG LAN-O (*Laughs*)   Aiya, seeing the two of you together, well, it truly seems like witnessing a reunion full of historic significance.

LIANG SHANG-CHÜN   Lan-o, have you been here long? Hua Yün, don't trouble yourself, we have to go right away. There's not much time left.

HUA YÜN   You've been writing quite a bit in these past few years. I really admire people like you who have accomplished something.

LIANG SHANG-CHÜN (*Glibly*)   Don't say that. I haven't done anything worth mentioning in recent years, partially because I've been working as an editor and that leaves me little time for writing, but also because things in general ... well, they just aren't very stimulating and so I'm not inclined to write. And if one wants to write something that will really "come to grips with life," it's not so easy to get it published; consequently, I don't write much of anything nowadays.

HUA YÜN   When I was in the south I read your articles and I thought they were very good.

LIANG SHANG-CHÜN (*Excitedly*)   No, those things were all very superficial. Now I feel very strongly about the importance of having pieces which boldly come to grips with life. Otherwise you publish something one day only to have it forgotten by the next and there's simply not much point to it. That's why I've been making plans recently to go down to the countryside for a while and then put some serious work into writing something truly worthwhile when I come back. As for being criticized, I've got that one pretty well figured out. Someone criticizes you, you criticize them right back. You can't get anywhere at all unless you're willing to struggle!

CHANG LAN-O (*Yawns, then suddenly remembers to look at her watch*)   Say, comrade writer, the performance is about to start, don't you think we'd better get going?

LIANG SHANG-CHÜN   Yes, yes, let's go. Hua Yün, you must come over to our place someday soon, okay?

CHANG LAN-O   Don't worry about that, she'll come over. Hua Yün, Liang Shang-chün is now renting a room from us, ahh, this tenant of ours, um, he doesn't pay rent but he has all kinds of critical suggestions about the place. We must go now or we won't see any of the first act. They've now made it a rule that no one will be admitted after the curtain rises.

LIANG SHANG-CHÜN   Well, let's be off then.

CHANG LAN-O   Hmmph, probably I'll have the dubious pleasure of seeing a play without its first act just because of this little reunion. We'll be seeing you, Hua Yün.

HUA YÜN (*Walking them to the door*)   Good-bye. I won't see you down the stairs if you don't mind. (CHANG LAN-O *takes* LIANG SHANG-CHÜN's *arm and is saying something to him as the two of them exit*)

(HUA YÜN *turns back and, heaving a sigh, goes to sit down on the sofa. She knows she will still have to wait awhile longer.* MENG HUA *comes bounding into the living room from the kitchen*)

MENG HUA   Mommy, I've had my dinner in the kitchen. How come Daddy ...

(*At this point the main door opens without warning and in walks* MENG

SHIH-CHING, MENG HUA's *father. He is thirty-nine years old and is the Assistant Director of the Party Committee's Rural Work Department. Tall and strongly built, he is wearing a black wool uniform. As usual he has ignored the proprieties not only by leaving the high, tight-fitting collar of his jacket unbuttoned but even by leaving his shirt collar open at the neck so that the rumpled neckline of his undershirt spills out into full view every now and again. He has a square-set face and because of his deep preoccupation with his work, his sideburns are becoming shaggy, while the wrinkles connecting the nose to the mouth corners, which indicate a determined will, are becoming ever more deeply etched into his face. Beneath the slender, arched eyebrows a pair of large eyes sparkle with intelligence and honesty. His is a mind that focusses on the important things and skips over trivialities and petty concerns. He works conscientiously and hard from dawn to dusk)*

MENG SHIH-CHING (*Carrying a large, brown briefcase under his arm while tearing open a big envelope, he enters, looking calm and unruffled*) How's my Little Hua? (*He bends down to look at his daughter*)

MENG HUA Daddy! Daddy's home. (*She reaches up to throw her arms around his neck and demonstratively, noisily covers his face with kisses*)

MENG SHIH-CHING (*Picks his daughter up in his arms and gives her a kiss*) Have you had your dinner?

HUA YÜN (*Becoming animated and cheerful*) She waited for you so long, she got hungry and ate ahead of us. (*Taking her husband's briefcase and papers out of his hands*) Let's eat right away, what time is it getting to be?

MENG SHIH-CHING (*Setting down* MENG HUA) I've already had dinner.

HUA YÜN Now, really, you agreed that we would wait for you and have dinner together and you didn't even call to let us know you wouldn't be back for dinner.

MENG SHIH-CHING We don't have our phone hooked up yet here, now do we? Several old comrades unexpectedly turned up and I had to go to dinner with them. If you haven't eaten yet, you'd better eat right away. (*So saying, he picks up his briefcase and papers and takes them over to the sofa, where he sits down and starts going over them*)

HUA YÜN (*Sighs softly, then walks over to switch on the lamp, pours out a cup of tea for her husband and takes it over to him*) Why don't you take a break when you've just gotten home?

MENG SHIH-CHING (*Has not yet understood the import of his wife's words*) Umm, I'm not tired. (*He takes the cup of tea and automatically puts it down on the floor while continuing to read*) Little Hua, wouldn't you like to come over here and keep Daddy company while he's working? Now don't squirm, just watch Daddy write, okay? (*He takes out his fountain pens and jots down comments in the margins of the papers he's reading*)

HUA YÜN (*Sits down facing her husband*) You don't have anything on for tonight, do you? I mean, you won't be going out?

MENG SHIH-CHING Uhh, that's right. Oh, no, wait a minute, it's nothing special but I do have to run over to the Agricultural Institute at nine o'clock just for a little while.

HUA YÜN At least I got the problem of transferring Hua into a new school here settled this afternoon.

MENG SHIH-CHING   Oh, really? That's nice. (HUA YÜN *still has something to say, but, noticing that her husband is completely absorbed in his papers, she is a bit put out and, getting to her feet, is about to leave him alone when he asks her*)

MENG SHIH-CHING   By the way, was there any mail for me today?

HUA YÜN   No, nothing. (*She stands there waiting for* SHIH CHING *to ask her something about her day*)

MENG SHIH-CHING   Little Hua, sit still there while Daddy goes to get something. (*He gets up and starts off toward the bedroom door.* HUA YÜN *can't take any more of this; tears well up in her eyes and she sits back down.* MENG SHIH-CHING *finally realizes something's amiss*) Why don't you have your dinner?

HUA YÜN   I'm not hungry.

MENG SHIH-CHING   Is something the matter?

HUA YÜN (*Won't look at him*)   What do you think? (MENG HUA *stares wide-eyed at her parents for a minute and then has the good sense to make herself scarce; she runs toward the bedroom*)

MENG SHIH-CHING   That's a good girl, Hua . . . you play by yourself awhile and Daddy'll come tell you a bedtime story by and by.

MENG HUA   All right. (*She exits*)

HUA YÜN   As soon as you get home, you throw yourself into your work. What about me? Do you even remember that there's still someone named Hua Yün in this world?

MENG SHIH-CHING (*Tenderly*)   Do you really think I could forget that?

HUA YÜN   But you haven't shown a bit of concern over the problem of my job. I'm just as serious about my work as you, you know?

MENG SHIH-CHING (*Walks over to stand behind his wife's chair*)   Isn't it all settled that you're to work in the main People's Hospital of this province?

HUA YÜN   But I don't want to be the head of some section in the hospital; I want to do professional work.

MENG SHIH-CHING   It's already more than a year ago that you raised this issue. If you don't meet all the requirements, I just don't see what can be done about it.

HUA YÜN   If I always have to do administrative work and sit in an office, how can I ever meet the requirements?

MENG SHIH-CHING (*Still very gentle and considerate of her feelings*)   Weren't you given the chance to take the medical school entrance exam? If you weren't one of those selected there's nothing anyone can do.

HUA YÜN   If I have no chance to study because I'm doing administrative work all the time, of course I'm not going to pass the entrance exam.

MENG SHIH-CHING   Hua Yün, every time I hear you talking like this, I feel you aren't seeing things as clearly as you might. I think you're placing too much emphasis on the external factors! You're not strict enough in the demanding of yourself . . .

HUA YÜN   So here it comes again, my subjective willpower is insufficient, is it? I'm so tired from my job at the hospital every day that I'm completely beat, and yet instead of being able to rest when I get home from the office, I still have a million and one housekeeping chores to do. You're certainly not about to take on any of the housework. Now you tell me just how in the world I'm supposed to be able to study up? Hmmph, we who are born to be women are always behind the eight ball anyway. Let's just take the question of changing jobs. Whenever you men get transferred or switch jobs, we women have to go right along with you. Why is it that I always have to give up my job and tag along with you?

MENG SHIH-CHING (*Laughs just like a kid*)   Okay, okay, from now on I tag along after you, how would that suit you? If you want to become a student and go back to school again, I'll go with you. Just think how amusing it will be for a woman student to be dragging her hubby along to class with her. (*He takes her face in his hands from where he is standing behind her*) You lovable little fool!

HUA YÜN (*Smiling through her tears*)   Don't touch me, someone might come in. (*She twists around to rest her cheek against her husband's chest*) Shih-ching, oh, don't always pontificate to me about those grand principles. I want you to talk to me about the feelings in our hearts. You know that I'm all stirred up and unsettled. But even so you won't help me find a way out. No, you only know how to be your same old Assistant Director.

MENG SHIH-CHING (*Caressing his wife's hair*)   What is it you'd actually like to do?

HUA YÜN   I'd like ... I'm thinking about switching into some artistic line of work. What would you think of that?

MENG SHIH-CHING   If you think it's feasible then go ahead.

HUA YÜN   Yes. I'm already thirty-one this year, and how I regret not having made up my mind sooner. Just think of all the old friends who've made a name for themselves and accomplished big things. Whenever I see any of them I really feel embarrassed.

MENG SHIH-CHING   There's no need for that. One does not do a job well for the sake of impressing other people!

HUA YÜN (*Pulls away from him*)   You always have the truth on your side, don't you?

(HSIU-LING *enters with two sealed envelopes*)

CHIA HSIU-LING   Comrade Hua Yün, let me give ...

MENG SHIH-CHING   Whose are they? Mine! (*He takes them from* HSIU-LING) When did these arrive?

CHIA HSIU-LING   Late this afternoon.

MENG SHIH-CHING (*Patiently*)   From now on I want you to give anything that has come that day to me as soon as I get home. Exactly! Whenever an envelope has a big red "urgent" stamped on it, you must give it to me right away, don't set it down anywhere, do you understand?

CHIA HSIU-LING   Yes, I do. That kind is a "special delivery."

MENG SHIH-CHING   That's right!

HUA YÜN   Hsiu-ling, you may serve the food now, I want to eat. (HSIU-LING *politely acknowledges this and exits, only to return in an instant with the food. As* HUA YÜN *sits down at the table,* SHIH-CHING *has again become engrossed in his work ... he tears open that letter and reads it.* HSIU-LING *goes back into the kitchen*)

HUA YÜN (*In a normal tone of voice*)   Shih-ching, that "darling" elder cousin of mine, Chang Lan-o, stopped by today. And besides her, there was also an old acquaintance, I wonder if you remember him? Liang Shang-chün dropped in for a bit too.

MENG SHIH-CHING   Oh, yes. (*As he turns over the pages with his attention riveted, pondering their contents, he gradually begins to talk out loud*) ... experience of rectifying the cooperatives ... cutting back, guard against the risks of rushing ahead too fast. ... This is just like Chekiang. Is the whole country in the process of pulling back? (*He picks up the document and writes comments on the margins*)

HUA YÜN (*Starting to eat*)   Shih-ching, you won't forget now, will you? You're going with me to the hospital tomorrow morning. The two of us will talk things over with the hospital and get it settled that I'm to enroll in classes in order to prepare for the med school exams. You promised to go with me.

MENG SHIH-CHING   Look at this, it's a directive, I'm afraid I won't be able to go with you, tomorrow morning the Party Committee is having a meeting to discuss the issue of decreasing the number of Agricultural Producers' Cooperatives. You go ahead and go by yourself!

HUA YÜN (*Half-beaten and feeling very let down*)   I just knew it was going to be like this.

MENG SHIH-CHING   This, now look, Yün, really there's ...

HUA YÜN (*No longer able to eat, she puts down her rice bowl and heads toward their bedroom*)   All right, all right! I wouldn't want to inconvenience you.

MENG SHIH-CHING   Hua Yün, look here, there's a letter from my mother. (*He rips open that smaller envelope*) Hmm ... the cooperative in our village had been operating very well. ... What's this? The county magistrate went down to our village and forced them to split up the cooperative. ... what the hell is going on there?

HUA YÜN (*She has gone over to him and, leaning from behind him, one hand resting on his shoulder, is reading it along with him*)   Hey, Grandma says she's going to come see us.

MENG SHIH-CHING (*Delighted*)   You're right! Ha, ha, leave it to old Mom to think things through like this. She says that if she doesn't see us now that we're here, who's to say we won't be transferred to some distant place again one of these days and then she won't be able to see us. (*He hands the letter to* HUA YÜN) To tell you the truth, I really have been missing Mom quite a lot. She had a pretty rough time of it after I left home. Ever since I was a little boy, I was the apple of her eye and she loved me something fierce! Even when I was naughty, so naughty I made her cry, she never could bring herself to give me even a little slap.

HUA YÜN   You hardly need to tell me about how devoted you and your mother are to each other. In all the years I've known you, I've never seen you cry except for two times when you were thinking about your mother.

MENG SHIH-CHING   That never happened.

HUA YÜN   Never happened? Think about it again. Back in 1945, that same year I met you (*She immediately abandons herself to these happy memories*) ... you were in that military hospital. We nurses were putting on that amateur theatrical performance to cheer up you wounded soldiers. I remember how after the performance was over and I had changed out of my costume, I went to see you. You were sitting there in front of the window thinking about something and the moon was so bright that night and when you saw me coming over to you, you started talking to me about the play and then you went on to talk about everything. When you spoke of your home village, you naturally talked about your mother and the tears ran down your cheeks. . . . I didn't know whether or not I ought to give you my handkerchief, I just automatically took it out and was fumbling with it in my hands, but you, you wouldn't make the first move and ask me for it; oh, no, you were too proud, you had to wait for me to make the first gesture . . . you certainly were acting the big shot, weren't you?

MENG SHIH-CHING (*Also thinking back to those days*)   Ai, wasn't it I who first reached out and took hold of your hand?

HUA YÜN   Yes . . . but it was I who first leaned over to kiss you. (*She starts to laugh*) Do you remember, I barely murmured that your whiskers were prickly and you were so quick on the uptake that the very next day there was no one in the whole hospital who was as smoothly shaved as you! Weren't you ever embarrassed?

MENG SHIH-CHING (*Embraces his wife and kisses her face*)   Oh, well, you know all of my past secrets anyway. Of course you have the right to say these things. It's really interesting to think back: going to school, afterwards teaching primary school in our county, fighting in the guerrilla forces, winding up in that hospital, meeting you, going to the northeast, then going down south, now doing this agricultural work, organizing cooperatives . . . it all sounds so simple when you talk about it. I'm almost forty now and yet I still feel as if I'm not yet grown up.

HUA YÜN   Have you looked at the clothes you're wearing? You need to change your undershirt and you never button up your jacket properly! . . . I really have something to regret too. Why didn't I change my profession back then and go into some type of work in the arts? Now it's been ten years since then, I bet I would surely have done something worth mentioning by now!

MENG SHIH-CHING   Back then everyone did say you had the talent for the stage, didn't they? Why, you even got lots of love letters and proposals in each day's mail. Hey, you were quite a big hit.

HUA YÜN   I was too, but the strangest thing was that you never wrote a single line to me, nor did you ever give me the pleasure of hearing a single word of praise from you; even so, I went right ahead and fell blindly, head-over-heels in love with you!

MENG SHIH-CHING (*Jokingly*)   If you regret that, you'd better figure out what you want to do about it pretty soon, it's still not too late.

HUA YÜN   Ai, let's not be too sure about that. (*She discovers there's still a piece of stationery in the envelope and when she takes it out and unfolds it, a snapshot falls out*)   Ooh, there's a photograph in here too! Who is this? I seem to have seen this face somewhere before. (*She reads the name on the back of it*) It's Meng Chen!

MENG SHIH-CHING (*Looks at it*)   It sure is! The rascal. He's practically a man now!

HUA YÜN   He says here in the letter that he's now in middle school. He writes a very good hand too! Your son's going to accompany Grandma up here. He knows how to say the right thing, this lad, says he's eager to see his younger sister but he doesn't mention anything about his mother. Uhh, I wonder how your "feudal missus"* has been getting along recently?

MENG SHIH-CHING [*Not at all happy to have this subject raised, reaches out, and* HUA YÜN *hands him the snapshot and letter from his son*] I don't know.

HUA YÜN   Meng Chen looks very much like you. Let's see, he's already fifteen or sixteen!

MENG SHIH-CHING   Yup.

HUA YÜN [*Teasing him*] I got it. Why don't you take back Meng Chen's mother and the two of you can live together like a good old happy couple. I'll take Little Hua and go back to Kiangsu.

MENG SHIH-CHING   If I could live with a woman like that who doesn't understand a thing, I wouldn't have ever gotten together with you. Just as in my decision to marry you, comrade, there was nothing casual or impulsive about my decision to divorce her.

HUA YÜN   But everything has to change someday. Perhaps you should marry the one you divorced and divorce the one you married.

MENG SHIH-CHING [*Laughs*] Do you know, this reminds one of the opening line from *The Romance of the Three Kingdoms,* which goes, "It is said that when the forces under heaven have been divided for a long time they must coalesce; when they have been united for a long time they must split asunder." (MENG HUA *comes running out from the bedroom*)

MENG HUA   Aiya, Daddy, I've been reading in there and have already read through two whole comic books and you still haven't come in. The two of you are talking on and on out here without stopping. Hmmph! You seem to have so much to say to Mommy and so little to say to me! (*Her little mouth again begins to curl into a pout*)

MENG SHIH-CHING   Aiya, sorry, sorry, I do apologize to this young lady of ours. Come and let me teach you a riddle.

MENG HUA [*Happy*] Yeah, Yeah! Mommy, you try it too!

HUA YÜN   I think we'll let father and daughter work out the riddle while I try to put away some of this mess. (HUA YÜN *straightens things up while* SHIH-CHING *and little* HUA *sit down to one side*)

MENG SHIH-CHING   Now listen, I'll tell you four things in the four lines of this riddle and you have to guess what they are, okay?

The eldest sister calls out up in the tree;
The second sister jumps high with fright;
The third sister carries a stick, you see;
The fourth sister lights her lantern bright.

MENG HUA   Ha, ha, what is it? Are the four sisters playing a game, Dad? Is that it?

*She is referring to SHIH-CHING'S former wife, whom she calls *feng-chien lao-p'o,* or "feudal missus," thereby connoting that the marriage had been arranged for them by their families according to the traditional, "feudal" custom in China prior to 1949. [J.B.]

MENG SHIH-CHING Mmm, no, each of the lines I spoke stands for a different thing, altogether there are four different things.

MENG HUA Ennn ... I can't get it. Won't you tell me the answer now?

MENG SHIH-CHING I'll tell you: "The eldest sister calls out up in the tree" stands for a cicada; "The second sister jumps high with fright" means a grasshopper; "The third sister carries a stick, you see" stands for the praying mantis; and "The fourth sister lights her lantern bright" ...

MENG HUA (*A naturally gifted child, she instantly figures this last one out*) It's a firefly, isn't it, Daddy?

MENG SHIH-CHING That's right, that's it, very clever of you. (*He again opens his briefcase and takes out more papers to work on*)

MENG HUA Who taught it to you? That's a great riddle, Dad.

MENG SHIH-CHING Your grandma taught it to me.

MENG HUA Grandma is really smart! (*She tries to repeat it to herself*) "The eldest sister calls out up in the tree" is a grasshopper, is that right, Daddy?

MENG SHIH-CHING (*His mind elsewhere*) Uh-huh, that's right, clever girl.

MENG HUA "The second sister jumps high with fright" is a praying mantis, right, Dad?

MENG SHIH-CHING (*Responds without thinking*) Absolutely correct, right.

MENG HUA Aiya, that "third sister" who carries a stick has to be a praying mantis, too. Then what is it that "jumps high with fright"?

MENG SHIH-CHING Huh? It's a firefly.

MENG HUA No, it's not! If it's like this, then you'd have eldest sister, second sister, and also third and fourth sisters all calling out, jumping around like crazy, carrying long sticks and everything!

HUA YÜN (*Losing patience, throws down the thing in her hand and leads* MENG HUA *toward the main door*) Come on, Little Hua, Mommy will take you outside to play. (*Remonstrating with her husband*) If you consider your time so damn valuable, don't bother to go through the false motions of paying attention to us!

MENG SHIH-CHING Don't talk like that, all right? Don't you know that cold porridge and cold rice are much easier to take than cold words and cold comments?

HUA YÜN Even a few cold words and comments are more than we're likely to get out of you during the whole day!

(MENG SHIH-CHING *is going to say something else but then restrains himself.* HUA YÜN *is just about to lead* MENG HUA *out the door when from the other side of their main door is heard the robust voice of an elderly woman*)

OLD MRS. MENG (*From outside the door*) Shih-ching! Yoo-hoo, Shih-ching! Aren't you home? Aren't you going to come out and help me carry in these things?

MENG SHIH-CHING (*Listens very attentively to that voice*) Hey, isn't that my mother's voice? Mom's here! Aiya, can it really be? (*He rushes past* HUA YÜN *and* MENG HUA *to the door, throws it open, and stands excitedly in the doorway greeting his mother*) Mom, dear old Mom, it's really you!

(OLD MRS. MENG, *smudged with the dust from her journey, enters carrying a big bundle of things tied up in a piece of homespun cloth with a floral pattern. She is already sixty years old, but because she does demanding labor all year long, she's still strong and vigorous. Her face is a large square one like her son's and her complexion has been burnished a ruddy red by the sun. There's still not much white in her hair. She's wearing a new outfit of clothing, and all this, combined with the fact that it's in her basic nature to be cheerful, makes her look not a day over fifty*)

MENG SHIH-CHING (*Hastens to take the large bundle from her*)　Come on in and rest yourself, Mom. How are you?

OLD MRS. MENG　I'm fine, just fine (*Her glance falls on* HUA YÜN) So this is young Hua Yün, is it? (*In her eyes practically everyone's name should be prefixed with "young"*)

HUA YÜN　....

MENG SHIH-CHING　Greet mother, Yün!

HUA YÜN　Mother, you're finally here!

MENG HUA　Daddy, what'll I call her?

OLD MRS. MENG (*Laughs heartily*)　As soon as I saw her, I knew she had to be my granddaughter. She looks like me, yes, she does, she looks like me! Granddaughter, come here and let Grandma have a good look at you. (*She picks* MENG HUA *up in her arms*) You call me Grandma, you silly little thing!

MENG HUA　Grandma? You mean you're Daddy's mother, you're my grandmother?

OLD MRS. MENG　Uh-huh, that's right. That's something that will never change in your whole life, I'm your "grandma"!

MENG HUA (*Not the least bit shy*)　Aiya, Grandma, Daddy just taught me that riddle about the four sisters and I've got it all jumbled up. Will you teach me how to get the four of them straightened out?

OLD MRS. MENG　Sure, I'll teach you lots and lots of them. (*She walks over to the large bundle she's brought with her from the countryside and, after poking about in it for a while, fishes out a large triangular steamed dumpling stuffed with brown sugar*) Granddaughter! Come over here and get this "t'ang-san-chiao" sugar dumpling from your old Grandma. Go ahead, silly girl, take it. Grandma gives it to you, you can eat it.

MENG HUA　Grandma, I'm full.

HUA YÜN　She's just had her dinner and we don't let her snack in-between meals!

OLD MRS. MENG　What diffence does that make? Little kids can eat one of these without any problem at any time of the day. Their tummies will digest them in no time at all. Take it.

(MENG SHIH-CHING *signals to* HUA YÜN. HUA YÜN *has no choice except taking it from the grandmother on behalf of her daughter*)

HUA YÜN　Say thank you to Grandma. (*She gives the steamed dumpling to* MENG HUA, *who takes it and stands there, fully aware of the situation, holding it in her hand but not eating it*)

OLD MRS. MENG　Oh, Shih-ching, you'd best go out now to meet her. She's carrying a great big basket and was coming on along behind me, she should be getting here by now.

HUA YÜN   Uhh, Mother, who are you talking about? Didn't Meng Chen come along with you?

OLD MRS. MENG   No, it's Meng Chen's mother who's come along.

MENG SHIH-CHING   Huh? . . . Oh, well then, I suppose I better go help her. (*He exits*)

(OLD MRS. MENG *looks unblinkingly at* HUA YÜN, *who becomes flustered and busies herself aimlessly arranging things here and there, her emotions in a whirl*)

OLD MRS. MENG   How are the two of you getting along?

HUA YÜN   Us? We're just fine, Mother.

OLD MRS. MENG   That's all right then.

MENG SHIH-CHING (*Offstage, his voice heard coming from the rear on the other side of the main door*)   Let me, let me give you a hand with that!

WOMAN'S VOICE (*of* LIU FANG-WEN *offstage*)   It's not necessary, we're already here, it's fine!

(MENG SHIH-CHING *pushes open the door and quickly steps aside to allow* LIU FANG-WEN, *his former wife, to enter carrying a large, heavy basket with netting serving as its lid.* LIU FANG-WEN *is thirty-seven, of medium height and a sturdy build. Her oval-shaped face is of a very ruddy complexion and she has a pair of bright, inquisitive eyes. Her hair is thick and black, no longer wound into a bun but cut short. She does farm work all year long and thus moves with the quickness and sureness of a man. However, she is very good-natured and obliging, and there's a certain special aura about her that appeals to people, which comes from her unassuming self-confidence and the iron will underneath her gentleness*)

OLD MRS. MENG   Set it down and have a rest, Fang-wen.* (*She turns to her son*) After we got off the train, I told her to hire a porter to carry it for us but she wouldn't hear of it, wouldn't consider spending any money for that.

LIU FANG-WEN   It's not so heavy. Mother, which room are you going to be using? Where should I put this?

OLD MRS. MENG   You silly, I've only just arrived here. I haven't had a chance yet to learn the frying pan from the stove, so how would I know where they're going to put me up? (*She glances out of the corner of her eye at her son and* HUA YÜN) Anyway, just as long as they don't expect me to sleep outside in the courtyard, anywhere will do. Just set the basket down for now and catch your breath. We'll worry about that later!

(LIU FANG-WEN *sets the basket down out of the way for the time being, straightens up, pats her hair into place and turns round to look at* SHIH-CHING. *He evades her glance. She transfers her gaze to* HUA YÜN. FANG-WEN *already knows full well who this must be and she says nothing.* MENG HUA *gives her mother a puzzled look and then looks again at* FANG-WEN. FANG-WEN *opens wide her arms in an inviting gesture to* MENG HUA, *who is instantly attracted by her motherly affection and goes over to cuddle up close to* FANG-WEN. *This child is very sensitive and since none of the grown-ups are*

---

*In the original, OLD MRS. MENG follows the traditional peasant form of address and calls LIU FANG-WEN by the kinship term, MENG CHEN'S MOTHER, or "Meng Chen chia niang." [J.B.]

saying anything, she also keeps quiet and just stands there gazing up intently into FANG-WEN'S *face. Everyone stands there awkwardly, all at a loss for something to say*)

MENG SHIH-CHING (*Breaking the ice*)   Mother, wouldn't you like to freshen up a bit? Hsiu-ling, Hsiu-ling, hurry up and draw some water!
(*Stage dims*)

SCENE TWO

A few hours later the same evening, the same place. OLD MRS. MENG *and her son,* SHIH-CHING, *are sitting on the sofa catching up on things. The living room has been straightened up a bit, and there now is a single bed set up, which* LIU FANG-WEN *is making up as* MENG SHIH-CHING *and his mother reminisce about the old days.* [He tells her that their old family friend Shuai Chien-hui, who once lived in their home and was so poor his toes stuck out of his shoes, has risen through the ranks to become vice-minister of logistics for the People's Liberation Army and is in Peking, only a few hours away by train. Awkwardness is in the air. LIU FANG-WEN tries to leave to spend the night elsewhere, but OLD MRS. MENG won't permit it. We learn that FANG-WEN, her first daughter-in-law, has stuck by her through the very hard times during the war with Japan when SHIH-CHING was off fighting in the guerrilla forces and that OLD MRS. MENG is convinced she would never have survived except for FANG-WEN'S loyalty and help. The old lady begins to assert herself and orders that everyone is to stay and be nice to everyone else.

HUA YÜN feels quite threatened at the sudden appearance of SHIH-CHING'S first wife, while he tries hard to avoid any conflict with his mother. He reassures her that he feels nothing toward LIU FANG-WEN and that FANG-WEN has nothing to do with them. But this totally unexpected event forces him to reveal to HUA YÜN for the first time that when he went back to his native village in 1952 and finally obtained a legal divorce from his first wife, he was pleasantly surprised to find LIU FANG-WEN quite amenable to the idea, and he felt constrained to honor her sole demand: that he not tell his mother about the divorce, since it would needlessly cause the old lady a lot of heartache. Thus OLD MRS. MENG still believes that both LIU FANG-WEN and HUA YÜN are legally married to her son. HUA YÜN is deeply hurt that SHIH-CHING has hidden this from her for more than three years.

We pick up the scene from the point where LIU FANG-WEN has come out from the kitchen, where she has been with OLD MRS. MENG. She and her former husband talk about the difficulties encountered in organizing and strengthening the Agricultural Producers' Cooperative in their home village. It turns out that LIU FANG-WEN is not at all the simple, subservient, traditional peasant woman in MENG SHIH-CHING'S memory. In fact, she has come up to the provincial capital not to see him and his family but rather to seek assistance from higher levels in opposing the county magistrate's high-handed efforts to disband their cooperative.]

LIU FANG-WEN (*Telling him all about their co-op in clear and well-ordered fashion*)   After we first organized the cooperative everything was going along just fine. Except for a few households of landlords and rich peasants, everyone was very much in favor of establishing the cooperative. A couple of weeks ago, our county magistrate, Magistrate Chou, uhh, he's none other than that old schoolmate of yours—later on I believe you and he taught for a time at the same school. His full name is Chou Ming-te. Well, to go on, Magistrate Chou led a work team down to our area to rectify the cooperative. First they rectified this and then rectified that and finally they rectified our co-op right out of existence.

MENG SHIH-CHING (*Extremely interested*)   Please sit down, sit, sit down right here on this sofa and tell me all about it.

LIU FANG-WEN (*Walks unabashedly to sit in a chair across from where he is sitting on the sofa*) Aren't you working here in the provincial government? Do you happen to know where I can find the offices of our province's Party Committee? Are they easy to locate?

MENG SHIH-CHING (*Surprised at discovering a totally new woman in his former wife*)   Sure, the Party Committee is easy to find. Uhh, would you please go on telling me about this matter of rectification of the cooperative in our village?

LIU FANG-WEN   From where I stand, Old Chou's way of doing things is highly questionable. As soon as he got to our village, he would only listen to what our backward elements had to say and he arrived at his conclusion just like that: he feels that the problems confronting our cooperative are simply too numerous. He says the presence of so many problems might disrupt production. That means the best thing to do is break up the cooperative as soon as possible.

MENG SHIH-CHING   What are the real problems in your cooperative?

LIU FANG-WEN   That's exactly the point at issue here! They never got things straight. Even if there were problems, they never even took the trouble to investigate whether or not these problems could be gradually resolved if we all got together to work at them. If you ask me, this was nothing but forsaking the spirit of positive leadership. As soon as old Chou arrived, he put forward the proposition that we were developing too fast, that we did not have a sufficient foundation of mutual assistance. In point of fact, the level of mutual assistance in our village can be considered damn good. Besides all the rest of it, he claimed that the masses are split into factions between the east and west ends of the village and that the Party members there are not united firmly enough, thus if we went ahead with the co-op, we wouldn't be able to sustain it. Since his work team had this kind of opinion, it was first proposed in the Party meeting that . . .

MENG SHIH-CHING (*Interrupts*)   Huh, you've been admitted to the Party?

LIU FANG-WEN (*Laughs*)   Yes, you haven't kept up with things back home. I was accepted by the Party in 1950.

MENG SHIH-CHING (*Just heard another surprise*)   Oh?

LIU FANG-WEN   Right, anyway, at the Party meeting he first proposed that if we're going to keep the cooperative we should split it into three little ones according to household. The majority of Party members were opposed to this idea.

MENG SHIH-CHING   Why?

LIU FANG-WEN   This would amount to disbanding the co-op! You've forgotten, I suppose, but in our village a great majority of the families living in the west end are poor peasants, the northern section is composed entirely of established middle peasants and the east end is where the landlords and rich peasants live. If we organize ourselves into three separate small cooperatives along these lines, the two in the northern and eastern sections of the village will lack leadership activists and inevitably these three co-ops will turn into one for the poor peasants, one for the middle peasants, and one for the rich peasants. If that happens, how would we ever be able to carry out the "class line"?

(SHIH-CHING *is lost in thought over what he has just heard.* HUA YÜN *has changed into her pajamas and comes out from the bedroom. She is stunned to see the two of them having such a cozy conversation. She struggles to control herself and pretends not to have noticed anything*)

HUA YÜN   Shih-ching, have you forgotten? Don't you have to run over to the Agricultural Institute for something this evening?

MENG SHIH-CHING   Hmm? Oh, ahh, I'm not going now. (*He doesn't even turn to look at her but continues listening to* LIU FANG-WEN. HUA YÜN *is about to say something else to him but catches herself and angrily whirls around to go back into the bedroom*)

LIU FANG-WEN (*With no interruption of her train of thought*)   Old Chou wasn't interested in anyone else's opinion; no, instead he considered us all ideologically deficient, and, indiscriminately lumping the green-topped turnips together with the purple-topped garlic, he leveled a barrage of criticism at all of us. He immediately followed this up with the proposal that anyone who wanted to drop out of the co-op be free to do so. Of course, there were those members who hadn't been firmly committed in the first place and who now began to "waver" at this point. As for the actively committed members, uhh, they felt that whereas we usually couldn't get the county to send any leadership cadre down to us, now we finally got one but he turned out to be a little tin buddha. He's full of pretentious airs and bent on giving us a hard time. He made them feel that no matter how we organized our co-op it was no good, and, well, this took the wind out of their sails. So our sunny skies got clouded all over right before our eyes and this one rumbling thunderclap shook our co-op apart at the seams.

MENG SHIH-CHING (*So completely drawn into her account that he totally forgets their former relationship and the unhappy atmosphere that had descended upon his home earlier in the evening. He talks with her now just as one old friend to another*)   Was everyone willing to accept this?

LIU FANG-WEN   About fifteen or sixteen households of active members in our cooperative are right now laying plans to reestablish it.

MENG SHIH-CHING   So you feel that old Chou's way of handling things was not the correct one?

LIU FANG-WEN   He did not actively lead everyone along the path to socialism. Even when everyone wanted to go in that direction he wouldn't let us. So what could be correct about it? (*She laughs*) I even told him off!

MENG SHIH-CHING   What is your role in the cooperative?

LIU FANG-WEN   The group elected me as . . . vice-chairwoman of the co-op. The chairman is Yü-hou.

MENG SHIH-CHING (*Another surprise*)   You? Well, a vice-chairwoman of the co-op?

(MENG SHIH-CHING *can hardly recognize her as that young woman who once was the cause of so much frustration for him—no, actually it was their arranged "feudal marriage" that had caused the trouble. This woman sitting there facing him was someone totally different; she was a vigorous and capable chairwoman, enormous vitality radiating from her very being*)

MENG SHIH-CHING (*Pouring a cup of tea*)   Have some tea, won't you?

LIU FANG-WEN (*Now this is also something completely new for her*)   My goodness! No, you have it. I'll help myself when I want some.

MENG SHIH-CHING (*Pouring out a second cupful*)   Go ahead, I'll drink this one.

LIU FANG-WEN (*Lifts the cup to her lips and takes a sip, then hurries to stop* MENG SHIH-CHING, *who is about to drink some too*)   It's boiling hot; you'd better put it down and let it cool off a while. You don't like to drink it so hot.

MENG SHIH-CHING   You still remember all my little peculiarities, don't you?

LIU FANG-WEN (*Lowering her head*)   How could I forget them? In the old days you wouldn't touch tea that was the least bit hot. That time I served you a hot cup of tea you pulled an ugly face and said that I must be trying to scald you to death giving you such a hot cup of tea. You really scared the wits out of me and I rushed to pour your tea from one bowl into another to cool it down for you. Only after I got back to my own room did I dare to cry my heart out.

MENG SHIH-CHING (*Embarrassedly*)   Actually I didn't know what I was doing then. It was that feudal marriage system that was to blame. I shouldn't have been so mean to you.

LIU FANG-WEN   I wasn't blaming you, was I? ... (*She takes something out of her basket and affectionately hands it to* SHIH-CHING)   Here's some of our homestyle steamed cake you love to eat so much. We came away in such a rush I didn't have time to make any more of it for you.

MENG SHIH-CHING   Thank you very much.

LIU FANG-WEN   You used to neglect your meals even when we served up the food you liked best. Now that you're so busy with your work I'm sure you're even more likely to forget to eat. Little Hua's mother should be told that she needs to constantly remind you to be sure and eat your meals.

[OLD MRS. MENG emerges from HSIU-LING's room to find her son and LIU FANG-WEN getting on famously, and she discreetly withdraws, a gratified smile on her face. FANG-WEN tells SHIH-CHING all about his childhood friend, CHAN YÜ-HOU, chairman of their village's cooperative, who has been so good to SHIH-CHING's mother over the years that he's now practically like an adopted son. SHIH-CHING tells her that he is the assistant director in the Rural Work Department that CHAN YÜ-HOU has told FANG-WEN to seek out in the provincial capital. She is quite relieved to learn this but is wondering whether he approves of what she and the other villagers are doing in going against the leadership of the county. Although still very new in the job here, SHIH-CHING tells her that he suspects she and the other activists have done the correct thing.]

MENG SHIH-CHING   When I was working in Chekiang Province, I took exception to the casual disbanding of cooperatives with the result that I was criticized just as you have been. But before I had time to gather more dramatic evidence to support my view, I was transferred up here. I think our village's experience in the rectification of the co-op will help to clarify this problem a great deal. We'll go together to the Party Committee tomorrow, but since the secretary of the Party committee has gone to Peking for a meeting and we don't know exactly when he'll be back, we'll first speak with Director Wang of the Rural Work Department.

LIU FANG-WEN (*with rising spirits*)   Okay, that's fine.

(HUA YÜN *enters again from the bedroom door. She has not fallen asleep and has been anxiously waiting up for* SHIH-CHING)

HUA YÜN   Say, Shih-ching, it's getting to be quite late, isn't it time to sleep?

MENG SHIH-CHING   No, you go ahead. I have to go tomorrow morning ... to go with her to the Party Committee, and there are still some matters that I must go over carefully with her.

HUA YÜN (*Very hurt*)   Tomorrow morning I have to go to the People's Hospital, so I won't wait up for you any longer, I'm going to sleep now.

MENG SHIH-CHING   Fine, fine, you go ahead and get a good night's sleep, okay?

(HUA YÜN *bites her lip very hard for a moment and then, with tears in her eyes, exits*)

MENG SHIH-CHING (*To* FANG-WEN *with great animation and enthusiasm*)   Go on, give me all the details of the problems in our village. I also want to hear about any problems you know of in the county leadership, the more detailed the better. (*He takes out a small notebook to jot things down*)

LIU FANG-WEN   Right!

(*Curtain*)

ACT TWO

[The same setting three days later. OLD MRS. MENG and HSIU-LING are enjoying a friendly contest of wills, in which the sprightly old lady, with her pungent and colorful peasant tongue, is protesting not being allowed to help out with the housework, and the servant, who already adores her, tries to keep her from lifting a finger. HUA YÜN returns early from work and learns that LIANG SHANG-CHÜN has stopped by looking for her and that her husband and his former wife have gone out on yet another attempt to have their meeting with DIRECTOR WANG. OLD MRS. MENG has no idea whether they'll be back for dinner or not. HUA YÜN receives a phone call from LIANG, who invites her out to dinner. He wants her to read something he's written that has appeared in the newspaper that day. She accepts the invitation and tells her mother-in-law that she will be dining out.

The messenger boy, CHI TA-CH'ENG, shows up with two more letters for Assistant Director MENG and wants to see HSIU-LING. This time she has some boiled water already prepared for him if he's thirsty, and he likewise reveals his romantic interest in her by giving her a "top priority special delivery" letter in a flowery pink envelope.

SHIH-CHING and FANG-WEN, both looking unhappy, enter just as HUA

YÜN is going out and there is another awkward moment between her and SHIH-CHING before she coldly walks out the door. SHIH-CHING and FANG-WEN have finally succeeded in seeing DIRECTOR WANG, and we learn that the county magistrate, CHOU MING-TE, has beaten FANG-WEN to the punch by first sending in a written report and then following that up by personally calling on DIRECTOR WANG yesterday.

MENG SHIH-CHING is deeply perplexed by the fact that his new superior, DIRECTOR WANG, has taken the side of COUNTY MAGISTRATE CHOU in regarding the co-op in his home village as a negative model. LIU FANG-WEN is angry and unwilling to back down. OLD MRS. MENG is a bit concerned to learn that FANG-WEN was so bold as to argue openly with their county magistrate. FANG-WEN explains to OLD MRS. MENG about CHOU.]

LIU FANG-WEN   Mother, you just can't imagine how that man speaks out of both sides of his mouth at once. He doesn't act a bit like a leader in the Communist Party—all he does is play the big shot and throw his weight around. He won't consider listening to anything the masses have to say, nor is there any lie that he wouldn't tell.

OLD MRS. MENG   What's all this? What did he say?

LIU FANG-WEN   He said . . . he said that Yii-hou and I are so charged up about organizing the co-op purely for the sake of personal gain, and, and he said that the two of us . . . the two of us are unwilling to split up!

OLD MRS. MENG   What sort of talk was that? This old Chou, hmmph! Well, how about that Director? Wasn't there a Director Wang who was also present? What did he say?

LIU FANG-WEN   As far as I can tell, Director Wang's bureaucratism is no joke either.

OLD MRS. MENG (*Sighs*)   Oh, dear me! When you reap wheat you get stiff at the waist, and when you carry a load on your carrying pole you get a sore shoulder; every occupation has its hazards and those who became officials are always going to have a touch of bureaucratism. A candy-peddler beats a gong —every line has its own way of doing business. There is always too much to be done in any job and you can't expect the stick to hit the exact center of the drum every time, now can you? We must try to be a bit more tolerant.

LIU FANG-WEN   Mother, I can be tolerant of anything else but just don't ask me to be tolerant of bureaucratism. Just think of it! Without investigating or seriously thinking through this matter, Director Wang just insisted that the way we organize the co-op is like weaving a dozen nets in your mind before having a single thread in your hand—it's futile. Therefore he completely agrees with old Chou in tearing down our co-op. And that's not all, today he even decided to have old Chou report on the experience of rectifying our cooperative!

OLD MRS. MENG   Say, Shih-ching, what's going on here? (MENG SHIH-CHING *is pacing back and forth deep in thought and does not make any response.* OLD MRS. MENG *continues looking at him*) Hey, Shih . . . (FANG-WEN *quickly signals her with her eyes not to ask him anything right then*) All right, all right, it's not my place to interfere and I don't understand all this anyway. (OLD MRS. MENG *walks out into the kitchen*)

LIU FANG-WEN (*Pours out a glass of water for* SHIH-CHING) Are you hungry? I could heat up some steamed cake for you. (SHIH-CHING *shakes his head*) When do you think the Party Committee Secretary will actually come back?

MENG SHIH-CHING (*Pacing up and down*) Uhhh, hard to say.

LIU FANG-WEN (*Growing more and more disgruntled all the time*) Hmmph! There seems to be no more point in waiting for him. These officials always find it easier to get together and work things out among themselves rather than with common people like us anyway. Even when the Secretary does come back he'll be just the same as the others and won't want cadres like us from the little villages to be giving reports. Like the others he'll no doubt say something like "Of course, it is unquestionably praiseworthy to take the initiative in moving forward to socialism, however ..."

MENG SHIH-CHING No, he would not!

LIU FANG-WEN What do you mean he would not? It's clear to me that all you officials stick up for each other.

MENG SHIH-CHING Don't talk nonsense.

LIU FANG-WEN (*Feels somewhat unfairly treated*) Well, just when I was being criticized by Director Wang and Magistrate Chou this afternoon, how come you, the Assistant Director, didn't have a single thing to say?

MENG SHIH-CHING Umm, that is ...

LIU FANG-WEN I understand.

MENG SHIH-CHING Don't let your imagination run wild and don't worry! Nothing's been settled yet and even if it were, we could still raise our objections and have things reconsidered. The higher levels have their own basis for making decisions.

LIU FANG-WEN (*Her determination surfaces*) You're trying to tell me they still haven't reached a final decision? Director Wang has already declared County Magistrate Chou's methods to have been the correct approach. All right, you have your approach and we have ours. When I get back home we're still going to proceed with the organization of our own co-op. I'm going to head back home today. You people way up here can just sit back and study and think things over all you want!

MENG SHIH-CHING No, I had already decided before this that I'd have to go myself.

LIU FANG-WEN Really? You? (*The phone rings and* SHIH-CHING *goes over to answer it*)

MENG SHIH-CHING Yes ... Oh, Director Wang, yes, what can I do for you? ... You want me to preside over the meeting to hear Magistrate Chou's report? ... I ... Director Wang, I was just meaning to consult with you on this. No, no, it's not that, it's just that I've only recently arrived and am not yet familiar with the situation, that's why I didn't say anything. I think it would be best for me to go down there and have a look.... The sooner the better.... If I could get away immediately that would be even better, yes.... You agree? In that case I wonder if the meeting to consider his report shouldn't be ... oh, you'll preside over it yourself? Yes, yes. Splendid.... No, I won't be taking anyone with me. All right then. I'll try to see you and discuss a few things with you before I head down there.... Right. Goodbye.

LIU FANG-WEN (*Has been listening all along*) You're going to go?

MENG SHIH-CHING (*Hanging up telephone*)   Yes!

LIU FANG-WEN (*With bated breath*)   Where will you be going?

MENG SHIH-CHING   To take a look at our village as well as our county seat.

LIU FANG-WEN   Really? (*So happy she's about to burst into tears*)   Aiya, this is really wonderful news, really wonderful. I haven't handled things very well on this trip up here, it's true, but if I've succeeded in getting the Assistant Director of the Rural Work Department to come down, that'll go a long way in making up for it with our villagers!

[LIU FANG-WEN suddenly realizes that in his dedication to his work, SHIH-CHING is forgetting about HUA YÜN's feelings. She tries to persuade him to delay his departure for several days, whereas she will leave immediately. SHIH-CHING, seeing his former wife in a totally new light, refuses to hear of her moving out to spend the night elsewhere and tells her how close he feels they are becoming. He asks her to forgive any of his past misdeeds.

FANG-WEN is touched; she cries as they address each other by their personal names for the very first time, while bitter memories of almost twenty years are laid to rest. Again it is FANG-WEN who catches herself up short as she realizes that this cannot be allowed to develop any further. She insists on returning to the village that very day. She goes out to purchase some things the villagers have asked her to bring back. OLD MRS. MENG enters in time to hear the last exchanges between SHIH-CHING and FANG-WEN.

HUA YÜN returns shortly after SHIH-CHING has disappeared into their bedroom. She is shocked by OLD MRS. MENG's insistence that all the Mengs, including FANG-WEN, move back to the village and live together as one big happy family.]

HUA YÜN   What are you saying?

OLD MRS. MENG   Haven't you figured it out yet? Well, don't worry about a thing. I'll take charge of everything for you and see to it there's no discrimination between who was the first and who was the second or between elder and younger wives. You'll both live with me and neither of you will have any cause to complain about the other. When three hearts live together in harmony, even dirt changes into gold. Since ancient times there have been countless examples of people living wonderful lives together like that!

HUA YÜN   But it's always been one husband, one wife ever since the ancient times just as it's always been one horse, one saddle. What you're talking about is against the law in our new society!

OLD MRS. MENG   Against what law? A family living together?

HUA YÜN   It's against the marriage law.

OLD MRS. MENG   Bah! We in the countryside have studied the new marriage law, too, and it's no use at all to us. It doesn't matter, if there's any trouble, I'll take care of it. You mustn't just pay attention to the law, child, heaven's justice and human nature are equally to be observed.

HUA YÜN (*Feeling humiliated herself and realizing the futility of explaining things to the old lady, speaks half to herself*) Humiliating, it's downright humiliating! I won't stand for it!

OLD MRS. MENG   My goodness, don't tell me you haven't noticed it? Shih-ching and Fang-wen have been coming and going everywhere together. Do you think they can be separated now?

HUA YÜN   Mother! Don't be silly! They got divorced years ago!

OLD MRS. MENG   What? Divorced? Who says so?

HUA YÜN (*A little regretful about her slip of tongue, but never willing to stop halfway in anything*) You're the only one who doesn't know!

OLD MRS. MENG   Can this be true? I certainly am going to have this out with Shih-ching! That heartless, ungrateful knave Ch'en Shih-mei!*

[OLD MRS. MENG upbraids her son for divorcing LIU FANG-WEN, who has been like a devoted daughter to her for all these years. MENG SHIH-CHING scolds HUA YÜN for upsetting his mother, who, in turn, accuses them both of conspiring to drive FANG-WEN away. FANG-WEN returns with her purchases, ready to to go back to the village. OLD MRS. MENG feels that even her "filial daughter" is abandoning her.

Quite beside herself now, HUA YÜN is very rude to LIU FANG-WEN, who picks up her luggage and leaves. The second act ends in a serious fight between HUA YÜN and MENG SHIH-CHING, both of whom are now questioning the viability of their marriage.]

ACT THREE

SCENE ONE

[A Sunday evening a little over a month later in the posh but garish living room of CHANG LAN-O's home. LIANG SHANG-CHÜN has invited HUA YÜN to come over for a visit and hints to CHANG LAN-O that he'd like to have an opportunity to discuss something very important with HUA YÜN alone. CHANG LAN-O is very bored, her husband being away from home on business most of the time, and she seems to take pleasure in telling LIANG SHANG-CHÜN things to build up his hopes of starting something with HUA YÜN.

From their conversation, we learn that SHIH-CHING has been back to his home village for over a month without writing to HUA YÜN. HUA YÜN has moved with MENG HUA and HSIU-LING into quarters at the hospital provided for employees there. LIANG SHANG-CHÜN has been writing articles filled with extravagant praise of the hospital and intended for HUA YÜN's eyes. His claim that he has no ulterior motive fails to convince CHANG LAN-O. He tells her the long story of how he had fallen for HUA YÜN back in 1945 in the liberated area where the three of them were at the time, but he lost out to MENG SHIH-CHING. LIANG goes on to recount a self-serving tale of how a second woman seduced and promptly abandoned him which made him hate all women—all except HUA YÜN. He

---

*A well-known character in traditional Chinese opera who casts aside and attempts to murder his loyal wife in order to marry a princess. [J. B.]

pretends to want CHANG LAN-O to keep his undying love for HUA YÜN a secret.

LIANG goes out to meet HUA YÜN and while he's gone she arrives. CHANG LAN-O behaves just as he knew she would: telling HUA YÜN many things that would appeal to her such as the new screenplay LIANG says he's written—a love story up to "international standards," for which HUA YÜN would be the most suitable female lead. Finally she tells HUA YÜN that LIANG is still in love with her.

Now it's HUA YÜN's turn to confide in her elder cousin and we learn of her great anguish since her husband had gone back with his mother to the MENGS' native village.

LIANG returns. He tells her that he's been down to the countryside gathering materials for his articles. As soon as CHANG LAN-O leaves, LIANG tells HUA YÜN that he's been to Chin-p'ing County and has even stayed two or three days in T'ung-lin Village, MENG SHIH-CHING's hometown.]

HUA YÜN   Really?

LIANG SHANG-CHÜN   Originally I went there to see whether or not Agricultural Producers' Cooperatives should immediately be set up on a widespread basis. The Rural Work Department of the Party Committee has been of two different minds and has been having intense debates over this issue, hasn't it? Moreover, Comrade Meng Shih-ching personally went down there.

HUA YÜN   According to what you saw, should the cooperatives be established there without further delay or not?

LIANG SHANG-CHÜN (*Shaking his head*)   Before long the newspaper will carry an article by me, you might want to watch for it. The opinions and methods of the Chin-p'ing County Magistrate, Comrade Chou Ming-te, are well worth serious consideration. I talked at great length with him for several days. That comrade is very capable, and having seen the worsening of the problems there, I'm in substantial agreement with his point of view, namely, that positive steps have still to be taken there in order to prepare the necessary conditions. This is especially true in T'ung-lin Village, which has rushed things in a reckless fashion. If not corrected, soon enough it's going to prove a great mistake.

[LIANG SHANG-CHÜN now proceeds to tell her that her husband's serious problem is not his devotion to the co-op, but rather his illicit relationship with a woman. LIANG gives her a photo showing SHIH-CHING and FANG-WEN together. HUA YÜN is crushed. LIANG consoles her and offers himself as a refuge for her. She tells him she will divorce SHIH-CHING but will never again love or marry another man.

MENG SHIH-CHING shows up at CHANG LAN-O's house looking for his wife. CHANG LAN-O and LIANG quickly leave HUA YÜN alone in the room just before SHIH-CHING enters. He is suntanned, thinner, and a bit gaunt. He tells her that his silence had been due to his illness and that he's had time to think things over on his sickbed. Now that they've both had time to cool off, they should try to talk things out. He starts an apologetic and serious analysis, but HUA YÜN is in no mood to listen.]

HUA YÜN   I have no time to quarrel with you. It is all very clear.

MENG SHIH-CHING (*Becoming stern*)   I must remind you that you've been doing the wrong thing!

HUA YÜN   What? Well, all right, let's just add things up, shall we? I completely gave you the best years of my youth. I sacrificed my own career in order to accommodate you, I . . . (*Begins to cry at the injustice of it all*) You're right! I have been doing the wrong thing! I married the wrong person!

MENG SHIH-CHING (*Angrily*)   Shut up! (HUA YÜN *has not expected* SHIH-CHING *to be so harsh and stares at him wide-eyed*) Aren't you ashamed to even say such things? (*He takes a couple of steps toward her and berates her*) You speak of sacrificing your youth, sacrificing your career very frequently, well, okay, you've made some sacrifices. But would you just stop and think about this calmly for once. You didn't make these sacrifices for anyone else, you made them for yourself! You're always blaming me for letting life slip by, for not caring enough about the way we live. But what about you, you who care about the way we live so much? Take a good look, why don't you, what kind of a life is it that you are so in love with? Paying no attention to our life at all is my mistake, but do you mean to tell me that being totally wrapped up in trivialities and petty concerns isn't your mistake? Just how have you spent your time, your youth? You've spent it trying to figure out how to find easier ways to make a bigger and better splash rather than buckling down to the long, hard process of really learning something thoroughly. You aren't willing to do the less demanding tasks and aren't up to doing the more demanding ones. The development of your career has come to a standstill while resting in your own hands and has *not* been thwarted by other people! You better wake up!

HUA YÜN (*Some of the things* SHIH-CHING *has just said would have struck home and made her take stock of herself, but other things have hurt her deeply and still others have produced a violent resentment in her; thus she sinks into a welter of very complicated and ambivalent emotions. For a moment she can't find any words to express herself, then she takes up one particular point out of context and fiercely counterattacks*)   Fine, fine! I'm overly concerned about trifles, I'm petty and superficial, I'm the one who's wrong! I'm wrong! I'll never be good enough for a big man like you who doesn't waste his time worrying about silly little things. (*She gets to her feet and is about to leave*) Let me go!

MENG SHIH-CHING (*Holds her back*)   Where are you going?

HUA YÜN   Is that any concern of yours? This is not your home. Get out of my way!

MENG SHIH-CHING   Hua Yün, why are you so pig-headed? (*He reaches for her hand*) Okay, I certainly don't expect you to think through all these problems at once or to correct all past mistakes in a single day. I've already explained to the chief of the People's Hospital and have requested a two-month leave of absence for you. Let's take Little Hua and go down to stay in the countryside together for a while. You've not been out in the rural areas for many years now, and if you go down there and take a look around, it will gradually broaden your perspective and ease your mind. You will be able to see what the working people are doing these days. Life is bubbling down there now!

HUA YÜN (*Dodges his hand*) What? You want me to go down there?

MENG SHIH-CHING Yes!

HUA YÜN You want me to go with you and be your concubine?

MENG SHIH-CHING What are you talking about?

HUA YÜN Aiya, you really are very liberal-minded! I'm amazed that after blatantly thumbing your nose at rules and breaking the law, your face doesn't show the least sign of blushing.

MENG SHIH-CHING What? What kind of crazy talk is this?

HUA YÜN You're not crazy, you're just pretending not to know. You hypocrite, go to hell!

MENG SHIH-CHING (*He's shocked by* HUA YÜN's *attitude yet he still imagines that she is merely blaming him for having any contact with* FANG-WEN) Oh, you're still upset over . . .

HUA YÜN You bet I'm upset. I cannot be anything but upset! It involves the law of the land. It involves my personal honor. I'm going to make it my business to be upset right through to the end!

MENG SHIH-CHING (*Unable to restrain his anger*) You really deserve a medal for narrow-minded petty jealousy!

HUA YÜN So I'm narrow-minded. Just exactly what have you done!

MENG SHIH-CHING (*Calmly*) Just because two people have gotten divorced, they can never say a word to each other again? They can't have any contact even though their work makes it necessary?

HUA YÜN Just listen to these pretty words, such eloquent and dignified things you say! (*To her, his calmness confirms her worst fears*) All right, from now on I will have nothing to say about your affairs, you can go talk to her until your tongue wears out and see if I care. You can go have contact with her for the rest of your life, it's none of my business. Comrade Meng Shih-ching, I'm telling you, you go right ahead! From now on I'll never ever make demands on you or complain; we're no longer husband and wife!

MENG SHIH-CHING (*Stung into uncontrollable rage*) That's fine with me! I've pampered you long enough. So it's good-bye! (*He sits down and searches in his briefcase for something*) When I was over at your place just before coming here, I told Hsiu-ling to pack your things for the trip—this is the train ticket I bought for you. I thought we'd go together, but now it was all for nothing! (*He tears the ticket into little pieces*) Good-bye then! (*He stands up and strides toward the door*)

HUA YÜN (*Tormented, she starts to say something, then stops*) You . . .

[But he halts before walking out, and Scene One of Act Three ends with a long sad farewell speech to HUA YÜN. He wistfully tells her of all the places in the village that figure so prominently in his memories of childhood; he was looking forward to showing them to her. He urges her to take good care of herself and to tell LITTLE HUA that her Daddy will come to visit her whenever he can, after his return to the city in a couple more months.

Hua Yün almost allows herself to cave in and make up with him but can't quite bring herself to forgive him, and he leaves.]

(*Curtain*)

[Act Three, Scene Two takes place two weeks later in the same Chang Lan-o's apartment. The living room has been specially decorated as if for some celebration, and there is a large round banquet table set up to one side. Chang Lan-o is happily getting things ready for a party. Her forty-five-year-old short, fat husband, Chao T'ao, just back from another of his commercial trips, sits on the sofa watching his wife bustling about. From them we learn that Liang Shang-chün is playing host this evening to many of his famous friends from literary and theatrical circles. They also talk about Liang Shang-chün's increased effort to win Hua Yün. Chao T'ao, a wily fellow, warns his wife not to be too sure that Meng Shih-ching is as bad as she has been led to believe or that Hua Yün feels anything more for Liang than simple gratitude for his attention. Chao suggests keeping out of this whole matter. Chao speculates that Liang Shang-chün is springing a "fait accompli" on her.

Chao is right in his prediction. In the middle of a very boisterous dinner, Hua Yün arrives. She is treated as the guest of honor and several of Liang's friends offer toasts for her engagement to Liang. Hua Yün, realizing the trap, is enraged. She slaps his face and storms out.]

[Acts Four and Five of the play bring it to a happy ending, with the help of an old and wise couple. Hua Yün goes to Peking to see Shuai Chien-hui and his wife, who are old family friends. Old Shuai, an outspoken high official in the PLA, points out many mistakes Hua Yün has made and questions whether Shih-ching has been the villain she believes him to be. Impressed by his good advice, she accepts his criticism and decides to go see Meng Shih-ching in his home village.

The higher levels right up to Chairman Mao have by this time overturned the rightist deviation of people like Director Wang and Magistrate Chou; thus activitists such as Liu Fang-wen have been vindicated. Meng Shih-ching and Liu Fang-wen also come to Peking to visit old Shuai after Hua Yün has gone out to find Shih-ching. While alone in the Shuai home Shih-ching causes Liu Fang-wen no little consternation by proposing that they remarry. Throughout Act Four old Shuai has resolutely advocated the obligation of marital loyalty, of sticking "Together through Thick and Thin," first to Hua Yün and then to Shih-ching.

Hua Yün arrives in Meng Shih-ching's village, meets his son, Meng Chen, and sees Liu Fang-wen expertly handle a couple of landlord elements trying to get into the cooperative. Hua Yün learns that Shih-ching has been living in the home of Chan Yü-hou all the time, except when he was sick and under his mother's care in her house.

Chan Yü-hou comes home; he and Liu Fang-wen have been secretly sweet on each other for years. Chan has been a widower for seven or eight years and his patient hopes for eventual marriage with FANG-WEN have been suddenly disturbed by the presence of SHIH-CHING in their village. FANG-WEN tries to explain her now somewhat confused feelings to YÜ-HOU and asks him to help her get through this situation.

HUA YÜN and LIU FANG-WEN finally have a heart-to-heart talk about their difficult situation. HUA YÜN now shows FANG-WEN the photograph of her and SHIH-CHING obtained from LIANG SHANG-CHÜN in Act Three, Scene One. It turns out to be a fake photo. After HUA YÜN and LIU FANG-WEN have made their peace with each other, MENG SHIH-CHING enters and he and HUA YÜN achieve their reconciliation, both admitting their mistakes to each other.

Old SHUAI comes in at the end for a visit to this model village cooperative and OLD MRS. MENG now supports the new generation's choosing their own marriage partners. She asks CHAN YÜ-HOU to be her "adopted son," thus giving her blessing to his marrying FANG-WEN. Everyone is reunited and even HSIU-LING, the governess, who had decided to return to agricultural life as member of the co-op, will continue to see CHI TA-CH'ENG, the messenger boy, on holidays. The curtain falls on a happy resolution.]

Translated by John Berninghausen

SUN CH'IEN
(1920?–)

Little is known of Sun Ch'ien's life. He seems to have achieved prominence as a filmwriter just after the Liberation, publishing his scripts in newspapers and magazines. Two of his scripts, *Harvest* and *When the Grapes Ripen,* were filmed in 1952 by the Northeast Film Studio of the Central Film Bureau. In 1955 a novelette, *Summer Story,* appeared, primarily aimed at the youth audience, and in 1964 a collection of his short stories, *The Lanterns of Nan-shan,* was issued. His bylines indicate that he was in Peking in the early fifties but from the late fifties on, he was writing from Tai-yuan, Shansi, where, in 1966, he produced a short story for newly literate workers and peasants, "The Heroes of Ta-chai."

Sun tends to focus on such themes as the struggle between progressive and conservative forces in the village, the tension between urban workers and rural peasants, and youth's search for commitment in collective life. Most of his works derive from his experiences living among the people he writes about, and he tends to view individual or local problems in the context of a national movement. The orthodoxy of Sun's Marxist thought is rooted in the simplicity of his material and psychological worlds, which is matched by the austerity of his descriptive prose. One is tempted to characterize his style as a kind of "verbal minimalism." But far from resulting in a banal reductionism, it endows his best pieces with a tone of primitivistic authenticity. In general, his work represents one of the more successful attempts to combine the inner struggles of realistic fiction with the didacticism of the socialist romance.

"The Story of a Scar" first appeared in the magazine *Sparks* in March 1958 and was reprinted in a 1959 anthology, *A Bumper Crop of Short Stories.* In it, Sun adopts the narrative persona of an ingenuous PLA soldier who returns to his village after ten years only to confront the human distances created by time and the ideals of the Revolution. Exploring the intersection of family tensions and socioeconomic change, the author charts the conflict between the brother's family and the pressures of the PLA demobilization, the state purchasing and distribution movement, and the collectivization of agriculture. The reader feels a fine, covert sympathy for the brother, whose traditional hopes for self-sufficiency are based on the experiences of genuine suffering and of small gains hard-won. The sister-in-law, however, is a stereotypical figure of petty-capitalist greed, so that the two of them come to symbolize the poles of sentiment and ideology within the narrator himself. The entire story of his progress through marriage and entry into the collectivist utopia involves the heroic transformation of his family and may be allegorized, in Maoist terms, as "solving contradictions among the people." —R.S.

The Story of a Scar

I've been a soldier in a lot of places, earned some scars and did a little bleeding. Take a look—here, on this arm, right where a Japanese sword cut a trench. Above the left calf here, Kuomintang bullets dug a couple of holes. And here, on my back, an American grenade tore out a piece of flesh.

I was discharged in '54 and went back home, figuring that I wouldn't get any more wounds for the rest of my life. But who could have known that last autumn I earned yet another scar—this time on my shoulder, when I was brutally struck with a shovel. If I hadn't ducked quickly enough, the blade would have split my skull in two.

When I was wounded before, it was with the army in battle; I might've gotten hit but we finished off the enemy. (You know in war, it's kill or be killed and no one ever wins who's afraid to bleed.) This time, though, the wound had nothing to do with the army or any battle. I got it in my own village. And the one who struck me wasn't a Japanese, Kuomintang, or American GI—it was my own brother!

You don't believe me? Well, it's true, really, my own brother struck me with a shovel. Sound strange? It sure does when you first hear it but if you think about it a bit, it isn't. I'll tell it to you from the start ...

I was discharged in the autumn of '54, which made it a full ten years since I had left my village. Ah, ten years ... no easy matter: when I left I was a fifteen-year-old kid; now I've become a full-grown man. I might have aged but my heart caught fire when I heard that I'd be returning home. Actually, I had no parents in the village, not even a wife. Just a brother.

My brother's name is Ch'en Hsiu-te and he's ten years older than me. My parents died young, so I was brought up almost entirely by him. Our family didn't do too well when I was young. My father left us only twenty *mu* of alkaline land, and, for a year, my brother and I barely scrounged out enough to survive on by our sweat alone. With no women in the house, we had to cook our own meals after returning from the fields and patch our own clothes too. You can pretty well see what a mess our lives were then. But my brother wasn't bowled over by hardship; all by himself, he shouldered the burden for both of us. Even now, I still remember how bitterly my brother struggled. While I slept, without my even knowing it, he would make breakfast, grab a few corn buns, and go out to the fields. He would never come back for lunch or even doze off in the afternoon. Only when it got dark would he return, sweat streaming down his face, his lips parched and cracked. Picking up a ladle, he would gurgle down a bellyful of cold water before lighting the fire to cook dinner.

He was never much for talking; when he did, it was in retaliation. He never scolded me and he never beat me. Still, I was always scared of him. Don't go thinking that he bossed me around—no, he never did. No matter how difficult things were, he would think of some way to see that I had enough to eat and some warm clothes. And for two years, when the harvests were pretty good, he even sent me to school.

Talk about the way he lived, well, it was frugal to the point where you just couldn't get any more frugal. He didn't smoke, drink, never bought a snack. Whenever we went to the temple fair, he would return with a hungry stomach. I remember that he was rather good-looking and had a strong body but he never mixed with the girls. Except for the necessary meals and sleep every day, his only pleasure was in working. That's the way he lived and that's how he raised me.

When I was fourteen, a flood overran the village. We hadn't stored up any grain and things were tough. The next year, there was no rain all summer long and the crops were baked dry. It was in the autumn of that same year that the guerrillas of the Eighth Route Army came to our village and I joined up.

When I was about to leave, my brother pulled out four silver dollars from under the *k'ang*—all we had—and handed them to me. He said, "Take these with you." I said, "There's no food left in the house. If I take them, what will you use to buy food?" He said, "I'll think of something, just take them." Of course, I couldn't, but my brother wouldn't listen to anything else. In my anxiety, I began to cry and he cried too. We cried a long time but I couldn't budge him—the only thing to do was to accept those four silver dollars. They were my brother's lifeblood, I don't know how much struggle he went through before he scraped them together; and how much he needed them then too!

With tears streaming, I left home and my brother . . .

Even in those ten years away, how could I forget him, my only relative? I would think about him and often write him letters. From his replies, I knew only that I had a sister-in-law and a little nephew. But I knew nothing about how they lived.

When I received my discharge orders, I immediately wrote my brother. How much I wanted to see him—and my sister-in-law and my nephew! I used my bonus to buy them a lot of presents so as to give my brother a chance to enjoy himself.

The end of September was threshing time. As soon as I entered the gate, I was dumbfounded. Gosh! The entire yard had been turned into a threshing floor—there were piles of grain everywhere, like a cluster of mountain peaks blocking even the path. Just think how my father left us only twenty *mu* of that alkaline land; to produce all these crops from that would have surprised anyone.

I looked up and was even more dumbfounded. My brother was really something. He had somehow had the means to build a new two-room house with a tile roof and glass windows. Compared to this, our old two-room shack looked squat and miserable.

The yard was unusually quiet. At the foot of the western wall was someone pumping a bellows—*"pa-ta pa-ta."* I walked into the yard towards the sound, circling around a pile of kaoliang and was further surprised . . .

There was a small awning by the wall and beneath it, a woman holding a child and pumping away. She was young—from the looks of her, not more than twenty—and pretty: large eyes, long lashes, and two shiny pigtails bouncing back and forth. I couldn't believe that this was my sister-in-law, but I couldn't doubt it either. To call that young girl "sister-in-law" was too much, but that's what I had to do.

I braced myself and yelled out, "Sister-in-law!" She just jumped up, startled, and looked all around. When she saw me, she blushed like a red lantern, so embarrassed that she could hardly utter a word. Her blushing embarrassed me as well. So we both just stood there stiffly. My little nephew got scared and started to cry.

After a while, the girl, while pacifying the child, asked me, "Are you thirsty?" I said, "Yes." "I'll boil you some water," she said.

I put down my pack and took out some pieces of candy, coaxing my nephew, "Come on, Uncle will hold you. Let Mama go heat some water." When I said this, the girl blushed again and said, all flustered, "I'm not his mama, I'm his auntie." I didn't get it clear so I asked, "His auntie? What auntie?" She laughed. "His mother is my older sister." I knew she didn't seem like my sister-in-law. She was really my brother's little sister-in-law. To tell the truth, she was pretty enough and though we'd just met, I liked her a lot; and from the looks of it, she seemed to like me. She asked me a lot of questions, such as how long I'd been travelling and so forth. We didn't waste any time but told each other our names: mine is Ch'en Yu-te, hers, Liang Hsiao-feng. And I found out from her much about how my brother got rich.

Liang Hsiao-feng's people lived in Hsi-chou Village, only about a third of a mile from us. They were originally middle peasants, quite well-off and living comfortably. Then, one year, both Hsiao-feng's parents died from a sudden sickness, leaving the two girls with no means to survive. So Ta-feng, the elder one, married my brother. At that time, Hsiao-feng was still small and couldn't get along on her own so she joined her sister in our house. Naturally, their land and household goods came along with them. Just think, with the property of two families combined, how could my brother not get rich?

Just as I was talking to Hsiao-feng, my brother and sister-in-law returned. How he'd changed, changed so much that even I wouldn't have recognized him. Agewise, he was in his prime, but one look at him and you'd think he was an old man. He had two bushy eyebrows, bloodshot eyes; wrinkles with sweat running down them lined his sallow face while a few wheat husks clung to his curly sideburns. And when I looked at what he was wearing, it wasn't much better than a beggar's outfit. That belt around his waist was made of torn rags; a piece of rope would have looked better to me.

I don't know what it was that struck me so painfully when I saw my brother's appearance. My eyes smarted and I couldn't bear it—I cried. My brother didn't cry; he sat down and barely sighed. I heard my sister-in-law chuckling loudly, "How interesting! Ten years as a soldier and you've become an old maid—stop crying, uncle, and take out those nice things you bought so we can have some fun opening them."

I held back my tears and looked up. Ah, how fat my honorable sister-in-law was, so fat she could hardly fit through the gate. Her eyes were small and puffy and her face, yellow and swarthy with dense clusters of freckles like specks of fly dung. It's strange, but she and Hsiao-feng were born of the same parents. How come one turned out so fine and the other, so repugnant? I could never figure it out.

I repressed my disgust and called out, "Sister-in-law!" and then opened up my pack, taking out the presents I'd bought them. There were quite a few, wrapped in all kinds of colors, which were spread out on the table. They attracted everyone—Liang Hsiao-feng also came over holding my little nephew. My sister-in-law's eyes lit up—she felt this one and poked that one. She seemed very excited. My brother chuckled as he gazed at the presents, continually saying, "Oh, no, you've bought so many things, so many things!" He couldn't have cared less about the quality, all he had to hear was that it cost money and he would look stunned, shaking his head. My two-year-old nephew was choking on the piece of candy and kept trying to cough it up. Liang Hsiao-feng picked up a piece of cloth to admire and seemed to like its pattern. Just as she was relishing it, my sister-in-law snatched it away and scolded her, "Go fix dinner! What are you looking at? There's nothing here for you!"

I didn't understand what my sister-in-law meant. Maybe she was really disciplining Hsiao-feng, maybe she was needling me for not bringing something for her. Normally, I wouldn't pay attention to this kind of thing, but I saw how Hsiao-feng just stood there, the red rushing into her face. I was moved, and normally I don't lie, but under these circumstances, I couldn't help it. I picked up the piece of cloth and said to my sister-in-law, "But this is for Hsiao-feng." She was startled, then broke out into a guffaw, saying, "Well, well —barely through the door and now he's in love. Hsiao-feng, he's given you this cloth—'From a thousand miles, he's brought but a feather; full of kindness though slight is the gift.' "

The blushing Hsiao-feng ran off with the cloth. My sister-in-law sat down to suckle the child while my brother pointed to the presents and asked me, "Yu-te, how much did you spend on all these things?" I told him the amount and he was not too pleased. He glanced at me and said, "So you spent your whole retirement pay?" I said, "I spent a bit of it and saved some, but not much."

Just as I was talking to my brother, my sister-in-law suddenly interrupted, "Ah, Yu-te, you were a soldier for ten years, how could you let them fire you?" I explained to her the reasoning behind the demobilization designed to increase production, but before I could finish, she cut in, "Well, sounds good enough, doesn't it?—'Build Socialism in Your Own Home Town'—but it's all phony if you didn't bring any money home!"

Aha! So she said building Socialism was phony! I expected my brother to sternly criticize her then and there. But who would have thought that when he heard it, not only didn't he get angry but he uttered "Hmm," in agreement. Then he added, "Right, you worked hard for ten years and got nothing back for it!"

What a letdown. It looked like my brother and sister-in-law didn't know what the Revolution was all about, as if I went off to fight in the army in order to make a fortune. If anyone else had said this to me, I would have gotten into a fight with him. But how could I start an argument after just coming home? I kept cool and said nothing.

I was lost in my thoughts for a moment when I saw my sister-in-law glance at my brother and he, as if obeying an order, looked over at me. Solemnly, he said, "So, Yu-te, you've come back . . . do you plan to set up your own household or work together with me?"

This came so suddenly, so unexpectedly, that for a minute I was struck dumb. I looked at him stupidly—then I realized how he'd changed, changed so that he wasn't even a shade of what he was ten years ago. Ten years ago, he could give me the only silver dollars he had for the road and now, now we were so distant, so far away from each other.

But I blamed my sister-in-law for everything because it was she who had thrown that first glance at him. I looked at my fat sister-in-law—she was anxiously awaiting my answer. So I controlled my anger, braced myself and said squarely, "I don't even have someone to cook for me, how can I set up house by myself? Naturally, I'll have to live and work with you."

My brother registered no particular emotion when he heard this. He simply said, "That's fine." My sister-in-law was different. She seemed to be delivering a speech to welcome me. "That's right, after all, two brothers—it should be this way! We're like the water helping the fish and the fish needing the water. If we become poor, you won't make much but if we become rich, you won't be left behind ..."

Just then, Hsiao-feng called us in to eat. It was a typical home-style meal: kaoliang noodles sliced like thin fish and topped with tomatoes. I hadn't eaten this kind of food for ten years. How much I had longed for this. But my home-cooked meal wasn't so tasty and when I thought about what my brother and sister-in-law had said, it stuck like a bone in my throat. No matter what I ate, it was hard to swallow.

That evening, I walked about the village visiting a few friends I had known as a kid. When I got back, Liang Hsiao-feng had already swept our old house clean. Though it was a little mildewed, I slept on a cloud that night. The next day, as soon as it got light, I went out with my brother and sister-in-law to the fields. Farming had been my livelihood, but I was a bit rusty after neglecting it for more than ten years. I couldn't keep up with my brother, not even with my sister-in-law.

Don't be deceived by how fat and swarthy she was—she was merciless when it came to earning a living and could succeed at anything; and there was that mouth of hers. Even when she was wrong, she'd make it sound as if she was right. As for her heart, well, naturally I couldn't see into her heart, but I had a feeling that it was as devious as an ant's. If she were buying parsley worth five cents, she would bargain it down to three; she never suffered nor did she have any idea what suffering was all about.

I hadn't been home for a few days when I realized that, in fact, my sister-in-law was the empress of the household. As for my brother, though he was the head in name, he was really just her executive. I hadn't understood it at first, for how could such a stubborn man like my brother be hoodwinked by a woman like that? Then I realized it. How had he become rich after all? Wasn't it all due to my sister-in-law? She had brought her property over to our family and, naturally, she brought along her ways as well. So the enterprise of the Liangs had merged with the frugality of the Ch'ens.

As for this frugality, I couldn't find another family in town to match ours. Don't think it was only my brother who wore such rags, my sister-in-law wasn't much better, you know. She was a woman not past thirty but she felt no shame running about the streets in clothes whose patches were patched. This was how she dressed. As for food, forget it!

When I was young, didn't my brother always refuse to come home for lunch? Now the whole family was like this. Every morning was like the *La-pa* Festival;* we had to eat before it got light and make it to the fields before sunrise.

*Considered the coldest day of the year, it is celebrated on the eighth day of the last lunar month, when the Buddha entered Nirvana. [R.S.]

At noon, every day, it was the same couple of cold, stiff corn buns no matter how hard you worked. Whether you felt like eating them or not, it was still just two corn buns. By the time night fell, your stomach would be growling, throat dry, and you'd long to race home on horseback. Ah, and at home, they would fix something "good to eat"—if not noodle soup, then wheat porridge. These elixirs would quench your thirst just fine and you'd pour bowl after bowl of it to fill up, then turn around and take a piss while your stomach would rumble again. Fortunately, that patterned cloth turned out to have been useful. If Hsiao-feng hadn't've deliberately scooped some thicker stuff from the bottom of the wok into my gruel at mealtimes, I'd've dropped dead from starvation that autumn for sure.

After the harvest, the village organized state purchasing and distribution for the first time and the masses elected me an inspector. As soon as I began the job, I realized what it meant to be put on the spot. Everyone else went along with it—only my brother was hard to manage. He refused to report the true figures of his harvest, but I knew what they were. So I expected what happened: his first report wasn't even half of what he had produced. What would you have done in such a case? There was nothing I could do but explain the "General Line" to him and urge him to follow along the Great Path of Socialism. But while I pushed my side, he had his own notions: we two just weren't striking the same chord. In the end, I had no choice but to try and frighten him. I told him, "If you've deliberately concealed your produce and it's found out, then all of it will be confiscated." After he heard what I'd said, he replied casually, "It doesn't matter—no one knows how much we have." I answered, "But I know."

He glared at me when he heard this and looked like he was going to throw me a few punches or at least yell at me. I waited a while but he didn't burst out—just spit, repressed his anger, turned and walked over to the Village Office.

My brother reported the full amount and I was glad, of course. But I didn't expect that at lunchtime my fat sister-in-law would start beating the child and banging the pots around; she deliberately found faults to provoke me. Women are typically narrow-minded, but I didn't get involved and kept calm. When she saw that I refused to get angry, it infuriated her even more—since she couldn't budge me, she vented her spleen on Hsiao-feng. Just as she was calmly washing the pots, my sister-in-law pulled the scrub brush from her hand, threw it far away and started shrieking, "How come you use so much water when you're washing? Are you afraid we won't be broke fast enough? Huh! Eat and drink like an animal! You'll be happy when the water's boiling and there's no more rice to put in it! I've reared a hairy devil in the house and now the evil days have arrived!"

Just listen to her. She's obviously yelling at me—comparing me to a hairy devil as if to say that I've stolen her family's fortune.

Now, Hsiao-feng was really a good girl. She didn't let it upset her just because she received these unfair accusations, nor did she answer her sister back. She just blushed and looked at me with those telling eyes, as if to say: "I am taking it along with you, you see?"

After the produce was handed over, vouchers were quickly issued. My brother and sister-in-law received their money and carefully reckoned it; the government had set farm prices fairly and the state purchasing and distribution hadn't hurt them a bit. They were both overjoyed and bought two pounds of fatty mutton for us, which we ate along with some fried rice-cakes in celebration of the harvest of '54.

After this operation was over, the Party branch planned to establish agricultural cooperatives. There was no question that I was to be actively involved, but I had no control over the situation in my own family; the matter had to be discussed with my brother. You see, state purchasing and distribution merely involved buying his produce and it was like cutting a piece of flesh off him. But the forming of cooperatives meant he had to give up his land and equipment and work together with everyone else. Do you think he wanted that? Of course not. Whenever this sort of thing came up, I had a hard job trying to convince him. I explained what the real reason for the poverty of the peasants was in the past, I explained about the instability of small economic units, I explained about the superiority of cooperativization and about the future prospects for socialist agriculture—I told him everything I knew.

It was just like when I tried to motivate him to report the actual amount of his crop: I pushed my side while he had his own notions, and we two just didn't strike the same chord. The last time, though, I had some room to maneuver and when we got to the crucial juncture, I could frighten him into agreeing. But this time, other than out-talking him, I had no chips to bargain with. Joining the cooperative was voluntary. If he'd rather die than join, no one could force him. But as for me, what had I fought and bled for? Wasn't it to enable the peasants of the country to enjoy a happy Socialist life? At this point, I was going to join the cooperative, of course, and firmly travel the Socialist road. So my brother and I locked horns and neither of us was about to budge.

My brother wasn't one to say much, was he? Still, when he did speak, it was his final decision. Unless you were to crack his skull, he never went back on what he said. This time he thought for a long while and not only refused to listen to my arguments but used that unique manner of his to try and persuade me. He said, "Yu-te, farming is not like setting off firecrackers. There's no room for a free-for-all. The saying goes, 'You plant your own crops and raise your own sons.' Enough said. I can't understand why you want to get mixed up with that mishmash?"

"In order to raise more food," I said.

"You mean that if we two worked together, we couldn't raise more than them? No way. We'd only harvest more, not less! The way I see it, you're willing to sweat and me—I'm not boasting—in anything else, maybe I'm not as good as the next, but when it comes to farming, I haven't seen anyone as good. With your sweat and my experience, in two years we could take this property and really turn it into something!" I said, "That's the capitalist road —our family may grow rich but the others will fail." He didn't understand what I was getting at, just blinked, stared at me uncomprehendingly and asked, "Then what do you think life is all about?"

"To work for your happiness, mine, everyone's," I replied. He half laughed, shaking his head and said, half jokingly, "Everyone says that but if anyone really tried it, they'd wind up starving."

I really became angry and could no longer hold it back. "You only think of yourself . . ." My words probably struck him in his most sensitive spot, for his expression instantly changed. I ought to say that my brother had great self-control. He didn't yell or start scolding me. He just stood up and, without a word, went toward the door. As he reached it, he suddenly turned around and said to me, "So you've decided to join those bunglers?" I said, "I hope we all do."

"So!—well, let me think about it a bit."

He left. That night, he didn't sleep too well. I kept hearing him cough and figured his thoughts were engaged in a terrible struggle. It must've been painful for his soul—cutting off the tail of capitalism is no easy matter. But I had faith that he would join us because we had chosen the right path.

The next morning I didn't see my brother, but right after breakfast he came back with my uncle. My uncle was an old man of more than sixty. I remember that after my mother died, we didn't have much to do with him aside from going over and paying respects at New Year's. Today was neither a holiday nor a family occasion. What was he doing here, clear out of the blue? Aha! I had it! My brother had brought him along according to the village custom to preside over the dividing of the family property.

In all honesty, I hadn't expected such a move from my brother. But I wasn't afraid—what of it? Was I going to wind up starving? All right, if he wanted to split up the family, then I'd go along with it. I am single and don't have to be bothered by a lot of those extra worries. But I was really unhappy inside. If I can't even convince my own brother, how could I persuade others? Still, since he was dead set against joining the cooperative, what else could I do? All that was left was to split things up and let him stand outside the great gate of Socialism, sniffing the aroma.

My uncle wasn't happy over the decision to divide the property: well, you know, its not so easy to split things up; the family had merged with the Liangs; I had spent a long time away involved in the Revolution and hadn't added anything to the property . . . I saw my uncle's problem and said, "I only want the share that my father left me. I'll accept whatever you decide to give. I'm not going to get angry even if you don't give me anything."

I had seen many brothers split up. In ninety-nine out of a hundred cases, they argue and even fight. After more than ten years of education in revolution, I naturally refused to upset family harmony over this. It's strange but the desire to possess is an obstinate enemy and I had to struggle hard to overcome it.

On the day when we were to separate officially, many people crowded into our yard—they figured there was going to be a good show: if not a fist fight, then at least a big quarrel between me and my brother. Even though we didn't fight or argue, it was enough of a spectacle, though. My brother, at least, tried to maintain some face. Only when dividing up the land did he spend some time picking and choosing; after that he was quiet. But my fat sister-in-law was really a greedy soul. If I picked up this, she said she had bought it; I picked up that and she said I had no use for it. But her best trick was when it came to choosing something good: she would claim it had come from her family every time. As for a silver locket I wore as a child (it was a present from my uncle), she insisted that it had belonged to some damn ghost of a brother of hers. Poison, isn't she? Never mind about how much she took, she had to call *me* a "damn ghost" as well.

After we separated, I continued to live in my old house, but my brother seldom spoke to me and I hardly ever asked about them. But I couldn't help going over to sit a while because there was a Hsiao-feng over there. I was like a piece of steel and she, a magnet. Unable to control myself, I would want to go over to my brother's house just to see her. Who could have known that as I grew closer to Hsiao-feng, my brother and sister-in-law hated me even more . . .

After more than two weeks of work, as we finally managed to make some progress in organizing the cooperative, my stomach had to act up, hurting me so that I couldn't eat well for two or three days. On the fourth day, it got a little better and I felt hungry. When night fell, I left the office to return home and cook something to eat.

I was startled as soon as I entered the gate: the light was on in my house and there seemed to be someone in there banging away at something. Who could have opened the door? Who would have lit the lantern? And what were they doing there?

I bounded into the house and there was Liang Hsiao-feng bent over a table cutting noodles. Surprised, I softly called, "You?" Hsiao-feng turned and looked at me with her face all blushing. Bashfully, she said, "I'm making some noodles for you . . . you've got to eat something!" I gazed at those light, fine noodles on the table and couldn't say anything. The expression on my face was probably pretty funny at that moment and Hsiao-feng giggled when she looked at me. After standing there forever, I at last found something to say. "How come you knew I hadn't eaten anything?"

"You used to go over to the pig sty every day to empty out your dish water but the last few days—its going on the fourth day now—I haven't seen you washing dishes."

Just think. A guy all alone finds a good woman who secretly cares for him. Who wouldn't have felt something deep? But just as I was about to say something to Hsiao-feng, that fat sister-in-law of mine hollered over in the new house, "Hsiao-feng, where the hell are you hiding? The kid has the runs!"

Strange, the child has the runs and Hsiao-feng has to take care of it—what are you being fed for?

Hsiao-feng didn't rush over. She finished cutting the last bit of noodles, then said to me, "When the water boils, cook them yourself, but boil them a little longer."

The moment she went into the new house, I could hear my sister-in-law yelling at her. I couldn't make out what it was about, but I felt that I was the one who had gotten her into trouble.

The next day, I didn't think Hsiao-feng would come looking for me and wasn't expecting her when she came over after dark to help me cook. It was like the day before—just when I wanted to say something important to her, there was hollering again from the new house. This time, it was from my brother himself.

Hsiao-feng still didn't leave right away. She kept glancing quickly outside and in a low voice said, "Do you know why they won't let me come to your room?"

"No."

"They're afraid that I might be taking away their property."

Really, I couldn't understand what she was talking about—here I was trying to get to know her, why would I take away my brother's property?

Hsiao-feng saw that I didn't understand at all and punched me in mock anger, saying, "You're really a melon-head! My family's property doesn't belong to my sister alone. If you and me get on well together, won't she have to give me my share?"

Aha! So that's what it was all about!

Before I could come up with a reply, Hsiao-feng said angrily, "As for them, they can't control me. If they get on my nerves, I'll serve them up something hot!"

Hsiao-feng left in a hurry. As usual, I heard my sister-in-law scold her and, as usual, it was a long time before I could fall asleep.

The next night, Hsiao-feng came over again. But this time, no one interrupted us early. About ten o'clock, that fat sister-in-law of mine "clop-clopped" over to my window and said furiously, "Hsiao-feng, why aren't you home in bed?"

"I'm busy."

"Busy with what?"

"Trying to get a man!"

Who would have expected Hsiao-feng to say something like this! I was dumbfounded and so was my sister-in-law. After a while, she started crying and screaming, "Ai-ya! Don't you have any shame?"

"If I did, I wouldn't be here!"

"You'd better get yourself back over to your room!" Hsiao-feng didn't yell but firmly replied, "I'm not going back any more!" My sister-in-law yelled back, weeping, "Then where are you going to sleep?"

"Right here."

My sister-in-law screamed like a slaughtered pig and ran off, "clunk-clunk" —I knew she was going back for reinforcements, so I quickly pleaded with Hsiao-feng. Ah, Hsiao-feng had the temperament of a pressure-cooker. Ordinarily, she could contain her frustrations, but just light a fire under her and she became a firebomb. If I hadn't thought of sending her over to my aunt's to hide from the storm, then the villagers would have really had a good show to watch.

The next morning, Hsiao-feng asked my uncle to mediate, just as my brother had, and arrange the dividing of the property between the sisters. Hsiao-feng wasn't like me. She didn't let anyone take advantage of her and made such a fuss that my sister-in-law had no choice but to give her her share.

After this, my brother and sister-in-law no longer acknowledged me; whenever they saw me, they looked away, as if they had run into an enemy. I can understand my sister-in-law's attitude, but that my brother should also act this way—well, I just couldn't figure it out. Hsiao-feng took her share with her. Wasn't this right? Why get so angry about it? But if my brother insisted on staying angry, what could I do?

The end of that year, I married Hsiao-feng and we continued to live in my old house. With two families sharing the same yard, it was impossible not to bump into each other. Secretly, I would tell Hsiao-feng to try and be patient and avoid anything that would provoke trouble. But there were things we couldn't dodge. Ah, that fat sister-in-law of mine; she loved money like her own life. Moreover, she had a disorder known as "having three hands." Those household things of ours, which had never sprouted wings, would somehow fly away without a trace. One time, I was shovelling coal and laid the iron shovel down when I went back inside. No sooner had I gone in than I heard someone walking about the pile of coal. Immediately, I turned and went out. My sister-in-law had already picked up the shovel and was walking back with it to her house. I called to her to stop and she turned around, looked at me (not even blushing) and put on an act, "Why, you young people, never knowing how to put things away. If you leave a shovel lying about here, someone will be tempted to steal it without your knowing it—I'm just going to borrow it for a while, I'll bring it back next time."

Sounds nice, doesn't it? Hah! If I hadn't've seen her and called out to stop her, it would have been as good as gone. So she needed to borrow it? She got three good shovels when we split up, why didn't she use her own? Did she really need to "borrow" mine?

But this was a small annoyance, the big problem came later ...

Wasn't there a small awning by the western wall of the yard? And wasn't there a small iron stove with a bellows? The bellows had been left by my father and the stove came from my sister-in-law's and wife's family. When I divided up the family property with my brother, we didn't divide these. Both families used the awning, the stove, and the bellows, which is to say, both families could cook on top of the stove under the awning. In the summer of '55, it was terrifically hot and we all moved outside to cook. Before long, we established the following procedures: breakfast and dinner, my brother's family cooked first and we cooked first at lunch. That's because my brother's family didn't eat lunch; even if they did cook something for lunch, it would be just a bowl of soup for my little nephew. During the summer harvest, Hsiao-feng and I were cutting wheat in the cooperative field, when one day, at noon, after we had finished working, we were both extremely thirsty. Hsiao-feng knew that I had stomach trouble and couldn't drink cold water, so she set down her sickle and went over to the awning to boil some water. I set mine down, wiped away the sweat, and was just striking a match to light up when I heard my sister-in-law shriek like a witch. "Are you blind? Can't you see the peas boiling on the stove? Why did you take my pot off? Put it back on!"

Hsiao-feng patiently replied, "You're not going to eat the peas until later. Let us boil some drinking water first, then I'll put yours back on." My sister-in-law answered meanly, "That won't do!" Now Hsiao-feng began to get angry. "Won't do? Well, you'll just have to put up with it! The fire doesn't belong to you alone!"

"If it's not mine, does that mean it's yours?"

I didn't get involved—when women argue, there's no pacifying them—the more you do, the more vicious they become. I knew enough to keep out of it and let them argue awhile. Anyway, I wasn't going to bother about them. Who expected my brother to come out and lend his voice? I heard him say to my sister-in-law, "What are you yelling about? Just take their pot off and that'll be the end of it!"

This was too much, but I held my peace and didn't go outside. My sister-in-law wanted to remove our pot. Hsiao-feng refused to give way. She screamed,

"Don't you dare move it!" Then all I heard was my brother say, "Why shouldn't we—I'll take it off then!"

I could have taken everything else, but I won't stand for anyone trying to push Hsiao-feng around. Unable to control myself, I ran out the door just as my brother was removing our pot. Thud! He threw it to the ground. The pot broke and the water spilled all over. I went berserk, picked up a pole, ran over to the awning, and, in a few blows, beat the iron stove into fragments. When my brother saw me, he reached for an ax and, with a few chops, pulverized the bellows. Hsiao-feng and my sister-in-law were scared stiff and kept screaming, "Help!" My brother and I faced each other with weapons and were panting angrily—if people hadn't run over and separated us, someone would have been killed that day.

I began to regret it right after the fighting stopped. I remembered how much I owed my brother; he raised me, and without him, I would have starved to death long ago. And no matter how backwards, conservative, and selfish he was, I had the responsibility to open his eyes. Sooner or later he would want to walk the Socialist road, and it was my responsibility to see that he changed. A Communist Party member taking arms against his own brother over peanuts and chicken feed—it still bothers me when I think of it, even now.

Okay, so we two brothers had destroyed our own stove and bellows. Now we had no place to cook and all we could do was each build a small outdoor stove near his house with some clay. Since there was no bellows, they weren't easy to use, and we fretted every time we wanted to cook. And whenever we did, it reminded me of that useless argument, weighing on me like a rock.

To tell the truth, I was thinking of apologizing to my brother right afterwards, but, frankly, I lacked the courage. When your heart's tied up in knots, you become agitated and for no reason at all, I got into an argument with Hsiao-feng. This made me even more upset. Somehow during this time, there had to be a drought. For the first ten days of summer there was no rain, nor any during the second ten. By the time autumn arrived, still no rain. The crops in the cooperative were so dry that their leaves began to curl, all yellowed, as if scorched by fire.

Since I was so involved with the work of the cooperative, I just put aside family troubles. I ran over to the County Committee to report on the situation and to the County Bank to borrow funds. After much effort, I was finally able to bring back two water pumps. Later, I had to go over to the Veterans' Agricultural Station to borrow another one. We set up the three machines by the riverside and pumped up water onto the land. For three solid days and nights, I didn't touch my bed. But by the morning of the fourth day, we had irrigated all the land. The crops thus watered turned colors again, like a patient who begins to recover; though his face isn't much to look at, there's life there.

At noon, I took a rest and had my fellow-workers irrigate the crops a second time as I went back to the village, exhausted and hungry. It felt like I couldn't move my feet anymore. When I reached the village, I could see my brother and sister-in-law hauling water to irrigate their corn fields. Though their land was close by, it was still about a third of a mile from the well. The sun was cruel that day and they were both sweating all over, their clothes drenched. I don't know why, but suddenly I felt pity for them. I decided I would help them.

I called out and my brother stopped dead in his tracks, staring at me. I said, "We've already finished irrigating our land. Why don't you use the water pumps in the afternoon?" My brother set down his water buckets and looked at me in disbelief; then he replied, "You people in the cooperative have support from backstage; you can afford to use those machines but our base is small— we can't afford those things." I said, "Brother, don't get ornery. You can't beat the cooperative. Right now, it's important to save the crops and with three water pumps, you can irrigate your fields in half the afternoon. Look, can't you see the superiority of the cooperative now?"

At my mention of "the superiority of the cooperative," his face suddenly fell. "Are you still trying to get me to join the cooperative?" he said. "I was thinking of something like that—you should join after the autumn harvest. Better early than late." He abruptly picked up the buckets, turned around, and went off. After a couple of steps, he turned and angrily said, "You hate it that I don't go broke fast enough—you're always trying to poison me!" I asked him, "When did I ever try to poison you?" He didn't answer my question but only spit and walked off, saying, "I figure I raised you for over ten years for nothing. If I had known it would turn out this way, I would have fed your food to the dogs." He walked off in a huff as I stood there, unable to say anything . . .

After five days, the heavy rain we'd hoped for fell and the crops were saved. There was a bountiful harvest for the cooperative that autumn because we had irrigated the land twice during the drought. Most of the household farmers suffered a shortage; the only exception was my brother. He had paid attention to farming techniques and put out a lot of sweat so that despite it all, he was able to raise a moderately good crop.

But the general harvest was not too good; there was a shortage of food and a black market quickly grew. At first, I thought it was those landlords, rich peasants, and profiteers who were stirring up the market. Hah! I never thought that my brother and sister-in-law were among those speculators.

Not long after the harvest, Hsiao-feng told me, "Today, brother brought back a cartload of grain—I think he must have gotten it from the black market." I said, "He has enough grain of his own, what does he need to buy more for?"

"How stupid can you be? If you buy in the autumn and sell in spring, you can get double the price."

"No, you see what a blockhead my brother is. How could he get involved in speculation?"

"Don't go treating him like a saint. If he were such a good old boy, he wouldn't have fought with you about dividing up the property and then when it was divided hid the cash away so that you didn't get a share. As I see it, they've lent out the cash for high interest."

"No way. They know well enough that the government won't allow any usury."

"They know well enough that the government won't permit a black market, but isn't that where they bought the grain?"

Hsiao-feng and I didn't reach any conclusions that evening, and, since we were still busy with the harvest, forgot the whole thing. Then, one night when it was already very late, I was just coming back from the office. Hsiao-feng hadn't gone to bed, which I thought was strange, so I asked her, "How come you're not sleeping?" She answered, a bit depressed, "I've been waiting for you."

"What's that? Is something wrong?"

"Of course there's something wrong. Do you know where Wang Yu-fu and Wang Yu-lu's work-checks are?"

"Certainly. In their house."

"In their house?—they've used their checks to pay off debts."

"What are you talking about?"

"Their checks were bought by their creditors. You're only concerned with distribution procedures. You have no idea whether they can get food or not!"

"Is this true?"

"You're still in the woods. By the time you figure the whole thing out, Wang Yu-fu and Wang Yu-lu will have been forced to let others take away their grain."

"Well, who would do such a dirty thing?—who's their creditor?"

"Who else? That honest brother of yours and my precious sister."

I cried out in surprise. Hsiao-feng went on, "They're thoroughly evil. Last summer, Wang Yu-fu's mother died. Your brother wanted to buy that piece of land of theirs east of the village, but they didn't want to sell, just mortgage it. Your brother was really vicious: he insisted on fifty percent interest and on including in the contract that if the money wasn't paid on time, then they must surrender the land. There was nothing the Wang brothers could do but sign, so they borrowed a hundred and twenty *yüan* from your brother. This summer the mortgage came due and the Wangs asked your brother to be lenient and wait until the autumn harvest for repayment. But your brother and sister wouldn't agree to anything except paying off their debt with their work-checks."

"Those rotten eggs!" I blurted out. Hsiao-feng said, "The rotten part is still to come. Don't we all get one-fifty a day for working? Well, their checks were accepted at eighty cents per man/day!"

A fire erupted inside me beyond control. I turned to run outside as Hsiao-feng asked me, "What are you going to do?" I said, "I'm going to find them."

"They're not home."

"Where did they go?"

"They must have gone again to collect their debt."

I ran out the gate toward Wang Yu-fu's house. I couldn't help wanting to grab them both right away—they've abused people too much. With their few dirty coins, they try to undermine our cooperative. Profiteering, exploiting, speculating—it was outrageous!

At the entrance to an alley, I saw a black shadow walking toward me. It seemed to resemble my fat sister-in-law, so I hid in a dark spot and observed her. As she got closer, I saw it was her all right, and, under the moonlight, I could see that she was shouldering half a sack full of grain. I called out, as if confronting an enemy, "Halt!" My sister-in-law cried out in surprise and fell down, flop! Just as I was about to grab her, she suddenly jumped up, threw off the sack and ran. But do you think that fat body of hers could run faster than me? Before she got two steps, I grabbed her by the collar. She turned around and as soon as she saw me, she bristled. "What are you trying to do?" she said.

"You know yourself—where did you get that grain?"

"None of your business. Anyway, I didn't steal it."

"You're worse than a thief. You've bought up work-checks from the cooperative. Do you know what law you've broken?"

"What law have I broken? When you kill someone, you pay with your life, and when you owe money, you pay it back. It's always been like this. Are you telling me that when you join the cooperative, you can run away from debts?"

Didn't she sound tough? As if she hadn't committed any crime at all but was involved in an honest deal. I ordered her to accompany me to the District Office. She said, without batting an eyelash, "Let's go then. One has to be reasonable no matter where. I'm not afraid of you!" I said, "Fine. Go reason with the District authority and let everyone listen to your dirty deeds."

I pulled my sister-in-law along over toward the District Office. Midway, my brother caught up with us. He was panting heavily and glared at me with his two giant bloodshot eyes, stared at me full of hatred, as if it wasn't they who were guilty of trying to destroy the cooperative but me. He asked me loudly, "Where are you taking her?" I said, "To the District Office."

"Are you going to let us live or not?"

"Who isn't letting you live?"

"Then let her go!"

"After she explains everything, she can go home, of course." My sister-in-law said angrily, "I'm not afraid no matter where we go—come on!"

After a few more steps, my brother caught up with us again. He said threateningly, "Are you going to let her go or not?" I said, "No."

"All right! If I can't make anything from this, you won't either—I'm going to kill you, you ungrateful thief!" He whipped out an iron shovel from behind him. It happened more quickly than I can tell. I could see the shiny blade in the moonlight come slicing toward my head. I ducked quickly—that is, my head ducked but not my shoulder. I felt the shovel fiercely strike me, then immediately fell unconscious . . .

When I came to, people were lifting me onto a stretcher. Hsiao-feng was bent over me, crying. I wanted to tell her that I wouldn't die, but I couldn't speak. My brother and sister-in-law along with my little nephew were lined up, kneeling beside the stretcher. From the looks of it, they seemed to be begging me not to accuse them in court. When I thought about how brothers could come to this, I felt bitter about it and couldn't stop the flow of tears. I remembered how good my brother once was to me and I wanted to give him a chance to live. So I nodded toward him in sympathy. I forgave him . . .

That winter, every village was caught up in hoisting high the banners of Socialism, and the cooperativization movement had reached its crest. When I returned from the hospital, my sister and brother-in-law had followed the tide and joined the cooperative.

Of course, my brother is a fine worker but not a very good member. But I think he will improve. He just needs time.

Nowadays, our two families still share the same yard, but we don't fight. My sister-in-law and Hsiao-feng even see each other a bit; but there's still a lot separating us.

And now I understand that Socialist reconstruction in the villages is no easy matter, nor is it much different from fighting on a battlefield. The only difference is that on the battlefield, you fight an enemy, while in the village, you fight not only enemies but also your own kind—and this struggle can sometimes be a bloody one.

So that's how I got the scar on my shoulder.

Translated by Richard E. Strassberg

CHOU YANG
(1908–)

For over twenty years—from the early 1940s to the mid-1960s—Chou Yang was the chief guardian and implementor of Mao Tse-tung's literary and cultural policies. He took charge of the series of relentless campaigns that ruthlessly purged the ranks of China's most creative writers. Then suddenly, in the summer of 1966, he, himself, became one of the chief victims of the Cultural Revolution.

His rise and fall from power can be explained by his personification of the Party organization man. Born in Hunan in 1908, Chou Yang attended Ta Hsia, Great China University, in Shanghai. In 1928 he went to study in Japan, where he became a student of nineteenth-century European literature. While there, he was arrested for participation in a leftist demonstration, and he returned to Shanghai at the end of the 1920s. Shortly thereafter, he became a Communist Party member and an organizer of the Party's cultural activities in Shanghai. In 1934 he was the Party representative in the League of Left-wing Writers. Though he had sharp clashes with Lu Hsün and some of his disciples, he was closely associated with the May Fourth Writers. He was not a creative writer, but, in addition to his organizational work, he wrote literary criticism and translated a number of Russian works, among them Tolstoy's *Anna Karenina* and the writings of the nineteenth-century populist Chunyshevski.

With the Japanese bombardment of Shanghai in 1937, he, along with a number of his colleagues, went to Yenan. There he quickly rose to power in the Party's cultural organs. He became director of education of the Communist-controlled Shensi-Kansu-Ninghsia Border Region, president of Yenan University, and dean of the Lu Hsün Academy of Arts. Soon after the 1949 Party takeover, he was listed as vice-chairman of several literary and cultural organizations and as deputy director of the Propaganda Department. But he wielded more power than his official positions signified. Unofficially, he assumed responsibility for tightening thought control not only in literature but in virtually every sphere of intellectual endeavor, particularly the humanities, social sciences, and creative arts.

Despite Chou Yang's efforts, dissident writers and intellectuals continued to express themselves. In the relative relaxation of the early 1960s, some May Fourth writers and intellectuals indirectly criticized Mao's policies of the Great Leap Forward in discussions of history, literature, and ideology—the very areas for which Chou was responsible. Mao, in 1962, 1963, and 1964, demanded a campaign to stamp out this criticism, but Chou and his associates responded only in a very superficial manner. Chou feared not only the dislocations of another campaign but also the fact that if he waged an intensive drive, it would have repercussions in his own bailiwick, from which the criticism had come.

When Mao delegated his wife, Chiang Ching, with the support of a group of young ideologues, to reform the traditional opera, which had been a medium for some of the criticism, Chou blocked her interference in his realm. Consequently, when Mao launched the Cultural Revolution against the Party hierarchy, the attack on Chou was second in ferocity only to that on Liu Shao-ch'i— perhaps because of the very personal nature of the previous struggle.

However, as can be seen in the piece reprinted below, "The Path of Socialist Literature and Art in China," Chou's purge was for reasons of ideology as well as power. This piece reflects his efforts throughout his career to balance a belief in mass literature with a concern for professional literature, a commitment to political standards with respect for artistic standards, and an interest in collective needs with an interest in individual needs. As Mao, in the mid-1960s, took a more radical course by calling for a new mass culture in conjunction with the Cultural Revolution, Chou's balanced approach, fashioned partly out of commitment and partly to follow every twist in the Maoist line, became subversive.

Shortly before his death, Mao approved the rehabilitation of Chou Yang along with other Party officials. He was listed in January 1978 on the Standing Committee of the Chinese People's Political Consultative Conference. Late in May of the same year he played an active role in the Third Congress of the All-China Federation of Literary and Art Circles in Peking. He is now deputy director of the Academy of Social Science. —M.G.

The Path of Socialist Literature and Art in China

(Report Delivered to the Third Congress of Chinese Literary and Art Workers on July 22, 1960)

Literature and art are a form of ideology belonging to the superstructure; they are a reflection of the economic basis and are the nerve center of the class struggle. . . . On the ideological front, we must raise still higher the revolutionary banner of Marxism-Leninism and oppose the reactionary ideological trends of modern revisionism; we must, by means of a protracted and unremitting struggle, make a clean sweep of the political and ideological influences of the bourgeoisie among the masses, and greatly enhance the communist consciousness and moral qualities of our people. Our literature and art should become keen instruments for educating the people in the spirit of socialism and communism, in the spirit of proletarian internationalism. . . . We should explain how sharp struggles have been waged, in the literary and art circles of our country, between the proletarian line and the bourgeois line, between the communist world outlook and the bourgeois world outlook.

SERVE THE WORKERS, PEASANTS AND SOLDIERS, SERVE THE CAUSE OF SOCIALISM

That literature and art should serve the workers, peasants, and soldiers is the proletarian line in literature and art. It is sharply opposed to the bourgeois line in literature and art. This is why it is looked upon with hostility and is hated by all reactionaries and revisionists both inside and outside the country. Hu Feng called this line "a Dagger"; the Yugoslav revisionists revile it as a "Persecution" of writers. . . . And in the eyes of bourgeois men of letters, literature and art are the monopoly of a small number of the "upper class," their private property; from their point of view literature and art should praise none but the bourgeoisie and bourgeois intellectuals, should prettify the corrupt way of life of the bourgeoisie and propagate bourgeois individualist ideas and low tastes. How can they, these "literary aristocrats," be willing to portray or serve the masses of workers and peasants? . . . This struggle started, e.g., with the criticism of the film *The Life of Wu Hsün** in 1951, proceeded to the criticism of the *Studies of the Dream of the Red Chamber*† and the repudiation of the ideas of Hu Shih and Hu Feng and the exposure of Hu Feng's counterrevolutionary clique, down to the struggle against Ting Ling and Ch'en Ch'i-hsia's anti-Party clique and other rightists in 1957, and following these, the repudiation of revisionist trends in literature and art. This series of struggles on the front of literature and art is a reflection in the realm of ideology of the class struggle in our country during the period of the socialist revolution and socialist construction. . . .

In our country, literature and art are no longer monopolized by a few, but have become the common undertaking of the broad masses of people of the various nationalities in our land.

. . . To open up the road for proletarian literature and art, Lu Hsün, Ch'ü Ch'iu-pai, and many other revolutionary writers and artists pioneered the way and even shed their blood or laid down their lives. Comrade Mao Tse-tung, on the basis of the actual practice in the Chinese revolution, has creatively developed the principles of Party literature formulated by Lenin by pointing out clearly that literature and art should serve the workers, peasants, and soldiers. As a result, our literature and art have undergone a fundamental, historic change. . . . The new age has set new tasks for our literature and art; the writers and artists of this new age cannot but take a new path in their life and creative activity, which is fundamentally different from that of writers and artists in the past—the path of integrating themselves with the masses of workers and peasants. This is the only way for writers and artists who are intellectuals not of proletarian origin to transform their former world outlook, establish a communist world outlook, *and become truly the spokesmen of the working class.*

Following changes in the foundation, the superstructure must change also. But changes in ideology that belongs to the superstructure take place much more slowly than changes in the foundation. This is why, after a socialist society has been established, the political and ideological influence of the bourgeoisie remains for a long time; while even in communist society there will

*The film based on the life of Wu Hsün (1838–97), a beggar who saved money to establish a tuition-free school, was a national hit in 1950 but was soon criticized by the Communist Party for upholding feudal values of traditional schooling. The controversy started a wave of ideological struggle in China. [K.Y.H.]

†The *Studies of the Dream of the Red Chamber,* a collection of essays by the literary scholar Yü P'ing-po (1899–), was severely condemned in a Party-directed campaign to expose Yü's antimaterialist and anti-Marxist viewpoints. The campaign started in September 1954 and lasted over a year. [K.Y.H.]

still be struggles between advanced and backward, between right and wrong. This determines that ideological struggle and ideological remolding are long-term tasks. During the last decade, bourgeois ideas have been under constant criticism in our country, and revisionism has not been able to occupy a dominant position in literary and art circles in our country; but this does not mean they do not exist—they take their cue from the climate. When there is the least trouble inside or outside the country, they will start creating disturbances again, rising like scum to the surface of the water to spread their poison once again.

LET A HUNDRED FLOWERS BLOSSOM, LET A HUNDRED SCHOOLS OF THOUGHT CONTEND

Regarding style, form, genre, and subject matter in art, however, we are for greater variety and encourage originality, while opposing monotony, rigidity, and narrowness. Our principle is the integration of uniformity in political orientation and variety in artistic styles. On the basis of his scientific analysis of the contradictions among the people in the socialist society, Comrade Mao Tse-tung put forward the policy of letting a hundred flowers blossom and a hundred schools of thought contend. . . .

The policy of letting a hundred flowers blossom and developing the new from the old not only has promoted the renovation of old traditions but also has made our new literature and art more national in character. More and more, our novelists and story writers are manifesting a national style in their language, characterization, and plots. Our poets, under the impact of the new folk-song movement, are striving to develop modern poetry on the basis of classical poetry and folk songs; hence there is a new trend in the style of poetry too. All kinds of painting and sculpture, in the same way, are demonstrating much more vivid national characteristics. Our modern operas have not only presented a new *revolutionary content but become more national in form too.*

Our literature and art not only put special emphasis on the portrayal of present-day struggles, creating images of contemporary heroes, but present outstanding characters in history from a new viewpoint.

As early as twenty years ago Comrade Mao Tse-tung proposed that we should evolve a fresh, lively Chinese style and Chinese flavor which the common folk of China love to see and hear. Our literature and art have a tradition dating back several thousand years; they reflect a rich fund of creative experience and they appear in our own national forms and styles that have developed over the past many centuries. If revolutionary literature and art possess no national features, if they cannot create new national forms suited to the new content on the basis of our own national traditions, they will not easily take root and blossom among the broad masses of the people. The national character and mass character of literature and art are interconnected and indivisible. Since the May Fourth Movement our literature and art have widely absorbed the experience of foreign literature and art, adopting many foreign forms and methods of expression; this was entirely necessary. . . .

However, all art forms and techniques of foreign origin when transplanted to China must be remodeled and assimilated till they possess national features and become our own. Now our literature and art are more and more manifesting their national character and mass character. Distinctive national originality in literature and art is the concentrated expression of the creativeness of the masses, the sign of maturity in the literature and art of an age and of a class.

... Our literature and art are composed of these two elements, the works of professionals and those of the masses who create in their spare time. These two component parts together make up the splendid variety and wealth of our literature and art. Letting a hundred schools of thought contend has promoted the lively activities of free debate and mass criticism in literary and art circles and throughout the world of thought. We have launched, through debates, the struggle between two paths in literature and art, and at the same time have held helpful discussions on many problems relating to literary and art creation and theory. Through these debates, the Marxist viewpoint has consolidated its position in literary and art theory and criticism. During the last two years, in the departments of literature in universities and the art colleges, criticism on bourgeois theory and ideas in the teaching of literature and art has been carried out; and on the basis of this criticism, the students and the teachers have collaborated to produce works of literary and art theory and histories of literature and art....

We have always held that letting a hundred flowers blossom means blossoming within the domain of socialism. The flowers to blossom are socialist flowers. We mean, through free emulation, to develop the socialist literature and art, and to oppose literature and art that are hostile to socialism. Letting a hundred schools of thought contend means contending under the guidance of Marxism-Leninism, means propagating and developing Marxist dialectical materialism and opposing *bourgeois idealism and metaphysics through free debate....*

Just as Comrade Liu Shao-chi has said, letting a hundred flowers blossom and a hundred schools of thought contend is an extremely firm class policy of the proletariat.

Bourgeois rightists and revisionists have tried to utilize the slogan of letting a hundred flowers blossom to bring forth their poisonous weeds hostile to socialism....

When men's world outlooks differ, their conceptions of beauty differ too. What we regard as fragrant flowers they consider poisonous weeds, while what we consider poisonous weeds they regard as fragrant flowers.

On the question of letting a hundred flowers blossom and a hundred schools of thought contend, we differ from the doctrinaires too. The doctrinaires are cut off from the masses, cut off from reality; they do not understand dialectics; they do not admit that multiplicity exists in the world. They want only uniformity in political orientation, not variety in artistic styles; they allow only a single flower to blossom, not a hundred flowers. This is extremely harmful.

We advocate literary and art works depicting present-day struggles, and we encourage and help writers and artists to do their best to get in touch and familiarize themselves with the people's new life and throw themselves into the heat of the people's struggle. At the same time, each writer and artist can, according to his sense of political responsibility, his personal experience of life, his interests and special talent, decide what theme to choose and what forms of expression to adopt. The readers and audiences of the new age like stirring works portraying the life and struggles of their contemporaries, as well as fascinating stories from history and legend performed on the stage. They like stirring militant marching songs; they also like fine and healthy lyrical music and dances. The new age requires more and better paintings of revolutionary history, revolutionary genre paintings and figure paintings, but shouldn't the new-style landscape paintings and flower-and-bird paintings also have a place in our galleries? The people need inspiration and encouragement in their spiritual life, but they also need things that give pleasure and delight.... We advocate using the methods of criticism and emulation to gradually eliminate works that are ideologically faulty or artistically inferior, in order to raise the ideological and artistic level of our works step by step. Socialist emulation in literature and art is the best way to encourage a multiplicity of artistic styles, develop various schools of art and expedite the raising of the quality of our works....

The elimination of poisonous weeds is a problem between us and the enemy. The existence of poisonous weeds is an objective reality. Their growth is decided by definite historical conditions. It is not possible to prevent them from existing and appearing. The problem is what is the most effective way to eliminate the harm caused by poisonous weeds. The revisionists are against fighting poisonous weeds; they are the protectors of all kinds of poisonous weeds; the revisionist current of thought is itself a poisonous weed, which does the greatest harm. They advocate the policy of liberalism and laissez-faire, "tolerance" and "compromise" on the cultural and ideological front, and their aim is to make socialist countries allow the capitalist reactionary culture to exist legally, to let it spread freely, to poison the people and youth. This, of course, we resolutely oppose. On the other hand, we do not approve of the method used by the doctrinaires either. They would ban poisonous weeds as soon as they appear; though the simple method of issuing administrative orders may have a temporary effect, it causes endless future trouble. It actually means allowing poisonous weeds to remain underground for a while, or allowing them to emerge in disguise to cause damage. This is another form of laissez-faire, which will not deal a mortal blow to the enemy. Our policy is: When poisonous weeds start to come out, we let them meet the masses as antagonists, and urge the masses to discuss them freely, so as to enable more people to recognize their true features, to sharpen the people's sense of discernment and fighting ability....

Therefore we are not afraid of poisonous weeds and opposite views; we are not afraid of open debates, not afraid that correct views may at one time meet with attacks and misunderstanding.

THE INTEGRATION OF REVOLUTIONARY REALISM AND REVOLUTIONARY ROMANTICISM

In order that literature and art may better reflect our age and more effectively serve the broad masses of laboring people and the great cause of socialism and communism, we advocate the artistic method of integrating revolutionary realism and revolutionary romanticism.... The putting forward of this artistic method is another important contribution made by Comrade Mao Tse-tung to the Marxist theory of literature and art. . . .

The fundamental difference between us Marxists and the mechanical materialists is that we, on the basis of a correct knowledge of objective reality, pay full attention to subjective activity, to progressive ideas and scientific foresight, and to the great significance of revolutionary vision. Is it not precisely because he is inspired by noble ideals that a proletarian revolutionary fighter braves all dangers with resolute fortitude? To us there is no limit to the revolutionary task of transforming the world; . . .

In the age of proletarian revolution, new heroic characters can only be the advanced elements of the proletariat and the revolutionary people. Hence the creation of new heroic characters has become the glorious task of socialist literature and art.

Our literature and art should create characters that can best embody the revolutionary ideals of the proletariat. These characters are not the products of the writers' fancy but new men and women emerging from the actual struggle. Their most admirable attribute is seen in the fact that they never are daunted by difficulties and shrink back, nor do they feel satisfied with the victories gained and so stop advancing.

Those writers with bourgeois prejudices have always held that the advanced characters among the masses of the people whom we describe are untrue to life and that only colorless "petty individuals" or low, negative characters are "true." Their argument is that every man has some faults and defects, that there is a struggle between darkness and light in the depth of every heart; this is what they mean by the "complexity of the inner mind." . . . Of course they must have worries, inner conflicts, and shortcomings of one kind or another, or make this or that mistake; but they always endeavor to use communist ideas and morality as the highest criteria for all their actions. What has the so-called complexity of the inner mind which the bourgeois writers advocate to depict, got in common with the rich inner life of the laboring people of this new age? The so-called secrets of man's mind that they want to reveal are nothing but an exposure of their own dark souls. Eager to depict weak-willed people and the petty affairs in which they are involved, they cannot see or are unwilling to describe the heroic characters and great struggles of today, or they force the low, empty souls of the bourgeoisie into the new socialist or communist men. Their works are shrouded in gloom, and they paint completely black the new life of socialist society and the fighting life of the masses. The result of this can only be to make people feel disappointed with socialist reality, and to foster a spiritual disintegration . . . and collapse among the people of the socialist countries.

Our understanding of the question of "truthfulness" and "realism" is completely different from that of the revisionist. The revisionists often oppose tendentiousness in socialist literature and art under the pretext of "depicting truth" and "realism." They deliberately set truthfulness in opposition to tendentiousness, claiming that tendentiousness hampers truthfulness; actually, what they oppose is only revolutionary tendentiousness in literature and art, and their aim is to replace it with the reactionary tendentiousness of the bourgeoisie. . . . How then are our literature and art to give a truthful reflection of this spiritual outlook of the masses, in other words, how are they to reflect the features of our age? Can we reflect it in melancholy tones, in pallid language and by petty, naturalistic methods? That is absolutely impossible. We must use heroic language, powerful tones, and vivid colors to praise and describe our age. The revolutionary romanticism in literature and art is the crystallization of the revolutionary romanticism in our people's life. . . .

Of course, life is full of contradictions. What is new in life always comes into being and grows up in a struggle against the old.

We face squarely the contradictions that exist within the ranks of the people in the socialist society; this keeps us from falling into the error of the nonconflict theory from the very start. Our literature and art must not evade defects and difficulties, ignore passive phenomena and negative characters, or water down the contradictions and struggles in life; such cheap optimism can only oversimplify life, presenting real, advanced people as lifeless men of straw. Works of this sort can arouse neither admiration for what is fine nor indignation against what is evil; they are still less able to induce men to think about life's problems, and once read they are immediately forgotten. . . .

Speaking of life and art, Comrade Mao Tse-tung further said, "Although both are beautiful, life as reflected in artistic and literary works can and ought to be on a higher level and of a greater power and better focused, more typical, nearer the ideal, and therefore more universal than actual everyday life." . . . Life in reality is the fount of literature and art, but literature and art should be on a higher level than reality; through images they reflect life and create characters; their aim is not passively to reflect reality for its own sake, but actively to reflect and impel reality forward and transform it. . . .

REFUTING THE BOURGEOIS THEORY OF HUMAN NATURE

At present the revisionists are desperately pushing the bourgeois theory of human nature, the false humanism of the bourgeoisie, "the love of mankind," bourgeois pacifism, and other fallacious notions of the sort to reconcile class antagonisms, negate the class struggle and revolution, and spread illusions about imperialism, and thus to attain their ulterior aim of preserving the capitalist old world and disrupting the socialist new world. . . . They use an abstract, common human nature to explain various historical and social phenomena, use human nature or "humanism" as the criterion of morality and art, and oppose literature and art serving the cause of *liberation of the proletariat and the laboring people.* . . . The old revisionist theorist Lukacs claimed that the humanistic ideal and principle are the "absolute criteria" in artistic criticism, and this so-called humanistic ideal or principle is "common human nature." In China, Hu Feng, the earliest pedlar of these theories of Lukacs, said, "The socialist spirit is the humanistic spirit"; in other words, "a profound compassion for all mankind." Feng Hsüeh-feng also claimed that man's basic demand is "the friendship of humanity as a whole." When the rightists were attacking us violently, Pa Jen once more brought out these old weapons to attack socialist literature and art, asserting that revolutionary literature and art lack "human interest" because they do not express "what men have in common" and "lack the humanism inherent in human nature." We consider that in a class society there is no abstract principle of humanism that transcends the age and classes. In a class society, humanism as an ideology always possesses a class content of a definite age.

A section of the positive romanticist writers and critical realist writers of the nineteenth century brought stirring accusations against the seamy side of capitalism. Many of them also appealed for humanism. But because they were not able to shake off the limitations of their bourgeois and petty-bourgeois views, the humanism they called for was unable to go beyond the confines of private property and individualism. . . . Now some people within the ranks of Marxism have confused communism with bourgeois humanism, claiming that communism is the "highest embodiment of humanism," the theory of social-ism the "most humane" theory, as if there were some mysterious "humanism" that is an immutable absolute truth, as if communism were simply an expres-sion of its final stage of accomplishment. . . .

No Marxist, no genuine revolutionary, will propagandize abstract "human-ism" and the so-called love of mankind. In a world where class antagonism exists, where there exist exploiters and exploited, oppressors and oppressed, there can be no "love of mankind" that transcends classes.

In their view, what is in keeping with bourgeois ideas, mentality, and way of life is human; anything else runs counter to human nature. If a work of literature describes the selfishness of certain characters, their schizophrenia or dual personality, then it accords with "human nature" and is "human." If a work describes men who are free from all thought of private ownership and possess communist moral qualities, if it describes the selfless nature of the proletariat, then it is "unnatural," lacking in "human interest," and contrary to "human nature." They have taken bourgeois human nature as the so-called common human nature.

Comrade Mao Tse-tung, dealing with the problem of how to approach the cultural heritage of China and other lands, has consistently opposed making a break with history and rejecting everything of the past, but at the same time he is against bolting things down raw and absorbing them uncritically. He proposes that, as regards past culture, we should take the fine essence and discard the dregs.

What we want to take over critically and develop is the tradition of progres-sive literature and art. The literature and art of eighteenth- and nineteenth-century Europe and Russia made a great contribution to mankind, producing a number of great writers like Goethe, Balzac, and Tolstoy. The good works of critical realism and positive romanticism expose the evils of feudalism and capitalism, and in varying degrees express the feeling and aspirations of the people of the time. . . . At the same time there is much worth learning in the artistic techniques with which these works describe life. However, even in the case of these works, we should adopt an analytical, critical attitude, and we must also see their negative side. Although the progressive works of literature of nineteenth-century Europe criticized capitalist society, the great majority of them did so from the standpoint of bourgeois democracy, bourgeois humanism and reformism. . . . Many of the characters described in these works are indi-vidualist "heroes," like Julien in *Le Rouge et le Noir,* who, because his personal ambition was frustrated, carried out a vengeful, despairing revolt against society, or like Jean Christophe, who relied on the strength of individual character and took the greatest pride in his loneliness. If young readers take these characters as their models, far from helping them to build up the new individuality with a collective spirit, this will serve only to destroy it, will simply strengthen old individualist ideas. . . . In the socialist society of today if anyone tries to pick up the old spears and javelins of bourgeois humanism and individualism, as the revisionists advocate, to "criticize" the new society and expose the "darkness" of the proletariat and the people, that is an act utterly opposed to the people and to socialism. . . . We should also analyze the ideas in these works that once played a progressive part, pointing out which of them still retain a positive significance today, which are no longer suited to the present, and which under the new historical conditions have become reactionary. We must be selective too when we learn from the technique of past masters, and not copy it mechanically.

The new age demands a new literature and art. We want to paint the newest, most beautiful pictures, write the newest, most beautiful poems—this is the demand made on us by the age. Thus we must have our own new ideas, new techniques, new artistic methods, and new path for creation. We should learn from our predecessors, but we must not think poorly of ourselves. . . . The ideological and artistic standard of many works falls short of the masses' level of appreciation, which is rising daily; some writings still have the shortcomings of formulism or writing according to abstract subjective ideas; modern revisionist views and various types of bourgeois ideas are still able to find a market among our intellectuals, writers, and artists; our heritage of literature and art still needs further reevaluation and editing; our experience in contemporary literature and art still needs to be further summarized, and our literary and art theory and criticism still need to be greatly strengthened.

In order to raise the level of our literary and art creations, we must at the same time raise the level of literary and art theory and criticism. . . . Our literary and art criticism is based on the standpoint of Marxism and takes the political standard as its first criterion, but at the same time we must make an accurate artistic analysis of the work and establish a scientific artistic standard of our new age on the basis of experiences summed up from our contemporary creative activities. . . .

We have all the prerequisites for the creation of a magnificent culture. . . . We have beloved and respected comrades like Kuo Mo-jo, Mao Tun, and many other outstanding veteran revolutionary writers and artists, as well as large numbers of talented and promising young literary and art workers who are emerging constantly from the masses. . . . The nation that has produced Ch'ün Yüan, Szu-ma Ch'ien, Tu Fu, Kuan Han-ch'ing, Ts'ao Hsüeh-ch'in, and Lu Hsün will certainly continue to produce thousands of brilliant writers and artists of genius.

Peking: Foreign Language Press, 1960

Excerpted by Merle Goldman

LIU CH'ING
(Liu Yün-hua, 1916–78)

Liu Ch'ing was born in Wu-pao, northern Shensi Province, and grew up during a time when China's national sovereignty was steadily eroding. Already a member of the Communist Youth Corps, he participated in the December Ninth Movement of 1935, when thousands of young Chinese rose in protest against their government's repeated concessions to Japanese expansionism. In 1936 he joined the Chinese Communist Party. Between 1937 and 1949 he worked in Northwest China, active in the cultural associations and as a cadre at the village level in the Shensi-Kansu-Ningsia Border Region. He took part in antilandlord struggles in the countryside, using this experience for his later novel, *Sowing*.

Throughout the 1950s Liu remained active as a writer, while holding office in several official literary and artistic organizations. In 1950 he published *Discussion of the Mass Line During Land Reform*. His novel *Wall of Bronze*, which deals with the fighting between Communist and Nationalist troops during the Sha-chia-tien campaign of 1947 in northern Shensi, appeared in 1951. Two years later, when he was serving as a member of the board of the Chinese Writers' Association, he published another piece of fiction describing the same campaign, *The Battle of Sha-chia-tien*, and in 1956 he began describing agricultural collectivization in *Three Years in Huang-fu Village*. Part One of *The Builders* was published in 1959, and the following year Liu served on the Presidium of the National Assembly of Writers and Artists and as a member of the National Committee, the Third Congress, All China Federation of Literary and Art Circles. Part Two of *The Builders*, begun in the later 1950s, was interrupted by the Cultural Revolution, when Liu and his work were severely condemned. He resumed his writing in 1976 and published the first twelve chapters of the second volume in spring 1977. Death in June 1978 prevented him from completing his ambitious novel.

The Builders, Part One, reflects a time of changing political and artistic priorities in China. By 1953, when the story takes place, the violence of civil war and the turbulence of Land Reform had blown over, and cooperation had taken priority over confrontation during the campaign to form mutual aid teams among poor and middle peasants.

As sociopolitical priorities shifted, the writer of socialist fiction was expected to adapt to new realities and goals. In the new stage of development, one did not see hero and villain meeting in open battle, and there were neither military engagements to galvanize the reader's attention nor open struggles against landlords to provide catharsis for frustration and anger. The immediate obstructions on the path to socialism were portrayed not as objectives to be attacked and smashed but rather as problems to be solved with patience and skill. As a reflection of this, characters in *The Builders* do not appear as purely good or purely evil, but as ordinary people, some likable, some very unlikable, whose positive and negative characteristics are closely correlated with the issues at hand in China's step-by-step plan for socialist development. It is through them that the author attempts to turn political issues into vicarious experiences and to make his vision of the struggle of his times affectively intelligible to the reader. —W.B.C.

449

from *The Builders*

[*The Builders* is concerned with events in 1953 in Frog Flat, a village in Shensi Province. Land has been redistributed, but the early spring grain shortage has left the poorest farmers without food to eat or seed for planting. The previous spring, short-term loans of excess grain had been made to needy farmers, but many of these are unpaid, and indebtedness poses a danger of dependency upon the wealthier peasants.

Liang Sheng-pao, an energetic young Communist Party member, is trying to mobilize support for his mutual aid team so that its members can increase productivity and break their cycle of dependency on the better-off peasants. Not everyone has unqualified sympathy for the project, however. Sheng-pao's stepfather, Liang the Third, a good-hearted, rough-and-ready old peasant, admires Sheng-pao's strength and determination but resents his pouring time and energy into projects that bring no visible personal gain. One such project is a trip to purchase a new quick-ripening variety of rice seed for the team members, which costs Sheng-pao precious hours of work time and brings no remuneration.

Kuo Chen-shan, the other Communist Party member in Frog Flat, considers Sheng-pao an upstart. Older and more experienced, Chen-shan has proved his zeal and effectiveness during Land Reform, but his leadership has been vitiated by concern with his own property and position.

Kuo Shih-fu, a well-to-do middle peasant, tries to undermine Sheng-pao's efforts. Working behind the scenes in league with the rich peasant Yao Shih-chieh, he tries to lure team members back into their pre-1949 state of dependency.

Hsu Kai-hsia, a pretty peasant girl, is emotionally involved in the events in Frog Flat. As a Communist Youth League member, she respects Chen-shan, but her respect is cooled somewhat as she senses the erosion in his zeal for socialist development. By contrast, her admiration and furtive affection toward Sheng-pao grow as she sees him struggling to improve the poor peasants' lot.

It is early spring, and the grain shortage among the poor peasants has become acute. A meeting is called to deal with the problem. Soon there develops a quiet struggle between two styles of leadership.]

After the gong fell silent, there was a burst of activity in the rice paddies and along the bank of the Kuan Canal. Shouts and answers, gates being pounded upon, dogs barking, and the conversations of people walking toward the school in a dusk not yet lighted by the moon all wove into a cacophony that covered the rice fields throughout the village of Frog Flat.

But as the smoke from evening cooking cleared above the fields, the village settled into silence. Those who wanted to attend the mass meeting had already arrived at the elementary school. Those who did not wish to go had already closed their gates tight, burrowed under their quilts, and could not be called out again no matter what.

The night was dark. The eye could no longer distinguish either the peak of Mt. Chung-nan from the valley below it or the cypress trees from the escarpment of Hsia-pao Village's North Flat. Farmers walking along paths in the paddies could only see rippling water to the north and south joined to a sky brimming with stars.

After Babbler Sun, the Village Affairs Committee member, had finished beating the gong, he lit the kerosene lantern. The lantern, fully pumped and hung up on the rafter of the first- and second-year elementary school, gave off a steady hissing sound. Its dazzling rays reached every corner of the room, illuminating a blackboard mounted on the whitewashed wall, color posters, charts, portraits of leaders, and desks and benches sitting on the brick-lined floor, just as plainly as if it were day. In the room there were only about twenty-odd farmers in tattered clothing, looking poor as mountain dwellers, despite the fact that they lived on the plain. Some sat smoking uncured tobacco or hunched over desks fretting and sighing, while others took advantage of the bright light and leisure for "bandit extermination"—opening their tattered jackets to capture lice. At the suggestion of Kuo Chen-shan, some of the fruits of the Land Reform struggle had been set aside to purchase as common property a kerosene lamp to provide light for these brows furrowed with worry over the early spring food shortage.

But there was no cause for alarm here. When these twenty-odd people were dispersed among over one hundred families of farmers, you might not take special notice of them. They were those who only a few years earlier had had the very marrow of their bones squeezed from them by the landlords and the mechanism of Old China. The People's Government could only give them land and loans to acquire draft animals and plant crops, and then call upon them to organize for production. It could not use sorcery to make them instantly rich. This point they themselves understood without explanation.

They could see that getting Incentive Grain Loans was a lost cause this year. The rich peasant Yao Shih-chieh and the leading well-to-do middle peasant, Kuo Shih-fu, had both failed to come, hadn't they? The other middle peasants, both prosperous and average, who had extra grain were peeking out from the peach orchard or from concealment behind mud walls. If the two richest farmers could not be summoned to the meeting, what could they, who could only lend out a few bushels of grain every spring, accomplish by attending the meeting? If you can't fell the large trees, you won't get much firewood! What good will twigs and bits of grass do? To bed, then! Off with our clothes and to bed! As they undressed for bed they told their wives, "If our representative calls again, you tell him I already left for the meeting a long time ago."

This was the most depressing mass meeting held in Frog Flat since Liberation!

After joining hands to sweep away the landlords, who had been cruel exploiters of poor peasants and a menace to middle peasants, farmers above the poverty level and those who were below it began to split off from each other. People like Yao and Kuo Shih-fu, who were powerful economically in the village, were doing their best behind the scenes to accelerate this split. The poor farmers sitting in the school couldn't have put into words just what was happening, yet they sensed it keenly.

Some farmers who were somewhat better off had left, one after another, when they saw that the meeting was not going to take place, but these twenty-some farmers were not going to leave, no matter what. They wanted to take no course other than that of reliance upon the Communist Party and the People's Government. Of course they could always get grain by writing a description of part of the land apportioned to them—its name, acreage, and limits—on a note for a grain loan and secretly giving it to someone with excess grain. But what a chilling, disappointing prospect that was! They felt that somehow it would be strange, awkward, and out of tune with the way their society was progressing, like a man turned around walking backwards down the road.

They sat in the schoolroom with righteous determination to follow the Party and the government, because they supported the Party and the government it led with all the determination and enthusiasm the hearts that beat beneath those tattered clothes could muster.

Look! To the east of the schoolroom, Township Party Branch Secretary Lu Ming-ch'ang and Kuo Chen-shan were standing in the shadows by a field of alfalfa having an animated conversation. Surely they were thinking of a solution. Perhaps they were discussing calling a mass meeting another day? Or perhaps they were discussing using agricultural loan funds to combat the spring food shortage? Perhaps ... at any rate, they wouldn't leave without thoroughly explaining the problem to the group. And then there was Liang Sheng-pao, who took the timid, hard-working Iron Man Kuo—the only middle peasant who attended the meeting—out to the peach orchard west of the schoolroom with militia leader Feng Yu-wan in tow. There they were, squatting in the shadows beneath a peach tree that was about to bloom, Sheng-pao and Yu-wan cornering Iron Man, wishing they could hold him down and pour certain thoughts into his head! Surely they were trying to talk him into something.

As the two Communist Party members of Frog Flat worked separately for the benefit of the recently liberated farmers, why shouldn't these poor farmers wait patiently? They had especially great hopes placed in Kuo Chen-shan, Chairman and village representative. With his quick and agile mind he would find a solution. Compared to Kuo Chen-shan, Yao and Shih-fu were like children. Their belief in Kuo Chen-shan was the concrete manifestation of their belief in the Communist Party. They were pragmatic people, unused to dealing with abstractions.

Those who avoided the meeting—the "go-it-alone" families—thought that since they had twenty or thirty *mu* of land, an ox, and two or three able-bodied men, they could get by on their own and so were masters of their own fates. There were even some who chatted condescendingly about the Communist Party actually having some good points: being reasonable, not abusing people verbally or physically, neither imposing a lot of taxes nor oppressing the common people. How absurdly nearsighted! They were hoping that history would stop in its tracks and that the New Democracy would last forever. They were afraid of the word "struggle" and hated to hear strange-sounding words like "socialism."

The group now sitting in the schoolhouse, the farmers who had formerly been pressed down at the bottom of the scale, would have been only too glad to put socialism into practice the very next morning. If history were to stop in 1953, after the redistribution of land and other means of agricultural production, then they would soon return to their tragic pre-1949 fate. The Communist Party would not allow it! Chairman Mao was brilliant: as he inventoried and redistributed all property and possessions, he rectified the party and prepared to advance. These poor peasants would march steadfastly forward behind the Communist Party. They could no longer be satisfied with a few acres of land, nor with having their stomachs only half full, nor with having a new padded jacket once every ten years, nor with shoulders bruised and swollen from the carrying pole. Such nonsense! Only fools wanted that. They believed that Chairman Mao Tse-tung would see them through.

They waited with perfect calm under the strong light of the kerosene lamp. Their calmness showed their inner composure, because they were quite free from anxiety. Even though their parents' blood and their childhood environments had made them different in temperament and character, poverty had made them one in thought, feeling, and bearing. This made more than twenty people like a single person. In their peasants' minds a single thought was forming, and in their hearts a single feeling was stirring.

Lean, solemn, and determined in bearing, Kao Tseng-fu sat on a bench behind the first row of desks. His arms, covered by sleeves through which the cotton padding showed, were wrapped around the sleeping Little Ts'ai. He sat there hating that crafty neighbor of his. He had rapped on Yao Shih-chieh's black gate until his knuckles ached before a distant answer to the effect that Yao had gone to Huang-pao Town had come from Yao's wife in the main building. The devil! He himself had seen Yao at nightfall. But what could he do? That large black gate was closed tighter than a drumhead without even a crack to peer through, and speaking to him through the closed gate was a woman. He hated himself for not being able to serve the people better as their representative. If it weren't for his having to take on the woman's work of cooking, if it weren't that caring for Little Ts'ai tied him down, that rich peasant Yao would never have escaped the meeting. He could have squatted in Yao's compound before nightfall and waited for him to finish dinner so they could go to the meeting together. If only he could get that wealthy peasant to the meeting, Kao would have plenty to say to him: "Why aren't you helping needy families get through the spring food shortage? *You* have no surplus grain? Where has your surplus grain gone? Could it be that you sneaked it into Huang-pao Town to lend out at high interest? Speak! Tell the truth! As soon as Land Reform has blown over, you've gone back to exploiting!" But what could he say now, with that rich peasant already sleeping with his wife on his fancy lacquered *k'ang*?

A disheartened expression appeared on Kao's thin, harried face. He didn't know how he was going to get through the spring, how he could get money for fertilizer before time for summer rice transplanting came. To him the coming months looked dark as the night outside. Yet, though Kao was suffering real privation, Fate could not defeat this unfortunate man, because he, like the poor peasants and former hired hands around him, placed hope in the government, which had given him land and a loan for a draft animal. While he was doing both a man's and a woman's work to keep alive, and carrying out the duties and errands of Township People's Representative, it was this hope that sustained him.

Kao was exhorting Jen the Fourth, who sat hunched over in the first row of desks: "Old Jen, your place is a long way from here, and you've got a bunch of kids there. You'd better leave early. Can't you see? Tonight's meeting isn't ever going to begin at all."

"No!" Old Jen looked upon attending meetings as a show of support for the government and the Party. Taking a pipe with a brass mouthpiece out of his thick-tongued mouth, he spoke, giving off a spray of saliva as he did: "Let's wait for our team leader and leave with him."

"Oh, yes. You're waiting for Sheng-pao. Right! With Sheng-pao's mutual aid team you don't have to worry," Kao said enviously.

"We aren't worrying," old Jen admitted. "It isn't that we can hold our own so well. We're relying on our good neighbors. They say 'A near neighbor is worth more than a distant relative,' and it's true! If it weren't for Sheng-pao taking the bunch of problems involved in a permanent mutual aid team onto his own broad shoulders, do you think I could keep from worrying? I'd be more worried than any of you, and that's the truth! After Spring Grave Visitation we're going into the mountains."

Old Jen's words and his satisfied air stirred up an intense interest among the shabbily dressed poor farmers in the schoolroom. They swarmed up from the desks in the rear and gathered at the front where they had detected a ray of hope.

But when they had found out all about the plan of Sheng-pao's mutual aid team for going into the mountains, all they could do was envy him. Their huts were scattered in every corner around the Kuan Canal and the upstream area. Their neighbors—tenant or semitenant farmers who had had a little bit of background in crop raising before—had gained or increased their holdings during the Land Reform, and this put them on an equal footing with the longer established middle peasants, whom they now imitated by devoting themselves to increasing their family wealth. They were only willing to join with their poverty-stricken neighbors in organizing seasonal, temporary mutual aid teams. They would not be like Sheng-pao, who put himself wholeheartedly into working for the common good.

Those twenty-odd men who had formerly suffered as hired hands or performed odd jobs for their livelihood were now together, discussing whether to form their own organization. "Let's organize a group and get Kao to lead us!" lean and lanky Wang Sheng-mao suggested, his eyes shining with excitement.

"Where are our draft animals?" interjected short, fat Iron Lock Wang. "Let's look before we leap!"

"We won't use animals. People can pull the plows, all right?" said Li Chü-tsai enthusiastically.

Then Yang Ta-hai, a stern ruddy-faced farmer with little tolerance for careless talk spoke: "Nonsense! I've seen two people plowing dry land, but that won't work in a paddy."

"Then what can we do?" several people asked in a discouraged tone of voice.

"This is really a bad spring!" Kao gave a depressed sigh, "Let's see what the Party members have to say."

"Anyway, Chairman Mao won't let anyone starve," someone in back said with an unconcerned air. When they looked back they saw it was not one of them. It was Pai Chan-k'uei, a former corporal in the Nationalist Army. When had he come in?

While they had huddled close together, rubbing ragged shoulders with each other, to discuss the "two-man plowing" technique, there had been two other people in the schoolroom. Babbler Sun was crouched against the north wall, busily filling out forms by the lamplight so that Party Branch Secretary Lu could take them back to the township office when he went. Pai was sitting on the bench nearest the back door smoking a cheap black cigarette. Sure! That was him with that nonchalant expression on his narrow face.

With Little Ts'ai still sleeping in his arms, Kao turned to Pai, who had been an assistant squad leader in a supply company stationed at Huang-pao Town during the first stage of the War against Japan, and asked him, "Pai, when did you get back?"

"Yesterday," Pai replied, puffing on his cigarette.

"From where?"

"Sian."

"On what business?"

"Collecting junk, as usual."

"You gathered junk during the day. Where did you stay at night?"

"In a friend's room."

"What friend?"

"The one who runs a junk shop. You think I have any high-class, distinguished friends?"

"What street in Sian does your friend live on?"

"Min-le Park." Pai was still responding, but his expression had changed from unconcern to unhappiness. Clamping his cigarette between his fingers, he demanded angrily: "What do you mean, anyway, interrogating me like this? You aren't a security officer, and you aren't a militia commander, either!"

"I'm a People's Representative," Kao said calmly, with a stern expression on his face.

"You don't represent the Upper Bank area, so you've no authority over me."

"I'm representative for all of Hsia-pao Township!"

Two pairs of eyes locked in opposition. A cold, penetrating glare shot forth from Kao's eyes and fixed itself on Pai's gaunt, ashen face. "All right, forget it!" the group advised. "Why get angry over nothing?" But the People's Representative, ever loyal to his social duties, didn't consider this getting angry over nothing. He didn't like a man of bad background, turned farmer late in life, mixing with his needy peasants year after year.

Before Liberation, when the Nationalists conscripted soldiers, and farmers could hire able-bodied men to take their places, Pai had "sold" himself five times. Each time recruits set out from the local division's area he had been able to escape. After Liberation, during Land Reform, he had shown a madman's zeal, but this former assistant squad leader had not been able at all to develop his talents in the new society. He had not reached his goal of becoming a village cadre.

This is the sort of "farmer" he was: In 1942, when the Nationalist troops stationed in Huang-pao Town had set out for the Chung-t'iao mountains in Shansi, his mistress, Turquoise, hid him until they were gone. Then he began to do odd jobs around Frog Flat. When setting up a grindstone he would put the shaft in backwards, as if the draft animal could push the grindstone with its head as it turned the mill! Once when he was plowing, he was not even aware when the plowshare dropped off. Finally, discovering what had happened, he had to dig through the whole field with his hands searching for the lost piece. Toward the end of the war against Japan, he drifted into selling himself into the army. After Liberation he brought home soybeans he had pulled up from the banks around his paddies and hung them, stalks and all, in the crotch of a tree in front of their hut. When the notoriously amorous Turquoise, by then his wife, wanted to cook some, she would take a stick and knock off as many as she needed. They had no children, so they went to the market in Huang-pao Town together and, just like "enlightened couples," man and woman would sit together in a restaurant sharing mutton and steamed buns like equals. The previous winter when the Property Inventory Team had come to the village to check on implementation of Land Reform, it was Pai who had taken the megaphone from Babbler Sun and announced to the whole village, "It's the second Land Reform! No need to go to the mountains now!" He had opposed having needy farmers go into the mountains for charcoal and wood after autumn planting and had agitated all over the village to have Yao Shih-chieh and Kuo Shih-fu reclassified as landlords, since they were making more of a killing than the "slender" landlords in former days. Only after Kuo Chen-shan had given him a severe talking to did he begin to behave a bit better. He and his wife had been given four *mu* of land during Land Reform, though Kao felt that they weren't real farmers. The soft full flesh of Turquoise's cheeks was too much like the flesh of her rump!

Right must triumph over wrong! Pai's droopy eyes retreated. Feigning contempt, he finally turned his head—upon which an old skullcap was perched—and faced another direction.

Kao pursued the spoils of victory: "I'm a township representative. Can't I ask you questions? You've collected junk in Sian, and now, since it's not planting time, or harvest, either, just what did you come back for?"

"Is that any business of yours?" Aroused once more, Pai glared with his heavy-lidded eyes at Kao.

"Whether it is or not," said Kao, "I'm asking you. You mean I can't ask?"

Humpbacked old Jen stood up. He plucked the pipe from his whiskered mouth, smiled and spoke, emitting a spray of saliva. "The truth, now! I'm not too blind to figure this one out! Pai, while you were in Sian you must have figured it was time to start maneuvering for new Incentive grain loans here. Right? Tell us!" Pai laughed through his tobacco-stained teeth. "There'll be no loans this year," said Jen. "You've come for nothing."

"Even if there were grain loans, you wouldn't get any, Pai," said Kao without a trace of sympathy. "Feeding you last year and the year before was a real mistake. How do you qualify as a needy peasant? At the market you've nothing better to do than stuff yourself at restaurants."

Pai could stand no more. His well-trained, agile body sprang to a standing position. The group thought he was about to have it out with Kao, but he stalked out of the room instead. The sound of his swearing came in from the courtyard: "Little bastard's getting big for his britches! What kind of a people's rep . . . !" The rest of what he said was cut off by the closing gate.

Kao was so angry that sparks shot forth from his eyes. It was all too obvious that he was the one being sworn at. He wanted to set out in pursuit, but he had Little Ts'ai sleeping against his chest. And the others advised him that there was no need to go up against someone of Pai's type. Furthermore, even though Pai wasn't a village cadre, after Liberation in movement after movement he had followed right behind the most active elements. He had been fearless, had moments of genuine enthusiasm and borne his share of hardships. But Kao was unconvinced. He said, "That fellow is no damn good! Two years ago when he got a grain loan, what did he say? 'We ate at the landlords' expense during Land Reform and at the rich and middle peasants' expense with the grain loans.' You can tell that when he took out that loan he had no intention whatsoever of repaying it. We can't let him mix in among us and pretend he's a needy peasant. And so what if he wasn't accepted as a village cadre? If he got accepted as a cadre, I'd quit being one!" Kao's responsible attitude aroused real admiration in the group. No matter how desperate his circumstances became, he remained upright and pure, like the white poplars along the T'ang River, which towered above all the elms, willows, and thorny locusts, their branches brushing the white clouds softly floating in the blue sky. By tacit consent he had become the representative figure of these needy farmers, and they were watching him to see how he got through the spring food scarcity, hoping then to follow his lead.

Time began to weigh on these farmers, and they became restless. Outside, over by the alfalfa field, Secretary Lu was still talking with Kuo Chen-shan. What were they saying? Were they thinking of how to call another meeting, or giving up on the grain loans, or thinking of another way to help the needy farmers? No! The two Party members over in the clover field had no solution other than grain loans and mutual aid teams. Their superiors had repeatedly stressed using certain funds only for certain purposes and would not allow agricultural loan funds earmarked for the promotion of seven-inch plows, "Liberation" model water wheels, chemical fertilizers, and insecticides to be lent to needy peasants so that they could buy grain. Such loans would violate policy, damage agricultural production, and bring charges of improper and illegal conduct against the perpetrators. The small relief fund had been established only for pitiful old people who through a sudden stroke of fate had lost their entire means of support. They were considered separately. There were only a couple such cases in the village, while there were ten times that number of needy families. How could relief funds be used to solve the problem? No, solutions would have to be devised in terms of more production.

Kuo Chen-shan's robust body loomed large in the shadows of the clover field. His whiskered cheeks were taut, and his teeth ground together in hatred toward Yao Shih-chieh and Kuo Shih-fu, two bastions of "go-it-alone" forces, one looming on the east side of the Kuan Canal, the other on the west. He was saying that if these bastions could not be stormed and taken, it would threaten his authority, and it would endanger every future project in all the five villages of Hsia-pao Township.

"If we could only get them to the meeting," said Chen-shan disconsolately to Secretary Lu, "I'd be able to solve this. The masses are with me, not them. A few words from this mouth of mine and they'd have to come up with some grain. And I'm not bragging either! Who'd have guessed that those two stick-in-the-muds would be slipperier than eels and not come to the meeting at all!"

Kuo Chen-shan stood hulking in the field, smacking his work-hardened hands together in anger. Two feet away, facing him with a flashlight in hand, was Secretary Lu. As he listened the expression on his wrinkled face betrayed disapproval of this monologue by Kuo Chen-shan. The Communist standing there in a gray padded uniform jacket was Hsia-pao Township's most uncompromising character, despite his unobtrusive manner. Even when work went successfully, Lu did not boast about the part he himself had played. Only those who wanted to cover up their failings when work went badly would boast. As Party branch secretary for Hsia-pao Township, he dealt with many people and had ample experience in observing this sort of person.

Lu was the same age as Kuo Chen-shan, but smaller and rather ordinary in appearance. Though his uniform was quite distinct from farmer's clothing, he could not alter his rustic appearance—thick hands, large feet, arms and legs sinewy from work, a curved back, and shoulders rounded from the carrying pole. China has millions upon millions of this sort of comrade. Whether they dress in coarse woolen clothing, generals' uniforms, or even field marshal's attire, they are still affable, straightforward, and entirely without affectation, men who stay close to the masses.

Secretary Lu chuckled quietly and said with frankness: "Chen-shan! Let's not get bogged down on Yao Shih-chieh and Kuo Shih-fu. If they were more progressive, what would be left for us Communists to do? Take a closer look at what you yourself have done. For example, after we held two meetings at the township level to set things up, you failed to do thorough groundwork here. You're being lax, Comrade, and you're not taking suggestions made at the township level seriously enough. If you had mobilized some ordinary middle peasants who have a few pecks of grain to lend out by talking to them individually, we never would have been caught in this stalemate, would we? Chen-shan, this won't do! From now on you must work harder and more painstakingly."

Kuo blew a long breath out through his hairy nostrils. "Ai! Lu, old friend, you can't clap with just one hand, you know! There are only two of us Communists in Frog Flat, and our comrade Sheng-pao is so wrapped up in production that he ignores politics. When the first meeting was called, he was off in Kuo-hsien buying rice seeds, so young Huan-hsi came to listen in. After he came back he didn't even contact me. That little rascal has gotten a bit arrogant since he joined the Party—"

Secretary Lu could not listen any longer. He spoke to this man, with whom he was on good enough terms to joke and tease, with considerable bluntness. "Ai-ya-ya! My dear Bomber [Kuo Chen-shan's nickname], your thinking is getting moldy! Even after the Party Rectification Campaign you say that cooperative farming has nothing to do with politics! Have you forgotten what Secretary Wang said at last winter's Huang-pao Township Party Branch meeting? Simply getting grain quotas delivered, continuing to issue agricultural loans, filling in statistical forms, writing introductions for people taking cases to court, witnessing applications for marriage certificates—that's not dynamic political activity. We Party members are often told not to get bogged down in administrative details, but to organize the masses and lead them in production. You should make a clear distinction between production by mutual aid teams and the go-it-alone variety. You say that Sheng-pao ignores politics and doesn't contact you? Well, you should take the initiative in helping him!"

A fine sweat broke out on the bridge of Kuo's nose, and his whiskery face turned red. His group was called a mutual aid team, but in actuality it was the private, "go-it-alone" form of production. Even in the darkness, Secretary Lu could detect his embarrassment.

Kuo stood speechless for a long time. With his large, coarse hands he rubbed the stubble-covered face under his skullcap, hoping thereby to control the feverishness he felt in his head. As he finished rubbing his face, he finally— thank heavens!—thought of a position he could take to cover his failings. "Lu," Kuo began, in a voice oozing patriotism, "I think that when our country declared an end to Land Reform, it was quite a mistake, wasn't it?"

"How so?"

"Ever since it ended, Yao Shih-chieh and Kuo Shih-fu have been on their way up again. In ordinary farmers' homes at New Year's and other festivals, they put food on the offering table for their ancestors' spirits. The rest of the time they worship the deed to their land. That makes it hard to get projects going."

"Then how would you do it? Have Land Reform every year? Get rid of all the middle peasants? Pull everyone down to the same level?"

"Look, you! Do you think I don't understand anything about policy? I'm not saying we should have Land Reform once a year, but we shouldn't declare Land Reform ended, either."

"So we can keep the whole countryside nervous?"

"Actually only the wealthy and well-to-do middle peasants would be nervous."

"Ordinary middle peasants wouldn't be nervous?"

"Well, they'd be nervous, but it wouldn't interfere with production."

"And would you keep the masses of poor farmers up in the air about the situation, unable to plan their next step forward?"

Quick-tongued Kuo Chen-shan was left without words. Controlling his anger, Secretary Lu admonished Kuo in a voice that was sharply critical yet more concerned than hostile. "Comrade! Don't start finding fault with the Party Central's line. We should take a closer look at how we ourselves are carrying out our work and whether our thinking has become corrupted. When you were peddling earthenware you travelled to a lot of places and saw a lot more than most farmers. But there's a distance of heaven and earth between your experience—mine, too, for that matter—and that of our comrades in the Party Central. We've seen pictures of Marx and Lenin so often that their faces are familiar to us. But just what did they actually say? Do you know? You don't? Well, let's take an honest look at ourselves. I've heard that you've had some business dealings with Han Wan-hsiang, who has the brick and tile kiln by North Gate in Huang-pao Town. You should remember who you are!"

"Who said I've had dealings with Han Wan-hsiang?" Kuo was getting tense and angry.

Secretary Lu calmly and patiently explained: "If you've had no dealings there's no cause for alarm. Now go to the classroom and announce that the needy peasants should go home. Tell them that after every village in the

Township has met we'll discuss possible solutions. Go on, now. I have a padded jacket and you don't. Be careful you don't get chilled."

"Who said I had dealings with Han Wan-hsiang?" Kuo persisted, ignoring the chill in the air.

"We'll talk about that later. Don't keep the needy peasants waiting!"

"No! I have to know who's spreading stories about me!"

"Don't worry! The Party Branch Office will get to the bottom of these stories about business dealings. Go adjourn the meeting now!" As he spoke, Secretary Lu flashed his light down a small path that led through the clover field, and, snuggling his padded jacket around his shoulders, he stalked off angrily.

Kuo handed an unexpected disappointment to the needy peasants who had such hope in him. He ran up to the classroom door, hastily announced cancellation of the meeting, and then ran off after Secretary Lu. He didn't even pause to pick up the form Babbler Sun had filled out. He wanted to find out just who in the township office was putting him in a bad light.

After Babbler Sun had taken the kerosene lamp away, the poor farmers gathered around Liang Sheng-pao in the darkness of the schoolyard. Several abruptly demanded that Sheng-pao's mutual aid team be expanded. This caught Sheng-pao unprepared, and he stood surrounded by his shabbily clothed neighbors, rubbing the back of his neck with his hand, a forced smile on his face. "Neighbors," he said in embarrassment, "The mutual aid team has just gotten organized. This is my first year as team leader, too. Next year—let me work at it for a year, and next year if you think I do my work well enough, we'll talk again. I'm young and untrained, so I'm afraid I might get everyone into a bad fix."

"We've got eyes. You did a good job buying the rice seeds," said Li Chü-ts'ai.

"Don't just be nice to the few neighbors around you," smiled tall, lean Wang Sheng-mao.

"Our huts may be far away, but our paddies are right next to yours!" said the solemn-faced Yang Ta-hai.

Sheng-pao really felt awkward. He felt closer to this group of people than he did to his own family. He was afraid that if he went ahead and took them into his team there would be too many to manage. Also, if he took several new members who had no draft animals into his team, working power would become a problem. No, it simply wouldn't do. He remembered the experience shared at the county meeting by Wang Tsung-chi, model peasant from Ta-wang Village, Tou-pao District: "To become good, mutual aid teams should be small at first." He couldn't be brash and begin something without a firm foundation. But, looking at it from another angle, he felt deep sympathy for these needy peasants who had weak draft animals—or none at all—and who could not plow and plant unless they teamed up with someone else. Their middle-peasant neighbors—former tenant or semitenant farmers—traded their draft animals' force for manpower in the seasonal mutual aid teams, getting real benefit from the bargain. During the slack time that followed planting these needy peasants became frantic with idleness, yet no one organized them to earn supplementary income. Thus they were unable to shed the label of "needy peasant," and every spring they ran short of food. Their demand not only aroused Sheng-pao's sympathy, it awakened his sense of obligation as a Communist to help the masses through their difficulties as well. He felt it would be shameful to sneak away from this group of men in ragged clothes.

"Yu-wan!" he shouted.

"Hey!" answered Feng Yu-wan from the darkness behind the group.

"Yu-wan, come here," said Sheng-pao. "Let's discuss whether we can revise this plan of ours."

Sheng-pao and Yu-wan had taken advantage of the time before the meeting to take Iron Man Kuo into a corner behind the schoolroom and talk him into lending two *tan* of grain to needy peasants in his election ward. This would allow those neighbors who were in dire straits to keep feeding their families for the time being, while they helped with the shipment of brooms, to be made from bamboo cut by the team, out of the mountains by Sheng-pao's mutual aid team. Now Sheng-pao was thinking of changing his plan. He could have those who were originally going to carry brooms cut bamboo for handles instead. Then another group could do the carrying. This way all the needy peasants in the village could be helped, and part of the problem at hand could be solved.

"Where will the new group get food for their families?" Yu-wan asked doubtfully.

"We'll think of a way!" Sheng-pao thought hard. Then he said again, even more emphatically: "I've got a way! As soon as we commit ourselves to delivery of the brooms, the marketing co-op will give us an advance. They won't make us wait until we've delivered a certain number of brooms to get the cash. No, a community project like the co-op will be more flexible than that. So if we do it this way, the food shortage won't be nearly as bad, and that'll give us a chance to think of our next step."

As they heard Sheng-pao and Yu-wan talk, the group began to bubble with happy excitement. With Sheng-pao lifting their crushing burdens, they suddenly felt free and light. In the light of the newly risen moon they gazed steadily at Sheng-pao's full face with joyful, grateful eyes. They felt like embracing him and kissing his face. There was such a good and sympathetic heart beating in his breast!

Each group member wanted to be first to join in:

"I'll go!"

"So will I!"

"You've got to take me!"

The school yard suddenly bustled with life and activity. Kao Tseng-fu, his tattered sleeves around a newly awakened Little Ts'ai, stood in the midst of the group, advising them to quit trying to outdo one another. Though he kept a calm exterior, he felt deeply moved. Like a spirited horse who sees another horse dashing away, he could not contain his own impulse to run forward. Seeing Sheng-pao's courage in doing what he knew to be right left a loyal, sincere man like Kao Tseng-fu so inspired that he trembled. With Little Ts'ai still in his arms, he nudged Sheng-pao, saying, "Sheng-pao, let me organize the men from the Kuan Canal area to carry brooms. You just handle the bamboo-cutting group."

The group voiced unanimous support for this, but Sheng-pao asked, "With Little Ts'ai tying you down, will you be able to go into the mountains?"

"You don't need to worry," Kao replied. "Don't worry about whether I can go into the mountains. That's my problem and I can solve it best myself. You just organize your bamboo cutters, and I'll take care of transportation!"

On the way home, Old Jen the Fourth let out sigh after sigh.

"Fourth Uncle," said Sheng-pao, "What's on your mind?"

"I'm thinking that you're young and full of imagination," Old Jen said, emitting his usual spray of saliva. "Taking on a project as ambitious as this—are you sure you know what you're doing?"

Sheng-pao spread his hands wide, and with an expression so full of grief he seemed about to cry, he said, "What could I do? Seeing those needy peasants about to starve was real torture for me. If a Communist didn't take care of them, who would?"

[The failure of Kuo Chen-shan to get grain loans for the needy peasants encourages the well-to-do middle peasant Kuo Shih-fu and his rich peasant crony Yao Shih-chieh to become bolder in cultivating disaffection among members of Chen-shan and Sheng-pao's teams. Chen-shan, though frustrated in his attempt to build up personal property—as a Communist his business activities are curtailed—dares not leave the Party, his only protection against retaliation from the enemies he made during Land Reform.

One day news comes that a competing mutual aid team has become self-reliant through a bamboo-cutting expedition. Feeling encouraged and challenged, Sheng-pao's team sets out for the mountains. They leave young Jen Huan-hsi behind to work with an agronomist who will arrive while the team is gone. The bamboo-cutting project is beset with hardship and danger—one member is hurt—but the group remains in high spirits and works harmoniously. By contrast, back in the village the visiting agronomist finds jealousy, mutual suspicion, and general noncooperation among the middle peasants, who bully and harass Jen Huan-hsi as he carries out his duties.

In his relation with Kai-hsia, Sheng-pao is a sterling model of Communist dedication but a rather reluctant suitor. Their romance almost bursts into flame late one balmy evening but ends on a tentative note after duty and devotion quickly reassert themselves.

Things are going well at the end of Volume One, with Liang Sheng-pao's ascendency as a leader established, the road toward self-sufficiency found for poor peasants, and the beginnings of improved agricultural productivity—the fast-growing seeds—introduced. The problems, though attacked successfully, are far from solved. Loose ends are left dangling, to be picked up and woven into Part Two, which deals with the next stage of agricultural collectivization, the establishment of agricultural cooperatives.]

Translated by William B. Crawford

CHAO HSÜN
(1920–)

When Chao Hsün finished his *Homecoming* in 1958, the Hundred Flowers thaw had already been chilled again and Party authorities promptly suppressed the manuscript. Two years later the antirevisionist movement was building toward another flood crest; the Party-directed editors of the *Drama Monthly* printed the play with a call for criticism to identify the "serious errors" in the author's line of thinking. Criticism indeed followed, in a series of denunciations attacking Chao Hsün for his failure to depict a single positive character in the entire four-act play, in which even the veteran Communist cadre, a rehabilitated People's Liberation Army officer, wavers when faced with a broken home and the chaos in a supposedly liberated village. The work, the critics claimed, was intended to expose the dark side of the new socialist society.

Homecoming fed the fire of the 1960 literary purge, but Chao Hsün returned to public life in the spring of 1978 after the downfall of the Gang of Four.

—K.Y.H.

---

from *Homecoming*

[This is a play in four acts, five scenes, a prologue, and an epilogue.

The prologue opens on a mountain trail, where TUNG SHU-LAN, a middle-aged village woman, reminisces with the old village head, WAN PAO-SHAN. TUNG has married MA HSING-WANG, her former husband's brother, because her husband, MA HSING-KUO, was reported killed in Red Army action nearly twenty years ago. WAN says he has just heard about an old Red Armyman returning to the village and wonders who he could be. A little later MA HSING-KUO enters and passes by TUNG, nearly rubbing shoulders with her, but they do not recognize each other.]

ACT ONE

SCENE ONE

That evening, immediately following the prologue. At MA HSING-WANG'S *house. On stage one sees the living room of his home, in which there are several pieces of rustic furniture. In the center are the ancestral tablets and the tablet of "Heaven, Earth, Emperor, Parents, and Teacher." One door leads outside; one side door leads to the bedroom; another side door leads to the kitchen.* MA HSING-WANG *and* TIAO SHIH-KUEI *are hiding grain.* SHIH-KUEI *is standing waist-deep in a hole in the ground, and* HSING-WANG *is bringing the grain to him bag by bag.*

TIAO SHIH-KUEI   How much more is there?

MA HSING-WANG   Only these two bags.

TIAO SHIH-KUEI   Come on, hurry up, there'll be people coming soon.
(HSING-WANG *gives him a bag. Someone knocks on the door. The knocking becomes more and more insistent*)

SUN ER-NIANG (*Calling from outside*)   It's just gotten dark. What are you two doing in there?

TIAO SHIH-KUEI   Sun Er-niang is here. Hurry! Hurry!
(HSING-WANG *gives* SHIH-KUEI *the last bag*)

TIAO SHIH-KUEI   Don't let her know I'm here.
(SHIH-KUEI *crouches down in the hole.* HSING-WANG *puts the cover on the hole, places some things on top of it, and goes to open the door*)

SUN ER-NIANG   My God! It sure was hard to get you to open the door! What are you doing behind a locked door?

MA HSING-WANG   It's dark, why shouldn't the door be shut? What do you want, Er-niang?

SUN ER-NIANG   Look, Hsing-wang, can the price be raised on that deal you were talking about?

MA HSING-WANG   The price is set. I'm only in this for other people. The price is a lot higher than the government's standard price.

SUN ER-NIANG   How you talk! If I weren't out for a little profit, would I be taking this risk? If I'm caught, then I'll be charged with selling grain on the black market, instead of selling it to the government as surplus.

MA HSING-WANG   Go sell it as surplus then! It's an honor and the price is high too.

SUN ER-NIANG   All right, you win. I'll sell it to you.
(SHIH-KUEI *knocks on the cover from underground*)

SUN ER-NIANG   What is under there?

MA HSING-WANG   A rat, a really fierce rat.

SUN ER-NIANG   That creature steals your grain. You'd better get a cat right away.

MA HSING-WANG   I advise you to sell, Er-niang. The price isn't low. Really, in a couple of days they're going to check very carefully, and you won't be able to sell even if you want to.

SUN ER-NIANG   You people are really something. All right, it's a deal, as long as it's cash on delivery—not a minute late in payment.

MA HSING-WANG   There won't be any mix-up. You won't be shortchanged a single cent.

SUN ER-NIANG   Then it's settled. You go and get it.

MA HSING-WANG   Okay! But you shouldn't talk about this matter with anyone else, because if it leaks out, we'll lose both our lives and money.

SUN ER-NIANG   You don't need to say that. I know I talk too much, but not about everything—for heaven's sake!
(SHIH-KUEI *sneezes underground*)

SUN ER-NIANG   What's that? That rat again? Your rat isn't afraid of people.

MA HSING-WANG   Yes . . . yes, it's the rat. I'll get a cat right away. You go on home. I'll go and get a cat this evening. No . . . no, I'll go and get the grain at your house.

SUN ER-NIANG   You're really sharp! In a few days, Hsing-wang, you're going to be very rich.

MA HSING-WANG   Yes, but I wish the money'd stay with me though. I ... (*Realizing that* SHIH-KUEI *has been shut up underground too long*) You'd better go!

(ER-NIANG *still doesn't want to leave. She wants to ask about something else, but* HSING-WANG *finally gets her out the door.* SHIH-KUEI *has been continually pounding on the underside of the cover.* HSING-WANG *comes back and takes the cover off the hole*)

TIAO SHIH-KUEI   God! You almost suffocated me! How come you got started with her on cats and rats and everything else at a time like this!

MA HSING-WANG   She wouldn't leave.

TIAO SHIH-KUEI   The tongues of people like her are too loose. Don't get too involved with them in the future.

MA HSING-WANG   She looked me up.

TIAO SHIH-KUEI   And besides, people like Ta Lao-niu are so poor that even an oil press can't squeeze a drop out of them. Why did you loan grain to him?

MA HSING-WANG   That day his wife was here crying her heart out ...

TIAO SHIH-KUEI   And you felt sorry for her? We're not running a charity.

MA HSING-WANG   They're willing to pay interest ...

TIAO SHIH-KUEI   Look, don't capsize the whole damn boat trying to catch the big one. We don't want to do it that way anyway. Let's get this grain off our hands immediately. This time we'll double our money.

MA HSING-WANG   Okay, let's get this batch together and go.

TIAO SHIH-KUEI   By the way, Hsing-wang, you see that this is such a good business, how come you don't chip in on it?

MA HSING-WANG   Where could I get the money?

TIAO SHIH-KUEI   Well, Shu-lan has ...

MA HSING-WANG   She doesn't have cash.

TIAO SHIH-KUEI   If she has valuables, that works just the same.

MA HSING-WANG   She probably has several bolts of cloth.

TIAO SHIH-KUEI   Cloth is all right too!

MA HSING-WANG   I'll see when she comes home. She's tight-fisted.

TIAO SHIH-KUEI   Okay, I'm going. Lao Chu will be here in a moment. We'll go to make contact together. Put that cover back on and make sure it looks all right. (*Takes a look*) Hm! Is this place safe?

MA HSING-WANG   Don't worry, everyone knows I haven't got a cent to my name. Who would imagine that I have grain stored in my home?

TIAO SHIH-KUEI   You still ought to be careful. (*Exits quickly*)

(HSING-WANG *covers up the hole and arranges things on top of it.* SHU-LAN *enters carrying firewood*)

MA HSING-WANG   Why haven't you cooked dinner yet?

T'UNG SHU-LAN   I went to cut firewood. You've just been sitting here doing nothing. Couldn't you start a fire?

MA HSING-WANG   Shu-lan, I happen to have something I want to talk to you about.

T'UNG SHU-LAN   (*Picking up some wild vegetables*) Would you sort these wild vegetables?

MA HSING-WANG   Are we going to have that wild vegetable mush again?

T'UNG SHU-LAN   If we don't eat that, what will we eat? You haven't gotten rich ...

MA HSING-WANG   Listen, we have a chance to get rich now. There's a business deal, an extremely profitable deal, but we are short of capital. Could you contribute some money?

T'UNG SHU-LAN   Where do I get the money?

MA HSING-WANG   You've been spinning and weaving all year. Isn't that money?

T'UNG SHU-LAN   It's all gone for the grain we ate.

MA HSING-WANG   You don't mean to tell me you are that generous—letting us eat it all up? Don't be pig-headed. If you give it to me, I'll guarantee that within a month you'll have two bolts for every one.

T'UNG SHU-LAN   This time I'm not going to be fooled.

MA HSING-WANG   But this time won't be like the other times, I guarantee ...

T'UNG SHU-LAN   No matter what you say, I don't have the money. (*Wants to go*)

MA HSING-WANG   Don't go. Tell me, where is the cloth you wove?

T'UNG SHU-LAN   I don't have any, I tell you.

MA HSING-WANG   All right, since you won't tell me, I'll go look for it myself. (*Goes into the bedroom*)

T'UNG SHU-LAN   Hsing-wang, don't mess things up. (*Exits with him*)

(*A rummaging noise comes from the bedroom*)

T'UNG SHU-LAN (*From the bedroom*)   What are you doing? I can't give it to you ... I can't.

(HSING-WANG *comes out of the bedroom carrying two bolts of cloth and some yarn on the bobbin.* SHU-LAN *comes on stage, clutching at him*)

T'UNG SHU-LAN   I won't give it to you no matter what. I worked hard to scrape up a little, and you squander it.

MA HSING-WANG   Let go! Let go! Or else I'll get rough.

T'UNG SHU-LAN   Give me back my cloth ... give me back my cloth.

MA HSING-WANG   Goddamn you! (*Forcefully throws her off.* SHU-LAN *falls down, then gets up again and runs straight at* HSING-WANG, *but is kicked away by him.* HSING-WANG *smugly exits.* SHU-LAN *lies on the ground weeping. The more she thinks about it, the more hurt she feels. Finally she bursts out wailing.* HSING-KUO *appears at the door. He halts there and looks around for a long time*)

MA HSING-KUO   Is this the home of Ma Hsing-wang?

(SHU-LAN *is crying sadly with her head bowed. She neither sees nor hears him*)

MA HSING-KUO (*After a while*)   Is this Ma Hsing-wang's house?

(*This time* HSING-KUO's *voice is a little louder, and he comes a step closer.* SHU-LAN *raises her head and looks at him with tear-filled eyes*)

T'UNG SHU-LAN   Who are you looking for?

(*Seeing that he seems to be a soldier, she is somewhat surprised*)

MA HSING-KUO   I'm looking for Ma Hsing-wang's house.

T'UNG SHU-LAN (*Seeing that a soldier has come to look for* MA HSING-WANG, *she wonders what he has done wrong now*)   He's not home. Why are you looking for him?

MA HSING-KUO   Not for anything in particular. (*Puts down his backpack*) I'm . . .

T'UNG SHU-LAN (*Sensing something*)   Who are you?

MA HSING-KUO   I'm his brother—Ma Hsing-kuo.

T'UNG SHU-LAN   Oh! (*Shocked, she steps back*)

MA HSING-KUO   Who are you? You're not . . .

T'UNG SHU-LAN   I'm Shu-lan.

MA HSING-KUO   Shu-lan, it really is you! (*He steps forward, eagerly trying to embrace her*)

T'UNG SHU-LAN   Hsing-kuo! (*Steps back*) Is it really you?

MA HSING-KUO   Yes, I've come back.

T'UNG SHU-LAN   Are you . . . a ghost, or a person?

MA HSING-KUO   Look (*Laughing*), how could I be a ghost?

T'UNG SHU-LAN (*Comes forward*)   Even if you're a ghost, I'm not afraid. I know you're dead. You sacrificed your life for the revolution. Everyone says so. I just don't believe . . .

MA HSING-KUO   Well, they've misinformed you.

T'UNG SHU-LAN   Hsing-kuo, I know that you saw I've been suffering, I've been miserable, and you came to comfort me.

MA HSING-KUO   I'm not a ghost; I'm alive!

T'UNG SHU-LAN   Even if only your spirit could come back and have a talk with me, my heart would be very comforted. Whenever I saw you in my dream, you never looked as real as today. Come closer, I want to take a good look at you.

MA HSING-KUO   Take a good look and see if I'm a ghost or a person.

T'UNG SHU-LAN (*Turning up the lamp wick*)   Yes, you're alive, not a ghost. Ghosts don't have shadows.

MA HSING-KUO   If I were a ghost, I wouldn't have come back.

T'UNG SHU-LAN   Hsing-kuo, this isn't a dream?

MA HSING-KUO   It's not a dream, it's real.

(T'UNG SHU-LAN *bites her hand hard*)

MA HSING-KUO   What are you doing? Shu-lan . . .

T'UNG SHU-LAN   (*Her hand is bleeding*) My God!

MA HSING-KUO   (*Abruptly grabs her hand*) It's all bloody. What's wrong with you? Shu-lan!

T'UNG SHU-LAN   This isn't a dream.

MA HSING-KUO   No, it's not a dream. It's real.

T'UNG SHU-LAN   You've come back alive! You've really come back! Hsing-kuo, I waited for you . . . it was so hard to wait! (*Falls on Hsing-kuo's chest crying*)

MA HSING-KUO (*Also unable to restrain his tears*)   Shu-lan, you see we're together again? You shouldn't cry anymore; you should be happy.

T'UNG SHU-LAN   Yes, I ought to be happy. (*Raises her head and smiles tearfully*) But I still can't help crying. (*Bursts out wailing*)

MA HSING-KUO   Then go ahead and cry to your heart's content. Oh, I left you all at home for twenty years. You can never get through crying about that hardship.

T'UNG SHU-LAN   Hardship—I wouldn't know where to start talking about that, but things were bad for you too while you were away!

MA HSING-KUO   It was both bitter and hard, but after all, we survived and we finally won the victory!

T'UNG SHU-LAN   Victory! Hsing-kuo, do you remember when you left you said, "Shu-lan, someday we'll fight our way back!"

MA HSING-KUO   Today I've fought my way back, but many of my comrades didn't come back.

T'UNG SHU-LAN   You've come back after all. You're not leaving again, are you, Hsing-kuo?

MA HSING-KUO   No, I'm not leaving. We'll be together forever. We'll build socialism together in our home village.

T'UNG SHU-LAN   Then these twenty years of hardships I've endured in your family haven't been in vain after all.

MA HSING-KUO (*Looking around*)   Is this house new?

T'UNG SHU-LAN   It was burned down three times by the Kuomintang. Afterwards we had to live in caves or ruined temples. The best places we had to live in were straw huts. After the liberation the government built these few rooms for us.

MA HSING-KUO   Shu-lan, how is everybody in the family?

T'UNG SHU-LAN   Dad passed away a long time ago. After you left, the White Troops often came to stir up trouble. They knew we were a Red Army family, so they arrested Dad and locked him up for quite a few months. He suffered a lot. They beat him until he almost died several times over. We had to pay to get him out, but he was already in terrible shape, and later he got sick and died.

MA HSING-KUO (*After a moment lost in thought, he asks indignantly*)   And Older Sister? After Mother died, Older Sister became our mother. When we were little, she saw that we were fed and clothed; when we grew up, she urged us to join the revolution. At that time she was the head of the Women's Organization of this area!

T'UNG SHU-LAN   Older Sister just died about a month ago. Her coffin is buried in the patch in back.

MA HSING-KUO   Older Sister suffered all her life. She managed to make it to the liberation, but she still didn't live to see any happy days . . .

T'UNG SHU-LAN   Older Sister had to beg for food for more than ten out of the last twenty years. Whenever she got some food, she gave a mouthful to the old folks, a mouthful to the youngsters, and often went hungry herself. At that time it was hard to beg for food too! The landlord's family wouldn't give us any. Sometimes they would even curse us, and call us bandit women, or communist women, and spit in our faces. . . . The other poor people didn't even have enough for themselves—how could they have any food to give us? Who knows how many times Older Sister cried about you. Afterwards, when she heard that you had died, she went blind from crying. When she was near death, she took my hand and told me never to leave the family. "If you leave, the whole family will disappear," she said.

MA HSING-KUO (*Wiping away his tears*)   When I was away I often thought of her. I hurried home and yet I won't even get to see her once. Mother brought eight children into this world, but there are only three of us left. What about Hsing-wang? Is he still okay?

T'UNG SHU-LAN   For the first several years after Hsing-wàng returned from the Red Militia, he didn't let out a peep. He just worked the fields, and behaved like a peasant. Later . . .

MA HSING-KUO   What happened later? He's still alive, isn't he?

T'UNG SHU-LAN   He's still alive, but his heart is dead.

MA HSING-KUO   What?

T'UNG SHU-LAN   He doesn't want to work. All he wants is to get rich. Just now he cheated me out of two bolts of cloth.

MA HSING-KUO   Does he live here?

T'UNG SHU-LAN   Um hm.

MA HSING-KUO   I heard he got married!

T'UNG SHU-LAN   Uh hm. (*Lowers her head*)

MA HSING-KUO   Does he have any children?

T'UNG SHU-LAN   Yes . . .

MA HSING-KUO   Where is his wife?

(T'UNG SHU-LAN *remains silent*)

MA HSING-KUO (*Realizing*) Oh . . .

T'UNG SHU-LAN   Hsing-kuo, you mustn't blame me . . .

MA HSING-KUO   No, Shu-lan, I'll never blame you. Twenty years . . . I couldn't expect you to remain a widow for twenty years.

T'UNG SHU-LAN   No, I could have waited for twenty years, or even longer, but they told me . . . they fooled my by telling me . . . (*Starts to cry again*)

(OLD VILLAGE HEAD *hurriedly enters.* SHU-LAN *sees him coming and steps aside, wiping her tears*)

WAN PAO-SHAN   Hsing-kuo! Hsing-kuo! You're really back. I was afraid that you were dead and that you wouldn't come back!

MA HSING-KUO   If I weren't alive, how could I have come back? Old Chairman, how have you been?

WAN PAO-SHAN   I'm an Old Ch'eng Yao-chin,* getting old but still hanging on. I've made it through even the very worst. If I were meant to die, I would have died several times already, but I wasn't meant to die. (*Sees* SHU-LAN) Shu-lan, why are you still wiping tears? (*Remembers*) Oh, Hsing-kuo, you can't mistreat Shu-lan. As a wife, she's even more virtuous than Chao Wu-niang.† Really, if it hadn't been for Shu-lan, your family wouldn't be here. She and Hsing-wang . . .

MA HSING-KUO   I know all about her and Hsing-wang, and I don't blame her at all.

WAN PAO-SHAN   During those awful days, the White Troops were really inhuman. If they didn't rape or slaughter our women here, they sold them. This child, Shu-lan, was determined, and for months and years on end she didn't come home. She lived in a cave like an animal.

MA HSING-KUO   That must have been awful for you, Shu-lan.

---

*Ch'eng Yao-chin's real name was Ch'eng Chih-chieh. He was a famous military hero of the T'ang dynasty. He also appears in such novels as the *Shuo T'ang*, where he takes on the aura of a legendary hero. [TRANS.]

†Chao Wu-niang is a legendary figure mentioned in such works as the *P'i-p'a Chi*. She is known as a paragon of wifely virture, who labors to care for her husband's parents during her husband's prolonged absence—a sort of Chinese Penelope. [TRANS.]

WAN PAO-SHAN   A while back, there was a person from this village named Ch'in Le, who became separated from his outfit and came home. He said that he saw you get killed while crossing the great Snow Mountains and Grasslands. Many people urged Shu-lan to remarry, and Hsing-wang agreed with them. I thought that if she were with Hsing-wang she would still be in your family, and it would still be the same people. At first Shu-lan wasn't willing. Afterwards, I had to come and urge her before she consented.

MA HSING-KUO   Shu-lan has done nothing wrong to me or my family. If there's any blame, I should take it for being very irresponsible toward Shu-lan and my family.

WAN PAO-SHAN   You can't be blamed either. If it weren't for you—some of you sacrificed your families, some of you sacrificed your lives—how could there be a today for us? (*To* SHU-LAN) Has Hsing-kuo eaten yet?

T'UNG SHU-LAN   Ah, you see I've been talking so much. I even forgot to fix dinner . . . (*Exits*)

MA HSING-KUO   I'm not hungry . . .

WAN PAO-SHAN   Hsing-kuo, come here and let me take a good look at you. You have aged a lot, son, and gotten thinner. What's this?

MA HSING-KUO   A wound.

WAN PAO-SHAN   Has it healed completely?

MA HSING-KUO   Completely.

WAN PAO-SHAN   Son, you soldiers suffered a lot away from home!

MA HSING-KUO   Didn't you often say that revolutions start with suffering but end in happiness?

WAN PAO-SHAN   You still remember that. I also remember what you said when you were leaving: "I'm determined to fight to the finish for the revolution. If the revolution doesn't succeed, I won't be back." You are quite a man; you kept your word. You really didn't come home until the revolution succeeded!

MA HSING-KUO   Old Chairman . . .

WAN PAO-SHAN   Now I'm not the chairman of the village soviet anymore. I'm the village head.

MA HSING-KUO   It doesn't make any difference whether you're called Old Chairman or Old Village Head. After all, you've been taking care of this area for the past twenty years. (*Takes a letter of introduction out of his backpack*) Here, according to the regulations, is my letter of introduction for my rehabilitation.

WAN PAO-SHAN   Don't you think I can recognize you without any letter of introduction?

MA HSING-KUO   It's not that, Old Chairman. When I joined the Red Army, it was you who gave me a letter of introduction. Now that I've come back from the army, I'm giving you another letter of introduction. That's leaving with everything in good order, and returning with everything in good order.

WAN PAO-SHAN   You are the only one of the soldiers I was responsible for who had a round trip ticket! (*Reads the letter*) Hsing-kuo, it says in the letter that you were wounded seven times, and your health is not very good. Now that you've come home, your duty, I'm afraid, will be to take care of your health first!

MA HSING-KUO   No, I can still work. I started out as a hired hand, and even though I haven't been doing it for such a long time I can still do some work in the fields.

WAN PAO-SHAN   You fought for the people for twenty years and your health isn't good. It's not too much for you to rest for a while. The people can afford to take care of you!

MA HSING-KUO   Old Village Head, if I had wanted to rest, I wouldn't have come back from Yenan. If I didn't do any work all day and just let our country take care of me, I'd get sick no matter how healthy I was.

WAN PAO-SHAN   Although land reform has been carried out here, there was too much destruction during the war, and in this short time we haven't been able to recover. We've got only a few people, but lots of rocky hills on our land. Life is still very hard now!

MA HSING-KUO   I didn't come back just to enjoy myself. There are still things I want to talk over with the county leaders. This letter of introduction is written to the county too. Do you think I should also make a trip to the county office?

WAN PAO-SHAN   You don't need to go. Just let us make contact and that'll do. (*Reads the letter*) Oh, Hsing-kuo, so you were a Red Army regimental commander too! That's not a low rank either.

MA HSING-KUO   Old Chairman, from now on, please don't ever tell anyone that I was a regimental commander.

WAN PAO-SHAN   This isn't a fake credential. It's a national rank. You earned it with your heroic, life-and-death exploits. Why can't I talk about it?

MA HSING-KUO   What's the point talking about being a regimental commander? I haven't had a hoe in my hand for so many years. When I try to be a peasant again, I won't be as good as other people. And there are also a lot of new cadres here. If you tell other people, they'll think I'm showing off my old rank. It gets in the way of our work.

WAN PAO-SHAN   Okay, we'll keep it a secret for the time being, but when it's necessary, we'll announce it.

MA HSING-KUO   This also involves my transfer to the Party unit here. When I go to the county to clear up my transfer, I will discuss my work assignment.

WAN PAO-SHAN   Why worry about work? I've already arranged work for you. Why should it be a problem?

MA HSING-KUO   No, Old Chairman, I still do have problems.

T'UNG SHU-LAN (*Enters*)   Dinner's ready. How about if I serve it out here? Why don't you have a snack here too, Old Village Head.

MA HSING-KUO   Let's eat in the kitchen.

WAN PAO-SHAN   I've already eaten. Let's talk while we eat.

(*The three of them exit together. After a while* HSIAO-SAN *and his mother,* HSIAO-SAN NIANG,* *enter*)

HSIAO-SAN NIANG   You saw an old Red Army soldier come here?

HSIAO-SAN   Um hm, he asked me the way and said he was coming back here.

HSIAO-SAN NIANG   Well, where is he? Hey, Shu-lan!

---

*The name "Hsiao-san Niang" literally means "Hsiao-san's Mother." This is how the woman is generally known around the village. [TRANS.]

T'UNG SHU-LAN (*Enters*) Oh, Auntie, how come you have time to drop by?

HSIAO-SAN NIANG Who has time to drop by for a visit? It's because I heard Hsiao-san say that an old Red Army soldier had come here, and I figured Hsing-kuo must have come back.

T'UNG SHU-LAN Hsing-kuo has come back.

HSIAO-SAN NIANG My God! Has Hsing-kuo really come back? It's really because Hsing-kuo's father was good to people all his life—he earned something for his children. Look! Hsing-kuo was gone for twenty years, but he finally came back.

T'UNG SHU-LAN You very seldom come here, Auntie. Come in and sit down for a while.

HSIAO-SAN NIANG All right. Hsiao-san, you take the ox home and then come back here!

(*Hsiao-san answers promptly, then exits*)

HSIAO-SAN NIANG I've come to inquire about the whereabouts of my brother, Ta-han. Didn't they join the Red Army together?

T'UNG SHU-LAN Auntie, didn't you find out a long time ago that Ta-han was dead? There was even a death certificate, and you've already received a survivor's pension.

HSIAO-SAN NIANG No, it's not that, Shu-lan. These reports are wrong as often as they're right. It's much more reliable to ask the people who left with them. Maybe my Ta-han is still alive! People used to say that Hsing-kuo was dead, and yet he has come back. Oh, Shu-lan, you don't know, but I dreamed last night that Ta-han came back, and today Hsing-kuo's come back. Perhaps this omen was fulfilled through him.

T'UNG SHU-LAN Hsing-kuo is eating. You can ask him later. Where is Uncle? Is he home?

HSIAO-SAN NIANG He's at home. He spends all day getting mad at people. Ah, Shu-lan, there's one thing I want to ask of you. Could Hsing-wang give us a few more days on that debt of ours? We don't even have food to eat. How can we pay you back?

T'UNG SHU-LAN What debt?

HSIAO-SAN NIANG Ta Lao-niu borrowed five pecks of grain from Hsing-wang. By now the principal plus the interest amount to one picul ...

CHIN PAO (*Enters carrying rice*) Auntie Shu-lan, I heard that Uncle Hsing-kuo has come back. The village government sent me to deliver twenty catties of rice.

T'UNG SHU-LAN We don't need it. We have rice.

CHIN PAO Don't refuse. To look after demobilized soldiers is also the responsibility of our village government.

HSIAO-SAN NIANG Shu-lan, did Brother Hsing-kuo bring anything back with him?

T'UNG SHU-LAN (*Pointing at a backpack*) Right here.

HSIAO-SAN NIANG He didn't bring back much stuff, but maybe he brought back a lot of money.

T'UNG SHU-LAN I didn't ask.

HSIAO-SAN NIANG Just think he's been gone fighting for the revolution for twenty years. He should be an officer of some rank or other. How come he didn't come back on horseback or in a car? I heard Hsiao-san say that he came back on foot.

CHIN PAO You're behind the times. Nowadays officers can't show off like that anymore. They are called the people's orderlies.

HSIAO-SAN NIANG Hm, that sounds good, but I've never seen an officer work the fields.

CHAO TA-K'UEI (*Swaggers in and says in a loud voice*) Shu-lan, I heard that an old Red Army soldier came to your place ... (*Sees* CHIN-PAO) You're really diligent, Sonny, when it comes to visiting your mother-in-law!

CHIN PAO Chao Ta-k'uei, what are you yelling about!

CHAO TA-K'UEI What? Did I say anything wrong? You've fallen for Hsiao-lan, hoping that her mother will arrange things for you. It's too bad you started too late. She's already been spoken for.

CHIN PAO I've come on serious business. Next time you shoot your mouth off I won't be so polite.

CHAO TA-K'UEI What?

T'UNG SHU-LAN (*Hurries to stop them*) Forget it. What's the use of dragging all that in? Didn't you come to see Hsing-kuo?

CHAO TA-K'UEI That's right. Where is Hsing-kuo?

(HSING-KUO *hears them and comes out. A crowd has come in from outside to watch*)

MA HSING-KUO Here I am, who is it?

CHAO TA-K'UEI It's me. You're Hsing-kuo ...

MA HSING-KUO And you are ...

CHAO TA-K'UEI My name is Chao Ta-k'uei, and they call me Chao Tzu-lung.*

WAN PAO-SHAN He's from Ta-k'uei's family. We used to call him Little Iron Pillar.

MA HSING-KUO Oh, Ta-k'uei, so you've been demobilized and come home too?

CHAO TA-K'UEI Yes, I've come back a veteran, but I left one of my legs at the front. They said I was supposed to come back to recuperate. Recuperate, my ass! Every day they make you angry. This village government doesn't take good enough care of demobilized soldiers!

CHIN PAO Ta-k'uei, what do you mean the village government doesn't take good enough care of demobilized soldiers! There's the disabled veteran's pension, help for plowing, new houses, what more could you want?

CHAO TA-K'UEI So what? Goddamnit, we fought for our country and shed our blood. After we come back, just to get a bite to eat they make you feel like you are freeloading from them. And we have to take the nasty looks from these young kids too. What are you so smart about? Where were you when I was fighting for the revolution?

CHIN PAO Don't try to pull any weight. There are people here with higher seniority than yours.

CHAO TA-K'UEI It's good that you came back, Hsing-kuo, you old Red Army soldier. Now we demobilized soldiers can stick together and stand up

*Chao Tzu-lung is another legendary hero, this time from the novel *Romance of the Three Kingdoms*. [TRANS.]

straight. But you have to be psychologically prepared. That village government gang are like temple bells. If you don't hit them they won't ring.

MA HSING-KUO   I don't have any problems to bother the government with.

CHAO TA-K'UEI   That's great, they're only afraid of problems. You've been in
the army for more than twenty years. What rank are you?

MA HSING-KUO   I don't have any rank. I'm an old footsoldier.

CHAO TA-K'UEI   Ha, we don't want to ride on your coattails. You're still an old
footsoldier after twenty years? You can't fool me.

MA HSING-KUO   Ask Old Village Head, it says so on the demobilization certificate.

CHAO TA-K'UEI   Oh, that's right! How about it, old Village Head?

WAN PAO-SHAN   Uh . . .

CHAO TA-K'UEI   Boy, I tell you, in this place people really care about these
things. They're not willing to listen to what a footsoldier has to say. They
don't even care much about what a former lieutenant like me says.
(*The crowd of people chimes in with "Big Brother has come back!" or "Uncle
has come back!" Some of them have brought pickled vegetables, some, firewood, and some, ricepuffs. People all exchange greetings with each other*)

MA HSING-KUO (*Sees a young woman holding a child*)   What family is that
young woman from?

WAN PAO-SHAN   She's the third daughter of your next-door neighbor, Lao-
chiu. When you left she was just a little taller than a table. Now this third
daughter is already holding her own third daughter in her arms.

MA HSING-KUO   So fast. And Lao-chiu?

SOMEONE IN THE CROWD   He was burned to death on the Wan-tzu Mountain.

WAN PAO-SHAN   Ah, when the Kuomintang burned the Wan-tzu Mountain
that time, twenty thousand of our people were burned to death all at once.

MA HSING-KUO   What family is this child from?

T'UNG SHU-LAN   This child is pitiable. His father, Ma Hsing-ch'u . . .

MA HSING-KUO   Is that the Ma Hsing-ch'u from the east side of the village, that
simple fellow who could only kneel down and kowtow when he couldn't pay
rent to Er Lao-yeh?

T'UNG SHU-LAN   Yes, that's the one. He was grabbed and taken away by the
Kuomintang soldiers, and he has never come back. When the child's mother
remarried, the child was left alone. He now lives with his uncle, but his
uncle has no food even for himself.

MA HSING-KUO   What a shame! This place of ours was so ravaged by the
Kuomintang!

WAN PAO-SHAN   In our village, several hundred families were wiped out and
their homes destroyed! In a gulch a little way from here, not a single person
or chimney was left in the whole village.

HSIAO-SAN NIANG   Brother Hsing-kuo, do you still remember me?

MA HSING-KUO   Aren't you Ta Lao-niu's wife? Yes, I remember. Didn't Ta-han
and I join the army together?

HSIAO-SAN NIANG   Yes, all you soldiers have come back. Only our Ta-han
hasn't come home. I've come to ask you if you know where he is.

MA HSING-KUO   We were together when we first joined the army. Later we
were transferred to different places. Ta-han went to the Plainclothes Division. He was very clever. The army announced a citation for him.

HSIAO-SAN NIANG   And then?

MA HSING-KUO   After that we never saw each other again. Didn't he ever write?

HSIAO-SAN NIANG   No he didn't. They said he ... (*Starts to cry*)

MA HSING-KUO   You should still try to find out about him. Perhaps you moved and the letters never reached you.

HSIAO-SAN NIANG   Some people said that they saw him killed. Oh, Ta-han, my life is so bitter. All the people who went with you have come back. Where are you? (*The more she cries, the sadder she becomes*)

TA LAO-NIU (*Calling from off stage*)   Hsiao-san Niang, Hsiao-san Niang, where the hell are you?

(HSIAO-SAN NIANG *is crying sadly and doesn't hear him*)

TA LAO-NIU   Goddamnit, where did that bitch go? Hsiao-san Niang!

SOMEONE IN THE CROWD   Ta Lao-niu, your wife is here.

T'UNG SHU-LAN   Auntie, Uncle is calling you.

TA LAO-NIU   Did you sell your goddamn ears to a lunch meat counter? I've been calling you like crazy and you didn't even hear.

HSIAO-SAN NIANG   Brother Hsing-kuo has come back and I came to ask him something ...

TA LAO-NIU   You ran over here to watch the excitement instead of cooking dinner. I called you but you didn't even answer.

HSIAO-SAN NIANG   I didn't hear you ...

TA LAO-NIU   So you even talk back to me. (*Goes up to her and slaps her face*) You're still arguing, still won't go home to cook dinner!

HSIAO-SAN NIANG   You want me to cook dinner. How could I cook dinner when there's nothing to cook? You get me some rice and I'll cook it.

TA LAO-NIU   You bitch! You're making me lose face here. You're asking me for rice here. Fine, I'll give it to you. (*Picks up a stool, about to hit her*)

HSIAO-SAN NIANG   You want to hit me! You can't afford to feed your wife and children, yet you still care about face! You're afraid of losing face, but I'm not. I've lived long enough. I would rather die and go with Ta-han ...

TA LAO-NIU   Goddamn you, you're still shooting your mouth off! You think I'm afraid to hit you. (*Before the crowd can stop* TA LAO-NIU, *the stool comes down on* HSIAO-SAN NIANG'S *head and blood flows*)

MA HSING-KUO   Uncle Lao-niu, what's the matter with you? How could you hit her so hard? (*Calls* SHU-LAN) Hurry, get some incense ashes and some clean cloth.

(*The crowd helps* HSIAO-SAN NIANG *to exit*)

WAN PAO-SHAN   You were wrong to do that, Ta Lao-niu.

TA LAO-NIU   I know I was wrong. If you think I should be beaten or punished or thrown in jail, Village Head, I'll accept it. This life isn't really worth living.

MA HSING-KUO   How can you talk like that, Uncle Lao-niu? Life nowadays is at least much better than before ...

TA LAO-NIU   Things are getting better for other people. I'm the only one with bad luck. What little grain I harvest isn't enough to pay back my debts.

MA HSING-KUO   How come you have so many debts?

TA LAO-NIU   I haven't had much luck. The year before last my ox died. Last year Hsiao-san Niang was bedridden for half a year. I alone couldn't keep the whole family alive even if I worked myself to death!

MA HSING-KUO   Say, Uncle Lao-niu, here are twenty catties of rice. Go ahead and take it.

TA LAO-NIU   I don't want it . . .

MA HSING-KUO   We're all brothers. Why should you turn it down?

TA LAO-NIU   I can't afford to take it. I've got debts coming out of my ears that I haven't paid back yet!

MA HSING-KUO   If you haven't got anything to pay back with, don't pay then.

TA LAO-NIU   Don't pay? If they didn't ask so much interest . . .

MA HSING-KUO   Interest? How much interest did they ask?

TA LAO-NIU   It's hard to be exact. Anyway, it's like a rolling jackass, you pay a picul on five pecks.

MA HSING-KUO   Oh! So such things are still going on. . . . Go ahead, Uncle, take this rice. You don't have to pay back anything, principal or interest.

TA LAO-NIU   I don't dare to take things from your family. Once it's eaten, my back'll be up against the wall. (*To* HSIAO-SAN NIANG *and* HSIAO-SAN) Go on, get a move on. Go home! both of you! (*Exits angrily*)

(HSIAO-SAN NIANG *and* HSIAO-SAN *exit together with him*)

MA HSING-KUO (*Not understanding*)   What was that all about?

WAN PAO-SHAN   Ta Lao-niu is throwing another one of his big temper tantrums. Let me go and see. (*Exits, following the trio*)

HSIAO-LAN (*Shoulders her way through the crowd*)   Mother, they say that Uncle has come back.

T'UNG SHU-LAN   That's right. Come and meet him.

HSIAO-LAN   Uncle.

MA HSING-KUO (*Joyfully*)   What a nice girl. (*Takes her hand*) How old are you?

HSIAO-LAN   Sixteen.

T'UNG SHU-LAN   This child is pitiable too. When she was eight years old, she was sent away as a child-bride.

A WOMAN   Sun Er-niang is known to be very harsh. Since this child has survived for eight years under her thumb, she really has come a long way.

MA HSING-KUO   How does your mother-in-law treat you?

HSIAO-LAN (*Doesn't answer. Tears well up in her eyes*)   Mother! (*Clings to her mother, crying*)

T'UNG SHU-LAN   What is it, child? Have you been beaten again?

HSIAO-LAN   She scolded me, scolded me really cruelly.

T'UNG SHU-LAN   She scolded you for no reason?

HSIAO-LAN   She saw Chin Pao carrying firewood for me and then scolded me. . . . I'm not going back to her family again, Mother.

T'UNG SHU-LAN   There you go again, child. Your father won't allow it. We don't have enough to eat ourselves . . .

HSIAO-LAN   I can work now . . .

T'UNG SHU-LAN   For these seven or eight years, you've eaten their food and worn their clothes and your father has used their money . . .

ER-MAN (*From offstage*)   Hsiao-lan, Hsiao-lan.

HSIAO-LAN (*Hides behind* SHU-LAN)   He's here again, like someone calling a ghost back.

ER-MAN   I see you. There's no use hiding. Mother wants you to come back.

HSIAO-LAN   I'm not going back.

ER-MAN   Mother wants you to come back right now!

HSIAO-LAN   I still won't go!

ER-MAN   All right, if you won't listen to me, I'll go get Mother! Oh, Mother's coming. (*Exits*)

HSIAO-LAN   Mother.

T'UNG SHU-LAN   Go on, child, you belong to them anyway.

A WOMAN   This child is pitiable. I wonder how many times she has been beaten.

SUN ER-NIANG (*Enters yelling*)   Hsiao-lan, Hsiao-lan!

(HSIAO-LAN *hears her and begins to tremble in fear*)

SUN ER-NIANG   What airs you're putting on! I sent someone to ask you to come back, and you wouldn't! All right, Hsiao-lan, I called you and you didn't answer. Your wings are getting stronger and you want to fly away, but it's not that easy. Even if I had raised a dog, it would still have to guard the house, Hsiao-lan . . .

MA HSING-KUO (*Goes up to her*)   Sister-in-law.

SUN ER-NIANG   So, who's this? Are you Brother Hsing-kuo? My God, you've been gone for ten or twenty years. You must have come back all loaded now! Come to think of it, we really have made a good match. From now on it'll be up to you to look after us a bit better . . .

MA HSING-KUO   Sister-in-law, since I left my family has gotten a lot of help from you.

SUN ER-NIANG   Don't mention it. From now on my family will be like a bald head following the moonlight, basking in your glory. Hsing-wang has a good head on his shoulders and he's skillful. He's really good at thinking of ways to get rich. Now with your influence, your family will really be rich and influential.

MA HSING-KUO   You've made a mistake about us, Er-niang. If we had money or influence, would we give a daughter away as a child-bride to another family?

SUN ER-NIANG   That was a long time ago! At that time, even though we say Hsiao-lan was given to our family as a child-bride, in fact she's just like my own daughter. I've never so much as laid a finger on her. That child was spoiled in her own family and has a bad temper. Even I have to put up with her a lot! Well, now that the country is liberated, we shouldn't be talking about getting child-brides. What they talk about is the equality of men and women!

MA HSING-KUO (*Not knowing what to say*)   I've just come home today and I would like to have Hsiao-lan back to help. I'll send her back tomorrow.

SUN ER-NIANG   Of course that's all right. Her uncle has come back. Naturally she should come home to see her uncle. But you also know that our family is short-handed. I can't get by by myself. I can't spare her for a single day. You know, our water jars are still empty. I would like to have her go home to carry two loads of water. She'll come back again tomorrow to see her uncle. (*She tugs* HSIAO-LAN *when she finishes talking*) Let's go, Hsiao-lan (*About to leave*) I'm really sorry, Brother Hsing-kuo. (*Pulls* HSIAO-LAN *out the door*)

You shouldn't think that because your uncle has come back, you can rely on his official position. Ha, if the King of Heaven himself came I wouldn't be afraid.

(*The sound of* Sun Er-niang's *scolding and* Hsiao-lan's *crying gradually fades away. The crowd discusses the matter among themselves.* Hsing-kuo *remains silent, lost in thought. Little by little the people in the crowd take their leave. In a moment,* Hsing-wang *bursts in*)

Ma Hsing-wang   Big Brother, you've come back.

Ma Hsing-kuo   Hsing-wang! (*The two brothers shake hands warmly*) How have you been doing all these years?

Ma Hsing-wang   Where should I start?

Ma Hsing-kuo   Come and sit down. Let's have a good talk. (*To* Shu-lan) You come and sit down too, Shu-lan. The whole family . . .

(*The curtain falls*)

[The next scene, a few hours later, sees Ma Hsing-kuo in the same room, unable to sleep, trying to decide if he should leave. T'ung Shu-lan comes out of the bedroom with a quilt to make him more comfortable. Back in the bedroom she has a bad fight with Hsing-wang. Hsing-kuo, after a long discussion, hands all his discharge pay to his brother to help him start all over again, clean. Still unable to sleep, Ma is joined by the old village head, whose mind is also troubled by the Ma family affair. He persuades Hsing-kuo to move to the village office and start working hard for the village.

Act Two takes place about two weeks later in the village office. The season is winter. The villagers gossip, suspecting Ma Hsing-kuo to have been a failure in the Army, perhaps even a deserter. The old village head is forced to tell them the truth, which surprises and awes them. Ma Hsing-kuo has been working hard to organize the village into an agricultural cooperative. With varying degrees of enthusiasm they all join except Ma Hsing-wang. Tension continues among the trio of the Ma family. Ma Hsing-kuo catches his brother trying to collect usurious debts from Ta Lao-niu.

Three years later, on the threshing ground, the younger cooperative members are harvesting with zeal. Sun Er-niang, the cruel mother-in-law, scolds the child-bride again for her contact with Chin Pao, the good young lad. Sun wants to cut wheat for herself, quarrels with Ma Hsing-kuo, and is finally criticized at a mass meeting.

Hsing-wang is bailed out of jail by the village head after a term served for his usurious and blackmarket activities. Hsing-kuo wants his brother to make a clean breast in the evening meeting and start afresh as a new man.

Three more months have passed. The final act returns to Hsing-wang's house, as in Act One. The two villains seen at the beginning of the play, Tiao and Hsing-wang, plot to burn the harvest and kill Ma Hsing-kuo. In the confusion of a roaring fire Hsing-wang is shot to death and Shu-lan is injured.

The Epilogue takes place on the mountain trail—the same setting as the Prologue. Spring has painted joyful colors over the bad memory of the fire and violence. SHU-LAN'S wound has healed; she supports her daughter's freedom of marriage. MA HSING-KUO, now a national labor hero, is leading the village ahead toward communization and modernization. Word begins to spread that he and T'UNG SHU-LAN should effect a reunion.]

Translated by the Seminar on
Contemporary Chinese Literature, Indiana University,
under the supervision of Prof. Leo Ou-fan Lee
(John Coleman, Lawrence Herzberg, Kenneth Koziol,
Gloria Shen, Eugene Teng, Ling-hsia Yeh, Jennie Chao)

WANG WEN-SHIH

(1921–)

Born to a family of grade-school teachers in Wan-jung, southwest Shansi Province, near the Shensi border, Wang Wen-shih spent his childhood in villages and small towns until the outbreak of the war against Japan, which thrust him into a life with the various resistance groups fighting behind enemy lines. He became active in youth organizations in North China. By 1938 he began his work and study at a middle school in Sian, where he joined the Communist Party.

His literary activities started upon his arrival in Yenan in 1942. He took part in cultural work troupes, staging folk drama and educating the peasantry in the land reform program.

Following the liberation in 1949, he served on editorial posts and worked for the association of Chinese writers in the north. His short stories won prompt recognition for his fine craftsmanship and his ability to capture the personalities and scenes of the tumultuous 1950s. A collection of these stories, *The Night of the Snowstorms,* was published in 1958. His novel, *Black Phoenix,* appeared in 1964.

Since 1953 he has been working at the county Party branch level in Shensi Province. There was no word about his involvement in the Cultural Revolution, though he published little in the late 1960s. In May 1978, he appeared at the third session of the Third Congress, All-China Federation of Literary and Art Circles, held in Peking.   —K.Y.H.

The New Production Brigade Leader

Late at night, when cackling hens were at roost and people normally would be sound asleep, not a single soul was in bed in the secluded village of Yen-chia-t'an. If you walked through the village now, you would hear excited whispers in the dark, where only lit cigarettes blinked. People were moving about and the noise of doors opening and shutting never ceased.

For ten days Yen-chia-t'an had been wrapped in the excitement created by the people's struggle, which climaxed in tonight's meeting. Yen Shu-p'ing, secretary of the Party branch and production brigade leader, had just been removed from his office and asked to prepare a full self-criticism. Yen San, who had been under the newly deposed Party branch secretary's pressure, was going to take over both positions. The whole village was in an uproar.

Under a persimmon tree near the edge of a cliff behind the village, two men stood shoulder to shoulder, scanning all the houses in the village below. One of them was the secretary of the commune Party committee, Lu Chiao, an able and determined man who organized the movement; the other was Yen San, a mild-mannered and simple farmer who used to be in charge of feeding the commune animals, and a member of the production brigade committee who originated the movement. Two weeks ago when he sent a brief report of accusation to the commune Party committee, it had never occurred to him that the thing would blow up so big.

For a long time Yen Shun-p'ing and his clique, under the manipulation of Yen Tzu-yü, who really controlled the village, had taken advantage of other commune members and embezzled commune funds. More recently they built for their selfish interest a so-called cadre mess hall without the commune Party committee's knowledge; they kept the best food to themselves. In production, they pushed the individual contract system against the collectivization movement, which led many commune members to revert to their capitalist frame of mind, all bent on doing some market speculating to get rich quick. Nobody bothered about the collectivized fields, even when the weeds there had grown taller than the planted crop. Yen Tzu-yü and his gang didn't stop at that; they further planned to assign the draft animals and tools permanently to the members' households, thus virtually splitting up the commune. It was the same night when the rascals were in the commune's stable discussing how to assign the animals that the animal feeder, Yen San, got desperate and spoke up to stop them. He had never practiced arguing with anybody. When he realized that he could not out-talk those guys, he and several of his fellow animal feeders grabbed the heavy sticks used for mixing the feed and stood ready to let the rascals have it. The rascals backed down and left. The next day the whole brigade found out about the incident. Many brigade members, worried about Yen San, dropped over to warn Yen San to be patient. Yen San said, "Okay, I've done it! So what?" Others in agreement with Yen San discussed it with him and whipped up a report to the commune Party committee secretary, requesting intervention. Right on the same day Party Committee Secretary Lu Chiao himself came down.

A man of action, resolute in making decisions, Lu Chiao had been studying the Yen-chia-t'an situation for some time already. He had talked about it before in standing committee meetings and all had felt that something had to be done about it. He postponed action only because he had not spotted the right person to carry it out, but he had been hoping for someone among the local poor peasants to emerge. The moment Yen San's report reached Lu, he didn't even take time to read it through. His assistant's oral summary of the case was enough to send him into action. Jumping off his chair he said, "Yen San, that's excellent, just perfect! Here's the man I've been waiting for! Yen-chia-t'an will soon shed its label of a backward village." He called the courier, Little Wu. "Hurry, get my bike. Pump up both tires!" Yen San in sending his report had only hoped for the commune Party secretary to arbitrate and stop the Yen Tzu-yü gang from perpetrating their misdeeds. Yen San never thought that Secretary Lu had understood the situation so thoroughly and made up his mind so firmly that a big revolution seemed to be descending upon the village. The shake-up campaign developed, and Yen San found himself swept into the surging waves of reform. Like a nonswimmer, he soon realized his own strength, because he had such a powerful coach, Secretary Lu, leading him on by the hand.

"Secretary Lu," Yen San said, "do you see what I see?" He pointed at several courtyards, all pitch-dark.

"What are you looking at?" Lu said, without paying much attention.

"You see there, the whole village is wide awake, only those houses of theirs have no lights!"

"They worked the whole day," Lu said, faking indifference. "And they were at the meeting the whole evening. Tomorrow is another working day. They should use this chance to catch some sleep."

"You think they can fall asleep?" Yen San said.

Lu said, with a wry smile, "They probably can't. They aren't having too good a time."

"That's right! Their houses are dark. Some kind of a ghost is walking there," said Yen San.

Are you afraid of ghosts?" said Lu. Yen San kept his naïve smile as his answer. "Why should living people fear ghosts? It's the ghosts that are afraid of living people," said Lu. "You need not be scared by them."

"No, I'm not scared."

"But only half an hour ago you begged me to let you off and find someone else to head up the brigade!" said Lu.

"I've been handling animals all my life. That's cutting feed and cleaning the stables. I've never been in charge of the whole business of agricultural production, Secretary Lu."

"You mustn't put it that way," said Lu. "You took the initiative in reporting their funny business of individual-contract production to the Party Committee."

"Right, I did."

"That proves you are one hundred times better than Yen Shun-p'ing!" Lu's tone was earnest. "You understand perfectly what socialist production is and what capitalist production is. Yen Shun-p'ing hasn't even begun to see these things!"

"But Shun-p'ing has been following the others' advice," said Yen San.

"This damn Yen Shun-p'ing!" The mention of him made Lu so angry that he had to pause a moment before continuing. "The Yen Tzu-yü's and the Yen Tzu-ts'ai's . . . are all really nothing much! The way to handle them is: one, don't be afraid of them, and two, be firm and strict with them. The rest will be easy. Now, you are the brigade leader; as long as you know how to exercise your power in dealing with those devils, there will be no problem!"

The energetic and enthusiastic Lu Chiao talked on as Yen San listened quietly. Each word reached Yen San's heart, making him burn with zeal. Just before Lu left him, he asked, "Are you coming back tomorrow?"

"The meeting will last two days. I'll try to be back in the evening the day after tomorrow. . . . You go ahead and handle the situation. Don't lose your courage and don't waver, you must remember!"

"Yes, I'll remember," Yen San said with confidence.

They were leaving, but a dark shadow suddenly appeared on the hillside running toward them. They halted their steps. Yen San shouted, "Who's there?"

"Me, it's me!"

"Is it a ghost?" Lu Chiao whispered, tugging Yen San's jacket.

"He's got something like a ghost about him," Yen San whispered back. "He sticks to you whenever you give him a chance, and he won't let you go."

"In that case," said Lu, "I'd better go. I'm not afraid of vicious ghosts, but the kind that hangs on you is quite another matter."

The dark shadow arrived before Yen San. It was Yen Chung-ho, about fifty, equipped with a sharp tongue that could turn black into white, and a sharp nose that stuck itself into anything of interest to him. He had been causing as much trouble as he'd helped to settle.

"How nice to be standing here doing nothing!" Yen Chung-ho said. "I looked all over for you."

"Looking for me?"

"Old San," said Yen Chung-ho, "let's go and have a seat at my house."

"Why go anywhere and have a seat at this time of the day? You should be in bed."

"You yourself have chosen good hours to sleep, apparently," Yen Chung-ho said. "Let's go, they all have been waiting for you."

"Waiting for me?"

"Who else? You are the principal party." Yen Chung-ho said.

Yen San didn't really care to go, but since the opponents had set up a challenge, his refusal would look cowardly. If he agreed to go, it would seem a bit humiliating. "You go ahead," he said. "If I feel like it, I'll join you later."

Yen Chung-ho left. Yen San purposely delayed awhile before walking down the hill. At the corner of the alley he ran into a group of people with lanterns and torches led by militia captain Yen Yung, around twenty-seven, a husky fellow with broad shoulders and big hands who had won a second-class citation as a demolition expert in the Korean War. He walked up to Yen San and said, "After the meeting, none of us wanted to go to bed. We talked about launching a night attack to deliver manure to the field, as a token of our support for you. Third Brother, you do a good job, you must!"

"Yes, we must!" Yen San seized Yen Yung's big hand. The sight of all those people there, with rakes, hoes and baskets and wheelbarrows ready for action, gave him much assurance. In their lantern light he saw the clear-featured, alert Yen Chao, now in charge of the public security committee; Yen Hsiu-o, a roofer's daughter, secretary of the Communist Youth Corps; several sturdy-hearted members of the Party branch committee and of the brigade committee. A few production team leaders were also there. "Come with me," Yen San said to them. "Let's go over there and talk a minute."

They went over to the big tree on the threshing ground. Yen San said, "It's this: Yen Chung-ho, that tricky devil, insisted that I go to his house. I thought that Yen Tzu-yü and his gang must have set up a confrontation for me. What do you say? Should I go or not?"

"Go, what are we afraid of?" the crowd said.

"Will it be all right?"

"It'll be all right," the crowd said.

"Then I can go?"

"Of course!"

"Fine, I'm going now!" said Yen San.

Yen Yung said, "Do you want me to post a few men at his door?"

"Shucks!" Yen San said, "we don't need that."

"Then let me stick around just in case," offered Yen Chao, head of the security committee.

Yen San thought it over for a moment, then said, "That won't be necessary either."

II

Yen Chung-ho and Yen Tzu-yü were neighbors. The adobe wall between their houses, taken down as topsoil for the fields last spring, had not been rebuilt yet. Lamp light and whispered conversation issued from the cracks in the closed door and windows of Yen Tzu-yü's house.

In Yen Chung-ho's main room, rather bright light shone on an old square dining table against the center of the back wall. Steam rose from tea wares, and tobacco was displayed on the table. Yen Tzu-yü and his gang were absent, only three old fellows from the village, known for their usual roles as mediators, sat around the table helping themselves to the amenities. One stood up to greet Yen San with respect, while another, claiming his status as a village elder, scolded Yen San for being a snob, now that he would refuse to come even upon an invitation. Yen San only smiled. He sat down next to the lamp, declined the tea and tobacco offered him, and bluntly asked Yen Chung-ho, "Where are your men? Who else are involved?"

"No one else," said Yen Chung-ho.

"Just these several uncles?"

"Yes, yes!"

Yen San cast a curious glance at the oldsters and shouted, his face straight, "What are you doing here?"

Like a bucket of cold water Yen San's words descended upon the oldsters, instantly silencing them. They thought to themselves: Just overnight Yen San has become a different man! What they had prepared to say was geared to the Yen San of yesterday.

In fact Yen San had not changed much in the last several days. He remained a sturdy fellow of medium height, with a bony head that resembled a raw chunk of dark brown iron ore. His face was dominated by the same knobby nose and thick lips, except that it seemed to radiate a newly acquired dignity. An alert, challenging light had been added to his usually smiling eyes. He sat there, calm as always, and yet in that calmness the people around him now sensed an aura of majesty. All this stunned his inquisitors, who thought in unison, "How come such a hired hand, who, for all his years of toil, never earned even the position of a foreman, who buried himself in the stable all year long, having nothing to say to anybody except his animals, suddenly rose and ascended the peak of the village's power structure—how come he could look with authority straight into the eyes of his opponents?"

Yen San was sizing up his opponents. He had prepared to encounter some tough ones there who had the powerline of the village in their hands. He had not expected to find only several poor and lower-middle old peasants there. One of them, Uncle Chi-mao, actually was one of those who had urged Yen San to fire off that explosive report. Yen San thought, "The Yen Tzu-yü gang's really full of devils! They thought they could send this team of poor peasants to march off against me as their vanguard. Fine," he said to himself, "since these dim-witted old fellows are here to talk with me, they must be on Yen Tzu-yü's side. I'd like to see what they have to say." Yen San dug out his own tobacco and started to smoke without saying another word.

The old fellows saw that Yen San refused to accept Yen Chung-ho's tea or tobacco and looked not at all conciliatory; they didn't know how to break the ice. They started gossiping about their neighbors, about this woman's short hair and that woman's patched pants . . . for a long time they just couldn't bring the topic anywhere close to their main business. Even Yen Chung-ho didn't know how to prompt them.

Yen San got impatient waiting for them to begin. He changed his tactics to seize the initiative. With a smile on his face he said, "Well, uncles, you people got me here just to listen to your gossip about our neighbor's dirty linen?"

Another shocked silence.

Yen San continued, "Excuse me for being a blunderbuss. Don't you people have any shame? You smoked their tobacco, drank their tea. Judging by the spots on this table you must have also eaten their fried eggs. How come? You mean to say they spent money getting you here just to gossip about our neighbors with you?" He turned to Yen Chung-ho. "Now, Chung-ho, you tell us. Why did you get these people here? How could you let them keep on chewing the fat like this? Even I can't help getting antsy for you!"

Yen Chung-ho's sharp tongue failed to serve him this time. Under Yen San's blitz attack his face turned red and he didn't know where to put his hands or feet. "Ah, Old San," he managed to say, "why did you put it that way? You don't mean that I am not allowed to invite people to sit down and just chat awhile?"

The old fellows all chimed in now. "That's it, that's it. You've just been made brigade leader, and you won't sit with the commune members just to chat awhile?"

Yen San laughed and said to Yen Chung-ho, "Chung-ho, guess you are a bit hard-pressed and you made a boo-boo. Just think, now that you have put it that way, what else can these people say besides gossiping? Just think for a moment . . . don't you wish you could take it back?"

The usually clever Yen Chung-ho certainly did not expect the usually clumsy Yen San to put him on the spot like that. What had Yen San got? Just a sense of honesty and a straightforward approach, and yet Yen Chung-ho got pinned down, couldn't even wiggle himself out of the hole.

Yen San followed up his own salvo. "Uncles," he said, "don't work yourselves into a dead-end street. They asked you to say something, why don't you people say it? I don't have much more time to stay here with you. If I leave before you've said what you meant to say, what are you going to do? Would they ever again treat you to tea, tobacco, and fried eggs?" He toyed with the tobacco on the table and said, taunting them, "Ah, what nice tobacco! Nice and thick leaves, beautiful color and the aroma, oh . . . what aroma! Who has saved up such nice stuff? It's not easy to get this kind of nice tobacco to smoke. Am I right, uncles?"

Embarrassment reigned among the old fellows. They sweated in panicky silence.

. . . . . .

After a long while, Yen Chung-ho said, "These several uncles here asked me to invite you here for a chat. Ah ... it's all for the sake of the masses of our village. Everybody is anxious to see the present incident settled quietly, without causing any disaster for our village, without spoiling the friendship among us."

"So, that's what it is," said Yen San, feigning nonchalance.

Yen Chung-ho said, "We all know, this time Secretary Lu came to our village because someone from here had sent in a report, and we've found out who that one was."

Yen San laughed. "Ha, ha, you are a smart fellow," he said. "How come this time you are so slow? You don't have to waste time trying to find out who reported. You forgot that I said in Yen Shun-p'ing's face at a meeting a month ago that I'd report on them."

"That's it," Yen Chung-ho said. "But only now they realized that you meant it. Anyway, let's not go into that now. Nobody is blaming you either. Let's hope that in the future we all cooperate and won't tear our village apart. That's all."

"I suppose I must thank you for your broad-minded attitude toward me," Yen San said, laughing again. "I would like to know, though, how do you figure on settling the thing at present, and in the future how are we going to cooperate with each other?"

Yen Chung-ho said, "Everybody feels that so long as there will be no repeated offense of those charges you enumerated in your report, that should do it. Those are small matters. What's important is to stick together in peace and harmony."

"Peace and harmony!" Yen San repeated these two words, as though he had never heard them before in his life.

"That's it. We are all together in a small family. If you don't run into them in the morning, you're bound to bump into them at night. Thank heaven that for many years there has been peace in Yen-chia-t'an. Let's hope nothing bad will happen in the future." Yen Chung-ho cast an apprehensive glance at Yen San before he continued. "At present, let's all give a helping hand to Shun-p'ing to tide him over this bad spot. During your term as acting brigade leader, we all guarantee to get the job done right for you. And then when the meeting is called to criticize Yen Tzu-yü, let us not single out his name. Later, you stay on the job of deputy leader to team up with Yen Shun-p'ing in handling our village affairs. Let us always talk things over first. With Yen Tzu-yü and his people supporting you, everything will be easy for you."

"Oh, ya!" said Yen San, as though pleasantly surprised by the great promise, "Even Yen Tzu-yü is going to give his support!"

Yen Chung-ho said, "Yen-chia-t'an has to have Yen Tzu-yü. Without him it's like a cart without wheels. You know what he can do, don't you?"

Now Yen San saw through his opponent's scheme: they realized that to knock Yen San over wouldn't be easy, so they were trying to drag Yen San over to travel along with Yen Shun-p'ing and to be under the latter's thumb in actuality. Yen San, angered to the bursting point, maintained his composure. He turned to the old fellows. "Then you people are here to make peace, right?"

"Right, right!" they said, "Peace comes first. We all are neighbors, we've been for generations sleeping on both sides of the same wall, you know."

Yen San turned to Chung-ho, "Tell me, if it is not settled the way you just suggested, something awful would surely happen?"

"Heaven forbid," Chung-ho said with a cunning smile, "Let heaven forbid anything bad happening to our village."

Yen San turned to the three old fellows, "Uncles, did you hear that? Something awful just might happen! Something awful, awful, uncles! You thought you were here just doing a bit of go-between, like the way we marry our daughters and sons in the village. So, you want to come here to speak for somebody! This tea and this tobacco are not easy to take. It may be easy to bite but hard to chew, you know. You'd better understand first what you are doing!" The three panicked; without knowing it they put down the tea and tobacco already in their hands.

Yen San approached a skinny old fellow. "Uncle Chi-mao," he said, "you of all people also came here to get involved in this business? You have joined me in signing that report, you remember!" The old man named Chi-mao stared at Yen San. Yen San said, "Uncles, you tell me. You've come here to sit across the table from me. For whom are you speaking? Did the commune members, the masses, send you here?"

Yen San continued in this vein, alternating harsh criticism with soft persuasion, until the three old fellows lost their tongues. They blushed, their heads bent low, and did not know how they should feel about the whole thing. Yen Chung-ho saw that he wasn't getting anywhere; he sneaked out of the room.

"You'd better go home and have a good rest, uncles!" Yen San wound up his speech with a broad grin. "If this won't do, I'll ask everybody at the open meeting tomorrow and see what the masses have to say to you people."

"No, please don't ask anything at the meeting!" the three old fellows said together. "We can only blame ourselves; we haven't studied well these days, haven't taken Secretary Lu's advice to heart." Then they proceeded to tell Yen San how Yen Chung-ho lured them there, urging them to say such-and-such. They asked Yen San to forgive them and promptly beat a retreat.

The moon had already gone down; it was all dark outside. Yen San hurried to help the old fellows get started on a safe journey home. Old Chi-mao pulled Yen San aside to whisper in his ear, "Yen San, to be honest with you, I came here hoping to settle this problem. I don't want to see it get bigger. You know what sort of a guy Yen Tzu-yü is. Nothing is beneath him. I'm worried about you; he could get you, you know. . . . Even when sleeping you'd better keep one eye open, and when you go out at night, you'd better carry that thing with you!"

"Don't worry, uncle," said Yen San. "Don't be scared by that devil!"

.   .   .   .

Footsteps sounded beyond the door. Several people appeared. First came a man, rather tall, sallow-skinned, with heavy eyebrows over big eyes, tall nose-bridge, a short moustache. Conceit and hypocrisy showed in his eyes; this was Yen Tzu-yü. During the land reform, he maneuvered to have himself classified as a wealthy middle-peasant. How he had managed to build a family fortune nobody knows, except that at seventeen he left home and knocked around for a long time. Everybody in the village knew about his calculating mean character and everybody stayed out of his way. This time, he had Yen Tzu-ts'ai and Yen Chung-ho with him. Bringing up the rear was Yen Shun-p'ing, his face lined with worry.

They walked into the room and sat around the table, Yen Tzu-yü facing Yen San. Yen Chung-ho busied himself with serving tea, but Yen Shun-p'ing kept his worry all to himself, shrinking behind the lamp, wordless.

Yen San took them all in with one glance and rested his eyes squarely on Yen Tzu-yü. Yen Shun-p'ing had no courage to face Yen San; he looked resentfully at Yen Tzu-yü for a brief moment and made his way to the door but was stopped by Yen Tzu-ts'ai's tug at his jacket. Yen Tzu-yü, as though nothing bothered him at all, talked casually and laughed loudly. He cracked jokes as he lighted a cigarette for himself. But Yen San quickly saw through him; his laughter couldn't quite cover up his worry, which actually weighed ten times more than anybody else's. Yen Tzu-yü had been around; he had sensed Secretary Lu's intentions, which would not stop at punishing Yen Shun-p'ing alone but would aim at a complete riddance of the power and influence of such people as Yen Tzu-yü and his gang. What lay ahead for him? How could Yen Tzu-yü avoid getting worried? Having seen through his opponent's problems, Yen San, too, laughed.

Yen Tzu-yü raised his head. He quickly suppressed the fleeting sign of panic in his eyes with a smile. "What, Old San," he said, "the whole village is about turned upside down, everybody is troubled, only you are having a good time, right?"

"What about you? Troubled also?" Yen San countered.

Yen Tzu-yü calmly waved his hand and said, "Forget it, Old San, we've had enough of this kidding. Let's be serious. The word Yen can't be split apart; we have all been tending one and the same ancestor's grave. All right, let's not talk about all that, just exactly what are you going to do?"

"What am I going to do?" said Yen San. "It doesn't seem right to tell you about it, does it?"

"Don't you want to settle it peaceably?" Yen Tzu-yü played with the cigarette between his fingers and said slowly, "The way I look at it, it would be best to make peace. It can only bring benefit to the revolutionary work in our village."

"What's that? What? Revolution, did you say?" Feeling quite amused, Yen San responded with a question.

"That's it. The way I look at it, it would be best to settle it quietly among ourselves," Yen Tzu-yü repeated.

"How shall we settle it? The way Chung-ho proposed?"

"No, not exactly. Chung-ho didn't quite get it straight. We want you to be the brigade leader and we'll support you to get the job done!"

"What else?"

"Nothing else," said Yen Tzu-yü. "If there is one more thing, it would be that we all try to get the commune business straightened out by discussing everything together, like old friends. We don't want to ruin the peace and harmony among us."

"Just like this?"

"Like what?"

"You got me here. You want me to do whatever you say. You want me to go wherever you want. Then your peace and harmony won't be ruined, right?" Yen San said; then he moved over to stand before Yen Shun-p'ing and addressed him sternly. "Shun-p'ing, to find you here is not exactly a nice thing. It makes me feel awful. What are you made of anyway—soft dough? Don't you have a single bone left in you?" Yen Shun-p'ing shot up abruptly and dashed out, after darting a hateful glance at Yen Tzu-yü, who looked stunned.

"Tzu-yü," Yen San turned to him, "let me ask you. Are you chairman of the commune's Party unit? Are you representing the commune membership? Or are you a cadre with any special assignment? That's right, you are none of these. Let me ask you, you got these people together here behind Secretary Lu's back. Don't you realize you are stepping way out of line when you do such things?"

"What?" said Yen Tzu-yü, his eyes popping out. "You are accusing me of . . ."

"Irregularity!" said Yen San.

"Ah, Old San," said Yen Chung-ho, trying to make peace, "you are charging other people with another offense? We are all here just for the sake of our common job; we want to exchange our views informally, that's all."

Yen Tzu-yü tried hard to sneer before he said, "Chung-ho, don't worry. After all is said, Old San is still from this same village of ours. His wife and child are living here; I don't think he wants to go too far!" He raised his eyes slowly to fix a gaze on Yen San. Lifting the corners of his mouth, he faked a confident smile. "Yen San," he said, "what do you say?"

Yen San stood up. "Let's wait and see," he said.

Yen Tzu-yü crushed the cigarette in his hand. "Fine," he said, his voice implying a dark threat, "I'll be waiting for you. I say, Old San, you'd better weigh the alternatives, you still have a little time left."

Yen San turned his head back in time to catch the undisguised look of hatred in Yen Tzu-yü's eyes. He snorted contemptuously and strode out. . . .

III

. . . The gong for breakfast had been struck; many commune members had started walking back toward the village. Yen San, engrossed in his job of spreading manure, had only two or three piles left. Suddenly Yen Hsiu-o, secretary of the Communist Youth Corps, ran breathlessly toward him from the west side of the village. Her shrill voice screamed in the air, calling, "Third Uncle! Your Kang-wa fell into the well! Third Uncle! Your Kang-wa . . ."

Shocked, Yen San's face turned pale. "Which well?" he shouted, dropping his shovel.

"Right near your own plot."

As though catapulted, Yen San flew across the road and the bean patch, and like a dark rocket he shot westward. Kang-wa was his only child, also the only boy in all the four branches of his clan. That boy was the jewel of jewels to him, like the only rice sprout in the whole of a ten-acre plot of land. . . .

Yen San plunged through the wall of humanity already gathered around the scene of a near tragedy to reach the edge of the well. Kang-wa, soaked all through like a rain-drenched little sparrow, drooped in the arms of a rescuer, who was equally soaked and muddy all over. Yen San snatched up the child, holding him tightly to his bosom. His ears and head were ringing; he could only vaguely make out somebody's voice saying to him, "Old San, don't worry. Kang-wa's all right. Nothing bad."

When Yen San's eyes slowly cleared, he noticed the child's eyes were turning. "Are you all right?" he asked.

"Yes."

"Where does it hurt?"

"Here," the child pointed at his right buttock.

Yen San pulled up the child's trousers to find a black and blue bruise. He touched it, but Kang-wa did not complain of pain. Feeling relieved, he heaved a deep sigh and started gently to rub his son. An image of a man which had been in his mind all these days surfaced: Yen Tzu-yü! Yen San looked up and scanned the crowd. In a flash his eyes engaged those of Yen Tzu-yü. This was not hallucination; that was really Yen Tzu-yü who was squatting right in front of him, in soaked clothes and with mud all over the legs. Yen San now realized that it was from Yen Tzu-yü's arms he had taken over the nearly drowned child. People around said, "Kang-wa was rescued by Yen Yung, the security committee head, and Yen Tzu-yü."

"Kang-wa," Yen San asked his son, "What were you doing?"

"I was picking apples. The branch broke."

"Ah, haven't I told you many times? You mustn't climb on the branch directly over the well!"

Yen Tzu-yü said, "Luckily, when the branch broke, Kang-wa grabbed onto it without letting go. The branch scraped the wall of the well and went down slowly. Otherwise just the fall would have been enough to smash him to pieces."

Yen San stared at Yen Tzu-yü in disbelief. He couldn't tell himself why, but he kept wondering, "It was he who saved my son?"

On his way home, Yen Tzu-yü walked behind him, carrying his plow on his shoulder. Yen Chung-ho trod by the side, mumbling, "In this area, there's a well just about every five or ten yards, and there is the Wei River in the north. It's too easy to lose a child." A little later, he mumbled again, "Let's hope there won't be any more trouble from now on!"

Yen San turned around to look at the two. He thought: "This guy's trying to use the accident to scare me? Sure, it's altogether very, very possible. The two children of the Party branch secretary at Hsüeh-chia-pao village, didn't they . . ." He felt his heart had been twisted into a tight knot.

Yen San didn't say a single word the whole morning. He just kept thinking about a way of handling this incident. Fellow commune members came in an endless procession to see him and his family, but his wife really had it bad— she kept walking out and in without knowing what she was doing.

In a little while, Yen Chao, the security committee head, and Militia Captain Yen Yung came in. Yen Chao threw a large broken tree branch on the ground. "Third Brother," she said, "take a good look at this." Yen San examined the branch; he discovered some ax marks where the branch broke off from the tree. "I've felt funny about the whole thing ever since it happened," Yen Chao said. "Why did both branches, the one Kang-wa stepped on and the other one he held in his hands, break off at the same moment? A little child like Kang-wa could not have weighed very much. . . . I looked around carefully. Aiya! There were ax cuts on the branch. I brought up the one Kang-wa had grabbed onto; it was the same."

Yen Yung said, "It must be that they had noticed Kang-wa climbing on the tree every day. It gave them a chance to plot against you, Third Brother."

Yen San turned the ax-cut branch over and over in his hand. He repeated under his breath, "Son of a bitch, I'm going to kill him . . . I'm going to kill that son of a bitch!"

Old Chi-mao hurried his way toward Yen San's house, with a cane's help, tumbling and tripping all the way. The moment he stepped inside the house he shouted, "Is Kang-wa all right? . . . Hai! it's all my fault . . . all my fault . . . I heard that my number three girl had taken ill, and I hurried to see her in the hospital. I forgot to tell you first . . ."

"What happened?" Yen San suddenly leaped to the door and grabbed the old man's arm in his pincer-like hands. His eyes seemed fearfully aflame as he stared at Chi-mao.

Chi-mao said, "You remember what I warned you about that evening? I've been worried all along. Yesterday I was with Yen Tzu-yü all the time. Evening came; we were all eating dinner in the mess hall. Nobody was in the field. Then I saw Yen Tzu-yü sneaking out of the village. I followed him. He started chopping at your fruit tree. He looked nervous. I thought since he hated you, he must be doing that to get even with you. And yet I was wondering why he didn't swing the ax at the base of the tree. I never imagined that . . ."

Looking fierce, Yen San yelled in a hoarse voice, "Uncle, are you sure of what you saw?"

"Of course!"

"You saw clearly?"

"I saw it clearly!"

"Is there any proof?"

"I can find it!" said Chi-mao. "As he chopped away at the tree I coughed in the corn field. That startled him and the ax slipped out of his hand and fell into the well."

It all became very clear to Yen Yung now. He said, "No wonder he insisted on going down the well first. He was afraid that I might discover the murder weapon down there myself."

"Okay, you son of a bitch!" Yen San said, shaking with rage. "Yen Chao, let's get the ax in the well, hurry! Yen Yung, you send a man to keep an eye on that devil; don't let him get away."

Before long the ax was brought home. They checked and confirmed that it belonged to Yen Tzu-yü. Yen San called the key members of the commune together behind closed doors. After they were all seated he said, "It's like this. Comrades, this time he resorted to such a criminal move all because he wanted to make us back down and bow to him. He wants to hurt me, scare me first, then he'd turn to scare all of you. Let's be frank now, is there anyone here who's afraid?"

"What are we afraid of?" everybody said in anger.

"Really? From the bottom of your heart?"

"From the bottom of our hearts!"

"Fine," Yen San continued. "Now, let's think a moment. I think we should hold a mass meeting first and arrest him right there in front of everybody and take him to the Public Security Station. Can we do that? What do you say?"

"Yes, let's do just that!" Everybody agreed.

Yen San turned to Yen Chao. "Yen Chao, you are in charge of security affairs. You know the rules. You think about this and tell us if it is according to the rules."

Yen Chao said, "We've got both the culprit and the material evidence; of course it's in accord with the rules. I said to you yesterday that we should deliver him to the Public Security Station."

"You are saying that it would be in accord with the rules for making an arrest?" asked Yen San.

"Yes, in complete accord!" said Yen Chao.

"Then we can arrest him?"

"We can!"

"The masses also have been suspecting a murder plot and they want the murderer caught and turned over to the law," Yen Hsiu-o said.

"That's the way they want it?"

"That's the way!"

"All right," said Yen San to Yen Yung. "Yen Yung, you hurry up and get our men together with their stuff ready. I'm going to talk to Secretary Lu on the phone!" He ran over to the next room for the phone call. When he returned, everything was ready. Yen San told Yen Chao, "Yen Chao, Secretary Lu instructed us to keep an eye on those chronic troublemakers when we take action."

"I'll see to that right away!" said Yen Chao.

"Yen Yung, are we all ready?"

Yen Yung said with a smile, "Third Brother, look, every one of them is a champ. We've got more than needed to over-fulfill the quota, if that's what you want."

"There mustn't be any over-quota in a business like this." Even Yen San smiled. Then he turned to Yen Hsiu-o, "You listen. The moment they've got the man, you go strike the bell to call for a mass meeting."

"Will do!" said Yen Hsiu-o.

Yen San raised his head and spoke with deep hatred, "Yen Tzu-yü, Yen Tzu-yü, damn you! We must kick you out of Yen-chia-t'an forever!" He pounded his huge fist on the table and announced, "Let's go get him!" A shower of dust came down from the beam overhead.

They rushed out the door.

Yen San kept Old Chi-mao behind. "Uncle," he asked the old man, "are you prepared to testify in court?"

"I'll use this to beat the hell out of him first before testifying against him," said Chi-mao, wielding his walking stick.

"You'd better keep your stick for walking. You swing it only when you have to, all right?" Yen San also smiled.

... The mass meeting lasted for over three hours. In Old Chi-mao's words, if the cadres hadn't stopped them, the people of Yen-chia-t'an would have long before torn the murderer Yen Tzu-yü to shreds.

That evening, Secretary Lu returned to the village after his meeting. Yen San reported to him in detail. Lu said, "It's good to have him arrested. In fact we did it a bit too late. We mustn't be soft in dealing with guys like him!"

Together they walked around in the village until they once again climbed onto the cliff behind it. Lights spread beneath them, both inside and beyond the village. The sound of whips cracking over draft animals, of rumbling motors, of drums and gongs filled the air and rocked the earth. The wind was still, yet a strong scent of ripening crops rushed toward them. A few minutes later, the bell suspended under a tall tree rang, and the kerosene lantern suspended over the open field was lit. The hour for the mass meeting had arrived. At tonight's meeting, the masses of Yen-chia-t'an would listen, in solemnity, to the first self-criticism by Yen Shun-p'ing. . . .

The time was the fall of 1959. The episode was only a short segment of the saga of commune rectification in Yen-chia-t'an. Let's pause here for now, though it's neither the beginning nor the end of the whole story.

Translated by Teng-ch'i Yeh and Kai-yu Hsu

CHAO SHU-LI
(1906–70)

Chao Shu-li, a native of Ch'in-shui, Shansi Province, came from a poor peasant family. Trained as a teacher, he was imprisoned by the Kuomintang for espousing radical ideas. He liked the folk theater of his home state; for a time he joined a local troupe and intended to make it his career. After 1940 he worked on cultural assignments in the Communist-dominated T'ai-hang Mountains and as a reporter for the *New China Daily.* Success came to him instantly upon the publication of his stories about the village folk, written in crisp, effective peasant language with honest and charming characterizations. Chao is endowed with a knack for the dramatic and a delightful sense of humor. Among his most popular works are the short story "The Marriage of Hsiao Er-hei," the novellas *Fu-kuei, The Rhymes of Li Yu-ts'ai,* and *The Changes in Li Village,* and the full-length novel *San-li-wan.* Chou Yang, the Party's literary authority for years, praised Chao highly and encouraged the nation's writers to follow the "Chao Shu-li direction."

From 1949 to 1966 Chao served on the editorial boards of many major literary journals. Frequently he returned to the countryside to work for the Party at the county level. He became a principal target of persecution in 1967, when the Cultural Revolution surged, and stories about the inhumane treatment that led to his death in 1970 did not surface until the beginning of 1979.

"The Unglovable Hands" is divided into three sections. The first stresses farmer Ch'en Ping-cheng's past, which includes what he did for the uncultivated land; the second, his purchase of five pitchforks; and the third, his experience in attending a Model Workers' Convention. In each episode his hands are emphasized: their appearance, their strength, and dexterity. Hence his hands are symbolic of the old farmer himself. Like his hands, Ch'en is indomitable, free in spirit, and inspiring to others; under no circumstances could he be affected by either the snicker of a young trainee, the kindness of his children and grandchildren, who want his hands protected from the elements, or his advanced age. To him, the gloves are cumbersome and unnecessary. At the very least they are something for him to worry about; at the worst, they restrict his movements and prevent him from doing his work. He sums up his own situation well: "My hands are unglovable."

In a 1962 review of the story published in *The Literary Gazette,* Lao She lavishly praised the author's simple but thoughtful choice of diction, accurate depiction of life in the country, and, in particular, his use of the gloves as "the thread" to link the story's many disparate elements into a coherent whole.

—K.M. and W.L.Y.Y.

The Unglovable Hands

The training corps of the Big Millstone Mountain Brigade, the White Cloud Ridge Commune, had been established when the brigade was still an advanced agricultural cooperative, and its goal was to teach skills to people who joined farm production for the first time. During that period of the advanced cooperative in 1956, a number of women and young students who had never participated in farming joined the work force, but their work was below standard. Hence Director Ch'en Man-hung proposed that a training corps be established, that two old farmers of high productivity serve as instructors, that some low-yield land be set aside as the training fields to train the unskilled. After the proposal was approved by the Administration Committee, a few scores of low-yield *mu* on top of the Big Millstone Mountain and several parcels of orchard land in the gulch on the southern side were designated as such; Ch'en Ping-cheng, father of Director Ch'en Man-hung, and old orchard-hand Wang Hsin-ch'un were selected as instructors. Ch'en served as coordinator and Wang as vice-coordinator, and the corps' members were assigned to various villagers as coaches. When commune members encountered unexpected difficulties with their work or when their coaches could not help them, they would then seek the advice of Ch'en or Wang. Even though the purpose of the corps was to train new workers, there were exceptions: (1) workers who had trouble with certain tasks might register for the classes when those tasks were taught; (2) those who could not perform certain tasks well or those recommended by the Evaluation Committee because of bad work attitudes were also included. Those in the last category, during this training period, would be denied full credit for each work day, which would be calculated on a 60 percent basis. It was a sort of token punishment for those who could have performed better but didn't.

Coordinator Ch'en Ping-cheng was already a man of seventy-six. In general, most men of his age should not participate in any major physical labor, but he was especially hale and hearty. As a young man, he could do the work of a man and a half; now in old age, he was the better of most young men in terms of strength. In the winter of 1958, when communes were established, the Big Millstone Mountain was classified as a brigade, and its leader was Ch'en Man-hung. The brigade soon had its Respect-Old-Folks Home, and the Evaluation Committee recommended that Ch'en Ping-cheng retire and live in the home. After three days in the home, the old man felt that light tasks such as stripping hemp stalks and picking cotton were not demanding enough to deplete his energy, so he asked to leave the home and to resume his job as coordinator of the training corps.

Old man Ch'en Ping-cheng's skill as a farmer was considered first rate, not only in the Big Millstone Mountain but also in the whole White Cloud Ridge area, which had cited him as an exceptional, exemplary worker. The stone dikes that he helped build never collapsed; the fire in the smoldering fertilizer pile that he had helped stack up never went out; and he was second to none in common tasks such as ploughing, seeding, hoeing, and harvesting.

When he taught in the training corps, he insisted not only on standards but also on proper style, claiming that if the style were not correct, the work would be below standard. For instance, in second-hoeing, he stressed that the tiller must bend his body to a certain degree, slant his body and feet to one side, and hold his feet steady. Also his hands must tightly hold on to the hoe, firmly strike the ground, and not allow the hoe to shake in any way. The standard was that the hoe must strike close to and around the seedling but not cover up any area yet undug. In piling dirt around the seedling, the tiller must, to the utmost extent possible, make a small mound with no more than three strikes of the hoe, and the top of the mound must be flat rather than pointed. As he lectured, he demonstrated to the trainees; sometimes he repeated the instructions more than ten times before he would allow them to do any work. Because of his many rules and regulations, they would remember one rule and forget another. Sometimes they stood too straight or moved forward incorrectly. Sometimes they hoed haphazardly, complicating simple chores. Old man Ch'en Ping-cheng kept reminding one trainee, then another; he also frequently interrupted their work by giving another demonstration.

A man named Ho Ho-ho had spent half of his life hoeing without ever bending his back. When he hoed, the hoe itself bounced around wildly; if it happened to bounce onto the weeds, then he cut the weeds, but if it happened to hit the seedlings, then the crop was damaged. After the founding of the training corps, the brigade's Evaluation Committee wanted him to have some training in the corps. When he came, Coordinator Ch'en Ping-cheng, as usual, taught him the proper hoeing style. The problem was that this man—nicknamed "Ha-ha-ha"—was indolent by nature. After bending down a little for hoeing, he would immediately straighten his back again. Old man Ch'en Ping-cheng had his ingenuity. Next day he brought a spare hoe from his own home and shortened it to a length of three feet, telling Ho, "Your habit of not bending down can only be cured with this short-handled hoe." Once he had a new hoe, his problem was corrected. He had to bend his back when using this three-foot hoe, otherwise, he could not touch the ground. Later other teams heard of this new method; they all prepared a number of short-handled hoes for those not accustomed to bending their backs.

When the trainees became tired from style exercises, Coordinator Ch'en gave them a break. Eight or nine terraced paddy-fields below, Vice-coordinator Wang Hsin-ch'un taught his class the planting of seeds. During the break the two groups met; the two old men smoked tobacco and chatted; the trainees read their newspapers or had a good time together. When the two old men met, Ch'en would extend his hand for a handshake, and Wang would always try to avoid it. Though younger than Ch'en by more than ten years and friendly with Ch'en, Wang abhorred shaking Ch'en's hand, because when Ch'en shook his hand, he felt as though he were being squeezed by pliers.

One day during the break Ch'en invited Wang for a smoke. Ch'en had a flint. Wang said, "How nice it would be to have a fire!" A new trainee, a high school student, quickly proceeded to look for twigs. But all he could find were two dry, two-inch-long persimmon twigs. Wang smiled and said, "You don't have to look for firewood. Grandpa Ch'en has some." Puzzled, the trainee looked around him but could not see any. Old man Ch'en added, "Yes, I have some." Leisurely he put down his flint; without looking he scratched the dirt around him for a while and, lo and behold, found two big handfuls of bark and twigs. Wang lit a match, while old man Ch'en scratched around and got more wood, which he put on top of the pile. The trainee exclaimed in amazement, "This is very good," and began to do likewise. Old man Ch'en tried to stop him: "Wait a minute; don't." But it was too late. The young man's middle finger had been pricked and he quickly withdrew his hand. Wang said, "Son, what kind of hands do you have? What type of hands does he have? His are like an iron-rake; brambles or thorns—nothing could hurt them."

While rubbing his middle finger, the student looked at Ch'en's hands, which were different from those of ordinary people. The palm seemed to be square in shape, the fingers short, stubby, and bent; the back and the palm of the hands were covered with calluses; and his round fingertips resembled half cocoons with nails attached to them. The hands looked like two small rakes made of tree branches. The student looked at the hands with contempt instead of admiration, as if he were saying, "How can you call them hands?"

The two old men sensed the young man's scornful attitude. Ch'en ignored him. Looking proud, Ch'en picked up his pipe to smoke. Old man Wang, after lighting his pipe, said to the young man, "Young fellow, don't you slight his hands. Without them, the present training field would still remain uncultivated. This land belonged to landlord Wang Tzu-yü. According to old folks, these ten and more sections of land on top of the Big Millstone Mountain were left uncultivated since the third year of Emperor Kuang-hsü [1877] until the third year of Emperor Hsüan-t'ung [1910]. In those days neither his family nor mine had any land; he was a field hand working for Wang Tzu-yü, and I was herd boy. Later he came here to cultivate the land; after I grew up, I was elevated from herd boy to field hand and followed him to plant rice seeds in the marsh. All these fields were cultivated by him and our present brigade leader, digging them hoe by hoe and building dike after dike. Without his hands, this whole area would still be wasteland."

Even though the student was a little sorry that he had despised Ch'en's hands, he was unwilling to acknowledge his mistake openly. Instead, he said in a mocking tone, "No wonder we are such slow learners; it is all because we don't have his hands."

In a serious voice, Ch'en lectured the young man, "We want your hands to learn to work like mine, not to be like mine. If I wasn't the first one to dig these fields for planting, my hands wouldn't be like this. Now, folks of the older generation have already plowed the land with their hands; soon everything will be mechanized, and your hands won't have to become like mine."

Even though old man Ch'en did not wish others to have hands like his, he, nonetheless, was proud of them. His hands were not only firm and tough but also dexterous. He loved weaving and frequently wove thorn vines into all types of farming tools and sometimes made children's toys out of stalks of kaoliang. When he made tools out of vines, he did not have to use an oxhorn wedge in splitting them. He divided a vine into three and used his index finger as the splitter—chi, chi, chi—the vine was split, and his hand was not even scratched. Yet he also did work of a very delicate nature. No one would guess that it was done by the same hands. The katydid cages that he made out of kaoliang stalks featured a door, windows, upstairs and downstairs rooms, and on the two-inch-square windows he made many decorative patterns from different angles, with holes so tiny that even bees would have difficulty crawling through them.

After the periods of land reform, mutual assistance teams, and cooperatives, communes were established. Old man Ch'en Ping-cheng's family income increased. In the winter of 1959, his children and grandchildren bought him a pair of knitted gloves to protect his hands. Upon receiving the gift, he said, "My hands have never enjoyed such luxuries before." As he tried them on, he found the palm not big enough, the fingers too tight and long. He barely drew them on before he stretched the palm into a square, stuffed the lower part of the fingers full and left the upper part of the fingers empty. His son Ch'en Man-hung said, "After a while, they will fit you nicely." He put them on, opened and closed his hands a couple of times, then took them off and gave them to his daughter-in-law. "Please keep them for me."

"Dad, please wear them. Don't your hands get cold when you work in the field?"

"We are building a storage shed in the gulch and it's not convenient to move stones with them on." As soon as he said this, he left his gloves and walked away. Not long afterwards, the work at the gulch was completed but other work followed—cutting hay, cleaning sheep-pens, storing turnips for winter, and thrashing corn, none of which went well with the use of gloves, and he soon forgot he had them.

One day the White Cloud Ridge held a goods exchange fair. His daughter-in-law said to him, "Now they don't really need you to teach them these odd skills, why don't you take the day off and visit the fair?" The old man agreed. He changed into his new cotton-padded jacket and tied a new sash around his waist. She then said, "This time you must wear your new gloves," and brought him his gloves. He drew them on and left.

The Big Millstone Mountain was a small village and had no consumer co-op. As the neighbors heard he was going to the White Cloud Ridge and saw him walking down the street in his new jacket and gloves, they asked him to buy things for them. One family wanted three ounces of oil; another family wanted two catties of salt. All those purchases would be more than his hands could carry, so he borrowed a basket from a neighbor. When he reached the White Cloud Ridge, he walked past half a street block and arrived at the consumer's co-op and purchased what he had been asked to buy. Then he walked to the commune and saw a carload of pitchforks being unloaded by a salesman. For two years new pitchforks had not been available in the area, and what the different brigades had was not enough to go around. He felt he could not miss the opportunity. Having no money, he remembered that his son, who was attending a meeting at the commune, might have some. So he went and told his son about the pitchforks. Man-hung said, "Yes, by all means. They are very precious. Go buy them quickly," and gave him fifty dollars. With the money he went to the mountain-goods section and looked over the pitchforks. Fastidious with tools, he could not bear to see any blemish on them. Removing his gloves and tucking them inside his sash, he picked up one pitchfork, put it on the floor to see if its three prongs were even and strong, and whether its head and handle were straight. Before he finished looking at one, more than ten people had gathered, everyone holding and examining a pitchfork. In no time, many more people came; even the brigade leader, who was conducting a meeting at the commune, temporarily halted the meeting to come over to buy some. No one was as fastidious as the old man; they merely asked the price and paid. Old man Ch'en Ping-cheng saw the situation getting out of hand. Forgetting his high standards, he chose five pitchforks at random, and the rest were grabbed by others. He paid, tied the pitchforks together, put them on his shoulder, carried his basket and jostled his way out of the congested market section. With his hands full, he had no interest in wandering around the other half of the street block and went home by the same road he had taken.

Once outside the White Cloud Ridge village, the congestion was gone, and the road was much wider. Then he felt for his gloves. He could only find one. He put down his basket, the pitchforks, loosened his waist sash, but he could not find the other glove. He knew he must have lost it at the market. He thought, "All right, so be it. I don't use the gloves much anyway." He tied the sash back around his waist, carried the pitchforks on his shoulder with one hand and his basket with the other, and walked toward home. After he had taken a few steps he thought, "The kids bought them especially for me. Now that one glove is lost, and if I don't go back to look for it, I am not being nice to them." Turning back he returned to the fair at the White Cloud Ridge. Fortunately, the salesman had found his glove and kept it on the counter. He returned it to him.

Some time later, old man Ch'en Ping-cheng was selected as the model worker of the year by the Evaluation Committee, and he had to attend the Convention of Model Workers at the county seat. It was another opportunity for him to wear his gloves. Besides his new cotton-padded jacket and his new sash, he wore his gloves.

The Big Millstone Mountain was about forty *li* from the county seat. Winter days are short, so Ch'en, after breakfast, left home and reached his destination at dusk. It was the registration day. Once in town, he registered for the convention, received his attendance permit, and started looking for a place to stay. He had not been in town for more than six months, and it had changed—the streets had been widened, the roads were smooth, the dilapidated place where he had stayed while attending the meetings before was replaced by rows of newly built brick and tile houses. It was dark when he entered the hostel. Rows of rooms in the rear section by the passageway were lit, indicating their occupancy; some of the rooms on the first three rows were lit also. He went to the reception desk, registered, and the receptionist took him to Room 5 of West Row Two. When he reached West Row Two, he saw that the only light came from Room 6, while the rest of the rooms were dark. He stepped on some objects, some of which were hard and others soft; he had no idea what they were. The receptionist told him, "Be careful. This row of rooms was just completed, no more than a week ago, and there are still a few things here and there. Walk on this side; the other side is a lime pit. Walk by the wall; there's some loose lumber around." As they got to Room 5, the receptionist snapped on the light before letting him into the room. What came into view were a clean room, a good fire in the fireplace, a table by the window, two chairs, a stool, two beds on each side of the room, an unpainted door and windows, and recently whitewashed walls. The walls smelled damp as they were heated by the fire. Looking at the beds, he asked, "Four in each room?" The receptionist replied, "Yes."

"Will you have all the rooms occupied during the convention?"

"Almost. Some participants from far places have not yet arrived. Take a little rest. Let me bring you some water to freshen you up." A while later the receptionist brought in the water. The old man washed his face, and people streamed in steadily, occupying all the rooms on West Row Two. Besides the old man, Room 5 had three young men. The four of them introduced themselves to one another.

The convention lasted for three and a half days. The old man either listened to reports or prepared to make his own; like everyone else, he was kept busy until the morning of the fourth day, when the County Party Chief made a summary report. In the afternoon those who lived nearby went home; those who lived some distance away had to stay one more night. Ch'en's home was forty *li* away—neither too far nor too near. A young man could probably cover the distance and reach home shortly after dusk. Since he was old, he did not want to walk in the dark and planned to spend an extra half day in town.

After lunch those who would stay the night all wanted to take a walk around town. The old man returned to West Row Two, Room 5, where his three roommates and another young man from Room 4 were playing poker. He said, "Don't you want to look around town?" One young man replied, "Grandpa, you just go ahead. We'll go later." The old man tied the sash around his waist, put on his gloves, and left. Since the courtyard was partially blocked by two big logs, he had to walk close by the wall of Room 3 after he passed the door of Room 4. He thought, "If only I could roll those logs aside, but to where?" Squatting by the door of Room 4, he sized up the situation, concluding that it would be best to roll the logs southwards to face the lime pit. Once he made up his mind, he took off his gloves, put them on the steps and proceeded to roll one of the logs. Cut off from both ends, this one log's middle section was unshapely, thick, short, bent, and flat. It was not easy to roll at all. It took him considerable strength to prop it up, but it turned over only once and was flat on the ground again. Seeking help, he first knocked on the door of Room 4, but no one answered. So he returned to Room 5 and said to the young people, "Comrades, would you please help me move the logs in the courtyard so people can walk more easily?"

"Surely, I tried to do that yesterday, but the logs won't budge," a young man replied, putting down his cards. The other three young men got up and stepped outside. The old man took off his new cotton-padded jacket, left it on his bed, and stepped out of the room.

The old man helped them move the logs. One young man said to him, "You just rest; let us do the work." The four young men took all the room around one short log. Unable to lay his hands on the same one, he started to move the other log. After they had moved the short log, they saw him struggling with the other one. One young man stopped him. "Grandpa, please don't. We can do it." A second young man helped the first one lift it up. This log was a little longer than the first, and one end was thicker than the other. Though the person holding the thin end had no trouble lifting it, the man supporting the thick end did, murmuring continuously, "No, no." Then he let go. The young man at the other end was also about to drop the log when the old man said, "Let me do it." Immediately he bent down. Using his hands to support the log, and with his legs apart as if he were riding on a horse, he stiffened his shoulders and lifted it up. When the first young man saw the second one sticking up his thumb in admiration of the old man, he joined his friend, saying, "Grandpa, you are really marvelous. But you are an old man. Let us do it."

A receptionist carrying a kettle of hot water came by. When he saw what went on, he hurriedly said, "Thank you all. Let us do it."

"It's nothing."

"Before the convention started, the only cleanup work remaining was the courtyards of the first three rows of rooms. During the convention we had no time. We're waiting for tomorrow morning to start cleaning up when all the guests will have moved out. The few of us can finish the work in just a couple of days." Old man Ch'en Ping-cheng said, "Why must you wait until we leave? The convention has ended. Isn't now a good time to help you clean up?"

"No, no, that would be too much trouble to impose on you all." Old man Ch'en and the young people all said that they didn't mind, and comrades from other rooms, who had not left for town, all came out of their rooms saying that they too would like to help in the cleanup. Seeing this, the receptionist hurried to consult the manager. Even before the receptionist returned, everyone looked for cleanup tools. Since the first two rows had not been thoroughly cleaned up, the tools were piled up in the courtyards between the west-east rows. They found shovels, brooms, open baskets, and poles, and they immediately started to work. Old man Ch'en wanted to haul the baskets for them, but everyone, upon seeing his white beard, insisted that he not do that type of heavy work. So he could only use a broom to sweep the courtyard along with the others. Model workers were truly model workers. When the people from the first three rows of rooms saw that the people on West Row Two were busy cleaning up, they immediately joined in the operation. In a short while, the receptionist and the manager came back. The manager advised everyone not to bother with the work; however, since he could not convince them, he called every staff member, including his assistant, the accountant, the receptionists, to join in the task.

Everyone used shovels to remove left-over bricks or tiles, bark, wood shavings, and other miscellaneous items; old man Ch'en followed and swept after them. He started from the southwest corner of the courtyard in West Row Two and swept northwards. When he reached the window of Room 6, he saw that there were mud cakes and wood shavings on the windowsill; he reached for the dirt with his broom. Because the windowsill was rather small, the broom was less than efficient; he put down his broom and brushed off the dirt with his ironlike hands. Then, looking toward the east, he saw every windowsill was similarly dirty. He started from Room 6 to Room 5, then to Room 4, and cleaned every windowsill before he returned to the west side to clean the courtyards.

Since there were many people, the work was done quickly. Within two hours, the six courtyards had been cleaned, and the garbage stood by both sides of the passageway; materials that could be used were left at the rear entrance of the storage room, to be hauled away by a truck that came by at night. After all the work had been completed, old man Ch'en felt satisfied, knowing that people could walk a lot more easily from then on.

The manager, his assistant, the accountant, and all the receptionists went to get water for the model workers to clean up. After that, some went into town; old man Ch'en once again put on his new cotton-padded jacket, tied the sash around his waist and planned to put on his gloves—only to realize that they had been lost again. He casually asked his young friends, "When you cleaned, did you see my gloves?" One man answered, "No, we didn't see them. Where did you leave them?"

"On the windowsill of Room 4." Another man said, "Yes, I seemed to remember one glove in a pile of wood shavings, all smeared with mud, and I thought it was someone's discarded old glove."

"Yes, probably when I pulled down the wood shavings of Room 4 the shavings covered them and you didn't see them and threw them in with the garbage pile." The old man went to look for his gloves in the garbage pile by the passageway, but the garbage from the row of West Two alone filled up more than several dozen baskets. How could he find his gloves right away?

When a receptionist saw him, he asked, "Grandpa, what are you looking for?"

"My gloves."

"Are you sure they are in there?"

"Yes, I am."

"Then you go into town and have a good time. We will find them for you."

"Don't bother; they are not of much use to me," the old man said firmly.

The old man strolled around several blocks in town. Other than admiring some new buildings, he had little interest in anything else, thinking, "I don't buy or sell. Why must I linger by the stores?" So he returned to the hostel. It was not yet dusk, and his roommates had not yet returned. A receptionist opened the door for him and told him that his gloves had been found. He entered his room; the fire in the quiet fireplace was still strong; and his gloves had been washed by a receptionist and put on the back of a chair to dry.

He returned home the next day. After changing his clothes, he returned the gloves to his daughter-in-law. "You'd better keep them. My hands are unglovable."

Enjoying the Short Stories of 1960, pp. 241–51

Translated by Nathan K. Mao and Winston L. Y. Yang

T'ANG K'O-HSIN
(1928–)

Along with Fei Li-wen and Hu Wan-ch'un, T'ang K'o-hsin emerged from a Shanghai factory to lead the younger generation of worker-writers. His first short story, published in 1953, attracted wide attention, and a year later he was pulled out of the production line to devote himself to writing full time for the labor unions. Before long he was transferred to the editorial office of the *Literature Monthly*. His stories concentrate on his factory experience, the changes the revolution has brought about in his and other workers' lives, and the new characters he has met.

By the mid-1960s T'ang had published several collections of short stories and articles, including *Spring in the Workshop* and *Seeds*. —K.Y.H.

The First Class

Just before the end of the shift, the machine shop foreman made an announcement: "There will be no overtime tonight. After work everybody will go to listen to the report of the new Party committee secretary."

Less than half an hour after work the workers had all left and the shop was deserted. But in the mechanics' change room in the spooling department, where the yarn on ring bobbins was transferred onto spools before being put onto the looms, there was still one man who hadn't left yet. He was puttering around, muttering to himself, his hands waving—just like an inexperienced actor reciting long and awkward stage lines from memory.

"Fellow students, today we, the staff and workers, are starting classes in our Red and Expert University,"* he said in half-baked standard Mandarin. "I will, speak on the subject of the safety and maintenance of the spooling department. I, myself, don't really know too much about this subject . . . " At that point he suddenly stopped, shook his head, and said, "Aii, what bunk! First it's 'I', then it's 'myself' . . . " He coughed, cleared his throat and then went on, "I don't know too much about this area, crude and unlearned as I am . . . " He felt that this last line had just a bit too much of an intellectual ring to it, but he couldn't think of any better way to express it. Then he looked at himself in the mirror again. Reflected in the wall mirror was the round face of a young man. He had a pair of lustrous black eyes; his two eyebrows were lined up like two of the Chinese characters for the word "one." Beneath his small nose was a pair of full lips that were surrounded by a luxuriant growth of soft brown hair. He looked and looked at himself, feeling somewhat deflated. No matter what, he felt that the face in the mirror could never be that of a teacher.

*Organized by the factory to upgrade the workers; classes are held at night and on weekends. [S.R.M.]

503

He reckoned that he was a plain and ordinary man—really too ordinary. In the history of his short life he had reaped no honor—much less accomplished anything spectacular. His father had been a worker at this same factory and had died two years before Liberation in a machinery accident, leaving him behind along with his blind mother. At that time he was only twelve, and neither he nor his mother had the capacity to earn their livelihood. Fortunately his father's coworkers at the factory figured out a way to get him in as an oiler's helper. From then on, wearing clothes splattered with oil, he carried an oil can from morning till night, worming his way from one machine to another. "Little Oiler"— these two words became his name.

After Liberation he was transferred to a repair team. He was one of the first batch of students in the crash campaign to eliminate illiteracy and was one of the first workers to be able to throw away the cap of illiteracy. Later he continued with upper elementary and junior high school; it was just as though he were a blind man opening his eyes, and in an instant he was captivated by the dazzling beauty of the world. He had never known just how many beautiful and interesting things the world held! He often asked himself why he never knew about these things in the past; he was interested in everything and eager to learn. After he graduated from junior high, he passed the entrance examination to enroll in a middle-level technological night school. In the technical aspects, he had his master's papers, sixth grade. But none of this was out of the ordinary, and he just took it for granted. To this point he still considered himself just a "Little Oiler." Even in a dream, he would never have imagined that today someone would ask him to serve as a part-time teacher in the Workers' Red and Expert University. So even when the director of studies of the school came to offer him the appointment, he still thought that it was a joke! It wasn't until later on, when, with all proper respect, they brought him the formal letter of appointment written on red stationery, that he finally believed them.

"Little Wu—aiya, you rascal. Don't you have your makeup on yet? The meeting is just about to start." A voice suddenly interrupted Little Wu's deep thoughts. He knew right away it was his assistant, Little Chin, and he replied without even turning his head, "I'm worried to death, and you're making wisecracks! I have to go to teach a class at 6:15; I don't even have half a minute to prepare myself."

"Don't talk nonsense! Whenever you have a minute, you're in here rehearsing." Then, imitating his manner, Little Chin recited, "Fellow students, today, we. . . . If that isn't rehearsing, then you must be going nuts!"

The two of them were quite a pair. Their teachers said that if there wasn't any noise when they were together, then the sun would most certainly be rising in the west. They never fought with each other; in fact they got along better than anyone else. But this time Little Wu didn't take any note of him; he locked his locker, turned, and walked out. Chin, following him closely behind, made a face and teased him, "Aiya! Now you're acting like a fortune teller. You haven't even started classes yet and here you are already putting on airs!" Actually, Little Wu had always been quick to snap back, but recently he had become more serious. The way he looked at things, if he didn't act more dignified as a teacher, how would the students ever be willing to listen to him?

When Wu and Chin stepped into the meeting hall, the proceedings had already begun. The hall was silent; only the voice of a man giving a report could be heard. Somehow the speaker's voice arrested Little Wu's attention; it sounded very pleasant and familiar. Before he had a chance to think about it, he raised his eyes toward the stage and was startled at what he saw. He rubbed his eyes in disbelief and looked up again. There was no mistake about it. Stunned, he stood there like a wooden statue. "Aiya, Little Wu, isn't that your old friend, Old Ch'u?" Little Chin spoke loudly as though there were no one else there.

Immediately a roomful of reprimanding glances were cast in their direction. But neither of them noticed. Someone in back of Little Chin reached out and tugged hard on his shirt tail and scolded, "Hey, isn't it enough that you guys don't know how to follow the rules; you've got to bother others as well?" At this the two of them hurriedly found nearby seats and sat down.

"Who's that on the stage?" Little Wu uneasily asked the person sitting next to him.

"He's the new Party committee secretary," the man answered, his eyes glued to the stage.

"What's his name?"

"Ch'u P'ing."

"See! Wasn't I right?" Little Chin mocked as though he had just won a bet.

How could he have been wrong? It had all just happened. It was only two weeks ago that the personnel department assigned a bunch of low-echelon cadres who had been reassigned from administration to each workshop. One had also been assigned to Little Wu's repair team so that the man could learn the job from him. He was about forty, very thin, and spoke with a northern accent. Although sharp bones seemed to be protruding from all over his longish face, that didn't stop people from feeling that he was very friendly and kind. No matter what task he was taught, his ingenious hands learned it quickly. Moreover he never waited for people to tell him what to do before he went and got the job done. From the beginning Little Wu took a liking to him, and it wasn't long before the two had become close friends. At first he called Little Wu "Old Wu." This made everyone laugh. Later on he began to call him "Master Wu" instead. As far as technical skills went, Little Wu had long since been qualified to be called "master," but nobody had ever called him that before, and so when anyone heard him called that, it still sounded quite strange. Some time later Little Wu said to him, "Please just call me Little Wu."

"That won't do," said Ch'u. "It's only logical that I should call you 'Master.'" Wu excitedly replied, "Aiya, where did you get all this logic stuff!" After that, Ch'u had no way out but to call him "Little Wu."

Ch'u regarded Little Wu as a very perceptive and straightforward person. As for his expertise in his craft, that went without saying, and he was full of little shortcuts in the daily production process. Even his oil can and tool box were different from everybody else's—easier to use and evergy saving. Ch'u often praised him as being a bit of an inventor. But he said he had done those things only for fun. This was in the autumn of 1959, when the tumultuous waves of the Great Leap Forward rose in a surging tide. The production rate of the spinning and weaving departments had jumped dramatically in a month's time, pressuring the spooling department, which was caught in the middle. The spooling machines had long been running at a fast clip, and the equipment was hardly ideal, which made it impossible to speed up any further. As a consequence they were naturally unable to satisfy the appetite of the weaving department and hindered their production, thus preventing the entire textile plant from stepping up the pace. Meetings and study sessions were held left and right; numerous experiments and innovations were tried, but they simply could not solve the basic problem. Once Ch'u asked Little Wu, "Could it possibly be that there really is no solution?"

"What do you mean, no solution?" Little Wu sharply replied. "If you want my opinion, we ought to take all these damn spoolers and throw them out. We don't need them!"

"Then what?"

"Just skip that step."

When he thought about it, Ch'u had to admit to himself that there was, in fact, a bit of duplication in the work procedures of the spooling department. He took Little Wu seriously and said with joy, "So there really is a way. Aii! Why haven't you mentioned it before?" Little Wu forced a laugh and said, "You're really too naïve. You believe whatever anyone says. I'm just talking nonsense. If we could really skip that step, they wouldn't need me, the Little Oiler, to tell them, would they?"

He then went on to say that once he had raised the problem at an informal discussion called by the chief engineer, but he had been immediately put down by the others. They said that the problem had been fully considered a hundred years ago by the people who had invented the weaving machine—it can't be done! Later on some of them teased him: "Little Wu, why were you born a hundred years too late?"

Ch'u tried to perk him up: "How can you compare the people of a hundred years ago with those of today? The engineers aren't always better than others in everything. When they say, 'It can't be done,' it doesn't necessarily mean that there is really no way to solve the problem. They still have a thing or two to learn from us workers."

"That's to say they should study the thoughts of the working class," Little Wu said.

"In technology, in production, in management . . . they can learn from us in all these areas. Not only the engineers, but the head of the factory, the section chief, the machine shop foreman . . . they all ought to learn from the workers."

"That's okay in theory," Little Wu said, still not quite agreeing with Ch'u's explanation. "Take me, for example. If you'd want me to tell you how many oil caps there are on a spooling machine or what spare part goes where . . . I could do it with my eyes closed. But I'm not sure about anything else . . . "

"According to what you just said, you're an expert," Ch'u said. Little Wu couldn't keep from laughing out loud as he chided good-naturedly, "Expert— ha ha, if you become the head of the factory, you can appoint me to be your chief engineer, okay?"

"That, I can't guarantee," Ch'u said, also laughing. "First, the factory head has no right to appoint the chief engineer; second, if you all become engineers, wouldn't that leave me, the head of the factory, to be the only worker? Actually, aside from the fact that your responsibilities are different from those of the engineers and the factory head, are there any real differences between you and them?"

"Any real differences? If the overall production problems of the entire factory are left to just you and me, do you think we can handle them?" Wu voiced his disagreement. "We'd still have to turn to the head of the factory, to the engineers ... "

"No, you're wrong!" A loud, clear voice suddenly interrupted Little Wu's train of thought. It sounded as though it were in the midst of an argument with him and scared him. He raised his head to look up on the stage; the Party committee secretary was speaking with gusto, "Comrades, this is only superstition. And whom should we depend on? On the masses. We should depend on the workers here, more than seven thousand strong. We can solve not only the small problems but the great ones as well. Not only do we want to discard one or two old techniques for new ones; we must bring about a revolution in the entire system of our industrial technology. We are the liberated people of China. We have gained control of the political power; we shall also master culture, science, and all technology!"

"Well put!" Little Wu thought to himself. It seemed to him that he had also said all of this to himself before. Although the words hadn't been the same, the thoughts were. But why hadn't he been able to keep them in mind?

"Did you hear that? The Party committee secretary was just talking about you!" Little Chin said as he gleefully nudged Wu.

"How did he put it?" Little Wu pressed.

"He didn't mention you by name, but he said he had met an excellent master worker from whom he had learned techniques as well as the real meaning of many principles."

"What else did he say?"

"He continued: 'Everyone has countless "atoms" hidden away in his heart, and he only has to devise a means to crush their "nuclei" in order to release a fantastic source of energy.' "

"Anything else?" Little Wu was as insistent as a child.

Chin was about to continue when suddenly a thunderous ovation rang out from the assembly. The meeting was over. The throng burst out of the four exits just like water gushing out of an opened sluice gate. The two of them could do nothing but follow the others flowing out of the hall.

Wu picked up his lecture notes and class record from the director of studies' office; the class bell had already rung. The director, who had helped him prepare his lessons, kept encouraging him. "You've been buried in the bowels of these machines since you were a child," he said. "You've been coming in contact with them day and night for more than ten years. You're as familiar with them as you are with your own hands, feet, eyes, and ears. Then on top of it you attended a technological night school. Now you have a great deal of practical experience as well as a good theoretical foundation. Besides, the students all come from your own factory. ... " But it was all still of no use. Either because of his excitement or his nervousness, he felt like there were scores of butterflies in his stomach. Even his hands were shaking.

When he got to the classroom, the students were all in their seats and very orderly. As he stepped into the room, someone—he wasn't sure who—called "Attention!" and everyone snappily stood up in salute. By that point he was really miserable and had no idea what to do next. His eyes swept the room for a second, but aside from Little Chin, who was sitting in the first row, he couldn't make out anybody else.

"Don't be too nervous; take it easy at the beginning . . . " He was remembering what the director had said. He paused slightly, calmed himself, and opened the class list to call roll. He called name after name. Suddenly he was speechless.

"Ch'u—P'ing."

"Here."

Wu's eyes looked out in the direction of the response. Indeed it was he, the Party committee secretary. Beside him was the chairman of the labor union's factory branch, the director of personnel, and a number of other Party committee cadres.

"Half an hour ago I was listening to his report along with several thousand others. Half an hour later he has become my student!" The thought flashed in his mind like a bolt of lightning on a stormy night. He still wasn't able to grasp it and mull it over, but this bolt of lightning lit up his eyes in a flash and let him see the expansive world and his own place in it. Immediately the blood throughout his entire body began to bubble and boil like the ocean's billowing waves, washing away the "opening remarks" that he had originally prepared to who knows where. In fact, now, he was no longer nervous. His excited voice had a slight tremor in it as he began his speech.

"Comrades, there's no need to introduce myself. You all know me, the Little Oiler. Right. But that was all in the past. I was like a dog buried in the works of my machines all day long; sleeping on the roadside. At that time I didn't get my share of anything. I never once entered the portals of a school and was never a student, not even for a day. I was never even able to walk along the streets without a care like others. . . . Today, not only have I graduated from a middle-level technological school, but here I am standing on this podium lecturing to others. Among those of you sitting here are my buddies, the Party committee secretary, the chairman of the trade union . . . they are all my leaders and my good comrades . . . "

As he spoke, he became more and more excited. Hot tears began to spill down his cheeks. The room was dead silent; everyone was touched by what he was saying as they watched him, their eyes speaking approval. His line of sight moved to a chair in the back where the Party committee secretary was smiling at him. He seemed to be encouraging Wu, saying, "Go on, you're doing fine."

His lecture was on the general principles of the spooling department. The class went well. He never thought that he would be able to deliver his lecture as skillfully and as fluently as he actually did.

The last ten minutes were devoted to questions from the floor. The first to stand up was the party committee secretary. "The yarn on the spools works about the same as the yarn on the ring bobbins. Why can't we eliminate the spools and use the small ring bobbins of yarn as they come from the spinning department and set them directly in the loom as the warp?"

That question again! Little Wu's face flushed instantly. He now considered the question again: the key to the matter of eliminating the spooling machines and using the ring bobbins of yarn to feed directly into the warp is that we can't solve the problems of connecting the ends and that of tensile strength. But is it possible that we, Chinese workers who have seized control of the political power of twentieth-century China, cannot solve these problems by using the scientific achievements of the twentieth century? Couldn't we use electronic bobbins, transistors, and those sorts of things to automatically control break-age? "Yes, it can be done. We can certainly skip that step," Wu said with confidence.

After class, as Little Wu stepped out of the room, he sensed that he had grown up, and that there were many things waiting for him to do. "Comrade Little Wu, when can we study the problem of eliminating the spooling machines?" Ch'u asked, catching up to him. Today he had added "Comrade" in front of "Little Wu."

"First thing tomorrow," he replied without hesitation.

"If you're going to form a small team, count me in."

"Will you be coming back again?" Wu asked, a little surprised.

Smiling, Ch'u replied, "Why not? I've only attended the first class!"

The two of them kept talking as they walked toward the men's dormitory.

First draft, December 7, 1959
Second draft, December 28, 1959
Enjoying the Short Stories of 1960, pp. 223–31

Translated by S. R. Munro

SHA TING
(Yang Ch'eng-fang, 1905–)

A Szechwan writer who was given early encouragement by Lu Hsün and Mao Tun, Sha Ting excelled in short stories depicting the life of impoverished peasants in the bleak, northern section of his native province. He attended school in Chengtu and later went to Shanghai, where he began his writing career in 1931. Within twelve months he had already published his first collection of short stories, *The Routes Beyond the Law,* which brought him wide acclaim. At the outbreak of the war against Japan he went back to Chungking in Szechwan but soon proceeded to Yenan to teach literature in the Lu Hsün Academy of Arts. His travels in war-affected areas and even behind the enemy lines produced a few volumes of fine journalistic writings, including a story about Marshal Ho Lung, one of the nation's ten most distinguished generals and a cofounder of the Red Army; the story was reprinted many times. The first postwar years saw his most prolific output: five novels (*Gold-panning, Homecoming, Caged Animals, Sowing Seeds,* and *Forced Passage*) and three collections of short stories which include some of his mature best. His "At the Teahouse Ch'i-hsiang-chü" remains a national favorite today.

A series of important assignments in the official writers' organizations in Szechwan prevented him from writing much after 1949. Only two more collections of short stories preceded his downfall during the Cultural Revolution, when his advocacy of a more liberal interpretation of the Party's literary policy incurred the wrath of the authorities then in power. He has since reemerged, and a few very short miscellaneous articles by or about him appeared in 1977. In 1978 he was named director of the Research Institute of Chinese Literature in the Academy of Sciences.

"Try and Catch Me" has been praised by Mao Tun as the best among the 1960 crop of short stories. It has retained much of the author's simple but effective language, persuasive portrayal of characters, and brisk pace, despite his apparent adherence to the official Party line about literature upheld at the time.

—K.Y.H.

Try and Catch Me

On all sides the hilltops were cloaked in mist. The rain pelted down intently. In the dining hall of the No. 1 production brigade of Shih-men administrative district in Ch'ih-shan Commune, things were busier than usual. Because the district office was inside the same compound as the dining hall, most of the cadres from the whole district had gathered together today in the compound.

The cadres assembled here to participate in the regular end-of-the-month cooperation-competition. Most of them were around the fire pits in the main hall, some sitting, some squatting, gabbing with one another about the production situation. The rest were either beating gongs and drums in the dining hall or watching the animal feeders taking care of the piglets in the feed lot near the gate. Altogether there were fifteen piglets, pure Lung-ch'ang hogs, born only the evening before.

Everyone was buzzing because, since the planting of the winter crops, Shih-men district had already walked off with the "satellite" three times, and they all felt sure that they would earn the "satellite" once more this time. After all, in the last month they had made terrific efforts. And besides, all the comrades in the inspection group, including the commune Party secretary stationed in this competition district, were well satisfied, and agreed unanimously that winter planting had been handled well. All the winter fields had been prepared —flooded and fertilized. Welfare activities and side occupations were running above average as well.

Now everyone noticed only one unusual thing. It was well past eight o'clock, and the commune members had all gone off to work despite the rain, but the responsible comrades from Yüan-pa and Chien-shan administrative districts who had gone to take part in inspection work still had not returned. When the group from Sai-ya district, the remotest one in the commune, came across the hilltops opposite them, everyone was getting uneasy about how late it was getting.

They all crowded together in the courtyard in front of the main hall, watching the team setting out for the commune headquarters in a flurry of banging drums and gongs and flying banners, until they passed out of sight. There they stood, braving the rain, caught up in all kinds of guessing. Amidst all the speculation, only one thing was sure: the Party branch secretary was late. When it came to inspection work, the branch secretary was always hardnosed, and nothing, however trifling, escaped his notice. Once he was off inspecting fertilizer collection at Yüan-pa, and because he figured the comrades there had overestimated their holdings, he called for a sample to be taken. But when none of the other inspectors agreed, he did it all by himself. . . .

When this old story came up, Pai Shou-ch'eng the guard let out a stifled sigh. He obviously meant to show his disapproval: the branch secretary was over-conscientious. Suddenly Old Lady Teng got to her feet grumbling and scolding. Old Lady Teng was named Teng Hsiu-lan, and she headed the women's brigade. Over fifty and skinny, she wore a blue cotton kerchief around her waist. "Stop your sighing," she barked. "Nowadays every bit of our work has got to be accountable. No funny business!"

"I'm afraid it may be dark on the road when he returns after his meeting," the sickly looking Pai Shou-ch'eng responded. "Besides, in this rain . . ."

"What difference does it make," someone else answered confidently. "The satellite is firmly in our hands anyway." The speaker was Kung Ch'i-yün, head of No. 1 production brigade, a stubby man with protruding eyes. After his comment, the conversation turned to the upcoming competition and people stopped worrying about the time. They talked animatedly and began moving back toward the main hall. But just then somebody called out happily, "Hey, isn't that Old Lung?"

The people who had already gone back toward the main hall swung back and joined the others on the edge of the threshing ground, craning their necks to see down into the valley below. A tall fellow with a wide rain hat, his pants hiked up to his thighs, was just crossing a little path and starting up the hill. This was the branch secretary, Lung Wei-ling, always popular with the masses. His work was always good, but more than that, he often reminded people of a marvelous revolutionary story.

In these red-earth Ta-pa Mountains, during the old revolutionary days, Lung Wei-ling's father had been chairman of a rural soviet. Later the whole family was killed by the reactionaries. Only Lung Wei-ling got away with his life. By the time the villagers brought word of the danger to his house, the reactionaries were already outside the main gate. So a young peasant woman deftly snatched up the infant Lung Wei-ling from a grain basket and stuck him into her backpack. Then she slipped out the rear door, pretending she was going off to gather pig fodder. This brave and ingenious woman was the same Old Lady Teng who now wore a blue cotton sash around her waist.

By now Lung Wei-ling was halfway up the hill. As he climbed, he answered the questions of the cadres gathered at the top. First they asked him if he had seen any sign of various other comrades. He called back that they were already on their way directly to the commune headquarters with Party Committee Secretary Wang. Most of the rest of the talk was about production news from the other two competition districts. Upset at the thought that the satellite might be grabbed by Yüan-pa or Chien-shan, stubby Kung Ch'i-yün called out excitedly, "You mean they're not all coming up here with you?"

"Who's to say they're going to be behind forever?" Lung Wei-ling answered with a spark of humor.

"That's not what I mean!" Kung Ch'i-yün replied peevishly.

"All right, all right," Lung Wei-ling said with a laugh as he sat down. "But don't get too worried; they still haven't made off with the satellite this time." Something about his brimming self-confidence brought hearty laughter.

Lung Wei-ling was not only strict about work, but severe in dealing with cadres, too. He earned their trust, though, not their dread. Not until he reached the top of the hill did people realize that his clothes were soaked, and they pressed him to go inside, warm up, and change. "Don't worry about me," he replied. "Hurry up and get ready to go!"

"I don't believe you're going off to your meeting like a soaked chicken," Old Lady Teng snorted. She turned around and went to dig up some fresh clothes for Lung Wei-ling. But by the time she got back with them, the cook working for the dining hall, a fortyish woman, had already made Lung dress again in her husband's new cotton jacket.

The group began to file out. By now the rain had slackened a little and the fog was beginning to lift from the hills all around. In this very hilly country, from the valleys below only steep mountain walls without a trace of cultivated land could be seen. But from the mountaintops, if you looked down where you had come from, countless terraced paddies and dry fields appeared, layer upon layer. By the time the group got to the top of Yün-tung Mountain, the sound of gongs and drums, which had hushed for a time, had started again and grown into a din, as though proudly announcing the latest victories in labor production work.

Altogether there were no more than twenty people in the group, but they seemed like a vast army of men and war mounts advancing along the path to victory. This was most striking in the sight of Lung Wei-ling himself. This young man of twenty-seven or twenty-eight, bearing the placard inscribed "satellite," strode firmly at the head of the column. His bright, cheerful face and clear features sparkled with the sweat of his heavy work. As he walked he discussed strategy with his comrades in a loud, clear voice. His words were military: "strategic point," "battle front," "concentrate our firepower," and so on. He had never been to war, but he understood nonetheless that they were engaged in struggle with Nature itself.

Ever since the Great Leap Forward, just about all rural cadres had talked about crop production this way. Even scrawny, sprightly Old Lady Teng was no exception. She strode up beside Lung Wei-ling and vigorously supported his views. She had gotten into the habit of calling him "Old Lung"; she really didn't think of him as her adopted son. Except for the few cadres playing the drums and gongs, most of the others listened intently and seriously, adding a comment now and then, expressing their doubts here and there. Once in a while someone would step out from the line and go up to Lung to make his point face to face.

Kung Ch'i-yün could never stay still. This short, sturdy young fellow was a drummer in the band, but now he had stopped playing the drum and had slung it over his neck and joined in the heated conversation. In this way the group quickly passed Heng-ling, Ta-p'ing, and T'ao-chia ya-k'ou and arrived at Ch'ih-shan, a bald little mound with a group of buildings clustered around its base. All the buildings housed commune-run activities and enterprises: the clinic, the book store, the general store, the factory, and the processing plant.

The commune committee's quarters lay against the side of the hill, in three levels that together looked like a temple. Lung Wei-ling led his column up the terraced slope and reached the stone-paved courtyard at the second level. Their arrival brought a burst of hearty greetings. Some of it was the usual hellos, and some of it was more lighthearted. K'o Feng-shan, the whiskered deputy head of the Shun-ho administrative district, stood in front of the assembly hall and guffawed.

"Hey, Lung! Ready to turn over the satellite today?"

"Sure, sure," answered Lung without concern, as he climbed the final steps leading to the hall.

"You watch out! You drool over it so much that pretty soon you're going to get drowned in your own saliva, if you don't watch out!"* Old Lady Teng called out with an offended look on her face.

"Don't count your chickens," retorted K'o Feng-shan, well known for his mischief.

"Listen," interjected Kung Ch'i-yün. "It doesn't matter what you think. The satellite isn't going anywhere."

The assembly hall was converted from a big old-style parlor, with more than ten fire pits built of stone slabs. Each burned bright red with a full load of charcoal. The faces of the people seated around them were flushed with the

*The original is an untranslatable homophonous pun used among villagers in some Szechwan areas. [K.Y.H.]

heat. No sooner had Lung Wei-ling stepped onto the raised platform than a group of comrades from his own district called him over to sit down by their fire with them. As the rest of the Shih-men district cadres filtered in, they all went over to join him.

This fire pit was on the left side of the hall. The two or three fires nearest it were already crowded with people. At one sat the cadres from Sai-ya district. Until now Sai-ya had always been rather backward. Two or three times they had lost ranking in the competition, and had come away with the "oxcart" placard. But in the last two months, their work had sped ahead. Not only had they moved up in the short-run competitions, but at the end of last month they had earned the "steam locomotive" award. Although they were still three steps away from winning the satellite, they had already become one of the commune's most dynamic districts.

Lung Wei-ling had only been sitting for a little while when Chang Fu-t'ai, the branch secretary from Sai-ya, turned to him and opened a conversation. Chang Fu-t'ai was a little over forty and had a bony face. Usually he said very little, but he listened hard to what those around him were saying, his eyes scanning the others' faces. He had learned many lessons from Shih-men and bore great respect for its fine work. In the midst of the conversation and laughter, Chang remarked seriously, "That labor allocation system of yours is really fine. But putting it into operation is no simple matter."

"Don't hurry it," Lung Wei-ling answered matter-of-factly. "I tell you, we've been tinkering with it for several months now. Like I said the last time, we've gotten the better of the problems time and again, but if you go over it with a fine-toothed comb you'll still find plenty of little troubles."

"Secretary Chang," interrupted Kung Ch'i-yün solemnly, "working out a system like this is not an easy matter."

"And whoever said learning from others was easy?" said Old Lady Teng with her usual bluntness.

Lung Wei-ling felt Kung and Teng starting to get rude to each other, and quickly added with a chuckle, "In a word, systems are well and good, but working on political thought still comes first."

"Right!" said Chang Fu-t'ai with a serious nod. "Right you are."

This middle-aged fellow from a hired-laborer's background liked to speak of what he intuitively understood. Because he had quickly understood Shih-men district's labor assignment system when it was under study, Sai-ya had not only learned it well but had improved upon it. But just when he was clearing his throat to talk about this, someone sounded the homemade bullhorn by the side of the chairman's platform.

The sound of the horn only increased the din in the assembly room. Here someone was saying, "Let's chat about it later!"; there someone called in a loud voice, "No little mini-meetings!" Soon everyone quieted down, and only the horn was heard, making a brief announcement for each cooperative competition district to hold its own meeting. There were four such districts in Ch'ih-shan Commune. In each district, a secretary of the Party committee was in charge.

Shih-men, Yüan-pa, and Chien-shan made up Competition District 1, and their meeting was held on the second floor of a smaller building. Below them, the hammering sounds of the farm implements factory continued without letup. The meeting was already on. The Party secretary, a thin, sallow, and sickly-looking fellow with half-closed eyes, was listening to leading members of the inspection team. The Party secretary was Wang Hsing-kuei, a slow talker. But he made people laugh with a few words of plain talk, and he got his points across too.

Now each administrative district conscientiously reported on the last month's production and living conditions. Yuan-pa and Chien-shan began to show, through their humble and modest reports, that Shih-men ought to retain the satellite, when Secretary Wang opened his eyes. His gaze swept over the crowd, and, smiling, he said in a low voice, "If it were only a matter for our three districts to settle, that would be fine ..." Someone piped up with some feeling, "Of course, it'll depend on how all other districts evaluate us!"

"Right, if the critique demotes us, we'll respectfully hand over the satellite," Lung Wei-ling went on crisply.

"It is good you are thinking like that." Secretary Wang voiced his approval. "That way we can avoid unpleasant surprises."

When Lung Wei-ling returned to his group, who were sitting around the fire chatting, many heads turned his way before he even sat down. Everybody knew how important the meeting Lung had just left was, and they all wanted to know just one thing: was the satellite still theirs? Some asked point blank, while others whispered; no one spoke loudly. "Aia," groaned Old Lady Teng, "I'm not going to believe that the satellite could run away from us."

"If we've lost it I'll fry a fish in my palm for you to eat," answered Kung Ch'i-yün with evident unconcern.

"Comrades!" Lung Wei-ling glanced at Teng and Kung. He spoke gravely, without looking at all the whisperers. "It's wrong to feel that way. Please remember what I have to say. If things go wrong, it will be because of our own arrogance and complacency."

"Complacency? We're on our toes all day long," protested Old Lady Teng.

But Lung replied sharply, "You're on your toes, but have the others been snoozing?"

Hearing his pessimistic tone, Old Lady Teng said no more. The others, waiting for the final verdict, also quieted down. But Old Lady Teng was clearly depressed. It wasn't because the boy she had raised had treated her rudely; they had learned long ago to be blunt about work. What bothered her was that until now she had been sure the satellite would not leave Shih-men, and now her faith was shaken.

Since the competition began, people had gotten more and more excited by it; the desire to win glory had grown more powerful. In these relatively large-scale end-of-month competitions, if one administrative district suffered a demotion, there were always some people who did not take the verdict well. Last spring, when Shih-men dropped from "airplane" to "oxcart" in the competition, Old Lady Teng had broken into sobs. But Lung Wei-ling had encouraged her, full of confidence, saying "Why cry? We can get up and try again!"

This time, not only Old Lady Teng but just about everyone was feeling uneasy. Some remained silent, some muttered to themselves, while others sat around trading opinons and guesses with their neighbors. Suddenly Kung

Ch'i-yün, who was always full of energy, burst out, "Hey, if we get demoted, we'll never fall all the way down to oxcart again!"

"What kind of lucky thought is that?" Old Lady Teng had finally found a target for her bluster. Old Lady Teng's voice was normally high, but now the people sitting around the fire and the others who had been exchanging predictions about the competitions suddenly stopped chattering and shot curious glances her way. This almost made Lung Wei-ling flare up. Lung's damp spirits made him seem reconciled to the loss of the satellite, but he answered her slowly, and with a smile. "When troops appear our warriors will halt them; when water floods we'll block it with earth," Lung quoted the old adage. "Keep calm, everybody, keep calm!"

"Now, didn't I tell you?" a chipper voice suddenly burst in. Lung Wei-ling turned to see who it was: K'o Feng-shan, the deputy head of the Shun-ho administrative district had already come in behind Lung. "In fact, it's about time the satellite moved to new quarters," K'o went on, "so you might as well get ready to hand it over."

"Don't you worry so much over nothing," Lung laughed. "If we have to hand it over, you won't need to make us."

"I don't care what you say, we'll never turn it over to you." Old Lady Teng lost control of herself.

"All we want is to avoid ever getting the 'doze-off' prize," Kung Ch'i-yün said with studied determination. Because Shun-ho's work had been consistently deficient, they had once earned for themselves the lowest-grade placard, which read "doze-off." Kung Ch'i-yün had meant to poke fun, but his tone was hard and quickly brought a burst of laughter from the others. But just then the bullhorn by the side of the chairman's platform sounded again.

This was to announce the opening of the critique session. The room suddenly fell silent, unlike the last time the horn sounded, when people had to shut each other up for a while. Everyone knew that once the representatives of each cooperative competition district had made their reports, the Party committee would announce the results of the competition. This was the most important part of the meeting. Even Pai Shou-ch'eng, who was old and sick and usually fell asleep, was now fully awake, afraid he might miss something.

The reports did not take long, but to those taking part in the meeting they were long enough. The responsible cadres from each administrative district listened intently. As the reports progressed, thoughts that had remained unspoken until now gradually came to the surface, and the comments grew blunt and frank. Here someone said, with admiration, "There's no argument; Ta-p'ing sure has improved," while over there someone remarked approvingly, "That's quite an effort!" Now and then someone else would say, in a tone of mixed determination and envy, "When you get back, figure out what caused this!"

Only the people from Shih-men district were still. From the work reports of the first three competition districts, it seemed that Shih-men still had the best record in land reclamation and that no other administrative district had outdone them. When the fourth competition district report opened with a discussion of production and living conditions in Sai-ya, everybody listened with rapt attention. Remembering the district's great recent efforts and thinking of the modest and practical Chang Fu-t'ai, the Shih-men people were even more anxious. Finally, Kung Ch'i-yün could stand it no longer; heaving a deep sigh, he said, "Ah, no problem!"

Hearing Kung's dispirited voice, Lung Wei-ling shot him a look of warning, but he said nothing. In their hearts he and Kung Ch'i-yün had the same feeling, but he didn't quite feel the satellite was lost yet. In this tumultuous, socialist labor competition a backward unit often leaped to the forefront in a single jump. Furthermore, this was a common occurrence; who knew what would happen with the other two administrative districts? But his spirits gradually sank anyway.

Next came the report of the Tung-shan administrative district. There was nothing special about their work record. Finally it was Shun-ho's turn. Now the hall grew noisy, as though everybody knew Shun-ho's foundation was weak, and it made little difference whether their report got heard or not. Discussions of how the contest was going spread around the room; now and then a little suppressed laughter could be heard.

Infected by this atmosphere, Kung Ch'i-yün made ready to talk. But out of the corner of his eye he caught sight of the color of Lung Wei-ling's face and shut up. Lung was once again absorbed, sitting stiffly with his head cocked to one side, listening seriously to the report. However, the house soon quieted down again, and everyone concentrated on hearing what was going on.

"We have compared conditions in the three administrative districts," Kung Ch'i-yün heard the reporter's hoarse voice going on. "This time Shun-ho deserves a big break. When it comes to land reclamation, as we see it, they've been more thorough than any of the others ..."

"What happened?" Kung Ch'i-yün muttered, staring at the reporter.

"A minute ago you said there was nothing to worry about," said creaky old Pai Shou-ch'eng.

"I don't believe they're going to take away our satellite," asserted Old Lady Teng loudly. She was as resolutely confident as before. When she got through speaking, she tugged on her blue cotton waist-sash, even though she didn't need to tighten it. Looking at her it seemed that if anybody, it didn't matter who, came and laid hands on the placard with *satellite* painted on it, she would put up quite a battle. "And no critique from the Party Committee?" she threw in for good measure.

"You're right on that score," Lung Wei-ling echoed approvingly. "We must all have faith in the Party committee."

By now all the reports were over and voices of the people had risen to a clamor. Here and there unrestrained arguments about the contest broke out. Some people were still talking about their own cases, some were comparing their administrative districts with others. Still other people, feeling strongly that their own work had been inadequate, were beginning to search for the reasons why.

As Lung Wei-ling went up to take part in the enlarged session called by the Party committee, he reminded his own district's cadres once again: this was a socialist competition, and correct attitude was more important than winning or losing. He knew that the enlarged meeting would call for opinions on the contest from all the districts, and he had the feeling that Shih-men was likely to lose the satellite. Everybody had better brace himself for the news.

The first person Lung saw, over by a file cabinet in the spacious room where the meeting would take place, was Party Secretary Wang Hsing-kuei, leaning on a rattan chair with his eyes half closed, as usual, pondering some problem. When Wang noticed Lung, he promptly opened his eyes. "It's not so bad to take your tumbles," said Wang in his usual phlegmatic way. "I generally think . . ."

"Rest easy, Secretary Wang," Lung replied quickly, "we won't give up."

"Right! As you said to our 'Lady General,' 'Get up and try again.' "

It was clear as day; Shih-men's satellite had already gone to Shun-ho. All that remained were the mechanics of the transfer. So as the first secretary of the Party committee made some final remarks about the debate and turned to the meeting for further opinions, Lung Wei-ling not only showed his agreement, but got up graciously and went around the table to shake firmly the hand of the Shun-ho branch secretary.

The Shun-ho branch secretary's name was Chang Yen, and he had been a correspondent for the district Party committee since Liberation, though he was younger than Lung Wei-ling. He was about twenty and smaller in size, so lots of people affectionately called him "little devil."

"Let's go through the transfer procedure in a little while," said Lung, pumping Chang Yen's hand. "Would it be too much trouble for you to keep that thing safe for us for a few days?"

"Why only a few days?" cried Chang with a laugh, his face flushed. "I'd say six months at least!"

"Not that long! You'll be passing it back to us at the end of next month."

The building seemed to shake as everyone burst into laughter. When it came time to announce the results formally in the auditorium and officially turn over the placards, the atmosphere was even more excited. The din of gongs and drums, of people talking and laughing, rose and fell in waves. But there were a few people around who felt that this month's contest had not come out right.

The ones who felt this way for the most part belonged to units who had been demoted in the debates. A minute before they had been voicing their protest, but they were soon swallowed up by the clamor of the applause and the din of drums and gongs. Above all they had their doubts about Shun-ho making off with the satellite. Some had no particular reason; they just could not figure out how an oxcart could suddenly be transformed into a satellite. But others had reason to doubt. A day or two before they had gone to Shun-ho's No. 7 production team and had come upon plenty of wasteland with nothing sown on it in the area of the bamboo grove.

Some of the Shih-men cadres were not too happy either; the satellite that they had held onto for three months had gone to Shun-ho, which had been so backward! On top of that, Sai-ya had made it up to "airplane," while Shih-men had fallen to "rocket"; that was painful too. Old Lady Teng had long since gotten too angry to talk, and the usually animated Kung Ch'i-yün wore a long face.

Now the room was quiet again, as people listened carefully to the Party committee's decisions on upcoming work assignments and took them down on paper. But as soon as the tasks were assigned, things perked up once more. The comrades who disagreed with the verdict of the contest started to feel more and more strongly that things were not right. Indeed, someone had already formally raised the matter of Shun-ho's unreclaimed land.

"They call that complete land reclamation?" Old Lady Teng said in a voice loud enough for all to hear. "They still have plenty of paddy and dry field unreclaimed."

"Why are you so excited again?" Lung Wei-ling asked with a smile. "Secretary Wang has already said . . ."

"If you have an opinion it's right to speak out!"

"Winning's important, but so is good sportsmanship." Lung set out to soothe not only Old Lady Teng but all the Shih-men cadres who had come to the meeting. He could tell that a lot of people with their own gripes were looking for a chance to complain about the contest results. Actually, they were trying to figure out a way to get the satellite back right away.

Lung's demeanor was serious, and he spoke calmly and placatingly. Every so often he cracked a joke. He moved from talking about the contest itself to the question of revolutionary cadres' behavior, hoping that everyone would cool off a little. He was just getting around to the idea that the overall benefit to the commune would not be served if the satellite stayed too long in one place, when the first secretary of the Party committee started to speak.

The first secretary was called I Ping-kuang. He was a lanky type, whose parents had both been killed during the revolutionary struggles. Just like Lung Wei-ling, he belonged to a martyr's family. In the last month, he had concentrated on Shun-ho's work, helping them allocate their labor resources and working for a number of days himself as a cook for them.

I Ping-kuang stood straight on the chairman's platform and said with determination, "I can see that many of you feel the inspection team missed Shun-ho's bamboo grove. I haven't been there of late myself. So let's face up to it and send a group down to have another look!"

"Right! The only thing to do is face facts," shouted a number of voices, supported by a round of applause.

"No!" K'o Feng-shan shouted jumping to his feet. "Who says the contest hasn't been strict enough?"

This usually sly operator now turned obstinate. Shun-ho had gotten hold of the satellite after much sweat, and he was afraid they might lose it after all, just because he himself had seldom inspected the bamboo grove. But at this point, those who approved the reinspection plan were all the more unwilling to let things lie.

"You must have a guilty conscience," came the answer from many mouths. "This is the Party committee's view!"

"Let me speak a few words on behalf of Shun-ho. We welcome reinspection . . ." This was the voice of Chang Yen, the branch secretary. He stood by on the stone edge of the fire pit, his voice rising to a high pitch. "Let's be strict about it this way," he went on more softly. "If the reinspection shows that there is unreclaimed paddy or dry field in the bamboo grove, we will deliver the satellite back to Shih-men with a band playing escort."

That really brought the room to a boil. Hand-clapping and laughter filled the air. The resentments of the dissatisfied minority vanished like smoke. And even though plenty of responsible cadres from the administrative districts saw no need for the reinspection, a team was quickly formed with the Party committee's support to do the job. The Party committee picked the team's members.

They came from the districts that had dropped in the rankings. Lung Wei-ling was one of them and was chosen to head the little group.

Lung was picked to head the team because people from the other two districts knew he would do a thorough job. No one put more hope in him than a few of the Shih-men cadres. They figured that since the baby-faced Chang Yen had spoken so rashly, all Lung Wei-ling had to do was discover a bit of unreclaimed land here and there and everything would be taken care of. Even if the plot were no bigger than a postage stamp, Shun-ho would have to give back the satellite.

Old Lady Teng typified this outlook. When Lung Wei-ling opened discussion with the Shih-men group on the Party committee's work assignments for the coming phase and was about to go off on the reinspection mission, the spry old lady got to her feet noisily. Grasping her adopted son tightly, she said to him with utmost gravity: "I want you to be as tough-minded as you were that time you went to Yüan-pa to inspect their fertilizer collection!"

"O.K.," said Lung with a grin. "I guarantee not a single inch of wasteland will escape unnoticed."

"That's the way to do it, "Kung Ch'i-yün piped up. "He certainly talks tough."

"All right, I'll do it," added Lung, "But you all should be seriously figuring out the reasons for what happened to us."

Neither Old Lady Teng nor Kung had really understood the branch secretary's words. If it had not been for the intervention of the little group's deputy branch secretary and the responsible cadres from the administrative district, they probably would have argued some more. But, at any rate, they felt satisfied.

When the small group meetings were over, the production teams went on trading challenges until at last the entire session came to an end. It was already well into the afternoon. A drizzle still floated in the sky. The people filed along the muddy mountain paths, to the sound of drums and gongs, returning to their home districts the same way they came. The Shih-men group got home just in time for dinner. After eating, without pausing to rest, they sat around the fire and prodded each other to figure out why Shih-men had lost. Why were there still little bits of unreclaimed land in the district?

Usually in these meetings, which seemed like investigations, Old Lady Teng took an active part and talked a lot. But this time, her heart was not in it. Sometimes, while a person next to her was speaking, she would mutter to herself "Hasn't he gotten back yet?" Or she would nudge Kung Ch'i-yün and whisper to him, "Go out and have a look!" And with no further prompting the stubby young man would catch her meaning, and quickly slip outside. He would stand at the lip of the hillside threshing ground with his flashlight shining and peer for a while into the darkness.

They were all waiting for Lung Wei-ling, hoping that he would bring them the good news they yearned to hear. But it wasn't until the next morning, after breakfast, when the commune members were getting ready to set out for work, that Lung suddenly appeared like a healthy tiger, his cotton jacket open and his face bright red.

"Hey! we waited for you long enough last night," people said as they got to their feet and gathered around him.

"I wanted to talk over some problems with that 'little devil.'" Lung was smiling like a victorious general returning from battle. "Their preparation for the winter crop planting is really good, but they did not stir enough fertilizer deep into the soil. I suggested they ..."

"What about your reinspection?" wailed Old Lady Teng, pulling on Lung's sleeve.

"Oh, you mean the unreclaimed paddy and dry field? We have to admit defeat. They were really thorough in eliminating their wastelands."

Kung Ch'i-yün let out a long, hopeless groan. "Ah, Shun-ho has the satellite in the bag now," he said softly.

"It's not that simple," Lung Wei-ling answered, grinning from ear to ear. "We'll make them give it back to us next month ..."

Enjoying the Short Stories of 1960, pp. 295–309

Translated by Robert A. Kapp

CHANG YUNG-MEI

Under the Banyan Tree

Big banyan tree, spreading shade,
Three new soldiers sit there and talk.

"Dirty clothes put in basin, but someone
Had washed them, just as I turned around.
The tear in my pants I was going to mend,
Overnight it was fixed up, as good as new."

"An apple appeared at the pillow of my bed
When I got sick, and a good-wish letter too;
The words gave strength to me and the apple
Is so red that it warms you like fire."

"A letter from home really touched me:
Dad is well now, can get back to the fields;
Don't know who sent him money in my name,
And also sent him medicines, time and again.
That kind of friendly concern, more than skin deep,
Reaches across hills and streams, far far away."

"Who can it be, who is he?
Seems like our squad leader, or platoon leader?
Or could be that old soldier who refuses to retire?"

The new soldiers are guessing,
Along comes the platoon leader, smiling,
"My comrades, that's nothing unusual
Among us soldiers of the people;
You need not try to guess his name.
Feeling close or not, it's a matter of class;
Among class brothers the bond is strongest.
And among the PLA, on the road to revolution,
Wherever you go you find people like that!"

Summer 1959
Conch-shell Bugle Call, pp. 98–99

Translated by Kai-yu Hsu

For a note on Chang Yung-mei, see p. 174.

CHAO P'U-CH'U
(1907–)

Chao was a successful businessman from Anhwei Province who managed a transport company while dabbling in Buddhism and classical Chinese poetry. He emerged as a leader of the liberals on the eve of Liberation, and in the 1950s he served as the president of the Buddhist Association in Shanghai while holding a high office in the government. Except during the years of the Cultural Revolution, he has been active in Buddhist organizations, often leading delegations to visit abroad.

Chao has earned a national reputation with his verse in the classical mode. Most of his poems collected in *Drops of Water* (1961) demonstrate his deft adaptation of traditional verse forms to accommodate current themes. The images are quite fresh and appealing. However, at times his lines can also be recondite and obscure; one very short verse published in the January 1977 issue of the *Poetry Journal* requires footnotes three times as long as the poem to explain four allusions involved. Such practices in writing poetry are indeed against everything the new literature of China is meant to be.

The latest collection of Chao's poems, *Chips of Stone,* was published in 1978.

—K.Y.H.

To the Tune "Partridge Sky"

—*Watching* Kuan Han-ch'ing, *Starring Ma Shih-tseng and Hung Hsien-nü*

Like trickling water the lingering song enters my dream,
A poet's mind and feeling entrusted to a tune.
Shocking grievance and blood and tears rage in the eastern sea,
The thunder and wind of justice rock all nine continents.
Rid the world of rats and lackeys,

Distinguish the right from wrong,
The case is settled today, settled forever.
A copper pea boiled in soup and fried in oil,*
Gladdens us with new green shoots sprouting all over.

Translated by Kai-yu Hsu

*The copper pea refers to a line spoken by Kuan Han-ch'ing in the play. (See pp. 767–80.)
[K.Y.H.]

CH'EN YI
(1901–72)

The call to arms and the call of the muse have been equally strong in Chinese tradition; every scholar used to feel, or make himself feel, ready to rise to the challenge of defending his country, and every soldier's highest aspiration was to write poetry like a Confucian scholar. It was in the blood of Mao Tse-tung; it was in the blood of Ch'en Yi—one of the ten meritorious marshals of the Communist armed forces, Chou En-lai's life-long comrade, and Foreign Minister until his death in 1972.

Ch'en had a rather legitimate claim to literature: he spent his two years in Paris (1919–21) studying French literature while working with Chou En-lai to organize communist cells. He completed his baccalaureate at a French-sponsored university while doing underground political work in North China in 1923–26. He wrote, while a student, on Anatole France, Romain Rolland, and proletarian literature, debating with the Chinese Bloomsbury poet Hsü Chih-mo.

Mao Tse-tung took Ch'en in as his poetry pupil, besides giving him tips on how to fight, guerrilla style. The lulls between campaigns gave Ch'en moments for reflection, and he committed his thoughts to verse. His heroic best came during the embattled years of Chinese Communist history, and his contemplative best during the years of peace, the late 1950s and early 1960s, when he was at the height of his success and still free from political attack. We have selected a few samples of the latter, all collected in *Selected Poems of Ch'en Yi*.

—K.Y.H.

Three Gorges of the
Yangtze River

When young I left home through the Three Gorges,
Day and night I watched the view.
Too confining, I thought of the whole thing,
And longed for the open world of the east coast.

I was young when I left home,
Forty years have since gone by.
The rills and hills, beautiful as ever,
But men have advanced, in long strides.

524

Szechwan's roads, truly hard as climbing heaven,
With the river snaking its way through mountains.
At each narrow gorge, one always faces
One more test, one more challenge.

The Min and the O mountains, thousands of feet high,
And the K'uei Gate and the Wu Peak lock in the west wind.
But none of them can stop the flow of the river,
As all waters rush forward toward the east.

November 1959
Selected Poems of Ch'en Yi, pp. 243–44

Blue Pines

Blue pine under snow,
The pine stands straight and strong
How unbending is it?—You want to know?
Just wait, when snow's gone.

Sensitive Plant

A plant named sensitive,
Only a plant it is, but man
How can he be less—to wit:
Many of old preferred death.

December 1960
Selected Poems, pp. 254–56

To My Children

Often I wish to rise to the sky,
Only to find myself earthbound,
I leap and I dash, but can't get away,
We are all together on this globe.

We are all together on this globe,
Now the East is free, the West enslaved.
If there could only be a blitz change overnight,
Turning the world into a place jewel-like and clean.

Turning the world into a place jewel-like and clean,
To fill with joy the hearts of all men and women.
Remember, it's man who decides, not heaven,
Just watch how China leaps higher and ahead.

Just watch how China leaps higher and ahead,
Replacing the old with the new in everything.
Communism soars afar beyond the horizon,
All nations do not have to be confined to this one globe.

All nations do not have to be confined to this one globe,
There are many suns outside the orbit of the sun.
Who can give a really new world?
With red rays shining all over the universe.

With red rays shining all over the universe,
When dreams and reality have come together.
Don't indulge only in idle words but no deeds
Don't just look under your nose but no further.

1961
Selected Poems, pp. 273–75

Translated by Kai-yu Hsu

HO CH'I-FANG
(1911–77)

Ho Ch'i-fang was born in 1911 (1910 by some accounts) in Wanhsien, on the Szechwan side of the Yangtze River Gorges. As a child he studied the traditional classics in the family school and read in secret the tales of fantasy and magic he found in the attic. Growing up he came into contact with Western and May Fourth literature at middle school in Chengtu and then at Shanghai, but when he entered Peking University in 1931 he elected to study Western philosophy in order to understand better what he thought was the basis of Western civilization. His first published poem dates from this year. In 1933, with Japanese troops only thirteen miles outside Peking, the universities sent their students home for an early vacation, but no signs of the crisis appear in Ho's early writings. In 1935, on graduation, he taught for a year at Nankai middle school in Tientsin, and here again refused even to acknowledge the student demonstrations that closed the school for a few days. Finally, on the eve of the Sino-Japanese war, he began to write about the twin evils of Japanese encroachment and social injustice. When war broke out, he returned to Szechwan but, in his new mood of social criticism, soon left for Yenan, from where he accompanied guerrilla forces in daring raids behind enemy lines, and where he later taught at the Lu Hsün Academy of Arts. In Peking, after the establishment of the People's Republic of China in 1949, he was given high academic posts and wrote several books of literary criticism; however, since 1942, very few poems by him have appeared. He was criticized during the Cultural Revolution, like many others, but in the early 1970s he was reinstated as director of the Institute of Chinese Literature at the Academy of Sciences. It was said that after the fall of the Gang of Four he was planning to set up a new poetry magazine. Unfortunately, he died on July 24, 1977, before such plans were able to materialize. The poems translated below include his last published work. They are written for the most part in a flowing, limpid vernacular, in Western quatrains with Western rhyme patterns, but on occasion he reverts to classical Chinese forms such as *lü-shih* and *chüeh-chü*.

Between 1936 and 1952 he published nine collections of poems and essays, of which the best known are *The Han Garden, Record of Painted Dreams, Prophecy,* and *Night Songs.*   —B.S.McD.

The Song

I hear a bewitching song,
So blithe, so young,
It seems like our young republic,
Singing her evergreen spring.

527

It seems like the dawn's golden rays
Trembling for joy on the waters,
Spring suddenly returns to the garden,
Dew laden blossoms unfold.

At times it sings low and sobbingly,
Like the fine spray of a fountain at night,
The round moon rises above the horizon,
A faint breeze lightly ruffles the leaves;

At times it sings high and loftily,
Like a huge billow touching the sky,
Transporting us from the earth's surface,
Towards the far-off blue ocean.

Then it sings soft and gently,
Like a maiden's eyes filled with sorrow,
And like plants which cleave the earth as they grow,
First love leaps in the heart.

Ah, it is so bewitching,
It's not music, it is life!
It's not something heard in a dream,
But the pulsating blood of spring!

> Peking, from the night of the 2nd to the
> morning of the 3rd, March 1957
> *People's Literature*, no. 10 (1961): 3

In March this year I met Yang Chi-fu at a conference in Peking. It turned out to be exactly twenty years since we had parted in the autumn of 1937. When I was working in Chungking in 1947, he was in Wanhsien running the Yü-ch'üan middle school. He sent me a regulated poem in five-word meter, entrusting it to a comrade to recite to me when he got to Chungking. Unfortunately, I only remember the final couplet now. He wanted me to write out a few lines for him. I wasn't able to write an old-style poem, since I happened to have contracted a slight illness, and my head was so dizzy I couldn't do anything; I just scribbled a few incoherent lines from my bed:

> Not content with private goals,
> You set up a school for the common good.
> Mo Ti grew anxious when silk was dyed,
> It was Confucius' wish that the way be shared.
> When tree roots reach deep into the earth,
> Leaves and branches will withstand the winds.
> Since parting there is much to say,
> When shall we two meet again?

After I had recovered I wrote these lines on a scroll for him. When we met again, he told me that the scroll was still hanging in his house in the country-side. In Chungking not long after sending it, I heard the news of his arrest. Because the school he ran was supported by the masses, he was eventually let out of jail. He suffered from TB for more than twenty years, and physically he was very weak, but he still worked resolutely. I also discovered at this time that he had high blood pressure, so that one topic of the poem is contempt for illness.

[Author's note]

For Yang Chi-fu

How could we know in twenty years
I would ascend your hall again,
At our former parting you weren't married,
Sons and daughters suddenly form a row ...

Tu Fu*

While you were talking,
You recalled Tu Fu's lines;
Just twenty years ago we parted,
Once more to meet again.

My temples are flecked with white,
You are thinner than before,
The hot blood in our breasts
Is yet the same as when we were young.

Pointing to your lungs,
You say the rotting spread,
You were kept in the enemy's prison,
And remained in danger after release.

Comrades urged you to rest,
You said, what does illness matter?
For the sake of our ideals,
How can one day pass without work?

Just as we held the enemy in contempt,
So did we look down on illness,
However great its strength,
Victory still was ours!

*From "For Wei Pa, the Recluse." [B. S. McD.]

While you were talking,
You recalled Tu Fu's lines;
Just twenty years ago we parted,
Once more to meet again.

Peking, night of the 8th, April 1957
People's Literature, no. 10 (1961): 4

In November 1958 I went to Honan on a tour of inspection. At a few places poems were demanded after the inspection, so that we were obliged to compose several pieces of doggerel. Afterwards I more or less forgot them. This is the only one I still remember. Fan Hai-liang was a peasant from Ma-kou village in San-kuan-miao in Teng-feng county, who was then a production team leader. His poem went like this—

Chairman Mao's eyes are like stars in the sky,
Even people living deep in the mountains see their light.
[Author's note]

For Fan Hai-liang

Of all the stars in the skies, Venus shines the brightest,
Among poets from the distant past, Li Po and Tu Fu are celebrated most.
Who is it writes the best poems today?
The multitudes of laboring people.

San-kuan-miao, Teng-feng county
in Honan, November 14, 1958
People's Literature, no. 10 (1961): 4

Night Passage through Wanhsien

The mountain town agleam with lamplight,
Loops around the river bank,
It looks much like Chungking at night,
Only the Chialing is missing.

Leaning on the boat railing,
I wanted to see it more closely;
This was my family home,
Nursed on its milk I grew up.

Where is the azure T'ai-po Cliff,
Where according to legend, Li Po once lived?
In the primary school at its foot,
I passed my childhood years.

Where is the bustling Southford Street?
Bombarded by British gunboats,
The street was once reduced to rubble,
But quickly filled again with shops.

Where are the streets along which
I raced together with my companions?
Shouting at the top of our voices
Anti-imperialist slogans.

I can't make out the places I knew so well,
Nor buildings that date from after Liberation,
I only see the lamplight gleaming,
Reflected in the river's midnight hue.

I only see the Yangtze's upper reaches,
Where night boats now can pass,
Like the pace of our reconstruction
Pressing on night and day.

I lean on the boat railing,
Until the mountain town is out of sight,
Red and green lamp-markers on the river
Seem to bid a reluctant farewell.

First drafted on board along the Yangtze,
December 9, 1958; revised in Peking, August 17, 1961
People's Literature, no. 10 (1961): 5

The First Morning in Vietnam

On June 27, 1961, the train arrived at Dongdang inside the Vietnam border, just as the sky was becoming light. The train continued forward. The flora and fauna in North Vietnam are similar to those in parts of South China and in my

native province of Szechwan. However, men and women do not dress like
Chinese. On the train some Vietnamese comrades were collecting signatures
from passengers in protest against the invasion and interference of American
imperialism in South Vietnam, and the Chinese comrades signed happily.

After the rain the mountain summit
Is wreathed by a ring of white mist.
Dawn has just awoken,
Laden with the cold dew of the night before.

Sunlight suddenly gleams:
Bamboo groves, lotus ponds, banana trees;
Like embroidered flowers stitched by hand,
Appear neat rows of rice paddies.

Peasants plough the fields with water buffalo,
Women labor in the fields and open country,
Everything is so touchingly familiar,
And yet so fresh and new!

But this is no Peach Blossom Spring.
In the south of the same peninsula
Under the same peaceful blue sky,
Americans and Ngo Dinh Diem still abide.

No evil power whatsoever
Can prevent the unity of Vietnam!
We say each of our fingers is attached to the heart,
How much more so each half of one body!

And so on this first morning,
I signed my name in the carriage,
Taking part in the Vietnamese people's
Struggle to unify their homeland.

Hanoi, June 30, 1961
People's Literature, no. 10 (1961): 5–6

Three Young Women from South Vietnam

I met three young women from South Vietnam:
One with short braids, cheerful and lively;
A thin one, with something sad in her face;
One with a pair of large eyes, grave and silent.

On an evening without moon or stars,
Only the sound of waves on the shore,
They rowed a boat across the sea
And stole away together to the north.

"At the time we made a fatal resolution,
If caught halfway we were ready to fight to the death."
Their life in the South was so hard,
So bitter it could not be borne.

"What oppressed us beyond bearing were too-heavy taxes,
Whatever kind of fish you caught, there was a fish-tax for them all.
Then there was the head tax. Then for building the district head's office
Each was assigned a contribution which cost us dear.

"The young men of the village were soon all conscripted,
All the work then fell to us.
A hint of discontent, one word of complaint,
They said you harbored communist ideas.

"They said the people's soldiers in the North were as thin as paper men,
They could stand on grass in water and the grass wouldn't sink.
Everyone knew that Ngo was America's running dog,
No one believed their ridiculous propaganda!"

They talked about their lives and homes,
But not about the people who arose in resistance,
Who might be burned alive or disembowelled,
Their villages wiped out by plane and cannon.

They had hardly any schooling but could till the soil,
And contribute their labor to their homeland's garden of flowers.
"Do you want to return home?" They answer:
"No, not until unification is realized."

They are three young women from South Vietnam,
Talking to me softly like little birds
Who have flown from their cage into the sun,
Both joyful and somewhat constrained.

Hanoi, July 15, 1961
People's Literature, no. 10 (1961): 7–8

Translated by Bonnie S. McDougall

HO CHING-CHIH

Song of the Landscape of Kweilin

O, gods of the clouds, immortals of the mist,
The mountains of Kweilin seem like gods and immortals!

O, deep as love eternal, beautiful as a dream,
The waters of River Li are like love and dreams!

O, how many folds of water, how many ranges of mountains?
The waters and mountains surround the city of Kweilin....

A mountain city or a water city?
All in the blue mountains and waters green....

O! These hills, these waters with me entwine,
At this moment, whence came this body of mine?

... The Yellow River's waves and desert winds
Have come over layers upon layers of frontier ranges.

On horseback I dream of a sand painting:
"The landscape of Kweilin is the best in the world"....

O! A dream world? An ethereal world?
I am as though on Tu-hsiu Summit right now!

O, is my heart intoxicated or still awake?
The waters and mountains usher me into their painted screen!

Painting in a painting—River Li reflects my thousand shadows,
Song in a song—mountain after mountain echoes my voice....

I wave at Old Man Mountain to ask,
How many thousands of years have the clouds stayed o'er the rivers and
peaks?

—In the Pearl Return Cave of Wave Subdue Mountain,
The pearl waited long for a knock at the door....

Chicken Coop Mountain sings and Folding Screen Mountain opens,
To let the green waters, white boat, and red flag come in!

For a note on Ho Ching-chih, see p. 361.

Spring rains wash away the earth's sad look,
Just look in Pierced Mountain's clear mirror—

O! The Mountains of Kweilin, the waters of River Li—
The smile of my motherland is so lovely!

The landscape of Kweilin enters my breast,
Such scenery, such feelings are the fighter's heart—

So lovely this land, and friendly the people,
My hair will be kept from ever turning grey!

Facing this land one's pride will naturally unfold,
My youth will be kept from ever growing old!

Seven Star Rock goes to a gathering of immortals
Calling Third Sister Liu to return from the skies....

A wide road opens between man and heaven,
Whoever wants to sing new songs, come follow me!

Third Sister has loads of mountain songs,
About this land, o, fighters, singing of our nation....

Red flags weave an intricate tapestry,
The sea's north and the sky's south are seen at one glance!

O, wind and sand of the frontier, waves of the Yellow River,
Bring spring to my hometown from thousands of miles away.

Under red flags: young heroes arise everywhere—
Too many to see: the many facets of "Tu-hsiu Summit"!

—O, thoughts crowd my mind, and feelings surge in my bosom,
Just like the rolling waters of River Li in spring!

O! A rain of profuse sweat paints a colorful picture:
May the landscape of Kweilin—be everywhere!....

First draft July 1959,
Revised August 1961
Singing Aloud, pp. 25–28

Translated by Hsin-sheng C. Kao

HSIAO SAN

[1896–]

Hsiao San went to school together with Mao Tse-tung and was one of the original dozen members of Mao's first Marxist study group in Changsha, Hunan Province. He joined the Communist Party upon its inception in 1921 and lived and studied in Russia for thirteen years. Since his return to China in 1939 he has been prominent in literary circles and has published over fifteen volumes under his name, including three books of verse: *Songs of Friendship, Selected Poems,* and *In the Stable.* He is best known for his stories of Mao Tse-tung's early life. —K.Y.H.

I Sing for My Fatherland,
Ten Years Old

They used to call us
In contempt like this:
For one, we are an inferior race,
And again, we are East Asia's sickly.

They used to name
Places in our country as they pleased:
The Lu-kou Bridge was Marco Polo,
The Princely Mansion Well was Morrison Street

They used to describe
The look of our country this was:
One rotten tree trunk, a cluster of weeds,
A broken bowl and a dilapidated temple.

Very much out of their habit,
They were stunned, speechless;
A thunderbolt out of the blue,
The Chinese people have stood up.

A giant walks out of the Huai-jen Hall,*
A giant steps on the Gate of Heavenly Peace;
"The People's Republic is hereby established!"
The five-star red flag rises high in pride.

*Chairman Mao's office in Peking. [K.Y.H.]

The Heavenly Peace Square remains hushed and solemn.
The 21-gun salute reverberates in the sky.
The song stirs the hearts of thousands gathered there,
"Rise, you who are unwilling to be slaves anymore."

They are very surprised,
They are very depressed,
We have wrestled away their swords;
Our destiny lies under our own control.

Then, still following their old habit, they think
China has always been a dish of loose sands.
Even though we may have unified our country,
We can't keep it safely in our hands.

Then they figure secretly,
China has always been stark poor*
When we are faced with this situation,
We surely would not know what to do.

And they have another habit:
When they see a young sprout issuing,
They'd hurry up to chop it down,
To avoid its growing into a big tree with spreading shade.

They are very uncomfortable,
They are really disturbed;
The Chinese really know how to take care of themselves,
And like iron, like steel, they are united.

We poked through that paper tiger,
We subdued fox fairies and demons.
If the enemy dares to stir again,
We'll wipe them out, to the last man.

Wiping out backwardness and poverty,
We rely upon our broad masses.
One leap forward after another,
Our 600 million, each a hero.

Each full of life and vigor,
Everyone shows his very best.
Great rivers must make way,
Towering mountains bow to us.

*A phrase in a 1958 speech by Mao Tse-tung that means that China is both economically underdeveloped and culturally blank—not without vestiges of ancient culture but lacking development into a modern Chinese culture. The nuance of the phrase, which admits China's deficiency without compromising her cultural pride, gives the expression national and lasting currency. [K.Y.H.]

Who's afraid of drought and flood?
Wet or dry we increase production.
People's communes stand unbending,
Our collective strength, unlimited.

Oil fields and steel capitals everywhere, and everywhere
Flows the precious liquid and dances the fire dragon;
An enormous bridge astride the Yangtze River,
A thoroughfare between Canton and Peking.

People no longer ask for
"Foreign cloth, matches and oil"....*
The "Red Flag," "East Wind," and "Hero" ...
Local products, too many to be counted.

We're happiest for our wise leadership,
We have a system of our own.
A great nation of socialism—
Wealth and strength, a certainty.

This system of ours is
truly miraculous,
It scares the enemy out of his wits,
And brings out broad grins from our friends.

This system of ours
Produces miracles.
In ten short years our record
Has exceeded many centuries.

Many statistical data become
History at the wink of the eye.
And many new books just off press
Already are outdated.

The giant that's our people has marched forth for ten years,
Today he returns once again to the Heavenly Peace Square.
Five-star red flags rise all around, all the way to the sky,
And our national anthem, and the "Internationale," ride the winds.

The People's Square, solemn, great, reflecting glory,
A brand-new assembly hall, flanked by huge museums.
The martyrs felled in the last 100 years will live forever,
As the towering memorial stands infallible in the Square.

*These items were called foreign in China because they were first introduced and
imported from overseas. Now China is producing Red Flag and East Wind passenger cars,
Hero fountain pens, etc. [Author's note]

Thousands upon thousands of good friends and distinguished guests
Have come from all directions of the earth.
"Our friends are all over the world,"*
We fear no lies or slander by a small "cluster."

We'll continue to make flying leaps forward,
Unafraid of the rightists' pulling our legs.
East wind rises to overwhelm the west wind completely,
The fortress of socialism is a rising sun.

October 1, 1959
In Stable, pp. 1–8

Translated by Kai-yu Hsu

*Chairman Mao's words. [K.Y.H.]

HSIEH CH'I-KUEI

Hsieh Ch'i-kuei published poems frequently in the early 1960s, but there is very little known about him.   —K.Y.H.

More

The factory staff try every way to save fuel and collect discarded scraps and used metal. With these they make a large quantity of farm implements to support the spring plowing in the commune. [Author's note]

Iron in furnace,
Hammer on anvil,
A hoe, each swing,
And a scythe, once more.

Our coal is "austerity coal,"
Our iron, scraps.
More hoes and more scythes,
More wheat, more rice.

Poetry Journal, no. 3 (1961): 36–37

Translated by Kai-yu Hsu

KUO HSIAO-CH'UAN
(1919–76)

When I spent a day with Kuo Hsiao-ch'uan in 1973 in Peking, he gave me a brief account of his earlier life without, however, acknowledging that he had been in jail at the height of the Cultural Revolution in 1967, as some sources claimed to be the case. But then, few people I saw that year in the People's Republic of China would even mention that subject.

Before the liberation of 1949, Kuo published poetry under several pen names, of which the best known was Ma T'ieh-ting. He was born to a teacher's family in a small town on the southern edge of Inner Mongolia, attended schools in Peking (then Peiping), and became actively involved in Communist-supported student movements. At the outbreak of the war against Japan, Kuo joined the political department of the Eighth Route Army in Shansi Province. From 1941 to the late 1960s he studied Marxism in Yenan, was assigned to the editorial offices of many regional and national publications, including the *People's Daily*, and held different political and administrative posts. He even served as the mayor of his hometown for a period. All the while he continued to write poetry. Collections of his verse and essays include *To Young Citizens, Old Hired Hand, Under the Moon, Songs of the K'un-lun Mountains*, and *Sugarcane Forest*. In style, his works are close to Ho Ching-chih's: both reflect Mayakovsky's influence. They are robust, throaty, and infectiously sonorous.

Kuo's poem "Gazing at the Starry Sky," translated below, was caught in the 1959 Anti-Rightist campaign and criticized for displaying bourgeois, individualistic sentiments.   —K.Y.H.

Gazing at the Starry Sky

. . . Starry Sky,
Only you
Deserve to be hailed, "Long Life Eternal!"
For how many times you have watched
The thawing of glaciers
And the eruptions of volcanoes!
How many times you have watched
The green oozing out of willow twigs,
And catkins, white as frost, take to flight.
At your lofty height,
From a place that staggers man's imagination,
You have seen all the beautiful sights in the world of man,
And witnessed all of its dramatic changes as well.

To you, time is—
Like space—
An infinite
And untamable flow.

Gazing at the starry sky above
Makes me feel sad.
However one might brag
About one's strength and ambition
Or about one's health and youth,
How can those things compare
With your permanence,
Your immemorial past and your unlimited future?
However one might claim
Possession of a hero's gusto and will,
And a hero's vision and courage,
How can those things compare
With the immensity
Of your capacity!

I love the world of man
As I have grown up there.
But in front of you
It is far less glittering.
Walking over a thousand mountains
And wading across ten thousand rivers
Do not bring one to your realm.
Even travelling over all the seas
And oceans on earth
Does not enable one to share your elixir.
And the myriads of bonfires
And lights and lanterns
Pale before just one of your tiny stars.
Putting all the roads
And bridges end to end
Won't measure up to even a section of your milky way.

I have journeyed over half the globe
From the east to the west.
The size of the earth
Has startled us and earned our admiration.
Yet who can tell
How many stars and planets the universe contains,
To which our earth is but a sibling?
Who has ever learned
How many lands there are in the sky
All capable of accommodating mankind?
Can't you see the moon?

—That huge expanse of space out there.
Those lands afar
—defy our imagination

Life is precious.
To sing praise of the life engaged in intense battles,
I have written volumes of verse.
But in the course of a man's life
How many chances does one have
To gaze at the starry sky?
And as one moves along in one's life,
How many nights like this does he have
To pass in the infinite space of the universe?
The life of man flickers no brighter than a falling star,
And in the endless flow of time
Life is but one of the faintest ripples.

I gaze at the starry sky.
It makes me feel sad.
And I carry this unnamed sorrow
As I walk toward the heart of Peking. . . .

People's Literature, no. 11 (1959): 90–93

Translated by Kai-yu Hsu

LI CHI

Soul Lamp

[This is a Northern Shensi legend about a light that is supposed to appear at night on the ruins of an ancient beacon tower facing the wilderness of Inner Mongolia. It is said that the lamp summons the soul of a man chased out to the wilderness to die. He had been in love with a woman, whose jealous husband organized the chase with the help of local police.]

A lamp was lit on top of the mountain
Its light seen all around.
On the thousands of miles of wilderness,
All dark, except this single spot of red.

It's not for chasing away vicious dogs,
Or warning the wolves that stalk the sheep;
Just for him, that one man alone,
Just for her lover, she lights the lamp.

One wick in the lamp, two ounces of oil,
When oil burns low she adds her tears,
The red lamp is her red, red heart,
Full of longing, full of fears.

In a shrill voice she calls out his name,
Why aren't you coming back?
If there are dogs on the ledge, take the grassland,
Dodge the police, follow the trail by the ditch.

Others going beyond the Wall always send letters,
But you are a needle fallen into the sea.
Are you a roadside sparrow, scared to death?
Or wandering out there in sickness and poverty?

Don't be afraid of the gleaming sword,
Don't be scared of the soldiers' bugle call.
You have an armor, your unlined sheepskin coat,
And your bare chest is stronger than a stone wall.

If you are dead somewhere beyond the Western Pass,
Send me a message in dream, anyhow, anyway.
I'll kill my husband at once; I will
Light the lamp at night, stay a widow during the day.

For a note on Li Chi, see p. 178.

The soul-summoning lamp lights up afar,
One by one all the saddened stars are gone;
She calls for none of the many wandering ghosts,
But only calls for her lover all night long.

April 1962
Poetry Journal, no. 3 (1962): 50–51

Translated by Kai-yu Hsu

LI YING

Red Willow, Sand Jujube, and White Caltrop

Red willows, sand jujubes, and white caltrops
Truly are the brave ones in the battle of life.

They are poor, very poor,
Adorned by no fleshy leaves, not a single one;
And humbly they stand, very humbly
Taking care to occupy little space, just a little space.

What they ask is infinitesimal,
For them there often is not even a single drop of rain;
Yet they offer their utmost,
Including their own shadows, that precious shade.

Look how they trample into surrender the acres of flowing sand,
Bearing on their shoulders thunderstorms, harsh and sudden.
They topple, but only for an instant, then they are up again,
In their eyes there is no defeat, but only victory.

To the travelers, dry and thirsty, trudging under the blazing sun,
They say, "Go on, don't stop!"
And to those long-buried cities under the sand,
They declare, "Get up, you cannot die!"

Their firm belief grips that day—there must be such a day,
When a chain of camels, or a chain of oxcarts' wooden wheels
Shall haul this wild stretch of sand, now clinging to the sky,
Away to a museum and deposit it there, forever there.

Yes, perhaps only an endless sky, just like this one above,
Can accommodate what they hold in their bosoms, their will and ideal,
And their unswerving devotion, their profound love, for life and the living,
And their undying loyalty to the people, their fellow men.

So I say, my young friends, my comrades,
If they aren't your shadows, what else could they be?

August 1961
Red Willow, pp. 133–34

For a note on Li Ying, see p. 371.

Sunrise over the Gobi

Settled is the cutting cold wind;
Settled, the immense Gobi, boundless and barren;
We mount our horses to start out at the break of dawn
Yearning for a touch of warmth, a touch of green.

Behold, there spouts a line of color on the horizon
Light blue, dark orange, then red, and purple.
Who has left an array of golden pheasant feathers
On this brown, desolate rocky plain?

The sun wakes and rises,
No, suddenly shooting up, pushing itself up with both hands.
It casts a glance at this sea of frozen rocks
And lengthens our shadows on it.

In haste we urge our horses along,
Towards the bright disk of a rising sun.
Only a few more steps, just a few steps
We'd plunge headlong into its bosom.

But in an instant the sun boils in wrath, and in an instant
It leaps over our horses' heads to land on our spines.
A sheet of blazing fire it spreads on the cold, cold land,
Along with a thousand, ten thousand golden shafts.

As suddenly rises a cloud of dust, hot and dry,
Rising higher and higher over the desert of Gobi.
Hot and dry all around, we pant and our horses pant;
Only a few hours, but passed were all four seasons.

From where comes a peal of singing, where?
Robust and sonorous it shakes the entire Gobi.
Men from our survey team are approaching us.
And I see the beauty of the people's will, right here.

August 1961
Red Willow, pp. 127–28

Dawn at Tun-Huang

At Tun-huang
Wind and sand wake up early,
So man snakes hugging the ground they are
Sliding along, hissing along.

But no roaring wind or flying sand
Can drown the songs on the country road.
And birds still sing on birch tree tops;
Water still chuckles in red willow clusters.

Along the creek comes a group of young people
Bundles of young trees piled on oxen's backs.
There is a small piece of the desert on each shoulder, yes, there is,
But they're going to plant peaches and apricots on the desert sea.

Whose flute is that, rising suddenly at such an early hour?
Where is it? In the fields, or tree clusters, over the dunes or hills?
I know that the flying sand can't cover up the holes in the flute,
Neither can any gusty wind sweep away that kind of hearty laughter.

Three young boys are coming up from down the road,
Their flute winds a string of musical notes around three shovels;
Three rosy faces, three blossoms of youthful health—
They're going to plant a tree-shaded path in their school.

People say at Tun-huang even the dawning is brown,
Brown wild clouds, brown ancient forts, and brown water in the river.
Yet why through the drape of sand thousands of miles wide I see now
Such a bright and cheery morning, dewy and green?

August 1961
Red Willow, pp. 122–23

Translated by Kai-yu Hsu

LIANG SHANG-CH'ÜAN

Floating the Raft

Mountains, bluer than the sky;
But bluer still, the waters lie
Under a sweep of silvery gleam.
Behold, a raft flows down the stream.

Man on raft, raft on sky
Where clouds and cooking-smoke fly,
And together drift afar with the wind
To the Nine-Step Rapids roaring in distance.

December 6, 1961, Ping-chang
The Mountain Stream, p. 172

A River of Colors

A hundred miles of river, a hundred miles of glen,
A hundred miles of plums red, and a hundred miles of bamboos green.
A hundred miles of sweet peaches and tangerines,
Each layer more beautiful than the last.

Orchards race rivers into the distance.
On both banks they stand, like guards of honor;
They greet the boats, waving them on toward the mountain,
Offering the passengers loads and loads of fruit.

Blooms of all colors smile on trees,
Winds of all colors shake the leaves,
Fish of all colors cavort in waves,
And feathers of all colors paint the sky.

Things in the commune, all full of life and vigor,
Sprouting, growing, multiplying, again and again.
Together they form a river of colors,
Racing the colorful life of the people here.

December 7, 1959, on the Ch'ing-chi River
Poetry Journal, no. 6 (1961): 16–17

Translated by Kai-yu Hsu

For a note on Liang Shang-ch'üan, see p. 180.

SHA PAI

Sha Pai's poems drew considerable attention during the 1960s, but very little has come to light about the poet himself.

The expression *chiang-nan,* south of the river, has been a rich, poetic image ever since the time of the Southern Sung Dynasty, when the imperial capital was moved for K'ai-feng on the Yellow Riverbank to Hangchow, south of the Yangtze River. Poets have used this image to summon to the mind a picture of the scenic Yangtze River delta area—lush green, rice-rich, and culturally prosperous. —K.Y.H.

People, Houses, South of the River

1. TRAVEL IN WATER COUNTRY

Roads of water country,
Paved by water and clouds;
Entering or leaving the village,
By an oar.

Fishing nets—door curtains,
Swing on trees;
Only upon approaching, you see
A cottage there.

Looking for anyone?
Go where rice blossoms are thick;
Footsteps, one by one,
Silence the frogs' drumming.

And the cicadas hush,
Evening haze rises over water,
The young ones take the visitors home,
Untying the boat, deftly handling the oar.

2. COTTAGES, SOUTH OF THE RIVER

Flowers before the door,
Melons behind the wall,
Beanstalks crawl under eaves,
Gourds hanging like bells.

550

Cabbage leaves wave green sleeves,
Eggplants lean on fences,
Half hidden in clouds of green,
These houses, South of the River.

Chickens call,
Ducks respond,
Baaing lambs
Chase after piglets.

Nobody home,
Only swallows carrying fallen petals.
And trumpet flowers on tops of trees,
Summon the villagers back, with kitchen smoke.

Poetry Journal, no. 2 (1961): 52–53

Translated by Kai-yu Hsu

WEN CHIEH
(1923–71)

In the 1940s, Wen Chieh was writing short tales published in miniature pamphlets for circulation among the guerrilla troops in North China. For that purpose he cultivated a simple, straightforward style of language, which he later adapted for his poetry.

Wen spent the 1950s in Kansu Province working for the Writers' Association and publishing poetry. He moved to Shanghai in the 1960s, and his writing career went on uninterrupted until the Cultural Revolution put a stop to it in 1966.

A recognized lyrical voice in contemporary Chinese poetry, Wen left several volumes of verse, including *Pastoral Songs of the T'ien Mountain Range*, *Motherland! the Glorious October*, *The First Spring Thunder* and *The Flame of Revenge*. The last is a long story-poem.   —K.Y.H.

To Water Buffalo

Dedicated to Li K'o-jan

Why do you like to paint water buffaloes?
Because they tread in wind and wind-driven rain;
Waves of mud chase after the plows they pull
And they bring forth the hands that plant rice.

Why do you like to paint water buffaloes?
Because they fear no difficulty, know no worry;
Relentlessly they scale the mountain, no matter how high,
And swim across any river that lies in their way.

Why do you like to paint water buffaloes?
Because their temperament is stubborn and yet kind;
Before the enemy they dart forth their twin swords,
But they bow to the little boy playing a short flute.

Why do you like to paint water buffaloes?
Because they demand very little of man;
When hungry they just chew some lush grass,
And to quench thirst they drink from any stream.

552

Why do you like to paint water buffaloes?
Because they step in cadence with the heart-beat of life;
Buffaloes! The essence of the revolutionary spirit,
Buffaloes! The best friends of laboring people.

October 27, 1961, Pei-tai-ho
Poetry Journal, no. 2 (1962): 42–43

Translated by Kai-yu Hsu

YEN CHEN
(1931–)

Born in Shantung, Yen Chen spent the war years in the guerrilla area on the eastern side of his native province. He started writing poetry after the liberation and success came to him quite promptly. As shown in his first widely applauded poem, "Old Chang's Hand" (published in *People's Literature,* January 1954), he is skillful in blending lyrical elements with story interest. He has an eye for the poetically exciting aspects of what might appear to the casual observer as a rather commonplace subject. *Songs South of the River* and *The Music Creek* are among his better-known collections of poems. —K.Y.H.

Night Song

Willow groves under the moon, brocades in green,
And the frozen clouds of blue hills stand in rows;
It's late at night, very late, ah, Doctor,
Why do you come to knock on the door?

The captain is in the room working on a design
Of an improved farm implement; the sound of sawing
Echoes the strings in a night song and the strings
Draw the doctor to the door, waiting.

The door opens and in steps the doctor along with
A stir of evening breeze, a whiff of flower scent.
"Comrade Doctor, whom are looking for?
Nobody is sick here, nobody at all."

The doctor's words, humorous yet earnest:
"I know your chronic disease of not going to sleep,
And I am here to give you a diagnosis ..."
The doctor gone, and the quiet of the night, calm and profound.

Songs South of the River, p. 42

Orchard

Trees full of blossoms, now all gone,
In the orchard, only green meets the eyes;
I laugh at the poets of the past era,
At a time like this, they'd heave long sighs.

Hundreds upon hundreds of new fruit
Peek out from behind the thick leaves;
Look, comrades, look at it now,
What a beautiful season this is!

The oriole is singing its very first song,
And on every branch, heavy, heavy dew;
And the glaring, bright sunshine serves
As the best gardener, most loyal and true.

I love this patch of intense green
For many happy dreams lie in its rich fold;
Who won't like to pick treefuls of ripe fruit,
When autumn mellows into rich gold?

Songs South of the River, p. 45

A Song of Spring South of the River

Ten miles of peach blossoms,
Ten miles of willow trees,
Ten miles of red flags fluttering in breeze,
Spring South of the River,
Heady like wine.

Hillsides draped in tender green,
In fields, juice flows;
Happy reports bulletined at crossroads,
Mountain songs,
Hovering about.

Some still in teens,
Others twenty-six at best,
They work as though in a muscle contest,
Plowshares fly in mud waves,
Clouds chase their carrying poles.

With a stream of laughter women emerge
From the village to work on their lands,
In front of the nursery they wave their hands,
Then they turn to embroider the fields in spring;
A flower in each of their hairpins.

Requests come from the old folks' home,
Many requests and more,
All say having no work is a bore;
Watching the buds crowd the willow twigs,
They wring their hands in anxiety.

Ten miles of peach blossoms,
Ten miles of willow trees,
Ten miles of red flags fluttering in breeze,
Spring South of the River,
Heady like wine.

Songs South of the River, pp. 35–36

The Frog's Croak

The frog's croak rings outside the village,
Pale moonlight fills the windowpane,
A sleepless captain of the production team
Treads on the moonlight to approach the riverside.

The moon, the frog's croak, and the river tide
Bring back to him a scene ten years old:
A soldier on scout duty, he sneaked across
The Yangtze River to come to the south side.

Pa, pa, pa ... flew the enemy's bullets,
Go, go, go ... he faked a frog's croak;
The enemy, though cunning, was fooled,
Towing his gun he slowly took to the road....

The frog croaks louder now, the village asleep,
The captain comes to a wheat field—all is calm;
He smiles and bends down to study carefully
That new ear of wheat lying against his palm.

Songs South of the River, p. 41

April Night

April night, sweet scent in the air,
Pale moonlight over the Yangtze River;

All lights and lamps are out now in the village,
Who is it that's knocking on the door?

Throwing a jacket on his shoulder, the old man opens the door,
To find the squad leader whose unit crossed the River,*
Still wearing the same smile as so many years ago, only
He has changed his uniform for a workman's overall.

The old man brews green tea in thawed snow,
And asks the squad leader of a time long past:
"You knocked once before in April ten years ago,
But now, what has brought you here again?"

The squad leader replies in his confident voice,
"I am a victory report personified,
Last time I came to liberate south of the river,
This time I'm here to build a long bridge."

In joy the old man beams all over,
He hugs the squad leader's broad shoulder;
At that moment he suddenly notices
The young man's temple is showing specks of grey.

Tenderly he touches the young man's forehead,
Words are choked by tears welling in his eyes;
He would like, very much like, to ask him:
Where have you been fighting these long, long years?

A whiff of soft spring breeze stirs,
Bringing a new kind of sound into the hut;
The drilling boat has started working in mid-river,
April night, sweet scent in the air.

Songs South of the River, p. 98

The Ink Maker

Soot-smeared arms, soot-smeared face,
Sweat never dries on your broad shoulder,
An iron hammer in hand you strike at the soot
Thousands of times you strike it, over and over.

*During the Liberation war. [K.Y.H.]

You keep pounding on it without stop,
Your blood and sweat turn into the famed Anhwei ink;
So many treasured poems, paintings and books,
Are all soaked through with your hard work.

During the hundreds of years in the past,
How many poems have been born in the Anhwei ink?
And yet none of them sing any praise of you,
None of them heed your labor, your hardship.

The Party has appraised your labor all anew:
Now you are an artist of the people,
And the people now dip in your sweet-scented ink
To paint the most beautiful pictures of our country.

Songs South of the River, p. 113

Translated by Kai-yu Hsu

PART FOUR

The Socialist Education
of the People

(1962–1964)

T he near famine of 1960–61 was officially blamed on a number of extrane-
ous issues, such as the withdrawal of Russian aid after 1959 and a general
lack of support for the Party's policy, but never on the policy of the Great Leap
Forward itself. Since Peking could not bring back Russian aid, the CCP turned
to address the problem of creating the "new man," totally selfless and dedicated
to a common socialist ideal. The campaign was called the socialist education of
the people.

But, as Shao Ch'üan-lin reminded us, the bulk of the population anywhere,
at any time, tends to stay politically in the middle. There are neither heroes
nor villains—just ordinary people with their faults and virtues. Shao was
promptly condemned. Ch'en Yün's play reflected the same theme by showing
the difficulty of persuading youths to go to the countryside and stay there. They
prefer urban amenities to the rigors of a frontier mining area. Ch'en Yün, too,
was condemned. In Ou-yang Shan's novel, the first part of his ambitious multivolume saga, the young intellectual hero of the 1920s showed interest in some
bourgeois ladies, but, according to his critics, the typical underground Communist comrade, even in the 1920s, should have been class-conscious enough to
reject such temptations. Li Ying-ju's novel was greeted as a model of socialist
literature when it first appeared in 1960, but now the critics found fault in its
depiction of some Communist underground workers fighting against the Japanese and Chinese traitors in the 1940s. Ma Feng had been enjoying great popularity with his proletarian stories, but the drive to root out the "middle
characters" attacked his characterization of the hero in "I Knew Three Years
Ago" as a satirical smear on the correct proletarian hero image.

Some writers, however, escaped the current round of condemnations. Liu
Chen was left alone to present us with a beautiful portrait of two female
characters: a wise older comrade and the brat of a "little red devil" whom she

patiently brings up. Hu Wan-ch'un, later one of the literary henchmen of the Cultural Revolution in Shanghai, gave voice to an aging worker troubled by alienation, a subtle problem not usually recognized in socialist literature.

On the eve of the Great Proletarian Cultural Revolution, the new literature, developed for over twenty years by two generations of trained writers, had reached a good measure of maturity. The following group of selections demonstrates that the harvest during this period was quite abundant—particularly in poetry, which had remained relatively free from controversy.

MA FENG
(1922–)

Ma Feng was born in Hsiao-yi, Shansi Province, to a poor peasant family. Before finishing his elementary school education, he joined the Communist anti-Japanese guerrilla forces at the age of sixteen. In 1943 he began writing for two newspapers in his home state. His first noted work, "The Story of Chang Ch'u-yüan" (1944), received a literary award. A year later came his novel *The Heroes of the Lü-liang Mountains,* which was organized episodically in the mode of the classical Chinese novel *Water Margin.* In 1949 Ma Feng was in Peking studying at the Central Literary Workshop directed by Ting Ling. During the next five years he worked for the Chinese writers organizations and published three collections of short stories on farm life. He returned to his home province in 1956 to assume the post of vice-chairman of the All-China Federation of Literary and Art Circles, Shansi branch.

The year 1958–59 was the most important period in Ma Feng's literary life. All his earlier stories were considered lacking in depth. "I Knew Three Years Ago," published first in *Sparks* (January 1958), marked the beginning of a new trend and style in his writings. His 1958–59 stories (published mostly in *People's Literature* and *Sparks*) dealt with the new agrarian society, and in them he began to emphasize plot development and character depth, trying especially to avoid stereotypes. He stressed the importance of writing on contemporary Chinese life; he disagreed with those who followed any foreign style of writing and insisted on writing with a Chinese, local flavor.

However, during the Great Proletarian Cultural Revolution, "I Knew Three Years Ago" became one of the prime targets for criticism because it exhibited the "middle-of-the-road characters" propounded by Shao Ch'üan-lin, who was under severe attack at the time. As a result, Ma Feng disappeared from the literary scene and was not cleared until 1973. By 1977, his new works began to appear. Among his well-known collections of short stories are *Chin-pao's Mother, Village Feud,* and *My First Superior.*

Since its first publication in 1958, "I Knew Three Years Ago" has undergone some minor changes, which bear no significance to the story's major theme or style. The following translation is based on a version published in *A Bumper Crop of Short Stories* (Peking, 1959). —L.D.

I Knew Three Years Ago

On my way to Chen Family Village, my mind rambled with thoughts of: "Have there been any changes during the four years since I've left it? Will my old friends still recognize me? And Uncle Chao, the stockman—how's he doing?"

The autumn harvest was already at its end and the fields were a deep autumn color. I didn't care to stop to enjoy the scenery but pedalled my bicycle hard so that I could fly to Chen Family Village in a flash.

After passing Red Bean Village, a newly built irrigation ditch appeared before me. From the distance, I saw three or four people along the bank busily working on something. As I got closer, I saw that they were patching up holes in the dike. Just as I was about to push my bicycle across the bridge, someone suddenly shouted to me, "Hey! Aren't you Old Ma? I haven't seen you in years!" He ran up to me, talking. I stopped.

The man was in his forties, slimly built with thin lips and a pointed chin. He wore a pair of old-fashioned, wire-rimmed dark glasses. His shoes, socks, and trouser legs were splattered with mud. He looked familiar; it seemed we'd met before but I just could not recall it at all. He reached me in three or four steps and shook my hand warmly. I asked him, "Is this a new ditch?"

"Yep. Today's the first day we're letting out the water," he said. "Are you going to our village? Great! We'll talk tonight then!" I racked my brains: he sounded like someone from Chen Family Village but who was he? What was his name? No matter how hard I tried, I just could not recall.

When I crossed the bridge and got on my bicycle, I heard him saying to the others, "Come on! Let's check the eastern side again. I knew all along the new ditch would not . . . " I did not hear the rest; the moment I heard the four words, "I knew all along," I immediately remembered—it was Chao Man-tun of the Chen Family Village Agricultural Cooperative. No wonder he looked so familiar! Whenever Chao Man-tun was mentioned, I would recall the many stories about him. He was really a character!

Chao Man-tun's nickname was "I Knew Three Years Ago." This phrase originated from a woodcut-printed farmer's almanac decorated with a water buffalo in spring plowing. In the old days it was sold near the end of the year. It was commonly referred to as "I Knew Three Years Ago" because a three-year lunar calendar was also printed in this booklet. As to how Chao Man-tun got this for his nickname, there was a story behind it:

He was a smart cookie and really knew how to manage affairs for himself. He was very calculating and nobody could take advantage of him. When sowing in the springtime, he could tell whether it would be better to harvest millet or *kaoliang* for that year; if you wanted to engage in some small business during the slack season, he could tell whether it would be more profitable to sell fruits or vegetables. Although such speculations had no guarantee, they were eighty to ninety percent accurate.

He was alert, sociable, and knew more than the average, simple-minded farmer. Therefore he frequently loved to show off in front of people. No matter what others would say—be it about cows or horses, or national affairs, or even about such matters as physiognomy—he could always put in his line and keep talking about it. One would think he knew everything, but this was not so. Sometimes he pretended to be an expert on things and would exaggerate wildly, making things up in order to fool people. But sometimes he would slip and make a fool of himself.

One year, he was going home with a group of young men after having seen an opera at Red Bean Village, which was five *li* away. While on the road, they talked about the opera, *The Wise Verdict of Judge Pao,* and praised Pao for his fairness and for his iron-faced impartiality. In order to reveal how well-read he was, Chao Man-tun said, "Of course! If Judge Pao didn't have such abilities, why would Emperor Ming of T'ang make him prime minister?"

They were overheard by Uncle Chao from behind. Now, Uncle Chao was well known as an opera fan and could be considered the historian in Chen Family Village. Although he had never read any history books, he had thoroughly memorized such historical romances as *The Three Kingdoms, Water Margin, The Cases of Judge Pao, The Five Girls of T'ang,* and *The Yang Family Generals.* So, after he heard Chao Man-tun's comments, he smiled and said, "Boy! That's really great!—making a Sung dynasty man into a T'ang dynasty minister!"

When Chao Man-tun realized that he had been caught, he immediately defended himself, "So what? T'ang and Sung are not that far apart in time!"

Not only did Chao Man-tun love to hold "big discussions" occasionally, but he sounded as though he had foresight and as though everything turned out the way he had predicted. Whenever something went well, he'd always say, "I knew all along it would be so!" But if something went wrong, he'd say, "I knew all along it would turn out bad!" Eventually, the phrase, "I knew all along," became his pet expression. So the people gave him that nickname.

"I Knew Three Years Ago" was the oldest member of the Chen Family Village Agricultural Cooperative. He voluntarily became a charter member when the agricultural cooperative was formed in the spring of 1951. Everyone thought it was strange, because the other eight charter members were either poor peasants or new middle peasants since the Land Reform of 1947–50, while Chao Man-tun had always been a middle peasant. Furthermore, when the village was in the process of forming an agricultural cooperative, he went around bad-mouthing it. Even up till the day before the eight families held their meeting, he was still saying to the people on the streets, "Even brothers split their homes. Now seven or eight families want to get together. See if they're not looking for trouble!" But on the evening of the next day, at the inaugural meeting, he signed up to join.

At first everyone thought he was kidding, but later, when they saw him put his fingerprint on the application form and pull his mule and donkey to the co-op stable, they realized that he was serious. This became the talk of the village for a long time; no one knew what he was really up to. Later, they discovered the secret from his wife.

It seemed that Chao Man-tun took action to join, but not without pressure. Early on the day of the meeting, he received a letter from his brother, a soldier in the Liberation Army for several years, who had been urging Chao Man-tun to join the cooperative. This last letter was especially strong, concluding with, "If you do not join, we will split our family holdings and I will put my portion in the cooperative." Chao Man-tun felt miserable the whole afternoon. After much thought, he decided that splitting the family holdings would be worse for himself. His wife and daughter were also urging him to join. So, gritting his teeth, he took the plunge—join!

Chao Man-tun's membership gave the cooperative a lot of trouble. He was a senior but the most backward member. His tricks and connivances were unsurpassed. If you heard of them, you would not know whether to laugh or cry.

At first, the cooperative assigned him as the stockman because he had some experience with livestock. At the end of the War of Resistance in 1945, he bought a young donkey for three pecks of grain. It was no bigger than a calf and as skinny as a skeleton. All the villagers said it would not live, but in less than three years the donkey grew big and strong and even foaled. Afterwards, whenever someone mentioned it, Chao Man-tun would gloat and say, "I knew all along it would turn out like this. Raising livestock depends on hard work!" He certainly did a lot for his two animals; he was more patient and considerate with them than with his own children.

Everyone thought it was appropriate to let such a person be the stockman, but who could tell that trouble would come the moment he started to work there? Soon the following ditty appeared on the blackboard bulletin:

> Cows, horses, donkeys, and mules complain,
> A profit the stockman sure has made of them.
> Mules and mares crowd together for feeding,
> Kicking here and biting there in chaos;
> The hay is unsieved, the feed uncooked,
> The trough half full of hay and half of mud;
> The pen is always unkempt,
> And the torn harnesses unmended;
> The co-op's livestock, all skin and bones,
> All need crutches to help them walk.
> His own donkey and mule on another trough are fed,
> Living as if in a palace;
> With the best in hay and feed,
> They're plump and strong like tigers.
> All are animals but treated differently,
> As the sweet stay sweet and the bitter stay bitter.
> Suffering like this,
> Why not quit the co-op when there's still time!

In less than half a year, the co-op members had much to say against him. Finally they held a meeting and subjected him to a good round of criticism. He was reassigned to be a cart-driver, and his two animals were assigned to pulling carts.

Everyone thought this would put him under control, but who was to know that this gave him an even bigger advantage? He would take the opportunity of delivering co-op grain to engage in some small business of his own. Today he'd bring some wine from the city and tomorrow some cigarettes. On the road, he would pick up passengers and pocket the fares. Once when he was sent to pick up charcoal that winter, he passed by a small town and found that they were selling suckling pigs at a cheap price. He had wanted for a long time to buy a sow, but he didn't have any money with him that day. So, he used the cooperative's charcoal money to buy a young sow for himself and returned with an empty cart. He told the co-op chairman, "The bridge outside the Li

Family Town has collapsed and I couldn't get through. I knew all along that this trip would be wasted!" But not long afterwards, the whole incident was investigated and the truth became known. The cooperative held a criticism meeting. Chao Man-tun was given a demerit and relieved of his post.

From then on, Chao Man-tun was to work in the fields, but then he turned to give the brigade leaders a lot of trouble. The co-op members wrote another ditty about this:

> Chao Man-tun, a corrupt mind,
> His work behavior, lazy.
> When the work's hard he feigns a tummy-ache,
> But works on vegetables in his private plot.
> He always picks the easy jobs,
> Not caring for quality but for speed:
> In three shovelfuls, he finishes a pile of fertilizer,
> And the place remains a jungle where he says he has
>   weeded.
> More wheat is thrown away than gathered,
> Don't you think that's weird?
> If the co-op's crops are poor
> Then everyone will suffer because of you!

There was no end to Chao's pickiness or tricks. The brigades also held meetings regularly to criticize him, but that didn't help any. Chao Man-tun had two ways of handling criticism. One was to joke about it. For example, whenever everyone criticized him for coming to work late, he would not discuss it or talk back, but would say with a smile, "Ah! It's obvious none of you have ever seen an opera. The best always comes on stage last!" Or he would take in everything, give no explanation, and stay calm. He would only say, "I agree completely." But the moment he left the meeting, he would have a lot to say, "Huh! Me grabbing for work points! Who doesn't want to earn a few more work-day credits? You keep saying the co-op is your family. Why don't you labor just for the co-op then?" Or, "Even if gold grew from the ground, if you don't earn any work-day credit, you could stare till your eyes pop out and still have no share in it!" He went to all three production brigades in the cooperative but no one wanted him. None of the brigade leaders could handle him and everyone called him "The Headache." They also wrote a ditty about him:

> "The Headache" knows only how to talk,
> To receive criticism is like drinking cold water;
> Always saying "I agree" at meetings,
> But never changing or repenting.

When I was here in the autumn of 1953, in less than three days I heard many such stories about Chao Man-tun from the people, especially from Uncle Chao, the stockman. Whenever Chao Man-tun was mentioned he would angrily say, "It's lucky that the co-op has only this one crafty devil. If there were more, then the whole country would certainly be in chaos!"

Later, when Chao Man-tun and I gradually became closer, I felt that this person was not as bad as others had said. I worked with him, cutting corn and breaking clods in the fields. He was full of energy when he worked. If he saw even just a little piece of a cob left on a stalk he would pull it off and put it in a pile. He was more meticulous than the young people. There was something else unique about him—he loved to talk and have fun. He was almost forty but he still liked to fool around with young people. When working together with him, you would not feel a bit tired. He always made everyone laugh and the day would be over before you knew it. I was quite bothered: Was he actually putting up a front for me? Or were Uncle Chao's remarks not true?

One night, I was talking about Chao Man-tun with Chen Ming-shan, the co-op chairman, and Chen said, "This person used to be very backward. There's not a bit of exaggeration in what everyone says about him. During the first two years he belonged to the cooperative, he was dying to see it fall apart. But he's progressed quite a bit this half year. Good or bad, he's an old member of three years' standing. Even a piece of cold stone warms up after you've carried it next to your skin for three years!"

Hu Feng-ying, Chao Man-tun's wife, also said he had changed recently. I was once assigned to eat with them at their house. The house was not too big but it was complete—the living quarters, the horseshed, the pigpen, the goatpen, and the outhouse—nothing was lacking. The house was neat and orderly. His wife, tall and plump, was almost the same age as Man-tun. She also loved to talk and have fun. They had a son going to elementary school in a small town and an unmarried daughter.

I was a bit late that night because I had some business at the cooperative. Man-tun had already finished dinner and had gone to the fields. While eating, I chatted with the wife. I don't remember how, but we got onto the subject of her husband. She said, "You've probably heard people say that he's the famous backward member of the co-op, haven't you?"

I nodded with a smile and she continued, "He was even more backward when he first joined the co-op that year. Every time he came home he would curse the co-op. 'Who in blazes came up with this damn thing! Even our Number Two Brother has joined the devil, forcing us to hell!' He talked about these things even in his dreams. Once he shouted, 'Save a little every day and next year we'll buy another two *mu* of land.' I woke him up and asked him what he was talking about. He sighed, 'Aw! What the hell can you buy?' At the time, he had joined the co-op but his heart was not in it. Afterwards, whenever the co-op held meetings to criticize him, he would come home to take it out on me."

She paused and then said, "It's much better now. For the past few years, our share at the end of the year has never been less than what we would get if we worked on our own. This has put his mind at ease. Nowadays, he only adds up his work points every few days. He hasn't been criticized for a long time."

Listening to his wife, I knew Chao Man-tun had really progressed. But shortly afterwards—a few days before I was to leave—Chao Man-tun got into trouble again. Autumn harvest was already over. The cooperative had just begun a well-digging project and planned to sink five wells before the ground froze. Chao Man-tun was somewhat experienced with well-digging. Before he joined the cooperative, he had supervised the digging of the well at his home.

The water was good and plentiful. So this time he was appointed as technical supervisor of the cooperative's well-digging project. The man was really something. He took responsibility for all the preparatory work of water prospecting and of starting the well holes. The work was managed in perfect order.

On the third day after the digging began, as the cooperative blackboard was about to write up his contribution, the diggers struck some shifting sand. They sent someone to the village to get Chao Man-tun, but he was nowhere to be found. When asked, his wife didn't know where he was either. She said he had left in a hurry before the crack of dawn. The co-op committee members were very angry. The project needed him now, but he had disappeared.

It wasn't until the second night that Chao Man-tun came back to the village. Immediately, he ran to the co-op office to apologize. Many people were in the office discussing the problem of the shifting sand. They saw him walking in and asked him where he had been. Chao Man-tun stuttered for a long time before saying he had gone to West Mountain to buy jujubes for sale. This infuriated everyone. They all started criticizing him at once and no one could hear what the others were saying. Chao Man-tun lowered his head, squatted on the floor, and just puffed on a cigarette. After everyone had calmed down, he stood up and said, "I know I'm wrong. The devil must have got me! When I was returning to the village from work that day, I bumped into a friend from T'ai-p'ing Village. He had just bought some jujubes from West Mountain. I heard him say that they sold for five to six cents a catty. I figured that by the eighth day of the twelfth lunar month, the price would rise to over ten cents a catty. If I could get a hundred catties, I could make five to six *yüan* with no effort at all. This should be enough to cover my New Year's expenses. Besides, I thought that since the digging was already well on its way, I might as well take a little time off . . . "

Uncle Chao, the stockman, came in to refill his lantern. He cut in, saying, "Your calculated plans are just great and your mind is really active. But you never think of the co-op!"

Chen Ming-shan, the co-op chairman, said, "The cooperative has assigned you to be the technical supervisor. This clearly shows that we trust you a lot and have great hopes in you. But you put aside your work to do some small business for yourself. Of course it's good for you because you can make five to six *yüan* in a couple of days. But if we stop the well-digging for a couple of days, do you know how much labor is wasted? And how much loss could result? Have you ever thought of this? Have you figured it out this way? You can abandon your work to make some money, but if others also follow your example, who's going to dig the wells? Chen Erh-ming is a new co-op member. Because he was afraid of delaying the digging, he didn't even go to his father-in-law's sixtieth birthday party. You're an old member and responsible for this project, yet you could do such a thing!"

Chen Ming-shan's face grew red. There wasn't a sound in the room. Chao Man-tun squatted by the table and lowered his head in silence. A cigarette with a long ash dangled between his fingers. He didn't smoke it or flick it; he just let it burn slowly. Chen Ming-shan said after a pause, "You joined the cooperative with reluctance but have you suffered since joining it? Has it been any worse compared to when you were on your own? You should know. During the hailstorm this summer, the ten *mu* of land that you brought into the cooperative were hit. If in the past you had met with such a disaster, would you have gotten so much grain this fall? When you were suddenly ill in July, co-op members went out in the rain all night long to get you a doctor and carry you to a hospital. They didn't want a cent from you or even a meal. Do you remember that? Also, over one-hundred *yüan* was spent on medicine and shots for you. You didn't have any money so the cooperative lent it to you. In the old society, whether it be a good or bad year, would you have been able to get such a large sum of money so fast? I know you manage your life very well, but to raise that much money you would have had to sell either your house or your land. Why is everyone so concerned with you? Why does the cooperative look after you? Because you're a member of the agricultural cooperative and a member of this big family. But how much have you done for this big family? Do you ever think of this big family at all?"

When Chen Ming-shen finished, Chao Man-tun lifted his head, looked at everyone with moist eyes, and said softly, "I know I'm wrong. I have not forgotten the good that the agricultural co-op has done me. I also want the co-op to grow, it's just that selfishness is still in me. The moment I heard that selling jujubes was profitable, I could only think of my own family. . . . I'm willing to accept any punishment."

Chao Man-tun was very sincere, so no one had anything more to say. Then his daughter came to call him home for dinner. The co-op chairman let him go for now, as the issue was to be discussed later. Man-tun nodded and left.

Uncle Chao whispered in my ear, "Just wait and see. He's going to swear when he gets out of the door."

His words aroused my curiosity. Quietly I followed Chao Man-tun. It was very dark in the courtyard. He walked with heavy steps and the light from his cigarette glowed on and off. I followed till he was outside the gate and only heard his daughter say with disapproval, "Dad, look at what you've done. It's really disgraceful!" Chao Man-tun didn't talk back. He heaved a long sigh and walked on. I did not know whether he hated himself or the others.

I left Chen Family Village the next day so I did not know how Chao Man-tun was to change afterwards.

I was on the road thinking of Chao Man-tun and, before I knew it, I had reached Chen Family Village. I noticed that many new willows had been planted outside the village, which was now surrounded by them. A few roofs could be seen above the trees. I remembered that this was once a nonproductive swamp area. Who could have dreamed that four years of labor could change it into this? I pedalled through the willows on my bicycle. Entering the village I saw many new houses lining both sides of the road. On the threshing ground, firewood and hay were piled up like mountains. The road was also crowded with heaps of grass and leaves. The village was very quiet; I didn't bump into a single person on the streets.

The managing committee office of the agricultural cooperative was still located at the same place. On the door hung a sign saying, "The Three-in-One Advanced Agricultural Cooperative." I pushed my bicycle into the courtyard and saw an old man, wearing a pair of spectacles, sitting on the steps of the west building. He was bending over his work—mending sacks. The sound of my bicycle made him raise his head, and I saw that it was Uncle Chao. I shouted, "Uncle Chao! How've you been?"

He started at me and beamed. "Oh, so it's you! I never thought you'd come here!"

He dropped his work and ran over with a limp to shake my hand. I asked about his leg; he said, "Even when one sits safely at home, disaster still may fall from the sky. The co-op bought a breeding horse this spring and I was rewarded with a kick. Who would have expected that one kick would turn me into a custodian?" Seeing my puzzled look, he explained, "The co-op chairman, Chen Ming-shan, saw that I was limping, so he said 'Forget about the stockman. How about a custodian instead?' I said, 'A custodian's okay with me. Besides, I can't jump anymore. Let the bald-head be the monk. It's just fitting for the part.' All I need is a job. It's better than eating free meals."

As he helped me with my baggage, he went on talking: "Managing our co-op is a big job now. When you were here last, the entire co-op had only fifty-two households, right? Now it's an advanced co-op of over five hundred households. Red Bean Village, T'ai-p'ing Village, and our village have joined together.... Let's go in and have a seat."

Carrying my baggage, I followed him to the office. It was like before, except the wall had a few more charts and banners, and a telephone had been installed. A worker whom I did not recognize was sitting at a table by the window, taking care of some forms. Uncle Chao introduced us; he was Liu Pin, an intern accountant. I asked about the former accountant, Hsiu-ying. Uncle Chao said, "She's the co-op's chief accountant now. She went to the cotton purchasing station in the city to settle the accounts there. Do you know that this year we have sold 120,000 catties of cotton alone to the government?"

When I asked him whether the autumn harvest was over, he said, "We're as busy as mules now, cutting corn stalks, picking leftover cotton in the field, gleaning, irrigating.... Everybody's helping in everything; there's a general mobilization of men and women, old and young. Even the co-op cadres have gone to the fields. Only us two, one old and one young, are left behind to guard the fort." He switched to singing in a gravelly voice, "Look at our fort, inside and out, up and down, left and right, in front and behind. There's only the two of us. Ha! Ha! Ha! ... How's that? Am I not like Ting Kuo-hsien, the opera singer? "

Liu Pin said, "Ting Kuo-hsien would surely bow to you as his master if he heard you."

"That won't do. I'm not even collecting any admission charge." Uncle Chao poured a cup of water for me and left.

Then Liu Pin turned to me. "This Uncle Chao is a very interesting person." Suddenly he asked, "Did you write that essay, 'Uncle Chao, the Stockman?' I read it at school." I nodded and asked him what grade he was in. He said he graduated last year from junior high school and that his home was in T'ai-p'ing Village. Originally a brigade worker, he was just transferred this summer to the managing committee.

As we talked, Uncle Chao carried in some torn sacks and said to me, "You might as well stay in the office and eat at the supply and distribution co-op. I've notified them already. The co-op is next door to Chao Man-tun's house. It's the new five-part structure."

"How's Chao Man-tun doing now?" I asked.

"Chao Man-tun has made a complete about-face. He's a member of the co-op's irrigation committee now and isn't doing too badly. You'd probably never have expected it, right? Neither would I. I used to hate Chao Man-tun the most and even suggested a couple of times to kick him out of the co-op. But the co-op chairman kept telling us to be patient and help him reform. I used to say, 'Even rivers and mountains are easy to change but one's basic nature is difficult to alter,' and that Chao Man-tun would change only if the sun rose in the west. But, this time I made the wrong bet."

I then asked, "What happened that time after he went to buy jujubes at West Mountain?"

Tilting his head, he thought for a long time. Then he suddenly clapped his hands and said, "My! You've got a good memory! That's right, there was such an incident. After our harsh criticism of him, he went to the well before dawn the next day. This guy is really something! He stopped the sand-shifting right away. Later we didn't have enough bricks for the fifth well; the kiln couldn't make any more. Everyone was worried to death, but again he came up with one of his clever ideas. One night, everybody was in the office worrying about it; some wanted to break down their houses and some wanted to tear down graves. Chao Man-tun then said, 'Why are the areas east of our village called Arch Bridge North and Arch Bridge South? There once must have been a brick bridge and it must have been buried long ago by earth and sand. If we dig up those bricks there would be enough for not only one well, but two.' No one believed him. The co-op chairman went to T'ai-p'ing Village the next day and asked a ninety-six-year-old man. It seemed to that old man that there was such a bridge when he was young. Afterwards, with the help of the old man, we actually dug up a brick bridge. This guy is really an 'I Knew Three Years Ago.' I'm over sixty now; even I can't remember such a thing. Who knows how he can remember such things? Don't you think it's strange?"

I was very happy to hear this and asked, "There was no problem after that?"

Mending his sacks, Uncle Chao said, "Think about it. Is it possible to have no more problems with him? Something happened again in the autumn of the year before. It was over the mating of sows." He then proceeded to tell me what happened.

What happened was this: After the autumn harvest of the year before, Chen Lan-ying, the pig-tender, suggested that we improve the breed of pigs by raising a lot of Russian Berkshires. The cooperative managing committee agreed but there were very few Berkshire boars at the time. Only the Ch'eng-kuan Agricultural Cooperative had one and they charged two *yüan* per mating. But they had already contracted with many other agricultural cooperatives; it would be at least two months if we were to wait our turn. For days Chen Lan-ying kept after the co-op chairman but nothing could be done about it. They had to put it aside for the time being.

One morning, Li Erh-kuei, the breeder for Ch'eng-kuan Agricultural Cooperative, was rushing the Berkshire boar on its way to an appointment at T'ai-p'ing Village. He passed by Chen Family Village. Chao Man-tun, squatting in front of the co-op office, saw Li Erh-keui and ran up to him and greeted him. He insisted on inviting Li into the office for a rest.

Li Erh-kuei said, "We can't let your co-op have the pig first. You have another month or so before it will be your turn!"

Chao Man-tun said, "Of course! Even if you gave us the pig to mate, we wouldn't want it anyway. We don't have any sows ready. Come on, come and rest in our co-op. The pig's tired even if you're not."

It was very cold that day and a big dust storm was brewing. Li Erh-kuei thought Chao Man-tun made sense so, without a worry in his head, he followed Chao. After the Berkshire boar was locked inside an empty house, the two went to the office. Chao Man-tun took out a cigarette from his own pocket and offered it to his guest. . . .

Speaking of Chao Man-tun and his cigarettes, there was a story behind that too. Not just anyone could smoke his cigarettes. Always afraid of people getting a free cigarette from him, he would often carry two packs in his pocket, one empty and one full. Every time he wanted to smoke with people around, he would put his hand in his pocket and slowly pull out a cigarette. If someone asked him for one, he would take out the empty pack and say, "It's empty. I only have the one left."

Once while threshing wheat, he took a break for a smoke and pulled his old trick again. Some youngsters made a fuss about it and wanted to search his pockets. Chao Man-tun said, "this pack is also empty," as he took out the other pack and threw it away. Everyone believed him but it was actually a trick. Chao Man-tun thought he'd wait until no one was looking and then pick it up. But, just at that very moment, there was a child playing by the threshing ground. He ran over and picked up the pack and said, "There are still five or six cigarettes left! Why are you throwing them away?" This ruined Chao Man-tun's trick. He had no choice but to smile and share his cigarettes with everybody there. So, every time Chao Man-tun offered you a smoke, it was either to borrow something from you or to ask you for help. His cigarettes were never "wasted." . . .

That day, Chao Man-tun lit a cigarette for Li Erh-kuei and also busied himself about boiling water for tea. He said he had to go out for firewood, but he sneaked over to the empty house and pushed the Berkshire boar into the sow pen next door. Then he got the firewood to boil water, while talking with Li Erh-kuei about everything under the sun. Those in the office thought the two were really friends.

The fire was low so the water was slow to boil. In fact, Chao Man-tun had purposely brought back green wood to delay everything. Li Erh-kuei was getting a bit impatient, but when he saw how nice Chao was, he did not feel right about leaving. By the time the tea was ready, an hour had already passed.

Chao Man-tun figured that by now the three sows should be finished with their mating business. So, pretending to go to the outhouse, he put the Berkshire back in the empty house. Li Erh-kuei didn't have the slightest idea as to what had happened; he even thanked Chao again and again before leaving.

When Uncle Chao reached this part of the story, Liu Pin and I were laughing uncontrollably. Uncle Chao was also laughing and said, "You see how devilish this guy is! When the co-op members heard about this, they were all very happy and thought that Chao Man-tun had done a good deed for the co-op, especially Chen Lan-ying, the pig-tender, who laughed so hard that she could not stop. Chao Man-tun also said proudly, 'I knew all along that after he finished mating at Red Bean Village yesterday, he had to go to T'ai-p'ing Village today. I can't let him pass our customs gate without paying a toll!'

"When the co-op chairman returned from the city and heard about this, he was extremely angry. He criticized Chao Man-tun, saying he was wrong, tricky, and taking advantage of others, and he had ruined the honor and credibility of the co-op. Many people did not understand this at the time. Neither did I. Feeling this was unjust, Chao Man-tun said, 'I gave up a cigarette and wasted half a work-day. Was it for myself? It was all for the co-op.'

"But the co-op chairman said, 'Is it right to harm our brothers' cooperative for the sake of our own? Forget for the moment that we've cheated Ch'eng-kuan Cooperative out of their six *yüan*. I ask you, how many sows can one boar mate a day? Li Erh-kuei did not know that halfway on his journey, the Berkshire had worked itself three times. When it went to T'ai-p'ing Village to mate again, could it impregnate the sows there? What if by chance the sows do not conceive. Won't this ruin T'ai-p'ing Agricultural Cooperative?' When he put it this way, everyone felt that something was wrong and didn't know what should be done. The co-op chairman suggested paying back the price of mating the three sows to Ch'eng-kuan Agricultural Co-op. He also wanted Chao Man-tun to go to T'ai-p'ing Village and apologize.

"This seemed to be a very good solution. But Chao Man-tun would rather die than go. He said, 'It's all right to pay back Ch'eng-kuan Co-op, but to apologize to T'ai-p'ing Village? No way! I didn't even use their co-op pigs to mate.' We were busy involving T'ai-p'ing Village and Red Bean Village to form an advanced co-op; so the matter was put aside."

"What happened afterwards? Did the T'ai-p'ing Village pigs mate?" I asked.

The sound of shuffling feet and laughter interrupted Uncle Chao. From the window I saw the women returning from picking cotton and gleaning the fields. The quiet courtyard suddenly became alive. Uncle Chao gathered the mended sacks. As he went out, he smiled and said, "Go ask Chao Man-tun about the sow incident. He's more clear on that than I am." He turned around at the door once again and said, "It's time for dinner. Go there yourself. It'll save someone a trip coming to get you."

I wanted to see Chao Man-tun after this, so when dinner was over I left the supply and distribution cooperative for Chao's house. I pushed the door and saw only Hu Feng-ying, his wife, washing dishes. When she saw me she smiled and said, "So, it's Old Ma! I've just heard from people on the streets that you've arrived. What wind has blown you this way? Please sit on the *k'ang.*" She poured some water and gave me a cigarette. I thought Man-tun had already left after dinner, but she told me he still had not returned. She said, "He's been busy irrigating the land these past few days. Today's the first day for the Harvest Ditch to release water—that's the one you'd see if you come from the city. I don't know when he'll be able to come home. Ai! He didn't even take any food with him when he left this afternoon."

I joked, "He's an irrigation committee member. If he's hungry he can just drink water."

Hu Feng-ying said in a complaint, "Don't ever mention water! Ever since he became an irrigation committee member, the land has water, of course. But if we at home want anything to drink, that's a different matter! The water jug is often empty. He's so busy he's got no time to fetch water and I'm stuck at home with a nursing baby."

Only then I noticed a baby sleeping in the corner of the *k'ang.* "You've added another member to your family," I remarked.

She smiled and said, "I married off my daughter last year, and this year I gave birth to a son—no loss, no gain, just even."

I asked her what her elder son was doing now; she said he was going to high school in the city and was already in the tenth grade. I chatted with her as I waited for Man-tun's return. She told me that he was quite a different man now from what he was before. His mind was always on the problems of the cooperative. Sometimes he could not sleep all night long because of the irrigation work. Last year his brother took a leave from the army to visit home. When he saw how enthusiastic his elder brother was about his work, he was very happy. After he went back, he sent many books on irrigation to Man-tun and even donated a level to the cooperative.

Proudly, Hu Feng-ying said, "You know, he wants to prove himself for Party membership! Sometimes when I complained to him about neglecting his family, he would criticize me for being backward and I would say, 'How long has it been since you became progressive?' He would answer, 'I knew all along you'd say that!' " Hu Feng-ying laughed loudly and so did I.

After an hour, Chao Man-tun still had not returned, so I left. When I stepped through the gate, a bright flashlight beam caught my face. It was so glaring I could not even open my eyes. I heard the familiar voice of Chen Ming-shan, the co-op chairman. I ran over, shook his hand, and asked him what he was doing. He said the tractor station had just called to say the Red Star Cooperative had already finished their own plowing and were coming tonight to help the Three-in-One Co-op. He had to go and supervise. I asked for permission to go along.

Chen Ming-shan and I talked about Chao Man-tun. He also said that Man-tun progressed a lot during these few years. The most important thing was that now there was a "cooperative" in his mind. Whenever he did something he would consider it on the basis of the "cooperative's" advantage. He no longer worked only for his family as he used to do. Chen Ming-shan continued, "Chao Man-tun was selfish in the past, which was not strange at all. He was a middle peasant pressured into the co-op to begin with; even if he were a poor peasant joining the co-op of his own free will, we could not expect him to become selfless overnight. For generations our peasants have been struggling, each one for himself. An agricultural cooperative is stronger than a single household. To join a cooperative does not mean one can make a turnabout in one stroke. Just like a rustic suddenly finding himself in the city. Even though everything in the city is much more convenient, it would still take the rustic some time to get used to it. It takes time to reeducate a person like Chao Man-tun."

"You certainly have worked a lot to reeducate Chao Man-tun," I remarked.

Chen Ming-shan said, "You are way off on that. Can one educate another all by oneself? If not for the efforts of the group, Chao Man-tun would still be Chao

Man-tun." He went on after a brief pause, "I went to a district Party committee meeting once. Secretary Liu of the committee gave a lecture and said, 'When individual output changes into collective output, then the economic foundations will change and the people's ideology and consciousness will gradually but surely change.' I did not think much of this when I heard him at first. Then I thought it over carefully. He actually makes sense."

The last time I came to Chen Family Village and met Chen Ming-shan, I felt he was not the type of co-op chairman who was concerned only with production. When I heard this from him, I knew then that he was a man with "ideology."

Our walk, punctuated by our conversation, had already taken us quite a way from the village. It was so dark that you could not even see the fingers of your hand stretched out before you. . . . When we reached Arch Bridge North, Chen Jen-ming, the brigade leader, and two machine operators were already waiting there. One of the operators was Chang Cheng-wan, who had raised livestock for two months, and the other, whom I did not recognize, was a high school student. The two tractors arrived shortly with four drivers, among whom was also a woman. Chen Ming-shan discussed the plowing with them and we then went back along the ditch.

Past the Chao Family Graveyard, several lanterns appeared ahead of us, where a few people were arguing about something. Fearing that a dike might have been broken, we ran toward the noise. But it turned out to be just a water diversion ditch; several people were talking excitedly there. We saw Chao Man-tun in the lantern light, shouting, "No! Hurry up and open it up! I knew all along that you would be up to your devilish tricks!"

"It's so dark now; what are you afraid of? The Red Star Co-op is not going to send anybody here," said an old man.

A younger man said, "Really! You want the horses to be strong but you don't want them to graze. You want us to irrigate the land more but you won't give us water!"

Chao Man-tun said, "We are in a hurry to irrigate our land; won't the Red Star Co-op want to do the same? Would you like what you are doing if the tables were turned?"

We found out that those two co-op members had diverted part of the water in the Red Star Cooperative's ditch into ours. Chao Man-tun discovered us. Without greeting me, he turned to the co-op chairman. "Here comes the co-op chairman. Let him tell you." Chen Ming-shan criticized the two co-op members and made them adjust the water diversion gate for the Red Star Cooperative.

The co-op chairman then turned to Chao Man-tun, "You'd better hurry home to eat; and don't you come out again tonight."

Chao Man-tun said, "I was just about to go home; otherwise my stomach would revolt." He cleaned the shovel in the ditch and wiped his eyes with a red handkerchief he had on his chest. No wonder he wore dark glasses during the day; there was something wrong with his eyes.

"You should go to the medic station and have that looked at," I said.

He replied, "I've already done that. It's okay, just a slight inflammation."

We waited until he put his things together. Then we started to walk back to the village. I asked Chao Man-tun about the pig-breeding incident. He smiled,

"Uncle Chao must have told you. I knew all along that this old man would tell you anything bad about me! What do you intend to do about it? Do you want to 'publicize' my faults in the papers again?"

I also smiled. "Not necessarily."

"Well, I might as well give you a complete confession," he said. He paused and then went on. "Not long after the pigs mated that day, our co-op joined Red Bean and T'ai-p'ing villages and formed an advanced cooperative. The new co-op decided to bring together all the Berkshires to be raised in Chen Family Village, because we had a flour mill which yielded better hog feed. The following spring, the sows were about to have piglets. The co-op chairman sent me to help Chen Lan-ying, the pig-tender. I agreed, but I didn't realize the chairman was trying to put me on the spot. Each of the four sows from Red Bean Village had about a dozen piglets. Each of ours had about seven or eight. But the two sows from T'ai-p'ing Village, well, let's not talk about it anymore! One of them had three, the other had only two. One piglet died at birth; the four surviving were no bigger than white rats. Boy, did my face turn red! Some of the people there said, 'Oh! Look what Chao Man-tun's done for our co-op!' Even if nobody said anything, I felt bad enough. That was really like picking up a rock and smashing it right on your own foot."

When Chao Man-tun finished his story, he talked to Chen Ming-shan about expanding Harvest Ditch. He wanted to build two more ditches next year, by which time 70 percent of the cooperative's land would be irrigated. He also wanted to plant two rows of willows along the banks of the ditch. Not only would this strengthen the dikes but it would also bring in a big crop of willow branches for weaving baskets. He went on, "Willows are easy to handle and grow. They don't grow tall and won't obstruct the crops growing along the sides. In one year we can get at least 35,000 catties of willow branches. Let's say one catty will get 2.5 cents; two times three is six and three times five is fifteen. That will be 750 *yüan*. If we add 5,000 catties, then two times five is ten and five times five is twenty-five. Altogether we'll have over 870 *yüan*. That's equal to over 2,000 catties of grain!"

Chao Man-tun was very excited and pleased with himself. It was as if he had an abacus in his brain. This expert in managing affairs was thinking only of the big family now. Chen Ming-shan liked his plans and said it would be proposed to the managing committee in a couple of days.

That was a night when autumn passed into early winter. The hour was late, but nothing was at rest yet in the countryside. Lanterns were ablaze, pumps rumbling and water rushing. The roar of the tractors completed this symphony. Chao Man-tun turned to me, "Old Ma, do you think we've changed at all?"

"Oh, yes, and how!" I said, thinking that not only has life changed, but more importantly, the people have changed.

He said, "I knew all along that we would change. Wait another three years and see!"

I responded, "I knew all along that you are an 'I Knew Three Years Ago.'"

The rest was drowned in laughter.

Translated by Lorraine Dong

OU-YANG SHAN

(Ou-yang Yang-i, 1908–)

Ou-yang Shan came from a poor family of Kwangtung. His involvement in the leftist student movement led to his dismissal from the Normal School of Canton, after which, with Kuo Mo-jo's help, he started as an auditor at the Sun Yat-sen University. He participated in the Kwangtung dialectal literary movement, one of the many promoting the use of vernacular language over the more formal classical idiom, which had not changed in centuries. His first successful novel, entitled *Faded Roses,* appeared in 1927. He moved to Shanghai to study under Lu Hsün, a signal figure in the "literary revolution" that had grown out of the May Fourth movement, and wrote "national defense literature," like so many others during the Sino-Japanese war. He attended Mao Tse-tung's Yenan Forum on Literature and Art in 1942 and, while still at Yenan, published the well-received novel about peasant life in the border areas, *Uncle Kao,* in 1946. Immediately following the revolution, he became a member of the National Committee of the All-China Federation of Literary and Art Circles, which he served until being branded a gangster and revisionist during the Cultural Revolution, in September 1966.

His downfall was the outcome of the criticism and controversy surrounding the first two volumes of his incomplete saga, *A Generation of Noble Souls,* a work intended to illuminate the failure of an idealistic generation of Chinese youth to achieve their revolutionary goals, torn as they were between personal survival and the urge to strengthen a war-torn, foreign-dominated China. The first volume, *Three-Family Lane,* was published in 1959. From the declining years of the Manchu dynasty through the Canton Insurrection of 1927, it chronicles the fortunes of members in three neighboring households that span the social spectrum of Republican China. The Chou family is headed by a blacksmith, the Ch'en family by a comprador-capitalist, while the Hos represent the upper end of society as landlords and high-ranking Kuomintang officials. The second volume, *Bitter Struggle,* published in 1962, follows the struggle of the young revolutionaries into the countryside near Canton from 1928 to 1931.

These two works fell under fire in 1964 as examples of erroneous thinking, of "commemorating a reactionary line" identified with the Liu Shao-ch'i clique during the Cultural Revolution. Ou-yang Shan's own son is said to have made a public denouncement of his father's criticism of the Great Leap Forward, manifest in such short stories as "The Remarkable Villager" (1960) and "In the First-Class Sleeping Car" (1961).

His *Generation of Noble Souls* did not conform to the Marxist notion of class antagonism, for the actions and sympathies of the characters are not wholly attributable to their class background. Indeed, the history of these three households that share the same lane is a tale of the constancy and essential unity of human nature. Ou-yang Shan was found guilty of writing a petty-bourgeois novel under revolutionary guise, of creating characters rather than characterizations, personalities rather than psychologies. Ultimately, *Three-Family Lane* remains one of the only fictional accounts of the failure of the urban revolution, and these two selections bring us to the China of the 1920s, as seen through the eyes of the youngest son of the working-class family, Chou Ping.

In January 1979 Ou-yang Shan announced that he had resumed writing his five-volume saga. He said that the manuscript of the third volume, of which only the first five chapters were serialized in a Canton newspaper in 1966, was seized by police during the Cultural Revolution. He further planned to revise the first two volumes as soon as he completed the last chapter of the entire project. —H.K.

from *Three-Family Lane*

Main Characters:

CHOU T'IEH, the father of Chou Ping, blacksmith and head of household on Three-Family Lane

CHOU PING, youngest son in the Chou family

CHOU YUNG, second son in the Chou family

CHOU CH'ÜAN, sole daughter in the family

CH'EN WAN-LI, comprador-capitalist, head of the second household on Three-Family Lane

CH'EN WEN-HSIUNG, only son of Ch'en Wan-li

CH'EN WEN-TI, second daughter of Ch'en Wan-li

CH'EN WEN-CHIEH, third daughter of Ch'en Wan-li

CH'EN WEN-T'ING, fourth daughter of Ch'en Wan-li

HO YING-YÜAN (or Fifth Master), landlord and high-ranking KMT official, head of third household on Three-Family Lane

HO SHOU-JEN, eldest son of Ho Ying-yüan

HO PU-CHOU (or Second Granduncle), bookkeeper and manager of the Ho estate in Chen-nan Village; also called "Unencompassable Ho"

HU YÜAN, a tenant farmer for Ho Ying-yüan

CHANG TZU-HAO, son of a landlord, husband of eldest daughter in the Ch'en family, Ch'en Wen-ying

LI MIN-K'UEI, son of a landlord

OU T'AO, younger daughter of a cobbler; sweetheart and cousin of Chou Ping

[In the language typical of the *pai-hua* fiction of the 1920s—particularly its dated mode of dialogues, which sounds rather quaint now—*Three-Family Lane* begins with the tale of how Chou Ping, youngest son of a blacksmith married to the sister of the wife of the Ch'en household, is taken under the wings of the Ch'en family, only to be booted out when he exposes Mr. Ch'en's attempt to seduce a maidservant. Victimized again and again by his impulsiveness and incorruptible nature, in this episode Chou Ping shows for the first time a concern for human needs, at the risk of self-incrimination under the rules of an oppressive society.]

THE COWHERD

Although the second daughter of the Ch'en family, Ch'en Wen-ti, was a schoolmate of the boy-next-door, Young Master Ho Shou-jen, they very rarely spoke to one another at school. Shou-jen had a delicate build, so the girls all snubbed him. Even though he had money and dressed himself handsomely, if she went over and addressed just a few remarks to him, the rest of the girls would certainly make her the laughingstock of the school. Shou-jen would typically spend an hour or two in her company at the library, on the playground, or just in the schoolyard, and never find the occasion to say so much as a single word. Yet now and then the opportunity did present itself.

On that day, they bumped into each other once again in the schoolyard. Wen-ti glanced in all directions to make sure no one was about, then turned toward him and said, "In your opinion, Master Ho, are the body and soul of a human being identical, or are they opposites? For instance, let's consider the case of Chou Ping, that little imp who lives on our Three-Family Lane. Everyone agrees upon his physical attractiveness, but opinions vary when it comes to his soul. If the body and soul are identical then he must be a good person, but if they are opposites then he must be a bad person. Won't you give me your advice on this matter, Master Ho?"

While speaking she flashed him an affectionate smile. Her hair was brown, the color of palm-tree fibers, her eyes were palm-brown, and her face was palm-brown too. In fact, her entire body seemed ablaze with the color of palm. While Ho Shou-jen gazed at her, he felt as though she had melted him on the spot—he could find the strength neither to move nor to answer her back. Seeing that he was so distressed, Wen-ti gave forth a self-satisfied giggle, and just walked away laughing.

Shou-jen was plunged into a state of complete remorse. Most of the time he could think of many things to talk about. But why was it that when it came time to use them, not even a simple sentence emerged? He was so ashamed that he tore at his hair.

After a while he thought back over every word Wen-ti had uttered. "Are the body and soul of a human being identical? Yes, what she said is correct, they must be identical. And what about that little imp Chou Ping? Why did she call that jerk a 'little imp'? I've got it—this means that she feels affection for him. Otherwise, why would she have said that everyone agrees upon his physical attractiveness? I've got it—feeling affection for someone and noting that someone is physically attractive are also identical!"

He finally deduced several things from her questions. He concluded that Wen-ti regarded Chou Ping as a good person. He concluded that Wen-ti was in fact enlisting his aid toward Chou Ping. He concluded that her questions were a kind of expression of her feelings for him. Because of this, he too began to regard Chou Ping as a good person. Moreover, he gradually developed a friendly feeling toward him, because he believed that such behavior would enable him to identify with Wen-ti.

Within a few days, he proposed to his father, Ho Ying-yüan, that Chou Ping tend water buffaloes for their family in their native village of Chen-nan. His father said, "Doesn't he steal the belongings of others?" Ho Shou-jen set the record straight: "Of course not. How could that be true! I have objectively concluded that he is a good person!"

After hearing his son defend Chou Ping, Ho Ying-yüan nodded his head and promised that it would be taken care of. Chou T'ieh and his wife had no recourse but to sigh and try to make the best of the situation. They waited for the bookkeeper to come from the country on one of his business trips, and when he arrived, he took Chou Ping back with him to Chen-nan Village.

That bookkeeper was named Unencompassable Ho, and was as plump as a fat pig. He was forty years old, the same age as Ho Ying-Yüan, but because he was elder in terms of clan seniority, everyone called him Second Granduncle.

Chen-nan Village is situated about twenty-five miles from the provincial capital, and one could get there by walking or by taking a train part way and walking the remainder of the distance. Walking, however, was the furthest thing from the mind of Second Granduncle, so he and Chou Ping journeyed by boat.

When they got aboard, he gave no instructions to Chou Ping, indeed said nothing to him at all, but instead fell fast asleep and began snoring loudly. It seemed as though he had entirely forgotten about Chou Ping. Ping for his part was glad not to be bothered. He took up the oars and helped the boatman with his rowing.

Along the way they passed by farmsteads and waterways, an unbroken landscape of trees and flowers, palms and mulberry . . . it was all very enjoy able.

Eventually they arrived at a secluded landing, where tree branches hung low upon the water. The boatman gave the oar a twist and guided the boat to rest against a miniature enclosed dock. They had reached Chen-nan Village. The village consisted of a sand bar that floated upon a river. Although winter had arrived, the trees were still lush with color and the chirping of birds was incessant. The full 2500 acres of land could not be taken in with a single glance, and now that the late-ripening crop of rice had been harvested, flocks of small birds were busy gleaning in the fields. Half of this land belonged to the Ho family. In addition to the part leased to tenant farmers for cultivation, the Hos worked on over thirty acres of the best water paddies, with the help of some ten-odd hired farmhands.

Every day Chou Ping set out early and returned late, tending water buffaloes for the Ho family. Among those hundred-odd families of tenant farmers, Chou Ping liked the family of Hu Yüan the best. This year Hu Yüan turned fifty, and his wife reached forty-three. They had two daughters and two sons. The eldest daughter, Willow, was twelve, the eldest son, Tree, was ten. The younger son, Pine, was eight years old, and the younger daughter, Apricot, was six just this year.

Hu Yüan was a distant cousin of the wife of Ho Ying-yüan, and at first he managed to eke out an existence upon a small plot of poor land he inherited. Then he took a wife and started raising children, and through a series of natural and other disasters his estate collapsed. Because of the Hus' relation to Mrs. Ho, Unencompassable Ho secured Ho Ying-yüan's special permission to lease some land to Hu to till without the usual security deposit.

The Hu children were all still young. The whole family depended on Hu

Yüan and his wife's working in the fields all year round. Hu Yüan was an honest and big-hearted fellow, and so took to looking after Chou Ping constantly. He saw to it that his clothes were washed and mended, and when there was soup or tea invited him to come and take a sip. The children, face-to-face with a city dweller of countless adventures and broad background, often surrounded him and asked about this and that. No matter whether it was an account of the sibling fights in the household of Ho Ying-yüan on Three-Family Lane, or gossip about the family of Ch'en Wan-li, or the incident involving that good-for-nothing junior proprietor of the Blue Cloud Shoestore, Lin K'ai-t'ai, whom Chou Ping once clobbered with a hammer for bothering the lovely Ou T'ao, or the episode in which Chou Ping was blamed by that deceitful clerk Kuo Piao for pilfering from the cash box in the Universal Deliverance Pharmacy, they were all held spellbound by his tales. As for the unearthly beauty of Ou T'ao, they all adored her and wished they too might see such a beauty. As for the illustrious past of Chou Ping, they envied his experiences no end and felt that their lives would be complete if they were to live through any one of those adventures. In a short time Chou Ping became a familiar guest in their home and soon came to be treated just like one of their own.

When winter came around there was no more work to do, so Unencompassable Ho instructed Chou Ping to go and clean out the granary. In his spare time, Chou Ping would go and amuse himself at the Hu household, where he learned all about planting and harvesting and the effects of wind and rain upon the crops, as well as chipping in with carrying water and fertilizer and planting vegetables.

One day the sky darkened and rain began to pour, and as the cold set in the family of Hu Yüan had not a grain of rice to put in the pot, so young and old alike became sullen and depressed. After spending the entire day pounding rice, Chou Ping was completely worn out, so he threw on a raincape and set off for the Hu household.

By this time it was already mid-afternoon, but as the daylight is short in winter, in every household he passed the stove had been lit and dinner was being prepared. Chou Ping pushed open the gate to the Hu household and, while removing his cape, yelled out "Willow . . . Willow." The entire household was gathered in the main room, but not one of them answered him. Hu Yüan was stretched out upon a plank-bed opposite the stove. It was hard to tell whether he was sleeping or awake. His wife sat on the edge of the bed, her head bent over the tatters she was mending with concentration. Willow was sitting upon a bamboo chair in front of the ancestral figures. She felt too lethargic to move, as if every ounce of strength had been drained from her body. The only sign of animation whatsoever came from Tree, Pine, and Apricot, who were sitting on the floor playing a game of bean-toss.

At first Chou Ping felt at a loss as to what to do. Then he strolled over to the stove and felt it with his hand—it was cold, so he asked, "How come, Uncle Hu, you haven't started the rice yet?"

"Not hungry!" was the grudging reply of Hu Yüan, accompanied with a long sigh. As Chou Ping observed that Hu Yüan was in a bad mood, and that none of the others felt like talking either, he, not knowing what had gone wrong, just slipped quietly onto a small stool and made no further remarks. After the amount of time it takes to smoke about half a pipeful of tobacco Hu Yüan began to speak again, "Ping, what kind of work did you do today?"

Chou Ping very cautiously replied, "Nothing much; I just pounded rice all day."

"For whom? For Second Granduncle?"

"No. It was for Fifth Master Ho Ying-yüan himself. New Year's is just around the corner, and he has been asking us to hurry up with the rice."

"Is there no rice sold in the city?" Hu Yüan said. "How is it that store-bought rice isn't good enough for him; instead he insists upon rice from his own paddies?"

"Uncle," Chou Ping answered, "you have no idea. Rice from neither Annam, Siam, nor Shanghai suits Fifth Master. The only rice he enjoys eating comes from his own village." This stirred the interest of Hu Yüan, who turned over and sat up nimbly and said with enthusiasm and pride, "It's so true. No matter what people say, rice from Annam, Siam, or Shanghai cannot compare in taste with rice from our village. But really, taking the rice to a mill to hull it is all he need do, what use is it wasting your time pounding it yourself?"

"That won't do at all!" Chou Ping said. "Neither adults nor children in the household of Fifth Master will eat machined rice at all. They say that it's got the smell of gasoline! They will only eat rice hulled at home."

While Hu Yüan was still mulling over the appetite of the family of Fifth Master Ho, his wife, listening by his side, completely lost her patience, and interrupted her husband. "You just stick to your own business. What has the kind of rice they like to eat got to do with you? First go out and bring back a little something to eat so I can fill up the bellies of our children, then let's talk about the rest!"

Hu Yüan opened wide both palms in despair and said, "And just how am I supposed to do that? We don't have any rice. We can't borrow any either. Perhaps we can eat another meal of boiled turnips like this morning!" When she heard him mention boiled turnips again, Mrs. Hu had nothing further to say. But Tree, Pine, and Apricot cried out in unison, "Mom! Dad! No more boiled turnips! Please, no more ... we want sweet potatoes, we want to eat sweet potatoes."

Willow, who was slightly older than the others, and a little more under-standing, knew that they hadn't any sweet potatoes either, and just cried, off to one side. Outside, a cold wind lashed and harsh rain poured down, and the spattering sound went on and on. Mrs. Hu thought and thought, then finally she too began to cry, and said, "How many days has it been since the last harvest? How long will we have to wait for the new year? for the next crop? Everyone else is busy celebrating the New Year, eating chicken, duck, fish, and pork; will turnips be all we have to eat? Even that won't help us to last through the middle of January. How can you expect us to go on like this! One would be better off dead! Yes, death itself would make the whole thing simpler! At least you wouldn't have to spend each month wondering whether you will live to see it end, or each year whether you will live to see the next!"

Chou Ping realized that they had nothing at all to eat. Without saying a word, he threw on his raincape and dashed out. He ran over to the kitchen, and seeing that the chief cook was oblivious to all else except preparing dinner, snatched a bowl and scooped out four bowlsful from the rice crock. He stashed two bowlsful in each pocket, which altogether weighed no less than five pounds. No one at all observed him. Having secured the rice, he again threw on his raincape and, in a single breath, ran back to the household of Hu Yüan. Upon arrival, he removed his shirt and emptied the contents of both pockets into a basket for washing rice, panting so hard that he could barely catch his breath.

The children leapt up with joy and surrounded him to take a look. They cried out, "There's rice, there's rice . . . we have food to eat, food to eat," without a pause. Even Mrs. Hu set down her tattered clothes, jumped off the bed, and lifted the rice basket to pour it into the pot. But the arm of Hu Yüan shot out and stopped her. "Hold on a minute!" he said, then turning to Chou Ping, "My good child, where on earth did you get this rice of yours?"

"It spilled out while I was pounding the rice." Chou Ping invented a story.

"I've never heard of such a thing!" Hu Yüan did not believe him. "How can rice be spilled when you are pounding it?"

Mrs. Hu became angry. She shoved away her husband's arm, saying, "Who cares whether it spilled out while he was pounding the rice or if it pounded out while he was spilling the rice! Let's eat first and discuss later." She emptied the basket with a whoosh into the pot. She added water and also cut up a few large turnips to throw in. The children scrambled over to light a crackling fire, and in a short while they could smell the aroma of cooked rice. Everyone invited Chou Ping to eat with them. He refused, but he tasted the good rice in his mouth just the same when everyone else was eating it with great relish.

The next day the sky had cleared, and it was even colder. When Chou Ping went to pound rice for the day, the first thing he did was to hide a small amount of it. After he had finished his hulling and his other chores, he took out the rice and stuffed it into a pocket on the inside of his shirt and then, pulling his old padded jacket over it, set off in the direction of the Hu family.

Hu Yüan was unwilling to accept it and would not say a word. Chou Ping scooped out one handful after another and put it in the rice basket, while Hu Yüan seized each handful as it came and tried to stuff it back into Chou Ping's pocket. "We cannot accept it," Hu said, "we cannot accept it, we simply cannot . . . " Meanwhile, a good quantity of rice had spilled out upon the ground, and groups of chickens in twos and threes flew in from next door and began pecking it up. Chou Ping was at the end of his wits and called out to young Apricot who had just turned six, "Come on, let's go outside and play." Once outdoors, he stuffed the rice into Apricot's pockets.

From that time on, Chou Ping used this method. Whenever he had spare time, he would come and ask the children to play. Then, he would stuff that snow-white grade-A rice into the pocket of one child or another. This situation produced fear in Hu Yüan as much as it elicited his gratitude. As a result, he began to find fault with his wife at the slightest provocation. One day, after a particularly violent spat, Hu Yüan sat off in a corner and muttered to himself: "It's all right to take what is yours to take, but don't you go taking what is not. When you do accept something, first you should try to find out who it belongs to. You think it's fun to take something! You think that family ever throws away anything? When you see something good to eat, you just gulp it down. You don't ever worry what's going to happen later, do you?"

Sometimes, when the rice was prepared and set out at the table piping hot, Hu Yüan would sit off to one side and mumble to himself, unable to bring himself to eat. His wife would say, "Go ahead and eat! Eat in peace what you have worked hard to earn. Do you mean to tell me it contains poison? Why sit there staring?"

"How I wish it were only poison," said Hu. "It's something much worse! I'm not concerned about myself; what worries me is the children."

Mrs. Hu began to cry again. She picked up a damp handkerchief and, covering her face with it, said, "Then you tell me how to go on living like this. May God help us all! If one is going to die, what difference does it make whether he eats poison or not? Let's eat well first, then let's all drop dead. It'd be much better than dragging on like this. Don't you tell me about worrying over the children, you heartless creature! Just look at how they've been starving—and you're still unwilling to let them eat!" Hu Yüan gazed at the children, who gazed back, each pair of eyes wide open, not daring to take a bite. Hu Yüan had no recourse but to let out a long sigh, lift up his chopsticks, and begin eating.

When Chou Ping heard the children's version of the events, he felt troubled. "Why do they feel I have done something wrong?" He thought and thought again but could not figure it out. On one occasion, he overheard Hu Yüan talking to the children, "Just you go ahead and eat. One day someone will find out about it, and when it comes to a tribunal in the ancestral shrine, won't we be looking pretty!" It was the original intention of Chou Ping to help the Hu family, but he had only succeeded in making them more miserable. He really hadn't the slightest idea why this matter would be brought up in the ancestral shrine, nor what the judgment would be—he could only keep the worry to himself.

Although the Hu household was not without its troubles, and each day seemed harder to pass than a whole year, time kept slipping by unnoticed, so that the year was out in the blink of an eye, and spring of 1921 had arrived. When it came time for spring plowing, Chou Ping tagged along with Hu Yüan and learned all about plowing, harrowing, and preparing the land for planting. Since the Hu family did not own any draft animal, young and old held on to ropes and pulled the plow themselves. Although Chou Ping was in charge of the Ho family's water buffaloes, he was not at liberty to lend them out, so he pastured the animals on a nearby embankment and joined the Hus in the plowing.

The time had come for soaking the rice seeds for sprouting, but the Hu family had no seeds. Again it was Chou Ping who thought of a way of obtaining some from the granary of Fifth Master Ho. A pocketful at a time, he did his best to accumulate enough for them. Hu Yüan stopped declining but simply said, "I swear before god that we will pay Fifth Master back in the future. Not a single grain less! If I can't pay it all up this life, I will do it the next life, even if it means coming back as a horse or a buffalo!" After all the seeds were planted, Chou Ping continued to sneak rice to the Hus from time to time for their food. Hu made no further refusals, but every time he accepted it he would make a vow, saying that in future generations they would simply have to pay back their debt.

Willow, Tree, Pine, and Apricot grew accustomed to playing with Chou Ping. They were all so close that if they missed being together for as much as a single day, everyone would feel terribly out of sorts. Willow once heard her parents lamenting the fact that they had no boys the age of Chou Ping, for such a lad would surely be a great help. She subsequently brought up the subject to Chou Ping, saying that she wished he'd become their brother. Apricot, who was standing by his side, brushed her fingers on her cheek to shame her elder sister, but after a while, she too began to call him elder brother. Hu Yüan and his wife, seeing how much their children adored Chou Ping, also wanted to have him as their adopted son but never found the occasion to tell him so.

The weather had turned warm. One day Chou Ping stuffed two pocketsful of rice inside his shirt, threw on his jacket, and walked out of the granary. On such a nice day as this, it would surely be uncomfortable to wear a padded jacket, but he had to keep it on to hide the rice. Who could have foreseen that, having walked only a few steps, he would suddenly run smack into that fatso Unencompassable Ho? When that Second Granduncle saw Chou Ping looking suspicious, wrapped in his winter jacket in such warm weather, he shouted out, "Where do you think you're off to?" He caught up with Chou and gave his jacket a yank. Chou Ping jerked away, freeing himself from the hand of Second Granduncle, but he could not prevent the rice from spilling out in a stream.

The situation turned sour. As expected, Unencompassable Ho beat him and coaxed him, but Chou Ping would not divulge the true circumstances. Finally, he said that he had lost in gambling and had no other recourse but to steal some rice to repay the debt. When questioned regarding his debtor, he was again unwilling to talk. Unencompassable Ho became so enraged that his entire bulk of fat began to quiver. Chou was kicked out of the house immediately without supper.

He tied all his belongings in a bundle on his back, went out to the main entrance of the Ho house, and sat down alongside the highway that ran through the village. He thought to himself, "Shall I go by the house of Old Master Hu to bid him farewell, and say a few parting words to Willow, Tree, Pine, and little Apricot? Mrs. Hu was so kind to me, will it do not to stop by?" But then he wondered how he could face them after getting himself into such a predicament over something so minor, and he decided not to go.

He reflected for about an hour, then tied the bundle upon his back again, brushed the dirt off his clothes, and followed the highway listlessly back toward Canton. It was well past the second watch when he arrived home.

[Four years pass, during which Chou Ping watches the youngsters on Three-Family Lane pledge their service to their country in her struggle to create a political identity strong enough to overcome warlord rule over the countryside and foreign control of the urban centers. The interaction between the rise and repeated setbacks of the Communist Party, founded in 1923, and the struggle against foreign domination sets the scene for the rest of the novel.

In the following episode, we are brought into the cynical, compromising world of the privileged Chinese. Ch'en Wan-li, comprador neighbor of the rich, landholding Ho family, enumerates the recent events, which terrify his businessman's heart, to the fascinated but undisturbed Ho Ying-yüan. Rallies protesting the brutality against Chinese workers, culminating in the violence of the May Thirtieth Massacre in Shanghai and the Shakee-Shameen incident that follows, result in massive work stoppages and embargoes of foreign goods. Shanghai, the stronghold of European colonization, is crippled by strikes.

On June 23, 1925, students and workers band together for a mass demonstration, in conjunction with a general walkout of Chinese seamen from British shipping companies. As the marchers approach Shameen, an island housing the firms and merchants involved in the foreign trade imposed upon Canton for well over a century, panic breaks out and fifty-two of their number are killed.]

THE STORM

The fluffy clouds upon White Cloud Mountain gathered together and drifted apart in succession, so that in the twinkling of an eye several months had passed, and it was now the last third of the month of June.

On the afternoon of the twenty-third day of the month, the sun broke through for a while, then the sky became cloudy and rain began to pour, creating an oppressive, humid heat. After Ch'en Wan-li finished lunch, he tried to take a brief nap but couldn't fall asleep, so he crawled out of bed and went to pay a visit on Ho Ying-yüan.

He strolled into the living room, but instead of Fifth Master Ho, he came upon the eldest son, Ho Shou-jen, seated along with Li Min-kuei and Chang Tzu-hao, the husband of his own eldest daughter. The room was extremely spacious. The north and south walls were lined with a set of rosewood formal chairs; marble-topped tables and stools were placed in the middle. Set against the center of the east wall was a glass hutch, in which assorted curios and jewels such as jade, agate, coral, and decorative rocks were displayed. Bookcases flanked the hutch, containing volumes of essays, fiction, and classical poetry and prose. Set against the west wall, underneath a window, was a large rosewood chaise lounge, complete with a matching tray and inlaid on three sides with marble. The window was framed in mahogany carved in the shape of sunflowers, holding panes of red, yellow, blue, and green glass. When viewed through the glass, the bamboo outside of the living room acquired an exquisite blue and green coloration.

Being a friend of the family, Ch'en Wan-li just sprawled out upon a rosewood couch to one side of a bookcase and struck up a conversation with the young people. "Today they're holding another demonstration march," he said. "Why aren't you young people getting into the act instead of hiding yourselves here?" Chang Tzu-hao and Ho Shou-jen just giggled and didn't speak a word, while Li Min-k'uei poked fun at him: "Now tell me, my fine man, why you yourself don't go and join in the festivities?" Ch'en Wan-li feigned an air of indignation and replied, "I was thinking of going, but I'm afraid you young people would knock me down. Aren't you the ones who spend the whole day talking about overthrowing the comprador class?" Li Min-k'uei picked up his line of reasoning and chimed in, "That's exactly why we decided not to go out and join the march. We do not find it fulfilling to lend our support to the Communist Party."

Ch'en Wan-li reflected upon this for a moment, then slowly stated, "According to that theory, the workers who came back from Hong Kong to participate in the strike are all Communists!" When Ho Shou-jen saw that no one attempted a rejoinder, he said, "Granted, you can't go around making irresponsible statements like that. Nonetheless, it cannot be denied that this particular strike was instigated by the Communist Party."

Ch'en Wan-li made a faint snort of acknowledgment, and said nothing more. Later on he turned and addressed his son-in-law, "Tzu-hao, I never really asked you about it before, but I'm curious about that warlord Ch'en Chiung-ming, whose influence extends across the eastern half of our province. If the Eastern Campaign of your Canton Revolutionary Army was so successful, why did you withdraw your troops?"

"Father," Chang Tzu-hao said, "you saw it yourself, didn't you? It's just that we want to overthrow the warlords Liu and Yang."

"The Yunnan and Kwangsi armies trafficked in opium and ran gambling joints; they are indeed warlords and should be overthrown. But have you overthrown that Ch'en Chiung-ming?" Ch'en Wan-li said.

"He's been taken care of," Chang Tzu-hao said, chuckling; then he quickly added, "Well, almost ... "

"Just as I said, a lot of work for nothing," said Ch'en Wan-li with a laugh. "If you can't even topple a single warlord, how can you talk about overthrowing something as vast as Imperialism? What do you know of Imperialism anyway? I personally would make a quick withdrawal of forces. The foreign airplanes, cannons, tanks, and warships are not coming here just to fool around with you!" At this point in the conversation, the group of young men had nothing further to say to him, and withdrew from the living room into the library.

Ch'en Wan-li lay down for a spell, alone in the room until Ho Ying-yüan made a dignified entrance, dressed in a diaphanous silk shirt and bead-sewn, straw-bottomed slippers. In his hand he held a fan made from goose feathers. When Ch'en Wan-li saw him, he sat up on the couch. "Fifth Master," Ch'en said, "it has only been a few days since I saw you last, how is it that you have grown thinner by the day?"

"Ah, to be like you instead," Ho Ying-yüan said, "who no matter what problems arise in this world of ours, never really takes them to heart. I saw you just a few days ago, and it seems you are getting plumper by the day!"

The two men engaged in such pleasantries for a while before turning to more pressing matters. "Fifth Master," Ch'en Wanl-li said, "what will come of the dispute over the post of counsellor in the provincial government?"

"I appreciate your concern," Ho Ying-yüan replied, "But what we're dealing with here is a movement that sparks up one day and dies down the next, never really coming to anything. For the moment, at least, the post will be kept. It's not that I crave the job or lust after the salary, it's simply that we cannot allow the Red elements to seize power and do with it as they please, not granting so much as a voice to the rest of the provincial assembly. Even if I permitted it, do you think that Sun Yat-sen's acting commander-in-chief, Hu Han-min, would stand for it?"

"That's right, of course you're right." Ch'en Wan-li clapped his hands in approval. "We businessmen cannot fathom the tricks of you politicians, but to tell the truth, I've spent the greater part of this year in fear and trembling, and rarely ever get a good night's sleep. It's been one crazy event after another. How can a man not be driven utterly mad? Just you count the incidents: in February of this year it was the Eastern Campaign, in March and April, memorial services for "Big Gun" Sun Yat-sen. When May came around we were sitting even prettier with the formation of both the Labor Congress and the Peasant Representative Assembly. A hundred thousand people took to the streets shouting and cursing, and it was none other than you and me that they were cursing! Next came the May Thirtieth Massacre, when those radical Chinese demonstrators, protesting against the abuses of the "Imperialists," were gunned down by the British in the International Settlement of Shanghai. Then the campaign against Liu and Yang, and now the Hong Kong worker's strike! What are we to make of all this? Haven't you seen how the young men in the household of that brother-in-law of mine, Chou Chin, Chou Yung, and Chou Ping, have developed a glazed look in their eyes, which soon turned red? If this isn't madness, then what is? Who allowed them to participate in such insanity? Has our police force locked itself away in an outhouse somewhere?"

Ho Ying-yüan remained unruffled. He just smiled. "What do businessmen know besides business?" he said. "A disturbance is not wholly undesirable, and may even contain certain advantages. It's only when things get out of hand that we have to worry. You'll see—there will come a day when they will tumble and fall very hard. There is every caliber of man in their very midst, including that Chiang K'ai-shek, who's got something in him. At the moment, he still seems to be a leftist. But don't you forget, between him and Hu Han-min lies a bit of the "one mountain ain't big enough for two tigers" problem—he's just too audacious. But if Hu Han-min can keep him in check, he too may be of some use.

Ch'en Wan-li did not particularly enjoy listening to the ins and outs of what he considered one big game of "hide-and-seek," so he changed the subject. "Fifth Master," he asked, "that group of bastards is planning to put on another ritual procession today, and I heard that they are going to march as far as the foreign compound at Shameen. Have you caught any wind of it yourself?"

"How could I avoid knowing?" Ho Ying-yüan said, with an impenetrable smile. "Isn't this just one more instance of those Commies stirring up trouble again? Well, the authorities over at Shameen are prepared for them. The moment they arrive, we're going to witness one hell of a 'roadside funeral service.' How those scores of souls wronged in the May Thirtieth Massacre will flock down upon Canton in search of fresh bodies! There's simply no way to escape what has been preordained!"

Ch'en Wan-li scratched his grey-haired scalp and thought it over, then said, as if he had come to a sudden realization, "If I understand you correctly, the British are still going to play tough."

Ho Ying-yüan looked smug, and, slashing the air with his goose-feather fan, he said, "Of course! Are you insinuating that they aren't permitted to act tough? Do you mean to tell me that they fear the likes of them? No, my friend, all we need do is watch the show, and what a pretty sight it will be!"

"Is your source reliable?" asked Ch'en Wan-li in a whisper. Fifth Master pretended to be angry, and said, "Reliable, unreliable, who the hell knows? You realize, of course, that my line is close to the foreign quarters!"

Ch'en Wan-li said no more. Upon returning home, he found his son, Wen-hsiung. "Hsiung, my boy," he said, "don't go back to the office this afternoon in Shameen. You needn't even go there to excuse yourself; a phone call will suffice." Ch'en Wen-hsiung had just put on an open-collar shirt and carried a Western-style jacket on his arm. He put down the jacket and asked, "Why? What have you heard?"

"They're prepared for action!" Ch'en Wan-li said in a low voice. "Haven't you had enough after that massacre on Nanking Road in Shanghai? Kissing one's life goodbye is no solution to any problem."

Wen-hsiung's face flushed and his heart began to palpitate. Finally, he managed to contain himself and said, "If that's how it is, I simply won't go back to work." He returned to his room and flopped down on the bed; he didn't stir for a long time. Then he got up and climbed up to the third floor, intending to break the news to his sisters Wen-ti, Wen-chieh, and Wen-t'ing. But they were out. He dashed over to the Chou household to discuss the matter with his cousins, but he only found Chou Ch'üan. Hearing the awful news, she became upset.

"Little Ch'üan," Ch'en Wen-hsiung said to her, "have no fear. In principle, we Chinese are in the right. All we need fear is that those Imperialists have no regard for principles . . . Do you know whether all the young people in both our families are going to participate in the march today?"

Chou Ch'üan shook her head, "I have no idea, but we can be sure that our mischievous Ping is going." She then placed a hand over her heart and said, "May God protect him."

By this time, upwards of a hundred thousand high-spirited demonstrators had already set forth from East Drill Ground. The leading contingent of marchers was composed of workers returned from the Hong Kong strike and resident Canton workers. They traversed the length of Yung-han street, then walked along the esplanade of Pearl River, heading toward the intersection of Hsi-hao-k'ou and Shakee boulevards. The rest of the column was composed of farmers, students, and patriotic residents who followed at their heels. Ou T'ao, Chou Ping, Ch'en Wen-chieh and Ch'en Wen-t'ing were all present in the ranks. But none had seen each other except for Ou T'ao and Chou Ping, who had exchanged a nod and smile at the very outset.

The demonstration was like a great river whose tumultuous waves whipped up to the heavens in anger. There was no sound in the air but a roar of anger, no desire save that of vengeance. Like a peal of thunder echoing in the skies above Canton, its rumble and quaking sent tremors through White Cloud Mountain, rocking London, Washington, Tokyo, and Paris alike.

Ou T'ao was marching and shouting along with the workers' contingent. She could not make out the sound of her own voice but instead heard a different kind of sound. Brute and majestic, it reverberated above her head with the force of a tempest, a hurricane. When she heard the sound, all at once she felt a surge of strength in her hands and feet, and no longer sensed that she was an individual marcher but rather a marcher one hundred thousand strong. What a powerful person she became! When she recognized such power, her courage increased a hundredfold. How she wished she had already arrived at Shakee Street. Ou T'ao believed with all her conviction that if the awesome force of these hundred thousand marchers were to weigh upon Shameen, the imperialists would have no recourse but to submit to the Chinese people.

Chou Ping felt the same way. He was marching in the student contingent about half a mile behind Ou T'ao. He too was shouting while marching along with the crowd. He too heard a brute and majestic sound reverberating above his head with the force of a tempest or hurricane. He too felt a surge of strength in his hands and feet, and no longer felt he was a single marcher but rather a marcher one hundred thousand strong.

He felt as though he could discern, somewhere in that deafening roar of a hundred-thousand marchers, the passionate, resonant voice of Ou T'ao. Chou Ping imagined that it was Ou T'ao herself conducting the voice of a hundred thousand demonstrators shouting out slogans. He tried with all his might to make his own voice audible, by thrusting forward his head and giving it his full throat, but it was never loud enough. To his great chagrin, the moment the words left his mouth they were engulfed by the voices of myriad others.

Before long they arrived at Sea Pearl Park, rapidly approaching Shameen. Chou Ping was overcome with a new sense of strength, a power more determined and fearless, which surged through the contingent from front to rear. His eyes were set open even wider, and his fists clenched even more tightly. He was no longer hearing any voices, but instead the sound of a raging storm exploding in his ears. Years later the sensation he felt at that moment would remain with him. He felt as though the contingent was no longer formed of even columns four abreast, bur rather that everyone was marching arm in arm, Ou T'ao's arm in his own, creating one long, horizontal line advancing upon the enemy . . . advancing mercilessly to crush the enemy . . .

Sure enough, a gust from the raging storm of anger was advancing mercilessly upon Shameen. The colonial settlement was terror-stricken from top to bottom. A certain low-ranking military officer who was standing upon the East Bridge of Shameen behind an iron fence and a row of sandbags was more frightened than most. He had already received orders stating, "If the situation so dictates you may open fire upon the Chinese pigs." By this point he was pulling out his handkerchief and wiping the sweat off his brow repeatedly. He saw with his own eyes that those heroic, valiant workers had already crossed the East Bridge and were heading straight toward the West Bridge.

As he sensed the awesome force of the raging storm, his legs turned to jelly and he felt as though he were about to faint. He sensed that Shameen was on the verge of siege, that the houses on Shameen were all tilting and about to topple over. He recalled that his son had just boarded a ship in his homeland bound for the Far East, to fill a post as assistant manager in a Western firm. He thought of the boots he had used to discipline a Cantonese rickshaw puller just the other night. Then he thought about the Chinese women he had fondled whenever he felt like exercising his right to fondle them any time he pleased. He called to mind all the opium, gold, and other smuggled goods amassed in his bedroom . . .

All this would perish before his very eyes. His heart beat so fiercely that his face turned pale in fear. He felt just like a mangy dog who had been driven into a blind alley, where there was no one to take pity on him, and where he would certainly be beaten to death. His corpse would be cast into the ocean, and floated back to his native land upon the lashing waves.

When his imagination got this far, he felt like crying, like screaming. Finally, he yelled out, "For the glory of our fatherland, for the glory of our fatherland —Forward March, boys . . . "

The foreign soldiers all understood the foreign words he uttered, but cast a bewildered glance in his direction, wondering what on earth would prompt a man like him to say such a thing. What is more, they saw no way to carry out his orders. In front of them was an iron fence tightly chained up, while sandbags barricaded the areas both behind the fence and on the side of the bridge. How were they to charge through?

The foreign military officer saw that no one had made the slightest motion, so he pulled out a pistol and fired it off in the direction of the crowd. The rest of the men followed suit ... It was in this manner that the vile, shameless, bloody massacre began.

The first to suffer casualties were marchers in the contingent of Cantonese workers with their glorious revolutionary tradition. Ou T'ao was marching in the center ranks of the group, and as it pressed closer to Shameen, she could feel her anger rise. She had a clear view of the foreign soldiers along East Bridge, whose guns were aimed in her direction. With all the strength she could muster, she shouted out, "Down with Imperialism!" For her this was no longer a slogan, but rather, it spelled out the message written upon her heart. Suddenly, there was a loud explosion some ten or fifteen yards away. This was followed by a rapid succession of gunfire. At once she understood what was happening. She looked on as one of her fellow workers fell to the ground at her side. She started screaming without thinking about anything else, "Let's go! Grab their guns! Kill them! Long live the workers! Long live China!" She continued to shout while marching forward.

The gunshots grew thicker, and their smoke obstructed the range of her vision. She suddenly realized that Chou Ping was not at her side. If only he were there, he would be able to jump up and snatch the guns from the enemy! But now it was up to her to do it.

Then, in the space of time it takes to blink an eye, she felt everything thrown into confusion. It seemed as though a heavy rock had struck her chest. Her eyes could no longer see, her ears could no longer hear. She wanted to scream, but no sound came out. She felt so odd, so very odd, where was she? Nothing remained but the summer sun, which she made out as a huge blur: that sun was always so bright, so very bright ...

At first, the demonstrators were thrown into chaos. Some continued to march forward, some wandered off to the sides, and some turned back in retreat. The entire group of a hundred thousand marchers halted for a moment, long enough for the meaning of the gunfire to sink in, then several seconds later the full wrath and fury of the crowd was unleashed as they broke away from their formation and pushed, shoved, or burrowed their way forward. Some marchers burst out with new extemporaneous slogans, "Raze Shameen!" "Annihilate the Imperialists!" and "Long Live the Workers of Canton!"

Chou Ping just followed the crowd forward as if he had lost all consciousness. He saw nothing and heard nothing, he only concentrated on locating the contingent of Cantonese workers. When he reached Hsi-hao-k'ou, he saw that the road ahead had already been sealed off by the police. The bulk of the crowd was just turning the corner to head north on Peace Road. Some of the demonstrators had already scattered, while others just stood around here and there in small groups, occasionally shouting out their slogans.

The atmosphere created by all the shooting kept igniting the crowd. Chou Ping looked everywhere, but the Cantonese worker's contingent was nowhere to be found, so he returned to the area that had been sealed off, pulled out a first-aid badge and fastened it to his sleeve in order to gain admittance into the prohibited area.

Just at that moment, a white red-cross ambulance zipped by and stopped right in front of him. In the vehicle, a man dressed in worker's garments motioned to him yelling out something. Chou Ping climbed aboard the ambulance and stood upon the running board at the side of the driver. The ambulance flew toward the scene of the incident at East Bridge as if it had sprouted wings. When they reached the end of the street, they all jumped down from the ambulance, sprinted over to Shakee Boulevard, and proceeded with their job quickly, solemnly, without speaking a word. The shops were all closed and locked up; Shakee Boulevard was still from one end to the other.

The only spectacle was the presence of men in grey and white coming and going. A passing shower had left small puddles of water gleaming upon the stone-paved street. Faint cries issued from the lips of the wounded. Their bright red blood trickled over the ground of their fatherland, spreading a brilliant color, and filtering at the same time down through the cracks between the stones deep into the soil below. The street appeared to be inlaid with rubies.

A foreboding sensation weighed upon the heart of Chou Ping. He suddenly caught a glimpse of a figure in white that had fallen facedown into a pool of blood. He believed that it was a woman. He seemed to recognize her and walked over to her. She was lying upon the ground, her two arms extended in front of her, as if she were preparing to leap up and continue to charge forward. Her jaw was perched upon a rock, her mouth contorted in anger, and her eyes staring wide open, as if keeping a watch upon the enemy.

Chou Ping bent over, and as he tried to help her stand up, he called "Ah-T'ao, Ah-T'ao ... " She made no response, but turned limp and buried herself, motionless, in his arms.

He raised his fist toward the murderers in Shameen and shook it a few times in anger, then carried her up with both his arms. But somehow, at his very first step, the two of them toppled to the ground in a rush of darkness.

[In the aftermath of what came to be known as the Shakee-Shameen Massacre, Chou Ping falls ill, while the city is paralyzed by a retaliatory strike. Following the heinous murder of his beautiful Cunégonde, we find our young Candide rudely awakened to the realities of the most corrupt of all possible worlds. After a long convalescence he emerges with the resolution to avenge Ou T'ao and her heroic companions and embarks upon the long road toward the revolution. Yet revolutionary ideals are turned into revolutionary illusion, as one by one his generation of noble souls become collaborators with the counterrevolutionary government. The end of the first volume of the saga finds Chou Ping aboard a ship to Shanghai in search of the Communist Party.]

Translated by Harry Kaplan

LIU CHEN
(1929–)

At the young age of nine, Liu Chen had already started working for the Communist Eighth Route Army in North China as a "little red devil," a courier delivering messages and doing propaganda work. Her brief schooling in 1941 ended in her arrest, and from then on she stayed in the T'ai-hang mountain region, sometimes masquerading as a boy to escape detection. There is much in the story "The Long Flowing Stream" that is autobiographical.

After 1949 she studied literature at the Lu Hsün Academy of Arts and in the literary workshop sponsored by the Chinese Writers Association. She published a great deal, mostly stories of her pre-1949 experience told in a refreshing style, brisk, nervy, and engaging. Very popular among younger readers, her works have been collected in *Treasure Hunt in the Western Realm, Paths in the Woods,* and other anthologies.

The veteran short-story writer Ai Wu has said of Liu Chen's works: "Her characters are never simple, though the language under her command adheres faithfully to the colloquial speech of the locale. It is real, lively, picturesque, humourous, and at times stunning."

In the 1960s she continued working in the countryside in North China. Like most of the writers, she also was criticized and remained silent during the Cultural Revolution. Her new writings started to appear in 1978.   —K.Y.H.

The Long Flowing Stream

I

How childish I was at thirteen!

My home was a small village on the North China plain, from which, no matter what direction you cast your eyes, the earth spread out flatly in front of you. I often wondered what mountains were like. Taller even than a poplar? And if you stood on the very tallest summit, how far from the sky would you still be?

In the spring of 1943, the Party sent me to the T'ai-hang Mountains; it was only then that I discovered that mountains were, after all, made of rock. In the mountains there were old temples and lush green woods. A long stream meandered down between the peaks and I wondered where it flowed. I thought myself to be in a dream world.

Our whole family had come from Shantung to southern Hopei to take part in the work of the revolution. It was infuriating how the enemy, in their various "mopping-up" campaigns of the previous year, had carved up the southern Hopei revolutionary base area into small pieces by constructing watchtowers and digging defensive moats. On the other hand, had they not done so, the southern Hopei party committee and school would not have moved to this small village in the T'ai-hang range, and I wouldn't have had the chance to see the mountains.

On the day after I arrived, cadre Wang of the Organizational Department called me in and asked me: "There is both a rectification team here and a regular school. Which would you prefer to join?" I thought it over awhile before asking him, "What will the older comrades who came with me be doing?" Cadre Wang said, "They'll be in rectification, of course." "O.K., then I'll be in rectification too," I said without hesitation. Whatever was most useful and most glorious was always done by the older comrades, so it wouldn't do to lag behind them.

A woman comrade seated beside me interrupted, "What would a child your age have to do with rectification—you belong in school!" I glared at her; her face was covered with freckles, and, by the look of her, she'd just come up from the plain as well. I gave voice to my displeasure with her remark: "Oh! so only *you* are allowed into rectification? Well, I'm going into rectification in spite of what you say and we'll just see what you can do about it!"

Cadre Wang laughed. "All right, all right, you go into rectification." He turned around and said to the woman comrade, "She's young, but she's been in the revolutionary ranks since she was nine. She's been in propaganda, a messenger—she's even been captured twice by the enemy. So it's just as well that she raise her consciousness through rectification."

I wished I could say to the woman comrade: "So there! Won't that shut you up for a while?" But instead, she smilingly stood up and took my hand: "Shall we go then?" I twisted away from her: "What do you think you're doing?"

Cadre Wang stood up quickly and said, "I haven't introduced you two yet. This is comrade Li Yün-feng, chair of the Tsao-nan county Women's Association to Save Our Country; now she's group leader in the Sixth Rectification Team. I'm assigning you to her group and you'll have to obey her from now on."

"What a mess I'm in now," I thought to myself.

When we arrived at the women's dormitory, you should have seen her go into action: borrowing a basin from the owner of the house, going to get hot water, getting out her washrag and soap, she said peremptorily, "Off with your clothes now. Wash!" Hey, what did they think they were doing with this big, steaming basin of hot water, slaughtering a pig? I stood there stuck in my tracks until she gave me a push: "Wash your hair first."

For convenience on the job, I had shaved my head when I became a messenger. I said indignantly: "Just what hair am I supposed to wash if I don't even have any?"

"Your head can still be dirty even without hair."

"But without dirt, where could crops grow?"

"So you're not only dirty, but naughty to boot."

"When I was in the enemy-occupied zone, I scrambled around all day long without anybody telling me to wash this or wash that. You're the only one who's ever been so picky."

Without further ado, she reached out her hand and pushed my head into the water and proceeded to wash me from head to toe, just about taking off a layer of skin while she was at it. She was winded when she had finished and she said, "There! That's much cleaner than the piglet you were."

"I brought that layer of dirt up with me from home and now you've cleaned off even the faintest smell of the old place," I pouted.

"You can go back and sniff at your hometown smell to your heart's content after you've finished your studies."

Suddenly, the main door opened and ten or so women comrades poured in, some with hair in braids, others with it short, all singing or talking and laughing loudly. They had cast off their false hairpieces and did not have to pretend to be bashful, young village matrons anymore. Once out from under the view of the enemy, it was as if they went wild; they could do what they pleased. When they caught sight of me, they gathered around and began to discuss me: "Our group has a new comrade, eh? Hey! So young?"

"But isn't this a young boy? Where's your hair?"

"You're going to participate in rectification? What if we criticize you and you break out in tears?"

I spoke out: "You're the one who'll cry!" I didn't choose to continue to be the subject of their chattering analysis, so I broke out of their encirclement.

Another comrade, who still had the air of a farm wife, came in with some food. She smiled at me and said, "We're in the same group, my name is Yü-chen. I've brought dinner, so why don't you and Yün-feng eat."

Yü-chen stared straight at me as we ate. Had I been thin-skinned it would have embarrassed me. Unprompted, she told me, "I'm from the third subdistrict's Women's Association. I came up into the mountains carrying a child on my back, but now he's staying with a farm family here." She spoke as if she couldn't suppress the information any longer.

At night all twelve of us slept on a large *k'ang.* They had squeezed out space enough for me, with Yü-chen on my left and Yü-feng on my right. Sitting in the light, Yü-chen was sewing a padded jacket for her child, while Yü-feng had gone to the room of the house's owner. I pointed at Yü-feng's empty bedding and softly asked Yü-chen, "Is she an all-right person?"

Yü-chen put on a grandmotherly expression and said, "She sure is; she's a senior-high graduate, a leader of the student movement in Tsinan before the war. She was put in jail three times by the warlord Han Fu-ch'ü. She had to be bribed out each time with her father's money. Her father is a businessman who finally asked her whether a well-brought-up girl like her wasn't ashamed of her continual trouble-making. He told her that they would support her at home, but if she were arrested again, he wouldn't waste his money to get her out. She told him that if he were ashamed of her he could keep his precious money at home and that if she were arrested again he didn't need to waste it on her. He was so mad his beard bristled and he smashed a huge teapot. She walked out then and never went back. Now she's on our county's Party committee."

Wow! That's quite something!

II

Of the ten or so comrades in our group, Yün-feng was the oldest and the most experienced, so everybody called her "Big Sister." In the rectification process some of the women comrades couldn't take it when they heard a slightly contrary opinion, and they would go back to the dorm and have a secret cry. I thought to myself, aren't you the ones who're the crybabies? I never cried even once. But Big Sister would just quietly call each of these women out and talk with them in low tones while sitting on the rock by the door. Sometimes they didn't come in to sleep until the middle of the night.

What I didn't know was why she insisted on being so strict with me. Everybody else got a big thick book to read, while all she found to give me was a primary school grammar or a math text book. She gave me volumes one through eight and told me brusquely, "Aside from reading the material on rectification, I want you to use your time wisely and read these texts. When you've mastered them down to the last punctuation point, I want you to learn multiplication and division. And don't be even the slightest bit careless about it."

You see! I had a mother-in-law before I'd even grown up.

The village in which we were staying happened to be undergoing a struggle against bad landlords. When the tenant farmers had a problem they would come and consult with her and she would stride off to help them solve it. She would go into the home of whoever was having difficulties and offer suggestions, even mediating marital squabbles or disputes between young women and their mothers-in-law. Without invitation or without even knowing the people she would march right in, as if going into her own home. She was only the head of a county Women's Association, but it was as if all China was hers to manage. But whenever the village people saw her they would break into smiles. The saying goes that two women are as loud as cymbals and three make a whole band, and when she and the other women got together she alone made as much noise as a whole opera. It was only when she saw me that her face would become stern and her voice icy, as if I'd owed her money in some previous life and had refused ever after to pay her back. She would leaf through my notebook and say, "Your characters are written so hastily! You must write them one stroke at a time. Don't try to run before you can walk."

That really got me angry: didn't *you* all just scribble things down as fast as you could go? So why should I be the only one who isn't allowed to write quickly? Young or old, I'm still a cadre and when I listen to a report how am I supposed to take notes? But she had an answer for everything: "All right, you can write more quickly when you're taking notes, but you have to make a clean copy later on." How could I disobey this? She was playing mother-in-law after all.

The long creek was behind the house we lived in. There were lots of pretty stones along its banks, rectangular ones, round ones, pink ones, and pure white ones. I filled my pockets so full that they bulged like toad's bellies and made a racket when I ran. I went out to gather stones every evening after supper and never came back before dark. By that time Big Sister would long since have opened up my textbooks and been waiting for me. When I came in she would ask, "Have you finished your cavorting? Time for study!"

If the truth be known, I had become accustomed to complete freedom of action in the zone occupied by the enemy. If I wanted to, I'd study for a while, but if I didn't, I'd just go out and play. The enemy would come every couple of days and we'd have to hide in underground tunnels; there had never been anyone like her, with her eyes constantly fixed on me. For anybody else, it was just rectification, but lucky me had this whole extra set of troubles. Well, no way out, I just had to sit down to study! But I always felt a bit victimized; I would stare at her and say, "You're so cutting when you speak, I don't like to listen to you."

Off to one side Yü-chen said, "She's hard on the outside, but a softy inside. She's a good heart." I turned my head and retorted, "Of course you'd say she's good; when your child didn't have any clothes, she used her own vest to make some. She won you over when she gave those little clothes to you."

"Hey, hey," said Yü-chen with a smile. "If you don't believe me just wait and see. If you're without clothes, so long as she has any, she'll give them to you."

"Well, I'm not a little baby, I wouldn't want any." Stifling a smile, Big Sister patted the text. "This is what I'm giving to you and you'll have to take it whether you want it or not."

So I sat there studying and pulling my long face, my mouth in a great pout. I always managed to make a few noises in order to irritate her. After we'd finished the lesson she stared at me for the longest time, finally sighing, "You really are the limit. You'll understand when you grow up." I gave her a sideways glance. "I'm not so young you know. I had cadre rank at the platoon level in my propaganda team even three years ago."

"Hmph! I don't know whether to laugh or cry about you."

I pointed at her face. "What about you? I don't know whether to laugh or cry about you." She laughed at that, grabbed hold of me and playfully hit me.

I asked her once, out of the blue, how many children she had. "Two," she replied.

"Who's taking care of them for you?"

"Their grandmother."

That evening I was wrapped in my bedding while she wordlessly patched up my worn-out padded jacket. It was true that autumn had passed and winter was coming. The leaves of the persimmon tree drifted down one by one into the creek, whose water had become somewhat chill. As she pulled on the thread she sang a very pretty song, which she said was a lullaby. At that moment I thought she was wonderful, and I asked her softly, "Do you miss your children?" Neither nodding nor shaking her head, she just grinned. I tried to encourage her. "You shouldn't worry. Their grandmother will take good care of them." The whole roomful of women burst out laughing. Yü-chen said to me in a soft voice, "You silly girl. She isn't even married yet." Well, I didn't believe that—how could there be a person still unmarried at age twenty-eight? I asked her huffily, "Are you married or not?"

"I was just teasing you," she giggled. I grabbed the quilt and yanked it over my head. "If you aren't ashamed of yourself, then I don't want to have anything to do with you." Yü-chen stuck her head under the covers and said softly, "She had a very fine boyfriend who was killed last year just after they agreed to get married." Oh! My heart sank as I stole a glance at Big Sister. Her face was calm. The small light of the lantern shone in her eyes as she began again to sing her lullaby:

Little baby, you sleep well,
The wind waits to carry you to the endless sea
The thunder will take you to the limitless sky . . .

"You hear?" Yü-chen whispered. "She made that up herself. She can write poetry too." I pondered that for some time. Poetry. What could poetry be?

III

After that I began to like Big Sister a bit more. Even the freckles on her face became agreeable. I thought once as I looked in the mirror how nice it would be for me to have freckles too, if my face were as pale as hers.

Whenever I made her angry, I thought of how her boyfriend had been killed and I quickly pulled my face out of its pout. But once when we were having a meeting, I just couldn't help myself. Whenever she criticized someone else, she would always address them as "comrade," but whenever it came to me it would be "Young Liu" this and "Young Liu" that, just as if I weren't a cadre at all. This was rectification, and all the others were dignified with words like "class consciousness," "standpoint," or this or that "ism." But me? She despised me, and didn't even grace me with so much as a single political term. It was as if I were a little ruffian who'd been caught stealing melons and was only worthy of having my crimes counted off against me: "Young Liu is lazy in her studying, she's not being realistic at all. She hasn't even mastered basic arithmetic, but she's still arrogant and self-satisfied and refuses to think about the long term. The revolution is going to require many things of us and we must continually take stock of ourselves."

When the meeting was over we took up with my lessons. My anger hadn't diminished at all, so I said to her nastily, "One Jap plus two Japs equals three Japs. If all you worry about is addition those three Japs will never be killed off." Angry and smiling at the same time, she said, "If that's the way you choose to think, don't bother learning anything at all; you'll see what happens to you." I said, "Of course I'll see what happens to me. What will happen to me tomorrow morning is that I'll eat four bowls of millet and drink five bowls of herb soup." I didn't care whether she objected to what I said or not—I ran out of the room.

I ran to the creek, took off my shoes and sat on a big smooth rock. I soaked my toes in the clear water and began to clap my hands and sing:

We're in the T'ai-hang Mountains
We're in the T'ai-hang Mountains
Mountains high and the woods so dense
Soldiers stout and our horses strong . . .

A little bird cocked its head and peered out at me from a crevice in the rock, as if to say, "That was good, let's have another." It didn't have to ask, as I sang one song after another, my enthusiasm growing with each one. It was as if I were conducting a chorus: the breeze blew, stirring up sparkling ripples of water like so many eyes gazing at me.

Altogether I sang fifteen songs. When it became dark and I returned to the dorm, I continued to sing as I unbuttoned my clothes and climbed into bed. Big Sister took hold of me. "Not so fast, you still have school work to do." I had no choice but to bring out my books and to let her teach me. As she began the lesson she stifled a laugh and said as she fixed her eyes on me, "It's no simple matter to eat all that millet and drink all that herbal soup, so why do you bother to learn all of this?" I immediately began to unbutton and said, "Fine! I'll hop straight into bed." She laughed and gave me a thump. "Now that we've fattened you up we can't slaughter and eat you, and since nobody's going to keep feeding you for nothing, hit the books."

In the eighth month of rectification, disaster struck. Big Sister developed lymphatic tuberculosis and was ordered to the infirmary to recuperate. She told Yü-chen, "You teach her the junior high curriculum. She's intelligent enough, but too frivolous. All she needs is a bit tighter control."

Big Sister said to me, "Sometimes I'm too quick-tempered and I say things that aren't very nice. It's all right with me if you hate me and shout at me, but what isn't all right is for you not to study."

I was not angry when I heard this, as I recalled that at home we called the kind of lumps that had appeared on Big Sister "trouble lumps." We thought that people only developed them from getting angry. I was very upset as I kept thinking about it and thus failed to hear her leave. I realized suddenly that she was gone and I stormed out the door in pursuit. I ran after her for about a kilometer or so, until she heard the sound of my steps and turned abruptly around. She stood still on the mountain path. I anxiously looked at the lumps on her neck and asked her, "Did you grow these because I made you angry?" She shed some tears as she took hold of my hand and said, "No!" She quickly opened up her case and took out a little black notebook. Handing it to me, she said, "Use this to keep a diary. If you write in it every day, it will develop your consciousness and your writing style." I nodded my head. She bent down and said to me very warmly, "You'll understand by and by that the revolution needs educated cadres."

This time I listened to her without any protest. The first thing I wrote in my diary was as follows: "Big Sister has gone. She got sick. This evening when I looked at her empty space on the *k'ang,* I only wanted to cry. I understand one thing: she was good to me."

IV

After the rectification I went on to a half year of high school. During the enemy's last "mopping-up" campaign in the T'ai-hang Mountains I was taken ill; I had a bout of malaria every day and was put in the infirmary as well, in the same room as Big Sister.

When I went in she hollered, "Young Liu!" and held out her arms to me. She had grown thin since, because we lacked the necessary medicines, the lymphatic tuberculosis had spread over her entire body. One of her legs was completely immobilized. I ran straight into her arms, feeling an inexpressible sadness. In the past eight or nine months I'd been such a fool, I hadn't even thought of coming to see her.

After being there only a day I realized that sitting all day on a plank-bed for so long had mellowed her. She was delighted to see me and she spoke to me much more nicely.

When my fever was up and I could neither stop vomiting nor sleep because of my aching head, I would say wild things like this to her: "There's a big rock outside our door at home," or "My mother makes the best rice noodles and fried cakes," or "My aunt has an apricot tree that gives big, ripe fruit." I didn't know it at the time, but I was homesick. Whenever this happened, she would come over on her crutches and sit on my bed. She would give me some hot water to drink and softly sing one of her pleasant songs:

> Sing, oh happy wind,
> You've been around the world's mountains and seas,
> The whole globe listens to your song . . .

She looked out the window at the mountain peaks both far and near. Two snow-white clouds coursed east across the blue sky; the tall mountains looked up at them as if to say, "Why can't we fly away too?" A gust of autumnal wind blew up, but the huge mountains did not move an inch. The wind also seemed to be speaking, "It won't work, you great rocks, you're too heavy." Big Sister was still singing to the wind.

The doctors were able to remit the fever with acupuncture, but they kept me there to recuperate. It was at this time that Big Sister wanted to see the black notebook that I had filled with diary entries. I was really embarrassed and a little bit afraid as I reluctantly handed it over to her. She smiled to herself as she began to read it. As she was about to turn the page, a stranger's voice came in from outside: "Is young Liu in here?" I replied, "I'm in here, who is it?" He came in.

I didn't know him. He was about thirty and dressed like a farmer, with a white fluffy towel wrapped around his head. He introduced himself: "I'm from the sixth subdistrict of southern Hopei and I'm passing through here on my way to Yenan. Your mother had me bring a few things for you." As soon as I heard the word "mother," my eyes filled with tears; it had been three years since I'd seen her. The man pulled from his pack two pairs of shiny white socks made of fine yarn and handed them to me, saying, "All your comrades in southern Hopei miss you. They hope you'll finish your studies and return as soon as possible to assist in the counterattack." As he finished speaking he began to stride out of the room. "Why don't you rest awhile," Big Sister interjected. "Can't. I have a long way to go."

"Did my mother give you any message for me?" I asked quickly. He turned his head around. "Oh! Yes, she did. She said that she is all right and that you shouldn't worry about her, that you should attend to your studies and not get sick." Holding the pairs of socks, I lowered my head and went back in the room. I felt inexpressibly sad. Big Sister was put out and said, "What a rash fellow, can't even stay a few minutes!"

Suddenly I thought about the socks. Because of the enemy blockade and two years of disastrous harvests, our comrades in southern Hopei had not been paid or issued any clothing in three years. I myself had no towel and had to wipe my face dry on my clothes when I washed. My winter jacket had long since lost its padding and become summer wear, and soon that, too, had been reduced to rags. With these two pairs of socks I really became a "millionaire." I immediately bounced up and lightly placed one pair in Big Sister's hand: "You wear these. You haven't had any socks to wear since last winter and, besides, you have a bad leg." Big Sister's eyes moistened as she nodded her head. She carefully looked at the socks and then contentedly laid them by her side. She opened up my diary once again and said, "You'll be going back pretty soon, so let's take a look at how your thinking has developed over the past six months."

She read it over page by page and when she suddenly frowned, my heart began to beat a little faster. Pointing at the notebook, she said, "Yes, you've progressed very quickly, but . . ." It was just that "but" that I was afraid of. And she would insist on saying, "But, look at what you've written here. I'll read it to you: 'High-school arithmetic is too hard. Since I plan to be neither a quartermaster nor an accountant, why should I learn it? When I grow up, I'm going to do something as mindless as possible . . .' " She looked up at me and asked, "What kind of work can be done mindlessly? Unless you plan to give up the revolution and become some sort of goddess."

You see? I knew her temper would never change, and here her old severity was coming out. I hung my head, but I still had to listen. She turned to another page and said, "When your teacher takes you to task, why must you abuse her so in your diary? If you can't take criticism, how will you be able to make any progress?"

Aren't you something! So everything's wrong with me from head to toe, each hair in the wrong place, toes too short, ears stuck on wrong, legs out of kilter. I pulled my face longer and longer; I didn't care how it looked since everything was wrong with me anyway.

With all her attention on the diary, she didn't notice me at all. "You see," she continued, "you make the same self-analysis every day: 'I'm not diligent, I don't make stringent enough demands on myself.' Why do you just analyze and never change? If you continue this way aren't you afraid you'll end up as a slacker?"

That was a real blow; I glared at her angrily. During the rectification I'd heard that "slackers" were the exclusive property of the KMT army. Caps askew, shuffling along, smoking opium, robbing people, inciting civil war, ambushing our own New Fourth Army: they were good-for-nothing bastards. How could she compare me to them? I was so furious that I broke into tears; I reached out and grabbed back the socks. I thought I'd give them to Young Hsi instead; after all, when we'd come up into the T'ai-hang Mountains together, the road had given her blood-blisters. She's an honest, straightforward sort of girl who doesn't pick at me like this.

Big Sister was startled for a moment and seemed on the point of smiling. But she resumed her serious look and, without another word, bent her head to the task of correcting the diary with her red pen. As far as I was concerned she could correct anything she pleased, because I didn't want the diary any more.

The call came for dinner; I brought it over to her and slapped it down roughly in front of her. She filled a bowl with millet and black beans and asked as she ate, "So you've completely forgotten the spirit of rectification? Are you a scorpion's tail again that can't be touched any more? All you want is soft breezes to massage you as you grow up? You want us to put you on an altar and kowtow to you as you grow up? Are we supposed to carry you around in a sedan chair as you grow up?"

"What business is it of yours how I grow up? Anyway, I'll keep growing up no matter what you do." Although I snapped in reply, I felt a bit guilty, since, according to the spirit of rectification, I *had* been acting immodestly. I didn't know why, but as soon as I heard someone criticizing me, I seemed to burn with rage. We didn't speak to one another for the rest of the evening.

That night, while everything else in the Tai-hang Mountains peacefully slept, I didn't. No wind blew and the leaves made no sound. The sliver of a moon kept watch over the earth, as if afraid someone would steal it. From far away came the sound of a waterfall that flowed and flowed, ever downward, day and night. Suddenly, from the farthest reaches of the east came the deep, thumping noises of cannons. Yes, they were fighting down on the plain. Which county seat were we attacking? Was it easy to cross the moats? Were the walls easy to breach? I thought of the plain.

A slight shadow appeared across the window as Big Sister lightly sat up on her plank-bed. Beyond the window, in the faraway sky, three small stars were blinking. She quietly gazed out the window and said to herself: "Cannon fire, cannon fire ... " Silence again. How nice it would be if she would only have said something to me. But she wouldn't; she was still angry with me. As I turned over she whispered to me, "Young Liu, are you asleep?" How good it was to hear her voice. I was on the verge of tears as I replied, "No."

"What are you thinking of?"

"The plain."

After a good while, she continued, "In Russia there was a man named Gorki, who had a very hard life when he was young. Once his grandmother brought him to the Volga River, where he boarded a ship ... "

From then on, whenever I couldn't sleep she told me stories. She told me *Pavel Korchagin,* the hero in *How Steel Was Tempered;* she told me *The Iron Flood,* and the story of Hsiang Lin's wife. She knew so many! Listening to her stories was like having something sweet slowly melt into my heart. It was as if the stars in the sky could speak and the very mountains and trees joined in. Her stories caused me to remember many events long past, from when I was little, and each one of them took on new significance, new perfection.

V

During the day when she would read or think her own thoughts, I would try to get her to tell me a story when I became bored. If she didn't, I'd pull at her arm and say over and over: "Tell me one, tell me one." Once, she sized me up, nodded, pulled out a big, thick book and stuffed it into my hands. "Here. Read it yourself."

The book was called *Son of the Working People* and I was enraptured with it. When I'd finished it, I borrowed a second and a third.... When I returned the fifth book to her, I threw it rudely down in front of her and complained, "No wonder you know so many stories, they're all in these books. But all you used to give me to read were text books, you never allowed me any of these."

"Who said you weren't allowed to read them? It was just that you didn't have the foundation."

"How many books as good as this are there, do you think? How many days would it take to finish reading them all?"

She quickly came down off her bed, and standing on one leg, she rolled up her mattress and bedding. Ho, good lord! Where did she round them all up? The area under her bed was completely paved with books. The one or two books that I had seen each comrade on the plain stash in their pockets or under their pillows all seemed to be gathered here. There were political books by revolutionary leaders, traditional Chinese novels, and I saw the name "Lu Hsün" for the first time. Dumbstruck for a time, I suddenly felt that I was just a pathetic little girl who'd climbed up out of our little village. Ahead of me, but at a great distance, stretched a wide and beautiful world, of which I knew nothing.

Big Sister spread out her mattress and sat on it. She stared at me for the longest time before saying, "Wait until we open up Peking and Shanghai and the other big cities. There are buildings and buildings full of books and they're all ours. How many days do you think it'll take you to finish them?"

"Oh, Big Sister!" I said as I embraced her, "I'm so ignorant!"

This was the autumn of 1944 and the trees were full of golden persimmons and red crabapples. The wild pepper was also ripe and it peeked out from among the dense leaves at the blue sky, the white clouds, and the mountain peaks. The local news-sheet carried the good news that we had won back eight county seats on the Hopei plain. Big Sister was happy as she anxiously called out, "Young Liu, go fetch the doctor as fast as you can!"

I ran as fast as my legs could carry me; I only wished there were something I could do to help cure her instantly. Dr. Sun came over, but there was nothing he could do without the necessary special medicines. As usual, he brought her some medicine and a few good books (it was only then that I understood that all those books were given to her by him). He stood there for some time whispering to her, comforting her, and he left only when she had calmed down.

The only way she could perform her work at all was by letter. So she wrote to the authorities of the county where she worked, wrote the secretary of the Party committee, wrote the chair of the Women's Association, wrote to all the women in the association. She asked if they were encountering problems and how their children were getting along. When she finished writing, she called me over and asked me to inquire whether anyone was going back to the plain and could take the letters along with them.

My health had been improving day by day. Just then, a messenger came in and called out in a loud voice: "Young Liu! Get your things together and get ready to set out for the plain with the last rectification team. You're to leave immediately."

"Oh!" I shouted as I leapt up. I looked around and saw Big Sister biting her lip and trembling all over. I went over to embrace her wishing only that I could carry her back with me to our jobs. She controlled herself with some effort, pushed me away and said: "Why don't you let me pack up all those old rags you're using for clothes." As I gave her all my things, I was seized by a combination of pain and joy; I stood there dumbly, not knowing what to do.

It was then that I came across those two pairs of white socks, gleaming like pearls in the midst of my tattered old clothes; I blushed. Big Sister was just about to stuff them in my pack when I reached out and grabbed her hand: "Keep one pair out for yourself."

"No," she said as she pushed me away. In tears, I went back and grabbed her hand again. "Won't you ever forgive me for that one mistake?"

"It's not that," she said, holding my face in her hands. "Who knows where you'll be assigned on your return, my dear? It may be some time before you see your mother again. And even if we defeat the Japs there's always Baldy Chiang eying us hungrily from his lair in Szechwan. Young as you are there's a hard road in front of you." We hugged each other tightly; I could not speak for my tears.

Outside, the bugle called us to fall in. As she pushed me toward the door, she helped me put on my pack, giving me at the same time a small purple notebook. "Use this for your diary. Keep as detailed a record as possible of the counterattack so that I can get some sense of it too." Her face was pale and serious as she silently waved to me.

I looked back at her as I walked out of the little stone building. My heart was heavy once we were on the road; the two pairs of socks felt as heavy as mountains.

After three days' march, we finally caught sight of the broad North China plain as we crossed the last ridge. Each small road led to the battlefield, led to my home by the river. My home, the great plain. I looked back at the dear T'ai-hang Mountains. Back there somewhere, over ridge upon ridge, in a deep little valley, a small stone building nestled in the shade of the persimmon and walnut trees. There Big Sister would be silently sitting by the window, listening to the waterfall on the mountain as it endlessly flowed down, down to the villages and faraway woods.

I looked down at myself, at my feet, my hands. I thought back on my words and actions of the past two years—dear me! Oh mountains, oh plain, what a silly child I was.

VI

For the next two years I returned to the plain to work in a performing troupe; I was so caught up in the invigorating but fatiguing work that I nearly forgot Big Sister. Later, when Chiang Kai-shek launched the full scale civil war, we were ordered to the battle front on the central China plain. The night before we set out an old man came to see me. When he arrived, he opened up his pack and took out two pairs of new, very white socks, as well as a sleeveless sweater made of heavy yarn. Holding out the sweater, he said, "This is made out of wool she spun herself while she was in the mountains." My heart leapt. "When did she return?" I asked. "She's been back a year. She lives in our village now."

"Did her legs get better?"

"Ah, how should I tell you this? They had to amputate one."

"Wha . . . " I cried out mournfully as I thought about those two pairs of socks. "Grandpa, was it because it was too cold in the T'ai-hang Mountains and she got frostbite in her foot because she had no socks?" The old man shook his head. "Well, whatever else, it was because the times were tough; it could have been anything." I sat right down on my bed and said to myself sadly, "She's crippled, she won't be able to work."

"Not so," said the old man, his eyes widening happily. "She's still the chair of our county Women's Association. And every day she goes out here and there on her crutches; she gets around pretty quickly, even in bad weather. Just now she's having the women make shoes and socks and organizing the men into stretcher-bearer battalions. While you're at the front lines, the villagers will provide support right behind you."

I went up to shake the old man's hand. I wanted to have him take my greetings back with him, but no words came out. All I could do was hand over in silence the purple notebook for him to take back.

During the next three years at the front much hardship came with the joys of victory. Whenever I saw the stretcher-bearers bravely running in the hail of rifle fire or saw the old men following us closely, delivering rations, it was like seeing Big Sister. On her crutches, even in bad weather, she was with us at the front in spirit, like millions of others.

After the victory of the war of Liberation, I returned north. My heart started to beat wildly as soon as I caught sight of the T'ai-hang Mountains. The dear old T'ai-hang Mountains! In the course of the war and of my life, I had gradually come to understand just what I had discarded and what I had gained while living in their embrace.

By 1960 it had been fifteen years since I'd seen Big Sister. One day, by chance, I heard from a district Party secretary that she was serving as the head of the district Party school. Diligently working and learning, all those years had passed for her as one day. She had come to the provincial capital to attend a Party plenum and was staying on the third floor of the National Hotel. Happy and excited, I bounded up the stairs and threw open the door. Big Sister was standing in front of the window. As she turned rapidly around, I ran over without a word and hugged her; I broke into tears. The tears were streaming down her cheeks as she said, "Don't cry, I'm fine."

Heart in my mouth, I ran my hand over her artificial leg. Standing up, I looked at her carefully; she had some grey hair, but her eyes were still lively and young and appeared to be even more profound and kindly. She pulled me over, took a look at me and said with a smile, "Do you still remember our little building in the T'ai-hang Mountains? My! So you've grown up after all." Recalling the business about the socks, I was between tears and laughter as I fell into her arms. Playfully slapping at my hands, she said, "And to think you've been writing with these dirty little hands. Everytime I'd read your writing, I'd think, 'You little devil, you! You still want to try getting by without using your brain?' " I concealed a smile and managed a put-upon expression. "But it's been much harder than ordinary schoolwork. Literature demands so much of a person."

"Of course, it's not simple at all," she said as she got up and walked across the room, "and when they first cut off my leg, I thought I'd never walk again.

But I kept at it and now I can walk. So I must believe that as long as you can take the first step, you can take a second; you shouldn't let anything tie you down ..." These few words brought illumination. If I closed my eyes it was as if I could see her, learning to walk again, step by step.

She suddenly thought of something, opened up her case, and brought out two little notebooks. "Hey!" I cried happily as I reached out to grab them. I held them tightly, as they were my first two diaries, one black-covered and one purple. I hastily opened up the first one. Big Sister said, "I've always wanted to give these back to you as I thought you might find them useful. You can get to know that naughty girl you used to be!"

I couldn't help but laugh as I leafed through them. The messy, often incorrect little characters and the wildly sprinkled punctuation marks had all been carefully corrected with red ink. It also contained my first self-analysis: "I am immodest, not diligent and this tongue of mine wags all day long ... "

I could just picture that wild and foolish girl again. In front of her were the fine poplars of the plain and the long flowing stream of the T'ai-hang Mountains; times of fierce struggle and of calm. Everything that Big Sister gave me in those days was precious. My youthful vanity had been washed away in the course of time and I could now love Big Sister's severity along with her warmth. I admired even more her spirit of loyalty to the people and to the revolution, as well as her ever-youthful striving for perfection.

I raised my head to look at Big Sister and became concerned once again: adult as I was, it was still so easy for me to think only of myself. "Big Sister, how have you been?"

"Do you remember Dr. Sun?" she said with a smile. I nodded. "Well, not long after you'd gone, he took his patient Comrade Huang Ching to Yenan and then went on to Manchuria. But after a few years he came back for me and we've had a good life together."

I jumped up and hugged her yet again. I whirled around a couple of times, wiped away my tears and said, "When you go back home give him a good scolding for me."

"What? Why?"

"Why? For not letting on to me when we were in the T'ai-hang Mountains that he'd fallen in love with my Big Sister. I only remember him standing around like a dummy, so it's hard to imagine that his mother had told him to take a bride!" Big Sister took hold of my clothes and said laughingly, "Let's go, you nasty girl. You come home with me and repeat to him in person what you've just said."

First draft, in Pao-ting, August 1, 1962

Translated by Ted Huters

LI YING-JU
(1913–)

The countryside of Hopei Province was the scene of Li Ying-ju's childhood, but he had the good fortune to study in a small town, where he learned to enjoy traditional Chinese literature, mostly classical novels and tales. His early exercises in poetry and prose appeared in local papers; his serious writing, however, did not begin until he plunged into life and action behind the enemy lines after the outbreak of the war against Japan in 1937. A stream of reports and short stories flowed from his pen, mostly retelling his experiences with the anti-Japanese guerrilla units and portraying the characters he encountered during that period.

He published two novels after 1949, *Fighting on the Hu-t'o River* and *Wildfire and Wind Vie in an Old City*. The second one was completed in 1958 after three years of work, then revised again in 1960. It won high acclaim for its well-developed structure and painstaking effort to delineate the principal characters. True, Li Ying-ju is a serious writer, always consciously striving for a high level of the art of fiction. He wrote essays in the early 1960s criticizing the crudity of proletarian stories that present stereotyped characters devoid of flesh and blood. A seasoned critic like Yeh Sheng-t'ao has praised Li's craftsmanship. But in his overly conscious effort to write differently, Li has not quite developed a personal style that flows and persuades. His language suffers from stiffness, and his inept juxtapositions of semiarchaic phrases and current vernacular are frequently jarring.

Along with most of the writers, Li disappeared from public life during the Cultural Revolution, and he has not yet returned after the fall of the Gang of Four. —K.Y.H.

---

from *Wildfire and Wind Vie in an Old City*

[In the early 1940s, when China was resisting the Japanese invasion, a Communist commissar, Yang Hsiao-tung, was assigned to work as an underground agent in a northern provincial capital occupied by the Japanese army.

The Communist liaison officer in the city was a young woman named Yin-huan, who adroitly used her cover as a nurse in the city hospital and her connection with Kao Tzu-p'ing, nephew of a government councillor, to aid Yang in setting up a base for underground activities. The puppet government, headed by a Japanese high official, was actually under the control of its military police commander, Kao Ta-ch'eng, and his nefarious followers, T'ien, Lan, and Fan. Although Kao exerted formidable pressure on the Communist resistance, it had little effect in stopping Yang from helping two senior cadres run the enemy's blockade, or Yin-huan from distributing revolutionary leaflets at an enemy's celebration party, or Han Yen-lai, a young impetuous comrade, from killing a Japanese officer. A strategic attack that destroyed the security police headquarters forced Kao to take desperate actions. He arrested Yang's aged mother and Yin-huan's elder sister, both of whom eventually died for the revolutionary cause.

In the meantime, Kao Tzu-p'ing, jealous of Yin-huan's increasing fondness for Yang, went to Commander Kao and told him where Yang could be found. Yang was taken captive. To get his signature on a defection paper, the enemies resorted to all forms of enticement and torture, but to no avail. The episode translated here (chapter 19) depicts the interaction between Yang, his mother, and their tormentors.

The hero survived. One of Kao's regimental chiefs, Kuan Chin-t'ao, was completely disillusioned over Kao's cruel deeds of exploitation and persecution and decided to join the resistance front. He, together with other Communist members, succeeded, after much tenacious effort, in rescuing Yang from his debilitating imprisonment. During a final close combat, Kao Ta-ch'eng was severely injured and his underlings, T'ien, Lan, and Fan, were all killed. The Communists safely withdrew from the city and returned in victory to the resistance base in the suburbs. There, Yang designated Han to be the officer-in-charge as he and Yin-huan, now his wife, were to leave for another, more challenging mission.]

CHAPTER 19

At the very moment when Yang Hsiao-tung was pushed into the car, neither fear of death nor thought of enemies crossed his mind. Instead, he was harshly blaming himself. "See what a terrible mess your leadership has made. No substantial results, only incessant troubles. The entire underground working force which the Party developed has slipped right through your fingers." But on second thought, he felt that such a view was biased. "Even though you have gone down, there are still Yen-lai and others. Besides, the Party will surely send a more competent comrade to take command. So, the situation is not completely hopeless. Furthermore, what lies ahead of you is another battle of hardship, and you'd better prepare yourself for the upcoming struggle."

The thought of a confrontation prompted him to open his eyes and look around. There were secret agents clustering all around him, so many that he couldn't even make the slightest move, let alone steal a look beyond them. He simply closed his eyes and tried to compose himself until they came to a stop.

The car pulled up in front of a row of tall barracks with a long walkway around the building. He was thrown into a cell that had iron bars dividing the room in half. The minute he was put behind the bars, both the iron gate and the cell door locked simultaneously. Though the cell was divided into two, it was still larger than an average dormitory room. Both the north and the south walls had small and narrow windows covered with wire mesh.

This could not be a real prison; it appeared more like a converted storeroom. Where was he? Yang tried to figure it out calmly. The car made a long turn when they started out, the sunlight streamed in from the right, and the road was bumpy all the way. With speed, time, direction, and all conditions taken into consideration, it seemed impossible for this to be the secret agents' headquarters. Neither could it be the military police station, which was in the city and a shorter distance than what they had travelled. The most likely possibility, then, was Kao Ta-ch'eng's headquarters outside the West Gate.

While still speculating, he heard footsteps outside the gate. They must have put a guard there. "But wherever this place is," he told himself, "take advantage of the time to rest up first." He lay down on the bed, which was nothing more than a few wooden planks.

He wasn't sure how much time had elapsed when he heard a clanking sound as the padlock on the gate opened. Lan Mao entered and cried in surprise when he caught sight of Yang. "Thank God! It's really you! It's been quite a while since our last encounter, hasn't it? You fooled me last time, but did you ever imagine that you'd fall into my trap?" Yang gave him a contemptuous look and turned around to face the wall. "Any case involving you Communists always stinks. But let me tell you something, Commander Kao is going to handle your case personally. If you're thinking of playing tricks on him, you'd better forget it. He'll beat you to a pulp. Guards, take him out!"

Yang was pushed out of the cell door and had walked about twenty or thirty steps when he saw a large room in front of him. Two ranks of soldiers spread out from the doorway like the wings of a wild goose, each man armed with at least two weapons. They had all kinds of guns, some held in hand and some stuck behind belts, but all of them were pulled out from their holsters, exposing gun barrels of various sizes. All seemed to be holding their breath, awaiting the coming of a mortal enemy. It appeared as though anyone who stepped into the room would never get out alive.

The soldiers made way for Yang to enter the room, where everything was prepared for his interrogation. He saw Kao sitting in front of him, howling, "Quick, bring me that bandit!" Hearing his shout, Lan hurried over and stood respectfully with Assistant T'ien on either side of the commander. For a moment, Yang was not sure how to react, but after a brief pause, he took a few swift steps, stood in the middle of the room, head lifted high, and said nothing.

Kao banged on the table loudly. "Look at him! Haughty and self-inflated. Who are you trying to impress? This is a place of law and order. Bow your head!" Yang stood there stone-faced as though he hadn't heard anything. "What's your name? Where do you live? What crimes have you committed? Speak up and tell me the truth!"

"Speak up!" roared the soldiers, echoing the threat and adding in their own abuses.

Yang had hoped to exercise self-control for a slow and persistent fight in the enemy's kangaroo court. But the situation unfolded so unexpectedly that he could no longer keep silent and maintain the dignity of being a Communist. Glaring at them, he said coldly, "Can't you show some respect, or are you a pack of mad dogs?"

"Look at this arrogant bastard! Who do you think you are, talking to us as an equal? How dare you make such a sarcastic remark!" Kao raved.

"Me? Equal to you? What could be more insulting?"

"Shut up! You must be out of your mind, you self-conceited lunatic. I can find better things to do than waste my time with you. Assistant T'ien, take him out, pump some lead in him and send him on his long journey!"

T'ien knew exactly what Kao had in mind. He took out his pistol and shouted, "Get going!" The guards swarmed over, pushing and pulling Yang out the door. T'ien scurried outside and stood waiting for him. Before Yang knew what had happened, two shots whizzed by his ears.

Ordinarily, T'ien's targets would completely collapse from his game of mock execution. Even a brave one would blanch in terror at the sight of a first-rate marksman like T'ien aiming at him. But this time things were different. When T'ien pulled his gun, the thought of "it's all over" did flash through Yang's mind, but when the shots were fired, he suddenly realized it was a trick. Sighing with relief, he threw a look of utter disgust at T'ien. Shocked by Yang's unperturbed expression, T'ien felt intimidated and bewildered. He knew he had failed to achieve his purpose. He signalled the guards to take Yang back to the room.

When Yang reached the middle of the interrogation room, a panicky figure emerged from the mob. It was Fan Ta-ch'ang. "Thank God, I made it in time! Commander Kao, do you realize who this gentleman is?" He lowered his voice and whispered into Kao's ear.

Feigning surprise, Kao said, "Oh! What a mistake! What a stupid mistake! I don't even know how it happened." First he berated himself, and then bombarded his guards with a tirade of obscenities. In a brazen manner, he came right up to shake Yang's hand, and told the guards to take him back for a rest.

"This must be the end of Act One!" Yang thought to himself.

Early the next morning, four or five orderlies brought over some household items: a teapot, some cups, a washbasin, a new quilt, cigarettes, tea leaves, and reading materials published by the puppet government. Yang was not at all pleased by the sight of these things because he saw them as the bait of a deadly trap. He merely eyed them while waiting for the situation to develop.

That afternoon Fan came to see him. He came across as a glib and amiable person, inquiring about Yang's health and engaging him in small talk as if they were old buddies. However, Yang grew bored listening to him and said, "If you have anything to say, spit it out! If not, just get out!"

Only then did Fan begin to divulge the plan. Kao had invited a few friends to a banquet especially designed to appease Yang for all he had gone through. Yang questioned Kao's sincerity but Fan denied any ulterior motive. "Commander Kao has great admiration for you and hopes to befriend you. That's why he has arranged for this meeting. When he greets you, he will open with a few welcoming words in the hope that you will respond in kind."

The enemies were obviously trying to set him up as a defector. Yang realized it and staunchly refused. But Fan persisted until he had no recourse but to give a deliberate cough. Immediately following the signal, five or six monstrous guards came in and threatened to drag Yang out by force. "Stop it!" Fan shouted. "Remember what Commander Kao said before we came? If we fail, he will come personally to invite Mr. Yang."

Sizing up the situation, Yang knew that the confrontation was unavoidable. "Stop harassing me!" he said. "Wherever it is, I'll go!"

"Will you say a few words then, too?" Fan said, testing how far Yang would go.

Exasperated, Yang answered evasively. "We'll see. If it's absolutely necessary I'll say something."

Fan and his men seemed satisfied with this response. "Why don't you get some rest now? I'll go telephone Commander Kao and announce your acceptance. I'll be in this evening to pick you up."

Kao Ta-ch'eng was the first to arrive at Epicurean Garden, the place where he planned to stage his performance. He was to be the star of the show, with his political and military sympathizers from the puppet government as the supporting cast. In the main parlor, under the brightly lit neon lights, a few round tables were set with an opulent spread of chicken and fish, fragrant wines, and dozens of tall-stemmed wine glasses stacked dense as a forest. At the table of honor, there was a loud speaker with two vases of fresh flowers on each side for decoration.

The distinguished guests were all there on time. News reporters carrying cameras had already selected the right positions for setting up spotlights. A speech had been prepared for Kao by his aides. He had practiced it a few times, underlined the words he didn't know, and spelled out the proper pronunciation. The final preparation was made while the guests awaited this important leader from the Communist side. Since he had consented to come, they planned to publicize the event by sending out telegrams, releasing his speech, printing his pictures, and making films. "He will not be able to pull himself out then," Kao and Fan surmised.

When Yang arrived, Kao did not detect any sign of reluctance, and thought to himself, "No one is void of vanity and love for indulgence in material things. Even a Communist is no exception." Feeling confident, he extended a few courteous words to Yang and explained that he had invited a few friends from military and political circles to join them at this informal gathering. This, he said, was an expression of his good intentions. The conversation took place in a private lounge. All along, Yang had a deadpan expression on his face, which Kao interpreted as silent approval. Exhilarated, he gave the order for the guests to be seated. The lounge door opened and he made a grand entry into the banquet hall.

As he appeared, all the guests rose to their feet. The spotlights were lit, and the two reporters knelt down by the door like two guardian dogs. They held their cameras close to their eyes and squinted while Kao's subordinates, the top echelon of the military, rolled up their sleeves and applauded with fervor. Quite out of keeping with his usual vulgar manner, Kao moved with an air of elegance toward the dais. He suddenly felt uneasy and turned around. Yang had not followed him out.

"Please join us!" Kao said, holding his speech with an outstretched hand while inviting Yang to come in.

"Get rid of these photographers first!" Yang shouted out, shocking the entire party even before making his entrance.

"What? A captive with such audacity?" many people in the audience thought. "Where did he get the courage to put his head in the lion's mouth?

Doesn't he know how ferocious Commander Kao is? Whoever falls into his hand loses at least his skin, if, luckily, not his life."

But none of them knew of the impression Yang had made on Kao during their first encounter the previous day. Kao tried to suppress his instinctive response and signalled to the reporters to leave. They picked up their cameras and left the hall in embarrassment. "Hey you! Turn off those damned spotlights. This place needs no illumination."

Assistant T'ien was standing by the doorway when Yang spoke out. He knew Yang was speaking to him and was unsure of how to react. Since his first round with Yang, he realized that this man was more frightful then he and his buddies, all decked out in scary getups, had tried to be. "Didn't Commander Kao submit to his demand to get rid of the reporters? What can I do?" Without even waiting for a nod of approval, he obediently went over and turned off the lights.

Finally, Yang strode out of the lounge and stood in front of the audience. "What kind of a game are you trying to play? You want to play it civil or play it rough? If it is rough, you outnumber me. But even if you take my life, you can't take my will. If it is civil, let's act like gentlemen. After all, there is no way you can force anything out of me."

Fan, afraid that things were taking a turn for the worse, hurriedly came forth and said in a compromising manner, "No one is trying to fight with you. Didn't I tell you that Commander Kao asked everybody over for a small get-together?"

Yang saw that even in his fury Kao was still holding on to the damned speech, which he was determined to give. He grabbed the chance to stand before the table and said, "If this is an informal gathering, I want to say a few words first. We Communists never try to hide where we stand. We dare to speak out in any situation ... You're all VIP's in this city, and in the eyes of the Japanese, you are courageous and your performance is exemplary." Yang showed no sign of anger. In fact, his words flowed with good rhythm.

With a false sense of confidence, Kao was pleased by what he had heard, misinterpreting the statement as indicative of a change of heart. Lan and Assistant T'ien also thought Yang had retreated from his unyielding stance. Their disappointment was now replaced with new optimism.

Kuan Chin-t'ao* was the only one among the officials who felt differently. He had no desire to come to the party until he heard from someone in the commander's headquarters that a Communist cadre had defected. Was it possible that someone from their side would surrender? How could a senior cadre be more cowardly than those two women comrades? Still incredulous, he decided to come to the party. When he first caught sight of Yang, he immediately recognized him to be the presiding officer he had met in Pa-li village. He shuddered.

---

*Kuan Ching-t'ao, the commander of Kao's First Regiment, was a capable and conscientious officer, who often took a dislike to Kao's ruthless and corrupt leadership. He was captured during a Communist attack and was brought to Pa-li Village, where Yang awakened him to the unselfish spirit and patriotic deeds of the Communist Eighth Route Army. This exposure aroused his sympathy for the Communist cause. The two female comrades mentioned in this passage refer to Chin-huan, a close friend of Yang's who was arrested soon after the Pa-li incident and was shot five times in her attempt to assassinate Kao during her trial, and Yang's mother, who was taken captive as bait for trapping Yang. [S.C. and L.G.]

As Yang's eyes pierced the audience, Kuan ducked behind Pockmarked Wolf, while listening with full concentration to every word Yang said.

"Speaking of your exemplary performance," Yang continued, "you supported Japanese devils to invade our country. . . . In the eyes of the Japs who have you to fight their war for them, you of course rendered them a meritorious service. As to your courage . . . you have the unconscionable courage to sell out your motherland and accept the Chinese people's most hated enemy, Japan's imperialism, as your friend, even your kin. Such courage has never been seen in Chinese history . . . "

"Take him out!" Kao yelled at the top of his voice. Pockmarked Wolf and a few other captains immediately swarmed over to form a barricade of guns around Yang.

Yang showed no signs of being nervous and said contemptuously, "You ass! These crummy guns couldn't scare anyone but a coward. Even if your military chief was here, I don't think he would dare handle my case all by himself, let alone your measly little security police unit. If you have guts, just go ahead and shoot." He pointed at his chest.

Eying each other, Pockmarked Wolf and the others made way for Kao, who was rushing toward Yang with a gun he had taken over from Assistant T'ien. "How dare you! If I wanted to kill you, all I'd have to do is bend my little finger."

"Then how would you account to your Japanese bosses?"

"I don't have to account for my actions. Your life is in my hands. A single word from me and you'll disappear without a trace."

"You could only murder a Communist in secrecy. But one day when you're captured, thousands of people will come to the square to judge you in broad daylight!"

"Bragging! That's all you Communists are good for!"

"Bragging? Huh! History will pass a verdict on you just the way I described."

Kao suddenly burst into loud laughter. "I'm no elementary school boy. I don't need a history lesson from you. I am the commander who has the power of life and death over you. A verdict on me—what rubbish! But I'll pronounce a verdict on you right now. Chief Lan, listen to his vicious tongue! Take him back and really fix him up!"

· · · · · · ·

When he came to, Yang was not sure where he was until he recognized the iron bars and the padlock obstructing his view. So, he was back where he started. The torture seemed to have taken place so long ago, and yet the scenes were still more or less clear in his mind. Kao Ta-ch'eng had personally supervised the punishment. First, rods were pressed against his flesh until he cursed at the top of his lungs; then he was forced to gulp down burning-hot chili juice. Electroshock came much later, but he couldn't recall exactly what had happened because by then he was already disoriented. But now, after some rest, he was wide awake and knew that he was still in one piece. Thinking he had control of his body, he tried to turn around, only to feel his loins so heavy that his entire body seemed to have been torn into bits. He struggled to get onto his feet, but his legs were burning with pain and could hardly support him. Grit-

ting his teeth, he hauled his legs around until he could finally sit up on the
wood bed. . . .

He closed his eyes and tried to get some rest until the prison door opened.
Fan appeared, removed the padlock, and came in. He inquired briefly about
Yang's condition. Having dismissed the guards, he came straight to the point
and said to Yang, "I must admit what Commander Kao did was a little reckless
and crude. He could have talked things over with you without resorting to
physical abuse. But, of course, Mr. Yang, your temper was a little too . . . "

"I've got no time for such frivolity. Why have you come?"

"I have something to discuss with you, but before we begin, let's try to be
more objective, put aside our individual beliefs, and talk to each other as
intellectuals. An intellectual should be flexible and willing to adapt to the
situation at hand. I myself have great respect for your courage and nerve. But
there are certain harsh realities that one must face . . . "

"Shut up! The last thing I need is propaganda."

"I'm not giving you any propaganda. I'm a practical man. Commander Kao
has left you several alternatives. Honestly speaking, your choice so far hasn't
brought you any closer to your goal. In fact, it has created even more obstacles
in your way. Take a look at this if you don't believe me!"

He took out a set of pictures from his briefcase and politely handed them to
Yang. Skimming over them, Yang recognized that they were pictures of all
kinds of unbearable brutal tortures. Infuriated by them, he yelled at Fan. "Do
you think you can scare me with this stuff? Only a maniac, an animal, would
resort to such a scheme. Anyhow, tricks of this kind would only work on a
coward. I'm telling you once and for all, I have no fear of death."

"It's true there are quite a few of you Communists who don't fear death." In
a contrived tone of soft voice, Fan drew out a couple of pictures and said, "Take
a look at what happened to these fearless guys!" One of them was a scene of
wilderness with the sun setting over a vast expanse. Bones were piled up by
the side of a decrepit tomb. They were obviously the remains of comrades
murdered for their anti-Japanese maneuvers. The couplet written in the picture
read:

> White bones scatter in the wilderness;
> Deserted tombs face the dusk.

Yang thought to himself, "These enemies are really malicious. Not only did
they kill our patriotic brothers, they desecrated their graves for propaganda
purposes. Worse than physical torture is the underhanded way they use these
pictures to break the will of the surviving comrades."

Seeing Yang deep in thought, Fan surmised his tricks had worked. In a
sarcastic tone, he asked, "What do you think of this couplet, Mr. Yang? Pretty
philosophical, eh?"

Yang snapped, "Hogwash! If there had to be a couplet, it should have been:

> Who on earth has ever escaped death,
> Let one's loyal heart forever illuminate history.

Why are you putting these dejected lines on the picture? To scare a man you threaten to kill? Don't you know I can't be broken?" He threw the pictures at him.

"If you think the pictures are depressing, there are more pleasant alternatives." He repeated over and over that all Yang would have to do was to make the slightest effort to cooperate and he'd be able to enjoy high prestige and a luxurious lifestyle. "You're over thirty now and still don't have anyone to take care of you. Don't you think this is something worth thinking about? We've tried to scout out some attractive candidates for you. Why don't you see which one you like best?" He displayed a dozen or so pictures of girls and pointing to each one he said, "This one is a clerk in the organization, that one is a young student, this one is . . . and they are all virgins. Should you be interested . . . "

Before he could finish his sentence, the entire pile of pictures was on the floor. Yang had already lain down on the bed and closed his eyes. Fan was on the verge of losing his temper at Yang's arrogance, but a second thought told him that it was too early to take any action. Having suppressed his anger, he grimaced, picked up the pictures, and left disheartened.

When evening came, Fan returned and went through the usual tricks of greeting him in a jovial manner. It seemed as if it must have been a different man that Yang had scoffed at in the morning, or, if it was the same man, he had somehow already put that insulting scene behind him. Fan didn't say very much, let alone ask any questions. It was the guards who coerced Yang to go with him. Yang could not figure out what the secret agents were up to. Though he tried to refuse, they forced him onto his feet. Staggering behind Fan, he soon came to a newly built partition with an iron gate that separated the building into two parts. Seeing that Fan was leading the way, the guard stationed outside the gate glanced at Yang and let him pass. The area was deserted, with only a few scattered houses. A few yards ahead, they reached a lawn connected to a man-made hill by a foot bridge over a stagnant pond. The hill was on a tilt, and on the left side there was a crooked pine tree standing in the wild grass. Under the tree lay the green and white tombstone of a martyr. Though the color of the characters had long since eroded, they were still barely legible in the hazy moonlight:

> Spirit of heroism engraves the crimson tablet,
> Blood of molten iron stains the burnt land.

Yang had been carefully observing his surroundings, which seemed faintly familiar, almost as if he had been there before. But it was not until he saw the tablet that all the disconnected memories strung together. Despite damages and alterations, the familiarity of the surroundings suddenly dawned on him. Anxiety begun to race through his body when he realized that he was standing in the courtyard of his old school. This was the place where he had devoured for the first time in his life a good book called *The Communist Manifesto.* The gray building illumined by the moonlight must be the library where Hsiao, the senior comrade, used to work; that kitchen close to the wall around the yard must be Old Han's bell tower; and below that high wall must be the open sewer that he himself once had squeezed through to deliver secret messages. Reminiscing about the past and realizing his present predicament, Yang inadvertently heaved a long sigh.

Fan seized what he thought was his chance and pressed the question, "Brings back old memories, doesn't it?" Yang was silent. "Mr. Yang, may I continue where I left off this morning? Women and wealth don't seem important to you. But let me ask you this, isn't life precious to you? Won't you feel reluctant to part with it?"

"Living in humiliation doesn't appeal to me at all. I didn't come into this world merely to reap personal profit."

"Is that right? Fine!" Fan continued confidently. "Even if you have no regard for yourself, perhaps you have some concern for your relatives."

"Relatives?" Yang paused and then continued, "All people are my relatives, but by the same token I could say that I have no relatives."

"Is that right? Please follow me over there!"

Fan led the way, circled the hill, walked around the lawn, and approached two newly constructed buildings standing parallel to each other. The houses, shimmering with a silver hue, squatted on the horizon, which was covered with a grey mist. Though the moon was obscured by dark clouds, the path was easy to follow. But even so, Yang struggled to keep up with Fan as he made his way to the front of the buildings. He bit his lip while trying to grab hold of the railing and climbed up the stairs to the second floor. Fan looked at the numbers on the doors and took him into a dark and dismal room. He told Yang to go up to the window and look to the north. On the north side about twenty yards away, there stood a building parallel to them. Not a light was on and the glass windows, even darker than the walls of the building, seemed to peer out like dozens of black eyes. Yang was not sure what Fan was up to, but he sensed that there was something behind the eye-socket windows.

Fan began, "Did I hear you say that you have no relatives? We both know that's not true. Just to prove it, take a look in the window across from us!" While saying this, Fan was feeling in the dark for the bell he had planted there. He rang the bell until all of a sudden the room across lit up. Yang saw a silhouette against the window pane and immediately realized that it was his mother. No words could describe his feeling at that moment. Fire was burning within him, his bones were disjointed and his ligaments strained. He had been leaning against the window until he felt so dizzy that he could no longer support himself and collapsed on the floor.

"Even a Communist has a father and mother. You can throw your own life away, but at least give a thought to your aged mother. No?" What a thrill for a secret agent to spot the Achilles' heel of an honest man. Fan was ecstatic and went off into an oration for more than ten minutes. Finally, he said that if Yang was willing to provide a list of his underground comrades, his mother would not be hurt and they would be allowed to have a family reunion in addition to monetary and material rewards. He went on until his voice was hoarse.

Yang thought it over again and again before he spoke, and this time he sounded ready to talk. "You can kill me and my mother. But if you understand the love between a mother and her son, please execute us separately and secretly, making sure she has no knowledge of what happened to me."

"Why, of course! We have humanitarian feelings too." Fan grabbed this chance to gain more ground. "Since fate has brought you and your mother together, why shouldn't we let you meet?" Yang desperately tried to refuse, but he was carried by the guards onto the terrace of the third floor. His mother was already on the other terrace facing him. They were only three yards apart.

In the dim moonlight, her white hair, pale face, and drooping posture showed how much she had aged and withered. But she seemed impatient and restless, staring under the terrace as if she were awaiting a happy and yet painful occasion. She obviously knew who was coming. Seeing her, all his feelings welled up and burst forth in a flood of emotion. He bent over the railing and cried out, "Ma . . . "

The old woman heard the familiar voice from the side of the balcony and turned her head. For a moment, she wasn't sure whether she felt surprise or joy, fear or sorrow. A mixture of all these feelings agitated her. It was quite some time before she was able to move her lips and utter, "Tung! Are you . . . "

"Ma!" The son cut right in. "We don't have much time, and we are not at home either. Let's say what we have to say and what we want to say!"

"Don't worry! I understand what you mean, son." She spoke, trying her best to suppress her feelings for fear that any sign of weakness would disgrace her son.

"Ma, as the situation now stands, we'd better not say anything about how we got here. Mentioning it would do us no good and only add to our sadness. So why don't we talk about something else?" Under such conditions, it was impractical and virtually impossible to chitchat. Unable to find the words, they both remained silent. Finally, Yang began. "Ma, let me say a few words first. Your son is an anti-Japanese warrior and Communist and has brought no shame to the revolution or the people. But when I think about all the caring you've given me and the disastrous end I've brought to you, that is my only regret."

"Stop it! I don't want to hear this." The elderly woman was about to say something when all of a sudden a car roared up. All the lights inside and out clicked on, including those directly above her and her son. A barrage of footsteps sounded on the staircase up to the terrace where Yang was standing. Kao appeared, followed by a mob including Lan Mao, Assistant T'ien, and some bodyguards who crowded around the entrance to the terrace. Yang winked at his mother and they both froze.

Fan took a couple of steps onto the terrace and said, trying to be smart, "I overheard your touching conversation. I'll repeat what I said an hour ago. You Communists have parents like everyone else; you should not ignore your filial obligations. Isn't this exactly why Commander Kao made this special trip? He has ordered both of you to be released as soon as you give us the list."

"If you're trying to make me betray my comrades, forget it!"

With a giant step, Kao came out on the terrace and grabbed the railing. Just as he was about to explode in anger, he reconsidered and said, "Yang Hsiao-tung, it was with good intentions that I arranged for you to see your mother. I did you a favor. So why be stubborn? Let me tell you something. We really don't need you. A three-legged toad is hard to find but a two-legged man is commonplace. Why do you think we tried so hard to convince you? Simply because we have respect for a man like you. If only you would give in, the car downstairs would take you and your mother out of this place. All right, I'll make a concession. You don't have to give me a list of Communists. All I want is your signature."

"You stupid bastard! Don't be ridiculous!" Kao's eyes bulged out. "How dare you insult me! Oh, forget it! Why should I trouble myself over this? Take him out and execute him right out there!"

Yang looked across the terrace. "Ma, don't worry about me! I'd rather be dead than alive." He marched with his head held high and followed the guards down the stairs.

Seeing that Yang showed no sign of fear, Fan thought a moment and whispered something into Kao's ear. At first Kao seemed annoyed, but just as Yang was going down the stairs, he yelled out, "Hold it! Bring the 'prisoner' back!" He strutted over to Yang and said viciously, "It would be too easy for you to die like that. I've got other ideas for you. You and your mother shall watch each other tortured. Whoever can't bear to watch will give in first. We'll see whether or not we'll get your signature."

The old woman became panicky, thinking to herself, "We could never give the names of those dedicated young men and women who work underground. But how much longer will the enemy grill us? Could I bear to watch my son suffer? Could I allow him to watch me ... ?"

She stood by, slapped her hands together, and shouted at them. "Move aside! I want to meet this Commander Kao of yours." The way she walked she seemed to have lost her balance. She hobbled to the edge of the terrace. Supporting herself by the railing, she said to Kao, "Do you think you can intimidate him with these few soldiers of yours? You misjudge him. He is still my son and will listen to me. If you were smart, you'd let me see him. Leave us alone for a while, and I'll try to persuade him." Kao glared at her with suspicion and said nothing. "We don't have wings to fly away. So what are you afraid of? All you want is a signature, right?" Kao and Fan exchanged glances, and reluctantly agreed to her suggestion. Everyone left the terrace. She was escorted over to her son's terrace.

The moment they were together, Yang embraced her and said in a hurry, "Ma, giving out my signature is not a small matter. Every word is going to make a world of difference. You understand, don't you, Ma?"

"No! It's you who don't understand." She turned ashen white. "Lift up your head and look me straight in the eye." He did what she said. "Now you understand?"

"Yes. You were trying to grab this last chance to be with me." She nodded her head.

"Say what is in your heart, Ma!" he urged her.

"What can I say, Tung? Don't ever think I'd blame a son like you for what he has brought upon me. No, never! I'm proud of you. I have no regrets. And I'd never hold you back.

"Oh! I almost forgot to tell you," she continued, her thin face suddenly aglow. Her voice was very low, almost unintelligible. Obviously she did not want anyone else to hear what she had to say. "I've picked a young woman that I know would make you happy. I gave her the ring with the red heart, and she didn't refuse. Oh ... " She suddenly felt enshrouded with fear as she thought about their future. She became silent. Then the terrace door opened and Lan

Mao came out to them because what they were saying had nothing to do with convincing him to give his signature. All the guards came back onto the terrace as Lan raised his voice and asked Kao for further instructions.

"Shall we take care of the son first or shall we start on the mother?"

Kao shouted, "Haul up both of them and beat them!"

The old woman screamed in despair. "Just a minute. Let me have another word with him." She held his head with both hands, and ran her fingers through his hair. Her bitter tears dripped silently over his face. But then she saw in his eyes that his only concern was for her. She pushed him aside. "Tung, my son! I won't be your burden. Fight to the end!" She rushed forward, threw herself over the railing, and plunged down from the top of the third floor.

Translated by Samuel Cheung and Linda Greenhouse

HU WAN-CH'UN

(1929–)

One of the foremost short-story writers on industrial themes during the 1950s and 1960s, Hu Wan-ch'un came from a poor family, apprenticed himself in a wineshop at the age of thirteen, and soon afterwards started working in a machine factory. Totally self-taught, he was encouraged by the Communist-supported labor union in Shanghai and rose rapidly to head up the Party branch in his factory after the liberation of 1949. His writing career, started in 1952, was accelerated by a literary prize awarded for his first published story, "Flesh and Blood." In rapid succession he produced several collections of short stories: *Youth* (1956), *Who Are the Creators of Miracles* (1962), *Family Problems* (1964), and *New Year* (1965). After 1958 he also added plays and motion-picture scripts to his writing accomplishments.

During the Cultural Revolution, he, Fei Li-wen, and T'ang K'o-hsin formed a trio in Shanghai as the most active proletarian writers who attacked older, well-established authors in that area. All three have stopped writing since the fall of the Gang of Four in 1976.

"Twilight Years" is representative of Hu's most artistically ambitious type of work, the depiction of the emotional difficulties of older workers when faced with the fact of their old age and retirement. In this story, and in a number of others, he explores the feeling of loss of identity and social role as a consequence of retirement from active labor. In the case of the central character in the story, Shun-fa, the author takes the problem of loss of social role a step further by presenting the issue of "generation link," the sense that one's life is a connection between past and future generations, that one's work is continued by succeeding generations and thus has meaning and significance.

At the outset, Shun-fa is a man suffering not only the "crisis of old age" but also the social isolation brought about by a lack of a sense of generation link. He equates himself with the symbolic barren old hen and perceives of himself as being contradictory to the symbol of agelessness, the pine tree. As the story progresses, we witness both a striking change in his mood (the author skillfully leads him through the emotional gamut from depression to exhilaration) and the onset of enlightenment regarding the broader aspects of generation link. He learns that one's contribution to the march of the generations need not be the mere production of natural offspring, but rather it can be the transmission of skills and experience to the representatives of the future. His contribution lives on in their achievements. In the large sense, his apprentices are his "children" just as the ducklings hatched by the old hen can be reckoned as her "progeny." This conception operates as the mainstay of all successful teachers.

The author also presents—but does not resolve—the problem of lack of communication between husband and wife. Shun-fa and Auntie Ch'en seem to be lost in separate worlds, neither really understanding or even perceiving the thoughts and feelings of the other. This results in Shun-fa's having to live through the experience totally on his own, his wife seeming to have no idea of the immensity of the problem or the wondrous joy of its resolution. The story ends on a note of Auntie Ch'en's complete alienation from all facets of the emotional events of Shun-fa's dramatic day. Whether or not the author has consciously added this extra problem in order to deepen the description of the complexity of the workers' daily life is open to debate; however, the fact remains that this particular husband and wife are missing out on the fullness of a relationship based on mutual understanding and shared emotional experience.

The story is very tightly structured, set within the bounds of a unity of time and place and focusing on a central theme and single character. There is a strict attention to realistic detail in the descriptions of the environment and an economy of style reminiscent of Hu Wan-ch'un's literary idol, Lu Hsün. All in all, in both content and form, it is a fine representative piece of working-class fiction.   —M.G.

Twilight Years

On the eve of the lunar new year, Master Shun-fa's mood underwent a slight change. He suddenly felt that there was something lacking in his life. That morning he had not taken his usual stroll down to the factory, nor had he gone around to the neighbors' to gossip; in the afternoon he had not gone to the Workers' Cultural Center to listen to chanted stories or to look at the newspaper. In fact, he had not been interested in going anywhere; he was not in particularly high spirits. He paced back and forth and all around his apartment, as though he wanted to find in some corner the thing that he lacked. The apartment, which ordinarily seemed not at all spacious, now suddenly became large, became empty.

It seemed exceptionally quiet in the apartment; the *tick-tock, tick-tock* of the clock on the five-drawer chest sounded clear and sonorous. Shun-fa paced slowly for a moment, then halted in front of the window. Outside in the dusk, standing straight and solitary, was a small pine tree. When Shun-fa's gaze fell on the pine, he involuntarily raised his hand to feel his own bald head: "Ah! I'm already sixty-six years old this New Year's! Already retired half a year."

Just then an old hen came clucking along outside in the courtyard, her head bobbing as she walked. When he saw this hen, Shun-fa got a bit angry, for ever since he had bought her, in the latter part of the year, she had not hatched a single egg. On the other hand, it so happened that the next-door neighbors raised ducks and had brought over a few eggs for the old hen to hatch—from which six ducklings were produced, split up evenly between the Chang, Li, and Wang families. But this old hen had not even let a fart, let alone laid a single egg of her own. The hen passed in front of the window, tilted her head to one side, blinked her small round eyes at Shun-fa, and gave out two prolonged *cluck-cluck* sounds, as if to say, "I'm going to lay an egg!" Shun-fa simply could not suppress his irritation, and his loud "Hmph!" startled the hen, who flapped her wings and scurried into the chicken coop.

Darkness gradually descended. Several trucks that had transported vegetables from the Wu-sung District people's communes were already racing along the highway towards home. The black cluster of towering blast furnaces at the steel factory emitted a bright red glow.

Master Shun-fa stood in the darkness, not caring to turn on the light. A *click-clack* noise came from the neighbor's back gate, and then the sound of people talking carried clearly: "Ah Mao's Ma, you've got lots of company today!"

"Oh, my boy Ah Mao has come to spend New Year's at home!"

"Was that your daughter-in-law wearing a short overcoat?"

"It sure was! Just married this year."

"Ha, ha, now you're a venerable old mother-in-law!"

Soon there came the hacking cough of old Mr. Wang. "Mr. Wang, has Ken-sheng come home for the holidays?"

"The work is heavy at his factory just now, so he'll be coming a bit late," replied Mr. Wang slowly. "But Ken-pao and Ken-fa have already been here for a while. Ordinarily, when they don't come around I feel lonely and deserted. But this morning they all came at once, and I'm beginning to feel a bit put out. Just think, three sons, three daughters-in-law, and four grandchildren—why the house is noisier than a tipped-over basket of frogs, *croak, croak, croak.*"

"Mr. Wang, that's your good fortune!"

Shun-fa had already caught snatches of this sort of chattering several times that day. Each time he heard it, he greatly envied his neighbors; at the same time it produced in him deep feelings of loneliness. When Shun-fa was in his mid-thirties he had also had a son. But he had been out of work for a long period of time, plagued by poverty and illness, and was fearful that his son would die of starvation. So Shun-fa and his wife, after much discussion and quarreling, decided to give their barely two-year-old boy away to another family. He remembered to this day the child's bright and flashing round eyes, his thick little lips—ai! For sure, if this son were still with him, Shun-fa could be holding a granchild in his arms today just like old Mr. Wang was doing. One time, when Shun-fa was forty-three years old or so, his wife told him she had heard of a poor family looking to give away a boy to the orphanage, and she wondered whether or not he might want to take the child in. He replied irritably, "We couldn't even feed our own son; don't let somebody else's child come here to suffer with along us." From that time on, his wife never brought up this matter again. After Liberation, he worked in the steel plant and his wife worked in a factory manufacturing stockings. They left home early and returned late; their thoughts were occupied with production, learning to read, and other pursuits. Who had time for other worries and concerns? Even if thoughts of his son should enter his mind on occasion, Shun-fa would rationalize to himself, "We're liberated now! These days old people enjoy workmen's insurance and have no anxieties over food and other needs, so it doesn't matter whether or not you have a son or daughter. It's not like before Liberation, when you lived by the old adage: 'Rear a son to support you in old age; store up grain in case of famine.'" So it was for Shun-fa, and the time passed day by day, year by year.

As Shun-fa stood idly before the window, memories of the past once more caused him a bit of vexation. From outside came the voices of old Mr. Wang's two small grandchildren hard at play, popping firecrackers. He exhaled softly, turning away from the window, but still he stood there motionless. In a moment, the pitter-patter of small children's footsteps resounded as they passed by the window, and then everything returned to silence.

Click. The electric light in the apartment suddenly flashed on. Shun-fa blinked his eyes several times before seeing clearly that it was his wife who had come in. Every evening it was the same old thing: "Auntie" Ch'en would return home from work, hastily throw her handbag onto the bed, then busy herself in the kitchen cooking dinner. But tonight it was different: seeing Shun-fa standing inertly in the darkness, not even bothering to turn on the light, she could not help feeling somewhat bewildered. As she fastened her apron she questioned him, "Old man, what's the matter with you?"

"It's nothing!" Shun-fa replied, suppressing his anger and annoyance.

"Well, then, why were you standing there looking dumb?" Auntie Ch'en, a bit puzzled, attempted to read his facial expression.

"Isn't tonight New Year's Eve?"

"Certainly."

"Don't you miss anything?"

"Oh-ho! Do I miss anything? We're too busy for that. . . . All of the electric looms need to be remodeled; the six manual looms belonging to our unit have just been refitted this afternoon." As she spoke, she took out one by one from the cupboard the various items and utensils she had bought only two days earlier for use on New Year's. "The new batch of synthetic fiber stockings are really beautiful, just as smooth and shiny as can be; it sure makes me feel good looking at them."

Once she got onto the topic of production it was like a rushing torrent; there was simply no stopping her. In this respect, the fifty-six-year-old Auntie Ch'en was no different from all of the younger girls working down at the factory. Usually while listening to his wife engage in this type of discourse, Shun-fa would nod his head in agreement. At this moment, however, he glared at her in astonishment, thinking to himself, "How is it she doesn't share my own feelings at all?" But gradually he began to understand: Shun-fa himself, during his long period of work preceding retirement, used to be just the same as his wife—when talking about production he would chatter unceasingly. In that period of his life he could not have felt such a deep sense of loneliness as he experienced today. As his wife talked on and on, he became a little impatient, and finally he blurted out, "All right, all right! Go on about your business."

Auntie Ch'en, thus interrupted, muttered darkly to herself, "I just don't know what's bothering this old man." She placed the New Year's goods in a basket, which she carried off into the kitchen. Soon, there came from the kitchen the sounds of frying food and clanging pots and pans.

Shun-fa sat down in a chair by the window, lit up a cigarette, and began to smoke slowly. Outside in the chicken coop the old hen, undoubtedly feeling very comfortable in the balmy weather, stirred about clucking loudly. Hearing this racket, Shun-fa suddenly shouted out angrily, "What are you cackling about, you eggless old hen?"

"What did you say?" Just at that moment his wife came in carrying the dinner plate. "Nothing, nothing. I was talking about the hen."

"Just so long as you weren't talking about me, it's okay," said his wife with a smile. "Come on, let's get ready to eat our New Year's Eve meal."

Shun-fa stood up and started wiping off the table. By the time his wife carried in the *huo-kuo* with boiling broth in it and a blazing charcoal fire underneath, he had already set out the bowls and chopsticks. Thereupon, the old couple sat down facing each other at the table and began drinking wine. From time to time, Shun-fa looked toward the two empty sides of the dinner table, as if to say, "If there were two more people sitting here with us, how lively it would be!" But his wife did not understand him at all; on the contrary, she went right on speaking energetically about factory matters. After eating their dinner, the old couple went to bed quite early.

Shun-fa could not get to sleep easily that night no matter what, and as it grew later and later, he could still hear sounds of laughter emanating from the neighbors' apartments. It was not until he heard the clock strike twelve that he drifted into a fitful slumber. The next morning, New Year's Day, he was startled awake bright and early by the sound of popping firecrackers. When he got out of bed, his wife specially cooked him up a bowl of New Year's rice-cake soup. He took no particular pleasure in eating this holiday fare. Just at that moment, there was a disorderly clattering of footsteps out in the corridor, and someone was laughing and joking with Auntie Ch'en: "Auntie! Happy New Year, a wealthy New Year—ha, ha! A prosperous New Year too!"

"You rascal! We're liberated now; who'd still talk about getting rich?"

"No more 'wealthy New Year'? All right, then I'll just kowtow before my Master's wife."

"Aiya! Why don't you drop dead, silly!"

"Ho, ho, ho! Talking about life and death on New Year's Day!"

"Ha, ha, ha."

Master Shun-fa knew immediately upon hearing the voice that the man talking to his wife was his number-three apprentice, Ah Fang. He thought to himself, "He's still the same old glib rogue." There was a sudden rapping at the door, and when he strode over and opened it, Shun-fa saw his number-one apprentice, Chü-sheng, standing respectfully in the doorway. Behind Chü-sheng stood Ah Fang; behind Ah Fang there were nearly ten young fellows. The smallest one of the group—perhaps only sixteen years old—had a very round face, resembling a rice-dough dumpling. As soon as he saw them, Shun-fa said, "What are you all just standing there for? Come in quickly and sit down!" The crowd burst inside like a flood, and the chairs, benches, and the edge of the bed were all filled with people. After Shun-fa sat down and Auntie Ch'en had poured tea all around, the number-one apprentice, Chü-sheng, said with a smile, "Master, we have come to pay our New Year's respects to you." Shun-fa laughed, "I'm afraid I don't deserve it."

The young men's animated conversation was generously punctuated with their affectionate and respectful reference to their master. Chü-sheng was over thirty years old, but he was still very shy and rather inept at conversation. Ah Fang, as always, became very well-mannered in the presence of the master. The number-five apprentice, Ta-k'uei, was still a bit dense in his appearance. Shun-fa had altogether eight apprentices, of whom three had come to pay respects this day. The rest of the visitors were the apprentices of these three. Only the round-faced youngster was a stranger to the old master. Shun-fa's gaze fell on this youth, and he casually pointed toward him asking, "Who is he? How is it I haven't seen him before?" The round-faced boy bashfully lowered his head. "Master," replied Ah Fang as he nudged a young man in his twenties sitting next to him, "he's apprentice Hsiao Mao's apprentice, newly arrived. We all call him 'Little Dumpling!' "

Someone in the group chuckled but promptly stopped himself. Shun-fa knew that Hsiao Mao was Chü-sheng's apprentice. Ah Fang made a motion with his mouth toward Shun-fa as he said to the round-faced youngster, "Hey, 'Little Dumpling,' how should you properly address my master?" Ta-k'uei interjected, "You ought to call him 'Great Grandmaster.' " 'Little Dumpling' blushed crimson. He said to Shun-fa in a feeble voice, "Uh, Great Grandmaster, my . . . my name is Hsiao T'ang-yüan." When everyone heard him take Ta-k'uei's bait and actually say "Great Grandmaster," they could not help bursting out laughing. Even Shun-fa laughed aloud.

Shun-fa glanced around, surveying the roomful of his apprentices and the younger workers. He could see in the eyes of these lively young men a great respect and affection for himself. Gradually, his mood became more relaxed, more open-hearted. A smile appeared on his face.

Ah Fang inquired, "Master, is your second apprentice still in Loyang at the tractor factory?"

"Now he's made foreman," Shun-fa said.

"Has he written you recently?"

"No. Probably he's overworked with work."

"How about your seventh apprentice, Ch'üan-ken?"

"He's still at the Ch'ang-ch'un automobile plant. I received a letter from him just this past month."

While Shun-fa spoke he stared unconsciously at his own hands, large and coarse and callused, hands that had worked with the tools in a metal shop for more than forty years. It seemed as if he were asking himself, "After all, how much experience have I already imparted to my apprentices?" His thoughts strayed onto one of the passages in Ch'üan-ken's letter: "Master! You really don't know how thankful I am to you right now. I think that even though you've retired, still in every ton of steel, every tractor, every Liberation brand automobile our country produces, you have a share of the credit!" Thinking about this passage, he felt a warm current flooding his heart, producing in him an indescribable joy.

"Master, what are you smiling about?" asked Ta-k'uei abruptly. "Nothing, really, nothing at all. I just feel very happy." Yes, Shun-fa had become quite happy. The loneliness of the day before, which had depressed him to the core, had dispersed like clouds in the wind, its whereabouts unknown. His face now bore a fresh and jolly expression, and he was talking and laughing. He asked about everybody's production and the situation of their lives.

Hsiao Mao spoke up, "Last month Master Ah Fang improved the container pulley of the blast furnace conveyer, eliminating steel-rolling accidents. He's now been elevated to an Advanced Worker."

"Oh! Ah Fang, that's no small achievement!"

"Master, what I did doesn't amount to much."

As Shun-fa continued to praise Ah Fang, he could not help turning his head to gaze out the window. Outside, the sunlight was bright and beautiful, and the sky was painted turquoise. Off in the distance atop the pitch-black giant blast furnace, he could make out the conveyer pulley gliding upwards and downwards. Shun-fa nodded his head, as if to say, "Oh! I can see it. Excellent! You clever rogue, you!" Ah Fang looked away, hinting that he did not care much about his achievement.

"Master, the lathe workers, fitters, and planers in our chief engineer's shop recently held a work performance competition." Ta-k'uei always spoke with great energy, and as he was talking his chair creaked and groaned. "Among the fitters, the most skilled was none other than our Master Chü-sheng. When it comes to fitting wedges into grooves, he's simply perfect. In handling a file, he has to be reckoned the best around; there's no fitter in the entire factory who can compare with him."

"Ta-k'uei! Don't ... don't talk nonsense!" Chü-sheng's usual modesty made him blush several shades of crimson. Ta-k'uei was not to be stopped. "You're as good as anyone can ever be with a file. And that's the truth!"

"If that's the case, then it's because my Master has taught me well."

While listening to this interchange, Shun-fa saw before him a mature, highly experienced Chü-sheng, but his mind conjured up the image of a scene that had occurred seventeen years ago: fifteen-year-old Chü-sheng wearing only a small and ragged cotton-padded jacket in the cold, dimly lit workshop, standing on tiptoes, wielding a file as though he were pulling on an oar. He was filing a metal wedge. He was so small that he stood no more than a head taller than the vise on the worktable; his hands were frozen like a steamed roll, all red and swollen. No matter how hard he tried he simply could not keep the file steady and straight, so that the wedges he made were all "big-bellied." When Master Shun-fa saw it, he curled his right forefinger and middle finger into a small fist the shape of a chestnut. He rapped little Chü-sheng soundly on the head, admonishing him, "Idiot! You ought to be spanked, so stupid! How many times have I told you—you must keep the file level and steady. Look at the way you're doing it, rolling from side to side like pulling on a sampan oar—hmph! What a good-for-nothing you are! Now look, you have to do it like this, see?" At the same time that he was scolding him, Shun-fa took the file himself and worked to correct Chü-sheng's error until it came out properly. However, little Chü-sheng was crying, using his finger to wipe his runny nose, ice-cold tears falling from the corners of his eyes, which were so full of the innocence of youth. At this point, Master Shun-fa's attitude softened, and he sighed as he said, "Ai! Child, if you don't become proficient at a trade, you're going to starve to death in the future; no one will give you a job—you must learn, learn for all you're worth!" Thereupon, little Chü-sheng once again began to file away in the very same "oar-pulling" manner. —Yes, indeed, this had happened seventeen years ago. Now, as Shun-fa gazed at the Chü-sheng who had become a skilled professional, his heart was filled with inexpressible emotion; he even began to reproach himself for having been too stern in those early years of Chü-sheng's apprenticeship.

"Do you still remember? In the beginning of your apprenticeship, I ... ai! ... I hit you so many times!" Much touched, Chü-sheng strode over to Shun-fa and said with the affection of a son for a father, "Master! I understand you perfectly now, why you scolded me so harshly, why you hit me with your knuckles. You did it for my own good; if you hadn't been so strict, I'd never be able to use the file as well as I do today." Chü-sheng's words warmed Shun-fa's old heart. The old master worker was too overwhelmed to smile; only warm tears trickled down his wrinkled cheeks. "Master, what's wrong?" asked Ah Fang. Hsiao Mao and "Little Dumpling" were also deeply moved; all the young men in the room were equally affected. They could sense in their hearts the old man's love for them—the noble and lofty class love felt by the older workers for the new generation. "I . . . I'm so very happy!" Shun-fa held Chü-sheng's hand tightly as he spoke, feeling that he was the luckiest man in the whole world.

The golden rays of the sun reached through the window and shone on Shun-fa's gleaming bald head, his rosy cheeks, and his thick grey eyebrows; he was the very picture of honesty and kindness. In the eyes of the young workers there, he became a strong and beautifully sculptured idol. A cool, fresh gust of wind blew into the room, causing a small, dark-green potted evergreen plant to quiver; like Shun-fa, it appeared lively and vibrant.

Ah-fang spoke out suddenly, "Oh, no! We've totally ignored our hostess!"

"I'm coming! I was making dumplings for all of you!" Auntie Ch'en was just on her way into the room carrying a tray on which were placed some ten bowls of steaming hot dumplings. She went around giving each a bowl, laughing and saying, "Let's eat dumplings on New Year's, and may we be reunited every year as we are today."

Hsiao Mao joked, "Oh! They're all 'Little Dumplings'!" Everyone in the room laughed.

After eating the dumplings the young workers took their leave. Just before departing they requested that if it were not too troublesome for Master Shun-fa, they would like to come to him for guidance whenever they ran into complex problems in production at the factory. Shun-fa assured them that he would be most happy and not in the least put out. Shun-fa saw them out himself, walking them clear out to the main road. It was not until the young men rode off on their bicycles or boarded the buses—just like a flock of sparrows dispersing in all directions—that Shun-fa turned around and strolled back, feeling very happy all the way home.

A happy man finds interest in everything. Shun-fa was just passing by the gate of the Lis' house when he saw inside the courtyard two ducks thrusting out their rear ends, flapping their wings to fly, and *quack, quack, quacking* noisily. He thought to himself, "Ah, how large the ducklings hatched by our old barren hen have grown!" Nearing his own gate he noticed his neighbor, Mr. Wang, his grandson in his arms, emerge smiling and chuckling from his duck-pen, where he had just picked up a large duck egg. Old Mr. Wang was playing with the child and saying, "Look! A large duck egg, how wonderful!"

"Congratulations to you, Mr. Wang!" called out Shun-fa with a smile.

"Oh, it's you! Take a look, the two duck eggs I got not too long ago have now produced eggs of their own!" replied Mr. Wang.

Shun-fa opened the door and went into his apartment, but seeing that his wife was in the kitchen washing dishes, he turned into the living room. The clock on the chest of drawers was just striking ten. The apartment had returned to its former quiet and lonely state; there was only the clock ticking in regular motion. Shun-fa stood before the window, lit a cigarette, and smoked slowly. His gaze once again fell upon the solitary small pine tree outside, yet this time he felt that the pine tree seemed suddenly to have grown a great deal taller. He looked at its surroundings, and he was slightly dumbstruck: that pine tree was not standing all alone after all, for it was included in the composition of a beautiful panoramic work of art. In the pine's background, weren't there the distant outlines of brand-new apartment buildings? Wasn't there also the tall furnace as well as the hot-blast furnace and the factory itself, with its roofline rising and falling against the sky? He once again saw in the courtyard the old hen come clucking along with head bobbing. Presently, the old hen passed in front of the window, tilted her head, blinking her round eyes. She then gave out two prolonged *cluck-cluck* cries, as if to say, "I'm going to lay an egg!"

Strange to say, Shun-fa could not help laughing. "Oh, if you don't lay an egg, it really doesn't matter." As he spoke, his wife entered the room carrying a wash basin, and she asked in disbelief, "Old man! What nonsense are you spouting now?"

"Nothing, nothing, I was talking about the hen." Auntie Ch'en breathed a sigh, "Ai! I really don't know what's the matter with you."

"Haven't you seen it? Our family's ducks have all grown up."

"The ducks belong to other families, not to 'our family.'"

This time, Shun-fa simply did not care to reply.

February 8, 1962

Translated by Michael Gotz

CH'EN YÜN, CHANG LI-HUI, HSÜ CHING-HSIEN

Not much is known about Ch'en Yün and Chang Li-hui, but Hsü Ching-hsien was a recognized young writer in the 1950s and 1960s and had a stormy political career.

Hsü published many articles and character sketches; some of the best were collected in *Life Is Like Fire* (1965). In 1966 he spearheaded a revolt in the Party structure in Shanghai and became a staunch supporter of the Gang of Four. He rose to the high status of a member of the Party Central Committee and vice-mayor of Shanghai. His Party assignments made him instrumental in the persecution of many noted authors during the Cultural Revolution in the Shanghai area. One report said that the fall of the Gang of Four in 1976 sent Hsü to prison.

The Young Generation, a four-act play treating the problem of getting young people to work in faraway places, touches a sore issue known as the "rustification of the young generation," or the endless task of fighting the corrupting influence of city life. It has continuing significance in the People's Republic.

—K.Y.H.

---

from *The Young Generation*

Main Characters:

HSIAO CHI-YEH, twenty-seven years old, graduated along with Lin Yü-sheng from the Geological Institute, now a member of a mining survey team assigned in the frontier region of Tsinghai Province. Hero of the drama, he is the model of loyalty to the Party and to the socialist revolutionary ideal, totally selfless, wise, enthusiastic, and capable. He is being sent back to Shanghai to report on the survey team's findings, as well as to persuade Lin to return to his duty in Tsinghai.

GRANDMOTHER HSIAO, over seventy, Hsiao Chi-yeh's grandmother, once a bond maid in a landlord's household, now a veteran Communist, a staunch and loyal partisan.

LIN YÜ-SHENG, twenty-four, classmate of Hsiao Chi-yen. Because his real parents were executed by the Kuomintang in the 1930s, he has been raised by the Lin family, his parents' old comrades. Spoiled by the bourgeois life in Shanghai and by his foster mother, Lin schemes to return to Shanghai for good in order to be with his girlfriend and enjoy city life.

LIN CHIEN, over fifty, Lin's foster father, veteran Communist, model partisan, who risked his life for the revolution many times. He is now head of a factory.

628

Hsia Shu-chüan, over forty, Lin's foster mother, aunt to Lin's girlfriend, Hsia Ch'ien-ju.

Lin Lan, eighteen, daughter of the Lin couple, graduating from high school.

Hsia Ch'ien-ju, twenty-three, Lin's girlfriend, graduating from the Geological College this semester. A bright and promising student, she is now torn between following better examples to accept what the country needs and go wherever the Party wants her and her boyfriend Lin's wish to stay in Shanghai to enjoy a better personal life.

Li Jung-sheng, sixteen, has done nothing for over a year because he cannot pass the high school entrance exam and is unwilling to work.

[In Act One, Lin Yü-sheng, egged on by Little Wu, a sort of playboy with a bourgeois family background, has forged a medical certificate about his arthritic leg in order to be allowed to return to Shanghai from his assignment in faraway Tsinghai. Lin buys expensive food and a Western-style dress to celebrate his girlfriend's birthday. Lin's foster mother, Hsia, while indulging Lin, hides the dress from the father's observation for fear that he might object to such bourgeois taste. Hsiao Chi-yen foils Lin's scheme to stay on in Shanghai by urging the Party authority in Shanghai not to assign him a job there. Lin learns about Hsiao's doing and suspects that Hsiao wants to get him away in order to steal his girlfriend. The birthday party is ruined because of the confrontation between Hsiao and Lin.

Act Two begins about a week later. Hsiao has just been told that his leg injury could be serious, but he does not take it seriously. Lin discusses his plan to stay in Shanghai with his girlfriend, urging her to marry him right away, which could persuade the authorities to let both of them stay. She scorns the idea. He switches his tactics; now he seeks his foster mother's intervention to get him a job in Shanghai. The mother reluctantly agrees but promptly regrets it, as Hsiao reminds her of the unethical nature of such "back-door" practice—influence-manipulation for personal gain. Lin's foster father returns in time to stop the mother from going to see the Party authorities, and the old couple starts to argue, with the mother still siding with Lin. Grandmother Hsiao enters to share with Lin's sister the bad news about Hsiao's leg: an amputation might be unavoidable. They hesitate, but eventually the grandmother breaks the bad news to Hsiao.]

ACT THREE

Follows closely upon the preceding act, with the same setting as the first act. [The small living room of the Lin family, in the suburbs of Shanghai. A staircase ascends to the second floor; there is a window through which the audience can see the scenery of suburban Shanghai, with factories in the distant background. A large door opens to the outside, one door to the kitchen, and another to the room shared by Lin Lan and Hsia Ch'ien-ju. The whole setting projects a feeling of simplicity and cleanliness.]

It is a breathlessly hot afternoon; the sun glares down mercilessly upon the earth. Even the chirping of the cicadas, showing fatigue, sounds heavy and dull.

From the window a few black clouds can be seen floating in the deep blue sky. One can faintly hear the deep rumble of far-off thunder.

(LIN LAN *is in the small living room repairing a wooden bucket. Her concern for* HSIAO CHI-YEH *makes her uneasy. She frequently goes out to look toward the road.* LIN YÜ-SHENG *sits on the sofa reading a magazine.* HSIA CH'IEN-JU *enters*)

HSIA CH'IEN-JU (*Toward inner room*)   Auntie, I'm going to the College. (*Exit*)
(*Just as* LIN YÜ-SHENG *is about to go into an inner room, the telephone rings*)

LIN YÜ-SHENG (*Answering the phone*)   Hello! Hi! . . . It's me . . . Go swimming? So you still feel like going swimming. I don't want to go . . . Look, things are really screwed up. Sure, I got my mother to go along, but my father found out . . . Yes . . . I simply don't have any alternative now . . . What? Write a letter to the school and use my father's seal? No, that's no good . . . No, anyway, I can't do that . . . Go to the college myself? . . . Yeah. Anyway, it's not against the law to express my opinion. OK, I'll go try and see . . . 'Bye.
(*Hangs up, and, pushing his bicycle, is about to exit*)

LIN LAN   Brother, who was that on the phone? . . . Little Wu again. Where're you going?

LIN YÜ-SHENG   There are some things I have to do. (*Exit*)

LIN LAN   Dad's coming; he wants to see you! (*Chases after her brother, shouting*)
(LIN CHIEN *enters, sees the broken bucket, starts to repair it*)
(LI JUNG-SHENG *enters*)

LI JUNG-SHENG   Lanlan! Lanlan! She's not home! (*Sees* LIN CHIEN) Oh, good. Just in time—a bucket repairman. We have a broken bucket, too. If you come over to our place in a while and fix it, we'll pay you.

LIN CHIEN (*Looks at him, laughs*)   Fine, Which house do you live in?

LI JUNG-SHENG   Number two in Workers' New Village. I'll take you there in a while. I ran into you just in time. Otherwise I'd have gotten yelled at.

LIN CHIEN   What do you mean?

LI JUNG-SHENG   My father would have come home and said, "All day long you do nothing. I tell you to fix the bucket and you won't. The only thing you know how to do is open your mouth to eat."

LIN CHIEN   What? Don't you go to school?

LI JUNG-SHENG   Last year I didn't pass the exam for senior high, so now I just hang around home.

LIN CHIEN   Why don't you find some work to do?

LI JUNG-SHENG   What is there good to do? Last year the Neighborhood Committee sponsored me to be a clerk, but I didn't want to be one. Now they're after me to go to work on a farm, but I don't want to.

LIN CHIEN   Why don't you go? I would if I were you.

LI JUNG-SHENG   It's OK if you want to go. You are a manual laborer, but I'm an intellectual.

LIN CHIEN (*Laughs*) Ha! What a big intellectual!

LI JUNG-SHENG Well, I've been through nine years of school, and they want me to do farm work! And they keep on saying how happy I ought to be to have grown up under socialism. What a pain!

LIN CHIEN Why aren't you happy? Isn't it good to go to the countryside to build socialism and new farm villages, and use your own hands to create a beautiful new life?

LI JUNG-SHENG Why should I be so happy about wallowing around in the mud all day, and getting all stinky and sweaty?

LIN CHIEN Well, what do you think you would be happy doing?

LI JUNG-SHENG A lot of things. Ha, like Lin Lan's father—a great leader. That must be impressive, and interesting!

LIN CHIEN No. It's no fun being a great leader.

LI JUNG-SHENG Come on, what's so hard about being a great leader?

LIN CHIEN Suppose I don't mention the past, when he used to fight as a guerrilla against the Kuomintang, but just stick to the present. If you're a great leader, you have to take part in the labor, you have to learn new jobs, and also have to get the work done fast and efficiently. There are quite a few things to worry about. And if you have a free moment, you still have to take care of other things like fixing this wooden bucket.

LI JUNG-SHENG Oh, come on, a big leader fixing a bucket?

LIN CHIEN Why not? Leaders are just regular people.

LI JUNG-SHENG From what you say, it isn't so much fun to be a leader.

LIN CHIEN The way you look at things, you wouldn't be satisfied no matter what you did.

LI JUNG-SHENG Ohhh. You seem to know quite a bit. How come? Did you go to school, too?

LIN CHIEN Did I ever go to school? I was an apprentice when I was quite young, but my education is only what I was able to piece together for myself, later on. How can I compare with you intellectuals? Back in the old days . . .

LI JUNG-SHENG Ohhh, you too! As soon as you start to talk, "Back in the old days . . . " Just like my father. These aren't the old days anymore. I'm sick of hearing about them!

LIN CHIEN If you don't know how bitter it was back in the old days, then you don't know how sweet it is today. Unless we talk about those times, you'll all think that the good life we have today just fell from the sky.

LI JUNG-SHENG Boy, you're a good talker. Why don't you get another job? You only fix buckets!

LIN CHIEN If nobody wanted to be a bucket repairman, then you'd have to fix your bucket yourself. And if you don't fix it, your father will yell at you, right?

LI JUNG-SHENG Then let somebody else fix it. Don't you have some education? It's really too bad for you to be doing this.

LIN CHIEN Is it? What do you think would be appropriate for me?

LI JUNG-SHENG Let me think. (*Thinking seriously*) That's it! You could be a store clerk.

LIN CHIEN But you didn't want to do that yourself, right?

LI JUNG-SHENG I've gone through nine years of school, but you've only . . .

LIN CHIEN   I only have a little bit of education, right?

LI JUNG-SHENG (*Satisfied*)   Yep.

(LIN LAN *enters*)

LIN LAN   Dad! Why are you back?

LI JUNG-SHENG (*Surprised*) "Dad?" He's your father, the one who is a big leader?

LIN LAN   I only have one father. (*Sees that* LI JUNG-SHENG *wants to run off*) What are you running away for? Come here, come here. Dad, this is Little Li.

LIN CHIEN   We've met.

LI JUNG-SHENG   So you're the one who won all those battles ... the ... great leader.

LIN CHIEN   Great leaders still fix buckets, right?

LI JUNG-SHENG (*To* LIN LAN)   Is it true that your father wants to go out to a farm?

LIN LAN   Why shouldn't it be true? Too bad his superiors won't let him go. (LI JUNG-SHENG *stares at* LIN CHIEN)

LIN CHIEN (*To* LIN LAN)   Well, how about you? Did you do well on the exam for Agricultural School?

LIN LAN   Dad, I didn't take the exam.

LI JUNG-SHENG (*Amazed*)   Didn't take it?

LIN CHIEN (*Surprised*)   Oh? What happened, you ...

LIN LAN (*Agitatedly explaining*)   No. Dad, I ran into something unexpected.

LIN CHIEN   An accident?

LIN LAN   Well, yes. This morning I thought that on the way over I'd go meet Wang Hsiu and go to the exam together with her, but when I got to her house, she had already left, and I found her mother having a relapse of her heart trouble. What could I do? There was nobody else at home. If I didn't help her, it'd be too late, so I took her right to the hospital. After the doctors saved her, and felt that the crisis had passed, I waited until they put her in a hospital room before I left. By that time, everybody had finished the exam.

LIN CHIEN   So that's what happened.

LIN LAN   Just now Wang Hsiu told me that she wanted to go explain the reason to the entrance examination committee, and request them to give me a make-up examination, but I wouldn't agree to it. Dad, I didn't plan to tell you, but I was afraid you'd be sad, so now ...

LIN CHIEN   You did the right thing! In order to help a person, you gave up your chance to advance your own education. That kind of spirit is commendable. But what do you plan to do later on?

LIN LAN   I plan to go to the Chingkang Mountain Farm in Kiangsi.

LIN CHIEN   Ah, good. You can learn by real work. Whether it's thought or agricultural science, in both you can learn something. But once you're there, you may run into a lot of difficulties. Have you considered that?

LIN LAN   Yes, I have. I think that no matter how big the difficulties are now, they can't compare with the ones you had when you were working for the Revolution. (*As though to herself*) Since the people in our parents' generation are all courageous, we better not be cowards!

LIN CHIEN   Well said!

LIN LAN   Mom'll never agree to this.

LIN CHIEN   Is she home?

LIN LAN   She probably went upstairs.

LIN CHIEN   Your mother will agree. She'll agree.

LIN LAN (*Happily*)   Little Li! Let's go there together!

LI JUNG-SHENG (*Hesitating*)   I ... I don't want to go.

LIN CHIEN   What? Oh, you can't find happiness as a farm worker, right?

(LI JUNG-SHENG *does not speak*)

LIN CHIEN   That's right, that's right. Young people always like to talk about this "happiness." As long as things are going along the way they want, they say, "I'm so happy." But when they run into the least thing that doesn't go the way they want, they say, "I'm not happy at all." But what is this "happiness?" They haven't even figured it out themselves.

LIN LAN   Dad, what do you say happiness is?

LIN CHIEN   Happiness is just an attractive-sounding word. (*To* LI JUNG-SHENG) Hey, come on, Little Li, sit down. Different people, different classes have different understandings of this word. Some people feel that happiness is just eating and playing without having to do any work. There are also people who feel that happiness is having fame and power. These views are both wrong. They do not correspond to the proletariat's view of happiness. We say that for a true revolutionary, happiness and struggle are inseparable. Before the Liberation, countless revolutionaries struggled heroically to overthrow the reactionary institutions. In their view, there was no greater happiness than that. Today, after Liberation, we don't suffer oppression and exploitation, but the struggle has not stopped at all. There is no greater happiness than for a young person to be able to take part in today's class struggle and production struggle, to contribute his or her share to the work of the Party and the people. (*Pointedly*) The kind of person who does not put out his or her best efforts can never achieve happiness. Right? Intellectual!

(LI JUNG-SHENG *does not speak*)

LIN CHIEN   You're not a child anymore! You have to use your brains. It'll be just terrible if you keep on muddling along like this!

(LI JUNG-SHENG *lowers his head and does not speak*)

LIN LAN (*To* LI JUNG-SHENG)   Well, how about it? You'd better come with me to the Chingkang Mountain.

LI JUNG-SHENG   I ... I'll think it over.

LIN CHIEN   Good. You have to consider it. If you aren't busy, come over often; and if there's time, we'll talk about it. How's that?

(LI JUNG-SHENG *nods*)

LIN CHIEN   You little imp.

LI JUNG-SHENG (*To* LIN LAN)   I'm going now. Here's your *China Youth*. (*Bows to* LIN CHIEN) Goodbye!   (*Exit*)

LIN CHIEN (*About to exit, turns to* LIN LAN)   Where's your brother?

LIN LAN   He went to the college about Ch'ien-ju's job assignment.

LIN CHIEN (*Severely*)   What, he went himself?

LIN LAN   Yes. Just now, that Little Wu called again, and after Yü-sheng took the call, he left.

(*Silence*)

LIN CHIEN   When he comes back, tell him to see me upstairs. (*Exit*)
(*After a slight pause,* HSIAO CHI-YEH *enters, walking with difficulty*)
LIN LAN   Chi-yeh! You're back!
HSIAO CHI-YEH   Where's your brother?
LIN LAN   How's your leg?
HSIAO CHI-YEH   Isn't he home?
LIN LAN   What'd the doctor say?
HSIAO CHI-YEH   He wants me to go to the hospital right away ... to have a biopsy.
LIN LAN   There's hope, isn't there?
(HSIAO CHI-YEH *does not speak*)
HSIAO CHI-YEH (*After a pause*)   Where'd Yü-sheng go?
LIN LAN   He went to the college.
HSIAO CHI-YEH   He went himself?
LIN LAN   Oh, my brother wants to stay in Shanghai himself, and he's also trying to keep our cousin here, too ... How could you have agreed to let him come back? Is his leg really that bad? That hospital must be crazy. They even gave him a medical excuse.
HSIAO CHI-YEH   That's just what I came to see him about.
LIN LAN   What for? Is ...
HSIAO CHI-YEH   I want to ask him about ... ask him whether he can go back to Tsinghai a little earlier.
LIN LAN   Yeah. That'll be good if you make him go back early.
(*After a slight pause,* LIN YÜ-SHENG *enters through the front door*)
LIN LAN   Hsiao Chi-yeh, my brother's back.
LIN YÜ-SHENG   Oh, you're here. I was just thinking of looking for you.
HSIAO CHI-YEH   I've been thinking of coming to see you, too. (*To* LIN LAN) I'd like to talk to your brother alone.
(*Exit* LIN LAN)
LIN YÜ-SHENG   Good. I hope you can give me an explanation.
HSIAO CHI-YEH   An explanation of what?
LIN YÜ-SHENG   Of why you want to create trouble between Ch'ien-ju and me, of why you're always trying to mobilize her to leave Shanghai. Why?
HSIAO CHI-YEH   Because the job requires you to leave this place. As an old classmate, I couldn't bear to see you going on like this.
LIN YÜ-SHENG   Thank you for your concern.
HSIAO CHI-YEH (*Sincerely*)   Yü-sheng, we were classmates for many years ... if I overstate myself, please don't get mad. We've been apart for almost a year now, and I really didn't expect you to turn out like this.
LIN YÜ-SHENG   May I ask how I've turned out?
HSIAO CHI-YEH   Just think, now. What have you done for the whole year? All day long you just stay hidden away in your petty individualist world, satisfied with your mediocre, trivial existence, hankering after the easy life, the only thing in your immediate view.
LIN YÜ-SHENG   Since you're so concerned about my life, I'll speak frankly with you. We do intend to make our life better, more comfortable, to make our life richer and more varied. Why is everybody working so hard? Isn't it just to make life better and happier?

HSIAO CHI-YEH   To make whose life happier? Is it just to make your individual life happier, or is it to give more happiness through your and everyone's labor, to the lives of hundreds of millions of people? You want your life richer and more varied. That's all right. Our life today *is* the richest, most varied in history. But it certainly is not in your little room, but in the ardent struggle of the broad masses!

LIN YÜ-SHENG   Don't talk to me about your high principles. I ask you, do you still admit the existence of individual happiness?

HSIAO CHI-YEH   In a socialist society, no worker is oppressed, no worker is exploited, and, while working in the collective, one can develop one's intelligence and abilities to the fullest and can create a more beautiful future. Isn't this the greatest individual happiness? Yü-sheng, the key to this question is just this: what kind of happiness is it that you're pursuing? If the whole country hadn't been liberated, then for sons of workers like you and me, it would be hard even to survive, not to mention graduating from college. And how could you even begin to discuss this kind of happiness that you're thinking of? When we think of happines today, we must never, never just pursue individual pleasure, or forget the responsibility that we young people bear toward the Party and the people. We must not forget to commit ourselves wholeheartedly to the magnificent work of building socialism.

LIN YÜ-SHENG   I haven't forgotten, and I can't possibly forget! If we do feel some interest in our own happiness, well, so what? We work and we labor like anybody else. We neither go around robbing and plundering nor do we exploit or interfere with others; we just spend our days according to our own wishes and our own ideals. May I ask what is illegal about this?

HSIAO CHI-YEH   There it is, over and over again, "ourselves," "ourselves." You start with yourself, and finish with legality, so where do you put the interests of the nation and the collective? Our country works according to plans, so when you put the interests of the individual before those of the collective, beyond the scope of national planning, how can this *not* interfere with others? How can you say it's "legal" not to respond to the needs of the country, not to obey your job assignment?! Why shouldn't you be criticized for it?

LIN YÜ-SHENG   Do you mean that the only thing in the interest of the nation is to go to some border area? Everyone has his own conditions. Surely you wouldn't go so far as to have everybody live the life of those in the mountain gulches!

HSIAO CHI-YEH   I'm sad for you when you talk this way. In the mountain gulches, you say? If it hadn't been for the vanguards of the Revolution struggling in the wild mountains, then there wouldn't have been any victory for the Chinese Revolution. If it weren't for the support from the mountain gullies and farming villages all over the country, our great cities and industries would have lost their life line. How can we achieve socialism, how can we gain happiness for the people, unless we arduously build up the country? Besides, the battle post for us geologists is right in the mountains! Yü-sheng, what's happened to that great ambition you had just after we graduated? You're on a very dangerous road!

LIN YÜ-SHENG (*Sneers*)   Dangerous road? What's the danger?

HSIAO CHI-YEH   The danger is that you aren't thinking of the Revolution any-more. The danger is that individualistic thought can corrupt your spirit without your being aware of it! It can destroy your ideals, erode your resolve, and make you fall deeper and deeper into the capitalist quagmire.

LIN YÜ-SHENG (*Contemptuously*)   Don't try to scare me. I did not come from a bourgeois family.

HSIAO CHI-YEH   As the postrevolutionary generation, we have to be even more careful. If we aren't, then despite the fact that we may have been born into the right family, bourgeois thought can still bore its way into our minds. (*Emphasizes*) It's up to you what path you take, but you're responsible for your behavior.

LIN YÜ-SHENG (*Counterattacking*)   What about you, then? It doesn't look like you've done any earthshaking deeds!

HSIAO CHI-YEH   That's right. Earthshaking deeds are done by the masses, not by any individual. I recall Chairman Mao saying something like, "An individual's abilities have a certain range. As long as one is not selfish, then one is a noble person, a pure person, a virtuous person, a person who has abandoned vulgarity, a person who is useful to the people." My abilities are very limited, but I'm willing to use all my strength to work in accord with the needs of the Party, and to be a simple, solid screw in the machine.

LIN YÜ-SHENG   Ah, what lofty ideals!

HSIAO CHI-YEH   No! Just the standard behavior for the busy life of the young people in the era of Mao Tse-tung. All of us ought to be like that. Yü-sheng, don't go on like this! Come back to Tsinghai!

LIN YÜ-SHENG   I have a bad leg. Don't you know?

HSIAO CHI-YEH   Is it really that bad?

LIN YÜ-SHENG (*Pretending to be tough, but actually afraid*)   What do you mean by that? The doctor gave me a medical excuse. You've seen it.

HSIAO CHI-YEH   Yes, I've seen it; it's in my pocket right now.

LIN YÜ-SHENG   What?

HSIAO CHI-YEH   But the doctor's added a few words.

LIN YÜ-SHENG   You ...

HSIAO CHI-YEH   See for yourself. (*Hands the certificate to* LIN YÜ-SHENG)
(*When* LIN YÜ-SHENG *looks at the certificate, his face immediately turns pale. He reaches out to take the slip of paper and, with shaking hands, looks at the doctor's repudiation, then collapses on a chair*)
(*Thunder rumbles*)
(LIN LAN *enters, sees the certificate on the table*)

LIN LAN (*Reads aloud*)   "This hospital never issued this certificate. It is a forgery."
(*Exit* LIN YÜ-SHENG, *hurriedly*)

LIN LAN   So this is how it is! (*About to go upstairs*)

HSIAO CHI-YEH (*Hurries to stop her*)   Lanlan! Don't tell your father about this for a while. We should try to help your brother.
(HSIA CH'IEN-JU *enters through the front door.* HSIAO CHI-YEH *takes the certificate from* LIN LAN'S *hands and hides it*)

LIN LAN   Cousin ... (*Stopped by* HSIAO CHI-YEH)

HSIA CH'IEN-JU (*Senses something amiss*)   What's going on?

HSIAO CHI-YEH   Nothing.

HSIA CH'IEN-JU (*To* HSIAO CHI-YEH)   What're you holding?

LIN LAN: It's ...

HSIAO CHI-YEH (*Immediately*)   A letter.

HSIA CH'IEN-JU   No. It looks like you're trying to hide something from me, Hsiao Chi-yeh. Let me see it.

HSIAO CHI-YEH   I can't let you see it.

HSIA CH'IEN-JU   Why?

HSIAO CHI-YEH   It has nothing to do with you.

(HSIA CH'IEN-JU *looks at them, suspecting something, then suddenly becomes worried*)

(LIN YÜ-SHENG *enters, unnoticed*)

HSIA CH'IEN-JU   Did he do something wrong? Why don't you say something? Give me the letter.

(*No one speaks*)

HSIA CH'IEN-JU   Ahhh. Don't torture me!

LIN YÜ-SHENG (*To* HSIAO CHI-YEH)   Give me the certificate. (*After receiving the certificate, he resolutely hands it to* HSIA CH'IEN-JU.) Ch'ien-ju, I've done something very wrong.

(HSIA CH'IEN-JU *tensely looks at the certificate, and then, downcast, walks toward the window*)

(*Outside, it begins to pour*)

HSIA CH'IEN-JU (*Softly*)   It's really pouring! ... (*For a long time she stands with her back to the audience*)

(LI JUNG-SHENG *enters, fleeing the rain, and takes in the scene with great amazement*)

(*Unbearable silence*)

LIN YÜ-SHENG   Well, what do you all say? What should I do?

HSIAO CHI-YEH   Go back to the prospecting team. If you've fallen down at some place, then you just get back up right there.

LIN YÜ-SHENG   No. I've got a bad leg. Even if I did exaggerate the trouble, it really is true that there is trouble.

LIN LAN   Your trouble isn't in your leg; it's in your head!

HSIAO CHI-YEH (*Sincerely*)   Yü-sheng, just think of how many people are struggling day and night for the success of the Revolution. For the past thirty years, your father has been risking his life for the Revolution. And now he's still at the front line of the effort to build socialism. My grandmother's almost seventy. But has she ever stopped working for the Revolution? If the older generation is still at the front line today, then what reason do we young people have to hide away in a little corner of individualism?

LIN YÜ-SHENG   It's easy to talk, but if your leg was like mine, then you'd ...

LIN LAN   Brother!

HSIAO CHI-YEH   Then I'd sneak away from the prospecting team? No, I never would.

LIN YÜ-SHENG   Sure, it's easy to talk, but if it were really that way ...

LIN LAN (*Sharply*)   Brother! Do you know that they're going to amputate Hsiao Chi-yeh's leg?

HSIAO CHI-YEH (*Trying to stop her*)   Lanlan!

LIN YÜ-SHENG (*At the same time*) What?
(*Everyone is shocked silent by this sudden news*)
(*Silence*)

HSIAO CHI-YEH It doesn't matter. If they do amputate, I'll go back to the prospecting team on crutches. If I can't climb mountains, then I'll just stay on the ground; if I can't go out into the field, then I'll just stay in the tent. But I'm going to work my whole life on the prospecting team, no matter what! (*Looks at his watch*) I have to go to a meeting.

HSIA CH'IEN-JU Well, don't go.

HSIAO CHI-YEH Yes, I have to go; they're going to evaluate our geological report today. They're all waiting for me!
(LIN LAN *brings out an umbrella*)

LIN YÜ-SHENG I'll go with you.

HSIAO CHI-YEH (*Warmly seizing* LIN YÜ-SHENG'S *hand*) No. You stay at home and think about this.

LI JUNG-SHENG (*Takes the umbrella from* LIN LAN) I'll go with you.

HSIAO CHI-YEH Okay, I'll let you come with me. (*To* LIN YÜ-SHENG) We'll talk again in a little while.
(HSIAO CHI-YEH, LI JUNG-SHENG *exit, with* LIN LAN *following.* LIN YÜ-SHENG *and* HSIA CH'IEN-JU *are left onstage*) (*Embarrassed silence*)

LIN YÜ-SHENG Why don't you say something? Well . . . let me have it. You have the right to.

HSIA CH'IEN-JU No, I don't have any right to yell at you. I can see in you now what I'd have been like later on. It's only after all this that I've been able to understand clearly what I've actually been doing for the past year . . . But you —I never would've thought . . .
(LIN LAN *enters, turns, and starts upstairs*)

LIN YÜ-SHENG You think that I didn't intend to do a good job? At the beginning I worked really hard, but later . . . There were the hardships of the life there, the difficulties in the work, and then my leg started up on me . . . The only thing I could do was . . .

HSIA CH'IEN-JU The only thing you could do was sneak away and come back here? And you even forged a medical certificate!

LIN YÜ-SHENG How else could I have managed it? You know what my family's like. If I came back the way the others do, could they have forgiven me? Then Little Wu gave me the idea.

HSIA CH'IEN-JU Little Wu again! Do you mean that you're not responsible for this?

LIN YÜ-SHENG No, of course not. I'm not trying to hide what my idea was at that time. At the time I thought that since I wasn't well, couldn't it be just the same to go back to Shanghai and work? Anyway, I wouldn't be able to come up with any great accomplishments out there.

HSIA CH'IEN-JU You were fooling yourself! Why was Hsiao Chi-yeh able to accomplish something out there? I never thought that you'd turn out like this! (*Painfully*) I'm really ashamed of you. (*Turns, about to exit*)

LIN YÜ-SHENG Ch'ien-ju, you . . .
(LIN CHIEN *enters, with* HSIA SHU-CHÜAN, LIN LAN *following*)

HSIA CH'IEN-JU Hello, Uncle!

LIN CHIEN   Don't go. Everybody sit down.

(*Silence*)

LIN CHIEN   Where's the certificate?

(LIN YÜ-SHENG *takes out the certificate*)

LIN CHIEN   Put it up on the wall.

LIN YÜ-SHENG (*Pleading*)   Dad.

LIN CHIEN   Put it up. Let everybody take a good look at it again and again. This is a lesson for you and for the whole family. How could our family produce a gutless loser like you?

(LIN YÜ-SHENG *hesitantly looks at his mother*)

LIN CHIEN (*Firmly*)   Put it up! Put it up yourself.

HSIA SHU-CHÜAN   Do what he says.

(*With no alternative,* LIN YÜ-SHENG *reluctantly walks over to the wall*)

LIN CHIEN   Afraid our family will lose face, are you? You've already made the whole working class lose face. (*Pained*) Doing what you did—a deserter! You've betrayed the Party that trained you, you've betrayed the teachers who taught you; but worst of all, you've let down your own departed parents.

(*Everyone starts*)

LIN CHIEN   Shu-chüan, it's time to tell him. (*Turns and goes upstairs*)

LIN YÜ-SHENG   My departed parents? Mom, you ...

HSIA SHU-CHÜAN (*Pained*)   No, we aren't your real parents. Your real parents died in a Kuomintang prison twenty-four years ago.

LIN YÜ-SHENG   Really?

HSIA SHU-CHÜAN   Your real parents worked in a factory with your father, joined the labor movement together and were also comrades-in-arms. During one strike, they were captured and put in jail. The enemy sentenced your real parents to death. Three days after you were born, they were killed.

(LIN CHIEN *comes downstairs carrying a box*)

LIN CHIEN (*Takes a letter out of the box*)   This is the letter your mother wrote for you just before she died.

LIN YÜ-SHENG   A letter from my mother. (*Takes the letter*)

LIN CHIEN (*Pained*)   Read it out loud; look at the hopes your parents had for you.

LIN YÜ-SHENG (*Reads aloud*)   "Dear Son: The executioner has already lifted his axe. All our comrades are singing heroically. We'll have to go up to the platform soon. You will never see your own parents again.

"Son, I'm writing this letter to remind you that your parents are workers and have sacrificed their lives for the Revolution of the Proletariat. You can forget your father and you can forget your mother, but you must never, never, forget that the world still harbors our class enemies! You must struggle for the sacred ideals of Communism.

"My child, hold the red flag high! Always advancing, always working for the Revolution, always loyal to the Party, always for the people!

"It is time, now. The prison doors are clanging. The executioner is coming. We part forever, my beloved child! We are going. Remember your debt. Don't forget your roots. Don't forget your roots ... " (*Toward the letter*) My mother! My own mother! (*He hunches over on the table, crying*)

LIN CHIEN   That's right, that's right. Don't forget your roots! Don't forget that you're the son of workers. Even more important, don't forget that throughout the world there is still a wide ... My old comrades-in-arms! You gave everything for the Revolution. Our life today is what we got with your blood, with your heads. But what can I say? ... I've let you down. I haven't brought him up to be the kind of person that you wanted. (*Painfully*) But I, I never imagined that he could ... Ohhh. (*Strikes the table with his fist and, after an emotion-choked pause, says sadly*) Yü-sheng, it wasn't easy for the proletariat to obtain power! The imperialists and reactionaries are just dreaming of a chance to get their wish to oppose the Revolution and restore the old order by using you young people. Son, you've got to be careful!

LIN YÜ-SHENG   Don't say any more, Dad. Please don't say any more! (*Runs off, crying*)

HSIA SHU-CHÜAN   Yü-sheng!

LIN CHIEN   It's all right, let him go run for a while in the rain and the wind. (*To* HSIA SHU-CHÜAN) You see? You can't be lax!

(HSIA SHU-CHÜAN *does not speak*)

LIN CHIEN   Of course, I'm responsible, too. The past few years, I've been rather insensitive to the problems of rearing our children. I always thought that in our society young people couldn't go too far astray. (*Forcefully*) No. The influence of the capitalist class is still extremely strong. Not every young person can correctly choose his or her own path!

(HSIA CH'IEN-JU *suddenly stands up, walks toward the door*)

LIN LAN   Where are you going?

HSIA CH'IEN-JU   I'm going to see Secretary Ho. (*Exits*)

LIN CHIEN   She ought to go.

(*Silence.* LIN LAN *is quietly looking at her father*)

LIN CHIEN   After every kind of hardship, our generation finally seized political power and established the regime of the proletariat; but Chairman Mao has repeatedly warned us that we have just taken the first step in our Long March! The way we are going is a road full of difficulties, but it is the road to victory! But what about the next generation? Will they be able to follow our path after all?

LIN LAN (*Resolutely*)   Yes, Dad. Don't worry. We can follow your path to the end!

LIN CHIEN (*Emotionally gazing at his daughter*) Good! You've got to be determined to obey the Party. Always keep to the Revolutionary road! (*Severely*) There are people who want to make our next generation corrupt and degenerate ... They can't! We'll never let them!

(*Curtain*)

[ACT FOUR. With his dishonesty exposed, LIN cannot bear the thought of returning in humiliation to his team in Tsinghai. However, the revelation of his real revolutionary Party parents has deeply touched him and he wants to go to the worst, most difficult place—partly to redeem himself and partly to run away from his girlfriend, now that he can no longer face her. HSIAO's patient but firm effort to educate LIN and his selfless act of yielding his own leading position on the team to Lin finally convince Lin that the comrades genuinely welcome back a prodigal son. The play closes with all the young people, including Li Jung-sheng and Lin Lan, gloriously and joyously setting off for the frontier areas to greet their new life and new assignments.]

Translated by Kevin O'Connor and Constantine Tung

Shao Ch'üan-lin (1905?–) and the "Middle Character" Controversy

It was the conviction of the May Fourth writers that public support for radical change would be mobilized when the truth about injustice and suffering in Chinese society was compellingly revealed in literature, particularly in fiction. And certainly, in retrospect, it was precisely the joining of a high degree of realistic integrity with a pragmatic intention that was one of the chief accomplishments of May Fourth literature. The new literature created to take its place after 1949 has retained the same belief in the pragmatic value of literature, but the shift has been away from realism toward the depiction of idealized characters who are to serve as role models, rather on the order of the exaggerations in the *Twenty-Four Paragons of Filial Piety* (or its female counterpart, *Biographies of Exemplary Women*) of the old society. That is, literary stories are used as a social tool for what psychologists call "alter casting."

Veteran writers did not shift easily to the new fiction, and rather than abandon their standards for realistic integrity, most stopped writing. Indeed, the history of Communist literature in China has been one of ever contracting boundaries, with sporadic attempts to break them down from the inside.

By 1962, long after the settling of the great confrontations with Ting Ling, Wang Shih-wei, Feng Hsüeh-feng, and finally, Hu Feng ("politics is the knife that killed literature"), the bureaucracy's problem became less one of holding its line on literature than one of finding some corrective to the problem of lifelessness and credibility. It was thus in the dual role of veteran writer and Party bureaucrat that Shao Ch'üan-lin addressed a conference of writers in Dairen in 1962 and argued persuasively for the return of a modest measure of realistic integrity to fiction. The context was not one of a challenge to government, such as Solzhenitsyn's letters to the Congress of Soviet Writers, but simply, it appears, a well-intended attempt by a Party member to get literature back on track, something to make it more effective while remaining within the basic Party guidelines. The key terms by which his views came to be known were "middle character" and "deepening of realism."

The inadequacy of the new literature, he argued, was a question not of subject matter but of treatment. The polished and buffed unreal new heroes who vigorously solved all problems and the protagonists who acted out the values the Party wanted propagated, threatened to reduce literary craftsmanship to simple Party spokesmanship. It was surely this tendency that provoked Shao to address the Dairen Conference in these terms:

> If there is merely diversity in the material, that still doesn't solve the problem. It is only when the characters themselves are diversified that we can widen the road of creativity. . . .

Stressing progressive and heroic characters is something we should continue to do, for it reflects the spirit of our age. However, speaking in terms of the overall situation, the reflection in our literature of people who are in the middle character situation in real life is relatively infrequent. The middle area is large and the tips are small; those who are good and those who are evil are relatively few. The largest number at every stratum are those in the middle; to depict them is very important because the contradictions invariably are centered upon such people. . . .

Shao's middle character views became highly controversial without their ever being published. What we know of them comes to us only indirectly, in the form of excerpts published in a curious *Literary Gazette* (Aug.–Sept. 1964) editorial that ostensibly attacked his views but in fact merely excerpted them one after another, with the occasional obligatory deprecating remark stitching them together. In the translation that follows, the *Gazette* editor's comments are in italics, Shao's are in ordinary type, and the translator's additions are in brackets and notes.

Shao was born around 1905, in Chekiang, and is himself the author of two short story collections dating from the Sino-Japanese war. He is mainly known for his long collaboration with Chou Yang in the literary bureaucracy, a relationship dating from their membership and activism in the League of Left-wing Writers in the 1930s. From 1953 to 1955 he was chief editor of *People's Literature* magazine. Conspicuously active in the antirightist campaigns of the late 1950s, which drove Ting Ling and others from power, he himself was purged as a rightist in the mid-1960s, when his middle character views were deliberately construed to be historically in a direct line with those of purged rightists, even including, ironically, his former enemies like Hu Feng. Those who silenced Shao pointed out that it was Hu Feng who over a decade earlier first observed that "Chinese society is small on both ends but big in the middle; the ends are hard, the middle, soft."

Recently the Chinese Writers' Association and its associated editorial office at the Literary Gazette *held a series of meetings to probe deeply into its errors and weaknesses, and especially into the error of the "middle character," whose chief proponent has been Shao Ch'üan-lin, former vice-chairman of the Association. From 1960 to the summer of 1962 the middle character was promoted in the editorial offices of the* Gazette *and its promotion in the pages of the* Gazette *itself was advocated. In the August 1962 meeting of the writers of short stories on rural subjects, held in Dairen and attended by sixteen writers and critics from eight provinces and cities, Shao Ch'üan-lin promoted the middle character idea and also advocated "the deepening of realism." After the meeting, the* Gazette *promoted the middle character.*

But comrades at subsequent meetings, based on overwhelming evidence, began a discussion and criticism of Shao Ch'üan-lin, whereupon it was decided that the middle character idea and the "deepening of realism" are bourgeois notions of literary theory, and that such notions oppose Party policy and oppose the principle of literature for the worker, peasant, and soldier. This will be discussed separately below.

In 1960 a series of long, critical articles in the Gazette *and other journals displeased Shao because of their discussion of the novel* The Builders *(by Liu Ch'ing) too much attention was paid to Liang Sheng-pao and too little to the middle character, Liang the Third. From 1960 on, at several editorial meetings sponsored by the* Gazette *and the Writers' Association, he said,*

In *The Builders,* Liang the Third is a more successfully drawn character than Liang Sheng-pao because he is a composite of the spiritual burden borne by the individual peasant over thousands of years. But almost no critic has analyzed this character, and therefore the analysis of the novel is inadequate. Even if one uses the struggle between the two paths, socialism and capitalism, and the new citizen as a means for analytically describing works on rural topics (such as Liu Ch'ing's *The Builders* and Li Chun's short stories), it remains inadequate....

Creativity at present is too narrowly channeled, and it appears that all our short stories are written exclusively in the Communist style.... Writers are hampered by some rules and regulations, and they are stifled. I hope critics can take up this question. At present writers do not dare to deal with the internal contradictions of the people. When the basis for realism is inadequate, then the romanticism will be superficial. As for the problem of creating heroic characters, writers also feel there are restraints. Ch'en Ch'i-hsia feels that writers should not cast characters to be either positive or negative, and this view of course is wrong. However, when this view of his is criticized, people seem to think that what is called for is a situation where if a character isn't depicted as positive then it has to be negative, which completely overlooks the middle character, and in point of fact, it is upon the middle character that all the problems are invariably concentrated....

Our creative works, generally speaking, are sufficiently revolutionary, but in their depiction of anguish and hardship, of the protracted nature of the struggle and its complexity, they remain inadequate. Characters are too pure, are exclusively heroic, daring to think and daring to act, while the complexity of struggle is inadequately reflected.... The task at present is to overcome difficulties, to describe contradictions. Merely describing model behavior and model conditions is too narrow....

Depicting a hero does not necessarily require that there be faults, only that there be a process of development. If we just write of a character's flawlessness then this becomes the theory of "one model for one class." In *The Builders* I feel that Liang Sheng-pao is not the most successful of characters, for, as a typical character, he can be found in any number of works. And is Liang the Third a typical character or not? I find him a highly typical character. Kuo Chen-shan is another. In *Keep the Red Flags Flying* Chu Lao-chung certainly is a typical character and so also is Yen Chih-ho. When present-day critics talk about *The Builders* they only talk about Liang Shen-pao [a poor peasant who becomes a model mutual-aid team leader and candidate for membership in the Party] and never any of the other characters; when they talk about *Keep the Red Flags Flying* they only talk about Chu Lao-chung and never about Yen Chih-ho.

Writers should have courage. But to have courage, to be sure, is no easy matter. When Chao Shu-li created My-calf-hurts [a woman who goldbricks] in the story "Get Some Training," there were many who took him to task for it. Writers have to withstand this. Amidst a diversity in the kinds of characters we create we still should create positive heroes, but positive heroes are not all of one kind, for they, too are diverse. If we can break out of this simplification, this dogmatism, this formulaic obsession, then it will let our creativity develop even further. On the one hand, this is the work of literary theory, but on the other hand, writers themselves must have their own ideas. . . . Write about whatever you know best, and so long as your standpoint is sound, the problems of "glorification" and of "magnification" will easily be solved. Glorification as it is now practiced is simply a single model for a single class, and is too far removed from reality, too far separated from the earthy qualities of real life. Magnification is still something we have to pay attention to; it is nothing but a generalization, a typicalizing of characteristics whereby we take very commonplace things and collect them together for a composite. . . .

The two tips of a pole are small, while the middle area is large. The heroes and the backward elements are the two tips; those situated in the middle are the majority, so we ought to write about the various kinds of richly complex psychological states of such people. The chief educational target of literature is the middle character. There is no need to indoctrinate those who are the most progressive and the most advanced. It is true that depicting heroes establishes a model; however, we should also pay attention to depicting characters who are situated in the middle. If we only depict the heroic models and not the contradictory and complex characters, then realism in fiction will be inadequate. When creating characters in fiction, the most important thing is to rely upon the character's own actions and psychology to reflect his or her contradictions. The fact that it was revisionists who wrote about the darkness of people's inner lives has caused us to shy away from doing the same thing. But the dark, inner life *is* something we can write about; it is only writing about darkness for the sake of darkness that is wrong.

Comrade Shao Ch'üan-lin feels that the reason why the middle characters that came to his attention are so well done is because of what the writers have placed upon such characters from past history. That is to say, the so-called "spiritual burden borne by the individual peasant for several thousand years." He said,

I feel Liang the Third is done better than Liang Sheng-pao, and Flourpaste T'ing in *Great Changes in a Mountain Village* made a deep impression on me too; such characters can most certainly progress, but they still have some of the old ways in them as well.

Another problem the short story runs into is this: within the compass of very little space the story raises a problem and resolves it. But what about problems that can't be resolved? For many years now there has been this sort of formulaic obsession. Some problems can be solved, but in some cases conditions are not yet adequate, so the problem cannot be resolved. When the process of solution cannot be completed, what then? For example, a story may deal with a time when the peasants are just beginning their transformation process, and yet, in order that all problems get solved within the story, they are described as if the transformation were already completed. And if the writer doesn't do it that way, then the critics will get on his back. For example, "Sister Lai" [by Hsi Jung] was censured by critics who felt that her thinking had not changed over to collectivisim. Especially in the theater, if the problem isn't solved, the critics are aroused. Is it that we absolutely must solve the problem? In the problem plays of the past the social problem was merely introduced and the audience was then allowed to form judgments for itself. Today we stress educating our people and pointing out the direction for them to take. However, is it true that fiction must solve problems on the spot? When all the preparatory conditions are met, then let there be a solution, or let there be a giving of direction to allow the readers themselves to seek a solution. But some contradictions cannot be resolved at once, as, for example, the changing over of peasants to collectivism. People asked of Comrade Hsi Jung's Sister Lai, "Why can't she change her attitude?" The answer is, "It's very difficult to do so. . . ."

The alteration of one's mental perceptions is an enormously arduous undertaking, even to the point where it is actually an anguishing process. Intellectuals who transformed from the old to the new underwent this anguish. As the saying goes, "Thrice-soaked in clear water, thrice-bathed in blood, then thrice-boiled in lye"—if that isn't hard and painful, then what is? Our own Lu Hsün also underwent this kind of process. Peasants who change over from individualistic economics to collectivist do the same. . . . Why is it that people say writing about people's internal contradictions cannot be stimulating? It is because they underestimate the long-term nature of the contradictions, the anguish involved, and the complexity of it.

On August 13, 1962, at a Literary Gazette *meeting, Shao Ch'üan-lin distorted Engels' letter to Margaret Harkness in order to form a theoretical basis for advocating his middle character.*[1]

Where Engels' criticism of Margaret Harkness' "City Girl" is concerned, it seems people have developed a misunderstanding, for it does appear that Engels is criticizing Harkness for not making Nellie, the heroine of the story, have a sufficiently high awareness. But in fact, Engels is criticizing the author for not adequately describing the relationship between Nellie and her total environment, with the result that the masses end up appearing negative. So far as Nellie is concerned, it doesn't make any difference whether she is described as aware or not. . . .

At the August 1962 conference Shao again distorted the original meaning of Engels' letter and he distorted also Chairman Mao's original meaning in the Yenan talks, to form a basis for his own personal theory. Shao said,

When Engels raised the issue of the typical character within the typical environment, the result was that people took the environment he was talking about to be within the era of socialism, and the hero's characteristics to be those of a socialist. Engels criticized Harkness for not describing a typical environment but the result has been for people to deduce from this the assumption that they were not to describe negative characters; a semiprogressive could not appear even in a minor role and except for the most perfect, heroic characters, none of the rest ever have even the slightest importance. From this, people have derived the theory of one class, one model, and throughout the world there can only be a certain few models—the proletarian model, which can only be heroic in struggle, fair-minded and utterly unselfish, etc.—which amounts to an extremely pernicious theory. Later, after reading "City Girl," one can see that this is by no means true. The story as it is written is the blandest of the bland. Engels is by no means censuring the author for having described the working girl to be so negative. At that time there were such working girls and it was not at all unusual. The problem was that no worker sympathized with her or was supportive, and this is insufficiently typical. This is a problem of the relationship between the character and the actual environment. That is to say, one must describe the changes that take place when a character is in a certain environment; it is not a question of whether a character in and of him or herself is or is not negative. If we were to take the heroine in "City Girl" and make her heroic, the entire story would vanish. In any environment there are various kinds of relationships, various kinds of people, including those who have no fear of hardship, but also those who waver; there are thieves, law violators, and disruptors, etc.—just all kinds of people who are related in some way to the specific environment. In the author's reflection of this, there will be a single aspect that is highlighted. In sum, the nature of typicality within a typical environment is diverse. Therefore, Chairman Mao wants us to analyze each and every person and each and every class; otherwise, we will develop the theory of one class, one model, which will produce a very great oppression.[2]

In the past few years there has been one kind of theory to the effect that writing about very commonplace things just isn't exciting enough, and I feel this theoretical position is biased. The first thing to look for is whether the artistry of the piece is such that it moves people. I still think the Hundred Flowers approach is best, and what we ought to do is see whether its roots have gone deep or not, and whether the foundation for realism is secure or not.

Short fiction is actually more difficult to write than long fiction: take a complex thing and then, through the generalizing of artistry, present it so that through the microcosm one sees the macrocosm, rather like the cross-section cut from a tree, whereby the annual growth rings and the characteristics of the tree are revealed. The relationship between the simple and the complex is this: through the simple one sees the complex; in a single grain of rice one sees the entire world. This is quite a different thing from mere simplification. Lu Hsün and Chekov are well worth our study in this respect. . . . The question of whether to write about commonplace or remarkable things gives way to the more fundamental question of whether the writing is based on real life or not. Each writer makes his own way, and each develops his own style. In the past few years each of our mature and seasoned writers has formed his or her own style. Each writer should be allowed to develop his own style, and it should be permissible if some use the commonplace to demonstrate the uncommon and the grand, and it should be permissible if others look at life with a smile, while still others do so with a frown. There is no need for us to become angry, nor need we interfere . . . .

Shao Ch'üan-lin wants a "deepening of realism" to take the place of the combining of revolutionary realism and revolutionary romanticism.

In short, the revolutionary quality of our creativity is quite strong, and yet I feel the depth with which reality is presented, the long-term nature of our social contradictions, and their complexity, are all inadequately presented. I feel our work shows that characterization is too simple, and that this simplistic quality is reflected in the description of an individual's character, in the area of interpersonal relations, and in the descriptions of the processes of struggle. This tells us that while the revolutionary nature of our works is quite high, the realistic integrity of them is too low. Take, for example, the story "The Unofficial Biography of Old Stand-firm" [by Chang Ch'ing-t'ien, in *Hopei Literature,* July 1962]. This story appeared in a regional literary journal, and for publication at that level it can still be approved, for it does have an educational function. But its weakness is in the oversimplification of its characters. The main character stands firm in every activity undertaken, exactly as his name implies. The other character, Big Cannon Wang, is even more simplistic. Now, a short story is very short, so the author can only stress one aspect of a character's personality. But this particular work makes readers feel it is too simplified; development from the introduction of the problem down to its resolution is very swift; there is no reflection of the complex nature of the people involved. . . .

Realism is the foundation of our creativity; without it there would be no romanticism. Our creative work should draw closer to real life; it should reflect reality with absolute fidelity. . . . The deepening of realism on this basis will develop an overwhelmingly powerful revolutionary romanticism, and from it, we can seek the path toward combining revolutionary realism with revolutionary romanticism.

At the conference, Comrade Shao Ch'üan-lin made a special point of praising the writing of Chao Shu-li. These past few years Comrade Chao Shu-li has not been able to muster a wholehearted revolutionary enthusiasm for describing the spirit of our revolutionary peasants. Comrade Shao not only failed to point out correctly this deficiency in Comrade Chao Shu-li's creative work, but he even went so far as to take this very deficiency and advocate it as a direction we should pursue. He said,

On this point of realism, some of our works have achieved rather good results, and I should point out that there are some writers who do have a penetrating knowledge where the protracted nature and the anguish of the struggle in rural villages is concerned. . . . Where the problems of rural villages are concerned, Comrade Chao Shu-li has a penetrating understanding. . . . In this conference we have talked much about Comrade Chao Shu-li and there have been those who feel he has been underevaluated these past two years, so that today we should reverse this. Why should we praise Old Chao? Because he has described the protracted nature and the anguish of the struggle in the countryside. As we see it now, he is even more penetrating in his view. This is a victory of realism.

The October 1962 issue of Sparks *published two articles advocating the middle character. One, by Shen Szu, is called "On Reading 'Sister Lai.'" This article advocates the educating of real-life middle characters by writing about middle characters in fiction. Shen says,*

If we take the grossness of the thinking and the character of real-life middle characters and graphically portray them in fiction so that things which are easily allowed to slip by and which are backward and appear to be minor are dramatically flashed before them as readers, then those very people who in real life take money and advantages to be the goal of life—those people, I mean to say, who, when there is no profit to be made, can never get out of bed early, yet when there is, can only long for the rooster's first crow—would they not all see themselves reflected in the images of Sister Lai and thereby realize that their own selfishness and advantage-seeking was under attack?

The other article is "Random Notes on 'Sister Lai'" by Comrade Hou Mo. This article expresses the view that writing about middle characters is one of the important topics for literary works to take up. The author defines a middle character as "one who is a member of the masses and yet still has weak and backward aspects."

The October 1962 issue of Hopei Literature *and the fifth issue of* Literary Criticism *in the same year simultaneously published Comrade K'ang Cho's "An Essay on Recent Short Stories," . . . in which he propagates the ideas of the "middle character" and "the deepening of realism" from the Dairen conference. In this article K'ang Cho raises some questions as he takes up certain characters in Chao Shu-li's works and compares them with a number of heroic images in other works, saying,*

Chao Shu-li's works and his characters always make one feel as though they are drawn from deep down in the real earth, and, moreover, even after the passage of time they retain their vividness undiminished; while with other works, when you read them you may feel they are full of a strength that can stir people to action, and yet, upon calm reflection, they make you think that the characters seem unreal and supernatural. Because of this, they cannot help but fade from the mind.

K'ang Cho believes that "Stubborn Ox Niu" (by Liu Shu-te, in Frontier Literature, *October 1959) [translated in* Chinese Literature, *1960, no. 1] and "I Knew All Along" (by Ma Feng, in* Sparks, *October 1958) [*Chinese Literature, *1959, no. 7] are clearly models of remarkably well-done middle characters in rural villages.*

Comrade K'ang Cho feels that so far as the short stories of the past few years are concerned, "Overall, their realism seems somewhat inferior to their revolutionary aspect." Because of this, he gave special emphasis to realism, saying,

The creative principle in the joining of realism and romanticism is, of course, that writing is to be based on real life. Therefore, this aspect of the realism in a work cannot help but form the central content of the overarching principle for creative writing. The mainstream of our short stories these past few years is, for the most part, derived from the principle of realism. . . . So far as the seeking of a combination of realism and romanticism into a single principle for creative writing is concerned, we must place realism in the primary position. I'm afraid this is the way it has to be if they are to form a better combination and if we are to achieve the rich diversity of the "Hundred Flower" ideal . . . . I am stressing here the spirit of realism, which is simply the same solid expertise and sincerity we find in the revolutionary realism of Chao Shu-li's work.

The overriding significance of the literature of our struggle has always been multifaceted, in that it provides people with education, influence, knowledge, appreciation, guidance in forming character, and pleasure. In this regard I was just thinking how few of our short stories are really well-wrought, light pieces for delight and esthetic appreciation. Why is it no Ch'i Pai-shih can appear on our literary scene?[3] Why is it we can't take a leaf from the pages of the T'ang tales, from the old vernacular storyteller's scripts, or the corpus of narratives on all kinds of ghosts and fox fairies in the collection *Strange Stories from a Chinese Studio* and emulate some of their diversity in our own works?

. . . .

The debate Shao touched off expanded from the discussion of the relationship of literature to reality (he was declared guilty of promoting "critical realism") to include the actual assessment of reality itself. "Just how many middle characters are there in China?" the critics asked, observing that Mao's own published analysis of rural society showed that seventy percent of the peasants were lower-middle or poor peasants who collectivized enthusiastically. The remainder "in the middle" was not a majority, they pointed out, and in any case constituted only a temporary phenomenon. "Promoting the middle character as Shao wants us to do will have us showing the masses to be pitiful, despicable, small-minded and thoughtless, while events in literature will be insignificant and frivolous," the critics charged. Moreover, advocates of a "deepening of realism," they said, "are critical of the reality of socialism. Shao says we have too many heroes, but we say there still are not enough. Heroes encourage us; middle characters make us feel unhappy and disquieted, and they erode our will to struggle."

Shao's "critical realism," they said, "is capitalistic, not proletarian. Critical realism is the product of capitalist society in its sunset. It had its value in its time, for Engels did say that it broke the optimism of capitalism and created doubts about the permanency of the existing order. But this is another time and another society." And finally, pointing out that Shao referred to collectivization as "an anguished process," they acidly observed that it was to most people a great liberation. His view, they concluded, was precisely that of the capitalistic petty bourgeois. Thus, once again, the position was reaffirmed that literature is not to reflect for the sake of reflection; it is to select what it reflects and to give it a high polish, for relatively narrow purposes. Literature is a lamp, not a mirror.

The problems that fenced writers in when Shao made his speech in 1962 were the same in 1942 after Mao's Yenan Talks, and they remain the same today: to describe things as they are ("critical realism"), and as they ought to be ("romantic realism"), at one and the same time without loss of realistic integrity. Some will argue that this cannot be done, but the name given to it is "revolutionary romanticism." Meanwhile, the need to square one's writing with fixed principles and day-to-day policies of Party leaders, which probably was the original purpose of the meeting at Dairen, leaves very little creative elbowroom. Liberalization in this atmosphere expresses itself only in the lifting, as Shao sought, of established taboos. Note, too, that the very fact of the Dairen-type meeting indirectly reveals the jobber-like role of Chou Yang and his bureau members, such as Shao Ch'üan-lin, in mediating between the demands and controls of the Party on the one hand, and the literary workers on the other.

The attacks on Shao and his middle character idea began in earnest in August 1964, and by November a history of the middle character concept was drawn up, with antecedents found as early as 1951 in selected quotations from such "rightists" as Ting Ling, Chou Yang, Feng Hsüeh-feng, Hu Feng, Ah Lung (I-men), Ch'in Chao-yang, T'ang Ta, Pa Jen, and Wang Hsi-yen. The half-tones that Shao had hoped to reintroduce into the communist literary art of black and white were rejected, and soon even the black was to be ousted, following the Cultural Revolution of 1966, in favor of a palette containing only shades of pure white, or rather, pure red. Sponsored literature after the Cultural Revolution, and particularly the short story, became wholly didactic and unimaginative, or, as they say of its counterpart in Russia, "the perishable output of safe writers."

NOTES

1. Engels wrote the English author Margaret Harkness in April 1888 to thank her for sending him a copy of her story "City Girl." He admired the courage of her realistic descriptions and he praised her for the "simple, unembellished way in which you make the cardinal point of the entire book the old story of how a proletarian girl is seduced by a man of the bourgeoisie." He goes on to say,

If I would venture to criticize something it would be that the story is still not realistic enough. Realism means, in my opinion, apart from faithfulness in detail, the faithful reproduction of typical characters in typical situations. Now, your characters are typical enough in their way, but the circumstances which surround them and which induce them to act are perhaps not typical to the same extent. In "City Girl" the working class appears as a passive mass which is unable to help itself and is not even endeavouring to help itself. All efforts to drag them out of their apathetic misery come from outside or from above. This may have appeared as a true description around 1800 or 1820 in the days of Saint Simon or Robert Owens, but it will not appear as a true description to a man who for fifty years has had the honor to participate in most of the struggles of the valiant proletariat. The rebellious mutiny of the working class against the environment of suppression which surrounds them, their endeavors—convulsive, semiconscious, or conscious—to regain their status as human beings, are part of history and therefore must claim a place in the sphere of realism. . . . "

The original letter was in English, but may now be lost. It appears only in German in Marx/Engels' Works, vol. 37, from which this translation is made.

2. The issue of Engels' letter to Harkness comes up again and again in Communist discussions of literary theory. The *Gazette* editor charges Shao with distortion, and Shao alleges that others have misunderstood Engels. It seems to me that careful reading of the letter will show that it is not simply that Harkness's masses are too negative (i.e., helpless and inert) for Engels. The thrust of his criticism is to encourage the author to go one stratum deeper in depicting reality by trying to describe not just the apathy but also the conditions that have made the masses apathetic. The intention is not to deflect writers away from realistic integrity, but in fact to deepen it. In the same letter he makes this quite clear: "It is far from my purpose to consider it a mistake that you did not write a novel which openly and directly is socialist . . . this is not what I mean. The more the convictions of the author remain hidden, the better for the piece of art." Misunderstanding of the letter seems to arise from the letter's most frequently quoted line, "typical characters in typical situations." Communist critics in China and Russia have come to use the word "typical" not in the sense of "the most often encountered," but in the sense of "that which most fully and vividly expresses the essence of a given social force." Deliberately magnified images (such as those we find in PRC writing and Russian tractor fiction) do not exclude "typicality"; rather, they are thought to reveal it more fully and to emphasize it. Typicality, in this sense, is regarded as the main sphere of partisanship in "realistic art." According to the theoretician G. M. Malenkov, the problem of typicality is always the problem of politicality. Naturally, anything a regime does not want written about becomes off limits as "untypical." (See Report to the 19th Party Congress, October 5, 1952, in *Soviet Literature,* May 5, 1956, 150–62.)

Shao seems to be on firm ground in sweeping aside the misinterpretations of Engels' letter, whereby people assumed "they were not to describe negative things," and he seems justified, too, in arguing that the letter does not disallow the kind of diversity in the depiction of reality that he would like to see appear in Chinese literature. But how he derives from this the highlighting of a single aspect and the analysis of "each and every person" is far from clear. However, the Engels letter certainly can be construed to justify writing of middle characters, providing the writer's realism penetrates the causes of their behavior and is careful to depict this. Shao, however, does not seem to base his case on the letter as well as he might have. But then we have to remember that Shao's arguments come to us only through a presumably hostile *Gazette* editor.

3. A twentieth-century painter (1863–1957), whose works delight people of all ages and political persuasions. Despite the fact his works are nonpolitical, he remains in good standing with Communist critics.

Translation and comments by Donald A. Gibbs

CHANG CHIH-MIN

(1918?–)

When Chang's long poem "Wang Number Nine Speaks Bitterness" appeared in 1949, the vivid description of how a poor peasant had suffered at the hands of merciless landlords drew lavish praise from the then leading Marxist poet, Hsiao San, who recommended it as a model for other poets to emulate. Fifteen years and about a dozen volumes of long and short poems later, he published another stirring story-poem, "The Contest Platform," translated below.

Starting with only a grade school formal education, Chang learned writing largely while serving in the army and in the Party. Since 1946 he has written about a good variety of characters and life experiences, with settings mostly in the western Hopei mountains. But it seems that he always finds the most impressive strength and inspiration in the tales of wrath and woe told by the abused peasants who have turned over a new page of history and changed their lot.

On the eve of the Cultural Revolution, "The Contest Platform" joined the ranks of the ten most popular poems delivered at poetry recitals. There was no news about Chang during the Cultural Revolution, but by mid-1978 he had returned to the active literary scene in Peking. Among his best-known collections are *Can't Kill Him* and *Characters on the Commune.*   —K.Y.H.

The Contest Platform

I

Go south of the Ch'in Mountain Range
—to the end of the earth!
Miles of lush green trees, miles of flowers in bloom.
How many kinds of trees are there?
Can't tell.

Can't remember so many names of flowers,
Can't tell about all the trees.
I only remember:
Old banyan trees, hundreds of years old
—found in every village,
And every village nestles under banyan trees.

Old banyan tree!
—stands in the street,
And under it unfolds a tense drama.
Look! A flock of ducks on this side,
Over there, a flock of chickens.
Puppies sleep in the tree shade,
And kids play "guerrilla war."

Look! The old aunt weaves palm fans,
Moving her stool to stay in the shade.
Listen! The production team
Discusses the water project around the tree.
Under the old banyan
—a drama unfolds
From morning to night, nonstop.

In the morning
The communers go to work
—they assemble here.
After dark,
Things no matter how large or small
—they talk over here.
Listen! Sometimes
Laughter resounds through the hills around.
Listen! Sometimes
Loud arguments break loose like a storm.

If we are to recall the past
—there is too much of that!
Poor peasants
Fleeing bad years, begging,
Selling their children under this tree....
Landlords
Take over houses and fields,
Rewrite the title deeds under this tree....
The drama under the banyan tree,
Who knows when it all started?

Old banyan tree
—huge and tall.
Thousands of branches, thousands of roots.
The thousands of roots of yours
Hug that high mountain
And embrace that creek.
Thousands of branches of yours
Form a picture of the village,
And of the people and their houses in it.

So tall!
Your roots sink into the bottom of the lake,
And branches hang on the clouds.
So old!
Your long hair drags on the ground,
And wrinkles crawl all over your face.
Old banyan tree, ah, old banyan tree,
No street or alley is as old as you,
No village dates before your start.

The moon on the wane
And the moon full.
How many times have you seen it
—the moon's waxing and waning?
Spring departs,
Winter comes.
How much have you been through
—the lashing wind and pounding rain?

Old banyan tree, ah, old banyan tree.
How much dramatic change
Of the present and the past
Has been recorded
—in your deep, deep folds?
And how many generations'
Life and death
Have rubbed the stone bench under you
Smooth and shining?
Under the banyan tree!
How is it to be painted?
Some say,
It shores up the clouds and hides the sun,
Like a pagoda of emerald.
Still others say,
It's an umbrella over the street,
Or a vine-clad arbor sheltering the alley.

The banyan tree's picture
Should not be painted this way!
It's not a vine-clad arbor, not an umbrella,
Neither a jade mountain, nor a pagoda.
To me
It is a village history of a thousand years,
A contest platform set up in the street.

II

A contest platform it is!
For many years
—and many generations
It has stood under a banyan tree in the south.
But no! Perhaps it also stands
—before an elm
In the north,
Or before a felt tent
On the grassland.

At a spot like this,
"Those wearing shoes"
"Those barefooted"
Were clearly separated out.
One writing brush dipped in red ink,
Drew a sharp line between the classes
—that was the color of the world of man.
The poor from the rich
Cut apart with a knife stroke

Look! On this side of the line
—men above other men.
In their pockets rested
Keys to paradises,
And whips to control other men
Swayed in their hands.
They summoned wind and rain
At their will,
And who was to live
Who was to die
—also up to them.

Look! On the other side of the line
—"ghosts," subhuman.
They let others ride on their necks,
And trample on their bodies.
Even if they lived to a hundred,
They would still be so many dumb animals.
Wanted to change their lot? Nothing doing!
They incurred a web of debts
—even long before they were born.

A contest platform, ah, a contest platform!
On that big tree over there
Used to be affixed, layer upon layer
"Imperial decrees" of the dynastic rulers,
"Injunctions" by county magistrates,
And "public notices" from village offices.
They demanded everybody
To keep his waist forever bent,
And his head, always bowed.

Contest Platform, ah, Contest Platform!
The sword and axe cuts
—on that tree,
They record:
Our uncompromising people
Have so many times
—rushed up,
And so many times
—been beaten back. . . .

. . . .

But the people did not accept defeat!
And the Contest Platform
Did not fold up its drama.
Look!
What's the burning light over there,
Shining on half of the country!
Ah, that was
The red flag of the "Autumn Harvest Uprising!"
Ah, that was
The beacon rising from the Chingkang Mountain . . . .

Look! The fire burned
From the shore of the Tung-t'ing Lake
To the Pearl River's delta.
Look! The fire engulfed the north and south
—shooting straight up to the sky!
The fire dyed the old banyan tree
Into a red banner of battle!
Look! So many people
Rushed out
From the fields, from fishing shacks,
From bullock sheds, from huts of hired hands,
—all rushed out.
They raised high their hoes, sickles,

Raised their fishing forks, fowling pieces. . . .
Right here, under this big tree
They wanted to bury the old society.

Look! Under this big banyan tree,
A hired hand's son
Hugged his father's bloodstained clothes,
And he demanded blood in repayment from
His landlord for generation after generation.
Look! Under this big banyan tree,
Red guards
Aimed their red-tasseled spears
At the chests of the local tyrants.
No longer would they be allowed
To lord over
This Contest Platform.

The sky changed color,
The earth changed color.
No more government, official
Laws and decrees
—affixed on the trees,
In their place appeared
Criminal charges
Against the landlord class.
The spreading square under the old banyan tree
Became the people's
Revolutionary court of trial,
No longer the landlord's
"Public hall."

"The barefooted people"
Have stood up, chests out.
But "those wearing shoes"
Have not yet retired.
Look! The white bandit army fought back.
Once again lights burned bright
In those huge courtyards behind red-lacquered doors.
Look! That bond maid who had briefly fled to freedom
Once again was tied up
Once again paraded under the big tree
To a water-filled dungeon.
Look! That hired hand, having broken his chain,
Once again paraded under this banyan tree
Back to the hut of the hired hands.

Under the banyan tree, ah, under the banyan tree,
Under the banyan tree—
It's still their execution ground.

Look! The landlord
Stood on the stone steps, hands on hips,
Shouting—
"Who dares to make any more trouble?"

Look! So many bloody bodies
Hanging under the big banyan tree.
That was a fifteen-year-old boy,
Only because he—
Had worn once an Eighth Route Army cap.
And that white-haired old man,
Only because he—
Had kept an arm band of the Red Guards. . . .

Once again so many people were chopped down.
Once again—
So many items of blood debt.
But the hope for victory
Did not leave the widows of the bamboo huts
Under the big banyan tree.
Because—
People under all the banyan trees everywhere
Had seen—
The red flag on the Chingkang Mountain.
Because we now
Have Chairman Mao
Have the Communist Party. . . .

III

Contest Platform, ah, Contest Platform!
How many years there have been,
—and how many generations!
The long river of history
Roared by under the big tree.
Friends or foe
Under that big tree
—clearly divided into red and white.
The past, our past,
What a past that was!
White sword blade going in,
And red sword blade coming out.

Struggle, and again struggle.
This word written in blood,

How is it to be explained?
The old fishermen of the "spear squad"
Told everybody:
If we didn't raise our spears
The landlords and the fishing bosses
Would never have bowed.
The veterans of the Red Fourth Army
Told everybody:
If we didn't wrest away
The enemy's machine guns
From their very hands,
We would never have struck down
—the white bandit's mountain holdout.

Struggle, and again struggle!
Yesterday passed in struggle,
And from struggle comes today.
Under the big banyan tree
Is a huge arena.
From the day our great grandfather
Seized a rock nearby
Hurling it—
Against the whip-lashing slave driver,
To the speak-bitterness meeting
During the land reform
When this generation's peasants
Cleared account with "Sun the Old Rich Man,"
There has not been a single day
Here, that was
—quiet, with the stage deserted.

Struggle, and again struggle!
History moves forward through struggle.
Who says
Today we may not need struggle any more?
And revolution is
A matter of yesterday,
And the exploiting class
Has already been delivered to
—an historical museum?
And today on the Contest Platform
All is peace and quiet?

Nonsense! Take back your
False claims
There is
No place in the world

Where your words could be confirmed.
Under the big banyan tree
People have not
—beaten swords into ploughshares.
People who have stood up
Through struggle
Understand thoroughly:
To keep the position gained
There can be no removal of the armors,
No troop withdrawal.

Look! Isn't it
Right under the banyan tree of today
That people argue
Whether to add a hundred-weight padlock
On the grave of the old world,
Or to leave a crack in its door,
Allowing the demons within to come to life
Again some day?
The poor old peasant says,
One thousand generations, ten thousand. . . .
Never, never again shall we allow
The landlord class to raise its ugly head.
But his landlord of yesterday says,
Some day, and there will be such a day,
When my son turns over his palm,
Then, "a chicken is a chicken,
And a phoenix, a phoenix. . . ."*

Look! Isn't it
Right under the banyan tree of today
That people are exposing:
A landlord's son turned village schoolteacher says,
"Landlords are also good people," with this
He intends to poison the souls of the kids. . . .
Look! Isn't it
Right under the banyan tree of today
That people are discussing
How that production team captain
Who responded to a landlord's wife
With a resounding box on the ear,
For she resorted to a shameless "plot of the flesh"
—to launch an attack on us.

*A common Chinese saying that means "those destined to be rich will be rich, and those meant to be poor will be poor." [K.Y.H.]

Under the banyan tree, yes, isn't it
Right here under today's banyan tree
That our militiamen are
Escorting away a group
—of "little Chiang Kai-shek's"
Who crawled over from offshore?
That a huge mass meeting of the communers is
Trying that antirevolutionary
Who sabotaged our electric water pump?

Under the banyan tree
The enemy has not laid down his arms.
Under the banyan tree
The people are still fighting.
If you say
There is no more enemy
Before us,
Let me ask you: Who killed
—our Liu Wen-hsüeh
If you say
The enemy today
Has already become "nice and kind,"
Let me ask you: Who it was
Who chopped away
Both of Hsü Hsüeh-hui's hands?

In a tough way, there is the sword;
In a soft way, there is the tongue.
Hard is the sword,
Soft is the tongue.
Look! That unconscionable merchant
So used to profiting by exploitation,
Is egging on a well-to-do farmer
To make some "small business" trips.
They are not carrying on
—just some friendly conversation!
Look! That old landlord
Is dragging away the cashier-accountant of our production team
To patronize a restaurant
And a teahouse.
He is not just making friends
—to pass time away.
What are these people after?
Can't you see it
From the gleam in their eyes?
From the nuances of their words?
What they want to chop down is
—the big mansion of socialism.

Under the banyan tree, ah, under the banyan tree,
Under the banyan tree we cannot
—relax and go to sleep!
We must never forget,
Under this banyan tree of today
The enemy has dragged down with him
—our Liu Chieh-mei.
We must never forget,
Under this banyan tree of today,
Many who have lost their alertness,
Fell into the enemy's
—ambush, trap. . . .

Contest Platform, ah, Contest Platform!
On the platform,
Battle drums have not yet hushed,
Battle banners have not yet furled.
Though on today's platform
We no longer see
The blood and severed heads of yesterday,
Each clash with the enemy still is
More than a minor skirmish.
Look! Each engagement with the enemy
Is a contest deciding
To whom belongs today,
And where we shall go tomorrow.

Look! Each of the contests is staged
To safeguard the world for the proletariat,
And insure a future for our children and grandchildren. . . .

IV

Under the banyan tree, ah, under the banyan tree.
How am I to paint a picture
—of the banyan tree?
Listen to the old poor peasant
And see how he answers:
He says—
You paint those branches and leaves
—hanging on clouds;
You paint that stone bench
—shining and smooth.

Right here, paint it right here.
The red and the white
—two opposing camps
Fought here yesterday, and
Will continue to fight here today.
You want to know how long they will be fighting?
Simple! In one word—
Until they surrender their guns
We'll stay on our horses. . . .

July 1963
Poetry Journal, no. 8 (1963): 4–16

Translated by Kai-yu Hsu

CHANG YUNG-MEI

The Bamboo Girl

Coconut wind, betel nut rain,
Viet Nam warriors go to war.
There is a little lady among the troops,
Her name is Bamboo Girl.

Little Bamboo Girl, little mounted trooper,
Has done much for the army transport and in actual combat.
Her mount is not a horse
But an elephant called Ah-hsi.

Ah-hsi, with its long trunk and huge ears,
Does its best hauling the guns.
And gazing at the flames leaping ahead,
Bamboo Girl hums a song to herself.

"Ah-hsi, my Ah-hsi, let's remember well
Our grievance when we charge against the foe.
Our bamboo hut has been leveled by their bombs,
And our blood stained our fields and ditches.

"Mother was burnt to death in front of the village,
And behind it lay my uncle, dying of poison gas.
My kid brother, most pitiful little brother,
A sword ended his life, less than one year old.

"Ah-hsi, you know American imperialism
Is our archenemy, our most deadly foe.
Let's follow Uncle Ho toward our liberation,
And fight to the bitter end, until victory is won.

June 11, 1964, Canton
Conch-shell Bugle Call, pp. 160–61

Translated by Kai-yu Hsu

For a note on Chang Yung-mei, see p. 174.

CHAO P'U-CH'U

To the Tune "Butterfly in Love with Flowers"

In December 1961, several members of the Writers' Association vacationed at a beach resort near Chan-chiang, Kwangsi Province. Comrade Ping Hsin [the woman poet] dreamed of butterflies. When she woke, she saw them in the garden, all orange-brown with black stripes like tiger's markings. We therefore called them tiger butterflies. The people of Chan-chiang resisted French imperialism for several decades. From this historical experience have come down many heroic and moving legends. It's befitting to see that even insects there reflect some heroic characteristics. Thus I wrote the following poem.—Chao

The scene of the southland forgets the year's ending,
Riotous green and joyous red,
Get caught up and stay with spring.
Waking up from a Chuang Chou Dream,* the dream still vivid
And a garden full of butterflies dances for you.

Why do their color and stripes resemble a tiger's?
Must be the heroes,
Whose souls turned into feathers and wings!
Hundreds of battles fought with pure loyalty bring glory to our homeland,
Now they fly and fly chasing around the memory trees.

To the Tune "West River Moon"

Red dirt and lush trees along the way,†
Three cups of thick milk and sweet tea.
The talk about battlefields is over, now let's talk about farm fields,
Which makes the mountains and rivers even more spirited.

For a note on Chao P'u-ch'u, see p. 523
*Chuang Chou, the legendary philosopher, dreamed of himself changing into a butterfly. [Author's note]
†Visit to the Red Light Farm on Hainan Island; saw thousands of *mu* planted in scented herbs. [Author's note]

Would like to summon Ch'ü Yüan here,*
To oversee these thousands of acres of scented herbs;
The minstrel has long departed from the Mi-lo River,
But here, dancing butterflies, hovering orioles—a riot of songs.

Poetry Journal, no. 2 (1962): 41

Translated by Kai-yu Hsu

*Ch'ü Yüan, poet-statesman of the third century B.C. author of *Li Sao,* who drowned himself in the Mi-lo River. [Author's note]

CH'EN YI

Gold Coast

—To the Tune of "All Red the River"

All gold
The coast,
Rising straight up to touch the sky.
Let'em plunder,
Let the storms over the ocean
Scream and whine as though possessed.
One million of the blacks here sold into slavery,
And the Indians on the other shore are nearing extinction.
Shocking indeed to know of man's inhumanity to man—
Two bloodstained continents.

Talk about forgiving,
Who'd agree?
Or about retribution,
No, not necessary.
Only the logic of struggle is merciless.
Now a free Africa starts from its northwest,
And the rest of it follows at once.
Look, how they cleanse their land to rise up in glory—
All of them, invincible.

January 1964
Selected Poems of Ch'en Yi, pp. 315–16

Translated by Kai-yu Hsu

For a note on Ch'en Yi, see p. 524.

HO CH'I-FANG

Revisiting Nankai

Before the War of Resistance against Japan, I taught at Nankai middle school in Tientsin. In January last year I revisited this scene from my past. Two school principals accompanied me on my tour and told me that the west building of the teachers' quarters, the south building of the junior middle school, and all the buildings of the girls' school were destroyed by enemy bombs at the beginning of the war. Afterwards I also strolled around the surroundings for a little while. A large stretch of wasteland behind the school had been filled and levelled and transformed into a public park. Ch'iang-tzu River used to be filthy and stinking because of the factory wastes which flowed into it, but now a drainage system has been installed and the waters are clean. The comrades accompanying me also told me that the notorious disorderly "San-pu-kuan" district* has now become a site for small-scale industry.

In my memory things remain
Which can no longer be seen,
A great mass of brand-new buildings
Now appear before my eyes.

A splendid sight, viewed for the first time,
Makes us stare in wide-eyed surprise,
When we can't recognize a place where we've been before,
It's more than amazement we feel!

This place, once a marshy wasteland,
A dumping-ground for coffins no one cared to bury,
Where stray dogs scavenged among the corpses,
And no one cared to drive the dogs away,

Is now transformed into a public garden,
With ponds, a shady bower, a trellis heavy with wisteria;
Birds twitter between the branches,
Children play games on the grass.

For a note on Ho Ch'i-fang, see p. 527.
*San-pu-kuan, meaning "three don't care," was an area in Tientsin claimed by neither the British, the French, nor the Japanese, who controlled the life of the city from their concessions (districts the Chinese government conceded to them with extraterritoriality). The area was therefore a refuge for criminals, prostitutes, and others who preferred to live outside the law. Ho also refers to this area in another poem, "North China Is Aflame!" [B.S. McD.]

669

The Ch'iang-tzu River once stank like the old society,
The thought of it invoked disgust,
Now in place of filth and garbage,
A layer of translucent ice has formed.

Green wheatfields stretch from either bank,
Alongside, a large tractor factory
Presses on to realize ahead of time
The mechanization of agriculture — our dream.

Written at Peitaiho while ill,
August 29, 1963

Poetry Journal, no. 3 (1963): 18–19

A Night in Chang Village

We kept watch round a kerosene lamp,
A roomful of cadres and peasants,
Plus a few from Hu Village who'd hurried over,
To bid me farewell on my return to Peking.

You fought at Shih-chia-chuang. You fought at Taiyuan.
You took part in the battle of Ta-ch'ing Mountain,
Until you were wounded in the shoulder
And sent home to farm the land.

A fragment of shell is lodged in your head,
Which often disturbs your sleep at night.
Son of poor peasants, you suffered since childhood,
Herding sheep for rich landlords, year after long year.

When the Japanese came you joined the Eighth Route Army,
And returned after Liberation with a disability card.
Now out at dawn, back at dusk, scorning wind and rain,
You herd sheep for the commune brigade.

Production brigade chief, praised by all,
Do you remember how tense it was during Land Reform?
You were a primary school graduate,
And helped me measure land and calculate production.

During Land Reform you were still a child,
You seemed to be lost deep in memories.
Now a still younger production team leader,
Are you thinking how your father died a hero?

On New Year's Eve the enemy pounced,
They slaughtered all the village resistance workers.
You were left an orphan, of your family the only survivor,
Your grandmother's care alone brought you to manhood.

Your old granny was so fond of me,
Because I was about the same age as your father.
When she saw me toiling in the village,
It was as if her son were living still . . . .

Those few months I can never forget,
Bonds from the heart tie me to this village.
I have eaten with every peasant family in their home,
I know the story of every peasant's life.

You say that my work was done carefully,
Enthusiasm about production fills every heart.
"Ho, old friend, you lost weight in Chang and Hu Villages!"
"There's not an inch of waste or barren land around us!"

We talk of the Land Reform of the past,
We talk of our motherland's present and her future.
Socialism spring-like ushers in
Dazzling colors under a radiant sun.

It's already past one. Early tomorrow
You have to take fertilizer to the fields.
You should rest. Good night to you all!
May you make this year's production better still!

February 22, 1964
Poetry Journal, no. 3 (1964): 22–23

Translated by Bonnie S. McDougall

HO CHING-CHIH

Our Great Motherland

I

The red sun rises in the east,
Its splendor shines upon the Four Seas,
Our great motherland
        Stands, towering and proud.
With the hands of a giant,
The spirit of a hero,
It rearranges the vast countryside.
Just look how spring fills South China,
        Flowers bloom beyond the borders;
A thousand wonders,
        Ten thousand spectacles.
The Three Red Flags* meet the east wind,
Gales and thunders of revolution come rolling forth.
O! Our great motherland
Advances toward the new age of socialism!
The great Mao Tse-tung,
The great Party,
Guide us
        Toward the bright and glorious future!

II

Mount Kunlun rises high, reaching the sky,
The Yangtze River flows into the East Sea.
A great people,
        Our hearts buoyant with revolutionary will!
The era's adverse current
And obstacles beneath our feet,
How could they stop the advance of our revolutionary troops?
Just look how many Ta-ch'ings,
        How many Ta-chais;
Heroes among our elders,
        Heroes in the next generation:
Thousands of Lei Fengs rise anew,

For a note on Ho Ching-chih, see p. 361.
*The General Line for Socialist Reconstruction (pronounced by Mao Tse-tung in 1957), People's Communes, and the Great Leap Forward campaign. (K.Y.H.)

A new generation comes up to continue the work!
O! Our great motherland
Advances toward the new age of socialism!
The great Mao Tse-tung,
The great Party
Guide us
          Toward the bright and glorious future!

III

The red sun shines all over the world,
The vast clouds and mist make way.
Our great motherland
          Holds up the great banner of Anti-Imperialism and
                    Anti-Revisionism!
Just look at the evil forces
          Being defeated one by one;
The east wind is rising, the west wind subsides.
Our shoulders touch the five continents,
          Our hearts link the whole world!
Friends from all over the world,
          Come from all directions.
Our suppressed brothers unite and march forward
A victorious tomorrow will surely come!
O! Our great motherland
          Advances toward the new age of world revolution!
The great Mao Tse-tung,
The great Party,
Guide us
          Toward the future of mankind's liberation.

August 1964
Singing Aloud, pp. 29–31

Translated by Hsin-sheng C. Kao

HSIAO SAN

Though I'm Old and Disabled

Though I'm old and disabled,
My will remains young and strong,
The thoughts of Marx, Lenin, and Mao
Have given me strength and force.
After forty years I know where to go,
My heart at peace and carefree.
I've rushed the enemy camp before,
Where swords gleamed in the light of flames.
What's left of me will be applied
To making truth prevail all over.
My bullets are now my short verses,
And in combat I rely on my prose.
Maybe it's just a glowworm's glow,
Flickering feebly in space;
Maybe it's only drops of water
Dripping into the immense ocean.
Be it a high note or low,
All can join in a great chorus.
Having been born in this great era,
My red heart shall never wilt.
Say not that time defers to nobody;
The spirit of revolution persists!
Happy to be a beast of burden,
Willing to toil and die for children.
But I frown at the thousands of foes,
To extend the right and expel the wrong..
The load is heavy, and the road long,
I steel myself without stop or rest.

Though I'm old and disabled,
An old horse lying in stable
Still dreams of the open space....

March 1963
In Stable, pp. 111–13

Translated by Kai-yu Hsu

For a note on Hsiao San, see p. 536.

JAO MENG-K'AN
(1901–)

In the late 1920s and 1930s Jao Meng-k'an delighted readers with his short, pristine lyrics in the *Crescent Monthly;* his success was derived largely from the new stanza forms in which he experimented. They were musically pleasing, compact, and not restricted to lines of exact length; they varied from the basic quatrains of classical Chinese poetry.

Jao has been writing very little since 1949. The Great Leap Forward movement following the Hundred Flowers campaign brought out a few of his poems, all cast in classical Chinese forms and diction. On at least one occasion, in 1962, he did participate in a forum discussing poetry, where he pleaded for the case for writing in the classical mold today. "Our country is a country of poetry," he said excitedly. "People like us can't compete with the youth, who can ride on long winds to sail the high seas, but to take over the relay stick and run a round or two occasionally is still within our reach. . . ." And he offered to the public his own recent verses.

First Snow of the Year

Suddenly flower-laden branches fill the window panes;
Unannounced, joyous flakes come fluttering down;
I know, all across the land, under clouds flaming red,
Each tree full of gem flowers is a tree full of verse.

Poetry Journal, no. 3 (1962): 66

July First

(Written for the wall bulletin of the International Relations Academy)
Purple haze enshrouds the rising sun on the horizon,
At dusk pomegranate blooms reflect the fire of sunset;
The people can't forget the occasion of July First.

More grain now for brewing liquor, more verse for songs,
They sing and dance, their joy overflows, as red flags unfurl
Over even the most secluded foothills and deserted riversides.

June 16, 1962
Poetry Journal, no. 5 (1962): 28

Translated by Kai-yu Hsu

JUAN CHANG-CHING
(1920?–)

Wartime activities in the rural areas of Shansi, North China, inspired Juan Chang-ching to write narrative poems in the folk-ballad mode. In many ways his development paralleled that of Li Chi, whose *Wang Kuei and Li Hsiang-hsiang* is often cited as representative of the genre.

After 1949 he traveled and worked for long periods of time in Inner Mongolia and Manchuria, which resulted in such works as *The Songs of the Surveyors* and the *White Cloud Obo Symphony*. From a trip abroad he brought back the poems that went into his *Havana in April*. In between these long trips, he also served on the editorial board of the *Poetry Journal* in Peking. Most of his poems won wide popularity with their rhythmic appeal; they are easily chanted and easily remembered.

In the spring of 1978 Juan was back in Peking, attending such public functions as the Third Congress of the All-China Federation of Literary and Art Circles and the People's Political Consultative Conference. He announced his progress in writing a long poem, "The Hai River," and a novel, *Layers of Mountains.* —K.Y.H.

In Praise of the New Yellow
River

The year before last I first visited the Yellow River,
A thousand miles of thunder rolling over the waves;
Gusty winds whistled through my strings, calling for songs;
My throat, scorching dry, yet the water was undrinkable.
In a hoarse voice I sang to the yellow sky
Where yellow clouds spread hiding the hills.

Last year I came to the Yellow River again,
Divers' pontoons afloat, locking the huge water course;
Underwater explosions lifted up the river
And dropped it down again. "What's going on?"
I asked. They were diverting the flow to tame
The wild current, forcing it to calm down.

This year I am here at the river once more,
Clear water, not muddy current, laps the shore;
I scoop a cup of water, on it float distant hills,
And over the hills fly wild geese in the sky.
I raise the cup to toast the hills and springs,
And sing for the new river, strumming my strings.

Songs of the Surveyors, pp. 6–7

Traveling in South Kiangsi

Going south along the Gan River,
Morning fog, covering the hills.
Willows along the river, green along the river,
And a river of green water, a river of white sails.

Distant hills blue, closer hills purple,
On them float green clouds of camphor trees;
Mustards bloom to greet the arrival of spring,
Spreading a golden carpet on the river.

I've been waiting for the ferry on the riverside,
Across the river eagles soar over peaks in clouds.
Under the willows a spirited horse's neigh recalls
How red flags crossed the river at night years ago.

Blue hills, green peaks, and the eighteen river bends,
Azaleas spot the hillside like bloodstains.
In the footprints left by the red fighters,
Proud pines extend their green shade all over the mountain.

February 12, 1962
Songs of the Surveyors, pp. 55–56

from *White Cloud Obo Symphony*

Nobody knows how long White Cloud Obo, a massive rocky knoll, has been
standing guard on the southern edge of the Eastern Gobi Desert in Inner Mon-

golia. The rocks are barren and the land stubborn. To eke out a living the early
steppe settlers had to struggle persistently. And when they triumphed, as in
the following story, a legend grew, looming ever larger in the minds and
memories of the inhabitants there until it took on sacred proportions:

> Old Grandfather Aersilang
> Walks down to the plain with his grandchildren.
> Ulantoya, holding a tiny lamb,
> Runs along, singing a song.
> Buergudeh herds his flock that rolls
> Over the knoll like so many clouds.
>
> A mountain creek flows on, quietly,
> A continuing bar of trickling music.
> Clear water mirrors the blue sky;
> Under the water white clouds fly,
> And the moss and weeds sway—
> Combed by the steady flow.
>
> Flowers and grass wave in colors and tender green,
> Bring out Ulantoya's pretty smile.
> Isn't it jealousy that makes some blooms pout,
> And gusts of wind wrinkle the water's face?
>
> The sheep baa at the sight of water,
> Lambs gambol; blossoms dangle from their mouths.
> Tears well up in Old Grandfather's eyes—
> Wonder what has welled up in his mind.
>
> "Ulantoya," he says, "you come here.
> And Buergudeh, you hold still.
> Listen to the creek, and do you know why
> It is called 'Red Spring'?
> The name has not dropped from blue sky.
> Now you let me sing you a 'Red Spring Song':
>
> "Many, many years ago—
> No rain for three hundred long days.
> No grass could grow, no flowers,
> A disaster gripped the entire steppe land.
>
> "They begged Heaven, but were not heeded;
> They begged Earth without any response.
> Drought split the rocks on that high mountain,
> And the land broke apart in ugly cracks.
> Day and night they prayed to Buddha, to all gods,
> But failed to get even a tiny patch of cloud.
> "Cattle and sheep hushed, horses wouldn't stir,

Everywhere strewn with the bones of their kind.
Immense though the land of Ulan Chabu,
Not a single line of cooking smoke rose
On the plain under the sun, that ball of fire.
Only cries of despair filled the tents.

"There was a brave man north of the mountain
They called him the son of a herdsman—
Fifteen he was that year, Aduchinfu,
He alone saved a calf from two preying tigers,
Blinding the eye of one of the clawing beasts
And breaking the teeth of the other.
Since very young he had nursed a hero's will
To risk his life for his people of the grassland.

"He walked all over the area, for 3000 *li,*
But still found no grass, or water.
He watched the animals drop dead,
And his beloved homeland dying every day.
Aduchinfu felt his heart stabbed by knives.
He came to this spot and, his sword drawn,
Swore to the blue sky above:

> 'The son of the herdsman, born here on this land,
> Aduchinfu is now kneeling here on this land.
> Mother Ulan Chabu,
> I'm giving back to you my warm blood.
> Please let it turn to clouds of rain
> To save our great grassland which bore me.
> The son of the herdsman kneels here,
> Aduchinfu is kneeling down here.
> Mother Ulan Chabu,
> I'm giving back to you my fresh blood.
> Please let sweet rain cut open a mountain creek,
> And save our great grassland that nursed me.'

"Having thus sworn, Aduchinfu
With a flash of his sword let flow his blood.
It shot up in the sky and turned into clouds,
And sweet rain began to pour and pour.
And then, a flash of lightning, a clap of thunder,
Split open the mountain into two halves.
Out from the middle flowed a creek,
A stream of water pure and clear.

"After giving the last drop of his blood,
Aduchinfu handed his sword to his fellow herdsmen,
And said:

'Don't let the wolves drink from it,
Or the foxes lap any drop of it!
Heavenly River must not be degraded in grassland,
Let no stranger intrude the creekside
We use our sword to protect our eyes,
And use swords we must to protect our good water.'

"Aduchinfu, Aduchinfu . . .
You live on in our hearts, from fathers to sons.
The sweet water bought with your precious blood
Named for our son's son forever, as the 'Red Spring.'"

"The Red Spring Song" taught by Old Grandfather
Soars up into the sky, and out of the valley,
Reaching beyond the heavens, and returns again
To nestle in the young hearts of the children—
Ulantoya and her little brother,
Their eyes, now four tearful streams.

The song finished, taught to the children,
Old Grandfather kneels on the creekside to kiss the ripples.
And then he rises and draws his sword
To sing that sacred song once more to the little ones.

"Don't let the wolves drink from it,
Or the foxes lap any drop of it!
We use our swords to protect our eyes,
And use swords we must to protect our 'Red Spring.'"

[Old herdsman Aersilang and his people thus engraved in their hearts the
sanctity of this precious spring. For generations they fought anything that
threatened to befoul their water source. And yet, it was the only source for
miles around and had to be tapped for the development of iron mines planned
there in the late 1950s. Aersilang's dilemma weighed him down when he
realized that for weeks the survey teams could not make any progress and no
work on the mines could be started. It was after much inner struggle that the
old herdsman finally allowed himself to lead the engineers to the water source,
and soon the mining began.

Much of the rest of the 2000-line poem describes how Old Aersilang had to
persuade, not entirely without use of force, some of his even more conservative
fellow herdsmen to yield to progress. Eventually an "electric dragon"—an
electric train—wound its way up the massive rocky mountain, White Cloud
Obo.]

The Yin Mountain Range greets the break of dawn.
All colors burst forth on grassland.
White Cloud Obo fires a salvo in salute
Cheering the rise of a golden sun!

Gold are the wings that hover over the land,
Carrying the Yin Mountain aloft, higher and higher.
Spring clouds float by, riding on rushing winds,
Carrying aloft the entire Yin Mountain Range.
They leave behind the old world
And cast away the months and years of poverty.
White Cloud Obo fires a salvo in salute,
As the grassland leaps forward in the era of steel.

December 1958–February 1963
White Cloud Obo Symphony, pp. 32–37, 88–89

Translated by Kai-yu Hsu

KO PI-CHOU
(1922–)

A prolific writer from Szechwan Province in the 1950s, Ko Pi-chou spent the years during and soon after World War II in the guerrilla area of North China. In the early 1960s he was a high Party functionary in writers' organizations in his native province, but the Cultural Revolution silenced him in 1966. There is still no word about his present situation.

His poetry collections include, among others, *Farewell to Yenan* and *The Yen River Flows On As Always.* —K.Y.H.

Mountain Eagle Gliding over Clouds

Crossing the Cuckoo Mountain in rainy season,
A landslide blocked our convoy.
Please just wait a minute, Comrades,
On top of the Cuckoo Mountain
There is our brave road crew.

Crossing the Cuckoo Mountain in mid-winter,
Waist-deep ice and snow seal off the pass.
Please just wait a minute, Comrades,
On top of the Cuckoo Mountain
There is our heroic road crew.

Crossing the Cuckoo Mountain in fine weather,
Spring blossoms red, but autumn leaves even brighter.
Pine spread in dark blue waves under white-capped peaks.
The grade is steep but the road, gradual,
And gradually it leads us to the blue sky.

Day after day, then spring, then fall,
Truck after truck, the caravan crosses the mountain.
The man is gone but his heart stays here,
While on top of the Cuckoo Mountain,
An eagle glides over the clouds.

October 5, 1962, Mi-ya-luo
Poetry Journal, no. 1 (1962): 45

July Morning Breeze

July morning breeze,
a clear cool stream
flows through my bosom.

Sky full of stars
all disappeared now,
except one,
blinking

And the dawn mist,
a streamer, milky white,
winds around
green trees.

The glow of sunrise,
that costumed girl
dances to her cheerful songs
to greet me.

Broad-leaved *wu-t'ung* trees*
and slender birches
paint a dark shade along the road
all the way to the valley
beyond the horizon.

Fields unlimited
roll in waves;
half-hiding houses in bamboo groves
like isles, dotting the plain.

Rice paddies hushed and still
connect mountains with rivers;
only the swelling tassels
sway in the sun.

Lively corn stalks
prop up white clouds in the sky;
music vibrates
on their red whiskers.

---

*A broad-leaved deciduous tree very commonly seen in China, perhaps paulownia. It brings a rich image to Chinese poetry because of its sensitive response to the arrival of autumn and the magic quality of its wood when it is used to make lutes. [K.Y.H.]

Aren't they the tassels
of red spears in battle?
We have won victory together
through the storms of the year.

July morning breeze,
a cool stream
flows through my bosom.

October 8, 1963, Chengtu
Poetry Journal, no. 12 (1963): 25–26

Translated by Kai-yu Hsu

KUO HSIAO-CH'UAN

Carved on North Wasteland

Carry on with it, our endless generations to come!
This is your perpetual heritage—forever new and young.
Till it, year after year, you, masters of the world of tomorrow.
This is a sacred land—never to be duplicated, on earth
    or in heaven.

This land pillows on frontier mountains, opening to the heart
    of our country,
In gusty winds and over trying distance, even ancient travelers
    dared not to explore it.
This land, with its back to virgin forests, stepping on
    many lakes,
And in deep water or snow, even the hoofs of the old pony-
    express stirred up no dust.

This land slumbers on, as in an immense dream.
No voice of man to be heard, only howling wolves, bears,
    and tigers;
This land, always covered in tall grass.
For days on end, no man casts any shadow on it, only the sky,
    and the water, and the red sun large as a cartwheel.

This land once was an abandoned mother
And the waters in the lake, her eyes glazing at the closing dusk.
This land once was an innocent exile
Cocking his ears, the empty valleys, to await the sound of
    every footstep.

Remember that time, always remember: the height of winter, 1954.
This land fell apart under the splitting north wind, and every
    fence gate, sealed by ice and snow.
Remember forever those warriors, those revolutionary soldiers
    then starting a new life,
Having just bid farewell to the battlefront, with blue smoke of
    war still haunting their memories.

For a note on Kuo Hsiao-ch'uan, see p. 541.

Flames of wild fire rose; they declared to the world with their
    red torches.
From now on, a forward march has started on the north wasteland.
The burning pine torches delivered an ultimatum to the roaming
    wild beasts,
From now on, the north wasteland shall tolerate your terror no more.

Who is there to bandage the bloody blisters and cuts under our
    feet, all over our bodies?
Let's start out at once, toward the heart of the grassland, to
    survey the soil and the water sources.
Who has the time to shave our beards or wait for the red clouds
    to clear away from our eyes?
Let's go on; let's break the all-devouring snow storm with the
    heat of our bodies.

Let the bugle calls resound to sweep away the various enemies
    in nature,
Let's blaze a wide trail and let our bayonets cut through the
    entangling grass.
Let the battle cries resound to summon forth springtime with our
    heartfelt voices,
Save some from our daily ration for seed grain; put plow straps
    on our shoulders where there used to be gunstraps.

No tractors, no motor caravans, no pack horses. . . .
But there is the land, tens of thousands of acres, turning
    over in the warm spring breeze.
No houses, no inns, no hamlets sending up wafts of smoke of
    evening cooking. . . .
There are several state farms, taking root among a forest of tents.

How can we price this inheritance? It's indeed difficult
As I write these lines, machines and buildings are already lined
    up, row upon row;
How can we measure this land? I really don't know how,
As I write these lines, green fields sown to wheat are
    stretching beyond the horizon.

This perpetual heritage, this broad way to happy life.
Every road cut through this land, a sober guide.
This magic land, this garden where truth is nurtured.
Every golden fruit grown there, a heart that glitters
    and shines.

Listen, fighting and happiness, revolution and youth—
In the song of life here, they forever strike out notes
    of strength.

Look, joy and work, harvest and cultivation—
In the historical pattern here, they forever contribute to
    an ever-rich design.

Listen, the twittering swallows and roaring winds, rustling pines
    and peals of thunder.
In the songs of life here, they never fail to move you and
    gladden your ears.
Look, the winter creeks and spring rain, the land under snow,
    then covered with blooms.
In the unfolding scroll of history here, they never cease to
    arrest your eyes and your heartbeat.

Our children, and children's children, new people of the Communist
    era
Your ancestors buried in this land retain in you their deepest trust.
The road before you will be smooth, any time and at all times,
Yet there shall be no time when you miss the soul of revolution.

You, masters of the future world, citizens of our socialist fatherland.
Your ancestors buried in this land, retain in you their infinite faith.
Though your life will be a thousand times better than today,
There shall be no day when you will forget the hardship of the present
    generation.

Yes, all forward-looking children, ever treasure the words of their
    revolutionary forefathers,
Not by falsely worshipping their ancestors' tablets, offering three
    tall incense sticks day and night;
Yes, all forward-looking good children, ever respect the will of the
    pioneers ahead of them,
Criticizing not their trivial blemishes that cling to them like dust.

... Carry on, and forever on, our future generations.
This is a perpetual endowment—always new and always young;
... Keep working on this land, you, masters of the world of tomorrow.
This is a magic land—not easily found in heaven or in earth.

                                January 24, 1963, Peking
                                Sugarcane Forest, pp. 3–7

Drinking Song

Rain in height of summer
Thunder after thunder
Battle at Chu-hsien-chen

Hammer against hammer.*
Tonight we drink
Cup to cup.

Cheering wine harms you not,
Even after a thousand cups.
Words from understanding friends,
Even ten thousand are not too many.
Tonight it is
The victory feast for a good year.

Drink and get rowdy—
That's a rotten guy
Drunk and talking nonsense—
That's a useless fry.
Toasting our bright future
Is this generation of new socialist heroes.

The money-bags get drunk
For their bad conscience;
Yamen† runners get drunk
For taking bribes.
For us, even if we get drunk,
That's because the wine of life is too strong and sweet.

Tigers in the mountain—
Beauty on their backs.
Larks on the tree—
Beauty in their beaks.
We, lumberjacks—
Our beauty inside.

Fill the cups,
Raise them high.
One cup,
Open your heart wide.
Heroic feeling and good wine
Have always gone side by side.

Our fatherland is a garden
And the north, its winter plum blossom;
The Lesser Hsing-an Range, a flower,
The virgin woods, its center.
The flower's scent
Fills our lungs.

*Famous legendary battle between two hammer-wielding heroes of the Sung dynasty (twelfth century). [K.Y.H.]
†Government compound in Imperial China. [K.Y.H.]

The warmth of our fatherland
Touches us like a spring breeze.
Our comradeship
Flows over here like so many rivers.
The Party is the sun
And we, the sunflowers.

Thousands of buildings
Await their door sills from here.
Thousands of railroads
Await our ties.
Our country's mission is the flag,
And we, the vanguards under it.

Spirited horses
Need no whipping.
Well-stretched drums
Need no heavy beat.
We, lumberjacks,
Know how to respond.

Let's drink,
Let's not stop.
Three cups,
Three cupfuls of happy tears.
Five cups,
More gusto than the water in the Yangtze River.

Snowflakes falling
In clusters like flocks of returning geese.
Pine forests lined up
Like gods of longevity marching to a banquet.
And these gods,
All white hair, white beard, and white eyebrows.

Snowflakes falling
Like stars raining down from the sky.
The birch trees standing
Like ancient warriors guarding the frontier.
These soldiers—
All white helmets, white armors, and white flags.

Sinewy horses on grassland
Their fastest is the Black Steed.*
Of the heroes in mountain fastness

*Famous steed belonging to the third century B.C. hero Hsiang Yü of the state of Ch'u.
[K.Y.H.]

The bravest is Li K'uei.*
The best of men on earth or in heaven,
Our generation holds the destiny.

The target lies afar,
Let's overtake it in long strides.
Treading on snow,
Like flying in clouds.
We, men on the mountain,
Are like fish in waves.

Heavy jobs
Leave a sweet taste.
Felling giant timbers
Like so many wheat stalks.
And we hoist the logs
As we raise our wine cups.

One shout,
A thousand echoes.
On tree-shaded trails
Machines whine in symphony;
And on lumber railroads,
Trains thunder along.

At one command,
Ten thousand trees surrender;
On the frozen chute
A stream of lumber flows,
And mountains of railroad ties
Rise in the yard.

Let's drink;
Let's not stop!
Seven cups,
Our feeling soars with the snowstorm
Ten cups,
Our hearts glow with the rising sun.

Peaks of the Lesser Hsing-an Range
Indestructible, even by thunderbolts.
The waters of the T'ang-wang River
Irresistible in spite of the many turns.
These lumberjacks
Specialize in meeting the troubles head-on.

*One of the 108 outlaws in the story *Walter Margin*. [K.Y.H.]

One day off,
Three days' fatigue.
Three days off,
Ten restless nights.
Ten days off,
One feels downright guilty.

Planning to leave the mountain,
He loses his appetite.
About to leave the mountain,
He can hardly move his legs.
Once out of the mountain,
He dreams of the mountain every night.

As the old saying goes,
Balance the stele on your back
So long as you remain a turtle.*
We say, so long as we
Take three feet of space each,
We each radiate our light, ten thousand fathoms long.

An old saying has it:
Keep taking orders until you stop
Being someone's errand boy.
We say now:
Drink three scoops of snowflakes,
Bloom ten thousand flowers.

Men in the mountain,
Lumber flows in all directions.
We stay in the woods,
But our will embraces all the hills and rills.
To our country we respond,
The way it wants us to respond.

Remember yesterday
The many tests and temperings.
Then look toward tomorrow,
The colorful blossoming.
Who doesn't wish to work like this for a hundred years
And live a hundred years like this?

*The base of a large tombstone, or stele, is traditionally carved in the shape of a turtle.
[K.Y.H.]

Cheering wine harms not,
Even after a thousand cups.
Words from understanding friends,
Ten thousand aren't too many.
Tonight it is
The pledge meeting for a good year.

December 1962–February 1963, Yi-ch'un to Peking
Sugarcane Forest, pp. 8–18

Translated by Kai-yu Hsu

KUO MO-JO
(1892–1978)

When Kuo Mo-jo died on June 13, 1978, he left a shelf full of volumes ranging from creative writing to history to archeology, with an equal number of tomes of translations from Western literature. His life of eighty-six years had been in many ways the embodiment of the development of modern Chinese literature.

A rebellious student in the out-of-the-way province of Szechwan, a romantic youth drunk with poetry, love, and revolution in the 1910s and early 1920s, introducer of Goethe and Schiller to the Chinese, a mature research scholar in ancient Chinese history and material culture—Kuo left his mark on every field he ventured into. As a founder of the Creation Society in 1921, he encouraged a rebellion against time-honored literary traditions and helped develop a purposive literature to advocate and guide the revolution.

In creative writing his first collection, *The Goddess* (1921), provoked all his contemporaries with its daring innovations: the use of the blank verse form and the adoption of Western images. Looking back at it now, its youthful experiments may be more significant as landmarks in the history of modern Chinese literature than for their own literary merit, but the arguments stimulated by them in Chinese literary criticism continue to find echoes even today.

In his later years Kuo's poetry was confined to occasional works, most of which used traditional Chinese prosody—regulated verse, quatrains, or the irregular meter lyric mode—and were written in response to state affairs or to the verses of such personages as Mao Tse-tung and Ch'en Yi. For years one of the vice-premiers of the government, he died in the presidency of the Chinese Academy of Sciences, an office he held longer than he held any other position. The bibliography of works by and about him is probably the most extensive among twentieth-century Chinese men of letters. Despite the fact that Kuo changed his political stances as frequently as the political tides changed, his apparent sycophancy does not seem to have seriously impaired his domestic or international reputation, which has remained on a par with that of Lu Hsün.

—K.Y.H.

Visit to Vietnam

HEAT AND FATIGUE

Comrade, are you hot?
No, I don't feel hot.
How can you not feel hot here, in the tropics?
Our friendship is warmer than the tropics.

693

Comrade, are you tired?
No, I don't feel tired.
You're getting on in years now, how come you don't feel tired?
No, I'm only fifteen.

FISH AND FLOWER

Water in the pond, warm now, like hotspring,
But teeming fishlings continue to cavort in the sun.

Water in the pot, hot now, like boiling soup,
Yet the flower in it still blooms, flaming red.

They struggle against the world of objective reality,
And fish and flowers thrive through the strife.

Poetry Journal, no. 9 (1964): 38–39

Translated by Kai-yu Hsu

LI YING

The Memory of a City

To a Korean comrade at arms

Remember that city?
Reduced to ruins at a wink of the eye?
Fallen on the bank of the Lin-jin River,
Fallen under the aggressor's gunfire?

Its flesh and skin scorched,
Its blood drained dry,
Its limbs blown away,
But its head, unconquerable, was held up high.

It said: bullets have pierced my bosom,
But left intact my confidence and strength.
You know it is this faith and this hate
That nurture my life, give me breath.

It said: look—
My heart still throbs and blood flows.
My flesh and skin are growing back and
In my handgrip still lies my weapon
    —to fight the enemy to the bitter end.

My comrades at arms, who have come from the Lin-jin
    River,
Today you brought me the sounds of rebuilding,
And a memory solemn and stern.
But without the blood bath of that year,
Today—
How could it bloom like a most beautiful flower
Smiling in the sun? . . .

Poetry Journal, no. 2 (1964): 38

For a note on Li Ying, see p. 371.

Passing a River of Pearls at Night

All day long, patrolling in wind and sand;
At night I find a glittering river.
Where have I ever seen such waters,
A bewitching beauty, impregnated with joy.

Are they not wild flowers in my memory,
Suddenly blooming all over the river's face?
Or fruits laden on trees covering the hills
All ripened tonight, waiting to be picked?

Are they leaping, flickering flames,
Single ones, in clusters, ever aglow?
Or thousands of birds, many-colored,
Chattering, gathering under water to build nests?

Perhaps it isn't any river, no, it isn't—
But the guardian mother of our land
Places her diamonds and other precious stones,
For the night in this cradle of a ditch.

I'd like to scoop up a handful for my comrades,
But they slip away between my fingers.
"Tonight the stars are really big and bright!"
These words of our captain cast sparks on the river.

If you never mounted a battle horse for our country,
How could you ever know the beauty of her hills and rills?
How could you ever know the stars on highlands in
     mid-autumn,
One brighter than another, each a story of thrills?

May 1962
Red Willow, pp. 55–56

Translated by Kai-yu Hsu

LIANG SHANG-CH'ÜAN

Flower Bridge

Songs on this side, the other side responds,
When the other side sings, this side follows.
The stone bridge arches a rainbow over the flow,
And under the rainbow the flow strums its strings.

The strings are ringing, forever ringing,
Keep telling an old story, very old and yet all new—
The bridge had just been done, the last stone set,
A flowered sedan chair brought in a young bride.

The young bride came from a farmer family,
But the stonemason was a lover of songs.
If songs were sung without proper match, he said,
She could not cross the bridge to see her bridegroom.

The farm girl was a folk-song singer,
If it was a folk-song match, hers burst out instantly;
Bursting out instantly was a well-wrought piece, startling the sun,
And the sun lingered on, unwilling to leave her.

The sun lingered on, and people lingered on,
Back and forth, thousands of songs exchanged,
The songs flowed with the water, reaching the sea,
Turning into clouds to fly back again.

Songs on this side, the other side responds,
When the other side sings, this side follows;
Today the sound of songs vibrates on both sides,
Sustaining the good name of the Flower Bridge.

May 19, 1961, Flower Bridge Commune
The Mountain Stream, pp. 175–76

For a note on Liang Shang-ch'üan, see p. 180.

Black Water and Reeds*

Water in Black River
Why so dark?
Virgin woods on both banks,
New leaves push the old.

Blooms at Reed Bloom Village
Why so white?
Winds bathed in frost
Have split the buds.

Tall houses near water
Built of stone;
Gun terraces amid the flowers
Rock-lined.

Between the rocks,
Plots of land have been planted.
Even the cracks and crevices
Are filled with crops.

Sturdy Tibetan people
Strong-willed, like rocks;
They spark easily when rubbed,
And are easily tempered into steel.

Black River, black.
Reed blooms, white.
Black as black gold,
And white like snow.

April 2, 1962, Chungking
The Mountain Stream, pp. 41–42

Translated by Kai-yu Hsu

---

*Name of a small frontier town in northern Szechwan, not far from Tibet. Most of the residents are members of ethnic minority groups speaking different dialects. [K.Y.H.]

LIU CHENG
(1925?–)

Liu Cheng is something of a mystery. He published a considerable number of satirical poems in the early 1960s, such as "The Tiger Posts a Decree," apparently with political immunity. Almost immediately after the resumption of the *Poetry Journal* in 1976, Liu's satire appeared again.

The "Tiger" poem was published in the fall of 1963 during a brief lull between two political storms. The reader may choose as the target of Liu's satirical barb either the authorities who pushed the Great Leap Forward campaign, which was nearing its end, or the Gang of Four, who were beginning to seize power. Either way, Liu was treading on very dangerous ground.

"The 'Wind' Clique," released in the spring of 1978, ostensibly comments on the Gang of Four headed by Chiang Ching. And yet the attack could be aimed at all those political turncoats, including such a luminary as Kuo Mo-jo, who always manage to sail along with the prevailing political wind.   —K.Y.H.

The Tiger Posts a Decree

I, the Tiger, hereby post a decree,
All ye animals, hear, oh, hear!

A policy of peace is what I, the Tiger
Pursue at all hours, every day.
To insure safety in the mountain,
I, the Tiger, won't shirk responsibility.
Therefore I declare three don'ts,
All ye animals must strictly obey.

First, don't grow horns on the head,
Thus end all clashes, once for all.
I, the Tiger, swear to high heaven,
On my top I grow only short hair.
You wild bulls and mountain deer
Logically should saw off your antlers.
No favoritism, no partiality, my decree—
May heaven and earth be my witness—is fair, very fair!

Second, don't fly in the sky,
To avoid disturbing the Lord on High.
I, the Tiger, pledge before everybody,
I shall never take off, no, not I!

You, big rocs and little wrens,
Pluck off your feathers completely.
When both animals and birds stay on the ground,
Equality of treatment can apply all round.

Third, don't swim in water,
'Cause sanitary drinks are at stake.
I, the Tiger, am well behaved,
Will never get into a lake.
You, fish and shrimp, crabs and clams,
Hasten to make a living on shore.
When all join in the free world,
The world will be peaceful forevermore.

As to sharp claws and teeth,
About them we need a liberal law,
Permitting free use of them
To bite, gnaw, tear, and claw.
I, the Tiger, will never monopolize,
Each will have his share of bites.
Go ahead and grow claws and fangs,
It's all hereby declared your rights.

Now that I've named the three don'ts,
Let's proceed to put them into practice.
For anyone daring to disagree and disobey,
Penalty will be severe, most severe penalty.
He'll be charged with disturbing peace,
And held responsible for all consequences.

It is hereby earnestly and earnestly announced!

Poetry Journal, no. 9 (1963): 36–37

The "Wind" Clique

Grass on top of the wall, always swaying
In all directions as the winds prevail.
The market is bearish, watch out!
Hurry up with a parting shot, hurry!
The market turns bullish, here he comes—
At a discount price, his soul on sale.

Who cares, human or devil.
Who cares, good or vile.
When there's milk, anybody's milk, the infant turns on a sweet smile.
Aha, but this time he bit on a hot pepper,
Bet he won't gamble on high stakes for a while.

Poetry Journal, no. 4 (1978): 50–51

Translated by Kai-yu Hsu

T'AI TEH-CH'IEN

T'ai Teh-ch'ien was a familiar name in the poetry of the late 1950s and early 1960s. His works, though a bit affected at times, brought a breath of fresh air to the poems then all too dominated by the sound of motors and the smell of gunpowder. He tended to be a little more intellectual than his contemporaries.

—K.Y.H.

In the Ta-pieh Mountains

ANCIENT RUINS, UNDERWATER

The Ta-pieh Mountains sway on water,
Ready to take off, ready to run.
In the valley, quiet, no man to be seen,
Only a pale yellow moon on the treetop.

An oar glistens, a boat sways on the lake,
One man drifts on it, alone,
Following the moonlight to trace
The traceless street, city, underwater.

Who knows how deep the water is, who?
A sinking pebble brings up a string of bubbles.
You call to the city, "How ... "
And "how ... " Is that the rusty bell down below?

Suddenly the oar flies, shattering
The moon's face and the lake's face;
A startled bird is the boat now, riding
On east wind that flutters a red flag

Of that old Red city, the Old Gold Castle,
Lying in fathoms of quiet cool water.
You still hear an aroused citizenry's shouts—
Golden carp leap, splash, and splatter.

And now a lake full of lights splashing,
From the power unleashed from the ancient city.
Old Gold Castle, a dynamo of revolution,
Its bugle calls still resound in the hills.

Waves surge in a lone visitor's heart, but
The valley remains quiet, quiet and serene,
Only the Ta-pieh Mountains sway on water,
Ready to take off, ready to spring.

FEBRUARY ORCHID

Without making a sound they bloom in deep mountain,
Without flaunting any bright red color in front of man.
Their sword-like blades and arrow-like buds in winter
Perfuming all the hills upon the first spring rain.

Humbly they hide behind the hundreds of spring blossoms,
Even at close range, not easily seen;
They yield the credit to other noisy wild flowers,
But continue to deliver scent to you, quietly and unfailing.

WILD FLOWER

In hidden mountains she blooms, her blossoms most plain,
Even the mountain folks think nothing of her work;
And winter comes, ordering her: "Get going, get going!"
She shakes her head and says, "There's a fire yet to burn."

Poetry Journal, no. 2 (1964): 56–57

Translated by Kai-yu Hsu

T'ANG TA-T'UNG
(1930?–)

A newcomer among the young poets of the 1960s, T'ang Ta-t'ung started with Tsang K'o-chia, T'ien Chien and several other experienced writers as his models. His imitative efforts suffered from too much restriction until he spent over six months pulling the cable and handling oars among the boatmen of the Chia-ling River in Szechwan. The result was a good number of poems in which he successfully captured the feeling and spirit of those living and straining their backs on the river: "In my whole life I've always liked to travel / No matter how wide the river is, it's still too narrow for me!" He took as his inspiration the best lines from the Tang dynasty poet, Li Po, written some twelve hundred years before:

> The Wu Mountains pinch the blue sky,
> And the Pa River flows like this.
> Soon the Pa River runs its course,
> But there's no time when the sky's reached.
> Three days it takes to go up the Yellow Bull Gorge,
> And for three nights the boat moves ever so slowly.
> Three days passed and again three nights,
> Not knowing his hair has turned into snow.

> Li Po, "Going Upriver to the
> Three Gorges"

How did T'ang Ta-t'ung see the same scene in 1962? His "Passing the Yangtze Gorges" tells us:

> Two mountains pinch the blue sky,
> Heaven is too small in the Gorges.
> I look up to find only one line,
> Too narrow for my pole.
> Two mountains embrace the river,
> The cliffs block startled waves,
> From a distance I see only a pinhole,
> Too small for my oar.
> . . . .
> Suddenly it all opens up, bright hills and shimmering water,
> Beyond the Gorges, the river widens and sky rises high;
> I can pole as I wish, and row as I wish.
> Looking back at the Gorges, no river to be seen;
> Only layers of mountains shield the waves,
> Only man's shouting is still heard in the mountain—
> The boatmen's songs that is, reverberating in the Gorges.

> *Szechwan Literature,* no. 10 (1962)

After that poem was written, the Cultural Revolution intervened, silencing the poet for a few years, but in 1977 his work appeared again in the revived *Poetry Journal* (no. 6, p. 58), still singing of the river.   —K.Y.H.

Boatman's Song on the Chia-ling River

The chant sets a cadence,
Our footsteps sound the drumbeat,
Ten thousand pull the cable together—
Hai-yo-hai ... hai-yo-hai ...
Our strength twisted into a rope
Pulls the sailboat up a swift river.

Our bent backs sore, our waists aching,
Hot drops of sweat prick our eyes,
Easy to go down the rapids, tough to go up!
Hai-yo-hai ... hai-yo-hai ...
We fear only the lack of unity,
Not the slow pace of progress.

Want to know the load we're pulling?
Just watch each of our trying steps.
We crush the gravel into water,
And the rocks into powder.
Hai-yo-hai ... hai-yo-hai ...
Our load is our country's rebuilding.

Wear out one cable after another,
Level off every cascade; for this
We boatmen have legs of iron.
Hai-yo-hai ... hai-yo-hai ...
As many rapids as there are in our country,
Our journey is as long.

Poetry Journal, no. 6 (1962): 23–24

June Flood Pours toward Chungking

June flood, a wild beast,
Rolls along, roars along ...
Threatens my boat to stop rowing
Frightens my sail a-tremble.

Who's afriad of mountain-sized waves,
Or of vicious whirlpools, those gaping jaws?
Shipping grain under stress and strain
As June flood pours toward Chungking.

Rain in buckets, sweat in buckets,
They flow together, sweat and rain.
You can soak my clothes, soak as you will,
But my bones, unchilled, defy the strain.

Wind cuts like sword, a sword ever sharp,
Things freeze, frozen to the core.
You can churn up waves, ugly waves,
But you can't take away my fighting oar.

Hard liquor, a bowl or two,
Keeps me warm to fight the storm.
Man used to worry while traveling by boat,
Now on waves' crests I freely roam.

Now good harbors shelter me during the day,
And at night docks offer me a restful shed.
Everywhere there's a home for us boatmen,
Everywhere friends come to our aid.

Thanks to the swift flow, swift as arrows
Fly over three days' journey in merely two,
Waves a thousand feet high reaching the sky
Carry my white sail to float in the clouds.

Poetry Journal, no. 6 (1962): 24

New Song of K'uei Men*

An awesome peak rises, piercing the clouds,
It seems to block the river and lock the Gate.

---

*K'uei Gate, a gorge on the Yangtze River at the entrance to Szechwan Province. Its majestic beauty and the historical events that occurred in the area have inspired many poems in Chinese literature. [K.Y.H.]

Hundreds of feet high it stands, higher than a bird can fly;
Below, the river writhes—a dragon, an angry sea serpent.
The warrior sighs as he gazes into the sky,
While boatmen's regret fills the valley:
Battle-axes and sails from ancient men of war sunk on the river's bottom,
And a hundred thousand troops swallowed up in the waves.
The river flows eastward to the sea, never to return,
Only the White King City stays perched on the rocks, lonely and in vain.

A signal tower has been erected on the cliff,
And buoys on the waves mark the channel,
Now K'uei Men has swung its doors open, wide open,
To let pass the soldiers of the transport corps.
Listen, in the cabins of the boats
Travelers are talking about Chu-ko Liang.*
Look, on the decks of the boats
Sailors talk and laugh, about things past and present.
We are the ones to judge the faults and merits of the past,
As the new era brings joy to fill our bosoms.

K'uei Men no longer cuts the new China into halves,
All one family now, those to its east and its west,
The mountains and rivers of Szechwan in spring delight our eyes.
The skies and waters of Hunan and Hupeh have donned new colors.
No longer is K'uei Men needed to guard our motherland,
In our hearts we keep the Gate of Heavenly Peace.
Let's move K'uei Men out to the country's frontier
To stand sentry for the battleline against revisionism,
Wearing a soldier's uniform, pine green and brand new,
To keep the lights burning in homes all over the land.

K'uei Men shakes its head, smiling,
Says it prefers to stay there to provide rear support—
Heroes like Huang Chi-kuang and Ch'iu Shao-yün . . .
Once started their journeys right here.
This is our bastion, richly endowed by Heaven,
With plenty of soldiers, and generals, and banners of war,
With bumper crops every season, every year,
And every month a new crop of soldiers in training.
All poised, all waiting for motherland's bugle call,
All the millions of heroes will march out of K'uei Men.

Poetry Journal, no. 6 (1977): 58

Translated by Kai-yu Hsu

---

*An historical hero, a superb military strategist of the third century A.D. He has been immortalized in the popular novel *Romance of the Three Kingdoms.* [K.Y.H.]

T'IEN CHIEN

Big Iron Man

A "talk-sing" poem, based on a legend circulating among members of the Wu-kung Commune, Jao-yang County, Hopei Province.

The days of gunshot are past,
It's gardens and flowers now.
Communes have changed the world, but
We must hold our rifles even more firmly.

Never, never to let our rifles go,
Keep our rivers and hills green.
The tree full of pear blossoms
Let me weave them into a story.

The Big Iron Man's name is Old Li. An old, poor peasant, a veteran militia-man, he has spent half his life with a rifle on his shoulder. They are inseparable, he and his rifle. His spine is unbending and his blood warm.

The commune is his home—its corridor, the lanes of trees. His straight spine bucks the evil winds, braves wild storms. Since coming to watch the orchard, he has won praise from everybody with his "all public no private" attitude, and they have all started calling him Big Iron Man, which is a supreme tribute.

An orchard on the edge of the village shelters a hut for Big Iron Man. He eats his meals in it, sleeps in it, and stands sentry duty in it. Be it a bright moonlit night, or one with a storm-darkened sky, Big Iron Man keeps his vigil at the open window, night after night. He knows the direction of the Revolution. He hunts well, and his favorite prey is fox. They say there was a "fox fairy" that failed to escape from him. Now let me tell this newly created legend....

No more idle talk, listen to my song:

The commune is a sea of flowers,
Pear blossoms, in April, are most sweet.
Some days ago, they told each other
About a fairy there, white as frost.
A white figure all over, even a white shadow,
Often comes out to comb her hair under moonlight.
Did she pick the flowers from the tree

For a note on T'ien Chien, see p. 182.

708

And make a dress out of them?
Did she steal water from the Milky Way
And stir up wind and waves around here?
The fairy goddess, pretty as a flower,
Who knows what she is up to?
They say she is a fox-turned-fairy,
Who wants Old Li for her bridegroom.
Thus every night she comes out under the tree,
Every night she shows herself at the window.
She stands near the window and looks in,
Sweet smile and sweet talk all the while.
This night, there is a bright moon above,
Big Iron Man sits on his *k'ang,* alone,
Both hands on the rifle, his old pal.

Big Iron Man says:
Outside the window, rustling wind rises,
The fox fairy must have scaled the wall.
Why does the fairy find me interesting?
Be guarded, ah, against secret plots of the foe.
Is she here to chop down trees in the orchard,
Or does she want me to surrender my weapon?
Look, is that a pear tree swaying, or
The gleam on the Milky Way's white water?
Suddenly there appears a white shadow,
Tapping the window, I can hear the sound

Fox Fairy says:
Big Iron Man, don't be so cruel,
Put down your rifle right now.
You've shot all the foxes, all of them,
What's the use of the gun in your hand?
Pear blossoms fall into the Milky Way,
And in the blooms has risen a bridge.
Out here the moon is so pretty tonight,
The Weaving Maid wants to meet her Ox-herder Boy.

Big Iron Man says:
Cunning fox, you stop dreaming,
Stop hoping for me to lay down my rifle.
You are a fox, and nothing more, and
You want to drag me into the mud pond.
I have shed blood for the Revolution,
I have been wounded defending my country.
I have planted trees for the commune.
Now these trees are grown, covered with blooms.
The moon should look only at red hearts,
As big trees should be timbers for the commune.

Don't think you can come here to tempt me,
I want to taste no honey on the tip of a sword.
Don't think you can come here to corrupt me,
What the Iron Man likes is his five-foot rifle.
Ghost and devil, don't try your clever disguises,
Big Iron Man here has had his mind all made up.
Look, here is a round which I load in my rifle,
And with this gun I am right at your chest!

Fox Fairy says:
Big Iron Man, don't shoot, please,
See the tears welling in my eyes.
I came to be with you, keep you company.
What's this disguise business, why did you say that?
Put your gun away, don't point it at me,
We can talk things over, very nicely.
A girl in your pear garden, very much in love with you,
Too bad for her to pick a heartless man.
Like a tiny boat the moon sails on water,
Which is the flowers—what a pretty picture,
And there is a fairy goddess waiting for you,
Why don't you come out and have a good time?

Big Iron Man says:
A long rifle in hand, I, the Iron Man,
Will keep vigil over this window and door.
My station is here, and here I stay,
A soldier doesn't leave his sentry post.
This window is the commune's nerve center,
Nobody can get by with any trick to harm it.
The commune's big banner is in my charge,
And I'll carry it through wind and rain.
We, poor peasants, flagpoles made of iron,
Can't be smashed up, can't be cut down.
The sky may shake, the earth may tremble,
I'll be a pillar, shoring up our commune.
No matter how sweet your smiles may be,
Can't fool the iron will of an iron man—me!

As they talk on, the day is dawning,
A ray of daylight mounts the windowpane.
After several clicks of the rifle bolt
The pear blossom girl is gone again.
The white pear blossoms remain, white as snow,
But the fox fairy is not under the tree.
He shakes his five-foot rifle in the wind,
Sunrise begins to paint the windowpane.
The old poor peasant's heart, red and radiant,

Matches the sun rising from the east.
Big Iron Man walks out of his door,
A wild stallion striding over the hills.
Suddenly his eyes are caught by the words:
          "The Grave of Big Iron Man"
Written clearly on a stone slab, straight and clear.
Big Iron Man, he bursts into laughter,
Ha, ha, here you are playing the game again.
I can see through all your devil's schemes,
But a stone can't fly, can't play many tricks.
All right, since you've drawn the battle line,
I'll take up you dare and see what you do.
Big Iron Man pauses and ponders a moment,
An idea occurs to him, and he keeps it to himself.
As the moon rises once more that same evening,
Big Iron Man hides behind a huge tree.
The same long rifle rests in his hand,
A long rope hides under his waistband.
As expected the fox fairy appears again,
A white veil on her face that turns toward him.
She picks a pear blossom and holds it high
In a low voice she mumbles a devil's charm.
Just as she approaches the step under the eaves,
Without knowing it she walks into a trap.
A rope is thrown over her, ties her down,
The fox fairy's disguise now falls exposed.
It turns out to be a bad element, so bad is he,
That he masquerades as a goddess to fool me.
He first spread the rumor about a fox fairy
Then acts that part dressed up as a she.
His (her) smile hides a knife and many tricks,
He dreams of taking over the pear orchard.
Now, let's see how he is going to transform,
Now, let's see where he is going to hide.
Today the fox fairy has fallen into a snare.
Everybody's eyes are clear, see the whole story.
Men of socialism, Wu-kung's blossoms,
With leaves ever so lush, and branches ever strong.
The pear blossoms dance to smiling red flags,
Dancing all the way across the Heng River and the
     Yangtze.
Let us paint a new portrait of Big Iron Man
With the colors and light of Wu-kung in spring.
Let us offer this orchard full of flowers and fruit
To Big Iron Man, as a reward, as a citation.

The *Poetry Journal* has been promoting poetry recitals and has published a
good number of poems to be sung. More recently the *Journal* has been encour-

aging talk-sing poems, and asked me to write one. This piece has been worked over twice with the actors of the Peking Youth Song Troupe and the editors of the *Journal*. I think it is not yet a definitive work. For the present I can only hope that it has some poetic significance as well as some capability of being sung and acted out on stage. . . .

Poetry Journal, no. 7 (1964): 4–7

Translated by Kai-yu Hsu

TSANG K'O-CHIA

Sun Island

Sun Island, Sun Island,
I knew your name even before we met;
Friends sent me off to Harbin,
Instructing me again and again to visit Sun Island.
Each day I stand on the river bank and confront you,
Watch the morning sun and the Lama Pagoda racing to reach higher
  in the sky.
And at dusk, the evening sun's afterglow
Lets me study your radiant face.
Small wooden barks, one by one,
Carry full loads of men and women, young and old,
Some of them to your vicinity to work
With spades and hoes in hand,
Some of them bringing sons and daughters along
To your place for relaxation.
You see off the little steamboat that sails up and down,
You hear the international train as it rumbles on its way,
You face the distant Martyr's Memorial,
You are separated from Harbin by the river.
You saw the tyranny of the new and old warlords,
You saw the Japs' mad destruction,
You saw the Resistance fighters' heroic action,
You saw the Russian Red Army's clean sweeps.
At that time, your face was dim,
At that time, the sun hid in dark clouds.

Sun Island, Sun Island,
How wonderful your shining name!
Sun Island, Sun Island,
Why are you called Sun Island?
I asked the old boatman,
He hesitated awhile, then said, "I don't know."
I asked the tour guide,
He just scratched his head.
Sun Island, Sun Island,
Never mind why you are called Sun Island,
Sun Island, Sun Island,
You look fine indeed.

For a note on Tsang K'o-chia, see p. 383.

Like a city, yet like a village, too,
Tall buildings and wood houses rival each other,
Families scattered here and there,
Yellow dirt roads, one after another,
Sunflowers grow to form a fence,
Hugh loofahs hang down their lengths,
Red-scarfed youngsters play on the swing in the yard,
Little squealing pigs scurry all over the streets.
Are the convalescents
Catching fish at the river's edge?
Not a soul in this one little courtyard,
An unfinished chess game spread out under the trees ...
No permanent residents here,
They all come and go like migrant birds.
I stand next to you,
Suddenly struck by a fancy:
Riding in a helicopter
Way up in the sky,
I cast my eyes downward,
You really are the sun, aren't you?
The river waters are your halo,
Casting off a greenish gleam,
Dirt mounds seem to be turning, so many revolving discs,
And the flow of people around them, as though in trance.
Looking up from the ground, the sun is in the sky,
Looking down, isn't that the sun on the ground?

"On the Sungari River"
People's Literature, no. 12 (1962): 13–14

The Well

—Visiting the Ancient Palace of the "Po-hai Kingdom" *

The well, more than a thousand years old,
The glazed tiles long gone from its octagonal top,
Quenches the thirst of July travellers
With its cool water limpid as melted ice.

Pairs of stone lions gaze into the wilderness,
Their huge eyes fixed in an astonished stare,
"Seaview Pagoda" cannot see the sea,
Only green crops extend to the sky's edge.

*An ancient palace in Niang-an, Kirin Province, kept as a monument marking the place where the founding emperor of the Manchu dynasty was born. [K.Y.H.]

Dust billows over the high road,
With carts rolling by and the bustling of people,
Jugs on their heads and skirts wind-blown,
The commune members walk on the once forbidden ground.

Sweet is the well water for the vegetable garden,
Tomatoes, one after another, red and fresh—
His hands pick them, his mouth explains them,
He thus becomes "the kingdom's" interpreter.

"On the Sugari River"
People's Literature, no. 12 (1962): 14

A Train Passing through Shanhaikwan

On a train passing through Shanhaikwan
In the depth of the night,
You can't see anything
Except for the brilliant platform lights.

One by one the passengers leave the car,
O, how peaceful this quiet night!
A mother holds her child's hand,
Her eyes searching out from the crowd.

A noise makes your mind think back,
The train stopped at "Station Sept. 18, 1931,"*
Suddenly the lights stirred into ghostly will-o'-the-wisps
Now and again a dark wind in the gloom before your eyes.

Just one enemy cannon report, our "great army" of three hundred
thousand paled.
Their military caps couldn't hide their ashamed faces.
Shanhaikwan, you are not the pass to retreat to,
But rather the ignitor of the nation's liberation.

A train passing through Shanhaikwan,
The earth's green rolls out to the eastern horizon,
The locomotive huffs, puffing out steam,
Like a swift horse, catching sight of the prairie ahead.

*Named to commemorate the Japanese occupation of Mukden on that day, an event
that signaled China's loss of all Manchuria. [K.Y.H.]

Sounds of crying, howling, and fighting
No longer can be heard,
In a warm voice the announcer on the train
Bids the passengers good evening.

Scenes of exile, gunsmoke, and battle charges
No longer can be seen,
Looking out of the window:
The mid-month full moon shines over the splendorous frontier
    hills.

November 17, 1962, Peking
"On the Sungari River"
People's Literature, no. 12 (1962): 16

Fearless

So young a child,
Already a martyr—
In peasant dress,
Face full of heroic spirit.

Homeless since very small,
Your Motherland is your home,
Parentless since very small,
You suffered all kinds of hardships.

With a whip you pastured the landlord's hogs,
With a whip the landlord flogged you,
You rebelled, you ran away,
And finally found your own people.

The Japanese devils got what they deserved at your hands,
You became Commander of the Children's Corps;
Wearing a uniform too big for you,
An awesome power shone in your little face.

I once stood before a portrait of Liu Hu-lan*
And compared your career with hers,
You both were children of poverty,
You both did deeds that shook the world.

*A martyr killed during the war of liberation. [K.Y.H.]

I think that were you alive today,
You'd have done a number of marvelous things;
Oh, but without yesterday's sacrifice,
How could there be today's good fortune?

Again and again I stand before your portrait,
For a long, long time unable to make myself leave.
Fearless, what an unyielding name!
Fearless, what an unyielding fighter!

"On the Sungari River"
People's Literature, no. 12 (1962): 12–13

An Old Woman

Blind in both eyes, hair white with age,
With no other wish but to see the Liberation Army,
A cane supports you as you shakily make your way here,
With your noble mother's heart.

With a pair of shrivelled hands for your eyes,
You touch the young soldiers' faces one by one;
And, as if somehow you are still not sure,
Again you measure their stature up and down.

"'Seven or eight Vietcong can't even break a twig,'
The enemy says this because he fears us!"
The cane supports you as you shakily move off,
With your heart full of joy and self-confidence.

The fighting men of the Liberation Army, tears in their eyes,
Watch your noble, gradually fading form,
The valor of killing the enemy fills their bodies,
Each drop of a tear, a pledge of action.

"In Praise of the Vietnam Heroes"
People's Literature, no. 6 (1964): 20

The Fight Will Never Be Done

You ask when the fight will be done?
The fight will never be done!
Not unless the whitecaps on surging waves cease to roll
And the waters of the Nine-dragon River cease to flow,
Not 'til the dark night comes to an end,
No, not 'til victory is firmly in our hands!

May 29, 1964
"In Priase of the Vietnam Heroes"
People's Literature, no. 6 (1964): 21

Translated by Hsin-sheng C. Kao

YEN YI

Yen Yi combines in himself something of both Hao Ran and Li Ying. A "Little Red Devil" running errands for the Eighth Route Army in the early 1940s, this son of a poor peasant soon found himself drawn to writing songs and rhymes for the cultural work teams in the Red Army. He traveled with different troops all over north and northwest China during the last phase of the War of Liberation, retracing many of the steps of the Long Marchers. A representative collection of his impressions of those years captured in verse is *Ode to the White Birch Tree* (1962).

As another fellow poet, Juan Chang-ching, said of Yen Yi's work, "Yen Yi's lines are filled with the genuine feeling of a soldier. . . . This characteristic is most precious." Yen Yi draws some images extremely well, such as that of steel in his "Musing on Steel," which sees the symbol of ultimate strength not in a bar of steel, but in the class of workers producing the steel. His pen often unrolls a scroll of fantastic landscape, as in his "Visit to the Asbestos County":

Look at those thousands of mountains
Each jade green, and yet
Each a cotton ball
Cloud-hidden . . .

Yen Yi was very much charmed by the kind of folks songs heard on stage in Honan province—a very free, colloquial, and at times daring form of rustic expression. Indeed the first book of verse he published after the fall of the Gang of Four, *The Story of the Purple Swallow* (1977), bears evidence of his development in that direction.   —K.Y.H.

Battleground Revisited

Village after village,
Where shall I go first, where?
New elms with old elms,
Which one shall I see first, which one?
Dear ones in every village
Whom shall I call on first, whom?

To Tan County,
My old Mom in Chung-hsing Village,
Quilts kept warm on the *k'ang*
And fire kept burning beneath it,
There under an oil lamp we talked,
And talked, through many stormy nights.

719

To Ch'eng-wu,
That fisherman's daughter on the Wan-fu River,
Once held my hand and called me "dear."
The Japs chasing her didn't know what to do.
Thus she escaped a disaster,
And we never even exchanged names.

At Chü-yeh,
Militiamen in jujube woods,
Have carried me on their backs,
Fed me with beans baked on campfire,
Let me drink from their cupped hands;
Near death, I survived again.

The sisters have washed clothes for me,
In winter, their hands chapped!
They made shoes for me,
Their fingers bled by needle pricks.
Even the trees here felt for me,
Giving me camouflage when I fought.

Seventeen years' absence, seventeen long years,
A swallow returns to find its old perch.
Wish I could grow ten thousand legs
To sing new songs to them, door by door—
Behind each of them, there are dear ones,
Behind each, there are warm hearts.

October 8, 1962, Chinan
Poetry Journal, no. 6 (1962): 18

Translated by Kai-yu Hsu

POETS OF THE EARLY 1960s

A peculiarity of the Chinese literary scene that vividly illustrates the interconnectedness of literature and politics is the abruptness of certain writing careers. This phenomenon was particularly evident in the 1960s, when a large number of young proletarian poets suddenly emerged and enjoyed success during the early years of the decade but then dropped out of sight during the Cultural Revolution.

We know very little about most of these poets. Chang Wan-shu wrote lyrical poems of fine quality. Chi P'eng excelled in writing about life in the navy. Like T'ang Ta-t'ung, Chiang Jih wrote poems about boatmen plying the inland rivers of Szechwan. Ko Fei was rated as one of the most promising of the younger poets. Kung Hsi, whose work first appeared in the 1950s, wrote about a soldier's life, as did Wang Shih-hsiang. Li Chia-hsün of Szechwan was one of the more outstanding new poets who first published during the Great Leap Forward campaign. Ning Yü was regarded as a skillful recorder of experiences in the shipyards, Shih Wen-hsiung was a full-time factory worker, and Shih Ying wrote about life on the commune. Most of these writers have not published anything in recent years. —K.Y.H. and R.C.G.

CHANG WAN-SHU

The Pines of Huang Shan

Good! The pines of Huang Shan,* loudly I applaud you, good!
Who can compare with you in your erect stature, firm grip, and lofty
    perch?
Ninety thousand miles of thunder, eight thousand miles of storms
Cannot push you down, cut you up, or knock you over.

If one is to stand up, then let it be on top of the clouds;
You climb over all the seventy-two famed peaks.
If one is to fly, then let the aim be at the zenith of the sky
Where one can watch enough, see enough of heaven's beauty.

You fear not the chilly winds assailing you from both ends of the valley,
You shake your arms, repelling the attacker sharply and with skill.
You fear even less the cold snow on high mountains, freezing one to the
    bone,
You break the foil of the frost and fold the cutting edge of the ice.

*Scenic mountain in southern Anhwei Province. [K.Y.H.]

721

Who can compare with you for your beginning in difficulty and poverty,
And you have straightened your back, shooting up from purple rocks.
Even your bare roots perpetually exposed to all sorts of weather
Cling to the boulders, tightly, and never let them go.

Your stance unshakable like the towering summits that endure eternity,
Pride glitters on every one of your thin and stiff needles.
You glance at the shady side, your eyebrows knit in anger,
But toward the sun you flex your muscular limbs, thousands strong.

Ah, pines of the Yellow Mountain, I sing fervent praise of you,
Wanting to learn your unyielding combat spirit, refusing to bend or break.
Look! On these ranges of mountain peaks, blue, purple and crimson red,
You stand like so many banners of battle, buffeting the wild wind.

Sunrise

Stepping over clouds and through fog I ascend the T'ien-tu Peak
To welcome you, the arrival of your noble and majestic life.
The sea whips up thousands of rows of waves, each mountain-high,
As though thousands of frightful thunderbolts explode underwater—
You come to life in grand style.

Bright rays of immeasurable length radiate the moment you rise above the
    sea,
Lighting up the clouds all around the sky, gilt and aflame.
Who can stop you?
The universe makes way for you in its immense space,
Lets you soar on wings, lets you freely fly.

Purple mountains, dark blue woods,
A locomotive of sheer force, a churning wheel of fire;
Thousands of mansions and thousands of chimneys,
Together sprout from this dear land of ours, together they pulsate,
Dashing toward you, rumbling toward you....

Everything turns golden in your light,
The spring tide of life surges, battle banner roll.
With heaven as an unlimited battlefield, and east wind directing the attack,
You fly ahead, fly toward the most ideal height
To issue forth your light, intense and strong.

Poetry Journal, no. 1 (1963): 25–26

CHENG CH'ENG-YI

Song of a Red Factory—An Ordinary Woman Worker

Bitter vines
Bear bitter squash.
In the factory's narrow alley,
I came into the world.

Mother sneaked me into the factory,
Hiding me under a loom.
She fed me with bitter tears
Mixed with cotton lint and dust.

Except Mother's lap,
I had no home of my own.
At six I learned to handle spindles,
By eight, I learned weaving.

Ten years in a "foreign textile mill,"
I grew up, pickled in bitter juice.
The year of Liberation
Saw me a girl of eighteen.

For the first time in my life,
I ate dinner sitting down,
I spoke without having to whisper,
I wore padded clothes, and learned to read.

Since then—
Fifteen years of spring sun glaring in my eyes,
Fifteen years of change, like wind sweeping clouds,
Fifteen years, I gradually became aware
Of the deep sea of bitterness, and of a wide, wide world.

Today, in many other countries
Many sisters of my class remain in fetters.
Today, there are still many mothers
Feeding their babies with bitter tears.

My yarn weaves the new world's baby buntings,
My yarn weaves a hangman's noose for the old society.
Today, I stand under the red flag,
I know what I should do....

Poetry Journal, no. 5 (1964): 15

CHI P'ENG

Tonight I Stand Guard

Tonight, sea breeze stirs, tiptoeing,
The blinker on the naval base tower, now dim, now bright;
With the moon on my arm I ascend the deck,
Tonight is my guard duty.

Blue haze covers the shoreline,
Thousands of lamps light up thousands of windows;
Boats return from offshore patrol
—bringing home loads of stars.

Salt crystals gather on the deck,
A blue light tops the mast;
A soldier's sleep marks only a brief pause in a long march,
By dawn he has to resume his journey, with starlight on his back.

A naval base never sleeps, any day, any hour,
My heart is on sentry duty, together with my gun.
Tonight, in how many harbors of our motherland
Are arrows poised on bowstrings tautly drawn?

Poetry Journal, no. 2 (1964): 55

CHIANG JIH

Sons and Daughters of Szechwan Rivers

Under each step, a cloud,
Man walks in clouds,
Pulls the boat up to the sky,
Holding on to the cliff as his handrail.

He starts the river chant,
The mountains echo him.
Standing on top of the Wu Mountain,
He leads the Yangtze River to flow backwards.

Mountain rain pours from above,
Mountain gale roars underfoot;
In wind and rain he passes the Three Gorges,
Feeling stronger than ever.

The rain lifts after dark,
Moonlight flows below his heels;
Where is the boat to dock tonight?
The dock, ah, the dock is the crescent moon.

Light a bonfire
Drink a cup of strong liquor,
Tomorrow, cross the Twelve Peaks
Toward the upper end of the upper Yangtze River.

Poetry Journal, no. 2 (1963): 39

KO FEI

Ascend White Cloud Obo

Our post is on the peak, the high peak!
Every morning I ascend it, with the sun in tow.
I climb! Pull up the thorny brambles in my way, by their roots.
I climb! Trample down and flatten the rocks tripping my feet.
Ha, shouldering the rain and bucking the wind I push forward,
And one trail after another emerges, bearing my footprints.

When I finally step on the top of the untamed White Cloud Obo,
The sun also ascends the sky, embracing all four corners of the earth.
And we, side by side, gaze afar, in the wind—the sun and I;
The city and the country, hand-in-hand, fly toward us—
My Motherland, be proud of your children, as we
Did it again, and again we conquered a forbidding height!
All the mountains in the world scorn the weak and bow to the strong.

To make them yield their treasures requires frontal attacks.
All pneumatic drills will drill through White Cloud Obo,
And detonating teams, press your buttons, blast it, blow ...
We'll drag the river of ore rocks, with one shout in unison—
Behold, our Motherland is soaring on wings of iron and steel.

I know, I know that there must be such a day, when—
This great White Cloud Obo shall be leveled, and drained;
But we also know our road ahead will unfold, continue to unfold,

And there will be countless more mountains for us to scale,
Ascend! We are vanguards of China's army of iron and steel;
Our post is on the peak, the high peak, the high, high peak.

Poetry Journal, no. 12 (1963): 15–16

KUNG HSI

Home of the Radar Soldier

An ocean framed in the window,
Sound of surf fills the room;
Seagulls rest under the eaves,
Shining red corals at the door.

A hurricane swoops down,
No more trace of the hut;
But well rooted is the radar soldier's heart,
Like a rock, he stays there, immobile.

The hut is like a bamboo shoot,
The old one blown away, a new one rises.
And seagulls come to rest as before,
Corals are bigger and redder than ever.

Small and deserted is the island,
Never has it received a name before.
Since the radar soldier made his home here,
They call it "The eye of our country."

January 3, 1962
Poetry Journal, no. 4 (1962): 13

LI CHIA-HSÜN

Backpacks

In the past the mountain folks carried packs on their backs,
One pack full of wind and rain, one pack full of sorrow.

High was the cliff, and steep the ledge, no place to go,
Three big mountains* weighed heavily on their backs.
They bent their waists, broke their muscles and bones—
The packs on their backs, filled with blood, tears, and hate.
Now they carry their backpacks on their shoulders,
They carry on their backs a pack full of bright sunshine.
They carry a new factory to their mountain region,
And sweet melons and fruits to the cities.
Farm equipment they bring in, all mechanized,
And books and papers for their new schools.
They carry a new era forward in long, long strides,
And step after step, each step greeting the rising sun.

Poetry Journal, no. 11 (1963): 31

LU CH'I

Willow Village Revisited

WILLOW VILLAGE REVISITED

Seeing Willow Village again,
My heart threatens to leap out of my chest.
Twelve years, ah,
Twelve years later, here I come again!
The willows on the creek
Have grown into shady rows.

That year I came for the land reform,
The creek side was bare,
For miles the waters were exposed to sun glare,
Mirroring the barren buffs and cliffs,
And the seeds of hate and anger
Still buried deep in hearts, just buried there.

Love and hate dawned on me the moment I entered the village,
The doors of rich mansions creaked shut in my face
As though grinding their teeth, wishing
To push me out and chase me away.
I ignored them, and settled down anyway,
As every straw-thatched hut invited me in to stay:

*Imperialism, feudalism, and bureaucratic capitalism. [K.Y.H.]

Sharing wild vegetables for me to eat
And tattered old quilts for me to sleep under.
The huts huddled close, their hearts strung together;
The water of bitterness, once joined in the creek, turned into angry waves!
Under today's willow shade there was
That struggle platform of yesteryear.

Those having shed tears at the "speak bitterness" meetings,
Remained clear-visioned; no dust could blur their eyes.
Once they have trodden the dirt of the Willow Village,
Their steps are steady, however wild the wind and waves.

In steady steps they marched forward,
Shoulder to shoulder they opened their road to happiness.
The fire they kindled to burn the land titles
Lighted up thousands of red flags, fluttering proud and tall,
And consumed the thousand-year-old poverty and hardship,
With the thousands of firewood bundles gathered by us all.

Twelve years, ah, twelve years have gone by.
When I left you, it was like leaving my own mother.
It was you who taught me how to walk steadily;
It was you who opened my eyes.
I sank my red roots in this village
And upon departure I planted a row of willows.

The willows are spreading their shade now, and here I come again,
Twelve years do not seem to have separated us at all.
I learned how to hate and I learned how to love,
So long as the enemy remains
I shall remain a willow in this village
To grow into a useful timber in fine or foul weather.

THE ABACUS CLICKS

Spending the night in Willow Village
I hear again the abacus clicks.
One click light, one click heavy,
Click, clack, click, clack . . .
Is it the pigs' feet trotting in the sty,
Or potatoes dropping into the storage pit?
Or perhaps that's not it,
But rice falling into the threshing tub
Like heavy rain, announcing a bumper crop?

Wonder how they got that bumper crop—
And the answer comes still from the abacus:
Click, clack, click, clack . . .
Is it drops of sweat falling to the ground,
Or the beat of dirt-tamping on a rising dyke?
Or perhaps that's not it,
But the footsteps of the captain on his nightly patrol?

Oh, no, no!
This abacus started clicking early:
That year we staged the struggle,
It computed exploitation, added up the lost lives,
Click, clack, click, clack . . .
It's the thousands of rifles firing salvos,
And the battle drums thundering together;
It added and added until
Heaven and earth turned over and man changed his fate!

It kept clicking till today, and today
It no longer computes the rent, but work points.
Yesterday it figured out whose hate was the strongest
Today it tells us whose love is the deepest.
Listen now, listen!
On that abacus
Throb the thousands of communers' hearts.

DOUBLE THE GUARD

A family chat in progress in Willow Village,
Around a warm, laughing fire.
Old Aunt brags about her daughter in-law;
Old Uncle scolds the "lazy bones";
Only the militia captain, in the best of moods,
Teases the young fellow and his girl:

"That year when the comrades came for the land reform,"
He says, "You were only this tall,
And she stood only that high.
You both wiped your noses sideways,
On your sleeves, already four shining patches!
You climbed on benches to watch the struggle,
Two black noses, side by side. . . .

"Then a few days back I went on guard duty
During the harvest, I saw you two under the haystack,
Whispering to each other, on and on and on.
I came back.
She started sewing flowery clothes and you

Painting your room. Hey, what are you two up to?
Hurry up and tell us all!"

Before the captain finishes speaking
A loud applause rises in the room.
All we hear is
Two shrill retorts followed by loud protests,
And pleased, not angry, fists
Hammer on the captain's broad back,
Rocking the room and shaking the lamp.

Laughing, the captain starts again,
Begging for mercy, but in words serious:
"Good brother, good girl!
Don't beat me up today,
Just punish me to stand sentry duty in front of your bridal
    chamber—
The original owner of your bridal chamber is still around,
Still peeping around with his two venomous eyes!"

Suddenly the whole room hushes,
Thoughtful eyes look at thoughtful eyes.
"The land reform comrades are back here tonight,
And tonight we must double our guard!"
And look!
A young couple responds immediately,
Raising the guns in their joyful hands!

March 1963, Chungking
Poetry Journal, no. 3 (1963): 4–7

NING YÜ

Ship Building

Too much snow, can't see the sky,
Ice wind howls, cuts like a knife blade.
River freezes stiff, earth freezes hard,
What a bitterly cold winter day!

Old Heaven picks a fight, we won't duck it,
Old Heaven gets angry, we'll buck it.
We'll shout down the howling winds,
And slice to pieces all the dark clouds.

In wind and snow our new ship grows,
Look, how beautiful, this silver world.
Plum blossoms bloom on the riverside,
Now, you listen to our words of pride:

"Our shipyard in winter has June weather,
Fire shoots from steel plates, smoke from the ground,
We ship-builders fight the battle, bathed in sweat,
Our hot breath warms the sky."

Poetry Journal, no. 3 (1962): 61

SHIH WEN-HSIUNG

A Chemical Fertilizer Worker's Lyrics

Like hard-working peasants in love with their land
Like weathered seadogs attached to their ship
We, Red workers in the chemical fertilizer plant
Give our hearts to the bustling shop of lathes and wheels.

Not very large, our shop is,
At one glance you can see all the machines there,
But the battledrum tapped by the motors is enough
To support the farmers' work for food grown on their land.

Not very old, our shop is,
Since the founding workers are still in their youth,
But the bulletins posted on the walls are enough
To start a war of crops across the river for the first prize.

So much in love are we with our shop,
For it is the source of endless food for crops.
Since the moment it collected our lofty ideals, every day
It's been offering poetry of good harvest to our fatherland.

Poetry Journal, no. 10 (1964): 51

SHIH YING

The Mountain Girl Likes to Talk

Where is the home of the mountain girl?
In the office of the production team,
At the broadcasting station of the village,
In the classroom of the village school . . .
She lives at all these places.

The mountain girl likes to talk,
When she starts, it's like a bubbling spring;
You can hear her even in Peking,
No mountain is tall enough to block her voice.

In the morning she goes home to the production team office,
Picks up the phone, and starts talking into it;
At noon she goes home to the broadcasting station to announce
The approaching storm of heavy snow and high winds at night;
But at night she goes home to the village school classroom,
Where an advanced class listens to her talk on a new poem.
A telephone messenger, a broadcaster, and a teacher,
All three rolled into one is she.

From her throat comes
The good news of bumper crops
And the dewy blossoms of apricot trees.
Her chatter makes even the illiterate old ladies so happy
That they want to remove their "cultural blinds."
This mountain girl of ours, ah,
She just likes to talk.

Poetry Journal, no. 2 (1963): 42

WANG SHIH-HSIANG

Target Practice in the Rain

In face-slashing wind,
Under skull-crushing rain,
On the rifle range we practice shooting.

Rain soaks our clothes,
Wind chills the bone,
Shall we do it or leave it alone?

How shall we explain,
If we call it off?
Bad weather tests the real stuff!

In water we crawl,
In mud we lie,
Through the rain screen we hit the bull's eye.

Bing, bing, bing!
Rifles ring,
In wind and rain red flags swing.

Winds slash us,
Rains inundate us,
But thunder and lightning come to congratulate us!

Poetry Journal, no. 3 (1963): 35

Translated by Kai-yu Hsu

ETHNIC MINORITY POETS

Besides Malchinhu, the nationally known Mongolian story writer, there are other ethnic minority writers whose works have been appearing in national publications. Some of them have had their works translated into Chinese; others have learned the language well enough to write in it. In either case, the works convey a strong flavor of their geographic origins, as the following selections will reveal.

We know something of the lives of two of these poets. Lutpulla Matallep was born in 1922 in Ili, Sinkiang Province, to a Uighur family. He was apparently killed in 1945 by the Kuomintang agents in Aksu because of his outspoken publications. The poems selected here were among his unpublished manuscripts. Rabchai Tsazang was born in Tibet in 1932. He learned Chinese there and started writing poetry in the 1950s. He has published a book of verse entitled *From the Grasslands.* —K.Y.H.

LUTPULLA MATALLEP

Untitled

Pain prepared a pen for me,
And sorrow, a well of ink,
Wanting me to write heartrending songs
About shabby thatched huts and faded flowers....

And about the filthy souls of the filthily rich,
  their devilish corrupt life with wine and women,
  and about the vagrants in streets pale with starlight,
  and about ravished young girls....

The passage of life is like that of a tiny boat,
Rocking along and yawing along in an immense sea;
The strong soon declined, the beautiful soon aged,
Leaving behind only tears and long, long sighs.

Some apply blood to their faces, like rouge,
Some drink tears to quench their burning thirst,
Still some pass nights sleeping on starved bodies,
But some others, sleepless, pace the floor in pain.

Are these what you want me to write about? No!
The pen is my will, and the inkwell, the source of my mind.
I want to cast my thought and will into a bugle.

Let pain and sorrow flee my bugle call,
Let them proceed toward total destruction;
I wish to be an accountant, loyal, and conscientious,
Recording all the sighs of the world, one by one.

New Year's Day, 1944

I Shall Never

Though the dark power has pressed me, deforming my back,
Though the devil's claws have grabbed me, seized my throat,
I shall never surrender—no, never!
Never in a cringing voice beg for the return to me of my life,
 the only thing that belongs to me,
 and belongs to me only once.
I shall never reach my two hands out to ask for forgiveness,
I hate those traitors sacrificing light before darkness,
I resent those faint hearts weeping in front of idols. . . .
I want to expose
 the dirty soul of the tyrant
 the bloodstained butcher's knife,
 and the noose that strangles truth and happiness.
The enemy may chop off my head, but the people will give it back to me.
The enemy may chop down our banner of revolution, but the people will
 put it back.
The enemy pushes us toward the gate of death that's rapidly collapsing,
And displays my head on top of a pole, as a warning to the people. . . .
But I shall never surrender—no, never!
I shall sing with all my strength and spirit,
And strum out my music with my unsoiled heart.
I shall let my blood flow into a torrent of revenge,
To sweep away the enemy's palaces,
And overrun the devil's tottering throne,
And ram ahead with resounding force
 and run, and run, and run . . . .

Poetry Journal, no. 2 (1962): 18–19

K'E-LI-MU HUO-CHIA (UIGHUR)

To My Party and My Country

I have found my tongue that's forever and ever free,
It is the door to the treasure trove of my wisdom;
This treasure trove is always open to my Party,
To praise the Party my kin will carry on even after my death.

Even if my body dissolves into a pinch of dust,
If only my poetry could endure the passage of time;
If only it could provide a spark in our battle,
My Party, ah, that will be my life's happiness.

Don't laugh at me, at my running always in wind and rain,
Don't say that I am poor with not a thread to my name;
So long as the Communist Party keeps guiding my country,
Wealth will grow from under our two laboring hands.

What a bat needs is not light but dark night,
We'll never give up our sun simply because of the bat's curse;
Let it stay blind, and forever blind be its eyes shunning truth,
My Party! We need you, we need your warmth and light!

Heavy dew adorns your many-colored skirt with a golden lace
And chilly frost leaves on your forehead a red beauty spot.
My country, ah, you are a sturdy and wholesome village girl,
Right now, back from the fields, your apron full of ripe fruits.

Poetry Journal, no. 3 (1963): 25–26

WANG CH'ENG-TUNG (T'U-CHIA TRIBE)

The Character of the Lhasa River

My father is the snowcapped mountain,
And my mother, the cloud-sealed peak;
Leaping off cliffs thousands of feet high,
Winding my way through miles of deep gorges,
I shaped my character, shown in my waves.

I love my land that has found a new life
—Flocks of sheep roam the grassland,
    Golden ears of wheat, red sheaves of barley,
    And the spring breeze chasing handsome steeds.
It's poetry, it's a painting, unfinished, unending.

I love my peaceful village
—Smoke from stoves, dancing clouds of gauze,
    The shepherd's flute leads the mountain people's songs,
    Laughter mingled with friendly conversation.
It's a sweep of brocade, of sunset, that unrolls on and on.

The Yellow and Yangtze Rivers are my sisters,
And my home, the broad land of my country.
I cheer, I sing, to greet my friends from abroad:
"Please stay," I say, "you guests from afar."
Enjoy my costume of red and green, and my flying pearly sprays,
Look at the half of my valley in orchards and woods,
And the other half, in crops.
I'm ready to pour out all I have
To water the flowers of friendship.

But none will dare to take advantage of my meekness,
As the wind and clouds change, so do I;
A thousand cresting waves, a thousand raised swords,
And each mounting wave, capable of exploding.
Who dares to steal water from my river
Or try to put me in manacles and fetters?
Look at the whirlpools in my swift current,
They would be my uncompromising reply.

On Earth and in Heaven

Grandpa, please go on telling
About the giant god Wei-teh-chin-kang,
How he flew thousands of miles on the wind,
And how he encountered the man-eating demon.

He drew his demon-slaying sword,
He shouted and the mountains shook;
His power stirred up a strong wind,
As his steed galloped forth to do battle.
A pool of blood spelled the end
Of the last of the highlands.

Grandpa, please go on and tell
About the hero Wei-teh-chin-kang,
How his sword split the darkness,
And brought joy to earth.

On bad waters rose a colorful arch of rainbow,
On barley fields sprinkled bright sunshine.
Sweet rain soaked all pastures and sowed
Seeds of hope in the hearts of men.
The hero patrolled the heaven and earth,
Guarding against buzzards and wolves.

In which cloud does he live, Grandpa?
I really wish I had a pair of wings,
So that I could offer him a pure white *hatta**
Together with our songs of worship.

The larks sing for him,
Happy flowers bloom for him,
Surely, you should offer him a *hatta*,
But you need not fly into the sky,
Just look at the frontier outpost,
There, a red star of the army shines bright....

November 1962, Lhasa
Poetry Journal, no. 1 (1963): 12–13

RABCHAI TSAZANG

Road

An order leads me to the mountaintop,
Further up only stars pave the trail;
It tells me to start climbing from there,
To scale the peak way above the starry sky.

Leaders order me up into the sky,
Pointing out to me a forward road;
They entrust to me the responsibility
Of digging a river of silver and moving a mountain of gold.

And my feet that know only pursuit of hopes,
Imprint a beginning point on the cliff;
One step after another, each step forward,
As the hills surge, all toward heaven.

As I move on, the stars gather thicker,
They dance and flicker to boost my morale;
The sky gets wider, immense, no border,
Just like the grassland under my horse.

*A piece of white material, like a scarf, offered by Tibetans as a token of respect and friendship. [K.Y.H.]

Immense is the night sky, stars countless—
Where is the zenith of these shining lights?
And the commander far away and high above,
In his wisdom what does he foresee?

When the first step starts pointing downward,
Pointing at the beginning of a descent;
In the midst of the stars surging all around me,
I see the landmark where a new journey starts.

Poetry Journal, no. 5 (1962): 23

Seashell

From the shore of the lake Er-hai, a few steps down lie the clusters of sails
on waterfront, and a few steps up you see immense fields of lush crops. But
what is sown in between, on the seashell-covered beach? No, it's not lying
fallow, the beach—young boys and girls often come here to sow their seeds of
hope. . . .

    Clear water in white seashell,
    A cup of toast to love—
        To her for her undying affection,
        And him, for undiminishing strength.

    A cup of toast to love,
    Holding heartrending memory—
        He said, this is the lake's bitter bile;
        This is the lake's tears, she said.

    Holding heartrending memory,
    Pouring it into lover's meeting here—
        Saying, around the lake it has been
        A world without love for years.

    Clear water in white seashell,
    A cup of toast to love—
        Now, in praise of love and life,
        It dispels bitterness in all hearts!

Poetry Journal, no. 6 (1962): 49–50

An Armed Race

A clear whistle sounded on the mountaintop,
It startled me, my heart pounding and pounding.
Did it come from a partridge's whisper to the stars,
Or from the moon, issuing a warning to wolves?

I looked up: Only trees towering on the ridge
Half covered the moon's bashful face;
Down below: Grass lush green in an open glen,
Yet no sheep dared to saunter around.

No sheep dared to saunter around,
They all scattered in panic—a defeated tribe,
Running toward where the whistle led them,
Having lost interest in this feeding ground.

A flock without shepherd, yet with one will—
They surged, like white clouds in the hills' folds;
The whistle sound lingered in the clouds and woods,
Was it foretelling fortune or misfortune?

Was it foretelling fortune or misfortune?
Where could I ask, where could I find it?
Several gunshots rang over my head,
I even saw the red lights trailing the bullets.

At the end of the trailing lights, two hounds barked
In ecstasy over a wolverine shot by the shepherd.
I picked a handful of wild flowers waiting for the shooter,
But I heard another whistle blow.

And I heard another whistle blow.
The shooter must be smiling now, look—
The surging white cloud again, the sheep returned
By the same trail, to the lush green grass.

The moon's lips touched the sheep's white coats,
Announcing, no more preying beasts around.
Who's that, who directed sheep's grazing at night,
With only those couple of simple whistle blows?

With only those couple of simple whistle blows,
You restored serenity to the moonlit night;
You, who stood guard on the craggy mountaintop,
Wove such magical touches into life.

Life's road, steep like a knife-blade mountain ridge.
Someone had to face the worst hardship,
Let me ask you, sentry in the moonlit night,
How many storms have you braved, all alone?

How many storms have you braved, all alone?
The answer came, in another whistle blow.
Ah, it was a young girl's signal from up there,
And her laughter dispelled all alarm.

In a night like this, meant for happiness,
Whose heart was not burning for love!
But you, with a long rifle on your shoulder,
Had on your mind only a lookout tower.

Ah, you, a member of your armed race, you stand
An undying flame on the road of the Red Long March.
I'd like to ask you to be a discerning guide
For the years ahead, solemn and stern.

Poetry Journal, no. 10 (1963): 24–25

CHANG CH'ANG (PAI TRIBE)

Thunder Crosses the Wilderness in Long Strides

Thunder crosses the wilderness in long strides,
Stamping its feet, pounding and shouting,
It whips the woods with its lightning;
Beneath, frightened trees shake and shiver.

Shame on you, disorderly thunder!
Don't you know what era we are in now?
Go to the power station, Nature's reformatory,
Go, you vagabond of the wild, go!

There you will meet many of your friends,
Wreckless storms, wandering streams . . .
The power workers will teach you and make you
Into commandoes in socialist reconstruction.

Then you will be sent to the cities and countryside,
To temper steel, weave cloth, mill rice and press oil . . .
Go!—the people having risen will change everything:
The old society, great Nature, and the entire universe. . . .

Lost Laughter

Springtime, white clouds wipe clean the mirrors in the paddies,
Barefoot communers step on the ledges to broadcast after rain;
Their hands stirring the seeds, then a shower of laughter
Falls and disappears and can never be found again.

Dusk in July, dawn in August,
The hoes turning the land, asking, still asking;
The rice plants only shake their heads in total silence,
The dewdrops only blink their eyes, hiding a secret.

A gust of autumn wind rises over the September plain,
And rice stalks laugh so hard—they bend and sway in gold;
Oh, that must be the spring seeds having stolen the laughter
From the communers, and now returning it one thousandfold.

Poetry Journal, no. 5 (1962): 35–36

Translated by Kai-yu Hsu

FOLK SONGS

The trend toward folk songs has been prominent since 1949; their flavor, in music, diction, and general style, is noticeable in the works of most new poets. However, the effort to collect, compile, and disseminate real, oral folk songs has continued, and from time to time newly collected pieces appear in print. The following are some examples. The names attached to the songs are either the collectors or, in some rare cases, the authors who created the lyrics to go with an extant folk-song mode in a particular locality. —K.Y.H.

CHIANG P'ING AND HUANG SHOU-CH'ANG

(KWEICHOW PROVINCE)

Many, Many Are My Songs
—A Duet

GIRL: Too many steps, hard to climb upstairs,
Too many songs, hard to begin;
Who, ah, who can start with one,
With him I will sing all year long.

BOY: Day after day I want to sing,
Many are my songs,
My sister, I only fear you can't sing,
I only fear you can't work with your hands.

GIRL: Frogs beat drums, guo ... guo ... guo,
Toads beat drums, ge ... ge ... ge,
If you have nothing to sing,
Don't talk like that to cover up.

BOY: No cover-up,
I understand what you say, sister,
A fox only brags about his big tail,
And a pheasant brags about its pretty feather.

GIRL: You talk too much,
Your nasty mouth insults people.
Don't believe me?
Let's try— We'll thresh, you cut the rice.

743

BOY: How can mud hill compare with rock hill?
      How can bamboo stick compare with steel rod?
      Your man here is an iron carrying-stick,
      Try as you may, sister, you can't bend it.

GIRL: An unhitched man, penniless, fakes rich,
      A little leech, spineless, fakes strength,
      You have hardly worked half a day,
      Talking big, you want to take a rest.

BOY: When a sunbird sings, she sounds swell,
      When a crow sings, she nauseates me,
      Golden finch has a hard, hard beak,
      But can't do anything, anything at all.

GIRL: To market down the valley people come and go,
      This one has left, but that one will arrive,
      If you are worn out, well, take a rest,
      Let me show you how to hold the fort.

BOY: You talk cute,
      You talked bare rocks into growing moss,
      Your man simply refuses to take a break,
      We'll see how you lose your style.

GIRL: Wish you would,
      Frogs land on banana leaves,
      Let's race in harvesting and cutting,
      The more the singing, the better the song.

Poetry Journal, no. 2 (1964): 28

TSENG CHI-NENG (KWANSI PROVINCE)

Rice Planting

Two lovers plant rice side by side,
Like flying needles, like running threads, line after neat line;
Too bashful to look up straight in his eyes,
She only steals glances at his reflection.

Carting Fertilizer

Two lovers carting fertilizer come up to a shady tree,
They take a break to talk about themselves;
Who knows that when they open up their chatterboxes
Everything they say is only about the spring plowing.

LIU HSÜEH-CHUNG
(ANHWEI PROVINCE)

Night Plowing

Ditches full of water, and sky full of stars,
A Milky Way falls across the rice fields;
The young fellow behind his plow treads on heaven,
His plowshare slices off half the moon.

Poetry Journal, no. 3 (1963): 30–32

KU LIU (KWANGTUNG PROVINCE)

Hope You Take Care to Stop
the Flow

I'm a mountain stream high up on a hill,
You're a field lying down below;
When the stream runs through the field,
Hope you'll take care to stop the flow.

CHIA CH'I-FENG (HOPEI PROVINCE)

Overnight Stop, under Bridge, I
Dream of Hurrying Along

Clear, clear water separates river banks,
Carries tons of songs and tons of grain;
Overnight stop, under bridge, I dream of hurrying along;
My heart arrives long before the shipment.

Poetry Journal, no. 1 (1963): 52

Translated by Kai-yu Hsu

PART FIVE

The Great Proletarian
Cultural Revolution

(1964–1970)

"Cultural Revolution" was not a term invented in 1964, or even in 1962. On June 9, 1958, the *People's Daily* had already proclaimed the beginning of a cultural revolution in China.

By 1962 the perpetual contention between the extremists (Shanghai-based hard-liners) and the moderates (Peking-based soft-liners) within the Party had once again intensified. Chiang Ching, Mao's wife, with the support of the Shanghai group, had started to purify the theater with her own revolutionary opera (*The Red Lantern,* 1963). Mao Tse-tung's orders regarding literature, as interpreted by Chiang Ching, were indifferently received. Teng T'o and his friends Wu Han and Liao Mo-sha were writing thinly veiled criticism against the arbitrary and sometimes ignorant leadership at the top level. In the country at large, resentment grew against the recently risen elite—old comrades now high up in the government—who, as the new privileged class, monopolized the comforts of the city and even the opportunity to give their children higher education. The cumulative failure to complete the Great Leap Forward and to educate the people as ideal Communists created a desperate situation. All this and more went into the making of the Great Proletarian Cultural Revolution.

Once Mao Tse-tung unleashed the fury of the Red Guards (high school students and some college students), instructing them to "bombard the headquarters," their action went beyond pasting large-character posters on Peking walls. By 1964, most of the students were trooping up and down the country; all schools were closed. By 1965, all the magazines were suspended and writers started going to the countryside under orders to learn from the peasants. By the end of 1966, all the Central leaders except Mao (and there was a rumored attack even on him) were denounced, and Chiang Ching and her close supporters reached the zenith of power.

Lao She is a tragic representative of the best-known authors killed by the Cultural Revolution. Since his post-1949 works were hitherto considered totally acceptable, *The Teahouse*, a three-act play written in 1957 about pre-Liberation life, is selected here to show the irony of his death. T'ien Han's historical play was accused of openly challenging the Party's authority. Hsia Yen's *The Lin Family Store*, a 1958 play based on Mao Tun's 1938 novel of the same name, was faulted because it did not pitch the shop clerk against his master. Yang Han-sheng, who based his 1963 screenplay on his experiences in a commune project to fight drought on the northern frontier, was charged with painting a gloomy picture of the new society. Along with Chou Yang, T'ien, Hsia, and Yang, all holding influential positions in the cultural and literary departments of the government, were now attacked as the Four Villains against the Cultural Revolution.

As the Cultural Revolution crested, nearly all the major works selected in this volume were one by one swept aside and buried, leaving only a lone *Red Lantern* (and six or seven other pieces also organized by Chiang Ching) to shine on the desolate stage of China. However, before all the bookstores boarded up their doors, a few works managed to appear and circulate because their authors were newcomers with neither a political past nor a current literary following to be shot at by the Red Guards. Lu Yang-lieh's story conveyed a good touch of frontier flavor. Wang Chia-pin, a member of a fishing fleet crew, demonstrated an excellent sense of the drama between man and nature, as well as a strong defense for the principle of writing from a proletarian's physical experience.

LAO SHE
(Shu Ch'ing-ch'un, 1899–1966)

Born to the modest family of a Manchurian soldier in the last imperial army of China, Lao She grew to be one of the most distinguished of the novelists who matured in the era of the May Fourth Movement. He was trained to be a teacher and taught school for some time before he went to England to teach Chinese for several years. It was there that he started writing. Except for the short period when he taught in universities and a yearlong visit to the United States (1949–50), Lao She divided his time between writing and leading writers' organizations. At the time of his death he was holding the influential and prestigious post of chairman of the Peking Federation of Literary and Art Circles.

The government of the People's Republic acknowledged in 1978 that Lao She died from the persecution of the Red Guards, and public rites were held to restore his memory to a position of honor. Early in 1979, details of his suffering were made public, but it is still unclear whether his death was a suicide or a murder.

Lao She published some thirty books—novels, plays, and collections of short stories. Among them the best remembered include *Divorce, Biography of Neu T'ien-szu, Rickshaw Boy,* and *City of Cats.*

Teahouse, written in 1957, is a three-act play centering on the vicissitudes of a teahouse in Peking. The time in the first act is 1898, right after the collapse of the Reformation Movement of the Manchurian Court, which will be followed by the collapse of the court itself. The second act occurs in 1916, after the death of the ambitious Yüan Shih-k'ai, who had briefly declared himself emperor, when the warlords are dividing up China. The third act follows thirty years later, around 1946, when World War II has just ended, and "the secret police of Kuomintang and the American soldiers are devasting Peking." In this play Lao She captures well the flow of history that has affected representative segments of the Chinese population during the first half of the twentieth century. The characterization is very persuasive, and the dialogues, typical of Lao She, realistic and lively. In February 1979, after thirteen years of suppression, the play was restaged in Peking with considerable fanfare. Here is Act I.

—L. C. and K. H.

Teahouse

ACT I

Characters (in order of appearance):
Sung En-tzu, in his twenties; an old-fashioned secret police agent.

WU HSIANG-TZU, in his twenties; a colleague of SUNG EN-TZU'S.

FIFTH MASTER MA, in his thirties; a local bully working for a Christian mission.

WANG LI-FA, in his twenties when he first appears; because his father died untimely, he, though young, has already become the manager of Prosperity Teahouse; a smart man, somewhat selfish, but kind-hearted.

T'ANG THE FORTUNE-TELLER, in his thirties; a professional fortune-teller; an opium addict.

SECOND MASTER SUNG, in his thirties; timid, but talkative.

FOURTH MASTER CH'ANG, in his thirties; a good friend of SECOND MASTER SUNG'S; both are regular customers of the teahouse; a conscientious man, physically fairly strong.

LI THE THIRD, in his thirties; waiter of the teahouse, diligent, sincere, and warm.

SECOND TE-TZU, in his twenties; a policeman.

LIU THE POCK-MARKED, in his thirties; a matchmaker, vicious and malevolent.

K'ANG THE SIXTH, forty years old; a poverty-stricken farmer, living in the outskirts of Peking.

FATTY HUANG, in his forties; the big boss of the ruffians.

OLD MAN, eighty-two years old; lonely and helpless.

CH'IN CHUNG-I, in his twenties; he is the landlord who leases the house to MANAGER WANG; from a wealthy family; later, becomes a Reformist-capitalist.

WOMAN FROM COUNTRYSIDE, in her thirties; so poor that she has to sell her daughter.

LITTLE GIRL, ten years old; daughter of the WOMAN FROM COUNTRYSIDE.

EUNUCH P'ANG, forty years old; now that he has amassed a fortune, he decides to take a wife.

LITTLE OX, a teenager; the page of EUNUCH P'ANG.

CUSTOMERS OF THE TEAHOUSE, A, B, C, AND D; all are men.

K'ANG SHUN-TZU, fifteen years old in Act I; daughter of K'ANG THE SIXTH; purchased by EUNUCH P'ANG as his wife.

WAITERS E AND F.

Time:
In the morning of an early autumn day in 1898, when the Reformist Movement led by Liang Ch'i-ch'ao and K'ang Yu-wei had just collapsed.
Place:
Prosperity Teahouse in Peking.
The curtain rises.

This kind of teahouse exists no more today. Decades ago, you could locate at least one of them in every city. The teahouse sold tea as well as simple snacks and meals. For bird lovers, after they had taken their thrush, oriole, etc. for a walk, this was the place where they could have a rest, drink tea, and let their birds demonstrate their singing. People would also come here to discuss busi-

ness or to work out deals of betrothal. In those days, group fighting* frequently occurred. However, there were always friends acting as mediators between the rival parties. After the mediators talked hurriedly to both parties, these thirty to fifty fighters would all come here to drink tea and eat pork noodles—a special dish of the teahouse, reasonably priced and taking only a few minutes to cook —and then, they would be reconciled amicably. In a word, this was an extremely important place in those days; here you could linger for hours no matter whether you were occupied or not.

Here you would hear the most absurd news, such as how a huge spider at a certain place had transformed itself into a spirit and was struck by a thunderbolt; or the most curious ideas, such as if a great wall was built along the coast, no foreign soldiers would be able to set foot on our land; or hear that a certain Peking opera singer had recently composed a new variation for a tune; or find out the best way to process opium. Here you could also take a look at newly discovered treasures such as an excavated pendant made of jade, or a snuff-box glazed in three colors. This place was so crucial that you could regard it as the locale of cultural exchange. Now, let us take a look at such a teahouse. Right by the entrance are the counter and the cooking stoves, or, to keep it simple, we can omit the stoves on the stage. Instead, we can make noisy clanks of dippers at the back of the stage. The room is enormous, with many rectangular and square tables as well as benches and stools, which are seats for the customers. Outside the window is the backyard, where many seats are scattered in the shade of the awnings. There are plenty of spots to hang birdcages inside the room or under the awnings. This poster is pasted everywhere: "Do not discuss affairs of the state."

Two customers, whose names we do not know, are humming to the beats of clappers; their eyes are narrowed to a slit, and their heads are swinging.

There are two or three more customers whose names we do not know either, absorbed in watching the crickets in an earthen jar. SUNG EN-TZU and WU HSIANG-TZU, wearing long grey gowns, are talking in a low voice. Their manner reminds you of the secret police from the yamen of the Northern Quarter.

Today a new dispute has brought group fighters here. The rumor says they fought over the ownership of a pigeon, and finally it seemed the strife could only be solved by force. If fighting should break out, bloodshed would be inevitable, for some of the fighters involved are men from the police station as well as from the guards of the Department of Finance, who are all fierce combatants. Fortunately, before both parties had assembled all the committed men, the mediators had already interceded. Thus, no war this time. The rival parties are holding a meeting here right now. Fighters are walking up, in groups of two or three, through the doors into the backyard. They roll their eyes ferociously and are dressed in shirts and pants.

FIFTH MASTER MA *drinks tea by himself in an inconspicuous corner.*

WANG LI-FA *sits on a high stool behind the counter.*

T'ANG THE FORTUNE-TELLER *enters, dragging his feet slipshodly. He wears a filthy long cotton gown; several small pieces of paper are stuck behind his ear.*

---

*Not as well-organized or sinister as gang fighting, though at times it could result in casualties. [K.Y.H.]

WANG LI-FA　Mr. T'ang, would you please go for a stroll outside?

T'ANG THE FORTUNE-TELLER (*Grins miserably*)　Dear Manager Wang, be kind to this fortune-teller. Give me a cup of tea free and, in return, I will now read your physiognomy. In addition, I will read your palm for free. (*Without waiting for* WANG's *reply, he snatches his hand*) This is the twenty-fourth reign year of Emperor Kuang-hsü, the year of the dog, and your age is . . .

WANG LI-FA (*Withdraws his hand*)　Forget about it! I'll give you tea free. Stop shooting off all that jargon. What's the use of telling me my fortune? Since both of us have to brave all sorts of weather to make a living, our lots will be equally tough for sure. (*Walks from behind the counter and directs* T'ANG *to sit down*) Sit down. Listen: if you don't break off opium, you'll be stuck with bad luck. This is my physiognomy. I assure you it is more reliable than yours.

(SECOND MASTER SUNG *and* FOURTH MASTER CH'ANG *enter, holding birdcages in their hands.* WANG LI-FA *greets them. After hanging up the cages, they sit down at a table. The bookish* SECOND MASTER SUNG *has an oriole in a small cage, while the vigorous, muscular* FOURTH MASTER CH'ANG *has a thrush in a large cage.* WAITER LI THE THIRD *comes over to them immediately, fills their bowls with boiling water, and covers them. They have brought their own tea leaves, as is customary. When the tea is ready,* SECOND MASTER SUNG *and* FOURTH MASTER CH'ANG *nod to the nearby customers in a courteous gesture, inviting them to drink first before they sip their tea*)

SECOND MASTER SUNG AND FOURTH MASTER CH'ANG (*To each other*)　Please. (*Then they take a look at the backyard*)

SECOND MASTER SUNG　I think there is trouble here.

FOURTH MASTER CH'ANG　They won't fight anyway! If they really meant it, they would all be outside the city. Why on earth should they gather in a teahouse!

(*Just then,* SECOND TE-TZU, *a fighter, enters. He overheard what* FOURTH MASTER CH'ANG *had said*)

SECOND TE-TZU (*Comes over to them*)　About whom are you making those wise remarks?

FOURTH MASTER CH'ANG (*Uncompromisingly*)　Are you speaking to me? I pay to drink tea here, not to be bossed around by anybody.

SECOND MASTER SUNG (*Carefully studies* SECOND TE-TZU)　Sir, you must be an officer in the police force. Please come, drink tea with us. We also get around and meet people, you know.

SECOND TE-TZU　Wherever I work is none of your business.

FOURTH MASTER CH'ANG　If you want to show off your stuff, go beat up the foreigners. Aren't they ferocious? You, who have been supported by the public, when the Anglo-French troops burned down the Full Bright Imperial Garden, you did not fight like a lion against them, did you?

SECOND TE-TZU　Whether or not I fought the foreigners is none of your business. I'll teach you a lesson first. (*About to hit him*)

(*Other customers have not paid any attention to them.* WANG LI-FA *runs to them*)

WANG LI-FA Gentlemen, we all are brothers of the street. Please don't fight.
Master Te, please come to the back.
(SECOND TE-TZU *ignores* WANG LI-FA. *He sweeps a cup to the floor. It breaks.*
He stretches his hand to seize the neck of FOURTH MASTER CH'ANG)

FOURTH MASTER CH'ANG (*Dodges the blow*) How dare you!

SECOND TE-TZU Well, I don't dare to touch the foreigners, but I certainly dare
to touch you!

FIFTH MASTER MA (*Still seated*) Second Te-tzu, you are quite a man, aren't
you!

SECOND TE-TZU (*Looks around and finds* FIFTH MASTER MA) Oh, Fifth Master
Ma, it's you. I am awfully sorry; I didn't see you. (*Goes over to greet him*)

FIFTH MASTER MA Can't you talk things over? Why did you pick a fight just
like that?

SECOND TE-TZU Yes, sir. You are right! I am going inside. Li the Third, I'll take
care of the bill here. (*Walks to the backyard*)

FOURTH MASTER CH'ANG (*Walks toward* FIFTH MASTER MA; *intends to unbur-*
den his mind to him) Sir, you are wise and understanding. I would like to
hear your views on this.

FIFTH MASTER MA (*Stands up*) I am busy. Good-bye. (*Leaves*)

FOURTH MASTER CH'ANG (*To* WANG LI-FA) That's strange! How oddly he acts!

WANG LI-FA You didn't know he is Fifth Master Ma! No wonder you have also
offended him.

FOURTH MASTER CH'ANG Did I offend him too? I've certainly picked the wrong
day to come.

WANG LI-FA (*Lowers his voice*) You just criticized foreigners, and he is precisely one of those who depend on the foreigners. He believes in foreign
religion and can speak the foreign tongue. He can go straight to the magistrate of Wan-p'ing County here when he needs to. That's why even the
officials yield to him.

FOURTH MASTER CH'ANG (*Walks back to his seat and sneers*) I have no respect
for the parasites of foreigners.

WANG LI-FA (*Points his head toward* SUNG EN-TZU *and* WU HSIANG-TZU *and*
whispers) Please watch your words. (*Loudly*) Li the Third, another cup of
tea here. (*Picks up the broken porcelain cup*)

SECOND MASTER SUNG Let's have a man-to-man talk. How much is this cup?
I'll pay for it.

WANG LI-FA No hurry. Let's work that out later. (*Walks away*)
(POCK-MARKED LIU, *the matchmaker, leads in* K'ANG THE SIXTH. LIU *greets*
SECOND MASTER SUNG *and* FOURTH MASTER CH'ANG)

LIU THE POCK-MARKED How early you have come today! (*Takes out a snuffbox*
and pours some snuff out) Please take a pinch. It has just arrived from Britain.
Fine and pure stuff.

FOURTH MASTER CH'ANG My word! We have to import snuff too! How much
silver has flowed into foreign hands!

LIU THE POCK-MARKED Our great Manchurian Empire possesses gold and silver piled up high like mountains. There is no way of spending it all. Please
enjoy yourself. I have some errands to run. (*Finds a table for himself and*
K'ANG THE SIXTH)

(LI THE THIRD *brings a cup of tea to him*)

LIU THE POCK-MARKED How about ten taels of silver? Give me a straight answer. I am too busy to wait on you.

K'ANG THE SIXTH Master Liu, a girl of fifteen is only worth ten taels of silver?

LIU THE POCK-MARKED If we sell her to the brothel, perhaps you can get several more taels, but you have already turned that down.

K'ANG THE SIXTH But she is my daughter! How could I . . .

LIU THE POCK-MARKED You cannot support your daughter. Could this be someone else's fault?

K'ANG THE SIXTH That's because we farmers cannot make a living in the countryside any more. If my family had as little as one meal of this porridge a day, and I still sold my daughter, I'd be a bastard.

LIU THE POCK-MOCKED I don't give a damn for the problems of you farmers. Since you entrust me, I've got you a good deal, and have found a place for your daughter where she'll be well fed. Aren't I fair enough?

K'ANG THE SIXTH Who is it anyway?

LIU THE POCK-MARKED When I tell you who he is, you'll give your consent from the bottom of your heart. He is serving in the palace!

K'ANG THE SIXTH Are you kidding? Someone serving in the palace would want a girl from the countryside?

LIU THE POCK-MARKED That's because your daughter is in luck.

K'ANG THE SIXTH Who is he?

LIU THE POCK-MARKED Imperial Steward P'ang. You must have heard of this Imperial Steward. He attends the Express Dowager. He is at the height of his career. Think about it: even the vinegar jar in his home is made of agate.

K'ANG THE SIXTH Master Liu, how could I give my daughter away to a eunuch? I should feel ashamed in front of my daughter.

LIU THE POCK-MARKED You should feel ashamed in front of her anyway, since you are selling her! It doesn't matter who is buying. What a fool you are! Think about it: after she is married into his house, she will eat delicious, delicate dishes, wear silk and satin dresses. How lucky! Well, tell me, yes or no, give me a straight answer.

K'ANG THE SIXTH In this wide world, I have never heard of such . . . He offers only ten taels of silver?

LIU THE POCK-MARKED I don't think all the families in your village can put together ten taels of silver. You know very well that now a child can bring only five catties of wheat flour in the countryside.

K'ANG THE SIXTH I . . . (*Sighs*) I have to talk it over with my girl.

LIU THE POCK-MARKED Listen, "Once you pass beyond the border of this village, you can't find the same shop any more." If you let this opportunity slip, don't blame me. Come back—the sooner the better.

K'ANG THE SIXTH (*Sighs*) I will be back in a moment.

LIU THE POCK-MARKED I'll wait for you here.

(K'ANG THE SIXTH *walks out slowly*)

LIU THE POCK-MARKED (*Pulls his stool toward* SECOND MASTER SUNG *and* FOURTH MASTER CH'ANG) It's very difficult to do business with bumpkins. They can never be straightforward!

SECOND MASTER SUNG This sounds like a big deal, right?

LIU THE POCK-MARKED   Not much in it for me. If it goes through, I'll earn a piece of silver, that's about all!

FOURTH MASTER CH'ANG   What has happened that's so drastic in the countryside that they have to sell their children?

LIU THE POCK-MARKED   Who knows what's going on! No wonder there is a saying: "Even a dog'd like to be born in Peking City."

FOURTH MASTER CH'ANG   Master Liu, making this sort of match, you must have a heart of stone.

LIU THE POCK-MARKED   If I don't take part in it, very likely they won't find any customers. (*Changes the subject*) Second Master Sung (*Takes out a small watch*), please look at this.

SECOND MASTER SUNG (*Takes the watch*)   What an impressive little watch!

LIU THE POCK-MARKED   Please listen to it. Tick-tock, tick-tock!

SECOND MASTER SUNG (*Listens to it*) How much is this?

LIU THE POCK-MARKED   You love it? You can have it. No haggling, five taels of silver will do. When you get tired of it and want it no more, I'll buy it back from you at the sale price. It is the genuine thing, good enough to hand down as a family heirloom.

FOURTH MASTER CH'ANG   Listen, I just realized how many foreign goods there are hanging off us! Liu, look at yourself: foreign snuffbox, foreign watch, gown made of foreign satin, shirt and pants made of foreign cloth....

LIU THE POCK-MARKED   But foreign stuff looks really super! If I wear local cloth, I'll look like a country yokel. Nobody will pay any attention to me.

FOURTH MASTER CH'ANG   Nevertheless, I feel our satin and Szechwan silk look much more impressive.

LIU THE POCK-MARKED   Second Master Sung, keep this watch. If you wear such a nice foreign watch, you will catch everybody's eye. What do you say?

SECOND MASTER SUNG (*Indeed loves the watch, but considers the price rather steep*)   I . . .

LIU THE POCK-MARKED   Wear it for a couple of days first. I'll collect the silver later.

(FATTY HUANG *enters*)

FATTY HUANG (*His eyes suffer from serious trachoma. Since he can hardly see clearly, he greets everybody in the room as soon as he enters*)   Brothers, lend your ears to me! How are you all? We are all kin, please do not spoil our good relations.

WANG LI-FA   These are other people. The ones you want are in the backyard.

FATTY HUANG   Pardon me, I cannot see clearly. Manager, prepare pork noodles. Since Fatty Huang is here, there will be absolutely no fighting! (*Walks inside*)

SECOND TE-TZU (*Comes out to greet him*)   Hurry up, please, the rival parties have already met each other.

(SECOND TE-TZU *and* FATTY HUANG *walk inside. The waiters bring tea to the backyard over and over again. An old man enters. He carries small goods such as toothpicks, beard combs, earpicks, etc. Lowering his head, he moves from table to table, but nobody buys his stuff. As he walks toward the backyard,* LI THE THIRD *blocks his way*)

LI THE THIRD   Old gentleman, why don't you take a walk outside? Since they are holding a peace negotiation in the backyard, no one will buy your stuff. (*Meanwhile he hands the old man a bowl of left-over tea*)

SECOND MASTER SUNG (*Whispers*) Li the Third (*Points to the backyard*), what on earth are they fighting for, with everybody's sword drawn and stick at the ready?

LI THE THIRD I heard it's for the sake of a pigeon. The pigeon of Chang's house flew to Li's house. The Lis refused to hand it over. (*Sighs*) We'd better keep out of it. (*Asks the old man*) Old gentleman, may I ask how old you are?

OLD MAN (*Drinks the tea*) Thank you. I am eighty-two. No one takes care of me. Nowadays a man means less than a pigeon. (*Sighs and walks out slowly*)

(CH'IN CHUNG-I *enters. His clothing is well tailored and his face beams with vigor and delight*)

WANG LI-FA Oh, heavens! Second Master Ch'in, you must be very free lately, or you would not honor this teahouse with a visit! And you come alone, without servants?

CH'IN CHUNG-I I come here to inspect how well you, my young fellow, are doing with your business.

WANG LI-FA Well, I am learning by practicing. I have to make a living from this. There is no other way out, for my dad died young. Fortunately, all the customers are my dad's old friends. When I fall short of hospitality, they won't raise their hands and they let me off the hook. To make a living in this tough world, good public relations are most important. I follow my dad's footsteps, his old tactics: always speak courteously, greet people frequently, and be sweet to everybody; then you will not get into a mess. Please sit down. Let me prepare a cup of fine tea for you.

CH'IN CHUNG-I No, no drink please. Nor am I staying.

WANG LI-FA Please sit down for a while. I feel very honored that you visit our humble shop. Li the Third, make a bowl of the very good. Second Master, how is your family? Is everything going well for you?

CH'IN CHUNG-I Not exactly.

WANG LI-FA Don't you worry. Your business has such a big turnover, "even your little finger is bigger than my waist."

T'ANG THE FORTUNE-TELLER (*Comes close to them*) This gentleman has a wonderful physiognomy. How prominent is your forehead! How full is your chin! Although you may not rise to the position of a prime minister, you will become as wealthy as Fan Li!*

CH'IN CHUNG-I Don't bother me! Go away!

WANG LI-FA Mister, now that you have drunk tea, please go and exercise yourself outside. (*He pushes* T'ANG *away a little.* T'ANG *sighs, lowers his head, and leaves*)

CH'IN CHUNG-I Li-fa, don't you think I should increase the rent a little bit? The small amount of rent that your father paid me in the past can't even pay my bill at the teahouse.

---

*Fan Li was a famous statesman of the Yüeh Kingdom in the fifth century B.C. After he retired, because of his talent in business he soon became a millionaire. He spent his last years at T'ao, and called himself T'ao Chu Kung. [L.C. and K.H.]

WANG LI-FA   Second Master, you are right, absolutely right! But I should not bother you with a trifle like this. Just send your manager here; I'll talk it over with him. Whatever increase there should be, I will comply for sure. Okay? Yes!

CH'IN CHUNG-I   You, young fellow, have become more slippery than your father. Well, just wait, sooner or later, I'll take back the house.

WANG LI-FA   Oh, please don't scare me. I know how much you care for me, how well you have been looking after me. You certainly won't have me carry a heavy teapot to sell hot tea on the street!

CH'IN CHUNG-I   Just wait. We'll see!

(*A woman from the countryside enters with a teenage girl. A straw is stuck in the girl's hair.* At first, LI THE THIRD intends to drive them out, but a soft spot in his heart checks him. They walk toward the center of the room slowly. The customers suddenly all stop chatting to watch them*)

LITTLE GIRL (*Stands at the center of the room*)   Mom, I am hungry! I am hungry!

(*The* WOMAN FROM COUNTRYSIDE *stares at the girl; then suddenly, her legs can no longer support her. She sits on the floor, weeping and covering up her face*)

CH'IN CHUNG-I (*To* WANG LI-FA)   Throw them out!

WANG LI-FA   Yes, sir. Go outside. You can't stay here.

WOMAN FROM COUNTRYSIDE   Gentlemen, please be charitable! Would someone take this child, two taels of silver only!

FOURTH MASTER CH'ANG   Li the Third, two orders of pork noodles. Take them outside to eat them.

LI THE THIRD   Yes, sir! (*Walks toward the woman*) Get up. Wait at the door. I'll bring the noodles to you.

WOMAN FROM COUNTRYSIDE (*Stands up, wipes her tears, and walks out as if she has forgotten her child. She turns back after walking away for two steps, embraces the little girl, and kisses her*)   My precious darling! My poor baby!

WANG LI-FA   Hurry up!

(WOMAN FROM COUNTRYSIDE *and the girl leave. After a while,* LI THE THIRD *carries two bowls of noodles outside*)

WANG LI-FA (*Comes over*)   Fourth Master Ch'ang, you are indeed kind and generous, to give them food. But, let me tell you: there are numerous cases like this. Can you take care of all of them? (*To* CH'IN CHUNG-I) Second Master, what do you think about what I just said?

FOURTH MASTER CH'ANG (*To* SECOND MASTER SUNG)   I think the Great Manchurian Empire will be finished!

CH'IN CHUNG-I (*An experienced know-it-all*)   Whether it will be finished or not does not depend on whether someone gives food to the poor. Li-fa, to tell you the truth, I really intend to take back this house.

WANG LI-FA   Second Master, please don't.

CH'IN CHUNG-I   I want not only to take back the house but also to sell the country estate as well as sell my business in the city!

---

*A sign to indicate that the bearer is for sale. [L.C. and K.H.]

WANG LI-FA   Why?

CH'IN CHUNG-I   To put all my resources together to start factories!

WANG LI-FA   Factories?

CH'IN CHUNG-I   Yes, gigantic factories! That's the only way to save the poor, to resist foreign import, to save our country! (*Talks to* WANG LI-FA, *while his eyes stare at* FOURTH MASTER CH'ANG) Well, why should I talk to you, you don't understand it anyhow.

WANG LI-FA   Why should you sell all your property for the sake of other people? How about yourself?

CH'IN CHUNG-I   You don't understand. This is the only way for our country to turn strong and wealthy. Well, time for me to go. Now that I see with my own eyes that you have a booming business, don't you play dumb when I increase the rent.

WANG LI-FA   Please wait a minute. Let me get a carriage for you.

CH'IN CHUNG-I   No, I prefer to take a walk.

(CH'IN *walks toward the entrance.* WANG LI-FA *sees him off. Supported by* LITTLE OX, EUNUCH P'ANG *enters.* LITTLE OX *carries a tobacco pipe*)

EUNUCH P'ANG   Hello, Second Master Ch'in!

CH'IN CHUNG-I   Master P'ang, you must have felt at ease these two days!

EUNUCH P'ANG   Of course I have. Peace is restored in our empire. The Imperial decree said: execution by beheading for T'an Szu-t'ung.* Let me tell you, anyone who dares to alter the old Manchurian ways will be beheaded!

CH'IN CHUNG-I   This sounds like nothing new to me.

(*Suddenly all the customers stop chatting. Holding their breath, they listen to them*)

EUNUCH P'ANG   Really smart, aren't you, Second Master Ch'in? No wonder your business is thriving.

CH'IN CHUNG-I   My small business is not worth mentioning.

EUNUCH P'ANG   How modest you are! Look, everybody in Peking knows your name! You are more influential than high officials. I've heard that quite a few rich men support the Reformation?

CH'IN CHUNG-I   Not exactly so. My influence reaches nowhere in your presence. (*Laughs*)

EUNUCH P'ANG   Well said, well said! Let each of us put up his own show just like when the Eight Immortals crossed the ocean.† (*Laughs*)

CHIN CHUNG-I   I'll visit you some other day, good-bye. (*Leaves*)

EUNUCH P'ANG (*Sneers and mutters*)   Such an insignificant moneybag dares to quibble with me! The way of the world has certainly changed for the worse! (*Asks* WANG LI-FA) Is Liu the Pock-marked here?

WANG LI-FA   Imperial Steward, please come to the back to have a seat.

---

*One of the leaders of the One Hundred Days Reformation Movement. The Reformists were supported by the Emperor, but the Empress Dowager wiped out the movement in September 1898. Six of them, including T'an Szu-t'ung, were executed. [L.C. and K.H.]

†While the Eight Immortals of popular Taoism ferried across the Eastern Sea to reach the Fairy islands, each displayed his or her magic power. They are Han Chung-li, Chang Kuo-lao, Lü Tung-pin, Ts'ao the Uncle of Empress, Li the Iron Staff, Han Hsiang-tzu, Lan Ts'ai-ho, and Ho the Goddess. [L.C. and K.H.]

(LIU THE POCK-MARKED *has seen* EUNUCH P'ANG *already, but he dares not come closer for fear of interrupting the conversation between* EUNUCH P'ANG *and* CH'IN CHUNG-I)

LIU THE POCK-MARKED   Hello, my good master, how are you! I have waited for you for a long time. (*Escorts* EUNUCH P'ANG *to a secluded table*)

(SUNG EN-TZU *and* WU HSIANG-TZU *come to greet* EUNUCH P'ANG. *He whispers to them. After a moment of silence, the customers start a heated discussion*)

CUSTOMER A   Who is T'an Szu-t'ung?

CUSTOMER B   It seems I have heard his name somewhere. Anyway, he must have committed a grave crime, or else he would not be beheaded.

CUSTOMER C   For these two months, those officers and gentry have been creating such havoc that I don't know what the devil they are doing!

CUSTOMER D   Great! I can keep my rations from the government now. Who cares what has been going on? T'an and K'ang Yu-wei proposed that the government should stop paying the rations of military ranks to all Manchurians,* and that the Manchurians should support themselves. How mean they are!

CUSTOMER C   We already had a hard time, because more than half of our rations were pocketed by our superiors.

CUSTOMER D   Well, it is better than nothing! To live on reduced rations is at least better than death. If I had to support myself, death would be the only way out.

WANG LI-FA   Gentlemen, please—"Do not discuss affairs of the state."

(*They quiet down and start to chat about their usual subjects*)

EUNUCH P'ANG (*Already sits down*)   What did you say? A girl from the countryside would cost two hundred taels of silver?

LIU THE POCK-MARKED (*Stands reverently*)   Though a country girl, she is extremely pretty! After she moves to the city, teach her how to use makeup and how to behave, I can assure you she'll look dazzling and act most properly. Whenever I am at your service, I strive for perfection in every minute detail, with even more devotion than when working for my father!

(T'ANG THE FORTUNE-TELLER *returns*)

WANG LI-FA   Why are you back again, Fortune-teller?

T'ANG THE FORTUNE-TELLER   I don't know what's going on. The troops are rushing all over the streets.

EUNUCH P'ANG   Of course, they are searching for the partisans of T'an Szut'ung. Don't worry, Fortune-teller, they aren't coming for you.

T'ANG THE FORTUNE-TELLER   Thank you, Imperial Steward; would you please also give me some opium pellets, for that will set my mind completely at rest.

(*Several customers leave quietly, as if they sense a forthcoming calamity*)

SECOND MASTER SUNG   We'd better go home too. It's getting late.

FOURTH MASTER CH'ANG   Okay. Let's go.

---

*Since the establishment of the Manchurian dynasty in the seventeenth century, all Manchurians had been given military rank and free rations. The Manchurians were the minority ruling class. [L.C. and K.H.]

(*Two men dressed in grey*—Sung En-tzu *and* Wu Hsiang-tzu—*come over to them*)

Sung En-tzu Wait a minute!

Fourth Master Ch'ang What for?

Sung En-tzu Did you just say: "The Great Manchurian Empire will be finished"?

Fourth Master Ch'ang I . . . I love the Great Manchurian Empire, so I fear that she will be finished.

Wu Hsiang-tzu (*To* Second Master Sung) Did you hear him? Did he say that?

Second Master Sung Gentlemen, we drink tea here every day. Manager Wang can guarantee that we are indeed peaceful citizens.

Wu Hsiang-tzu I asked you, did you hear him say that?

Second Master Sung Well, let's talk about it. Please sit down.

Sung En-tzu If you don't answer the question, I'll arrest you too! Since he said "The Great Manchurian Empire will be finished," he is a partisan of T'an Szu-t'ung.

Second Master Sung I . . . I heard it. He . . . he said . . .

Sung En-tzu (*To* Fourth Master Ch'ang) Come!

Fourth Master Ch'ang Where are we going? We should clear up the fact first.

Sung En-tzu Do you dare to resist arrest? Here is "the imperial law"! (*Takes the manacles from his belt*)

Fourth Master Ch'ang Listen, I am a Manchurian myself!

Wu Hsiang-tzu It's a far more serious crime for a Manchurian to turn into a traitor. Handcuff him!

Fourth Master Ch'ang Don't. I cannot escape anyway.

Sung En-tzu I agree, you can't. (*To* Second Master Sung) You come with me also. If you tell the truth in the court, you will be released.

(Fatty Huang *comes in from the backyard with four or five men*)

Fatty Huang How splendid! The sky has cleared up; so have the troubles. I did not run my feet off in vain.

Second Master Sung Master Huang, Master Huang!

Fatty Huang (*Rubs his eyes*) Who is it?

Second Master Sung It's me, Sung the Second. Please come over here! Please help us.

Fatty Huang (*Recognizes them*) Oh, Master Sung, Master Wu. You two gentlemen are investigating a case, aren't you? Please go on.

Second Master Sung Master Huang, please give us your hand. Spare some kind words for us.

Fatty Huang I take care of the cases when the government does not. But I will keep my hands off when the government does. (*Asks everybody*) Shouldn't it be so?

Everybody on Hand Yes, sir.

(Sung En-tzu *and* Wu Hsiang-tzu *take* Fourth Master Ch'ang *and* Second Master Sung *outside*)

Second Master Sung (*To* Wang Li-fa) Please look after our birds.

Wang Li-fa Don't worry, I will deliver them to your homes.

(FOURTH MASTER CH'ANG, SECOND MASTER SUNG, SUNG EN-TZU *and* WU HSIANG-TZU *leave*)

(T'ANG THE FORTUNE-TELLER *tells* FATTY HUANG *that* EUNUCH PANG *is here*)

FATTY HUANG   Oh, my good master is here too? I heard that you are taking a bride. Please accept my congratulations.

EUNUCH P'ANG   You just wait for the wedding party.

FATTY HUANG   I am grateful for your invitation. (*Leaves*)

(WOMAN FROM COUNTRYSIDE *carries the empty bowls in and places them on the counter.* LITTLE GIRL *enters also*)

LITTLE GIRL   Mom, I am still hungry.

WANG LI-FA (*Sighs*)   Go outside!

WOMAN FROM COUNTRYSIDE   Let's go, my darling.

LITTLE GIRL   Aren't you going to sell me again? Mom, are you?

WOMAN FROM COUNTRYSIDE   My darling. (*Weeping, leaves with* LITTLE GIRL)

(K'ANG THE SIXTH *enters with* K'ANG SHUN-TZU. *They stand in front of the counter*)

K'ANG THE SIXTH   My girl, Shun-tzu, your father is a bastard. A bastard I am. But what can I do? If you don't find a place to feed yourself, you will starve to death. If I don't get some taels of silver, I will be beaten to death by my landlord. Shun-tzu, you'd better accept your fate. Help me.

K'ANG SHUN-TZU   I ... I ... (*Too agitated to speak*)

LIU THE POCK-MARKED (*Rushes to them*)   Here you are! You give your consent, right? Okay. Come to meet Imperial Steward. Come, kowtow to Imperial Steward.

K'ANG SHUN-TZU   I ... (*About to faint*)

K'ANG THE SIXTH (*Supports his daughter*)   Shun-tzu, Shun-tzu!

LIU THE POCK-MARKED   What's the matter?

K'ANG THE SIXTH   She is so hungry and disturbed that she has passed out! Shun-tzu, Shun-tzu!

EUNUCH P'ANG   I want one alive, not a dead one.

(*Everybody turns quiet*)

CUSTOMER A (*Playing chess with* CUSTOMER B)   Check! You are finished!

(*End of ACT I*)

Translated by Ling Chung and King Hu

TENG T'O
(1912–66)

Teng T'o belonged to the younger, more progressive-minded generation of Communist leaders: people who were as committed to revolutionary ideals as their older comrades, but who had benefited from a higher education and showed a broader, more urban-oriented and internationalist outlook. After 1949, their qualifications should have enabled them progressively to take over the Party. With their revolutionary credentials and their intellectual sophistication, they could have considerably eased China's entry into the modern world. However, through the Cultural Revolution, Mao managed to wipe out nearly all of this small enlightened elite, thus inflicting upon the country a grievous harm whose ultimate consequences are still to be fully assessed.

The son of a successful Mandarin from Fukien Province, Teng T'o taught school for a time before he began his Party activity in the Shansi-Chahar-Hopei guerrilla zone, where he was editor of a newspaper, *Resistance News.* After 1949 his political and journalistic career rose swiftly. By 1952 he had become editor-in-chief of the *People's Daily.* In 1959, however, he had to relinquish his influential position; it was a political setback on the national scene, but it did not prevent his ascent inside the Peking municipality, where, under the protection of P'eng Chen, he became one of the secretaries of the municipal Party committee. As a member of the Academy of Sciences (department of philosophy and social sciences) and regular contributor to various newspapers and journals (*Peking Daily, Peking Evening News, Enlightenment Daily, Frontline, Historical Research*), he remained very active in the fields of culture, education, and journalism. In the spring of 1966, his influential newspaper column brought disaster upon him and his close associates, Wu Han and Liao Mo-sha. Unable to bear the severe persecution, Teng killed himself in May of that year. Wu Han, an accomplished historian and for many years vice-mayor of Peking, also committed suicide. Thirteen years later, both Teng and Wu were publicly exonerated.

The disastrous column Teng wrote under the title "Evening Talks at Yenshan" was published in the *Peking Evening News* in 1961–62. It became tremendously popular among intellectuals. Foreign observers were puzzled: why should these modest little articles dealing with various historical literary anecdotes arouse such enthusiastic interest? The answer was provided in 1966, with the first stage of the Cultural Revolution. Violent attacks were launched against Teng T'o as part of a broader offensive aimed at P'eng Chen and the Peking clique, which led to the downfall of Liu Shao-ch'i and most of the Central Party leadership. The attacks included a detailed exegesis of Teng's writings, identifying the hidden meaning of each of his articles. Actually they had constituted so many parables, transparent to the initiates, which daringly criticized the person, style, and policies of Mao Tse-tung.

When reading Teng T'o, Westerners may feel that his short essays hardly reach beyond the level of commonplace and commonsense observations. However, in a totalitarian system, banality can become the last refuge of sanity and decency; to make commonsense observations requires the greatest of courage, since it challenges directly the ideological dogma. Teng T'o did it with unparalleled daring, wit, and elegance. In affirming that intellectuals owe their first unconditional allegiance not to the Party but to truth, in asserting the primacy of rationality and informed criticism over raw political power, he committed the ultimate sin, the unforgivable crime (like Hu Feng had done before him) —he questioned the absolute authority of the Party.

The following article, first published in the *Peking Evening News* on August 24, 1961, and later collected in his five-volume *Evening Talks at Yenshan,* bore the brunt of the attack in 1966. Without specifically saying that Teng had identified Wang An-shih, the Sung Dynasty prime minister in the article, with Mao Tse-tung, the Party-directed critics condemned Teng for inciting people to oppose the Party's General Line and the Great Leap Forward.

—Pierre Ryckmans

Study More, Criticize Less

Study more and criticize less. This is a correct attitude toward learning, worthy of promotion. We must be humble about anything if we lack specific knowledge about it or about its circumstances. We must apply ourselves seriously to studying it and we must never thoughtlessly criticize it, which would often lead to mistakes, exposing ourselves to ridicule, or even causing irreparable damages. It is a lesson handed down to us by generations of scholars in the past through their experiences of learning and working. Whoever chooses to ignore the lesson is doomed to defeat.

In general, to sit down and actually write a whole book, or to lay hands personally on a certain matter, is rather difficult, but it is always easy to be an uninvolved spectator and to criticize. Those writers in the past often devoted their whole lives to the completion of their books without feeling that they had done everything possible in their work. Along came the fault-finders, just enough to douse the writers with cold water and make them shudder in despair. Liu Yüan-ch'ing of the Ming Dynasty cited an example in his book *The Saintly Company* to illustrate the problem. He said,

> Liu Chuang-yü often picked bones in Ou-yang Hsiu's [1007–72] *History of the Five Dynasties* and showed them to Su Tung-p'o [1036–1101]. Su said to him, "When Ou-yang completed his Five Dynasties history, Prime Minister Wang An-shih [1021–86] asked me why I did not take up the history of the Three Kingdoms, something Ou-yang should have done but did not. I bowed and declined the weighty assignment. After all, writing a book of history involves collecting data that cover tens or even hundreds of years; it is impossible not to miss a minor point here and there. I dared not to accept the assignment precisely because I dreaded the gleaners like you who would follow my footsteps to pick and criticize."

Ch'en Chi-ju [1558–1639], also of the Ming Dynasty, quoted the same anecdote in his *A Mirror for Studying,* with the comment, "My teachers told me not to make irresponsible criticism against those ahead of us unless we have read all the books in the world. I rather think that if I could finish reading all the books in the world, I would know better not to criticize those ahead of us casually."

Actually none of us can deny that Ou-yang Hsiu's *New History of the Five Dynasties,* only about half as long as Hsüeh Chü-cheng's [912–81] old *History of the Five Dynasties,* offers many insights. Just the same, there have been fault-finders throughout the ages whose picking would not have convinced Ou-yang Hsiu at all. Could it be that there are so many people who are born with an addiction to criticizing others but are not necessarily equipped with either the knowledge or the ability even to focus on a real issue?

Many people feel sure about themselves, confident about their knowledge, and look down upon those whom they criticize, forgetting that they themselves are never infallible and their targets may be making progress every day. The result is that the critics blunder all too often. Lu Yu [1125–1210], the poet-statesman of the Sung Dynasty, mentioned in his book *Notes Taken in the Studio Where I Study Even When Old* the instances when Wang An-shih slipped in his criticism against others because of his own carelessness:

> Wang An-shih had always slighted Shen Wen-t'ung, thinking that Shen had not read enough. He sent Shen a poem, "You relax pillowing your head on a pile of books / Until sundown when you go home on horseback / . . . ." And then when Wang wrote Shen's epitaph, he said, "Though he seldom read any book. . . ." Someone saw it and remarked that perhaps Wang ought to think about that line; after all Shen had won the number one position in the ultimate imperial examination. Whereupon Wang changed the phrase "read any book" to "kept any book in sight." Once Wang An-shih read Cheng Yi-fu's poem on dreaming of an immortal, ". . . He gave me a book written on green jade / In unusual archaic script red and serpentine / I looked at it but could not understand a thing / But he had turned and soared up to the purple clouds." Wang guffawed and said, "This man admits his illiteracy without anybody questioning him about it." Yi-fu said, "No! I am only using Li Po's [701–62] line."

Wang An-shih himself failed to recognize Li Po's poetry, and yet he turned to ridicule others, only succeeding in exposing himself to ridicule. . . .

As a creative statesman of the Sung Dynasty, Wang An-shih had many innovative ideas but not enough practical experience or knowledge. Chang Lei of the Sung Dynasty wrote in his *Miscellaneous Comments on Attainment of Wisdom,*

> Prime Minister Wang An-shih liked to talk about irrigation systems for the country. At that moment he was thinking of draining Lake T'ai [in Chekiang Province] to create thousands of acres of fertile land, which provoked much chuckling among others. Wang spoke of it one day with his visitors. One of them, scholar Liu Kung-fu, said, "That's easy." "How," asked Wang. Liu said, "Just open up another Lake T'ai on the side to drain the water into, that's all you need." Everybody laughed.

Anecdotes like this about Wang An-shih's blunders are legion. All of them point up one fact: Wang was impractical and arrogant—his two failing traits.

We need to derive from past experiences the principle that we must maintain a humble attitude to learn more and criticize less about anything and everything. How much more and how much less is, of course, a relative matter. To us, we should be ready all the time to study more about Marxism-Leninism and humbly learn from the masses through actual practice. Here I am not talking about the resolute struggle against any and all erroneous and reactionary things; that is a separate question.

Let us all honestly own our ignorance when confronted with what we do not know and openly admit our error when one has been committed. Ch'en Chi-ju, who also wrote *What I Have Heard and Seen,* said,

> Hsü Wen-chen was in Chekiang examining candidates. One of them had a line in his composition, ". . . Yen Hui (Confucius' best student) was troubled by Confucius' lofty wisdom. . . ." Commissioner Hsü wrote a comment on it, "Where did you invent this one?" Upon reading the comment, the candidate approached the commissioner and said, "The line, sir, came from the book *Fa-yen* by Yang Hsiung [53 B.C.–18 A.D.]." The commissioner immediately responded from his rostrum, saying, "Too bad this commissioner passed his own examinations too early, thus having lost the chance to do some hard studying." He then stood up and saluted the young candidate, adding, "Thank you for your enlightenment!" Everybody there was greatly impressed by the commissioner's attitude.

It's true that at the end of the very first chapter of *Fa-yen* there is such a line. The prestigious commissioner that day admitted his error on the spot, which act did not cause him to lose face but, on the contrary, earned him much admiration. Isn't that a great example for posterity to observe?

Evening Talks at Yenshan, Vol. I, pp. 82–85

Singing of Lake T'ai

Discussing state affairs, the Eastern Foresters followed Master Turtle Hill,*
Their concern covered everything between the earth and the sky.
Do not say, please, the eggheads indulged only in empty talk.
Where their heads braved the sword, fresh bloodstains lie.

Enlightenment Daily, September 7, 1960

Translated by Kai-yu Hsu

*Yang Shih (1053–1135), who first established the Eastern Forest Academy at Wusih near Lake T'ai. Revived by loyal scholars toward the end of the Ming dynasty, the academy was the target of bitter political persecution for decades. [K.Y.H]

T'IEN HAN
(T'ien Shou-ch'ang, 1898–1968)

It would be difficult to imagine a native playwright who has had as great an impact or has played as central a role in the development of drama in modern China as T'ien Han. T'ien Han was born in 1898 to a declining gentry family in Changsha, Hunan. In 1916 he travelled to Japan to study medicine and there met Kuo Mo-jo. Together with Yü Ta-fu and others, he organized the famous Creation Society. When he returned to China in 1922, T'ien Han and his wife founded the South China Society, one of the earliest companies in China devoted to the study, writing, and performing of modern drama. The South China Society continued, off and on, until it was formally disbanded by the Kuomintang in 1930. It was during this time that T'ien Han wrote such plays as *Night Talk in Soochow* and *The Death of a Famous Actor,* which were among the first experiments with romanticism in Chinese spoken drama (*hua-chü*), and which continued to serve as popular models throughout this early period. After the founding of the League of Left-wing Writers, T'ien Han changed the direction of his plays from their earlier romanticism and experimentation with "Art for Art's Sake" to a more political commitment. His socialist plays of the 1930s were among the first to incorporate the concept of a "mass" hero. And under the Party's aegis he continued to rise to a position of considerable power and influence in post-Liberation Chinese theater; in 1958, when *Kuan Han-ch'ing* was published, he was head of the national Drama Association and the controlling force in the Peking theater world. It was after a long silence that T'ien Han wrote this "historical play." The "historical play" is a long-established dramatic tradition used by Chinese playwrights to mask an attack on the regime in power under the somewhat safe guise of retelling history. *Kuan Han-ch'ing* was the forerunner in the revival of the tradition in the crucial period just prior to the Cultural Revolution. Later, in 1961, it was republished together with his *Hsieh Yao-huan,* another "historical play" using the Chinese opera form, thus presenting a most explosive pair to the Chinese public. Similar works followed on stage, such as Meng Ch'ao's *Li Hui-niang,* and of course Wu Han's now famous *Hai Jui Dismissed from Office.* During the Cultural Revolution Wu Han fell because of his play. In April 1979 Ts'ao Yü, the celebrated playwright and director of the People's Art Theater in Peking, revealed that T'ien died in jail in 1968 under persecution by the Gang of Four—mainly because of *Kuan Han-ch'ing.*

The hero of the play, Kuan Han-ch'ing, was a leading playwright during the Yüan dynasty. He was moved by the corrupt conditions prevailing in China to write a historical play, *The Injustice to Tou O,* which directly attacked the evil officials and ministers. T'ien Han, in his play excerpted here, speaks through Kuan Han-ch'ing's mouth to encourage his audience to "speak out" against injustice.

I have translated here two scenes from the play, the first and the sixth. The latter scene gives us a partial glimpse of the technique that T'ien Han revived from his earlier successful play, *The Death of a Famous Actor.* Not only are we the audience for T'ien Han's play, but also, with the actors backstage, we share in the performance of Kuan's play, *The Injustice to Tou O.* The scene also demonstrates the overwhelming power a seasoned playwright such as Kuan Han-ch'ing or T'ien Han has at his command, and why T'ien Han and the others had to be so rigorously condemned during the Cultural Revolution.

—E.J.B.

from *Kuan Han-ch'ing*

SCENE 1

Characters:
MRS. LIU, wineshop proprietress.
ERH-NIU, MRS. LIU's daughter.
KUAN HAN-CH'ING, famous Yüan Dynasty dramatist.
HSIEH HSIAO-SHAN, friend of KUAN HAN-CH'ING's and fellow Drama Society member.
CHIEN SHUA-CH'IAO, friend of KUAN HAN-CH'ING's and fellow Drama Society member.
YOUNG GENTLEMAN, Lord Akham's twenty-fifth son.
MAN WITH CROOKED HAT, or, as MRS. LIU calls him, "FOURTH MASTER TS'UI."

Cambaluc (today's Peking), the capital city in the eighteenth year of the reign of Kublai Khan (1281). On a street corner next to a small wineshop on the edge of the city are gathered a great many people, watching the execution procession. Amidst the long wailing of a trumpet, a Mongolian official in charge of the execution comes rushing in on horseback, followed by runners sounding bamboo clappers and shouting: "Out o' the way! Out o' the way!" In a moment the executioner, accompanied by the beating of gongs and drums, appears, a feather perched high on his hat and the official sword in his hand. He is escorting a donkey cart bearing a female prisoner, head bowed, hair askew, and carrying on her back the notice of her impending execution. An old woman trails close behind, shouting at the top of her voice: "Child, child! Oh, Heavens! Save my child! This can't be!" She is repeatedly abused by the runners, who, like fierce tigers, snarl at her: "Get away, old woman! Get away, or they'll cut your head off too!" The proprietress of the small wine shop, MRS. LIU, is carrying a bamboo basket, in which is concealed wine, meat, and some sacrificial paper money. Originally it seems she had thought to squeeze through and stop this pitiful procession, but, seeing it is impossible, she withdraws and murmurs softly: "Poor child!" And tears flow like rain. Just then a few household servants in Mongolian dress pass by. Alarmed, she chokes back her cries and wipes dry her tears. She calls to her daughter,

ERH-NIU, *in the street.* ERH-NIU, *though dressed in common everyday clothes, is without doubt a beautiful young lady.*

MRS. LIU   Erh-niu! What good does it do to keep watching? There are household duties that need your attention!

ERH-NIU   I'm coming, Mother. (*But she continues watching*)

MRS. LIU   She says "I'm coming," but she doesn't move. Ai, you can see this kind of excitement on the street at least once or twice a month. What's so interesting about it?

ERH-NIU (*Only now forcing herself to turn back, grabs hold of her mother's hand*)   Mother, it's so pitiful! How could such a young woman be a murderess?

MRS. LIU   Who said she was a murderess! She's a good child, just like you. You've forgotten about Hsiao-lan who came to visit us in spring the year before last.

ERH-NIU   Hsiao-lan? You mean Mrs. Ch'en's daughter-in-law?

MRS. LIU   That's the one! (*Wiping away tears*)

ERH-NIU   She's completely changed! Mother, is there some way we can save Hsiao-lan? Is there?

MRS. LIU   Silly child. How can we save her! (*Indicating the bamboo basket*) I prepared some wine and things, thinking to sacrifice them to her spirit, but even this I'm afraid to do. Hsiao-lan has truly had a sad life, and then this ... (*She stops abruptly*)

(KUAN HAN-CH'ING—*a great playwright*—*at first standing behind the crowd watching, now, hearing* MRS. LIU'*s and her daughter's voices, pushes his way through to them*)

KUAN (*In a low voice*)   Mrs. Liu, do you know her?

MRS. LIU   Aiya! Master Kuan, you too have come to watch the show?

KUAN   No. I was going out of town to see a friend. When I was passing by here, the streets had been cleared, and I ran into it.

ERH-NIU   Ah, Uncle Kuan is here. Come in and sit awhile, won't you? (*She hurriedly makes tea*) Please have some tea.

KUAN   Thank you. Erh-niu is growing more and more beautiful. You still remember Uncle Kuan?

MRS. LIU   We're old neighbors. You moved away barely two years ago; how could she have forgotten! Please have a seat.

KUAN   All right. (*Sitting down*) Business still good?

MRS. LIU   Not bad. It's just that I need more help and I can't afford any. My husband is usually in the countryside at Wan-p'ing. He hardly comes back more than once or twice a month.

KUAN   That doesn't matter. Erh-niu is certainly a great help to you.

MRS. LIU   That's right, but if she were a boy it would be better. For a girl to be seen too much in public, it's asking for trouble.

KUAN   Oh, that's true. Mrs. Liu, do you know that prisoner who just went by?

MRS. LIU   Yes. I'm distantly related to her mother-in-law's family. Ai, to see with my own eyes that child, totally innocent, come to such an end, and no way to help her—Oh ... (*Dries her tears*)

KUAN   What happened to her? Still so young, and yet having committed such a serious crime?

Mrs. Liu   What crime? She's a good child.

Kuan   Then why?

Mrs. Liu (*Watching the people on the street slowly disperse; in a low voice*) Master Kuan. This child's mother-in-law told me all about it, and she spoke the truth. If you can't save her life, perhaps in the future you can avenge the dead.

Kuan   Oh, tell me about it.

Mrs. Liu   This unfortunate child is Chu Hsiao-lan. Her family were originally farmers in Hsiang-yang. As you know, that area had seen battles for a good many years. The city destroyed, Lord Alihaiya* staked out ranches for raising his horses. He seized her family's few *mu* of land and even conscripted her father to take care of the horses. Her father, in a fit of rage, ran away, leaving behind Hsiao-lan and her mother. Unable to make a living, they came to the city to search for an uncle. Unfortunately, her uncle was away, and so they took lodging with a Mrs. Ch'en, who had come from the same town. Hsiao-lan's mother became ill and was sick for more than half a year. To pay for the doctor and the medicine, they had to borrow ten taels of silver from Mrs. Ch'en. Mrs. Ch'en had a son named Wen-hsiu. He was a good boy, but since childhood had suffered from poor health, and no betrothal had yet been set for him. One day Mrs. Ch'en asked Hsiao-lan's mother for the ten taels of silver. But where was she to get the money? There was no other way. She gave Hsiao-lan to Mrs. Ch'en to be her daughter-in-law, partly to repay the debt. Hsiao-lan's mother's illness continued, off and on, till last fall she passed away.

Kuan   Oh. And Hsiao-lan?

Mrs. Liu   Later, Hsiao-lan and Wen-hsiu were married. The two got along quite well together. Mrs. Ch'en loved her as if she were her own flesh and blood. In their modest way, they managed to be very comfortable. Who could have known trouble would arise right within the household.

Erh-niu   Mother, don't talk about these things now. What can be done to save Hsiao-lan? I'm going to die from worry! Can't we ask Uncle Kuan to think of a way? Hurry! Hurry!

Mrs. Liu   Silly, child. Uncle Kuan is a doctor and can only save people from colds and coughs. How can he save someone from getting her head chopped off? Mother's talking. Don't bother us.

(Erh-niu, *seeing there is nothing that can be done here, rushes out*)

Kuan   Mrs. Liu, tell me how it happened, that trouble right within the household?

Mrs. Liu   Mrs. Ch'en's own family was named Li. She had a cousin on her father's side called Liu-shun. He was quite old and lived in Mrs. Ch'en's house. Mrs. Ch'en had to run the house herself, so she entrusted him with certain household matters. The year before last, Liu-shun's son, whom he had not seen in many years, turned up. His son was named Li Yi, but everyone called him Donkey Li. He was a restless scoundrel, who had gotten mixed up with the army for many years. They say he went with Commander Sa to fight down South. When he reached Lin-an† he got himself a good haul

---

*A cruel warlord who served under Kublai Khan.
†Lin-an was the capital of the Southern Sung dynasty. [E.J.B.]

and then came back. When he got back, he saw Hsiao-lan and wanted to marry her. But Hsiao-lan paid no attention to him. Later, after she and Wen-hsiu were married, Donkey Li still would not give up. One day Wen-hsiu went out and didn't return. Only two days later did it come to light that he had been drowned. Some say Donkey Li did it.

KUAN (*Striking the table*) Imagine such disgusting vermin! He actually got away with chewing up good and meek people! (*Turning to Mrs. Liu*) Of course he did this in order to get Hsiao-lan, right?

MRS. LIU Right. After Wen-hsiu was buried, Hsiao-lan cried bitterly day and night. Donkey Li shamelessly brought up the matter of marriage again to Hsiao-lan. She said she would not marry and would rather spend her life taking care of her mother-in-law. Mrs. Ch'en, because her son had died, cried till she became ill. One day, she felt like having some lamb tripe soup. Hsiao-lan prepared the soup. Donkey Li found an excuse to send Hsiao-lan out of the room, and put arsenic into the soup. He had decided to poison Mrs. Ch'en and then take Hsiao-lan. Who could have known that Mrs. Ch'en would suddenly lose her appetite for the soup. Li Liu-shun, being a glutton, took the bowl and ate the broth. Immediately he started to throw up blood and he died. Donkey Li intimidated Hsiao-lan, saying if she agreed to marry him, he wouldn't say a word; if she didn't, he would seize her and take her to face the magistrate. Hsiao-lan, with a clear conscience, said: "If I'm to face the magistrate, then I'll face him." Who could have known this child's fate was to be so bitter; she had to cross paths with a corrupt official.

KUAN Ai, nowadays uncorrupted officials are all too few. Who was the official she ran up against?

MRS. LIU (*In a low voice*) The case was brought to Ta-hsing Prefecture. The prefect, Lord Khoshin,* as you know, is money-hungry; but he's also very concerned with his good name, and is continuously ordering the people to present him with "ten thousand signature" umbrellas.† He's a Semu,‡ and when he saw Hsiao-lan was a "barbarian's"** daughter and also had fled her native village, he was prejudiced against her. Donkey Li gave him a letter from Commander Sa, and also some silver, so how could he avoid ruling in his favor? During the trial Hsiao-lan explained what had happened from start to finish, but the prefect didn't listen to a thing she said and mercilessly used cruel tortures to force her to confess how she poisoned to death Donkey Li's father. But Hsiao-lan would rather die than plead guilty.

KUAN Right! No matter what, she shouldn't plead guilty.

MRS. LIU Finally, Lord Khoshin said, "Since she won't confess, then her mother-in-law must have administered the poison." He then ordered Mrs. Ch'en to be dragged out and given eighty lashes. Hsiao-lan, seeing that the judge intended to flog her mother-in-law, thought, "Mother-in-law is so old, how can she withstand the beating?" She steeled her heart and submitted a confession.

*Lord Akham's eldest son.

†An umbrella with 10,000 signatures given by the people as a tribute to popular officials.

‡Name used to refer to the national minorities in Northwest China then under Mongol Rule.

**The Mongols referred to the Han people as "southern barbarians." [E.J.B.]

KUAN   That's awful! Why did she admit what she hadn't done!

MRS. LIU   If she hadn't done so, wouldn't that corrupt judge have beaten her mother-in-law to death?

KUAN   She should never have pleaded guilty. Once she does, she has to forfeit her life. Didn't she think of that?

MRS. LIU: How could she not think of that?! But she wanted to save her mother-in-law, so she did it, regardless of the consequences. Hsiao-lan, that child, had just that sort of character.

KUAN   She truly is a noble woman. But weren't there any conscientious judges to hear an appeal?

MRS. LIU   Ai! Master Kuan, who was there to give her a fair trial? Nowadays, a donkey's life is worth more than a Han's. The day before yesterday, Hsiao-lan was given only one hearing, and today wasn't she sentenced to be executed?

KUAN   It's all these jackals of judges who treat human life as if it were nothing more than weeds!

MRS. LIU (*In a low voice*)   Master Kuan, you had best not say such things. (*The people on the street again rush past.* ERH-NIU *comes running back*)

ERH-NIU (*Pulling her mother*) Mother, hurry and think of something. (*To* KUAN HAN-CH'ING) Uncle Kuan, hurry! Don't you know a lot of people? Hurry! Think of something!

(*In the distance the sound of a cannon is heard*)

MRS. LIU   What is there left to do! She's already gone. Poor Hsiao-lan! (*Sinking into a chair, she hides her face and cries*)

(ERH-NIU, *at her side, also cries*)

KUAN (*With immeasurable sorrow*)   What kind of a world is this! (*Getting up*) Mrs. Liu, thank you. I'm going. (*To himself*) Ai, can I do nothing more than save people from colds?

MRS. LIU   Good-bye, Master Kuan. Come and visit us when you have time. Going home?

KUAN   Uh, no. I'm going out of town to visit a friend.

(*With heavy and measured steps, he is about to go on his way out of town, when his friends and fellow Drama Society members* HSIEH HSIAO-SHAN *and* CH'IEN SHUA-CH'IAO *emerge from the crowd on the other side of the street.* HSIEH HSIAO-SHAN *catches sight of* HAN-CH'ING *and grabs him.* KUAN HAN-CH'ING, *lost in thought, is startled*)

HSIEH   Aiya! Old Kuan. I was just looking for you. I went to your house, but you weren't there. So you were here drinking.

KUAN   I wasn't drinking. I was talking with Mrs. Liu about the prisoner who just went past.

HSIEH   I know a little about the case myself. I hear she was falsely accused.

CH'IEN   They say someone wanted to marry her, but she was unwilling, so he implicated her.

KUAN   Mrs. Liu just told me the whole thing. It made me furious.

HSIEH   Ai, what were you getting mad for? Nowadays, nine out of ten cases are misjudged. If you're going to take them all so seriously and get angry about them, then there's no way you can go on living. I've something I want to discuss with you. Come over to my place and have a drink.

KUAN   No. I'm on my way out of town. What is it?

HSIEH A certain man has asked me to teach him to sing your piece "Four Pieces of Jade, in Nan-lü mode." The first line, I remember, is "When thirsty, drink, when hungry, eat, when drunk, sing." But Ch'ien Shua-ch'iao insists it's "When thirsty, drink, ah, when drunk sing," without the three words "when hungry, eat." Good. Now we'll let the "original edition"—you—testify to the truth. Which one of us is wrong?

KUAN You're both right.

CH'IEN That doesn't make sense. Which one is right?

KUAN Originally, you are. "When hungry, eat" was added on later, to make it easier to sing. Some say the addition changed the flow of the melody and was not as subtle as the orginal.

HSIEH Yes, that's true. I think I'll use the original version. That gentleman is especially fond of those lines of yours that come later: "To till the land in the South, to retire in the mountains in the East, the ways of the world, I have seen plenty. In leisure to consider the things that have gone before, he may be wise and I a fool. What is there to fight about?" He said what you wrote is really beautiful.

KUAN (*From the bottom of his heart, he disagrees with that kind of easy, idle life*) No! It's completely wrong! He's not necessarily wise, and I'm not necessarily a fool. We have to fight. We have to fight to distinguish the wise from the foolish, the right from the wrong. I think, Hsiao-shan, you had best not teach that line.

HSIEH What? You've changed your mind? Then, what about the section "Passionate Mode"? Do you still want to learn it or not?

KUAN I do. I'll come over and see you later. (*To* CH'IEN SHUA-CH'IAO) Is Fourth Elder Sister Chu* in today?

CH'IEN Probably.

KUAN "Probably"? And Sai Lien-hsiu? Has she recovered?

CH'IEN (*Shaking his head*) I don't know.

KUAN You don't know? Aren't you and Sai Lien-hsiu rather involved?

HSIEH Their affair has blown away. This fellow got drunk and forgot his lines on stage, and Sai Lien-hsiu bawled him out. He couldn't take it, so he ran off for quite a few days.

KUAN Ch'ien Shua-ch'iao. No matter how good an actor you are, do you think a performer should forget his lines on stage? Do you?

CH'IEN Of course he shouldn't.

KUAN Well, then, if a person bawls you out for your own good, tell me why you lost your temper?

CH'IEN Because, because ...

KUAN Because the person is a woman, right? There is only one truth under Heaven. Is there a male truth and a female truth? I'm going to see Fourth Elder Sister. Come with me and apologize to Sai Lien-hsiu. (*To* MRS. LIU) Mrs. Liu, Erh-niu, we're leaving now.

MRS. LIU Good-bye.

    (*They go off together*)

KUAN (*At the corner of the street, taking his leave from* HSIEH HSIAO-SHAN)

---

*Kuan is referring in a familiar way to Chu Lien-hsiu. [E.J.B.]

Hsiao-shan, will you arrange for me to meet with the drummer Old Jen-szu and the flutist Yü Mei? I'm thinking of writing a new play, and I want to talk over with them the scene divisions and the melodies.

HSIEH   Fine. (*He exits in the direction of town*)

(KUAN HAN-CH'ING *and* CH'IEN SHUA-CH'IAO *exit in the opposite direction. Just at this time, the servants in Mongolian dress who passed by a while ago are returning, followed by a richly outfitted young gentleman and a man with his hat on crooked. They enter* MRS. LIU*'s wine shop*)

MRS. LIU   Young masters, please sit down.

YOUNG GENTLEMAN   No, thank you. (*To the man with the crooked hat*) You tell her.

MAN WITH CROOKED HAT   Mrs. Liu. The matter that I raised with you yesterday—what about it?

MRS. LIU   The matter you raised yesterday? Oh, Fourth Master Ts'ui, didn't I tell you? Our Erh-niu has already been betrothed. Sixth Master Chang was the go-between. The boy's family are the Chous from Wan-p'ing. Although they are farmers, the boy, Chou Fu-hsing, is employed at the home of Lord Horikhosen. They're only waiting for this year's fall harvest, and then they'll be married. (*Motioning for her daughter to go inside*)

(ERH-NIU *runs inside the house*)

MAN WITH CROOKED HAT   It's useless to argue. I know all about this, and I've told our young lord. He says: "This isn't important. Who cares if he is employed at the Minister's residence. Even if he were the Minister's son himself, he would still have to give in. Give some money to this fellow named Chou to pick another woman for a wife."

MRS. LIU   When a girl has already been betrothed, decency will not allow this.

MAN WITH CROOKED HAT   Where do you find that much decency? Our young lord, the twenty-fifth son of Lord Akham, has taken a fancy to your daughter. This is the greatest decency. Others aspire but cannot reach this height. You, on the contrary, have made our young lord pay several personal visits to your house. Don't spoil it when someone is doing you a great honor. Now, are you agreed or not?

MRS. LIU   Fourth Master, please say a few words on my behalf to the young lord. Erh-niu's betrothal has already been settled. She doesn't have this measure of good fortune.

MAN WITH CROOKED HAT   (*To the young gentleman*) You see, sir?

YOUNG GENTLEMAN   Don't waste words with her. Get the young woman!

MAN WITH CROOKED HAT (*To the servants*)   Get the young one!

(*The servants drag* ERH-NIU *out of the house*)

ERH-NIU   (*Resisting*) Mother! Help! Help!

MRS. LIU   Fourth Master, Young Lord, you can't do this! Her father has gone to Wan-p'ing. I can't make this decision. Wait for her father to return. Fourth Master, Fourth Master, I'm begging you. (*She kneels*)

MAN WITH CROOKED HAT   It can't be done, but it shall be done!

(*Without another word they drag off* ERH-NIU, *the* MAN WITH CROOKED HAT *following last.* MRS. LIU *leaps up and grabs hold of the corner of his robe and won't let go*)

MRS. LIU   How can you kidnap a person's child in broad daylight! Can you ignore the Emperor's Law?!

MAN WITH CROOKED HAT   Don't be so obstinate, Mrs. Liu. For twenty years our Lord Akham's family has done things this way. If you want the Emperor's Law, go to Ta-hsing Prefecture and tell them about it. You make enquiries. The governor of the Capital Region, who is also the prefect of Ta-hsing Prefecture, Lord Khoshin, is the eldest young lord of our family. (*Pushes* MRS. LIU *away and swaggers off*)

MRS. LIU   Heavens! What am I to do? What am I to do? I must die! (*Falling to the ground, she wails*)

[In Scenes 2–5, KUAN is persuaded by his close friend, the famous actress CHU LIEN-HSIU, to show his outrage at the unjust execution of CHU HSIAO-LAN by writing a dramatized version of the incident. She herself has volunteered her services for the performance of the controversial play. After long hours of painstaking efforts, and with the kind assistance of his solicitous friends and colleagues, *The Injustice to Tou O* is completed, a theater is secured, and all is ready for the premier performance.]

SCENE 6

Characters:
KUAN HAN-CH'ING
CHU LIEN-HSIU, famous Yüan Dynasty actress.
WANG HO-CH'ING, old friend of KUAN HAN-CH'ING's.
DIRECTOR HO, director of the Jade Goddess Theater.
WANG CHU, Yi-tu troop commander.
YEH HO-FU, scoundrel in the theater circles of the time.
HO CHEN, assistant to the Prime Minister.
IMPERIAL BODYGUARD, BACKSTAGE MANAGER, ACTORS, PUPILS OF CHU LIEN-HSIU.

Backstage at the Jade Goddess Theater. KUAN HAN-CH'ING *and* MA ERH, YEN SHAN-HSIU, *and* SAI LIEN-SHIU, *all of whom have removed their makeup, are positioned behind the doorway curtain of the embroidered backdrop, eagerly watching the action on stage and the audience's response. From time to time they exchange a few whispered comments. The backstage attendants and the Mongolian guards constantly mill about. Onstage Act 4 of* The Injustice to Tou O *is approaching the end.*

FEMALE GHOST (*Sings the Coda*)   Destroy all these transgressing ministers and officials. Take into your hand the sword of authority which the emperor has bestowed on you, rid the people of this evil.
(*The audience cheers. Some shout, "Rid the people of this evil!"*)

FEMALE GHOST (*Speaks*)   Father, my mother-in-law is old. There is no one to take care of her.

T'IEN CHANG   What a dutiful child!

FEMALE GHOST (*Sings*)   I charge you, Father, to exhume my grandmother's body and see that it has a more fitting burial, and with kindness take care of my mother-in-law. Take pity on her old age. Finally, reopen my case and reverse the unjust verdict that sent me to death.

(*The audience shouts approval*)

T'IEN CHANG   Dawn has broken. Go and bring to me every official from the Yanchow Prefecture who took part in trying the case of Tou O.

ATTENDANT   Yes, sir!

(*While the final act is still in progress onstage*, CHU LIEN-HSIU, *dressed in the part of the Ghost of Tou O, leaves the stage.* KUAN HAN-CH'ING, *visibly moved by her performance, is helping her as she enters backstage. Her disciples rush to her side.* HSIANG-KUEI *gives her some tea to drink*)

KUAN   Rest, Fourth Sister! Your acting was tremendous. Even I never dreamed this play was so powerful.

CHU LIEN-HSIU (*Removing the "ghost" trimmings on her costume*)   There seemed to be people shouting.

KUAN   Some were calling: "Rid the people of this evil."

(WANG HO-CH'ING *and Director of the theater* HO, *full of exuberance, rush in*)

WANG HO-CH'ING   Aiya! Lien-hsiu, you acted beautifully. In such a short time to produce such a marvelous performance! (*To* KUAN HAN-CH'ING) Han-ch'ing, you are quite a writer of tragedies. Still, I must say that if it weren't for this opportunity, there would be no way for this play to be staged.

KUAN   I'm truly grateful to you.

WANG HO-CH'ING   No need to thank me. Just don't drive me away next time I visit you. (*All burst into laughter*)

KUAN   Fourth Sister, hurry and remove your makeup. You must be exhausted.

HO   Don't take it off. Change into the costume you wore in the first act, and come with me to Her Ladyship. She was so delighted tonight that she cried through one yellow silk handkerchief after another. She said: "I've never seen such a wonderful play! I *must* have a look at that pitiful little daughter-in-law. Give her a little something. And mind you, treat her properly." When Madame Po Yen saw how pleased Her Ladyship was, she too said: "This play isn't bad." Well, it looks like I did well this time as a program manager.

(*An Imperial Bodyguard dressed in Mongolian attire anxiously rushes in*)

BODYGUARD   Hurry up. Her Ladyship is anxiously waiting.

HO   We're coming. Put a few more flowers in your hair. Pat on a little more powder. Her Ladyship doesn't like a young lady without any makeup. (CHU LIEN-HSIU *is engulfed by a flurry of her pupils hurriedly applying fresh makeup. A backstage manager enters*)

BACKSTAGE MANAGER (*To* HO)   Director, Commander Wang would like to see Miss Chu and Master Kuan.

HO   Is he Wang Chu of Yi-tu, Commander of a Thousand Men?* Please invite him in! (*After the* BACKSTAGE MANAGER *leaves, to* KUAN HAN-CH'ING) He's rather a straightforward and hot-blooded person. A while back someone in the audience shouted, "Rid the people of this evil"—that was him. Why don't you see him?

*In the Yüan dynasty commanders were ranked according to the number of men in their command. [E.J.B.]

KUAN   All right.

(WANG, *an immensely imposing army officer, accompanied by the* MANAGER, *enters.*)

WANG CHU (*To* HO.)   Director Ho, which one is the actress that just acted Tou O?

HO (*Pointing to* CHU LIEN-HSIU, *who is just touching up her makeup*) She's the one.

WANG CHU   You acted beautifully. You spoke what is in our hearts. "The officials have no wish to uphold the law. The people want to speak out, but dare not."

CHU LIEN-HSIU   You're very kind, but the credit is really due to Master Kuan's excellent writing. (*Indicating* KUAN HAN-CH'ING)

WANG CHU   Nevertheless, it was your singing that carried so much feeling, so much power. Every word struck deep into our hearts.

BODYGUARD (*To* CHU LIEN-HSIU)   Hurry up. Her Ladyship is waiting.

CHU LIEN-HSIU (*To* WANG CHU)   I hope you will honor me with more of your criticism. Please excuse me. I'm going to see Her Ladyship. (*Once more straightening her outfit in the mirror, to her pupils*) All of you go home.

(DIRECTOR HO *and* BODYGUARDS *assisting* CHU LIEN-HSIU *exit. Her pupils are tidying things up. Some leave*)

WANG CHU (*To* KUAN HAN-CH'ING)   Mr. Kuan. I've seen many of your plays. But this play moved me more than all the others. It moved quite a few people today. If I may be so bold as to inquire, was this play of yours inspired by Chu Hsiao-lan's case?

KUAN (*With great difficulty*)   Uh, no. It's taken from a historical tale.

WANG CHU   Oh. You really should write more of these historical plays.

(*The* BACKSTAGE MANAGER *and* YEH HO-FU *enter, leading the swaggering* HO CHEN, *assistant to the Prime Minister*)

HO CHEN   Where is Chu Lien-hsiu?

BACKSTAGE MANAGER   Your Excellency. Director Ho just escorted her to see Her Ladyship.

HO CHEN   Oh. Which one is Kuan Han-ch'ing?

KUAN   ...

YEH HO-FU (*Indicating* KUAN HAN-CH'ING)   He is.

HO CHEN (*Sizing* KUAN *up*)   You then are the playwright Kuan Han-ch'ing? Do you recognize me?

KUAN   ...

YEH HO-FU   His Excellency, Lord Ho, the Assistant to the Prime Minister.

KUAN   Oh. Ho ...

HO CHEN   Weren't you a member of the Imperial Medical Academy? You write plays too?

KUAN   Not very well, I'm afraid.

HO CHEN   Why so modest? It wasn't bad. Her Ladyship, among others, was moved by it. Ha, Ha, Ha! Even our Lord Akham watched part of it. I'm afraid we're going to trouble you again tomorrow. We don't want *Gazing at the River Pavilion;* instead, we want *The Injustice to Tou O.* Understand?

KUAN   ...

HO CHEN   The substitution has been made, but I'm afraid we must impose upon you to alter a few things. (*To* YEH HO-FU) Did you mark down all the places His Lordship indicated?

YEH HO-FU   They're all written down.

HO CHEN   The list?

YEH HO-FU   Right here.

HO CHEN (*Taking it, gives it to* KUAN HAN-CH'ING)   Kindly have a look at these and correct them all. All right?

KUAN (*Accepting the list and hurriedly glancing over it*)   I'm afraid I can't do that. If I make all these changes, then it won't be a play.

(WANG HO-CH'ING *takes the list and also looks at it*)

HO CHEN   It wasn't a play to begin with. You even curse heaven and earth and the demons and gods, to say nothing of us government officials. You call that a play? If it weren't for fear of offending Her Ladyship, our Lordship would have lost his temper. I was the one who . . .

YEH HO-FU   Right. It was His Excellency who made excuses for you. Finally His Lordship ordered: "Tell Kuan Han-ch'ing to change the play and perform it again tomorrow night."

KUAN   No. It can't be changed.

HO CHEN   "Can't be changed"? That's a bold answer. But His Lordship has ordered: "If it isn't changed, it can't be performed."

WANG HO-CH'ING   Han-ch'ing, why don't you make the changes.

KUAN   No. I'd rather see the play banned than change it.

HO CHEN   You're stubborn as a mule. Didn't your venerable sage Confucius say: "If you have made mistakes do not shrink from correcting them"?

KUAN   He was speaking of mistakes.

HO CHEN   Do you mean to say you haven't made any mistakes?

(DIRECTOR HO *returns, assisting* CHU LIEN-HSIU, *who is carrying in her arms quite a few gifts*)

HO   Aiya! Her Ladyship was certainly happy today. Look at all the presents she gave! There's never been anything like this before!

HO CHEN (*To* DIRECTOR HO)   Ho!

HO (*Sensing something amiss*)   Yes, sir, Your Excellency.

HO CHEN   Tomorrow at this same time . . .

HO   Yes, sir.

HO CHEN   In this same theater . . .

HO   Yes, sir.

HO CHEN   This same play—Our Lordship troubles you to perform it again. Understand?

HO   Yes, sir. I understand.

HO CHEN   But the play must be sung in accordance with all the changes. I've given the list to Kuan Han-ch'ing.

KUAN (*With determination*)   Lord Ho, please go back to Lord Akham and say I would rather that this play never be performed again. It can't be changed. If it were changed the way he wants it to be, it would be a completely different thing. It would no longer be the original *Injustice to Tou O.*

HO CHEN   Ha, Ha! Kuan Han-ch'ing, you really are a fool. Do you think Our Lordship wants to see your original *Injustice to Tou O?* There's nothing more to be said. The play will be changed and performed accordingly. If it isn't, your heads will roll!

(HO CHEN, *with his bodyguards in attendance, storms off.* YEH HO-FU *remains behind*)

YEH HO-FU   Han-ch'ing, didn't I tell you from the outset there would be trouble with this play? A wise man doesn't walk into certain disaster. Change it! Just now Lord Khoshin told his father about all the parts in the play where you held him up to ridicule. Some of those remarks of yours were aimed directly at His Lordship himself. How could he not get angry? Those of us in the trade know full well we're merely "playing a game." So—make a few changes, cut out a few lines, then the storm will blow over. Good. Han-ch'ing, take the advice of an old friend!

KUAN (*Unable to restrain himself*)   What kind of friend are you! You're a traitor!

WANG HO-CH'ING (*Fearing he's going too far*)   Han-ch'ing!

YEH HO-FU   See, a person with the best of intentions tries to help you. You and your temper—you haven't changed.

WANG HO-CH'ING   Old Yeh, don't say any more. Han-ch'ing is in a fit of temper.

YEH HO-FU   His Lordship is also in a fit of temper. We'll just see who gets burned. Good-bye! (*His real character finally reveals itself as he exits*)

WANG HO-CH'ING (*His eyes following* YEH HO-FU *out*)   I really never imagined he was that vile a scoundrel!

(WANG CHU *comes out from an inner room and enthusiastically grasps* KUAN HAN-CH'ING*'s hand*)

WANG CHU   Mr. Kuan. Today really is a lucky day. Not only have I seen your play, but I've also seen what kind of a man you are. The way you respect your play, protect it with your life, it moves us even more profoundly. It makes us love your play even more. Right! Better not to produce it. No matter what, it can't be changed. But a great play like this must be produced everywhere. If it can't be put on in Cambaluc, you can take it to some other place. You could go to the South and produce it there. China is a big place. When will you come and perform it in Yi-tu? I'll host all of you, you can be sure of that. When I was watching your play, I couldn't stop myself from speaking out. If you go among the people and perform your play, even more people will speak out. Right! We must by all means "rid the people of this evil." We cannot easily let go of these depraved ministers and corrupt officials. Take care of yourselves. Good-bye! (*Shouting good-byes to everyone, he walks off with bold, determined steps*)

WANG HO-CH'ING   When you compare the two, *that* is a man. Yeh Ho-fu is nothing more than a mouse.

CHU LIEN-HSIU   Han-ch'ing, what are we going to do? When I heard the shouts coming from the audience, I knew there was going to be trouble. Not only that, but Sai Lien-hsiu got carried away today. It seemed to me she added a few lines. My heart was in my mouth.

DIRECTOR HO   Mr. Kuan, there's no other way. Put up with it a little. Make the corrections on the list. Tomorrow morning Lien-hsiu and the others will have to have a rehearsal or two to make sure it will go well in the evening. What Yeh said was right. You needn't make a whole lot of changes. Just omitting a few lines would suffice. For example, "The ministers and officials have no intention to uphold the law," etc., can be left out. As for cursing heaven and earth, the way I see it, if the singing will go better with it in, then leave it in. It won't send anyone to the chopping block. To speak frankly, these men of position, they fear you're striking out at those in office. They don't care if you attack heaven and earth. They feel it has nothing to do with them and would as soon let it go.

WANG HO-CH'ING   You're absolutely right.

HO   Good. All of you go home! Lien-hsiu, producing such a show in only a few days, you must be exhausted. Go home and have a good rest. You have to conserve a little energy for tomorrow's performance. Although we had this big blow-up, still, Her Ladyship gave you so many lovely gifts, and was so taken by you, she even spoke of adopting you. That should make you happy. Well, see you tomorrow.

EVERYONE   See you tomorrow.

HO (*Glancing back*)   Mr. Kuan, a great man can bend. Make a few changes, all right?

(DIRECTOR HO, *followed by attendants, exits.* CHU LIEN-HSIU, *her makeup removed,* KUAN HAN-CH'ING, *and* WANG HO-CH'ING *are left onstage*)

CHU LIEN-HSIU   Well, Han-ch'ing and Mr. Wang, hurry up and think of something.

WANG HO-CH'ING (*After a moment of silence*)   Today's was really a moving performance. There were even some among the officials who were moved; Commander Wang, for example. But the more you move people, the harder it is for them to live with their guilty consciences. Akham is the most powerful man at court. Many have fallen under his hands. How could he be willing to let us off easily? Luckily, Han-ch'ing is a famous scholar. They dare not take action lightly. Also, Lord Po Yen's mother very much liked the play and even received Lien-hsiu. I hate to think what would have happened otherwise. It's good of Han-ch'ing to stand firm. On the other hand, if the play isn't changed, it can't be produced. The theater has already been booked. It has to be produced. Whether we live or die, succeed or fail, all depends upon what we ourselves decide to do now.

KUAN   I've already decided. I would rather see it banned. It will not be changed under any condition!

WANG HO-FU   But we've just said it has to be produced.

CHU LIEN-HSIU (*Having made up her mind*)   Then we'll put it on the way it is, without change.

WANG HO-CH'ING   And how will you then satisfy these sly old foxes? Didn't you hear Ho Chen say "If it's not changed and staged, your heads will roll!"

CHU LIEN-HSIU (*After considering it a moment*)   We'll do it this way, Mr. Wang. Please devise a way of getting Han-ch'ing out of the city tonight. (*To* KUAN HAN-CH'ING) Han-ch'ing, you go. I'll take care of things here. Don't worry. I would rather lose my head than see your play lose a single line.

KUAN   How can that be right? If you're going to lose your head, let's all lose ours, together!

[In the last five scenes of the play, as decided, *The Injustice to Tou O* is performed again the following night for Lord Akham and the other officials, without change. Outraged, Akham wants the entire company executed on the spot but is persuaded from taking such drastic action against KUAN and CHU. The young impetuous actress, SAI LIEN-HSIU, however, without a patron, has her eyes gouged out by Lord Akham's men. KUAN and CHU are taken to prison, where they await punishment. Thanks to the repeated petitions of KUAN'S many friends and admirers, he is sentenced to permanent exile rather than execution. On the day of his departure, his friends gather to see him off. And there, at the Marco Polo Bridge, KUAN HAN-CH'ING and CHU LIEN-HSIU bid a tearful farewell.]

Translated by Elizabeth Jeannette Bernard

HSIA YEN
(Shen Tuan-hsien, 1900–)

Hsia Yen grew up in Hangchow. He left school after his primary years to help support his family by working as an apprentice in a dyeing mill. Two years later he found the chance to enter a provincial technical high school, where he performed outstandingly and won a government scholarship to study electrical engineering in Kyushu, Japan.

In addition to engineering, which he dutifully pursued, literature and politics gradually awakened deeper interests in the youthful Hsia Yen. During the intellectual ferment of the May Fourth movement, while he was still in high school in Hangchow, he joined in editing two student magazines that promoted "the new tides in thought." During his Japan years he began reading Western literature and social science, including Marxism.

In 1927 Hsia Yen returned to China, taught school for a while, and moved increasingly into literature and politics. He joined the Communist Party in Shanghai at a time when doing so involved great risk and participated in the planning of the League of Left-wing Writers. As part of his heavy responsibilities within the league after its founding in 1930, Hsia Yen moved to create an important subsidiary, the League of Left-wing Dramatists. Film held a particular fascination for him, partly because of its potential to reach large masses of people. His chance to extend his influence to filmmaking circles came in 1932, when the Japanese bombing of Shanghai shocked that city's film industry into a more radical view of China's historical situation. Hsia Yen became an advisor to the Star Film Company, which began to produce leftist movies almost exclusively. In 1933 he founded a united front group called the Association for Cinematic Culture in China, which contributed film reviews to newspapers and provided scripts and personnel to the main Shanghai studios.

It was not until 1936, when the League of Left-wing Writers disbanded, that Hsia Yen made his own name as a creative writer. In that year he produced a piece of "reportage literature" (*pao-kao wen-hsüeh*) called "Bonded Labor," which Communist critics promptly hailed as a masterpiece of the genre. Shortly thereafter he turned to plays. His *Story of Ch'iu Chin, Sai Chin Hua,* and *Under Shanghai Eaves* all achieved success both among critics and at the box office. Some performances were closed because they satirized government policies. During the war years Hsia Yen fled Shanghai and moved between Kweilin, Chungking, Hong Kong, and Singapore, working as an editor at various newspapers.

After 1949 he returned to his old home base—Shanghai—and reshouldered heavy responsibilities in the administration of the new regime's literary and filmmaking enterprises. In 1954 he was appointed Party secretary of the All-China Federation of Cinematic Workers, a position that certified his preeminence in China's film industry.

He was also appointed vice-minister of culture in 1954. The minister of culture was Mao Tun, a prolific writer from the 1920s and 1930s and author of the short story "The Lin Family Store" (1932), upon which Hsia Yen's filmscript

781

was based. The film was produced for the screen in 1958. Released the following year, it was warmly received among critics and movie-goers until, six years later, it became the object of severe criticism, which led to the removal of Hsia and Mao Tun from their official posts.

Early in 1978 Hsia, his health much impaired, was appointed advisor to the Ministry of Cultural Affairs. He has resumed some filmmaking activities.

—P.L.

from *The Lin Family Store*—A Filmscript and a Controversy

[The story is about a Mr. Lin, the proprietor of a small general store in a town not far from Shanghai in 1931. He has a wife, who is subject to bouts of hiccoughs when under stress, and a teenage daughter named Ming-hsiu. They live modestly in rooms that adjoin the Lin family shop. Mr. Lin's chief assistant in the shop is a young man named Shou-sheng. There are also two hired shophands, one identified as "No. Four" or "Ah-szu," and another simply referred to as "the shophand."

The shop is described as an example of the in-between status of the petty bourgeoisie. On the one hand, it is deeply in debt to banks and wholesalers; on the other, it is a creditor to some smaller shops which themselves are on the brink of insolvency. Hsia Yen introduces the setting as "a society of cannibals ... [in which] big fish eat little fish and little fish eat shrimp."

The opening scenes show how Proprietor Lin, as a little fish, finds himself severely pressed after the Japanese bombing raids on Shanghai in late January 1931. His wholesaler in Shanghai, worried that passage to the countryside may be in jeopardy, sends a collector to demand a clearing of accounts from the Lin family shop. Local moneylenders, fearing that Lin will go bankrupt, refuse him credit. To make matters worse, a boycott is developing against Japanese goods, which Mr. Lin stocks. His daughter, Ming-hsiu, has been taunted at school for wearing clothes made in Japan.

The numbers below refer to the scenes of the filmscript.]

20

(*Fade in*) The evening of the fourth day after New Year's, in the living quarters adjoining the rear of the Lin family shop.

New Year's scrolls, as is the custom, still hang on the main wall, and a tablecloth that has been worn to a deep red hangs from the front edge of a table. Tin plates on the table are laden with tangerines, sugar cane, nuts, and so on.

The scrolls are all the kind of thing in which "businessmen" take pride. Hanging them is merely an observance of custom; it has nothing to do with "refinement."

It appears they have just finished the evening meal—the three Lins, the shophands, and Shou-sheng. Ah-szu brings Mr. Lin a thermos bottle and pours him a cup of tea. Mrs. Lin, seeing that they are going to talk business, retires to the back room.

Mr. Lin presses his hands together and faces Shou-sheng: "What to you think we should do? (*He pauses a moment*) If we stay open, where are we going to get merchandise? If we close up, then the four or five hundred dollars people owe us just 'dries up,' right? It says in the paper the fighting in Shanghai is something fierce . . ."

The shophand sits clenching his scalp, unable to utter a word. Ming-hsiu suddenly breaks the stillness: "Papa, Japanese aircraft have bombed Hangchow."

As the atmosphere grows heavier still, the shophand says: "I hear that Chapei in Shanghai is all burned out, and most of the hundreds of thousands of people are running away, leaving everything. The foreign concessions are crammed with people and rents have skyrocketed . . . an awful lot of people are flocking to the countryside. (*He pauses*) One bunch got here just yesterday, and they looked like pretty high-class types. Quite a few of them were crowding into the Shrine of Sage Confucius. . . ."

Shou-sheng suddenly has a thought. Putting down his teacup he asks the shophand: "Wait a minute—we still have a lot of those small items—washbasins and towels and stuff—stored in the shop, don't we?"

"Yeah, quite a few," the shophand answers, uncomprehending.

Shou-sheng continues proudly: "Mr. Lin, there's a way out of this."

Mr. Lin is startled: "And what is that?"

"We can sell every item in that whole batch of merchandise—like the washbasins, the towels, the soap, toothpowder, toothbrushes. . . ."

"Who'd buy it?" Mr. Lin is skeptical.

Standing up, Shou-sheng continues with confidence: "This is a great chance to do business, Mr. Lin. The people fleeing Shanghai must still have a pretty penny on them. But they can hardly have run away carrying washbasins and soap. When they settle in they're sure to need all the daily necessities. . . . So the market's in the bag!"

Mr. Lin is still somewhat skeptical, but Ming-hsiu, who is busy eating peanuts and melon seeds at the table in the rear, becomes interested and pulls up a stool to listen.

"Can you be sure of it?" asks Proprietor Lin. "Other shops have washbasins and towels, too, you know."

Shou-sheng speaks quickly: "Mr. Lin, you're forgetting that we're the only ones with any real supply of these items. Yü-ch'ang-hsiang [the competing shop across the street] can't even come up with ten washbasins, and the ones they have are all odds and ends." (*Proudly*) "We've got this market in the palms of our hands, Mr. Lin. If we sell the stuff as a 'one-dollar package' at a dollar apiece, it's sure to sell."

Feeling as if snatched from the jaws of disaster, Mr. Lin smiles and pats

Shou-sheng's shoulder, saying, "Right you are . . . you really are the sharpest man we've got. Well then, let's get things moving. . . ."

The shophand is happy too, and quickly says, "I'll go get the stuff out and start checking it over." Then, calling back over his shoulder to Ah-szu, "Hey, come gimme a hand!"

By the time the shophand and Ah-szu have exited, Shou-sheng has come up with another idea.

"Let's get right on it, Mr. Lin. The refugees will be either in the Shrine of Sage Confucius or else in that empty building in the silk factory outside the west gate. Let's make plenty of posters and paste them up right this evening."

Ming-hsiu feels there is work for her as well, and excitedly joins in: "I'll help you do the posters, Shou-sheng." She dashes to get out the inkstone and brushes. Shou-sheng is busy too, procuring a stack of paper from inside the shop. When Ming-hsiu has rubbed up some ink, Shou-sheng takes a brush and begins to write. Mrs. Lin, forgetting about the stomachache she had, pitches in by cutting paper and mixing paste.

Mr. Lin rushes into the shop to assist in checking the merchandise. Ah-szu and the shophand are assembling washbasins, towels, toothbrushes, and tooth-powder into matched sets. Mr. Lin helps by matching soap, towels, and glass cups into sets. He calculates the price as he goes, dully mumbling "fifty cents . . . thirty-two cents . . . plus forty-eight cents . . . less twenty percent. . . ."

Sheet by sheet the advertisements are written: "Grand Sale—One Dollar Package," "Below Wholesale Clearance," "Slashed Prices Unmatched Any-where," and so on and so forth.

The kerosene lamp begins to flicker, and Mr. Lin turns it up a bit. As he counts up the items, suddenly something occurs to him: "Oh, yeah—those things we released to Ch'en the Seventh's shop on commission basis last year —there was a lot of small merchandise in there, too. (*Shou-sheng nods*) Okay, let's go get those things back." He prepares to leave.

Shou-sheng is hesitant: "But it's New Year's. How could we do a thing like that?"

Proprietor Lin puts his scarf around his neck. In an accusing voice, and with a touch of sarcasm, he says: "What a fine conscience you have, caring whether it's New Year's or not. Let's go! If they've sold anything, we collect; if not, we take the stuff back!" Beckoning the shophand, he leaves.

21

In the evening, at Ch'en the Seventh's little general store.

Turning a deaf ear to all protestations, Proprietor Lin is busy removing some small items of merchandise. Ch'en the Seventh is beseeching him to desist, but Proprietor Lin is stony-faced. The shophand is placing washbasins, towels, and the like into the bamboo basket they have brought along.

22

(*Fade in*) Shou-sheng, Ming-hsiu, and the others are still writing advertise-ments. The sound of firecrackers can be heard in the distance.

"Ah-szu!" Shou-sheng calls out. And then to Ming-hsiu: "They're already saluting the god of wealth . . . it's almost dawn. Why don't you go and rest?" Ming-hsiu shakes her head, but cannot fight off another yawn. When Ah-szu comes running in, Shou-sheng says to him: "Go start pasting—at the gate of the Shrine of Kuan the Divine, at the Shrine of Sage Confucius, and all around the silk factory. I'll be there in a minute."

Ah-szu excitedly grabs a stack of paper and a jar of paste and runs out.

A string of firecrackers goes off near by. As Mr. Lin rubs his eyes, the rays of dawn are already seeping under the front door.

23

(*Fade in*) At the gate of the Shrine of Kuan the Divine, early in the morning. Refugees are clustered here and there, three or four to a group. Some are buying breakfast snacks. They quickly notice the advertisement on the walls:

—Special to our Displaced Countrymen: Items for Daily Use at Unheard-of Low Prices.
—Also the "One-Dollar Package."
—Supply is Limited, First Come First Served.

A hubbub of discussion ensues.

24

The inner rooms of the Lin residence. Mrs. Lin is implanting three sticks of lit incense before a porcelain image of Kuan Yin. She prostrates herself and kowtows vigorously, mumbling some indistinct phrases.

25

At the morning market. Sure enough, all kinds of refugees are crowding around in front of the Lin family shop. Though obviously travel-weary, they nevertheless are dressed much more stylishly than the "local yokels."

The shophand and Ah-szu are busy selling one after another of the "one-dollar packages." An unexpected smile appears on Mr. Lin's face.

These Shanghai people, from the big-time city, make their purchases with little nonsense. They pick something up, glance over it, pull out their cash, and pay. They don't pick through the merchandise or want to knock a few pennies off the price.

Remarkably enough, people are also buying umbrellas, galoshes, and things like that.

26

At the Yü-ch'ang-hsiang shop [across the street]. The storefront is decked out in splendid fashion, with even a vase on the counter filled with winter sweet blooms and nandina leaves. Yet business is slow.

The proprietor of Yü-ch'ang-hsiang is in an agitated state. He runs out in front of the counter and peers at the Lin family shop. His little clerk is pointing and gesticulating.

There is much bustle at the Lin family shop.

The proprietor's expression is one of surprise, then suspicion—mixed with an element of swelling jealousy. He ponders a moment, then gives a slight wave of his hand to his accountant. He goes up to the cashier's counter and the accountant follows.

The two men huddle together, whispering stealthily. The accountant alternately nods and appears to be deep in thought. In a moment the proprietor says, "So that's what we'll do. You yourself (*With emphasis*) make the arrangements." The accountant nods his head, picks up his felt hat from the counter top, and walks out. (*Fade out*). . . .

[In scenes 27 and 28 it becomes clear that a nasty rumor has been planted about the Lin family shop. Mr. Lin grows increasingly desperate.]

29

In the home of President Yü of the Merchant's Guild. Yü and his family are playing "hit the jackpot" with dice. When he sees that Mr. Lin has come, Yü leaves the table and rises to greet Lin, clasping his hands in the New Year's salute: "Best wishes, Lin my friend, and every prosperity in the New Year! You started this year with a real bang, old boy—your business was fantastic when you opened today!"

Mr. Lin, preoccupied with his own worries, returns the salute, mumbles "thank you," and extends perfunctory civilities to all present. Then he pulls Yü aside and says, "I must impose upon your kindness again, President . . ."

"No problem, no problem. Have a seat."

The two sit down and talk privately.

Mrs. Yü and the children go on rolling dice. While continuing to play, Mrs. Yü calls out, "Amah Wang, make some sweet tea! Company's here."

Mr. Lin is whispering, and his voice is drowned out by the sounds of the dice and the children's laughter.

President Yü listens to him and guffaws: "That's possible, but hardly a foregone conclusion. Take it easy, old boy. Tomorrow I'll . . . go get in touch with them. Just take it easy."

Mr. Lin feels relieved and smiles as he replies, "That's wonderful. Thank you so much." He rises and prepares to excuse himself when Amah Wang comes in with sweet tea. Yü grabs hold of him: "What's your hurry? Let's chat some more—it's great to have you here."

Mr. Lin reluctantly sits down again. Yü, bubbling with laughter, gives the impression of one about to reveal a bit of good news. "There's something I've wanted to tell you for a long time, only haven't had the chance. (*He pauses, rubbing his chin*) Somewhere or another Commissioner Pu [of the local Kuomintang Party branch] has noticed your daughter, who very much suits his fancy. The commissioner is nearly forty and still without a son. His wife has never given birth, but if your daughter were to go over . . ."

At this point Mr. Lin begins to panic. He tries to speak, but Yü cuts him off:

"If she can just produce a child or two, she's a ready-made Madam Commissioner! Ha, ha! When that happens even I can ride on her coattails."

This bolt from the blue leaves Mr. Lin scared silly. He is totally at a loss for what to say. "President Yü ... you ... must be kidding!"

But Yü is still the picture of seriousness. "We're old friends, so we can be quite frank. When it comes to things like this—from an old-fashioned point of view —one might feel a loss of face or something. But it needn't be so. It's the style these days, and there'd be nothing improper if your daughter made this move. . . . What's more, since Commissioner Pu's already got this in his head, if you go against him it'll be hard for you to get along around here. (*He pauses to allow the import of this statement to sink in*) But if you agree, you'll have something to look forward to. I've looked at all this from your own point of view, believe me, or I never would have brought it up."

"No, no, President Yü, we are modest folk—we couldn't be such social climbers! My little daughter is unrefined and ... ah ... we really couldn't. . . ."

"Ha, ha! You're not climbing—someone else is stooping, that's all! What fault of yours is it? Let's leave it this way: you go back and talk it over with the missus, and I'll just hold off for now. If I see Commissioner Pu, I'll just say I haven't had a chance to mention it, okay? But you'll have to let me know pretty soon."

"Uh-huh—" Mr. Lin arises with a ghastly expression on his face. His legs are unsteady.

As Yü sees him to the door, a volley of laughter and the rattling of dice are heard from within the room.

30

Mr. Lin's bedroom in the interior of the Lin residence. It is late at night, and Mrs. Lin obviously has been weeping for some time. She is outraged and, despite efforts to keep her voice down, she indignantly bursts out: "A right and proper family ... hic!* ... has a pure and innocent girl be somebody's concubine! (*Mr. Lin gestures that she should lower her voice*) Hsiu's the only one I've got—even if it were good people with a proper proposal, I wouldn't let her go!"

"I feel the same way, but ..."

" 'But' you say?! But I won't have it! See if they can steal her from me!"

"Steal they won't—but they're sure to hatch some kind of evil scheme. These people are more vicious than thieves." Mr. Lin is also on the verge of tears.

"If they get her, it'll be over my dead body!" ...

A few days later police come to the Lin family shop and arrest Mr. Lin. He is jailed on the strength of rumors that he intends to abscond with borrowed funds. Shou-sheng learns that a bribe of $200 will release Mr. Lin. At the same time the proprietor of the Yü-ch'ang-hsiang shop offers to buy the Lin shop's marketable merchandise.

---

*Here she makes a sound between hiccoughing and burping because of her chronic stomach trouble. The author himself deleted this in his 1959 revision for the screen. See *Treatises on the Motion Picture* (Peking 1963), p. 260. [K.Y.H.]

37

Five o'clock P.M. The inner quarters are already dark and gloomy. Shou-sheng is standing before Mrs. Lin. Ming-hsiu enters carrying a lit kerosene lantern.

Shou-sheng says: "The way it looks now, things are pretty clear. A moment ago, Guild President Yü told me that to get somebody out you have to spend two hundred dollars or more. Now the accountant from the Yü-ch'ang-hsiang shop comes across the street to gouge some merchandise for a sum of one hundred and fifty or sixty. It looks like they're all in cahoots. (*He becomes somewhat agitated*) Just look—the Party branch and the Merchant's Guild want money, Yü-ch'ang-hsiang wants merchandise, Commissioner Pu wants a certain person. . . ."

Mrs. Lin, who has been weeping continuously, manages a sentence: "It's . . . it's like picking the softest of the steamed buns out of a bamboo steamer. Your master was too gentle a person, that's all—everybody took advantage of him. . . ."

Shou-sheng scratches his head, then says: "Mrs. Lin, I think we'd better let them gouge this batch of stuff. We can take their hundred and fifty or sixty dollars of cash, add in the fifty or sixty in the shop, and get Mr. Lin out before going any further."

Mrs. Lin is both grieved and upset at the idea of spending so much money. She merely weeps (*A noiseless weeping*) and says nothing.

Seeing that his suggestion is getting nowhere, Shou-sheng feels obliged to withdraw. But just as he steps through the swinging door to the shop, Ming-hsiu catches up with him. The color is gone from her face and her voice is trembling. "Oh, Shou-sheng! Mama's too upset to think! She keeps saying . . . that they've already killed Papa. You . . . you must hurry up and settle it with Yü-ch'ang-hsiang, hurry up and get Papa out! You . . . better take charge of things."

So saying Ming-hsiu suddenly blushes and runs back inside. Shou-sheng's eyes follow her as she goes. He stares dumbly for a moment, then slowly turns again to leave, mustering his determination.

38

Shou-sheng returns to the shop area and takes a packet of cash out of the teller's drawer. He speaks to the shophand in a firm voice: "Close the front door, Ah-szu. (*Hands a list of inventory to the clerk*) Please check these items to see if they are all there. I'm going over to give Yü-ch'ang-hsiang his answer."

Ah-szu and the shophand are unaware of what is happening. They look startled as they reach to receive the inventory list.

39

(*Fade in*) The inner quarters. In front of two candles, Mrs. Lin is kowtowing before the bodhisattva Kuan Yin.

Ming-hsiu yawns and stretches, then glances at the old-fashioned clock on the table in front of the bed.

It is 11:40. Mrs. Lin stands up after finishing her obeisances to the bodhisattva.

Ming-hsiu says, "Why don't you go rest, Ma? I'll stay up."

Mrs. Lin shakes her head and sits down. One can hear the distant tolling of the night watch.

A moment later the sound of the outside door opening sends Ming-hsiu dashing out. Mrs. Lin also turns to rise.

Sure enough, it is Shou-sheng bringing Mr. Lin back. Mrs. Lin can hardly believe her eyes. Ming-hsiu's worried expression rapidly disappears and is replaced by a look of joy. Mrs. Lin examines her husband in every detail, seeking to satisfy herself that he has not been abused. She then hastens back to offer incense before the bodhisattva Kuan Yin.

The dazed Mr. Lin sits down as Ming-hsiu drapes a padded gown over his shoulders and pours him a cup of hot tea.

Shou-sheng digs a paper packet out of his clothing and places it on the table. "This is a bit of left-over money. We still have fifty or sixty."

Mr. Lin heaves a sigh. His voice is listless as he says, "You might as well have let me die over there. Spending money to get me out means our money is all used up. And the shop is empty. Isn't this the end of the line?"

Mrs. Lin moves to her husband's side. Seeing him in this mood she cannot help weeping again. Mr. Lin continues, fighting back sobs. "They've gouged all our stuff ... our debts are piled high ... what can we do with ... this shop?"

"Mr. Lin, sir." The speaker is Shou-sheng, who then dips his finger in his tea and writes a character on the table.

(*Close-up on the character "Leave"*)

Mr. Lin is startled; then tears gush from his eyes. He glances at Mrs. Lin, glances at Ming-hsiu, and can only sigh.

Shou-sheng lowers his voice: "This is the only way out, Mr. Lin. If we scrape together everything in the shop, it'll come to a hundred dollars or more. Take it with you—it should get you by for a month or two. Let me handle what happens here."

His words are overheard by Mrs. Lin, who quickly interjects: "You go, too —you and Hsiu. Leave me here by myself; I'll fight to the last."

Mr. Lin waves his hand in an effort to calm her, but, suddenly seeming healthy and vigorous, she dashes into the bedroom. Ming-hsiu cries out "Ma!" and runs after her.

Mr. Lin is dazed. In his indecision he sits tapping his head with his hand.

Shou-sheng lowers his voice again. "You and your daughter leave together, Mr. Lin. Mrs. Lin will never feel comfortable if the young lady stays here, since that guy Pu is sure to try something.

Mr. Lin still cannot make up his mind. Shou-sheng, at a loss, walks aimlessly around the table.

At this point Mrs. Lin enters in a burst of tears. Both Mr. Lin and Shou-sheng jump with surprise. Cupped in the lady's hands is a little "gift box." The sight of Mr. Lin's and Shou-sheng's startled expressions brings her to a stop. "You two come in here, too," she says, "and listen to my idea."

Mr. Lin and Shou-sheng follow her in.

She opens up the little box, removes from it a paper packet, and says, pointing at the packet: "These are my private savings, about two hundred and some dollars. I'm going to give half to you. Hsiu—(*With emphasis*) I hereby betroth you to Shou-sheng. Early tomorrow morning Hsiu will leave with her father ... hic! ... I'm not going. Shou-sheng will stay with me a few days until we see what happens. There's no telling how many days I have to live ... hic! ... (*Pointing to Ming-hsiu and Shou-sheng*) If you'll kowtow together in front of me, I can set my mind at ease."

Mr. Lin is astonished at his wife's decision but, at the same time, feels it to be a relatively fitting solution. He wants to speak, but Mrs. Lin is busy grabbing Ming-hsiu with one hand and Shou-sheng with the other, requiring them to "do their kowtows."

The two of them oblige and kowtow before the elder Lins. Ming-hsiu inclines her head, blushing profusely. Shou-sheng steals a glance at her.

At this point Mr. Lin finally has decided what to do.

"All right," he says, "so be it. (*He pauses*) But Shou-sheng—if you stay behind to deal with those people, be extremely careful at every turn."

Mrs. Lin now has found her confidence: "Go get your things ready, Hsiu!" (*Fade out*)

40

(*Fade in*) The Lin family shop has finally closed down. It is early morning, and a sheet of paper pasted on the front door bears the message: "Clearing Accounts—Going Out of Business."

A group of people gather around and clamorous gossip breaks out.

"There was wind of this a few days back."

"The boss took off two days ago."

One woman sighs. "Times are really hard."

All of a sudden Ch'ien the Monkey [from a local bank] crowds his way in, accompanied by a clerk. Barging to the front, he pastes a poster next to the one that reads "Clearing Accounts—Going Out of Business":

Public Announcement of the Heng Yüan Money Shop:
"In order to protect the interests of all creditors, any ..."

Having pasted the notice, Ch'ien the Monkey pounds savagely on the door.

Lu the Monk comes rushing over with the tottering Mrs. Chu [a small creditor]. When she sees what has happened, she nearly faints.

Ch'en the Seventh comes running as well. The crowd outside the door gets bigger and bigger....

[A few final scenes depict outraged creditors and the lonely image of Proprietor Lin fleeing in a small boat.]

The film about the Lin family shop was attacked for "prettifying the bourgeoisie," meaning that it wrongly allowed a person like Lin to appear honest and pitiable.[1] Its detractors objected less to the film's subject matter than to the viewpoint from which it was presented. In the words of one critic:

If we really want to depict the image of an exploiter like Proprietor Lin, we must pay attention to the relationships between the exploiter and those he exploits. We must reveal how it happens that the blood and sweat of the working people turn into his profit; this means we must reveal the oppressive and exploitative relationships between him and his shophands and must deal with the conflicts and struggles between those two classes. But ... in the film we see nothing whatever of class conflict, or the clash between labor and capital. What we see is how very kind and concerned the proprietor is toward his shophands, as if they were his own family; what we see is how loyal and true the shophands are toward the proprietor, planning and scheming on his behalf. In the film the proprietor's interests are made into the common interests of these two types of people. ... .[2]

Scenes 20 and 39 above include obvious examples of the mutual concern between Shou-sheng and Proprietor Lin that Hsia Yen's critics found unacceptable. Would a shophand really have thought of the "one-dollar package" to save his boss's skin? Would the boss really engage his daughter to a shophand?

Mao Tun's original story in 1932 had been an attempt at "naturalistic" description, a kind of combination of Zola's concern for scientific detail with a Communist concern to reflect current social theory. The fact that the story was attacked thirty-three years later hardly implies that it was out of step in its time. Consider the following description of the petty bourgeoisie written by Mao Tse-tung in 1926:

The petty bourgeoisie ... fall into three different sections. ... The third section consists of those whose standard of living is falling. Many in this section, who originally belonged to better-off families, are undergoing a gradual change from a position of being barely able to manage to one of living in more and more reduced circumstances. When they come to settle accounts at the end of the year, their debts mounting and their life becoming more and more miserable, they "shudder at the thought of the future." They are in great mental distress because there is such a contrast between their past and their present. *Such people are quite important for the revolutionary movement;* ... not only will [the left-wing of the bourgeoisie] join the revolution, but the middle section too may join, and even the right-wingers. ... [Emphasis added.][3]

Given this background, how could Hsia Yen's critics have held it to be grossly wrong to put the Lin family story on a movie screen in 1959? Had Hsia Yen distorted Mao Tun's theme? Such distortion was never charged—in fact Hsia Yen's critics were quite ready to concede that the film was "faithful to the original work."[4]

A close comparison of the filmscript with Mao Tun's text reveals that Hsia Yen, far from adding bourgeois sympathies to the story, actually altered it in a "left" direction. The original story, for example, does not include the episode in which Lin cruelly retrieves his merchandise from the little shop of Ch'en the Seventh (end of scene 20 and scene 21). This and other touches were added by Hsia Yen in order to stress the exploitative side of the petty bourgeoisie. "In one respect," Hsia Yen wrote, "[Lin] is oppressed, is exploited; but in another he is an exploiter quite capable of oppressing others."[5]

Despite his efforts to make Proprietor Lin seem less sympathetic, it was Hsia

Yen, and not Mao Tun, who in May 1965 came under direct attack for the bourgeois sympathies that remained in the story. Mao Tun was punished only to the extent of a quiet removal from office in late 1964.

Hsia Yen's critics, aware of this apparent inconsistency, explained by saying that times had changed. Chang T'ien-i, a fellow writer from the thirties, put it this way: "Regarding any piece of writing from the past (from the thirties, for example), to ask what effect it had in its time is one thing, but what effect it is likely to have when transplanted before the eyes of today's readers and viewers (especially youth) is quite another matter."[6] Others argued that sympathy with Proprietor Lin was appropriate in the thirties because the correct course at that time was to unite with people like Lin in a joint struggle against the Kuomintang and the Japanese. In the fifties, however, there was no need to sympathize or ally with capitalism in any form.

It is almost certain that there were other, more crucial reasons for the attack on Hsia Yen, reasons related to the struggle for power by those who were later known as the "Gang of Four." Mao Tun, though formally outranking Hsia Yen in the Ministry of Culture, was not a member of the Communist Party and was, to some degree, only a ceremonial figure.[7] But Hsia Yen was a long-standing member of the Party who had wielded a strong influence in the Party's film circles ever since the early thirties. Thus anyone attempting a turnover of power would naturally need to concentrate on Hsia Yen.

Hsia Yen's association with the "revisionist" wing of the Party leadership—those who became prominent public enemies during the Cultural Revolution—can be traced back at least as early as 1962. In that year he contributed periodically to a column in the *People's Daily* called "Ch'ang-tuan Lu" ("Long and Short Records," or "Sizing Things Up"), which soon gained a reputation for thinly veiled but astute criticism of national policies. Other contributors to this column included Teng T'o, a prominent journalist, and Wu Han, a historian and Deputy Mayor of Peking. In 1966 Teng and Wu were denounced for anti-Party activities in an attack whose ultimate targets were such leading "revisionists" as P'eng Chen, Mayor of Peking, and Liu Shao-ch'i, Chairman of the People's Republic. To some degree the criticism of Hsia Yen must be viewed as an opening sally of the larger campaign.

From 1966 until 1977, Hsia Yen and Mao Tun were not heard from publicly. A year after the fall of the "Gang of Four" both reappeared. They participated at a state banquet on September 30, 1977, the eve of the eighteenth anniversary of the People's Republic. In subsequent months they published some brief reminiscences, mostly denouncing the Gang of Four, and met occasionally with foreign visitors.

Translation and comments by Perry Link

NOTES

1. *Literary Gazette,* no. 6 (1965): 2–14; *Film Criticism* (May 20, 1967): 3–4; *Current Background,* no. 766 (July 15, 1965).
2. Hu K'o, "What Has the Film 'The Lin Family Shop' Propagandized?" *Literary Gazette,* no. 6 (1965): 4.

3. Mao Tse-tung, "Analysis of the Classes in Chinese Society," *Selected Works of Mao Tse-tung,* Vol. I, pp. 15–16.

4. Su Nan-yüan, " 'Lin's Shop' is a Picture for Prettifying the Bourgeoisie," *People's Daily* (May 29, 1965); *Current Background,* no. 766 (July 15, 1965).

5. Quoted in Chang T'ien-i, "A Critique of the Revision of 'The Lin Family Shop,' " *Literary Gazette,* no. 6 (1965): 7.

6. Ibid., p. 6.

7. Some sources identify Mao Tun as a Communist Party member. For example, see Ting Wang, *Critical Introduction to Chinese Writers of the 1930s,* p. 15. But Mao Tun has not been behaving like one with weighty Party responsibility. [K.Y.H.]

REVOLUTIONARY PEKING
OPERA

The Red Lantern is perhaps the best known of eleven model "Modern Revolutionary Peking Operas" written during the Cultural Revolution under the aegis of Chiang Ching. From the moment of its important debut at a drama festival in Peking in 1964, it attracted widespread attention from critics, who praised it for its ideological, literary, and musical qualities.*

The creation of a new form of opera was advanced as a fulfillment of the guidelines set down by Mao Tse-tung in his famous *Talks at the Yenan Forum on Literature and Art* delivered in 1942. The main principle was that art must serve the people—that is, the workers, peasants, and soldiers. In contrast to traditional Peking Opera, which represented ideal worlds of emperors, ministers, scholars, and beauties, Revolutionary Opera turns to the proletariat and the historical theme of liberation through struggle. The events of the War of Resistance and the civil war against the Nationalists form the core of this new mythology. Revolutionary Opera is designed to present positive images of the people as well as to enable the audience to reexperience the revolutionary process through the catharsis of the theater.

One of the key aesthetic problems of the genre is characterization, wherein a tension is perceived between the function of typifying the masses and the fulfillment of the emotional and artistic need for a heroic figure who is somehow extraordinary. This is solved theoretically by the doctrine of "combining revolutionary realism with revolutionary romanticism" and practically by allowing heroes such as Li Yü-ho to express human emotions in the midst of crises and to suffer mortality.

As a result of Soviet influence in the 1950s, many techniques of Western ballet and socialist realism have been assimilated. The actors themselves, however, conceive of their craft more in terms of attitude. Personal struggle against the temptations of self associated with the Stanislavsky system, and the emphasis on the collective life of the troupe as it identifies with the masses through labor, enable the actors to grasp the essence of their role from an enhanced socialist life offstage.

Musically, Revolutionary Peking Opera is built on the aria forms of traditional Peking Opera. However, a number of new aria types have been created by amalgamating melodies from local operas. The orchestra has been enlarged and often includes Western instruments for more power, while the greater precision of the Western scale has been adopted to enable better tuning. Incidental music plays an expanded role and is often excerpted for concert use. In addition, scenery and realistic props link this genre to Wagner and other Romantic proponents of a "total theater."

*Forty such essays have been collected in *Critical Essays on the Peking Opera 'The Red Lantern'* (Peking, 1965). A complete text including musical scores, dance patterns, and detailed pictures of costumes, scenery, props, and lighting can be found in *The Red Lantern* (Peking, 1972).

The two principal musical modes involved are *hsi-p'i* and *erh-huang,* the former somewhat higher pitched and crisper than the latter. A "standard beat" consists of the regular rhythm of 2-2-3, or 3-3-4, usually set parallel to a trocha-ic-trochaic-dactylic or dactylic-dactylic-trochaic-trochaic pattern in the text. "Swaying beat" is slower and more lyrical than "fast beat," and "flowing-water beat" suggests a narrative mood. There is also a more vigorous flowing beat in frequent use. "Scattered beat" gives the singer greater freedom to vary the metrical arrangement of each line. "Two-six" suggests something like a tro-chaic pattern.

The arias usually have one end-rhyme sustained throughout a passage. As in traditional Peking opera, arias can also function as asides.   —K.Y.H. and
Richard Strassberg

---

from *The Red Lantern*

A REVOLUTIONARY PEKING OPERA IN ELEVEN ACTS

[The opera presents a page from the Chinese Communist guerrilla war against Japan in the early 1940s in North China.

In Acts I–IV, old Communist revolutionary railroad worker LI YÜ-HO lives with GRANDMA, who has accepted LI as her son, and a young girl, T'IEH-MEI, who calls him her father. All three of them work together to aid the guerrillas. An underground messenger jumps a train to deliver a secret code book to LI, who is to transmit it to a guerrilla unit. A spineless comrade, WANG, when threat-ened by the Japanese, betrays LI. Still unaware of the crucial turn of events, LI returns home after an unsuccessful attempt to deliver the code book, as the curtain rises on Act V.]

ACT V: Relating the Story of a Revolutionary Family

Evening, at LI's house. The audience can see both the living room and the area outside the door to the house. As the curtain rises, GRANDMA LI *is in the room waiting for* LI YÜ-HO

GRANDMA (*Sings*—hsi-p'i *swaying beat*)
The time grows late
And Yü-ho has not yet returned.
(T'IEH-MEI *comes out of the back room. A siren sounds*)
T'IEH-MEI (*Sings—vigorous flowing beat*)
There's so much commotion in the streets,
I worry about my father.
(LI YÜ-HO *enters holding his lunchbox and a signal lantern. He knocks on the door*)
LI (*Offstage*)   T'ieh-mei!
T'IEH-MEI   Daddy is home.
GRANDMA   Hurry up, open the door.

T'IEH-MEI (*Opens the door*) Daddy!

GRANDMA   Yü-ho!

LI   Mother!

GRANDMA   You're back. Did you make the connection? (*Takes his lunchbox and the lantern*)

LI   No. (*Takes off his coat*)

GRANDMA   What happened?

LI   Mother! (*Sings* hsi-p'i *flowing beat*)

At the porridge stall, as I contacted the knife-sharpener,
Police car sirens sounded, and Japanese swarmed out to search.
But the knife-sharpener covered me by luring away the wolves.
Seizing the chance, I opened the lunchbox and hid the secret code.
I hid it at the bottom of the porridge where it can't be found . . .

T'IEH-MEI   Uncle Knife-sharpener was wonderful!

GRANDMA   Yü-ho, so where is the secret code?

LI   Mother! (*Confiding in her, he continues singing*)   To prevent any slip, I've stored it in a safer place.

T'IEH-MEI   Daddy, you really are resourceful.

LI   T'ieh-mei, now you know all about it. It is more important than our lives. We would rather have our heads cut off than reveal the secret. You understand?

T'IEH-MEI   Of course I understand.

LI   So you do understand. Just look at this good child!

T'IEH-MEI   Oh, Daddy . . .

LI   Ah . . .

(*It gradually gets dark.* GRANDMA LI *brings over a kerosene lamp*)

GRANDMA   Ah . . . look at you two.

LI   Mother, I have something to do. I have to go out again.

GRANDMA   All right. Be careful! Come back quickly.

LI   Okay. Don't worry.

T'IEH-MEI   Daddy, put this scarf around you. (*She puts a scarf around his neck*) Daddy, be sure you come back early.

LI (*Lovingly*)   Don't you worry. (*He goes out the door, exits*)

(T'IEH-MEI *closes the door.* GRANDMA LI *polishes the signal lantern with great care as* T'IEH-MEI *gazes at her intently*)

GRANDMA   Come, T'ieh-mei. Let me tell you the story about this red lantern.

T'IEH-MEI   Ai. (*Very happily, she goes over to the table and sits down*)

GRANDMA (*Seriously*)   This red lantern has, for many years, lighted the paths upon which we poor people have trod. It has lighted the paths for us workers. In the past, your grandpa held it. Now your father holds it. My child, you already know what happened last night. At crucial junctures, we cannot part with it. You must remember: this red lantern is our family's treasured heirloom.

T'IEH-MEI   Oh, the red lantern is our family's treasured heirloom?

(GRANDMA LI *looks at* T'IEH-MEI *with confidence and trust, then she walks into the back room.* T'IEH-MEI *picks up the lantern, examines it carefully, and ponders it.*)

T'IEH-MEI (*Sings—hsi-p'i scattered beat*)

I heard Grandma tell

(*Switches to swaying beat*) About the red lantern,
Her words were few, but their meaning, profound.
Why don't my father and uncles
(*Switches to standard beat*) Fear any danger?
Because they want to save China, save the poor and defeat the Japanese devils.
I think: what they do everyone should try to do;
What they are we all should try to be.
Oh, T'ieh-mei!
(*Switches to vigorous flowing beat*) You are seventeen, and no longer young.
Why don't you help father to lighten his worries?
For instance, if father carries a thousand catty load,
You, T'ieh-mei, should bear eight hundred.
(GRANDMA LI *comes out of the back room*)
GRANDMA   T'ieh-mei, T'ieh-mei!
T'IEH-MEI   Grandma!
GRANDMA   My child, what are you thinking about?
T'IEH-MEI   Nothing.
(*A child's cry is heard from the neighbor's house*)
GRANDMA (*Sighs*)   Ai! They have nothing to eat again. We still have some cornmeal left. Hurry and take it over to them.
T'IEH-MEI   Yes, Grandma. (*She puts the cornmeal into a container*)
(HUI-LIEN *enters and knocks at the door*)
HUI-LIEN   Grandma Li!
T'IEH-MEI   Cousin Hui-lien is here.
GRANDMA   Hurry up, open the door for her.
T'IEH-MEI   Yes, Grandma. (*She opens the door.* HUI-LIEN *enters*)
GRANDMA (*With concern*)   Oh, Hui-lien, how is the baby?
HUI-LIEN (*Sighs*)   How can I afford to take the child to a doctor? These days, fewer and fewer people send me clothes for mending or washing. In our house, we've been living from meal to meal, but now there's nothing left, nothing at all.
T'IEH-MEI   Cousin Hui-lien, here, take this. (*She hands her the cornmeal*)
HUI-LIEN (*Extremely touched*)   . . .
GRANDMA   Go ahead, take it. I was just sending T'ieh-mei to bring it over to you.
HUI-LIEN (*Accepting the flour*)   You are so kind to us!
GRANDMA   Don't say that. The wall is the only thing separating us—otherwise we would be one family.
T'IEH-MEI   Grandma, we are one family even if we don't tear the wall down.
GRANDMA   T'ieh-mei is right.
(*The child cries again*)
AUNTIE T'IEN (*Calling from offstage*)   Hui-lien, Hui-lien!
(AUNTIE T'IEN *enters*)
T'IEH-MEI   Hi, Auntie.
GRANDMA   Auntie, come here and sit down.
AUNTIE T'IEN   I can't. The child is crying again. Hui-lien, go home and look after the child.

(*Seeing the flour in* HUI-LIEN's *hand, she is very touched*)

GRANDMA   Make some food for the child first.

AUNTIE T'IEN   But you yourselves don't have enough to eat.

GRANDMA   Ai! (*Warmly*) Between our two families, whatever is ours is also yours. So don't even think of it.

AUNTIE T'IEN   We have to get back.

GRANDMA   Don't hurry. Take care!

(AUNTIE T'IEN *and* HUI-LIEN *exit*)

T'IEH-MEI (*Closing the door*)   Grandma, Cousin Hui-lien and her family have suffered too much!

GRANDMA   Yes. In the past, her father was a porter working on the railroad. He was crushed to death by a train. The Japanese devils not only didn't give them any compensation, they even seized her husband to work for them without pay. T'ieh-mei, our two families are working people sharing the same hatred and bitterness. We must take good care of them.

(FAKE LIAISON MAN, *an enemy agent in disguise, enters, knocks at the door*)

T'IEH-MEI   Who is it?

FAKE LIAISON MAN   Does Li Yü-ho live here?

T'IEH-MEI   Someone looking for daddy.

GRANDMA   Open the door.

T'IEH-MEI   All right! (*She opens the door*)

(FAKE LIAISON MAN *enters the room and hurriedly closes the door behind him*)

GRANDMA   You are . . .

FAKE LIAISON MAN   I sell wooden combs.

GRANDMA   Do you have one made of peachwood?

FAKE LIAISON MAN   Yes, I do, but I want cash.

T'IEH-MEI   All right. Wait.

(FAKE LIAISON MAN *puts his pack down and turns around.* T'IEH-MEI *is about to get the signal lantern.* GRANDMA LI *stops her. Instead, she picks up the kerosene lamp to test the man.* T'IEH-MEI *suddenly understands*)

FAKE LIAISON MAN (*Turns back, sees the lamp*)   So I finally found you, thank Heavens. It wasn't easy, believe me!

(T'IEH-MEI's *surprise turns to anger; she is unable to control herself*)

GRANDMA (*Realizes the plot, very calmly*)   All right, my man. Come on, show us your wooden combs so we can choose one.

FAKE LIAISON MAN   What are you talking about, old lady? I came here to get the secret code.

GRANDMA   Child, what is he talking about?

FAKE LIAISON MAN   Don't interrupt, grandma. The secret code is a very important document of the Communist Party. It has a great deal to do with the future of the revolution. Come on, give it to me, hurry up.

T'IEH-MEI (*Angrily chasing him out*)   Don't talk nonsense here. Get out.

FAKE LIAISON MAN   Don't, don't . . .

T'IEH-MEI   Get out!

(T'IEH-MEI *pushes the man out of the door, throws his pack at him, and slams the door with a bang*)

T'IEH-MEI   Oh, Grandma!

(GRANDMA *quickly stops* T'IEH-MEI *from talking.* FAKE LIAISON MAN *calls two plainclothes agents over to watch* LI's *house, and then exits*)

T'IEH-MEI Grandma, I almost fell into his trap.

GRANDMA My child, there must be someone who has turned traitor and betrayed us.

T'IEH-MEI In that case, what shall we do?

GRANDMA (*Whispers*) Hurry, tear off the signal.

T'IEH-MEI What signal?

GRANDMA That red butterfly on the window.

T'IEH-MEI (*Understands*) Oh. (*About to tear it off*)

GRANDMA T'ieh-mei, open the door and use it to block the light. You tear the signal off, I'll sweep the ground to cover you. Hurry, hurry!

(T'IEH-MEI *opens the door, and* LI YÜ-HO *enters in haste. He closes the door.* T'IEH-MEI *is frightened and* GRANDMA LI *drops her broom to the ground*)

LI (*Sensing something wrong*) Mother, has something happened?

GRANDMA There are "dogs" outside.

(LI YÜ-HO *shows no fear. He quickly arrives at a conclusion about the enemy situation*)

GRANDMA Oh, my son, my son!

LI Mother, it is possible that I'll be arrested. (*Instructs his mother very cautiously*) The secret code is hidden under the stone tablet by the old locust tree on the western bank of the river. You must try your best to deliver it to the knife-sharpener. The password remains the same.

GRANDMA The password remains the same.

LI Right! You must be very careful.

GRANDMA Don't you worry, son.

T'IEH-MEI Daddy ...

(*Auxiliary warrant officer* HOU *of the Japanese military police enters, knocks on the door*)

HOU Is Li *Shih-fu* home?

LI Mother, they're here.

T'IEH-MEI Daddy, you ...

LI T'ieh-mei, open the door.

T'IEH-MEI Yes, Daddy.

HOU Open the door!

(T'IEH-MEI *opens the door, seizing that moment of activity to tear off the red butterfly*)

HOU (*Entering*) Oh, you must be Li *Shih-fu.*

LI Yes, I am.

HOU Captain Hatoyama invites you to a party. (*He hands the "invitation" over*)

LI Oh? Captain Hatoyama invites me to a banquet?

HOU Correct.

LI My goodness! What an honor! (*Scornfully he throws the invitation on the table*)

HOU To make friends. Li *Shih-fu,* shall we?

LI After you, please. (*To his mother, firmly and solemnly*) Mother, take care of yourself! I am going now.

GRANDMA Just a minute. T'ieh-mei, bring some wine here.

T'IEH-MEI   Yes, Grandma. (*She goes to the back room to get wine*)

HOU   Hey! Old lady, there's lots of wine at the banquet, more than enough for him to drink.

GRANDMA   Ah ... poor people are used to drinking their own wine, because drop by drop it soaks deep into their hearts. (*She takes the wine* T'IEH-MEI *has brought in and bids* LI YÜ-HO *farewell, dignified yet emotional*) Now, my son, this bowl of wine ... you, you, you drink it down.

LI (*Solemnly receives the wine*)   Mother, with this wine at the bottom of my heart, I can cope with whatever wine they may offer me. (*Drinks it up in a gulp*) Mother, thank you, thank you, thank you!

(*Heroically sings—hsi-p'i two-six beat*)

Upon parting I drink a bowl of Mother's wine,

Courage fills this whole body of mine.

"To make friends with me?" Hatoyama invites me to dine;

I can handle him now, whatever his line.

Time is awry, storms descend without warning—Mother,

You must always be mindful of the changing weather.

T'IEH-MEI   Daddy! (*She throws herself onto the bosom of* LI YÜ-HO, *sobbing*)

LI (*Continues singing his covert message, with intense affection and feeling*)

Little T'ieh-mei, watch the weather when going out to sell.

"Accounts," coming in and going out, you should remember well.

When tired, watch the door, beware of stray dogs roaming free;

When depressed, wait for the magpies to sing on the tree.

You should take over the family affairs

And share with grandma her concerns and her cares.

T'IEH-MEI   Daddy! (*Sobs on her father's bosom*)

HOU   Li *Shih-fu,* shall we go?

LI (*To* T'IEH-MEI)   My child, don't cry. From now on, listen to your grandma.

T'IEH-MEI   Yes, Daddy.

GRANDMA   T'ieh-mei, open the door. Let your father go to the "banquet!"

LI   Mother, I am leaving now.

(LI *holds his mother's hands tightly, and each encourages the other to keep struggling.* T'IEH-MEI *opens the door. A cold wind blows in. In heroic and majestic stride with head held high,* LI *goes out against the wind.* HOU *follows*)

(T'IEH-MEI *picks up the scarf, chases her father, shouting, "Daddy!"* ENEMY AGENTS A, B, *and* C *rush in, stopping* T'IEH-MEI.)

AGENT A   Stop. Get back!

(*He forces* T'IEH-MEI *back. The agents enter the house*)

T'IEH-MEI   Oh, Grandma ...

AGENT A   Search! Don't move!

(*The agents search and mess up the household. One of them finds a copy of an almanac, opens it up and then throws it away*)

AGENT A   Let's go.

(*Exit the* AGENTS)

T'IEH-MEI (*Closes the door, pulls down the window curtain, looks about*)   Grandma! (*She throws herself into her grandma's arms and sobs. A little while later*) Grandma, my daddy ... will he return?

GRANDMA   Your father . . .

T'IEH-MEI   Oh, Daddy! . . .

GRANDMA   T'ieh-mei, your tears cannot save your father. Don't cry. Our family . . . It is time you should know about our family.

T'IEH-MEI   Know what?

GRANDMA   Sit down, child. Let Grandma tell you.

   (GRANDMA *gazes at the scarf, and all the past revolutionary events come back to her. Old hatred and new hatred bubble up in her mind.* T'IEH-MEI *moves a tiny stool and sits by her grandmother*)

GRANDMA   Child, your father . . . is he nice?

T'IEH-MEI   Daddy is nice.

GRANDMA   But your daddy is not your real father!

T'IEH-MEI (*Shocked*)   Ah? What did you say, Grandma?

GRANDMA   I am not your real grandmother either!

T'IEH-MEI   Ah? Grandma, grandma, you must be crazy.

GRANDMA   No, I am not. My child, we three generations are not from one family. (*Stands up*) Your family name is Ch'en, mine is Li, and your father's is Chang. (*Sings*—erh-huang *scattered beat*)

These past seventeen years have been stormy times, and I'm afraid to talk about the past.

I fear that you are too young and your will is not strong.

Several times I have tried but I just couldn't open my mouth.

T'IEH-MEI   Grandma, tell me. I won't cry.

GRANDMA (*Sings*—*slow three-beat*)

It looks as though your dad will never come home again this time.

And I, your grandmother, will be arrested and put in jail.

I see the heavy burden of the revolution soon falling on your shoulders.

(*Switches to vigorous flowing beat*) I've told you the truth. Oh, T'ieh-mei! Don't you cry, don't be sad!

You must stand firm, you must be strong!

(*Switches to standard beat*) Learn from your father, to have a red, loyal heart and a will as strong as steel.

T'IEH-MEI   Grandma, please sit down and tell me everything slowly.

   (T'IEH-MEI *helps her grandmother sit down*)

GRANDMA (*Sighs*)   Hai! It is a long, long tale! In those early years, your grandfather worked as a repairman in the locomotive shop on the river banks in Hankow. He had two apprentices. One was your real father, Ch'en Chih-hsing.

T'IEH-MEI   My real father, Ch'en Chih-hsing?

GRANDMA   One was your present father, Chang Yü-ho.

T'IEH-MEI   Oh? Chang Yü-ho?

GRANDMA   At that time, the warlords fought each other and the whole country was in turmoil. Later (*She stands up*), Chairman Mao and the Communist Party led the Chinese people to revolt. In February of 1923, the railroad workers organized an all-China union at Chengchow. Wu P'ei-fu, that running dog of foreign devils, would not permit them to form a union. So the union headquarters called a strike; all the workers of that line walked off their jobs. More than 10,000 workers along the river banks marched in demonstration. That evening, the weather was just as cold and the sky just as dark as today. I worried about your grandfather. I could neither sit still nor sleep. By the lamp light I mended old clothes. Suddenly I heard someone knocking at the door, shouting, "Mother Li, open the door, hurry!" So I quickly opened the door, and a man rushed in.

T'IEH-MEI Who was he?

GRANDMA He was your dad.

T'IEH-MEI My dad?

GRANDMA Your present dad. I saw he was wounded all over, holding this signal lantern in his left hand.

T'IEH-MEI Signal lantern?

GRANDMA He held a child in his right arm.

T'IEH-MEI A child ...

GRANDMA A baby not quite a year old ...

T'IEH-MEI That child ...

GRANDMA It was no one else ...

T'IEH-MEI Who?

GRANDMA It was *you!*

T'IEH-MEI *Me?*

GRANDMA Your daddy held you tightly in his arm; with tears in his eyes, he stood in front of me and cried, "Mother Li, Mother Li!" Then he just stared at me, unable to utter any words. I was so upset I urged him to speak up, fast! He ... he ... he said, "My *Shih-fu* and my brother Ch'en ... they ... they all sacrificed their lives. This child is the only heir of my brother Ch'en ... a second generation of the revolution. I must raise her so that she can continue with the revolution!" Then he repeatedly called out, "Mother Li, Mother Li! From now on, I will be your own son, and this child will be your own granddaughter." At that moment, I ... I ... I took you over and held you tightly in my arms!

T'IEH-MEI Oh, Grandma! (*She rushes to her grandmother's bosom*)

GRANDMA Now, stand up, and stand straight! Listen to your grandma.
(*Sings*—erh-huang *standard beat*)
During a labor strike your parents' blood the devils' hands did stain;
Since then Li Yü-ho has worked hard so the Revolution may obtain;
He's vowed to carry on for those martyrs that the red lantern may shine again;
He wiped the blood off, buried the dead and went back to the fireline.
Now the Japanese bandits have come to loot, kill, and burn;
You've watched your father taken to jail, never to return.
Note this "account" of blood and tears, note it down well,
(*Switches to vigorous flowing beat*) You must set a heroic goal, steel your will, get even with the foe,
For a blood debt can only be with blood redeemed.

T'IEH-MEI (*Sings*—erh-huang *standard beat*)
Hearing Grandma talk about revolution, oh, how sad yet heroic!
I now realize I've grown up in the midst of these storms.
Oh, Grandma, for seventeen years of rearing the debt I owe you is deep as the ocean.

(*Switches to vigorous flowing beat*) From now on I'll aim high and keep
my eyes clear.
I'll demand an eye for an eye; I must carry on the task left by the martyrs.
Now I raise the red lantern, let its light brighten all four corners.
Daddy!...
(*Switches to fast beat*) My father's will is, like the tall pine, unbending
and strong.
A brave Communist he is, a pillar between the earth and the sky.
Daddy, I shall follow you forward without any hesitation.
Now the red lantern is raised high, its light, bright as day.
For my father to slaughter those beasts, it will light up the way.
Generation after generation, in the battlefield we shall remain
Until all the vicious wolves have been slain.
(T'IEH-MEI *and* GRANDMA *raise the red lantern high, striking a dramatic
stance. The lantern shines bright.*
(*Stage dims*)

(*Curtain*)

[In Acts VI–XI, LI faces the Japanese captain who has known him before.
Tortures follow LI's refusal to cooperate. Meanwhile, his house is under surveillance, but T'IEH-MEI sneaks out the neighbor's door. The Japanese arrest
GRANDMA and T'IEH-MEI in order to coerce LI. That failing, GRANDMA and
LI are executed after much heroic declaration, while T'IEH-MEI is allowed to go
home, secretly tailed. Again the neighbor aids T'IEH-MEI's escape. She finally
succeeds in delivering the code book to the guerrilla leader as the Japanese and
the traitors all die in a clash with the guerrilla unit.]

Translated by Richard F. S. Yang

YANG HAN-SHENG
(Ou-yang Chi-hsiu, 1902–)

Yang Han-sheng was born in Kao-hsien, Szechwan Province, and graduated in sociology from the University of Shanghai. He joined the Communist Party in 1925 and served under the command of General Yeh T'ing. After participating in the unsuccessful Nanchang Uprising of 1927, which was led by Chou En-lai, Yang went to Shanghai to work with the leftist literary groups. Between 1930 and 1937 he was a key member of the League of Left-wing Writers, serving for a period as the head of the Party branch in that organization. In 1936 he supported Chou Yang's National Defense Literary Movement in opposition to Lu Hsün, who castigated Yang as one of the Band of Four Ultra-leftists, ironically anticipating his own downfall as one of the "four rightist villains" thirty years later.

While in Shanghai, Yang, using the pen name Hua Han, wrote three stories published in one volume under the title *The Underground Spring.* These stories deal with the peasant problem in the late 1920s. The leftists greeted the book with enthusiastic acclaim, praising it as a model for progressive literature. Yang also wrote movie scripts for the Star Company, including such romantic and melodramatic pieces as "Life's Melancholy Tune," "The Tide of Wrath in the China Sea," and "Loyalty in Life and Death," which were very popular.

During the war, Yang held posts in the political-cultural agencies of the Nationalist government, working with Kuo Mo-jo and other leftist writers. He produced a good number of very successful plays, including *The Wind and Cloud on the Frontier, The Spring and Autumn of the Taiping Kingdom of Heaven,* and *The Death of Li Hsiu-ch'eng.* After the war, he returned to Shanghai, where he continued to work for the Communist cause and at the same time wrote more screenplays for the K'un Lun Motion Picture Company.

The Communist take-over of 1949 sent Yang Han-sheng to the Cultural and Educational Commission of the State Council as its deputy secretary-general, holding simultaneously the position of chairman of the screenwriters guild, vice-chairman of the Federation of Literary and Art Circles, and secretary of its Party branch. His writing activity was much reduced. His screenplay *The Northland and South of the River,* written in 1962 from his fresh experience of participating in the north in the Great Leap Forward, drew wide attention for a time but brought him severe criticism during the Cultural Revolution. The charge pointed out his failure to uphold the Communist Party's efficient leadership, because the film tends to emphasize the interrelated forces in society at any given moment in history. Of his earlier works, *The Death of Li Hsiu-ch'eng* (a hero in the Taiping Rebellion) was denounced for its alleged stress on defeat and surrender—a traitor's attitude.

Yang dropped out of sight in 1965 and did not reappear in public until the very end of 1978. In January 1979, he was reported to have regained an important assignment in the government, handling cultural affairs.   —D.D.

from *The Northland and South of the River*

[The People's Republic of China is a very late comer in cinematics; even her best footage exhibited in the United States in August 1978 failed to impress the seasoned reviewers in New York. But the screenwriters in Peking understand the power of the screen in mass education and they are making their cinema serve, quite effectively, their political and revolutionary causes. *The Northland and South of the River* is no exception.

First, the plot:

Tung Wang, a poor and bankrupt man, is fleeing from a tyrannical landlord. In his flight, Tung asks his brother, Tzu-chang, to care for his son, Hsiao-wang. The brother refuses; luckily Wu Ta-ch'eng, a poor peasant but progressive and generous, offers to care for Hsiao-wang as the pursuers draw near. Tung Wang barely escapes, but Wu Ta-ch'eng is implicated; and after a fierce struggle, he too finds himself a fugitive, fleeing from home.

Years pass. Wu Ta-ch'eng and his family have long since settled in a rural farm community; Wu is the village leader and has raised Hsiao-wang into a strong young man. The days go by peacefully and happily. Hsiao-wang and Kuei-fen, the daughter of a local villager, fall in love. Then, in this particular year, the weather has been exceptionally dry; the villagers are worried about their crops. As their leader, Wu makes plans to have wells dug. The work begins and progresses; but gradually, as winter approaches, the work becomes increasingly difficult. To add to the hardship, other disasters occur, the weather turns worse, and Ch'ien San-t'ai, a counterrevolutionary, sabotages their efforts, bringing the work to a halt.

Chang Chung, a man who has appeared on several timely occasions to assist Wu Ta-ch'eng, comes again and brings to Wu's attention where his problems lie. The sabotage is discovered and soon thereafter the work returns to a normal pace. Again, the community is at peace. But Tung Tzu-chang, Hsiao-wang's worthless uncle, has been living in the village and constantly acting contrary to the people's ideals and purposes. In addition to trying to do business for private gain, he finally persuades Hsiao-wang to leave the community for the city to seek excitement and a better life-style.

A new conflict is created in Wu Ta-ch'eng's household as Hsiao-wang, against the advice of everyone, including the girl he loves, decides to leave, having been poisoned by his uncle's deceit. Fortunately, Tung Tzu-chang, in a moment of drunken stupor, shows his villainy. He is apprehended and forced to make a public confession and apology. The film ends as Chang Chung returns with Wu Ta-ch'eng's wife, blinded earlier, now completely healed through successful treatment. Once again, happiness is the order of the day.

From the first frame, the film's unmistakable atmosphere is noticeable, identifying its national origin and tradition. Even in revolutionary times and with such a remarkably scientific medium, the initial setting is reminiscent of scenes from such Chinese classics as *The Songs of the South* and *Water Margin*. The mood of desolation, its poetic qualities, indeed the very words used to begin the filmscript are familiar to countless such settings, dramatically highlighted and coupled with a mournful song, resembling the weaving together of poetry with prose, found in centuries of popular drama and fiction.

A cold and desolate embankment.
The skies barely glimmer with light, their colors still hidden; and opaque is the
    mist riding low on a morning breeze, sweeping across a field. On the fields,
    once growing pastures show withered and desiccated.
Large patches of agricultural fields appear to have been put to the torch and
    now lie completely blackened and dead.
September, just when autumn is cold.
From the distance comes the mournful song of shepherds:

> Ten years, drought and famine; nine without harvest:
> Even fires are cold, and chilling smoke oppresses each home.
> The landlords are wolves; the officials are like tigers!
> And on countless miles of fields are harbored the sounds of crying.
> Endless chains of mountains, and endlessly circling waters—
> A life, a generation! Working like beasts.
> Ceaseless flow tears, inadequate to speak the suffering,
> In times like these, is there never an end?
> In times like these, is there never an end?

[The film begins by making direct use of action and suspense to heighten interest and provide the necessary narrative exposition. At the same time, it establishes the contrasting environments needed to give appropriate commentary to life before and after the revolution; we must first witness the social ills that led to necessary change. A destitute father, chased by the gang of a tyrannical landlord, is forcibly separated from his son.]

TUNG WANG   So, let's go!
HSIAO-WANG   Dad, I don't want to go . . .
TUNG WANG (*Desperate*)   Hurry up! Let's go. Don't make me mad.
HSIAO-WANG (*Still chewing a potato, stares at his father*)   I . . . I don't want to
    go . . .
TUNG WANG (*Stamps his feet and with tears in his eyes*)   You don't want to
    come with me? Where would you go? You don't have a mother! Now, come
    on!
(HSIAO-WANG, *deeply hurt, starts to cry.* TUNG WANG *drags* HSIAO-WANG
    towards the door)

[The separation of parent from child suggests a melodramatic prototype common in Chinese literature even before the flowering of drama in the Yüan dynasty; its prevalence continues unabated, in the absence of such other forms as tragedy or the more sharply distinguished categories of the comic and the serious. The primary response the above scene hopes to elicit is "What kind of society would allow this to happen?" rather than "What kind of person would do something like this?" since the villain has not been adequately revealed to us. At the same time, this act of melodrama provides an opportunity to depict virtue. Wu Ta-ch'eng, at whose home the above scene takes place, intervenes and persuades Tung Wang to leave the son to his care. The charity is expressed in clichés: "As long as I have food, your son will have food," and "as long as I have life, he will be taken care of."

Yang Han-sheng is fully aware of the fact that melodrama depicts well-defined and predictable entities of character and action, while the overall plot structure may often be extremely circuitous and episodic. It is a form that communicates well to the masses and is hence well suited for promulgating for popular consumption ideologic and sociologic points of view. In view of the requirements for the arts at this time, we can expect to find in Yang's melodrama some expression of the greatest national fears and the greatest national commitments. We note further that pathos, in addition to an association with the matter of social injustice, relates to the "complaint motif," a device traditional to Chinese poetry since the *Shih Ching*, the earliest Chinese anthology. To that extent the revolutionary art of the People's Republic shows important ties to the past.

The virtue thus depicted is, more often than not, a homely virtue and not the awesome acts of Greek tragic heroes. Wu Ta-ch'eng's charity is revealed in the exchange translated above, but a more glaring and more typical example of heroism is illustrated by the following excerpt, taken from about the middle of the film. The scene is night in the midst of a severe winter storm with temperatures well below zero. The villagers have assembled to discuss the problems of digging the wells, a task that has become frustratingly difficult. Before solutions can be raised, Ch'ien San-t'ai brings word that the dynamite sticks have been used up in a remote mountain area, and someone voices the opinion that the work must now come to a stop. Wu Ta-ch'eng retorts that the suggestion is unacceptable and then asks for volunteers to bring more dynamite to that area on foot, a difficult and dangerous task.]

(*There is a moment of silence*)

LAO CHENG (*Suddenly comes forward*)   I'll go! If I can't get the dynamite back in any other way, I can at least use my own back to carry it.

T'IEN LU   You've got to be kidding. Look, Associate Director, don't you understand? If you drop the stuff, it'll explode! Have you lived too long to care about life any more?

K'UNG SZU (*Sarcastically*)   Heh, Lao Cheng, even if just for the sake of your young wife, I think you ought to live a while longer.

LAO CHENG   You spineless mice! What do you know? You think I'm bragging, don't you? Among us, who besides me has ever handled the transport of dynamite? Have you all forgotten? During the Liberation struggle, it was I who delivered dynamite to the front line! If I don't do it, who will?

CHENG'S WIFE (*Anxious and torn at the same time, scolds him in a low voice*)   Look at you! You want to go, just like that. Didn't you think at least to talk to me about it first?

LAO CHENG   This is not a matter for discussion with you.

CHENG'S WIFE (*Angrily*)   I won't let you go!

LAO CHENG (*Imploring*)   Oh, please, let me go.

CHENG'S WIFE (*Ignores her husband and suddenly steps forward. She points to* LAO CHENG *and says in a loud voice*)   Don't listen to him. He's just bragging. . . .

LAO CHENG (*Changes his attitude, his voice serious*)   I'm sorry, Er-sao, I'll listen to you about anything, except this. On this, you've got to listen to me. I'm not careless of life. But since this is for the sake of all of us, for the sake of our children and our grandchildren, so that they might see the light of happy days . . . How can I not go?

(CHENG'S WIFE *is too angry to say anything*)

WU TA-CH'ENG   You may go, Lao Cheng, but . . .

[In view of the socio-political climate of 1962 in the People's Republic, we can, without even seeing the film, make reasonably accurate assumptions about the manner of presentation, the nature of the acting, and perhaps even the view the cameraman seeks, all of which render a relatively heroic but rather formal posturing of characters, speeches, ideas, and acts. At no time would it seem necessary, desirable, or possible for the audience to ponder over the righteousness of an ideal, the moral label of each character, or the relative merits of the decisions and actions embraced. Hence, the film's artistic aims are found in the conviction, the degree of sincerity and poignancy, with which characters and deeds are presented. If the plot outline given earlier suggests a complexity in the narrative development, it is, after all, not unusual for melodrama to rely on a number of twists and turns of story as its main source of complication.

It would appear that the necessary compliance to making statements about the State's cause would have been adequately, if not nobly, performed by such scenes as the above; Yang Han-sheng, however, did not appear totally insensitive to the one-dimensional nature of such heroic expostulations, and he portrayed convincingly the nagging doubts, the uncertainty, and the weariness present in such singular devotions.

In the final complication of the film, we see Hsiao-wang's decision to leave the village. Poisoned by his uncle's deceit, he is torn between his desire to leave for the city and his love for Kuei-fen. What makes his dilemma convincing is both the screenwriter's art in portraying with restraint Hsiao-wang's inner struggle and our own ability to relate to this problem; the appeal of the city and its magnetic attraction to the young growing up in small rural areas are universal problems. There are three brief scenes which deal with this situation, all coming near the end of the film.]

(HSIAO-WANG *and* KUEI-FEN *are alone, secluded behind a rock pile. They are quarreling*)

HSIAO-WANG (*Interrupting her*)   You must be the one who told them! Let me ask you, did you tell them everything?

KUEI-FEN   What are you afraid of? You seem already set on leaving. If you are right, you should talk things over with Brother Ta-ch'eng.

HSIAO-WANG   How can I talk with him now? I haven't even settled the matter with you. What's there for me to say to him at this point?

KUEI-FEN (*Surprised*)   Me? What are you talking about?

HSIAO-WANG (*Very touchingly*)   I . . . I need you to go with me! Since sooner
or later we'll live together. Why don't you go quickly and get permission
from your father!

(KUEI-FEN, *shocked by the suddenness of all this, shakes her head, speechless*)

[Shortly after the above scene, Hsiao-Wang is confronted by Ming-hsin, who
grew up with him under Wu Ta-ch'eng's care.]

(*In the woods*)

MING-HSIN (*Annoyed*)   Don't give me that! You're only thinking of getting
away! You're afraid of hardship and you yearn for ease and comfort!

HSIAO-WANG   No! It's not that I'm just thinking of myself! I don't want to risk
my life recklessly. Here, it's . . . A period of wind, a period of snow . . . After
the planting, drought; after the drought, planting . . . more drought, more
planting; more planting, more drought . . . over and over and over again,
without ever an end! We start working before daybreak and end it after dark
every day; we shoulder our loads; we push the carts; we work our backs,
burden our shoulders! What time do we have for ourselves? The irrigation
system needs work; a tree belt is needed as a windbreaker! Here we're flying
kites under the table—you can't get anything up high no matter how you try!

(*Upon the last words, a slapping sound interrupts from* MING-HSIN's *hand
against* HSIAO-WANG's *face. Thereupon, the two begin to fight*)

[The dilemma Hsiao-wang finds himself in seems convincingly portrayed;
and, presumably, it accurately points to existing conditions and problems in his
society. We may wish to credit Yang Han-sheng with both honesty and artistic
sensitivity, but we should not be surprised to discover that the movie fell under
critical attack: Yang's presentation of the more "negative" aspects of life in the
rural communities of the People's Republic of China was said to undermine the
people's enthusiasm toward laboring in the outlying areas. Yang more thoroughly belabored the problems than he shed light on solutions.

It is also interesting to evaluate Yang's attitudes toward that age-old di-
chotomy of town versus country. His interest in the rural setting has been
nearly life-long. To a great extent, he embraces the traditional writers' stance,
which portrays the country as the seat of innocence, purity, and honest dili-
gence. The town, on the other hand, has typically been viewed as the locus of
deceit, evil, and parasitic sloth. It is true that Yang focuses our attention on the
problems of life in the rural community, the unending hardships, the constant
struggle against natural elements; and typical to melodrama, which introduces
problems and complications seemingly from out of nowhere, this selection of
locations most hostile to human survival easily provides a stream of conflicts
for the characters to react against. But Yang's presentation of life's hardships
in the villages is nevertheless given from the perspective of an artist concerned
with showing the dynamics of human struggle and courage as well as ultimate
triumph. Nowhere is there an unsympathetic condemnation of farm life in
favor of the glitters of the city.

The translation that follows is taken from the latter part of the film (Part IV, section 3). It is not a part of the film which advances the plot. Instead, the scene is like a short, independent movement, a segment of life showing yet another facet of the people and their lives in this small community. Yin-hua, Wu Ta-ch'eng's wife, is blind due to eye disease; courageously she makes herself useful by taking care of the village children on behalf of the working parents. But more important than this characterization of a rustic heroine and her contribution to the community's cause is the following more developed sequence of Yang's artistic techniques, his presentation of a touching village scene, showing the basic humanity of a community and its participants, a scene that presumably would be castigated by Yang's critics for not making his art speak forcefully of social solutions or the more positive aspects of life in this new society.]

(WU TA-CH'ENG's *home*)
(*Outside, a heavy, freezing snow storm; the wind cuts like knives. It is bitterly cold*)
(*Inside,* YIN-HUA *is speaking to a 12-year-old child*)
YIN-HUA   Hsiao Li, I've already talked it over with your family ... from now on, you're to come every day and help me take care of these young friends. How do you feel about it?
HSIAO LI (*Reluctantly*)   All right.
YIN-HUA (*Turns and speaks to the other children*)   Your families are all very busy now, so from now on, you're to come here and play. I'll be here to play with you, and to tell you stories. How about it?
CHILDREN   Good.
(MRS. CHENG *brings* T'IEH-SHU *in*)
MRS. CHENG (*to* YIN-HUA)   I've already mended your sister-in-law's clothes; I must get them to her right away, but this child simply won't let go of me.
YIN-HUA   You go on ahead. Leave the child here with me.
T'IEH-SHU   Grandma, I want to go see Mommy with you. I want to go! I want to go!
MRS. CHENG   It's snowing much too hard out. Why don't you play here with Auntie Wu. Grandma will be back soon, so be good.
(MRS. CHENG *takes her winter garment and leaves.* YIN-HUA *takes* T'IEH-SHU *by the hand*)
YIN-HUA   T'ieh-shu, would you like to hear a story? Come children, let's all sit close together. Hsiao Li, will you please help the children move some chairs?
(T'IEH-SHU *and several other children sit around* YIN-HUA, *facing her. But before everyone has settled down, two older children stealthily come in from outside. As soon as they enter, they gesture to the children sitting in front of* YIN-HUA; *they try to get them to go out and play in the snow, build snowmen, and have snowball fights.* HSIAO LI *and* T'IEH-SHU *as well as a few other children nod their heads to show they understand. And the two older children then quietly sneak back out*)
YIN-HUA (*Smiling*)   Is everyone seated? All right, then ... Let's first talk about some of the differences between a wolf and a dog. Then, I would like to tell you a story about a wolf hunting expedition. Would you like that?
CHILDREN   Yes!

YIN-HUA   Has anyone here ever seen old Mr. Wolf?

T'IEH-SHU   I haven't, but I've heard the wolf howl, and it's very frightening!

YIN-HUA   Do you think the wolf looks at all like the dog?

T'IEH-SHU   Yes, indeed!

YIN-HUA   But you've just said that you've never seen Mr. Wolf? How would you know that he's like a dog?

T'IEH-SHU   I've seen him in a picture.

(YIN-HUA *smiling, nods her head*)

(*The children, one and two at a time, begin to sneak out. The first is* HSIAO LI *and the last to follow is* T'IEH-SHU)

(*However,* YIN-HUA *continues to speak to the children happily*)

YIN HUA   Now listen carefully. The wolf is actually the early ancestor of the dog. Dogs and wolves do have many points in common; but they also have some important differences. And you should remember what they are. For example, old Mr. Wolf has a tail that always hangs down, while Mr. Dog's tail is always curled up. The wolf's neck is extremely long, whereas the dog's neck is quite short. Mr. Dog makes a sound that goes like "wow!" "wow!" "wow!" The wolf makes a sound that seems like some strange creature crying, "woooo!" "woooo!" When you hear it, it's very frightening.

(*Just as* YIN-HUA *finishes her imitation, the cry of a real wolf suddenly bursts forth.* YIN-HUA *hears this and responds with an unavoidable cold shiver*)

YIN-HUA   Did you hear that? What was that?

(*There is no answer. And* YIN-HUA *immediately realizes that there is not the usual commotion from the children*)

(*She is suddenly frightened and calls out*)

YIN-HUA   T'ieh-shu! T'ieh-shu!! Why don't you answer? Hsiao Li! Hsiao Li!

(*The house seems cold and quiet. As she does not hear the children, she is very upset and proceeds to grope about in search for them, until finally it dawns on her that* T'IEH-SHU *and the other children have gone outside. She feels a quick sensation of cold terror; and in haste she grabs a cane, then proceeds to call out* T'IEH-SHU*'s name while stumbling about to get to the outside*)

(*Outside the village in the distant snow-covered wilderness, a lone, hungry wolf cries out for a moment; then it heads straight towards the village*)

(*Outside the village*)

(T'IEH-SHU *and the other children are making snowmen and having snowball fights*)

(*They hear the cry of the wolf and are frightened. Turning about, they run and scream*)

CHILDREN   The wolf is coming! The wolf is really coming!

(*When* T'IEH-SHU *hears the wolf's cry, he too runs with the others; but because of his age, he cannot run fast; and in running, and falling, he is left farther and farther behind*)

(*The wolf is coming towards the village at a fast pace.* T'IEH-SHU *is running slowly*)

(YIN HUA *hears the screams of the children; she heads towards the edge of the village: she is running, and crying out, and asking for* T'IEH-SHU ...)

YIN-HUA   T'ieh-shu! T'ieh-shu! Hsiao Li! Hsiao Li! Where are you? Children, where is T'ieh-shu? Why did you children leave him behind?! T'ieh-shu! T'ieh-shu! Has anyone seen T'ieh-shu?!

(*One group of children, while running, respond*)

CHILDREN T'ieh-shu is still behind us—he can't run.

YIN-HUA (*Trembling*) Oh, heavens! T'ieh-shu! T'ieh-shu!

(*Up and down she scrambles toward the edge of the village.* TIEH-SHU *sees* YIN-HUA *coming toward him ...*)

T'IEH-SHU Auntie Wu!

(TIEH-SHU *rushes toward* YIN-HUA. YIN-HUA *dashes forward a few more steps and embraces* TIEH-SHU *in her arms, crying with tears of relief*)

YIN-HUA T'ieh-shu, don't be afraid, don't be afraid! I'm here; and that nasty wolf won't come here.

(*And indeed, as the hungry wolf rushes near, it turns and runs away upon seeing others*)

(MRS. CHENG, WU TA-CH'ENG, HSIAO-WANG *have all arrived*)

Comments and translation by Donald Dong

LU YANG-LIEH
(1931–)

Lu Yang-lieh is a soldier-writer in the ranks of the People's Liberation Army. After he studied at Chekiang College in Hangchow, he joined the army at the age of eighteen and worked in a cultural troupe. In 1953 he joined a semiprofessional group of writers, and wrote several short stories about army life.

The story "Star" is from Lu Yang-lieh's *Slave Girl Chin-chu,* a collection of eight stories describing Tibetan life in the old days and after Tibetan Liberation (1951). The title story has a "White-haired Girl" motif in which a slave girl is forced to live in a mountain cave, and years later is released to expose the evildoers.

The setting of "Star" is the Red Army on their historic Long March (1934–35), passing through Sikang Province. Combining intrigue and adventure, the story begins and ends with the same blind bard playing his Sgrian sitar; thus it revives the literary convention of a storyteller who participates in the action of his own narration. The star is the badge awarded to a slave for his heroic exploit in aiding the Red Army.   —M.T.

Star

I

The All-deities Festival is a joyous occasion for Tibetans. This auspicious day is also observed as the anniversary of the establishment of the Nima People's Commune.

At daybreak, the courtyard in front of the Nima Lama Temple is already congested with people. Staunch militiamen in traditional armor on horseback with swords at their waist are getting ready for the annual parade. Long-skirted girls, adorned in dresses of brocade silk, prepare to present their best dances. Peasants and herdsmen, production heroes from various villages, have brought their finest wool sheep, cows that give the sweetest milk, and barley seeds as big as beans.

Suddenly the sound of a samisen* is heard in front of the Great Scripture Hall. Hurray! The minstrel is here! He is immediately surrounded by the crowd. Seeing that he is a blind bard, the crowd quietly sits down and looks at him reverently.

The wandering minstrel sits upright in great dignity. Holding his *sgra-snyan,* a homemade samisen, he begins to play the familiar "Socialism is Wonderful" as a prelude. Then he sings a saga . . .

*A type of three-stringed banjo. [K.Y.H.]

813

II

Today I am going to tell about neither deities nor sprites. I am going to reveal to you the saga of the Sacred Mountain of Nima [the Sun], on which today you can see woodsmen, drilling machines, an electrical power station, and all the rest. In the past, it was a dark hell!

Black pines covered the whole mountain. Anyone venturing into it would most likely fall astray and be doomed by the vipers or bears, or venomous vapor from the decaying underbrush.

Yet, this black pine forest is a treasure land with an abundance of bears' gall, musk, fox furs, precious medicinal herbs, and the like, but it is not easy to get them. The Living Buddha of the temple used to force his *wa-tzu* [bondman, slave] to make an expedition for the treasures in the forest; the *wa-tzu* seldom came back. The rare survivors returned empty-handed.

Half a century ago, a *wa-tzu* named Bawu was born in the temple. Everyone said that he must be an incarnated mountain deity, or else he could not travel unharmed within the forest. Amazingly, he always came out with abundant treasures.

One day, on his tall white horse, Bawu returned from the Black Forest. He wore a long sword at his waist and an old English rifle slung across his shoulder, the fork supporting the gun barrel sticking up like two long swords. His iron-like right arm was free from the sleeve of his robe, thus revealing half his bare, bronze chest. Behind his saddle he carried a sack heavily filled with precious ginseng and worm-herb. It was not yet dark, but strangely the lights in the village were already lit. Even more strangely, the streets, which had been cluttered and smelly, were clean and tidy. Riding forward, Bawu could see brightly colored posters on the walls. But since he was illiterate, he did not know the themes of the posters. He was sure, however, that they were not incantations.

On a small open lot by a street intersection, a group of children, hand in hand, had formed a circle and were singing:

> Red Army brothers are going on the Long March,
> With clapping hands we bid them farewell.
> They will defeat the Japanese aggressors,
> So the nation can enjoy peace.

Bawu found this very curious. How had these children, who usually gathered only to quarrel and fight, become so civilized? What was the song?

Bawu got off his horse and walked over to watch the gathering. What had happened during his absence from the village for the past five or six days? Suddenly he beheld many Chinese soldiers in blue uniform, equipped with rifles and swords, walking on the village streets. Bawu was surprised and frightened. Two years ago some Chinese soldiers had camped in the village. Bawu hated them because they were the meanest men in the world. When they were happy, they would shoot yaks and sheep as living targets; when they were depressed, they would whip the villagers. They took the villagers' property any time, any place, as they wished.

Now Chinese soldiers were here again! The only difference was that they had had yellow uniforms two years ago.

"No matter how they dress, they are all alike," Bawu thought. He decided to avoid the Chinese. He walked his horse quickly past the soldiers.

Down the street, Bawu caught a glimpse of twenty or more villagers surrounding two Chinese soldiers. One of them stood on a rock, talking energetically. There was no indication that the villagers were frightened or disgusted. Instead, they listened attentively.

Bawu could not help but glance at the two Chinese soldiers. Something red caught his eye. Looking more carefully, he saw a red star fixed on the cap of each soldier.

Bawu proceeded to Nima Temple, which stands at the center of the village. As he arrived at the yellow outer wall, a little lama called to him, "Bawu, the Chief Steward wants to see you in the Great Scripture Hall."

Bawu could guess that the Chief Steward's summons was not auspicious; he wondered what sort of trouble he would encounter.

Bawu walked down the central approach to the temple. He became more amazed at each step he took. Many butter lamps were lighted. He wondered which Bodhisattva was celebrating a birthday today.

Under the staircase of the well-lit hall stood the big, greasy Chief Steward. As soon as he saw Bawu, he greeted him with a broad smile. Then he embraced Bawu in a solemn salute.

"Bawu, you must have had a wearisome journey."

This unusual courtesy struck Bawu dumb. He could not believe what he had heard. But the Chief Steward continued, "Bawu, your luck has come! The Living Buddha has sent for you!"

The upper stories of the Great Scripture Hall were the most sacred part of the temple. Even the lamas who were living in the temple, not to mention a *wa-tzu,* were not allowed to intrude. Today the Living Buddha wanted to see Bawu in his chamber. How could Bawu be at ease? He did not know his fate—he had to wait and see.

Following the Chief Steward, Bawu carefully watched his own feet ascending the steps to the inner sanctum.

The thick, heavy drapes and screens were rolled aside at the entrance. Brilliant lights projected from colorful glass lampshades. The floors, waxed with butter, appeared as clear as mirrors. The demoniac designs and figures lacquered on the wall gaped and stared. Bawu was giddy, not knowing whether he had come to Heaven or Hell.

The drapes were parted at the last doorway, to admit Bawu and the Chief Steward, who walked bending low in reverence. Bawu had to follow the example. The Chief Steward prostrated himself toward the yet unseen Living Buddha; Bawu did likewise, sticking his tongue out once and shaking himself, as the ritual required.

The salute over, Bawu lifted his head. To Bawu's surprise, the Living Buddha was not at all as he had imagined. He was not handsome and dignified like the Buddhas in the paintings or the scripture illustrations. What was this? The Living Buddha was an ugly old man sitting on a chair lined with tiger-skin. His bald head gleamed in the light. His sagging face was too big to match his short, dumpy stature.

"Living Buddha, Bawu is present by your command," the Chief Steward said, carefully pronouncing the words.

The Living Buddha opened his droopy eyes slightly and cast a glance upon Bawu. Then he pointed to the floor near his seat, saying, "Come here!"

The Chief Steward gestured to Bawu. Bawu walked on his knees to the place.

Bawu sat on the floor. The Living Buddha reached over and touched Bawu's forehead, chanting some Buddhist texts. Bawu never dreamed that he would receive such blessing! He was bewildered.

"Bawu," the Chief Steward said, "you have found favor with the Living Buddha. He is going to give you twenty yaks, fifty goats, a horse, and the rifle which you've been carrying on your shoulder. You may choose any one of the women from the village as your wife. Hereafter, you are going to lead a comfortable life, and you won't be required to serve in the temple."

Bawu could not believe what he had heard. This day was indeed a strange day full of strange events. Was the Mountain Sprite Nima really revealing His divine power? However, Bawu's thirty years of life told him that this game of reward without labor was a precursor to some imminent catastrophe.

As he expected, the Chief Steward said to him, "Bawu, since the Living Buddha is so kind to you, how are you going to repay his grace?"

"From my head to my toe, every hair and every inch of this skin of mine belongs to the Living Buddha. I will listen only to what the Living Buddha wills," Bawu said without any feeling.

The Chief Steward stretched his neck and came closer to him. "Did you see the Chinese soldiers in our village?"

Before Bawu could answer, the Chief Steward gnashed his teeth and added, "These Chinese soldiers are the most wicked among the wicked!"

Bawu could not understand the Chief Steward. Two years ago when the villagers hated the Chinese soldiers in yellow uniforms, the Living Buddha, the Chief Steward, and the Chinese *benbu* [officials] acted like dear brothers. But now ...

While Bawu was trying to puzzle it out, the Living Buddha screamed, "You must guide them to the Devil's Cliff!"

The Chief Steward immediately added an explanation: "These Chinese soldiers are going to the North tomorrow. They are bound to go through the Black Forest and climb Nima Peak. They do not know the way, so you must offer to guide them! But," the Chief Steward grinned, "you have to remember the words of the Living Buddha."

"Oh, the words bid me to kill," Bawu realized at once.

When confronting those who deserved death, Bawu's hand, holding a gun or a sword, never trembled, but the brave never kill without justification. Judging from the reactions of the villagers, the Chinese soldiers he had seen did not appear to be bad men. Why did the Living Buddha want to murder them?

Bawu was thinking to himself when a lama reported from the doorway, "The Chinese *benbu* has arrived."

As the Living Buddha and the Chief Steward rose to greet the guest, Bawu withdrew at once. When he passed through the big reception hall, he saw lamas preparing a large banquet. He realized that the Living Buddha wanted to hold a feast for the ranking Chinese official. He suspected that the food might be poisoned.

Bawu was thinking about what he, entrusted with a special mission, should do on the following day. Deep in thought, he descended the steps and collided with someone coming the opposite way, losing his balance. The other man reached down to help him. Bawu lifted his eyes and saw a Chinese soldier, who said apologetically, "Forgive me. Are you hurt?"

A little Chinese soldier who accompanied the other man stepped forward and bent to brush the dirt from Bawu's clothes. Bawu was embarrassed because the collision was his fault. While he struggled to say something polite to the soldiers, the Chief Steward appeared at the top of the staircase shouting, with an exaggerated smile, "Ah-ha, Mr. Political Commissar, the Living Buddha wishes to receive your honor. Please come in."

Bawu turned to watch the middle-aged Chinese military man with whom he had collided climb the stairs toward the Chief Steward. He asked himself, "Is he a *benbu*?"

III

With the permission of the Chief Steward, Bawu returned to his own home the following morning. Bawu's mother, who was old, thin, and weak, lived alone in a small tattered nomad's tent. Such a tiny tent! The Chief Steward had commented that the Bodhisattvas could not endure looking at it. Therefore, she was kept two miles away from the decent village.

Ordinarily, Bawu had to get special permission from the Chief Steward before he could go home at night, after his long day's servile work in the temple, to carry some water and grind some barley to feed his mother. Every spring, he had to arrange several nights to work on that small plot of land in front of his mother's tent, planting barley.

Now the barley was ripe. Bawu decided to harvest it before he set out to guide the Chinese soldiers through the Black Forest to Nima Peak.

Bawu hurried out of the village and down the road. In the fields on both sides of the road, full ears of barley pressed against one another, waving gently in the cool morning breeze, rippling all the way to the horizon.

The villagers had gotten up early today and were at work, harvesting in the fields. As he walked past them, Bawu wondered why people looked so cheerful today.

The sun rose with spreading rays from the eastern valley. Innumerable reflections of shining red flashed in Bawu's eyes. Standing on tip-toe, he saw red stars shining throughout the fields.

Bawu was hypnotized by the sight; he stood there gazing for a long while before resuming his run toward his mother's tent. As he approached, he heard the stone mill grinding and his old mother talking and laughing. He also saw a heap of threshed barley beside the mill near the opening of the tent.

"Who helped mother thresh all the barley?" he asked himself. He was about to ask the question aloud when he entered the tent and saw a little Chinese soldier working at the mill. He recognized him as the very man who had brushed the dirt from his clothes the previous evening.

"Bawu, how are you?" The little Chinese soldier called him by name, and greeted him warmly.

His old mother stood up, smiling, and called to her son: "Bawu, these are dear friends of mine. How nice they are! They helped me harvest, carry water, chop wood, and make dung cakes for fuel. They have done everything." His mother suddenly changed her tone. "But in one thing they are no good. Like this boy, none of them will accept even half a bowl of barley mush as payment for their help."

Suddenly Bawu heard the sound of hooves approaching. Someone shouted, "Is Bawu at home?"

Bawu left the tent. A *wa-tzu* on horseback and carrying a rifle pointed to a horse he was leading, and shouted, "The Chief Steward wants you to return to the temple immediately. We are departing!"

Bawu's mother and the little Chinese soldier followed Bawu out of the tent. The mother looked apprehensive. The little Chinese soldier raised his hand, shouting to Bawu, "Bawu, I am Mengleh. We are going to work together."

It was high noon. The Chinese troops were about to leave. Holding sheepskins which contained butter and cheese, and brazen pots of milk and tea, the villagers congregated at the roadside to see them off. A singer, shaking his finger bells and beating his small drum, began to sing with feeling:

> The eagles fly from afar
> On their ten-thousand-mile journey;
> I pray the deities in Heaven and on earth,
> Provide them with cloudless days . . .

Bawu and the political commissar walked ahead of the troops. The villagers saluted Bawu because he represented the whole village in repaying the Chinese soldiers for their help. But Bawu remembered the Chief Steward, who had summoned him and reiterated his assignment that morning. Bawu was worried and rueful. He wished desperately that he could just disappear from the scene.

Suddenly the song came to an end and the crowd grew silent. The Chief Steward, as an envoy of the Living Buddha, had come to say farewell to the troops. Holding a Buddhist scripture, the Chief Steward smiled and said to the political commissar, "May you have a fair journey and a bright future."

Having said this, he closed his eyes and chanted some benedictory verses. The henchman of the Living Buddha made Bawu feel nauseated, as though he had swallowed a scorpion. He tried to turn away, but he was too late to dodge the Chief Steward's stare, which shot at Bawu like two daggers. It seemed to be saying, "The Devil's Cliff! The Devil's Cliff!"

IV

The sky was clear and the trees swayed in the wind. The soldiers sweated and struggled against the hot sun. Because of the heat they had stripped to a thin underwear, but they were still panting and out of breath. The road on which they marched extended to the edge of the Black Forest, and then turned westward. Near the entrance to the deep forest, Bawu came to a stop and said to the political commissar, "It is cold within the forest. You should tell the men to put on their sheepskins."

It was irrational that they should put on fur while they were still sweating, but without hesitation, the commissar took his own jacket from his pack and put it on even though he was dizzy from the heat. He told Mengleh to pass the word: "I order all of you to put on your fur jackets immediately."

To Bawu's surprise, the troops acted in one accord. It was the first time he had had the experience of his word being so respected and producing such an effect.

As soon as they stepped into the Black Forest, a current of cold air swooped against them. The commissar found he could hardly breathe in the sudden chill. With his broad shoulders and chest, Bawu purposely strode before the commissar to shelter him from the blast of icy air. The men began to sneeze.

The Black Forest was indeed like a dungeon. Ahead of the troops, it was dark as far as one could see. The rotten leaves and decomposed plants threw off a dank, overpowering odor. The severe blast of cold air almost turned the men into pillars of ice. The political commissar felt dizzy and weak. Bawu supported him and helped him walk, saying "No one can stop here."

The commissar told Mengleh to pass along the order that everyone should march forward without pause. Despite the fact that they were almost breathless and were stumbling, the commissar and the soldiers still forced themselves to accelerate their pace along the forest path.

After they had pushed ahead five or six *li*, the day grew brighter. Over their heads, the leaves were thinning. Small patches of blue sky appeared among the boughs of the huge trees. Bawu stopped and then guided the commissar to a resting place on a rock. He plucked some wild leaves growing from a crack in the rocks. He chewed a leaf and then handed it to the commissar. Following Bawu's advice, the commissar sniffed the herb. He immediately felt rested and invigorated as he breathed in the strange soothing fragrance. Bawu told him, "We call this herb *Hsüeh-tan-cha,* which means longevity. In the forest I eat them when I run out of food. It tastes good if you make tea with them." Bawu put a small bunch into his mouth. The commissar also chewed a leaf and exclaimed, "Umm, very good. Now we don't have to worry about starvation!"

The commissar gave a handful of the leaves to Mengleh and told him to distribute some to each battalion so that everyone could collect and fill his pocket with the magic herb. Bawu rose and said with joy, "I'm going to fill my pockets so that I can boil some tea for you later."

He started calling the big Chinese *benbu* simply "you."

The troops continued their march. Another mountain range stood before them. The dense, primeval black pine trees of the forest, growing on both sides of the valley, gave way to the rocky crags of a barren mountain range which blocked the way. When the troops completed their climb to the top of the mountain pass, dark, ominous clouds rolled across the sky, spreading in every direction. The sun was hidden. A gale blew and a thunderstorm crashed down upon the men. It seemed that the strong wind and rain were competing with all their force to hurl the troops off the mountain. The men, not dressed for such weather, were drenched to the skin. When they tried to move on the loose, slippery ground, they felt as though they were walking perilously on a ship deck without railing, being tossed in the surging sea. Fortunately, the storm soon subsided. Once again the sky was blue. The setting sun painted the treetops golden, and a rainbow leaned against the peak of the mountain. Everything was quiet, fresh and clean.

When the sun sank behind the mountain into the deep pine forest below, the men of the Red Army began to make camp. They built fires around their campsite. Burning pine cones and branches crackled in the midst of a milk-white fog. While the political commissar gathered the soldiers around him to hold a discussion, Bawu and Mengleh sat watching a small pot of the magic herb boiling over the fire. Bawu was adding wood to the flames, and Mengleh was cleaning his rifle. They began to talk softly.

"Mengleh, my friend, where is your home?"

"The Golden Sand River runs for a thousand miles. It flows through the valley of your village and then comes to the forest of my home," Mengleh chanted his answer like a song.

"You live in Liang-shan?" exclaimed Bawu. "Are you a Yi? You are not a Chinese?"

"No. No."

Bawu realized how impolite and abrupt he was, but he had to finish what he wanted to say. He touched Mengleh's rifle. "I meant I was surprised that you were a Yi, and yet they trusted you with this gun."

Someone's voice interrupted them, "Who are 'they'?"

Bawu and Mengleh turned around and saw that the political commissar had come over to them. Bawu felt uneasy. The commissar sat down between them and took out a small pipe into which he stuffed some fresh tobacco.

"I never expected that we could still find tobacco left in the pleats of a regimental commander's tobacco pouch. He generously gave me half of it," the commissar said cheerfully as he lighted the pipe. He handed it to Bawu, saying, "Come, have a puff."

Like all brave Tibetans, Bawu loved to smoke. He, Mengleh, and the commissar took turns smoking the pipe. The tobacco smoke erased the cares and uneasiness from Bawu's mind. The last shred of tobacco had burned; the commissar put away his pipe. He remarked, "Among the three of us, one is a *wa-tzu* of Tibet, one is a slave from Liang-shan, and one is a Han worker. Indeed, we are brothers in need."

"What is a worker?" Bawu asked.

"A worker eats the same food as you do, dresses the same as you do, and lives in a shabby place just as you do. We workers build tall buildings, but never live in them," said the commissar.

"Do you have a Living Buddha and a Chief Steward where you live, Mengleh?" Bawu asked.

"Of course," Mengleh said, angrily. "That is why I joined the revolution."

The *Hsüeh-tan-cha* herb in the pot began to send out its aroma. The night fog gradually dispersed, leaving the men's clothes damp. Pine cones still crackled in the fire, and the flames lit the red faces of the men clustered around the blazing warmth. Bawu reflected upon the commissar's words. The pine forest was so intensely quiet that even the lowered voice of the commissar echoed distinctly throughout the valley.

It was late. Bawu closed his eyes, but inside him a tempest was rising. He had lived for more than thirty years, but not until tonight had he come to the realization that a *wa-tzu* was not predestined to suffer. There are two kinds of people in the world. Some people are enslaved to work like animals and die like dogs, but another kind of people squeeze and oppress others to fatten themselves. Bawu now understood why people in his village had no milk to drink —butter was used to polish the floor of the temple.

Bawu had been like a yak, carrying goods and eating grass, and then falling asleep, day in and day out. It had never occurred to him that the world was beautiful. Now as he remembered the troops putting on the fur jackets as they entered the Black Forest, the *Hsüeh-tan-cha* herb, and the pipe which he had smoked, Bawu was restless and lay awake, thinking.

V

Bawu did not know when he fell asleep. When he awoke, he found himself covered by the commissar's fur coat and squeezed in between the commissar and Mengleh. Day had dawned. He sat up and saw a world of whiteness; it had snowed during the night. The two men beside him were not completely covered because they three had been sharing the one fur coat that belonged to the commissar. Bawu was deeply touched and felt even more uneasy. When he tried to get up and cover the commissar and Mengleh so that they could sleep warmly, the commissar opened his eyes.

"Good morning, Bawu. Will our journey be rough today?"

At that instant, it occurred to Bawu that today they would come upon the first and second of the Devil's Cliffs. If they were to bypass them, they would have to pass under a waterfall and over a steep precipice. "The journey today is very dangerous," he said. "Commissar, you will have to be very careful."

The pine forest had thinned out in this area. The trees were replaced by vast marshes covered with broad-leaved grass that grew to a man's waist. The rank grass had very sharp edges, like sword blades. Even worse, one could hear snakes hissing everywhere, slithering through the grass.

"Don't worry," Bawu shouted reassuringly.

Holding a long stick in his left hand and a knife in the right, Bawu led the way, slashing forward, making the sound "wu-hsü-wu-hsü."

The soldiers followed him, pushing ahead, their swords clearing a path. The reptiles' hissing was all around, but the knives and sticks frightened the snakes away. Bawu led the troops directly to the foot of a great waterfall that thundered two hundred feet down a cliff, sounding like exploding ammunition and clashing armies on a battlefield . . .

The creek below the waterfall ran no more than a hundred paces and then shot down to another precipice. There was only one way to cross the waterfall: by wading across the rapid creek.

"Commissar, let me try first," shouted Bawu. He took off his boots and tightened his belt. Tying one end of a rope to a pine tree and holding the other, he slipped down into the torrent of icy-cold water. He was nearly swept away despite his hold on the rope. His face paled and then turned purple in the freezing cold. Bawu clenched his teeth and struggled in the thigh-deep water. The trust and expectations of his fellow villagers came to mind, and steeled him with the awareness of the importance of his mission. He moved slowly, step by step, and finally reached the other side; the rope was pulled taut and now spanned the river. Clinging to the rope, and with great difficulty, all the troops crossed the creek.

After the waterfall, the path came to an end. They faced an overhanging cliff about two hundred feet high; even monkeys would not attempt to climb that! The troops halted under the cliff and built fires for their meal. Meanwhile, the commissar had more than forty leather belts put together. After eating a few bites, Bawu walked up to the cliff. All eyes were riveted on him as he climbed to a tree which protruded from the rocks. He then threw the rope he had brought with him at another tree growing above him; the loop caught the tree and he pulled himself up to it. From tree to tree he ascended. Then he lowered one end of his rope for the chain of leather belts. From the top he waved at those below. The soldiers applauded, then started to follow him.

Again Bawu felt that it was his fellow villagers who were looking at him. He felt like shouting, "Don't worry, I will never fail you. I, Bawu, am a man to be trusted!"

The adventure, which had lasted for three days and three nights, thus came to an end. The terrifying Black Forest was now far behind them. On the fourth day, when the sky spread its colorful sunrise all over, the magnificent Nima Peak rose before them. Like a dignified old man with disheveled white hair, it stood straight up, greeting the travelers.

Bawu would have joined the Red Army as Mengleh had done if he did not have to care for his old mother at home. He held back his tears and said goodbye to the commissar and his soldiers. The commissar took the red star from his own cap and held it in his left palm. His right hand tightly gripped Bawu's hand as he gravely said to him, "Bawu, my friend. There is one thing I hope you will remember. It is not that the insurmountable Nima Peak is a sun which never sets. The real sun that never sets is this star. Someday it will rise on top of the summit of Nima, and your village will be radically changed."

With great excitement Bawu received the red star and carefully put it into the amulet hanging on his chest. He was very touched as he said, "Dear Red Army men, my friends, as long as I live, my tongue will tell my fellow villagers all about you."

The sun was rising as the Red Army climbed toward the mountain's summit. Thousands of golden rays were reflected on the glaciers. The commissar and his comrades turned back to wave goodbye to Bawu, who stood at the edge of the Black Forest watching the troops ascending like so many eagles soaring with extended wings. Hot tears flowed down his face. He heard them calling from the far distance: "We shall return!"

Bawu returned to his village, but without saying anything to the villagers, he disappeared. A few days later his old mother mysteriously disappeared also. From that time, no one in the village of Nima ever saw the mother or her son again. Some yak caravans, returning from a temple festival elsewhere, reported that they had seen a minstrel, with eyes gouged out, who resembled Bawu. It was said that the blinded minstrel wandered from village to village with his samisen, singing the story:

> A flock of eagles flew in from afar,
> Leaving me a red star.
> It is a sun which never sets,
> Illuminating the heart of a *wa-tzu* ...

The wham of the huge brass gong in the courtyard of the temple interrupts the song of the blind bard. The festival ceremony is about to start.

The minstrel puts away his *sgra-snyan* and takes out his amulet, from which he produces a five-pointed red star.

Translated by Meishi Tsai

WANG CHIA-PIN

Very little is known about Wang Chia-pin. In *Selected Creative Writings by Young Workers, Peasants, and Soldiers,* the collection in which "The Whale Trough" appears, he is referred to simply as "a worker." He is very likely assigned to a fishing fleet, since his latest short story, which appeared in *People's Literature* in May 1977, is on the same subject.

Among the writings of his peers, Wang's prose stands out with its descriptive power which brings the reader close to the scene of the action. He is a promising young writer who bears watching. —K.Y.H.

The Whale Trough

The fish run was in full swing. Boats plied the waters of the harbor like shuttles, ceaselessly darting back and forth, and the sounds of whistles, anchor chains, motors, and shouting people blended into the steady humming pulsation of a busy fishing port, a bustling, cheerful arena of collective endeavor.

In the harbor area, huge wooden cases freshly unloaded from returning boats were lined up, forming a great wall of fish and shrimp. The odor threatened to take away the breath of any casual visitor.

Expedition I and *Expedition II* were docked against the pier. Having just completed a joint run and unloaded their catch, they were now preparing for their next run.

Szu-ma the Flying Dragon, captain of *Expedition I,* stood almost six feet tall, big hands, big feet, a broad face matching his square head. He flipped down from the bridge, landed on the deck, and crossed the gangplank in a few nimble strides. The second skipper, a tiny bit of a shriveled, wiry old man named Old Root, called out to Flying Dragon from the bridge: "Hsiao-lung, about our request to run the Whale Trough, you'd better talk to your dad nicely. Don't get excited if he does. Don't get angry either when he gets angry at you. I don't believe his head is so full of dried cement that he can't turn around, ever . . ."

Behind Old Root stood a line of his crew, all sturdy calves ready to prance at the first word that their captain had secured permission to run the Whale Trough.

"Comrade Crewmen," the loudspeaker on the dock suddenly blared. "The 'Learn from Ta-ch'ing and Ta-chai' special forum now begins.* You are listen-

---

*From time to time since the early 1960s, campaigns have been conducted to rally all industries to emulate the spirit and practice of Ta-chai, a model commune in southwestern Hopei Province, and Ta-ch'ing, a model oil field in Manchuria. [K.Y.H.]

ing to a message from Szu-ma the Flying Dragon, captian of *Expedition I.* . . . "
Flying Dragon stopped, moved by his own words over the loudspeaker: "I was
raised exclusively by the Party. In the old society, a man like me could not
possibly dream of being a captain. Now, we workers are the masters, and we
must listen to the Party and to Chairman Mao. The oil workers have developed
a Ta-ch'ing; why can't we develop another Ta-ch'ing, a Ta-ch'ing of the sea . . .
We request permission to run the Whale Trough, to expand our fishing waters. . . ."

Flying Dragon's blood boiled. Whale Trough, a mysterious place haunted by
sharks and other huge denizens of the deep, beckoned all the members of the
Expedition fleet to uncover its secret. Like their leader Flying Dragon, no longer
content with the familiar waters close to shore, they were dying to venture out
into the unknown.

Last year Flying Dragon drafted a plan to conquer the Whale Trough, a plan
which drew much attention from the leadership. Party Branch Secretary Chi,
who also headed up the Deep Sea Bureau of the Marine Products Commission,
was called back to commission headquarters to study the project and prepare
for it. Months had gone by and no word came from the commission, yet the
fish run had just about reached its peak now. Any further delay would see the
fish run move northward, and the chance for getting into the Whale Trough
would be missed. Flying Dragon quickened his steps, hoping to have another
heart-to-heart talk with Fishing Fleet Director Szu-ma the Big Sea.

Szu-ma the Big Sea was Flying Dragon's father, an old sea dog. Several years
before, the leadership thought Big Sea was getting old, and fleet headquarters
needed someone to take charge, to sort of keep things on an even keel. Big Sea
was transferred from his boat to assume the local directorship. He took his desk
job as seriously as he did any assignment he had had, leading his fleet always
one step ahead of the others. As his old pal Old Root said of him, the only
trouble with Big Sea was that he tended to look only at the immediate returns.
On this matter of running the Whale Trough, for example, he would not back
down from his disagreement with his son. He opposed the project because he
himself had tried it once some nineteen years before. At that time his capitalist
boss had forced him to risk it against his better judgment; they brought back
not a single fish, lost their net, and almost did not come back at all. No, he was
not interested in taking that kind of risk any more; he would rather do the safe
thing, by staying in familiar waters to realize a bigger catch for the government. The father and son argued on and on. Finally the father said, "I have no
time to exercise my vocal cords with you. If I had time, I'd rather spend it
figuring out how to get a bigger catch from spots close to shore. . . ."

Flying Dragon reviewed their arguments in his mind while rushing headlong toward his father's office. He didn't see the archway fashioned out of fish
cases covered with decorations to boost morale and forecast an "Overflowing
Catch" until he bumped into it, nearly knocking it off its base.

"What are you doing? Trying to knock down the dragon gate?"

Flying Dragon turned around and found himself facing Bureau Chief Chi,
whom he had wanted to see for all these long months. He walked up to the chief
and said, "Hi, Chief, what about our plan to run the Whale Trough?"

"It's been approved," Chi said. "The commissioner even commented that this
is the direction in which we should all be moving in the future."

Flying Dragon would have leapt for joy if the thought of his father's objection had not followed this cheering news. "Ah, I see," he said, his brow tightly knitted. "But the lower echelon lacked steam!" He stressed the words "lower echelon." "The lower echelon leadership would not support us. We even quarreled several times, but each time it was me who got criticized!"

"Ah," said Chi, suppressing a secret chuckle. "Shame on you to talk that way! What's the use of quarreling? Will that settle anything? If you've got a point, let's bring it out into the open and discuss it fully. If you quarrel, that's exactly what he wants. He's your dad, and you're his son. He's got a bit of advantage there!"

The humorous way Chi put it drew a smile from Flying Dragon. He pressed his question: "All right, when do we go? The very next trip out?"

"What do you think?" Chi half closed his eyes to study the husky young man in front of him.

"We're ready to move, even today."

"You are ready, but what about your dad?" Chi patted the young man's broad shoulder. "You mustn't quarrel with your dad. Your dad has been doing a good job overseeing the production. The commission is very pleased with him. You have to be patient with him, help him to see our long-range interest."

Flying Dragon felt reassured, and his steps became lighter as he walked along with the bureau chief. The chief studied this young captain, who had grown up under his very eyes. The young man bore strong resemblance to his father in the way he frowned and walked, and yet he had something about him not to be found in his father.

The fleet director's office was a small wood hut overlooking the entire harbor across a row of willow trees.

As the two men approached the hut, they could hear Big Sea's loud, hoarse voice yelling. "... Hey, Old Root! You listen to me first! You old rascal, your mouth is just like a machine gun, rattling nonstop ... You don't have to give me that sort of stuff, all empty big talk! We are fishermen, you understand? Not explorers. It's the best season now in the waters close to shore. Don't you ever think of that? ..."

Big Sea was heavy and fat. He stooped over the desk, shouting into the phone. Old Root, on the other end, must have said something that annoyed him, for he stamped his foot and yelled, "What? Me, conservative? What sort of nonsense are you spewing? The older you get the crazier you become, eh? ..."

He slammed the phone down, but another phone on the desk started ringing. Angrily he snatched it up. "This is Szu-ma! ... What information? ... What? You are the research institute? This is the fleet director's office, not the information resource room. Damn it ..."

Flying Dragon pushed the door open and rushed toward the phone. "Dad!" He only had time to grab the receiver from his father's hand before he excitedly rattled off, "Comrade, I asked for the information! ... Oh, thank you, thank you ..." He turned to his father and said, "Dad, you see, the theoretical aspect ... Hello!" He had to turn back to the phone again. "I was talking to someone else here. I wanted to tell you that if you people can take care of the theoretical aspect of the project, we can catch the fish and uncover the Whale Trough's secret for you—our boat gives you our word of honor!"

"You ask them," interjected Bureau Chief Chi, "if they have any new information on the present status of the geology of the Whale Trough."

Big Sea, who had been ignoring the two visitors by gluing his eyes on a wall map, turned around, startled by what he had just heard.

". . . That's it! That's it!" Flying Dragon relayed Chi's question. He seemed to be even more excited. "We are with you on that. Comrade, I pledge my head on this thing. We will never let you down!"

Flying Dragon put the phone down. "Chief, now everything is ready," he said, grinning broadly and rubbing his hands. "All we need is that gust of east wind!" He glanced at his father.

"What did the research institute say?" Chi asked.

"They have checked every source except those of the fifteenth century. Everything they went through said the same thing: the Whale Trough is a basin with no direct current through it. It's got a mud bottom." Flying Dragon continued: "They also said there is no record of any wreck or shoals in that area. Lots of sharks. Whales during June and July. These things seem to dovetail well with the fish runs near here. It's really very promising."

"That's enough!" Big Sea interrupted his son. "It's all a lot of paper work!" His eyes fixed on Bureau Chief Chi, asking the unspoken question: Have we decided to try the Whale Trough?

"Yes, we are going to try it!" Chi guessed Big Sea's question and answered with a smile. "I'm back this time just to talk it over with you. How about sending *Expedition I* and *II* on this exploratory mission?"

"Right in the middle of the fish run here?"

"Yes, right at the height of this best season."

Big Sea started pacing the floor. Pulling out his best team, the Expedition boats, at this moment would wreck his production plan. To him, this would be worse than being hit by a hurricane.

Flying Dragon stared at his father's stiff neck, hoping that somehow he would see it bend into a nod of the old man's head.

"How about it, Old Hai?" said Chi, who knew the temperament of this old sea dog very intimately. "We've got to work the waters close to shore, of course, but we've got to look further. You are not just a captain of one boat now, you are the leader of an entire fleet. You have to stand higher and see farther . . ."

Chi kept talking, about matters from pre-Liberation days to the present, and from the present to the distant future. But Big Sea was troubled. He figured how much fish he would lose if he missed his main strength during the season, which came only once in a year. He couldn't make up his mind.

Flying Dragon watched his father's face as it turned lighter, then darker, then lighter again. Since the senior Szu-ma said nothing, his son didn't know what to do. Finally he hit upon an idea. "Dad," he said, "recently many comrades out there have been talking about you."

"What about me?" The father stopped pacing.

"The young fellows out there say, 'The director had a bad time in the Whale Trough some nineteen years ago; that's why he doesn't dare to do this, doesn't dare to do that—he is plain scared!' "

Big Sea blushed in anger. He glared at his son for a moment without saying anything. His reddened eyes seemed to be saying, "I know, I know, it's you, and nobody else, who said I am scared!" Then he turned inquiringly to Bureau Chief Chi.

Flying Dragon left his father's office without further argument.

The leadership had approved the project, and Bureau Chief Chi continued to work at the preparations. Big Sea relented and agreed to let *Expedition I* and *Expedition II* start out in three days. Grudgingly he walked the bureau chief out of his office, saying, "Look, we are so busy this year. All three of my managers have gone out to sea to be where the frontline action is. I'm left alone to man this show. It's bigger than I can handle."

"We're prepared to assign two deputy directors to help you."

"Two? When will they be here? Are they cadres from commission headquarters?"

"They have been here for a while already, out there aboard a boat somewhere."

"But who are they?"

"One is Old Root."

Big Sea was disappointed. He had hoped he would get some reliable help. Of course, Old Root was quite a fisherman, but something had gotten twisted between these two old sea pals; they seemed to quarrel every time they got together.

"Who is the other one?"

Chi laughed. "The other one? Well, we'll have to watch and see. Look here, Old Hai, we can't just dig around our own threshold forever; we have to expand into more distant seas. You have to adapt your strategy somewhat . . ."

Returning to his office alone, Big Sea stared at the wall map showing the fishing waters in the vicinity. The adventure forced upon him nineteen years before by his capitalist employer once again passed before his eyes.

Nineteen years ago, Big Sea had been second in command on a small, beat-up fishing boat. The captain was a worthless foreigner who knew nothing except bossing people around. He was determined to go treasure-hunting in the remote, mysterious Whale Trough.

It was the same kind of windy season as this year. After leaving the fog-bound harbor, the rickety boat coughed and shook, moving three knots forward and two back. It took them three solid days and two full nights to reach the Whale Trough.

From a distance, the water of the Trough looked murky, black, and eerie. The sharks, those huge black shadows of death, shot through the waves. Whale spouts, measuring over thirty feet high, shot up all around. The size and sight of the Trough unnerved the foreign skipper. His courage, fit only for risking a high stake in a gambling joint, fled.

"First Mate," the foreigner called, "God has led us into this heavenly place! Let's light the firecrackers."

The old fishermen followed a superstitious tradition. When they saw a huge marine object, they would beat gongs and drums and light firecrackers to drive away the devil and ensure luck. At that time, Flying Dragon, only thirteen years old, was on board with his father, and the young boy enjoyed enormously the assignment of carrying a string of popping firecrackers as he walked around on the deck.

The boat approached Flying Shark Lane on the edge of the Trough. A swift current caught the feeble boat and held it captive for a time. Somehow no map had shown the tight, rocky spot in the middle of Flying Shark Lane, and when the foreign skipper saw it, he turned pale.

It was a good thing that Old Root, already a famed pilot, was on board. He sweated with Big Sea to steer the boat through the jutting rocks to reach the Trough. In the middle of the Trough they dropped their net, then they full-throttled the engine. But the boat stood still, as though glued to the bottom of the ocean. Was it some marine monster that held the net in its claws? Strong winds rose. Schools of sharks, like wolf packs, gathered around. At each toss of the wave the boat missed capsizing only by a couple of inches. The fear-crazed foreign captain scurried around, spreading panic among the crew.

"Let go of the net!" the foreign captain kept yelling. A succession of huge waves smashed against the boat, breaking the thick boards kept ready for fencing off the sharks.

The situation was critical. Big Sea seized an axe from the emergency rack, thinking, "If I don't do it, it will be almost certain death, but if I risk it, there might still be a chance." He darted to the net platform and chopped away at the cable. The steel cable broke, freeing the boat from the drag net, and they managed to get back to port after a tough struggle. Even now, Big Sea still could not understand why the net got stuck. . . .

It was settled now—about running the Whale Trough.

During the three days remaining, Flying Dragon hurried with the preparations. He called a meeting of the crew, and they discussed all the unexpected situations they could think of and mapped the necessary countermeasures. They studied the eyes of the net, which seemed small and would make the net too heavy to drag when too much mud was caught in it. So they changed it, installing a net with larger eyes. What with the net-changing and others jobs, the crew, including the cook, all pitched in to work an extra night in order to start out as scheduled.

Big Sea had his own preparation to do for the fish run in waters close to shore. He ran breathlessly between the customs office, the telegraph bureau, and back to the boat dock, with no time to spare for watching how the Expedition team was getting along. When he heard that the bureau chief had transferred Old Root away from Flying Dragon to take charge of the auxiliary boat, *Expedition II,* he was stunned. "Don't forget that Flying Dragon is still just a kid!" he complained to Bureau Chief Chi on the telephone.

"In your eyes he is still a kid, but I see in him a little tiger," said Chi.

"Chief," pleaded the senior Szu-ma, "you trust him too much."

"Don't worry, I'll be with them. Old Hai, drop over to commission headquarters. Let's talk about this thing some more. . . ."

"I can't make it now. There are still five teams of boats yet to go out."

By dusk, Big Sea finally found time to go to the dock again. *Expedition II* had already been iced and was now anchored outside the harbor. *Expedition I* was packing its last load of ice.

Like a gleaming arm, the ice bridge reached out from the cold-storage tower, its rumbling conveyor belt delivering huge boulders of ice into the ice smasher. As each crystal boulder disappeared into the machine, a loud crash resounded and then a flood of crushed ice rushed to the hold of *Expedition I* by way of the elevated funnel.

Big Sea mounted the net platform of *Expedition I;* there he saw a huge nylon net caught in golden sunlight. It felt nice and soft. "How many fish would such a net mean if it were used in our familiar sure-fire waters," Big Sea thought, and he felt unhappy about the prospect of casting the net into the Whale Trough.

Back on the dock, Big Sea saw his son, naked except for a pair of sweat-soaked shorts, running among the crew who were loading the empty fish tubs. Muscles rolled under the young man's tanned, almost black, skin as he shouted encouragement to his fellow crewmen: "Let's step it up—we've pledged to start out on time!"

"Dad," Flying Dragon greeted his father, "are you here to inspect our preparations?"

"How many tubs have you loaded?" said the old man.

"A thousand."

"A thousand?" The old man obviously thought it was too much. "What are you trying to do? Move the whole house? You really don't have any idea yet what you may run into, and here you are, going big guns already. I don't think you know what you're doing. That ice and those tubs have been prepared for the boats working around here."

The young man pouted. Big Sea looked at his son, who stood half a head taller than himself now; he looked at his broad shoulders, at the wrinkles on his forehead, and at the stubble of beard around his mouth. Ever since the boy had lost his mother when he was thirteen, he had been with his father on a fishing boat. Nineteen years had passed, and only now Big Sea seemed to notice for the first time that the boy had grown up.

And the thought melted the old sea dog's heart.

"Put your clothes on," he said.

Obediently, Flying Dragon put on his clothes. With his hand, the father brushed away the few pieces of fish scale stuck on the young man's back.

"With your Uncle Old Root gone, you'd better be twice as careful about everything," the father said.

"Yes, dad."

"Whenever anything happens, send me a message first."

"I know."

"If things don't look right, pull back quickly. Don't miss the fish run in this area also."

Big Sea was talking his way back into that old rut about protecting production by sticking closer to home base. The young man had no interest in listening to that again. He smiled and interrupted his father: "Dad, it's time to go." Then he shouted to his crew, "Make ready to cast off!"

The crew followed Flying Dragon on board. Turning back to his father, Flying Dragon said, "Dad, don't worry. We guarantee we'll open up the Whale Trough for us!"

The gangplank was removed; each crewman assumed his station. In the red light, Flying Dragon stood on the bridge, looking like a bronze statue. He made sure everyone was in position before he pulled the whistle to signal a start. "Front cable off!" he called. The engine bell rang and *Expedition I,* with all its lights ablaze, steamed out, followed closely by *Expedition II.*

As soon as the boat left the harbor area, Flying Dragon urged his men to get some sleep, to rest up for the next day's battle. Activities on board subsided. Only the engine rumbled on steadily, indefatigably.

From the chart room, Flying Dragon found a set of maps, which he took to the captain's cabin. He slipped off his shoes, spread the maps on the floor, and crawled from one end of the room to the other, reviewing the underwater topography. The tiny cabin suddenly seemed immense, and he felt he was watching his father, old Big Sea, doing exactly the same thing some years back.

The gossamer-thin lines, the sesame-like dots, each informed Flying Dragon something of this sea and posed for him a complex problem. He pushed the magnifier back and forth until he found Flying Shark Lane, which would present the first test for his boat. If successful, they would be directly approaching the Whale Trough. His eyes followed the Lane until they came to the Trough, which was marked in three large characters, near his left toe. He examined that area with care, and realized that the net he and his father had abandoned nineteen years before must be just about in the center of the Trough.

Something moved under the map. "Who's that?" Flying Dragon asked.

"Open up here," answered Hsiao Hsu, who had been transferred from *Expedition II* to assist Flying Dragon. Hsiao Hsu wanted to come up through the trapdoor which opened to the crew's cabin. Flying Dragon folded up his maps and let the visitor in. About a dozen crewmen followed Hsiao Hsu.

"Captain Szu-ma," Hsiao Hsu said, "these comrades are too excited to sleep. They all want to hear from you once again the story of how you were forced to go to the Whale Trough nineteen years ago."

"Tell us about how the foreign idiot made a fool of himself," said one crewman.

"Tell us about those huge sharks," said another.

Flying Dragon scratched his head. "Haiya, all of you know that story already. Why should I tell that again?"

"We'll never get tired of hearing it. Why don't you tell us again, exactly the way it happened."

"Yes, tell us, captain!"

Flying Dragon had to tell the story once again, from the very beginning, and it was not an unwelcome task. He always got carried away with his own story. Toward the end, he was overcome with emotion. "This happened nineteen long years ago," he said. "It's an old calendar, worn out and worm-eaten. Comrades, we are a new generation of crewmen raised by Chairman Mao himself. Only we can conquer this ocean and uncover its mystery!"

"This time," said Hsiao Hsu, "we are going to put a stranglehold on the neck of the Whale Trough and demand that it give up its fish."

"Ya!" said another crewman. "Let's convert the Whale Trough into a Ta-ching of the sea."

Excitement over the anticipated battle filled the tiny cabin. Outside, cold wind had started to blow. It was past midnight. Patches of fluorescent green blinked around the boat on the dark sea's face, as microscopic marine life glowed like so many fireflies heralding the approach of a storm. . . .

After the departure of *Expedition I* and *II,* Big Sea walked back to his office, where a staff member on duty handed him a letter. It was from Bureau Chief Chi.

"Old Hai," the letter said, "both you and I have been busy these days. We haven't had much chance to chat. I wonder if you have any further thought about developing the fishing waters of the Whale Trough. The current mission of *Expedition I* and *II* will have much to do with our future marine production. Just to make sure things will be all right, I have decided to go with *Expedition II,* where I will have Old Root's wise counsel. You don't have a thing to worry about. But you do have a heavier responsibility at headquarters overseeing the work in near-shore waters. I believe the picture of our production is about to embark on some dramatic changes. All right, you keep direct contact with the commissioner whenever you need any help."

The letter warmed him. He felt the leadership's concern over the entire operation; not a single link or a single person was overlooked. He bent over the desk, and before he knew it, he had started to snore. . . .

The rustling leaves of the willow trees and the resounding surf outside awakened him. The sky was pitch-dark. He jumped up and grabbed the phone. "What's the position of the expedition?" he asked the radioman. "Closing in on Flying Shark Lane," came the answer. "Oh? What about the weather there?" "High wind expected," said the radioman, followed by a spell of the transmitter's ticking sound.

Experience told Big Sea that the approaching storm would be a whopper. He thought of the Whale Trough, and the scene he witnessed nineteen years before returned to haunt him.

Anxiously he awaited the dawn, when he would phone the commissioner to order the expedition back to port. But the phone rang, and from the other end came the commissioner's voice. "I was at your office," said the commissioner, "but you were sleeping so soundly that I didn't want to wake you up . . . Old Hai, I'm at the radio station. Can you come over? The devil of a weather is playing tricks on us; I need your help. . . . "

"Yes, yes, right away!" said Big Sea. He had forgotten his request for the return of *Expedition I* and *II.*

Expedition I had already reached dark and unfamiliar waters. Black clouds pressed down, hovering just over the tip of the ship's mast. But the boat kept its energetic course, darting ahead, splitting a threatening ocean. The engine roared as tirelessly as the fluttering red flag above.

Captain Flying Dragon stood unperturbed on the bridge, feeling no need of sleep at all. "Our position?" he asked Assistant Skipper Hsiao Hsu.

"Five knots to Flying Shark Lane."

A telegram was brought over. It was from the commissioner, saying, "Captain of *Expedition I,* you are doing very well. Keep up the fearless revolutionary spirit. High wind expected. Be extra alert. Hope you will overcome all difficulties and insist on victory. Wish you success in charting a new channel for the marine products industry of our country...."

The wind gained strength at dawn, and the boat gained knots, biting into Flying Shark Lane. A brilliant flash of lightning split the sky, followed by sustained peals of thunder.

Dodging skillfully the visible shoals, *Expedition I* was rapidly closing in on the critical "throat" of the lane. Suddenly Hsiao Hsu called out, "Whirlpool ahead!"

Flying Dragon squinted. In the distance he spotted a large area of churning water, a funnel-shaped maelstrom with a deep, sunken center. That was the throat of the lane. He felt the boat begin to shake as though it had contracted a case of malaria. The waves breaking against the hull of the boat thudded dully as a windstorm caught up with them.

Flying Dragon asked for full speed ahead. The boat leapt forward. He recalled what Old Root had told him just before their departure: "For the throat, you aim at its center and rush it." To the right of the whirlpool's center he saw a straight line—a through current. He headed his boat toward that current.

But, as the old sailors say, it takes only a lamb of wind to bring on a tiger of waves—the pounding wind had stirred the Lane into a deafening chaos. At a moment like this, if a man were anything less than perfectly calm, his knees would have buckled long ago. Flying Dragon thought of the people waiting for the results of what he was doing, waiting and watching him; the thought steeled his nerves and he signaled for reduced speed, to proceed with caution.

"Left, further left, still more ... " he gave orders. Like a hunter spotting his prey, he squinted at the course ahead. Without warning, *Expedition II* shot up from behind, pulled even with *Expedition I,* then passed it. During that one moment when it was abreast with the lead boat, Flying Dragon heard Old Root call out to him from the bridge of the second boat, "Be steady now! ... " Flying Dragon realized that Old Root had found the throat of the Lane and had aimed straight at it. He followed suit. At fast-forward three, *Expedition I* wedged forth, caught up with the second boat, and together they sliced the mountainous waves and buffeting wind until they cleared the critical passage.

"Relax," Flying Dragon said to the pilot, a young crewman with beads of sweat all over his face. "That was only the first dry run, a sort of initial greeting extended by the Whale Trough."

Leaving Flying Shark Lane behind, *Expedition I* headed toward where Big Sea had left his net nineteen years before. The boat rocked and yawed, fighting the storm, at times her mast almost touching the peaks of waves. Each wave seemed higher than the last until the plexiglass window of the wheelhouse threatened to give way to the relentless pounding of angry water. Inside the wheelhouse, the pilot's stool toppled and rolled from one end of the floor to the other.

Flying Dragon secured his foothold on the bridge. His legs, which had weathered years of storms on the sea since he was only thirteen, held him straight as though they were two pillars screwed to the board. Undaunted, he clung to the charted course without deviation.

But a wall of seawater rose directly in front of the bow and crashed on the wheelhouse, causing the windows to break their clasps and slide down the slots. Water rushed in. The pilot was knocked over. For a split second the boat slid helplessly sideways into the gaping trough of the second wave. Flying Dragon leapt to the wheel and, giving it a sharp spin, turned the boat back onto its course. He pushed the windows back into position, wiped the glass top of the compass. Hsiao Hsu, his assistant, ran into the room to take over the wheel. "Captain," he said, "you keep watch. Let me handle this for you."

"She wants to show us some color," Flying Dragon smiled, looking at the churning sea. "Ah, but she doesn't know us!" He flipped on the sonar screen. Sixty feet below the surface it was all calm; a huge black shadow remained immobile in the center of the screen. It could not be fish, for there was no movement, he thought. Weeds would not look like that either. Flying Dragon was puzzled.

According to his chart, that must be just about where his father had lost the net. The thought stirred him; he had to swallow hard before ordering "Net down!"

The nylon net rolled off the platform. *Expedition II* closed in to catch the other end of the cable. Together the two boats started dragging.

But there was no drag, much to Flying Dragon's surprise. The boats proceeded as though nothing were happening. The crew looked at each other, wondering. In their minds, they, too, were reviewing the story of what had happened to the captain's father years back.

"Captain Hsu," Flying Dragon said, "you keep the wheel. I'll go astern to take a look." He went to the rear of the boat. The cable was taut; the net must have behaved properly underwater. Upon returning to the bridge, Flying Dragon sent a message off: "*Expedition I* net down. Drag normal."

An hour passed, with no change in the boat's speed. What could have happened nineteen years before that had pinned down the boat? None of the crew had anything to say.

"Look! The cat!" the crew yelled suddenly. Flying Dragon turned back. There in the midst of boiling whitecaps flashed the dark shadow of a large shark, followed by a looming black mound, the back of a whale, its tail flopping some distance away. In between, another chunky shark flashed its jaw at the hovering sea gulls above. The crew held on to the heaving rail, transfixed by this show of movement and power.

Before Flying Dragon could reflect on this ominous sight so like the prelude to what happened to his father seconds before the senior seaman had had to abandon his net, *Expedition I* stopped, just like the other ship nineteen years before! Flying Dragon sucked in some cold air; his heart skipped a beat.

"Aiya! ... The ship is not moving!" someone yelled.

"Don't yell!" Flying Dragon ordered, as much to stop any panic as to calm himself. "All right," he thought, "you scared the foreign idiot nineteen years ago, but you're going to come clean this time ... for a while I thought you weren't going to show up. All right ..."

"What has caught the net down below?" he reflected. "What has drawn those cats of the sea and the birds above?" He ordered full-speed-forward, as he and Old Root had agreed to do before departure.

"Signal *Expedition II*, increase-five!" The signalman manipulated his flags

nimbly, and Flying Dragon read from the other boat a flag saying the order had
been received and complied with. He turned to his talk-tube. "The horse isn't
running," he spoke into the tube. "Whip her five—hard!"

Still the boat was glued to the same spot.

"Give her five, again!" he called.

Still nothing happened.

"Again ..." But Flying Dragon checked himself as he noticed the spray
splashed onto the net platform by the propeller of his own ship. The cable
strained dangerously, and the ship yawed like a struggling fish itself, trying to
get free. The cable could snap any minute, and that beautiful new net would
be lost forever. He bit his lips, his face flushed purple. If the net was lost, how
would he face anybody back at the harbor? He fought hard to stay calm.

"Back to normal-forward," he ordered.

He had an emergency huddle with Assistant Captain Hsu, then returned to
the deck himself to direct the battle. The crew on the deck waited for his orders,
their black plastic suits glistening in the pale dawn.

"Comrades," Flying Dragon said, "the Whale Trough is challenging us to a
fight now. The situation is tough. She wants to swallow our net. Are we going
to let her do that?"

"No!" the crew shouted.

"Right! Let's bring up our net. The storm is ugly, and we don't know what's
going on down there. Be extra careful! We're going to get back our net at all
cost!"

Expedition II closed in again to hand back the other end of the cable. The
cable wrench squeaked and *Expedition I* backed up toward that something
down below. Prancing sharks thickened around the ship.

A huge wave swooped down on the water tank astern, clawing its way onto
the ship. The deck tilted sharply, throwing the crew off-balance. The board on
the net platform flew up and landed on the forward deck. Flying Dragon
jumped at it, caught it, dragged it back to the platform and latched it down
again.

Another wave tried its turn to smash the ship. This time a huge belt of
shining sparkles emerged above the crest for a moment and sank down into the
murky water again.

"The net is full! ... It's bubbling up now!" the crew yelled, overjoyed.

Flying Dragon grinned. Wiping the brine off his face, he shouted, "The
bastard! Ha, you almost fooled us, didn't you? Fellows, hurry up with the
machine gun."

A burst of rattling gunfire subdued the sharks somewhat. "Perhaps the net
is safe from their sharp jaws now," Flying Dragon thought. On calmer days the
net would "bubble up" to the surface when full of fish, and one could see it from
a distance, but today the rough sea had kept the crew guessing until the net
had been pulled quite close. The wrench was whirring, pulling ... its speed
increased.

Smoke rose from the wrench spool—too much load! The spool began to act
funny: turn and stop, turn and stop, as the long dragon of a net neared the ship.
Then one end of the net was hauled over the side of the ship. The thing was
too full for the two-ton capacity of the crane; they had to use the load divider,

a cable noose which could be drawn over the sausage-like net to divide it roughly into two-ton sections so that each section could be pulled up and emptied one after the other.

The divider noose was lowered, and it caught the net-sausage nicely. But then another huge wave tossed the whole thing up, sky-high, and when it dropped down again, Flying Dragon's heart sank—the rope attached to the divider noose had snapped. What could they do now? The broken rope dangled on the net several yards from the ship; it was caught in a section of rusted old cable that twisted around the net like a rotten, dead sea serpent. And the net, pulled and shoved in the waves, was slipping off the ship.

Flying Dragon leapt to the chain on the deck, tossed it around one end of the net, and twisted it tight on the railing. The net was momentarily secured to the railing. "Give me the hook!" Flying Dragon shouted. He waited for the huge sausage to be tossed close to the side of the ship and then stabbed the net with the hook, hoping to catch the broken rope. The rusted cable tangled around the sausage refused to give. A few more twists and turns, and another high wave knocked the hook into two pieces.

Each wave now clawed at Flying Dragon's heart as it washed away that much farther his chance of securing that bulging netful of fish. He dropped his section of the broken hook-stick with a curse and wrung his hands. The crew's eyes all were fixed on his angry face.

The old cook ran out from the kitchen, a meat cleaver in hand. "What's caught? Where?" he shouted, panting. "Let me get it with this thing!" This comical outburst reminded everybody of something they had not thought of. "Yes, let's chop it off, yes ... " One young crewman gave voice to everybody's flash discovery.

"Ya, somebody go and chop it!" said someone.

"Captain, let me go!" another responded.

Flying Dragon's eyes did not leave the floating sausage for one second as he thought about this last risky suggestion. Suddenly he swiveled around.

"Give me the file and pliers! Hurry!" he ordered one crewman nearby.

In a second he had stripped naked, donned a life jacket, and belted on it the file and pair of pliers. He had one hand on the end of the net, one foot already seeking a foothold on the sausage, when the crew rushed around him, all shouting, "Captain, let me go." "Let me ... " "Captain, you are the head of the ship, you let me ... "

"Yes, and because I am the head of the ship ... stand back!"

Expedition II pulled closer, its whistle screaming. Flying Dragon saw Old Root shouting something from the bridge, but he could hear nothing for the wind. He saw, too, Bureau Chief Chi on the bridge, waving a safety belt at him. The crew on *Expedition I* got the message. They hurried to bring out a safety belt and quickly attached it over their captain's safety jacket. In a moment he was gone, washed under the waves.

From the ship, the floating fish sausage seemed a stable island, at least stable enough for one to walk on it. But the sausage was not solid. It gave under each step. Flying Dragon clung to it like a lizard, holding his breath when it was awash, and struggled forward a few inches at a time between waves.

Some of the crew also put on life jackets, ready to reinforce their captain;

others were dropping shark repellent around the sausage to shield their captain from those predatory jaws. Assistant Skipper Hsu whirled the wheel this way and that, trying to keep the ship as steady as possible. *Expedition II* turned in circles around this arena to help scare the "sea cats" away.

Inch by inch, Flying Dragon got closer to the rotten cable tangled in the net. How many times he was tossed up into the sky and dropped down to the bottom of the sea's trough he didn't know and didn't care. All he wanted was that rotten cable. And when he finally got within reach of it, he was stunned. There, attached to one end of the rotten cable, was a broken piece of pulley which he immediately recognized as having belonged to his father's boat. Nineteen long years! The net had rotted away, but its skeleton, its ghost, remained, waiting here to give him another bad time! He felt like biting it with his own teeth. . . .

. . . .

The senior Szu-ma stayed on land, but he was dying to be in the Whale Trough.

At first the message that *Expedition I* had entered the Whale Trough and that the drag was normal jarred him only a little. Then word about the net "bubbling up" exploded in his ears. For a long while he couldn't believe the radio message in his hand.

Then he was thrust back into gnawing anxiety as he pictured in his mind how his son crawled toward the broken rope. He couldn't help but feel that he, Big Sea, should have been on *Expedition I.* After all, to him Flying Dragon was still a boy!

As Szu-ma wallowed in his own emotional waves, the door of the radio room opened and out stepped the radioman. His mouth trembled, and it was only with difficulty that he managed to mutter the figure, "Two hundred thousand!"

"What?" the senior Szu-ma jumped. "Two hundred thousand?"

" 'Trouble removed. Net lift normal. Estimate two hundred thousand *catties* in net.' " The radioman handed the message from *Expedition I* to the old man.

As though a mirror vividly reviewed a page of old history for him, Big Sea saw in a flash the mystery that had nearly cost his life nineteen years before. His net, then, had also dragged a full load—too full for his rickety boat to handle. That was long ago, he thought, and that was when someone forced him to risk his life. But today, ah, today, what kind of people are we dealing with now, and what kind of ships are we handling now! Big Sea thought of his attitude, and regretted his timidity. . . .

Out in the Whale Trough, *Expedition I* continued to load the fish, two tons at a time: tighten the noose, haul up, swing over the deck, and drop. . . . The net bulged, bursting in a few places. The live fish swam away; the stunned and half-dead fish lured even more gulls to swarm around. Two birds struggled together with a huge fish, carried it aloft for a few feet, then slipped and dropped it right on Flying Dragon's head. "Look, even they want to help," someone yelled and laughed.

Four big shovels, four pairs of strong arms, kept pouring fish into the gaping mouth of the hold. Still too slow. The fish piled up higher and higher on deck.

What would have taken the two boats ten days to net from waters near shore, even at the peak of a run, was here in this one haul. The crew laughed and hopped on the pile of fish. Hopping together with them were the live catch, all sizes, shapes, and colors, their dancing rhythm accentuated by the engine's roar. Seeing this, who could fail to recognize that it's better catching fish than eating them?

Evening came. The winds stilled and the sea's face resumed a joyous calm. The Whale Trough looked even more immense than before. Miles of shining brocade dyed by the sunset was cut only occasionally by the black scissors of sharks' fins. Further away stood columns of white spout; the whales roamed, ever so casually.

The crew gathered further information about the Trough, proving that it was really an ideal fishing area as they had projected, and the message reaching Flying Dragon from his father the following day applauded their finding. "Congratulations!" the message read. "Now the fleet is organizing teams to plunge right into the Whale Trough for its treasures. . . . "

On the bridge, Flying Dragon took in the scene of infinite beauty around him as the engine of *Expedition I* hummed a triumphant tune on a smooth homeward journey. The setting sun continued to burn the western sky. He turned to look at Assistant Skipper Hsu, who was equally absorbed in the intoxicating view. "Who knows how far it is to the South Pole?" he said to Hsu. "At least several thousand knots," someone answered. "Only several thousand? Much farther than that . . . " someone else chimed in with a comment.

In Flying Dragon's ears sounded a song, " . . . let us open up a new world . . ." And he saw himself piloting a boat in all the corners of mystery, over all the immense oceans on earth.

Selected Creative Writings by Young Workers,
Peasants, and Soldiers, pp. 130–155

Translated by Kai-yu Hsu

HO CHING-CHIH

Answer the World of Today

—On Reading the Diary of Wang Chieh

Write like this,
Write like this —
Our diaries
Should be written like this.

Write like this,
Write like this —
Our history
Should be written like this.

Write of our
Splendid red flag,
Write of our
Great achievements.

With
All our lives,
With
All our warm blood.

Life —
Write it like this,
Death —
Write it like this.

Revolution!
Revolution! —
In every line,
Every page.

The people!
The people! —
In every chapter,
Every stanza.

For a note on Ho Ching-chih, see p. 361.

The world,
In our hearts.
The heroes,
In our ranks.

We are
Comrades at arms of Huang Chi-kuang and Lei Feng,
We are
Thousands and thousands of Wang Chiehs!

Who says Wang Chieh
Already made the sacrifice?
Who says Wang Chieh
Has already bid us good-bye?

See the thousands and thousands of hearts of Wang Chieh
Beating in unison,
See the thousands and thousands of diaries of Wang Chieh
Still being written . . .

O, write,
We shall write!
We shall write this way,
We must write —

Face
The ten-thousand beacon fires,
Respond
To the world of today!

Revolution —
Never retreat!
Struggle —
Never cease!

How can we tolerate
The traitor's betrayal?
How can we allow
The thief's rampancy?

Our red flag —
Never shall fall!
Our torch —
Never shall die!

Who is
A "good breed of revolutionary"?
The people
Can tell!

Please look
At the revolutionary troops,
Just this moment
Regrouping ...

We are
Mao Tse-tung's fighters,
We are
Heroic Wang Chiehs!

Come, see the enemy:
Are they not crazed?
Come, let the storm
Blow more fierce!

We have already
Made preparations,
Ready to meet
All that must come!

We shall sing loudly:
"This is the last struggle ..."
Fight forever
In the very front line!

We shall
Open our diaries
To write down boldly —
The truth of Mao Tse-tung's thought

Write: the sky
Will never fall!
Write: the earth
Will never be destroyed!

Write: the imperialist bandits,
Must be all buried!
Write: the revisionist traitors,
Must pass the final judgment!

O, write: to peoples of the world,
Final victory!
O, write: on the whole earth,
The season brings blossoms everywhere ...

O, our diaries,
Our history,
Shall be written down: tomorrow
A newer, a more beautiful page!

November 11, 1965
Singing Aloud, pp. 149–154

Translated by Hsin-sheng C. Kao

MAO TSE-TUNG

Return to Well Ridge Mountains (1965)

To climb once more the Well Ridge Mountains:
Pilgrimage devoutly planned.
Thousand-mile journey, and here the old haunts
All changed in aspect, smiling and bland.
Song of oriole, dance of swallow,
Purling streams on every side,
Trails pierce the clouds where we stand.
Perilous heights over Yellow Vale —
These we leave behind.

With storm and thunder
Banners surging
The people have taken this land.
Passage of thirty-eight years
Drumming fingers, a wave of the hand.
We can pluck the moon from the nine-fold heavens,
Seize the great turtle from five oceans' depths,
Then back with cheers and a band.
No task on earth too difficult:
We have only to stretch out our hand.

Dialogue of the Birds (1965)

Leviathan-roc spreads his wings,
Rises ten thousand miles
By the whirlwind's force propelled.
The sky on his back, he surveys below
Walled cities where humans dwell:
Horizons lit by gun-flash,
Shell craters all around
Startle a sparrow from bramble dell.
"Whatever to do?
Oh! I want to fly off as well!"

For a note on Mao Tse-tung, see p. 373.

"And whither, sir, shall you journey?"
Now comes the sparrow's reply:
"There's a fairyland, I hear tell,
Where a year or so back, when the moon was bright
Three clans contracted in peace to dwell.
They've lots to eat there, too,
Potatoes piping hot,
Plenty of beef to sell."
"Bullshit, my friend:
Just watch heaven switch with hell."

MAO TSE-TUNG'S POEMS

Return to Well Ridge Mountains (1965), to the tune "Water Music Prelude." The Well Ridge Mountains (Ching-kang shan), on the Hunan-Kiangsi border, were the earliest base of Mao's Communist armies. Now, almost forty years after the fierce battles fought there, Mao celebrates peace and looks forward to ever greater achievements.

Dialogue of the Birds (1965), to the tune *Nien-nu chiao,* "Charms of Nien-nu." "Leviathan-roc" is an image borrowed from the Taoist philosopher Chuang Tzu, of a creature of vast powers beyond the comprehension of the blinkered sparrow. Here the roc stands for the Chinese people, or perhaps the Communist Party. The sparrow is the revisionist or capitalist-roader who looks enviously toward the West. There, the lands of beef and potatoes—the United States, Russia, and Great Britain—have entered into a detente to preserve their prosperity. Mao's roc makes an earthy comment, literally "quit farting": the prosperity of the West is only temporary, the "heaven" of the future will be China.

Translation and notes by Cyril Birch

PROLETARIAN POETS OF THE EARLY 1970s

The dust of the Cultural Revolution was barely beginning to settle; poetry journals were still suspended. But in some regions a few small pamphlets of verse had begun to appear. The following selections come from one of these pamphlets, recommended highly by a senior professor of literature at Sun Yat-sen University, Canton, as a worthy sample of proletarian writings in recent years. The professor's judgement is supported by the fact that the poems had been screened by a contest held in Kwangtung Province in honor of the thirtieth anniversary of Mao Tse-tung's "Yenan Talks." —K.Y.H.

CH'IU YEN

My Sword, Eversharp

Night rain, pouring in buckets,
The mountain village locked in by a windstorm.
A bugle sounded,
Men came running from all directions.

Several squads of militia—several walls,
Standing erect on mountain slope, braving wind and rain.
"Count off!" "One, two, three . . ."
Ah, why one too many?

A flash of lightning
Lit up Uncle Hung Sung:
Silver eyebrows on bronze face,
And a glistening sword in hand.

"Uncle Hung Sung!" "Here!"
"Fall out!" "Yes!"
"Go home!" "No!"
There was fire in his words:

"Time was when White dogs came at us,
Blood flowed in streams in our village.
The Red Guards counterattacked at night,
I wielded this very sword, and enemy heads rolled."

845

"Until the class struggle ends
My sword will keep singing under my pillow,
Its blade eversharp, and its heroic spirit ever high;
Though my hair is frosty, my heart stays red."

"Fall in!" A new order rang,
Uncle Hung jumped in joy, like a young fellow.
He felt weightless, stepping on air, in wind and rain,
His silvery hair reflected on his gleaming sword.

March 1972, at Tzu-chin
New Poetry from Southern Kwangtung, pp. 151–52

SHEN JEN-K'ANG

Spring Rain

Thick and downy, spring rain
Sprinkles on the plain;
Soft, gentle breeze
Wakes up the sleeping households.
And the doors and windows, one after another
Open to the sky still dark grey before dawn.
The communers
Ready their plows to greet a new day.

Long threads of rain
Hang down from the sky;
A vigorous choral music
Has been struck on these strings;
Lively, vocal raindrops
Nurture our sprouting crops.

From up there
Come rain and wind day by day;
And on earth
Spread the signs of spring everywhere.

Riding on the wind, spring rain arrives,
And the newly terraced fields at La-tzu-k'ou
Stand vertical, a pagoda of a thousand stories.

In sunny March
The freshly turned soil blooms.
Riding on the wind, spring rain arrives.

The plot at Yang Chia-ling which Chairman Mao once tilled
Shines forth,
And the glittering plowshares
Ease the Red seeds into the soil.

Spring rain, falling, falling,
Riding on ceaseless wind.
Waves of green water churn in the rivers and streams,
While on the hills, unrolls a misty screen.

From the Ta-ts'ang range to T'ien-shan,
From the Yangtze River to southern Yunnan,
Every inch of land heralds the arrival of spring,
Every inch of land
Sprouts the young shoots of Ta-chai.

Early March, the rivers thaw,
Mid-March, wild geese return from the south,
Spring rain has soaked through the land now.
At the meeting to discuss spring plowing
The production brigade stays until sunrise.
This year, they declare,
Let's beat the quota and break the 1000-catty miracle limit,
Let's mold a world abundant in food and clothes.

Willow catkins fly, peach blossoms glow,
Spring rain brings noisy cheer to earth,
Noisy rumbles of farm machines,
Noisy commands to the draft animals.
This year, we say,
We want to rise several further stories high,
And for that men are racing, everywhere.

Revised in Canton, spring 1972
New Poetry from Southern Kwangtung, pp. 66–68

WEI CHIH

Greeting the New Year before
the Furnace

The hour is late, the Last Eve approaching,
In the furnaces, flames leap and reel;
Before them we fight, wiping sweat like rain,
Locked in close combat with molten steel.

Say, you want to view flowers on New Year's Eve,
This is not a bad place, not bad at all;
A rainbow in the sky, a sunrise spreads
Where the steel sparks rise and fall.

Say, you want to watch the old year's passing
Around a fire, then come right over here;
Most satisfying to face such roaring blazes
And hold battle positions without wavering or fear.

Say, you want to toast the arriving spring,
Let us race with time, hurry and speed up;
Let each crucible be our drinking glass,
Let's pour bucket after bucket, cup after cup.

Arms of iron wielding rods of steel,
Sketch heroic designs and visions ahead;
As crimson light and heat wave rise to the sky,
We write our unending poetry, fiery and red.

New Poetry from Southern Kwangtung, pp. 38–39

Translated by Kai-yu Hsu

PART SIX

The Aftermath:
The Fall of the Gang of Four
—Returns and Reversals

(1971–)

After the Cultural Revolution, a few works not condemned during the movement reappeared; Wei Wei's and Malchinhu's stories of the 1950s and Hao Jan's of the 1960s were among them. Hao Jan also resumed writing, and his long novel *Broad Road in Golden Light* soon appeared. The worker-poet Li Hsüeh-ao published some new verses, but Yang Mo, author of *The Song of Youth,* was encouraged only to rewrite her once-denounced old novel. Premier Chou En-lai's death in 1976 triggered a return of the moderates to power. By October of that year, the Gang of Four, led by Chiang Ching, had been officially ousted. The fall of the Gang of Four gave rise to such a work as "White Bone Demon"; its satire is all too blunt, and its humorous quality is too easily lost without masterful performers to bring it before an audience, but it dramatically illustrates the political change.

The thaw became more convincing each day with the return of writers and works once condemned and the resumption of long-interrupted works (Yao Hsüeh-yin's *Li Tzu-ch'eng,* Liu Ch'ing's *Builders*). Most of the old-timers are back on stage now, except for those permanently removed by the Cultural Revolution (Lao She, Chao Shu-li, Teng T'o, Shao Ch'üan-lin, and others) or by the indiscriminating passage of time (Kuo Mo-jo).

By the end of 1978, a group of new writers had come into the limelight. Their works, mostly short stories, give detailed accounts of the injustice perpetrated by the Gang of Four. These works expose the evil of the anti-intellectual radicalism that has produced a generation of mindless youth, and record the cruel treatment meted out to the loyal comrades who stood in their way. Adequate exploration with these new works clearly requires another volume.

Meanwhile, side by side with the new and vigorous voices of such worker-poets as Feng Ching-yüan, one hears of some whispered stories not so enthusiastically praising the new life or new politics. They indicate that a dissenting voice exists, though its magnitude and significance still remain to be seen.

849

WEI WEI
(1920–)

Son of a poor family in Chengchow, the rail center of Honan Province, Wei
Wei joined the Eighth Route Army in 1937 and spent most of the war years in
the Shansi-Chahar-Hopei border area, fighting and writing reports and stories
about his experience. A long poem entitled "The View at Dawn" was circulated
widely and rallied several other young poets in that area who together spearheaded a new poetry movement. Some of their well-remembered works have
been collected in *Shansi-Chahar-Hopei Poems* (1959). These verses—unpol-
ished, unadorned, but quite impressive and moving—flowed from the hearts
and mouths of the embattled people.

But Wei Wei's writing career did not reach its peak until the Korean War,
when he served as a war correspondent. His dispatches were warmly received,
and a collection of them, *Who Are the Most Loveable People,* established his
reputation as a worthy model in this genre. The book is among the first to be
reissued after the Cultural Revolution.

As shown in the story translated below, the works collected in that volume
won their readers with their simple but effective language. The narrator purposely addresses the young reader, but the stories possess an appeal to readers
of all ages.

Wei Wei served in the editorial offices of several national publications. He
is among the very few who survived the Cultural Revolution with no mishap.
Toward the end of September 1978, reports from Peking identified him as chief
of the political department in the military command of the Peking district. His
new full-length novel *The East,* also based on his Korean War experience, was
scheduled for publication in the winter of 1978.

His published works include *Two Years* (poetry), *To the Battlefront* (poetry),
The View at Dawn (long poem), *The Flowers of Happiness Bloom for the Brave*
(essays), *Red Storm* (screen play), *Angry Winds in Open Sky* (another novel),
and other writings. —K.Y.H.

In a Snowstorm

When I heard this story, there was intense fighting on the Han River front.
The volunteer army was marching column by column toward the front
through heavily falling snow. As the comrades hurried along, no one noticed
a twelve- or thirteen-year-old Korean girl following close behind.

As soon as the troops came to a halt, this young girl, no one knows how, found
her way to the machine-gun company. The comrades took one look at her and

851

wondered where on earth she had come from, on a day as cold as this, wearing only unlined pants and jacket, a filthy little white skirt, and a pair of low-topped thin-soled rubber shoes that were falling apart. Her hair was kneaded into a messy bun, with a few stalks of grass sticking to it and, on a closer look, a shrapnel wound on her neck could be seen. First she took this comrade's hand, held it and talked awhile, then she took that comrade's hand, held it and talked awhile. But the interpreter was not there, so no one had any idea what she was saying or where she had come from.

It was only after the arrival of the interpreter that everyone found out that this child had lost her entire family. She had already wandered two or three hundred *li*, searching here for food and shelter today, tomorrow seeking elsewhere. On this particular day, she had just dug herself into a hay nest to sleep when she saw our volunteer army unit going by, and she had come running to catch up.

Hearing this, our volunteer army comrades all strove to arrange for her to wash and eat, and prepared a place for her to sleep.

Who could have guessed that the next day the young girl would not leave! She said to the company commander, "Uncle, I want to go with you."

He smiled and replied, "If you were to go with us, what would you do?"

She said, "If I couldn't do anything else, I could boil water and serve meals for you, couldn't I? I used to help my mother cook at home."

"But we start fighting in a day or two."

"Start fighting!" the girl said. "What is there to be afraid of? If I can't fight, I can watch, can't I? Seeing you kill the American devils with my own eyes would make me very happy!"

But think about it, my young friends. How could the volunteer army take a young girl with them to the line of fire to fight? They were certainly unwilling simply to cast her aside, but what was to be done?

The company commander went to consult with the political officer. And they came up with a solution: have one of the local people, at whose house they were billeted, take her in. This person agreed to the plan, and after discussing the pros and cons with the young girl, she was installed in this person's home.

To everyone's surprise, she came running back to the company in the middle of the night. She said that the person had shut her into a tiny, cold room and had told her that after the troops left she would be beaten to death. . . . It turned out that this person was not a peasant, as they had supposed, but a landowner. In all, there were only three families in this village and all the members of the other two families were gone. The company commander and the political officer were unable to come up with another plan and so were quite concerned.

At noon the next day, the battalion commander telephoned to say that the troops should step up preparations, because fighting could begin that very night. This made the company commander and the political officer even more worried. One's brows knit into a knot, and the veins in the other's forehead began throbbing. These two, even in the midst of the most dangerous battle, had never been so upset.

But the young girl was still there, saying, "Good uncles, I know you've agreed to take me with you. When do we start?" She pointed to the machine guns sitting nearby and continued, "Rat-a-tat-a-tat, kill those American 'salamis'!"

This made the two men want to laugh and cry at the same time. The company commander looked at his watch. It was ticking so lightly and quickly that it seemed to be running away.

II

In the end, the company commander had to telephone battalion headquarters for instructions. The battalion political officer weighed the situation for a long while before answering: "About the problem of the Korean girl, don't worry, just take good care of her. I will come over soon to take care of the situation."

And indeed, after a short while the battalion political officer showed up.

He was a tall young man, very friendly and likable. The company commander, and all the rest, rushed over and saluted him. The Korean girl was a very intelligent child; she imitated everyone else and saluted too.

The company headquarters was packed with people.

"Is this the young girl you were talking about?" said the tall political officer, pointing at the girl.

The company commander nodded. "Yes, she's the one, and she absolutely insists on going with us."

The young girl saw that they were talking about her and she ran over to the senior political officer. As if she were greeting her mother, she put her tousled head in his lap and grasped his belt in her two small hands. Then she raised her head and pointed to the wound on her neck, her large eyes fastened on the tall officer. She started talking about how she had been wounded by American bombers, how she had managed to run out of her burning house. She went to find her father and saw him collapsed outside the ox shelter, the fodder he had been cooking for the ox thrown to one side. She shook him. He didn't respond. The bomb had killed him. She found her mother in the kitchen. She had been in the midst of washing rice. The rice was scattered all over. The girl shook her mother, but her mother didn't respond. Her mother could never respond to her again. The girl went to find her big brother. He was still holding the hempen rope he had been splicing, his face now a sheet of blood. She went looking for her sister-in-law, and found her still holding the new clothes she had been making for her. She had also collapsed on the floor—dead. And thus out of her once beautiful family there remained only herself. She wept in front of her parents, wept in front of her brother and sister-in-law, then finally dried her tears and came away.

While the interpreter, also a Korean, was translating to all assembled, big tears rolled down his cheeks. All heads were lowered. The political officer's eyes too were moist. He forced back his tears and sighed deeply.

The girl raised her head again and with her big eyes fixed upon the officer, continued to implore.

"Uncle, you absolutely must allow me to go with you. I must avenge my family! I can learn anything. I can even sing Chinese songs. If you don't believe me, I'll sing one for you." She glanced around at all the people in the room and started singing,

> The east is red, the sun is rising,
> From China has come forth Mao Tse-tung . . .

She sang on . . . The political officer suddenly reached out and hugged her to him, no longer able to keep his tears from flowing. At this point the whole roomful of volunteer army comrades were weeping. Some turned their faces away to wipe away their tears, and others were sniveling.

"Comrades!" the political officer said sternly to all present. "Would you say this child is lovable?"

Was there anyone who could say she wasn't?

The political officer continued, "That's right. This child is extremely lovable. She is just like the thousands and thousands of lovable children of our own homeland. But this child has been so bitterly hurt by the enemy. If the American robbers battled their way into our homeland, what would happen to those lovable children of our homeland . . . ?"

All were listening in silence. Those thousands and thousands of children of our homeland, in the cities, in the countryside, wearing red neckerchiefs, or with no red neckerchiefs, like grain in a field whose boundaries cannot be seen, all leaping and dancing about before everyone's eyes.

All had their minds fixed on these images as they stared at the senior political officer, their eyes open wide.

He went on: "But comrades! We will not allow those fortunate children of our homeland to become like this child. We must make this child—make all of Korea's thousands upon thousands of children—as happy as those of our homeland. Isn't that right?"

"Right!" said everyone with one voice.

"All right, comrades! It is for them that we are fighting. Tonight we start action. Have you finished polishing the machine guns?"

"Yes, we have."

"What about the 60mm howitzers?"

"Those are ready too."

"Good. Now, comrades, when you fight, you must fight with all you've got, the more the better. You must pile the corpses of those wild animals mountainhigh and drain their blood like a river. They must all die on our battlefield."

"But, what about the child?" the company commander interrupted to ask.

The political officer replied, "You have all done a wonderful job taking care of her. I want to commend you for it. Now, let her go with me, I'll think of something." As he spoke, he took her hand and stood up.

When she saw that the tall officer was going to take her with him, she was so happy that she couldn't stand still, her smiling small face a flower in bloom. She said, "Good Uncle, let's go. Even if you were taking me to the edge of the sky, I would still want to go."

III

The mountain roads were filled with snow. The entire sky had been blown into a whirlwind of feathery whiteness. And it was cold! The tall political officer took off his overcoat and put it around the shoulders of the little girl. At first, she wouldn't wear it. It was only when he acted angry that she put it on. The overcoat dragged on the ground, so she stumbled a bit as she walked, but she was truly happy. If they had walked by other people on the road, she would surely have said with pride, "Hey, look! I too am a part of the volunteer army!"

They arrived at battalion headquarters. The commander and his deputy were both there; only the assistant political officer was absent. The tall officer made the introductions and the young girl bounded over to shake their hands. The deputy commander's eyes were very sharp. He immediately saw the wound on her neck and shouted, "Hey, couriers, what are you doing? Run and get the medic to take care of this child's wound."

The tall political officer asked if all the combat preparations were complete. After making sure that everything was ready, he chuckled lightheartedly and said, "Well, what shall we do to welcome our young guest?"

The commander patted the girl on the head and laughed merrily, saying, "Young lady, you are in luck! I just bought a small chicken. We were going to eat it to gain strength for action. Now that you've come, it will be to welcome you!"

After the medic had cleansed the wound and applied some medicine, the courier carefully carried in the food. The chicken was done to a turn and piping hot!

The little girl was embarrassed to eat. She would only pick up a tiny piece, causing the battalion commander to burst out laughing again. "Ha, so you're still being polite! To be a soldier you have to be able to eat, march, and fight. Come on!" He picked up a fat, juicy chicken leg and placed it all glistening and dripping in her bowl.

How could she express the happiness that was in her heart on this day!

By the time they'd finished eating, it was getting late. The regimental courier brought in an order: they were to set off at eight o'clock that night. The battalion commander whispered into the political officer's ear, "Well, what are we going to do, Old Liu? You plan to ... "

The political officer whispered back, "A while ago, I told the assistant political officer to go and make arrangements for her."

And indeed, before he left to visit the machine-gun company, he had told his assistant to make arrangements for the girl to stay in the home of one of the local people.

Everyone was laughing and talking in the room when suddenly "weng—weng—weng— ... ," enemy planes began circling over the village. The brave little girl stood up and shouted, "Uncles, lie down, lie down!" But these volunteer army uncles were all used to fighting American planes; no one was afraid. Seeing that none of them moved, she went up, and pushing on them, forced them to lie down. She loved those volunteer army uncles so much!

Just as the American planes were leaving, the assistant political officer came back, with several Korean people following behind. Among them was a white-bearded old man bent over at the waist and also an old woman holding a small padded jacket in her hands.

As soon as the assistant political officer entered the room, he said excitedly, "Sir! Mission accomplished! All of these families are arguing over which of them will be allowed to take in the girl." He patted the little girl on the head and squeezed her hand. The old woman hurriedly came forward to put the padded jacket on the girl. The bent old man also pushed his way forward, waving his hands, saying, "No, no, comrade, let her go with me."

As soon as the young girl saw what was going on, she ran over to the senior political officer, and, so upset that she was about to cry, said, "Uncle, didn't you say that I could go with you? Why do you want to send me away again?"

The tall officer and the commander said, almost in unison, "Good child! We are going to fight right away."

"But I left home to avenge my family!"

Ai! This really stumped all the people in the room. No one had thought that this young girl could be so strong-willed.

At this point there suddenly came the sound of a woman's voice from outside the door. "Is this the battalion headquarters?" Presently a short-haired young woman in uniform with a bag over one shoulder entered and said, "I am the Women's League cadre for this area. I've come to take care of your food supplies."

The battalion commander burst out laughing again and said, "Terrific! You've come at just the right time. Our food supply has already been taken care of. But how about seeing to the problem of our young friend here?" Then he went out to check the preparations for setting off.

After the woman cadre had heard the story, she put her arms around the little girl, kissed her, and said tenderly, "All right, you want to avenge your family, why don't you come and work with our group."

The political officer, taking advantage of this opportunity, said, "That's right. Working with them is fighting against the American devils too!" He acted as if he were angry, saying, "And if you don't obey, the next time I see you, I won't talk to you!"

This time the little girl said slowly in a low voice, "All right. I'll do what Uncle says. But later on I still want you to take me to go fighting."

The piercing fall-in bugle call sounded. The soldiers assembled and set off. During those last moments the little girl ran up and shook hands with the battalion commander, the political officer, and many of the soldiers. Even after the troops had marched far off into the distance, she still stood on a high slope calling in a loud, clear voice, "Goodbye uncles, goodbye uncles ... "

June 1951
Who Are the Most Loveable People, pp. 23–31

Translated by Natasha Wild

HAO JAN
(Liang Chin-kuang, 1932–)

Born into a poor peasant family in a village thirty miles east of Peking, Hao Jan was orphaned before he was ten. Running errands for the Eighth Route Army guerrillas in his early teens and becoming a village cadre at fourteen and a member of the Chinese Communist Party at sixteen, he took part in the War of Resistance and the Civil War and, along with millions of Chinese peasants, lived through long years of poverty and deprivation. From early 1949 to mid-1954, he helped organize, first as a district cadre, then as a county cadre, nearly two hundred mutual-aid teams and agricultural cooperatives, witnessing thus the land reform and collectivization movements in North China.

According to Hao Jan, his experience as a newspaper reporter and his reading of Marxist writings further enriched his knowledge of rural China and deepened his understanding of its transformation through agricultural collectivization. As he worked successively through the fifties for the *Hopei Youth,* the *Hopei Daily,* and the *Friendship Daily,* reporting on life in the Chinese countryside, he extended his contact with the peasants, from village, to region, to an entire province, and finally to all of China. His enrollment in 1952 at Party and Youth League schools, where he read for the first time Chairman Mao's "Talks at the Yenan Forum on Literature and Art," and his association from 1961 to 1964 as a literary editor with the Party journal *Red Flag* gave him the opportunity to study political and literary theories from a Marxist perspective. As a result he was better able to grasp the true significance of class struggle and relate it to his own experience in his writing.

With folk and traditional literature his main link to culture, and with only three and a half years of formal schooling, Hao Jan never aspired to become a writer. The success of a propaganda skit he wrote in 1949 convinced him of the effectiveness of literature as a political weapon, however, and he began to write newspaper reports, little songs and poems, as well as short plays and stories. After *Peking Literature* published his first story, "Magpies Lighting on the Bough," in 1956, Hao Jan took fiction writing seriously, and in 1964 became a professional writer. By 1975 he had written over thirty books of essays, reportage, children's stories, juvenile fiction, short stories, and novels. Outside China he is best known for his two long novels, *Bright Sunny Sky* and *The Broad Road in Golden Light.* Recently, after the fall of the Gang of Four, he has been criticized for glorifying Chiang Ching and her esthetic theories in his 1974 novella, *Sons and Daughters of Hsisha.* But the criticism has been rather mild, and by January 1979 he, though still not publishing anything, was seen at public functions.

Bright Sunny Sky (Vols. I–III, 1964–66) is a story about class struggle in the Chinese countryside, set in the context of a summer harvest and the Hundred Flowers campaign in 1957. By dramatizing this struggle through an interlocking network of romantic, personal, and intergenerational relationships, Hao Jan makes an otherwise abstract concept tangible and meaningful. And by portraying peasants from their own point of view in a language and literary convention familiar to them, he creates a multitude of truly memorable characters—among them middle-of-the-road middle peasants who are fully capable of initiative, analysis, and ideological development. In *The Broad Road in Golden Light,* a novel projected to be in four parts (Vol. I, 1972; Vol. II, 1974), Hao Jan combines class and line struggle to underscore the historical significance of agricultural collectivization in China. By correlating the cognitive process the characters undergo under the Party's guidance, with a patterning of details and images associated with symbols in the title (road, light, and the color of gold), he depicts vividly and compellingly the vulnerability of poor peasants shortly after Liberation and their determined efforts to free themselves from the stranglehold of individual small peasant economy through the organization of mutual-aid teams and cooperatives among themselves and through alliance with workers.

As a story celebrating self-reliance, "The Wheels Are Flying" (1961) offers insights into how China proceeded with mechanization of its agriculture at a time of simmering Sino-Soviet conflict. As an example of Hao Jan's art, it typifies his way of joining a Marxist world view with a lyrical approach to fiction writing. Li Chu-fang learns—with his two personality traits reacting and uniting in a dialectical interplay—to fix the wheels by repeatedly going through the cognitive process in a practice-knowledge-practice pattern. And as he overcomes one after another increasingly more difficult problems, he acquires not only greater proficiency in mechanical skills, but also deeper understanding of the meaning of self-reliance. His progress, technical, emotional, and ideological, is highlighted at crucial points by the recurrent images of moonlight, the quails, the wild lilies, the Party branch secretary, and the turning wheels. Such a procedure, lyrical by virtue of its affinity with the formulaic progression so pervasively evident in the first, 2500-year-old anthology of Chinese poetry, *Book of Songs,* is characteristic of Hao Jan's fiction as a whole. It becomes a prominent structuring device in *The Broad Road in Golden Light,* and at times comes precariously close to being a formalistic exercise in *Sons and Daughters of Hsisha.* —W.K.M.

The Wheels Are Flying

PROLOGUE

Li Chu-fang was quite famous in his brigade for his two personality traits: (1) he drooped, and (2) he drilled. On the surface he drooped like a wilting rice stalk, never excited and always half asleep; underneath, however, he drilled like a sharp bit, boring to the bottom of things and figuring them all out without making any fuss. These two traits, drooping and drilling, were of course always bound up together in him. He was only twenty-five, belonging to an age group right in the prime of youth and health. These young ones—they are like a bonfire started on a wild mountain which gets more splendid the longer it burns and can even scorch the whole mountain till it is red all over. But Li Chu-fang was an exception. He was like a "choke stove,"* whose leaping flames are concealed within its belly and which, unknown to others, quietly radiates its scorching heat.

There was even something droopy in the way he looked. Short in limbs and body, with a chubby round face, sparse faint eyebrows, and small eyes, all day long he half drooped his upper eyelids and seemed always deep and far away in thought; when he walked, it was usually with lowered head, and hands clasped behind his back; when he spoke, he did it softly and slowly, in a somewhat hoarse voice, and when he got going in earnest, if you should barge in and interrupt him, he would not get upset but would wait till you finished before he spoke again.

No amount of analogy or talking about his appearance can clearly describe someone like Li Chu-fang. Let's give a little example.

Once the mess hall was carrying out a campaign to remodel the cooking facilities, and one of the projects was to crank up a homemade running water system. The method itself had been learned from the Pi-tu Production Brigade, but halfway through, the project ran into a snag. The pipes the Pi-tu Production Brigade used were all metal, fruit of victory won at the capture of Chang T'ien-tso's blockhouse years back. The Li Village didn't have even an inch of it. People were sent everywhere to find and to buy such pipes, but they came back empty-handed; all they could do was to stop the running water project halfway. One morning after a long time had passed, it was suddenly discovered that a peculiar water pipe had connected the kitchen with the well. Several sunflower stalks had taken the place of the metal pipes. These sunflower stalks are very tough and long, hard on the outside but soft inside. All you have to do is to hollow them out with an iron rod and join them together—you have a water pipe.

The discovery of this peculiar water pipe sent the whole brigade into an uproar. No one could guess who had done it. First of all, the youth team work-point recorder, Liu Chin-hsiang, got extremely excited. More than anything else she worshiped people who were more advanced and made greater contributions than she. Such a remarkable person and marvelous job! If she did not immediately publicize and praise them, if she did not quickly submit a report and ask the brigade committee to grant an award, she wouldn't be at peace with herself. Moreover, since she was both the editor-copyist of the blackboard newspaper and the broadcast announcer, if she didn't transmit news in the brigade to the outside soon, she would be considered remiss in carrying out her responsibilities!

The lanky young woman, not bothering to eat her breakfast, nor taking time to comb her hair, flew all over the street, with a notebook in one hand and a fountain pen in the other. First, she pushed open the door of Carpenter the First, and all smiles asked, "Carpenter the First, did you put up that water pipe in the

---

*The popular name the peasants have for a kind of large coal-burning stove. [Author's note]

dining hall?" Completely bewildered by the question, Carpenter the First shook his head. The young woman then came to Blacksmith the Second's house, "It must be you who put up the water pipe in the dining hall!" The response was again no. She put the same question to the head of the technical team, all the well-known innovators, several middle-school students who had returned to the village to take part in production, the cadres who had come down from the city, and even the health worker, but still she could not find the inventor. Finally, Liu Chin-hsiang went to ask the Party branch secretary, Mother Ch'ü. She said, "Mother Ch'ü, it must have been a god who put up the water pipe!"

Smiling, Mother Ch'ü said, "Actually gods are simply human beings who are willing to use their brains. My guess is that it was probably Li Chu-fang."

The young woman pressed her thin lips together and thought to herself: "Could a cotton ball softy like him have thought up such a clever method?"

But that was only the way she thought; in the end she still ran to Li Chu-fang's place. Li Chu-fang was hard at work in the courtyard, pumping air into the tire of a wheelbarrow. She asked in a hurry, "Was it really you who put up that water pipe in the dining hall? Yes or no? Tell me quick!"

Without raising his head, Li Chu-fang only let out a soft "hm—."

She laughed: "I felt it must have been you. If it were someone else, I would have known about it a long time ago. When you were into something that important, why didn't you say a word or two to me about it?"

Still without raising his head, the young fellow said, "What do you mean by 'something important'? I have not tempered steel or cast iron. All I did was to take the stalks, hollow them out, and join them together. That's all."

She opened her notebook, took off the cap of her patterned fountain pen, and said, "Though this matter is small, it reveals the wisdom of us commune members—tell me quickly, how did you come up with this idea?"

Only then did Li Chu-fang realize that the young woman had come on an assignment. He put down the air pump. He blushed, and his thick lips quivered for quite a while before he began: "I saw how very worried they were when they went everywhere and could not get the pipes, and I started wondering why we always had to rely on outside purchases? Why can't we think of a solution ourselves? . . ."

She abruptly interrupted him, closed her notebook, replaced the pen cap, and said, "You go on with your work. You could never explain it anyway. I'm going."

At noon that day, the full, sweet voice of Liu Chin-hsiang rose from the loudspeaker, and her new article also appeared on the blackboard bulletin. She even drew a portrait over her article. People praised her for her art work, but said that she had drawn Li Chu-fang a bit too handsome. . . .

I

Not long after autumn harvest began, as the contests among the various wheelbarrow teams reached a point of flaming fervor, something went wrong with the axle of Li Chu-fang's wheelbarrow. Every push made it squeak, and sometimes it simply stopped and would not turn. Sent to the commune repair shop, it had stayed there for five days without any action. He was sick with impatience.

The slogan the commune Party committee proposed for this autumn harvest was: swift harvest, swift transport, swift threshing. The commune members' enthusiasm was very high; only on the point of swift transport had obstacles developed. This is a mountain region, and small wheelbarrows are a principal means of production and transportation. The kind of wheelbarrow handed down from ancient times had wooden wheels and axles; the villagers call it a "quacky cart," because when in motion it squeaks like a grunting old lady. In the year of communization, the "quacky carts" were fitted out with ball bearings and rubber tires. When you push these carts, they sail and sing along like spring wind swishing through the willow branches. The advance in the means brought with it many advantages, as well as a little problem: whenever something—just about anything—went wrong with the cart wheels, there was no way to fix them. The wooden wheels used in the past were very easy to fix. All you had to do was to find a carpenter to hammer it over a few times; if it still didn't work, you simply threw it away, sawed off a piece of wood and made a new wheel. With rubber-wheeled carts, however, it is different.

[The parts were made in the cities far away; nobody dared to touch them. The commune had set up a repair shop, but with so many carts breaking down at the same time when harvesting was in full swing, the waiting line got longer and longer, and only those who yelled loudest managed to get theirs repaired in time to reenter the transportation contest. Liu Chin-hsiang egged Li Chu-fang on to use the same pressure tactics, but when Li got to the repair shop and saw how hard the comrades there were working, he lost heart. He left the shop, agreeing to wait his turn to get his wheelbarrow fixed.]

Once on the street, he walked around aimlessly a bit, feeling empty, his heart tumbling nonstop. He thought: "If I go back again empty-handed like this, there's no telling how much longer I will have to wait. That repairman said there was nothing seriously wrong. Since there is nothing seriously wrong, I'd better not add to their work load. Let me try to make do by pushing it the way it is." He decided to return to the shop to retrieve the cart.

The moment Li Chu-fang pushed the cart out of the town of T'ang-wu, he regretted it. Since the wheel did not turn, there was no way at all of making do. He squatted down, and looked the cart over; he wrung his hands in despair. An idea suddenly surfaced: since the repairman said there was nothing seriously wrong, why couldn't Li Chu-fang try to fix it himself?

As he got home, Liu Chin-hsiang ran in like a gust of wind. The sight of the cart parked in the courtyard stopped her short. Happy beyond expectation, she said, "Eh, I just went there to ask about it. They insisted that it would take several more days. Look, they have given in to your pressure and fixed up your cart. It pays to be a bit tough, doesn't it?"

Li Chu-fang said, "It has not been fixed. I pushed it back exactly the way it was."

"How are you going to use it?"

"I'm thinking of fixing it myself."

"Good heavens! But this is not as simple as sunflower stalks or mulberry roots. You're really being ridiculous! When you take it back again, you'll have to start all over to wait for your turn from the very beginning!"

Li Chu-fang did not say a word, but got a wrench out of the tool box and immediately set to work to take the wheel apart. Liu Chin-hsiang glared at him a couple of times behind his back, stamped her foot, and took off.

A crescent moon rose over the ridge of the eastern hill; the catalpa tree was like a sieve, sifting the moonlight onto the ground, sifting it onto a youth, silent, dripping with sweat. With one hand holding that rusty wrench and the other grasping the wheel he had taken off the cart, he didn't know where best to begin. He would turn something a few times, then stop for a while, feeling helpless and yet unwilling to give up. . . .

At that moment someone's silhouette appeared over the western wall; in the moonlight, the hair, intermixing white and grey, appeared silvery. After a while, she called softly to him, "Chu-fang, come over here; I'll have a few words with you."

Li Chu-fang was startled; he could tell it was Mother Ch'ü's voice. This old Party branch secretary was his neighbor; because the houses of the two families were exactly back to back, whenever they talked to each other they always did it conveniently over the wall. The old woman's son had been in the army; in the years when the Communist Party was leading the masses of this area to fight as guerrillas in the Ta-ku Mountains, she went through thick and thin risking her life, delivering messages, spying on the enemy, and made great contributions. She was the first Communist Party member that Li Chu-fang knew, and having grown up by her side since childhood, he took her as the model in everything. Her presence that moment made him happy.

Still wringing his hands, Li Chu-fang slowly walked over to her, the moonlight casting his elongated shadow on the earthen wall. Mother Ch'ü leaned over the wall toward him, and with a smile said, "A moment ago, Chin-hsiang came again to tell on you. The cart has not yet been fixed but you already brought it back. What's on your mind?"

"I'm thinking of fixing it myself."

"Yes, that is a good idea. I was about to talk to you about it. Ah, Chu-fang, in our socialist construction we have to depend on hard struggle and self-reliance. Let's leave out the big projects and talk only about the pigs our brigade has been raising. At first, we could not buy enough piglets, but we didn't beg for aid, and we didn't sit and wait. We ourselves rounded up a few old sows for breeding. And look, now in our village is a whole flock of fat pigs and they have become a treasure house . . . At a meeting yesterday, the commune Party committee proposed that the repair shop do all it can, and that the masses also start doing repairs themselves—that we walk on two legs. You are usually good at figuring things out. You should give it a try in this area and blaze a trail."

An upsurge of warmth coursed through Li Chu-fang's breast and a flame spread before his eyes. After a brief moment, he murmured, "I didn't think of it as that important; I was afraid that it wasn't like sunflower stalks or mulberry tree roots . . ."

Mother Ch'ü said, "Even the sunflower stalks are not a small matter. That method you have invented—as soon as I introduced it at the enlarged meeting of the commune Party branch, a lot of brigades went back to experiment with it . . ."

They talked for a long time before Mother Ch'ü left; her voice, however, lingered in the young man's heart. . . .

When he returned to the wheel, his courage grew, his strength multiplied, and his mind and eyes became keen. In a short time, he took the axle assembly apart.

Liu Chin-hsiang returned to the courtyard. She hesitated for a moment, then mischievously asked Li Chu-fang, "Mother Ch'ü criticized you, didn't she?"

"No."

"I don't believe that!"

"She encouraged me to hurry up and give it a try." He repeated for her what Mother Ch'ü had just told him, plus his own understanding of it.

At first Liu Chin-hsiang pretended to be totally unmoved, but later she couldn't help nodding her head, and then she started to laugh. "Out with it," she asked, "are you sure you can fix it yourself?"

"Yes."

She laughed and said, "Then let's light a lamp quickly and get going."

Li Chu-fang said, "I have the lamp, but no oil. We also need machine oil for the axle assembly."

"What if we don't have machine oil?"

"Lard will do."

"We have some at home. I'll go steal some for you."

A hurricane lamp hung from the catalpa tree, a small dish of lard had been placed on the ground, and four eyes were riveted on the axle assembly that had been taken apart. Li Chu-fang held the ball-bearing cup before Liu Chin-hsiang's eyes and said, "You see, here's the trouble. The ball bearings have jammed together. We'll have to wipe them clean, and lay them out properly. We'll also have to tighten the cover. It has to be neither too loose nor too tight. If it's too loose, the ball bearings will again be jammed together; if it's too tight, the cart will drag and will be hard to push—Ah, my mom has locked up the cabinet. We don't have a rag."

Liu Chin-hsiang said, "Use my handkerchief."

Seeing that the printed handkerchief was new and still gave off a faintly perceptible aroma of scented soap, Li Chu-fang couldn't bear to shove it on the grimy black grease. He said, "Wouldn't that be a pity?"

She pouted and said, "What difference does it make? You always have your quiet way of putting me down anyway!"

Like a mouth drawn into a broad smile, or someone on the lookout for some secret, the crescent moon inched its way towards the two young people hard at work. Before long the moon moved directly over head; it was bedtime. Outside the door some people were passing by, talking and laughing, but no one noticed, indeed could know, that in the courtyard these two young people were doing something extraordinary. Only Mother Ch'ü quietly took a look over the wall. Then the old woman returned to her room and put on her reading glasses. Just as she finished reading an editorial in the newspaper, she was startled by Liu Chin-hsiang's unrestrained laughter.

"It's turning!"

II

Li Chu-fang's wheelbarrow was loaded with golden rice stalks, like a small mound. The heavy, drooping grain spikes rubbing against each other made a pleasant sound. On the flat, smooth, narrow road, the fully inflated, fully greased cart wheel was rolling, rolling ...

The moment he arrived at the threshing ground, Li Chu-fang was surrounded by the others. "Chu-fang, did you really fix this cart?" someone said. "Ho, ho, you sure are a sharp drill-bit—digging deep without a sound."

"How about fixing my cart for me!" said another.

Team member Li the Roller, pulling his cart and forcing his way through the crowd, shouted, "You all back away a little first. Team leader, you have to fix mine first!"

Without waiting for Li Chu-fang to speak, Liu Chin-hsiang joined in. "There is nothing wrong with your cart," she said. "Why should you come barging in when we're all so busy? Is there a free-for-all over meat dumplings or something?" Making a face, Li the Roller said, "To tell you the truth, even if my cart went on the blink, I'd sooner push harder to keep it going than let it go to the repair shop and sit idle in the storeroom."

Liu Chin-hsiang said, "The way you're ruining the cart—for that alone we wouldn't bother fixing it up for you."

Waving his hand, Li the Roller said, "But I didn't even ask you. Why all this yakety-yak!? Is Li Chu-fang yours now?"

Liu Chin-hsiang flew at him, blushing and yelling, "You good for nothing, don't you run away! I'm going to tear up your mouth!"

When everybody burst out laughing, Mother Ch'ü, covered all over with chaff, came over to them. Also laughing, she said, "Chin-hsiang, don't tear up the Roller's mouth. If you really tear it up, Li Chu-fang won't be able to fix it."

Everybody broke into even heartier laughter.

Mother Ch'ü took a look at the cart that had been fixed and, turning around, saw that Li Chu-fang had not joined the rest in their chatter, but was squatting alone on the side. With his half-closed eyes staring at the cart, he was thinking his own thoughts. "Chu-fang," she asked, "was it difficult to fix the cart?"

Li Chu-fang was turning over in his mind what Li the Roller had just said.... Now hearing Mother Ch'ü ask about it, he raised his head and said, "Not difficult. We can handle little things and fix them all ourselves." He paused and went on: "Mother Ch'ü, I have an idea, but I don't know if it will work!"

"Let's hear it. Let's talk about it and see whether it will work."

Everybody crowded around, wanting to hear what kind of clever idea this quiet drill-bit was going to come up with this time. Liu Chin-hsiang also forced her way to the front. But Li Chu-fang's words seemed to have jammed in his throat, and for a long time could not come out. Liu Chin-hsiang felt for him and urged him, "Come on, out with it!"

Li Chu-fang said, "I was thinking of getting another person to set up a small repair and supply team with me. That way, we will send our carts to town only for big troubles. Little things we'll fix ourselves."

Almost everyone crowding around shouted "Hooray!" Some were clapping.

Mother Ch'ü said, "Good, let's do it right away. Go ahead and pick whoever you want to be your partner."

Li Chu-fang looked up, turning his half-closed eyes to his teammates one by one.

Liu Chin-hsiang's heart was pounding, as she thought: "Wouldn't it be great if he points at me." The night before, Li Chu-fang had told her all those important things, and together with him she had fixed the damaged cart. She was particularly interested in the project. If it weren't for the nasty remark Li the Roller had just made about her, she would have pulled Li's cart over and fixed it for him to see right then and there . . . She then thought: "They all say behind my back that Li Chu-fang's afraid of me. Doesn't 'afraid' mean the same thing as 'dislike'? He won't pick me, he . . . why doesn't he say something? He sure is a cotton ball character . . ."

It so happened that at this very instant Li Chu-fang cast his eyes on Liu Chin-hsiang, and taking his time, said, "Liu Chin-hsiang will do. I don't know whether she wants to do it or not?"

Liu Chin-hsiang's face went red all of a sudden, all the way down to the bottom of her neck. Muttering, she said, "You want me . . ."

Li the Roller forced his way forward and said, "If you don't want to do it, I will!"

Liu Chin-hsiang shot him an angry look and hurriedly said, "It's for Chu-fang to pick. No volunteers. You think you'll have a turn?"

The tiny cart-repair team came into being. . . .

[Li went for some training and provisions and, together with Liu, set up the workshop in a toolshed. He prepared a board and she wrote a sign for the door. He even brought in his pet quails and a potted flower.]

Seeing the two quails in the cage, she let out a cry. "Why don't you raise a skylark? Beats me that you should be raising such a stupid thing!"

"I like them. They're trustworthy and simple. I dislike the endless chattering of the skylark."

She stole an angry look at him, and when she took a look at the flowers she cried out again. "Why don't you grow cassia instead of this wild lily?"

"Wild lilies are not as pungently sweet-smelling as cassia flowers, but their scent lasts a long time. They don't blow hot this moment and cold the next."

"Phew! You're calling me names in a roundabout way!"

Holding back his laughter, he said seriously, "You insisted on questioning me. Now that I told you, you accuse me of calling you names. From now on I'll just be cotton ball."

She said with a smile, "Everyone says you are straightforward, but it seems to me you are not the least bit trustworthy inside—well, let's be serious now. Should I go out to the streets and call them to bring in their carts?" . . .

[They realized that they had to have some parts, especially some spare ball bearings. He said he couldn't find any. She said she could do better but returned equally empty-handed. She smashed their shop sign in frustration.]

Smiling helplessly, he asked, "You didn't get any, did you?"

"Since you knew it was impossible to get the ball bearings, you should have said something earlier when you came back. I could have told Mother Ch'ü that I wouldn't come here with you and I would have washed my hands of you. Now that we have, after a lot of hullabaloo, stirred everybody up, you still haven't got a thing to work with. How am I supposed to talk to the others?"

He shook his head, and still in a conciliatory tone, said, "This temper of yours is really no good."

"Since you knew it was no good, why didn't you find someone else? Why did you have to pick me?"

He stood up. "Comrade Liu Chin-hsiang, first of all please don't get angry. Would you listen if I were to offer you a suggestion?"

She glanced at him through the corner of her eye, and seeing that he looked very serious and that the veins of his temples seemed to be throbbing, she thought to herself: "He is going to get angry." "Is it criticism?" she asked.
"Yes."

Turning around, she fetched a stool and sat down. "Go ahead," she said.

Li Chu-fang also sat down, but said gently, "My suggestion consists of only one sentence. There are in you good points that I lack, and I want to spend more time with you in order to learn from you; there are also in you weaknesses that I don't have—it's easy for you to be happy, but just as easy for you to get discouraged . . ."

"Everybody can be happy or unhappy at times."

"When are you happy? When everything is going smoothly. When do you get distressed? When your work runs into difficulties . . . Can you say this is not a major shortcoming? What do you think?"

The proud young woman unconsciously nodded her head . . .

[He went on, patiently and in great detail, describing his thought, his outlook on life and work.]

Originally she had her neck turned and her head lowered; but drawn by his voice, she gradually raised her head. Her anger-filled fiery gaze began to soften, changed to surprise, then to respect. They were little companions who had been playing together from a very young age . . . Now, they were gradually growing up, and as they got older, their concerns of heart and mind became more numerous, and the young woman, in spite of herself, grew fond of this young fellow. If she did not see him for a few days, she would think of him; yet the moment she saw him, she wanted to quarrel with him. But there seemed to be in the young fellow a piece of magnet, holding her fast, making it impossible for her to leave. Why had she grown fond of such a person? She couldn't explain it; he was like a lock which couldn't be opened. More recently, she seemed to have discovered the key; today, she actually got hold of the key in her hands; the door to his inner mind and spirit had opened toward her, allowing her to look into the burning light and heat inside. . . .

The two quails stood in the cage, their heads side by side; the wild lilies held still in the pot, bearing beads of water, giving a faint scent. They all looked as if they were listening to the heart-to-heart talk of the young couple. . . .

[They made peace. He learned a way of substituting homemade steel rings for the ball bearings. The young couple worked happily together to fix carts for their brigade. She even learned to be calm and patient with everybody. But that lasted only about five or six days, and the young lady was pouting again.]

That morning, he suddenly laid down his work and left without saying a word. When he came back around noon, he said to her, "If there are any more damaged ball bearings, let's not replace them with steel rings. We'll just make do with old ball bearings. If we cannot make do, we'll just have to send the carts to the commune repair shop."

"What's the matter with you?" She could not make head or tail out of what he said.

"Just now I went to the threshing ground to see several commune members with carts. They said that carts fitted with steel rings were hard to push. When I gave it a try, it was really a bit heavy."

The young woman pouted and said angrily, "These monkeys, if you gave them cookies to eat they would find them too crispy. What is so terrible about some extra weight! Having it this way is after all better than not having any."

Li Chu-fang brought over the cart wheel he had left half finished, and putting it before Liu Chin-hsiang, said, "Take a look at this place. When I took it apart for repair, I discovered this problem: steel rings do not turn as freely in there as ball bearings. When in use they not only weigh the cart down, but also keep biting into the ball bearing cup. After a while, the axle would be ruined."

Now the young woman understood; but she sighed and said, "We cannot use steel rings and cannot buy ball bearings anywhere; are we going to stop working again?" . . .

[They solved the problem by casting ball bearings themselves, but not before they had gone through much trouble and withstood much hardship. Their dedication and selflessness moved all the villagers to pitch in and help them.]

III

[The harvesting season reached its peak.]

That afternoon, many people crowded into the small room of the cart wheel repair team, setting off a raucous hue and cry, turning the whole shop into a deafening frog pond.

"Really, when are you going to fix it for me? Give me a definite date!"

"No matter what, you have to fix it for me first!"

The placid Li Chu-fang was besieged in the midst of a crowd. One pair after another, the agitated, angry eyes were all riveted on him. It looked as if he had changed places with that worker at the commune repair and supply shop a month ago; but the people encircling him now were even more unrestrained because they were all close friends. Lowering his head, Li Chu-fang swiftly but calmly went on working.

After the problem of ball bearings was solved, another difficulty stubbornly pressed in on this young man. There were no more ball bearing cups and axles. He had written letters everywhere and thumbed through newspapers, but nowhere could he find anyone with the experience of making these things in the backyard. At the hardware store in T'ang-wu, every so often there would come a shipment of them, but as soon as they arrived they were sold out, and Li Chu-fang and Liu Chin-hsiang were never—not even once—able to buy any.

People were still shouting and clamoring; some of them were provoked to greater anger by Li Chu-fang's quiet composure. Li the Roller was among those shouting the loudest. He forced his way before Li Chu-fang, brandished his big hand and cried out, "Man, if you don't have a diamond drill, you shouldn't have taken on this porcelain work. All the two of you care about is to act big!"

As luck would have it, he was heard by Liu Chin-hsiang on her way in. For the fifth time in seven days she had gone to T'ang-wu for news. People at the hardware store had told her that a shipment of goods would arrive that night and would be on sale the next day at the market. Happily she rushed back, not expecting in the least to have such remarks flung in her face. How could she not lose her temper? Arms akimbo and face tightly drawn, she yelled at Li the Roller. "What are you trying to do? Want to gobble up people or something?"

"Whether I gobble up people or not, if we cannot complete our work, you two will be held responsible!"

"If I cannot complete my work, will it do if I go take it out on you?"

"This is your job."

"It is my job all right, but even so I have not signed a contract to let you cuss me out!"

Seeing that the quarrel was getting out of hand, Li Chu-fang stood up. He pushed this one and pulled that, earnestly entreating everyone to forget it. He said, "Comrades, please go home first. The carts have not been fixed in time; it's our responsibility. We'll have to figure something out. What good does it do to keep on bickering?"

All the people there felt that Li Chu-fang had said everything there was to be said. The only thing they could do was to restrain themselves a little longer. So they all left.

Li Chu-fang saw them to the door. When they were a long way off, he turned around, and just as he was going to ask Liu Chin-hsiang about the supply situation, she plunked herself down on the stool and turned her back on him.

Chuckling, he circled round to her front. "Are you mad? Who are you mad at now?"

"I'm mad at you—mad at you and no one else!"

"What have I done to you?"

"Has your mouth been sealed off? There they were, pointing at your nose, cussing you out, and you didn't throw a single word back at them!"

"They are worried to death!"

"They are worried! We are having an easy time, aren't we?!"

He sighed, turned around and sat down on his little stool, and as if talking to himself said in a low voice, "You probably feel that I was too soft. Why is it that as soon as someone gets angry at me, I must get angry at him in return? If that is the case, we don't have to talk about anyone else, just the two of us. We might as well forget about doing any work—we would be quarreling all day long, wouldn't we? Is that what you want? . . ."

[She relented and told him about the scheduled arrival of a new shipment of the parts they needed. The next morning he got up early and ran to the hardware store in town, only to find a long line ahead of him. Fortunately she had gotten there even earlier than he had. She gave her place in line to him. When his turn came to buy the parts, out of sympathy for a comrade behind him who was in a worse fix, he yielded his turn and lost the chance to buy any. She ran home in a huff and swore never to see him again. But she still wanted to finish repairing the one wheel she had started the day before, as a gesture to wind up her association with him. She went back to the repair shop, and found him going through the discarded worn parts removed from broken wheels. But she was determined to say nothing to him, no matter how he entreated her.]

"How come you have also turned into a cotton ball?" he said.

Even this joke did not arouse any response. But the young fellow went on cheerfully; "After I returned, I thought of picking through these discards to see if there were any parts we could use as makeshifts. As I was going through them, I suddenly discovered a secret. You see this cup can no longer grab onto the small axle; but if we replace it with this old thick axle, it will grab quite tightly, won't it? You see the threads on this axle have been worn out; they can no longer hold big cups. But if we fit them to a smaller cup, they will grab all right. When we match them up like this, I think that except for axles whose threads have been completely worn out, the majority of these discards can all be used . . ."

While she was trying to finish repairing that one last wheel, Liu Chin-hsiang was thinking: "No matter what you say, I won't listen. I won't say anything either. Before I leave I'll say only this: 'I've already given my word of honor. I will not get angry with you again. I have not quarreled with you over what happened today. You go ahead with what you're doing. No matter what, I'll never have anything to do with it again.' " But, try as she would to think this way, every word he said found its way into her ears. She felt that he was holding up his hands behind her back, gesturing for her to see. She really wanted to turn her head, but she did her best to keep her neck stiff and, biting her lips, refused to look. She was determined not to look.

But he went on. "Do you still remember what I said the day you got angry at me over the problem of ball bearings? If we can handle certain things, why must we go out and buy them? Haven't we made up our minds to be stronger and to rely on our own efforts?" . . . She froze for a moment, and her hands, busy at work as they were, also came to a stop.

"You still remember," he continued, "when I returned from learning at the Hsia-shan Reservoir, we wanted to make ball bearings, but did not have steel molds. You said, 'We sure have enough problems, but we must keep going!' Yes, you were right to say that. From the beginning to now, how many difficulties have we overcome! In the future, there will still be difficulties. But we are not afraid, because revolution is nothing but struggle against difficulties. We should bear in mind the whole situation, give up conveniences to others, and keep the difficulties for ourselves. . . ."

Past events, one by one, reappeared before her eyes. Mulling over the whole thing, she could no longer contain herself, and suddenly swinging around, she took hold of Li Chu-fang's hands and muttered, "I—I am in the wrong again!"

Translated by Wong Kam-ming

MA CHI AND
T'ANG CHIEH-CHUNG:
COMIC DIALOGUES

Not much is known about T'ang Chieh-chung, who plays a subordinate role when performing in this selection, but Ma Chi has been ranked among the greatest in *hsiang-sheng,* a unique form of comic stage dialogues developed in China. A little plump in stature and always witty whether on or off stage, Ma had been a key member of the Ch'ü-i (song and dialogue) Troupe of Peking until the Cultural Revolution. Since 1976, however, he has reappeared in the revived Troupe and has been performing with increasing acclaim.

Hsiang-sheng relies on quick repartee between two performers. Puns and clever proverbs are used extensively. The Chinese speech, rich in homonyms and metaphorical wordplay, lends itself to the art of *hsiang-sheng* particularly well.

In the following selection, a fifteen-minute performance, the subject is a satirical, blunt, frontal attack on Chiang Ching, Mao Tse-tung's widow, leader of the Gang of Four. It employs all the traditional trappings of this art form, including the homophonic pun between *T'ai-hou* (the title "Empress") and *t'ai-hou* (literally, "too thick"). Such wordplays bring instant response from the audience, but defy translation into another language.

Although the all-too-bare references to Chiang Ching's ridiculous behavior and political crimes deprive the "White Bone Demon" of much subtle charm, the audience in China today is still ready to respond to its fun-making because of the familiarity of the subject. The title of the piece comes from a character in the Ming dynasty allegorical novel *Journey to the West,* or *Monkey* as Waley translated it. In that novel, the demon is eventually overpowered by the Monkey; at one time Mao Tse-tung praised Monkey for this victory. Hence the popularity of the title in China today. —K.Y.H.

White Bone Demon

A. Have you ever seen a ghost?

B. A ghost? That's just something handed down by tradition, folklore. Actually there is no such thing.

A. Sure there is. I've seen one.

B. Oh? You've seen one? What did it look like?

A. Well, it was neither man nor demon; half the face was smiling and half crying, its long claws were extended, and, normally it walked sideways.

870

B. Wow! Where was this?

A. It would be difficult to say actually where. It usually is leaping about all over the place. It wears a red hat on its head; it has a Marxist overcoat on; it is made up to look like a representative of the most orthodox way of life; it infiltrates the ranks of our revolutionary troops, and carries out nefarious activities of all kinds. Its crimes have added up to the limit of Heaven's tolerance!

B. Ohhh! You must be talking about the White Bone Demon of the Gang of Four.

A. Exactly! It's that female ghost that I'm talking about.

B. How come she is neither human nor demon?

A. Well, what would you say she is, a person or a demon?

B. I'd say she's a person.

A. Well, if she's a person, why is she so full of the devil? Always grasping for power, destroying our great leader Mao Tse-tung, and betraying our beloved Premier Chou?

B. Hmmm! This creature isn't human. She's purely and simply a demon.

A. Then, if that's the case, how is it that she dares to come out in the bright daylight and carry out her nefarious schemes?

B. Well then, I guess she's a person.

A. If she's a human being, then why is she afraid of the sun, always hiding in the shadows and conducting the secretive affairs of the Gang of Four?

B. Then she's still a demon, all right, no question about it.

A. If she's a demon, then why does she have a human yet doglike appearance? Disguises herself as a proper ladylike person, talks like a human being, but doesn't do the things that human beings do?

B. Then she must be a demon . . . .

A. What . . .?

B. No! She's human after all.

A. Is she human or is she a demon?

B. She's . . . .

A. She's human to your face and a demon behind your back, so, she is neither human nor a demon.

B. Well, what about that bit where you said half her face is smiling and the other half is crying?

A. This White Bone Demon goes around everywhere with her evil scheming designs, and she puts on a tricky act in whatever she does. One minute she's crying and the next minute she's laughing. When she's crying she's like a crocodile shedding tears, and when she's laughing she's like a mad dog barking in the sun.

B. She's really crafty. How far are her claws extended?

A. The White Bone Demon has ambitions that extend over the entire earth, everywhere. She grabs for Party power, grabs for political power, grabs for cultural power, grabs for military power, grabs for financial power, grabs for labor power, grabs for . . . (*Grabs his partner*)

B. Let's stop all this grabbing! Her claws are extended much too far.

A. Her hands reach out everywhere.

B. How about her walking sideways?

A. The White Bone Demon makes her own laws. She relies on her position of power to carry out acts of wickedness and perversion and "walks sideways" in encroaching on the rights of others.

B. She must belong to the crab family.

A. The most brutal aspect yet of the whole thing is the creation of the Gang of Four. They violated the principles of Marxism and oppose the thoughts of Mao. They defy the basic principles of the "Three Do's and Three Don'ts."* In reaching for power, they secretly changed Chairman Mao's directive; they brutally opposed the man whom Chairman Mao selected to succeed him, our venerated Chairman Hua, and sought to bring down a whole raft of responsible people in the Central government as well as local comrades.

B. Truly the Gang of Four have the appearance of human beings but the hearts of beasts.

A. Lest the whole world did not fall into total confusion, they screamed "Attack with reason, but defend with force," but they actually incited beatings and lootings in all levels of society to interfere with Party-directed campaigns and to interrupt production. If you didn't look right to them, they just arbitrarily put a hat on you, or charged you with violating the Party line.

B. Oh my! They were really the greatest manufacturers of lines and hats!

A. Take someone like you, for example; they would make it so that you could neither climb up nor climb down, they would neither let you live nor let you die.

B. I would obstinately oppose them.

A. They'd accuse you of hating the Party.

B. Then I'd stay out of their way.

A. They would accuse you of lack of enthusiasm toward the Party.

B. I would pretend to go along with them but be neither close nor distant.

A. They would say that you weren't taking a firm stand.

B. Then in that case I would be forced to become intimately involved with them?!

A. They would accuse you of persecuting them, hurting them, and opposing the revolution.

B. Ouch!! In that case how can I go on living?

A. Now you see why the Gang of Four are a calamity for our Party and the great enemy of the Chinese people. There's no peace in the nation so long as they're around. Before his death, Chairman Mao made his wise move, and now Chairman Hua has heroically taken charge and has carried out the ideals of Chairman Mao's revolution. In one stroke he has wiped out the Gang of Four and achieved a great historical victory.

B. Good! Get rid of the Party's traitors; cut down the nation's enemies; and do justice to the people's grievances! This truly brings joy to the hearts of everyone.

A. Just so, and particularly with our commune production brigade.

B. Right!

A. When Chairman Hua saved us from the Gang of Four everyone was delighted.

---

*Do practice Marxism, unite, and be open and aboveboard; don't practice revisionism, split, nor intrigue and conspire. [K.Y.H.]

B. Everyone was happy.

A. The oldsters were so happy at the time that they all had a few extra drinks.

B. Right!

A. The youngsters set off firecrackers and the children leaped and danced around.

B. Yeh!

A. The old ladies were so happy, they were grinding their teeth and stamping their feet.

B. What?? Grinding their teeth and stamping their feet? How was that?

A. Because the Gang of Four were even worse than "Old Baldy," Lin Piao.

B. Right. Everyone loathed the Gang of Four.

A. Just so.

B. Say, where was it that you saw the White Bone Demon?

A. Right in our brigade.

B. She wormed her way right into your brigade?

A. She knew the importance of creating antirevolutionary public opinion. She came into our midst; she played all kinds of tricks, using both carrots and sticks; she dreamed of seizing the Party apparatus and the power.

B. That was a daft hope!

A. That day we were all working the fields when we heard this strange wailing sound .... Wooooooo ...!

B. Whew! What was it?

A. The black clouds in the sky were boiling about, and sand and rocks were blowing around on the ground.

B. A tempest had sprung up!

A. The White Bone Demon had arrived.

B. Wow! She brought a ghostly wind with her.

A. As she got out of her car, she looked all around her. Musicians opened up the way in front of her; her shrewd chief of staff brought up the rear. A man on her left and a woman on her right side to guard her, and in the middle she swayed back and forth three times each step she took.

B. What kind of weird behavior was that?

A. Behind her entourage there was still a large group of her factotums, pressed into her service.

B. How many had she forced into working for her?

A. Well, there was one to carry her cape, one with her parasol, another carrying her bed, a further one carrying food, others carrying flower pots, carrying cushions, leading horses, dragging dogs, pulling monkeys along ...

B. Wow! It must have been a really lively scene.

A. When we all saw it we were thunderstruck. "Wow!" everyone said, "This must be the advance omen of an earthquake coming."

B. Huh! It was more like the queen of the rats coming out of her hole.

A. The children were the most fun. They said, "Daddy, daddy, give us a dime."

B. What did they want the money for?

A. They wanted to buy a ticket to watch the monkey show!

B. Huh ...

A. I was busy at the time pumping up my bicycle tire, and looking over my shoulder I saw the White Bone Demon with her look of false benevolence on her face, and I cursed her under my breath.

B. What were you cursing her for?

A. Look at that act! What a snob! She cannot farm the land, she can't work, she can't fight. All she knows how to do is ride on top of the heads of the people in pomp and majesty. What do you think you are, capitalist bloodsucker! Just a typical . . . . "BANG"

B. What happened!!?

A. My tire exploded!

B. Yes??

A. When the White Bone Demon heard the bang she was actually delighted. She said, "I've come here to learn from you. There's no need for you to welcome me with firecrackers."

B. Boy! She really had no sense of shame.

A. Then she asked urgently that all the commune members gather around for a meeting so that she could personally address them.

B. What did she have to say?

A. I'll mimic her for you. (*High falsetto quavering voice*) "Comrade members of the commune . . ."

B. What kind of a voice was that?

A. How can a ghost sound pleasant?

B. Oh!

A. (*Continuing*) "I've come to visit you. I've brought study materials with me to give you."

B. Chairman Mao long criticized her practice of taking materials all over the place.

A. Right. "I've traveled thousands of miles coming here to show my concern for you!"

B. We have Chairman Mao's leadership, the Party's concern for us, and we have authorized documents from the Central government, so there's no need for *you* to come here with your materials for us.

A. "What I've brought for you is a complete set of materials so that you can shoot 'three arrows simultaneously in a volley.' Without my three arrows you won't be able to accomplish the goal of the 'three arrow volley.' "

B. This "three arrow volley" is illicit and unauthorized material that you are shoving on us.

A. "Oh dear! I think it would be best if you all sat down nicely and studied. How can anyone accomplish anything without studying? When I was young I loved to study. Even now I've maintained this habit. Every day I study three hours of Marx's and Lenin's books, five hours of Chairman Mao's works. I've read through four volumes. I can repeat by heart Marx's *Capital* and the complete works of Lenin."

B. Come off it! Cut out all that nonsense.

A. "Comrades, you must study. It won't do if you don't. Our struggle is a complicated matter. Don't you see that I am opposed by many in the Polit-buro?"

B. Long ago they spotted you as a conspirator with wild ambitions.

A. "I'm not afraid of opposition. The truth is not in their hands. For many months they've tried to get me. They said I had a wild scheming heart. They viciously attacked me. Comrades, how could I have a wild scheming heart? All I have is this little heart of a thief."

B. That's true. You've the heart of a thief that won't die.

A. "They also started rumors. They said I wanted to seize power. I give you my oath I've never wanted to seize power."

B. What *have* you tried to do?

A. "I've just held my breath until I can usurp the Party leadership."

B. Isn't that the same thing?

A. "They also said I openly opposed the Central regime. Comrades, that's just slanderous, because in my opposition to the Central government I never dared to be open."

B. That's enough ... You just blew it. You and your Gang of Four are nothing but a group of ambitious and conspiring characters.

A. "Comrades," (*weeping*) "Don't listen to them. I tell you ... uh ... uh ... uh ... I'm not going to say anything more ..."

B. Why aren't you going to say anything more?

A. (*His own natural voice*) Everyone had left the place.

B. Right! No one wanted to listen to that any more.

A. (*In his natural voice*) After the White Bone Demon left, everyone gathered around and started to debate the issue. "Elder brother, what do you think this White Bone Demon really came here for?"

B. Why ask that? It is simple, it is just like the weasel visiting the chicken to wish her a happy new year ... Evil designs in his heart.

A. Right. She's setting out by herself to destroy the great Anti-Lin, Anti-Confucius movement started by Chairman Mao himself. What are these three tidy packages of arrows that she has brought us? Isn't this simply a ruse to strike down a large segment of those cadres loyal to Chairman Mao's revolution?

B. She's made herself out to be an expert on Marxism. Who's going to believe what *she* says?

A. That's so. But there are always those bad elements who will echo what she says. For example the old woman landowner who said, "Oh my, what she said really appeals to my thinking. Her 'three arrows in a volley' ideal. Wonderful, but wouldn't it be much better if there was a volley of 10,000 arrows?"

B. Oh, stop it!

A. But the Party branch secretary of the commune brigade immediately started to criticize her severely. "Ms Ch'en, you're being enthusiastic a little too prematurely. Do you expect to take advantage of the ghostly wind in order to create wild waves? You can't do that. We can distinguish between what smells good and what smells foul. We can clearly see who is a true revolutionary and who is a false revolutionary. We long ago perceived the false pretenses and evil designs of the White Bone Demon."

B. That's right. Poke a hole through her fake Marxist claims; expose her ambitions against the Party.

A. The White Bone Demon rested for a while and then sauntered towards our pigpen, and as she walked she talked....

B. What did she say?

A. She said, "I hear that your secretary rebuked Ms Ch'en behind my back. What is this? Are you working against me? Do you hate me that much? Oppose me? Open your eyes and see who I am."

B. You're the White Bone Demon.

A. "I am the celebrated champion of the Cultural Revolution. I have labored long and bled much for the revolution. Today I brought down one group, tomorrow I'll bring down another group. Stealing documents, confiscating materials, blowing a cold wind and creating disorder; it hasn't been easy for me, you know!"

B. You are evil incarnate, piling up crimes to excess.

A. "Open your eyes and see who I am. I am the trumpeter for the literary revolution."

B. You're an ambitious political climber.

A. "In the 1930s I threw in my lot with the revolution. I acted in the film 'Sai Chin-hua'* and they wanted me to take the part of the little prostitute. I opposed them. I fought for the right to be the star of the film."

B. She performed as Sai Chin-hua! What shame she brought to the Chinese race.

A. "Furthermore, how about the revolutionary operas that are now being performed. Which one of them was not brought about by me personally?"

B. Those were the fruits of Chairman Mao's revolutionary line for literature, and *you* want to take the credit?

A. "Let me tell you, from the 1930s to the 70s it was I who filled the gap in the literary revolution."

B. It was you who went about tearing down everything about Chairman Mao's revolutionary line.

A. "At the First General Assembly of the Party, you were not there."

B. Were you there?

A. "No, I didn't make it either, and I didn't make it to other important assemblies, but I have been to the liberated areas and I have participated in the labor effort. When I went back to the city I had five calluses on my hand. If you don't believe me you can come here and feel them. They're still hard."

B. Where are they?

A. "Here, see?"

B. Oh, you're talking about your fingernails!

(*After further expression of disapproval of the attitude of her audience and a demonstration of her lofty power, she stops talking and her voice falters. . . .*)

B. What's going on here?

A. (*His own voice*) She's squeezing tears from her eyes, but they're all false. While she is doing this, one of her minion clowns suddenly leaps forward and says: "Hey, you there, look what you've done! You've pushed our leader into the pigpen. All of you are going to be severely punished for this." (*He proceeds to make a show of strength, makes some loud noises, then falters as he runs out of words and ideas.*)

*A fabulous woman whose controversial involvement with the German commander during the Boxer Rebellion (1900) has been the subject of a number of works of fiction and theater pieces. [K.Y.H.]

B. His own speech knocks him down.

A. (*His own voice*) Just at this point the White Bone Demon crawls out of the pigpen and saunters out onto the threshing floor.

B. Boy! She really pokes her nose into everything.

A. She says: "Comrades, I've come to be one of you. . . . Let me help you do the corn. But then, I'm afraid of sunlight, and if I help you winnow the grain I'm afraid of the wind. Perhaps I could help you load the sacks, but then I'm afraid of sunburn. I'll tell you what I'll do. I'll do whatever I can within my own limitations."

B. What *can* she do?

A. "Let's play some poker."

B. Going to have some fun, eh?

A. "Let's play right here. But I get to deal first, O.K.? . . . Comrades, I am really feeling concerned these days. When we look at our country, who is going to take over the responsibilities? If we look at the way things are arranged at present, I am a little unhappy about it all. My feeling is that women are better than men."

B. Even in her dreams she wants to take over power.

A. "I remember that in history there were some powerful and very great personages who were women; among these was Lü Hou."

B. Lü Hou was one of the most ambitious characters in history.

A. "Was she a woman, or wasn't she?"

B. Yes, she was a woman.

A. "Then there was Wu Tse-t'ien."

B. Yes, she was a woman.

A. "Then there was Hsi T'ai-hou."

B. Yes, she was a woman.

A. "Then there was Sai Chin-hua."

B. Yes, she was a woman.

A. "Then there was Sung Chiang."

B. Right, she was a woman . . . No, wait a minute, she wasn't a woman. Sung Chiang, that "surrendering type," was a man.

A. "Well, even if he was a man, he was born of one of us women."

B. That's absolutely ridiculous!

A. "All these outstanding women! Some were intellectual types, others were military. Some became Emperors, and others became Empresses. Do you think I look like an Emperor? Or am I like an Empress?"

B. I think you look like an Empress Dowager [*T'ai Hou*].

A. "What about me is like an Empress Dowager [*T'ai Hou*]?"

B. (*Play on homonyms*) The skin of your face is too thick [*t'ai hou*].

A. "All these great political figures, I really admire them. Take Wu Tse-t'ien, for example. All she did was devote herself to national affairs and she became a great Emperor. Everybody called her the Great Sage Emperor. They say that my actions and behavior will sooner or later deserve this title."

B. The Great Sage Emperor —— a big shot!

A. (*Chiming in*) Yes, ought to be shot!

B. That would be just deserts for a crime.

A. "Then there was Lü Hou. I really respected her. She . . . er, she . . . (*stammering*) That's done it!"

B. What's the matter?

A. "I've got all the poker cards in my hand."

B. There you go again, grasping for power and authority.

A. "Let's go. We'll go over and take some photographs. We'll take some pictures of labor on the threshing floor."

B. For what purpose?

A. "So that they can see that not only can I carry out intellectual and military tasks, but I can also work in the fields."

B. How about erecting a couple of monuments and writing up your biography?

A. "We'll go out into the fields and do some hoeing, and let's compete and see who hoes the best and fastest. (*To her minion, Hsiao Tu*) Come take some photographs. And let's do it the way we always do; put me in the middle. And hurry it up, I can't hold out much longer. This is all very tiring. Oh, oh, dear oh dear, what's the matter? Why can't I hoe this grass out?"

B. The hoe couldn't have been very sharp.

A. (*His natural voice*) She was using a carrying pole.

B. Oh come on, don't just put on an act.

A. "I say, you women commune members over there, come on over and the old lady, me, will have her picture taken with you. Don't be so coy about it, the female emperor here is about to take power."

   (*His own voice*) At this point the ugly little minion came up and most officiously said, "Hurry up, all of you. Wash your faces and change your clothing. You are going to have your pictures taken with our leader." When the White Bone Demon heard the words "wash your faces and change your clothes," her face suddenly paled.

B. What was the matter?

A. The one thing she feared was to hear people talking about hygiene.

B. Why is that?

A. As soon as hygiene is brought up, people want to get rid of the four great evils.*

B. So, that's what it was!!

Translated by Robert Tharp

---

*Implying "Gang of Four," while speaking of the national campaign in the early 1950s to berid the nation of mosquitoes, flies, sparrows, and rats. Bedbugs replaced sparrows in a later campaign in 1960. [K.Y.H.]

YANG HSING-WANG

Yang Hsing-wang, a member of the People's Liberation Army, writes about a type of hero and heroism that best illustrates the ideal championed by the Communist Party—revolutionary realism plus revolutionary romanticism. The principal character in the following selection, Commander Tsou, exemplifies all the virtues required of such an abstract hero, and yet there is enough characterization to make Tsou seem a real human being. "Carry On" is among the best of this type of story. —K.Y.H.

Carry On

The tires of the truck hungrily devoured the mountain road.

June, in the hilly region south of the Yangtze River, blue pines and white birches stood on diligent sentry duty along the ridges. Pink carnations accentuated the yellow of wild chrysanthemums, with patches of gentian blue all over the hillside—a beautiful rug was spread over the land.

But, absorbed in my own thinking, I sat in the cab, unmoved by the view outside the window.

I had just completed an assignment at a remote station to "support the left" to overcome the rightist tendency there, and now the leadership wanted me to return to take over the Sixth Company from Commander Tsou. The Sixth Company, my own company, had a glorious record and was characterized by some as "the company with big gongs on its legs"; wherever it goes there is a loud wham. Particularly during the past seven years under Tsou Ch'iang's command, it has stood firmly on Chairman Mao's proletarian revolution line, bucking the evil wind of "open and free competition" and obstructing the vicious tides of "restoration of capitalism." The company has earned for itself a name, "the vanguard company," and the feats and anecdotes I have heard completely justify this honor.

To tell the truth, the moment I knew I was coming back I started hoping for a return to the Sixth Company, but the news that I was to take over the command got me twisted up inside. Could I take that responsibility? Didn't the commissar remind me, as I was boarding the truck, that I must try to be a worthy successor to Commander Tsou, to carry on and further develop the enviable tradition of that company? Yes, there must be a lot about Commander Tsou that I should learn. But where would I begin?

A squeak of the brake, then the truck halted, jerking me awake from my daydream. I realized we had arrived at the work site of the Sixth Company.

It had been two years since I last saw that work site, and now the familiar sights greeted me like so many old friends, old, and yet fresh. Jumping off the truck, I drew a deep breath of the air heavily filled with dynamite smoke and machine oil. In one glance I took in two huge placards; on one of them was written, "The angry roar of our pneumatic drills frightens American imperialists," and on the other, "As our dynamite blasts, Russian revisonists fall apart." On the air, Chairman Mao's May 20th statement was being broadcast. The sounds of the bustling activities told me that Commander Tsou must be somewhere close by.

"Comrade messenger, go find Third Platoon Leader!" a sonorous voice called. Tracing the voice, I saw a tall man wearing a safety helmet; he stood on a boulder, facing the work site. Isn't this Commander Tsou, I asked myself as I ran toward him.

He leapt off the boulder. Before I could salute him, his hands had already seized mine and were shaking them vigorously. His hands felt strong as ever, but the calluses seemed much thicker now.

The third platoon leader brought over by the messenger astounded me. I could see immediately that he was Chang Yung, and yet how he had changed. His pale face that used to characterize him as an old-fashioned scholar had acquired a reddish brown tan, and he had lost his rather fragile physique altogether. He greeted me warmly first before turning to Commander Tsou. "Commander," he said, "are you looking for me?"

"You made me look you up!" Tsou said, sternly.

"Anything happened?"

"First let's go look at the blackboard bulletin you have put out, then we'll talk." Tsou and Chang Yung raced toward the tea room. After a few steps, Tsou looked back at me and said, "The commissar is in a study session. You go back to headquarters first and rest. We'll have a long chat this evening."

On the way to headquarters, I asked the messenger, "What do you think has happened that involved Chang Yung?"

"I am not sure, but perhaps the commander's ruler has measured out problems again this time." He smiled, adding, "Our commander has a special 'ruler' which he ordinarily keeps to himself. But once he takes it out and catches somebody with something not quite right, that guy is in for some trouble."

"What sort of ruler is that? Could it be that sharp?"

"You'll find out in time," he said. "But you don't need to be so scared. The commander's ruler is sharp, but not scary. When he catches you with it, he makes you feel that you deserve it. Nobody really bears him any grudge."

Several years ago when I worked with Commander Tsou, I had learned about that man's sharpness, which never failed to catch our serious slips. He had used it on me once, when I slipped in my assignment to help Chang Yung.

That was when I was still serving as leader of the Eighth Squad. Chang Yung came to us as a new recruit from a big city. I thought in him we finally got someone with lots of ink—from then on we wouldn't have to worry about writing or drawing something any more. Soon I was to find out what we were getting into with him. He had been going to school all those years; his fair skin and tender hands simply could not take our life of rocks and shovels. Several days of pushing the rocks made him feel he could not stick to that kind of schedule. As he put it, he had found the right road but walked into the wrong door—in other words, he should not have chosen to be in the Engineer Corps. He worked less than one man but talked more than ten, causing more trouble than the credit he earned for our squad. Every day he got just that much more on my nerves and I began to needle him every chance I found. "Next time, can you talk a little less?" I'd say to him, but he would answer, "What's a mouth for, if it's not for talking?" "All right, but you're all talk, no work!" I said. "Who's all talk, no work?" he protested, "I'm not spending my days in bed, am I?" He was like that, always ready with the last word. I went to look for the company commander.

The commander was wielding a hammer in the iron workshop. The moment I stepped inside the shop I said, "Commander, will you transfer Chang to some other squad? This puddle of ours is too small for a big fish like him."

Commander Tsou looked at me for a moment. He pointed to the large hammer and said to me, "Come, give a hand here. You swing that, I'll handle the tongs." Then after a pause, he added, casually, "What happened now?"

"What happened!" I said, after spitting into my palm and trying the handle of the hammer. "I can't handle this 'man of letters.' "

"Ho! That's some temper you've got there. Now, let's talk first. How is he doing these days?" They said Commander Tsou had a firecracker temper, that's true, but when you got angry, he became a perfect picture of patience.

"He can't work," I said, "but he has a mouth bigger than anybody else's. I just don't know what to do with him."

"There's nothing wrong with being able to talk well, is there?"

"But his is all talk, no work."

"Don't be in such a hurry. It takes patience to help others to learn." He tapped the piece of iron in his tongs. "Even iron requires repeated tempering before it can be useful. This thing takes a lot of hammering. A person takes even more."

"Company Commander, I am not putting him down. He is not going to amount to very much."

"What did you say? Why can't he amount to very much? Every piece of iron can be tempered into steel." His expression became severe. I glanced at him and realized immediately that I had been caught by his "ruler."

He stopped his work with the tongs, and, looking straight at me, spoke very deliberately. "Squad Leader, when you look at a person, you look at all his aspects; you look at his basic stuff. You have to look at both sides. Don't stick to your own prejudice. Chang came from the worker class. He has a deep-set hatred against the old society. He grew up under the red flag; he has the warmest affection for the Party, for Chairman Mao. These are his bases. As to his present physical inferiority, his soft muscles that can't take much hard work, and some errors in his way of thinking now, these are the lingering poison of the old educational system. I'm confident that he will turn out to be a full-fledged warrior after he has been through the furnace of revolution. Of course, this process will require his own voluntary effort, but it also depends on how thoroughly we do our work in giving him ideological education."

I had had a feeling that to suggest a transfer of Chang Yung would not be the best solution, but I had been too fed up to think of anything else. Before Commander Tsou finished what he was saying, I hurried to own my mistake. "Commander," I said, "it's my mistake. I withdraw my request. Let's not transfer Chang Yung."

"You mean to wipe out your mistake by just withdrawing your request?" He put down the tool and took a step toward me. "My good leader of the Eighth Squad," he said, his voice very stern though not hostile, "your mistake was not only in your request. Listen, Comrade, Chang is not only a soldier in your squad, but a brother in our proletarian class and a successor to carry on the proletarian revolution. It's not a question of whether you can or can't handle Chang, it's rather whether you have a deep proletarian class feeling toward him. We don't help Chang just to improve the record of work performance for your squad. It's a job required for our revolution, for communism. Have you ever thought about the whole thing that way? Don't you think that is the way it should be?"

Just as the messenger comrade said a moment ago, the commander's "ruler" was strict, but would not hurt anybody's feelings. On the contrary, it convinced and persuaded the one "measured" by it. Now, you go ahead and try to analyze that short statement of his. There is a high degree of awareness about what the correct Party line is, intense warm feeling for class brotherhood, an organic application of the Chairman's principle of "dividing any one thing into two" . . . all these and more are there. After he put it that way, everything became clear to me. "Commander," I said, "I understand now. In the past I set the standard too low for helping Chang."

I thought that the commander must be through with "measuring" me, but no, he was not. After pausing in deep thought for a moment, he added, "It's good that you now understand. Tonight let's call a squad leaders meeting. You explain to them your real understanding of this issue; let them all learn a lesson."

Then I realized that our commander's "ruler" really had a few more notches than any others I had seen. . . .

Though that was quite a few years ago, I could never forget that experience. Now I heard again the mention of our commander's "ruler," and I wondered what the commander had spotted today and how he was going to measure Chang Yung with it.

Sunset dyed in crimson the whole western sky and all the mountains beneath it. It was time to call it off for the day.

I had gone back to company headquarters, found my bunk, and was chatting with the messenger comrade about this and that when Commander Tsou's loud laughter rang in the yard outside. "Hey," he was saying, "don't think it's just a small blackboard bulletin; if you think hard about it, it's not a simple problem. And this Chang Yung . . ."

He walked in and immediately started stripping off his work clothes, hanging them on the wall. "How was it?" he asked me. "Learned a lot from this assignment to 'support the left'?" Only now I had the chance to study him, noticing his slightly thinner cheeks. Otherwise he remained the same strong, husky soldier, always optimistic and always confident.

I briefly described my experience of the past couple of years and turned the subject back to Chang Yung. "There's a problem in the blackboard bulletin that Chang Yung edited?"

"Not only is there a problem—it's a big problem!" He became thoughtful again. After a pause, and a sip of tea from the cup on the table, he said, "Chang Yung is doing all right now at work, always keeping up with everybody, but his way of thinking is still too simple. Just because his platoon fell behind the Second Platoon in rock tonnage, he became desperate and, blinded by impatience, he lost his direction again...."

Chang Yung had been promoted to platoon leader early this year. His morale had been high, and he was always striving to get ahead in his work and was taking every assignment very seriously. But he was too stubborn and too competitive, easily peeved if he was not recorded as the number one. These last few days, the Second Platoon wedged ahead of Chang Yung's Third Platoon; Chang couldn't take that. He exercised his well-trained hand in a cartoon, showing a rocket on the one side, and an ox-cart on the other. The caption he wrote was a rhymed stanza in the impromptu style,

> The Second Platoon rides on a rocket now.
> What shall we do?
> Work hard, work solidly, and stake our lives on it,
> This challenge we must break thru.
> Who's the hero, and who the best?
> The difference lies in this very shift—
> and your strength, your zest.

Commander Tsou got hold of Chang Yung at the work site, pointed out to him where the problem was, and asked him to think it over to discover the root of the trouble. Chang said nothing at the moment, but silently he was protesting. "In order to get more done," he thought, "I see nothing wrong in promoting competition. All right, I admit there might be a suspicion of 'fighting to be number one,' but how serious a mistake is that? Why do you make a mountain out of a molehill?"

Commander Tsou explained the problem in just a few words, then stopped promptly. I knew he was waiting for my comments. "You plan to write something on the blackboard bulletin?" I asked.

"Right! We have to write something. But, I will just assign a topic. The write-up ... well, we'll let you do that," he said, glancing at me.

"Let me do that?"

"Yes, we'll let you do that. I'll be your assistant."

I stared at him. Things started churning inside me. My good old commander, I said to myself, are you already training me on the job now?

That evening, I handed to the commander the draft of a plan of education which I had thought over, worked over time and again until I felt that the statement should pass his measurement. He read it with a smile.

"We are using the method of analyzing just one model case to teach the entire company a lesson on the Party line with life experience," he said. "That's very good. This will more than resolve the problem of Chang Yung. But how high do you intend to push your analysis?" He looked at me, pointing at one statement in my draft which said, "From this model case study, we expect everybody to take a step forward in understanding the importance of 'politics takes command,' and in overcoming the 'only military' viewpoint in our minds."

"It's not enough to make everybody understand," he added. "We have to mobilize everybody to dig for the roots and search for the causes. Why is there such an 'only military' concept budding in our minds? Is it because we don't recognize what that is, or is there some other reason? That's the top priority real question which we must solve first. You think it over some more ..."

"Ah ..." I slapped the back of my head and said, "that's right! We have to develop the right style of integrating theory with practice. And if I revise this statement that way, the analysis would have been pushed higher, wouldn't it?"

"Ha, ha ..." he laughed. "Your head is not sleeping, no, not sleeping at all. This must be one of the things you gained from your support-the-left assignment."

At the meeting on the following day, we discussed the subject, "What can we use to stimulate revolutionary morale?" The Second Platoon leader started out with a thorough critique in which he expounded on the importance of political education among the troops. "... What is this advanced political spirit?" he asked. "It's the lofty ideal of liberating the peoples of the world to achieve communism. And what's this advanced political work? It's the integration of each shovel of earth we dig and each rock we move with China's revolution and world revolution ..."

One speaker after another followed up with contributions on this theme until it became evident that the entire company was seeing more clearly what the Party line was and how we should behave in order to stay on it. I watched Chang Yung from my chairman's vantage point. He listened intensely, scratching his scalp and pulling his hair all the while as though determined to pull something out of his head. His face began to redden and, when he seemed to be on the point of bursting, he shot up from his seat. "Comrades," he shouted, "it's not that our company commander is making a mountain out of a molehill; it's my own political awareness that's too low!"

Everybody was a bit stunned by this outburst, but the stunned silence facilitated Chang Yung's explanation. He spoke in a hurry, as if too many things were rushing out of his mind and throat all at once. He praised the Second Platoon leader for having led his group on the right path, always focusing on the revolutionary purpose of each action, while he on his own part slipped into the "only military" viewpoint when he urged his platoon to race for the glory of being the best among one's own comrades. As he reached his conclusion, declaring that his study of Marxism-Leninism-Maoism stopped short of actual practice, his voice came close to breaking under the emotional strain.

Commander Tsou followed Chang Yung's impassioned speech carefully, nodding his head from time to time. He stood up immediately upon Chang's conclusion and said, "Very good. Comrade Chang's understanding has penetrated way beyond the surface, and he has dug up the root of the problem...."
He exhorted the entire company to learn from this case study so that in the future each one would be able to discover deep meaning about a great principle

even from the most trivial event. ". . . As to the minor flaws in our thinking and work," he said, "we must follow the example of Comrade Chang to keep vigil over even the slightest flaw and dare to correct it wherever we find it to prevent it from spreading and worsening. We must be good at going thoroughly after the roots, reaching all the way to the bottom . . ."

The meeting was over. I hoped to corner the commander to chat with him for a while longer, but a phone call from regimental headquarters called him away.

The moment of Commander Tsou's departure arrived. Yesterday he spent the whole afternoon explaining to me the situations of the different squads in the company and taking me on a final tour of the work site to familiarize me with the various aspects of the project. We did not return to company headquarters until after dark. Then almost immediately he found Chang Yung and talked with him until very late. Still he would not take time out to get a haircut or take a bath. He walked through the sleeping quarters to do his last bed count; he finished his shift of sentry duty.

Breakfast was over. I found the barber and literally forced Commander Tsou to submit to a haircut. Then I asked him to go with me to the bathhouse. He would not go no matter how I entreated him. The messenger comrade offered a comment, saying that the commander would not go to any bathhouse because bathing would make him dizzy; he would only take sponge baths. I was puzzled. He and I used to go to the bathhouse together; we had done that many times. Why all of a sudden had he developed such a peculiar ailment? Since he was adamant, I did not insist.

It was about time to start the day's work, but the car from regimental headquarters had not arrived to pick up Commander Tsou. I urged him to stay back and rest while I would proceed to the work site. He said, "Perhaps I should go also, to take another look at the machine shelter, which is located in a gulch. It may need some reinforcing because the weather is acting funny; soon there may be heavy rain."

"How could there be rain on a clear day like this?" I said, noticing the cloudless blue sky above.

"You can never tell," he said, smiling, and at the same time he proceeded to put on his work clothes. I knew in a situation like that any further argument with him would be a sheer waste of words. I let him come with me.

The blackboard bulletin at the work site today was again prepared by Chang Yung. On one side he had drawn a map showing the situation of the people's revolution in the various parts of the world. On the other side he had sketched several Russian-made tanks disabled by gunfire; standing above these wrecks were our comrades heroically handling pneumatic drills. The contrast made the ruined tanks look extremely pitiful. There was also an impromptu verse to go with the cartoon:

> The enemy is whetting his sword.
> What shall we do?
> Work hard, work solidly, and stake our lives on it,
> To accomplish our missions before war begins.

With one more detonation hole,
We destroy the imperialists, revisionists, and antirevolutionaries;
With one more load of gravel,
We support Asia, Africa, and Latin America.

We read the bulletin. Commander Tsou nudged me and said, "What do you think of this? Chang Yung's brains have been limbered up, eh?"

The weather in the mountains was as unpredictable as a monkey's whim. All morning the sky had been spotless blue, but suddenly a mushroom of black cloud rose in the southeastern sky, rolling and unfolding, accompanied by rumbling thunders. As Commander Tsou had predicted earlier, a sheet of rain raced toward us on the tail of gusty winds only a few minutes after our arrival at the work site. And there a tough but exciting battle began, with the team of comrade drillers bearing the brunt of the weather front. Many of them were precariously anchored on sheer cliffs, their footholds threatened by each gust of strong wind, their eyes blinded by the torrential rain. Commander Tsou went right into their midst, hooking himself nimbly onto a safety rope.

A flash flood broke loose.

The pneumatic pressure pump station perched in a gulch soon came under the joint assault of several cascades of water. The shelter started to lean dangerously on one side. A group of comrades rushed over to drive stakes around it while others dug channels to divert the stream. But the flood was one step ahead of them. One wave rammed the front of the shelter, knocking it off its base, pulling the stakes and ropes along with it.

"Shut her off!" the drill squad leader shouted.

On the far end of the line, Commander Tsou noticed the drills suddenly stopping. "The pump! . . ." he yelled, and dropping the drill he started running toward the pump shelter.

I followed close behind him. After a few yards he suddenly started panting and his steps fumbled. I rushed over to steady him. His face had turned ghastly pale and the veins bulged on his forehead. "Commander," I said recalling his old case of tuberculosis, "are your lungs hurting again?"

"Nothing wrong with me," he said, "hurry up and save the pump!" He pushed me away.

I obeyed and ran to the shelter, where I directed an operation to drag the pump out of the collapsing structure, which was almost gone with the relentless waves.

"Comrades, protect our country's property!" Commander Tsou had also reached the shelter. "Save the pump!" He plunged ahead of everybody else to put his shoulder against the machine, trying to push it out of the flood-washed shelter. But the flood came down faster, and another high wave knocked down the two corner posts under which two comrades had been straining to push the machine. Commander Tsou saw the falling posts—he jumped right down under them in an attempt to break their fall and save the two comrades. He did, but the posts crushed him under, and a downpour of mud and flood water followed.

"Commander! . . ." shouted the two comrades who had been pushed aside by the commander, thus escaping the disaster.

Everybody was shocked; everybody was calling the commander as they reached under the waist-deep water to try to pull him up. We found him and dragged him, soaked and unconscious, out of the shelter and carried him to a ledge a few steps away. I put his head in my lap and tried to revive him. The two comrades stood before him, too choked to say anything. After a few minutes, he stirred a little bit and opened his eyes. "Don't you worry, commander," I said to him. "You have saved these comrades, and they are right here. The pump is also safe . . ." He seemed to smile faintly, and the corners of his mouth trembled a little, but no sounds came from him.

An ambulance arrived and rushed him to the hospital.

That night, I sat alone in company headquarters, thinking back to the days when I first worked with him. We were also pushing a strenuous project at a work site. His tuberculosis was not getting any better, but despite repeated suggestions from the leadership for him to remain in the hospital, he stayed on the job, always saying that he felt all right. It was not until the very end of the project that the leadership discovered that his illness had been aggravated to a dangerous degree. Only then was he ordered to the hospital. At that time, our unit received orders to start a new project at a place even more remote and primitive. I went to the hospital to say goodbye to him. Tears welled up in his eyes as he seized my hands and said, "When you get back to our unit, you tell the leaders that I'll try very hard to rush back to our company!" I went to the new work site, but soon I was transferred to a third place for a support-the-left assignment. Since the hospital had said that his case was serious, I didn't think he would be back to the company so soon, but he went back. . . .

The phone rang, shaking me out of my reminiscence. From the other end came the commissar's voice. I asked in a hurry, "How is the commander?"

"His injury is not too bad."

"Oh, that's good . . ." I heaved a long sigh of relief.

"You find his disability certificate and deliver it here right away, will you?"

"What? Commander Tsou's disability certificate?"

"Didn't you know? The last time he was hospitalized, the central portion of his right lung was removed."

The revelation left me speechless. No wonder he gasped for breath, and no wonder he would not take a bath in the bathhouse. . . . I rushed over to the side of his bed, dug into his bag, and found his certificate and the discharge paper issued by the hospital. With pain I read every word on those papers, carefully. Under the army doctor's notation saying "lost ability for heavy physical labor," there was a line in red ink: "To safeguard the revolutionary line of Chairman Mao, I'll keep up my forward attack, as long as my heart continues to throb."

These few words brought back to my mind, wave upon wave, the various scenes involving him; some I witnessed myself, others were told to me. A sallow skinny boy, fists clenched, glared at his tyrant landlord . . . then he was pulling a cart-load of coal, straining under a thick, black rope, alongside a tottering old man . . . suddenly he appeared in a liberation army uniform, his face full and ruddy now, chatting merrily with his kin in the village, under unfurled red flags with music in the air . . . then he appeared on the China-India border, leaping out of a trench toward the enemy . . . finally he was jumping into the flood water to save two comrades and that pump, meeting the collapsing shelter with his own shoulder.... There were also his deliberate and thoughtful talks, his hearty laughter, this disability certificate decorated in red ink, and a ruler with a few extra notches....

"I shall keep up my forward attack, as long as my heart continues to throb!" Isn't this the only way I can carry on the legacy of this man and his company? I asked myself, and suddenly I knew, like a flash of lightning across the dark sky outside, that I had found the answer.

In the Red-rock Mountain, pp. 31–48

Translated by Kai-yu Hsu

YAO HSÜEH-YIN
(Yao Kuan-san, 1910–)

With only three years of grade school and one semester of junior high school, Yao Hsüeh-yin, the son of a farmer in Teng-hsien, Honan Province, from 1929 through 1932 taught himself by reading assiduously in the Peking Library. Soon after that, he began writing for a living. His short story "Short of Half Carload of Wheat Stalks" (1938) catapulted him into prominence, and a number of novels followed from his pen, including *Nui Ch'üan-te and the Red Carrot, When Flowers Appear in Warm Spring, Love and War,* and *Long Night.*

Yao taught in colleges in Shanghai (1946–51), then returned to his native province to concentrate on writing. An ambitious historical novel based on the life of Li Tzu-ch'eng (1606–45) was taking shape in his mind and he had actually started writing it when politics intervened in 1957 to send him to live and learn from the peasants in the countryside of Wuhan. Two years later he returned to continue his work on Li Tzu-ch'eng and completed the first of five parts in 1963. Though it was said that Mao Tse-tung saw it and thought well of it, the first volume of the novel failed to attract much attention. But Yao persisted, in spite of another brush with the political authorities, who ordered him to undergo reeducation in 1967. Completion of the second part and republication of the first part of *Li Tzu-ch'eng* in 1977 was accompanied by a story about how Mao Tse-tung personally intervened to reinstate Yao among the few state-supported writers so that he could continue the novel. The eminent modern Chinese writer Mao Tun praised *Li Tzu-ch'eng* as the first long historical novel since the May Fourth movement (1919) worthy of that designation.

As the work of a single author, *Li Tzu-ch'eng* differs from the traditional Chinese historical novel, which grew out of the genius of the common people. When finished, *Li Tzu-ch'eng* will run to some three million words. Yao is conscious of the gargantuan assignment he has undertaken, particularly in view of his advancing age. He therefore maintains a rigorous schedule, rising at three in the morning, writing until lunch, and spending the afternoon doing research in the library. For Yao's attitude toward literature, one need only refer to his complaint published in the *Wen-hui Daily* of Shanghai on January 10, 1957. Yao applauded the move to send the writers to experience life with the proletariat (he himself went to a factory), but decried the narrow-vision glasses worn by these writers, who left large segments of reality outside their field of view. Yao's complaint brought Yao himself under subsequent political attack.

The story of Li Tzu-ch'eng unfolds during the last few chaotic years of the Ming dynasty (1368–1644). Li, one of the most successful leaders of popular rebellion, came close to establishing a new dynasty, but was prevented from doing so by the Ming general, Wu San-kuei, who ushered in the Manchus from the north. Yao has made exhaustive use of historical evidence to give us a novel informed by the new Marxist perspective. Li Tzu-ch'eng is presented as fighting for the poor disenfranchised peasantry, while Wu San-kuei represents the interests of the gentry oppressor. The important characters in the novel, an impressive array of heroes as well as villains, are all well endowed with the complexities of living human beings and are described in an equally rich language.

In the following excerpt, Li, having suffered a major defeat, has gone to the camp of Chang Hsien-chung for help. This is a bold move in two ways: Li is putting himself under the control of an erstwhile rival, and further, that rival has ostensibly given up the rebellion and surrendered. The episode gives us a sample of Yao Hsüeh-yin's art of fiction at its dramatic best.   —W.L.

from *Li Tzu-ch'eng*

A FORK IN THE ROAD REQUIRES A DECISION

(from Chapter 19)

While Chang Hsien-chung and Li Tzu-ch'eng were upstairs talking things over, Hsü Yi-hsien and several of his men were hurtling through the night toward Wang-chia-ho, whipping their mounts every inch of the way. By the time they had arrived and entered Chang K'o-wang's camp, it was close to two in the morning. Hsü routed Chang out of bed and explained to him his idea that they ought to take advantage of the chance they had now to get rid of Li Tzu-ch'eng once and for all. Now this K'o-wang, though only twenty-two, had already outdone his foster father, Chang Hsien-chung, in duplicity and cruelty. Before Lady Ting had presented Hsien-chung with a son of his own, he had always looked upon K'o-wang as his proper heir and K'o-wang had always thought of himself in the same way. But now that Hsien did have a son of his own flesh and blood, K'o-wang still continued to believe that he would be the one to inherit the mountains and rivers that his foster father would conquer. For the peasantry had traditionally honored the status of an adopted son, and added to that was the fact that few babies born in the field ever survived into adulthood. After he had heard Hsü Yi-hsien out, K'o-wang lost every last trace of drowsiness, leaped to his feet, and shouted, "Right! We mustn't let the tiger get back to his mountain lair!"

"Then we can't afford to dilly-dally, my young commander. The quicker we act, the better."

"Why all the hurry? He's not going to disappear into thin air, you know."

"But suppose he does—it'll be too late to do anything about it then."

"Since he's come all this distance to get here, he's certainly not going to be in any hurry to get back. He'll stay here and rest up four or five days at the very least. Don't worry, I'll personally see to it that he *is* killed, but let me first sit down and talk the whole thing over calmly with my foster father, the senior commander."

"You err, my general. It's absolutely inconceivable that Li-Tzu-ch'eng will linger here any longer than necessary. If we don't strike immediately, we'll miss by a hair."

"How can you be so sure that he won't stay for a while?"

"Well, the way I see it, Li Tzu-ch'eng is busy regrouping his defeated men, and he's also trying to locate his wife, daughter, and generals. He's on pins and needles, as they say, to get on with all that. What's more, he knows that Lin Ming-ch'iu has come to Ku-ch'eng. There's no reason in the world why Tzu-ch'eng should want to stay. You've got to remember that Li's very alert. It could well be that he'll get your foster father to agree on the date for another concerted uprising and then suddenly vanish before the sun is even up tomorrow."

"You're really convinced that he'll leave so soon?"

"Look at it this way. He's famous for being able to shift his troops around with lightning speed. The government forces can't lay a hand on him. If he's that sharp ordinarily, do you think he's going to be careless now that he's far away from his own forces and his life is on the line?"

Chang K'o-wang mulled this over for a bit and answered, "All right, we'll do as you say. No matter how sharp he is, he's not going to evaporate into thin air *this* time."

Turning responsibility for the morning drill over to his younger brother, Chang Wen-hsiu, he immediately picked the best two hundred and fifty crack cavalrymen of his entire force and, accompanied by Hsü Yi-hsien, set out for Ku-ch'eng. By the time they had galloped out of the stockade at Wang-chia-ho, the cock had already crowed a second time.

At the first crow of the cock Chang Hsien-chung sent a servant girl to wake Li Tzu-ch'eng. Li rose and had just finished the business of rinsing his mouth and washing his face and hands when Chang Hsien-chung came up the stairs.

"Brother Li, I got you up ahead of time. I'm a man who likes to get things done. Let's go. We'll have a cup of wine in the Flower Hall first to perk you up and then you'll be able to set out before daybreak and get a head start on things. You came in secret and you'll go in secret. Lin Ming-ch'iu, close by as he is, won't know a damned thing about any of this."

"Has Shang Chiung come?"

"Yes, I sent for him and he's waiting for you in the Flower Hall right now." While accompanying Prince Valiant downstairs, Hsien-chung continued. "So as to maintain secrecy, I've ordered some troops to set out during the night; they'll wait for you at Kuang-hua-hsien. Your personal company of fifty men is having breakfast at this very moment."

"Good. You think of everything."

Chang Hsien-chung slapped his friend on the shoulder and said half in jest, "If the day ever comes when I have to shelter myself under *your* eaves to keep out of the rain, I hope you won't let me get my clothes too wet."

Tzu-ch'eng took Hsien-chung's hand. "Hsien-chung, if there ever is such a day, I certainly won't leave you standing out there under the eaves. You'll come in, and if your clothes are wet, I'll take mine off and put them on you."

"Do you really mean that?"

"Of course I do."

Chang Hsien-chung shook his head from side to side and laughed heartily. Tzu-ch'eng felt a chill grip his heart, for in that instant he realized, more clearly than ever before, that it would be exceedingly difficult for him to work together with Hsien-chung over any long period of time.

"As the days accumulate, you come to see what's really in a man's heart; when the time comes you'll believe what I've said," said Li.

After a hurried farewell meal and a parting cup of wine, Prince Valiant led his entourage—the medical doctor, Shang Chiung; the prince's son, Shuang-hsi; and his personal company of fifty men—out through a side gate. They mounted their horses and moved out. Hsien-chung, accompanied by twenty-odd of his own men, escorted them on their way.

Dawn had not yet broken. Night curfew was still in effect and the streets were deserted save for Chang Hsien-chung's sentries and patrol squads. Hsien-chung accompanied his guests for three or four miles out of town. It was only after they crossed a pontoon bridge called "Crossing of the Taoist Immortals" and had come to a fork in the road that he finally bade them all farewell. He spoke to the doctor, Shang Chiung: "Cousin, all the time you were here I kept thinking about keeping you on, but I knew that Tzu-ch'eng wouldn't stand for it, so I just didn't bring it up. Wang-chia-ho isn't far from here, you know. You'll go right past it. Do you think you'll have a chance to see your goddaughter and godson-in-law?"

"Not this time. Prince Valiant and I are in a hurry. And if things work out for us, I'll have all the time in the world to see them later on anyway."

Shang Chiung's words were no more than out of his mouth than a rumble of hooves was heard thundering down from the north. A stand of trees cut off most of the view so that they could not see exactly how many horses there were. Their experienced ears told them, however, that two or three hundred were involved. Hsien-chung was completely taken aback and wondered to himself what under the sun could have happened over there at Wang-chia-ho. Prince Valiant could not help but feel somewhat apprehensive. He exchanged glances with the doctor, who, in turn, gave a secret sign to Tzu-ch'eng's two young generals, Shuang-hsi and Chang Nai, and the men under their command. In a flash every sword was drawn. Startled by this show of arms, Hsien-chung smiled and said, "Hey, what is all this? Why should you do such a thing in an area under my control? There are no government troops around here and no one else would even dare to pull anything against you. Those men are coming from the direction of my foster son's camp. You haven't a thing to worry about."

Tzu-ch'eng returned Hsien-chung's smile. "Well, you see, my men are so used to being on guard against the unexpected that such immediate reactions have become ingrained." Then Li Tzu-ch'eng turned his head to the right and left and shouted to both wings, "Sheath your blades!"

Though this command was loud and clear and though Shuang-hsi acknowledged it with one "Yes, sir!" after the other, he didn't sheath his sword. Chang Nai and fifty men of the guard took their cue from him and kept their swords firmly in hand too. Everyone was prepared against the long shot that something might go amiss. From the expression in Tzu-ch'eng's eyes, Shuang-hsi knew that the order was not meant to be taken seriously; furthermore, the doctor had winked at him while Tzu-ch'eng was shouting. Therefore, Shuang-hsi was not only unusually on the alert, but was even thinking of how, if the need should arise, he would bound over to Hsien-chung to get in that half-the-battle first blow.

In no time at all Chang K'o-wang and his men had made their way through the trees. It had already grown so light out that immediately upon clearing the edge of the forest, K'o-wang was able to tell right off that Tzu-ch'eng was taking his leave of Hsien-chung. He told Hsü Yi-hsien, his aide-de-camp, "Just in the nick of time, a moment later and he'd have gotten away. Now, when we meet him, don't be in a hurry to start anything. My foster father is still Commander-in-Chief and we must have his agreement before we make our move."

"I understand."

As soon as they arrived at the fork in the road, Chang K'o-wang and Hsü Yi-hsien diligently saluted and greeted the guests; they even went through the motions of exhorting them to stay a while longer, but neither of them dismounted to perform the proper ceremonies that would have been required if they had been serious about it. Shang Chiung asked, "K'o-wang, what kind of business do you have to do that made you gallop so fast?"

Hemming and hawing, K'o-wang replied evasively, "Well, you see, Hsü Yi-hsien, my aide-de-camp, arrived in Wang-chia-ho during the night. When I learned from him that both Commander Li and you, my honored elder, had graced Ku-ch'eng with a visit, I made it a special point to go to the city to pay my respects. Who would have expected that you'd be in such a hurry to leave? If I'd been a moment later, I wouldn't have set eyes on you."

"But it worked out all right in the end," Hsü Yi-hsien continued, "and we did catch up in time to see you off."

"Thank you. You flatter us too much," Li Tzu-ch'eng responded. Wasting no time, he gave Hsien-chung and the others a final salute, whipped his mount and, taking the lead, rode off at the head of his cavalrymen.

As soon as they had gone, Hsien-chung asked his foster son, "K'o-wang, my son, why did you come galloping like a bat out of hell just now? And why did you bring so many men?"

K'o-wang motioned to the officers and men around him and ordered, "Fall back a few paces." Once they were out of earshot, he hurriedly told his foster father of the plan to take advantage of the chance they now had to get rid of Li Tzu-ch'eng and asked permission to strike immediately.

Hsien-chung responded, "Although Tzu-ch'eng and I don't piss in the same pot and though it's true that sooner or later we are bound to have a falling out, still he *is* down on his luck right now and he did make a special trip here to ask me for *my* help. Now how do you expect me to wipe him out? No!"

"But my father and commander, since you yourself realize that sooner or later you are going to come to a parting of the ways, why not take advantage of the opportunity you have to get rid of him here and now? Why leave a potential enemy around who may do you harm in the future? Better to be a murderer than a victim any day!"

Chang Hsien-chung seemed at a loss for words. Signs of contradiction and indecision showed in his eyes. To be sure, he had last night sworn a solemn oath that he would join Li Tzu-ch'eng in a new uprising next year after the wheat harvest was in—still, he had never considered his cooperation with Tzu-ch'eng in any other light but as something temporary during a period when their interests happened to coincide. And just a few minutes ago when Li Tzu-ch'eng's men had heard that sudden rumble of hooves, they had drawn their swords without even thinking. Wasn't that an unmistakably clear indication that whatever misunderstandings stood between them they were too deep to be resolved? And just suppose that it *was* the Will of Heaven that Hsien-chung accomplish great things in the future; then eliminating Tzu-ch'eng *now* would accord with the Will of Heaven above and also fit in with the wishes of his own aides here on earth below. In that case, the oath he had taken would not really be worth serious consideration. But on the other hand, if, for the time being, he made no move, then Tzu-ch'eng would tie up a portion of the government troops in Shensi and that would be advantageous to Hsien-chung's own present position. When all was said and done, what should he do? *What* should he do?

Hsü Yi-hsien could see that Hsien-chung's stance on this issue was not so firm as it had been last night and that he was at this very moment beginning to waver. Thereupon he immediately went into an analysis of the pros and cons of the plan and asked that Hsien-chung consent to it right away in order to keep this golden opportunity from slipping through their fingers. He wound it all up by saying, "If you refuse my loyal advice now, then someday in the future you are sure to suffer defeat at the hands of Tzu-ch'eng. And if that's the way it's to be, then there's no point in my remaining at my commander's side and I request permission to retire into the mountain fastnesses and live in seclusion."

Chang Hsien-chung's expression remained exactly as it had been. He studied Chang K'o-wang's face once again, and then turned and gazed off in the direction of Li Tzu-ch'eng and his cavalry. By now the sky was very light, and soon Hsien-chung's eyes adjusted to the distance and focused in on Prince Valiant's small band. They were riding along the highway that fronted the north bank of the Hsiang River. In the soft rays of the morning sun he was even able to see the whip in Li Tzu-ch'eng's hand.

"If we make our move right away, we can still get them," urged K'o-wang excitedly, a murderous glow radiating from his reddened eyes. "My father and commander, why don't you let me take the troops and go after them? Let me go! Now!"

Ever since the Great Conference at Jung-yang in Honan Province during the seventh year of the Ch'ung-chen Emperor's reign [1634],* Hsien-chung had watched Li Tzu-ch'eng's reputation mount by the day. A few years later, when Tzu-ch'eng was elevated to the status of Prince Valiant,† Hsien-chung had become even more jealous. Yet last night, seeing Tzu-ch'eng defeated and seeking refuge in his camp, Hsien-chung's jealousy, along with all the ill-feeling that had accumulated in his heart as the two men struggled for leadership, was for the moment suppressed. What's more, Tzu-ch'eng's attitude had been so frank and open and his talk had been so straightforward that Hsien-chung had been genuinely moved, and that was the reason he had shown his rival such generosity and warmth. But now, after hearing the exhortations of Chang

---

*It was attended by thirteen rebel leaders representing seventy-two bands of followers. [W.L.]

†Kao Ying-hsiang, an uncle of Li Tzu-ch'eng's, was the first to lay claim to the title. When Kao was decapitated by government forces in 1636, Tzu-ch'eng's followers chose him to succeed to it. [W.L.]

K'o-wang and Hsü Yi-hsien, a sudden storm of conflicting feelings erupted in his heart.

He looked over the two or three hundred crack cavalrymen led by K'o-wang, and then gazed into the distance at the small group under Tzu-ch'eng's command. A plan for wiping Tzu-ch'eng out completely flashed across his mind like a shimmer of summer lightning. It was as though he saw the whole bloody business from beginning to end. It would be quick and simple: he would catch up with Tzu-ch'eng and then ride bridle to bridle with him, pretending that he had something important to discuss. Tzu-ch'eng would be completely off guard. Hsien-chung would suddenly raise one hand and before Tzu-ch'eng had time to call out, he would fell him. While Shuang-hsi and the others were still figuring out what was going on, K'o-wang and his men would have mopped up the rest of the small band.

"Would my commander be so good as to decide now while the opportunity is still ripe. Hesitate no longer." There was a savage look on Hsü Yi-hsien's face as he spoke, and he had already unsheathed his sword.

But Chang Hsien-chung still couldn't bring himself to make the decision that they wanted. Among the numerous leaders of the peasant armies, Hsien-chung was famous for his decisiveness in the thick of things; K'o-wang had never seen his foster father hesitate like this in deciding whether or not to kill a man.

Chang K'o-wang was so eager that he could no longer contain himself; "In another minute they'll be so far away that pursuit will be a waste of time!" With his eyes he signaled his personal troops and the sentries to be on the ready. The Mongol stallion he was riding was fully as eager as he; snorting impatiently, it pulled tight against its reins and pawed the dirt. If the rider had relaxed his hold on the reins for a single instant, the horse would have shot forward like an arrow freed from its bowstring.

Chang Hsien-chung neither nodded his head in agreement nor shook it in refusal. While slowly stroking his brownish beard, he looked off in the distance at the gradually receding shadows of Tzu-ch'eng's horses. Every man held his breath in tense anticipation. Every eye was glued to Chang's right hand. They all knew his peculiar habit: whenever he was wavering as to which way to go on an important issue, or whenever he was deciding whether or not to kill someone of note, he would grab his long beard in the right hand and begin to stroke slowly downward. If when halfway down he suddenly tightened his hand or finished the stroke with an abrupt downward motion, it meant that he had decided to go through with whatever it was he was considering. If he suddenly relaxed his grip when halfway through the stroke, however, that meant that he had decided to call the whole thing off. This time, as he reached the halfway point on the first stroke, Chang K'o-wang thought that he had already agreed to the attack and, drawing his sword, quietly ordered his men: "On the ready!"

Every sword was unsheathed and the head of every horse was pointed westward; every man was ready to gallop off in pursuit as soon as Hsien-chung's horse moved. But the head of Hsien-chung's horse remained perfectly still. Hsien-chung's left hand was drawn tight against the reins, while the right hand continued to stroke his long beard. It neither moved suddenly downward nor did it let go.

Li Tzu-ch'eng let his horse, Black Dragon, proceed westward at its own leisurely pace in the early dawn light, pointedly refraining from whipping him to a gallop. The appearance of Chang K'o-wang and Hsü Yi-hsien with so many mounted men had made him very suspicious. He had quickly deduced that K'o-wang's arrival had come as a surprise to Hsien-chung, and that made him confident that Hsien-chung had not turned against him. Because of that deduction, he had decided to take a bit of a risk and move out slowly rather than gallop off at full tilt and thereby stir up doubts in Hsien-chung's heart. He realized quite clearly that if he did take off at a gallop, not only would the results of his meeting last night vanish into the morning mists, but his own life and the lives of his men would be in jeopardy as well.

The doctor rode beside Prince Valiant and he too was apprehensive about their present situation. He addressed the prince in quiet tones. "It seemed to me that Hsü Yi-hsien and Chang K'o-wang were up to no good. Did you feel that way too?"

"I did to a certain extent, but I don't think it's too serious. Even if Hsien-chung were to change his mind, I doubt very much that he'd do it this quickly. All we have to do is to keep our reins slack and move out with calm and assurance. We must avoid any sort of movement that could be taken for nervousness."

He spoke a bit more loudly than usual so that his two young generals, Shuang-hsi and Chang Nai, along with his personal troops would also hear him. And, sure enough, although every man was in a hurry to get out of there, they all refrained from using their whips to urge their horses forward.

The doctor asked, "In the beginning you had intended to rest up for a few days at Hsien-chung's place. Why was it that as soon as you set eyes on him you were in a hurry to leave? Did you sense right off that he was unreliable, or were you afraid that there were too many agents from the government army in Ku-ch'eng?"

"The large number of agents there was a factor, but besides that . . ."

"Besides that you could tell that Chang Hsien-chung was unreliable."

"No, it was because I sensed that that eagle-beaked advisor of his who was forever waving a goose-feather fan was something less than a good and honest man. Last night at the banquet I noticed that Eagle Beak's smiles were only skin deep and the expression in his eyes was uneasy. He had very little to say—another Fan Tseng, apparently.* Seeing him, I thought to myself that since my primary purpose in coming here had already been accomplished, there was nothing to be gained by lingering any longer and it would be best to leave."

"You left at just the right time—a wise decision, a wise decision. While it is intolerable to harbor thoughts of doing injury to others, it is equally inadmissible not to have the good sense to be on one's guard against them, for on the off

---

*Fan Tseng lived at the end of the Ch'in dynasty [221–206 B.C.]. He was an advisor to Hsiang Yü [one of two main contenders in the struggle to establish a new dynasty] and was honored by him with the title "Second Father." During a banquet at Hung-men, he vigorously exhorted Hsiang Yü to kill Liu Pang [the other main contender, who was eventually successful in establishing a new dynasty, the Han]; Hsiang Yü [like Hsien-chung] did not accept the suggestion. [Author's note]

chance that anything unexpected did happen, you'd not only have lost what you gained in coming here this time, but you'd have sacrificed all your past accomplishments as well."

"On the other hand, if you are going to accomplish anything really great, there are times when you have to gamble. If I had listened to the advice of Pu-chih and the others rather than coming here in person, then Chang Hsien-chung would never have agreed to join us in the rising next year after the wheat harvest is in." Having said this much, Tzu-ch'eng felt very pleased with himself and added, "In retrospect, it would seem that taking an occasional wild risk is well worth it."

"To be sure," said Shang Chiung, "I wasn't as intent on trying to talk you out of coming here as Pu-chih was, but I *have* felt anxious about the entire trip all along. As the saying goes, 'a tiger's hide conceals the heart inside and a human skin hides what lies within.' Who could tell *what* was going through Chang Hsien-chung's mind after he threw in with the government forces at Ku-ch'eng?"

"You weren't the only one who was anxious. I was just as concerned as anyone that Chang might use the opportunity to take advantage of us, but on the other hand, I did know the man's character inside out. As I had it figured, after he threw in on the government side at Ku-ch'eng, he'd probably been treated rather poorly. Surely the imperial court did not trust him and it was quite likely that his officers and men had suffered slights at every turn, so much so that they probably couldn't put up with it any longer. And then I came along with a plan that gave Chang a way of getting back at them. Under those circumstances, why should he want to do me any harm? But on the other hand, if I had stayed around too long, then it would be hard to say what might happen." Tzu-ch'eng looked at the doctor and asked, "Do you agree?"

Shang Chiung nodded his head and replied, "Last night when you left every last one of your personal troops outside the city wall and took only Shuang-hsi and Chang Nai with you to see Chang, I was really worried. I saw that your expression, however, was perfectly calm—didn't seem to have a care in the world. It's true that you really *are* different from ordinary people in being able to face danger with equanimity."

Tzu-ch'eng laughed and said, "Since I was already inside the city, what use would fifty soldiers have been if Chang had taken it into his head to do me in? In a situation like that a small number of personal troops isn't going to do any good. You have to depend on the courage that comes from the rightness of your cause and on your own ability to take advantage of opportunities as they present themselves."

As they came to the outskirts of a village, Tzu-ch'eng turned around and looked back. He saw that they were now somewhat over a mile from the fork in the road. Chang and the others stood there watching them from afar. Seeing that mass of horses and men still there at the fork in the road, Tzu-ch'eng was even surer now that Chang K'o-wang and the others were up to no good and that Chang Hsien-chung was still wavering. Li Tzu-ch'eng's face betrayed not a single trace of fear, but as soon as he and his men had wound through to the other side of the village, he raised his whip and brought it down against Black Dragon's flanks with a loud crack.

Chang Hsien-chung had his last glimpse of Li and his men as they entered the village. The opinion that Li should not be harmed had carried the day.

Hsien-chung knew that his own strength at present was not sufficient for him to go it alone and that he'd have to cooperate with other commanders in order to be a match for the government forces and, he hoped, create a new situation in the future. If he were to kill Tzu-ch'eng, then Lo Ju-ts'ai and other potential allies would be forever wary of him. He would be left with one hand and it is not easy to do much clapping that way.

When Chang had gotten this far in his musing, his heart gave a sudden start as he realized something else: the Manchu soldiers would not be likely to remain within the passes for very long, and since the imperial court was less than convinced of his own sincerity, then as soon as the Manchus left, the two government commanders now fighting them would be free to divert their attention to Chang. They might very well return to Ku-ch'eng with a mass of troops; what's more, they might even transfer a large number of frontier troops to join in an attack against him. Clearly, if he got rid of Tzu-ch'eng, he would be in a tough spot.

"Yes, I must let Tzu-ch'eng live," he said to himself, "so that he can stay in Shensi and tie down one leg of the government forces."

"Commander, what are you hesitating for?" Hsü Yi-hsien asked and then winked at K'o-wang.

"Let's make our move right now. Don't let the tiger slip back to his mountain lair," urged K'o-wang as he picked up his reins and moved his horse to the fore.

Chang Hsien-chung looked at him sternly, threw the beard he had been stroking with his right hand to one side, and said in harsh tones, "K'o-wang, son, what do you think you're doing being so goddamned impetuous? . . . Back to town, back to town!" Barking out his command, Chang swung his horse's head around, dug his stirrups into its side, and galloped off in the direction of the pontoon bridge.

Chang K'o-wang and Hsü Yi-hsien looked at each other but did not dare disobey the command. Discouraged and disappointed, they swung their horses' heads around, sheathed their swords, and followed behind Hsien-chung, riding toward the pontoon bridge.

Translated by William Lyell

MALCHINHU
(1930–)

Malchinhu's interest in literature was nurtured early by his peasant mother, who taught him folksongs and told him folktales in Mongolian. Later he joined a cavalry unit and worked in a cultural troupe. His writing, first appearing in 1951, drew wide attention with its frontier flavor and soon made him one of the foremost non-Han Chinese writers. By 1962, his short stories had been collected in popular anthologies, including *On the Kolchin Grasslands* and *The Flowering Steppe*. More recently his two movie scripts, *Spring in the Desert* and *Oh, My Motherland!* have been screened and received with enthusiasm.

Vivid local color of his homeland enriches his depiction of the lives and loves of his own people, mostly contrasting the pre-1949 misery of their enslavement and the joyful change since Liberation. His stories record the brief but bloody Japanese invasion, as well as the struggle between rich, conservative Mongolian herd-owners and the People's Liberation Army units.

Since 1973, Malchinhu has been deputy chief of the Cultural Affairs Commission, Inner Mongolia Autonomous Region. He was a delegate to the Third Congress of the All-China Federation of Literary and Art Circles (Peking, 1978).

—K.Y.H.

On the Kolchin Grasslands

An amazing drama was enacted on the Kolchin grasslands last August.

The evening sun was being swallowed up by the far horizon. A northwest wind was stealthily ruffling the grass till the plain looked like a racing sea, while the dark clouds gathering overhead resembled the calfskin roof of a tent. Everybody knew the autumn rain was at hand.

Sarin-Gua had driven her cattle back from further than the eye could see. She was riding a big roan horse, accompanied by her favorite hunting dog, little Galu, who followed his mistress wherever she went.

Although the herd strained forward against the high wind, Sarin scolded them for being too slow. She cracked her whip continuously and shouted: "Giddup!" But how could the cattle know this treatment was due to the fact that their mistress was anxious to meet her lover?

When Sarin had driven the herd to a sand dune not far from the village she suddenly reined in her horse and swept the plain for some time with disappointed eyes. "Sanbu! Sanbu!" she called. But there was no one in sight, and no answer to her call. She could do nothing but round up the cattle on the sand dune and wait for Sanbu in the high wind.

Presently a gray horse came flying like an arrow from the east. Then Sarin's heart gave a leap and her face lit up like a blooming flower. Hurriedly jumping down from her horse she took from her breast a pink tobacco pouch with long ribbons, which she waved over her head in welcome. However, as the new-comer drew nearer, her enthusiasm was damped.

It was not her long awaited Sanbu.

A bearded old man galloped up to Sarin and reined in his horse.

"What are you doing here, lass?" Actually he knew quite well why she was there, and was simply teasing her.

"What's the hurry, Grandad, that your horse is in such a lather?" she parried his question.

"Very urgent business, and I must call a mass meeting to announce it."

"After the meeting this evening will you go on with the story you didn't finish yesterday?"

"It probably won't be possible. Didn't I say there's very urgent business?"

"Urgent business indeed! Say you won't and have done with it."

"It's true; take my word for it. All right, I must be getting on. You'd better go back soon too, young woman."

The horse galloped off.

This old man, whose name was Amugulan, was both village head and an old Party member. Because he was honest and kind, and because he was the first to accept hardship and the last to take his ease in the service of the people, he had won the confidence and love of the masses. All the youngsters in the village called him Grandad Amugulan.

After Amugulan had left, Sarin started worrying again over Sanbu's delay. She also wondered about the urgent business of Grandad Amugulan.

Just then the northwest wind brought the booming of thunder, and the distant horizon was lit by golden lightning—the prelude to a downpour. But since she had promised to meet her lover, Sarin had to wait on.

"Good evening, comrade!" A low, deep voice sounded behind her. "Would you please tell me the name of the village ahead?"

She turned to confront a man lean as a brown goat. His long, unkempt hair seemed to be swarming with lice, his pock-marked face was stained with sweat, and he had over his shoulder a brown blanket. Suspicious of this unexpected arrival, Sarin asked rather nervously:

"Who are you, and where are you from?"

"I've come from the Zharut-Hushu because of the drought there." He deliber-ately withheld his name.

"Where are you going, and who are you looking for?"

"When I set out, Malhei of our village asked me to bring a message to Galsan in Bayan-undur village of the Kolchin-Hushu. Tell me, please, how far Bayan-undur village is from here." Awaiting her answer he eyed her cunningly.

The words "Galsan of Bayan-undur" aroused Sarin's suspicion. Galsan of their village had been a platoon leader of the Kuomintang troops, and was under surveillance. . . . And now a suspicious character like this had come expressly to ask about another suspicious character. For a long time Sarin said nothing. Galu, the little hunting dog beside her, pricked up his ears and looked steadily at the stranger.

"Where is your home in Zharut?"

"Altan-obo village." He paused, then added hastily: "Only very soon we'll be moving away, because the drought there's terrible. Tell me, comrade, do you know how far Bayan-undur village is or not?"

"Bayan-undur village? Very close," she said slowly. "But we've a rule in Kolchin that travellers must produce their identity cards before they've the right to ask the way. Otherwise people won't tell them."

"Hah!" He gave a crafty smile. "Identity card? I have one all right. Only when I left home my wife was afraid I might lose it on the road, so she sewed it into my pants. It would be rather awkward getting it out here. All right, it's growing dark and I must be moving on. Goodbye!" And he started off.

As Sarin watched him go she felt very uneasy. She knew he was a suspicious character, yet she had no means of stopping him. She remembered the Mongolian proverb, "Whoever lets a wolf go sins against the grasslands," and thought: "Since I've met a suspicious character I mustn't on any account let him slip away." At once she hit on a plan, and hurried after the stranger, calling: "Wait a moment, comrade!"

The rascal slowly came to a standstill.

"It's late, and sure to rain by the look of it. Come to my house for a bowl of tea and a rest."

The fellow said nothing, only looked up at the sky reflectively. Just then, as luck would have it, a sudden gust of wind switched the brown blanket he had over his shoulder. A shiver ran down Sarin's spine as she saw with amazement the glittering barrel of a gun.

Sure now that he was up to no good, she thought, "I simply must find a way to get him back to the village. No, that's no good; he's so crafty that he'd be able to see through my plan, and then it'd be too late. Now he's looking up at the sky, what's to stop me snatching his gun from him?"

Darting fiercely forward she laid hands on the rogue's gun. He twisted round and struggled desperately with her. However, Sarin had a firm grip on the gun, and the two of them tugged wildly this way and that.

As she struggled for the gun, Sarin shouted: "A saboteur! Come quick!" hoping this would summon the villagers. Little Galu came to her aid, biting the scoundrel till his hands and face ran with blood. For a moment the stranger relaxed his guard and Sarin, giving a fierce tug at the gun, succeeded in wresting it from him. Frenzied with rage he kicked her savagely in the stomach. Although the pain was agonizing, she realized this was a matter of life and death, and that on no account could she let the enemy get the better of her.

Dogs are the most intelligent creatures on the plain. By now the dogs in the distant village had been aroused and were barking wildly. This alarmed the scoundrel even more, and he thought: "I've lost my gun, and soon a pack of dogs from the village may be after me. I could never hope to get away from those Mongolian dogs. Better go while the going's good." He turned and jumped onto Sarin's big roan horse. The horse gave a start, but under the pressure of the stranger's legs, it flew off.

It was a Czech gun Sarin had seized. Since she was only used to hunting guns, she was unable to manipulate it. In her agitation she took a few steps forward, then fell down. Only little Galu pursued the stranger, biting the roan horse's hind legs and making it buck like a crazy thing until the rascal was thrown. He scrambled up at once, and, not able to catch the horse again, dropped the brown blanket and took to his heels. Once more Galu gave chase, but gave up when he saw his mistress was not following.

The rascal had spent the last few days on the grasslands, in the desert and wilderness, without a square meal all that time. The fierce struggle with Sarin had exhausted him. He had scarcely left the sand dune before his head started reeling. However, he ran on desperately until he saw in front of him a stretch of marshland, where reeds were tossing like ocean waves in an evening gale. He stopped for a moment, then produced a box of matches from his pocket, and dived into the reeds.

By the time little Galu and the big roan horse reached Sarin's side again, she was just getting unsteadily to her feet, thinking to herself: "Although I've captured a gun, the enemy's escaped. It's as bad as shooting rabbits and only nicking their fur."

She lowered her head, frowning, to fumble with the gun. There was a sudden click as the safety catch was released. In her joy she forgot her pain and fatigue. Mounting the roan horse, she led little Galu northward in pursuit.

As soon as she had crossed the sand dune she smelled smoke. Sarin gave an exclamation on seeing a sea of fire ahead. She reined in her horse. Consternation made great drops of perspiration run down her forehead.

Fanned by a strong north wind, a raging fire was roaring and crackling furiously. Because it was August, the reeds were dry, and they blazed so fiercely that even a wild duck could not have flown over.

Although Sarin was still nearly three hundred yards from the fire, the dense smoke already made it difficult for her to breathe, and her face stung in the fierce heat. She could not understand how this fire had started.

Marshland is one of the treasures of the plains. Those who live nearby take the reeds to town each year to exchange for cloth, boots, tea, flowered silk, and brocade. Some indeed depend on this for the whole year's food. And now their marshland was a sea of fire. As a Mongolian saying goes: "Fire is the plain's worst enemy."

"That rogue must have started this fire. But he's wrong if he thinks he can get away with it!" Thereupon Sarin brought her whip smartly down on the horse, and without hesitation headed for the blaze.

Flames and smoke formed a lurid line of fire closing in upon her from all sides. Yet her one thought was: "I must break through! The saboteur mustn't get away!" She bent down to call Galu to jump onto the horse. Fearing he would be burnt as they dashed through the fire, she wrapped him in the folds of her skirt. By now sparks were raining on her head. She saw that the belt of fire was narrower to the west, and decided to break through there. Given free rein the roan horse, like a mad wolf, hurtled through the fiery inferno. The intense heat made Sarin faint and fall limply over his neck, her headdress on fire and white smoke wreathing from her clothes. The roan horse was burnt too, and blood dripped from his mouth. As if sympathizing with his mistress, he slackened his pace and walked on with lowered head. However, at that critical moment, his strength failed him. His front legs suddenly buckled under him, his head dropped, and he sank onto the scorched black ground.

As night fell, the wind dropped. Sarin felt a refreshing coolness, as when one takes off furs in June to plunge into the river. She recovered consciousness. Her eyes opened weakly, then closed again. However, when she remembered she was chasing a counterrevolutionary she shook herself and straightened up. She found the heavy Czech gun still slung over her left arm. Only then did she become conscious of the pain in her face, and when she put her hand up to her cheeks, her fingers came away stained with blood. "The roan horse has been hurt in the fire, and I'm still dizzy," she thought. "It would be better to let Galu go first." So she released Galu from her lap, saying: "Go on! Off with you!" Not a hair on his body had been hurt, and he jumped down and dashed in the direction pointed out by his mistress.

Then Sarin extinguished the sparks in her clothing, adjusted her dress, and pulled the horse to his feet. After leading the horse for a few steps she mounted once more to gallop across the boundless plain through the black, illimitable night.

By now drops of rain were beginning to fall from the dark sky, pelting noisily on the grass.

Sanbu had been to town that day to have his horse shod. Since he was late coming home, he knew Sarin must have waited for some time. He bolted his meal and hurried out again. Riding the snow-white horse Baby Rabbit, a fast runner with staying power, he reached the sand dune in next to no time. To his surprise Sarin was not there. There was not even a sign of her. "Hang it, she's let me down," he thought. Looping his whip he started for her home, but he had no sooner passed the sand dune than he saw a thick pall of smoke to the north, and flames leaping high. At once he put aside all thought of Sarin, and turned back to report to Grandad Amugulan.

Grandad Amugulan had just called a mass meeting and was reading an announcement to the villagers:

"The meeting this evening is for an announcement. First I'll read you the circular from the Hushu Security Office." The old man started reading in a grave, deep voice:

People's Government of Tunutug-gacha.

Yesterday we received a notice from the League Security Office regarding the counterrevolutionary Boyan. This criminal joined the Kuomintang in 1947 and held the post of deputy commander of a unit of the puppet cavalry. He lorded it over the Ar-Kolchin-Hushu, committing every conceivable crime, plundering the people of over five hundred horses, over seven hundred cattle, and over three thousand sheep. He also raped more than twenty women. . . . His crimes aroused the wrath of the people. Hence when our army liberated the Ar-Kolchin-Hushu, this criminal changed his name and escaped to a district in the Zharut-Hushu, where for a long period he carried out subversive activities. The great movement to suppress counterrevolutionaries has struck fear into the hearts of evil-doers, and on the fifteenth of this month he fled. A description of his appearance follows: . . .

Amugulan had just finished reading this announcement and was pausing a moment before embarking on a simple explanation when Sanbu burst into the meeting like a two-year-old colt, completely out of breath. Everybody was taken aback.

"A fire's started, Grandad Amugulan!" he gasped.

"What? A fire!" The whole room was agog.

"Speak plainly, Sanbu, where is the fire?" asked Amugulan.

After Sanbu had given Amugulan a clear account, everybody rose from their seats. Some of those standing in the doorway had already left.

Two simple words—"grasslands fire"—yet what an impression they create! There had been many such fires in the past. Homes had been reduced to ashes, while cattle, sheep, and camels had perished in the flames. Since Liberation, however, each district had a fire prevention organization, and clauses on fire prevention had been included in patriotic compacts, with the result that no fire had broken out during the past three or four years. Now that the fearful words were heard again, they naturally caused alarm.

On hearing Sanbu's account Amugulan knitted his brows and paced to and fro. Then, he turned to the others:

"Today's meeting is temporarily adjourned. Our first job is to fight the fire. Go home at once to get what's needed, and gather when the bell rings under the old elm east of the village."

Everyone rushed off to carry out the orders.

Amugulan held an emergency meeting with the village cadres and some of the militiamen, at which he said:

"We've had no fire on the Kolchin plain for three or four years, have we? Then what a coincidence that today—just after receiving an urgent notice from the Hushu Security Office—such a fierce fire should suddenly break out. There's more to this than meets the eye. We must be very much on our guard."

They all agreed with Amugulan, and immediately posted guards about the village. Amugulan took out his pencil and wrote a few characters in his diary, then he tore out the page, folded it in three, and gave it to Sanbu, saying:

"Deliver this directly to the District, and bring back a receipt." And to another militiaman he said: "You go and ring the bell."

All the villagers gathered under the old elm tree, men and women, old folk and youngsters who had just laid down their school books. Most of them had brought brooms, others had hoes and sopping wet rugs.

About eight hundred yards from the fire was a hillock like a pyramid of cow dung. Amugulan stood there and waved his arm, and the villagers came to a pause. Old Bayar, who towered a head above the crowd, noticed that the rain was coming down faster and faster, and muttered as if it were an incantation: "When thirst burns your vitals, may you find a peach orchard. When a grassland fire starts, may the north wind bring a downpour."

"Comrades!" shouted Amugulan. "The fire's just ahead. We must learn to fight the fire. We must first break up the enemy forces, then annihilate the different sectors, so to speak."

"But it seems to me this fire is so fierce, if we grapple with it directly we're bound to fail," Old Bayar put in before Amugulan had finished. "That means we must burn a fire-ditch in front of the fire, where all the grass is burnt at once so that by the time the fire reaches the ditch, it cannot pass. That way we can put it out safely. This is a lesson we learned through many years in dealing with fires." He made his proposal very confidently.

"Old Bayar's right, that's the best way—let's do it!" said Amugulan.

"Right! That's the way to deal with grassland fires!"

A roar of approbation rose from the crowd.

"All right, don't shout! We'll carry out Old Bayar's proposal. First we must systematically burn a strip in front of the fire. When the fire reaches the passage we have burned out, we'll divide into teams to cope with the different sections. Fortunately it's going to pour all evening. We're in luck. It just goes to show that we people of the Kolchin plain are Fortune's favorites! Get to work, comrades! When we've finished putting out the fire, our pretty girls will sing to us."

Organized into a big fire-fighting force, the three hundred or so villagers attacked the fire as if they were besieging a city. All persons, regardless of age or sex, were confident of victory as they charged toward the fiery sea.

Sanbu braved the pouring rain to deliver the letter to the District, but in his eagerness to return and fight the fire, hurried off without waiting for a receipt. Flying like the wind, Baby Rabbit galloped for dear life over the muddy turf. But when he galloped past the eastern sand dune and turned north, the horse suddenly pricked up his ears and stopped, as if frightened. Sanbu looked in front and saw not far away a dark object. Surprised, he jumped off his horse to have a look at it. It was a brown blanket, soaked through with water. Picking up the blanket he had only taken a couple of steps when he saw another object like a black clod. His flashlight showed it to be a new pink tobacco pouch with long green brocade ribbons embroidered with twining petunias. He gave a puzzled smile: "Who could have had a rendezvous here and dropped this? Well, no matter what pretty girl made it, it's mine now. Still, my Sarin can embroider a hundred times better than this." Then he thought: "Fighting the fire's the main thing." He rolled up the pouch and blanket, fastened them to his saddle, and moved on.

Presently he could hear the distant shouts of the fire-fighters and see that the fire was rapidly being extinguished. Only a few minor sections remained, but these also were under control. He was just heaving a sigh of relief when he noticed a line of fire in the south, which was stealthily burning across. That looked bad, because to the east was the largest haystack in the whole district. If the fire were to spread here, the cattle would have nothing to eat that winter. Filled with anxiety he leapt down from his horse and tried to call the others to help, but his voice was lost in the sizzling of the flames. Thereupon thrusting the tobacco pouch into his pocket, he took the wet blanket from the saddle, and dashed toward the conflagration which was spreading eastward.

Baby Rabbit retreated a little further from the fire, to wait for his master.

Sanbu was very brave, yet it would be interesting to know what he was thinking when he leapt into the fire. He was not so mad as to seek death by burning. Far from it. He was a level-headed, intelligent youngster. But he was a twenty-two-year-old Youth Leaguer. When he saw the raging fire thrusting like a poisonous snake toward the big haystack, and it looked as if presently the towering goat grass would be ablaze, he leapt into the fire without any thought of the danger.

A wet blanket is the best thing to put out fire. Sanbu used it to extinguish flames right and left. However, it is not easy to move in a raging fire. The thick smoke suffocated him, the flames seared him agonizingly. But he paid no attention to them, thinking, "If only I can put out this fire, I don't care if I'm burned."

Exhausted and dizzy from the dense smoke, he pulled himself together for a spell, but then all went black before his eyes and he staggered and fell. Little tongues of flame still darted around him.

Amugulan hurried from east to west and back again, encouraging the villagers and inspecting the work of each team, until he was ready to drop. Thanks to the villagers' efforts and the pouring rain the great fire was finally extinguished.

"Hey, look! There's still fire in the east!" shouted Old Bayar.

"How could a fire have started there too?"

Amugulan looked eastward and saw another blaze there. Gasping for breath he hurried over, and was able to make out a black form lying in the flames. He exclaimed, "Someone's lying in the fire. Hurry up and get him out!"

The villagers ran forward, Old Bayar at their head. He rushed into the fire with eyes closed and bated breath, picked up the unconscious form and darted back again. Then the others helped carry the injured man some distance from the fire, and discovered it was Sanbu.

Led by Amugulan, the villagers put out this fire too.

Then Amugulan went over to Sanbu to call him by his name, but the lad remained unconscious and there was no reply.

"We'd better hurry up and carry him back," said a youngster.

"No, that doesn't matter," said Amugulan. "He's been overcome by the smoke. As soon as he breathes fresh air he'll come round."

Sure enough, very soon Sanbu recovered consciousness. Still feeling weak and dizzy, he made no answer to Bayar's friendly questions. Bayar knew his daughter and Sanbu were in love, and he himself was fond of the lad.

"He's come to," said Amugulan to the villagers, "and the fire has been extinguished. The rain's getting heavier, we'd better go back. Only the captain of the militia must post some militiamen as guards to see that no further fires break out."

Black night covered the boundless grasslands. Although the fire had been put out, the treasure of the plains—the reeds of the big marsh—had been burnt to the ground. Tired and sick at heart, they all walked home in silence.

On the way back, Sanbu's head cleared. He gave Amugulan and Bayar a complete account of how he picked up the blanket and the tobacco pouch on his way back from delivering the message, and also of his experience later in fighting the fire.

"You say besides picking up a blanket, you picked up a tobacco pouch?" said Bayar, as they entered the village administration office.

"See, here it is." Sanbu produced the pouch from his pocket and handed it to Amugulan.

"Aha! This is very interesting," said Amugulan as he took the pouch and opened it. "There's a paper inside. Why, it's a letter."

"Whose letter? What does it say?" asked Sanbu and Bayar simultaneously.

After glancing through the letter, Amugulan looked bewildered.

"Strange! What can it mean?" he wondered. "The blanket, the letter ... and on such a dark and rainy night. Very odd."

"What does it mean?"

"Do you see whose letter this is?" He handed it to Sanbu.

"Why, it's a note to me from Sarin," Sanbu cried.

"What's happened to my Sarin?" exclaimed Bayar.

"Did your daughter bring the cattle back this evening?" asked Amugulan.

"I didn't see her, but she may have gone to fight the fire with the others. She's one of the women activists, and wouldn't shirk!"

"Better go home and see whether she's really back or not."

"What could have happened? Right, I'll go and have a look." As he spoke Bayar departed.

Dear Sanbu,
    This tobacco pouch is not very pretty, but I tired my fingers out sewing it. It's for you.

                                                Sarin.   August 24.

As Sanbu read the letter, his eyes grew round as saucers, and he looked completely at sea.

"Don't you think it strange?" asked Amugulan.

"Strange! Very strange!" Cold sweat was pouring down Sanbu's face. "This suspense is terrible."

"Don't get worked up, lad. When Bayar comes back we'll know."

The door of the outer room slammed as Bayar rushed in with a number of villagers at his heels. Failing to find Sarin at home he had called at several houses.

"She left this morning and hasn't been back since," Bayar told Amugulan. "We've looked all over the village, but no one knows anything about her."

"No, when I was coming back from the District at sunset, I saw her on the east sand dune. I thought she must be waiting for Sanbu."

"Yes, we had arranged to meet today, but when I got to the east sand dune she wasn't there."

"Why should she stay out for no reason? What else did you say to her, Sanbu? Why does it happen just today she hasn't come?"

Although Bayar trusted Sanbu, his anxiety made him speak very sternly. It was the first time he had treated Sanbu like this.

Sanbu felt as if he had been given a slap in the face. Unable to speak he stared at the light for a time, then tears came to his eyes.

After a moment's reflection Amugulan took up the brown blanket and said: "I take rather a different view of this. Look at this blanket—a brown blanket. When I read the notice from the Hushu Security Office at the meeting just now, it said that escaped felon Boyan was carrying a brown blanket. It's strange too that those fires broke out this evening. If instead of considering these questions we just quarrel among ourselves, we won't get anywhere."

Bayar looked up in embarrassment, glanced at the company, and said to himself: "The proverb says: 'A blind man can crawl all his life without getting out of the Kolchin grasslands.' I'm an old fool. Although my hair's white I'm still muddleheaded. Amugulan's quite right. Sanbu can't be blamed for Sarin's disappearance. I know he loves her." Then turning to Sanbu he asked, "Are you still angry with me, lad?"

Sanbu got up slowly, and said: "No, I'm not angry with anyone. What worries me is how to get Sarin back quickly. I tell you, I can't be at ease for a single second while she's disappeared."

Just then the militia captain and security officer, who had heard of Sarin's disappearance, hurried in perspiring.

"Good, you've come just at the right time," said Amugulan. "I was about to send someone for you."

When Amugulan had studied the situation with the militia captain, the security officer, Sanbu, Bayar, and the others, he decided to divide the village militiamen into several groups to search different parts of the plain for Sarin. He also wrote a report to the District.

Amugulan, Sanbu, and three other militiamen formed one group, to search northwards.

Sarin had kept after the counterrevolutionary.

The storm raged violently over the grasslands, crashes of thunder and flashes of lightning were making people feel the end of the world was near. Before Sarin stretched the black, empty wilderness. She could only guess at the direction and terrain, guided by her years of experience in cattle herding here. But it is difficult to advance so much as an inch on the grasslands in the rain because everywhere is a mass of mud. Occasionally the roan horse floundered, and horse and rider fell together into the muddy water. But Sarin did not lose heart, and after each fall got up again to go on with the chase.

When her burns came in contact with the water the pain was agonizing. "How far will I have to chase him on this vast plain?" she wondered. Just then a flash of lightning enabled her to see footprints in the mud, and this encouraged her to go on, thinking: "Shar-mringol River is to the west, and because of this heavy rain it will be in flood. He won't go there. The north's the only possible way."

She could dimly make out a small hill ahead, with some young elms on it. Not only had Sarin often brought the cattle here in the past, but it was on this hill Sanbu had first proposed to her. All kinds of flowers grew on the hill, and she remembered how once Sanbu had put two blossoms in her headdress. . . . In her mind's eye she saw Sanbu's handsome mouth and gay smile, and was lost for a moment in memories of their love.

Suddenly, short barks were heard from the hill, and Sarin's heart missed a beat, though whether from pleasure or fear she herself could hardly say.

"Galu must have found the saboteur," she thought.

Ascending the hill she did her best to make the horse go slowly and quietly, trying to pierce the darkness with her eyes. She hoped little Galu would give her another sign, but he was silent.

"Ha! Let's see you bite again, damn dog!" A man's deep voice sounded triumphantly from the slope seven or eight yards away. Straining her eyes Sarin could see a black figure climbing the hill, and behind it another black form lying on the ground.

"The scoundrel must have killed Galu!" she thought, and in a fit of fury rushed toward him and fired. The black figure flew like the wind. "He has no gun," she thought. "I needn't kill him; better capture him alive!" She caught up and struck him with the butt of the gun. Sarin heard him give a cry and fall. With her finger on the trigger she shouted: "Don't move!" (She remembered this · was something soldiers said.) The black form neither spoke nor stirred. "I may have knocked him out," she thought. Alighting from her horse she was just going over to tie him up, when she heard the click of a rifle behind her, and then a shout: "Don't move! If you move we'll fire!"

Sarin trembled all over, and thought: "It's all up! I've fallen into a trap and been surrounded! But I must be a true Mongolian and show no fear."

"Who are you? If you come any nearer I'll fire!" she shouted at the top of her voice.

"Hi! Is that Sarin?" It was a man's voice which Sarin knew and loved. Then the bright light of an electric torch lit up her mud-stained figure.

"It's really you, Sarin, dear child!" cried Amugulan, jumping down from his horse. There were others behind him.

"Grandad Amugulan! Sanbu!" Never before had these names sounded so dear and wholly admirable to Sarin. With tears in her eyes she ran forward and grasped Amugulan warmly.

"Good girl! Hold on a bit. Tell me, was it you who fired just now?"

"Yes. I'd seized the saboteur's gun, and I knocked him out with it."

Sarin embraced Sanbu too, then took his torch to shine on the prostrate black form. They looked where she turned the torch, and saw a pock-marked man getting up and ready to make off.

"Want to escape, you wretch? Halt!"

Amugulan strode over to the frightened rogue, and asked: "Who are you? What are you doing?"

"I—I'm an ordinary citizen." Gold teeth flashed as he spoke.

"Oh, I know you, you're Deputy Leader Boyan of the Ar-Kolchin-Hushu."

"That's not true, I'm of the Kolchin-Hushu."

"Think you can talk your way out of this? Then think again."

"It was this rogue who set fire to the northern marsh," said Sarin indignantly. Boyan rolled his eyes and said nothing.

"No more reasoning with a counterrevolutionary," said Amugulan to the militiamen. "Tie him up and take him off."

The sight of the enemy being tied up made Sarin inexpressibly happy. Then Sanbu came up and gripped her hand, saying, "You've had a tough time, Sarin."

"No, it was my duty."

They laughed.

"Sarin's quite right: this is the duty of every Mongolian."

"Grandad Amugulan! My little Galu had been with me for four years, and killed three wolves who were after the cattle; but today ... " She faltered and stopped.

Amugulan stroked her hair and said: "I feel for you, child. Your hair's been scorched, your face is swollen with burns, and your favorite dog's been killed. But I don't think this is sad. You ought to understand, that man you caught is Boyan, the counterrevolutionary most hated by the people of the Zharut and Kolchin-Hushu, and all Mongolians. . . ."

Boyan hung his head as Amugulan spoke.

The black clouds overhead rolled southwards, and in the eastern sky dawn appeared. The flowers carpeting the grasslands raised their heads, smiling, while high in the sky wild geese cried.

The sun had risen.

Chinese Literature, no. 1 (1953): 297–312

THE DISSENTING VOICE

During my six-month visit to the People's Republic of China in 1973, I interviewed, both officially and informally, a good number of writers. One of my conclusions then was that no underground literature was possible under the pervasive system of control that Peking exercised with such disturbing thoroughness and efficiency. But I was wrong. As Howard Goldblatt and Leo Lee have noted in the following essay, writings of one form or another were in surreptitious circulation even during the most tumultuous days of the Cultural Revolution. Goldblatt and Lee take pains to differentiate those works written by exiled authors outside China from others written by residents of China, whose criticism of the regime, if too blunt, could easily invite dire consequences. The latter works perhaps deserve to be considered as real underground literature, and reports on their existence have been persistent since October 1976. In January 1979, the authorities in Peking even acknowledged the existence of one such hand-copied novel and indicated approval for its wider circulation. Unfortunately, thus far no authentic samples of such literature have become available outside the People's Republic and Goldblatt and Lee can only report what they have learned about them indirectly.   —K.Y.H.

THE DISSENTING VOICE

The writer's position in twentieth-century China has often proved to be precarious and sometimes dangerous. Prior to the Yenan declaration by Chairman Mao that the writer's responsibility was to serve the people in ways determined by the Party, writers as often as not were the nation's foremost critics; as such they found themselves cast in the unenviable role of dissidents. Once Party control was established, the openly dissident writer all but ceased to exist, replaced by a new breed of literary worker committed to the proposition that China had stepped out of the dark tunnel of bourgeois tyranny and stood at the threshold of the millennium. The new literature, known as socialist realism and revolutionary romanticism, has held a virtual monopoly in creative writings over most of the last three decades. The situation has not remained static, however, for each shift of the political winds has altered the face of literature and affected the status of writers, old and new. In recent months, for example, even the highly acclaimed revolutionary novelist Hao Jan has been the subject of critical attacks following the fall of the Gang of Four.

911

What this means is that the writings of the past thirty years have been highly short-lived—few of the selections in the present anthology have been immune to criticism in the People's Republic of China. It is not so much a matter of changing literary tastes as it is the protean nature of political orthodoxy. As a consequence, some of the writers represented here have stood accused of counterrevolutionary ideologies, their works labeled as "poisonous weeds." However, among them one will search in vain for broad anti-Party attacks such as those associated with writers like Solzhenitsyn, Koestler, or Silone; rather, one finds oblique, veiled criticisms of personality cults, of Party elitism, and of bureaucratic insensitivity. But the situation is changing with the appearance—or at least the knowledge—of new samples of literature that go beyond the limited dissentist stance of earlier writers.

UNDERGROUND LITERATURE

If during the 1950s and early 1960s the literary scene was somewhat kaleidoscopic, as the writers' fortunes rose and fell in concert with the mutable political scene, there was, nonetheless, fairly constant creative activity. This came to an abrupt end with the outbreak of the Cultural Revolution. A sweeping renunciation of practically every creative work written before 1966 resulted in the near elimination of creative literature for the next decade. The Cultural Revolution thus had the ironic effect of bringing cultural activities to a virtual standstill. Not surprisingly, the term "underground literature" and the phenomenon it describes date from this period.

According to reports emerging from China in recent years, the earliest examples of underground literature belong to the oral tradition—stories told and retold, expanded and improved. Eventually, many of the more popular stories were written down and clandestinely circulated, some of them growing in length and sophistication until they evolved into full-length novels. The existence of this body of subterranean literature has gone largely unnoticed outside of China until very recently; in fact, not until an article in Chinese appeared in late 1977 was there any indication that a fairly large corpus of underground writings existed in China. Prior to that, a collection of poems, essays, and short stories, some of which were reportedly smuggled out of China by former Red Guards, appeared in Hong Kong under the title *Who Dares to Sing a Song That Moves the Earth?* but the acclaim accorded it in some circles was attributable more to its novelty than to its literary excellence or sociopolitical significance. There were, reports had it, far more popular and impressive works that had not reached beyond China's borders, but in the absence of the manuscripts themselves, our information has thus far remained largely secondhand.

In general terms, as Fox Butterfield has indicated, the underground literature that has gained widespread popularity is very much in the escapist vein: tales of espionage and agents provocateur, family feuds, romance and illicit sex, and cops-and-robbers thrillers abound in these writings.[1] On their face these works do not appear to be treasonous anti-Party diatribes, nor do they call for the overthrow of the government, but their circulation is every bit as secret and the penalties of discovery every bit as severe as if they were,[2] most likely because the tone of despair, anxiety, and pessimism, and the manifestations of "bourgeois" mentality that permeate these works are viewed with alarm and total disapprobation by the Party, especially by senior cadres and security forces.[3] Authorship of these works is attributed to soldiers, factory workers, resettled urban students, and junior cadres. Many of the stories are regional in nature and popularity, while others have a much broader geographical base, though variations of detail often appear from region to region.

The fountainhead of most of this literature is the Cultural Revolution. One of the longest (reputedly in excess of 400 pages) underground novels, "The Hsiang River Runs Red," written by a resettled Hunanese student in 1969, is a depiction of the Cultural Revolution in Hunan, focusing on the conflict between a father and son, the latter a Red Guard activist who commits suicide out of a sense of betrayal. According to one reader of the novel, "It shows how the young people were used, by both Mao and the bureaucrats."[4] A complex novel entitled "The Pearl River Runs Long" recounts the intertwined lives of three generations of two families, and takes the reader through the dizzying political changes of contemporary Chinese history from Liberation to the Cultural Revolution. Like "The Hsiang River Runs Red," this novel also points the finger of accusation at the excesses of the Cultural Revolution.

Another popular type of *samizdat* (self-published) literature deals with love, licit and otherwise. Though there has been a slight lessening of restrictions on the depiction of romantic love in aboveground literature in China,[5] available reports show that underground writings go far beyond the official sanctions. In "Ah-hsia," a first-person narrative that by contemporary Western standards is mildly pornographic (some versions are reportedly illustrated), the heroine is a jilted lover who comes to realize that if men can take their pleasure with her body, she should be able to do the same with theirs. The social message in this story is the debasement and manipulation of women in New China, while in the story "Big Shoes," the blame for an adulterous romance is laid at the doorstep of the Party and its policy of forced prolonged separation of spouses. One romantic story, reputedly smuggled out of China, has appeared in a Hong Kong magazine: "The Strange Encounter of a Drifter" is a soap-opera story of romance between a spectacularly beautiful and dedicated worker (a woman in the proletarian mode) and a beggar-pickpocket. With only an incidental reference to a lecherous bureaucrat at the end, there seems little in the story to keep it "underground" for long.

Among the most popular themes in underground fiction is espionage and political power struggles. This is best represented by "The Plum-Flower Gang," a complex novel synthesized from various popular oral tales about contemporary political intrigue. Peopled with characters both real and fictional, most versions deal with a spy network (the Plum-Flower Gang) with Taiwan connections, which is infiltrated and crushed through the efforts of a counterespionage agent released from his labor-reform camp for this particular mission. A variation on this theme appears in the recently published retelling of a story entitled "Incident at the Yangtze River Bridge." The incident in the title is the attempted assassination of Chairman Mao as his special train crosses the Yangtze River Bridge at Nanking. Though the plot is foiled, the enormity of the attempted act deals a staggering emotional blow to Mao and other government leaders, particularly Hsü Shih-yu, the Nanking Garrison Commander.

Premier Chou En-lai takes personal charge of the campaign to root out the conspiracy, and enlists a man who is China's answer to James Bond to take on the mission single-handedly (a follower of Lo Jui-ch'ing, he must first be released from a labor-reform camp). What follows is a cloak-and-dagger tale of derring-do by the protagonist and ruthless Machiavellian determination on the part of the conspirators he is stalking. Complete with Bond-like devices, a cold-hearted femme fatale, and a hideout with underground passages, the bulk of the story is concerned not with politics per se, but with high adventure. In the end most of the conspirators barely escape Hsü Shih-yu's troops and their identity is not revealed. But in the final paragraph the narrator discloses what the reader has suspected—the enemies of the people were the Air Force Commander Wu Fu-hsien in league with Lin Piao.

A released criminal figures prominently in yet another story, "The Nine-Dragon Vase," in which the observed theft of a national treasure by a member of Nixon's entourage, identified as Hei-ke (Haig?), presents a touchy problem of protocol: how to recover the treasure without causing a diplomatic cause célèbre. The feat is accomplished by a released convict during a magic performance when he causes a specially crafted look-alike vase to disappear, then tells his audience, which includes Nixon himself, that the vase has reappeared in Haig's briefcase. A variation on this theme appears in a recently published story from Hong Kong, "The Thief in Hai-chu Square." Here, too, foreigners figure prominently in the story, but as the victims, not the culprit: a pickpocket is operating among foreign businessmen attending the Canton Trade Fair, much to the consternation of officials worried about the image of the new "crime-less" China. A member of a smashed gang of pickpockets is released from prison to catch the malefactor and restore the visitors' property (less patriotic than most of his fictional counterparts, his acquiescence is based on the promise of a commuted sentence), which he accomplishes by plying his old trade. True to the code of honor among thieves, however, he does not expose the thief to the authorities; rather, he convinces him to give up his dangerous line of work (a capital crime), then invents a story that results in his own return to prison.

Officially the Cultural Revolution is now history, but the disillusionment and trauma it produced throughout the nation, particularly among the youth, have been manifested in underground writings of considerable popularity. The continuing shock waves of the Lin Piao Affair, the T'ien-an-men Incident (a riot over the memorial service for the late Premier Chou), the death of Mao, and the fall of the Gang of Four will quite possibly be mirrored in subsequent underground literature as expressions of the authors' yearning for more personal freedom, individual identity, and an end to political excesses.

DISSENT LITERATURE BY EXILES

With the appearance of two significant works written by recent exiles, the phenomenon of dissent now begins to attract worldwide attention. These two works—*The Execution of Mayor Yin* (Yin hsien-chang) by Chen Jo-hsi and *The Coldest Winter in Peking* (Pei-ching tsui han-leng ti tung-t'ien) by Hsia Chih-yen—have just been published in their English translations.[6]

The Execution of Mayor Yin is a collection of eight short stories, most of which are based on the author's personal experience during her seven-year stay in China (1966–1973) as an "overseas intellectual" who had returned to China to serve the people. These stories present a gallery of characters, all ordinary people, mostly in the urban milieu of Nanking and Peking, who were caught in the maelstrom of the Cultural Revolution. Chen's approach is essentially humanistic: with a technique of understatement and indirection (through the subtle use of a seemingly passive narrator), she succeeds in bringing out the irony of human sacrifice for a cause whose changing nature in the confusion of slogans and campaigns rendered it incomprehensible to most Chinese people. The protagonist of the title story, for instance, is erroneously executed by Red Guards as an alleged "counterrevolutionary"; at the last moment before his execution he cries out, again and again, "Long Live Chairman Mao!"

Hsia Chih-yen's novel, though less well written than Chen's stories, is more explosive. Cast in the form of a political thriller (and predicting a fictional coup by the Gang of Four *before* it allegedly took place in real life), this sprawling novel comes closest to a clear dissentist stance by frontally attacking Mao Tse-tung for his policies of "socialist-fascist" dictatorship during the Cultural Revolution. Hsia's protagonists are mostly real figures, including China's highest-echelon leaders; other "fictional" characters not readily identifiable with real personalities are nevertheless personifications of political positions. Hsia's own sympathies are reserved, however, for a group of underground youths who feel betrayed by Mao's Cultural Revolution. The novel ends in a massive demonstration by the "people" led by this underground group in a futile contest for power with other groups in Peking's T'ien-an-men Square, under the shadows of the abortive coup by the Gang of Four.

The Coldest Winter in Peking is the first novel by a former official and member of the Academy of Sciences, now in exile in Japan. His nom-de-plume, Hsia Chih-yen (literally "flame of summer"), when compared with his book's title, connotes somewhat melodramatically a clear message concerning his deep-seated political commitment. Hsia is a loyal follower of the late Premier Chou En-lai and considers the T'ien-an-men Incident of April 5, 1976 as marking the first awakening of the Chinese people in their demand for democracy and freedom. This dissentist cause, which casts Mao as a betrayer of the true meaning of the socialist revolution, is to some extent also shared by Chen Jo-hsi (not to mention the anonymous authors of some of the underground novels). In Chen's most recent work, a long novel titled *Kuei* (*Repatriates*), she echoes Hsia's sentiment by making her vaguely autobiographical heroine announce that Mao, "this last Chinese emperor," will "step down" sooner or later.[7] And in a revealing reversal of her real-life experience, the heroine in the novel does not choose to leave China but rather decides to stay on after the trauma of her husband's death (the result of an accident which may also have been suicide). Like Hsia, Chen sees renewed hope in the younger generation who, seasoned by the very crucible of the Cultural Revolution and, ironically, attaining a higher level of consciousness by the very success of the Maoist political education, will eventually be China's future masters.[8]

This idealistic—perhaps even naive—vision may seem premature. But its dynamic assertion by two exile writers who left China out of bitter disillusionment gives us reason to believe that the underground writers inside China may have harbored an even stronger feeling concerning the future. When some of the underground works eventually surface, they will probably be valedictory documents to a prolonged national nightmare which is, for the moment, over.

September 1978
Howard Goldblatt and Leo Ou-fan Lee

NOTES

1. Fox Butterfield, "Literature of Dissent Rises in China," *The New York Times,* Dec. 13, 1977, p. 1.
2. Chen Jo-hsi, "Ta-lu ti k'ou-t'ou wen-hsüeh" (Oral Literature in Mainland China), *Chung-kuo shih-pao* (*China Times*), June 9, 1978, p. 12.
3. The clandestine publication and circulation of non-approved works is in itself an overt political act, irrespective of the themes and contents.
4. Fox Butterfield, p. 8.
5. *San Francisco Examiner,* April 25, 1978, p. 10.
6. Chen Jo-hsi, *The Execution of Mayor Yin and other Stories from the Great Proletarian Cultural Revolution,* tr. Nancy Ing and Howard Goldblatt (Bloomington: Indiana University Press, 1978). Hsia Chih-yen, *The Coldest Winter in Peking,* tr. Liang-lao Dee (New York: Doubleday, 1978).
7. Chen Jo-hsi, *Kuei* (*Repatriates*) (Taipei: Lien-ching, 1978), pp. 410–411.
8. The ranks of exiled dissident writers have been swelled in recent months by another writer, Lin Ye-mu, whose stories are reminiscent in theme, setting, and tone of Chen Jo-hsi.

H.G. and L.O.L.

AI CH'ING

The Red Flag

Red fire,
Red blood,
Red the wild lilies,
Red the azalea blooms, a red flood,
Red the pomegranate in May,
Red is the sun at the birth of day.

But most beautiful of them all,
      the red flags on forward march!

The red flag
Born behind prison walls, a thousand years old.
Fighting for Truth
Sickles shining like gold
Hammers shining like gold,
Proclaiming the laborer's glory
      and the victory of united workers and peasantry.

In the dark and long night,
      in stifling darkness a thunderbolt has struck—
"Proletarians of the world, unite!"
Then,
Following lightning flashes in the sky, many miles long,
The red flag ascends the stage of history.

  . . . .

The red flag is fire,
The fire of the revolt of the oppressed,
The fire of the anger of the exploited,
The fire of all suffering ones under the sky,
Now striving for freedom and liberation.

For a note on Ai Ch'ing, see p. 354.

Dancing fire,
Galloping fire,
Blazing fire,
Fire that destroys the private property system,
Fire that wipes out the old world.

Symbolizing the ideal,
Signaling a faith,
A summoning battle cry,
An unconquerable drum call,
With it we stay victorious forever.

Its undying glory
Matches the red clouds at dawn;
Bullets may pierce it but
Can never knock it down.

Alert, responding quickly, and resourceful,
It stands ready to do battle,
Always prepared, always awake,
Even during moments of complete quiet.

A war mount shaking its mane,
It waits for the bugle call
To leap from the trench instantly
And dart toward the smoke-covered battlefield ahead.

The red flag flutters on forward march—
Forward, assault!
Sweep aside all obstacles;
Forward, assault!
Blast all the stubborn field defense;
Forward, assault!
Take all the strategic heights;
Forward, assault!
Occupy all the enemy's territory.

. . . .

Red flags, thousands upon thousands,
Red waves in the sea,
Unfolding in front of us, always
Leading us
        to dash toward communism,
        shouting victory cheers.

from the *Wen-hui Daily* (Shanghai, April 30, 1978)
Translated by Kai-yu Hsu

CHEN YANG

Chen Yang, identified only as a worker, wrote poems with gusto in response to the official call for literary production to observe the thirtieth anniversary of Mao Tse-tung's "Talks at the Yenan Forum on Literature and Art." The following selection was included in a volume entitled *People Sing on the Long Island*, edited by the Committee on Proletarian Literature of Hunan Province. The title was taken from a line in a poem by Mao Tse-tung, "People sing on the long island, their song moving the earth." The long island refers to the sandbar (Orange Isle) in the middle of the Hsiang River outside the city of Changsha, a scenic spot frequented by Mao in his youth. —K.Y.H.

To a Chingkang Rock

—A friend gave me a rock from the Chingkang Mountain

This is an ordinary rock
That has been through great battles.
It has shared much hardship with Red Army fighters,
And struggled against many enemies of our class.

When the enemies rushed us in droves,
When red soldiers ran out of ammunition,
This rock, whistling, darted against our foes,
Hitting them, scattering them, making them tremble.

When red soldiers gave their lives in combat,
Their blood dyeing red the unconquerable hills,
This rock, filled with the martyrs' vengeful hatred,
Flew down the mountain gulch to smash the enemy's skulls.

Perhaps at dawn just before the action began,
It had supported the kettle to cook our soldiers' breakfast;
Perhaps at night after a bloody engagement,
It had served as a pillow for a weary red hero ...

A little rock nestled in my palms,
A towering Chingkang Mountain in my heart.
My thoughts rage like the surf in the sea,
Many are the associations, many the mixed feelings.

919

Forty years of stormy change altered the world,
Now the sky paints an artist's dream, and the land spreads a brocade.
How much wind and rain has this rock withstood through history,
And how many springs and autumns of fighting has it survived!

Ah, if without Chairman Mao's thought to direct our battle,
How could there be red flags flying all over the country?
If anyone dares to encroach upon our sacred motherland,
Every rock will rise in anger along with every revolutionary soldier.

People Sing on the Long Island, pp. 23–25

Translated by Kai-yu Hsu

CH'EN KUAN-HSÜAN

A native of Szechwan Province, Ch'en Kuan-hsüan started publishing poems in the early 1970s and was among the young writers tempered in the furnace of the Cultural Revolution. Like T'ang Ta-t'ung, Ch'en finds moving poetry in the spectacle of boatmen pulling a sampan upstream against the swift Yangtze current. —K.Y.H.

Boatman in Szechwan Rivers

Man walks in clouds,
Masts buried in fog;
He carries the Yangtze on his back,
And under his feet lies the Wu Mountain.

His pulling straightens a thousand river bends,
His pulling opens up ten thousand gorges,
He pokes the moon with his pole, eighteen feet long,
As the east wind sends him to the four seas.

He tucks away the sharp curves in his heart,
And folds in his bosom all the rapids;
One stride, he steps over the twelve peaks,
Three lines of river chant, and the K'uei Gate makes way.

Moving Shanghai to Chungking, and back
To unload Shanghai on Chungking docks;
A boatload of cotton and grain, a boatload of coal,
Each boat a load of laughter, a load of love.

River chants soar up to the sky,
His boat sails toward the rising sun;
One rope on a river boatman's shoulder
Links the snow-capped mountains with the sea.

Enlightenment Daily (Peking, April 22, 1973)

Translated by Kai-yu Hsu

FENG CHING-YÜAN

Feng Ching-yüan has the distinction of being the only poet, up to this writing, whose life is discussed in the newly revived *Poetry Journal.* In an autobiographical sketch, we learn that he was born in the early forties in San-t'iao-shih, an industrial area just north of the old city in Tientsin. His family was employed in the steelworks, but Feng still speaks of hunger which kept him awake at night, and scavenging by day in garbage dumps. He was still illiterate when he started work in the steelworks after Liberation, but soon started to write poetry for broadcasting over the local radio. By the time he joined the army, around 1960, he was sending his poems to literary magazines. It was then he made the discovery that the poems his fellow soldiers praised were being rejected by editors, while the poetry appearing in those magazines did not appeal to his comrades. (This, in 1976, he attributed to the "black line in literature and art.") He therefore began to write two sorts of poetry, one straightforwardly describing the life around him, the other more consciously literary. This tendency, he claims, was to some extent checked during the "socialist education campaign" of the early sixties, when one of his more simple poems, as he recounts, proved able to move people deeply:

At dinner that day I didn't eat well and I couldn't sleep that night, my heart was in turmoil; looking at the pen in my hand, I thought of San-t'iao-shih, I thought of steel. The pen nib was made of steel, it was forged in furnace and machine, and thus its purpose, grasped in the hands of the proletariat, is to battle, shout, and roar for the revolution! Under the care of the Party I went to school and received an education, and recently I've been able to use my pen to write a few poems. What has changed? Why can't I take the revolution's needs as my measure instead of making publication my goal? There is steel in the nib, but is there any steel in the poems I write with this pen? As I turned over the pages of Chairman Mao's "Talks at the Yenan Forum on Literature and Art," the teaching that I had read and written down more than a dozen times, that revolutionary literature and art should become "a powerful weapon to unite and instruct the people, and to attack and destroy the enemy," seemed now so extraordinarily fresh and clear that every word, every stroke, engraved itself in my heart.

In 1973 he returned to San-t'iao-shih, where he continued to write and develop his ideas on the nature of poetry and creative writing:

Good steel must be wrought, good poetry must be worked. In its course from ore to finished product, a piece of steel undergoes a constant process of furnace firing; it is pressed and stretched, and blended in with the blood and sweat of many people. A good poem is similarly forged from a drawn-out battle in life, informed by a host of people and things, by unceasing study and realization, and by repeated hammering. The accidental does happen, but is not on any account a product of "inspiration" but similarly is the result of repeated actualization.

Steel is refined in the struggle in production, by unceasing cleansing of impurities and elimination of sulphur, and poetry should also be refined and honed in class struggle. Steel is reality striking reality, it has solid weight; poetry is the same, it cannot be light and airy but must embody a vigorous fighting spirit. Every line of poetry should be bursting with enthusiasm, soaked with sweat, cast from the heart.

Steel rings when it is dropped on the ground, and vibrates when struck; poetry must also resound in the mouth, it must be rich in music, easy to read and to memorize.

Steel comes in all shapes and sizes, in an infinite variety of long, square, flat, and round pieces, even in combinations such as round inside and square outside, or convex on one side and concave on the other: but every single shape is manufactured to meet the needs of socialist industrial and agricultural development and battle; the forms of poetry, on a foundation of revolutionary political content, should also come in many different kinds, each with its own hue.

In steel there is poetry, and the turbulent life of struggle provides the inexhaustible source for our progress in creating poetry; steel in poetry is the goal after which we should strive, which I should be able to achieve but have not yet accomplished . . .*

The autobiography concludes with the then obligatory diatribe against Teng Hsiao-p'ing, but the restoration of Teng to power some months later does not seem to have prevented Feng Ching-yüan from appearing in *Poetry Journal,* *People's Daily,* and *People's Literature* in 1977. Feng has now left the factory and works for the Tientsin Metallurgy Bureau.

Feng's poems are written with an unusually dense syntax, and he employs an extensive and powerful vocabulary. His fondness for repetition, perhaps excessive, gives his poems weight and tension, which he modulates on occasion with more subtle parallelism in the manner of traditional regulated verse. His favorite poetic form is a kind of controlled free verse, without regular line lengths or rhyme patterns yet not without structure. To squeeze the maximum impact from each line, he frequently resorts to classical prosody and scansion; as a proletarian poet, Feng fuses traditional techniques with a modern sense of freedom. A collection of his works appeared in 1975 as *We Temper the Steel the Revolution Needs.*   —B.S.McD.

Cable Song

A thousand steel rods converge and mingle,
Ten thousand steel wires join to form a cable.
You'd like to know their mettle?
    Hauling mountains—mountains topple!
    Tugging the sun—the sun goes sprawling!

*Excerpts from "Steel and Poetry" (Kang yü shih), *Poetry Journal*, no. 8 (1976), pp. 80–85

Steel cables, twist and twine, hey!

Each wire has been pulled and twanged,
Each one is filled with class feeling,
Plunging vigorously into the collective:
    Wind blows, it won't break,
    Thunder strikes, it won't collapse,
    Waves break, it won't loosen,
    Water soaks, it won't slacken!

Steel cables, twist and twine, hey!

Link hands above and below, front and back,
North, south, east, and west, all face the center,
    Twist and turn a force,
    Twist and turn a cable,
    Twist and turn a heart,
Twist and turn tight and smooth!

Steel cables, twist and twine, hey!

The crane's waiting to raise ten thousand ton,
The winch's waiting to hoist the load,
The capstan's waiting to haul the iron anchor,
The derrick's waiting to drill the earth's layers ...
Revolutionary construction urgently needs them,
Every minute every second we must mightily contend!

Steel cables, twist and twine, hey!

A thousand twists and turns in unbroken line,
Kilometer after kilometer, the direction is clear.
    Oppose dissension and retreat,
    Surrender and revisionism.
    Ascend the mountain, descend the mine,
    Thrust into the ocean and mount the skies,

Steel wires in single purpose have a force without rival,
People in unity have strength beyond compare!

Steel cables, twist and twine, hey!

For revolution's sake we splice the cable,
Day and night sing loud in praise of unity:
    Unity gives strength,
    Unity is our guarantee,
    Unity gains victory,
    Unity scales the heights.

The entire party and army twine to form a steel cable,
The IRR quail craven-hearted!*
When eight hundred million people twine and form a steel cable,
Even the sun and moon must alter course!

Poetry Journal, no. 1 (1976), pp. 61–62

The Age Sings Out: Two Themes

1. LAY THE RAILS DOWN!

Iron is amassed here,
And steel lies here in rows.
Fire which smelted nine times and heated twice as much again,
The hammer which roared a hundred times and then a thousand more,
The gleaming red-hot sweat of smelting workers,
The red-flushed hearts of foundrymen,
All together in the solid metal
—Boil and bubble, melt and fuse ...
Lay down, lay the railway tracks down!

There is ore in the rails,
There is coal in the rails,
There is electricity in the rails,
There is water in the rails,
The resolution of a million proletarians,
The daring of a million revolutionaries,
Are in these rails which stretch uninterrupted
—Solidified into steel particles, iron fibres!
Lay them down, lay the tracks down!

To mountain and forest, to seashore and frontier lands,
The clanging rails resound,
No direction they cannot conquer,
No fortress they cannot smash!
A backbone, hard and strong,
Bearing the sun and moon, lightning and thunder ...

Who fears that thorns will block the way,
Wrapped in mist and fog,
Who fears the rivers deep and wide,

*Imperialists, revisionists, and reactionaries: contracted to a three-syllable expression
in Chinese, it frequently appears in Feng's poems. [B.S.McD.]

The path encircles peaks,
Singing, "The working class must lead in all things,"
"We will be masters of the world."
—Forward, forward!
Riding on the east wind of the Cultural Revolution,
Welcoming the morning radiance of socialism,
—Lay down the rails, lay them down!
Lay them down, hey, lay the tracks down!
Nature's defenses disappear in front of the revolution's tracks,
Selfless and fearless under the steel!
Lay them down, hey, lay the tracks down!
Cross a hundred mountains, ford ten thousand rivers,
Obeying always Chairman Mao's summons,
Following always the Party's direction!

2. DRILL! RR-RR-RR-RR FORWARD

To stride forward is to go on the offensive,
To start drilling is to open battle,
The tougher the opposition the harder we drill,
The more complex the substrata the harder we strive!
Never look back once we set our course,
          Zz-zz-zz-zz: dig in,
          Rr-rr-rr-rr: forward!

There's no subject in the world that can't be drilled,
There's no mountain on earth that can't be drilled,
When problems arise then drill to the truth,
When troubles loom then drill them through!
Be steel strong, iron hard,
Be rock thick, stone stubborn,
Even granite rock a hundred layers deep
Can still be drilled through till you see the sky!

The drill chips twirl in one direction,
The drill blade spins at the same angle,
The point shatters metal and stone,
The bit takes aim—
Rr-rr-rr-rr, rr-rr-rr-rr,
A hundred setbacks won't make us retreat, a thousand twists won't
      bend us!

Thick steel plate—drill!
Steep cliff rock—drill!
Lofty mountains—drill!
Mysterious substrata—drill!
Railway tracks—
Like our workers' propaganda teams,

According to Chairman Mao's directives,
We march into schools and hospitals, far and wide ...
March into every realm in the superstructure!
Railway tracks—
Like our workers' theoretical groups,
We study Marx and Lenin, criticize "the rites," oppose retreat,*
Our strength cannot be checked,
With savage fury we beat the drums of war against revisionism!
Railway tracks—
Like our workers' militia companies,
We shoulder guns, sing battle songs, tread the storm,
Counterattack the evil rightist trend to reverse the verdicts,
In front of T'ien-an-men,
Defend the five-starred flag ...

Oh, the rails reach up to heaven in rainbow ribbon dance,
The Cultural Revolution has set up a noble monument.
Every new-style workers' organization
Is a wheel carrying forward the trains of the age,
Each revolutionary worker's shoulder
Is a section of track along history's highway.

Mount "Eagle's Sorrow Brook,"
Tread "Wolf Fang Awl,"
Ride "The Tiger's Back,"
Penetrate "The Lion's Mouth" ...
Wherever the enemy stirs up trouble,
The iron fist of class extends,
Wherever a stubborn rock blocks our path,
It gets smashed to pieces!
Those petty clowns who go against the age
Aren't worth a heap of dogshit,
But clay and stones that meet the need of revolution
Together contribute to form—
The substratum of proletarian dictatorship.
There's a red flag on the drill shank,
The blade point's beneath the drill chuck;
Clamp on tightly the rotating-plate of the Three Great Revolutionary
     Struggles.
Penetrate beyond the layers of mire and stagnant water,
Break through the tiers of fierce impeding waves,
The distorted doctrines of revisionism,
The weird talk of the bourgeoisie within the Party,
Completely without mercy
—Pierce them through and through!

*Confucius upheld the rites of the ancient Chou Dynasty. Hence the anti-Confucius
campaign criticized "the rites." [K.Y.H.]

Who says it's difficult to break long-standing habits?
Who says it's hard to make a move?
The revolution advances along the highway,
Breaking through ten thousand double-barred gates!
See us drill through a million meters daily,
Ten mountains in one night—
Drill forth ore deposits, drill forth treasure,
Drill forth oil wells, drill forth fountains,
Drill forth a new horizon in our thinking,
Drill forth resolution to breach the heavens!

Drill!—Believe no evil spirits!
Drill!—Fear no hardship.
Beneath the drill bit, water and oil are inexhaustible,
Beneath the drill bit, metal and coal beyond measure.
The drill bit opens forth—the proletariat's future;
The drill bit brings to light—communism's tomorrow!

Oh, gaze at this sacred realm, behold this great land,
Here and now,
How many drill bits are thunderously turning!
Steel drills, iron drills, oil drills,
Driven by water, wind or electricity . . .

In front of every drill: a team of iron men,
In front of every drill: a row of comrades in steel,
Fired in the Cultural Revolution, ah,
Forged in the Cultural Revolution,
Each one has a drill-like style,
Each has a drill-like daring—
Study Marx and Lenin,
Climb the mountain of theory;
Reform ways of thinking,
Establish a firm proletarian outlook . . .
Drill, drill, drill!

Oh, to stride forward is to go on the offensive,
To start drilling is to open battle!
Criticize deeply Liu, Lin, and Teng,*
Struggle bravely against the IRR;
Break through old ways of thinking,
And overcome old ideas . . .
        Zz-zz-zz-zz: dig in,
        Rr-rr-rr-rr: forward!

Poetry Journal, no. 7 (1976), 31–34

*Liu Shao-ch'i, Lin Piao, and Teng Hsiao-p'ing. [B.S.McD.]

The Fire's Roar

Fire, raging in the heart,
Fire, roaring in the workshop:
    Press on, press on! Stoke the flames, stoke the flames!
    Dash forward, dash forward! Advance, advance!

Time, hey, fire presses fire speeds,
Force, hey, fire races fire flees,
Hearts, hey, fire ignites fire blazes,
Iron and steel, hey, fire fuses fire melts.

"Wash away the Gang of Four's fiascos with our burning sweat!"
"Cast a year of progress and good order in iron and steel!"
"Marshal all positive factors to shoulder—
    the entire burden Chairman Mao entrusted to us!"
    The sound of fire rolls in every furnace.

Seize the steel in front of the furnace, toil till the sweat goes flying—
    fiery sparks are aflutter,
Rush to mend the red-hot crucible, conquer difficulty and danger—
    the fiery glow's agleaming,
Steam- and fire-driven conveyer carts shuttle steel and brick—
    fiery dragons are dancing,
Team A issues a challenge team B responds—
    the fiery torch's ablaze . . .

It's not that the smelting shop can't carry on without fire,
The meeting to study Ta-ch'ing sets the air here aflame,
It's not that we steelworkers are easily set on fire,
Chairman Hua's great speech goes straight to our hearts!

One study session under the lamp: bodies toughen, fists clench,
One passage read in front of the furnace: hearts churn, blood boils,
    Oh, life is like fire, it burns again,
    Look, light and victory lie ahead!

Poetry Journal, no. 4 (1977), 41

Hey, Let the Steel Flow

Let the steel flow—! Let the steel flow—!
Yes, a mighty river gushes forth,
Crash! it rolls from the bowels of the rock-melting, iron-smelting
    furnace.

At high temperatures, a hundred tons of glowing, flaming steel
Races out in uniform response to the summons of our motherland,
A truly unprecedented, irresistible force!

Look at the river's surface: smoke rolling, lightning flashing,
        incandescent showers,
The rushing torrent pours from the furnace mouth, billows flying,
—How can the Heaven-sent waters of the Yellow River compare with this!

Gaze at its banks: thunderclaps burst, footsteps pass, flags signal,
Press forward three troughs of molten steel for casting, a spectacle
        of sound and color,
—More impressive than the Yangtze River Gorges!

The scene is so dazzling brilliant,
People who grappled with fume and smoke under the blows of the Gang of
        Four
Now beam with pride and joy as they behold this boundless vista!

Remember when black clouds and heavy fog took over, did we ever forget
        steel?
Facing flying "labels," beating breasts,
"Come, we stand firm unto death on top of the furnace!"

Now our hearts beat fast as the furnace quickens,
The winged boat of our ideals bravely embarks in the wild current of
        the steel,
The intoxicating joy in our hearts explodes in the steel sparks.

To the devil with those ghouls and misfits who shrink from heat and light!
Let those cheats and petty thieves who play tricks with smoke and fog
Tear their guts out in the company of their ancestors, the IRR!

Under the leadership of Chairman Hua, we—
Are advancing, burning, smelting steel,
Listen, the sound of the bell to tap the steel strikes urgently once again!

Hey, let the steel flow—! let the steel flow—,
Its source is eight hundred million red hearts, three million Party members
        its protectors,
The molten steel brims with strength enough to push the age ahead!

Poetry Journal, no. 4 (1977), p. 42

Translated by Bonnie S. McDougall

HO CH'I-FANG

Reminiscence

*In commemoration of the 33rd anniversary of the "Talks at the Yenan
Forum on Literature and Art"*

I remember former days reading at night in the attic,
Alone with a book of T'ang verse and an earthenware lamp,
The angry howl of the wind in the pines was trying to lift off the roof,
The sobbing cry of the cuckoo seemed like a string of pearls.
I began to realize the majesty of nature;
Lingering deep inside, this feeling never faded.
As a child I didn't understand the meaning of song,
A seed planted in a wintry grave returns to life in spring.

June 1–6, 1975
Poetry Journal, no. 9 (1977), 70–75

Translated by Bonnie S. McDougall

For a note on Ho Ch'i-fang, see p. 527. "Reminiscence" is the first of fourteen poems
by Ho, all written in the traditional regulated verse (*lü-shih*) form with eight lines of
equal length in each poem. [K.Y.H.]

HSÜ YÜ AND HUO HUA

Hsü Yü and Huo Hua are a team of young writers of verse, close comrades in one of the army units assigned to work on communes or construction projects in such far-flung areas as Inner Mongolia, Sinkiang, or Manchuria. Together with a few other comrades having similar assignments, they have published a volume of poems entitled *New Songs of Soldier-tillers* (1973). Their lines dance with energetic rhythm; their diction flows, incisive and sonorous. The following selection stands as one of the very best ever written by a Chinese proletarian poet. —K.Y.H.

Battle in a Rainy Night

A clap of deep thunder,
A streak of lightning,
Hurried whistles all over the encampment.
Quick! To the drying field!
Lanterns, a moving line.
Shadows, a flickering file.

A clap of fearful thunder,
A streak of lightning,
Like the flashes of a camera,
Catches the various scenes of a battle.

Upon the sea of grain, a thousand hands.
Beyond the sea of grain, a million spades.
Wood-scrapers hurry on grain waves.
Brooms roll up golden billows.
Before rains' arrival, sweats sprinkle.
In no time, gold sea changed into gold mountain.

A clap of fearful thunder,
A streak of lightning,
Sacks, upon shoulders, fly.
Roads, under feet, flee.
Young lads of seventeen, eighteen,
Shoulder two hundred pounds, moving jet-fast.
A long dragon flying-dancing,
Head at granary, tail at drying field.

A clap of fearful thunder,
A streak of lightning,
Woman lieutenant soars up the wheat battlements
          —like an eagle upon the peak,
Her arms holding black clouds,
Her feet stepping on lightning.
One wave of her hand:
"For the revolution, wrest the grains from the dragon's
     mouth!
               Quick! Cover them!"

One clap of thunder follows another clap of thunder,
One streak of lightning follows another streak of lightning,
Like the flashes, flashing-flashing, of a camera,
Taking down a documentary of the battle.
You ask what title this movie?
     —"Battle in a Rainy Night"!

New Songs of Soldier-tillers, pp. 37–39

Translated by Wai-lim Yip

KUO HSIAO-CH'UAN
(1919–1976)

A Poem in the Old Style

No more tears of the old peasants,
Ever-present is the zeal of the young.
For an ardor-filled heart,
The pen is mightier than the sword.

Gossips are but to be laughed at,
Undaunted spirit flows into literary art.
Oh when shall we return to the North,
To talk about the great river, over a cup of wine?

Poetry Journal, no. 7 (1977), 64

Translated by Mark McCarvel and others

For a note on Kuo Hsiao-ch'uan, see p. 541.

KUO MO-JO

I Sing of the Third Plenum of the Central Committee of the Tenth Congress of the Chinese Communist Party

—to the tune "All Red the River"

The governance of a country:
        grasping the essentials,
Acting in accord with the will of the people,
        adopting firm policy.
Drums resound,
From the East a gentle wind blows,
And the Red Flag flutters.

In a flash the Gang of Four
        is smashed to pieces!
The entire country bursts forth
        with "The Internationale."
The time for men of talent
        has arrived,
The Eight Hundred Million become
        one in heart,
Together, to build up the nation!
Clouds and rivers swell,
Winds and thunder mount,
Together, they all take action
Against the pair of American and Soviet bullies.
The people of the Third World are united:
Firm as a steel wall.

For a note on Kuo Mo-jo see p. 693.

Accomplish the Four Modernizations of our country,
Carry out the Three-year Program of peace and prosperity.
If we unyieldingly persist for twenty more years,
What a grand scene will emerge!

July 20, 1977
Poetry Journal, no. 8 (1977), 13

Translated by Mark McCarvel and others

LI YING

Lookout Post on Mountaintop

Since when
This immense sea suddenly ceased rolling;
Severe, majestic, and craggy at their extreme
Are the mountains, those frozen waves.

Ho! Look at them, each thrusting into the sky,
Black, dark brown, and through them, patches of steel grey.
Over there, on the steepest peak
Perches in majesty an outpost of our warriors.

No, that's not just an outpost,
That's a threatening cliff, a cluster of thorns,
Or a floating cloud, lingering,
Or a mountain eagle, resting its wings.

From the mountain's foot to the outpost, it's too far, too far away,
Won't you look at it through these glasses—
You'll see wild flowers blooming at its door
And wild berries grow red below its window.

Let me tell you: the bright sun, clear moon, and cool breeze,
Come to be our best neighbors; they come and stay.
And flowers and bushes together with wild birds
Also stay with us, in the same family.

Thunder and rain often rock the outpost,
But the shelter is held firm by pine roots and weathered vine;
Around the outpost it's too quiet, too lonely, but
We know the music of the streams, and mountains' songs.

There five pairs of eyes forever wide awake,
Day and night they scan the valleys and skies.
And there throb five hearts, five red hearts,
Their rhythm is the real life of the great mountains.

For a note on Li Ying, see p. 371. *Red Flowers All Over the Mountain* is a collection
of his post-Cultural Revolution poems.

937

Full, intense, vigorous is our life,
A solemn mission stamped in our hearts;
Be proud, hold your head up high, fatherland,
We remain always your devoted soldiers.

We stand on mountain high, very high mountains,
At times it seems we're standing in the sea;
Look, are not the mountains surging against the sky?
And roaring, the sound of surf in the clouds, in the wind?

Ho! This tiny outpost of ours up on the mountain,
Perhaps is a small sailboat floating on the sea.
When you, our beloved ones at home, gaze at the night sky,
That farthest star, way out there, is the lantern on our mast.

Red Flowers All Over the Mountain, pp.6–8

Sound of the Flute

One by one the stars appear
On the banks of the milky way, a bonfire ablaze;
Look, over the edge of the amber cloud
Stands our lookout post.

From where comes a flute tune
Echoing back and forth in these deserted mountains?
Clear and crisp, better than a secluded stream,
More ethereal than the oriole's song in clouds.

The commissar steps out of his camp room,
He looks up, he can't hold back a smile;
"Listen to those young fellows up there," he mutters,
"They are making music, out of a piece of bamboo."

Little tunes from beyond the Great Wall, one after another
Fill up the valleys and gulches south of the river;
A wealth of feeling flows from the flute holes,
A wealth of fuel feeding that bonfire.

The commissar turns around, steps into his room,
His hand on the phone, a smile on his face.
"Squad Leader No. 5," he says, "encore, please, encore!"
"But remind the sentries to watch out for signals!"

Red Flowers All Over the Mountain, pp.19–20.

In a Storm

Through the rain, through the wind, came an infant's cry,
A baby has been born to the woman over the hill.
—Thus the mountain has gained a lusty son
—And the country, a husky soldier.

"Squad Leader, what gift shall we give?"
The squad leader's eyes blinked, once and again,
"Let's give them one quiet night first,
And let's go, the patrol unit, fall in."

To greet this new life—brand new life—
The mountains have bathed themselves green and clean;
To protect this little life—tiny little life—
One conviction is shared among the comrades' hearts.

The patrol reached over the hill, the storm lifted.
Overhead a bright moon lit up the sky;
Three bayonets, three streaks of silver,
And silvery was the windowpane on the young mother's room.

The mother fell asleep, the infant fell asleep,
The night over the valley, peaceful and quiet;
And the hills, like a resting new mother
In comfort and ease now, after that spell of tension.

Dawn breaking now, we wound our way back to camp,
From all four directions rose roosters' calls;
Squad Leader said, "Let us give the whole mountain to them,
Plus the drums of battle, and chimes of cheer ..."

Red Flowers All Over the Mountain, pp.35–36

Our Army Cook

Lighter than the deer's is his step,
Earlier than the eagle rises he;
And when he pushes open the door to look at the sky,
The mountains have disappeared, fog, fog, everywhere.

From a pocket hidden in his jacket he draws a match,
One strike, he lights up another day.
In the lamplight his shadow moves about,
A bundle of firewood burns, and a meal is ready.

Hills around embrace our small lookout post,
And our cooking smoke embraces all the hills;
But our cook is busy running out and in,
No time to bother about the cloud or fog engulfing him.

Vegetables before the window dye the rocks green,
Pigs behind the hut, round and fat.
These keep him smiling, all day long,
And all day long he sings, his songs fill the air.

Two instruments of music adorn his window,
Within, a samisen, and without, a waterfall.
On him grow two tireless wings,
One is the song of revolution, the other, a carrying pole.

Ah, comrades on night patrol are about to return,
He hurries to fill up each one's wash basin;
In two buckets he brings home a colorful world,
One bucket full of red sun, and the other, blue hills.

Red Flowers All Over the Mountain, pp.42–43

The Lamp

An ink bottle holding a wick
Lights up this cozy home,
This little lamp in our mountain lookout post,
Is a blossom that never fades.

Has it captured the essence of the sun and the moon?
Has it been nurtured by the water in Heavenly River?
Thus all year round it blooms without fail,
Every night on mountaintop it bursts open, wide open.

The rising whirls of fog affect it not,
And insuppressibly it burns under downpouring clouds.
Thousands of mountain peaks hold it up high,
As it converses with thousands of stars.

Under the lamp we study books and papers,
Under the lamp we mend our shoes and socks;
The lamplight shines on our youth, full of life,
As we loyally guard our country's frontier pass.

Our bosom houses the entire world, the universe,
Our eyes scan the land from extremity to extremity;
This era of revolution unfolds with resounding forces,
And the lamp lights up our way forever forward.

It is the loftiest flower of our land, perhaps;
Perhaps in the most remote area this flower lies;
Perhaps it's really as small as a tiny bean, but
It kindles the clouds and reddens the skies.

Red Flowers All Over the Mountain, pp. 104–105

Translated by Kai-yu Hsu

Spring Song

Windbreak, files and files of bamboo fences
Like waves rolling toward sky's brim.
Harken: flights and flights of songs.
Who knows under which row of surges?

Upon the south ditch, we till once and again.
The ditch soil, we rake and rake.
The manure, we sieve and sieve.
Clear water, we sprinkle and sprinkle.

One rack of greenhouses after another,
Cozy warm, no fear of blowing wind.
Mat after mat covering tightly,
Solid, thick, no fear of biting frost.

Grow fresh vegetables for our nation.
Sweating and sweating—so what?
Only a few days, small seeds
Will burst into sprouts in orderly rows.

Hey! phalanx under the windbreak;
The commune deploys soldiers and horses,
From the end of the village, children call out: Dinnertime!
Everybody ignores the slanting sun ...

All sisters carry a broad smile;
Under the windbreak, fresh greens, trellis of flowers,
All flow into their dreams,
Harken: spring songs fill the horizon!

Jujube Tree Village, pp.30–31

Translated by Wai-lim Yip

PA SHAN

Pa Shan is a member of the People's Liberation Army who prefers anonymity behind a pen name. His poems, however, stand out noticeably among many others published after the Cultural Revolution. He incorporates in his poetry the best images created by the proletarian heroes since the Liberation. He uses them effectively and writes with ease. —K.Y.H.

Alpining

Mountain—high
High—into the sky.
Mountain—dangerous
Like a piercing dagger.
Stars pass their night here,
Piercing, breaking cloud-buds into petals.

See: we, the camping squad
Devoted to climbing this high mountain.
Thorns cut our feet;
Our nose-tips are sore from hitting the overhanging cliffs, again and again.
Red stars glitter in the moonlight
Like frisking stars, a huge spread of them.

Our shoulders carry rifles.
In our bosoms, four precious volumes.
We have strength we can never exhaust,
Pushing through clouds, parting mist up the summit.
To protect our country, we train ourselves: all tiger's guts.
From bitter fatigue, we taste the fragrant, sweet victory.

Raising our hands
To tear a piece of white cloud to wipe our sweat.
Lowering our head
Excited to see lines and lines of fishing boats, full load
        homeward bent.
Oh! The camping squad lines up to sing.
Against the silver lake we take a color picture to keep.

Red Flag Unfurling in the Wind, pp. 158–159

Translated by Wai-lim Yip

PING HSIN
(Hsieh Wan-ying, 1900–)

After having published nothing in twenty years, Ping Hsin is writing again. As she herself explains in the following pages, she had felt unworthy and lacking in things important and appropriate enough to say. During the same twenty years, other writers had turned to other callings—research, mostly. But Ping Hsin stayed closer to her interest: young people. She worked with grade school pupils, at times teaching them but mostly just living with them. She also went to the countryside to learn from the poor peasants, as did everyone else.

Born to wealthy, indulgent parents in Fukien, Ping Hsin spent her childhood marveling at the forms and colors of the shells, kelps, waves, at everything about the sea. Adolescence in an aristocratic Christian mission school in Peking and intense reading of Tagore's verse laid a foundation for what she called her philosophy of love, love for mother and child, trees and birds. All these peopled her very early collections of verse, *The Stars* (1921) and *Spring Waters* (1922), which brought her instant fame. Three years at Wellesley College in the United States (1923–26) furthered her development in the same direction, though she turned to prose—rather, poetic prose—addressed to young readers. She wrote about her travels abroad and her homesickness. After she returned to China, she taught for years at Yenching University. Her setback during the Cultural Revolution, which froze her pen, was not severe.

Now between official visits to friendly countries as a representative of China's older generation of writers, between receiving foreign dignitaries in the same role and reciting poetry, in English, on festive occasions, Ping Hsin writes "letters to my little readers" and other essays to sing the glory of the new society, and an occasional verse or two. Her pen is still facile, and her tone is as cheerful as a three-year-old who has just found a new toy.   —K.Y.H.

Because We Are Still Young

"Because we are Still Young" has not yet been published anywhere except on the wall bulletin of the Central Ethnic Academy in Peking. I have made a copy for Li Cheng-tao [the Nobel laureate physicist]; now I'm making a copy of it for you. It isn't a good poem, but you do whatever you see fit with it . . .

Ping Hsin
New Year's Day, 1973

Yesterday, a young man came to see me,
He read his new poem aloud for me to hear;
The first one was entitled:
"Because we are still young."

This title touched off my yearning for poetry;
As I gazed at his face full of youth and life,
I repeated, in a low voice, after him,
"Because we are still young."

I said, "Young man,
Who said the age of seventy is hard to attain since time of old?
It's nothing rare in the Mao Tse-tung era;
Look how many people beyond seventy there are
Who continue to work, nonstop, for socialism.

"When I was young, I never really had any time of youth!
At that time, all around me were
Beacons of war, fanned by imperialism to reach high in the sky,
And devils of feudalism all over the land,
Bleached bones piled up like mountains, blood and tears flowed in streams,
More anniversaries of national humiliation than any other festivals,
That, my friend, was China when I was young.

"I dared not struggle, I only wondered and waited,
I could see neither the future, nor the people's might;
I only locked myself in a tiny study with my books,
Though I had ears, I heard not the gunshots of people's revolution.

"The east is red, and the sun rises,
In China emerged a Mao Tse-tung.
This one triumphal thunderclap split the sky,
And the revolutionary peoples of the world all cheered,
The great leader mounted the Gate of Heavenly Peace,
Solemnly he proclaimed the success of China's revolution.

"I wiped my tears of joy and stood up,
Looking up to the blue sky of my motherland;
A brilliant sun filled every corner of the earth,
Thousands of sickles waving, thousands of axes raised,
Millions of faces overflowing with heartfelt joy.
I watched and felt anxiety in my heart,
'What can I do?' I asked myself.

"Half a century passed in wondering and waiting,
The second half of my life mustn't be wasted any more,
I must seriously reform myself, so that
I can successfully serve the people.

"Whom shall we serve,
And why shall we serve?
Chairman Mao has explained both very well,
And has pointed out for us the road ahead.

"We must merge ourselves with the new masses,
We mustn't ever hesitate again.
Share their lot, and breathe with them,
Be familiar with their life
And know what they say,
Write their hate and their happiness,
Smash the enemy, unite ourselves,
Let literature and art be a powerful weapon.

"The baptism of the Cultural Revolution,
Washed away from me the capitalist mud and dirt.
Resolutely I marched on the bright May Seven* road,
Honestly learned from the proletariat, from the very beginning.

"Over one year at the May Seven cadre school, I really learned,
I don't do labor work as well as others, so I learned to work in the field,
          planting vegetables, watching the crops, and picking fruit.
I picked sweet potatoes, I picked peanuts . . .
Each periodic review of my experience, I rose that much higher,
In my main curriculum—learning from the workers and peasants.

"The oil worker said,
'Revolution plus persistence, persist to carry out revolution,'
The poor-middle peasant said,
'Pick one more basket of flowers to support Asia, Africa, and Latin
          America.'
The awareness of liberated people is high, their strength, great.
United they listen to Chairman Mao,
And armed with Mao Tse-tung thought,
Their radiant red hearts are concerned over the whole world.

"Look, young man,
These people don't say much, but they say it well,
And their heroic words educated me.
In the Mao Tse-tung era we must live this way,
Live, learn, and work, until we grow old,
And the youth of revolution never grows old.

*Mao Tse-tung's directive dated May 7, 1966, exhorted every Chinese to learn lines of
productive work in addition to his or her principal career.

"Therefore, young man,
You are the sun at eight o'clock in the morning,
But I am not just a golden sunset either.
We both strive to grasp Mao Tse-tung thought,
Which stands like the sun that never sets."

New Evening News (Hong Kong, Jan. 14, 1973)

Translated by Kai-yu Hsu

SHEN YUNG-CH'ANG

Signaling a change in direction, Peking authorities late in 1970 started calling for greater literary output in an attempt to repeat the Great Leap Forward campaign that had harvested hundreds of volumes of homespun verses in 1958–59. Every anniversary was used as an excuse to rally the writers to write. One of the volumes thus produced, to commemorate the fiftieth anniversary of the founding of the Party, was a book of verse entitled *Thousands of Songs Dedicated to the Party* (1971); it includes the following selection.

Shen Yung-ch'ang is identified as a member of the Shan-yang Commune in Chin-shan County. His simple verse, cast in the folksong style, reflects the spirit of the time very well.   —K.Y.H.

Homespun Correspondent

All quiet late at night,
In the room, under a lamp light,
The homespun correspondent of our team
Seizes his pen in earnest.

Reports, page after page,
Make clear our line of work,
Singing praise of Chairman Mao,
Describing to him our new farm life.

Red hearts turn to the sun;
Broad shoulders bear heavy tasks.
He holds firmly his literary power,
To serve as our responsible spokesman.

Imitate not the ephemeral showing of the night-blooming cereus,
But rather learn from the plum blossoms which shun crowded springs.
He keeps to his heart the meaning of the "homespun,"
And always writes to serve revolution.

Thousands of Songs Dedicated to the Party, pp. 64–65

Translated by Kai-yu Hsu

947

Glossary

agricultural producers' cooperative: the intermediate step between redistribution of land and the commune system, or between the 1940s and 1957, depending on the locality

All-China Federation of Literary and Art Circles: established soon after 1949 to rally the cultural forces behind the Party and the government

anti-revisionism: opposition to the policy supposedly followed by Russia since 1959, a relaxation of Marxism-Leninism

anti-rightist campaign: any movement billed as combating tendencies toward capitalism in behavior or in way of thinking

brigade committee (production brigade committee): the controlling element in a production brigade in a commune

cadre: originally a key member of any organization, now loosely used for anybody who is somebody in the PRC, usually a Party member

catty (*chin*): a weight measure, about 1.33 pounds

chang: a length measure, 10 Chinese feet, approximately 10.9 American feet

cheng-feng: literally "straighten out the prevailing style of doing something"; a reform movement, used for the repeated drives to correct erroneous tendencies in the work and living style of the people involved; each of the movements (Three Antis, Five Antis, anti-rightist, etc.) is a *cheng-feng* movement

chin (see *catty*)

Chinese Writers' Association (national, with local branches): established soon after 1949, suspended during the Cultural Revolution (1964–70), recently revived

chüeh-chü: a standard Chinese verse form; a quatrain, or a cut-short verse, four lines of equal length, with five or seven syllables in each line

commune committee: the controlling element in a commune

co-op, or cooperative (see agricultural producers' cooperative)

Five Antis campaign, or Five Antis: begun in 1952 to oppose bribery, tax evasion, theft of state property, skimping on work and cheating on materials, theft of state economic information

Four Great Evils: four pests to be eliminated—in the early 1950s, mosquitoes, flies, sparrows, and rats; in 1960, after successful eradication of sparrows, bedbugs became the fourth pest

Four Villains: in literary circles, Hsia Yen, T'ien Han, Yang Han-sheng, and Chou Yang, purged during the Cultural Revolution

Gang of Four: Chiang Ching (Mao Tse-tung's wife) and her three close supporters Chang Ch'un-ch'iao, Wang Hung-wen, and Yao Wen-yüan, politically powerful in the mid-1960s, disgraced in 1976

General Line (short for General Line of the State): a guideline pronounced by
the government in 1953 for the period of transition to socialism, roughly
parallel to the first five-year plan, then modified in 1957 by Mao Tse-tung to
pave the way for the second five-year plan

Great Leap Forward: policy for an all-out drive to develop the country, pronounced by the Sixth Plenum of the Central Committee of the CCP's Eighth
Congress, in November 1958

Great Proletarian Cultural Revolution: official dates, 1966–69, but possibly 1962–
76; ostensibly waged to keep the revolution from backsliding, but it actually
caused a near civil war

hsieh-hou-yü: a figure of speech in Chinese colloquial, with the last word of
a familiar proverb omitted for the reader or listener to supply

hsiang: subdivision of a county

Hsiao: meaning "small," prefixed to a name as a form of friendly address

Hundred Flowers movement: drive to encourage literary and artistic activity,
(sometimes also applied to other areas of endeavor), first officially launched
in January 1956 by Chou En-lai; the phrase was introduced by Lu Ting-yi on
June 26 of the same year and was quickly applied to the movement.

huo-kuo: fire-pot, a sort of fondue with boiling broth instead of melted cheese

jenminpi: monetary unit; literally, "people's money"

k'ang: heated adobe or brick platform used as a bed or sitting place in winter
in North China

kaoliang: a main sorghum in North China

Kuomintang: short for Chung-kuo kuo-min-tang, the Chinese Nationalist Party,
founded by Sun Yat-sen in 1912 and stewarded by Chiang Kai-shek until his
death in 1975

Lao: meaning "old," prefixed to a name as a form of friendly address

League of Left-wing Writers: established in 1930 by Lu Hsün, disbanded by
Chou Yang in 1936

li: a length measure, about one-third mile

Long March: the Communist forces' 8,000-mile trek to escape Kuomintang siege
and to consolidate scattered Communist bases in China, started in Juichin,
Kiangsi Province, in October 1934, and ended in Yenan, Shensi Province,
December 1935

lü-shih: a classical verse form; eight lines of equal length, with five or seven
syllables in each line; also known as regulated verse

May Fourth movement: On May 4, 1919, students in Peking demonstrated
against the Versailles decision to give to Japan former German possessions
in Shantung; the movement was a dramatic expression of complex intellectual, social, and political undercurrents that began toward the end of the
nineteenth century; in literature, the movement brought forth writings on
modern themes in *pai-hua* (vernacular). The May Fourth era generally refers
to the 1920s and 1930s.

May Seven (May Seven school for cadres): Mao Tse-tung's directive dated May 7, 1966, exhorted every Chinese to learn other lines of productive work in addition to his or her principal career. Schools were subsequently established for this purpose. Some critics say the schools are but a modified form of reform through labor.

mu: an area measure, about one-sixth of an acre

pai-hua: vernacular, daily speech; its adoption in written language was promoted around the beginning of the twentieth century in an effort to create a new Chinese literature

Party branch secretary: head of a branch of the Chinese Communist Party, usually in an institutional unit, such as a commune or a factory

Party committee secretary: the committee of the CCP branch, usually in a political subdivision, such as a province, a county, a district (*hsiang*)

picul: a weight measure, equal to 133.33 pounds

"poisonous weeds": a metaphor in circulation at the end of the Hundred Flowers movement, diligently used by those in power to label any writing they could not accept as a "fragrant flower," but would rather reject as a poisonous weed

red-faced hero: exaggerated red makeup is always found on the stereotyped hero on the revolutionary opera stage; the expression is now used to denote a suntanned, fearless, almost superhumanly powerful model hero

Red Guard: a term used before Liberation for the Communist militia or guerrilla member (*ch'ih-wei-tui*); now rephrased *hung-wei-ping,* used for high school, even grade school students organized to serve the Communist cause; the Red Guards (school pupils) were called out by Mao Tse-tung during the Cultural Revolution to protect their leader and safeguard the revolution

Repatriates: landlords and village bullies who fled their villages at the advent of the Communist forces; after the Nationalist forces retook those areas, they returned to their village

Shensi-Kansu-Ningsia Border Region: the Communist sphere of influence in North China in the late 1930s and the 1940s, with the Kuomintang's acquiescence

shih-fu: form of address, for a teacher of a trade, the master of a shop, a foreman, etc.

struggle meeting: a meeting, usually public, called to punish an offender, with the penalty ranging from gentle reprimand to physical abuse or even lynching, depending on the situation and the charge

Ta-chai: a model commune in southwestern Hopei Province

Ta-ch'ing: petroleum center in Manchuria, a model industrial development

tan: a weight measure, about 135 pounds

Three Antis: a movement begun in 1952 to oppose corruption, waste, and bureaucratism; cf. Five Antis

T'ien-an-men Incident: On April 5, 1976, supporters of the late Premier Chou En-lai insisted on holding a public memorial in his honor at the historic square in Peking, the Gate of Heavenly Peace (T'ien-an-men). Wreaths were laid and poems were posted. A riot ensued when police took down the tokens of grief. It has been said that the incident is as important as the May Fourth incident of 1919.

tz'u: Chinese classical verse forms popularized toward the end of the T'ang dynasty, set to tunes of some 400 modes

wok: chinese cooking pot, in Cantonese; in standard Mandarin speech, *kuo*

yüan: monetary unit, value varying throughout the years, worth about 50¢ (one-half dollar) U.S. money after the Chinese monetary system had been stabilized toward the end of the 1960s

Translators and Contributors

Barlow, Tani Ph.D. candidate in modern Chinese history, University of California, Davis. Research interest: Ting Ling.

Bernard, Elizabeth J. B. A., Princeton, 1973; M.A., School of Oriental and African Studies, London, 1975; Ph.D. candidate, Chinese literature, University of California, Berkeley. Research interest: modern Chinese drama.

Berninghausen, John (b. 1942, Iowa) B.A., Spanish and Chinese, University of Minnesota; Ph.D. candidate in Chinese, Stanford University. On faculty, Chinese and Asian Studies, Middlebury. Co-editor, *Revolutionary Literature in China.*

Birch, Cyril (b. 1925, England) Ph.D., Chinese literature, School of Oriental and African Studies, London. On faculty, Oriental Languages, University of California, Berkeley, since 1960. Seven books, including *Studies in Chinese Literary Genres* (1974) and *Peach Blossom Fan* (1976), and many articles on Chinese literature.

Bjorge, Gary J. Ph.D. in Chinese, University of Wisconsin, 1977. Articles on Chinese literature in anthologies and journals. Research interest: twentieth century Chinese literature.

Boler, Lucy O. Yang (b. 1939, China) B. A., sociology, University of California, Berkeley, 1963; M.S., sociology, San Jose State University, 1967. Instructor in English as a second language, San Francisco Community College District, since 1969. Currently M.A. candidate, Chinese language and literature, San Francisco State University.

Chang, Richard F. (b. 1921, China) J.D., LL.M., Associate Professor of Chinese, University of Illinois. Publications: *Read Chinese* II, III, *Modern Chinese Poetry,* and *Under the Eaves of Shanghai.*

Cheng, George C. T. (b. China) B.A., literature, National Ch'eng Kung University, Taiwan; M.L.S., University of Oregon; M.A., San Francisco State University. Librarian, San Francisco State University, since 1971. Articles and translations in *Ming Pao Monthly, China Monthly,* and *Perspectives.*

Cheung, Dominic (b. 1943, Macau) B.A., Western literature, National Chengchi University, Taiwan, 1966; M.A., English, Brigham Young University, 1969; Ph.D., comparative literature, University of Washington, 1973. Assistant Professor of Chinese and Comparative Literature, University of Southern California. Author of *Feng Chih,* eight books in Chinese poetry, and other works.

Cheung, Samuel B.A., Chinese University of Hong Kong, 1967; Ph.D., University of California, Berkeley, 1974. On faculty, Department of Oriental Languages, University of California, Berkeley, since 1974. Many articles on Chinese linguistics.

Chun, Doris Sze (b. Taiwan) B.A., Chinese, 1974; M.A., San Francisco State University, 1977. Teaching in Foreign Language Department, San Francisco State University. Main interest, Chinese language and literature.

Chung, Ling (b. 1945) B.A., English, 1966; M.A., Ph.D., comparative literature, University of Wisconsin, 1969, 1972; advanced study, University of Michigan, 1974. Teaching: State University of New York. Articles on and translations of Chinese literature in two anthologies and many journals. Current research: Li Ching-chao, Han Shan.

Crawford, William B. (b. 1940) Studied Chinese literature, San Francisco State University and Taiwan University; Ph.D., Chinese language and literature, Indiana University, 1972. On faculty, Chinese and Comparative Literature, Pittsburgh University, since 1972.

Dong, Donald D. (b. 1939, Hong King) B.A., Harvard, 1962; M.A., San Francisco State University, 1966; advanced study in Taiwan, 1967; Ph.D. candidate, comparative literature, University of Washington. Teaching: National Cheng-chi University, University of Washington, San Francisco State University. Awards for playwriting, 1966, 1969; two dramatic productions; articles on modern Chinese poetry.

Dong, Lorraine B.A. and M.A., Chinese, San Francisco State University; Ph.D. candidate, Asian languages and literature, University of Washington. Dissertation: Evolution and Life of Ts'ui Ying-ying (c.803–963).

Gibbs, Donald Ph.D., Chinese language and literature, University of Washington. Taught at National Normal University, Taiwan, and at Harvard; Chairman, East Asian Studies, University of California, Davis. Publications: *A Bibliography of Modern Chinese Literature, 1918–1942, Index to Chinese Literature,* and others. Current research: *Wen-hsin tiao-lung.*

Goldblatt, Howard (b. 1939) M.A., San Francisco State University; Ph.D., Indiana University, 1974. On faculty, San Francisco State University, since 1974. Residence and research in Taiwan and Japan. Publications: *Hsiao Hung;* translator, *The Execution of Mayor Yin,* by Ch'en Jo-hsi; many articles on Chinese literature. Current research: Northeast Chinese authors.

Goldman, Merle Faculty, Chinese history, Boston University; research associate, Fairbank Center for East Asian Research, Harvard. Publications: *Literary Dissent in Communist China* and other books and articles on modern Chinese ideology.

Gotz, Michael Ph.D., Oriental languages, University of California, Berkeley. Founder, editor, *Modern Chinese Literature Newsletter.* Articles and translations, modern Chinese literature.

Greenhouse, Linda B.A., Chinese language and literature, University of California, Santa Barbara, 1973; Chinese studies, Taipei; M.A., Asian studies, University of California, Berkeley.

Haft, Lloyd (b. 1946) B.A., Harvard, 1968; Ph.D., University of Leyden (Netherlands), 1973. Researcher, Documentation Center for Contemporary China, University of Leyden, since 1973. Publication in Dutch periodicals. Current research: Pien Chih-lin.

Hom, Marlon K. B.A., San Francisco State University; M.A., Indiana University; Ph.D. candidate, University of Washington. Dissertation on *Liao-chai chih-i* by P'u Sung-ling.

Hsu, Raymond S. W. University of Nanking, China; Ph.D., linguistics, Cambridge University. On faculty at Cambridge University, University of Malaya, and currently University of Hong Kong. Publications: *The Style of Lu Hsün* and many articles on Chinese literature.

Hu, King (Hu Chin-ch'üan) (b. 1931, China) Peking Academy, 1958. Stage acting, production, scriptwriting, 1950–70; director, King Hu Film Productions. Teaching: Baptist College, Hong Kong. Produced eight films; won twelve international citations and awards. Publication: *Lao She and His Writings.* Research interest: contemporary Chinese literature.

Huters, Ted Ph.D., Chinese, Stanford University, 1977. On faculty, University of British Columbia. Co-editor, *The Revolutionary Literature in China.* Current research: Ch'ien Chung-shu.

Kao, Hsin-sheng C. Ph.D., University of Southern California, 1977. Assistant Professor of Asian Studies, University of La Verne. Research interest: Chinese fiction, translation of Chinese poetry.

Kaplan, Harry A. (b. 1954) B.A., University of California, Berkeley, 1976; M.A., Harvard, 1978; Ph.D. candidate, Harvard. Research interest: literary interpretation and the evolution of fiction.

Kapp, Robert A. B.A., Swarthmore; M.A., Yale; Ph.D., history, Yale. Assistant Professor, Rice University; on faculty, East Asian Studies, University of Washington. Editor, *Journal of Asian Studies* (1978–81). Research in England, Japan, and Taiwan. Publications: *Szechwan and the Chinese Republic,* articles and reviews.

Kinkley, Jeffrey C. (b. 1948) B.A., University of Chicago; M.A., Ph.D., history and East Asian languages, Harvard, 1977. Lecturer, History Department, Harvard. Research interest: Shen Ts'ung-wen.

Koziol, Kenneth G. (b. 1952) B.A., classics, Xavier University; advanced study, Sorbonne, Middlebury, and Taiwan; Ph.D. candidate, East Asian languages, Indiana University.

Lai, Jane (b. 1939, Hong Kong) B.A., M.A., Hong Kong University; M.Litt., Bristol University, 1973. Lecturer, English and comparative literature, Hong Kong University.

Lee, Leo Ou-fan (b. China) B.A., National Taiwan University; M.A., Ph.D., Harvard University. Teaching: Dartmouth College; Chinese University of Hong Kong; Princeton University; Associate Professor, East Asian languages, Indiana University. Publications: *The Romantic Generation of Modern Chinese Writers,* several critical essays in the *Ming Pao Monthly.* Research interest: twentieth century Chinese literature.

Link, Perry (b. 1944) Ph.D., history and East Asian languages, Harvard. Research in Asia. On faculty, University of California, Los Angeles, since 1977. Many articles, book reviews, and translations. Research interest: modern Chinese literature.

Lyell, William A., Jr. M.A., University of Chicago; Ph.D., University of Chicago, 1971. On faculty, Stanford University. Publications: *Lu Hsün's Vision of Reality, Cat Country,* and articles on Chinese literature. Research interest: *Li Tzu-ch'eng.*

Mao, Nathan K. Studied at New Asia College (Hong Kong), Yale; Ph.D., English, University of Wisconsin; on English faculty, Shippensburg State College. Translator of Li Yü's *Twelve Towers* and Pa Chin's *Cold Nights;* co-author, *Classical Chinese Fiction: Essays and Bibliographies.*

McCarvel, Mark M.A., Chinese, San Francisco State University, 1978; currently advanced study in Taiwan.

McDougall, Bonnie S. (b. 1941, Australia) Studied and taught at University of Sydney; currently research fellow, Fairbank Center, Harvard. Publications: *Paths in Dream: Selected Prose and Poetry of Ho Ch'i-fang,* articles on modern Chinese literature.

Munro, Stan Studied Chinese at Yale, in Hawaii, and in Taiwan; studied linguistics at Alberta and Toronto; residence in different parts of Asia. On faculty at University of Alberta, East Asian Studies, since 1966. Publications: *The Function of Satire in the Works of Lao She, Genesis of a Revolution,* and others.

O'Connor, Kevin (b. 1950) B.A., East Asian studies, Princeton; M.A., Asian languages and literature, University of Washington, 1975; now studying medicine at University of Rochester.

Palandri, Angela C. Y. Jung (b. Peking) B.A., Fu Jen University; Ph.D., University of Washington. Professor of Chinese, University of Oregon. Publications: critical analysis of Yuan Chen; two volumes of translations of Chinese poetry. Research interest: contemporary Chinese women writers.

Pickowicz, Paul Gene B.S., Springfield College, 1967; M.A., Tufts University, 1968; Ph.D., University of Wisconsin, 1973. Assistant Professor of History, University of California, San Diego. Publications: fourteen monographs on contemporary Chinese intellectual currents in various anthologies and learned journals. Research interest: Ch'ü Ch'iu-pai.

Robyn, Philip (b. 1943) B.A. and advanced studies, Chinese language and literature, San Francisco State University. Translator, Joint Publication Research Center, San Fransicso. Research interest: contemporary China.

Ryckmans, Pierre (Simon Leys) (b. 1935, Brussels) Ph.D., art history, University of Louvain. Taught at Chinese University of Hong Kong; reader, Chinese studies, Australian National University. Books include *The Life and Work of Su Renshan (1814–1849), Images Brisées, Chinese Shadows, Les Propos sur la Peinture de Shih T'ao;* many articles on contemporary China. Current research: Chou Tso-jen.

Strassberg, Richard E. Ph.D., Princeton; Assistant Professor of Chinese, Yale. Translated Revolutionary Peking Opera; published articles on traditional drama. Research interest: seventeenth-century playwright K'ung Shang-jen.

Tharp, Robert N. (b. 1913, Manchuria) Taught Chinese, Defense Language Institute, Yale University. Bilingual education, New York. Currently advisor to Defense Language Institute, Monterey, California.

Ting, Wang Associated general editor of the Min Pao publications, journalist, mass media specialist. Wrote and edited eleven books and many articles on contemporary China, including *Chinese Writers in the 1930s, Biography of Chiang Ching, Treatises on the Cultural Revolution, A Preliminary Appraisal of the Personnel of the New CCP Central Committee.*

Tsai, Meishi (b. 1942, Taiwan) B.A., Tunghai University, Taiwan; M.A., English, University of California, Los Angeles; Ph.D., comparative literature, University of California, Berkeley, 1975. On faculty, Chinese and Asian Studies, Pomona College, since 1973. Publications: *Contemporary Chinese Novels and Short Stories, 1949–74,* and other works in contemporary Chinese literature. Research interest: Taoism and medieval Chinese literature.

Tsau, Shu-ying B.A., Peking University, 1958. Assistant Professor of Chinese, York University, Toronto. Contributor to *Revolutionary Literature in China.* Research interest: contemporary Chinese literature.

Tseng, Maurice H. (b. 1927, China) B.A., George Washington University, 1952; advanced study, University of California, Berkeley. Teaching: Army Language School, Monterey; Yale University; Associate Professor of Chinese, San Francisco State University. Author of and contributor to four books on Chinese language and literature.

Tung, Constantine B.A., San Francisco State University; M.A., University of California, Berkeley; Ph.D., Claremont Graduate School. Associate Professor of Chinese at State University of New York. Author of several articles on modern Chinese literature. Research interest: drama in the PRC.

Wild, Natasha M.A., Chinese, San Francisco State University; advanced study, Chinese language and literature, Taiwan. Taught in the Chinese program, San Francisco State University. Research interest: modern Chinese literature.

Wong, Kam-ming (b. China) Ph.D., Cornell University. Taught Chinese language and literature, University of Iowa and Cornell. Publications: many studies on *Hung-lou-meng,* Lu Hsün, and Hao Jan. Research interest: Chinese fiction.

Yang, Lucia (b. China) B.A., San Francisco State University; M.S., Ph.D., Chinese and linguistics, Georgetown University, 1975. On faculty, University of Oregon, since 1976.

Yang, Richard F. S. B.A., Yenching University; Ph.D., University of Washington. Teaching: University of Washington, University of Southern California, University of Pittsburgh. Publications: *Fifty Songs of the Yüan, Four Plays from the Yüan Drama, Eight Colloquial Tales of the Sung.*

Yang, Winston B.A., English, National Taiwan University; Ph.D., Chinese, Stanford University. Professor of Chinese, Seton Hall University. Publications: *Classical Chinese Fiction and Modern Chinese Fiction* (with Nathan Mao and Peter Li); *Studies in Traditional Chinese Fiction; Mao Tsung-kang;* and many articles and reviews in Chinese literature.

Yee, Edmond (b. 1938, China) M.Div., Pacific Theological Seminary; M.A., modern Chinese literature, San Francisco State University; Ph.D., Oriental languages, University of California, Berkeley. On faculty, Pacific Lutheran Theological Seminary, Berkeley. Research interest: Ming dynasty Chinese drama.

Yeh, Teng-ch'i (b. 1940, Taiwan) B.A., Taiwan University; advanced study, Chinese literature, San Francisco State University.

Yeung, Ellen Lai-shan Graduate study, San Francisco State University. Teacher, curriculum writer, San Francisco School District.

Yip, Wai-Lim (b. 1937, Kwangtung) B.A., National Taiwan University, 1959; M.F.A., University of Iowa, 1964; Ph.D., comparative literature, Princeton, 1967. Professor, University of California, San Diego. Bilingual poet. Wrote and edited more than a dozen books, including *Chinese Poetry: Major Modes and Genres, Modern Chinese Poetry, Hiding the Universe, Ezra Pound's Cathay.*

Yuan, K'o-chia   B.A., foreign languages and literature, Tsing Hua University, 1964. Advanced study and teaching, writing, and editing in the field of literature, in Peking since 1946. Research in Western literature, Academy of Sciences, Peking, since 1950s.

In addition to the translators and contributors listed above, **Jennie Chao, John Coleman, Lawrence Herzberg, Kenneth Koziol, Gloria Shen, Eugene Teng, and Ling-hsia Yeh** participated in a group translation project as part of a seminar on contemporary Chinese literature, under the direction of Leo Ou-fan Lee at Indiana University.

Chinese References

Across (1949). Tsou Ti-fan.
跨過　鄒荻帆　上海

As the Ice and Snow Melt (1956). Li Chun.
冰化雪消　李准　北京

At the Bridge Site (1956). Liu Pin-yen.
在橋樑工地上　劉賓雁　北京

Auntie Kuan (1959). Ju Chih-chüan.
關大媽　茹志鵑　北京

Autumn Harvest (1956). Mao Tun.
秋收　茅盾　北京

Autumn Rhymes (1963). Chün Ch'ing.
秋色賦　峻青　北京

Battle Fires Spread (1951). Liu Pai-yü.
戰火紛飛　劉白羽　北京

The Battle of Sha-chia-tien (1953). Liu Ch'ing.
沙家店戰鬥　柳青　北京

Before Daybreak (1959). Ju Chih-chüan.
黎明前的故事　茹志鵑　北京

Before the New Bureau Director Came. Ho Ch'iu.
新局長到來之前　何求
初級中學課本：文學，第五冊
245至276頁

Biography of Niu T'ien-szu (1935). Lao She.
牛天賜傳　老舍　上海

The Birth of a Person (1931). Ting Ling.
一個人的誕生　丁玲　上海

Bitter Struggle (1963). Ou-yang Shan.
苦鬥　歐陽山　北京

Black Pheonix (1964). Wang Wen-shih.
黑鳳　王汶石　北京

The Blood-stained Clothes (1962). Chüan Ching.
血衣　峻青　北京

Blue Sky and the Forest (1942). Tsou Ti-fan.
青空與林　鄒荻帆　重慶

The Brand (1934). Tsang K'o-chia.
烙印　臧克家　上海

Bright Sunny Sky (1972). Hao Jan.
艷陽天　浩然　北京

Broad Road in Golden Light (1972). Hao Jan.
金光大道　浩然　北京

The Builders (1960). Liu Ch'ing.
創業史　柳青　北京

A Bumper Crop of Short Stories (1963).
短篇小說的豐收　北京

Caged Animals (1963). Sha Ting.
困獸記　沙汀　上海

The Carpenter Shop (1948). Tsou Ti-fan.
木廠　鄒荻帆　上海

The Carter's Story (1949). T'ien Chien.
趕車傳　田間　上海

Cart Wheel Tracks (1959). Li Chun.
車輪的轍印　李准　北京

The Changes in Li Village (1950). Chao Shu-li.
李家莊的變遷　趙樹理　北京

Cheers (1959). Tsang K'o-chia.
歡呼集　臧克家　北京

The Children of Hsi-liu-shui (1956). Chou Erh-fu.
西流水的孩子們　周而復　上海

Chin-pao's Mother (1962). Ma Feng.
金寶娘　馬烽　北京

Chinese Ballads (1936). T'ien Chien.
中國牧歌　田間　上海

City of Cats (1933). Lao She.
貓城記　老舍　上海

Coal Mines in May (1955). Hsiao Chün.
五月的礦山　蕭軍　北京

The Coldest Winter in Peking (1977). Hsia Chih-yen.
北京最寒冷的冬天　夏之炎　台北

Colorful Clouds (1964). Hao Jan.
彩霞集　浩然　北京

The Conch-shell Bugle Call (1973). Chang Yung-mei.
螺號　張永枚　北京

The Countryside, on High Tide (1956).
農村在高潮中　北京

Critical Essays on the Peking Opera "The Red Lantern" (1965).
京劇紅燈記評論集　北京

Critical Introduction of Chinese Writers of the 1930s (1978). Ting Wang.
中國三十年代作家評介　丁望
香港

The Death of a Famous Actor (1960). T'ien Han.
名優之死　田漢　北京

The Death of Li Hsiu-ch'eng (1959). Yang Han-sheng.
李秀成之死　陽翰笙　北京

Decay (1947). Mao Tun.
腐蝕　茅盾　哈爾濱

Defend Yenan (1954). Tu P'eng-ch'eng.
保衛延安　杜鵬程　北京

The Diary of a Suicide (1929). Ting Ling.
自殺日記　丁玲　上海

Discussion of the Mass Line During Land Reform (1950). Liu Ch'ing.
雜談土地改革運動中的羣眾路綫
柳青　新華書店

Disillusionment (1927). Mao Tun.
幻滅　茅盾　上海

Divorce (1933). Lao She.
離婚　老舍　上海

Dripping Water Wears Away the Rock. K'ang Cho.
水滴石穿　康濯　收穫
一九五七年七月廿四日

Drops of Water (1961). Chao P'u-ch'u.
滴水集　趙樸初　北京

The East (1978). Wei Wei.
東方　魏巍　北京

East is Red (1963). K'ang Cho.
東方紅　康濯　北京

East Shantung Stories (1959). Chün Ch'ing.
膠東紀事　峻青　北京

Enjoying the Short Stories of 1960 (1961). Tu P'eng-ch'eng et al.
1960短篇小說欣賞　杜鵬程等
北京

Evening Talks at Yenshan (1963). Teng T'o.
燕山夜話　鄧拓　北京

The Execution of Mayor Yin (1978). Chen Jo-hsi.
陳若曦

Faded Roses (1929). Ou-yang Shan.
玫瑰殘了　歐陽山　上海

Family Problems (1964). Hu Wan-ch'un.
家庭問題　胡萬春　上海

Farewell to Yenan (1951). Ko Pi-chou.
別延安　戈壁舟　北京

Field Combat Verses (1951). Li Ying.
野戰詩集　李瑛　漢口

Fighting on the Hu-t'o River (1959). Li
Ying-ju.
戰鬥在滹沱河上　李英儒　北京

Fighting on the Plain. Chang Yung-mei.
平原作戰　張永枚　紅旗
一九七三年七月號

Fish's Eye (1935). Pien Chih-lin.
魚目集　卞之琳　上海

Flames Ahead (1952). Liu Pai-yü.
火光在前　劉白羽　北京

The Flames of Revenge (1962). Wen Chieh.
復仇的火燄　聞捷　北京

Flood (1936). T'ien Han.
洪水　田漢　上海

Flood (1932). Ting Ling.
水　丁玲　上海

The Flowering Steppe (1962). Malchinhu.
花的草原　瑪拉沁夫　北京

The Foothills of the Pamir Plateau (1940).
Yang Shuo.
帕米爾高原的流脈　楊朔　桂林

Forced Passage (1946). Sha Ting.
闖關　沙汀　上海

From the Grasslands (1960). Rabchai
Tsazang.
草原集　饒階巴桑（藏族）　北京

Fu-kuei (1953). Chao Shu-li.
福貴　趙樹理　北京

A Generation of Noble Souls (1959).
Ou-yang Shan.
一代風流　歐陽山　香港

The Goddess (1921). Kuo Mo-jo.
女神　郭沫若　上海

The Gold-panning (1947). Sha Ting.
淘金記　沙汀　上海

Great Changes in a Mountain Village
(1962–63). Chou Li-po.
山鄉巨變　周立波　北京

Hai Jui's Dismissal from Office (1962). Wu
Han.
海瑞罷官　吳晗　北京

The Han Garden (1936). Pien Chih-lin, Ho
Ch'i-fang, and Li Kuang-t'ien.
漢園集　卞之琳，何琪芳，李廣田
上海

Havana in April (1964). Juan Chang-ching.
四月的哈瓦那　阮章競　北京

The Herald of Dawn (1948). Ai Ch'ing.
黎明的通知　艾青

Homecoming. Chao Hsün.
還鄉記　趙尋　劇本一九六〇三月號

Hometown (1947). Ai Wu.
故鄉　艾蕪　上海

Hsieh Yao-huan. T'ien Han.
謝瑤環　田漢
劇本一九六一第七、八合期

Hurricane (1949). Chou Li-po.
暴風驟雨　周立波　北京

In Darkness (1928). Ting Ling.
在黑暗中　丁玲　上海

In Peace Time (1958). Tu P'eng-ch'eng.
在和平的日子裏　杜鵬程　西安

In Stable (1963). Hsiao San.
伏櫪集　蕭三　北京

In the Countryside, Forward—March!
(1956). Ch'in Chao-yang.
在田野上——前進　秦兆陽　北京

In the Red-Rock Mountain (1972).
紅石山中　北京

It Happened in the Reed Pond (1950). Yang
Mo.
葦塘紀事　楊沫　北京

It Is Not Yet Dawn (1936). T'ien Chien.
未明集　田間　上海

Jujube Tree Village (1972). Li Ying.
棗林村集　李瑛　北京

Keep the Red Flags Flying (1958). Liang Pin.
紅旗譜　梁斌　北京

Kuan Han-ch'ing (1961). T'ien Han.
關漢卿　田漢　北京

The Land Beautiful as Brocade (1953). Yang Shuo.
錦繡河山　楊朔　北京

The Lanterns of Nan-shan (1964). Sun Ch'ien.
南山的燈　孫謙　北京

Leaves of Three Autumns (1933). Pien Chih-lin.
三秋草　卞之琳　上海

Li Tzu-ch'eng (1978). Yao Hsüeh-yin.
李自成　姚雪垠　北京

Life is Like Fire (1965). Hsu Ching-hsien.
生命似火　徐景賢　上海

The Lin Family Store (1961). Hsia Yen.
林家舖子　夏衍　北京
（中國電影劇本選集）
　　三至四六頁

The Lin Family Store (1938). Mao Tun.
林家舖子　茅盾　上海

The Long Flowing Stream (1963). Liu Chen.
長長的流水　劉眞　北京

Love and War (1946). Yao Hsüeh-yin.
戎馬戀　姚雪垠

The May Festival (1959). Li Chi.
五月端陽　李季　北京

Midnight (1933). Mao Tun.
子夜　茅盾　上海

Moonless Night (1954). Yang Shuo.
月黑夜　楊朔　北京

Morning in Shanghai (1958). Chou Erh-fu.
上海的早晨　周而復　北京

Morning Lights (1964). Liu Pai-yü.
晨光集　劉白羽　北京

The Morning Sun (1961). Liu Pai-yü.
早晨的太陽　劉白羽　北京

Mother (1933). Ting Ling.
母親　丁玲　上海

Motherland! the Glorious October (1958). Wen Chieh.
祖國！光輝的十月　聞捷　北京

Mount Wang-nan (1950). Yang Shuo.
望南山　楊朔　上海

The Mountain Stream (1963). Liang Shang-ch'üan.
山泉集　梁上泉　北京

Mountain Wilderness (1962). Ai Wu.
野山　艾蕪　北京

The Music Creek (1963). Yen Chen.
琴泉　嚴陣　北京

My First Superior (1959). Ma Feng.
我的第一個上級　馬烽　北京

A New Home (1955). Ai Wu.
新的家　艾蕪　北京

New Poetry from Southern Kwangtung (1972).
南粵新詩　廣東

New Songs of Soldier-Tillers (1973). Hsü Yü, Huo Hua, et al.
軍墾新曲　旭宇，火華等著　北京

New Spring (1956). Chang Yung-mei.
新春　張永枚　北京

New Year (1965). Hu Wan-ch'un.
過年　胡萬春　上海

Night in South China (1935). Ai Wu.
南國之夜　艾蕪　上海

The Night in the Village (1957). Ho Ching-shih.
鄉村的夜　賀敬之　北京

The Night of the Snowstorms (1958). Wang Wen-shih.
風雪之夜　王汶石　北京

Night Scenes (1936). Ai Wu.
夜景　艾蕪　上海

Niu Ch'uan-te and the Red Carrot (1942).
Yao Hsüeh-yin.
牛金德與紅蘿蔔　姚雪垠

Nocturnal Songs (1950). Ho Ch'i-fang.
夜歌　何其芳　上海

Northland and South of the River. Yang
Han-sheng.
北國江南　陽翰笙　電影劇作
一九六三　六月號
十至四二頁

The Offspring (1958). Wang Yüan-chien.
後代　王愿堅　北京

On Poetry (1952). Ai Ch'ing.
新詩論　艾青　北京

On the Kolchin Grasslands (1959).
Malchinhu.
科爾沁草原的人們　瑪拉沁夫
北京

On the Writing of Short Stories (1959).
Chün Ch'ing.
談談短篇小說的寫作　峻青　上海

One Year (1956). Fei Li-wen.
一年　費禮文　北京

An Ordinary Laborer (1959). Wang
Yüan-chien.
普通勞動者　王愿堅　北京

Party Membership Dues (1956). Wang
Yüan-chien.
黨費　王愿堅　北京

The Past Generation (See The Third
Generation)
過去的年代（見第三代）　蕭軍

Pastoral Songs of the T'ien Mountain Range
(1956). Wen Chieh.
天山牧歌　聞捷　北京

The Path of Socialist Literature and Art in
China (1960). Chou Yang.
中國社會主義文學與藝術之道路
周揚　北京

Paths in the Woods (1957). Liu Chen.
林中路　劉眞　北京

Peian-Heiho Line (1950). Liu Chen.
北黑綫　楊朔　上海

People Sing on the Long Island (1972).
長島人歌　長沙

The Petrel (1961). Chün Ching.
海燕　峻青　上海

Pledge (1953). T'ien Chien.
誓詞　田間　上海

Pledge to Peace (1954). Liu Pai-yü.
對和平宣誓　劉白羽　北京

Poems of the Last Ten Years (1957). Feng
Chih.
十年詩抄　馮至　北京

Poems of the War of Resistance (1956).
T'ien Chien.
抗戰詩抄　田間　上海

Poems on the Seashore (1955). Chang
Yung-mei.
海邊的詩　張永枚　北京

Prophecy (1954). Ho Ch'i-fang.
預言　何其芳　上海

The Quiet Maternity Ward (1962). Ju
Chih-chüan.
靜靜的產院　茹志鵑　北京

Rainbow (1929). Mao Tun.
虹　茅盾　上海

Record of Painted Dreams (1936). Ho
Ch'i-fang.
畫夢錄　何其芳　上海

Red Flag Unfurling in the Wind (1972).
風展紅旗　工農兵詩選　北京

Red Flowers All Over the Mountain (1973).
Li Ying.
紅花滿山　李瑛　北京

The Red Lantern (1970).
紅燈記　北京

Red Rock Hill (1949). Yang Shuo.
紅石山　楊朔　上海

Red Star—A Jewel (1953). Ai Ch'ing.
寶石的紅星　艾青　北京

Red Willow (1965). Li Ying.
紅柳集　李瑛　北京

Repatriates (1978). Chen Jo-hsi.
歸　陳若曦　台北

Return by Night (1958). Ai Wu.
夜歸　艾蕪　北京

Rickshaw Boy (1937). Lao She.
駱駝祥子　老舍　上海

Romance of the Coal Mine of Black Stone Hill (1950). K'ang Cho.
黑石坡煤窰演義　康濯　北京

The Route (1932). Sha Ting.
航綫　沙汀　上海

The Rhymes of Li Yu-ts'ai (1962). Chao Shu-li.
李有才板話　趙樹理　北京

Sai Chin Hua (1936). Hsia Yen.
賽金花　夏衍　上海

San-li-wan (1963). Chao Shu-li.
三里灣　趙樹理　北京

The Seeds (1965). T'ang K'o-hsin.
種籽　唐克新　上海

Selected Creative Writings by Young Workers, Peasants, and Soldiers (1965).
工農兵青年創作選　北京

Selected Plays by Lao She (1959). Lao She.
老舍劇作選　老舍　北京

Selected Poems of Ch'en Yi (1977). Ch'en Yi.
陳毅詩詞選集　陳毅　北京

Selected Short Stories (1956).
短篇小說選　北京

Selected Works of Mao Tse-tung (1965). Mao Tse-tung.
毛澤東選集　毛澤東　北京

Seventeen Short Poems (1952). Li Chi.
短詩十七首　李季　漢口

Shachiapang (1970).
沙家浜　北京

Shansi-Chahar-Hopei Poems (1959). Wei Wei.
晉察冀詩抄　魏巍　北京

Short Songs on the Highland (1949). Chou Erh-fu.
高原短曲　周而復　上海

Singing Aloud (1973). Ho Ching-chih.
放歌集　賀敬之　北京

Slave Girl Chin-chu (1965). Lu Yang-lieh.
女奴金珠　陸揚烈　上海

Snow and the Village (1943). Tsou Ti-fan.
雪與村莊　鄒荻帆　成都

The Songs of the Kunlun Mountains (1965). Kuo Hsiao-ch'uan.
崑崙行　郭小川　北京

Songs of the Surveyors (1963). Juan Chang-ching.
勘探者之歌　阮章競　北京

The Song of Youth (1960). Yang Mo.
青春之歌　楊沫　香港

Songs South of the River (1961). Yen Chen.
江南曲　嚴陣　上海

Sons and Daughters of Hsisha (1974). Hao Jan.
西沙兒女　浩然　北京

Southern Journeys, II (1964). Ai Wu.
南行記續編　艾蕪　北京

Sowing (1963). Liu Ch'ing.
種谷記　柳青　北京

Sowing Seeds (1946). Sha Ting.
播種記　沙汀　上海

Spring (1956). Ai Ch'ing.
春天　艾蕪　北京

The Spring and Autumn of the Taiping Kingdom of Heaven (1946). Yang Han-sheng.
天國春秋　陽翰笙　上海

Spring Famine (1946). Chou Erh-fu.
春荒　周而復　上海

Spring in the Valley (1955). Chou Erh-fu.
山谷裏的春天　周而復　北京

Spring in the Workshop (1956). T'ang
K'o-hsin.
車間裏的春天　唐克新　北京

Spring Planting, Autumn Harvest (1956).
K'ang Cho.
春種秋收　康濯　北京

Spring Silkworm (1933). Mao Tun.
春蠶　茅盾　上海

Spring Waters (1922). Ping Hsin.
春水　冰心　上海

The Stars (1921). Ping Hsin.
繁星　冰心　上海

Steeled and Tempered (1962). Ai Wu.
百鍊成鋼　艾蕪　北京

The Story in Song of the Horse-headed
Fiddle (1956). T'ien Chien.
馬頭琴歌傳　田間　北京

The Story of Ch'iu Chin (1951). Hsia Yen.
秋瑾傳　夏衍　北京

The Story of Li Shuang-shuang (1961). Li
Chun.
李雙雙小傳　李准　北京

Sugarcane Forest (1963). Kuo Hsiao-ch'uan.
甘蔗林——青紗帳　郭小川　北京

The Sun Shines Over the Sangkan River
(1948). Ting Ling.
太陽照在桑乾河上　丁玲
光華書店

Swallow Cliff (1954). Chou Erh-fu.
燕宿崖　周而復　上海

Taking Tiger Mountain by Strategy (1970).
智取威虎山　北京

Tall, Tall Poplars (1964). Ju Chih-chüan.
高高的白楊樹　茹志鵑　上海

Teahouse (1959). Lao She
茶館　老舍　北京
（見老舍劇作選）

The Third Generation (1937). Hsiao Chün.
第三代　蕭軍　上海

A Thousand Miles of Lovely Land (1953).
Yang Shuo.
三千里江山　楊朔　北京

Thousands of Songs Dedicated to the Party
(1971).
千歌萬曲獻給黨　上海

Together through Thick and Thin. Yüeh
Yeh.
同甘共苦　岳野　北京
劇本一九五六十期

Three-Family Lane (1959). Ou-yang Shan.
三家巷　歐陽山　廣州

Three Years in Huang-fu Village (1956). Liu
Ch'ing.
皇甫村的三年　柳青　北京

To the Fighters (1954). T'ien Chien.
給戰鬥者　田間　北京

To Young Citizens (1956). Kuo
Hsiao-ch'uan.
給青年公民　郭小川　北京

Treatises on the Motion Picture (1963).
電影論文集　北京

Triumphal Return (1962). Tsang K'o-chia.
凱旋集　臧克家　北京

Uncle Kao (1949). Ou-yang Shan.
高乾大　歐陽山　上海

Under Shanghai Eaves (1946). Hsia Yen.
上海屋簷下　夏衍　上海

The Underground Spring (1932). Yang
Han-sheng.
地泉　陽翰笙　上海

Up and Down the Great River (1977). Li
Chun.
大江上下　李准　（電影）

Village Feud (1956). Ma Feng.
村仇　馬烽　北京

Village in August (1935). Hsiao Chün.
八月的鄉村　蕭軍　上海

Author Index

966

Title Index

971